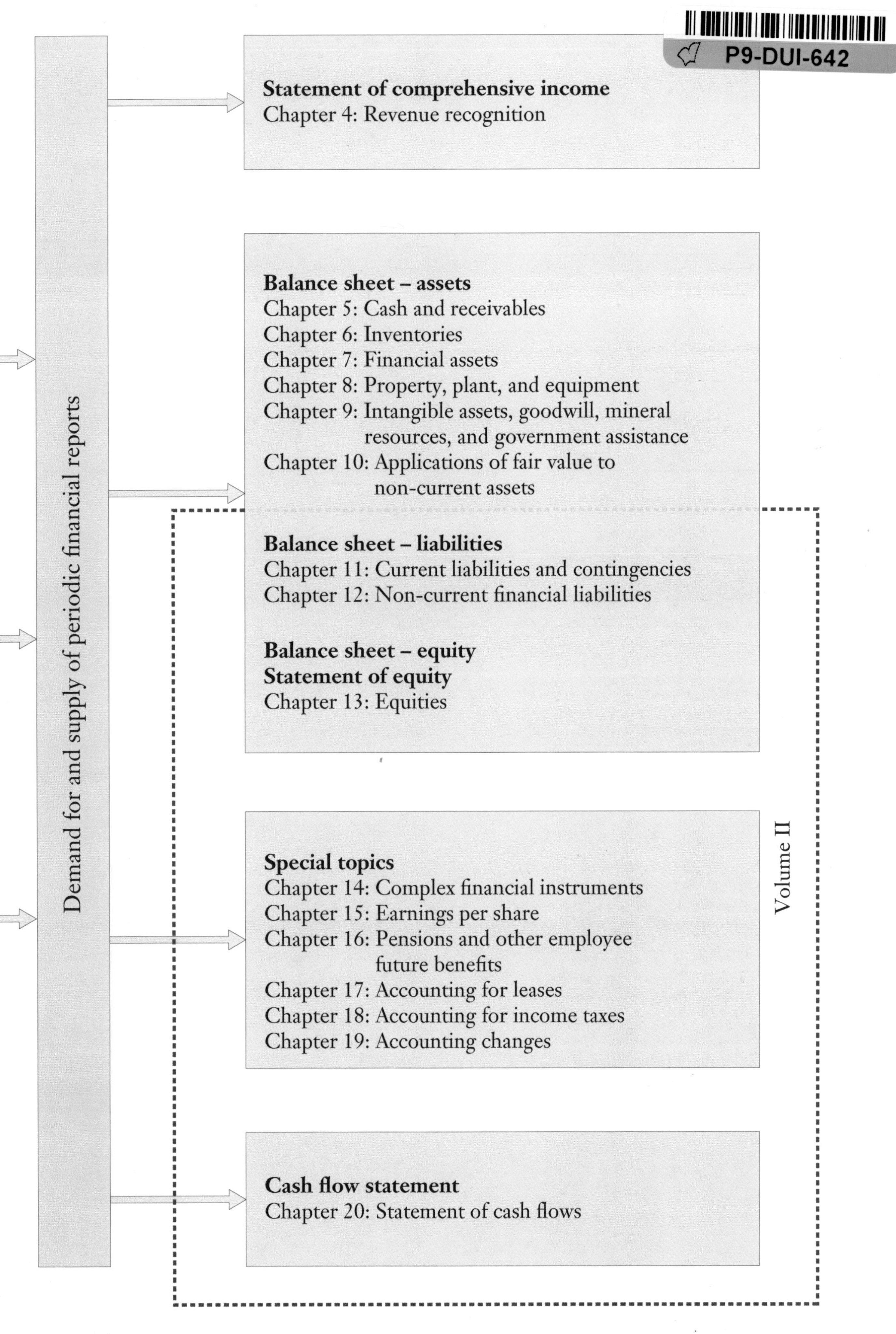

P9-DUI-642
Demand for and supply of periodic financial reports
Statement of comprehensive income
Chapter 4: Revenue recognition
Balance sheet – assets
Chapter 5: Cash and receivables
Chapter 6: Inventories
Chapter 7: Financial assets
Chapter 8: Property, plant, and equipment
Chapter 9: Intangible assets, goodwill, mineral resources, and government assistance
Chapter 10: Applications of fair value to non-current assets
Balance sheet – liabilities
Chapter 11: Current liabilities and contingencies
Chapter 12: Non-current financial liabilities
Balance sheet – equity
Statement of equity
Chapter 13: Equities
Special topics
Chapter 14: Complex financial instruments
Chapter 15: Earnings per share
Chapter 16: Pensions and other employee future benefits
Chapter 17: Accounting for leases
Chapter 18: Accounting for income taxes
Chapter 19: Accounting changes
Cash flow statement
Chapter 20: Statement of cash flows
Volume II

INTERMEDIATE ACCOUNTING

FOURTH EDITION

INTERMEDIATE ACCOUNTING

FOURTH EDITION

KIN LO
University of British Columbia

GEORGE FISHER
Douglas College

WITH CONTRIBUTIONS BY

TREVOR HAGYARD
Concordia University

ZVI SINGER
HEC Montréal

Pearson Canada Inc., 26 Prince Andrew Place, North York, Ontario M3C 2H4.

978-0-13-482007-1

1 20

Library and Archives Canada Cataloguing in Publication
Lo, Kin, 1970-, author
Intermediate accounting / Kin Lo, George Fisher. — Fourth edition.

Includes index.
Contents: v. 1. Chapters 1-10 – v. 2. Chapters 11-20.
ISBN 978-0-13-482008-8 (v. 1 : softcover).–ISBN 978-0-13-482007-1 (v. 2: softcover)

1. Accounting–Textbooks. I. Fisher, George, 1957-, author II. Title.

HF5636.L6 2019 657'.044 C2018-903284-7

Kin:

In memory of my mother, who did not have the benefit of schooling, but gave me the freedom to question, unconditional support of my pursuits, and the humility to know that there is always more to learn.

George:

My passion for teaching has been richly rewarded by many opportunities including the privilege of co-authoring this text. I dedicate this book to my wife, Gail, and my family, friends, colleagues, and students who have encouraged me along the way.

About the Authors

Kin Lo, PhD, FCPA, FCA is the Senior Associate Dean—Students at the Sauder School of Business, University of British Columbia. He holds the CPA Professorship in Accounting established by the Chartered Professional Accountants of British Columbia (CPABC). After receiving a Bachelor of Commerce from the University of Calgary, he articled at PricewaterhouseCoopers and subsequently earned his doctorate from the Kellogg School of Management at Northwestern University in Chicago in 1999. His research has been published in the most important accounting journals, including *The Accounting Review*, *Journal of Accounting Research*, and *Journal of Accounting and Economics*, and he served as an Associate Editor at the *Journal of Accounting and Economics* from 2003 to 2011.

Since joining UBC in 1999, Professor Lo has taught extensively in intermediate-level financial accounting for undergraduates, as well as master and doctoral-level courses. He has coached numerous winning teams in regional, national, and global case competitions. His outstanding teaching has been recognized by the Killam Teaching Prize. Kin has also been a visiting professor at MIT Sloan School of Management and the University of California at Irvine's Merage School of Business.

Aside from research and teaching, Kin is also active in the professional accounting community, serving on provincial and national committees and contributing as a columnist to the Institute of Chartered Accountants of British Columbia's magazine *Beyond Numbers*. From 2008 to 2011, Professor Lo was a member of the Board of Evaluators for the Chartered Accountants' national Uniform Final Evaluation (UFE). He is a member of the Academic Advisory Council for the Accounting Standards Board of Canada. In recognition of his contributions to accounting education, he was awarded Fellowship by the CPABC in 2013. Kin is also an avid sailor.

George Fisher, MBA, CPA, CGA is the coordinator for the accounting option in the Bachelor of Business Administration degree program offered by Douglas College. He teaches financial reporting in the College's BBA and Post-Degree programs and facilitates financial reporting courses for the Chartered Professional Accountants' Western School of Business.

Mr. Fisher has been actively involved in the development of curriculum for CPA Canada since its inception. His publications for CPA Canada include *IF1, Intermediate Financial Reporting 1*; *IF2, Intermediate Financial Reporting 2*; and *AFR, Advanced Financial Reporting*. Mr. Fisher previously co-led the development of the finance elective for the CPA Professional Education Program.

Mr. Fisher was associated with the Certified General Accountants for more than 15 years in several roles, including authoring the final exams for CGA Canada's Financial Accounting 3 course (Financial Accounting: Liabilities & Equities). Other publications for CGA Canada include the domestic and international versions of *Financial Accounting: Assets (FA2)*, *Financial Accounting: Consolidations and Advanced Issues (FA4)*, and *Corporate Finance Fundamentals (FN1)*.

Brief Contents

Preface		xix
CHAPTER 11	Current Liabilities and Contingencies	517
CHAPTER 12	Non-Current Financial Liabilities	580
CHAPTER 13	Equities	638
CHAPTER 14	Complex Financial Instruments	690
CHAPTER 15	Earnings per Share	750
CHAPTER 16	Pensions and Other Employee Future Benefits	800
CHAPTER 17	Accounting for Leases	840
CHAPTER 18	Accounting for Income Taxes	917
CHAPTER 19	Accounting Changes	966
CHAPTER 20	Statement of Cash Flows	1003
APPENDIX A	Time Value of Money and Simple Valuation Techniques	A1
APPENDIX B	Case Solving, Comprehensive Cases, and Capstone Cases	B2
APPENDIX C	Canadian Tire Corporation 2016 Consolidated Financial Statements	C2
Glossary		G1
Index		I1

Contents

Preface xix

CHAPTER 11 Current Liabilities and Contingencies 517
- A. Introduction 518
- B. Definition, Classification, and Measurement of Liabilities 519
  1. Liabilities defined 519
  2. Recognition 520
  3. Financial and non-financial liabilities 520
  4. Current versus non-current liabilities 520
  5. Initial and subsequent measurement 521
- C. Current Liabilities 522
  1. Trade payables 522
  2. Common non-trade payables 524
  3. Notes payable 529
  4. Credit (loan) facilities 532
  5. Warranties 532
  6. Deferred revenues 534
  7. Customer incentives 535
  8. Other current liabilities 540
- D. Contingencies 542
  1. Contingencies involving potential outflows 543
  2. Contingencies involving potential inflows 546
  3. Treatment of contingencies under ASPE 548
- E. Commitments and Guarantees 549
  1. Commitments 549
  2. Guarantees 550
- F. Presentation and Disclosure 551
- G. Substantive Differences Between Relevant IFRS and ASPE 551
- H. Standards in Transition 551
- I. Summary 552
- J. Answers to Checkpoint Questions 553
- K. Glossary 554
- L. References 554
- M. Problems 555
- N. Mini-Cases 573

CHAPTER 12 Non-Current Financial Liabilities 580
- A. Introduction 581
  1. Overview 581
  2. Financial leverage 582
  3. Debt-rating agencies 583
- B. Common Non-Current Financial Liabilities 584
  1. Notes payable 584
  2. Bonds 585
- C. Initial Measurement 587
  1. Debt exchanged for non-cash assets 588
  2. Debt issued at non-market rates of interest 588
  3. Compound financial instruments 588
  4. Interest rates and how they impact the selling price of bonds 589

5. Determining the sales price of a bond when the market rate of interest is given 591
6. Timing of bond issuance 591
D. Subsequent Measurement 593
1. Effective interest rate 593
2. Amortization using the effective interest method 593
3. Amortization using the straight-line method 598
E. Derecognition 600
1. Derecognition at maturity 600
2. Derecognition prior to maturity 600
3. Derecognition through offsetting and in-substance defeasance 603
F. Putting It All Together—A Comprehensive Bond Example 604
G. Other Issues 606
1. Decommissioning and site restoration obligations 606
2. Off-balance-sheet obligations 609
3. Bonds denominated in foreign currency 610
H. Presentation and Disclosure 612
I. Substantive Differences Between Relevant IFRS and ASPE 613
J. Standards in Transition 613
K. Summary 614
L. Answers to Checkpoint Questions 615
M. Glossary 615
N. References 616
O. Problems 617
P. Mini-Cases 633

CHAPTER 13 Equities 638
A. Introduction 639
B. Components of Equity for Accounting Purposes 640
1. Contributed capital 640
2. Retained earnings 643
3. Accumulated other comprehensive income (AOCI) 643
4. Summary 645
C. Equity Transactions Relating to Contributed Capital 645
1. Issuance of shares (recognition and initial measurement) 646
2. Stock splits (subsequent measurement) 649
3. Reacquisition of shares (derecognition) 649
D. Equity Transactions Relating to Retained Earnings 652
1. Cash dividends 652
2. Stock dividends 653
3. Property dividends (dividends in kind) 654
4. Dividend preference 654
E. Statement of Changes in Equity 656
F. Presentation and Disclosure 658
G. Comprehensive Illustration of Equity Transactions 660
H. Substantive Differences Between Relevant IFRS and ASPE 661
I. Appendix: Par Value Shares and Treasury Shares 662
1. Par value shares 662
2. Treasury shares 663
J. Summary 666
K. Answers to Checkpoint Questions 666
L. Glossary 667
M. References 668
N. Problems 668
O. Mini-Cases 687

CHAPTER 14 Complex Financial Instruments 690
A. Introduction 691
B. Types of Financial Instruments 692
1. Basic financial assets, financial liabilities, and equity instruments 692

2. Derivative financial instruments 693
3. Compound financial instruments 695
C. Accounting for Compound Financial Instruments 696
1. Initial measurement 697
2. Subsequent measurement 698
3. Derecognition of debt prior to maturity or conversion into equity 700
4. Derecognition of debt through exercise of the conversion option 703
5. Derecognition of debt at maturity 705
D. Accounting for Warrants 705
1. Initial measurement 705
2. Subsequent measurement 706
3. Derecognition through exercise of the warrants 706
4. Derecognition when the warrants expire 707
E. Accounting for Stock Compensation Plans 707
1. Employee stock option plans (ESOPs) 708
2. Stock appreciation rights (SARs) 710
F. Presentation and Disclosure 716
G. Substantive Differences Between Relevant IFRS and ASPE 716
H. Appendix: Derivatives and Hedging 717
1. Derivatives—Forwards, futures, and swaps 717
2. Accounting for derivatives 719
3. Hedging overview 720
4. Hedge accounting 722
5. Fair value hedges 722
6. Cash flow hedges 724
I. Summary 726
J. Answers to Checkpoint Questions 726
K. Glossary 727
L. References 728
M. Problems 729
N. Mini-Cases 748

CHAPTER 15 Earnings per Share 750
A. Introduction to Basic and Diluted Earnings per Share 751
B. Calculating Basic EPS 752
1. Numerator: Net income available to ordinary shareholders 753
2. Denominator: Weighted average number of ordinary shares outstanding 755
3. Complicating factors 756
4. Basic EPS 759
C. Calculating Diluted EPS 760
1. Identify all potential ordinary shares 761
2. Compute incremental EPS for all potential ordinary shares 762
3. Rank order incremental EPS 764
4. Sequentially compare incremental EPS to provisional EPS to determine diluted EPS 764
5. Effect of discontinued operations 769
6. Diluted EPS when basic EPS is negative 770
7. Other considerations 771
8. Putting it all together: A comprehensive example 772
D. Presentation and Disclosure 774
1. Presentation 774
2. Disclosure 774
E. Substantive Differences Between Relevant IFRS and ASPE 775
F. Summary 775
G. Answers to Checkpoint Questions 776
H. Glossary 776
I. References 777
J. Problems 778
K. Mini-Cases 797

CHAPTER 16 Pensions and Other Employee Future Benefits 800
A. Introduction 801
B. Nature of Pension Plans 802
1. Defined contribution plans 802
2. Defined benefit plans 803
C. Accounting for Defined Contribution Plans 803
D. Accounting for Defined Benefit Plans 804
1. What to account for in defined benefit plans 806
2. Implementing pension accounting for defined benefit plans 811
3. Presentation and disclosure 816
E. Other Issues 818
1. Settlements 818
2. Asset ceiling 818
3. Multi-employer plans 818
4. Other long-term employee benefits 819
F. A Practical Illustration: Canadian Tire Corporation 819
G. Substantive Differences Between Relevant IFRS and ASPE 821
H. Summary 821
I. Answers to Checkpoint Questions 822
J. Glossary 822
K. References 823
L. Problems 823
M. Mini-Cases 837

CHAPTER 17 Accounting for Leases 840
A. Introduction 842
B. Economics of Leasing 842
C. Classification of Leases—Lessor 846
1. The primary consideration when classifying leases 846
2. Indicators supporting the classification of leases 847
3. Additional considerations for classification of real estate leases 849
D. Accounting for Operating Leases—Lessor 849
E. Accounting for Finance Leases—Lessor 851
1. Recognition and initial measurement 852
2. Subsequent measurement 860
3. Derecognition 864
4. Lessor's preference for classifying leases as finance leases, rather than operating leases 865
F. Presentation and Disclosure of Leases—Lessor 865
1. Presentation 865
2. Disclosure 866
G. Accounting for Leases—Lessee 867
1. Recognition and initial measurement of lease liabilities 867
2. Recognition and initial measurement of right-of-use assets 869
3. Applying the recognition and initial measurement criteria for right-of-use assets and lease liabilities 870
4. Subsequent measurement of lease liabilities 873
5. Subsequent measurement of right-of-use assets 873
6. Applying the subsequent measurement criteria for right-of-use assets and lease liabilities 874
7. Practical expedients 879
8. Derecognition 882
H. Presentation and Disclosure of Leases—Lessee 885
1. Presentation 885
2. Disclosure 885
I. Accounting for Sale and Leaseback Transactions 885
1. Accounting for a sale and leaseback transaction—Sales criteria met 887
2. Accounting for a sale and leaseback transaction—Sales criteria not met 889

J. Substantive Differences Between Relevant IFRS and ASPE 891
1. Lessor's lease capitalization criteria 892
2. Lessor's classification of finance (capital) leases 892
3. Lessee's lease capitalization criteria 892
4. Lessee's discount rate for present value calculations 893
5. Lessee's inclusion of residual value guarantees in the determination of lease payments 893
6. Lessee's accounting for the lease and related non-lease components in the lease contract 893
K. Summary 894
L. Answers to Checkpoint Questions 895
M. Glossary 895
N. References 897
O. Problems 897
P. Mini-Cases 915

CHAPTER 18 Accounting for Income Taxes **917**
A. Introduction 918
B. Methods of Accounting for Income Taxes 919
1. Taxes payable method 920
2. Tax allocation methods 920
3. Summary of alternative approaches 924
C. Applying the Accrual Method: Permanent and Temporary Differences 925
1. Permanent differences 925
2. Temporary differences 927
3. Disposals of depreciable assets 930
4. Schedule for analyzing permanent and temporary differences 933
D. Changes in Tax Rates 934
E. Tax Losses 936
1. Carryback of tax losses 937
2. Carryforward of tax losses 938
F. Measurement: No Discounting for Time Value of Money 940
G. Presentation and Disclosure 940
1. Presentation and disclosure of income tax expense 940
2. Presentation and disclosure of income tax assets and liabilities 941
H. A Practical Illustration: Canadian Tire Corporation 941
I. Substantive Differences Between Relevant IFRS and ASPE 943
J. Summary 944
K. Answers to Checkpoint Questions 945
L. Glossary 945
M. References 946
N. Problems 946
O. Mini-Cases 963

CHAPTER 19 Accounting Changes **966**
A. Types of Accounting Changes 967
1. Changes in accounting policy 967
2. Corrections of errors from prior periods 968
3. Changes in accounting estimates 969
4. Summary 970
B. Treatments for Accounting Changes 971
1. Prospective adjustment 971
2. Retrospective adjustment 973
C. Changes in Accounting Standards 975
D. Implementing Retrospective Adjustments 976
1. Retrospective adjustments involving only presentation 977
2. Retrospective adjustments affecting only temporary accounts 977
3. Retrospective adjustments affecting both permanent and temporary accounts 978
E. Summary 984

F. Answers to Checkpoint Questions 984
G. Glossary 985
H. References 985
I. Problems 985
J. Mini-Case 1002

CHAPTER 20 Statement of Cash Flows **1003**
A. Introduction 1004
B. Presentation of the Statement of Cash Flows 1005
1. Cash and cash equivalents defined 1005
2. Classifying cash flows 1006
3. Format of the statement of cash flows 1010
4. Format of the statement of cash flows under ASPE 1014
C. Preparing the Statement of Cash Flows 1016
1. Sources of information 1017
2. The process—Indirect method 1017
3. The process—Direct method 1027
4. Effects of specific items on the statement of cash flows 1031
5. Putting it all together—Comprehensive examples 1036
D. Presentation and Disclosure 1047
E. Substantive Differences Between IFRS and ASPE 1048
F. Summary 1049
G. Answers to Checkpoint Questions 1049
H. Glossary 1050
I. References 1050
J. Problems 1051
K. Mini-Cases 1075

APPENDIX A Time Value of Money and Simple Valuation Techniques **A1**

APPENDIX B Case Solving, Comprehensive Cases, and Capstone Cases **B2**

APPENDIX C Canadian Tire Corporation 2016 Consolidated Financial Statements **C2**

Glossary **G1**

Index **I1**

Preface

"There is too much material to learn!" is a complaint commonly heard among both students and instructors of intermediate-level financial accounting. The current environment in Canada involving multiple accounting standards certainly adds to the problem. However, this sentiment was prevalent even before the splintering of Canadian generally accepted accounting principles (GAAP) in 2011. So what is the source of the problem, and how do we best resolve it?

Regardless of one's perspective—as an instructor of intermediate accounting, as a student, or as a researcher reading and writing papers—often *the problem of too much content is an illusion.* Instead, the issue is really one of *flow*, not just of words, but of *ideas.* Why does a class, research paper, or presentation appear to cover too much, and why is it difficult to understand? Most often, it is because the ideas being presented did not flow—they were not coherent internally within the class, paper, or presentation, or not well connected with the recipients' prior knowledge and experiences.

Connecting new ideas to a person's existing knowledge and efficiently structuring those new ideas are not just reasonable notions. Modern neuroscience tells us that for ideas to be retained they need to be logically structured and presented in ways that connect with a person's prior knowledge and experiences.

OUR APPROACH

How can we better establish the flow of ideas in intermediate accounting? One way is to apply more accounting theory to help explain the "why" behind accounting standards and practices. Inherently, humans are inquisitive beings who want to know not just how things work, but also why things work a particular way. When students understand "why," they are better able to find connections between different ideas and internalize those ideas with the rest of their accumulated knowledge and experiences.

This approach contrasts with that found in other intermediate accounting textbooks, which present accounting topics in a fragmented way, not only between chapters but within chapters. For example, how is the conceptual framework for financial reporting connected with other ideas outside of accounting? How do the components such as qualitative characteristics relate to the elements of financial statements? Fragmented ideas are difficult to integrate into the brain, which forces students to rely on memorization tricks that work only for the short term. For example, a frequently used memory aid for the conceptual framework is a pyramid; this is a poor pedagogical tool because the concepts within the diagram are not logically connected and the pyramid shape itself has no basis in theory. In contrast, we anchor the conceptual framework on the fundamental notions of economic demand and supply.

Also different from other textbooks, we do not aim to be encyclopedic—who wants to read an encyclopedia? This textbook is designed as a learning tool for students at the intermediate level, rather than as a comprehensive reference source they might use many years in the future. Being comprehensive burdens students with details that are not meaningful to them. At the rate at which standards are changing, books become outdated rapidly, and students should learn to refer to official sources of accounting standards such as the *CPA Canada Handbook*.

ARE INTERMEDIATE ACCOUNTING STUDENTS READY FOR ACCOUNTING THEORY?

Most programs that offer an accounting theory course do so in the final year of their programs, with good reason—concepts in accounting theory are difficult. Thorough exploration of these concepts requires a solid grounding in accounting standards and practices and higher-level thinking skills. However, not exposing students to these concepts earlier is a mistake.

Other management (and non-management) disciplines are able to integrate theory with technical applications. For example, when finance students study investments and diversification, the capital asset pricing model is an integral component. Finance students also learn about firms' capital structure choices in the context of Modigliani and Miller's propositions, the pecking order theory, and so on. Students in operations management learn linear programming as an application of optimization theory. Relegating theory to the end of a program is an exception rather than the rule.

Accounting theory is too important to remain untouched until the end of an accounting program. This text exposes students to the fundamentals of accounting theory in the first chapter, which lays the foundation for a number of *threshold concepts* (see Meyer and Land, 2003[1]).

THRESHOLD CONCEPTS

While by no means perfect, this textbook aims to better establish the flow of ideas throughout the book by covering several threshold concepts in the first three chapters. Threshold concepts in this case are the portals that connect accounting standards and practices with students' prior knowledge and experiences. As Meyer and Land suggest, these threshold concepts will help to *transform* how students think about accounting, help students to *integrate* ideas within and between chapters, and *irreversibly improve* their understanding of accounting. Introducing these concepts is not without cost, because threshold concepts will often be troublesome due to their difficulty and the potential conflict between students' existing knowledge and these new concepts.

The previous two pages of this Preface identify the threshold concepts and the layout of the chapters in both volumes of this text. Crucially, the first chapter in Volume 1 begins with the threshold concepts of *uncertainty* and *information asymmetry*. The need to make decisions under uncertainty and the presence of information asymmetries results in *economic consequences of accounting choice*. Those consequences differ depending on whether the accounting information interacts with *efficient securities markets*. These concepts open up the notion of *supply and demand for accounting information*, which forms the basis of the conceptual frameworks for financial reporting (Chapter 2). Decision making under uncertainty leads to the issues surrounding the *timing of recognition* under accrual accounting (Chapter 3), which in turn lead to the concept of *articulation* between financial statements. Accounting choices having economic consequences leads to considerations of the *quality of earnings* and the potential for earnings management (Chapter 3).

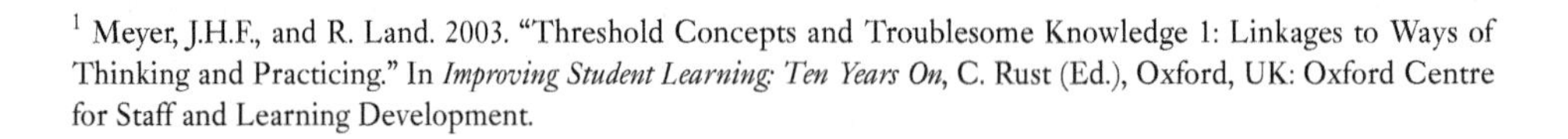

[1] Meyer, J.H.F., and R. Land. 2003. "Threshold Concepts and Troublesome Knowledge 1: Linkages to Ways of Thinking and Practicing." In *Improving Student Learning: Ten Years On*, C. Rust (Ed.), Oxford, UK: Oxford Centre for Staff and Learning Development.

These concepts then resurface at different points in the remaining 17 chapters. For example, the concept of information asymmetry is fundamental to understanding the reasons that companies issue complex financial instruments (Chapter 14). Another example is the important role of the moral hazard form of information asymmetry in explaining why accounting standards do not permit the recognition of gains and losses from equity transactions through net income. A third example is the influence of uncertainty and executives' risk aversion on the accounting standards for pension plans, which allow the gains and losses to flow through other comprehensive income rather than net income. A fourth example is the application of information asymmetry to the accounting for leases (Chapter 17).

As an aid for students, we have put threshold concepts icons in the margin to identify when these concepts appear in the various chapters. To further clarify these icons, we include the name of the specific concept next to the icon to ensure students understand which concepts are being referenced.

ACCOUNTING STANDARDS AND PRACTICES

Along with the unique approach of introducing and integrating theory through the use of threshold concepts, this text also provides thorough coverage of accounting standards and practices typically expected of an intermediate accounting course. This edition reflects recently issued standards, including IFRS 15 on revenue recognition and IFRS 16 on leases.

Following an overview of the four financial statements in Chapter 3 in Volume 1, Chapter 4 explores revenue and expense recognition to highlight the connection financial reporting has to enterprises' value-creation activities. Chapters 5 to 10 in this book then examine, in detail, issues involving the asset side of the balance sheet.

The second volume begins with coverage of the right-hand side of the balance sheet in Chapters 11 to 13. Coverage in Chapters 14 to 18 then turns to special topics that cut across different parts of the balance sheet and income statement: complex financial instruments, earnings per share, pension costs, leases, and income taxes. Chapter 19 revisits the topic of accounting changes introduced in Chapter 3. Chapter 20 examines the statement of cash flows, which integrates the various topics covered in Chapters 4 through 19.

INTEGRATION OF IFRS

This is the first Canadian text written with International Financial Reporting Standards (IFRS) in mind throughout the development process, rather than as an afterthought. For example, we devote a separate chapter (Chapter 10) to exploring issues surrounding asset revaluation and impairment because these issues cut across different asset categories under IFRS. The complete integration of standards in the development process adds to the smooth flow of ideas in and between chapters. Another example is Chapter 10's coverage of agriculture activities, a topic covered by IFRS but not by past Canadian standards.

COVERAGE OF ASPE

While this text puts emphasis on IFRS, we do not neglect Accounting Standards for Private Enterprises (ASPE). Near the end of each chapter is a table that identifies differences between IFRS and ASPE. In contrast to other textbooks, we identify only substantive differences rather than every detail. In addition to the summary table, we carefully choose to discuss certain important differences in the main body of the chapters to create opportunities for understanding the subjective nature of accounting

A·S·P·E

standards, and the advantages and disadvantages of different standards. For example, Chapter 8 discusses the different treatments of interest capitalization under IFRS and ASPE. In the end-of-chapter Problems, we have placed icons in the margin to identify questions that apply ASPE instead of IFRS.

REFERENCE TO ACCOUNTING STANDARDS

Consistent with the threshold concepts described above, this textbook avoids treating accounting standards as written in stone and with only one interpretation. Ultimately, it is people who make accounting standards and it is important to analyze and evaluate the choices that standard setters make to understand the rationale behind the standards. Where appropriate, the chapters provide specific quotations from authoritative standards so that students begin to develop their ability to interpret the standards themselves rather than rely on the interpretations of a third party.

INTEGRATION OF LEARNING OBJECTIVES

To enhance the flow of material, each chapter fully integrates learning objectives from beginning to end. Each chapter enumerates four to six learning objectives that the chapter covers. The end of each chapter summarizes the main points relating to each of these learning objectives. We have also organized the Problems at the end of each chapter to match the order of these learning objectives as much as possible.

INTEGRATION OF CPA COMPETENCIES

To ensure students are building the knowledge and skills required for the CPA designation, we have integrated the competencies outlined in the CPA Competency Map and Knowledge Supplement. Each chapter now opens with a list of CPA Competencies, related Knowledge Items, and levels that are covered in that chapter; also, a master list of all the financial reporting Competencies and Knowledge Items is available at the end of this textbook. As well, all the Problems on MyLab Accounting for *Intermediate Accounting* 4e are mapped to the Competency, Knowledge Item, and level that is being assessed. These features will allow students and faculty interested in the CPA designation to become familiar with the Competency Map and the material covered in the book.

CHAPTER FEATURES

This text contains a number of features that augment the core text. We are mindful that too many "bells and whistles" only serve to distract students, so we have been selective and have included only features that reinforce student learning. The result is an uncluttered page layout in comparison to competing textbooks. We firmly believe that clean design supports clear thinking.

Opening Vignettes

Each chapter opens with a short vignette of a real-world example that students will easily recognize and to which they will relate. These examples range from household names such as Bank of Montreal, Bombardier, and Telus, to car shopping and Christopher Columbus. As mentioned earlier, this connection to existing knowledge and experiences is crucial to learning new concepts. Each vignette serves to motivate interesting accounting questions that are later addressed in the chapter.

Charts and Diagrams

We have chosen to use graphics sparingly but deliberately. These graphics always serve to augment ideas in a logical way rather than to serve as memory "gimmicks" that lack meaning. For instance, it has been popular to use a triangle to organize the Conceptual Framework for financial reporting. We eschew the use of this triangle because that shape has no logical foundation or connection with the Conceptual Framework. Instead, we develop the Conceptual Framework from fundamental forces of supply and demand, so we provide a diagram that illustrates the interaction of those forces:

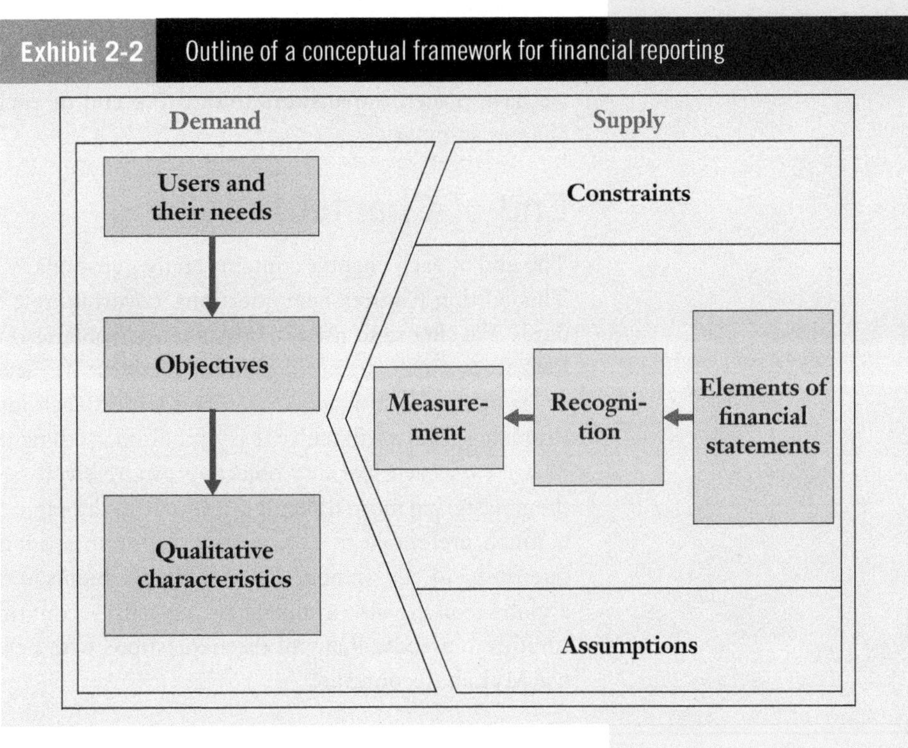

Exhibit 2-2 Outline of a conceptual framework for financial reporting

Feature Boxes

When warranted, we provide more in-depth discussions to reinforce the core message in the main body of the chapters. These discussions often take the form of alternative viewpoints or surprising research results that serve to broaden students' perspectives on the issues. Compass icons identify these feature boxes to denote the different perspectives on various issues.

STILL WAITING...

In 1670, an incorporation under the British royal charter created "The Governor and Company of Adventurers of England trading into Hudson's Bay." The charter gave the company exclusive rights to the fur trade in the watershed flowing into Hudson Bay. The company continues to operate today as The Hudson's Bay Company. It was publicly traded until January 2006, when it was purchased by private equity firm NRDC Equity Partners. In late 2012, the company became a public company again by issuing $365 million of shares on the Toronto Stock Exchange (ticker HBC). If investors had to wait until dissolution to find out what happened to their investments, they would have been waiting for three and a half centuries—and counting!

Checkpoint Questions

At important transitional points in each chapter, we pose "Checkpoint Questions" to engage students to reflect upon what they have just read, and to review, if necessary, before proceeding to the next portion of the chapter. These questions appear at the end of sections and there are five to ten such questions within each chapter. To encourage students to think about these questions before looking at the answers, we have placed the answers toward the end of each chapter, immediately after the chapter summary.

End-of-Chapter Problems

The end of each chapter contains many questions to help students to hone their skills. This edition features new questions, covering new chapter material and IFRS standards. We choose to use a single label—Problems—for all questions. This choice follows from our focus on learning objectives. We have organized the Problems in the order of the learning objectives, and within each learning objective according to the Problem's level of difficulty (easy, medium, or difficult). This approach allows students to work on each learning objective progressively, starting with easier questions and then mastering more difficult questions on the same learning objective. This approach is much preferable to having students jump around from "exercises" to "discussion questions" to "assignments," and so on. Problems in the textbook that are marked with a globe icon are also available on MyLab Accounting. Students have endless opportunities to practise many of these questions with new data and values every time they use MyLab Accounting.

MyLab Accounting Make the grade with **MyLab Accounting:** The problems marked with a globe icon can be found on **MyLab Accounting.** You can practise them as often as you want, and most feature step-by-step guided instructions to help you find the right answer.

Cases

We have included Mini-Cases that are based on, or mimic, real business scenarios. The distinguishing feature of these cases is their focus on decision making. While they are technically no more challenging than Problems, cases bring in additional real-world subjective considerations that require students to apply professional judgment.

We have also included an appendix that provides case solving tips to students, as well as three comprehensive cases that cover topics across multiple chapters. MyLab Accounting for Volume 2 also contains two capstone cases that cover many of the topics in both volumes of the textbook. These cases simulate those on professional exams that require four to five hours of an entry-level professional accountant.

TECHNOLOGY RESOURCES

MyLab Accounting

MyLab delivers proven results in helping individual students succeed. It provides engaging experiences that personalize, stimulate, and measure learning for each student, including a personalized study plan.

MyLab Accounting for the fourth edition of *Intermediate Accounting* includes many valuable assessments and study tools to help students practise and understand key concepts from the text. Students can practise an expanded number of select end-of-chapter questions, review key terms with glossary flashcards, and review accounting fundamentals with the online, interactive Accounting Cycle Tutorial.

MyLab Accounting can be used by itself or linked to any learning management system. To learn more about how MyLab Accounting combines proven learning applications with powerful assessment, visit www.pearson.com/mylab.

Pearson eText

Pearson eText gives students access to their textbook anytime, anywhere. In addition to note taking, highlighting, and bookmarking, the Pearson eText offers interactive and sharing features. Instructors can share their comments or highlights, and students can add their own, creating a tight community of learners within the class.

Learning Solutions Managers

Pearson's Learning Solutions Managers work with faculty and campus course designers to ensure that Pearson technology products, assessment tools, and online course materials are tailored to meet your specific needs. This highly qualified team is dedicated to helping schools take full advantage of a wide range of educational resources, by assisting in the integration of a variety of instructional materials and media formats. Your local Pearson Canada sales representative can provide you with more details on this service program.

SUPPLEMENTS

These instructor supplements are available for download from a password-protected section of Pearson Canada's online catalogue (www.pearsoncanada.ca/highered). Navigate to your book's catalogue page to view a list of those supplements that are available. Speak to your local Pearson sales representative for details and access.

- **Instructor's Solutions Manual.** Created by Kin Lo and George Fisher, this resource provides complete, detailed, worked-out solutions for all the Problems in the textbook.
- **Instructor's Resource Manual.** The Instructor's Resource Manual features additional resources and recommendations to help you get the most out of this textbook for your course.
- **Computerized Test Bank.** Pearson's computerized test banks allow instructors to filter and select questions to create quizzes, tests, or homework. Instructors can revise questions or add their own, and may be able to choose print or online options. These questions are also available in Microsoft Word format.
- **PowerPoint® Presentations.** Approximately 30–40 PowerPoint® slides, organized by learning objective, accompany each chapter of the textbook.
- **Image Library.** The Image Library provides access to many of the images, figures, and tables in the textbook, organized by chapter for convenience. These images can easily be imported into Microsoft PowerPoint® to create new presentations or to add to existing ones.

ACKNOWLEDGMENTS

During the development of this book, we obtained many helpful and invaluable suggestions and comments from colleagues across the country. We sincerely thank the following instructors who took the time and effort to provide thoughtful and meaningful reviews during the development of this fourth edition:

Ann-Marie Cederholm, Capilano University
Kathy Falk, University of Toronto Mississauga
Jing Lu, University of Guelph
Kelsie McKay, Georgian College
Jean Pai, University of Manitoba
Dal Pirot, MacEwan University
Zvi Singer, HEC Montreal
Barbara Wyntjes, University of British Columbia

Thanks also go to Desmond Tsang of McGill University and Zvi Singer of HEC Montreal for their hard work in creating many of the end-of-chapter Mini-Cases, and to Kim Trottier of Simon Fraser University and Trevor Hagyard of Concordia University for their creative and challenging Comprehensive Cases.

We would also like to acknowledge the assistance of the many members of the team at Pearson Canada who were involved throughout the writing and production process: Megan Farrell and Keara Emmett, Acquisitions Editors; Nicole Mellow, Program Manager; Anita Smale, Developmental Editor; Sarah Gallagher, Project Manager; Tania Andrabi, Production Editor; Laura Neves, Copy Editor; and Spencer Snell, Marketing Manager.

Kin Lo
George Fisher

INTERMEDIATE ACCOUNTING

FOURTH EDITION

Smereka/Shutterstock

CHAPTER 11

Current Liabilities and Contingencies

CPA competencies addressed in this chapter:

1.1.2 Evaluates the appropriateness of the basis of financial accounting (Level B)
1.1.4 Explains implications of current trends and emerging issues in financial reporting (Level C)
a. emerging trends in accounting standards and recent updates
1.2.1 Develops or evaluates appropriate accounting policies and procedures (Level B)
1.2.2 Evaluates treatment for routine transactions (Level A)
g. Provisions, contingencies, and current liabilities
k. Financial instruments
p. Foreign currency transactions
1.3.1 Prepares financial statements (Level A)
1.3.2 Prepares routine financial statement note disclosure (Level B)
1.4.1 Analyzes complex financial statement note disclosure (Level C)

Fortis Inc. is the largest investor-owned utility engaged in the distribution of natural gas and electricity in Canada. In British Columbia, the company's operations are known as FortisBC, which includes what was previously Terasen Inc. In 2000, Terasen built a natural gas pipeline through the interior of British Columbia. To facilitate the construction, Terasen purchased millions of dollars in equipment. Terasen carefully structured its affairs to avoid paying the 7% provincial sales tax (PST) on the equipment purchase. Avoidance techniques included reselling the equipment to a trust it created for this purpose and leasing the equipment back.

In 2006, the BC government reassessed Terasen and ordered the company to pay an additional $37.1 million in PST, which through negotiation was reduced to $7 million including interest. In 2009, the trial court found in favour of Terasen, setting aside the BC government's reassessment. In 2010, the BC Court of Appeal upheld the trial court's decision.

How do companies such as Terasen determine the amount to report as liabilities at the end of a fiscal year? What is required when the amount originally estimated is subsequently found to be incorrect? What do they do when the amount owed depends on the outcome of a future event?

LEARNING OBJECTIVES

After studying this chapter, you should be able to:

L.O. 11-1. Describe the nature of liabilities and differentiate between financial and non-financial liabilities.

L.O. 11-2. Describe the nature of current liabilities, and account for common current liabilities including provisions.

L.O. 11-3. Describe the nature of contingent assets and liabilities and account for these items.

L.O. 11-4. Describe the nature of commitments and guarantees and apply accrual accounting to them.

11 CONTENTS

A. INTRODUCTION 518
B. DEFINITION, CLASSIFICATION, AND MEASUREMENT OF LIABILITIES 519
1. Liabilities defined 519
2. Recognition 520
3. Financial and non-financial liabilities 520
4. Current versus non-current liabilities 520
5. Initial and subsequent measurement 521
C. CURRENT LIABILITIES 522
1. Trade payables 522
2. Common non-trade payables 524
3. Notes payable 529
4. Credit (loan) facilities 532
5. Warranties 532
6. Deferred revenues 534
7. Customer incentives 535
8. Other current liabilities 540
D. CONTINGENCIES 542
1. Contingencies involving potential outflows 543
2. Contingencies involving potential inflows 546
3. Treatment of contingencies under ASPE 548
E. COMMITMENTS AND GUARANTEES 549
1. Commitments 549
2. Guarantees 550
F. PRESENTATION AND DISCLOSURE 551
G. SUBSTANTIVE DIFFERENCES BETWEEN RELEVANT IFRS AND ASPE 551
H. STANDARDS IN TRANSITION 551
I. SUMMARY 552
J. ANSWERS TO CHECKPOINT QUESTIONS 553
K. GLOSSARY 554
L. REFERENCES 554
M. PROBLEMS 555
N. MINI-CASES 573

A. INTRODUCTION

In simple terms, liabilities are obligations to provide cash, other assets, or services to external parties. However, this perspective suffices for only simple transactions and balances. For anything other than rudimentary transactions and balances, we must look to the framework and specific standards in IFRS (International Financial Reporting Standards). As alluded to in the opening vignette regarding Terasen, substantive challenges can exist in determining the amount that must ultimately be paid, because a number of different factors can affect the value of the indebtedness. These factors include whether:

- the obligation is a financial liability or a non-financial liability;
- the market rate of interest is different from that recorded in the loan documentation;
- the market rate of interest has changed since the liability was incurred;
- there is uncertainty about the amount owed;

- the amount owed depends upon the outcome of a future event; or
- the obligation is payable in a foreign currency.

In this chapter and the next, we will examine how these (and a few other) factors affect the value of the indebtedness reported on the balance sheet.

The amount reported for liabilities is important to creditors, investors, suppliers, and other interested parties. Information on how much the company owes, to whom, and when the amounts are due is useful to stakeholders in their decisions to lend to the firm, to invest in the company, or to extend trade credit.

CHECKPOINT **CP11-1**

List four factors that can affect the value of indebtedness.

B. DEFINITION, CLASSIFICATION, AND MEASUREMENT OF LIABILITIES

L.O. 11-1. Describe the nature of liabilities and differentiate between financial and non-financial liabilities.

Financial statements convey information. For any communication to be effective, the receiver must understand the sender's message. Imagine that you are travelling in Italy and ask, in English, for directions from a passerby. If that person speaks English, he or she will comprehend your request and will probably assist you. However, a person who speaks only Italian will not understand you and will not be able to help. This example extends to communicating information of a technical nature, like accounting, even when a language barrier does not exist. For instance, if a physicist summarizes Einstein's theory of relativity as "$E = mc^2$; energy and mass are equivalent and transmutable," you will have little chance of understanding what the scientist is trying to communicate unless you know that E stands for energy, m for mass, and c for the speed of light. To enhance the quality of communication between preparers and users of financial statements, IFRS defines key terms in each of its standards. We will now discuss some of these definitions pertaining to liabilities.

1. Liabilities defined

IAS 37 defines a liability as follows:

> ¶10 A ***liability*** is a present obligation of the entity arising from past events, the settlement of which is expected to result in an outflow from the entity of resources embodying economic benefits.[1]

liability A present obligation of the entity arising from past events, the settlement of which is expected to result in an outflow of resources.

This definition includes three key elements, as elaborated on in Chapter 4, of IFRS *The Conceptual Framework for Financial Reporting* paragraphs 4.15–4.17:

1. it is a present obligation;
2. arising from a past event; and
3. expected to result in an outflow of economic benefits.

This is an "and" situation, as all three criteria must be satisfied. Present obligations are normally legally enforceable but can also be constructive in nature (i.e., obligations that arise from recurring practice). For example, a company that regularly repairs products after the warranty period to maintain good customer relations would report a liability for the amounts that are expected to be expended both in the warranty period and in the period afterward.

The past event criterion is fairly straightforward: present obligations normally arise from past events rather than a decision to do something in the future. For example, if you borrowed money from a bank last week—a past event—you incurred a liability and have a present obligation. If, however, last week you simply resolved to borrow money from the bank next week—a decision to do something in the future—you have not yet incurred a liability.

The expectation of an outflow of economic benefits is also relatively uncomplicated. For a liability to exist, you must have an expectation that you are going to give up something in the future to satisfy the creditor's claim. That "something" could be cash, other assets, or services.

CHECKPOINT **CP11-2**

What are the three criteria of liability?

2. Recognition

The definition of a liability set out above does not require that we know the precise amount of the obligation. Just as for assets, recognition on the financial statements requires a liability to be measured reliably (IAS 37 paragraph 14). However, IAS 37 suggests that it would be rare that a reliable estimate cannot be obtained. This presumption differs from the treatment of assets, which may or may not be measured reliably (e.g., research and development).

The fact that there is uncertainty over the amount or timing of payments does not imply that a liability cannot be reliably measured. For example, payments for warranty costs are uncertain in terms of both amount and timing, yet we would still record a liability for the estimated cost of fulfilling warranties. **Provision** is the IFRS terminology used to refer to liabilities that have some uncertainty with respect to the timing or amount of payment. All provisions are liabilities.

provision A liability in which there is some uncertainty as to the timing or amount of payment.

3. Financial and non-financial liabilities

In the introduction, we suggested that whether an obligation is a financial or non-financial liability may impact how the debt is valued. A **financial liability** is a contractual obligation to deliver cash or other financial assets to another party. For example, a loan from the bank is a financial liability of the company that borrowed the money. Non-financial liabilities are obligations that meet the criteria for a liability, but are not financial liabilities. Non-financial obligations are typically settled through the delivery of goods or provision of services. For instance, magazines routinely sell subscriptions for one or more years. The publisher's obligation to the subscribers is to provide the magazine for the agreed-upon period. This is a non-financial liability as it will be settled by delivering the periodical, rather than paying cash or providing a financial asset. Warranties are another example of non-financial liabilities. Lastly, liabilities established by legislation such as income taxes payable and provincial sales tax payable are also non-financial liabilities as they are not contractual in nature. For example, if Terasen had lost the court challenge, its resultant PST payable would have been non-financial in nature.

financial liability A contractual obligation to deliver cash or other financial assets to another party.

From an accounting perspective, it is important to distinguish between financial and non-financial liabilities as IFRS requires that some financial liabilities be measured at their fair value rather than amortized cost. Amortized cost is discussed in Chapter 12.

4. Current versus non-current liabilities

Current liabilities, the primary focus of this chapter, are obligations that are expected to be settled within one year of the balance sheet date or the business's normal operating cycle, whichever is longer. As most businesses' operating cycles are one year or less, we will simply refer to current liabilities as those due in the following year. In addition to these criteria, IAS 1 paragraph 69(d) also requires that an entity shall classify a liability as current if it does not have an unconditional right to defer settlement of the liability for at least 12 months after the reporting period. IAS 1 paragraph 60

current liabilities Obligations that are expected to be settled within one year of the balance sheet date or the business's normal operating cycle, whichever is longer. Also includes liabilities at fair value through profit or loss, and liabilities that the entity does not have an unconditional right to defer settlement of for at least 12 months after the reporting date.

normally requires that current liabilities be presented separately from non-current liabilities in the balance sheet.[2]

In addition to the length of time until maturity, certain financial liabilities classified as "at fair value through profit or loss (FVPL)" would also be reported as current liabilities.[3] In practice, relatively few companies elect to report financial liabilities as FVPL.

Note that the distinction between current and non-current liabilities is made during the financial reporting phase, rather than the recognition process. For example, when a company takes out a five-year bank loan, it *records* a debit to cash and a credit to the loan account in its general ledger. When it prepares its financial statements, it then *reports* the principal amount of the loan due in the twelve months following the balance sheet date as a current liability, and the remainder as a non-current liability.

5. Initial and subsequent measurement

The process of measuring a liability, both initially and subsequently, is determined to some degree by the nature of the obligation. Broadly speaking, we have three categories of indebtedness:

a. *Financial liabilities at fair value through profit or loss (FVPL)* should be initially and subsequently measured at fair value. (Recall that **fair value** is the price that would be received to sell an asset or paid to transfer a liability in an orderly transaction between market participants at the measurement date.) As discussed in Chapter 12, for liabilities at FVPL, transaction costs are expensed.

fair value The price that would be received to sell an asset or paid to transfer a liability in an orderly transaction between market participants at the measurement date.

b. *Other financial liabilities* (i.e., not FVPL) should be initially measured at fair value minus the transaction costs directly associated with incurring the obligation, so this is no different from recording assets at their acquisition cost. However, subsequent to the date of acquisition, financial liabilities not FVPL are measured at amortized cost using the effective interest method. The effective interest method is discussed in Chapters 7 and 12.

Determining the fair value of longer-term debt obligations is usually fairly straightforward. In many cases, fair (market) values are readily available, as in the case for bonds issued in public markets. Determining the fair value of shorter-term liabilities can be more difficult, though, as normally these types of obligations are not actively traded (e.g., a trade payable to a supplier). Moreover, the time to maturity may be uncertain. Recognizing the inherent difficulties in accurately determining the fair value of short-term obligations, and given that the time value of money is usually immaterial in the short term, accounting standards permit many current obligations to be recognized at their maturing face value.

c. *Non-financial liabilities:* The measurement of non-financial liabilities depends on their nature. For instance, warranties are recorded at management's best estimate of the future cost of meeting the entity's contractual obligations.[4] In comparison, the liability for prepaid magazine subscription costs are valued at the consideration initially received less the amount earned to date through performance. For example, a publisher that received \$75 in advance for a three-year subscription and has delivered the magazine for one year would report an obligation of \$50 (\$75 – \$25).

In a somewhat circuitous manner, IFRS provides an exception to the requirement to initially recognize liabilities at fair value and permits many short-term payables to

---

2. Alternatively, liabilities may be presented in order of liquidity when this style will result in more reliable and relevant information. Financial institutions typically use the liquidity style of presentation.

3. There are certain exceptions to this, as set out in IAS 1 paragraph 71. Discussion of these exclusions is beyond the scope of this text.

4. When the time value of money is material, "best estimate" refers to the present value of the obligation (see IAS 37—Implementation Guidance).

be measured at the undiscounted amount owing (the transaction price). Specifically, IFRS 13 stipulates that:

> ¶37 When a quoted price for the transfer of an identical or a similar liability . . . is not available and the identical item is held by another party as an asset, an entity shall measure the fair value of the liability . . . from the perspective of a market participant that holds the identical item as an asset at the measurement date.[5]

IFRS 9 then establishes that:

> ¶5.1.3 . . . an entity shall measure trade receivables that do not have a significant financing component . . . at their transaction price . . . .[6]

The collective consequence of these two standards follows:

- Because quoted prices for most payables are not available, the debtor should measure the obligations in the same way that the corresponding receivables are measured by the creditor.
- The creditor measures accounts receivable at their transaction price (invoice amount), provided that they do not include a significant financing component.
- The exception applies to trade and many other common payables, as the debtor's payable is (usually) reported as a trade receivable by the creditor.

C. CURRENT LIABILITIES

L.O. 11-2. Describe the nature of current liabilities, and account for common current liabilities including provisions.

This chapter includes a wide-ranging discussion of accounting for current liabilities (in this section), contingencies (Section D), and guarantees (Section E). Long-term liabilities will be the focus of the next chapter (Chapter 12). Before getting into the specifics, it may be helpful to think of these obligations in terms of the "big picture," specifically:

- Current liabilities arise from past events: the amount to be paid is known or can be reasonably estimated.
- Contingencies arise from past events: the amount to be paid is determined by future events.
- Financial guarantees arise from contracts previously entered into: the amount to be paid is determined by future events.

The focus of this section is current liabilities, several of which are common across almost all entities and a few that are relatively unique. Some of the more universal obligations include trade payables, notes payable, revolving credit facilities, taxes payable, provision for warranties, and deferred revenues. An entity generally uses its **current assets** such as cash to pay its current liabilities when due.

current assets Assets that are expected to be consumed or sold within one year of the balance sheet date or the business's normal operating cycle, whichever is longer. Also includes assets held primarily for trading purposes.

Distinguishing liabilities that are current from those that are long term is important because financial statement users frequently use this information. For instance, financial analysts often use the relationship between a company's current assets and current liabilities in the form of the current ratio (current ratio = current assets ÷ current liabilities) or working capital (working capital = current assets − current liabilities).

The following discussion examines the pertinent features of current liabilities commonly encountered.

1. Trade payables

trade payables Obligations to pay for goods received or services used.

Trade payables and accruals are obligations to pay for goods received or services used. Trade payables are also commonly called accounts payable or trade accounts payable. Due to processing delays, not all invoices for trade payables will have been received at the end of a year (or another reporting period). In such instances, an enterprise needs to record an "accrued liability" for invoices not yet received but for which

5. Copyright © 2015 IFRS Foundation.

6. Copyright © 2015 IFRS Foundation.

the enterprise owes an obligation. Trade payables and accrued liabilities are typically reported as one total on the balance sheet.

As the amount owing is usually known with a high degree of certainty, there are few concerns that arise in accounting for trade payables. There are two issues that must be considered, however:

THRESHOLD CONCEPT
INFORMATION ASYMMETRY

1. *Cut-off:* Caution must be exercised near the end of a reporting period to ensure that the obligation is properly reported in the period to which it pertains. Intentionally recording obligations in the wrong period so as to manipulate financial results is an example of moral hazard discussed in Chapter 1.
2. *Gross versus net:* Some suppliers offer discounts to encourage early payment by purchasers; for example, they may sell on terms of 2/10 net 30. These trade terms mean that buyers will be entitled to a 2% discount if they pay within 10 days (2/10); otherwise, they have 30 days to pay the face amount of the invoice (net 30). The question is, should a buyer report an obligation for the full value of a $100,000 invoice (for example), or the net amount of $98,000?

The answer is not clear-cut, and both methods are seen in practice. From a theoretical perspective, the net method should be used, as $98,000 is the cost of the goods and $2,000 is the cost of financing the purchase for 20 days (from days 11 to 30). This approach is supported by IAS 2—Inventories, which indicates that trade discounts are deducted in determining the cost of inventory. From a practical perspective, though, it is much easier to record invoices at their face value. Moreover, when the net method is employed and discounts are not availed of, entities should report a finance expense for "purchase discounts lost." Managers are loath to do this, as forgoing available discounts is usually considered a poor business practice.[7] Given these considerations, it is not surprising that businesses predominantly use the gross method, which can usually be justified on the basis of cost–benefit and materiality factors. This is another example of moral hazard. Exhibit 11-1 contrasts the journal entries for the two methods using a hypothetical invoice of $100,000, assuming that the entity uses a perpetual inventory system.

Exhibit 11-1 Supporting journal entries for the gross and net methods for a $100,000 trade payable with terms of 2/10 net 30

	Gross Method		Net Method	
Purchase date				
Dr. Inventory	100,000		98,000	
Cr. Trade payables		100,000		98,000
If discount taken				
Dr. Trade payables	100,000		98,000	
Cr. Cash		98,000		98,000
Cr. Inventory		2,000		
If discount not taken				
Dr. Trade payables	100,000		98,000	
Dr. Purchase discounts lost (an expense)			2,000	
Cr. Cash		100,000		100,000

CHECKPOINT **CP11-3**

From a theoretical perspective, should the gross method or net method be used to account for trade payables?

7. While trade terms vary considerably, 2/10 net 30 is relatively common. The effective cost of not taking this discount on an annualized basis is 44.59% $\{[(1 + 2/98)]^{(365/20)} - 1 \approx 44.59\%\}$.

2. Common non-trade payables

Companies regularly incur obligations of a short-term nature that do not arise from ordering goods or services on account. Since IFRS is largely silent on this matter, the level of aggregation and disclosure differs widely amongst firms. In this section, we explore some of the more common non-trade payables, including sales taxes payable, income taxes payable, dividends payable, and royalty fees payable.

As set out in the opening vignette, Terasen was ultimately successful in avoiding having to pay provincial sales tax on the equipment in question. The company accomplished this by strictly complying with tax laws. Most entities are not so fortunate, however. Indeed, Benjamin Franklin (1706–1790) uttered these famous words: "In this world nothing can be said to be certain, except death and taxes," highlighting the difficulty in avoiding taxes. In Canada, we have many different forms of taxation, but by far the most common are sales taxes and income taxes.

Federal and provincial statutes require people and corporations to pay taxes on various activities such as the purchase of goods and services or earning income. As the obligations to pay are legislative in nature, rather than contractual, they do not fit the definition of a financial liability set out in IAS 32 paragraph 11 and hence are non-financial liabilities. A brief overview of the nature of these obligations follows.

a. Sales taxes payable

Depending on the province or territory they sell in and the nature of the good or service sold, vendors may be required to collect provincial sales tax (PST), goods and services tax (GST), or harmonized sales tax (HST). The vendor is required by law to charge the appropriate amount of tax on the transaction and remit the funds to the government at a later date.

Historically, the provincial governments levied PST and the federal government charged the GST. The result was that in many jurisdictions, businesses were required to collect two separate taxes on most sales. Subsequently, the federal government entered into agreements with some provinces to impose only one tax—the HST—and to split the proceeds on a predetermined basis. As at January 1, 2018, the rates applicable in the provinces and territories were as follows:

Exhibit 11-2 PST, HST, and GST rates as at January 1, 2018

	PST	GST	HST
Alberta	—	5%	—
British Columbia	7%	5	—
Manitoba*	8	5	—
New Brunswick	—	—	15%
Newfoundland	—	—	15
Northwest Territories	—	5	—
Nova Scotia	—	—	15
Nunavut	—	5	—
Ontario	—	—	13
Prince Edward Island	—	—	15
Quebec**	9.975	5	—
Saskatchewan	6	5	—
Yukon	—	5	—

*In Manitoba, the PST is known as the Retail Sales Tax (RST).
**In Quebec, the PST is known as the Quebec Sales Tax (QST).

The concept of sales tax is fairly straightforward: the business charges and collects taxes on its sales and remits the tax portion to the government(s). However, the application is not as simple, for a number of reasons:

- Taxes are not uniformly applied to all sales. Some products are exempt from PST and others are exempt from GST.
- The regulations and rates in each province differ somewhat, including which products are exempt.
- Businesses are generally permitted to deduct the GST and HST paid on their purchases from the GST and HST collected and to remit the net amount owing to the federal government. In the case of PST, goods purchased for resale are exempt from PST, but businesses generally cannot recover PST paid on other purchases.

With the forgoing in mind, we have provided only a general overview here. Exhibit 11-3 illustrates the accounting for the collection and subsequent remittance of PST.

Exhibit 11-3 Journal entries to record the collection and payment of PST related to the sale of goods

Facts: Company A, which employs a perpetual inventory system, sells goods on account for $5,000 in British Columbia subject to 7% PST. The cost of the goods was $3,000. The company subsequently remits the sales taxes collected to the government.

Note: The obligation to collect GST has been deliberately ignored.

Sale of goods		
Dr. Accounts receivable	5,350	
Cr. Sales		5,000
Cr. PST payable ($5,000 × 7%)		350
Dr. Cost of goods sold	3,000	
Cr. Inventory		3,000
Settlement of sales tax obligation		
Dr. PST payable	350	
Cr. Cash		350

With respect to GST and HST, businesses generally establish two general ledger accounts: GST or HST recoverable, and GST or HST payable. Assuming that the company is doing business in an HST jurisdiction, it debits the asset account, HST recoverable, for HST paid on purchases and credits the liability account, HST payable, for HST charged on sales. Typically, the HST collected exceeds the amount paid (because revenues usually exceed expenses), resulting in a current liability for the net amount, payable to the Canada Revenue Agency (CRA). It is possible that the recoverable amount exceeds the payable amount, for example, when a company has paid HST on a large purchase of capital assets. In these circumstances, the net amount would be reported as a current asset for the HST refund due from the CRA. Unlike the general prohibition against the netting of assets and liabilities under IFRS, netting of the tax receivables and payables is acceptable because the relevant tax laws permit this offsetting.

In the forgoing example, for expository purposes, we ignored the GST that the vendor would have had to collect. Exhibit 11-4 is based on the same facts, except that the vendor now also charges and remits the GST.

Exhibit 11-4 Journal entries to record the collection and payment of PST and GST related to the sale of goods

Facts: Company A, which employs a perpetual inventory system, sells goods on account for $5,000 in British Columbia subject to 7% PST and 5% GST. The cost of the goods was $3,000. The company subsequently remits the PST and GST collected to the government.

Sale of goods		
Dr. Accounts receivable	5,600	
Cr. Sales		5,000
Cr. GST payable ($5,000 × 5%)		250
Cr. PST payable ($5,000 × 7%)		350
Dr. Cost of goods sold	3,000	
Cr. Inventory		3,000
Settlement of tax obligations		
Dr. GST payable	250	
Dr. PST payable	350	
Cr. Cash		600

Exhibit 11-5 demonstrates the payment, collection, and remittance of the net amount of HST payable.

Exhibit 11-5a Journal entries to record the payment and collection of HST and the remittance of the net HST payable

Facts: Company B, located in Ontario, purchases $40,000 inventory on account. It subsequently sells goods that cost $30,000 on account for $50,000. And last, the company remits the net HST owing to CRA. The HST rate in Ontario is 13%. The company uses a perpetual inventory system.

Companies pay HST when they purchase goods or services, but they are entitled to recover the amount spent. HST recoverable, an asset account, is debited for the amount of HST paid.

Exhibit 11-5b Purchase of goods

Dr. Inventory	40,000	
Dr. HST recoverable ($40,000 × 13%)	5,200	
Cr. Accounts payable		45,200

Companies collect HST when they sell goods or services and are required to remit this amount to CRA. HST payable, a liability account, is credited for the amount of HST collected.

Exhibit 11-5c Sale of goods

Dr. Accounts receivable	56,500	
Cr. Sales		50,000
Cr. HST payable ($50,000 × 13%)		6,500
Dr. Cost of goods sold	30,000	
Cr. Inventory		30,000

Companies are required to remit the net HST owing to CRA on a monthly, quarterly, or annual basis; the required payment frequency is determined by the estimated amount owed. When the monies are paid to CRA, an entry is made to record the outflow of cash and the reversal of the amounts previously posted to the HST payable and HST recoverable accounts.

Exhibit 11-5d Settlement of sales tax obligation

Dr. HST payable	6,500	
Cr. HST recoverable		5,200
Cr. Cash		1,300

b. Income taxes payable

The federal government and all of the provinces require businesses to pay tax on the taxable income they earn. The amount of income tax owing is normally recorded as a current liability. However, there are additional amounts to be recorded in addition to the amount currently due. Chapter 18 discusses the accounting for income taxes in detail.

c. Dividends payable

When the board of directors declares a cash dividend on ordinary or preferred shares and they are not immediately paid, this gives rise to a dividends payable liability. As dividends are normally paid a short time after declaration date to the shareholders that owned the shares at date of record, they are classified as current liabilities.

As will be discussed in Chapter 13, companies can issue stock dividends instead of paying out a cash dividend. Unlike cash dividends, the declaration of a stock dividend does not give rise to a liability as it does not result in an outflow of resources embodying economic benefits. Moreover, unlike cash dividends, stock dividends are revocable by the board of directors at any time before they are issued. When an entity declares a stock dividend that is not immediately distributable, they may, but are not required to, prepare a journal entry that debits retained earnings and credits stock dividends distributable or some similar equity account.

The declaration of dividends is at the discretion of the board of directors, and therefore undeclared dividends in arrears on cumulative preferred shares are not a liability. Rather, the company's obligation to pay these amounts before any distribution to the ordinary shareholders is disclosed in the notes to the financial statements.

d. Royalty fees payable

A common way of starting a business in Canada is to purchase a franchise. A franchise arrangement is one in which one party (the franchisor) licenses its trademark, business practices, and so on to another (the franchisee). This arrangement gives the franchisee the right to sell specified goods or services in a designated area. For example, Tim Hortons, Subway, and A&W all sell franchises. Most franchise agreements require the franchisee to pay the franchisor a royalty fee based on sales or some other metric and stipulate how often this fee must be paid. Unpaid royalty fees are recorded as a current liability.

Dr. Royalty fee expense	XXX	
Cr. Royalty fee payable		XXX

Royalty fees also arise from other areas such as oil and gas and can be a significant cost of doing business. For example, the oil and gas industry pays the Province of Alberta a (maximum) royalty rate on conventional oil wells of 40% of revenues and 36% on natural gas for the right to extract petroleum products. Royalties are a major expense for publishing companies as well. For example, in 2016, Pearson PLC, the parent company of the publisher of this book, paid £264 million in royalty fees to its various authors.

CHECKPOINT **CP11-4**

Can a company report its HST receivable and payable as a net amount on the balance sheet? Why or why not?

Using Financial Calculators

It is very important that you understand how to use a financial calculator, as you will need one to solve many of the problems related to time value of money (TVM) in this textbook. The financial calculator keystrokes illustrated in this text are for the Texas Instruments BA II Plus, given its widespread use. Most other financial calculators employ a similar methodology; however, the required keystrokes may differ slightly across brands and models of calculators. Refer to your owner's manual for specifics.

The abbreviations that follow are used throughout the text in TVM illustrations:

- PV — present value
- FV — amount due at the end of N periods (i.e., the future value)
- PMT — amount of the annuity payment
- I/Y — interest rate per period
- N — number of periods

To solve for (compute) the unknown variable, press these keys:

CPT **PV** or **CPT** **FV** or **CPT** **PMT** or **CPT** **I/Y** or **CPT** **N**

BGN — You need to set your calculator to BGN to compute the value of an annuity due. An annuity due is one in which the payments are made at the beginning of the period, rather than at the end of the period. To do this, press these keys: **2ND** **PMT** [BGN] **2ND** **ENTER** [SET] **CE/C**. Your calculator's display will now include a small BGN in the upper right-hand corner. Repeat the same keystrokes to return to the mode for payments at the end of the period.

For the sake of consistency, we enter present values (PVs) as negative values using the (+|−) key, and payments (PMTs) and future values (FVs) as positive values. (Alternatively, you can enter PVs as positive values and PMTs and FVs as negative values. What is important is that the signage of the PVs differs from that of the PMTs and FVs, to distinguish cash inflows from cash outflows.)

When you follow the methodology in the text and input PMTs and FVs as positive values, the calculator's output will display a negative number when you solve for PVs, such as −1.074.257426. The negative sign is ignored when using this information to prepare journal entries.

(Continued)

CAUTION: The Texas Instruments BA II Plus allows you to specify the number of interest-compounding periods per year. Before you start, it is important to check the factory default setting by pressing **2ND** **I/Y** [PY] and verify that it shows 1. If the compounding frequency (number of payments per period) is set at 1, do not change it as the examples in this text assume P/Y = 1 and use the number of periods to maturity. If the compounding period is other than P/Y = 1, reset the compounding period to 1 by following the instructions in your owner's manual on how to make this change.

There are a couple of reasons why we set the compounding period at 1 irrespective of the number of payments in a year:

1. Conceptually, many people find it easier to think in terms of an interest rate per period and the number of periods to maturity.
2. It is consistent with the format for entering the data into an Excel spreadsheet.

Note that the **CE/C** key does not clear the data in your TVM registry keys (**N** **I/Y** **PV** **PMT** **FV**). The required keystrokes to clear this information are **2ND** **FV** [CLR TVM].

3. Notes payable

Trade payables arise in the normal course of business. While a legally enforceable obligation, trade payables are not supported by a written promise to pay. In some instances, suppliers who provide credit terms over an extended period require the purchaser to sign a promissory note. Loans from banks and finance companies are invariably supported by a note payable as well. The note will normally detail the amount owed, the interest rate, the payment due date(s), and the security provided. The classification of notes payable as current, non-current, or a combination thereof is based on the payment due date(s). Notes payable can be interest bearing or non-interest bearing.

In the absence of transaction costs, interest bearing notes are recognized at the fair value of the consideration received, which is normally the transaction price.[8] Thus, if an enterprise issues a note to a supplier in exchange for $200,000 in inventory, a liability of $200,000 is recognized, as set out in Exhibit 11-6.

Exhibit 11-6 Interest bearing note

Journal entry to record the issue of an interest bearing note at the market rate of interest		
Dr. Inventory	200,000	
Cr. Note payable		200,000

The fair value of non-interest bearing notes is normally estimated using other valuation techniques, the most common of which is discounted cash flow analysis. For example, if an enterprise issues an $80,000, one-year, non-interest bearing note in exchange for a luxury automobile of uncertain worth, you must determine the note's present value before recording the transaction. Assuming a market rate of

8. This assumes that the interest rate stated in the note approximates the market rate of interest for similar transactions. If otherwise, the value of the note would be determined using present value techniques similar to that discussed in conjunction with valuing non-interest bearing notes.

interest of 5% for similar transactions, the enterprise would recognize an obligation as follows:

Exhibit 11-7 Non-interest bearing note

Journal entry to record the issuance of a non-interest bearing note for $80,000 due in one year

Dr. Automobile	76,190	
Cr. Note payable ($80,000 ÷ 1.05)		76,190

Using a BA II Plus financial calculator: 1 **N** 5 **I/Y** 80000 **FV** **CPT** **PV** → PV = −76,190 (rounded)

As previously discussed, the governing standards do provide a limited exception to the requirement to initially recognize liabilities at fair value. In this respect, many enterprises measure the obligation at the face value of notes originally payable in 90 days or less, and at a discounted amount for longer periods. The aspect of materiality, though, remains a matter of professional judgment and must be applied on a case-by-case basis.

Having established the fundamentals, we will now illustrate accounting for a variety of notes payable from inception to liquidation in Exhibit 11-8.

Exhibit 11-8a Accounting for the issuance and retirement of notes payable[9]

	Scenario 1	Scenario 2	Scenario 3
Face amount of note issued	$100,000	$100,000	$100,000
Date issued	May 1, 2020	May 1, 2020	May 1, 2020
Due date	June 30, 2020	May 1, 2021	May 1, 2021
Interest rate in the note	0%	0%	6% (payable at maturity)
Market rate of interest	6%	6%	6%
Consideration received	Inventory	Equipment	Cash
Company year-end	Dec. 31	Dec. 31	Dec. 31

In the first scenario, the obligation may be recorded at face value, as the effect of discounting is immaterial given the short time to maturity:

Exhibit 11-8b Scenario 1 journal entries

Issuance:	Dr. Inventory	100,000	
	Cr. Note payable		100,000
Payment:	Dr. Note payable	100,000	
	Cr. Cash		100,000

In the second scenario, the fair value of the note must be estimated using present value techniques. The discount is charged to interest expense over the life of the note using the effective interest method.

9. For ease of illustration, assume that the company does not prepare interim financial statements.

Exhibit 11-8c Scenario 2 journal entries

Issuance:	Dr. Equipment	94,340	
	Cr. Note payable ($100,000 ÷ 1.06)		94,340
Using a financial calculator: 1 **N** 6 **I/Y** 100000 **FV** **CPT** **PV** → PV = −94,340 (rounded)			
At year-end:	Dr. Interest expense		
	($94,340 × 6% × [245/365] = $3,799)	3,799	
	Cr. Note payable		3,799
Payment:	Dr. Interest expense		
	($94,340 × 6% × [120/365] = $1,861)	1,861	
	Cr. Note payable		1,861
	Dr. Note payable	100,000	
	Cr. Cash		100,000

In the third scenario, the obligation is recorded at face value, as the stated interest rate in the note approximates the market rate of interest. Interest is accrued at year-end and paid at maturity.

Exhibit 11-8d Scenario 3 journal entries

Issuance:	Dr. Cash	100,000	
	Cr. Note payable		100,000
At year-end:	Dr. Interest expense		
	($100,000 × 6% × [245/365] = $4,027)	4,027	
	Cr. Accrued interest payable		4,027
Payment:	Dr. Interest expense		
	($100,000 × 6% × [120/365] = $1,973)	1,973	
	Dr. Accrued interest payable	4,027	
	Dr. Note payable	100,000	
	Cr. Cash		106,000

Note that when a note payable is issued at a discount, accrued interest arising from the amortization of the discount is credited to the note payable. This process is followed to ensure that at maturity, the book value (carrying cost) of the note equals the face value of the note. At maturity, the borrower then pays the note holder the face amount of the note, which includes the original (discounted) principal amount and accrued interest.

When a note payable is issued at face value (par), however, accrued interest is credited to accrued interest payable. This is because, at maturity, the borrower must pay the note holder the face amount of the note plus all accrued interest not previously paid.

CHECKPOINT **CP11-5**

Why are short-term trade payables normally valued at the original invoice amount rather than the fair value?

4. Credit (loan) facilities

Companies frequently arrange to borrow money on an ongoing basis by way of a line of credit with their financial institution to fund their day-to-day operations. The revolving line of credit can take many forms; a common one is an overdraft facility in which the company can borrow up to an agreed-upon limit and pay interest only on the amount actually borrowed. Lines of credit are particularly useful for seasonal businesses that require financing that varies through the year according to the levels of sales and purchasing activity. The terms of a credit facility, including collateral (security pledged), interest rate and fees, financial covenants (promises), and other conditions, are formally documented in a credit agreement. Most revolving credit facilities are payable on demand, meaning that the company must repay the indebtedness if the bank issues a demand for repayment.

Outstanding lines of credit are a financial liability governed by the various standards covering accounting for financial instruments, including IFRS 7—Financial Instruments: Disclosures, IFRS 9—Financial Instruments, and IAS 32—Financial Instruments: Presentation. Due to the demand feature discussed above, the outstanding amount of the line of credit is reported as a current liability. These standards require that the terms and conditions of the credit facilities be disclosed. Exhibit 11-9 reproduces select disclosures made by Canadian Tire Corporation in its 2016 financial statements pertaining to its credit facilities.

Exhibit 11-9 Excerpts from the 2016 financial statements of Canadian Tire Corporation

Note 22. Long-term debt

Senior and subordinated notes

Asset-backed senior and subordinated notes issued by GCCT are recorded at amortized cost using the effective interest method.

Subject to the payment of certain priority amounts, the senior notes have recourse on a priority basis to the related series ownership interest. The subordinated notes have recourse to the related series ownership interests on a subordinated basis to the senior notes in terms of the priority of payment of principal and, in some circumstances, interest. The asset-backed notes, together with certain other permitted obligations of GCCT, are secured by the assets of GCCT. The entitlement of note holders and other parties to such assets is governed by the priority and payment provisions set forth in the GCCT Indenture and the related series supplements under which these series of notes were issued.

Repayment of the principal of the series 2012-1, 2012-2, 2013-1, 2014-1, and 2015-1 notes is scheduled for the expected repayment dates indicated in the preceding table. Subsequent to the expected repayment date, collections distributed to GCCT with respect to the related ownership interest will be applied to pay any remaining amount owing.

Principal repayments may commence earlier than these scheduled commencement dates if certain events occur including:

- the Bank failing to make required payments to GCCT or failing to meet covenant or other contractual terms;
- the performance of the receivables failing to achieve set criteria; and
- insufficient receivables in the pool.

None of these events occurred in the year ended December 31, 2016.

Debt covenants

The Company has provided covenants to certain of its lenders. The Company was in compliance with all of its covenants as at December 31, 2016.

Source: From Canadian Tire Corporation 2016 Report to Shareholders.

5. Warranties

There are two common forms of warranties: those provided by the manufacturer included in the sales price of the product and those sold separately, either by the manufacturer itself or by another party. Warranties sold separately are accounted for in accordance with IFRS 15—Revenue from Contracts with Customers, which was discussed in Chapter 4 and therefore is not repeated here. The following discussion focuses on manufacturers' warranties.

To facilitate the sale of their merchandise, manufacturers often include a guarantee that products will be free from defects for a specified period, agreeing to fix or replace them if they are faulty. This obligation, known as a **warranty**, is accounted for as a provision in accordance with IAS 37. Recall from above that a provision is an obligation that is uncertain in either amount or timing. Subsequent claims are charged against the provision, rather than expensed.

warranty A guarantee that a product will be free from defects for a specified period.

We estimate warranty provisions using **expected value** techniques, which weight possible outcomes by their associated probabilities. The computations are similar to those used in the accounting for bad debts under the aging method. While neither the exact amount of the obligation nor the customers that will require warranty work are known with certainty, the provision represents a reasonable estimate of the amount that will ultimately be provided in goods or services.

expected value The value determined by weighting possible outcomes by their associated probabilities.

Although we discuss warranties as part of current liabilities, warranties can often extend beyond one year. For example, manufacturers' warranties on automobiles often provide coverage for three, five, or even ten years. The expected obligation for the year following the balance sheet date is reported as a current liability, and the remainder would be classified as a non-current provision. Exhibit 11-10 illustrates the accounting for warranties.

The required provision is estimated using expected value techniques. Note that the provision for all three years of the warranty is expensed in the year of sale. This is an application of the matching concept. At the end of 2020, Vanderhoof will report provisions for warranties on its balance sheet totalling $4,000,000 [(1% + 1% + 2%) × $100,000,000]; $1,000,000 would be reported as a current liability and $3,000,000 as a non-current liability.

Exhibit 11-10a Example of accounting for warranty provisions, accrual basis

Facts:

- In 2020, Vanderhoof Automobile Manufacturing Inc. manufactured and sold $100,000,000 of specialty cars.
- Vanderhoof provides a three-year warranty on each new car it sells.
- Using expected value techniques, Vanderhoof estimates that the cost of the warranty obligation will be 1% of sales in each of the first two years following the year of sale, and 2% of sales in the third year following the sale.
- In 2021, the cost to Vanderhoof of meeting its warranty obligations was $900,000 ($500,000 for parts and $400,000 for labour).

Exhibit 11-10b Journal entry to recognize the provision in 2020

Dr. Warranty expense	4,000,000	
Cr. Provision for warranty payable		4,000,000
$100,000,000 × (1% + 1% + 2%)		

In 2021, the cost to Vanderhoof of meeting its warranty obligations is debited to the provision for warranty payable (liability) account, rather than being charged to an expense account.

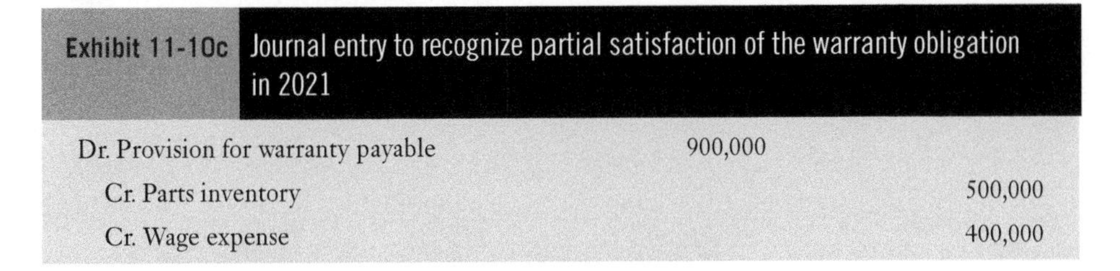

Exhibit 11-10c Journal entry to recognize partial satisfaction of the warranty obligation in 2021

Dr. Provision for warranty payable	900,000	
Cr. Parts inventory		500,000
Cr. Wage expense		400,000

THRESHOLD CONCEPT
TIMING OF RECOGNITION

If management's estimate subsequently proves to be incorrect, the change in estimate should be adjusted prospectively in the manner discussed in Chapters 3 and 19.

If warranty obligations are immaterial, the costs can be expensed as the enterprise incurs them. This is often referred to as the cash basis of accounting for warranties. The process is fairly straightforward, as illustrated in Exhibit 11-11.

Exhibit 11-11 Example of accounting for warranties, cash basis

Facts:

- In 2020, Zander Lynn Inc. manufactured and sold $10,000,000 of steel shelving.
- Zander Lynn provides a one-year unconditional warranty on all shelving it sells.
- Due to the nature of the product, few clients have occasion to claim under the warranty and the amount of the claims are immaterial. Accordingly, Zander Lynn accounts for its warranty expenses using the cash basis.
- During the year, the costs of Zander Lynn meeting its warranty obligations for replacement shelving totalled $10,000.

To recognize partial satisfaction of the warranty obligation in 2020		
Dr. Warranty expense	10,000	
Cr. Shelving inventory		10,000

CHECKPOINT **CP11-6**

What techniques are used to estimate the required provision for warranties?

6. Deferred revenues

deferred revenue A non-financial obligation arising from the collection of revenue that has not yet been earned.

Deferred revenue is a non-financial obligation arising from the collection of assets that have not yet been earned.[10] Many companies require a partial or full payment prior to delivery of the agreed-upon good or service. For instance, if you order a new car from the dealership, you have to make a down payment (deposit) before they will procure the car from the manufacturer. Similarly, when you book a cruise or flight, the travel agent collects the full fare from you before departure. Companies' reasons for requiring full or partial prepayment are many, but include encouraging performance on the purchaser's part and cash flow considerations. Whatever the motive, the accounting outcome is the same: the company has incurred a non-financial obligation alternatively referred to as deferred revenue, unearned revenue, or deposits.

Deferred revenues also arise from customer loyalty programs. This topic is discussed in the section that follows, because the nature of this obligation warrants independent coverage. Moreover, the manner in which the current portion of the customer incentive liability is determined differs from that outlined in the paragraph that follows.

Like warranties, deferred revenues may have both a current and a non-current portion. For example, a publisher that sold a three-year subscription would report its obligation to provide the magazines in the year following the balance sheet date as a current liability and the remainder of the commitment as a non-current liability.

10. See, for example, IFRS 15 paragraph 31, which establishes that revenue is recognized when the goods are delivered.

When the good is delivered or the service provided, the seller recognizes revenue in the normal manner, as per Exhibit 11-12.

Exhibit 11-12 Accounting for deferred revenues

Facts:

- In December 2020, Kamlona Airlines Co. sold a \$3,000 one-way ticket for a flight from Vancouver, British Columbia, to Repulse Bay, Nunavut, for passage in January 2021, and a \$3,500 ticket from Toronto, Ontario, to Kugluktuk, Nunavut, for passage in February 2021.
- Kamlona does not maintain a customer loyalty program.
- The passengers fly at the scheduled time.

Journal entries

To record the receipt of cash in December 2020		
Dr. Cash	6,500	
Cr. Deferred revenue		6,500
To recognize partial satisfaction of the obligation in January 2021		
Dr. Deferred revenue	3,000	
Cr. Revenue		3,000
To recognize satisfaction of the remaining obligation in February 2021		
Dr. Deferred revenue	3,500	
Cr. Revenue		3,500

CHECKPOINT **CP11-7**

Are deferred revenues a financial or non-financial liability? Briefly describe how deferred revenues arise.

7. Customer incentives

Businesses frequently use a number of marketing incentives to increase sales including customer loyalty programs, discount vouchers, and rebates. Accounting for inducements can be complex, and an in-depth study of this material is beyond the scope of this text. What follows is a rudimentary explanation of the requisite accounting for incentives.

a. Customer loyalty programs

Customer loyalty programs include arrangements offered by retail outlets that award points for purchases that can be subsequently redeemed for merchandise, and airline frequent flyer plans that award miles that can then be exchanged for future flights or other products. Popular Canadian loyalty programs include Aeroplan™, HBC Rewards™, Shoppers Optimum™, and Scene™.

Accounting for customer loyalty programs is governed by IFRS 15—Revenue from Contracts with Customers. While the various programs differ in their terms, they share two essential commonalities, specifically:

1. they grant the customer a material right to future goods or services for free or at a discount; and
2. the underlying transaction involves at least two performance obligations: (i) fulfilling the terms of sale; and (ii) meeting the loyalty plan commitment. These collective obligations are commonly referred to as multiple deliverables.

These programs thus give rise to downstream performance obligations as the customer may exercise his material right to the good or service. Factors to be considered when determining the amount of the liability to be recognized for unsatisfied performance obligations include:

- The liability recognized should reflect the portion of the transaction price allocated to the future performance obligation. Recall from Chapter 4, that in the absence of complicating factors, the transaction price is allocated based on the relative observable stand-alone sales price of the performance obligations. This methodology is commonly referred to as the relative fair value method or the proportional method.
- If the stand-alone selling price is not directly observable, then the entity must estimate this amount following the methodology prescribed in paragraphs 78 and 79 of IFRS 15. The supporting application guidance outlined in paragraph B42 provides that the estimate should factor in the likelihood that the option to the material right might not be exercised.
- IFRS 15 normally requires that the transaction price be adjusted to incorporate the effects of the time value of money if the contract includes a significant financing component. IFRS 15 paragraph 62(a), however, exempts customer loyalty programs from this requirement.

There are three common ways to offer awards:

1. Companies offer awards that they supply themselves. This is fairly common in the airline and hotel industry but is not always the case.
2. Businesses offer awards that are supplied by a third party. For example, Air Canada offers Aeroplan miles to its customers. Aeroplan, Canada's largest loyalty marketing program, is owned and operated by an independent firm, Groupe Aeroplan Inc., doing business as Aimia.
3. Firms offer customers the choice of receiving awards from their own programs or those of a third party. For example, guests staying at Marriott hotel properties have the choice of receiving Marriott points or frequent flyer points on their favourite airline.

The accounting for loyalty programs differs depending on who supplies the awards:

- *Awards supplied by the entity:* The transaction price must be allocated to the performance obligations in accordance with the guidance in paragraphs B42 and 73–75 of IFRS 15. Using a frequent flyer point program as an example, the airline ticket has two distinct components. The first is the customer's right to fly the specified route at the indicated time; the second is the customer's material right to services, specifically, the entitlement to miles that can be used toward future travel. From an accounting standpoint, these two sources of revenue must be accounted for separately, as the airline will earn the income at different points in time. Initially, the entire sales price of the ticket is unearned. The airline first earns the flight portion when the passenger takes the scheduled trip, and later earns the award segment when the customer redeems the miles. Exhibits 11-13 and 11-14 illustrate accounting for awards supplied by the entity.
- *Third-party awards:* Accounting for third-party awards does not pose any special challenges. The enterprise records the full transaction price as revenue at the time of sale. In accordance with IFRS 15 paragraph 98, the enterprise contemporaneously recognizes an expense for the cost of purchasing the points from the third party.[11] The rationale here is that the reporting entity has satisfied both performance obligations and has no downstream commitment to the customer after the sale.

[11] A determination must be made as to whether the selling firm is acting as an agent for the third party or as a principal. A full discussion of this aspect is beyond the scope of this text.

- *Choice of awards:* IFRS 15 does not provide specifics on how to account for loyalty programs that provide customers with the option of receiving awards supplied by the entity or a third party, although the supporting Basis for Conclusions briefly discusses this aspect. In the absence of definitive guidance, considerable professional judgment must be exercised. A full discussion of this issue is beyond the scope of this text.

Exhibit 11-13a Accounting for customer loyalty programs, own awards

Facts:

- Frank's Hotel Inc. maintains a customer loyalty program that grants members points for each hotel stay. Members can redeem these points, which do not expire, for future hotel stays.
- In 2020, the hotel received $5,000,000 in room-related revenue and awarded 50,000 points. The proportional stand-alone sales price of the room revenues and the points were estimated to be $4,950,000 and $50,000 respectively. Management anticipated that 80% of the points will eventually be redeemed.
- In 2021, customers redeemed 30,000 of these points.
- In 2022, customers redeemed 10,000 of these points.

The first step is to allocate the transaction price of $5,000,000 to the performance obligations and record the requisite journal entry. While this information has been provided in the question, in practice, management would determine this amount in accordance with the guidance in paragraphs B42 and 73–75 of IFRS 15. Once the stand-alone value of the performance obligations has been estimated, the journal entry to record the sale can be made.

Exhibit 11-13b Journal entry to recognize the room-related revenue in 2020

Dr. Cash	5,000,000	
Cr. Room revenue		4,950,000
Cr. Unearned revenue (award points)		50,000

On an ongoing basis, the amount of award revenue earned during the period must be determined and recorded as a journal entry.

To determine the amount of award revenue to be recognized, the denominator is the number of points expected to be converted rather than the number awarded. The hotel expects 40,000 points to be redeemed (50,000 × 80% = 40,000), so the value per point is $50,000 ÷ 40,000 points = $1.25/point. In 2021, 30,000 points were redeemed × $1.25/point = $37,500.

Exhibit 11-13c Journal entry to recognize award point revenue in 2021

Dr. Unearned revenue (award points)	37,500	
Cr. Award revenue		37,500

In 2022, 10,000 points were redeemed × $1.25/point = $12,500.

Exhibit 11-13d Journal entry to recognize award point revenue in 2022

Dr. Unearned revenue (award points)	12,500	
Cr. Award revenue		12,500

THRESHOLD CONCEPT
TIMING OF RECOGNITION

Management's estimate as to the redemption rate may subsequently prove to be incorrect. If so, the change in estimate must be adjusted prospectively in the manner discussed in Chapters 3 and 19. Exhibit 11-14 illustrates accounting for goods supplied by the entity.

Exhibit 11-14a Accounting for customer loyalty programs, own awards

Facts:

- Amber's Mercantile Ltd. offers a customer loyalty program whereby customers earn points each time they shop. Customers may redeem points, which expire after five years, for a select group of small kitchen appliances.[12]
- In 2020, Amber's sales totalled $20,000,000; cost of goods sold was $16,000,000; and it awarded 50,000,000 points. Management allocated $19,910,000 of the transaction price to the sale of products and the remaining $90,000 to the reward plan obligation. The allocation was based on the relative stand-alone sales price of the component parts, including an expectation that only 60% of the points will be redeemed before expiry.
- In 2020, Amber purchased 3,000 blenders, paying $60,000 cash. The normal retail sales price of the blenders is $30 each.
- In 2021, customers redeemed 10,000,000 points (1,000 blenders).
- In 2022, customers redeemed 9,000,000 points (900 blenders).

Similar to the example in Exhibit 11-13, the first step is to allocate the revenue to the performance obligations and record the requisite journal entry. Recall that $90,000 has been allocated to the reward plan obligation. The purchase of the blenders must also be accounted for.

Exhibit 11-14b Journal entries for 2020

Dr. Cash	20,000,000	
Cr. Sales		19,910,000
Cr. Unearned revenue (award points)		90,000
Dr. Cost of goods sold	16,000,000	
Cr. Inventory		16,000,000
Dr. Award point inventory (blenders)	60,000	
Cr. Cash		60,000

On an ongoing basis, the amount of award point revenue earned during the period must be determined and recorded as a journal entry. Note that the cost of the blenders must also be accounted for at time of delivery.

Amber expects 30,000,000 points to be redeemed (50,000,000 × 60% = 30,000,000), so the value per point is $90,000 ÷ 30,000,000 points = $0.003/point. In 2021, 10,000,000 points were redeemed × $0.003/point = $30,000.

Exhibit 11-14c Journal entry to recognize award point revenue in 2021

Dr. Unearned revenue (award points)	30,000	
Cr. Award revenue		30,000
Dr. Premium expense (1,000 blenders × $20)	20,000	
Cr. Award points inventory (blenders)		20,000

12. For ease of exposition, we will assume that the only appliance available is a multi-speed blender. To acquire the blender, customers must redeem 10,000 points.

In 2022, 9,000,000 points were redeemed × \$0.003/point = \$27,000.

Exhibit 11-14d Journal entry to recognize award point revenue in 2022

Dr. Unearned revenue (award points)	27,000	
Cr. Award revenue		27,000
Dr. Premium expense (900 blenders × \$20)	18,000	
Cr. Award points inventory (blenders)		18,000

The customer incentives obligation will be classified as a current liability if the points (or other tracking mechanisms) can be redeemed at any time at the discretion of the holder. This is in keeping with the requirements set out in paragraph 69 of IAS 1 that stipulate that a liability be reported as current if the entity does not have the unconditional right to defer settlement of the liability for at least 12 months after the reporting period.

b. Discount vouchers (coupons)

On occasion, entities enter into contracts that include the sale of goods or services and a voucher that entitles the customer to a discounted price on future purchases. The essence of the transaction is that the customer is paying in advance for the right to subsequently purchase goods or services at a discount. Providing that the voucher offers the customer a material right,[13] the requisite accounting parallels that of the "awards supplied by the entity" described above. Specifically, the transaction price is allocated to the performance obligations on the basis of relative stand-alone sales prices adjusted for the probability of exercise and any discount that would otherwise be available. Revenue is recognized for the voucher obligation when the future goods or services are delivered or the option expires.

c. Rebates

A *common form of rebate* requires buyers to submit evidence of purchase to the manufacturer, who then sends the customer a cheque for the agreed-upon amount. The manner in which rebates are accounted for differs fundamentally from that of customer loyalty programs. Briefly, accounting for customer loyalty programs involves recognizing a separate performance obligation for the award portion of the sale whereas accounting for rebates does not.

Accounting for rebates is governed by IFRS 15 paragraphs 50–54, "variable consideration." The essence of this guidance is that in accordance with paragraph 48, the transaction price (sales revenue) recognized must be downwardly adjusted for the envisaged rebate to be disbursed (variable consideration). The entity's obligation for rebates is typically estimated using expected value techniques and a liability established for the amount it expects to refund. The refund liability is subsequently updated each reporting period based on current facts and circumstances with the resultant adjustment accounted for prospectively as a change in estimate.

Obligations pertaining to customer incentives will be reported as a current liability if the incentive can be redeemed at any time at the holder's discretion. This classification is in accordance with IAS 1 paragraph 69's requirement to report obligations as current if the entity does not have an unconditional right to defer settlement for at least twelve months after the reporting period.

---

13. The voucher offers a material right if the discount offered is greater than that available to parties that do not enter into a similar contract.

CHECKPOINT **CP11-8**

What are the three common ways of offering customer loyalty awards?

8. Other current liabilities

There are many other types of current liabilities, including certain obligations to employees. Rather than attempt to compile an extended list of other current liabilities, we shall discuss some liabilities that warrant special consideration given their unique characteristics.

a. Obligations denominated in foreign currencies

Accounting for obligations denominated in foreign currency, both current and non-current, is fairly straightforward and governed by IAS 21—The Effects of Changes in Foreign Exchange Rates. The standard requires:

1. translation of the foreign currency debt into the functional currency at the exchange rate evident on the transaction date;[14]
2. revaluation of the foreign currency obligation at the end of a period using the exchange rate at that time; and
3. recognition of the gain or loss from revaluation in the income statement.

Also, as illustrated in Chapter 12, interest is charged to expense at the average rate for the period, rather than the spot rate paid at the time of the payment. The difference is recognized as a gain or loss on the income statement.

Exhibit 11-15 illustrates the accounting for a foreign currency obligation.

Exhibit 11-15a Accounting for a foreign-denominated liability

Facts:

- Langleed Corp. purchases inventory from a US-based company on December 20, 2020. The invoice is for US$80,000. The spot exchange rate at the transaction date was C$1.00 = US$0.92.
- Langleed's year-end is December 31. The spot exchange rate at December 31, 2020, was C$1.00 = US$0.91.
- Langleed paid the obligation in full on January 20, 2021, when the spot exchange rate was C$1.00 = US$0.93.

The trade payable is recorded at its Canadian dollar equivalent using the exchange rate evident (the spot rate) on the date of acquisition.

Exhibit 11-15b Journal entry to recognize the purchase of inventory

Dr. Inventory	86,957	
Cr. Trade account payable		86,957
US$80,000 × C$1.00 / US$0.92 = C$86,957		

[14] The functional currency is that used by the company when it prepares its financial statements. For Canadian companies it is usually the Canadian dollar.

The trade payable must be revalued at the end of each reporting period using the spot rate at period end. The resultant gain or loss is reported on the income statement.

Exhibit 11-15c Journal entry to revalue the obligation at period-end

Dr. Foreign exchange loss	955	
Cr. Trade account payable		955
US\$80,000 × C\$1.00 / US\$0.91 = C\$87,912		
\$87,912 − \$86,957 = \$955 (a loss)		

The trade payable is revalued when settled using the spot rate at payment date. Again, the gain or loss, if any, is reported on the income statement.

Exhibit 11-15d Journal entry to revalue the obligation at payment date and recognize payment of the payable

Dr. Trade account payable	1,890	
Cr. Foreign exchange gain		1,890
Dr. Trade account payable	86,022	
Cr. Cash		86,022
US\$80,000 × C\$1.00 / US\$0.93 = C\$86,022		
\$86,022 − \$87,912 = −\$1,890 (a gain)		

b. Maturing debt to be refinanced

Term loans by their nature have a maturity date. At maturity, the company must either repay the indebtedness or make arrangements with the lender to refinance the obligation. If a company does not reach an agreement to refinance the maturing debt before the balance sheet date, then the obligation is classified as a current liability irrespective of whether arrangements are made to refinance before the financial statements are authorized for issue. In the latter case, the fact that arrangements had been made to refinance the obligation subsequent to the balance sheet date should be disclosed as a non-adjusting event.

c. Non-current debt in default

If the borrower defaults on the terms of a non-current liability before the balance sheet date and, as a result, the loan becomes payable on demand (which is very common), then the obligation is classified as a current liability. If the lender agrees before the end of the reporting period to provide a grace period extending at least 12 months after the balance sheet date, then the loan can be classified as non-current. If agreement is reached after the statement date but before the statements are issued, the liability must be presented as a current obligation with the details of the grace period disclosed (IAS 1 paragraphs 74–76). Exhibit 11-16 summarizes the treatment of maturing debt and loans in default.

Exhibit 11-16 Classification of maturing debt and loans in default

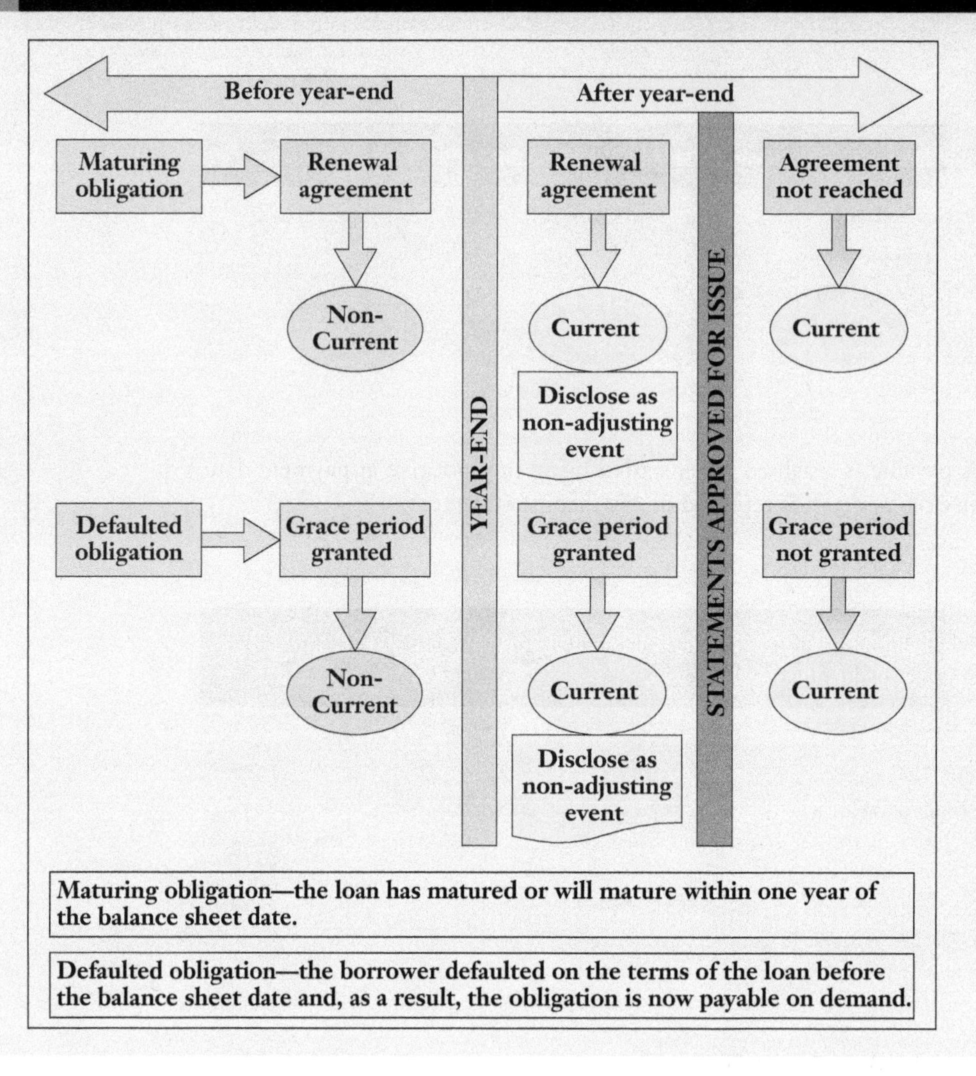

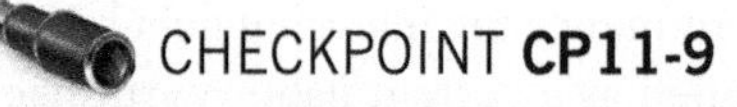
CHECKPOINT **CP11-9**

How are liabilities denominated in foreign currencies accounted for at the transaction date? At period end(s)?

D. CONTINGENCIES

L.O. 11-3. Describe the nature of contingent assets and liabilities and account for these items.

In this section. we address one of the questions posed in the opening FortisBC vignette: what should companies do if the amount owed depends upon the outcome of a future event? The short answer is that they report a contingency. The word "contingent" simply means "depends upon," and a **contingency** is an existing condition that depends on the outcome of one or more future events. A contingency can involve either a potential future inflow or outflow of resources.

contingency An existing condition that depends on the outcome of one or more future events.

The nature of a contingency is that it involves one or more uncertain future outcomes. Thus, the probability of those future outcomes is crucial. IFRS refers to three ranges of probabilities that are important for accounting purposes:

- **Probable:** the probability of occurrence is greater than 50% (IAS 37 paragraph 23).
- **Remote:** is not numerically defined in IAS 37, but rather uses the common meaning of the word, which is "a very low probability." What constitutes "very low" is a matter of professional judgment, with each case being decided on its own merits.
- **Possible:** This term is also not explicitly defined in IAS 37. However, given that IAS 37 defines "probable" as being greater than 50%, "possible" is 50% or less, but greater than remote.[15]

probable The probability of occurrence is greater than 50%.

remote A very low probability of occurrence.

possible A probability of 50% or less, but more than remote.

Exhibit 11-17 The probability continuum

Remote	Possible		Probable
0%	≤50%	>50%	100%

The fact that a contingency depends on a future outcome raises a second issue: are the amounts of the potential future inflows or outflows measurable with sufficient reliability? Amounts that cannot be reliably quantified pose obvious problems for accounting. However, IAS 37 paragraphs 25–26 assert that only in extremely rare cases will the entity be unable to determine a range of possible outcomes by which to estimate the extent of the obligation. The combination of measurability and probability of the future inflows or outflows jointly determines the accounting treatment for the contingency. We first address potential outflows followed by inflows.

1. Contingencies involving potential outflows

Contingent outflows can result in one of three accounting treatments: recognition of a liability through a provision, disclosure of a contingent liability, or no action. (We defer the definition of a contingent liability, as it can only be appreciated after the following discussion.) Exhibit 11-18 summarizes these three possible accounting treatments and the conditions that would lead to those treatments. The cells in the table have been labelled 1 through 6 for ease of reference below.

Exhibit 11-18 Accounting for contingent outflows

		Likelihood		
		Remote	Possible	Probable
Measurability	Obligation can be reliably measured	No action required (3)	Disclose a contingent liability in the notes to the financial statements (2)	Recognize a provision for the obligation (1)
	Obligation cannot be reliably measured (rare)	No action required (6)	Disclose a contingent liability in the notes to the financial statements (5)	Disclose a contingent liability in the notes to the financial statements (4)

15. These are mutually exclusive categories for accounting purposes. In ordinary language, "possible" means anything that has non-zero probability, which includes both remote and probable events.

a. Recognition of a provision

Refer to cell 1 in the top right corner of Exhibit 11-18. When the future outflow is probable and measurable, the enterprise should record a provision for the obligation. For example, a manufacturer that includes a warranty with its products would normally fall into this scenario. The reason is not that there is a greater than 50% probability that any single unit is defective, but that the probability that at least some of the products have a defect is likely to be greater than 50%; the company would also likely have sufficient information to estimate the cost of fulfilling the warranty. Thus, companies generally need to record provisions for warranties, as previously discussed in Section C.

The manner in which the best estimate of a provision is measured is governed to some extent by whether the provision relates to a large population (e.g., a warranty covering thousands of products) or a single item (e.g., a lawsuit). As discussed in Section C, the best estimate of the provision for warranties and other large populations is determined using expected value techniques. The best estimate of the provision required for a single item, such as a lawsuit, though, is less clear.

The IASB is aware of the issue, having written a research paper on the matter in July 2015, observing that the lack of specific guidance in IAS 37 on how to measure provisions for single items has contributed to a wide divergence in practice amongst the "big four" accounting firms. In this respect, observed practices include using: expected value techniques, the most likely outcome approach, and a modified version of the most likely outcome approach.

This issue is not likely to be resolved in the near term as, at the time of writing, the IASB had not scheduled further research on the matter. For the sake of consistency, throughout the text and supporting materials, we will measure all provisions for lawsuits using the most likely outcome approach, as illustrated in the example that follows: Suppose a company is facing a lawsuit and its legal counsel believes that a loss is probable. Counsel estimates that there is a 70% probability that the courts will award $500,000 and a 30% probability that they will award $300,000. In this case, the company will record a $500,000 provision, as this is the most likely outcome.

Note that when there is a range of possibilities and all outcomes in the range are equally likely, the most likely outcome is the midpoint of the range.

b. Disclose as a contingent liability

When the probability of the contingent outflow is only possible but not probable, then the enterprise would not be required to recognize a liability. Instead, it would just disclose the fact that it has a contingent liability. This situation includes cells 2 and 5 in Exhibit 11-18. In addition, even in situations when the future outflows are probable but cannot be measured reliably, the standard criterion for recognition fails; therefore, such situations also result in the disclosure of a contingent liability. This is cell 4 in Exhibit 11-18.

While somewhat obtuse, IFRS defines contingent liabilities as those contingent outflows that require disclosure. Specifically, IAS 37 states the following (with bracket references to Exhibit 11-18 added):

contingent liability Is (a) a possible obligation that arises from past events and whose existence depends on one or more future events; or (b) a present obligation that arises from past events that is not recognized as a liability because: (i) it is not probable that an outflow of economic resources will be required to settle the obligation; or (ii) the amount of the obligation cannot be measured with sufficient reliability.

> ¶10 A ***contingent liability*** is
>
> (a) a possible obligation that arises from past events and whose existence will be confirmed only by the occurrence or non-occurrence of one or more uncertain future events not wholly within the control of the entity; [i.e., cells 2 and 5] or
>
> (b) a present obligation that arises from past events that is not recognized because:
>
> (i) it is not probable that an outflow of resources embodying economic benefits will be required to settle the obligation; [i.e., cells 2 and 5] or

(ii) the amount of the obligation cannot be measured with sufficient reliability [i.e., cell 4].[16]

It should be noted that this use of "contingent liability" in IFRS is narrower than a plain English interpretation of the two words, which is how Canadian standards have traditionally used the term.

c. No action required

When the probability of the contingent outflow is remote, then neither recognition nor disclosure is warranted. This outcome is reflected in cells 3 and 6 in Exhibit 11-18.

Exhibit 11-19 sets out various situations that serve to illustrate how to apply the information just discussed and summarized in Exhibit 11-18.

Exhibit 11-19a Illustrations of accounting for contingencies—Scenario 1

Frieda Hengemolen slips on a wet floor in Fred Geotechnical's office, falls, and breaks her arm. Frieda sues Fred Geotechnical for $2 million in damages, alleging negligence. Fred's law firm advises that the company is indeed liable and that the courts will likely award damages to the litigant. The lawyers suggest that it is very unlikely the courts will award the full $2 million sought as the normal settlement for this type of injury is $100,000 to $200,000. In their opinion, all payouts within this range are equally likely.

Required accounting: In this instance, Fred Geotechnical provides for a $150,000 liability (the midpoint of the range) as the payout is probable and can be reasonably estimated.

Dr. Lawsuit settlement expense	150,000	
Cr. Provision for liability settlement costs		150,000

[($100,000 + $200,000) ÷ 2 = $150,000]

Exhibit 11-19b Illustrations of accounting for contingencies—Scenario 2

Zulu Geothermal sues Roxanne Geothermal for patent infringement, seeking $10 million in damages. The matter is a highly technical one that hinges upon the judge's understanding of the testimony of a number of scientists. Roxanne's lawyers are unsure as to the outcome but estimate the plaintiff's probability of success to be about 25%.

Required accounting: In these circumstances, Roxanne Geothermal discloses the details of the contingent liability in the notes to its financial statements but does not make provision for a liability as payout is estimated to be possible, but not probable.

Exhibit 11-19c Illustrations of accounting for contingencies—Scenario 3

Angel Smith, who lives close to the ZMEX radio station, sues for $100 million in damages. Smith alleges that the radio waves broadcast by ZMEX caused his wife's brain cancer and ultimately led to her death. ZMEX's law firm advises the company that this is a nuisance lawsuit that is unlikely to succeed. They are confident that the courts will dismiss the case as being without merit.

Required accounting: Given these circumstances, ZMEX does not provide for a liability nor does it disclose the lawsuit in the notes to its financial statements. No action is required as the litigant's probability of success is remote.

In the context of contingent liabilities, think back to the opening vignette. The purpose of this anecdote was to illustrate the inherent uncertainty and imprecision in valuing obligations, particularly those for which the amount owing is determined by future events. During the period discussed, Terasen prepared its financial statements in

---

[16] Copyright © 2012 IFRS Foundation.

accordance with Canadian GAAP, which differed from IFRS with respect to accounting for contingencies. Nevertheless, it is instructive to look at how Terasen accounted for this contingent liability during the process:

- 2000–2005: Terasen believed that they owed nothing, a view subsequently upheld by the courts. Moreover, they had not yet been reassessed. As such, they neither provided for a liability nor disclosed a contingency.
- 2006: Terasen was reassessed and ordered to pay $37.1 million in PST and interest. Terasen disclosed a contingent liability in its notes to the financial statements, stating that the amount had not been provided for as they did not believe that they were liable and the company was appealing the settlement. The company initially made a good faith payment of $10 million pending resolution of the appeal, establishing an "other" asset for this amount. The reduction in the assessment to $7 million in March 2007 was disclosed as a subsequent event; the overpayment was refunded to the company, reducing the recorded asset.
- 2007: The province refunded the overpayment to the company. Terasen reduced the asset account and disclosed a contingent liability of $7 million.
- 2008: Terasen disclosed a contingent liability of $7 million.
- 2009: The trial court agreed with Terasen's challenge of the province's assessment. It continued to disclose a contingency, however, as the BC Court of Appeal granted the province leave to appeal.
- 2010: The BC Court of Appeal upheld the trial court's decision. Terasen disclosed this fact and recorded that in the third quarter of 2010 it received a refund from the province of the balance of the good faith payment made in 2006.

Throughout the continuing period of uncertainty, Terasen's note disclosure provides its readers with information to alert them to the possibility that the company may have to expense the reassessed amount at a later date. Note that if Terasen had been ultimately unsuccessful in its appeal, it would have had to record an expense as an error requiring retrospective restatement or as a change in estimate, as discussed in Chapters 3 and 19.[17]

THRESHOLD CONCEPT
TIMING OF RECOGNITION

This example clearly illustrates the inherent uncertainty in estimating liabilities. In the Terasen example cited above, it took the company 10 years and considerable effort to fully resolve that it was not indebted to the provincial government for PST on the equipment used to construct the pipeline.

2. Contingencies involving potential inflows

The treatment of contingent inflows does not mirror the treatment of outflows just described. This difference arises because management has a tendency to overstate assets and income, so the concept previously referred to in IFRS as prudence (conservatism) requires stronger evidence before contingent inflows are recognized.

a. Recognition as an asset

IAS 37 states that contingent assets are not recognized in the financial statements. However, it then reasons that when the realization of income is virtually certain, then the related asset is not a contingent asset and recognition is appropriate. "Virtually certain" is not numerically defined in IAS 37, but the term is commonly used to indicate that something is so nearly true that for most purposes it can be regarded as true. What constitutes "virtually certain" is a matter of professional judgment, with each case being decided on its own merits. In contrast, a contingent outflow would be recognized as a provision if it is simply probable (i.e., greater than 50% likelihood).

17. It is difficult to be definitive as to whether this loss on appeal would result in an error or a change in estimate, because we do not have access to all the facts of the lawsuit. IFRS and the then-current CICA standards both provide that errors include misinterpretation of facts. Based on what we know, if Terasen ultimately lost, it could be because they misinterpreted the facts of the case (an error) or the court had a different interpretation of the law than the company's lawyers (a difference of opinion).

b. Disclose as a contingent asset

When the contingent inflow is probable (>50%), IFRS recommends disclosing a contingent asset, which IAS 37 defines as follows:

> ¶10 A *contingent asset* is a possible asset that arises from past events and whose existence will be confirmed only by the occurrence or non-occurrence of one or more uncertain future events not wholly within the control of the entity.[18]

contingent asset A possible asset that arises from past events and whose existence will be confirmed only by the occurrence or non-occurrence of one or more future events.

c. No action required

When the contingent inflow is not probable, the enterprise should neither recognize nor disclose such potential inflows.

To visualize a situation involving virtual certainty, consider the example of Zedco, in which Zedco is awarded damages by the courts and the judgment is no longer subject to appeal. This constitutes virtual certainty,[19] as Zedco has a legally enforceable right to collect the monies due after the appeal process has been exhausted. Assuming that Zedco was awarded $1,000,000, the company would report a pre-tax gain on the settlement of lawsuit of $1,000,000.

When realization is probable, the contingency should be disclosed in the notes to the financial statements. *Probable* has the same meaning as that described above for the contingent liabilities subsection (i.e., a probability in excess of 50%).

To illustrate the disclosures pertaining to contingencies, Exhibit 11-20 sets out select disclosures made by Canadian Tire Corporation in its 2016 financial statements. Observe how the information provided regarding legal proceedings lacks specifics. This is deliberate and quite normal. Companies do not want to admit liability or disclose the amount provided for in its financial statements as the claimant could potentially use this information against the defendant if the matter goes to trial.

Exhibit 11-20 Excerpts from the 2016 financial statements of Canadian Tire Corporation

Note 19. Contingencies

Legal and regulatory matters

The Company is party to a number of legal and regulatory proceedings. The Company believes that each such proceeding constitutes a routine matter incidental to the business conducted by the Company. The Company cannot determine with certainty the ultimate outcome of all the outstanding claims but believes that the ultimate disposition of the proceedings will not have a material adverse effect on its consolidated earnings, cash flow, or financial position.

Source: From Canadian Tire Corporation 2016 Report to Shareholders. Copyright ©2016 by Canadian Tire Corporation, Limited. Reprinted by permission.

CHECKPOINT **CP11-10**

In the context of accounting for contingencies under IFRS, what do the terms *probable, possible,* and *remote* mean?

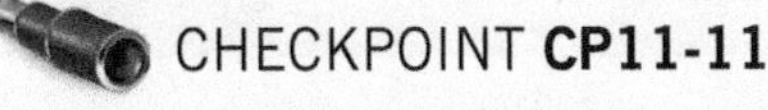

CHECKPOINT **CP11-11**

When is a provision recognized for a contingency involving potential outflows?

---

18. Copyright © 2012 IFRS Foundation.

19. Assuming that the defendant has sufficient assets for Zedco to collect the monies due.

3. Treatment of contingencies under ASPE

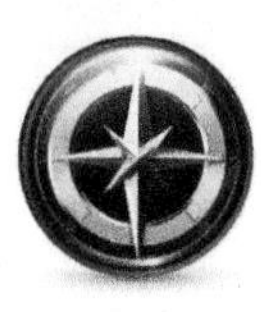

THRESHOLD CONCEPT
TIMING OF RECOGNITION

Similar to IFRS, ASPE treats contingent inflows differently from contingent outflows. However, ASPE (Section 3290) uses a different range of probabilities for future events. Instead of "probable," ASPE uses the word "likely," which means that the chance of occurrence is high. In common usage, "likely" infers a probability of greater than 50% but is often interpreted as a probability of around 70% in the context of the governing standards. As "high" is not defined in the standards, professional judgment must be exercised with each case being decided on its own merits.

Another difference relates to the terms used to describe contingent inflows and outflows. Whereas IFRS uses terms focused on the balance sheet (contingent assets and liabilities), ASPE focuses on the income statement (contingent gains and losses).

For example, if an enterprise determines that there is an 80% chance of losing a lawsuit, ASPE would require recognition of this contingent loss in the financial statements. If the probability is only 60%, the enterprise would disclose that contingent loss. In this latter case, IFRS would require recognition of a provision because 60% is within the meaning of probable.

A third difference relates to instances when the enterprise is required to recognize a contingent loss and there is a range of estimates for the dollar amount of contingent outflows. Within this range, if there is one estimate that is most probable, the enterprise would use that estimate. However, when no one estimate is better than any other in the range, the enterprise would only need to recognize a contingent loss for the minimum in the range and disclose the remainder. In contrast, under IFRS, the mid-point of the range is the most probable outcome of a range in which no one estimate is better than any other. The example in Exhibit 11-21 contrasts the difference in accounting treatment required by IFRS and ASPE for a particular set of facts.

Exhibit 11-21a Contrasting the required accounting under IFRS and ASPE for a contingent loss when there is a range of estimates of the dollar amount of contingent outflows

Facts:

Frieda Hengemolen slips on a wet floor in Fred Geotechnical's office, falls, and breaks her arm. Frieda sues Fred Geotechnical for $2 million in damages, alleging negligence. Fred's law firm advises that the company is indeed liable and that the courts will likely award damages to the litigant. The lawyers suggest that it is very unlikely the courts will award the full $2 million sought as the normal settlement for this type of injury is $100,000 to $200,000. In their opinion, all payouts within this range are equally likely.

The company's lawyer advises that Fred Geotechnical is liable, hence under ASPE a loss is likely and under IFRS a loss is probable.

Under ASPE, a loss is provided for as payout is likely and can be reasonably estimated. As no one estimate in the range is better than any other, the company need only recognize the minimum in the range—$100,000. Fred Geotechnical is required to disclose the remainder of the contingent outflow in its notes to the financial statements.

Exhibit 11-21b Journal entry under ASPE to provide for the potential outflow

Dr. Lawsuit settlement expense	100,000	
Cr. Lawsuit liability settlement costs		100,000

Under IFRS, a loss is provided for as payout is probable and can be reasonably estimated. The amount of the provision is determined using the most likely outcome, which in this case is the midpoint of the range. As the estimated loss has been provided for, note disclosure is not required.

Exhibit 11-21c Journal entry under IFRS to provide for the potential outflow

Dr. Lawsuit settlement expense	150,000	
Cr. Provision for liability settlement costs		150,000
[($100,000 + $200,000) ÷ 2 = $150,000]		

E. COMMITMENTS AND GUARANTEES

1. Commitments

Companies enter into legally binding contracts, both oral and written, on an ongoing basis. Many of these are mutually unexecuted contracts in that neither party has yet completed any part of the agreement. You may recall from your introductory financial accounting course that we do not report the assets and liabilities that will eventually arise from mutually unexecuted contracts until they meet the IFRS criteria for these items (either assets or liabilities). However, this does not mean that enterprises can ignore mutually unexecuted contracts for accounting purposes. Since commitments require companies to do certain things in the future, users of financial statements should be made aware of these future obligations. Consistent with this demand for information, accounting standards require companies to disclose certain commitments in the notes to the financial statements and to explicitly recognize other commitments on the balance sheet.

L.O. 11-4. Describe the nature of commitments and guarantees and apply accrual accounting to them.

If an enterprise commits to buy property, plant, and equipment, it must disclose this fact (IAS 16 paragraph 74). This requirement applies equally to mutually unexecuted and partially executed contracts.

IAS 37 paragraphs 66–69 require companies to recognize the cost of onerous contracts on the balance sheet, including onerous contracts with customers governed by IFRS 15—Revenue from Contracts with Customers (discussed in Chapter 4). Briefly, an **onerous contract** is one in which the unavoidable costs of fulfilling the contract exceed the benefits expected to be received. Note that the comparison uses the expected future benefits to be received from the goods or services acquired in the contract rather than the current market value of the item. Accordingly, a contract to buy assets for more than the current market price is not necessarily onerous, because the future benefit could be higher. ASPE does not provide specific guidance on this matter.

onerous contract A contract in which the unavoidable costs of fulfilling it exceed the benefits expected to be received.

Exhibit 11-22 illustrates how a drop in the market price may or may not lead to an onerous contract, and whether a liability needs to be recognized in the financial statements.

Exhibit 11-22 Example of onerous contracts

Facts:

- Zeppy Distributors Inc. entered into a non-cancellable contract to buy 100,000 litres of paint for $4 per litre from the manufacturers for resale to retail outlets. Zeppy intends to resell the paint at $5 per litre as it typically charges a 25% markup.
- Subsequent to the contract being entered into, and before delivery is taken, the manufacturer reduces the price to $3 per litre due to weak demand.
- In situation 1, Zeppy must reduce the resale price to $3.75 per litre (the current market price plus the 25% markup) to remain competitive.
- In situation 2, Zeppy is able to maintain the resale price at $5 per litre as it is the sole distributor of the product.

(*Continued*)

Exhibit 11-22 Continued

	Situation 1	Situation 2
Expected economic benefit	100,000 × \$3.75 = \$375,000	100,000 × \$5.00 = \$500,000
Less: Unavoidable costs	100,000 × \$4.00 = 400,000	100,000 × \$4.00 = 400,000
Profit/(loss)	\$ (25,000)	\$100,000
Result	Onerous contract for which the expected loss must be provided	Non-onerous contract

Situation 1 would require the following journal entry:

Dr. Loss on onerous contract	25,000	
Cr. Provision for loss on onerous contract (a liability)		25,000

2. Guarantees

IFRS includes guidance with respect to the measurement and disclosure of guarantees. Guarantees come in many forms, including financial guarantees, performance guarantees, indemnities, and letters of credit. An extended discussion of the various types of indemnities and how to account for each is beyond the scope of this text. However, the following provides a brief discussion of accounting for financial guarantee contracts, and Chapter 14 considers guarantees that meet the definition of a derivative financial instrument.

financial guarantee contract A contract that requires the issuer to make specified payments to reimburse the holder for a loss it incurs because a specified debtor fails to make payment when due.

Appendix A of IFRS 9 defines a **financial guarantee contract** as:

> ¶A . . . a contract that requires the issuer to make specified payments to reimburse the holder for a loss it incurs because a specified debtor fails to make payment when due in accordance with the original or modified terms of a debt instrument.[20]

A common form of guarantee, particularly for two companies under common control, involves one entity (company A) guaranteeing the bank loans of another entity (company B). The essence of the commitment is that if company B defaults upon the loan, company A will pay the creditor the principal and interest due. For accounting purposes, the guarantor (company A) must initially recognize a liability for the fair value of the guarantee of company B's indebtedness (IFRS 9 paragraph 5.1.1).[21] Company A must also disclose details of the guarantee in accordance with IFRS 7:

> ¶B10(c) [An entity shall disclose] the maximum exposure to credit risk [from granting financial guarantees, which] is the maximum amount the entity could have to pay if the guarantee is called on, which may be significantly greater than the amount recognized as a liability.[22]

Refer to Appendix C for the Report to Shareholders of Canadian Tire Corporation for the year ended December 31, 2016. Note 34, Guarantees and commitments, illustrates the company's disclosure pertaining to various guarantees that it has issued.

---

20. Copyright © 2012 IFRS Foundation.

21. Subsequently, the guarantee is measured at the higher of the best estimate to settle and the remaining provision recorded in the financial statements. Discussion of this point is beyond the scope of this text.

22. Copyright © 2012 IFRS Foundation.

F. PRESENTATION AND DISCLOSURE

Throughout the chapter, we have discussed some of the more important presentation and disclosure requirements for current liabilities. The disclosure requirements for liabilities, particularly financial liabilities, are quite complex. Indeed, these wide-ranging requirements are one of the main reasons why the notes to the financial statements of publicly accountable enterprises (PAEs) are so extensive, often in excess of 100 pages!

Disclosure standards that must be observed include the following:

- IAS 1—Presentation of Financial Statements
- IAS 32—Financial Instruments: Presentation
- IAS 37—Provisions, Contingent Liabilities and Contingent Assets
- IFRS 7—Financial Instruments: Disclosures

As many of these requirements apply to both current and non-current obligations, we will defer further discussion of the particulars until Chapter 12.

The Accounting Standards Board (AcSB) has long recognized that such extensive disclosure requirements, while perhaps appropriate for PAEs, are difficult and overly costly for many private companies to comply with relative to the benefits to users. Recognizing the different environments of PAEs and private enterprises, the disclosure requirements in the ASPE standards are substantively reduced.

G. SUBSTANTIVE DIFFERENCES BETWEEN RELEVANT IFRS AND ASPE

ISSUE	IFRS	ASPE
Contingencies—focus on balance sheet or income statement	Standard refers to contingent assets or liabilities.	Classified as contingent gains or losses.
Contingencies—terminology	Contingent assets and contingent liabilities refer to contingencies that are not recognized as provisions.	Contingent gains and contingent losses refer to the potential for gains or losses that depend on future events, irrespective of accounting treatment.
Contingencies—range of estimates for recognition of contingent loss	Use the amount of the most probable outcome in the range. If no estimate in the range is more likely than another, recognize the midpoint of the range as a provision.	Use the amount for the most probable outcome in the range. If no estimate in the range is more likely than another, recognize the minimum value in the range as a contingent loss and disclose remainder.
Customer loyalty programs	IFRS 15 requires sales transactions to be segregated into components: earned revenue arising from the sale of goods or service, and unearned revenue for the obligation to provide an award credit at a later date.	ASPE does not specifically address accounting for customer loyalty programs.
Disclosures for liabilities	Disclosure requirements are complex. Relevant standards that must be observed include IAS 37 and IFRS 7.	Disclosure requirements are much less demanding because users have the ability to obtain additional details from the reporting enterprise.
Onerous contracts	IAS 37 requires companies to provide for the cost of onerous contracts.	ASPE does not specifically address accounting for onerous contracts.

H. STANDARDS IN TRANSITION

In May 2015, the International Accounting Standards Board (IASB) issued an exposure draft (ED) to amend The Conceptual Framework for Financial Reporting. Proposed changes include changing the definition of a liability from *A liability is a present obligation of the entity arising from past events, the settlement of which is expected to result in an outflow from the entity of resources embodying economic benefits*[23] to *A liability is a present obligation of the entity to transfer an economic resource as a result of past events, and that an obligation is a duty or responsibility that the entity has no practical ability to avoid.*[24]

The revisions were approved by the IASB in March 2018. They are effective for annual periods beginning on or after 1 January 2020 for preparers who develop an accounting policy based on the Conceptual Framework.

The immediate impact of the amended definition of a liability is expected to be minimal as the proposed change is minor in nature and as the Conceptual Framework is not a governing standard and does not override specific standards (e.g., IFRS 9 or IAS 37). Moreover, the IASB has advised that it will not automatically change existing standards as a result of amendments made to the Conceptual Framework.

---

[23] Conceptual Framework paragraph 4.4(b). Copyright © 2012 IFRS Foundation.

[24] ED/2015/3 Conceptual Framework paragraph 4.24. Copyright © 2012 IFRS Foundation.

I. SUMMARY

L.O. 11-1. Describe the nature of liabilities and differentiate between financial and non-financial liabilities.

- Liabilities are present obligations of the entity arising from past events that are expected to result in an outflow of resources.
- Financial liabilities are contractual obligations that will be settled in cash or by transferring another financial asset to the creditor.
- A non-financial liability is an obligation that meets the definition of a liability but is not a financial liability. Non-financial liabilities are often settled through the provision of goods or delivery of services.

L.O. 11-2. Describe the nature of current liabilities, and account for common current liabilities including provisions.

- Current liabilities are obligations that are expected to be settled within one year of the balance sheet date or the business's normal operating cycle, whichever is longer. Liabilities at FVPL, and liabilities that the entity does not have an unconditional right to defer settlement of for at least twelve months after the reporting date are also classified as current obligations.
- Current liabilities are reported separately from non-current liabilities in the balance sheet unless they are presented in order of liquidity to provide more reliable and relevant information.

L.O. 11-3. Describe the nature of contingent assets and liabilities and account for these items.

- A contingent liability is:
  - a possible obligation whose existence can be confirmed only by future events that are not wholly controlled by the entity; or
  - it is possible (> remote) but not probable (≤ 50%) that the obligation will have to be paid; or
  - the obligation cannot be measured with sufficient reliability.
- Contingencies that are probable (>50%) are reported as provisions.

- Contingencies that are possible are disclosed in the notes to the financial statements.
- A contingent asset is a possible asset whose existence can be confirmed only by future events that are not wholly controlled by the entity.
- Contingent assets are not recognized in the financial statements. However, when the realization of income is virtually certain, then the related asset is not a contingent asset and its recognition is appropriate.

L.O. 11-4. **Describe the nature of commitments and guarantees and apply accrual accounting to them.**

- Contractual commitments pertaining to the acquisition of property, plant, and equipment must be disclosed.
- Enterprises shall record provisions for onerous contracts, including those arising from IFRS 15—Revenue from Contracts with Customers.
- Enterprises shall record provisions for financial guarantee contracts and disclose such guarantees.

J. ANSWERS TO CHECKPOINT QUESTIONS

CP11-1: Factors that can affect the value of indebtedness include whether:

- the obligation is a financial liability or a non-financial liability;
- the market rate of interest is different from that recorded in the loan documentation;
- the market rate of interest has changed since the liability was incurred;
- there is uncertainty about the amount owed;
- the amount owed depends upon the outcome of a future event; or
- the obligation is payable in a foreign currency.

CP11-2: The three criteria of a liability are that it is (i) a present obligation, (ii) arising from a past event, and (iii) expected to result in an outflow of economic benefits.

CP11-3: From a theoretical perspective, the net method should be used to account for trade payables.

CP11-4: IFRS permits a company to report its HST receivable and payable as a net amount on the balance sheet as relevant tax laws permit this offsetting.

CP11-5: Short-term trade payables are normally valued at the original invoice amount rather than fair value because the effect of discounting is immaterial.

CP11-6: Warranty provisions are estimated using expected value techniques.

CP11-7: Deferred revenues are a non-financial obligation arising from the collection of assets that have not yet been earned.

CP11-8: The three common methods of offering customer loyalty awards are:

1. Companies offer awards that they supply themselves.
2. Businesses offer awards that are supplied by a third party.
3. Firms offer customers the choice of receiving awards from their own programs or those of a third party.

CP11-9: Liabilities are accounted for at the transaction date by translating the foreign currency obligation into the functional currency at the exchange rate evident at the transaction date. The obligation is revalued at period end(s) using the spot exchange rate with the gain or loss reported on the income statement.

CP11-10: The terms *probable, possible,* and *remote,* as they pertain to contingencies, collectively describe the likelihood of a possible liability or asset being confirmed as a liability or asset. Probable is a likelihood of occurrence greater than 50%. Remote has a very low probability of occurring. The likelihood of possible falls between probable and remote.

CP11-11: A provision is recognized for a contingency involving potential outflows when the obligation is both probable and measurable.

K. GLOSSARY

contingency: An existing condition that depends on the outcome of one or more future events.

contingent asset: A possible asset that arises from past events and whose existence will be confirmed only by the occurrence or non-occurrence of one or more future events.

contingent liability: Is (a) a possible obligation that arises from past events and whose existence depends on one or more future events; or (b) a present obligation that arises from past events that is not recognized as a liability because: (i) it is not probable that an outflow of economic resources will be required to settle the obligation; or (ii) the amount of the obligation cannot be measured with sufficient reliability.

current assets: Assets that are expected to be consumed or sold within one year of the balance sheet date or the business's normal operating cycle, whichever is longer. Also includes assets held primarily for trading purposes.

current liabilities: Obligations that are expected to be settled within one year of the balance sheet date or the business's normal operating cycle, whichever is longer. Also includes liabilities at fair value through profit or loss, and liabilities that the entity does not have an unconditional right to defer settlement of for at least 12 months after the reporting date.

deferred revenue: A non-financial obligation arising from the collection of revenue that has not yet been earned.

expected value: The value determined by weighting possible outcomes by their associated probabilities.

fair value: The price that would be received to sell an asset or paid to transfer a liability in an orderly transaction between market participants at the measurement date.

financial guarantee contract: A contract that requires the issuer to make specified payments to reimburse the holder for a loss it incurs because a specified debtor fails to make payment when due.

financial liability: A contractual obligation to deliver cash or other financial assets to another party.

liability: A present obligation of the entity arising from past events, the settlement of which is expected to result in an outflow of resources.

onerous contract: A contract in which the unavoidable costs of fulfilling it exceed the benefits expected to be received.

possible: A probability of 50% or less, but more than remote.

probable: The probability of occurrence is greater than 50%.

provision: A liability in which there is some uncertainty as to the timing or amount of payment.

remote: A very low probability of occurrence.

trade payables: Obligations to pay for goods received or services used.

warranty: A guarantee that a product will be free from defects for a specified period.

L. REFERENCES

Authoritative standards:

IFRS	ASPE Section
IAS 1—Presentation of Financial Statements	1400—General Standards of Financial Statement Presentation 1505—Disclosure of Accounting Policies 1521—Balance Sheet
IAS 21—The Effects of Changes in Foreign Exchange Rates	1651—Foreign Currency Translation
IAS 32—Financial Instruments: Presentation	3856—Financial Instruments
IAS 37—Provisions, Contingent Liabilities and Contingent Assets	3290—Contingencies

IFRS	ASPE Section
IFRS 7—Financial Instruments: Disclosures	
IFRS 9—Financial Instruments	
IFRS 15—Revenue from Contracts with Customers	3400—Revenue

MyLab Accounting Make the grade with **MyLab Accounting:** The problems marked with a 🌐 can be found on **MyLab Accounting.** You can practise them as often as you want, and most feature step-by-step guided instructions to help you find the right answer.

M. PROBLEMS

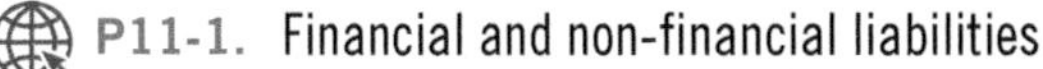

P11-1. Financial and non-financial liabilities (L.O. 11-1) (Easy – 10 minutes)

A list of liabilities follows. For each item, indicate by using the letter F that it is a financial liability or N that it is a non-financial liability. For obligations that are non-financial in nature, briefly explain why they do not meet the criteria of a financial liability.

Item	Liability	Financial or non-financial obligation?	Explanation
1.	Accounts payable		
2.	Warranties payable		
3.	USD bank loan		
4.	Bank overdraft		
5.	Sales tax payable		
6.	Notes payable		
7.	Unearned revenue		
8.	Finance lease obligation		
9.	HST payable		
10.	Bank loan		
11.	Bonds payable		
12.	Obligation under customer loyalty plan		
13.	Income taxes payable		

P11-2. Liabilities defined—the nature of liabilities (L.O. 11-1) (Easy – 10 minutes)

What are the three criteria of a liability? Describe how trade accounts payable meet each of the criteria.

P11-3. Liabilities defined—provisions and financial and non-financial liabilities (L.O. 11-1) (Easy – 10 minutes)

a. Explain what provisions are.
b. Explain what financial liabilities are and how they differ from non-financial liabilities.
c. Provide three examples of financial liabilities and three examples of non-financial liabilities.

P11-4. Measurement

(L.O. 11-1) (Medium – 10 minutes)

a. Identify the three broad categories of liabilities.
b. Explain how each of these three classes of liabilities is initially measured.
c. Explain how each of these three classes of liabilities is subsequently measured.

P11-5. Current and non-current liabilities

(L.O. 11-1) (Medium – 15 minutes)

A list of liabilities follows. For each item, indicate by using the letter C that it will be reported as a current liability, N that it will be reported as a non-current liability, or B that it potentially can be reported as either or both a current and non-current liability. For obligations that you determine to be N or B, briefly explain why this is the case.

Item	Liability	Current or non-current liability, or potentially both?	Explanation
1.	Accounts payable		
2.	Warranties payable		
3.	Deposits		
4.	Bank overdraft		
5.	Sales tax payable		
6.	Bank loan maturing in five years was in default during the year; before year-end, the lender grants a grace period that extends 12 months after the balance sheet date.		
7.	Five-year term loan; amortized payments are payable annually		
8.	Unearned revenue		
9.	Finance lease obligation		
10.	HST payable		
11.	90-day bank loan		
12.	Bond payable that matures in two years		
13.	Obligation under customer loyalty plan. (Customer's discretion as to when to redeem.)		
14.	Income taxes payable		
15.	Bank loan that matures in five years that is currently in default		
16.	Three-year bank loan that matures six months after the balance sheet date		

P11-6. Accounting for taxes payable

(L.O. 11-2) (Easy – 15 minutes)

Select transactions and other information pertaining to Best City in the World Inc. (BCW) are detailed below.

Facts:

a. BCW is domiciled in Charlottetown, Prince Edward Island, and all purchases and sales are made in PEI.
b. The HST rate in PEI is 15%.
c. The balances in BCW's HST recoverable account and HST payable account as at March 31, 2018, were $8,000 and $12,000, respectively.
d. BCW uses a perpetual inventory system.
e. Inventory is sold at a 100% markup on cost. (Cost of goods sold is 50% of the sales price.)

Select transactions in April 2018:

1. BCW purchased inventory on account at a cost of $10,000 plus HST.
2. BCW purchased equipment on account at a cost of $20,000 plus HST. It paid an additional $500 plus HST for shipping.

3. Cash sales—BCW sold inventory for $15,000 plus HST.
4. Sales on account—BCW sold inventory for $20,000 plus HST.
5. BCW paid the supplier in full for the equipment previously purchased on account.
6. At the end of the month, BCW remitted the net amount of HST owing to the Canada Revenue Agency.

Required:

Prepare summary journal entries to record the transactions detailed above.

P11-7. Accounting for taxes payable (L.O. 11-2) (Easy – 15 minutes)

Select transactions and other information pertaining to Bedford Whale Watching Ltd. (BWW) are detailed below.

Facts:

a. BWW is domiciled in Bedford, Nova Scotia, and all purchases and sales are made in Nova Scotia.
b. The HST rate in Nova Scotia is 15%.
c. The balances in BWW's HST recoverable account and HST payable account as at June 30, 2018, were $20,000 and $22,000, respectively.
d. BWW uses a perpetual inventory system.
e. Inventory is sold at a 25% markup on cost. (Cost of goods sold is 80% of the sales price.)

Select transactions in July 2018:

1. BWW purchased inventory on account at a cost of $12,000 plus HST.
2. BWW purchased equipment on account at a cost of $15,000 plus HST. It paid an additional $1,000 plus HST for installation.
3. Cash sales—BWW sold inventory for $11,000 plus HST.
4. Sales on account—BWW sold inventory for $20,000 plus HST.
5. BWW paid the supplier in full for the inventory previously purchased on account.
6. At the end of the month, BWW remitted the net amount of HST owing to the Canada Revenue Agency.

Required:

Prepare summary journal entries to record the transactions detailed above.

P11-8. Accounting for taxes payable (L.O. 11-2) (Easy – 10 minutes)

Select transactions and other information pertaining to Anne Greene Ltd. (AGL) are detailed below.

Facts:

a. AGL is domiciled in Vancouver, British Columbia, and all purchases and sales are made in BC.
b. The PST rate in BC is 7%. The GST rate is 5%.
c. The balances in AGL's GST recoverable, GST payable, and PST payable accounts as at June 30, 2018, were $21,000, $20,000, and $22,000, respectively.
d. AGL uses a perpetual inventory system.
e. Inventory is sold at a 50% markup on cost. (Cost of goods sold is two-thirds of the sales price.)

Select transactions in July 2018:

1. AGL purchased inventory on account at a cost of $40,000 plus applicable taxes.
2. Cash sales—AGL sold inventory for $30,000 plus applicable taxes.
3. Sales on account—AGL sold inventory for $60,000 plus applicable taxes.

4. At the end of the month, AGL remitted the net amount of GST owing to the Canada Revenue Agency and the PST payable to the Province of BC.

Required:

Prepare summary journal entries to record the transactions detailed above. Remember that the purchase of inventory for resale is PST exempt.

P11-9. Accounting for taxes payable (L.O. 11-2) (Easy – 10 minutes)

Select transactions and other information pertaining to Flat and Fertile Inc. (FFI) are detailed below.

Facts:

a. FFI is domiciled in Saskatoon, Saskatchewan, and all purchases and sales are made in Saskatchewan.
b. The PST rate in Saskatchewan is 6%. The GST rate is 5%.
c. The balances in FFI's GST recoverable, GST payable, and PST payable accounts as at August 31, 2018, were $15,000, $18,000, and $14,000, respectively.
d. FFI uses a perpetual inventory system.
e. Inventory is sold at a 33.33% markup on cost. (Cost of goods sold is 75% of the sales price.)

Select transactions in September 2018:

1. FFI purchased inventory on account at a cost of $30,000 plus applicable taxes.
2. Cash sales—FFI sold inventory for $20,000 plus applicable taxes.
3. Sales on account—FFI sold inventory for $50,000 plus applicable taxes.
4. At the end of the month, FFI remitted the net amount of GST owing to the Canada Revenue Agency and the PST payable to the Province of Saskatchewan.

Required:

Prepare summary journal entries to record the transactions detailed above. Remember that the purchase of inventory for resale is PST exempt.

P11-10. Accounting for dividends payable (L.O. 11-2) (Easy – 10 minutes)

The following is an extract from the balance sheet of Zach's Fashion Inc. as at December 31, 2018:

Shareholders' equity	
Preferred shares A, 100,000 authorized, $1 per share cumulative dividend, 10,000 issued and outstanding	$ 100,000
Preferred shares B, 50,000 authorized, $2 per share non-cumulative dividend, 5,000 issued and outstanding	50,000
Common shares, 1,000,000 authorized, 100,000 issued and outstanding	1,000,000
Retained earnings	5,000,000
Total shareholders' equity	$6,150,000

The company did not declare dividends in 2018.

On October 31, 2019, Zach's declared the stipulated dividends, including arrears, on both classes of preferred shares payable on December 1, 2019, to holders of record at the close of business on November 15, 2019.

On November 30, 2019, Zach's declared cash dividends of $0.50 per common share payable on January 2, 2020, to holders of record at the close of business on December 15, 2019.

Required:

Prepare the journal entries to record the above transactions.

P11-11. Accounting for dividends payable (L.O. 11-2) (Easy – 15 minutes)

The following is an extract from the balance sheet of Belle Beauty World Ltd. as at December 31, 2020:

Shareholders' equity	
Preferred shares A, 500,000 authorized, $2 per share non-cumulative dividend, 50,000 issued and outstanding	$ 500,000
Preferred shares B, 250,000 authorized, $1 per share cumulative dividend, 25,000 issue and outstanding	250,000
Common shares, 10,000,000 authorized, 200,000 issued and outstanding	2,000,000
Retained earnings	10,000,000
Total shareholders' equity	$12,750,000

The company did not declare dividends in either 2019 or 2020.

On October 31, 2021, Belle declared the stipulated dividends, including arrears, on both classes of preferred shares payable on December 1, 2021, to holders of record at the close of business on November 15, 2021.

On November 30, 2021, Belle declared a 10% common stock dividend distributable on January 2, 2022, to holders of record at the close of business on December 15, 2021. The ex-dividend price of the common shares was $15.

Required:

Assume that Belle elects to prepare a journal entry at the declaration date of the common stock dividend to record the impending distribution. Prepare the journal entries to record the above transactions.

P11-12. Accounting for royalty fees payable (L.O. 11-2) (Easy – 15 minutes)

Gail Fisher signed a five-year franchise agreement that gave her the exclusive rights to sell Yummy Yoghurt products in Cloverdale, British Columbia. The terms of the agreement require Gail to pay the franchisor an ongoing royalty of 5% of net sales and contribute 2.5% to the sales and marketing fund, both payable on the 15th of the month following. Gail opened the Yummy Yoghurt franchise on January 1; her sales for the first three months of operations were $50,000, $40,000, and $60,000, respectively.

Required:

Prepare journal entries to record the accrual and payment of the franchise and marketing fees.

P11-13. Accounting for royalty fees payable (L.O. 11-2) (Easy – 15 minutes)

On January 1, 2020, Zoe Robinson signed a 10-year franchise agreement that gave her the exclusive rights to sell Exclaim donuts in Halifax, Nova Scotia. The terms of the agreement required Zoe to pay the franchisor $30,000 upon signing the agreement and an ongoing royalty of 7% of net annual sales payable on the 15th of the month following year-end. Zoe must also contribute 2% of her net sales to the Exclaim sales and marketing fund, again, payable on the 15th of the month following year-end.

Zoe amortizes the franchise agreement on a straight-line basis. Her net sales for 2020 totalled $850,000.

Required:

a. Assuming that Zoe prepares adjusting entries only at year-end, prepare the required journal entries for 2020.
b. Prepare journal entries to record the payment of the franchise and marketing fee in 2021.

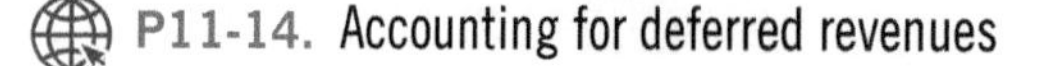

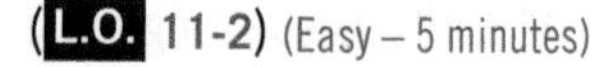

P11-14. Accounting for deferred revenues (L.O. 11-2) (Easy – 5 minutes)

Build a Deck Inc. (BaD) enters into a contract to construct six decks adjacent to a commercial building. The purchaser has agreed to pay $5,000 for each deck (total $30,000). The terms of the contract call for a 40% deposit ($2,000 per deck) at time of contract signing and payment of the balance ($3,000 per deck) as each deck is completed. The contract is signed on October 1, 2018. Two decks are completed in 2018 and the balance in 2019. BaD has a December 31 year-end. The cost to BaD of constructing each deck is $2,300, which it pays in cash.

Required:

a. Prepare summary journal entries for 2018 and 2019.
b. What is the balance in the deferred revenue account as at December 31, 2018?

P11-15. Accounting for warranties (L.O. 11-2) (Easy – 5 minutes)

In 2020, Surinder's Cycles Inc. sold 2,500 mountain bikes. For the first time, Surinder offered an in-store, no-charge, two-year warranty on each bike sold. Company management estimates that the average cost of providing the warranty is $5 per unit in the first year of coverage and $7 per unit in the second year.

Surinder's warranty-related expenditures totalled $6,000 for labour costs during 2020.

Required:

a. Prepare the summary journal entry to recognize Surinder's warranty expense in 2020.
b. Prepare the summary journal entry to recognize the warranty service provided in 2020.
c. Determine the total provision for warranty obligations that will be reported on the company's balance sheet at year-end. Assuming that all sales transactions and warranty service took place on the last day of the year, how much of the warranty obligation will be classified as a current liability? As a non-current liability?
d. Briefly explain why companies offer warranties.

P11-16. Accounting for obligations denominated in foreign currencies (L.O. 11-2) (Easy – 5 minutes)

On May 1, 2020, St. John's Brew Supplies Inc. borrowed US$140,000 from its bank. St. John's year-end is December 31, 2020. Exchange rates were as follows:

May 1, 2020	US$1.00 = C$1.02
December 31, 2020	US$1.00 = C$1.04
Average rate May 1–December 31, 2020	US$1.00 = C$1.03

Required:

Prepare the required journal entries to record receipt of the loan proceeds and for any adjustments required at year-end. Ignore the interest component.

P11-17. Accounting for obligations denominated in foreign currencies (L.O. 11-2) (Easy – 5 minutes)

On December 15, 2020, Edmonton Horticulture Society (EHS) received supplies on account costing US$5,000 from a vendor in Washington. EHS, whose year-end is December 31, 2020, paid the account in full on January 3, 2021. Exchange rates were as follows:

December 15, 2020	US$1.00 = C$1.04
December 31, 2020	US$1.00 = C$1.01
January 3, 2021	US$1.00 = C$1.03
Average rate December 15, 2020–January 3, 2021	US$1.00 = C$1.02

Required:

Assume that EHS expenses supplies when received. Prepare the required journal entries to record receipt of the supplies inventory, any adjustment required at year-end, and payment of the accounts payable.

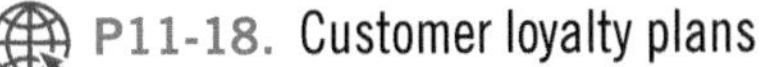

P11-18. Customer loyalty plans (L.O. 11-2) (Easy – 5 minutes)

The text identified three primary methods of offering awards under customer loyalty programs:

1. The company offers awards that it supplies itself.
2. The business offers awards supplied by an outside party.
3. The firm offers its customers a choice of receiving awards from its own program or those of a third party.

Required:

a. When is revenue recognized for the award portion of sales under the first two methods?
b. How is the price charged for the good or service in the underlying transaction apportioned between sales revenue and awards revenue?

P11-19. Accounting for rebates (L.O. 11-2) (Easy – 10 minutes)

In an effort to stimulate lagging sales of its XLT converter, Rchris Enterprises Corp. implemented a manufacturer's rebate program at the beginning of 2020. Customers that purchased an XLT converter during the year were entitled to a $50 rebate providing that they submitted an application that included a copy of the sales receipt and the UPC code.

During the year, Rchris sold 20,000 converters for $600 cash each. The company only provided rebates to 30% of the purchasers, however, as it routinely rejected applications that were not properly supported by the required documentation. The cost of manufacturing the XLT converter is $350 per unit. The rebate cheques were all mailed on January 15, 2021.

Required:

a. Prepare summary journal entries to record revenue in 2020.
b. Prepare summary journal entries to record the issuance of the rebate cheques in 2021.

P11-20. Accounting for notes payable (L.O. 11-2) (Easy – 10 minutes)

On January 1, 2018, GFF Transmission Services Co. issued a $20,000, non-interest bearing note, due on January 1, 2019, in exchange for a custom-built computer system. The fair value of the computer system is not easily determinable. The market rate of interest for similar transactions is 4%. GFF's year-end is December 31.

Required:

a. Prepare the journal entry to record the issuance of the note payable.
b. Prepare the journal entry to record the accrual of interest at December 31, 2018, assuming that GFF prepares adjusting entries only at year-end.
c. Prepare the journal entry to record the retirement of the note payable on January 1, 2019.

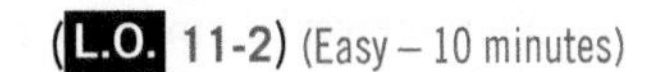

P11-21. Accounting for notes payable (L.O. 11-2) (Easy – 10 minutes)

On July 1, 2020, XXT Satellite Services Ltd. purchased an automobile for $40,000. The company paid $10,000 cash and issued a $30,000 note due on April 1, 2021, for the balance. The 4% annual interest rate on the note, which approximates the market rate of interest for similar transactions, is payable at maturity. XXT's year-end is December 31. XXT computes interest accruals based on the number of days, rather than months.

Required:

a. Prepare the journal entry to record the purchase of the automobile.
b. Prepare the journal entry to record the accrual of interest at December 31, 2020, assuming that XXT prepares adjusting entries only at year-end.
c. Prepare the journal entry to record the retirement of the note payable on April 1, 2021.

P11-22. Accounting for notes payable and trade payables

(L.O. 11-2) (Medium – 25 minutes)

North Vancouver Laundry (NVL) recently hired Fred as its payable clerk, a position that has been vacant for two months. While the other accounting staff have taken care of the "must do's," there are a number of transactions that have not yet been recorded:

November 15, 2020—NVL purchases $5,000 of supplies inventory on account. The terms offered are 2/10 net 30.

November 22, 2020—NVL purchases 10 washing machines. NVL issues an $8,000 non-interest bearing note payable due on January 15, 2021.

November 28, 2020—NVL borrows $20,000 from the bank. NVL signs a demand note for this amount and authorizes the bank to take the interest payments from its bank account. Interest is payable monthly at 4% per annum.

December 18, 2020—NVL purchases $4,000 supplies inventory on account. The terms offered are 2/10 net 30.

December 21, 2020—NVL purchases 15 dryers. NVL issues a $10,000 non-interest bearing note payable due on December 21, 2021.

December 22, 2020—Fred pays the November 15, 2020, and December 18, 2020, invoices.

December 31, 2020—Fred processes the payroll for the month. The gross payroll is $20,000; $1,400 is withheld for the employees' Canada Pension Plan and Employment Insurance premiums.[25]

Other information

- NVL uses the net method to record accounts payable.
- NVL's year-end is December 31 and interim statements are normally prepared on a monthly basis.
- Due to the vacancy in the accounting department, NVL's latest interim statements are for the period ended October 31, 2020. The necessary accruals were made at that time.
- The market rate of interest for NVL's short-term borrowings is 4%.

Required:

a. Prepare journal entries to record the documented events and the necessary accruals for the months of November and December. Compute interest accruals based on the number of days, rather than months.
b. Contrast the gross and net methods of accounting for trade payables.

P11-23. Accounting for notes payable and trade payables

(L.O. 11-2) (Medium – 20 minutes)

Ranjit was recently hired by Montreal Express Inc. (MEI) to assist its payable clerk in bringing the accounts up to date. Ranjit was asked to record the following transactions:

August 15, 2020—MEI purchases a new inventory monitoring system. MEI issues a $6,000 non-interest bearing note payable, due on October 15, 2020.

August 18, 2020—MEI borrows $10,000 from the bank by way of demand note. MEI pledges its accounts receivable as security and authorizes the bank to take the interest payments from its bank account. Interest is payable on the last day of each month at 4% per annum.

August 21, 2020— MEI purchases $8,000 inventory on account. The terms offered are 3/10 net 45.

---

25. While accounting for payroll withholding taxes has not been dealt with explicitly in this chapter, it is assumed that students were introduced to this topic in their introductory accounting course(s).

September 20, 2020—MEI purchases a waste management system. MEI issues an $8,000, non-interest bearing note payable due on September 20, 2021.
September 23, 2020—MEI purchases $3,000 in inventory on account. The terms offered are 3/10 net 45.
September 24, 2020—Ranjit pays the August 21 and September 23 invoices.
September 30, 2020—Ranjit accrues for unbilled utilities totalling $1,700.

Other information

- MEI uses the gross method to record accounts payable.
- MEI's year-end is December 31 and in-house, interim statements are normally prepared on a monthly basis.
- MEI's latest interim statements are for the period ended July 31, 2020. The necessary accruals were made at that time, except that MEI only records depreciation expense at year-end.
- The market rate of interest for MEI's unsecured short-term borrowings is 5%.

Required:

Prepare journal entries to record the documented events and the necessary accruals for the months of August and September. Compute interest accruals based on the number of days, rather than months.

P11-24. Current versus non-current liabilities—balance sheet classification of maturing liabilities (L.O. 11-2) (Medium – 5 minutes)

Explain how a long-term loan maturing within one year of the balance sheet date is reported in the financial statements, assuming that the company intends to renew the liability for a further five years.

P11-25. Balance sheet classification of non-current obligations in default (L.O. 11-2) (Medium – 5 minutes)

Explain how a non-current obligation in default is reported in the financial statements.

P11-26. Accounting for deferred revenues (L.O. 11-2) (Medium – 10 minutes)

HF Magazines Corp. sells three-year magazine subscriptions for $180 cash each. The cost of producing and delivering each magazine is $2 paid in cash at the time of delivery. HF's sales activity for the year follows:

- On January 1, 2020, HF sells 10,000 subscriptions.
- On April 1, 2020, HF sells 5,000 subscriptions.
- On November 1, 2020, HF sells 12,000 subscriptions.

HF delivers the magazines at the end of the month. HF's year-end is December 31.

Required:

a. Prepare journal entries to record the subscription sales during the year.
b. Prepare summary journal entries to record the revenue earned during the year and the related expense.

P11-27. Accounting for deferred revenues (L.O. 11-2) (Medium – 10 minutes)

MVD News Inc. sells one-year newspaper subscriptions for $72 cash each. Newspapers are delivered daily. The average cost of producing and delivering papers each month is $3 paid in cash at the time of delivery. MVD's sales activity for the year follows:

- On January 1, 2020, MVD sold 8,000 subscriptions.
- On February 1, 2020, MVD sold 6,000 subscriptions.
- On August 1, 2020, MVD sold 9,000 subscriptions.
- On December 1, 2020, MVD sold 12,000 subscriptions

MVD's year-end is December 31.

Required:

a. Prepare journal entries to record the subscription sales during the year.
b. Prepare summary journal entries to record the revenue earned during the year and the related expense.

P11-28. Accounting for warranties (L.O. 11-2) (Medium – 10 minutes)

SST Jetski Corp. has sold motorized watercraft for a number of years. SST includes a three-year warranty on each watercraft they sell. Management estimates that the cost of providing the warranty coverage is 1% of sales in the first year and 2% of sales in each of years two and three. Other facts follow:

- SST reported a $260,000 provision for warranty payable on its balance sheet at December 31, 2020.
- SST's sales for 2021 totalled $4,800,000 spread evenly throughout the year.
- The cost to SST of meeting their warranty claims in 2021 was $240,000: $150,000 for parts and $90,000 for labour.
- SST's sales for 2022 totalled $5,400,000 spread evenly throughout the year.
- The cost to SST of meeting their warranty claims in 2022 was $300,000: $180,000 for parts and $120,000 for labour. Based on recent claims history, SST revises their 2022 warranty provision to 7% of sales.

Required:

a. Prepare summary journal entries to record warranty expense and warranty claims in 2021 and 2022.
b. Determine the provision for warranty payable that SST will report as a liability on December 31, 2022.

P11-29. Accounting for obligations denominated in foreign currencies (L.O. 11-2) (Medium – 10 minutes)

On December 1, 2018, Joy Vasek Importers Inc. borrowed US$1,000,000 from its bank. The loan is payable in full on July 1, 2019. Interest is payable each month end at 5% per annum. Pertinent exchange rates in 2018 follow:

December 1, 2018	US$1.00 = C$1.08
December 31, 2018	US$1.00 = C$1.10
Average rate December 1–31, 2018	US$1.00 = C$1.09

Required:

Prepare the required journal entries to record receipt of the loan proceeds; payment of interest on December 31, 2018, and for any adjustments required at year-end.

P11-30. Current liabilities–note disclosures (L.O. 11-2) (Medium – 15 minutes)

Refer to the 2016 financial statements for Canadian Tire Corporation in Appendix C.

Required:

a. What was the amount of current liabilities reported in Canadian Tire's financial statements as at December 31, 2016? What was this amount comprised of? Use the same categories that the company reports on its balance sheet.
b. The company had several categories of provisions. What were they and what was the current portion of each?
c. Did Canadian Tire report its liability for commercial paper at fair value through profit or loss or at amortized cost?
d. What was the company's current ratio as at December 31, 2016? How much working capital did it have?

P11-31. Accounting for customer loyalty programs (L.O. 11-2) (Medium – 15 minutes)

Winnipeg Air Corp. offers a customer loyalty program that grants members award miles for each flight taken. Members can redeem the miles, which expire 10 years after issuance, for future flights. Members must redeem 15,000 miles to obtain a return flight within Manitoba under the reward program (short-haul flight) and 25,000 miles to fly elsewhere in Canada. Other facts follow:

- Winnipeg Air's experience has been that 50% of the award flights taken are short-haul flights.
- In 2021, Winnipeg Air received $8,000,000 cash in flight-related revenue for flights taken in 2021.
- Winnipeg Air expects that 75% of the 8,000,000 miles awarded in 2020 will be redeemed before they expire.
- The performance obligation pertaining to the miles is estimated to be $90,000.
- During 2022, 60 short-haul award flights and 60 award flights for travel elsewhere in Canada were claimed.
- During 2023, 75 short-haul award flights and 75 award flights for travel elsewhere in Canada were claimed.

Required:

a. Prepare a summary journal entry to record the flight-related revenue in 2021.
b. Prepare summary journal entries to recognize award revenue in 2022 and 2023.

P11-32. Accounting for customer loyalty plans (L.O. 11-2) (Medium – 15 minutes)

Zoebug's Emporium Inc. rewards its frequent shoppers with gift cards. The premium program awards members one point for every dollar spent. Zoebug's provides members with a $10 gift card for every 1,000 points redeemed, which can then be used to purchase additional merchandise at Zoebug's. Pertinent facts follow:

- Points expire six years after they have been earned. Historically, 70% of the points will be redeemed.
- Zoebug allocates $14,895,000 of the contract amount to sales and $105,000 to the reward program.
- Zoebug's markup on cost is a constant 50% [items costing $1 are sold for $1 × (1 + 50%) = $1.50].
- In 2018, Zoebug's cash sales totalled $15,000,000. Zoebug's never sells on account.
- In 2019, customers redeemed 3,000,000 points.
- In 2020, customers redeemed 4,500,000 points.

Required:

a. Prepare summary journal entries to record sales-related revenue in 2018.
b. Prepare summary journal entries to recognize premium revenue in 2019 and 2020.
c. Provide a brief explanation as to why companies offer incentive programs.

P11-33. Reporting current liabilities (L.O. 11-2) (Difficult – 15 minutes)

Hacker's Superstore Inc. (HSI) borrowed $4,000,000 on January 1, 2020, at a fixed rate of 4%. The loan was repayable over five years at $898,508 per annum. The loan agreement included various covenants and stipulated that in the event of default the loan became immediately payable on demand. HSI had a December 31 year-end and reported its financial results in accordance with IFRS. The December 31, 2020, financial statements were approved for issue on March 5, 2021. Four independent situations follow:

1. The first payment on the loan, due on December 31, 2020, was paid as agreed.
2. The first payment on the loan was due on December 31, 2020. The payment was not made by HSI until January 12, 2021, due to the late receipt of a large receivable. While the lender did not take any precipitous action, it did not agree to amend the due date.
3. The first payment on the loan was due on January 1, 2021.

4. The first payment on the loan was due on January 1, 2021. HSI was in breach of the current ratio covenant at the December 31, 2020, year-end. In January 2021, the lender agreed to waive the default until January 2022.

Required:

For each of the four scenarios above, indicate the amount that HSI should have reported as a current liability on its balance sheet as at December 31, 2020.

P11-34. Accounting for warranties (L.O. 11-2) (Difficult – 15 minutes)

Stanger Educational Services Corp. sells multimedia presentation systems. In its first year of operations in 2018, the company sold 1,000 units for $5,000 cash each, representing a 25% markup over cost. Stanger provides a one-year parts and labour warranty on each system they sell; the estimated cost of providing the warranty coverage is $400 per unit.

The cost to Stanger of meeting their warranty claims in 2018 was $170,000: $50,000 for parts and $120,000 for labour.

For part (a), assume that Stanger properly provides for the warranties on an accrual basis. For part (b), assume that Stanger erroneously concludes that the warranty costs are immaterial and elects to account for the warranty obligations on a cash basis.

Required:

a. Prepare journal entries to record the forgoing events on an accrual basis.
b. Prepare journal entries to record the forgoing events on a cash basis.
c. Discuss why the cash basis cannot normally be used to account for warranty expenses.
d. Warranty claims in 2019 related to 2018 sales were $300,000, raising the total cost to $470,000. How should Stanger account for the $70,000 claimed in excess of that previously provided for?

P11-35. Accounting for deferred revenue (L.O. 11-2) (Difficult – 20 minutes)

GHF Computer Systems Inc. maintains office equipment under contract. The contracts are for labour only; customers must reimburse GHF for parts. GHF's rate schedule follows:

	One year	Two years	Three years
Photocopiers	$240	$420	$600
Fax machines	180	320	450

GHF's 2018 sales of maintenance agreements is set out below:

	One year	Two years	Three years
Photocopiers	24	12	36
Fax machines	24	24	36

Required:

Assuming that sales occurred evenly throughout the year:

a. What amount of revenue will GHF recognize for the year ended December 31, 2018?
b. What amount of deferred revenue will GHF report as a current liability on December 31, 2018?
c. What amount of deferred revenue will GHF report as a non-current liability on December 31, 2018?

P11-36. Accounting for deferred revenue (L.O. 11-2) (Difficult – 25 minutes)

Muscles Gym Corp. offers a variety of fitness packages to its members:

- A pay-as-you-go membership for the use of the fitness facilities costing $40 per month
- A one-year, non-cancellable membership costing $420 per year
- A two-year, non-cancellable membership costing $720 ($360 per year)
- A personal trainer package (PTP) of 10 coupons for one-hour sessions costing $750

The chart that follows summarizes Muscles' membership numbers and relevant financial information at December 31, 2021:

	# of Customers	Liability	Current Liability	Non-Current Liability
Pay as you go	220	$ 0	$ 0	$ 0
One year	180	40,950	40,950	0
Two year	120	45,000	33,300	11,700
Unused personal training sessions	352	26,400	26,400	0
		$112,350	$100,650	$11,700

Other information:

- All fees are payable in advance. One- and two-year memberships are effective from the first of the month following sale.
- 15 one-year memberships were sold every month in 2021.
- Five two-year memberships were sold every month in 2020 and 2021.
- Historically, all personal trainer session coupons are redeemed within one year of purchase.
- To simplify their accounting somewhat, and as the amounts are not material, Muscles recognizes the pay-as-you-go membership fees as revenue in the month charged even if they are purchased during the month.

Transactions during January 2022:

- 34 pay-as-you-go members cancelled their memberships before paying for January.
- Muscles attracted 45 new pay-as-you-go members.
- Muscles sold 20 new one-year memberships.
- Muscles sold 10 new two-year memberships.
- 112 coupons for personal training sessions were redeemed.
- 10 new personal trainer packages were sold.

Required:

a. Prepare journal entries to recognize the receipt of cash and recognize revenue in January 2022.
b. What is the total deferred revenue that Muscles will report as a liability as at January 31? How much of this will be reported as a current liability? [*Hint:* It is easier to determine the non-current portion and subtract this from the total obligation to determine the current portion.]

P11-37. Accounting for customer loyalty programs (L.O. 11-2) (Difficult – 15 minutes)

Halifax Air Shuttle Inc. offers a customer loyalty program that grants members award miles for each flight taken. Members can redeem the miles, which expire five years after issuance, for future flights. Members must redeem 15,000 miles and pay a $100 service charge to obtain a flight under the reward program. Other facts follow:

- In 2018, Halifax Air received $10,000,000 cash in flight-related revenue for flights taken in 2018.
- Halifax Air expects that 80% of the 9,375,000 miles awarded in 2018 will be redeemed before they expire.
- The performance obligation pertaining to the award miles is estimated to be $75,000.
- During 2019, 200 award flights were claimed.
- During 2020, 150 award flights were claimed.

Required:

a. Prepare a summary journal entry to record the flight-related revenue in 2018.
b. Prepare summary journal entries to recognize award revenue in 2019 and 2020.

P11-38. Accounting for contingencies and customer loyalty programs

(L.O. 11-2, L.O. 11-3) (Medium – 10 minutes)

It is early in February 2021 and you are conducting the audit of Adventuresome Airlines Ltd.'s 2020 financial statements. Through discussion with Adventuresome's chief financial officer, you learn of matters that have not yet been incorporated into the 2020 financial statements:

- In July 2020, 57 passengers on board Adventuresome Airlines Flight 007 were seriously injured when the plane missed the runway on final approach. In January 2021, the injured passengers launched a class action lawsuit against Adventuresome seeking damages of $10 million. Adventuresome's internal investigation of the incident determined that the pilot was intoxicated during the flight. The company's solicitors suggest that if the matter goes to court, Adventuresome will be found liable and ordered to pay the $10 million.

  In an attempt to reduce its loss, Adventuresome's solicitors made a settlement offer of $8 million to the plaintiffs. The litigants' attorney has not provided a formal response but has indicated that the offer is being seriously considered. Adventuresome's lawyers estimate that there is an 80% probability the plaintiffs will accept the offer.
- During 2020, Adventuresome began a customer loyalty program. For each aeronautical mile that a passenger travels on a paid flight, the passenger accrues one flight mile. Passengers can redeem accrued flight miles for free air travel. Earned miles do not expire.

  Adventuresome's analysis of its competitors' programs suggests an average redemption rate of 80%. In 2020, Adventuresome awarded 30,000,000 flight miles, 4,800,000 of which were redeemed. Management estimates the performance obligation pertaining to the flight miles is $720,000.

Required:

Prepare the journal entries to record the required adjustments for the above events, assuming that Adventuresome reports its financial results in accordance with IFRS.

P11-39. Describe the nature of contingent assets and liabilities

(L.O. 11-3) (Medium – 10 minutes)

a. Explain what contingencies are.
b. Describe how to account for contingent liabilities.
c. Describe how to account for contingent assets.

P11-40. Accounting for contingencies

(L.O. 11-3) (Medium – 10 minutes)

Discuss the terms "probable," "possible," and "remote" in relation to contingencies. In what circumstances are contingencies provided for in the financial statements, and when are they simply disclosed?

P11-41. Accounting for contingencies

(L.O. 11-3) (Medium – 15 minutes)

The following are six independent situations. The underlined entity is the reporting entity.

1. The Supreme Court of Canada ordered a supplier to pay Pangay Strobes Inc. $100,000 for breach of contract.
2. Ynot Pharmaceuticals Inc. sued Xbot Agencies Ltd. for $20 million alleging patent infringement. While there may be some substance to Ynot's assertion, Xbot's legal counsel estimates that Ynot's likelihood of success is about 20%.
3. Environment Canada sued Canless Isotopes Ltd. for $10 million seeking to recover the costs of cleaning up Canless's accidental discharge of radioactive materials. Canless acknowledges liability but is disputing the amount, claiming that the actual costs are in the range of $5 million to $6 million. Canless's $10 million environmental insurance policy includes a $1 million deductible clause.
4. Calfed Cattle Inc. sued Toropost Feed Ltd. for $2 million alleging breach of contract. Toropost's legal counsel estimates that Calfed's likelihood of success is about 70%. Based on its experience with cases of this nature, the law firm estimates, if successful, that the litigants will be awarded $1,000,000 to $1,200,000, with all payouts in this range being equally likely.

5. Helen Threlfall broke her leg when she tripped on an uneven floor surface in Montpearson Co.'s office. On the advice of legal counsel, Montpearson has offered Threlfall $100,000 to settle her $300,000 lawsuit. It is unknown whether Threlfall will accept the settlement offer. Montpearson's legal counsel estimates that Threlfall has a 90% probability of success, and that if successful, she will be awarded $200,000.
6. The courts ordered a competitor to pay $500,000 to Winfland Boxes Corp. for patent infringement. The competitor's legal counsel indicated that the company will probably appeal the amount of the award.

Required

a. For each of the six situations described above, and assuming that the company reports its financial results in accordance with IFRS, indicate whether the appropriate accounting treatment is to:
   A. recognize an asset or liability.
   B. disclose the details of the contingency in the notes to the financial statements.
   C. neither provide for the item nor disclose the circumstances in the notes to the financial statements.
b. For each situation that requires the recognition of an asset or liability, record the journal entry.

P11-42. Accounting for contingencies (L.O. 11-3) (Medium – 10 minutes) A·S·P·E

Aaron Robinson's Architecture Ltd. (ARAL) is a private company that reports its financial results in accordance with ASPE. Unfortunately, a three-storey apartment building that ARAL designed recently collapsed. The owners of the apartment complex are suing ARAL for $10,000,000 in damages. ARAL's legal counsel estimates that the plaintiff has an 80% likelihood of success, and that if successful the litigants will be awarded $6,000,000 to $8,000,000, with all payouts in this range being equally likely. ARAL's $5,000,000 errors and omissions liability insurance policy includes a $500,000 deductible clause.

Required:

For the situation described above, indicate the appropriate accounting treatment. If the circumstances require the recognition of a liability, record the journal entry.

P11-43. Accounting for contingencies (L.O. 11-3) (Medium – 20 minutes)

The following are two independent situations. The underlined entity is the reporting entity.

1. Broken Horse Stables Inc. sued Topnotch Equestrian Inc. for $1 million alleging breach of contract. Topnotch's legal counsel estimates that Broken Horse's likelihood of success is about 55%. Based on its experience with cases of this nature, the law firm suggests that if the litigant is successful then it will be awarded $600,000 to $800,000, with all payouts in this range being equally likely.
2. Meagan Morton broke her arm when she slipped on the ice in front of the office of Boondoggle Inc. On the advice of legal counsel, Boondoggle has offered Morton $200,000 to settle her $400,000 lawsuit. It is unknown whether Morton will accept the settlement offer. Boondoggle's legal counsel estimates that Morton has a 75% probability of success, and that if successful, she will be awarded $200,000 to $300,000, with all payouts in this range being equally likely.

Required:

a. Assuming that the reporting company prepares its financial statements in accordance with IFRS:
   i. For each of the two situations described above, indicate whether the appropriate accounting treatment is to:
      A. Recognize a liability.
      B. Disclose the details of the contingency in the notes to the financial statements.
   ii. For each situation that requires the recognition of a liability, record the journal entry.

A·S·P·E

b. Assuming that the reporting company prepares its financial statements in accordance with ASPE:
   i. For each of the two situations described above, indicate whether the appropriate accounting treatment is to:
      A. Recognize a liability.
      B. Disclose the details of the contingency in the notes to the financial statements.
   ii. For each situation that requires the recognition of a liability, record the journal entry.

P11-44. Accounting for guarantees (L.O. 11-4) (Easy – 5 minutes)

ZSK Interiors Ltd. guarantees SIL Exterior Co.'s $150,000 bank loan. Describe how ZSK will initially account for the guarantee and discuss the nature of the required disclosure.

P11-45. Accounting for commitments (L.O. 11-4) (Easy – 5 minutes)

Explain what onerous contracts are and how they are accounted for.

P11-46. Accounting for commitments (L.O. 11-4) (Medium – 10 minutes)

Kitchener Distributors Inc. entered into a non-cancellable contract to buy 10,000 litres of linseed oil for $3 per litre for resale purposes. Kitchener intends to resell the oil to retail paint outlets for $4 per litre. The contract was entered into on October 31, 2020, for delivery on January 15, 2021. Kitchener's year-end is December 31.

On December 12, 2020, Kitchener's supplier reduced the price to $2 per litre due to adverse market conditions.

Required:

a. Outline the required accounting treatment assuming that Kitchener expects it can sell the oil for $3.20 per litre.
b. Outline the required accounting treatment assuming that Kitchener expects it can sell the oil for $2.75 per litre.

P11-47. Accounting for commitments (L.O. 11-4) (Medium – 10 minutes)

Waterloo Wholesale Corp. entered into an irrevocable contract to buy 1,000 kilograms of amorphous silica for $40 per kilogram for resale purposes. Waterloo intends to resell the silica to local cosmetic manufacturers for $60 per kilogram. The contract was entered into on November 30, 2020, for delivery on January 15, 2021. Waterloo's year-end is December 31.

On December 18, 2020, Waterloo's supplier reduced the price to $24 per kilogram due to adverse market conditions.

Required:

a. Outline the required accounting treatment assuming that Waterloo expects it can sell the silica for $36 per kilogram.
b. Outline the required accounting treatment assuming that Waterloo expects it can sell the silica for $45 per kilogram.

P11-48. Accounting for various situations (L.O. 11-2, L.O. 11-3, L.O. 11-4) (Difficult – 20 minutes)

A number of independent situations are set out below.

1. A former employee of Moncton Minimarket Inc. sued the company for $500,000 alleging that the company's owner sexually harassed her. Moncton's lawyers suggest that the lawsuit has a 20 to 30% probability of success and that, if successful, the plaintiff will be awarded between $100,000 and $200,000.
2. Calgary Pyrotechnics Ltd. received a $5,000 fee to guarantee the $500,000 bank indebtedness of Edmonton Fireworks Inc. The fair value of the guarantee is initially estimated to be $5,000.
3. Humboldt Syringes Co. sued a competitor for $300,000, alleging corporate espionage. Humboldt's legal counsel believes that the company will be successful and will be awarded somewhere in the range of $250,000 to $300,000.

4. A customer sued Cache Creek Tractor Corp. for $100,000 for breach of contract. Cache Creek's solicitors advise that they will almost certainly be found liable. Based on previous results, counsel estimates that there is a 50% probability that the courts will award the $100,000 being sought; a 30% probability that $90,000 will be conferred; and a 20% probability that the judgment will be $80,000.
5. Saskatoon Conveyor and Clutch Ltd. is in the midst of preparing its financial statements for the year ended December 31, 2018. Saskatoon has been in ongoing discussions with its bankers about renewing its $5,000,000 loan maturing on June 30, 2019. While nothing had been finalized by year-end, the bank did agree to extend the maturity by five years on January 15, 2019.

Required:

For each of the above situations, assuming that the entity reports its financial results in accordance with IFRS, describe how the event should be dealt with in the financial statements of the underlined entity and explain why. Prepare all required journal entries.

P11-49. Accounting for various situations

(L.O. 11-2, L.O. 11-3, L.O. 11-4) (Difficult – 20 minutes)

A number of independent situations are set out below.

1. Truro TV Superstore Inc. received 20 52" XZT widescreen televisions from its supplier in New York, shipped on an FOB destination basis. The contract price was US$500 each. The exchange rate on the day of receipt was US$1.00 = C$0.99.
2. Regina Chromatography Inc.'s year-end is December 31. On November 30, 2020, it entered into a non-cancellable contract to purchase 1,000 litres of solvent at a price of $2.50 per litre, for delivery on January 5, 2021. Prior to year-end, and due to a recent glut in supply, Regina's supplier reduced the price to $1 per litre. While solvent is an essential component in the lucrative, high-margin, chromatography business, it is a relatively low-cost component, accounting for less than 1% of the process cost.
3. Prince Albert Amusement Inc. has a long-term loan facility with Saskabank that becomes payable on demand in the event of default. One of the loan covenants stipulates that Prince Albert will ensure that its year-end current ratio does not fall below 1.5:1. In early December, the company anticipated that its current ratio would be less than the required minimum at its year-end of December 31, 2022. Prince Albert discussed this matter with Saskabank and on December 29, 2022, the bank agreed to waive this covenant until December 31, 2023. Prince Albert's current ratio at December 31, 2022, was 1.3:1.
4. A customer of Red Deer Heavy Equipment Ltd. was injured on the company's premises when a shipping crate fell on him. The injured party is suing the company for $500,000 for pain and suffering and loss of income. Red Deer's solicitors advise that the company will almost certainly be found liable. Based on previous verdicts, counsel estimates that there is a 60% probability that the courts will award $300,000, and a 40% probability that the judgment will be $200,000.
5. A former employee of Edmonton Bison Inc. fired for incompetence has sued the company for wrongful dismissal. The plaintiff is seeking $100,000 in damages. Edmonton's lawyers advise that the lawsuit has a 10 to 20% probability of success and that, if successful, the plaintiff will be awarded between $10,000 and $20,000.

Required:

For each of the above situations, assuming that the entity reports its financial results in accordance with IFRS, describe how the event should be dealt with in the financial statements of the underlined entity and explain why. Prepare all required journal entries.

P11-50. Accounting for various situations (L.O. 11-2, L.O. 11-4) (Difficult – 20 minutes)

A number of independent situations are set out below. The underlined entity is the reporting entity.

1. Montreal Pool and Skeet Corp.'s debt to equity ratio is 1.6:1, based on its draft financial statements for the year ended December 31, 2019. This leverage ratio exceeds the 1.5:1

maximum stipulated in Montreal's loan agreement pertaining to a $1,000,000 loan maturing on March 15, 2022. The loan agreement stipulates that the loan becomes payable on demand upon breach of any of the loan covenants. Montreal's creditors agreed on December 15, 2019, to waive their right to demand payment until December 31, 2020, for reason only that the firm's leverage ratio exceeds the stipulated maximum.

2. Bathurst Piano Storage Inc. issued a $20,000, 30-day, non-interest bearing note to Len's Crating for storage bins. The market rate of interest for similar transactions is 2%.
3. On November 30, 2021, Port Mellon Fertilizer Ltd. entered into a non-cancellable agreement to buy 10 tonnes of phosphorus for $1,000 per tonne for delivery on February 28, 2022. Phosphorus is a key component of the custom fertilizer that Port Mellon produces. The market price of phosphorus is extremely volatile, as evidenced by the $700 per tonne that it could be acquired for on December 31, 2021. Notwithstanding the premium price paid for the phosphorus, the company expects that fertilizer sales will remain profitable. Port Mellon's year-end is December 31.
4. Gander Airport Parking Ltd. awards customers 250 award miles per stay in a well-known airline mileage program. Gander pays the airline $0.02 for each mile. Gander, which is not an agent for the airline, estimates that the fair value of the miles is the same as the price paid—$0.02. Parking revenues on May 24, 2020, were $25,000. Gander awarded 50,000 airline points to its customers.
5. On October 15, 2020, Charlottetown Windows and Sash properly recorded the issue of a $20,000, 6% note due April 15, 2021. Charlottetown is preparing its financial statements for the year ended December 31, 2020. Charlottetown does not make adjusting entries during the year.

Required:

For each of the situations described above, prepare the required journal entry. If a journal entry for the underlined entity is not required, explain why.

N. MINI-CASES

CASE 1

Cool Look Limited

(40 minutes)[26]

Cool Look Limited (CLL) is a high-end clothing design and manufacturing company that has been in business in Canada since 1964. CLL started as an owner-managed enterprise created and run by Hector Gauthier. Its ownership has stayed within the family and is now in its third generation of management by the Gauthier/Roy family. Martin Roy, Hector's grandson, is the newly appointed president, chief executive officer, and chairman of the board of CLL, and wants to modernize the company.

You are the audit senior on the CLL audit for its fiscal year ended November 30, 2021. Today is December 9, 2021, and you are reviewing correspondence from CLL's bank. You come upon a letter dated November 1, 2021, from the bank credit manager, that causes you some concern (Exhibit I). After you finish reviewing the letter, you recall the other issues that are causing you concern in the audit (Exhibit II). You pull out your notes from your review of board minutes (Exhibit III) and the November 30, 2021, management-prepared draft financial statements (Exhibit IV) to clarify your thoughts further.

As you contemplate the work to be completed, you decide to write a memorandum to the file that discusses the outstanding accounting issues that are currently facing CLL, the audit procedures that are required to gain adequate assurance over those issues, and other areas of concern you want to raise with your partner.

Required:

Prepare a memo that (i) discusses the going concern assumption as it relates to this case, and (ii) identifies and discusses the accounting issues that need to be resolved before the financial statements can be finalized.

Exhibit I Letter to CLL from bank

November 1, 2021

Dear Sir:

We have reviewed CLL's internal third-quarter financial statements, dated August 31, 2021. As a result of this review, we have determined that your financial ratios continue to decline and that you are in default of the covenants in our agreement for the second consecutive quarter.

However, since the bank and CLL have a long history, and because CLL continues to make required debt payments on time, we are willing to extend the $6,000,000 secured operating line of credit until the end of February 2022.

Based on CLL's February 29, 2022, internal financial statements, we will expect CLL to meet the following financial ratios. If this is not done, we reserve the right to call the loan at that time.

Ratios:

Current ratio no less than 1:1

Maximum debt-to-equity ratio [Debt / (Debt + Equity)] of 80%; debt is defined as total liabilities.

We thank you for your business.

Yours truly,

Mr. Vuiton Burbery

Credit Manager

[26] Uniform Final Examination 2005, with permission Chartered Professional Accountants of Canada, Toronto, Canada.

Exhibit II Excerpts from audit file regarding outstanding issues

Capital Assets

At a physical inspection of the CLL factory, audit staff noted that only about one-half of the equipment at the factory was being used, even though it was 2 o'clock on a Wednesday afternoon. The rest was covered by tarps. The plant manager explained that the equipment covered by tarps was outdated and unable to manufacture products in its current condition. Senior management is investigating whether it can be refitted with updated technology to make it usable. This refitting would cost approximately $1.5 million and would take three to six months to complete. The equipment covered by tarps cost $2.9 million and has a current net book value of $1.3 million.

Maintenance expenses are currently about 25% of last year's amount. The plant manager indicated that some of the functioning equipment is not running at full efficiency due to the need to perform maintenance soon. He stated that, while there would normally be some safety issues when maintenance is reduced, his staff consists of well-trained, seasoned employees, and he is not concerned.

Inventory Transaction

Finished goods inventory at a cost of $565,000 was shipped by CLL to Big Bargain Clothing (BBC), a national retail clothing outlet store, on November 29, 2021. The shipment was recorded as sales revenue of $1,000,000, generating a gross profit of $435,000. CLL and BBC signed a special agreement stating that BBC can return unsold goods to CLL at any time after February 1, 2022.

Long-Term Debt

CLL's long-term debt includes the $6,000,000 secured operating line of credit. The line of credit is a revolving loan callable on three months' notice by the bank if certain financial covenants are not met. It had been classified as long-term debt in 2020 because the bank waived its right to call the loan before December 1, 2021.

Exhibit III Excerpts from notes taken during review of board minutes

August 7, 2021—Management presented a document discussing the temporary cash crunch at CLL. Management presented options to conserve cash until the Christmas buying season, when a new large contract with a US chain of stores begins. One alternative was to discontinue making required contributions to the CLL pension plan. Another alternative was to delay remitting GST and employee withholdings. The board passed a resolution to temporarily delay remitting GST and employee withholdings until cash flows improved.

September 5, 2021—The board received information from management regarding an incident at the factory. Some dirty rags had caught fire in a metal garbage can. The fire was put out quickly and no damage was done. Management and the board were quite relieved that the fire had not spread, because CLL has not renewed its fire and theft insurance this year due to the need to conserve cash. For the same reason, CLL has not renewed the directors' liability insurance. The board decided that the renewals would be done immediately after cash flow improved.

November 10, 2021—The board passed a motion to allow Martin Roy to postpone repayment of his interest-free shareholder loan by another six months to May 31, 2022. He owes CLL $500,000. The board also received a report from management on the letter from the bank dated November 1, 2021.

The board is concerned that, even with its efforts to conserve cash, CLL may be unable to meet the ratio requirements. The board is curious to know whether CLL's efforts thus far have produced results.

Exhibit IV Draft financial statements

CLL
Extracts from the draft balance sheet
As at November 30
(in $000's)

	2021 (unaudited)	2020 (audited)
Current assets		
Cash	$ 1,094	$ 1,376
Accounts receivable	1,148	736
Inventory	2,241	2,358
Prepaid expenses	184	134
Due from shareholder	500	500
	5,167	5,104
Property, plant, and equipment (net)	9,392	9,719
	$ 14,559	$ 14,823
Current liabilities		
Accounts payable	$ 2,315	$ 995
Current portion of long-term debt	821	803
	3,136	1,798
Pension benefit liability	208	236
Long-term debt	9,149	9,234
	9,357	9,470
Share capital	10,386	10,386
Deficit	(8,320)	(6,831)
	2,066	3,555
	$ 14,559	$ 14,823

CLL
Extracts from the draft income statement
For the year ended November 30
(in $000's)

	2021 (unaudited)	2020 (audited)
Operating revenues	$ 16,620	$ 16,285
Cost of sales	9,321	8,995
Gross profit	7,299	7,290
Selling and administrative expenses	6,580	5,900
Depreciation and amortization	1,310	1,485
Operating loss	(591)	(95)
Interest expense	898	902
Net loss	$ (1,489)	$ (997)

CASE 2 Earth Movers Ltd.

(60 minutes)[27]

Earth Movers Ltd. (EML) is in the business of supplying heavy equipment and work crews for landfill operations, road construction, and gravel pit operations. Kevin Donnelly started the company 28 years ago with a small inheritance. EML has contracts with several municipalities in two provinces and recently obtained a contract in a third province. In addition, EML owns and operates two landfill sites.

Kevin owns 50% of EML's shares; his wife, Leslie, owns 25% of the shares; and his daughter, Brenda, owns the other 25% of the shares. Brenda, who graduated with a business administration degree four years ago, joined the company in February 2018 after leaving her job as a buyer for a department store chain. Her current responsibilities as assistant controller include payroll administration and supervision of the billing clerk. It is anticipated she will move into the controller's role when the controller, Betty Wylie, retires in two years.

EML has recently appointed White & Bean (WB), Chartered Professional Accountants, as auditors for the year ended June 30, 2018. Fred Spot, CPA, a good friend of Kevin Donnelly, was the auditor for the past several years. Mr. Spot has advised WB that he is not aware of any reason why they should not accept the appointment of auditor.

In early June, the company had been served notice by its bank, the Dominion Royal, that the interest rate charged on its loan will be increased from prime + 1% to prime + 3%. Interest is payable monthly and principal is repayable over 10 years. Kevin has approached several banks to obtain new financing and only one, S&L Bank, has offered a lower rate. It will supply financing at prime + 1% pending receipt of audited financial statements. The amount of financing provided, some of which will be long term and some short term, will depend on certain asset balances and financial ratios (see Exhibit I). Kevin would like EML to repay the loan he made to the company and has asked WB to determine how much financing EML can expect to obtain. Kevin wants to be fully informed of any accounting concerns WB may have in determining the financing available.

Terry Mitchell, the engagement partner, has asked you to prepare a report that provides the information requested by Kevin including all necessary explanations and assumptions.

It is now July 2, 2018, and you are back in your office after attending the spare parts inventory count and verifying the existence of fixed assets. Your notes from this visit are attached (Exhibit II). You have reviewed and discussed the draft financial statements with Betty Wylie and made some notes (Exhibit III).

Required:

Prepare the report to the client.

Exhibit I S&L Bank financing offer

1. No financing is available if the working capital ratio is below 1.0. Calculation of the working capital ratio excludes any financing from S&L Bank.
2. Subject to 1 above, S&L Bank will provide financing to EML based on the following formulae:

Formula 1

If the working capital ratio is 1.0:1.25, S&L Bank will advance funds equal to (70% × accounts receivable) + (30% × inventory) due on demand, and (50% × land, building, and equipment, net) as long-term debt.

Formula 2

If the working capital ratio is greater than 1.25:1.0, S&L Bank will advance funds equal to (80% × accounts receivable) + (40% × inventory) due on demand, and (70% × land, building, and equipment, net) as long-term debt.

3. EML will supply S&L Bank with monthly unaudited financial statements, accompanied by comments from management.
4. Credit limits and long-term debt renewal will be based on the annual audited financial statements.
5. Interest on the loans will be payable monthly.

[27] Uniform Final Examination 1994, with permission Chartered Professional Accountants of Canada, Toronto, Canada.

Exhibit II Notes from inventory count and asset existence test

1. One of the trucks in the sample was not on the client's premises. Betty explained that it was at a repair shop because there had been a fire in the cab. Kevin has not decided whether it is worthwhile to repair the truck but is expecting to receive $90,000 from the insurance company. At his insistence, Betty recorded $90,000 as a current receivable and as a gain on asset disposition.
2. Spare parts inventory includes the spare metal wheels for the earth mover vehicles, as follows:

Size 250H	7 wheels	$570,000
Size 350H	5 wheels	150,000

The metal wheels are used until the tracks wear down. Each earth mover has three wheels that must be replaced approximately every five years. The old wheels are removed and rebuilt, so the number of wheels in inventory is fairly constant. EML's fleet includes two old earth movers that use size 250H wheels. The other 19 earth movers use size 350H wheels.

Two earth movers were scrapped in fiscal 2018. Six size 250H wheels were transferred to spare parts inventory at the book value of the scrapped vehicles, which was $550,000. No entry has been recorded for the remaining parts from the scrapped vehicles, which will be sold to a scrap metal dealer for about $60,000.

Kevin said that he plans to change the method of depreciation for all heavy equipment. In the past, the declining-balance method was used. He has decided to use the straight-line method, as he had heard that one of his main competitors has been using this method for years. He suggests adding a note to the financial statements explaining the straight-line method and the average useful life of the equipment.

Exhibit III Draft financial statements

Earth Movers Ltd
Balance sheet
As at June 30, 2018
(unaudited, in $000's)

Assets	
Cash	$ 84
Accounts receivable	585
Spare parts inventory	907
Land, building, and equipment (net)	2,759
Landfill sites	415
	$ 4,750
Liabilities	
Accounts payable	$ 347
Current portion of long-term debt	89
Income taxes payable	53
Long-term debt	2,428
Due to Kevin Donnelly	300
Deferred taxes	47
Shareholders' Equity	
Common shares	1
Retained earnings	1,485
	$ 4,750

CPA's notes from review of the financial statements

1. EML owns and operates two landfill sites. The Banbury site has an estimated remaining life of nine years and a book value of $290,000. The Eckleforth site has a remaining life of two years and a book value of $125,000. Kevin plans to offer the Eckleforth site to the City of Eckleforth for use as a recreational area in exchange for the city taking the responsibility for cleaning up the site. In this way, he is hoping to avoid spending $250,000 to $350,000 in cleanup costs.
2. Income taxes payable relate to Kevin and Leslie's personal taxes. The amount is large, as they recently lost an appeal regarding the tax treatment of some personal property. Fred Spot, CPA, has prepared the Donnelly's tax returns for a nominal fee for several years.
3. During the winter, several staff painted and generally cleaned up the interior of EML's office and shop building. Kevin says the place looks "as good as new" and therefore told Betty to record the $9,700 cost of their labour as an addition to land, building, and equipment.
4. Repairs and maintenance expense includes $15,800 worth of parts and labour for the overhaul of a 350H earth mover. Kevin bought the machine at an auction this year for the low price of $95,000 since he knew that Mack Jacobs, the shop foreman, would enjoy the challenge of making it operational. The machine is now in use at the Banbury site.
5. Accounts receivable include $85,000 in disputed invoices relating to the operation of a gravel pit. Kevin has not been pressing for collection because the contract to operate the gravel pit is up for renewal and he feels he can use the receivable as a bargaining tool.
6. Accounts payable include $146,000 due to Fred Spot, CPA, for consulting services and for the annual audits for the fiscal years 2015 to 2017.

CASE 3 Lisa's Insurance Services Ltd.

(20 minutes)

Lisa Ramage, who owns a number of businesses, opened an insurance agency called Lisa's Insurance Services Ltd. (LISL) at the beginning of the year. Year-end (December 31, 2021) is fast approaching and Lisa has asked you, the company accountant, to prepare a report outlining how the following items should be reported in LISL's financial statements. LISL has various obligations, including a $500,000 overdraft facility and a $2,000,000 three-year term loan with its bank, GFF Financial Inc.

1. On July 1, 2021, LISL took advantage of a vendor-provided financing offer to acquire computer equipment. LISL signed a $20,000, note payable in full on July 1, 2024. Interest is payable annually at a rate of 2% per annum. LISL's bank previously advised that it would charge an interest rate of 8% per annum for a loan on similar terms.
2. LISL has been sued by S. Berg Ltd. (SBL), a client, for unspecified damages. The lawsuit alleges negligence and contends that LISL sold SBL an insurance policy that was inadequate for its needs. When SBL's premises were destroyed by fire, the insurance proceeds were $1 million less than that required to reconstruct the facilities. LISL's legal counsel believes that the courts may possibly find in favour of SBL, and if they do so the range of the award will likely be between $600,000 and $800,000 with no one estimate better than the rest.
3. LISL has guaranteed $100,000 of the indebtedness of Kaitlyn's Studios Inc. (KSI), a related corporation. KSI has a long record of profitability and the probability of default is thought to be remote.
4. LISL's loan agreement with GFF Financial Inc. includes a covenant that the company will maintain its current ratio of no less than 1.30:1. If LISL fails to meet this or any of the other covenants at year-end, all loan facilities become immediately due and payable. As it appears that LISL's current ratio at year-end will be slightly less than this, LISL obtained a letter from GFF dated December 15, 2021, agreeing to provide until December 31, 2022, for LISL to remedy this defect.

Required:

Prepare the report.

CASE 4

ElectroTools Ltd.

(30 minutes)

You are Ranjit Sidhu, the CFO (chief financial officer) of Electro Tools Ltd., a Canadian public company that manufactures electronic appliances. Electro Tools sells its products to major retailers such as Future Shop and Best Buy. The company's CEO (chief executive officer), Robert Watt, visited your office in early 2021 and advised that at the recent board of directors' meeting he was told to look for ways to increase the company's revenues. He is considering making changes to the company's warranty and reward programs to achieve this goal.

The company currently offers warranties separately from the products it sells. This means that a consumer purchases the product without a warranty. They are then offered (by the retailer on Electro's behalf) the opportunity to purchase a three-year warranty on the product. Approximately 70% of consumers currently purchase the warranty. Mr. Watt is considering changing this practice to bundling the two products such that the downstream customer is automatically provided with a warranty when they purchase Electro's product. The new price of the bundled product would be the sum of the current sales prices of the appliance and warranty purchased separately.

To encourage retailers to purchase the company's products, Electro Tools employs a reward program. Retailers that reach pre-specified levels of purchases in the current year are provided with a cash discount the following year. For example, if a retailer makes purchases of between $1 million and $2 million during the year, then it is entitled to a 2% discount on all purchases in the following year. Purchases in the range of $2 to $5 million entitle the retailer to a 4% concession, and purchases in excess of $5 million entitle the retailer to a 6% reduction. Mr. Watt is considering replacing the discount program by contracting with Rewards Plus Inc., an independent company that offers a points-based rewards program to its clients. Electro Tools will award points to the retailers based on their level of purchases; the points can then be used to acquire a variety of communications products and services (e.g., iPhones and cell phone plans) from Rewards Plus. Electro will pay a fee to Rewards Plus for this service based on the number of points it awards. Mr. Watt intends to build the reward system such that the cost of the rewards provided under the new program will be equivalent to the discounts provided under the old program.

Mr. Watt has asked you to analyze the effect of these potential changes. Specifically, he wants you to address the following issues:

1. Will there be changes to the way warranties and rewards are recorded? If so, how will the changes affect the financial statements?
2. Will the changes allow Electro Tools to report increased revenues?
3. What other issues should be considered?
4. What are the potential negative aspects of those changes?

Required:

Write a memo to Mr. Watt, addressing the issues raised.

GerryRousseau/Alamy Stock Photo

CHAPTER 12
Non-Current Financial Liabilities

LEARNING OBJECTIVES

After studying this chapter, you should be able to:

L.O. 12-1. Describe financial leverage and its impact on profitability.

L.O. 12-2. Describe the categories and types of non-current liabilities.

L.O. 12-3. Describe the initial and subsequent measurement of non-current financial liabilities and account for these obligations.

L.O. 12-4. Apply accrual accounting to the derecognition of financial liabilities.

L.O. 12-5. Apply accrual accounting to decommissioning and site restoration obligations.

L.O. 12-6. Describe how non-current liabilities are presented and disclosed.

CPA competencies addressed in this chapter:

1.1.2 Evaluates the appropriateness of the basis of financial accounting (Level B)

1.2.1 Develops or evaluates appropriate accounting policies and procedures (Level B)

1.2.2 Evaluates treatment for routine transactions (Level A)
h. Long-term liabilities
k. Financial instruments
p. Foreign currency transactions

1.3.1 Prepares financial statements (Level A)

1.3.2 Prepares routine financial statement note disclosure (Level B)

1.4.1 Analyzes complex financial statement note disclosure (Level C)

TransLink is Metropolitan Vancouver's regional transit authority. Among TransLink's responsibilities are operating the public transit system and sharing responsibility with municipalities for major roads in the region.

On December 9, 2016, TransLink announced that it had issued an additional $150 million in bonds to finance capital projects. TransLink proudly reminded readers that it is Canada's only transportation agency to raise funds directly through Canadian debt capital markets and that it had raised $1.33 billion since 2010. On a related note, Moody's Investors Service and Dominion Bond Rating Service (DBRS) respectively reaffirmed TransLink's Aa2 and AA credit ratings in October 2016.

Long-term debt is an important source of financing for enterprises. For organizations such as TransLink, what are the mechanics of issuing (selling) bonds? Who determines the creditworthiness of the issuer? How is the interest rate to be offered to investors determined? What are the key issues that accountants should be aware of in relation to debt financing?

12 CONTENTS

A. INTRODUCTION 581
1. Overview 581
2. Financial leverage 582
3. Debt-rating agencies 583
B. COMMON NON-CURRENT FINANCIAL LIABILITIES 584
1. Notes payable 584
2. Bonds 585
C. INITIAL MEASUREMENT 587
1. Debt exchanged for non-cash assets 588
2. Debt issued at non-market rates of interest 588
3. Compound financial instruments 588
4. Interest rates and how they impact the selling price of bonds 589
5. Determining the sales price of a bond when the market rate of interest is given 591
6. Timing of bond issuance 591
D. SUBSEQUENT MEASUREMENT 593
1. Effective interest rate 593
2. Amortization using the effective interest method 593
3. Amortization using the straight-line method 598
E. DERECOGNITION 600
1. Derecognition at maturity 600
2. Derecognition prior to maturity 600
3. Derecognition through offsetting and in-substance defeasance 603
F. PUTTING IT ALL TOGETHER—A COMPREHENSIVE BOND EXAMPLE 604
G. OTHER ISSUES 606
1. Decommissioning and site restoration obligations 606
2. Off-balance-sheet obligations 609
3. Bonds denominated in foreign currency 610
H. PRESENTATION AND DISCLOSURE 612
I. SUBSTANTIVE DIFFERENCES BETWEEN RELEVANT IFRS AND ASPE 613
J. STANDARDS IN TRANSITION 613
K. SUMMARY 614
L. ANSWERS TO CHECKPOINT QUESTIONS 615
M. GLOSSARY 615
N. REFERENCES 616
O. PROBLEMS 617
P. MINI-CASES 633

A. INTRODUCTION

1. Overview

Non-current liabilities are obligations expected to be settled more than one year after the balance sheet date or the business's normal operating cycle, whichever is longer. As discussed in Chapter 11, many current liabilities arise from financing the firm's day-to-day operating activities. Borrowing comprises the major portion of non-current liabilities, although other significant liabilities do exist, as we will see in other chapters.

There are two key reasons why companies borrow to acquire assets: (i) they have insufficient cash available to pay for the acquisition, or (ii) they expect to profit by investing in assets that will generate income in excess of borrowing costs.

L.O. 12-1. Describe financial leverage and its impact on profitability.

non-current liabilities
Obligations that are expected to be settled more than one year after the balance sheet date or the business's normal operating cycle, whichever is longer.

It is helpful to think of these motives in personal terms. People routinely take out loans to buy new cars or mortgages to purchase real estate when they do not have enough of their own cash. Similarly, individuals borrow money to buy stocks or other investments expecting that the return generated will exceed the cost of borrowing.

2. Financial leverage

financial leverage Quantifies the relationship between the relative level of a firm's debt and its equity base.

Whatever the underlying reason, when a business borrows money its total debt level increases, and so too does its financial leverage. **Financial leverage** is one measure of solvency. While there are different ways to calculate financial leverage, in simple terms it quantifies the relationship between the relative level of a firm's debt and its equity base. Financial leverage offers shareholders an opportunity to increase their return on equity (ROE) when the business performs well but exposes them to an increased risk of loss as well. For this reason, leverage is often referred to as a double-edged sword. Moreover, increased financial leverage also amplifies the risk of bankruptcy as the company has additional payments (interest and principal) that must be made on an ongoing basis. See Exhibit 12-1 for an illustration of how financial leverage affects the return to the shareholders.

A natural question to ask is, "What is a safe level of debt?" This is a very difficult question to answer as opinions vary widely. While a full discussion of this issue is beyond the scope of this text, considerations include the nature of the industry, degree of operating leverage, stability of cash flows, competitive factors, and economic outlook.

Exhibit 12-1 An illustration of financial leverage's impact on profitability

Facts: Vernon Hydroponics Services Inc. is a new company. Its only asset is $100,000 of cash raised by issuing common shares.[1]

	Scenario 1 (unlevered)		Scenario 2 (levered)	
	Vernon invests the **$100,000** in a venture that will pay out either **$75,000** or **$130,000** at the end of one year, depending on the success of the venture.		Vernon **borrows $200,000** at 6% interest and invests **$300,000** in the same project outlined in Scenario 1. The payout will be **$225,000** ($75,000 × 3) or **$390,000** ($130,000 × 3) because it invests three times as much.	
	Unsuccessful	Successful	Unsuccessful	Successful
Opening equity	$ 100,000	$100,000	$ 100,000	$100,000
Loan proceeds	—	—	200,000	200,000
Investment	$ 100,000	$100,000	$ 300,000	$300,000
Payout expected	$ 75,000	$130,000	$ 225,000	$390,000
Repay loan	—	—	(200,000)	(200,000)
Pay loan interest	—	—	(12,000)	(12,000)
Closing equity	75,000	130,000	13,000	178,000
Opening equity	100,000	100,000	100,000	100,000
Profit (loss)	$ (25,000)	$ 30,000	$ (87,000)	$ 78,000
Return on opening equity (ROE)	−25%	30%	−87%	78%

Commentary: This example demonstrates how leverage can increase investors' returns while concurrently exposing them to large losses.

(Continued)

[1] IFRS uses "ordinary" shares to refer to common shares.

Exhibit 12-1 Continued

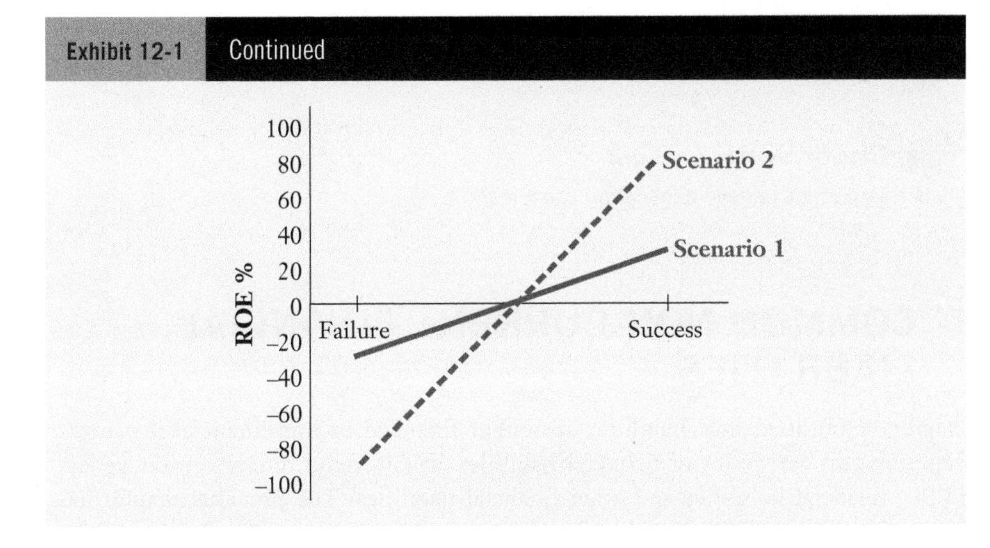

 CHECKPOINT **CP12-1**

What is the primary advantage of leverage, and what are two disadvantages of leverage?

3. Debt-rating agencies

There are literally thousands of bond issues outstanding at any one time in Canada. Most investors do not have the resources to evaluate the financial strength of the hundreds of issuers[2] or research the nuances of the plethora of bond issues to facilitate making an informed investment decision. For this reason, investors often rely on debt-rating agencies to assess the risk for them.

The TransLink opening vignette posed the question, "Who determines the creditworthiness of the issuer?" Debt-rating agencies such as DBRS (also known as Dominion Bond Rating Service) and Moody's Investors Service evaluate the financial strength of governments and companies that issue publicly traded debt and preferred shares. Their role is to provide an independent and impartial evaluation of the riskiness of debt securities to assist investors in making educated decisions. The credit rating conferred is the agency's assessment of the borrower's ability to pay the obligation when due. Similar to an external audit, this evaluation by independent rating agencies helps to reduce information asymmetry between bond issuers and investors, which in turn can reduce the cost of financing.

THRESHOLD CONCEPT
INFORMATION ASYMMETRY

The higher the ranking awarded, the lower the perceived probability of default. For example, DBRS's bond ratings range from AAA to D. On November 30, 2016, DBRS confirmed the AAA rating previously awarded to the Business Development Bank of Canada, Canada Mortgage and Housing Corporation, Canada Post Corporation, Export Development Canada, and Farm Credit Canada. This seldom-conferred rating signifies that there is virtually no chance of default; in contrast, a company awarded a D rating has announced its intent to default on its obligations—or has defaulted already. As set out in the opening vignette, Moody's Investors Service and DBRS respectively reaffirmed TransLink's credit ratings as Aa2 and AA prior to the bond issuance. Long-term debt such as TransLink's that earns a AA rating, while

[2] There are far more bond *issues* outstanding than there are bond *issuers* because most companies and governments (*the issuers*) have more than one bond *issue* outstanding. For example, the bond issue referred to in the opening vignette is TransLink's ninth bond issue.

slightly more risky than that of the CMHC's AAA rating, is still considered to be of superior credit quality with a very low probability of default.

 CHECKPOINT **CP12-2**

Why is it important to have debt-rating agencies?

B. COMMON NON-CURRENT FINANCIAL LIABILITIES

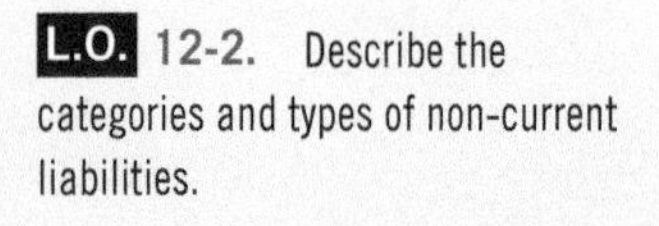
L.O. 12-2. Describe the categories and types of non-current liabilities.

Chapter 11 outlined how liabilities are either financial or non-financial in nature. There are two categories of financial liabilities: at fair value through profit or loss (FVPL) financial liabilities and other financial liabilities. The previous chapter has already considered FVPL financial liabilities (current obligations) and many of the more common non-financial liabilities including warranty obligations and deferred revenue. This chapter will focus primarily on non-current financial liabilities, including notes payable and bonds such as those issued by TransLink. Recall that **financial liabilities** are contractual obligations to deliver cash or other financial assets to another party at a future date.

financial liability A contractual obligation to deliver cash or other financial assets to another party.

Exhibit 12-2 summarizes the topical coverage of Chapters 11 and 12.

Exhibit 12-2 Topical coverage

	Financial	Non-financial
Current	Chapter 11	Chapter 11
Non-current	Chapter 12	Chapter 11

While financial liabilities at FVPL are current liabilities, we include a discussion of accounting for related transaction costs in Section C, to contrast that with the accounting for transaction costs of other financial liabilities.

Similarly, obligations arising from decommissioning and site restoration costs, while non-financial in nature, are dealt with in Section G of this chapter because of the similarity of its treatment with non-current financial liabilities. Moreover, due to their specialized nature, separate topical coverage is provided for pension obligations, lease liabilities, and deferred income taxes in Chapters 16, 17, and 18, respectively.

1. Notes payable

The remaining time to maturity differentiates non-current and current notes payable. For most privately owned companies, notes are issued to a bank or supplier and are not publicly traded. A mortgage is a special type of note payable specifically secured by a charge over real estate. Many large, well-known companies such as Ford Credit Canada issue (sell) notes directly to the investment community, who then trade these notes on recognized exchanges and over-the-counter (OTC) markets.

Banks and other institutions are financial intermediaries using deposits by some customers to make loans to other clients. At the risk of oversimplifying a complex business model, banks make money by charging a "spread"—an interest rate on loans that is higher than the rate they pay on deposits. One reason why companies sell notes directly to investors is to lower interest costs by reducing or eliminating the spread. For example, assume that Bank A is paying 1% interest on one-year deposits and charging 3% on one-year loans. Borrower B and depositor C are both better off if they are able to bypass the bank and deal with each other directly, with B paying C 2% for the use of its money.

Exhibit 12-3 Reducing the spread

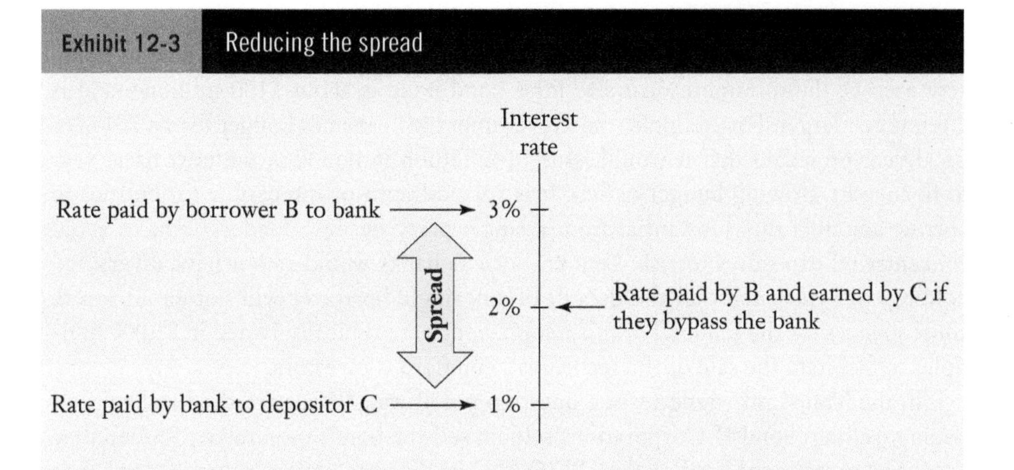

Of course, banks do not earn a spread without good reason—the spread is compensation for value-added services. Banks are able to offer a low rate on deposits because they offer a safe place for depositors to put their funds, whereas someone buying a note from a company faces significant information asymmetry about the company. On the lending side, banks have developed specialized processes to evaluate the creditworthiness of borrowers.

CHECKPOINT **CP12-3**

Why do companies sell notes directly to the investing public?

2. Bonds

a. Overview

Governments and publicly traded companies issue (sell) bonds directly to investors to raise large amounts of long-term funds. Bonds are a very common form of long-term debt. For these reasons, much of this chapter is devoted to accounting for bonds. Many of the ideas will also be applicable to other kinds of long-term debt.

Lending money to a company entails moral hazard, since the company's management has control of the funds lent by the creditors (see Chapter 1). To reduce this moral hazard, bonds include **covenants**, which are restrictions on the borrower's activities. Covenants can be positive or negative, respectively requiring or forbidding certain actions. An example of a positive covenant is the borrower pledging to maintain its current ratio in excess of 1.5:1; a negative covenant is agreeing not to pay dividends in excess of $1,000,000 per year.

covenant The borrower's promise to restrict certain activities.

A **bond indenture** is the contract that outlines the terms of the bond, including the maturity date, rate of interest, interest payment dates, security pledged, and financial covenants. Provided that the borrower strictly complies with the covenants, lenders cannot otherwise restrict its activities.

bond indenture A contract that outlines the terms of the bond, including the maturity date, rate of interest, interest payment dates, security pledged, and financial covenants.

By convention, the coupon return on bonds is quoted as a nominal annual rate, while interest payments are usually paid semi-annually. For example, 6% bonds pay interest of 3% every six months, resulting in an actual annual return of 6.09%.[3]

[3] $(1 + 0.03)^2 - 1 = 0.0609 = 6.09\%$

Reasons for issuing bonds (instead of using a bank loan, for example) include reducing the cost of borrowing and accessing large amounts of capital. Due to transaction costs, the minimum deal size for a bond issue is about $100 million—and is often much larger. For example, the Government of Canada's budget for its 2017–18 fiscal year projected that it would issue $142 billion in bonds in the next fiscal year to finance its growing budget deficit. It is very difficult or impossible for entities to borrow amounts this substantial from a single party because lenders want to avoid concentrated exposures to risk. Lenders such as banks would rather have diversified holdings of loans such that the default of any single borrower will not entail severe consequences for the lender. For this reason, bonds are typically issued in $1,000 multiples to facilitate the sale of the securities to numerous investors.

In the TransLink vignette, one question posed was, "What are the mechanics of issuing (selling) bonds?" Corporations seldom sell the bonds themselves. Rather, they engage an **investment bank** such as BMO Nesbitt Burns to underwrite (sell) the bonds on its behalf.[4] As part of the underwriting process the investment bank typically provides a wide range of services to the borrower. These include providing advice with respect to structuring the bond issue (term, interest rate (yield), security, and covenants) and regulatory and legal issues.

investment bank A financial institution that acts as an agent or underwriter for corporations and governments issuing securities.

The more common method of underwriting is a **firm commitment underwriting**, where the investment bank guarantees the borrower a price for the securities, expecting to resell them to its investment clients at a profit. A lesser-used arrangement is a **best efforts approach**, where the broker simply agrees to try to sell as much of the issue as possible to investors.

firm commitment underwriting Occurs when the investment bank guarantees the borrower a price for the securities.

best efforts approach Occurs when the broker simply agrees to try to sell as much of the (debt) issue as possible to investors.

New bond issues are sold at the offering price in what is known as the *primary market.* This market is dominated by institutional investors; small investors are seldom able to purchase new bond issues at the offering price. Subsequent to issue, bonds trade in a decentralized, secondary, over-the-counter (OTC) market, rather than in a common location like the Toronto Stock Exchange.

In the OTC market, dealers carry inventories of bonds. They earn a profit by selling the bonds for more than they paid for them. The price differential is referred to as the spread. Trades are typically conducted between brokers via phone or proprietary electronic systems. Individual investors cannot participate in the OTC market directly, rather they must arrange to buy and sell bonds through a broker such as CIBC Investor's Edge.

b. Types of bonds

Once a corporation decides to raise capital by issuing bonds, it must determine the characteristics (features) of the indebtedness, such as the maturity date. While the company's investment bank will advise the firm in this respect, the business must consider a number of factors, including investor preferences, projected cash flows, desired capital structure, and minimizing its cost of capital. Reflecting these various considerations, there are many different types of bonds to satisfy these diverse needs. Some of the more common bonds are described below:

secured bonds Bonds backed by specific collateral such as a mortgage on real estate.

debentures Unsecured bonds.

stripped (zero-coupon) bonds Bonds that do not pay interest; stripped bonds are sold at a discount and mature at face value.

serial bonds A set of bonds issued at the same time but that mature at regularly scheduled dates rather than all on the same date.

- **Secured bonds** are bonds backed by specific collateral, such as a mortgage on real estate.
- **Debentures** are unsecured bonds.
- **Stripped (zero-coupon) bonds** are bonds that do not pay interest. Stripped bonds are sold at a discount and mature at face value.
- **Serial bonds** are a set of bonds issued at the same time but that mature at regularly scheduled dates rather than all on the same date.

[4] It is common for the lead investment bank to form a syndicate with other investment banks to help sell the bonds to institutional and private investors.

- **Callable bonds** permit the issuing company to "call" for the bonds to be redeemed before maturity. A **call premium** is the excess over par value paid to the bondholders when the security is called.
- **Convertible bonds** allow the holder to exchange or "convert" the bond into other securities in the corporation, usually common shares. Convertible bonds are an example of compound financial instruments, discussed in Chapter 14.
- **Real-return or inflation-linked bonds** protect investors against inflation. While the mechanics differ slightly across issues, the basic premise is that the cash flows are indexed to the inflation rate. Real-return bonds are not that common in Canada, although the Bank of Canada does issue them occasionally. Most real-return bonds are held by bond funds, rather than by individual investors.
- **Perpetual bonds** are bonds that never mature. Perpetual bonds are seldom issued in Canada.

callable bonds Bonds that permit the issuing company to "call" for the bonds to be redeemed before maturity.

call premium The excess over par value paid to the bondholders when the security is called.

convertible bonds Bonds that allow the holder to exchange or "convert" the bond into other securities in the corporation, usually common shares.

real-return (inflation-linked) bonds Bonds whose cash flows are indexed to the inflation rate.

perpetual bonds Bonds that never mature.

C. INITIAL MEASUREMENT

L.O. 12-3. Describe the initial and subsequent measurement of non-current financial liabilities and account for these obligations.

Non-current financial liabilities, like all financial statement elements, must be assigned a value when they are first recognized on the balance sheet. In general, enterprises should initially record financial liabilities at fair value minus debt issue costs (IFRS 9 paragraph 5.1.1). Examples of transaction costs include fees charged by investment banks and regulatory agencies, legal and accounting fees, and outlays for promotion. For example, if an enterprise issues a bond for gross proceeds and fair value of $100 million and incurs $2 million of bond-issue costs, it would record the bond at the amount of the net proceeds of $98 million.

The one exception to the inclusion of transaction costs is FVPL financial liabilities. Enterprises should initially recognize these liabilities at fair value with all transaction costs expensed. This exception to the general rule makes sense to the extent that FVPL financial instruments must be measured at fair value at each balance sheet date, so any transaction costs included in the initially recognized amount would be expensed when the item is re-measured at fair value. For instance, using the example just given, if the bond is classified as FVPL, the company would record $100 million for the liability and expense the $2 million. If at year-end the bond still has a fair value of $100 million, no additional income or expense would be recorded. However, if the bond had initially been recorded at the amount of net proceeds ($98 million), then the $100 million fair value at year-end would result in a $2 million increase in liability and a corresponding $2 million expense. The outcome is the same: both treatments result in $2 million of expense.

In many cases, the fair value of the debt is easily determinable. For example, if a company issues a standard bond at par value for cash, and the timing matches the interest payment date, then the fair value of the note equals the cash received. Not all situations are this straightforward, however. Some common departures include receiving non-cash assets, bonds issued at premium or discount, issuance of hybrid financial instruments, and debt issuance dates that differ from the interest payment dates. We discuss these issues next.

CHECKPOINT CP12-4

A bond indenture includes covenants. What is a bond indenture and what are covenants?

CHECKPOINT CP12-5

How are bonds traded subsequent to issue? How do the dealers earn a profit?

1. Debt exchanged for non-cash assets

Notes or other debt instruments exchanged for assets are recognized at fair value. This treatment is supported by IAS 16—Property, Plant, and Equipment, which reads in part:

> ¶6 *Cost* is the amount of cash or cash equivalents paid or the fair value of the other consideration given to acquire an asset at the time of its acquisition . . .[5]

IFRS 13, supported by paragraph B2 of the application guidance in Appendix B, provides guidance on determining the fair value of financial liabilities given in exchange for non-cash assets.

2. Debt issued at non-market rates of interest

If the liability is non-interest bearing or the stated rate of interest is different from the market rate of interest, the fair value of the debt will differ from the face (maturity) value. This includes bonds issued at a premium or discount, discussed later in this chapter. If the note is issued for consideration other than cash, the fair value must be estimated employing the fair value hierarchy set out in paragraphs 72–90 of IFRS 13. In the absence of similar market transactions, discounted cash flow analysis is normally used to determine the liability to be recognized.

Exhibit 12-4 illustrates two scenarios accounting for the issuance of debt in exchange for cash or non-cash assets, and a third scenario involving debt issued at a non-market interest rate.

Exhibit 12-4 Accounting for the issuance of debt

	Scenario 1	Scenario 2	Scenario 3
Face amount of note issued	$150,000	$150,000	$150,000
Date issued	Jan. 1, 2021	Jan. 1, 2021	Jan. 1, 2021
Due date	Jan. 1, 2023	Jan. 1, 2023	Jan. 1, 2023
Interest rate in the note	4%	0%	4% (payable annually)
Market rate of interest	4%	Unknown	6%
Consideration received	Cash	Equipment	Land
Value of similar transaction	not applicable	$140,000	not applicable
Fair value determination	Cash received	Level 2 input	Discounted cash flow analysis
Journal entry on issuance	Dr. Cash 150,000	Dr. Equipment 140,000	Dr. Land 144,500
(NP = Note payable)	Cr. NP 150,000	Cr. NP 140,000	Cr. NP 144,500

Comment—Scenario 3

The note payable consists of two types of cash flows: an ordinary annuity for the periodic coupon payments and a single sum due at maturity for the principal. The value of the note is the sum of the present value of the two parts.

Using a BA II Plus financial calculator: 2 **N** 6 **I/Y** 6000, ($150,000 × 4%) **PMT** 150000 **FV** **CPT** **PV** → PV = −144,500 (rounded)

3. Compound financial instruments

A compound financial instrument is one with both debt and equity features. For example, a bond that can be exchanged for common shares in the issuing company has elements of both debt (the bond) and equity (the right to exchange the bond for shares).

When initially recognized, the component parts must normally be accounted for separately, as detailed in Chapter 14.

4. Interest rates and how they impact the selling price of bonds

The **coupon or stated rate of interest** on a bond is the interest rate specified in the bond indenture (contract).[6] The coupon rate is expressed as a percentage of the bond's face value and governs the amount of interest paid by the borrower at each payment date. For example, a $1,000, 5-year, 6%, semi-annual bond pays $30 ($1,000 × 6%/2) interest to the investor every six months.

coupon (stated) rate of interest The interest rate specified in the bond indenture.

The **market rate of interest** or **yield** is the rate of return (on a bond) actually earned by the investor.[7] The market rate of interest factors in the interest payments received over the life of the bond, and any discount received or premium paid at the purchase date. For example, the market rate of interest for a $1,000, 5-year, 6%, semi-annual bond purchased for $990 is:

market rate of interest (yield) The rate of return (on a bond) actually earned by the investor.

990 [+I−] [PV] 1000 [FV] 10, (5 × 2) [N] 30 [PMT] [CPT] [I/Y] → I/Y = 3.1179% *per period* (rounded).

Similarly, the market rate of interest for a $1,000, 5-year, 6%, semi-annual bond purchased for $1,010 is:

1010 [+I−] [PV] 1000 [FV] 10 [N] 30 [PMT] [CPT] [I/Y] → I/Y 2.8835% *per period* (rounded).

For the borrower, the **effective interest rate** is the rate of interest paid (on a bond). The effective interest rate factors in the interest payments made over the life of the bond, discounts given or premiums received at the issuance date, and the borrower's transaction costs that are directly attributed to issuing the bonds (e.g., investment bank and legal fees).[8] For example, the effective interest rate for a $1,000, 5-year, 6%, semi-annual bond sold for $990 with $5 in directly attributable transaction costs is:

effective interest rate The rate of interest paid by the borrower that factors in premiums or discounts at issuance and transaction costs.

985, ($990 − $5) [+I−] [PV] 1000 [FV] 10 [N] 30 [PMT] [CPT] [I/Y] → I/Y = 3.1774% *per period* (rounded).

Similarly, the effective interest rate for a $1,000, 5-year, 6%, semi-annual bond sold for $1,010 with $5 in directly attributable transaction costs is:

1005, ($1,010 − $5) [+I−] [PV] 1000 [FV] 10 [N] 30 [PMT] [CPT] [I/Y] → I/Y = 2.9416% *per period* (rounded).

Note that in the absence of transaction costs, the effective interest rate paid on the bond by the borrower equals the market rate of interest earned by the investor.

When the coupon rate is less than the market rate, bonds will sell at a discount. Conversely, when the coupon rate exceeds the market rate, bonds will sell at a premium. The inverse relationship between bond price and the market rate of interest is illustrated in Exhibit 12-5a. The impact of transaction costs is then considered in Exhibit 12-5b.

---

6. "Coupon" is a historical term from when bonds were printed and issued to the purchaser. The bond was composed of the body, which had to be surrendered at maturity, and a coupon for each interest payment—hence the name. On the interest due date, the investor would detach the coupon and submit it to the borrower for payment. Today, bond certificates are seldom printed; most interest payments are electronically credited to the investor's account.

7. In the absence of transaction costs paid by the investor (Chapter 7).

8. As illustrated elsewhere in this chapter, over the life of the bond, the total amount charged to interest expense equals all interest paid (the coupon), plus directly attributable transaction costs, plus the discount or minus the premium at issuance.

Exhibit 12-5a Illustration of the inverse relationship between bond prices and the market rate of interest

Facts

A $100,000, 5-year, 12% bond that pays interest semi-annually dated January 1, 2018, is offered for sale on January 1, 2018.

	Scenario 1 $100,000 in bonds are sold for **$99,000**	Scenario 2 $100,000 in bonds are sold for **$100,000**	Scenario 3 $100,000 in bonds are sold for **$101,000**
Inputs			
Maturity value	$100,000	$100,000	$100,000
Interest payments ($100,000 × 12%/2)	$ 6,000	$ 6,000	$ 6,000
Number of payments (5 × 2)	10	10	10
Price received for the bond	$ 99,000	$100,000	$101,000
Solve for market rate*	6.1367%	6.0000%	5.8650%

*Scenario 1: 99000 **+I–** **PV** 100000 **FV** 6000 **PMT** 10 **N** **CPT** **I/Y** → I/Y = 6.1367% *per period* (rounded)

*Scenario 2: 100000 **+I–** **PV** 100000 **FV** 6000 **PMT** 10 **N** **CPT** **I/Y** → I/Y = 6.0000% *per period*

*Scenario 3: 101000 **+I–** **PV** 100000 **FV** 6000 **PMT** 10 **N** **CPT** **I/Y** → I/Y = 5.8650% *per period* (rounded)

From Exhibit 12-5a we can conclude that:

- Bonds will sell at a discount (less than par value) when the coupon rate is less than the market rate (Scenario 1).
- Bonds will sell at **par value** (the amount to be repaid to the investor at maturity) when the coupon rate equals the market rate (Scenario 2).
- Bonds will sell at a premium (more than par value) when the coupon rate is greater than the market rate (Scenario 3).

par value The amount to be repaid to the investor at maturity.

Exhibit 12-5b Impact of transaction costs on the effective rate of interest

Facts

The borrower paid $500 in transaction costs to issue the bonds in Exhibit 12-5a.

	Scenario 1 $100,000 in bonds are sold for **$99,000**	Scenario 2 $100,000 in bonds are sold for **$100,000**	Scenario 3 $100,000 in bonds are sold for **$101,000**
Inputs			
Maturity value	$100,000	$100,000	$100,000
Interest payments ($100,000 × 12%/2)	$ 6,000	$ 6,000	$ 6,000
Number of payments (5 × 2)	10	10	10
Price received for the bond	$ 99,000	$100,000	$101,000
Market rate	6.1367%	6.0000%	5.8650%
Less: Transaction costs	$ 500	$ 500	$ 500
Net cash received	$ 98,500	$ 99,500	$100,500
Solve for effective rate*	6.2058%	6.0682%	5.9323%

*Scenario 1: 98500 **+I–** **PV** 100000 **FV** 6000 **PMT** 10 **N** **CPT** **I/Y** → I/Y = 6.2058% *per period* (rounded)

*Scenario 2: 99500 **+I–** **PV** 100000 **FV** 6000 **PMT** 10 **N** **CPT** **I/Y** → I/Y = 6.0682% *per period*

*Scenario 3: 100500 **+I–** **PV** 100000 **FV** 6000 **PMT** 10 **N** **CPT** **I/Y** → I/Y = 5.9323% *per period* (rounded)

From Exhibit 12-5b, we can conclude that when the borrower incurs directly attributable transactions costs, the effective rate of interest paid on the bonds by the borrower will always be higher than the market rate of interest earned by the investor.

Companies normally aim to issue the bonds at par by setting the coupon rate to equal the prevailing market rate of interest. Recall from Section B, subsection 2 that one of the services provided by the investment bank is guidance as to the required yield. Due to the issuer having to obtain regulatory approval for the bond sale and other factors, there is inevitably a time lag between when the company determines the coupon rate and the time of sale. Fluctuations in the market rate in the intervening period cause the actual sale price to change so as to provide investors with the required market rate of return. Such price changes result in the bond selling at a discount or a premium.

5. Determining the sales price of a bond when the market rate of interest is given

Much of the discussion in this chapter focuses on determining the effective rate of interest from the sales price and other information such as the coupon rate and term. Nevertheless, it is sometimes useful to determine the sales price of a bond from a given market rate. The reason is that investors normally demand a certain yield—and their requirements drive the price, not the other way around. Having received the price that the investors agreed to pay, the company then uses this information to determine the effective rate of interest that they are paying.

Determining the sales price of a bond when the market rate of interest is known involves computing the present value of the coupons and the present value of the maturity amount. The sum of these two amounts is the sales price of the bond, as demonstrated in Exhibit 12-6. These two calculations can be combined when using a financial calculator or computer spreadsheet.

Exhibit 12-6 Determining the sales price of a bond when the market rate is known

Facts: A $100,000, five-year, 6% bond that pays interest semi-annually dated January 1, 2018, is offered for sale on January 1, 2018. The bond is sold to yield a 7% return to the investors.

Required: Determine the selling price of the bonds.

Maturity value	$100,000
Interest payments	$3,000 ($100,000 × 6% / 2)
Number of payments	10 (5 × 2)
Effective rate (yield)	3.5% (7% / 2)
Price paid for the bond	$95,842 as per the computations below

Calculation of sales price when the market rate of interest is known

100000 **FV** 3000 **PMT** 10 **N** 3.5 **I/Y** **CPT** **PV** → PV = −95,842 (rounded)

6. Timing of bond issuance

a. Selling bonds on the issue date specified in the indenture

Exhibit 12-7 illustrates the journal entries the issuing company would make in each of the three situations detailed in Exhibit 12-5a and the first scenario in Exhibit 12-5b.

b. Selling bonds after the specified issue date

The preceding examples assume that the bonds were sold on their issue date. On occasion, though, due to adverse market conditions or regulatory delays, a company may not sell its bonds until after the issue date. Consider a $1,000, five-year, 6% bond dated January 1, 2018, that pays interest on June 30 and December 31 and is sold at par on

Exhibit 12-7 Accounting for the issuance of bonds, using facts established in Exhibits 12-5a and 12-5b

	Exhibit 12-5a			Exhibit 12-5b
	Scenario 1	Scenario 2	Scenario 3	Scenario 1
Maturity value	$100,000	$100,000	$100,000	$100,000
Sales price	99,000	100,000	101,000	99,000
Transaction costs	0	0	0	500
Journal entry on issuance (BP denotes bonds payable)	Dr. Cash 99,000 Cr. BP 99,000	Dr. Cash 100,000 Cr. BP 100,000	Dr. Cash 101,000 Cr. BP 101,000	Dr. Cash 99,000 Cr. Cash 500 Cr. BP 98,500

Comment—Exhibit 12-5b, Scenario 1
The obligation is measured at the net of the fair value ($99,000) and transaction costs ($500) as required by IFRS 9 paragraph 5.1.1.

March 1, 2018. The bond indenture assumed that the bonds would sell on the issue date and provided that the purchaser receive $30 ($1,000 × 6% × 6 / 12), representing six months of interest on June 30, 2018. The problem is that the investors are only entitled to $20 ($1,000 × 6% × 4 / 12), as they have owned the bonds for only four months.

By convention, when bonds are sold between interest payment dates, the purchaser pays the seller the agreed-upon price for the bond plus interest that has accrued since the last payment date. In the example above, this would be $10 ($1,000 × 6% × 2 / 12), bringing the total consideration received to $1,010 accounted for as set out in Exhibit 12-8.

When bonds are sold on other than their issue date, the premium or discount, if any, is amortized over the length of time between when they are actually sold and their maturity date. In the example just given, the two-month delay would reduce the amortization period from 60 months (five years) to 58 months.

Exhibit 12-8 Accounting for the issuance of bonds between interest payment dates

On date of sale:		
Dr. Cash	1,010	
Cr. Bonds payable		1,000
Cr. Accrued interest on bond payable (balance sheet)[9]		10
On date of first interest payment:		
Dr. Accrued interest on bond payable	10	
Dr. Interest expense	20	
Cr. Cash		30

CHECKPOINT **CP12-6**

On what basis are notes and other debt instruments valued when exchanged for non-cash assets?

CHECKPOINT **CP12-7**

In the absence of similar market transactions, what method of valuation is normally used to determine the liability to be recognized for debt instruments issued at non-market rates of interest?

9. Alternatively, the company may credit interest expense on the date of sale, in which case the debit to interest expense on the date of the first payment would be $30. This is a bookkeeping matter much like the payment for insurance policies that can be debited to prepaid insurance or insurance expense. The key is that the company should adopt a policy, apply it consistently, and make appropriate adjusting entries at period end.

CHECKPOINT **CP12-8**

If investors demand a market rate on a bond issue that is greater than the coupon rate, will the bond issue sell at a premium or a discount?

CHECKPOINT **CP12-9**

When bonds are sold between interest payment dates, how does the purchaser compensate the seller for interest that has accrued since the last payment date? If a new 10-year bond issue is sold at a discount one month after the issue date, how many months would the discount be amortized over?

D. SUBSEQUENT MEASUREMENT

After initial recognition, all financial liabilities, except those FVPL, are measured and reported at **amortized cost**, which is the amount initially recognized for the debt adjusted by subsequent amortization of the net premium or discount.[10] There are two essential steps that must be taken to determine the amortized cost of a financial liability:

amortized cost (of debt) The amount initially recognized for the debt adjusted by subsequent amortization of the net premium or discount.

1. establish the effective interest rate; and
2. amortize the premium or discount using the effective interest method.

The following discussion explores these two steps in more detail.

1. Effective interest rate

In IFRS, the effective interest method must be used to determine amortized cost. Applying this method requires the effective interest rate, which is the rate of interest paid by the borrower that factors in premiums or discounts at issuance and transaction costs.[11] Exhibit 12-5b demonstrated the procedure for calculating the effective interest rate.

In Canada, the method used to calculate interest, by established convention, depends to some degree on the nature of the financial instrument. For example, in this chapter and Chapter 17, you will see that interest on bonds and leases is usually calculated based on the number of months outstanding, without regard to the number of days in each month.

The method used to calculate interest on notes payable depends on their nature. If the term note includes a set payment amount that includes principal and interest, as is done for bonds and leases, interest is usually calculated based on the number of months outstanding. If, however, the note is repayable on a principal plus interest basis or does not include an established repayment schedule (i.e., is repayable on demand), interest is calculated on a daily basis.

2. Amortization using the effective interest method

a. Interest payment coincides with fiscal year-end

After determining the effective interest rate, the process of applying the effective method is shown in Exhibit 12-9.

Companies frequently use spreadsheets to compute interest expense and determine the amortized cost of bonds to be reported at each balance sheet date. Exhibits 12-10 and 12-11 demonstrate the process outlined above and include select journal entries to record the issuance of the bonds and subsequent payment and accrual of interest. In both

10. The net premium or discount includes the premium or discount and transaction costs.

11. IFRS 9 Appendix A technically defines the effective interest rate as the rate that exactly discounts estimated future cash payments or receipts through the expected life of the financial instrument.

examples, the fiscal year-end is December 31, which coincides with an interest payment date. To ease understanding, we have broken these two exhibits into their component parts.

While working through the two examples that follow, you should observe the following:

- At maturity, the amortized cost of the bond (the carrying value or net book value) equals the maturity (face) value of the bond.
- The original discount or premium and transaction costs are charged to interest expense over the life of the bond. Amortizing bond discounts and transaction costs increases interest expense relative to the coupon payment; premiums decrease interest expense.
- For bonds sold at a discount, the interest expense per period increases each period. This is because the amortized cost of the bond increases each period and interest expense is a function of the bond's book value. Conversely, for bonds sold at a premium, the interest expense decreases each period.

Exhibit 12-9 Applying the effective interest method of determining amortized cost

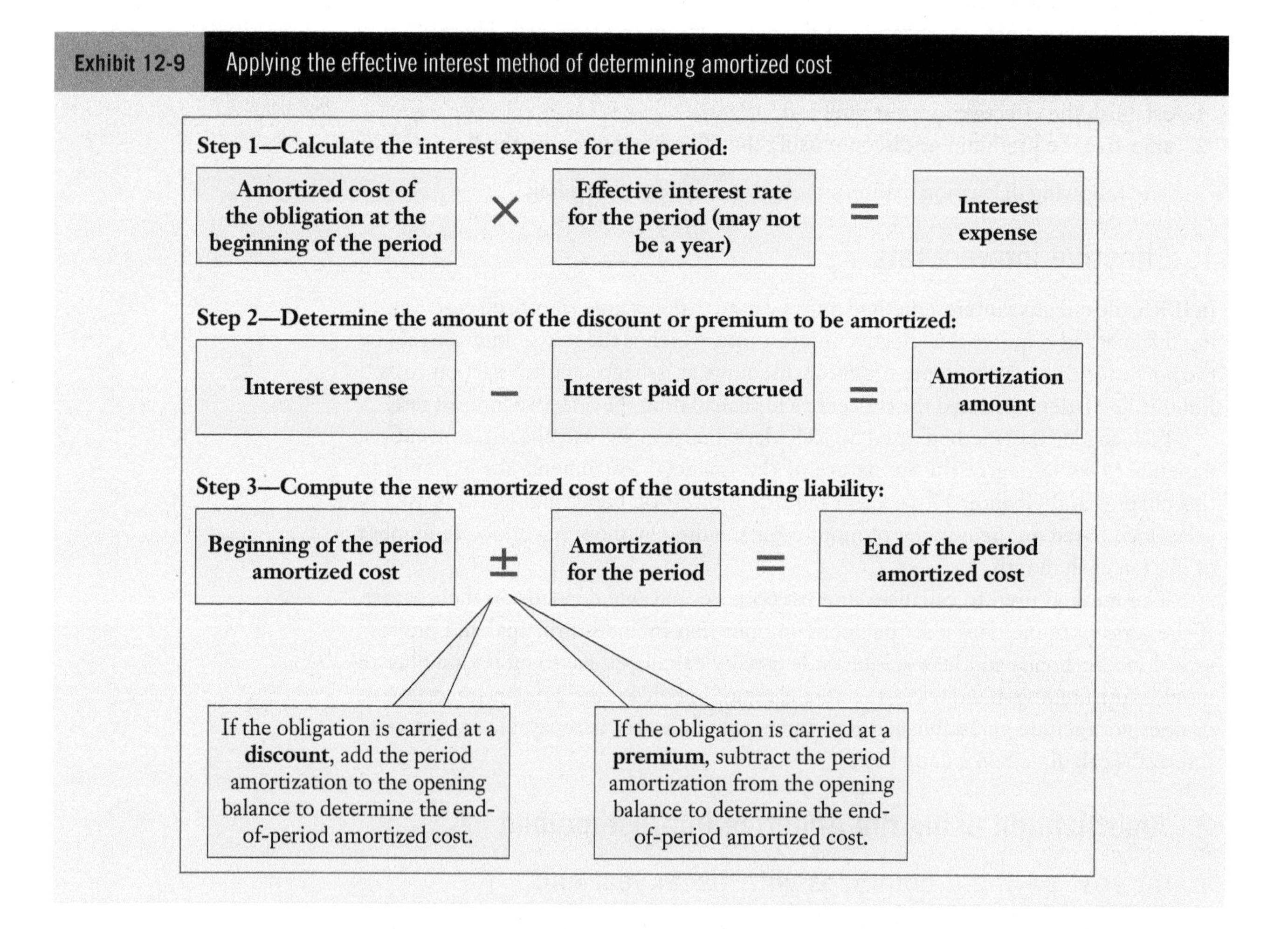

Exhibit 12-10a Example for determining the interest expense and amortized cost of a discount bond

Facts:

- Port Bay Inc. sells $1,000,000 of three-year bonds on January 1, 2018, for **$981,000**.
- The coupon rate on the bonds is 6% payable on July 1 and January 1.
- Transaction costs directly attributable to issuing the bonds total $15,000.
- Port Bay Inc's fiscal year-end is December 31.

Step 1: Determine the effective interest rate using a financial calculator or spreadsheet. The process is illustrated in Exhibit 12-10b.

Exhibit 12-10b Computation of effective interest rate

- The net proceeds *(PV)* to Port Bay are \$981,000 − \$15,000 = \$966,000
- The maturity value *(FV)* of the bonds is \$1,000,000
- N = 3 years × 2 payments/year = 6
- PMT = \$1,000,000 × 6%/2 = \$30,000

Using a financial calculator: 966000 **+/−** **PV** 1000000 **FV** 6 **N** 30000 **PMT** **CPT** **I/Y** → I/Y = 3.6410% per period (rounded)

Step 2: Use the facts given in Exhibit 12-10a and the effective rate determined in Exhibit 12-10b to construct an amortization schedule like the one shown in Exhibit 12-10c.

Exhibit 12-10c Amortization schedule for Port Bay's discount bond

Date	Interest expense @3.6410%	Interest paid	Discount amortized	Amortized cost
Jan. 01, 2018				\$ 966,000 (a)
Jul. 01, 2018	\$ 35,172 (b)	\$ 30,000 (c)	\$ 5,172 (d)	971,172 (e)
Jan. 01, 2019	35,361	30,000	5,361	976,533
Jul. 01, 2019	35,556	30,000	5,556	982,089
Jan. 01, 2020	35,758	30,000	5,758	987,847
Jul. 01, 2020	35,968	30,000	5,968	993,815
Jan. 01, 2021	36,185	30,000	6,185	1,000,000
	\$214,000	\$180,000	\$34,000	

Calculations

(a) \$981,000 − \$15,000 = \$966,000 (initial proceeds net of issuance cost)

(b) \$966,000 × 3.6410% = \$35,172

(c) \$1,000,000 × 6%/2 = \$30,000

(d) \$35,172 − \$30,000 = \$5,172

(e) \$966,000 + \$5,172 = \$971,172

Step 3: Use the information from the facts in Exhibit 12-10a to prepare the journal entry when the bonds are sold on January 1, 2018:

Exhibit 12-10d Journal entry for bond issuance

Issuance	Dr. Cash (Sales proceeds – transaction costs)[12]	966,000	
Jan. 01, 2018	Cr. Bonds payable (\$981,000 – \$15,000)		966,000

[12] Alternatively, cash could be debited \$981,000 for the sales proceeds and credited \$15,000 for the payment of transaction costs. In practice, the amount received from the investment bank (sales proceeds less its fees) would be debited to cash. Transaction costs paid separately (e.g., to legal counsel) would be recorded separately. For ease of exposition, we will normally debit cash with the net proceeds from the bond issue.

Step 4: Use the information from the amortization schedule in Exhibit 12-10c to prepare the journal entry for the first interest payment on July 1, 2018:

Exhibit 12-10e Journal entry for first interest payment

Interest payment	Dr. Interest expense	35,172	
Jul. 01, 2018	Cr. Cash		30,000
	Cr. Bonds payable ($35,172 − $30,000)		5,172

Step 5: Use the information from the amortization schedule in Exhibit 12-10c to prepare the year-end accrual for interest expense on December 31, 2018:

Exhibit 12-10f Journal entry for year-end accrual of interest expense

Year-end	Dr. Interest expense	35,361	
Dec. 31, 2018	Cr. Interest payable		30,000
	Cr. Bonds payable ($35,361 − $30,000)		5,361

Step 6: Record the second payment of interest on January 1, 2019:

Exhibit 12-10g Journal entry for second interest payment

Interest payment	Dr. Interest payable	30,000	
Jan. 01, 2019	Cr. Cash		30,000

Steps 4, 5, and 6 are repeated until the bonds mature on January 1, 2021, at which time the liability will be derecognized, as illustrated later in Section E.

The above example illustrated a discount bond. The following example in Exhibit 12-11 illustrates a premium bond.

Exhibit 12-11a Example for determining the interest expense and amortized cost of a premium bond

Facts:

- Port Bay Inc. sells $1,000,000 of three-year bonds on January 1, 2018, for **$1,025,000**.
- The coupon rate on the bonds is 6% payable on July 1 and January 1.
- Transaction costs directly attributable to issuing the bonds total $15,000.
- Port Bay Inc's fiscal year-end is December 31.

Step 1: Determine the effective interest rate.

Exhibit 12-11b Computation of effective interest rate

- The net proceeds *(PV)* to Port Bay are $1,025,000 − $15,000 = $1,010,000
- The maturity value *(FV)* of the bonds is $1,000,000
- $N = 3$ years × 2 payments/year = 6
- $PMT = \$1,000,000 \times 6\%/2 = \$30,000$

Using a financial calculator: 1010000 **+I−** **PV** 1000000 **FV** 6 **N** 30000 **PMT** **CPT** **I/Y** → I/Y = 2.8165% per period (rounded)

Step 2: Construct the amortization schedule.

Exhibit 12-11c Amortization schedule for Port Bay's premium bond

Date	Interest expense @2.8165%	Interest paid	Premium amortized	Amortized cost
Jan. 01, 2018				$1,010,000 (a)
Jul. 01, 2018	$ 28,447 (b)	$ 30,000 (c)	$ 1,553 (d)	1,008,447 (e)
Jan. 01, 2019	28,403	30,000	1,597	1,006,850
Jul. 01, 2019	28,358	30,000	1,642	1,005,208
Jan. 01, 2020	28,312	30,000	1,688	1,003,520
Jul. 01, 2020	28,264	30,000	1,736	1,001,785
Jan. 01, 2021	28,215	30,000	1,785	1,000,000
	$170,000	$180,000	$10,000	

Calculations

Small differences due to rounding

(a) $1,025,000 − $15,000 = $1,010,000

(b) $1,010,000 × 2.8165% = $28,447

(c) $1,000,000 × 6%/2 = $30,000

(d) $28,447 − $30,000 = $1,553

(e) $1,010,000 − $1,553 = $1,008,447

Step 3: Journal entry for bond issue on January 1, 2018.

Exhibit 12-11d Journal entry for bond issuance

Issuance	Dr. Cash (Sales proceeds – transaction costs)	1,010,000	
Jan. 01, 2018	Cr. Bonds payable ($1,025,000 – $15,000)		1,010,000

Step 4: Journal entry for interest payment on July 1, 2018.

Exhibit 12-11e Journal entry for first interest payment

Interest payment	Dr. Interest expense	28,447	
Jul. 01, 2018	Dr. Bonds payable ($30,000 − $28,447)	1,553	
	Cr. Cash		30,000

Step 5: Journal entry for accrual of interest on December 31, 2018.

Exhibit 12-11f Journal entry for year-end accrual of interest expense

Year-end	Dr. Interest expense	28,403	
Dec. 31, 2018	Dr. Bonds payable ($30,000 − $28,403)	1,597	
	Cr. Interest payable		30,000

Step 6: Journal entry to record the payment of interest on January 1, 2019.

Exhibit 12-11g Journal entry for second interest payment

Interest payment	Dr. Interest payable	30,000	
Jan. 01, 2019	Cr. Cash		30,000

Again, Steps 4, 5, and 6 are repeated until the bonds mature on January 1, 2021.

b. When interest payments do not coincide with fiscal year-end

In Exhibits 12-10 and 12-11, the second interest payment date coincided with Port Bay Inc.'s year-end. However, this often is not the case. If the interest payment and fiscal year-end dates differ, it is necessary to prorate the amortization of the discount or premium. Exhibit 12-12 is based on the facts previously given in Exhibit 12-11 with the exception that Port Bay Inc.'s fiscal year-end is now assumed to be October 31 (instead of December 31). Recall that we determined that the effective semi-annual rate of interest was 2.8165% and constructed the following amortization schedule (in part):

Exhibit 12-12a Amortization schedule (excerpted from Exhibit 12-11c)

Date	Interest expense @2.8165%	Interest paid	Premium amortized	Amortized cost
Jan. 01, 2018				$1,010,000
Jul. 01, 2018	$28,447	$30,000	$1,553	1,008,447
Jan. 01, 2019	28,403	30,000	1,597	1,006,850

The journal entries to record the issuance of the bond on January 1, 2018, and interest expense on July 1, 2018, remain the same as that previously illustrated in Exhibits 12-11d and 12-11e, respectively. On October 31, 2018 (Port Bay's revised fiscal year-end), four months have passed since interest was last expensed. It is now necessary to prorate the interest costs that will be paid on January 1, 2019 [$28,403 × (4 months ÷ 6 months) = $18,935 interest to be accrued].

The journal entry for the accrual of interest on October 31, 2018, is:

Exhibit 12-12b Journal entry to record accrual of interest at year-end

Year-end			
Oct. 31, 2018	Dr. Interest expense	18,935	
	Dr. Bonds payable	1,065	
	Cr. Interest payable		20,000

 CHECKPOINT **CP12-10**

How are at fair value through profit or loss liabilities measured subsequent to issue? How are the remainder of financial liabilities measured subsequent to issue?

3. Amortization using the straight-line method

IFRS unambiguously requires that amortized cost be determined using the effective interest method. Canadian standards, however, permit use of the straight-line method by some companies. A brief history follows:

- Prior to the adoption of Section 3855, Financial Instruments—Recognition and Measurement, the standards permitted all companies to amortize debt discounts and premiums using either the effective interest or straight-line method.
- The Accounting Standards Board (AcSB) issued Section 3855 effective for fiscal years beginning on or after October 1, 2006. Like IFRS, this standard mandated the use of the effective interest method to determine amortized cost. Adoption of this section was mandatory for publicly accountable enterprises but optional for private companies.

- The AcSB issued Accounting Standards for Private Enterprises (ASPE) effective for fiscal periods beginning on or after January 1, 2011. These standards include Section 3856—Financial Instruments, which does not specify the method for determining amortized cost, so this standard implicitly permits straight-line amortization of premiums and discounts.

The straight-line method of determining amortized cost continues to be widely used by private enterprises in Canada. Advocates of the straight-line method assert that it is simple to use and note that the results do not usually differ materially from those obtained under the effective interest method. We have included an illustration of the application of the straight-line method in Exhibit 12-13, contrasting it to the effective interest method.

Exhibit 12-13a Example comparing the straight-line and effective interest methods of amortizing a bond discount

Facts:

- Sointula Educational Services Ltd. sells $1,000,000 of three-year bonds on January 1, 2018, for $973,357.
- The coupon rate on the bonds is 6% per year, payable on July 1 and January 1; the bonds yield 7% per year, or 3.5% per period.
- Sointula Educational Services' year-end is December 31.

The process for determining the amount of the discount or premium to be amortized using the straight-line method differs materially from that used for the effective interest method. Exhibit 12-13b describes the application of the straight-line method.

Exhibit 12-13b Computation of bond amortization using the straight-line method

- Determine the amount of discount (or premium, as the case may be), which is $1,000,000 − $973,357 = $26,643.
- To determine the amount to be amortized each period, divide this discount by the number of periods until maturity: $26,643 ÷ 6 = $4,441 (rounded).
- Interest expense for each period is the sum of interest paid or accrued and the discount amortized: $30,000 + $4,441 = $34,441.

The outcomes of applying the straight-line and effective interest methods are contrasted below. As you compare the results, note that total interest expense over the life of the bond is the same under both methods. Application of the straight-line method results in interest expense remaining constant each period, whereas under the effective interest method the amount charged to interest expense is a function of the bond's amortized cost.

Exhibit 12-13c Amortization schedules for the straight-line and effective interest methods

	Straight-line method				Effective interest method			
Date	Interest expense	Interest paid	Discount amortized	Amortized cost	Interest expense	Interest paid	Discount amortized	Amortized cost
Jan. 01, 2018				$ 973,357				$ 973,357
Jul. 01, 2018	$ 34,441 (a)	$ 30,000 (b)	$ 4,441 (c)	977,798 (d)	$ 34,068	$ 30,000	$ 4,068	977,425
Jan. 01, 2019	34,441	30,000	4,441	982,239	34,210	30,000	4,210	981,635
Jul. 01, 2019	34,441	30,000	4,441	986,680	34,357	30,000	4,357	985,992
Jan. 01, 2020	34,441	30,000	4,441	991,121	34,510	30,000	4,510	990,502
Jul. 01, 2020	34,441	30,000	4,441	995,562	34,668	30,000	4,668	995,170
Jan 01, 2021	34,438	30,000	4,438 (e)	1,000,000	34,830	30,000	4,831	1,000,000
	$206,643	$180,000	$26,643		$206,643	$180,000	$26,643	

(*Continued*)

Exhibit 12-13c Continued

	Straight-line method				Effective interest method			
Date	Interest expense	Interest paid	Discount amortized	Amortized cost	Interest expense	Interest paid	Discount amortized	Amortized cost

Calculations

Small difference due to rounding

(a) \$30,000 + \$4,441 = \$34,441

(b) \$1,000,000 × 6%/2 = \$30,000

(c) \$1,000,000 − \$973,357 = \$26,643; \$26,643/6 = \$4,441 (rounded)

(d) \$973,357 + \$4,441 = \$977,798

CHECKPOINT **CP12-11**

Under IFRS, which method must be used to determine amortized cost? What alternative method does ASPE permit?

E. DERECOGNITION

L.O. 12-4. Apply accrual accounting to the derecognition of financial liabilities.

To derecognize a financial liability is to remove it from the entity's balance sheet. For the most part, firms can derecognize liabilities when they extinguish the obligations. IFRS 9 paragraph 3.3.1 provides that an obligation is extinguished when the underlying contract is discharged, cancelled, or expires. Paragraph B3.2.4 of IFRS 9 clarifies that extinguishment occurs when the entity pays off the debt or when it legally no longer has primary responsibility for the liability. Obviously, the most common way to extinguish an obligation is by paying the creditor cash or providing goods and services as specified in the contract. We look at this typical method as well as other transactions that would lead to derecognition in this section.

1. Derecognition at maturity

The customary way to extinguish obligations is to settle them when due. For example, a \$100,000 bank loan maturing on June 22, 2019, will be extinguished when you pay the bank \$100,000 plus interest on the due date. Accounting for the derecognition of a matured obligation does not provide any special challenges as there will not be a gain or loss on retirement; amortized cost equals the principal amount due.

Refer back to the bond obligation introduced in the spreadsheet in Exhibit 12-11c. The journal entry required for derecognizing the obligation on January 1, 2021, is shown in Exhibit 12-14.

Exhibit 12-14 Journal entry to record the derecognition of a maturing obligation

Jan. 01, 2021	Dr. Bonds payable	1,000,000	
	Dr. Interest payable	30,000	
	Cr. Cash		1,030,000

2. Derecognition prior to maturity

Companies sometimes pay off their obligations prior to maturity. For example, a company may use surplus cash to purchase its own bonds in the financial markets or exercise a call provision that requires the bondholders to tender their bonds for redemption. The process to extinguish the liability is the same in both cases and is analogous to recording the disposition of a depreciable asset. Derecognition of a financial liability should follow these steps:

1. The company updates its records to account for interim interest expense, including the amortization of discounts or premiums up to the derecognition date.
2. The entity records the outflow of assets expended to extinguish the obligation.
3. The entity records a gain or loss on debt retirement equal to the difference between the amount paid and the book value of the liability derecognized. Exhibit 12-15 demonstrates this process.

Exhibit 12-15a Example for derecognition prior to maturity

Facts:

- On October 1, 2019, Port Bay Inc. repurchases the bonds issued in Exhibit 12-10.
- Port Bay repurchases the bonds on the open market for total consideration of $980,000 cash.

Step 1: The company updates its records to account for interim interest expense. Prior to the repurchase, the bond discount was last amortized on July 1, 2019.

Exhibit 12-15b Amortization schedule up to the date of repurchase and related journal entry

Date	Interest expense @3.6410%	Interest paid	Discount amortized	Amortized cost
Jan. 01, 2018				$966,000
Jul. 01, 2018	$35,172	$30,000	$5,172	971,172
Jan. 01, 2019	35,361	30,000	5,361	976,533
Jul. 01, 2019	35,556	30,000	5,556	982,089
Oct. 01, 2019	**17,879** (a)	**15,000**	**2,879**	**984,968** (b)

Calculations

(a) Interest for three months: $982,089 × 3.6410% × 3/6 = $17,879

(b) This line records the effects of Port Bay updating its records on Oct. 1, 2019

Journal entry to update Port Bay's records (October 1, 2019)		
Dr. Interest expense	17,879	
Cr. Interest payable ($30,000 ÷ 2)		15,000
Cr. Bonds payable ($17,879 − $15,000)		2,879

Steps 2 and 3: Port Bay records the outflow of assets expended to extinguish the obligation and records the gain on retirement on October 1, 2019.

Exhibit 12-15c Journal entry to record repurchase

Dr. Interest payable (given)	15,000	
Dr. Bonds payable (from schedule)	984,968	
Cr. Cash (given)		980,000
Cr. Gain on bond redemption ($15,000 + $984,968 – $980,000)		19,968

If the entity retires only a portion of a liability, the obligation is derecognized on a pro rata basis. For example, if a company retires 40% of a bond, it would derecognize 40% of the book value, including 40% of the unamortized premium or discount. The example in Exhibit 12-16 illustrates such a case.

Exhibit 12-16a Derecognition prior to maturity

Facts:

- Port Bay Inc. repurchases the bonds issued in Exhibit 12-10.
- Ignore the repurchase demonstrated in Exhibit 12-15. Assume instead that Port Bay calls the bonds and pays each holder the face amount of the bonds, plus accrued interest ($15,000), together with a 2% call premium ($20,000). The total consideration paid is $1,035,000.

Step 1: The company updates its records to account for interim interest expense. The journal entry required to update Port Bay's amortization of the discount from July to October is the same as that illustrated in Exhibit 12-15b. For ease of reference it is replicated here.

Exhibit 12-16b Amortization schedule up to date of bond retirement

Date	Interest expense @3.6410%	Interest paid	Discount amortized	Amortized cost
Jan. 01, 2018				$966,000
Jul. 01, 2018	$35,172	$30,000	$5,172	971,172
Jan. 01, 2019	35,361	30,000	5,361	976,533
Jul. 01, 2019	35,556	30,000	5,556	982,089
Oct. 01, 2019	17,879 (a)	**15,000**	**2,879**	**984,968** (b)

Calculations

(a) Interest for three months: $982,089 × 3.6410% × 3/6 = $17,879.

(b) This line records the effects of Port Bay updating its records on Oct. 1, 2019.

Journal entry to update Port Bay's records (Oct. 01, 2019)

	Dr.	Cr.
Dr. Interest expense	17,879	
Cr. Interest payable ($30,000 ÷ 2)		15,000
Cr. Bonds payable ($17,879 − $15,000)		2,879

Steps 2 and 3: Port Bay records the outflow of assets expended to extinguish the obligation and records the gain on retirement on October 1, 2019.

Exhibit 12-16c Journal entry to record bond retirement

	Dr.	Cr.
Dr. Interest payable (given)	15,000	
Dr. Bonds payable (from schedule)	984,968	
Dr. Loss on bond redemption ($1,035,000 − $15,000 − $984,968)	35,032	
Cr. Cash ($1,000,000 + $15,000 + $20,000)		1,035,000

In practice, the outstanding bond balance ($984,968 in Exhibits 12-15c and 12-16c) can be quickly determined by referring to the general ledger. In a classroom setting, the net book value (amortized cost) can be determined in a number of ways:

- Manually compute the bond amortization on a period-by-period basis. This is a time-consuming task and prone to error, especially if the number of payment periods is large.
- Construct a spreadsheet. While not difficult to do, many students do not have access to a spreadsheet program in the classroom and even fewer can use one in an examination.

- The most feasible method is to use your financial calculator to determine the amortized cost. We explain this method more fully here.
   i. The necessary starting point for preparing the journal entries is the bond liability balance at the interest payment date prior to the redemption (July 1, 2019, in this example).
   ii. When originally sold on January 2018, there were six periods until the bonds mature. On July 1, 2019, the bonds have been outstanding for three periods and accordingly there are now only three periods left until maturity (July 1, 2019, is 18 months or three periods before the maturity date of January 1, 2021).
   iii. Using a financial calculator: 1000000 FV 30000 PMT 3.6410 I/Y 3 N CPT PV → PV = −982,090 (rounded). Note how this amount corresponds to the amount derived using the spreadsheet method. The $1 difference is due to rounding.

3. Derecognition through offsetting and in-substance defeasance

a. Offsetting

Offsetting is the practice of showing the net amount of related assets and liabilities on the balance sheet, rather than showing each of the components separately. For example, Company A has a receivable of $10,000 owing from Company B as well as a payable of $7,000 owing to the same company. If offset against each other, Company A would report a net asset of $3,000 as opposed to an asset of $10,000 and a liability of $7,000. Offsetting usually improves key financial ratios, making it easier to meet lenders' restrictive covenants. Moreover, it may also free up borrowing capacity as loan agreements typically limit the maximum debt a company can carry. In the simple receivable/payable example above, offsetting may permit Company A to borrow an additional $7,000.

IFRS asserts that separately reporting assets and liabilities generally conveys more information than reporting the net amount, and that offsetting compromises the user's ability to correctly interpret the financial results. Consequently, IAS 1 paragraph 32 prohibits offsetting generally, unless specifically allowed by another standard. One such exception is IAS 32:

> ¶42 A financial asset and a financial liability shall be offset and the net amount presented in the statement of financial position when, and only when, an entity:
> (a) currently has a legally enforceable right to set off the recognized amounts; and
> (b) intends either to settle on a net basis, or to realize the asset and settle the liability simultaneously.[13]

In other words, the reporting entity must be both willing and legally able to offset the amounts against each other.

An example of when these tests would normally be met occurs when an entity has two chequing accounts with the same bank, one of which is overdrawn. Offsetting is appropriate in this instance because it better reflects the economic substance of the situation.

b. In-substance defeasance

Companies may want to satisfy a liability before the maturity date but are precluded from doing so by restrictions in the loan agreement or onerous prepayment penalties. In an effort to avoid reporting the liability, firms may indirectly extinguish their debt.

[13] Copyright © 2012 IFRS Foundation.

in-substance defeasance An arrangement where funds sufficient to satisfy a liability are placed in trust with a third party to pay directly to the creditor at maturity.

In-substance defeasance is an arrangement where funds sufficient to satisfy a liability are placed in trust with a third party to pay the creditors directly. (See Chapter 1 for a case study on this issue.) While popular for a period of time in the 1990s, current accounting standards make this type of arrangement ineffective. In particular, IFRS 9 specifies the following in its application guidance set out in Appendix B:

> ¶ B3.3.3 Payment to a third party, including a trust (sometimes called 'in-substance defeasance'), does not, by itself, relieve the debtor of its primary obligation to the creditor, in the absence of legal release.[14]

The essence of this guidance is that the borrower cannot usually derecognize the obligation through in-substance defeasance, which is a unilateral arrangement put in place by the debtor. The defeasance would result in derecognition of the liability only if the creditor also formally confirms that the entity is no longer liable for the indebtedness.

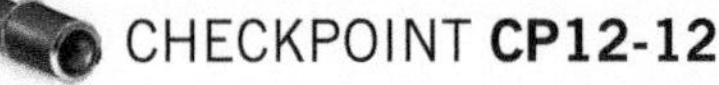

CHECKPOINT **CP12-12**

When is offsetting (the practice of showing the net amount of related assets and liabilities on the balance sheet) allowed?

F. PUTTING IT ALL TOGETHER—A COMPREHENSIVE BOND EXAMPLE

Creative Conundrums Ltd. (CCL) raised $9,500,000 before expenses by selling $10,000,000 of five-year, 5% bonds dated January 1, 2018. CCL used part of the proceeds to pay its investment bank's fee of $200,000 and related legal and accounting fees of $300,000. Interest is payable on June 30 and December 31 each year. CCL can call the bonds on January 1, 2020, at 102 ("102" means 102% of the face value, so for each $1,000 bond outstanding CCL will pay the holder $1,020 plus accrued interest). The company exercises this privilege, redeeming 60% of the bonds on the call date. The company's year-end is December 31.

Required:
Prepare journal entries to record the following:

a. The issuance of the bonds on January 1, 2018.
b. Payment of interest and related amortization on June 30, 2018.
c. Payment of interest and related amortization on December 31, 2019.
d. Repurchase of the bonds on January 1, 2020.
e. Retirement of the remaining bonds on December 31, 2022, assuming that the final interest payment has already been recorded in the company's books.

Note: You will need to use a financial calculator or a computer spreadsheet to determine the effective rate. The suggested solution is based on the use of a financial calculator to determine the effective rate and the use of a spreadsheet to determine interest expense, discount amortization, and the amortized cost of the bonds.

Solution:
The first step is to determine the effective interest rate and use this to prepare a spreadsheet that details period interest expense and discount amortization.

Exhibit 12-17a Determining the effective interest rate

Using a financial calculator:

The net proceeds *(PV)* are \$9,500,000 − \$200,000 − \$300,000 = \$9,000,000
$N = 10\ (5 \times 2)$;
$PMT = (\$10{,}000{,}000 \times 5\% \times 6/12) = \$250{,}000$
Using a financial calculator: 9000000 **+|−** **PV** 10000000 **FV** 250000 **PMT** 10 **N** **CPT** **I/Y** → I/Y = 3.7155% per period (rounded)

Spreadsheet

Effective rate per period: 3.7155%

Date	Interest expense	Interest paid	Discount amortized	Amortized cost
01/01/2018				\$ 9,000,000 (a)
06/30/2018	\$334,396	\$250,000 (b)	\$84,396 (c)	9,084,396 (d)
12/31/2018	337,532	250,00	87,532	9,171,928
06/30/2019	340,784	250,000	90,784	9,262,712
12/31/2019	344,157	250,000	94,157	9,356,869
01/01/2020	Redeem and derecognize 60% of outstanding bonds			(5,614,121)
				3,742,747
06/30/2020	139,062	100,000 (e)	39,062	3,781,810
12/31/2020	140,514	100,000	40,514	3,822,323
06/30/2021	142,019	100,000	42,019	3,864,342
12/31/2021	143,580	100,000	43,580	3,907,922
06/30/2022	145,199	100,000	45,199	3,953,121
12/31/2022	146,879	100,000	46,879	4,000,000

Calculations
Small differences due to rounding
(a) The net sale proceeds of the bonds (\$9,500,000 − \$200,000 − \$300,000 = \$9,000,000)
(b) \$10,000,000 × 5%/2 = \$250,000
(c) \$334,396 − \$250,000 = \$84,396
(d) \$9,000,000 + \$84,396 = \$9,084,396
(e) \$250,000 × (1 − 60%) = \$100,000 or
\$10,000,000 (1 − 60%) × 5%/2 = \$4,000,000 × 5%/2 = \$100,000

The information in the questions, supplemented by the spreadsheet, can then be used to answer the question. On January 1, 2018, CCL records the journal entry to report the issuance of the bonds and the net receipt of cash.

Exhibit 12-17b Journal entry to record bond issuance

Dr. Cash (Sales proceeds – transaction costs)	9,000,000	
Cr. Bonds payable (\$9,500,000 – \$200,000 – \$300,000)		9,000,000

On June 30, 2018, CCL records the payment of interest and the related amortization of the bond discount. Recall that interest expense is determined using the effective interest method (interest expense = amortized cost × the effective interest rate for the period).

Exhibit 12-17c Journal entry to record interest on June 30, 2018

Dr. Interest expense (from spreadsheet)	334,396	
Cr. Cash		250,000
Cr. Bonds payable		84,396

The company would have recorded the December 31, 2018, and June 30, 2019, payments in the normal manner.

At the year ended December 31, 2019, CCL again records the payment of interest and the related amortization of the bond discount.

Exhibit 12-17d	Journal entry to record interest on December 31, 2019	
Dr. Interest expense (from spreadsheet)	344,157	
Cr. Cash		250,000
Cr. Bonds payable		94,157

On January 1, 2020, CCL records the redemption of 60% of the outstanding bonds. As interest was just paid, there is no need for CCL to update its records to reflect the passage of time.

Exhibit 12-17e	Journal entry to record repurchase of bonds on January 1, 2020	
Dr. Loss on bond redemption ($6,120,000 − $5,614,121)	505,879	
Dr. Bonds payable (from spreadsheet)	5,614,121	
Cr. Cash ($6,000,000 × 102%)		6,120,000

CCL would continue to record interest expense in the normal course until the bonds mature. On December 31, 2022, CCL would then record the retirement of the bonds.

Exhibit 12-17f	Journal entry to record retirement of bonds on December 31, 2022	
Dr. Bonds payable	4,000,000	
Cr. Cash		4,000,000

G. OTHER ISSUES

1. Decommissioning and site restoration obligations

L.O. 12-5. Apply accrual accounting to decommissioning and site restoration obligations.

As discussed in Chapter 8, the acquisition of property, plant, and equipment often entails an obligation to incur the future costs of dismantling and removing the item, as well as restoring the installation site to a predefined condition. For example, once the ore body is exhausted, mining companies are usually required by government regulation to dismantle all structures, reclaim the land, and return it to a useful purpose such as a park or wildlife reserve. The costs of decommissioning and restoring a site to meet an entity's legal and constructive obligations are provided for in accordance with IAS 37. The non-financial provision must be recognized for the estimated future obligation discounted by an appropriate interest rate that reflects the risk of the obligation (IAS 37 paragraph 47).

To understand the accounting required, suppose Gail's Gold Mines Inc. (GGMI) purchases a piece of land for the purpose of developing a gold mine. GGMI is legally required to remove all structures and convert the mine site to a wildlife sanctuary at the end of its estimated 10-year useful life. GGMI estimates that it will have to spend $10,000,000 to decommission the site and reclaim the land when operations cease. The present value of this $10,000,000 site restoration cost, assuming a discount rate of 5%, is $6,139,133. To recognize this site restoration cost, the company would record the following entries upon initial acquisition and subsequently (assuming straight-line depreciation[15]):

Exhibit 12-18	Journal entries for GGMI's site restoration costs		
Acquisition:	Dr. Land[16]	6,139,133	
	Cr. Obligation for future site restoration cost		6,139,133
Each year:	Dr. Depreciation expense ($6,139,133/10 years)	613,913	
	Cr. Accumulated depreciation—land		613,913
Year 1:	Dr. Interest expense ($6,139,133 × 5%)	306,957	
	Cr. Obligation for future site restoration cost		306,957
Year 2:	Dr. Interest expense [($6,139,133 + 306,957) × 5%]	322,304	
	Cr. Obligation for future site restoration cost		322,304

By the end of 10 years, the accumulated depreciation will total $6,139,133 ($613,913/year × 10 years), which is the present value of the $10,000,000 at the beginning of the 10 years. The amount of interest expense will increase each year, along with the balance of the obligation. By the end of 10 years, the account "Obligation for future site restoration costs" will be $10,000,000. The following table shows the amount relating to the site restoration costs:

Exhibit 12-19 Schedule of expenses and balance sheet amounts related to GGMI's site restoration

Year	Interest on obligation for site restoration at 5% (a)	Obligation for future site restoration at end of year (b)	Depreciation expense	Accumulated depreciation at end of year
0		$ 6,139,133		$ 0
1	$306,957	6,446,090	$613,913	613,913
2	322,304	6,768,394	613,913	1,227,827
3	338,420	7,106,814	613,913	1,841,740
4	355,341	7,462,155	613,913	2,455,653
5	373,108	7,835,262	613,913	3,069,567
6	391,763	8,227,025	613,913	3,683,480
7	411,351	8,638,377	613,913	4,297,393
8	431,919	9,070,295	613,913	4,911,306
9	453,515	9,523,810	613,913	5,525,220
10	476,191	10,000,000	613,913	6,139,133

Calculations

(a) Interest = Prior year balance of obligation × 5%

(b) Obligation − Prior year obligation + Current year's interest

IFRIC 1—Changes in Existing Decommissioning, Restoration, and Similar Liabilities provides additional guidance on how to account for decommissioning liabilities and restoration costs, particularly with respect to a change in the estimated outflow of resources required to satisfy the obligation or a change in the current market-based discount rate. While a full discussion of the implications of IFRIC 1 is beyond the scope of this text, the essence of this guidance is as follows:

- Changes in a decommissioning liability resulting from either a change in estimated cash flows or a change in the discount rate are offset by increasing or decreasing the related asset account by the same amount.

15. We have assumed straight-line depreciation for ease of exposition. Reclamation and site restoration costs for a gold mine would normally be depreciated using the units-of-production method.

16. While land is not normally depreciated, IAS 37 paragraphs 58 and 59 allows for this in limited circumstances such as those set out in this example.

- If the reduction in the liability exceeds the carrying amount of the related asset, the asset is reduced to $nil with the remainder recognized in profit or loss. It thus follows that once the related asset has been fully depreciated, changes in the liability are recognized in profit or loss.
- If the carrying value of the asset is to be increased, the entity shall consider whether the revised book value is fully recoverable, and if otherwise, shall account for any shortfall as an impairment loss.
- The revised book value of the asset is depreciated over its remaining useful life. That is to say that the change in estimate is accounted for prospectively.

The forgoing assumes that the related asset is measured using the cost model. If the related asset is measured using the revaluation model, changes in the liability are recognized in either other comprehensive income or profit or loss as established by IFRIC 1.

Exhibit 12-20 illustrates accounting for a change in the market-based discount rate building upon the initial facts in the Gail's Gold Mines Inc. (GGMI) example above.

Exhibit 12-20a An illustration of a change in the market-based discount rate on decommissioning liabilities

Facts:

- GGMI originally estimated that it would have to spend $10 million to decommission the site and reclaim the land when operations were projected to cease in 10 years' time.
- In Year 6, the market-based discount rate increased from 5% to 6%.

From Exhibits 12-18 and 12-19, we established that at the end of Year 5 the obligation for restoration was $7,835,262 and the cost of the land was $6,139,133. We know that $7,835,262 is the present value of $10,000,000 discounted at 5% for five years. By changing the discount rate to 6%, we derive the required balance of the liability—$7,472,582 ($10,000,000 $\div$ 1.06^5 = $7,472,582). Hence, both the liability and the asset account must be decreased by $362,680 ($7,835,262 − $7,472,582 = $362,680).

Exhibit 12-20b Journal entry

Dr. Obligation for future site restoration (from above)	362,680	
Cr. Land		362,680

The revised net book value of the land of $2,706,886 [$6,139,133 (original cost) − $362,680 (revision to cost) − $3,069,567 (accumulated depreciation) = $2,706,886] must be depreciated over the five remaining years at a rate of $541,377 per year ($2,706,886 $\div$ 5 = $541,377).

Exhibit 12-20c Revised schedule of expenses and balance sheet amounts related to GGMI's site restoration

Year	Interest on obligation for site restoration at 5% (a)	Obligation for future site restoration at end of year (b)	Depreciation expense	Accumulated depreciation at end of year (c)
0		$ 6,139,133		$ 0
1	$306,957	6,446,090	$613,913	613,913

(Continued)

Exhibit 12-20c Continued

Year	Interest on obligation for site restoration at 5% (a)	Obligation for future site restoration at end of year (b)	Depreciation expense	Accumulated depreciation at end of year (c)
2	322,304	6,768,394	613,913	1,227,827
3	338,420	7,106,814	613,913	1,841,740
4	355,341	7,462,155	613,913	2,455,653
5	373,108	7,835,262	613,913	3,069,567
Adjustment		(362,680)		
Revised obligation		7,472,582		
6	448,355	7,920,937	541,377	3,610,944
7	475,256	8,396,193	541,377	4,152,321
8	503,772	8,899,965	541,377	4,693,699
9	533,998	9,433,963	541,377	5,235,076
10	566,038	10,000,000	541,377	5,776,453

Calculations
(a) Interest = Prior year balance of obligation × 5% for Years 1–5 and 6% for Years 6–10
(b) Obligation − Prior year obligation + Current year's interest
(c) $6,139,133 (original cost) − $362,680 (revision to cost) = $5,776,453 net cost to be depreciated

ASPE standards (Section 3110) are essentially the same as those in IAS 37 and IFRIC 1. Differences include:

- Section 3110 refers to decommissioning responsibilities as asset retirement obligations (AROs).
- IFRS recognizes decommissioning and site restoration obligations for both legal and constructive obligations whereas ASPE only recognizes AROs for legal obligations.
- ASPE requires that the increase in the provision for the future site restoration cost due to the passage of time be charged to accretion expense, rather than to interest expense.

2. Off-balance-sheet obligations

We previously suggested that a company may be motivated to keep debts off its balance sheet so as to improve key financial ratios and free up borrowing capacity. These incentives may also encourage management to structure its affairs in a manner that ensures certain obligations need not be recognized.

The IASB appreciates that the true extent of an entity's debt is very relevant to financial statement users. Over the years, the IASB has developed increasingly stringent requirements governing the recognition of obligations, with its goal being to ensure that entities recognize all of their liabilities on the balance sheet. Obligations that were previously left off-balance-sheet but now have to be recognized include those emanating from derivative contracts, special purpose entities (SPEs), decommissioning costs, and leases.

The nature of the obligations arising from derivatives, decommissioning costs, and leases and how to account for each are discussed in this and other chapters; accounting for SPEs, other than the brief discussion below, is beyond the scope of this text.

SPEs gained notoriety in the Enron debacle in 2001. Enron, a US-based energy company (once named "America's Most Innovative Company" for six consecutive years by *Fortune* magazine), used non-consolidated SPEs to hide debt and inflate reported earnings. As a direct result of the Enron scandal, both the Canadian Accounting Standards Board and the US Financial Accounting Standards Board introduced stringent standards mandating the consolidation of nearly all SPEs.

Briefly, SPEs are entities that are created to perform a specific function such as undertaking research and development activities. The reasons for creating SPEs are many, and include tax considerations and isolating the backer from financial risk. A distinguishing feature of SPEs is that control is usually achieved by the sponsoring firm through a beneficial interest rather than owning more than 50% of the voting shares. IFRS 10—Consolidated Financial Statements, requires the consolidation of most SPEs.

3. Bonds denominated in foreign currency

Given its proximity to the United States and the relatively small capital markets in Canada, many Canadian entities, including the federal and provincial governments, issue long-term debt denominated in US dollars. As discussed in Chapter 11, accounting for obligations denominated in foreign currency is fairly straightforward and governed by IAS 21—The Effects of Changes in Foreign Exchange Rates. Recall that the standard requires the following:

1. translation of the foreign currency debt into the functional currency at the exchange rate evident on the transaction date[17];
2. revaluation of the foreign currency obligation at the end of a period using the exchange rate at that time; and
3. recognition of the gain or loss from revaluation on the income statement.

Also, interest is charged to expense at the average rate for the period, rather than the spot rate paid at time of payment. The difference is recognized as a gain or loss on the income statement.

Exhibit 12-21 illustrates the accounting for a bond denominated in US dollars.

Exhibit 12-21a Accounting for a bond denominated in US dollars

Facts:

- Belle Inc. issues US$1,000,000 of two-year bonds on January 1, 2018, at par that mature on December 31, 2019.
- The coupon rate on the bonds is 4% payable annually on December 31.
- Belle's year-end is December 31. It does not accrue interest throughout the year.
- Exchange rates:
  - January 1, 2018, C$1.00 = US$0.99
  - December 31, 2018, C$1.00 = US$0.97
  - December 31, 2019, C$1.00 = US$1.01
  - Average rate 2018, C$1.00 = US$0.98
  - Average rate 2019, C$1.00 = US$0.99

The bond payable is recorded at its Canadian dollar equivalent using the exchange rate evident (the spot rate) on the date of acquisition.

[17] The functional currency is that used by the company when it prepares its financial statements. For Canadian companies it is usually the Canadian dollar.

Exhibit 12-21b	Journal entry to recognize the issuance of the bond	
Dr. Cash	1,010,101	
Cr. Bonds payable		1,010,101
US$1,000,000 × C$1.00/US$0.99 = C$1,010,101		

The bond must be revalued at the end of each reporting period using the spot rate at period end. The resultant gain or loss is reported on the income statement.

Exhibit 12-21c	Journal entry to revalue the obligation at period-end (December 31, 2018)	
Dr. Foreign exchange loss	20,827	
Cr. Bonds payable		20,827
US$1,000,000 × C$1.00 / US$0.97 = C$1,030,928;		
$1,030,928 − $1,010,101 = $20,827 (a loss)		

The Canadian dollar equivalent of the interest payment is determined using the spot rate on the interest payment date (C$1.00/US$0.97); however, interest expense is determined using the average rate for the period (C$1.00/US$0.98). The difference between the amount paid to purchase the US dollars and the amount charged to interest expense is reported on the income statement as a foreign exchange gain or loss.

Exhibit 12-21d	Journal entry to record the payment of interest (December 31, 2018)	
Dr. Interest expense	40,816	
Dr. Foreign exchange loss	421	
Cr. Cash		41,237
US$1,000,000 × 4% = US$40,000 × C$1.00 / US$0.97 = C$41,237 (spot rate)		
US$40,000 × C$1.00/ US$0.98 = C$40,816 (average rate)		
$41,237 − $40,816 = $421 (a loss)		

We repeat the process in 2019 and record the derecognition of the liability.

Exhibit 12-21e	Journal entry to revalue the obligation at period-end (December 31, 2019)	
Dr. Bonds payable	40,829	
Cr. Foreign exchange gain		40,829
US$1,000,000 × C$1.00/ US$1.01 = C$990,099		
$990,099 − $1,030,928 = $40,829 (a gain)		

Exhibit 12-21f	Journal entry to record the payment of interest (December 31, 2019)	
Dr. Interest expense	40,404	
Cr. Foreign exchange gain		800
Cr. Cash		39,604
US$1,000,000 × 4% = US$40,000 × C$1.00/ US$1.01 = C$39,604 (spot rate)		
US$40,000 × C$1.00 / US$0.99 = C$40,404 (average rate)		
$40,404 − $39,604 = $800 (a gain)		

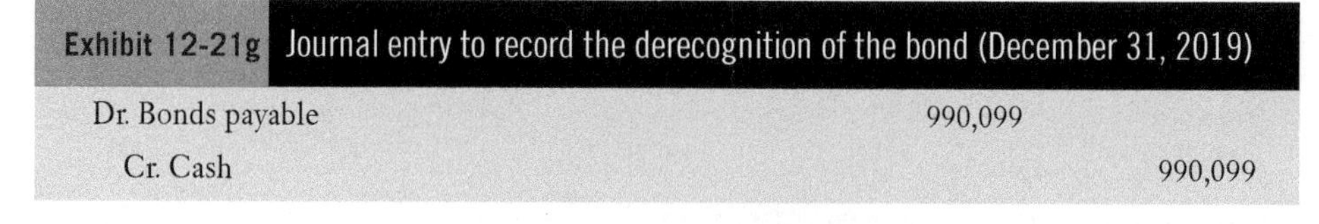

Exhibit 12-21g Journal entry to record the derecognition of the bond (December 31, 2019)

Dr. Bonds payable	990,099	
Cr. Cash		990,099

CHECKPOINT **CP12-13**

Why might a company be motivated to keep its debts off its balance sheet?

H. PRESENTATION AND DISCLOSURE

L.O. 12-6. Describe how non-current liabilities are presented and disclosed.

As suggested in Chapter 11, IFRS requires extensive disclosure as to the nature of an entity's liabilities. The company is required to disclose information that enables users to evaluate the significance of financial liabilities on its financial position and performance. Standards that must be considered include the presentation and disclosure requirements in:

- IAS 1—Presentation of Financial Statements
- IAS 32—Financial Instruments: Presentation
- IAS 37—Provisions, Contingent Liabilities and Contingent Assets
- IFRS 7—Financial Instruments: Disclosures

We will not reproduce the complete list of the requirements here, but the disclosures should cover the following essential aspects:

- the nature of contingent liabilities;
- a summary of the accounting policies used to determine the measurement basis of valuing liabilities—for example, amortized cost;
- pertinent details of the indebtedness, including collateral pledged and call or conversion privileges;
- the fair value of each class of financial liability and how this was determined—for example, discounted cash flow analysis; this information need not be provided for financial instruments whose carrying value reasonably approximates their fair value—for example, trade payables;
- total interest expense on liabilities other than those valued at fair value through profit or loss;
- a schedule that details the contractual maturity dates of financial liabilities;
- the nature and extent of risks arising from financial liabilities, including credit risk, liquidity risk, and market risk; and
- details of any obligations in default, including the carrying amount of loans in default at statement date and whether the default was remedied before the financial statements were issued.

The format and extent of disclosure differs between companies. To gain some insight into the level of detail provided, please refer to disclosures made by Canadian Tire Corporation in its 2016 financial statements contained in Appendix C. Exhibit 12-22 sets out specific areas to review.

Exhibit 12-22 References to notes in the 2016 financial statements of Canadian Tire Corporation

Note	Title	Pertinent disclosure
4	Capital management	Composition of capital under management and a description of the key covenants included in the company's debt agreements.
5	Financial risk management	Qualification and quantification of the various financial risks faced by the company together with an explanation as to how they manage these risks.
17	Trade and other payables	Composition of trade and other payables.
18	Provisions	Composition of provisions.
19	Contingencies	General disclosure with respect to ongoing litigation against the company.
20	Short-term borrowings	Description of the nature of the company's short-term borrowings.
21	Loans payable	Description of the nature of the company's loans payable.
22	Long-term debt	Description and quantification of the company's long-term debt, including segregation into the current and non-current components.
30	Net finance costs	Composition of finance costs.
32	Financial instruments	Description of measurement methodology, a schedule contrasting the carrying value and fair value of financial liabilities, and a reconciliation of the amounts arising from financial instruments that were recognized in net income and equity.
34	Guarantees and commitments	Description and quantification of guarantees and other commitments.

Source: From Canadian Tire Corporation 2016 Report to Shareholders. Copyright ©2016 by Canadian Tire Corporation, Limited. Reprinted by permission.

I. SUBSTANTIVE DIFFERENCES BETWEEN RELEVANT IFRS AND ASPE

Issue	IFRS	ASPE
Amortization of premiums and discounts on financial liabilities	Enterprises must use the effective interest method.	Enterprises may use either the effective interest method or the straight-line method.
Increase in the provision for site restoration costs (AROs) due to the passage of time	Charged to interest expense	Charged to accretion expense
Decommissioning and site restoration obligations (AROs)	Recognized for both legal and constructive obligations	Recognized only for legal obligations

J. STANDARDS IN TRANSITION

In May 2015, the International Accounting Standards Board (IASB) issued an exposure draft (ED) to amend The Conceptual Framework for Financial Reporting. Proposed changes include changing the definition of a liability from *A liability is a present obligation of the entity arising from past events, the settlement of which is expected to result in an outflow from the entity of resources embodying economic benefits*[18] to *A liability is a present obligation of the entity to transfer an economic resource as a result of past events.*[19]

The revisions were approved by the IASB in March 2018. They are effective for annual periods beginning on or after 1 January 2020 for preparers who develop an accounting policy based on the Conceptual Framework.

The immediate impact of the amended definition of a liability is expected to be minimal as the proposed change is minor in nature and as the Conceptual Framework is not a governing standard and does not override specific standards (e.g., IFRS 9 or IAS 37). Moreover, the IASB has advised that it will not automatically change existing standards as a result of amendments made to the Conceptual Framework.

[18] Conceptual Framework paragraph 4.4(b). Copyright © 2012 IFRS Foundation.

[19] Conceptual Framework paragraph 4.24. Copyright © 2012 IFRS Foundation.

K. SUMMARY

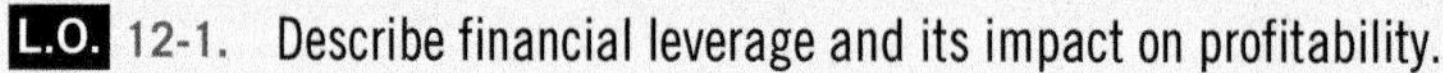

L.O. 12-1. Describe financial leverage and its impact on profitability.

- Financial leverage quantifies the relationship between the relative level of a firm's debt and its equity base.
- Financial leverage offers shareholders an opportunity to increase their return on equity (ROE) when things go well but exposes them to an increased risk of loss as well.

L.O. 12-2. Describe the categories and types of non-current liabilities.

- Non-current liabilities are expected to be settled more than one year after the balance sheet date.
- Non-current liabilities are either financial or non-financial in nature. Examples of financial liabilities include bonds and notes payable. Examples of non-financial liabilities include deferred revenue and warranty payables.

L.O. 12-3. Describe the initial and subsequent measurement of non-current financial liabilities and account for these obligations.

- Financial liabilities are initially recognized at fair value less costs directly attributable to issuing the debt.
- Financial liabilities are subsequently measured at amortized cost, excepting those at fair value through profit or loss.

L.O. 12-4. Apply accrual accounting to the derecognition of financial liabilities.

- Liabilities are derecognized when they are settled or when the debtor is legally released from primary responsibility for the liability.
- Retiring an obligation prior to maturity may lead to a gain or loss on retirement, which flows through income.

L.O. 12-5. Apply accrual accounting to decommissioning and site restoration obligations.

- The costs of decommissioning and restoring a site to meet an entity's legal obligations are provided for in accordance with IAS 37.
- This non-financial provision must be recognized for the estimated future obligation discounted by an appropriate rate of interest that reflects the risk of the obligation.

L.O. 12-6. **Describe how non-current liabilities are presented and disclosed.**

- IFRS requires extensive disclosure as to the nature of an entity's liabilities.
- Standards that need to be complied with in respect to presentation and disclosure include IAS 1, IAS 32, IAS 37, and IFRS 7.
- Required disclosure includes detailing the essential aspects of contingent liabilities, a summary of accounting policies pertaining to the measurement basis of valuing liabilities, pertinent details of the indebtedness, the fair value of each class of financial liability, and details of obligations in default.

L. ANSWERS TO CHECKPOINT QUESTIONS

CP12-1: The primary advantage of leverage is the opportunity to increase the firm's return on equity (ROE). Disadvantages of leverage include that it exposes the shareholders to an increased risk of loss and increases the risk of the company going bankrupt.

CP12-2: It is important to have debt-rating agencies because they provide an independent and impartial evaluation of the riskiness of debt securities to assist investors in making informed decisions. This function reduces information asymmetry between issuers and debt investors, thereby decreasing the cost of financing.

CP12-3: Companies sell notes directly to the investing public to lower their interest costs by reducing or eliminating the spread.

CP12-4: A bond indenture is a contract that outlines the terms of the bond including the maturity date, rate of interest and interest payment dates, security pledged, and financial covenants. Covenants are restrictions on borrower's activities. They can be positive or negative, respectively requiring or forbidding certain actions.

CP12-5: Subsequent to issue, bonds are traded in a decentralized, secondary market referred to as an OTC (over-the-counter) market. Dealers carry an inventory of bonds. They earn a profit by selling the bonds for more than they paid for them.

CP12-6: Notes or other debt instruments exchanged for non-cash assets are valued at fair value.

CP12-7: In the absence of similar market transactions, discounted cash flow analysis would normally be used to determine the liability to be recognized when debt instruments are issued at non-market rates of interest.

CP12-8: When the effective interest rate is greater than the coupon rate, bonds will sell at a discount.

CP12-9: When bonds are sold between interest payment dates, the purchaser pays the seller the agreed-upon price for the bond plus the interest that has accrued since the last payment date. If a 10-year bond issue is sold at a discount one month after the issue date, the seller would amortize the discount over the remaining 119 months ($10 \times 12 - 1$) until maturity.

CP12-10: After initial recognition, at fair value through profit or loss liabilities are measured at fair value. The remainder of financial liabilities are measured at amortized cost.

CP12-11: IFRS requires that amortized cost be determined using the effective interest method. ASPE additionally permits the use of the straight-line method to determine amortized cost.

CP12-12: Offsetting is only allowed when the reporting entity is willing and legally able to offset the asset and liability against each other.

CP12-13: A company may be motivated to keep debts off its balance sheet so as to improve its key financial ratios and free up borrowing capacity.

M. GLOSSARY

amortized cost (of debt): The amount initially recognized for the debt adjusted by subsequent amortization of premium or discount.

best efforts approach: Occurs when the broker simply agrees to try to sell as much of the (debt) issue as possible to investors.

bond indenture: A contract that outlines the terms of the bond, including the maturity date, rate of interest, interest payment dates, security pledged, and financial covenants.

call premium: The excess over par value paid to the bondholders when the security is called.

callable bonds: Bonds that permit the issuing company to "call" for the bonds to be redeemed before maturity.

convertible bonds: Bonds that allow the holder to exchange or "convert" the bond into other securities in the corporation, usually common shares.

coupon (stated) rate of interest: The interest rate specified in the bond indenture.

covenant: The borrower's promise to restrict certain activities.

debentures: Unsecured bonds.

effective interest rate: The rate of interest paid by the borrower that factors in premiums or discounts at issuance and transaction costs.

financial leverage: Quantifies the relationship between the relative level of a firm's debt and its equity base.

financial liability: A contractual obligation to deliver cash or other financial assets to another party.

firm commitment underwriting: Occurs when the investment bank guarantees the borrower a price for the securities.

in-substance defeasance: An arrangement where funds sufficient to satisfy a liability are placed in trust with a third party to pay directly to the creditor at maturity.

investment bank: A financial institution that acts as an agent or underwriter for corporations and governments issuing securities.

market rate of interest (yield): The rate of return (on a bond) actually earned by the investor.

non-current liabilities: Obligations that are expected to be settled more than one year after the balance sheet date or the business's normal operating cycle, whichever is longer.

par value: The amount to be repaid to the investor at maturity.

perpetual bonds: Bonds that never mature.

real-return (inflation-linked) bonds: Bonds whose rate of return is tied to the inflation rate.

secured bonds: Bonds backed by specific collateral such as a mortgage on real estate.

serial bonds: A set of bonds issued at the same time but that mature at regularly scheduled dates rather than all on the same date.

stripped (zero-coupon) bonds: Bonds that do not pay interest; stripped bonds are sold at a discount and mature at face value.

yield: See **market rate of interest (yield)**.

N. REFERENCES

Authoritative standards:

IFRS	ASPE Section
IFRS 9—Financial Instruments IAS 32—Financial Instruments: Presentation	3856—Financial Instruments
IAS 16—Property, Plant, and Equipment	3061—Property, Plant and Equipment
IFRS 13—Fair Value Measurement	
IAS 1—Presentation of Financial Statements	1400—General Standards of Financial Statement Presentation 1505—Disclosure of Accounting Policies 1521—Balance Sheet
IAS 37—Provisions, Contingent Liabilities, and Contingent Assets IFRIC 1—Changes in Existing Decommissioning, Restoration, and Similar Liabilities	3110—Asset Retirement Obligations
IFRS 10—Consolidated Financial Statements	AcG 15—Consolidation of Variable Interest Entities
IAS 21—The Effects of Changes in Foreign Exchange Rates	1651—Foreign Currency Translation

MyLab Accounting Make the grade with **MyLab Accounting:** The problems marked with a 🌐 can be found on **MyLab Accounting.** You can practise them as often as you want, and most feature step-by-step guided instructions to help you find the right answer.

O. PROBLEMS

P12-1. Off-balance-sheet obligations (L.O. 12-1) (Easy – 5 minutes)

a. Provide two reasons why companies may be motivated to keep debt off the balance sheet.
b. Give three examples of obligations that IFRS now requires to be reported on the balance sheet when this was previously not the case.

P12-2. Financial leverage (L.O. 12-1) (Medium – 15 minutes)

I Love Debt Inc. is in the process of acquiring another business. In light of the acquisition, shareholders are currently re-evaluating the appropriateness of the firm's capital structure (the types of and relative levels of debt and equity). The two proposals being contemplated are detailed below:

	Proposal 1	Proposal 2
Estimated EBIT*	\$ 300,000	\$ 300,000
Long-term debt	\$2,000,000	\$3,000,000
Market value of equity	\$2,000,000	\$1,000,000
Interest rate on long-term debt	4%	4%
Tax rate	30%	30%

*Earnings before interest and taxes

Required:

a. Calculate the estimated return on equity (ROE) under the two proposals. [ROE = net income after taxes ÷ market value of equity; net income after taxes = (EBIT − interest on long-term debt) × (1 − tax rate)]
b. Which proposal will generate the higher estimated ROE?
c. What is the primary benefit of adopting the capital structure that generates the higher estimated ROE? What are two drawbacks to this approach?

P12-3. Financial leverage and other aspects of borrowing (L.O. 12-1, L.O. 12-2) (Easy – 5 minutes)

a. Describe financial leverage and outline the principal benefit and drawbacks of borrowing funds to finance the acquisition of assets.
b. What is the function of debt-rating agencies like DBRS and Moody's Investors Service?
c. What are financial liabilities?
d. What is the primary advantage to corporations of selling notes directly to the investing public, rather than borrowing from a financial institution?

P12-4. Bonds (L.O. 12-2) (Easy – 10 minutes)

a. What is a bond indenture?
b. What are covenants? What are the two general categories of covenants?
c. Why do companies issue bonds instead of borrowing from a bank?
d. How do companies normally sell a new bond issue to the investing public?

P12-5. Types of bonds (L.O. 12-2) (Medium – 10 minutes)

Briefly describe the distinguishing characteristics of the bonds listed below:

- Callable bonds
- Convertible bonds
- Debentures
- Real-return bonds
- Perpetual bonds
- Secured bonds
- Serial bonds
- Stripped (zero-coupon) bonds

A·S·P·E

P12-6. Issuing bonds at a discount

(L.O. 12-3) (Easy – 5 minutes)

Shangri-La Inc. reports its financial results in accordance with ASPE and employs the straight-line method of amortization. The company issues $5,000,000 of five-year, 4% bonds dated January 1, 2018. Interest is payable on January 1 and July 1 each year. The proceeds realized from the issue were the $4,900,000 sales price less the $50,000 fee charged by Shangri-La's investment bank. Shangri-La's year-end is December 31.

Required:

Prepare journal entries to record:

a. The issuance of the bonds.
b. Payment of interest and related amortization on July 1, 2018.
c. Accrual of interest and related amortization on December 31, 2018.

P12-7. Accounting for notes payable (L.O. 12-3) (Easy – 5 minutes)

On May 1, 2019, Ripley Ltd. purchases a new automobile for $36,000 from the dealer who provides the financing. The three-year, interest-free loan is repayable at $1,000 per month. The market rate of interest for similar transactions is 0.5% per month.

Required:

Prepare journal entries to record:

a. The purchase of the automobile.
b. The accrual of interest and the loan payment at the end of May 2019.

P12-8. Accounting for notes payable (L.O. 12-3) (Easy – 5 minutes)

Patrice Wall Accounting Inc. takes advantage of a well-known office furnishings store's low interest rate financing. Patrice buys furniture on the first day of its fiscal year, signing a $10,000, three-year note. The note is payable in full at maturity. Interest is payable annually at 2%. The market rate of interest for similar transactions is 4%.

Required:

Prepare journal entries to record:

a. The purchase of the office furniture.
b. The payment of interest and related amortization of the discount at the end of Year 1.

A·S·P·E

P12-9. Issuing bonds at a premium (L.O. 12-3) (Easy – 8 minutes)

Utopia Corp. reports its financial results in accordance with ASPE and employs the straight-line method of amortization. The company issues $5,000,000 of six-year, 6% bonds dated January 1, 2019. Interest is payable on January 1 and July 1 each year. The proceeds realized from the issue were the $5,200,000 sales price less the $20,000 fee charged by Utopia's lawyers. Utopia's year-end is December 31.

Required:

Prepare journal entries to record:

a. The issuance of the bonds.
b. Payment of interest and related amortization on July 1, 2019.
c. Accrual of interest and related amortization on December 31, 2019.
d. Briefly describe the difference between a firm commitment underwriting and a best efforts approach.

P12-10. Selling par bonds after the specified issue date (L.O. 12-3) (Easy – 10 minutes)

On the River Co. (OTRC) sells $1,000,000 of 10-year, 4% bonds at par plus accrued interest. The bonds are dated January 1, 2021, but due to market conditions are not issued until May 1, 2021. Interest is payable on June 30 and December 31 each year.

Required:

Prepare journal entries to record:

a. The issuance of the bonds on May 1, 2021. Assume that OTRC has adopted a policy of crediting accrued interest payable for the accrued interest on the date of sale.
b. Payment of interest on June 30, 2021.
c. Payment of interest on December 31, 2021.

P12-11. Measurement of non-current financial liabilities  (L.O. 12-3) (Easy – 10 minutes)

Discuss how non-current financial liabilities are initially and subsequently valued.

P12-12. Issuance of bonds (various)  (L.O. 12-3) (Easy – 15 minutes)

Golf for Life Inc. issues three series of $1,000,000 six-year bonds dated January 1, 2018, on the issue date. Interest is payable on June 30 and December 31 each year. Series A has a coupon rate of 5%; series B is 6%; and series C is 7%. The market rate of interest at time of issue is 6%.

Required:

a. Prior to making any numerical calculations, comment on whether:
   i. Series A will sell at a discount, par, or premium and briefly explain why.
   ii. Series B will sell at a discount, par, or premium and briefly explain why.
   iii. Series C will sell at a discount, par, or premium and briefly explain why.
b. Prepare journal entries to record the issuance of:
   i. The series A bonds.
   ii. The series B bonds.
   iii. The series C bonds.

P12-13. Issuing bonds at a discount (L.O. 12-3) (Medium – 10 minutes)

Escape to Egypt Travel Inc. issues $4,000,000 of five-year, 4% bonds dated January 1, 2021. Interest is payable on January 1 and July 1 each year. The proceeds realized from the issue were the $3,900,000 sales price less the $40,000 fee charged by Escape's investment bank. Escape's year-end is December 31.

Required:

Prepare journal entries to record:

a. The issuance of the bonds.
b. Payment of interest and related amortization on July 1, 2021.
c. Accrual of interest and related amortization on December 31, 2021.

P12-14. Issuing bonds at a premium (L.O. 12-3) (Medium – 10 minutes)

Australian Balloon Rides Ltd. issues $4,000,000 of five-year, 4% bonds dated January 1, 2018. Interest is payable on January 1 and July 1 each year. The proceeds realized from the issue were the $4,200,000 sales price less the $20,000 fee charged by Balloon's lawyers. Balloon's year-end is December 31.

Required:

Prepare journal entries to record:

a. The issuance of the bonds.
b. Payment of interest and related amortization on July 1, 2018.
c. Accrual of interest and related amortization on December 31, 2018.

P12-15. Issuing bonds at a discount (L.O. 12-3) (Medium – 10 minutes)

Really Really Cheap Vacations Ltd. issues $2,000,000 of five-year, 5% bonds dated January 1, 2021. Interest is payable on January 1 and July 1 each year. The proceeds realized from the issue were the $1,900,000 sales price less the $10,000 fee charged by Really's investment bank. Really's year-end is December 31.

Required:

Prepare journal entries to record:

a. The issuance of the bonds.
b. Payment of interest and related amortization on July 1, 2021.
c. Accrual of interest and related amortization on December 31, 2021.

P12-16. Issuing bonds at a premium (L.O. 12-3) (Medium – 10 minutes)

Outstanding Accountants Co. sells $1,000,000 of 10-year, 4% bonds priced to yield 3.9%. The bonds are dated and issued on January 1, 2018. Interest is payable on January 1 and July 1 each year. Outstanding's year-end is June 30.

Required:

Prepare journal entries to record:

a. The issuance of the bonds.
b. Accrual of interest and related amortization on June 30, 2018.
c. Payment of interest on July 1, 2018.
d. Payment of interest and related amortization on January 1, 2019.

A·S·P·E

P12-17. Selling bonds at a discount after the specified issue date (L.O. 12-3) (Medium – 15 minutes)

Cloverdale Country Rodeo Inc. (CCRI) sells $1,000,000 of 10-year, 6% bonds for $980,500 plus accrued interest. The bonds are dated January 1, 2021, but due to market conditions are not issued until April 1, 2021. Interest is payable on June 30 and December 31 each year. CCRI elects to report its financial results in accordance with ASPE and uses the straight-line method to amortize the bond discount.

Required:

Prepare journal entries to record:

a. The issuance of the bonds on April 1, 2021. Assume that CCRI has adopted a policy of crediting accrued interest payable for the accrued interest on the date of sale.
b. Payment of interest on June 30, 2021.
c. Payment of interest on December 31, 2021.

A·S·P·E

P12-18. Selling bonds at a premium after the specified issue date (L.O. 12-3) (Medium – 15 minutes)

In the Burbs Ltd. (ITBL) sells $5,000,000 of eight-year, 4% bonds for $5,009,400 plus accrued interest. The bonds are dated January 1, 2018, but due to market conditions are not issued until

March 1, 2018. Interest is payable on June 30 and December 31 each year. ITBL elects to report its financial results in accordance with ASPE and employs the straight-line method to amortize the bond premium.

Required:

Prepare journal entries to record:

a. The issuance of the bonds on March 1, 2018. Assume that ITBL has adopted a policy of crediting accrued interest payable for the accrued interest on the date of sale.
b. Payment of interest on June 30, 2018.
c. Payment of interest on December 31, 2018.

P12-19. Amortizing a premium using the effective interest method and the straight-line method (L.O. 12-3) (Medium – 15 minutes)

A·S·P·E

Golf Is Great Corp. sells bonds to friends and families to finance the acquisition of a driving range. On January 1, 2018, Golf Is Great sells $3,000,000 in four-year, 5% bonds priced to yield 4% for $3,109,882. Interest is payable on June 30 and December 31 each year. The corporate year-end is December 31.

Golf Is Great is a private corporation and the bonds are not publicly traded. As such, Golf Is Great may elect to use either the straight-line or effective interest method to amortize the premium.

Required:

a. Complete a bond amortization spreadsheet that contrasts the use of the straight-line method and the effective interest method. Use the format that follows as employed in Exhibit 12-13c.[20]

Straight-line method					Effective interest method				
Date	Interest expense	Interest paid	Premium amortized	Amortized cost	Date	Interest expense	Interest paid	Premium amortized	Amortized cost

b. Review your results tabulated in part (a). Does the choice of methods affect:
   i. Cash flow for each of the periods, and if so how?
   ii. The total interest expense over the life of the bond, and if so how?
   iii. Reported profitability on a year-to-year basis, and if so how?

P12-20. Accounting for notes payable (L.O. 12-3) (Medium – 20 minutes)

You are the accountant for Simply the Best Fireworks. The company has been negotiating with various car dealers in an attempt to get the best deal on a new Vroom Vroom XKY. The purchasing manager provides you with a summary of three offers and asks you to analyze them to determine the best arrangement. The options available are to:

i. Pay $40,000 cash.
ii. Issue an interest-free note for $43,200 repayable in 36 equal monthly installments.
iii. Issue a 9% note for $38,000 repayable in 36 equal monthly installments.

For a car loan, Simply's bank will charge the company a nominal rate of 6% per annum, payable monthly.

Required:

a. Analyze the offers in terms of the cost of the purchase expressed in present value terms.
b. Independent of part (a), prepare the journal entry to record (i) the purchase of the automobile assuming that Simply issued the $38,000 note, and (ii) the first payment on the loan.

---

[20] Exhibit 12-13c illustrates the amortization of a discount. This question requires you to amortize a premium and the spreadsheet computations must be adjusted accordingly.

P12-21. Accounting for notes payable (L.O. 12-3) (Medium – 25 minutes)

You are the chief financial officer for Outstanding Interiors Ltd. The company has been negotiating with suppliers in an attempt to get the best deal on a new data management system. Three suppliers have provided quotes and you have been asked to analyze them to determine the best arrangement. The options available are to:

i. Pay $250,000 cash.
ii. Issue an interest-free note for $278,400 repayable in 48 equal monthly installments.
iii. Issue a 6% note for $240,000 repayable in 60 equal monthly installments.

The market rate of interest for similar transactions is 0.4% per month.

Required:

a. Determine the cost of the purchase for each of the three options expressed in present value terms.
b. Based on your analysis in part (a), which option should Outstanding Interiors Ltd. choose?
c. For the second and third options, prepare the journal entries to record (i) the purchase of the data management system, and (ii) the first payment on the loan.

P12-22. Accounting for notes payable (L.O. 12-3) (Difficult – 20 minutes)

Stanger Corp. purchases a new automobile and takes advantage of a low interest rate loan offered by the manufacturer's financing division. Stanger buys the car on July 1, 2018, paying $10,000 cash and signing a $48,000, four-year note repayable at $1,050 per month including interest at a nominal rate of 2.4% per annum (0.2% per month). The market rate of interest for similar transactions is 0.3% per month. The first loan payment is due on August 1, 2018. Stanger estimates that the residual value of the car will be $8,500 at the end of its four-year useful life. Depreciation is accounted for monthly on a straight-line basis.

Required:

Prepare journal entries to record:

a. The purchase of the car.
b. Depreciation expense on July 31, 2018.
c. Interest expense on July 31, 2018.
d. The loan payment on August 1, 2018.
e. Interest expense on August 31, 2018.

P12-23. Amortizing a discount using the effective interest method and the straight-line method (L.O. 12-3) (Difficult – 25 minutes)

Buy Low Sell High Corp. issues bonds to finance the acquisition of marketable securities. On January 1, 2019, Buy Low sells $1,000,000 in three-year, 5% bonds for $970,000. Interest is payable on June 30 and December 31 each year. The corporate year-end is December 31.

Buy Low's junior accountant, Bob Blades, has been asked to prepare a bond discount amortization spreadsheet. Bob is not sure whether he should use the straight-line or effective interest method to amortize the discount, so he prepares both.

Required:

a. Complete a bond amortization spreadsheet that contrasts the use of the straight-line method and the effective interest method. Use the format that follows as employed in Exhibit 12-13c.

Straight-line method					Effective interest method				
Date	Interest expense	Interest paid	Discount amortized	Amortized cost	Date	Interest expense	Interest paid	Discount amortized	Amortized cost

Prepare journal entries to record:

b. The issuance of the bonds on January 1, 2019.
c. Payment of interest and related amortization on June 30, 2019, under the straight-line method.
d. Payment of interest and related amortization on June 30, 2019, under the effective interest method.
e. Retirement of the bonds on December 31, 2021, assuming that the final interest payment has already been recorded in the company's books.
f. Compare and contrast the two methods. Interest expense in the first period is higher under which method for bonds sold at a discount? For bonds sold at a premium? Why does IFRS require public companies to use the effective interest method? Why do the Accounting Standards for Private Enterprises allow companies to use the straight-line method?

A·S·P·E

P12-24. Derecognition prior to maturity—refinancing a bond issue

(L.O. 12-3, L.O. 12-4) (Medium – 10 minutes)

Adler Corp. issued $4,000,000 of 10-year, 4.5% bonds on January 1, 2018, at par. Interest is due annually on December 31. The market rate of interest has since increased dramatically to 8%. As such, Adler can repurchase its bonds on the open market for $3,441,000. They decided to take advantage of this situation, and on January 1, 2023, issued a new series of bonds in the amount of $3,441,000 (five-year bonds, 8% interest payable annually). The bonds were sold at par and the proceeds were used to retire the 4.5% bonds.

Journal entry for the sale of the new bonds		
Dr. Cash	3,441,000	
Cr. Bonds payable		3,441,000
Journal entry to retire the old bonds		
Dr. Bonds payable	4,000,000	
Cr. Cash		3,441,000
Cr. Gain on bond redemption		559,000

Adler has recorded a gain on the retirement, which increases its net income for the year.

Required:

Ignoring transaction costs and taxation effects, is Adler any better off? Discuss.

P12-25. Selling bonds after the specified issue date; derecognition prior to maturity

(L.O. 12-3, L.O. 12-4) (Medium – 10 minutes)

Legally Yours, a law firm, sells $5,000,000 of four-year, 6% bonds priced to yield 4.2%. The bonds are dated January 1, 2018, but due to some regulatory hurdles are not issued until March 1, 2018. Interest is payable on January 1 and July 1 each year. The bonds sell for $5,315,703 plus accrued interest.

In mid-June, Legally Yours earns an unusually large fee of $7,000,000 for one of its cases. They use part of the proceeds to buy back the bonds in the open market on July 1, 2018, after the interest payment has been made. Legally Yours pays a total of $5,400,000 to reacquire the bonds and retires them.

Required:

Prepare journal entries to record:

a. The issuance of the bonds—assume that Legally Yours has adopted a policy of crediting interest expense for the accrued interest on the date of sale.
b. Payment of interest and related amortization on July 1, 2018.
c. Reacquisition and retirement of the bonds.

A·S·P·E

P12-26. Accounting for bonds; various topics (L.O. 12-3, L.O. 12-4) (Medium – 15 minutes)

Exclusive Golf Vacations sells bonds to friends and families to finance the acquisition of a small tropical island on which it intends to build a golf resort. On January 1, 2018, the company sells $10,000,000 of 5% bonds at 103. The three-year bonds mature on January 1, 2021, with interest payable on June 30 and December 31 each year.

Exclusive Golf Vacations' year-end is December 31. As it is a private corporation and the bonds are not publicly traded, Exclusive has elected to report its financial results in accordance with Part II of the *CPA Canada Handbook*—Accounting (ASPE) and uses the straight-line method of amortization.

Required:

a. Complete a bond amortization spreadsheet using the format that follows:

Straight-line method				
Date	Interest expense	Interest paid	Premium amortized	Amortized cost

b. Prepare the journal entry to record the issuance of the bonds.
c. Prepare the journal entry to record the payment of interest and related amortization on June 30, 2018.
d. Prepare the journal entry to record the derecognition of the bonds at maturity.

P12-27. Accounting for bonds; various topics (L.O. 12-3, L.O. 12-4) (Medium – 15 minutes)

Jane's Steel Inc. sells bonds to the investing public to finance the acquisition of a new foundry. On July 1, 2018, the company sells $8,000,000 of 3% bonds priced to yield 3.5% for $7,887,020. The bonds mature on July 1, 2021, with interest payable on June 30 and December 31 each year. The corporate year-end is December 31.

Required:

a. Complete a bond amortization spreadsheet using the format that follows:

Effective interest method				
Date	Interest expense	Interest paid	Discount amortized	Amortized cost

b. Prepare the journal entry to record the issuance of the bonds.
c. Prepare the journal entry to record the payment of interest and related amortization on December 31, 2019.
d. Prepare the journal entry to record the derecognition of the bonds at maturity.
e. Briefly explain the difference between the primary market for bonds and the over-the-counter (OTC) market.

P12-28. Non-current financial liabilities denominated in foreign currency (L.O. 12-3, L.O. 12-4) (Medium – 15 minutes)

On January 1, 2018, Jakeman's Chiropractic Corp. (JCC) borrowed €100,000 from its bank. JCC signed a note payable due on December 31, 2019. Pertinent details follow:

- The interest rate on the note was 5% payable annually each December 31. The market rate of interest for obligations of this nature was also 5% on the issue date.
- JCC's year-end was December 31. It did not accrue interest throughout the year.
- Exchange rates of consequence were:

	Euro	Canadian dollar
January 1, 2018	€1.00	C$1.44
December 31, 2018	€1.00	C$1.47
December 31, 2019	€1.00	C$1.42
Average rate 2018	€1.00	C$1.45
Average rate 2019	€1.00	C$1.43

Required:

Prepare journal entries to record:

a. Issuance of the note payable on January 1, 2018.
b. Revaluation of the liability on December 31, 2018.
c. Payment of interest on December 31, 2018.
d. Revaluation of the liability on December 31, 2019.
e. Payment of interest on December 31, 2019.
f. Derecognition of the liability on December 31, 2019.

P12-29. Issuance and derecognition of bonds (L.O. 12-3, L.O. 12-4) (Medium – 20 minutes)

On July 1, 2018, Inuvialuit Golf Corp. issued $5,000,000 of five-year, 6%, semi-annual bonds for $5,040,000. At time of issue, Inuvialuit paid its investment bank a $40,000 sales commission. On July 31, 2021, Inuvialuit calls $3,000,000 of the bonds, paying 102 plus accrued interest, and retires them. On March 31, 2022, Inuvialuit purchases the remaining bonds on the open market for $1,980,000 including accrued interest and retires them. Inuvialuit's year-end is August 31. The company does not use reversing entries.

Required:

a. Prepare journal entries to record:
   i. The issuance of the bonds on July 1, 2018.
   ii. Repurchase of the bonds on July 31, 2021.
   iii. Payment of interest on December 31, 2021.
   iv. Retirement of the remaining bonds on March 31, 2022.
b. Provide a brief explanation as to the most likely reasons that Inuvialuit was able to repurchase its bonds at a discount.

P12-30. Issuing bonds (various); derecognition prior to maturity (L.O. 12-3, L.O. 12-4) (Medium – 25 minutes)

There are three independent situations summarized below. In all three cases the bonds are sold on January 1, 2018, and the issuing company has a December 31 year-end. In Situation 3, the bonds were all repurchased at par on January 1, 2022.

	Situation 1	Situation 2	Situation 3
Face value	$10,000,000	$20,000,000	$40,000,000
Coupon rate	14%	10%	12%
Coupon dates(s)	6/30; 12/31	12/31	12/31
Market rate	12%	12%	14%
Time to maturity	6 years	12 years	8 years

Required:

Prepare journal entries to record:

a. The issuance of the three bonds.
b. Payment of interest and related amortization on December 31, 2018.
c. Retirement of the Situation 3 bond on January 1, 2022.

P12-31. Issuing bonds at a discount; derecognition prior to and at maturity (L.O. 12-3, L.O. 12-4) (Difficult – 20 minutes)

Fredericton Aerospace Inc. raised $10,500,000 by selling $10,000,000 of six-year, 4% bonds dated January 1, 2021. Fredericton used part of the proceeds to pay its investment bank's fee of $400,000 and related legal and accounting fees of $200,000.

Interest is payable on June 30 and December 31 each year. Fredericton can call the bonds on January 1, 2024, at 101. The company exercises this privilege, redeeming 40% of the bonds on the call date and retiring them. The company's year-end is December 31.

Required:

Prepare journal entries to record:

a. The issuance of the bonds on January 1, 2021.
b. Payment of interest and related amortization on December 31, 2023.
c. Repurchase of the bonds on January 1, 2024.
d. Retirement of the remaining bonds on December 31, 2026, assuming that the final interest payment has already been recorded in the company's books.

P12-32. Accounting for bonds; various topics

(L.O. 12-3, L.O. 12-4) (Difficult – 20 minutes)

On March 15, 2018, Candoit Inc. sold $10,000,000 of five-year, 3% bonds for $9,972,469. From the proceeds, Candoit paid its investment bank a $200,000 sales commission. Interest is payable semi-annually on March 15 and September 15. On March 16, 2022, Candoit buys back $2,000,000 of bonds on the open market for their face value.

Required:

a. What are the nominal and effective rates of interest that Candoit is paying on the bonds expressed as an annual percentage rate?
b. Assuming that Candoit records the bond liability at amortized cost, what is the net book value of the bonds outstanding on March 16, 2020? On September 16, 2020? Use your financial calculator to determine these amounts and then verify them by constructing a schedule of interest expense and bond amortization during the life of the bond. For this part, ignore the redemption of bonds on March 16, 2022.
c. On the date of the open market purchase, had market interest rates increased or decreased since the bonds were issued? Explain.
d. Did the repurchase result in an *economic* gain or loss for either Candoit or the investor? Explain.

P12-33. Issuance of bonds (various); derecognition prior to maturity

(L.O. 12-3, L.O. 12-4) (Difficult – 20 minutes)

Two independent situations follow:

1. On January 1, 2018, Cute Koalas Inc. issued $4,000,000 of 7%, 12-year, callable bonds priced to yield 6%. The bonds may be called at 102 on or after December 31, 2023. Interest is payable on June 30 and December 31. Cute Koalas calls the bonds on January 1, 2025.
2. On January 1, 2021, Cuddly Kangaroos Ltd. issued $6,000,000 of 5%, eight-year bonds priced to yield 6.5%. Interest is payable on June 30 and December 31. Cuddly repurchases the outstanding bonds on July 1, 2024, at which time the market rate of interest is 6%.

Required:

Prepare journal entries to record:

a. The sale and retirement of the bonds in Scenario 1.
b. The sale and retirement of the bonds in Scenario 2.

P12-34. Issuance of bonds (various); derecognition prior to maturity

(L.O. 12-3, L.O. 12-4) (Difficult – 20 minutes)

Two independent situations follow:

1. On January 1, 2018, Alligator Inc. issued $6,000,000 of 5%, eight-year, callable bonds priced to yield 6%. The bonds may be called at 101 on or after December 31, 2021. Interest is payable on June 30 and December 31. Alligator Inc. calls 40% of the outstanding bonds ($2,400,000) on January 1, 2023.
2. On January 1, 2019, Crocodile Ltd. issued $5,000,000 of 6%, six-year bonds priced to yield 5.5%. Interest is payable on June 30 and December 31. Crocodile repurchases the outstanding bonds on July 1, 2022, at which time the market rate of interest is 7%.

Required:

Prepare journal entries to record:

a. The sale and retirement of the called bonds in Scenario 1.
b. The sale and retirement of the bonds in Scenario 2.

P12-35. Non-current financial liabilities denominated in foreign currency

(L.O. 12-3, L.O. 12-4) (Difficult – 20 minutes)

On January 1, 2018, Marianne's Massage Inc. (MMI) issued US$5,000,000 of five-year bonds at par that matured on December 31, 2022. Pertinent details follow:

- The coupon rate on the bonds was 6% payable annually on December 31.
- MMI's year-end was December 31. It did not accrue interest throughout the year.
- Exchange rates of consequence were:

	Spot rates			Average rates	
Date	US dollar	Canadian dollar	Year	US dollar	Canadian dollar
Jan. 1, 2018	US$1.00	C$1.10			
Dec. 31, 2018	US$1.00	C$1.08	2018	US$1.00	C$1.09
Dec. 31, 2019	US$1.00	C$1.06	2019	US$1.00	C$1.07
Dec. 31, 2020	US$1.00	C$1.11	2020	US$1.00	C$1.08
Dec. 31, 2021	US$1.00	C$1.09	2021	US$1.00	C$1.10
Dec. 31, 2022	US$1.00	C$1.07	2022	US$1.00	C$1.08

Required:

Part I
Prepare journal entries to record:

a. Issuance of the bonds on January 1, 2018.
b. Revaluation of the liability on December 31, 2018.
c. Payment of interest on December 31, 2018.
d. Revaluation of the liability on December 31, 2022.
e. Payment of interest on December 31, 2022.
f. Derecognition of the liability on December 31, 2022.

Part II
Over the life of the bond, what was the total foreign exchange gain or loss reported due to borrowing in US dollars? Identify the amount that is attributable to: (i) the change in exchange rates between the time the bonds were issued and derecognized; and (ii) purchasing US dollars for payment of interest at rates that differed from those used to determine interest expense.

P12-36. Selling bonds after the specified issue date; derecognition prior to maturity

(L.O. 12-3, L.O. 12-4) (Difficult – 30 minutes)

Avoiding Faux Pas (AFP), a leading international school of etiquette, sells $3,000,000 of six-year, 6% bonds priced to yield 7.2%. The bonds are dated July 1, 2020, but due to some regulatory hurdles are not issued until December 1, 2020. Interest is payable annually on June 30 each year. AFP can call the bonds on July 1, 2024, at 102. The bonds sell for $2,838,944 plus accrued interest.

AFP sells shares to the public for the first time in early 2023. They use part of the IPO (initial public offering) proceeds to buy back $1,000,000 (face value) of the bonds in the open market on July 1, 2023. AFP pays a total of $950,000 to reacquire the bonds and retires them.

On July 1, 2024, AFP calls the remaining bonds and retires them. The company's year-end is June 30.

Required:

a. Complete a bond amortization spreadsheet using the format that follows, the use of which was illustrated in Exhibit 12-10c. Include the partial redemption of bonds on July 1, 2023.

Date	Interest expense	Interest paid	Discount amortized	Amortized cost

Prepare journal entries to record:

b. The issuance of the bonds on December 1, 2020, assuming that AFP has adopted a policy of crediting interest expense for the accrued interest on the date of sale.
c. Payment of interest and related amortization on June 30, 2021.
d. Payment of interest and related amortization on June 30, 2023.
e. Repurchase of the bonds on July 1, 2023.
f. Payment of interest and related amortization on June 30, 2024.
g. Repurchase of the bonds on July 1, 2024.

P12-37. Accounting for bonds; various scenarios

(L.O. 12-3, L.O. 12-4) (Difficult – 30 minutes)

Three independent situations follow:

1. I'm Alive Ltd. (IAL) issued $5,000,000 in stripped (zero-coupon) bonds that mature in 10 years. The market rate of interest for bonds of a similar nature is 3.6% compounded monthly. Five and a half years after issue, when the market rate was 4.8%, IAL repurchased $2,000,000 of the bonds on the open market. IAL accrues interest monthly. Bonds are carried at amortized cost.
2. Creative Accountants sold $2,000,000 of five-year bonds that pay the then-current market rate of interest of 6% annually on December 31. The bonds are dated January 1, 2018, but were not issued until February 1, 2018. Creative's year-end is December 31. Creative has adopted a policy of crediting interest expense for the interest accrued up to the date of sale.
3. On January 1, 2020, Able Minded Professors Corp. (AMPC) sold $3,000,000 of three-year, 5% bonds priced to yield 4.5%. Interest is payable on June 30 and December 31 each year.

Required:

a. Prepare journal entries to record:
   i. The sale and retirement of the bonds in Scenario 1.
   ii. The sale of the bonds in Scenario 2 and payment of interest on December 31, 2018.
   iii. The sale of the bonds in Scenario 3.
b. Prepare a schedule of interest expense and bond amortization during the life of the bond in Scenario 3.

P12-38. Accounting for bonds; various scenarios

(L.O. 12-3, L.O. 12-4) (Difficult – 30 minutes)

Three independent situations follow:

1. Second Time Around Corp. (STAC) issued $7,000,000 in stripped (zero-coupon) bonds that mature in eight years. The market rate of interest for bonds of a similar nature is 4.8% compounded monthly. Four and a half years after issue, when the market rate was 3.6%, STAC repurchased $3,000,000 of the bonds on the open market. STAC accrues interest monthly. Bonds are carried at amortized cost.
2. The Friendly Car Dealer sold $4,000,000 of five-year bonds that pay the then-current market rate of interest of 3% annually on December 31. The bonds are dated January 1, 2019, but were not issued until March 1, 2019. Friendly's year-end is December 31. Friendly has adopted a policy of crediting interest expense for the interest accrued up to the date of sale.
3. On January 1, 2019, Creative Geniuses Ltd. (CGL) sold $3,000,000 of three-year, 5% bonds priced to yield 5.5%. Interest is payable on June 30 and December 31 each year.

Required:

a. Prepare journal entries to record:
   i. The sale and retirement of the bonds in Scenario 1.
   ii. The sale of the bonds in Scenario 2 and payment of interest on December 31, 2019.
   iii. The sale of the bonds in Scenario 3.
b. Prepare a schedule of interest expense and bond amortization during the life of the bond in Scenario 3.

P12-39. Accounting for bonds; various topics

(L.O. 12-3, L.O. 12-4) (Difficult – 30 minutes)

On April 1, 2019, Illustrious Inc. sold $8,000,000 of four-year, 4% bonds for $8,298,101. From the proceeds, Illustrious paid its investment bank a $150,000 sales commission. Interest is payable semi-annually on September 30 and March 31. On October 1, 2021, Illustrious buys back $3,000,000 of bonds on the open market for their face value.

Required:

a. What are the nominal and effective rates of interest that Illustrious is paying on the bonds expressed as an annual percentage rate?
b. Assuming that Illustrious records the bond liability at amortized cost, what is the net book value of the bonds outstanding on October 1, 2019? April 1, 2020? Use your financial calculator to determine these amounts and then verify them by constructing a schedule of interest expense and bond amortization during the life of the bond. For this part, ignore the redemption of bonds on October 1, 2021.
c. Assuming that Illustrious records the bond liability at amortized cost, prepare the journal entry to record the issuance of the bonds.
d. Assuming that Illustrious records the bond liability at amortized cost, prepare the journal entry to record the redemption of the bond on October 1, 2021.
e. Assuming that Illustrious designates the liability as at fair value through profit or loss, prepare the journal entry to record the issuance of the bonds.

P12-40. Offsetting and in-substance defeasance

(L.O. 12-4) (Easy – 5 minutes)

a. What is offsetting? When is it allowed? What are some benefits to the company of offsetting?
b. What is in-substance defeasance? When do defeasance arrangements qualify for offsetting?

P12-41. Derecognition prior to and at maturity

(L.O. 12-4) (Easy – 10 minutes)

Mississauga Wheels Ltd. (MW) sold $5,000,000 of five-year, 6% bonds at par on January 1, 2021. Interest is payable on June 30 and December 31 each year. The bonds can be called at any time at 101 plus accrued interest. On April 1, 2022, MW bought back $1,000,000 of bonds on the open market for $984,736 including accrued interest and retired them. On August 1, 2023, MW called $500,000 of bonds and retired them. MW prepares accrual entries only at year-end.

Required:

Prepare journal entries to record:

a. The open market purchase of the bonds on April 1, 2022.
b. The calling of the bonds on August 1, 2023.
c. Retirement of the remaining bonds on December 31, 2025, assuming that the final interest payment has already been recorded in the company's books.

P12-42. Accounting for site restoration obligations

(L.O. 12-5) (Easy – 8 minutes)

Meagan's Metals Corp. (MMC) has been granted a licence to use an abandoned limestone quarry as a dump for old and abandoned motor vehicles. The terms of the licence require MMC to replace the mined limestone with scrap metal, and once the quarry is returned to its original grade, to construct a nature park. MMC estimates that it will take 20 years to fill the dump site and that downstream remediation costs will be $15 million. An appropriate interest rate for this obligation is 6%.

Required:

a. Prepare the journal entry to record the site restoration obligation, assuming that MMC reports its financial results in accordance with IFRS.

A·S·P·E

b. Prepare the journal entry to record the site restoration obligation, assuming that MMC reports its financial results in accordance with ASPE.

P12-43. Accounting for site restoration obligations (L.O. 12-5) (Easy – 8 minutes)

Jane's Oil Inc. (JOI) installed an offshore oil drilling platform. The terms of the government's approval to drill requires JOI to dismantle and remove the platform upon completion of drilling. JOI estimates that it will take eight years to exhaust the proven reserves of oil at the site. Dismantling and removal costs are estimated to be $3 million. An appropriate interest rate for this obligation is 4%.

Required:

A·S·P·E

a. Prepare the journal entry to record the site restoration obligation assuming that JOI reports its financial results in accordance with IFRS.
b. Prepare the journal entry to record the site restoration obligation assuming that JOI reports its financial results in accordance with ASPE.

P12-44. Accounting for site restoration costs  (L.O. 12-5) (Medium – 10 minutes)

Refer to part (a) of problem P12-43. At the beginning of Year 6, JOI determined that the appropriate market-based interest rate for this obligation was 5%. JOI depreciates the asset on a straight-line basis.

Required:

a. Prepare a journal entry to record the change in the liability amount.
b. Prepare a journal entry to record depreciation expense at the end of Year 6 on the asset related to site restoration costs.

P12-45. Accounting for site restoration obligations (L.O. 12-5) (Difficult – 20 minutes)

During 2021, Surinder's Copper Mine Inc. (SCMI) built the infrastructure for an open pit copper mine in a remote area in Northern British Columbia at a total cost of $20 million, paid in cash. The mine is expected to produce 800,000 tonnes of copper over its estimated useful life of 10 years.

The BC government's approval granted to SCMI was conditional upon the company remediating the site and establishing a wildlife reserve. The estimated cost of remediation is $5 million. An appropriate interest rate for this obligation is 5%.

Assume that SCMI has grouped the $20 million construction costs and the remediation asset in an account called "Mine assets" and that it uses the units-of-production method to depreciate this asset. SCMI began mining operations in January 2022 and during the year it mined 60,000 tonnes of copper. In 2023, it increased its production to 90,000 tonnes of copper. While SCMI is a private company, it elects to report its financial results in accordance with IFRS. Its year-end is December 31.

Required:

a. Prepare a journal entry to record the site restoration obligation and a summary journal entry to record the cost of construction. Date both entries December 31, 2021.
b. Prepare the adjusting entries pertaining to the mine asset and site restoration obligation for the year ended December 31, 2022.
c. Prepare the adjusting entries pertaining to the mine asset and site restoration obligation for the year ended December 31, 2023.

A·S·P·E

P12-46. Accounting for asset retirement obligations (L.O. 12-5) (Difficult – 20 minutes)

Refer to problem P12-45. Assume that SCMI elects to report its financial results in accordance with Accounting Standards for Private Enterprises (ASPE).

Required:

a. Prepare a journal entry to record the asset retirement obligation and a summary journal entry to record the cost of construction. Date both entries December 31, 2021.
b. Prepare the adjusting entries pertaining to the mine asset and asset retirement obligation for the year ended December 31, 2022.
c. Prepare the adjusting entries pertaining to the mine asset and asset retirement obligation for the year ended December 31, 2023.

P12-47. Accounting for asset retirement obligations (L.O. 12-5) (Difficult – 30 minutes)

Refer to problem P12-45. At the beginning of 2028, SCMI determined that the appropriate market-based interest rate for this obligation was 4%. Management determined that the revised book value of the asset was fully recoverable; an impairment test was not conducted. During its six years of production to the end of 2027, the mine produced 600,000 tonnes of copper; 200,000 tonnes remained to be mined. During 2028, SCMI mined 50,000 tonnes of copper.

Required:

a. Prepare a journal entry to record the change in the liability amount.
b. Prepare the adjusting entries pertaining to the mine asset and site restoration obligation for the year ended December 31, 2028.

P12-48. Disclosure (L.O. 12-6) (Easy – 5 minutes)

List five types of disclosures made regarding companies' indebtedness.

P12-49. Non-current financial liabilities—note disclosures (L.O. 12-6) (Medium – 15 minutes)

Refer to the 2016 financial statements for Canadian Tire Corporation in Appendix C.

Required:

a. What was the amount of long-term liabilities reported in Canadian Tire's financial statements as at December 31, 2016? What was this amount comprised of? Use the same categories that the company reports on its balance sheet.
b. The company had several categories of provisions. What were they and what was the long-term portion of each?
c. What were the company's "other long-term liabilities" comprised of? Use the same categories that the company reports in its notes to the financial statements.
d. What was the company's total long-term debt to (total) equity ratio as at December 31, 2016?

P12-50. Accounting for notes payable and disclosure (L.O. 12-3, L.O. 12-6) (Medium – 25 minutes)

Sarah Bower is the owner of Sarah's Shameless Boutique Corp. (SSBC), a newly incorporated company. Sarah believes that she has a great concept but does not have a lot of money to start the business. Sarah is fairly resourceful, though, and has been able to arrange the following:

1. On July 1, 2018, SSBC provides a vendor with a $10,500 non-interest bearing note due on July 1, 2019, in exchange for furniture with a list price of $10,000. Sarah Bower guarantees the debt.
2. On August 1, 2018, SSBC buys a photocopier listed for $3,400. The office supply store agrees to accept a $500 down payment and a $3,000, three-year note payable at $1,040 per year including interest at 2% with the first payment due on August 1, 2019. The loan is secured by a lien on the photocopier.

3. On September 1, 2018, SSBC borrows $10,000 from its bank for working capital purposes. The loan, plus interest at 6% per annum, is due on June 30, 2019. SSBC grants the bank a security interest in its accounts receivables and inventory.

Unfortunately, SSBC's target audience is a bit more prudish than Sarah anticipated and sales have been slow. While the company was able to retire the bank loan on the due date, it had insufficient cash to pay off the furniture loan. The vendor agrees to accept 1,000 common shares in SSBC in settlement of the obligation. Sarah believed that the shares are worth $15 each, but as this was the first time that SSBC had issued shares to anyone other than Sarah, a fair market price was not yet established.

SSBC's year-end is June 30. The company's banker has suggested that an appropriate market rate for SSBC is 6% per annum for loans that mature in one year or less and 8% for loans with longer maturities.

Required:

a. Prepare journal entries to record:
   i. The purchase of the office furniture.
   ii. The acquisition of the photocopier.
   iii. The receipt of the loan proceeds.
   iv. Payments and accruals on June 30, 2019.
   v. The retirement of the office furnishings loan on July 1, 2019.
b. Briefly describe the note disclosure that would be required with respect to the forgoing liabilities.

P. MINI-CASES

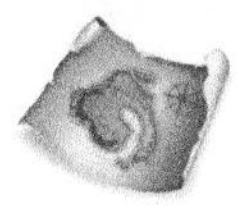

CASE 1
Jackson Capital Inc.
(45 minutes)[21]

Jackson Capital Inc. (JCI) is a new private investment company that provides capital to business ventures. JCI's business mission is to support companies to allow them to compete successfully in domestic and international markets. JCI aims to increase the value of its investments, thereby creating wealth for its shareholders.

Funds to finance the investments were obtained through a private offering of share capital, conventional long-term loans payable, and a bond issue that is indexed to the TSX Composite Index. Annual operating expenses are expected to be $1 million before bonuses, interest, and taxes.

Over the past year, JCI has accumulated a diversified investment portfolio. Depending on the needs of the borrower, JCI provides capital in many different forms, including demand loans, short-term equity investments, fixed-term loans, and loans convertible into share capital. JCI also purchases preferred and common shares in new business ventures where JCI management anticipates a significant return. Any excess funds not committed to a particular investment are held temporarily in money market funds.

JCI has hired three investment managers to review financing applications. These managers visit the applicants' premises to meet with management and review the operations and business plans. They then prepare a report stating their reasons for supporting or rejecting the application. JCI's senior executives review these reports at their monthly meetings and decide whether to invest and what types of investments to make.

Once the investments are made, the investment managers are expected to monitor the investments and review detailed monthly financial reports submitted by the investees. The investment managers' performance bonuses are based on the returns generated by the investments they have recommended.

It is August 1, 2021. JCI's first fiscal year ended on June 30, 2021. JCI's draft balance sheet and other financial information are provided in Exhibit I. An annual audit of the financial statements is required under the terms of the bond issue. Potter & Cook, Chartered Accountants, has been appointed auditor of JCI. The partner on the engagement is Richard Potter; you are the in-charge accountant on this engagement. Mr. Potter has asked you to prepare a memo discussing the significant accounting issues, audit risks, and related audit procedures for this engagement.

Required:

Prepare the memo requested by Mr. Potter pertaining to issues with respect to the company's debt, equity, and cash flow.

Exhibit I Draft balance sheet and other financial information

Jackson Capital Inc.
Draft balance sheet
As at June 30, 2021
(in $000's)

Assets	
Cash and marketable securities	$ 1,670
Investments (at cost)	21,300
Interest receivable	60
Furniture and fixtures (net of accumulated depreciation of $2)	50
	$23,080

(*Continued*)

[21] Uniform Final Examination 2002, with permission from Chartered Professional Accountants of Canada, Toronto, Canada.

Exhibit I Continued

Liabilities	
Accounts payable and accrued liabilities	$ 20
Accrued interest payable	180
Loans payable	12,000
	12,200
Shareholders' equity	
Share capital	12,000
Deficit	(1,120)
	10,880
	$23,080

Jackson Capital Inc.
Summary of investment portfolio
As at June 30, 2021

Investments	Cost of investment
15% common share interest in Fairex Resource Inc., a company listed on the TSX Venture Exchange. Management intends to monitor the performance of this mining company over the next six months and to make a hold/sell decision based on reported reserves and production costs.	$ 3.8 million
25% interest in common shares of Hellon Ltd., a private Canadian real estate company, plus 7.5% convertible debentures with a face value of $2 million, acquired at 98% of maturity value. The debentures are convertible into common shares at the option of the holder.	$ 6.2 million
Five-year loan denominated in Brazilian currency (reals) to Ipanema Ltd., a Brazilian company formed to build a power generating station. Interest at 7% per annum is due semi-annually. 75% of the loan balance is secured by the power generating station under construction. The balance is unsecured.	$ 8.0 million
50% interest in Western Gas, a jointly owned gas exploration project operating in western Canada. One of JCI's investment managers sits on the three-member board of directors.	$ 2.0 million
50,000 stock warrants in Tornado Hydrocarbons Ltd., expiring March 22, 2023. The underlying common shares trade publicly.	$ 1.3 million

Jackson Capital Inc.
Capital structure
As at June 30, 2021

Loans payable

The company has $2 million in demand loans payable with floating interest rates, and $4 million in loans due September 1, 2025, with fixed interest rates.

In addition, the company has long-term 5% stock-indexed bonds payable. Interest at the stated rate is to be paid semi-annually, commencing September 1, 2021. The principal repayment on March 1, 2026, is indexed to changes in the TSX Composite Index as follows: the $6 million original balance of the bonds at the issue date of March 1, 2021, is to be multiplied by the stock index at March 1, 2026, and then divided by the stock index as at March 1, 2021. The stock-indexed bonds are secured by the company's investments.

Share capital

Issued share capital consists of:

1 million 8% Class A (non-voting) preferred shares redeemable at the holder's option on or after August 10, 2025	$ 7 million
10,000 common shares	$ 5 million

CASE 2
Total Protection Limited
(30 minutes)[22]

Total Protection Limited (TPL) was recently incorporated by five homebuilders in central Canada to provide warranty protection for new-home buyers. While most homebuilders provide one-year warranties, TPL offers 10-year warranties and includes protection for a number of items not usually covered. For example, if a problem arose as a result of faulty construction or construction materials, TPL would protect its customers against any resulting decline in the market value of their property and would provide for the costs of restoring the property. TPL does not, however, cover general declines in market value.

The five shareholders believe TPL will increase their home sales and at the same time minimize their individual risks. The idea for TPL originated with Safe-Way Builders and, therefore, this shareholder will receive a royalty payment of 5% of income before income taxes. The shareholders have engaged your firm to prepare a report that will assist them in managing TPL to maximize its long-term profitability. In addition, as a separate report, the shareholders would like your firm to recommend appropriate financial accounting policies for TPL.

You and the partner on the engagement meet with Gus Filmore, president of Safe-Way Builders. Gus is currently operating TPL from the offices of Safe-Way Builders, for which TPL will be charged rent. Gus provides you with the following information on TPL's operations:

- TPL's revenues consist of an initial fee paid at the time of purchase of the warranty and an annual maintenance fee paid over the term of the warranty. Currently, the initial fee and annual maintenance fee depend on a number of factors, including the cost of the home, reputation of the builder, construction design of the home (e.g., brick versus aluminum siding), and the home's location. The warranties are sold through each builder, who can adjust the initial fee and annual maintenance fee if an adjustment is considered necessary to make the sale. The builder receives a commission of 10% of the total warranty revenue, which should ensure that the builder will try to maximize the initial fee and annual maintenance fee. Typically, a buyer of a brick house worth $250,000 that was constructed by a good quality builder should expect to pay an initial fee of $2,000 plus an annual maintenance fee of $250.
- To date, TPL has been doing very well, primarily as a result of two factors: (i) central Canada has been experiencing a boom in the residential construction industry, and (ii) TPL has expanded to offer coverage for homes built by builders other than the shareholders. "Quite frankly," explains Gus, "an increasing share of our business is from these outside builders, many of which have entered the industry just to try to capitalize on the demand. We don't think that permitting these homebuilders to sell coverage will hurt our home sales since most of these builders are in the low-price segment of the market, keeping costs down by employing new, less expensive construction methods and materials. We require that their initial fee must be at least $1,500 per home to ensure that they don't lower the price just to make a sale."
- "Our real problem is keeping up with the paperwork," continues Gus. "I have my own business to run and cannot devote much time to TPL. We haven't even had time to get organized or set up any system for TPL. Lately, I must admit that I've lost track of what's going on. All I know is that we're making money. In just 11 months, TPL has collected about $1.6 million while paying out only $224,000 in repair costs. Keep in mind, however, that I've been able to keep these repair costs down by having Safe-Way Builders do the repairs. Business will only get better since we plan to expand within the next month to offer coverage in western Canada and the southwestern United States. We don't know what to do with all this cash. We're considering investing it all in real estate for future development. After all, that's what we're good at! On the other hand, some shareholders are looking forward to receiving the cash themselves."

Just before you leave the client's premises, you manage to collect some additional information on the operations of TPL (see Exhibit I).

When you return to the office, the partner asks you to prepare the reports requested by the shareholders.

[22] Uniform Final Examination 1990, with permission from Chartered Professional Accountants of Canada, Toronto, Canada.

Required:

Prepare a report recommending appropriate financial accounting policies for TPL.

Exhibit I Information gathered from client records

	TPL Shareholders						
	Larkview Estates	Towne Homes	Granite Homes	Kings Road	Safe-Way Builders	Other Builders	Total
Number of warranties sold	50	85	190	250	175	465	1,215
Warranty revenue ($000's)	$120	$165	$395	$90	$160	$705	$1,635
Repair costs incurred ($000's)	$ 6	$ 9	$ 21	$42	$ 39	$107	$ 224

CASE 3 Kaitlyn's Cats Inc. (20 minutes)

Kaitlyn's Cats Inc. (KCI) is a chain of pet stores that specializes in the sale and veterinary care of *felis catus,* more commonly known as domestic cats. On October 1, 2021, KCI raised a net of $523,973 by issuing $500,000 in 10-year, 6% bonds that pay interest on April 1 and October 1. The market rate of interest at time of issue was 5%. Transaction costs directly attributable to the debt issue totalled $15,000. KCI elected not to designate the liability as at fair value through profit or loss.

Kaitlyn Reid, owner of KCI, is contemplating how to present the bond indebtedness on KCI's balance sheet at issue date. She has set out her initial thoughts as to some possibilities below in advance of her meeting with the company accountant to discuss this matter.

Possibility		
1.	Bonds payable	$523,973
2.	Bond issue costs (report as a non-current asset)	15,000
	Bonds payable	500,000
	Premium on bonds payable	38,973
3.	Bond issue costs (expensed)	15,000
	Bonds payable	538,973

Required:

a. Discuss the advantages and disadvantages of each of the three methods being considered. Which of the three options complies with the requirements of IFRS 9?
b. What is the effective rate of interest on this obligation? Why is this rate used to determine interest expense rather than the stated coupon rate?
c. Why were investors willing to pay $538,973 for a debt instrument with a maturity value of $500,000?
d. Assume that KCI designated the liability as at fair value through profit or loss. Would your answer to part (a) change? If so, how would it change?

CASE 4 Non-current liabilities (30 minutes)

LowTolerance Ltd. is a Canadian public corporation that manufactures high-precision tools used by companies in the semiconductor industry. Recently, demand for LowTolerance's tools has been on the rise, and the company is looking to expand its business. The company did not have the cash needed for the expansion; to raise capital, management issued bonds to the public. On August 1, 2021, it sold $8,000,000 of five-year bonds at 92.46. The bonds have a stated interest rate of 9%, and pay interest semi-annually on January 31 and July 31. The company incurred direct costs related to the issue of the bond (e.g., legal and accounting fees and the investment banker's commission) of $280,010.

On August 1, 2025, LowTolerance retired 30% of the bonds. At that time the bonds' market price was $99.

Required:

(Round the numbers in your answers to the nearest dollar.)

a. What were the gross proceeds from the bond issue? What interest rate did the investors require on the bonds? What were the net proceeds from the bond issue?
b. Another bond of LowTolerance Ltd. is traded based on a market rate of 10%. Is the rate on both bonds the same? If not, what might cause the difference?
c. IFRS mandates the use of the effective interest method for determining interest expense. In your opinion, what might be the problem(s) with the use of the straight-line method?
d. Prepare the journal entry for the issuance of the bonds on August 1, 2021.
e. Prepare the original bond amortization schedule—do not include the partial redemption on August 1, 2025.
f. Calculate the gain or loss on the partial bond retirement on August 1, 2025, and prepare the journal entry to record this event.

Adrian_ilie825/Fotolia

CHAPTER 13

Equities

LEARNING OBJECTIVES

After studying this chapter, you should be able to:

L.O. 13-1. Describe the characteristics of different types of share equity and identify the characteristics that are relevant for accounting purposes.

L.O. 13-2. Identify the different components of equity for accounting purposes that apply to a transaction and analyze the effect of the transaction on those equity components.

L.O. 13-3. Apply the accounting standards and procedures for transactions relating to contributed capital.

L.O. 13-4. Apply the accounting standards and procedures for transactions relating to the distribution of retained earnings.

L.O. 13-5. Prepare a statement of changes in equity.

CPA competencies addressed in this chapter:

1.1.2 Evaluates the appropriateness of the basis of financial accounting (Level B)

1.2.1 Develops or evaluates appropriate accounting policies and procedures (Level B)

1.2.2 Evaluates treatment for routine transactions (Level A)
i. Owners'/shareholders' equity

1.3.1 Prepares financial statements (Level A)

1.3.2 Prepares routine financial statement note disclosure (Level B)

1.4.1 Analyzes complex financial statement note disclosure (Level C)

Canadian Tire (Toronto Stock Exchange tickers CTC and CTC.A), the iconic retailer known for having Canada's unofficial second currency (Canadian Tire "money"), has grown from its first store in 1922 to more than 1,700 retail locations and gas bars today. The company has two classes of shares: Common and Class A. In its 2016 Report to Shareholders, the company reported the following information regarding its share capital:

($ millions)	2016	2015
Authorized		
3,423,366 Common Shares 100,000,000 Class A Non-Voting Shares	$ 0.2	$ 0.2
Issued and outstanding	647.9	671.0
3,423,366 Common Shares (2015—3,423,366) 67,323,781 Class A Non-Voting Shares (2015—70,637,987)		
	$ 648.1	$ 671.2

Why do companies such as Canadian Tire have different classes of shares, and how do we account for them? What are the distinctions among "authorized," "issued," and "outstanding?" How do we account for differences between shares authorized and shares issued, or between the number issued and the number outstanding?

The company also disclosed that it issued and repurchased Class A shares. How do we account for such equity transactions?

13 CONTENTS

A. INTRODUCTION 639
B. COMPONENTS OF EQUITY FOR ACCOUNTING PURPOSES 640
1. Contributed capital 640
2. Retained earnings 643
3. Accumulated other comprehensive income (AOCI) 643
4. Summary 645
C. EQUITY TRANSACTIONS RELATING TO CONTRIBUTED CAPITAL 645
1. Issuance of shares (recognition and initial measurement) 646
2. Stock splits (subsequent measurement) 649
3. Reacquisition of shares (derecognition) 649
D. EQUITY TRANSACTIONS RELATING TO RETAINED EARNINGS 652
1. Cash dividends 652
2. Stock dividends 653
3. Property dividends (dividends in kind) 654
4. Dividend preference 654
E. STATEMENT OF CHANGES IN EQUITY 656
F. PRESENTATION AND DISCLOSURE 658
G. COMPREHENSIVE ILLUSTRATION OF EQUITY TRANSACTIONS 660
H. SUBSTANTIVE DIFFERENCES BETWEEN RELEVANT IFRS AND ASPE 661
I. APPENDIX: PAR VALUE SHARES AND TREASURY SHARES 662
1. Par value shares 662
2. Treasury shares 663
J. SUMMARY 666
K. ANSWERS TO CHECKPOINT QUESTIONS 666
L. GLOSSARY 667
M. REFERENCES 668
N. PROBLEMS 668
O. MINI-CASES 687

A. INTRODUCTION

Equity refers to the ownership interest in the assets of an entity after deducting its liabilities. In other words, equity is a residual amount that is determined by assets and liabilities through the balance sheet equation: equity = assets − liabilities. Indeed, if the balance sheet equation is to hold, equity must be a residual amount rather than defined independently, since the Conceptual Framework already defines assets and liabilities. The residual nature of equity, however, does not mean that we can be cavalier about it—it is still necessary to provide information useful to financial statement readers. The questions are, then, who uses information about equity, and what information about equity would be useful?

First, equity has legal **priority** below that of liabilities in general, meaning that available funds go toward paying off liabilities prior to paying equity claims should the enterprise be liquidated. As a result, debtors have little interest in the specifics of what happens with equity beyond the overall amount of equity to assess solvency of the enterprise. In contrast, equity holders are concerned about both liabilities and equity accounts. Thus, information about equity is primarily geared toward equity holders themselves.

priority The rank of a liability or an equity claim when a company liquidates, where higher priority confers preferential payout before other claimants.

Second, equity holders who do have residual claims on the enterprise are concerned about the size of their claims, and they need to be aware of changes to their share of profits. Consequently, accounting reports need to provide detailed information about the composition of equity and changes in equity that can result in the dilution

of owners' stakes in the business. This information asymmetry between management and owners is particularly high, and the information need is particularly strong, when there are multiple types of equity and when there are many equity holders such as public companies.

Third, equity holders are interested in distinguishing (i) changes in equity due to direct contributions or withdrawals of capital from (ii) changes in equity derived from return on equity capital (i.e., income). This categorization is natural because it separates capital transactions with *owners* from the entity's income-generating transactions with *non-owners* such as customers, employees, and suppliers.[1] This chapter follows this categorization by first discussing contributed capital, followed by two equity accounts that accumulate income: retained earnings and accumulated other comprehensive income (AOCI). We then discuss the effect of various transactions on equity: stock issuances, stock splits, stock reacquisitions, dividend payments, and transfers to reserves.[2]

L.O. 13-1. Describe the characteristics of different types of share equity and identify the characteristics that are relevant for accounting purposes.

From this point forward in this chapter, we will focus on the incorporated form of business, so we will refer to shareholders rather than the more generic "equity holder." However, the material is equally applicable and therefore transferable to other forms of organizations such as proprietorships, partnerships, and trusts.

L.O. 13-2. Identify the different components of equity for accounting purposes that apply to a transaction and analyze the effects of the transaction on those equity components.

B. COMPONENTS OF EQUITY FOR ACCOUNTING PURPOSES

As noted in the introduction, accounting separates equity into three components: contributed capital, retained earnings, and AOCI. Within each of these three components are sub-components that differ from each other in a variety of ways.

1. Contributed capital

contributed capital The component of equity that reflects amounts received by the reporting entity from transactions with its owners, net of any repayments from capital.

Contributed capital refers to amounts received by the reporting entity from transactions with shareholders, net of any repayments from capital (rather than accumulated income). In a simple case where a company issues 10,000 shares for \$20 each, and later repurchases 1,000 of these shares at the same price, the contributed capital would equal 10,000 shares × \$20/share − 1,000 shares × \$20/share = \$180,000. (Section C will consider other cases when the share price changes from issuance to repurchase.)

Shares have a number of characteristics, including whether they have residual claims, par value, cumulative dividends, or voting rights, and whether they are authorized, issued, or outstanding. We discuss these characteristics below and any accounting implications involved.

a. Common shares (or ordinary shares)

common (ordinary) shares An equity interest that has the lowest priority and represents the residual ownership interest in the company.

In Canada, the shares that represent the ultimate residual interest in a company are usually called **common shares**. The equivalent term for common shares in IFRS is **ordinary shares**. These are the shares that have lowest priority, but claims to all residual assets after the entity satisfies all other debt or equity claims. These shares have the most upside potential should the enterprise be successful, but also the most downside

1. In some cases, an owner can also engage in transactions with the reporting entity as someone other than an owner (e.g., a customer). For instance, many shareholders of large financial institutions such as Bank of Montreal or Royal Bank of Canada will also have deposits or loans with these banks. In such cases, we need to identify whether these individuals are acting as owners or non-owners.

2. Caution—the term "reserves" is used in two different contexts in this chapter. The first is as above, which refers to the appropriated portion of an entity's retained earnings. This terminology is used in this context in both Parts I and II of the *CPA Canada Handbook*—Accounting. The second, used later in the chapter, refers to an equity account to describe the balance sheet account used to accumulate the balance of other comprehensive income (OCI) and other items (e.g., contributed surplus). This terminology is used only in the context of Part I of the *CPA Canada Handbook*—Accounting.

should the business fail. Because common shares represent the ownership interest, every corporation must have at least one class of common shares.

b. Preferred shares

While every corporation must have a class of common shares, some corporations also have additional classes of shares. Any share that does not represent the residual interest in the company is called a **preferred share**. For example, a company may have, in addition to a class of common shares, "Class A shares" and "Class B preferred shares." For accounting purposes, these other classes are all considered to be preferred shares to reflect their economic substance, whether the company literally labels them as "preferred" or not. Preferred shares have priority over common shares with respect to the receipt of dividends and a claim on the entity's net assets in liquidation.

preferred shares Any shares that are not common shares. Preferred shares have priority over common shares with respect to the receipt of dividends and a claim on the entity's net assets in liquidation.

It is important to note that "preferred" only refers to the preferred shareholders' claims over those of the common shareholders. Preferred shareholders *do not* have preference over debt holders' claims on the entity's net assets. In liquidation, all debt holder claims must be fully satisfied before any monies are distributed to the preferred shareholders.

For preferred shares, dividends may be stated as a fixed amount or as a percentage of a benchmark value (usually \$25) established in the terms of the preferred share agreement. For example, a preferred share with a benchmark value of \$25 per share could either specify a dividend rate of \$1.25 per share or 5%; that 5% is expressed relative to the benchmark value, so that \$25/share × 5% = \$1.25/share.

c. Par value and no par value shares

The par value of a share is a legal term referring to the nominal value of a share, in contrast to the amount the share was sold for. The *Canada Business Corporations Act* (CBCA) no longer permits companies to issue shares with par value.[3] However, provincial laws such as those in Ontario and British Columbia permit the use of par value for companies incorporated under those laws.[4] Shares issued with a stated par value are simply called **par value shares**. Shares issued without a stated par value are called **no par value shares**.

par value shares Shares with a dollar value stated in the articles of incorporation.

no par value shares Shares that do not have a stated par value.

The discussion in this chapter focuses on accounting for no par value shares, as given the restrictions outlined above, par value shares are seldom issued. Accounting for par value shares is discussed in Section I, the appendix to this chapter.

d. Cumulative vs. non-cumulative dividends

Regardless of whether a share is a common or preferred share, dividends, which are usually paid quarterly, are always discretionary payments. A corporation need only pay dividends when it declares them to be payable. This discretion applies even if there is a stated dividend rate on the shares. As an added measure of protection, many preferred shares will require *cumulative dividends*, meaning that the company must pay for any past dividend payments that it missed (i.e., those scheduled but not declared) prior to paying any dividends on common shares. In other words, a company can defer but not avoid a cumulative dividend on preferred shares if it is to pay dividends on common shares. However, there is no interest to compensate for the time value of money lost on the deferral. Shares with non-cumulative dividends do not have any rights to missed dividend payments.

In either case, companies are loath to miss dividend payments even though dividends are discretionary. A dividend schedule is a commitment to disburse cash to

3. *Canada Business Corporations Act* (R.S.C. 1985, c. C-44) Section 24 Paragraph (1). The CBCA previously allowed companies to issue par value shares. The revised Act states that a par value share issued before the change in rules is deemed to be a share without nominal or par value.

4. *Ontario Corporations Act* (RSO 1990, c. 38) Section 25 Paragraph 1 and *British Columbia Business Corporations Act* (SBC 2002, c. 57) Section 52 Paragraph 1.

shareholders on a regular basis, and breaking that undertaking is a strong signal that the company is in financial difficulty.

e. Voting rights

A corporation may assign voting rights in a variety of ways according to its articles of incorporation. The vast majority of large, publicly traded enterprises will have one vote per common share, so that decision rights match economic ownership (in terms of rights to future cash flows). A small minority of public companies deviate from this practice. However, private companies use shares with a variety of voting rights to suit their needs.

The opening vignette outlined the contributed capital for Canadian Tire, which has two classes of shares: 3,423,366 common shares and 67,323,781 Class A non-voting shares. It turns out that, while the voting rights differ between these two classes, they are both common shares and are practically identical to each other economically. Specifically, Canadian Tire's 2016 financial statements indicate the following:

> In the event of the liquidation, dissolution, or winding-up of the Company, all of the property of the Company available for distribution to the holders of the Class A Non-Voting Shares and the Common Shares shall be paid or distributed equally, share for share, to the holders of the Class A Non-Voting Shares and to the holders of the Common Shares without preference or distinction or priority of one share over another.[5]

The common shares, which have the voting rights, are closely held by the Billes family, who founded the company in 1922. Holding the two classes of shares is the family's way of maintaining voting control of the company while allowing them to secure additional capital from the stock market.

f. Number of shares authorized, issued, or outstanding

shares authorized The number of shares that are allowed to be issued by a company's articles of incorporation.

shares issued The number of shares issued by the corporation, whether held by outsiders or by the corporation itself.

shares outstanding Issued shares owned by investors.

treasury shares Shares issued but held by the issuing corporation; treasury shares are not outstanding.

There are three figures that refer to the number of shares, two of which are important for accounting purposes. The number of **shares authorized** is the number of shares that the corporation is permitted to issue as specified in the articles of incorporation. This is a legal detail that has no practical significance. Indeed, many companies specify an unlimited number of authorized shares.

The two important figures are the number of shares issued and outstanding. **Shares issued** has the intuitive meaning—the number of shares issued by the corporation. However, some issued shares may not be outstanding. **Shares outstanding** are shares of the corporation owned by investors, including the company's officers and employees. Issued shares owned by the issuing corporation are called **treasury shares**. Treasury shares are issued but not outstanding. Accounting for treasury shares is discussed in the appendix to this chapter, Section I.

Based on this discussion, the following relationships always hold:

Exhibit 13-1 Relationship among numbers of shares authorized, issued, and outstanding

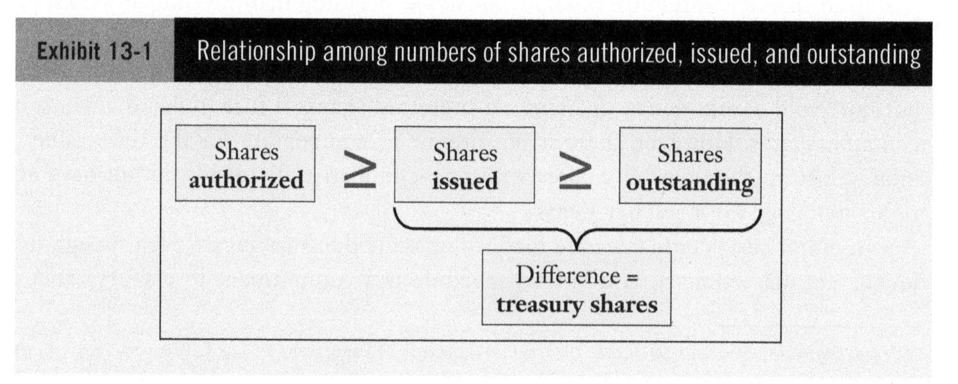

[5] *Source:* From Canadian Tire Corporation 2016 Report to Shareholders. Copyright ©2016 by Canadian Tire Corporation, Limited. Reprinted by permission.

CHECKPOINT **CP13-1**

Briefly describe the primary difference between common and preferred shares.

CHECKPOINT **CP13-2**

When is a corporation legally obligated to pay cash dividends?

CHECKPOINT **CP13-3**

Briefly describe the difference between cumulative and non-cumulative dividends.

CHECKPOINT **CP13-4**

Briefly describe the difference between issued and outstanding shares.

2. Retained earnings

Recall from introductory accounting that **retained earnings** reflect the cumulative net income (profit or loss) minus dividends paid. Retained earnings does not represent cash available to the corporation. Rather, it is an element of equity that does not have any particular relationship to cash or any other asset. Some companies allocate a portion of retained earnings as reserves to identify amounts in equity that they do not intend to pay out as dividends. In some instances, the reserves are required by laws or regulations. **Appropriation** is the term for the process that allocates a portion of retained earnings to an appropriated reserve. For example, most universities have a portion of their net assets[6] set aside as reserves for the endowments that they have received from donors, when the donors specify that the university should spend only the income and not the capital from those donations. The use of an endowment reserve account ensures that the university does not spend the donated capital. Another common example is the appropriation of retained earnings for the purpose of repaying a long-term bond that requires the bond issuer to maintain a "sinking fund." Suppose a company issues a $50 million bond due in 10 years, and the bond indenture specifies that the company must set aside $5 million per year in a sinking fund so that the company will have funds to repay the bondholders at the end of 10 years. Assuming that the company complies with the contractual requirements, the journal entry would be as follows for each of the 10 years:

retained earnings A component of equity that reflects the cumulative net income (profit or loss) minus dividends paid.

appropriation The process that allocates a portion of retained earnings to a reserve.

Exhibit 13-2 Journal entries for the annual appropriation of retained earnings of $5 million for a sinking fund reserve

Dr. Retained earnings	5,000,000	
Cr. Sinking fund reserve (or appropriated retained earnings)		5,000,000
Dr. Restricted cash	5,000,000	
Cr. Cash		5,000,000

Notice that two journal entries are required. The first one appropriates the retained earnings, while the second one shows the actual cash being set aside.

3. Accumulated other comprehensive income (AOCI)

Under IFRS, accumulated other comprehensive income (AOCI) accumulates other comprehensive income (OCI) from all prior periods, similar to the manner in which

6. "Net assets" for a not-for-profit organization has the same meaning as "equity" for a for-profit entity.

realized profits and losses are accumulated in retained earnings. AOCI is then reported on the balance sheet as a component of equity. AOCI is not reported under ASPE, however, as this latter set of standards does not include provision for either OCI or AOCI.

contributed surplus The component of contributed capital in excess of the amount allocated to share capital.

It should be noted that IFRS uses the generic term "reserves" to refer to AOCI as well as to other types of reserves (e.g., **contributed surplus**). While AOCI is not specifically defined in IFRS, it remains acceptable to use this terminology in financial statements.

Accounting for investments in financial assets was detailed in Chapter 7. As discussed there and in Chapters 3 and 10, OCI usually represents the unrealized change in the fair (market) value of select assets including FVOCI investments. For example, a $25,000 investment in bonds classified at fair value through OCI, whose market value subsequently increases to $27,000 by balance sheet date, results in an unrealized gain of $2,000 being reported in OCI. The $2,000 in OCI would then be closed out to AOCI at year-end as part of the closing entry process.

"Recycling" is an issue unique to OCI. Recall that items recorded through net income impact retained earnings in the same period. For example, ignoring related expenses and tax effects, recording revenue of $100 in 2018 results in an additional $100 of net income and therefore an extra $100 of retained earnings in 2018. The same does not apply to OCI, as this is closed to a reserve account within equity (AOCI) where it is "parked" until a future date when it may be recognized through net income and retained earnings. **Recycling** refers to this process of initially recognizing amounts through OCI, accumulating that OCI in AOCI (reserves), and later removing those amounts from AOCI by recognizing them in net income and retained earnings.

recycling (of OCI) The process of recognizing amounts through OCI, accumulating that OCI in reserves, and later recognizing those amounts through net income and retained earnings.

OCI arising from investments in debt securities at fair value through OCI is recycled through net income and retained earnings, whereas OCI arising from investments in equity securities[7] is not. Rather, an entity may (but is not required to) reclassify the accumulated other comprehensive income directly to retained earnings. Essentially, the entity would process a journal entry debiting AOCI and crediting retained earnings, thus bypassing the income statement.

Consider again the previous example of the $25,000 investment in bonds. When the value of the investment increased to $27,000, the $2,000 unrealized gain was reported in OCI, which was then closed out to AOCI. Assuming the investment was subsequently sold for $28,000, prior to derecognizing the investment, the company would first update its carrying value to $28,000. The gain of $1,000 is reported in OCI, which will be closed out to AOCI at period end. The company then "recycles" the total gain of $3,000 through net income, offsetting this with a debit to AOCI. "Recycling" is somewhat descriptive in that the $3,000 is recognized twice: first through OCI and a second time through net income.

It is important to note that AOCI needs to be distinguished by its source. For example, a company needs to distinguish AOCI arising from at fair value through OCI investments separately from amounts arising from revaluation.[8]

CHECKPOINT **CP13-5**

Where is accumulated other comprehensive income reported and what does it represent?

CHECKPOINT **CP13-6**

Briefly describe recycling as it pertains to other comprehensive income.

---

7. Recall from Chapter 7 that normally investments in equity securities are classified at fair value through profit or loss. The entity may, however, irrevocably elect to present subsequent changes in fair value through OCI.

8. In practice, AOCI needs to be even more specifically identified. For example, we would specify "AOCI from the revaluation of Land at 333 Yonge Street, Toronto, ON" due to the need to track the revaluation reserve according to the item (or group of items) being revalued.

4. Summary

The following diagram summarizes the accounting classification of the different components and sub-components of equity:

Exhibit 13-3 Equity and its components

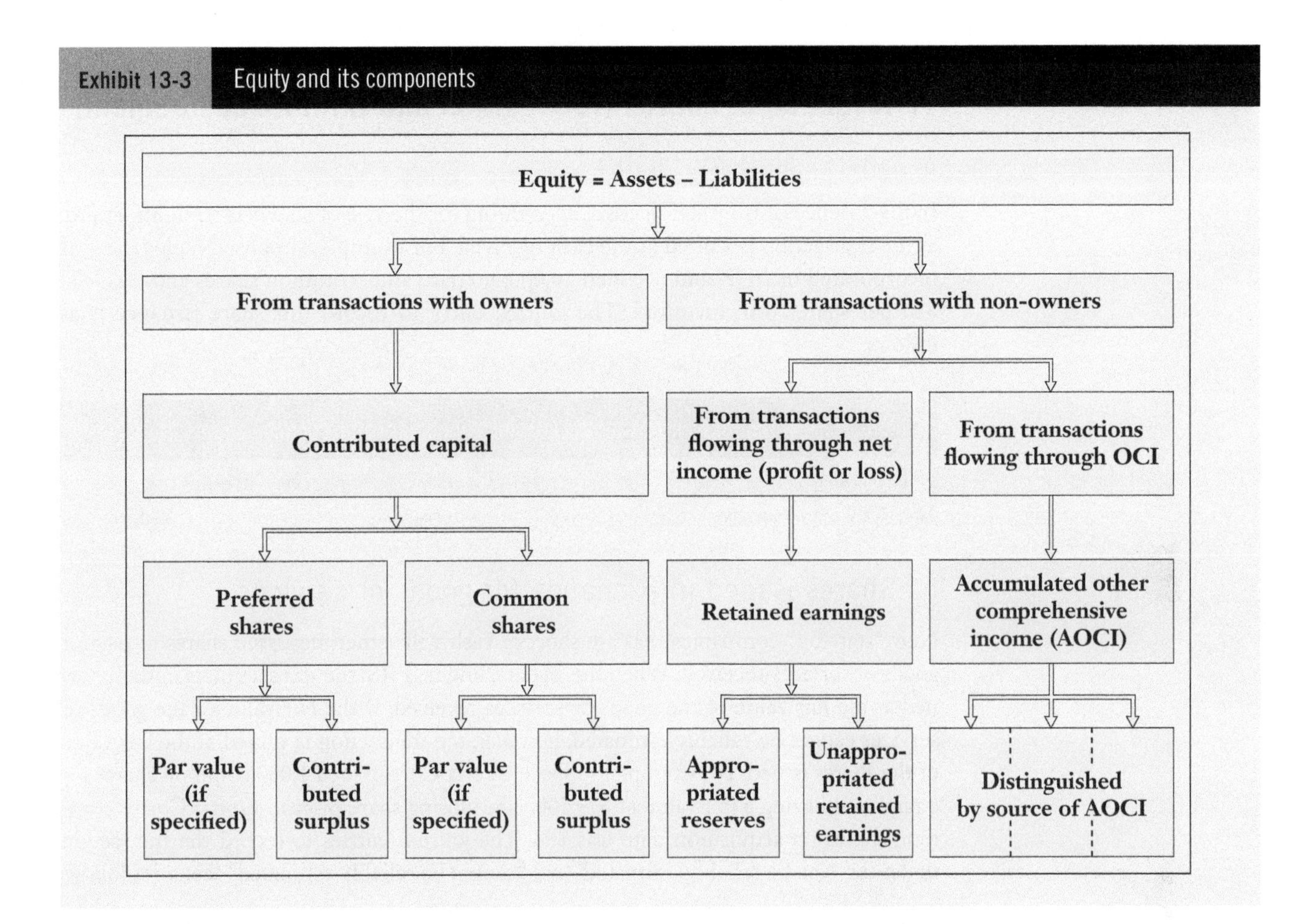

The next two sections will examine the accounting for transactions relating to contributed capital and retained earnings.

C. EQUITY TRANSACTIONS RELATING TO CONTRIBUTED CAPITAL

L.O. 13-3. Apply the accounting standards and procedures for transactions relating to contributed capital.

This section discusses the accounting for transactions primarily affecting contributed capital, although in some transactions there will also be ancillary effects on retained earnings.

IFRS provides little guidance with respect to specific categories of equity to be used for transactions relating to contributed capital, as international standards are unable to deal with the wide variety of country-specific laws that affect business ownership. Indeed most standards simply use the encompassing term "equity." The three broad classifications within equity are share capital, retained earnings, and reserves. What modest direction there is in this respect is set out in IAS 1:

- Paragraph 54(r) requires that an entity provide information in the statement of financial position (balance sheet) pertaining to issued capital and reserves attributable to the parent.

- Paragraph 78(e) provides that, if warranted by the size, nature, and function of the amounts involved, equity capital and reserves should be disaggregated into various classes, such as paid-in capital, share premium, and reserves.
- Paragraph 79(b) mandates that a description of the nature and purpose of each reserve within equity be provided in the statement of financial position, the statement of changes in equity, or the notes to the financial statements.

1. Issuance of shares (recognition and initial measurement)

a. Shares sold for cash

In the absence of transaction costs, accounting for the sale of shares is straightforward, as the transaction is valued at the cash received. For example, suppose Naples Inc. was incorporated in 2022, and it issued 10,000, no par value, common shares and received $20 per share from investors. The journal entry to record this share issuance is as follows:

Exhibit 13-4 Journal entries for the issuance of no par value common shares

Dr. Cash	200,000	
Cr. Common shares		200,000

b. Shares issued in exchange for goods or services

New "start-up" companies that are short of cash will sometimes issue shares to pay for goods or services received. When this occurs, under IFRS, the transaction is initially valued at the fair value of the goods or services received. If the fair value of the goods or services cannot be reliably estimated, however, the transaction is valued at the fair value of the shares issued. For example, suppose Gretta Corp. issued 1,000 common shares for equipment having a fair value of $79,500. The closing share price of Gretta Corp.'s common shares on acquisition date was $80. The journal entries to record the transaction under the "can be reliably estimated" and "cannot be reliably estimated" scenarios follow:

Exhibit 13-5 Journal entries for the issuance of common shares in exchange for goods

Can be reliably estimated			Cannot be reliably estimated		
Dr. Equipment	79,500		Dr. Equipment	80,000	
Cr. Common shares		79,500	Cr. Common shares		80,000

The accounting treatment for shares issued in exchange for goods or services received differs slightly under ASPE, in that the transaction is initially valued at the fair value of the consideration received or the shares given up, whichever can be more reliably measured.

c. Shares sold on a subscription basis

Occasionally, companies will sell shares to the public or employees on a subscription basis. While the terms of the sale will vary between issues, the commonality is that the subscriber makes a down payment toward the cost of purchasing the shares and agrees to pay the remainder at a later date. Accounting for the sale of shares on a subscription basis is not complicated, as illustrated in Exhibit 13-6. Golf Is Good Inc. sells 10,000 no par value common shares for $8 each on a subscription basis. Terms of the sale require the purchaser to pay $3 per share when the contract is signed and the balance in three months' time.

The first step in the process is to establish a common shares subscribed account and record the initial receipt of cash. The balance is debited to a subscriptions receivable account.

Exhibit 13-6a Journal entry at date of contract signing

Dr. Cash (10,000 shares × \$3/sh)	30,000	
Dr. Subscriptions receivable [10,000 shares × (\$8/sh − \$3/sh)]	50,000	
Cr. Common shares subscribed (10,000 shares × \$8/sh)		80,000

When subsequent payments are received, cash is debited and subscriptions receivable credited.

Exhibit 13-6b Journal entry for subsequent payment

Dr. Cash (10,000 shares × \$5/sh)	50,000	
Cr. Subscriptions receivable		50,000

When the shares are paid for in full, the common shares subscribed account is closed and the shares are issued to the purchaser.

Exhibit 13-6c Journal entry to record the issuance of the shares

Dr. Common shares subscribed	80,000	
Cr. Common shares		80,000

A question that arises from accounting for shares sold on a subscription basis is how to report the subscriptions receivable on the balance sheet. Logically, it makes sense to report subscriptions receivable as a contra equity account so as to prevent manipulation of financial statements. The contra account treatment ensures that only the amount received (\$30,000 in the example just given) enters equity. The alternative of treating the \$50,000 subscriptions receivable as an asset and the full \$80,000 as equity can improve leverage ratios. This issue becomes more important with the size of the share subscription program and the time lag between subscription and payment.

The contra equity treatment is the approach that the FASB has taken in the United States. ASPE, however, does allow some limited discretion in this respect, as Section 3251 provides the following guidance:

> ¶10 Share purchase loans receivable shall be presented as deductions from shareholders' equity unless there is substantial evidence that the borrower, not the enterprise, is at risk for any decline in the price of the shares and there is reasonable assurance that the enterprise will collect the full amount of the loan in cash.[9]

IFRS does not directly address the matter, leaving it as a matter of professional judgment.

Another issue that results from selling shares on subscription is how to account for defaulted contracts. Essentially, there are three potential outcomes: (i) refund the cash paid and cancel the contract, (ii) issue a lesser number of shares to the subscriber

9. Uniform Final Examination 1990, with permission from Chartered Professional Accountants of Canada, Toronto, Canada.

that reflects the amount paid, or (iii) keep the money paid as a penalty for the subscriber defaulting on the contract. The outcome will depend on any relevant legislation regarding share subscriptions and the provisions of the subscriptions contract. In the case of outcome (iii), the funds retained are recorded through contributed surplus; this is a capital transaction and does not flow through net income.

d. Bundled sales

Companies will occasionally sell a bundle or basket of securities that includes two or more equity instruments. The question is how the issuer should allocate the proceeds to the individual instruments. One approach is the relative fair value method, also called the proportional method, as described in Chapter 8 for bundled purchases of property, plant, and equipment. Recall that under this method, the sales price is allocated proportionally to the components based on the estimated fair value of each component. A second method is the residual value method, also called the incremental method. Briefly, the enterprise estimates the fair value of the components and then allocates amounts to these components in descending order according to the reliability of each component's fair value (i.e., most reliable first).

Exhibit 13-7 illustrates the application of the two methods. Sailing Boats Ltd. sold 1,000 packages of equity security consisting of one common share and one preferred share. Each package was sold for $100; total proceeds were $100,000. At time of sale, the market price of the common shares was $91 and the estimated fair value of the preferred shares was $10. In Scenario 1, the company uses the relative fair value method. In Scenario 2, the company uses the residual value method and considers the market price of the common shares to be measured more reliably than the estimated fair value of the preferred shares.

Exhibit 13-7a Scenario 1—Use the relative fair value method

The sum of the fair values is $101 ($91 + $10). Proportional allocation results in 91/101 of the sales price being allocated to the common shares and 10/101 being allocated to the preferred shares.

Dr. Cash (1,000 packages × $100/package)	100,000	
Cr. Common shares (91/101 × $100,000)		90,099
Cr. Preferred shares (10/101 × $100,000)		9,901

Exhibit 13-7b Scenario 2—Use the residual value method

The common shares can be more reliably measured at their market price of $91, so the common shares pick up the first increment of $91. The preferred shares pick up the residual value of $9 ($100 − $91).

Dr. Cash (1,000 packages × $100/package)	100,000	
Cr. Common shares ($91 × 1,000)		91,000
Cr. Preferred shares ($9 × 1,000)		9,000

Note that bundled sales are different from compound financial instruments, which will be discussed in Chapter 14. Bundled sales are for two or more equity instruments that are normally sold separately, but sold together in the particular instance. Compound financial instruments are those that are not normally sold separately as components but are rather sold jointly. The difference is analogous to a bundled sale of two cars versus the sale of a single car, which has many different components (frame, engine, tires, etc.).

e. Share issuance costs

Accounting for share issuance costs does not provide any special challenges. Expenses that are directly associated with issuing stock, including underwriting, accounting, and legal fees, are charged directly to equity as they represent a capital transaction.

Entities may elect to deduct the issue costs from the related share capital account, reporting the net amount raised (the offset method), or charge them directly to retained earnings (the retained earnings method). For example, suppose that Gidget Inc. sold 1,000 common shares for grossing $100,000 cash. The net proceeds received by Gidget were $95,000, as its investment bankers charged $5,000 for underwriting the share issue. The journal entries to record the transaction under the offset method and the retained earnings method follow:

Exhibit 13-8 Journal entries for the issuance of common shares with share issuance costs

Offset method			Retained earnings method		
Dr. Cash	95,000		Dr. Cash	95,000	
			Dr. Retained earnings	5,000	
Cr. Common shares		95,000	Cr. Common shares		100,000

2. Stock splits (subsequent measurement)

Equity is subsequently measured at historical cost. Accounting for stock splits is an application of this measurement principle.

stock split An increase in the number of shares issued without the issuing company receiving any consideration in return.

A **stock split** is an increase in the number of shares issued without the issuing company receiving any consideration in return. For instance, a company can double the number of shares issued by undergoing a two-for-one stock split. The economic positions for the company as well as every single shareholder remain the same. It is no different from having, say, either five $20 bills or ten $10 bills—the total value is still $100. Because there are no changes in economic substance, no journal entry is required, other than a memo entry to note that the number of shares has changed.

Companies engage in stock splits typically to bring their share price to a desired range. Typical trading rules on exchanges require multiples (called “lots”) of 100 shares, so a share price of $200 per share is often considered too high because trades would involve a minimum value of $20,000. A more modest price of $20 per share would lower the minimum trading value to $2,000, which can increase trading volume and improve liquidity in the market for the company’s shares.

Companies can also engage in reverse stock splits to reduce the number of shares issued and increase the stock price correspondingly. Reverse stock splits are also called share consolidations.

CHECKPOINT **CP13-7**

Briefly describe the primary reason why companies declare a stock split.

3. Reacquisition of shares (derecognition)

Companies buy back their own shares for a number of reasons. First, share repurchases are a tax-efficient alternative to dividend payments to return cash to shareholders. The tax advantage arises from the fact that companies choosing to pay dividends must pay them equally to each share in a class, whereas in a share buyback, shareholders can choose whether (and when) to sell their shares back to the company. Investors’ ability to choose when to sell allows for better tax planning.

THRESHOLD CONCEPT
INFORMATION ASYMMETRY

Second, buying back shares alleviates information asymmetry by providing a credible positive signal to the market similar to the positive signal from the announcement of dividend increases. (See Chapter 1 for a discussion of signalling.) The signal is credible because it is costly for the company to expend cash to buy back its own shares. From the buyback, we infer that corporate executives believe their company's shares to be undervalued.

Third, many companies offer stock compensation to executives and other employees. To make these shares available, the company can either issue new shares or buy back existing shares that had been previously issued.[10] The latter is often administratively less cumbersome.

Finally, share buybacks decrease the number of shares outstanding, which lowers the denominator in the calculation of earnings per share (EPS), so it is possible to increase reported EPS. (See Chapter 15 for details of calculating EPS.)

There are other reasons for buying back shares, but the above discussion suffices to show that companies have many reasons for engaging in these transactions, and therefore we expect these transactions to be fairly common. As the opening vignette notes, Canadian Tire in 2016 did in fact repurchase some of its Class A non-voting shares.

The accounting for share repurchases can be complex and depends on whether the shares are cancelled once repurchased or held in treasury. We discuss the cancellation scenario below, deferring discussion of accounting for share repurchases held as treasury shares to Section I, the appendix to this chapter.

As previously mentioned, to avoid contradicting country-specific laws, IFRS provides little guidance on how to account for equity. Paragraph 33 of IAS 32—Financial Instruments: Presentation reads in part: *"No gain or loss shall be recognized in profit or loss on the purchase, sale, issue or cancellation of an entity's own equity instruments. . . . Consideration paid or received shall be recognized directly in equity."*[11] So while it is clear that gains and losses arising from a company dealing in its own shares are not reported on the income statement, IFRS does not provide any details on which equity accounts are to be used to track the gain or loss arising from share repurchases. In light of this, the following discussion is based on ASPE.

a. Cancellation of reacquired shares

A business that is incorporated under the *Canada Business Corporations Act* is not permitted to hold its own shares.[12] Therefore, any repurchased shares must be retired.

Paragraphs 11–14 of ASPE Section 3240—Share Capital outline the accounting treatment for repurchased shares. For the retirement of no par value shares, the required accounting can be summarized as follows:

- For each share redeemed and cancelled, the pertinent class of share capital (e.g., common shares) is debited for the average cost[13] of all shares in that class, irrespective of when the shares were issued or how much they were sold for.
- Contributed surplus must be separately tracked and disclosed for each class of shares, including the sources of the contributed surplus (e.g., repurchase of shares).
- Gains are credited to the contributed surplus account for that class of shares.
- Losses are debited to the contributed surplus account for that class of shares to the greatest extent possible. The remainder, if any, is charged to retained earnings.
    - o Contributed surplus for that class of shares can be debited to the full extent that the surplus was created by previously repurchasing shares for less than their average cost.

10. Assuming that the company is permitted to hold treasury shares.

11. Copyright © 2012 IFRS Foundation.

12. *Canada Business Corporations Act* (R.S.C. 1985, c. C-44) Section 30 Paragraph (1).

13. "Cost" in this instance refers to the net proceeds credited to the share account when issued.

- o Contributed surplus can be debited on a proportional basis for a surplus that was created by transactions other than repurchasing shares for less than their average cost.
- Debits to contributed surplus for one class of shares (e.g., preferred Class A shares) cannot be debited to contributed surplus of another class of shares (e.g., preferred Class B shares).

To illustrate the accounting for share repurchases, we continue the example of Naples Inc. from Exhibit 13-4. Recall that we credited the common share account for $200,000, reflecting the original share issue price of $20 per share ($20 × 10,000 shares). Now suppose that Naples Inc. purchases 1,000 of its own shares at $18 each in January 2023 and immediately cancels them, and then subsequently repurchases and cancels an additional 1,000 shares for $23 each in February 2023. We account for these repurchases as shown in Exhibit 13-9.

Exhibit 13-9 Journal entries for the repurchase and cancellation of 1,000 shares at $18/share and 1,000 shares at $23/share

January 2023		
Dr. Common shares (1,000 shares × $20/share)	20,000	
Cr. Cash (1,000 shares × $18/share)		18,000
Cr. Contributed surplus—from repurchase of common shares		2,000
February 2023		
Dr. Common shares (1,000 shares × $20/share)	20,000	
Dr. Contributed surplus—from repurchase of common shares*	2,000	
Dr. Retained earnings ($23,000 − $20,000 − $2,000)	1,000	
Cr. Cash (1,000 shares × $23/share)		23,000

*Cannot exceed the credit balance arising from past transactions in the same class of shares.

Observe that the repurchase price of $18 in January 2023 is below the issue price. In other circumstances, we would consider this to be a "gain" because the sale price exceeds the purchase cost by $2 per share. However, accounting standards do not allow this "gain" to flow through the income statement like other gains. Instead of a gain, we record the $2 per share difference as a credit to contributed surplus.

To summarize the accounting for share repurchases and cancellations, when the repurchase price ($18) is less than the average common share value ($20), the "gain" is recorded in contributed surplus, increasing equity. When the repurchase price ($23) is higher than the average common share value ($20), the "loss" goes to reduce contributed surplus and retained earnings.

WHEN A GAIN IS NOT A GAIN

A commonly given reason for why accounting does not recognize gains on share repurchase transactions is that it involves a company buying its own shares from its shareholders rather than a transaction with an external party. However, this is not a satisfactory explanation because the (former) shareholders who sold the shares on the other side of the transaction would have recorded losses had they purchased at the issue price of $20 per

(Continued)

THRESHOLD CONCEPT
INFORMATION ASYMMETRY

share and sold back to the company at $18 per share. Instead, there are two other explanations that are more compelling. First, a drop in a company's share price is hardly good news for shareholders, so recording a gain in this situation would be inconsistent with the underlying economics. Second, permitting the recognition of gains creates a moral hazard (see Chapter 1). Since management has superior information relative to shareholders, management could record gains by judiciously timing share issuances and repurchases to the detriment of shareholders if accounting standards permitted the recognition of such gains.

D. EQUITY TRANSACTIONS RELATING TO RETAINED EARNINGS

L.O. 13-4. Apply the accounting standards and procedures for transactions relating to the distribution of retained earnings.

In this section, we discuss transactions that result in the distribution of retained earnings. We do not discuss accumulations of retained earnings, which have been dealt with in other chapters (such as Chapter 4, which dealt with recognition of revenues and expenses).

Very few companies would pay all of their retained earnings as dividends, as there are cash flow implications, uncertainty as to the future performance of the business, contractual restrictions, and signalling effects. However, the amount of retained earnings does serve as a ceiling as to how much can be paid in dividends. On the other hand, it is commonly misunderstood that retained earnings represent funds available—that is not the case! Retained earnings may have been spent on equipment, for example, and not be available as cash. *Retained earnings is not cash.* To pay cash dividends, cash must be available.

THRESHOLD CONCEPT
INFORMATION ASYMMETRY

1. Cash dividends

Cash dividends are by far the most common kind of dividends. These require attention to some relevant dates.

a. Declaration date

Dividends are discretionary payments, even for preferred shares that have cumulative provisions. Prior to declaration, a company has no obligation to pay, and therefore it records no liabilities for dividends. However, once the board of directors declares a dividend, the company then has an obligation to pay and should record a dividend payable.

b. Ex-dividend date and date of record

These two dates are closely related. The date of record is the date when the company compiles the list of shareholders to determine who should be paid how much in dividends. This date is specified at the time of dividend declaration. For shares that are publicly traded, the ex-dividend date will be several days before the record date. For the Toronto Stock Exchange, the ex-dividend date is currently two business days prior to the date of record. The ex-dividend date is the date on which a share trades without the right to receive a dividend that has been declared. Prior to ex-dividend, an investor who holds the share would be entitled to receive the previously declared dividend. For example, a dividend record date falling on a Monday would have an ex-dividend date on the previous Thursday (in a regular five-day work week). Investors who buy and hold the shares on Wednesday would be entitled to the dividends, whereas those who buy on Thursday would not receive the dividend.

c. Payment date

This is the date when the funds for the dividend are transferred to shareholders.

d. Summary

For accounting purposes, only the declaration date and payment date are relevant. The ex-dividend date is important to investors who need to know whether they should pay a price that includes the dividend or not. The date of record is a matter of administrative necessity to identify whom the company should pay. Refer to Exhibit 13-10.

Exhibit 13-10 Summary of relevant dates and accounting for cash dividends

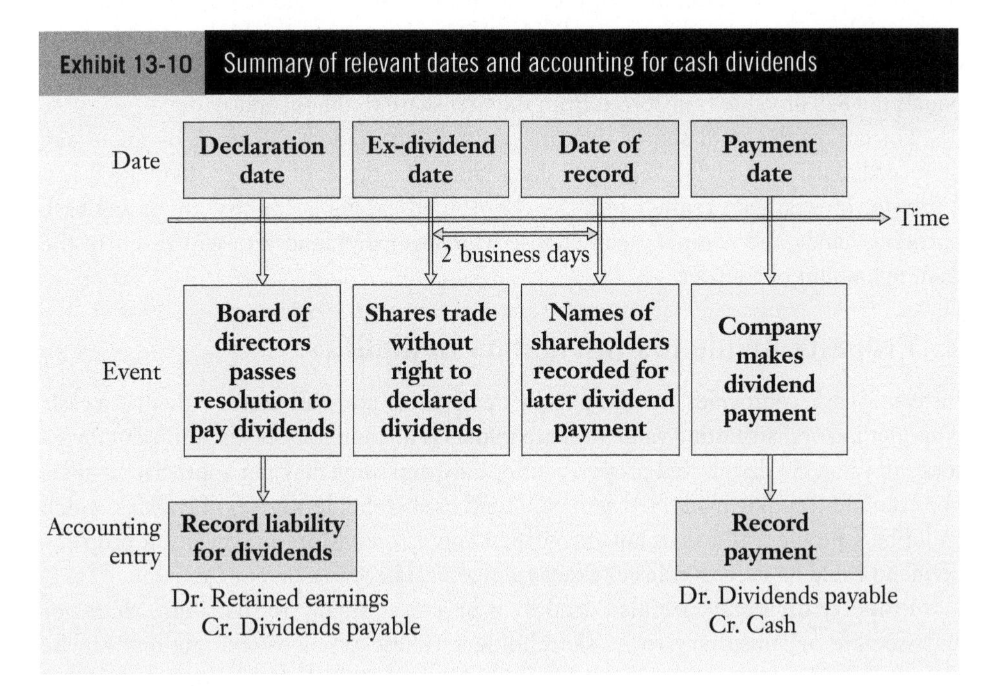

2. Stock dividends

Companies can issue stock dividends instead of paying out a cash dividend. However, doing so simply increases the number of shares issued and there is no cash outflow. Each shareholder owns the same fraction of the company as before the stock dividend. For example, suppose Trail Company has 800,000 no par value shares outstanding and it declares a 5% stock dividend. Before the stock dividend, the shares traded at \$11.55. If you were a shareholder who owned 8,000 shares (1%) of Trail before the dividend, you would own 8,400 shares afterward, again 1% of 840,000 shares outstanding. Economically, stock dividends have the same effect as stock splits: both increase the number of shares without any change to the company's resources. The value of the company's shares before the stock dividend was \$9,240,000 (800,000 shares × \$11.55). We would expect no significant change in the company's value due to the dividend, so we would expect the ex-dividend stock price to be \$9,240,000 ÷ 840,000 shares = \$11.

As noted above in Section C, we make no journal entries for stock splits. However, we do record a journal entry for stock dividends. The difference in accounting treatment between stock splits and stock dividends is largely a result of legal and tax requirements. For tax purposes, stock dividends are treated as income to the shareholders just like cash dividends, but no tax consequences arise in stock splits. Stock dividends also result in an adjustment to the shares' tax basis (technically called paid up capital), which is relevant in the windup of a company.

Assuming that the ex-dividend stock price is \$11 as expected, we would record the following journal entry:

Exhibit 13-11 Journal entry to record a stock dividend of 40,000 shares at \$11/share for Trail Company

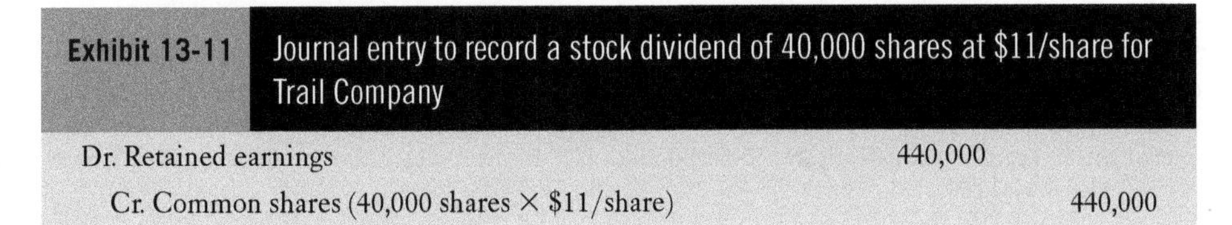

Dr. Retained earnings	440,000	
Cr. Common shares (40,000 shares × \$11/share)		440,000

This transfer from retained earnings to the contributed capital (common share) account explains why stock dividends are sometimes called "capitalization of retained earnings."

In general, the ex-dividend price of $11 is the appropriate price to use. To see why, consider a simpler but more extreme scenario where the stock dividend is 100%, so that the number of shares doubles. Suppose the market value of the shares outstanding is $100 and there is only one share pre-dividend. The share price should therefore be $100 per share before the stock dividend, and $50 per share afterward. This ex-dividend price equals the $50 of value transferred from the first share to the second share.[14]

For companies with shares that are not publicly traded, the stock dividend can be recorded using the book value per share. Since the result of a stock dividend is just a transfer of retained earnings into the contributed capital account without any cash changing hands, the company can choose whichever dividend rate will result in the desired amount of transfer.

3. Property dividends (dividends in kind)

Instead of cash, companies can also pay dividends using non-cash assets rather than cash. This method of distributing value to shareholders is uncommon because different investors will value the distributed property differently, and some may not appreciate it at all. For example, a cookie manufacturer could send its shareholders boxes of cookies, which could be a problem if a shareholder owned many shares. More practically, a property dividend could be used to transfer assets from a subsidiary to a parent company.

Property dividends are also used by a parent company to distribute shares of an associate or subsidiary to its shareholders. These types of transactions can be significant. The largest distribution of this kind in Canadian history was in May 2000 when Bell Canada Enterprises (BCE) spun off its 35% ownership in Nortel Networks Corp. in a transaction valued at $88 billion. At the time, the now defunct Nortel was the world's second largest telecom equipment supplier. More recently in 2006, BCE, in a transaction valued at $8.5 billion, spun off its shareholdings in Alliant Inc. into an income trust, distributing the trust units to its shareholders by way of a property dividend.

South of the border, Altria Group spun off 89% of Kraft Foods to its shareholders in 2007 in a transaction valued at US$47 billion. In 2008, Altria then distributed its majority holdings in Philip Morris International Inc. to its shareholders.

Since the assets being distributed are non-monetary, it is normally necessary to estimate the fair value of those assets for purposes of recording the value of the dividend. The difference between the book value and fair value is recorded in profit and loss (see IFRIC 17—Distribution of Non-cash Assets to Owners).

ASPE treatment differs from that in IFRS. ASPE 3831.15 specifies the use of book values, and hence no gains or losses, when an entity distributes to its owners shares of a subsidiary or investee accounted for by the equity method.

4. Dividend preference

When a company declares dividends it must consider dividend preference as discussed in Section B, subsection 1d earlier in this chapter. Recall that dividends in arrears on cumulative preferred shares together with the current dividend entitlement on cumulative and non-cumulative preferred shares must be paid before any monies can be

14. For Trail Company, the 40,000 shares distributed will be part of the 840,000 shares outstanding after the dividend, or 40/840 = 1/21 = 4.762% of shares outstanding. The value of these 40,000 shares at the ex-dividend price of $11 is $440,000, which is equal to 1/21 of the market value of equity (1/21 × $9,240,000 = $440,000). In contrast, the pre-dividend price of $11.55 would result in a dividend value that is too high (40,000 shares × $11.55/share = $462,000).

distributed to common shareholders. The exhibits that follow illustrate the effect of various dividend preferences.

In 2019, Gail Robinson Inc. declared $1,000,000 in cash dividends. Its capital structure includes 200,000 common shares; 100,000 cumulative preferred shares "A," each entitled to an annual dividend of $1; and 50,000 non-cumulative preferred shares series "B," each entitled to an annual dividend of $3. The series A shares must receive their dividend entitlement for the year, including any arrears, before dividends can be declared on the series B shares.

- In Scenario 1, the prescribed dividends on both series of preferred shares were paid in 2018; there are no dividends in arrears.
- In Scenario 2, the prescribed dividends on both series of preferred shares were last paid in 2017.
- In Scenario 3, the prescribed dividends were paid on the series A preferred shares in 2018 but not on the series B preferred shares. There are no dividends in arrears on the series A preferred shares.

Exhibit 13-12a Example of dividend preference—Scenario 1

	Preferred A	Preferred B	Common	Total
Pfd A entitlement 2019—100,000 × $1	$100,000	$ 0	$ 0	$ 100,000
Pfd B entitlement 2019—50,000 × $3	0	150,000	0	150,000
Remainder	0	0	750,000	750,000
	$100,000	$150,000	$750,000	$1,000,000

In Scenario 1, there are no dividends in arrears, so only the current year's entitlement must be paid to the preferred shareholders. The balance of the dividends declared is distributed to the common shareholders.

Exhibit 13-12b Example of dividend preference—Scenario 2

	Preferred A	Preferred B	Common	Total
Pfd A entitlement 2019—100,000 × $1	$100,000	$ 0	$ 0	$ 100,000
Pfd A arrears 2018—100,000 × $1	100,000	0	0	100,000
Pfd B entitlement 2019—50,000 × $3	0	150,000	0	150,000
Remainder	0	0	650,000	650,000
	$200,000	$150,000	$650,000	$1,000,000

In Scenario 2, dividends were not paid on either class of preferred shares in 2018. The series A shares are cumulative, so both 2018 and 2019's entitlements must be paid before monies can be distributed to the common shareholders. The series B shares are non-cumulative in nature, however, so only the current year's entitlement needs to be paid.

Exhibit 13-12c Example of dividend preference—Scenario 3

	Preferred A	Preferred B	Common	Total
Pfd A entitlement 2019—100,000 × $1	$100,000	$ 0	$ 0	$ 100,000
Pfd B entitlement 2019—50,000 × $3	0	150,000	0	150,000
Remainder	0	0	750,000	750,000
	$100,000	$150,000	$750,000	$1,000,000

In Scenario 3, while dividends were not paid on the series B shares in 2018, there are no dividends in arrears as the series B shares are non-cumulative in nature. Therefore, only the current year's entitlement must be paid to the preferred shareholders.

E. STATEMENT OF CHANGES IN EQUITY

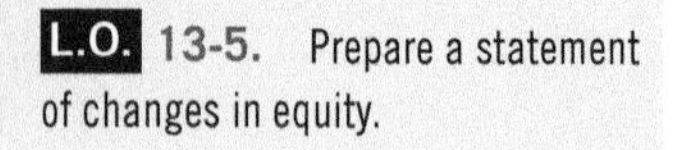
L.O. 13-5. Prepare a statement of changes in equity.

ASPE 1000—Financial Statement Concepts establishes that profit-oriented enterprises normally prepare a statement of retained earnings, whereas IAS 1—Presentation of Financial Statements stipulates that a complete set of financial statements includes a statement of changes in equity for the period. You should be familiar with the statement of retained earnings from your previous study of financial accounting, but may not be familiar with the statement of changes in equity. This latter statement also reconciles the change in retained earnings but is much more comprehensive than the statement of retained earnings. As discussed in Chapter 3, the statement of changes in equity provides information about the changes that took place during the period in all equity accounts. For ease of reference, much of this material is reproduced below.

Presentation of the statement of changes in equity is governed by IAS 1, most notably paragraphs 10, 47, 79, and 106–110. This standard requires that companies present a statement of changes in equity that includes the following items:

- For each component of equity (e.g., contributed capital, unappropriated retained earnings, reserves, AOCI), a reconciliation of the opening and closing balances, separately disclosing changes resulting from profit or loss; OCI; and capital transactions
- The total comprehensive income for the period
- The effect of retrospective changes in accounting policies

The standard provides options with respect to certain disclosure; the following may be presented in either the statement of changes in equity or in the notes to the financial statements:

- For each component of equity, an analysis of OCI by item
- The change in an entity's equity between the beginning and end of the reporting period
- The amount of dividends declared, including dividends per share amounts

Lastly, the reporting entity should also disclose, either in the balance sheet, the statement of changes in equity, or in the notes to the financial statements:

- Equity disaggregated into its components (par value, contributed surplus, retained earnings, by class of shares, etc.)
- The number of shares authorized, issued, and outstanding for each class of shares; a reconciliation of shares outstanding at the beginning and end of the year; whether the shares have par value; and any rights, preferences, or restrictions on the shares
- A description of the nature and purpose for each reserve

One of the objectives of financial statements is to provide information on changes in financial position. The statement of changes in equity aims to achieve this objective by identifying the reasons for the change in total equity and its components from the beginning to the end of the period. Exhibit 13-13 shows an example of such a statement.

Exhibit 13-13 Statement of changes in equity for Illustrator Ltd.

Illustrator Ltd.
Statement of Changes in Equity
For the year ended December 31, 2020

In $000's	Share capital	Accumulated OCI on FVOCI securities*	Retained earnings	Total	2020 Total
Profit for the year	–	–	2,393	2,393	1,386
Other comprehensive income					
Net gains on available-for-sale securities	–	420	–	420	240
Total comprehensive income	–	420	2,393	2,813	1,626
Issuance of common shares	2,000	–	–	2,000	–
Dividends declared	–	–	(200)	(200)	(200)
Net change in equity	2,000	420	2,193	4,613	1,426
Balance at January 1	13,000	240	23,400	36,640	35,214
Balance at December 31	15,000	660	25,593	41,253	36,640

Classes of transactions:
1. Profit or loss
2. Other comprehensive income
3. Dividends
4. Capital transactions
5. Effect of changes in accounting policy and correction of errors

Components of equity

*OCI = other comprehensive income
FVOCI = at fair value through OCI investments

There are three components of equity shown in Exhibit 13-13 that we will consider:[15]

1. *Contributed capital*—the amount of funds provided by owners, net of any repayments to the owners or repurchases of ownership units (shares).
2. *Retained earnings*—the amount of cumulative profits (or losses) recognized through the statement of comprehensive income less dividends (and a few other adjustments as noted elsewhere in this chapter).
3. *Reserves*—amounts accumulated from events or transactions increasing equity that are not transactions with owners and which have not flowed through profit or loss; an example of a reserve is "accumulated other comprehensive income," or AOCI.

There are potentially up to five classes of transactions that explain the change in these three components:

1. *Profit or loss*—income and expenses as recognized on the statement of comprehensive income, other than (2) below
2. *Other comprehensive income* (OCI)
3. *Dividends*

15. A fourth component is non-controlling interest, which is beyond the scope of this text.

4. *Capital transactions*—transactions with owners such as share issuances or repurchases
5. *Effect of changes in accounting policy and correction of errors*

Exhibit 13-14 summarizes the typical relationship between the five classes of transactions and the three components of equity, along with the two presentation options.

Exhibit 13-14 Content and alternative presentations of the statement of changes in equity

Class of transaction	Component of equity affected
1. Profit or loss (also called net income)	Retained earnings
2. Other comprehensive income	Accumulated other comprehensive income (a component of reserves)
Total comprehensive income (1 + 2)	
3. Dividends*	Retained earnings
4. Capital transactions (e.g., share issuance or repurchase)	Contributed capital and sometimes retained earnings
5. Effect of changes in accounting policy and correction of errors	Contributed capital or retained earnings

*Dividends may be disclosed outside the statement of changes in equity.

It is important to note that there can be several types of contributed capital, such as when a company has more than one class of shares. Also, each type of OCI needs to be tracked as a separate component of reserves. Because there are five different classes of transactions and multiple components of equity, it is usually most convenient to use a matrix-style presentation as illustrated in Exhibit 13-13.

F. PRESENTATION AND DISCLOSURE

As noted in the introduction, the information relating to equity is primarily to serve the needs of the shareholders (rather than creditors or other parties). Consequently, the presentation and disclosure rules are geared toward enabling shareholders to understand the different equity claims and categories, and changes in them. As discussed in Section E above, companies are required to prepare a statement of changes in equity to facilitate shareholder understanding of this area.

To illustrate the presentation of these items, Exhibit 13-15 reproduces the 2016 Consolidated Statements of Changes in Equity for Canadian Tire Corporation.

Note that Canadian Tire has shown the opening and closing balances of each component of equity, and the transactions that explain the changes in these balances. In addition, it must also disclose the additional information detailed in Section E, including:

- Equity disaggregated into its components (par value, contributed surplus, retained earnings, by class of shares, etc.)
- The number of shares authorized, issued, and outstanding for each class of shares; a reconciliation of shares outstanding at the beginning and end of the year; whether the shares have par value; and any rights, preferences, or restrictions on the shares
- A description of the nature and purpose for each reserve
- The amount of dividends declared

Refer to Appendix C for the Report to Shareholders of Canadian Tire Corporation for the year ended December 31, 2016. Note 25, Share capital, and Note 26, Share-based payments, illustrate the company's disclosure pertaining to its equity.

Exhibit 13-15 Canadian Tire Corporation Consolidated Statements of Changes in Equity

(C$ in millions)	Share capital	Contributed surplus	Total accumulated other comprehensive income	Retained earnings	Equity attributable to shareholders of Canadian Tire Corporation	Equity attributable to non-controlling interests	Total equity
Balance at January 2, 2016	$ 671.2	$2.9	$ 148.1	$ 4,172.0	$ 4,994.2	$ 795.5	$ 5,789.7
Net income	–	–	–	669.1	669.1	78.4	747.5
Other comprehensive (loss) income	–	–	(111.4)	(2.9)	(114.3)	1.2	(113.1)
Total comprehensive (loss) income	–	–	(111.4)	666.2	554.8	79.6	634.4
Contributions and distributions to shareholders of Canadian Tire Corporation							
Issuance of Class A Non-Voting Shares (Note 25)	9.3	–	–	–	9.3	–	9.3
Repurchase of Class A Non-Voting Shares (Note 25)	(449.4)	–	–	–	(449.4)	–	(449.4)
Excess of purchase price over average cost (Note 25)	417.0	–	–	(417.0)	–	–	–
Dividends	–	–	–	(170.3)	(170.3)	–	(170.3)
Contributions and distributions to non-controlling interests							
Issuance of trust units to non-controlling interests, net of transaction costs	–	–	–	–	–	2.0	2.0
Distributions and dividends to non-controlling interests	–	–	–	–	–	(78.4)	(78.4)
Total contributions and distributions	(23.1)	–	–	(587.3)	(610.4)	(76.4)	(686.8)
Balance at December 31, 2016	$ 648.1	$2.9	$ 36.7	$ 4,250.9	$ 4,938.6	$ 798.7	$ 5,737.3

(C$ in millions)	Share capital	Contributed surplus	Total accumulated other comprehensive income	Retained earnings	Equity attributable to shareholders of Canadian Tire Corporation	Equity attributable to non-controlling interests	Total equity
Balance at January 3, 2015	$ 695.5	$2.9	$ 82.0	$ 4,075.1	$ 4,855.5	$ 775.3	$5,630.8
Net income	–	–	–	659.4	659.4	76.5	735.9
Other comprehensive income (loss)	–	–	66.1	1.9	68.0	(2.5)	65.5
Total comprehensive income	–	–	66.1	661.3	727.4	74.0	801.4
Contributions and distributions to shareholders of Canadian Tire Corporation							
Issuance of Class A Non-Voting Shares (Note 25)	8.3	–	–	–	8.3	–	8.3
Repurchase of Class A Non-Voting Shares (Note 25)	(434.6)	–	–	–	(434.6)	–	(434.6)
Excess of purchase price over average cost (Note 25)	402.0	–	–	(402.0)	–	–	–
Dividends	–	–	–	(162.4)	(162.4)	–	(162.4)
Contributions and distributions to non-controlling interests							
Issuance of trust units to non-controlling interests, net of transaction costs	–	–	–	–	–	1.8	1.8
Distributions and dividends to non-controlling interests	–	–	–	–	–	(55.6)	(55.6)
Total contributions and distributions	(24.3)	–	–	(564.4)	(588.7)	(53.8)	(642.5)
Balance at January 2, 2016	$ 671.2	$2.9	$148.1	$ 4,172.0	$ 4,994.2	$ 795.5	$ 5,789.7

The related notes form an integral part of these consolidated financial statements.

G. COMPREHENSIVE ILLUSTRATION OF EQUITY TRANSACTIONS

This section provides a comprehensive example that illustrates most of the equity transactions discussed in this chapter. Suppose Flatrock Kitchen Decor Ltd. was incorporated on January 1, 2019. The incorporation documents authorized an unlimited number of common shares and 100,000 preferred shares. During the following fiscal year, the company engaged in the following transactions relating to its equity:

a. On January 1, the company issued 10,000 no par value common shares at $10 per share. On the same day, it issued 2,000, $2, cumulative preferred shares for proceeds of $25 per share.
b. On March 15, the company issued an additional 10,000 common shares at $20 per share.
c. On April 20, Flatrock repurchased and cancelled 2,000 common shares at a cost of $12 per share.
d. On September 1, a common shareholder donated artwork with a fair value of $18,000 to the company for no consideration. The gain was credited to contributed surplus on common shares.
e. On September 2, the company repurchased and cancelled 2,000 common shares at $20 per share.
f. For the fiscal year ended December 31, 2019, the company had net income of $30,000 and $0 OCI. The board of directors declared the dividends payable to preferred shareholders and $15,000 of dividends for the common shareholders.

To analyze these transactions, it is often useful to use a spreadsheet. Similar to inventory accounting, it is necessary to keep track of both the dollar amounts and the number of units (shares). In addition, it is necessary to separate the equity components among common and preferred shares, any contributed surplus for each class of shares, as well as retained earnings. Exhibit 13-16 shows such a spreadsheet for Flatrock's transactions in 2019.

Exhibit 13-16 Analysis of Flatrock's equity transactions

	Common shares			CS—repurchases	CS—other		Preferred shares			Retained earnings
Trx	# sh	$	$/sh	$	$	$/sh	# sh	$	$/sh	$
a.	10,000	$100,000	$10				2,000	$50,000	$25	
b.	10,000	200,000	20							
	20,000	$300,000	15							
c.	−2,000	− 30,000	15	6,000						
	18,000	$270,000	15	$6,000						
d.	–	–	–	–	18,000	$1				
	18,000	$270,000	15	$6,000	$18,000	1				
e.	−2,000	− 30,000	15	−6,000	− 2,000	1				−$ 2,000
	16,000	$240,000	15	$ -	$16,000	1				
f.	Net income									30,000
	Preferred dividends ($2 × 2,000 shares)									− 4,000
	Common dividends									−15,000
										$ 9,000

Repurchase at $12/share. Withdraw at average carrying value of $15/share. Difference ("gain") of $3/share goes to contributed surplus—repurchases.

$18,000 / 18,000 shares = $1/share.

Repurchase at $20/share. Withdraw at average carrying value of $15/share. Difference ("loss") of $5/share or $10,000 total first comes out of CS—repurchases as much as is available. $1 per share comes out of CS—other. Remainder comes from retained earnings.

Note: CS = contributed surplus

The journal entries that accompany these transactions would be as follows as shown in Exhibit 13-17.

Exhibit 13-17 Journal entries for Flatrock's equity transactions

a. Jan. 1	Dr. Cash	100,000	
	Cr. Common shares (10,000 sh × \$10/sh)		100,000
	Dr. Cash	50,000	
	Cr. Preferred shares (2,000 sh × \$25/sh)		50,000
b. Mar. 15	Dr. Cash	200,000	
	Cr. Common shares (10,000 sh × \$20/sh)		200,000
c. Apr. 20	Dr. Common shares (2,000 sh × \$15/sh)	30,000	
	Cr. Cash (2,000 sh × \$12/sh)		24,000
	Cr. Contributed surplus on common shares (repurchases) (2,000 sh × \$3/sh)		6,000
d. Sep. 1	Dr. Artwork	18,000	
	Cr. Contributed surplus on common shares (other)		18,000
e. Sep. 2	Dr. Common shares (2,000 sh × \$15/sh)	30,000	
	Dr. Contributed surplus on common shares (repurchases) (amount as needed)	6,000	
	Dr. Contributed surplus on common shares (other) (2,000 sh × \$1/sh)	2,000	
	Dr. Retained earnings (remainder)	2,000	
	Cr. Cash (2,000 sh × \$20/sh)		40,000
f. Dec. 31	Net income—not explicitly journalized; results from the net of revenues, expenses, gains, and losses		
	Dr. Retained earnings	19,000	
	Cr. Preferred dividends payable		4,000
	Cr. Common dividends payable		15,000

As this example shows, it is very important to maintain clear records of each class of shares and the different components associated with each class. It is not acceptable to intermingle different types of contributed surplus and amounts for different classes of shares.

H. SUBSTANTIVE DIFFERENCES BETWEEN RELEVANT IFRS AND ASPE

As indicated earlier in the chapter, IFRS does not provide specific recognition and measurement standards for items of equity. Therefore, preparers of financial reports for public enterprises need to consult guidance outside of IFRS. In Canada, the most relevant guidance is contained in ASPE (Part II of the *CPA Canada Handbook*—Accounting).

ISSUE	IFRS	ASPE
Accounting for repurchase and resale of shares	No specific guidance.	ASPE prescribes the allocation of repurchase costs and proceeds from resale of shares.
Accounting for treasury shares[16]	No specific guidance.	ASPE permits the use of the single-transaction or the two-transaction method, although the former is preferred.

(Continued)

16. This item refers to a topic covered in Section I.

ISSUE	IFRS	ASPE
Accumulated other comprehensive income (AOCI)	AOCI is a component of equity.	There is no concept of "other comprehensive income" in ASPE, and therefore no AOCI.
Dividends in kind	Distribution to the owners of shares of a subsidiary or investee is normally measured at fair value.	Distribution to the owners of shares of a subsidiary or investee is measured at book value unless the asset is impaired.
Presentation	A statement of changes in equity presents balances and transactions for all equity components.	A statement of retained earnings presents balances and transactions for retained earnings. Information relating to other equity components should be disclosed.
Shares issued in exchange for goods or services received	If fair value can be reliably estimated, the transaction is initially valued at the fair value of the goods or services received. Otherwise, the transaction is valued at the fair value of the shares issued.	The transaction is initially valued at the fair value of the consideration received or the shares given up, whichever can be more reliably measured.

I. APPENDIX: PAR VALUE SHARES AND TREASURY SHARES

1. Par value shares

As previously established, the par value of a share is a legal term referring to the nominal value of a share, in contrast to the amount that the share was sold for. Shares issued with a stated par value are simply called par value shares.

For common shares, par value has no particular economic significance because common shares do not have a pre-specified dividend rate. For both common and preferred shares, the par value has no bearing on the price at which shareholders buy or sell the shares. Actual prices can be higher or lower than par value.

Under ASPE, the proceeds from the sale of par value share capital must be segregated in equity into share capital for the par value amount and into contributed surplus for the excess of the sale price over the par value.[17] For example, suppose Naples Inc. and Parksville Company are both incorporated in 2018 and they both issue 10,000 common shares and receive $20 per share from investors. Naples's shares have no par value, while Parksville's have a par value of $1. The journal entry to record this share issuance is shown in Exhibit 13-18.

Exhibit 13-18 Journal entries for the issuance of common shares with or without par value

Naples Inc.—no par value			Parksville Company—par value of $1/share		
Dr. Cash	200,000		Dr. Cash	200,000	
Cr. Common shares		200,000	Cr. Common shares—par value		10,000
			Cr. Contributed surplus		190,000

As noted previously, the par value in this case has no economic significance. Therefore, we should consider the effect of the above two journal entries to be the same. In other words, we should think of the amount from the par value ($10,000) and

17. We do not consider instances where issue price is below par because this rarely occurs in practice.

the contributed surplus ($190,000) for Parksville Company together as a single amount of $200,000 for contributed capital.

Suppose that each company repurchases 1,000 of its own shares at $18 each in 2019 and cancels them immediately. How would we account for this repurchase?

First, note that the amounts for contributed capital before the repurchase are as shown in Exhibit 13-19.

Exhibit 13-19 Contributed capital for Naples Inc. and Parksville Company before share repurchases

Naples Inc.—no par value		Parksville Company—par value of $1/share	
Common shares (10,000 sh × $20/sh)	$200,000	Common shares—par value (10,000 sh × $1/sh)	$ 10,000
		Contributed surplus	190,000
		Total contributed capital	$200,000

Observe that both companies' accounts reflect the original share issue price of $20 per share ($200,000 ÷ 10,000 shares). Also observe that the repurchase price of $18 is below the issue price. In other circumstances, we would consider this to be a "gain" because the sale price exceeds the purchase cost by $2 per share. However, accounting standards do not allow this "gain" to flow through the income statement like other gains. Instead of a gain, we record the $2 per share difference as a credit to increase contributed surplus (Exhibit 13-20).

Exhibit 13-20 Journal entries for the repurchase and cancellation of 1,000 shares at $18/share

Naples Inc.—no par value			Parksville Company—par value of $1/share		
Dr. Common shares (1,000 sh × $20/sh)	20,000		Dr. Common shares—par value (1,000 sh × $1/sh)	$ 1,000	
			Dr. Contributed surplus	19,000	
Cr. Cash (1,000 sh × $18/sh)		18,000	Cr. Cash (1,000 sh × $18/sh)		18,000
Cr. Contributed surplus—from repurchase of shares		2,000	Cr. Contributed surplus—from repurchase of shares		2,000

Notice that, in both cases, a total of $20,000 is removed (i.e., debited) from contributed capital, amounting to $20 per share. In addition, it is important to note that the $2,000 credited to contributed surplus needs to be identified as arising from share repurchases and, for Parksville Company, separated from the contributed surplus that previously arose from share issuance. Under ASPE, the $19,000 debit and $2,000 credit to contributed surplus have not been and *cannot be netted out* because they relate to two different types of contributed surplus.

2. Treasury shares

While a company incorporated under the *Canada Business Corporations Act* is generally not permitted to hold its own shares, companies incorporated in other jurisdictions may be allowed to do so. For example, the *British Columbia Business Corporations Act* allows companies to hold repurchased shares.[18] Shares in treasury are issued but not outstanding. Treasury shares do not have voting rights and do not receive dividends.

---

18. *British Columbia Business Corporations Act* (SBC 2002, c. 57) Section 82 Paragraph 1.

IFRS does not provide specific guidance on how to account for treasury shares. Under ASPE, there are two methods that can be used to account for treasury shares: the single-transaction method and the two-transaction method. The single-transaction method treats the reacquisition of shares and the subsequent selling off of shares as two parts of the same transaction (see Exhibit 13-21). The two-transaction method treats the two parts as components of two transactions: the repurchase is the close of a transaction that began with the initial issuance of the shares, and the subsequent resale is the beginning of the next sale-repurchase pair.

Exhibit 13-21 Two methods for treasury share transactions

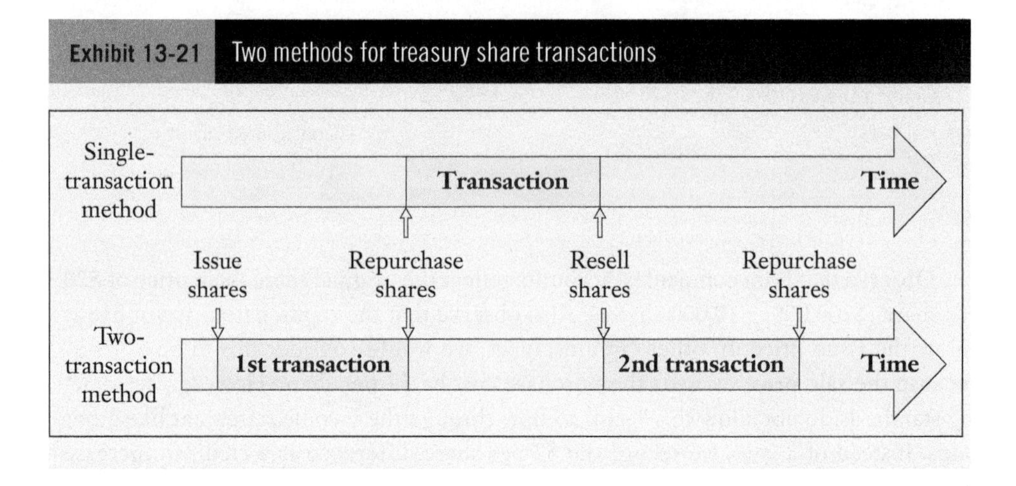

Accounting standards indicate a preference for the single-transaction method over the two-transaction method, although both methods are acceptable (see ASPE 3240.06).

To illustrate the accounting for treasury stock transactions, suppose Smithers Company reacquired 3,000 no par value shares at $8 per share and subsequently sold 1,000 of these shares at $12 per share. Assume that the average price of shares outstanding is $10 and there is no contributed surplus before this transaction. The journal entries for each method would be as shown in Exhibit 13-22.

Exhibit 13-22 Journal entries for the repurchase of 3,000 shares at $8/share and subsequent resale of 1,000 shares at $12/share

Single-transaction method			Two-transaction method		
Repurchase 3,000 shares @ $8/share					
Dr. Treasury stock	24,000		Dr. Common shares (3,000 sh × $10/sh)	30,000	
Cr. Cash (3,000 sh × $8/sh)		24,000	Cr. Cash		24,000
			Cr. Contributed surplus		6,000
Resell 1,000 shares @ $12/share					
Dr. Cash (1,000 sh × $12/sh)	12,000		Dr. Cash	12,000	
Cr. Treasury stock (1,000 sh × $8/sh)		8,000	Cr. Common shares		12,000
Cr. Contributed surplus—from repurchase or resale of shares (repurchases)		4,000			

As this example shows, the two methods have different effects on contributed surplus, in terms of both amount and timing. In the single-transaction method, we increase contributed surplus when the repurchased shares are later resold (i.e., when the single transaction cycle is complete). In the two-transaction method, we increase contributed surplus at the time of repurchase.

For the single-transaction method, we have a separate treasury stock account. The amount recorded in treasury stock is a contra account in equity until these shares are sold.

In instances where companies resell treasury shares for less than the repurchase cost (akin to a loss), the difference first comes out of contributed surplus from prior repurchases to the extent available and then out of retained earnings. We do not involve contributed surplus from other sources because shares in treasury are issued but not outstanding, so none of the contributed surplus (other) can be attributed to these non-outstanding shares. ASPE Section 3240 indicates the following (italics in original):

> ¶16 *When a company resells shares that it has acquired, any excess of the proceeds over cost shall be credited to contributed surplus; any deficiency shall be charged to contributed surplus to the extent that a previous net excess from resale or cancellation of shares of the same class is included therein, otherwise to retained earnings.*[19]

To illustrate this accounting, suppose Smithers Company from Exhibit 13-22 resells the other 2,000 shares that it previously repurchased. The resale price is only $5 per share. Prior to these transactions, the relevant balances in Smithers's accounts are as follows under the single-transaction method shown in Exhibit 13-23.

Exhibit 13-23 Smithers's account balances prior to the second treasury stock transaction

Treasury shares	16,000 Dr
Contributed surplus—from repurchase or resale of shares (repurchases)	4,000 Cr

The journal entry for the resale would be as shown in Exhibit 13-24.

Exhibit 13-24 Journal entry to record Smithers's second resale of 2,000 shares of treasury stock at $5/share

Dr. Cash	10,000	
Dr. Contributed surplus—from repurchase or resale of shares (repurchases)	4,000	
Dr. Retained earnings	2,000	
Cr. Treasury shares		16,000

In this repurchase and resale, the cost of $8 per share exceeds the sale price of $5 per share. The difference of $3 per share on 2,000 shares totals $6,000. We first allocate this amount to contributed surplus arising from repurchases to the extent that it is available ($4,000). The remainder of $2,000 goes to reduce retained earnings.

CHECKPOINT **CP13-8**

Which is the preferred method to account for treasury shares? Briefly describe the mechanics of this approach.

---

19. Uniform Final Examination 1990, with permission from Chartered Professional Accountants of Canada, Toronto, Canada.

J. SUMMARY

L.O. 13-1. Describe the characteristics of different types of share equity and identify the characteristics that are relevant for accounting purposes.

- Shares can have a variety of characteristics involving par value, preference for dividends, the accumulation of dividends, and voting rights.
- For accounting purposes, par value affects how we record the proceeds received from the issuance of shares. Different classes of shares need to be separately recorded.

L.O. 13-2. Identify the different components of equity for accounting purposes that apply to a transaction and analyze the effect of the transaction on those equity components.

- We can divide equity into two broad components: contributed capital and accumulated income.
- Contributed capital consists of amounts received from the issuance of shares. In the case of par value shares, contributed capital has two components: par value and contributed surplus.
- Accumulated income consists of the accumulation of comprehensive income less dividends paid. The retained earnings portion derives from profit or loss, while amounts from other comprehensive income accumulate separately as accumulated other comprehensive income. Certain amounts of retained earnings may be set aside as reserves.

L.O. 13-3. Apply the accounting standards and procedures for transactions relating to contributed capital.

- Proceeds from the issuance of shares affect contributed capital and, in some instances, retained earnings.
- For accounting purposes, contributed surplus needs to be identified by source, arising from the issuance of shares with par value, repurchase and resale of shares, and other transactions.

L.O. 13-4. Apply the accounting standards and procedures for transactions relating to the distribution of retained earnings.

- Cash and property dividends reduce retained earnings when they are declared.
- Stock dividends require a transfer from retained earnings to contributed capital, in contrast to stock splits, which require no journal entry. Generally, the ex-dividend price provides a fair measure of the value of the dividend.

L.O. 13-5. Prepare a statement of changes in equity.

- The statement of changes in equity provides information about the changes that took place during the period in all equity accounts.
- Preparation of the statement of changes in equity is governed by IAS 1.
- The opening and closing balance of each class of equity must be separately reconciled on the statement of changes in equity.
- The statement of changes in equity must include the total comprehensive income for the period.

K. ANSWERS TO CHECKPOINT QUESTIONS

CP13-1: The primary difference between common and preferred shares is that common shares represent the residual interest in the company while preferred shares do not.

CP13-2: A corporation is legally obligated to pay cash dividends when it declares them to be payable.

CP13-3: The difference between cumulative and non-cumulative dividends is that for cumulative dividends, the company must pay any past dividend payments it has missed (i.e., dividends scheduled but not declared) prior to paying any dividends to common shares. This differs from shares with non-cumulative dividends, which do not have any rights to missed dividend payments.

CP13-4: Issued shares are the net number of shares that the corporation has issued; outstanding shares are issued shares that are not held by the company as treasury shares. Outstanding shares + Treasury shares = Issued shares.

CP13-5: Accumulated other comprehensive income (AOCI) is reported as a component of equity in the balance sheet. AOCI represents the accumulation of other comprehensive income (OCI) from previous periods.

CP13-6: Recycling of OCI refers to the process of recognizing amounts through OCI, accumulating that OCI in reserves, and later recognizing those amounts through net income and retained earnings.

CP13-7: The primary reason companies declare a stock split is to bring their stock price to a desired trading range.

CP13-8: The preferred method of accounting for treasury shares is the single-transaction method. The mechanics of this method are that the cost of the repurchased shares are held in the treasury stock account—a contra equity account—until the shares are either resold or retired. The amount to be allocated to contributed surplus and/or retained earnings is not determined until the shares are removed from treasury.

L. GLOSSARY

appropriation: The process that allocates a portion of retained earnings to a reserve.

common (ordinary) shares: An equity interest that has the lowest priority and represents the residual ownership interest in the company.

contributed capital: The component of equity that reflects amounts received by the reporting entity from transactions with its owners, net of any repayments from capital.

contributed surplus: The component of contributed capital in excess of the amount allocated to share capital.

no par value shares: Shares that do not have a stated par value.

ordinary shares: See **common shares.**

par value shares: Shares with a dollar value stated in the articles of incorporation.

preferred shares: Any shares that are not common shares. Preferred shares have priority over common shares with respect to the receipt of dividends and a claim on the entity's net assets in liquidation.

priority: The rank of a liability or equity claim when a company liquidates, where higher priority confers preferential payout before other claimants of lower priority.

recycling (of OCI): The process of recognizing amounts through OCI, accumulating that OCI in reserves, and later recognizing those amounts through net income and retained earnings.

retained earnings: A component of equity that reflects the cumulative net income (profit or loss) minus dividends paid.

shares authorized: The number of shares that are allowed to be issued by a company's articles of incorporation.

shares issued: The number of shares issued by the corporation, whether held by outsiders or by the corporation itself.

shares outstanding: Issued shares held by investors.

stock split: An increase in the number of shares issued without the issuing company receiving any consideration in return.

treasury shares: Shares issued but held by the issuing corporation; treasury shares are not outstanding.

M. REFERENCES

Authoritative standards:

IFRS	ASPE Section
Framework for the Preparation and Presentation of Financial Statements	1000—Financial Statement Concepts
IAS 1—Presentation of Financial Statements	1400—General Standards of Financial Statement Presentation
IAS 32—Financial Instruments: Presentation	3240—Share Capital 3251—Equity 3260—Reserves
IFRIC 17—Distribution of Non-cash Assets to Owners	3831—Non-monetary Transfers

MyLab Accounting Make the grade with **MyLab Accounting:** The problems marked with a 🌐 can be found on **MyLab Accounting.** You can practise them as often as you want, and most feature step-by-step guided instructions to help you find the right answer.

N. PROBLEMS

P13-1. Types of share equity and their characteristics

(L.O. 13-1) (Easy – 5 minutes)[20]

Identify whether the following statements are true or false.

Statement	T/F
a. Common (ordinary) shares have priority over preferred shares.	
b. A share with cumulative dividends must be a preferred share.	
c. Investors favour purchasing preferred shares.	
d. Common shares always have voting rights.	

P13-2. Types of share equity and their characteristics

(L.O. 13-1) (Easy – 5 minutes)

Identify whether the following statements are true or false.

Statement	T/F
a. The number of shares issued > number outstanding > number authorized.	
b. A share with a fixed dividend rate (i.e., a preferred share) is more valuable than one without (i.e., a common share).	
c. All issued shares are eligible to vote for the board of directors.	
d. All outstanding shares are eligible to vote for the board of directors.	

P13-3. Types of share equity and their characteristics

(L.O. 13-1) (Easy – 10 minutes)

Having a cumulative dividend is a common feature of preferred shares.

Required:

a. What does it mean to have a cumulative dividend feature?
b. Why do preferred shares commonly have this feature?
c. Can common shares have a cumulative dividend feature? Explain briefly.

---

[20] Based on CGA-Canada FA3 examination, 2009.

P13-4. Accounting standards for share equity (L.O. 13-1) (Medium – 15 minutes)

Preferred shares are defined as being a form of equity by the *Canada Business Corporations Act* (CBCA). Preferred shares generally have a specified dividend rate and in the event of bankruptcy or liquidation have priority over common shares. However, preferred shares do not have a residual interest in the entity.

Required:

a. Why is residual interest central to the value of common shares?
b. Identify qualities of preferred shares that make them similar to debt financing; identify qualities that make them similar to equity financing.
c. Discuss three reasons why management would want to use preferred shares as a source of financing.

P13-5. Accounting standards for share equity (L.O. 13-1) (Medium – 10 minutes)

A major objective of IFRS is to harmonize accounting rules and procedures around the world. Yet for the details and specifics of accounting for equity accounts (e.g., repurchase of the company's own shares), there are no international rules; rather, countries like Canada are defining the accounting standards for equity accounting and reporting.

Required:

a. Why are there no specific IFRS standards relating to equity accounts?
b. Is it a problem that there are not uniform standards for equity accounting and reporting?

P13-6. Share equity characteristics relevant for accounting (L.O. 13-1) (Medium – 10 minutes)

For accounting purposes, of the following characteristics, which distinguish a common share from a preferred share? Explain your answer briefly.

- The share has no par value.
- The share has voting rights.
- The share has a residual claim.
- The share does not have cumulative dividends.
- The share is issued and outstanding.

P13-7. Components of equity (L.O. 13-2) (Easy – 5 minutes)

Financial reporting distinguishes equity into two broad components: contributed capital and accumulated income; the latter is further separated into retained earnings and accumulated other comprehensive income (AOCI).

Required:

Briefly explain why equity needs to be separated into these categories.

P13-8. Components of equity (L.O. 13-2) (Easy – 5 minutes)[21]

Which of the following are accounts reported in the equity section of the balance sheet?

Account	Equity section	Asset or liability
Preferred shares		
Investment in Company A common shares		
Accumulated other comprehensive income		

(Continued)

[21] CGA-Canada FA3 examination, June 2010, with permission Chartered Professional Accountants of Canada, Toronto, Canada.

Account	Equity section	Asset or liability
Bonds payable		
Donated assets		
Appropriated reserves		
Provision for warranties		

 P13-9. Components of equity (L.O. 13-2) (Easy – 5 minutes)

Which of the following are accounts reported in the contributed capital section of equity?

Account	Contributed capital	Not contributed capital
Common shares		
Retained earnings		
Preferred shares		
Accumulated other comprehensive income		
Appropriated reserves		
Equity in associate		
Contributed surplus—common shares		

 P13-10. Components of equity (L.O. 13-2) (Easy – 5 minutes)

Which of the following transactions have the potential to directly affect the retained earnings portion of equity? Exclude indirect effects such as the transfer of income into retained earnings at the end of a year.

Account	Has potential to directly affect retained earnings	No direct effect on retained earnings
Declaration of a cash dividend		
Issuance of common shares		
Issuance of preferred shares		
Appropriation for a reserve		
Stock split		
Declaration of a stock dividend		
Omission of a cumulative dividend on preferred shares		

 P13-11. Accounting for contributed capital (L.O. 13-3) (Easy – 5 minutes)[22]

When shares are repurchased and cancelled at more than their original issue price, the journal entry to record the retirement potentially includes which of the following components?

Account	Transaction potentially affects this account in the manner indicated (Yes / No)
Debit to cash	
Debit to retained earnings	

(Continued)

22. CGA-Canada FA3 examination, June 2009, with permission Chartered Professional Accountants of Canada, Toronto, Canada.

Account	Transaction potentially affects this account in the manner indicated (Yes / No)
Credit to share capital	
Debit to loss on share retirement	
Debit to contributed surplus	

P13-12. Accounting for contributed capital

(L.O. 13-3) (Easy – 5 minutes)

Lisa's Yoga Inc., a publicly accountable enterprise, issued 1,000 no par value common shares to a supplier in full payment for machinery that normally sells for $50,000. Lisa's Yoga Inc.'s common shares were trading at $51 on the transaction date.

Required:

Prepare the journal entry to record the acquisition of the equipment.

P13-13. Accounting for contributed capital

(L.O. 13-3) (Easy – 10 minutes)

A·S·P·E

Storoshenko Corp. (SC) is a private corporation that elects to report its financial results in accordance with ASPE. SC issued 2,000 no par value common shares to a scientist in exchange for a patented process that she had developed. The patent is estimated to be worth $50,000. A chartered business valuator recently valued SC and estimated that the common shares were worth $24 each.

Required:

a. Assume that the fair value of the patent can be more reliably measured than that of the common shares. Prepare the journal entry to record the acquisition of the patent.
b. Assume that the fair value of the common shares can be more reliably measured than that of the patent. Prepare the journal entry to record the acquisition of the patent.

P13-14. Accounting for shares sold on a subscription basis

(L.O. 13-3) (Easy – 15 minutes)

Wedding Boutique Corp. sells 20,000 no par value common shares for $20 each to employees on a subscription basis. Terms of the sale require the employees to pay $12 on contract signing and the balance in one year's time. Wedding Boutique Corp. has a policy of refunding employees their initial payment if they subsequently default on the contract.

Required:

a. Prepare the journal entries required at time of contract signing.
b. Assume that all employees make the scheduled payments. Prepare the required journal entries.
c. Independent of part (b), assume that contracts representing the sale of 5,000 shares are defaulted upon. Prepare the required journal entries pertaining to the default.
d. Given the facts at hand, how would Wedding Boutique Corp. report the subscriptions receivable account on its balance sheet?

P13-15. Accounting for bundled sales and share issuance costs

(L.O. 13-3) (Easy – 10 minutes)

Walt's Antique Cars Inc. issued equity securities. The offering included 100,000 bundles of one no par value common share and one no par value preferred share. Each bundle sold for $50. Walt's has adopted a policy of charging share issuance costs to retained earnings.

Required:

a. Assume that the fair values of the common shares and preferred shares are $42 and $10, respectively. Prepare the journal entry for the issuance of the equity securities using the relative fair value (proportional) method.
b. Assume that the fair value of the common shares is $42 each but the value of the preferred shares is not known. Prepare the journal entry for the issuance of the equity securities.
c. How would your answer to part (a) change if Walt's incurred $20,000 of costs directly related to the issuance of the securities? Prepare the journal entry.

A·S·P·E

P13-16. Accounting for shares sold on a subscription basis

(L.O. 13-3) (Medium – 20 minutes)

In January 2021, Rita Inc. sells 50,000 no par value common shares for $20 each to the investing public on a subscription basis. Terms of the sale require the investors to pay $11 on contract signing, $5 in July 2021, and the balance in December 2021. The subscription contract provides that Rita Inc. is not required to reimburse investors who default on their contract.

In July 2021, investors that subscribed to purchase 40,000 shares make the agreed-upon payment; the remainder default on the contract. In December 2021, investors that subscribed to purchase 35,000 shares make the agreed-upon payment; the remainder default on the contract.

Required:

Prepare the journal entries required in January 2021, July 2021, and December 2021 assuming that Rita Inc. follows ASPE pertaining to accounting for equity transactions.

P13-17. Accounting for bundled sales and share issuance costs

(L.O. 13-3) (Medium – 20 minutes)

Shangri-La Inc. raised additional capital by selling equity to investors. The package of securities included one no par value common share, one cumulative Class A preferred share, and one non-cumulative Class B preferred share. Shangri-La sold 200,000 packages for $100 each. It incurred $25,000 in costs directly related to the issuance of the securities. At the time of sale, the market value of the common and cumulative preferred shares was $60 and $35, respectively. The Class B preferred shares are a new class of shares so they did not have a market price. Shangri-La has a policy of charging share issuance costs to retained earnings.

Required:

a. Assume that the fair value of a Class B preferred share is $7. Prepare the journal entry for the issuance of the equity securities using the relative fair value (proportional) method.
b. Assume that the fair value of a Class B preferred share is $7. Using the relative fair value (proportional) method, prepare the journal entry for the issuance of the equity securities on the basis that Shangri-La had adopted a policy of allocating the share issuance costs to the related capital accounts.
c. Assume that the fair value of the Class B preferred share is not reliably measurable. Prepare the journal entry for the issuance of the equity securities.

P13-18. Accounting for contributed capital

(L.O. 13-3) (Medium – 10 minutes)

Accounting standards do not permit the recognition of capital transactions (those involving owners acting as owners) to flow through net income. Explain why accounting standards prohibit the recognition of gains or losses on capital transactions on the income statement.

P13-19. Accounting for contributed capital (L.O. 13-3) (Medium – 20 minutes)[23]

When a corporation engages in a capital transaction (those relating to its contributed capital), the journal entry may involve either a debit or a credit to contributed surplus. While not permitted by accounting standards, *if these debits or credits were to be recognized through income*, a debit would be called a "loss" and a credit would be called a "gain."

Consider the following sequence of transactions:

January 1, 2021: Company issues 10,000,000 no par value common shares at $10 each.

January 1, 2022: Company reacquires 100,000 common shares in the open market at $8 each and cancels them immediately.

There were no other capital transactions and the company had not paid any dividends.

Required:

a. Prepare the journal entries for the two transactions.
b. Review the journal entry for January 1, 2022. How much was credited other than cash? Does this credit reflect good or bad management? As a shareholder, would you be happy or unhappy about this credit entry?
c. What would have been the journal entry for January 1, 2022, had the repurchase price been $30?
d. In the journal entry for part (c), explain why the debit goes to reduce retained earnings. How would a shareholder interpret the reduction in retained earnings?

P13-20. Accounting for contributed capital (L.O. 13-3) (Medium – 15 minutes)[24]

A·S·P·E

Cambridge Corp. has a single class of shares. As at its year ended December 31, 2021, the company had 2,500,000 shares issued and outstanding. On the stock exchange, these shares were trading at around $10 per share. In the company's accounts, these shares had a value of $30,000,000. The equity accounts also show $450,000 of contributed surplus from previous repurchases of shares.

On January 15, 2022, Cambridge repurchased and cancelled 100,000 shares at a cost of $10 per share. Later in the year, on August 20, the company repurchased and cancelled a further 300,000 shares at a cost of $15 per share.

Required:

Assume that Cambridge follows the guidance in ASPE pertaining to accounting for equity transactions. Record the journal entries for the two share transactions in 2022.

P13-21. Components of equity (L.O. 13-2, L.O. 13-3) (Medium – 15 minutes)

Refer to the 2016 financial statements for Canadian Tire Corporation in Appendix C.

Required:

a. What was the amount of equity reported in Canadian Tire's financial statements as at December 31, 2016? What was this amount comprised of? Use the same categories that the company reports on its balance sheet.
b. The company had two categories of share capital. What were they and what was the closing balance of each?
c. What were the opening and closing balances of the company's contributed surplus?
d. What were the opening and closing balances of the company's accumulated other comprehensive income (loss)? What were the four categories of AOCI reported in Canadian Tire's financial statements?

23. CGA-Canada FA3 examination, December 2009, with permission Chartered Professional Accountants of Canada, Toronto, Canada.

24. CGA-Canada FA3 examination, June 2010, with permission Chartered Professional Accountants of Canada, Toronto, Canada.

P13-22. Accounting for retained earnings (L.O. 13-4) (Easy – 5 minutes)[25]

Mark Corporation declared and distributed a 5% stock dividend. Mark had 400,000 common shares outstanding and 1,000,000 common shares authorized before the stock dividend. The board of directors determined the appropriate market value per share as $7.

Required:

How much should be recorded for the stock dividend? Record the journal entry (if any) for the shares distributed.

P13-23. Accounting for retained earnings (L.O. 13-4) (Medium – 10 minutes)

Belmont Corporation has a December 31 year-end. On December 15, 2021, the board of directors declared a cash dividend of $0.50 per common share, payable on January 30, 2022. The date of record for this dividend is January 14, and the ex-dividend date is January 12, 2022. Additional information relating to the shares follows:

	No. of common shares at end of day	
Date	Issued	Outstanding
December 15, 2021	4,000,000	4,000,000
January 11, 2022	4,000,000	3,800,000
January 14, 2022	4,000,000	3,600,000
January 30, 2022	3,600,000	3,600,000

Required:

a. Determine the dollar amount of dividends to be paid as a result of the dividend declaration on December 15, 2021.
b. Record all the journal entries related to this dividend in 2021 and 2022.

P13-24. Accounting for retained earnings (L.O. 13-4) (Medium – 20 minutes)

Cardiff Corporation is a public company traded on a major exchange. Cardiff's common shares are currently trading at $20 per share. The board of directors is debating whether to issue a 25% stock dividend or a five-for-four stock split (i.e., a shareholder who holds four shares would receive a fifth share). The board is wondering how shareholders' equity would be affected, and whether the value of the typical shareholder's investment will change.

Details of Cardiff's equity section of the balance sheet is as follows:

Common shares, no par value, 10,000,000 shares issued and outstanding	$ 56,500,000
Retained earnings	170,000,000
Total shareholders' equity	$226,500,000

Required:

a. At what price would you expect the shares to trade after either transaction? Explain with calculations.
b. Show what the equity section of the balance sheet for Cardiff would look like after the stock dividend. Do the same for the stock split alternative.
c. Assume that an investor has 4,000 common shares before the stock dividend or stock split. What would be the value of the investor's holdings before and after the stock dividend or stock split?
d. What is your recommendation to the board of directors?

---

[25] CGA-Canada FA3 examination, June 2010, with permission Chartered Professional Accountants of Canada, Toronto, Canada.

P13-25. Dividends in kind (L.O. 13-4) (Medium – 15 minutes)

Jamie Bleay Inc. (JBI) has an at fair value through profit or loss investment in which it owns 200,000 common shares of Richard Ramey Ltd. (RRL). JBI distributes its shareholding in RRL by way of a property dividend. Other information follows:

- The current book value of the RRL shares is $580,000.
- The market value of the RRL shares is $600,000.
- JBI's capital structure includes 50,000 issued and 40,000 outstanding common shares.
- The dividend is declared on December 15, 2021, and distributed on December 18, 2021.

Required:

a. Prepare the required journal entries to record the declaration and payment of the dividend in kind assuming that JBI prepares its financial statements in accordance with IFRS.
b. What is the fair market value of the RRL shares that each JBI common shareholder receives?

P13-26. Dividends in kind (L.O. 13-4) (Medium – 10 minutes)

A·S·P·E

Peter Quitzau Inc. (PQI) owns 200,000 common shares of Margaret Thornton Ltd. (MTL), a private company. PQI distributes its shareholding in MTL to PQI's shareholders by way of property dividend. Other information follows:

- PQI exercises significant influence over MTL. It accounts for its investment using the equity method.
- At dividend declaration date, the cost of the MTL investment was $400,000; the book value $500,000; and the estimated market value $600,000.
- The dividend was declared on December 15, 2018, and is distributed on December 18, 2018.

Required:

Prepare the required journal entries to record the declaration and payment of the dividend in kind, assuming that PQI prepares its financial statements in accordance with ASPE.

P13-27. Accounting for contributed capital and retained earnings (L.O. 13-3, L.O. 13-4) (Medium – 20 minutes)

A·S·P·E

As of January 1, 2021, the equity section of GFF Educational Inc.'s balance sheet contained the following:

Preferred stock, $4 non-cumulative dividend, 2,000,000 shares authorized, 10,000 issued and outstanding	$1,000,000
Common stock, unlimited shares authorized, 1,000,000 issued and outstanding	4,000,000
Contributed surplus—from repurchase and cancellation of common shares	450,000
Contributed surplus— from repurchase and cancellation of preferred shares	10,000
Retained earnings	3,540,000
Total shareholders' equity	$9,000,000

- On March 1, 2021, GFF repurchased and cancelled 1,000 preferred shares at $120 per share.
- On June 30, 2021, GFF spent $500,000 to repurchase 100,000 common shares. These shares were cancelled immediately.
- On November 15, 2021, GFF issued a 15% stock dividend on common shares. GFF's stock traded at $8 per share after the dividend.
- On December 15, 2021, GFF declared the annual cash dividends on the preferred shares, payable on January 2, 2022.

Required:

Assume that GFF follows the guidance in ASPE pertaining to accounting for equity transactions. Record the journal entries for the above transactions occurring in 2021.

P13-28. Accounting for contributed capital and retained earnings

(L.O. 13-3, L.O. 13-4) (Medium – 30 minutes)

As of January 1, 2021, the equity section of Gail and Samson Inc.'s balance sheet contained the following:

Class A preferred stock, $3 cumulative dividend, 500,000 shares authorized, 2,000 issued and outstanding	$ 200,000
Class B preferred stock, $5 non-cumulative dividend, 200,000 shares authorized, 5,000 issued and outstanding	500,000
Common stock, unlimited shares authorized, 20,000 issued and outstanding	1,300,000
Contributed surplus—from repurchase and cancellation of common shares	100,000
Contributed surplus—from repurchase and cancellation of Class A preferred shares	25,000
Contributed surplus—from repurchase and cancellation of Class B preferred shares	20,000
Retained earnings	1,890,000
Total shareholders' equity	$4,035,000

- Dividends were last paid in 2018. There were no arrears at that time.
- On February 1, 2021, Gail sold 1,000 common shares for $65,000 cash.
- On March 1, 2021, Gail issued a 5% stock dividend on common shares. Gail's stock traded at $65 per share after the dividend.
- On April 1, 2021, Gail declared $50,000 in cash dividends, payable on April 15, 2021.
- On April 15, 2021, Gail paid the dividends declared on April 1.
- On May 1, 2021, Gail repurchased and cancelled 1,000 Class B preferred shares at $110 per share.
- On June 1, 2021, Gail spent $75,000 to repurchase 1,000 common shares. These shares were cancelled immediately.
- On July 1, 2021, Gail declared and distributed a two-for-one stock split on the common shares.

Required:

a. Assume that Gail and Samson Inc. follow the guidance in ASPE pertaining to accounting for equity transactions. Record the journal entries for the above transactions occurring in 2021.
b. Briefly describe the procedure for recording the two-for-one stock split.
c. How much was the dividend per share amount paid to the common shareholder?

A·S·P·E

P13-29. Accounting for contributed capital and retained earnings

(L.O. 13-3, L.O. 13-4) (Medium – 20 minutes)

As of January 1, 2019, the equity section of BC Marine Co.'s balance sheet contained the following:

Common shares, 10,000,000 authorized, 2,000,000 issued and outstanding	$5,000,000
Contributed surplus—from repurchase and cancellation of common shares	150,000
Contributed surplus—expired options on common shares	200,000
Preferred shares, $2 cumulative dividend, 5,000,000 authorized, 50,000 issued and outstanding	1,050,000
Retained earnings	2,400,000
Total shareholders' equity	$8,800,000

- On May 1, 2019, the company spent $500,000 to repurchase 100,000 common shares. These shares were cancelled immediately.
- On July 15, 2019, the company repurchased and cancelled 1,000 preferred shares at $20 per share.
- On November 1, 2019, the company declared and paid the annual cash dividends on the preferred shares. On the same day, the company issued a 10% stock dividend on common shares. BC Marine's stock traded at $6 per share after the dividend.

Required:

Assume that BC Marine follows the guidance in ASPE pertaining to accounting for equity transactions. Record the journal entries for the above transactions occurring in 2019.

P13-30. Dividends in kind (L.O. 13-4) (Difficult – 30 minutes)

A·S·P·E

Ron Tidball Corp. (RTC) owns 100,000 shares in Scott Austin Ltd. (SAL). RTC distributes its shareholding in SAL by way of a property dividend. Other information follows:

- The current book value of the SAL shares is $450,000.
- The market value of the SAL shares is $500,000.
- The dividend is declared on June 15, 2021, and distributed on June 30, 2021.
- Scenario 1—SAL has 10,000,000 shares outstanding; the investment is designated as at fair value through profit or loss (IFRS) and is quoted in an active market (ASPE).
- Scenario 2—SAL has 50,000 shares outstanding. RTC has significant influence over SAL and accounts for the investment using the equity method.
- Scenario 3—SAL has 15,000 shares outstanding. RTC controls SAL.

Required:

a. For each of the scenarios, prepare the required journal entries to record the declaration and payment of the dividend in kind. Assume that RTC prepares its financial statements in accordance with IFRS.
b. For each of the scenarios, prepare the required journal entries to record the declaration and payment of the dividend in kind. Assume that RTC prepares its financial statements in accordance with ASPE.

P13-31. Dividends preference and distribution (L.O. 13-4) (Difficult – 30 minutes)

Della's Garden Delight Corp.'s capital structure includes the following equity instruments:

- No par value common shares, 2,000,000 shares issued and outstanding
- Class A, non-cumulative preferred shares, each entitled to an annual dividend of $5, 80,000 shares issued and outstanding
- Class B, cumulative preferred shares, each entitled to an annual dividend of $4, 40,000 shares issued and outstanding

The dividends on the Class A and B shares are *pari passu* (equally ranked) with respect to current dividend entitlements. (Dividends declared are applied firstly to arrears, if any. If the remaining dividend is insufficient to pay the current year's entitlement on the A and B shares, then that amount is distributed on a pro rata basis.) On December 31, 2021, Della's declared $744,000 in dividends, payable on January 15, 2022.

- Scenario 1—there are no dividends in arrears.
- Scenario 2—dividends were neither declared nor paid in 2020.
- Scenario 3—a total of $280,000 in dividends were declared and paid in 2019; dividends were neither declared nor paid in 2020.

Required:

a. Determine how much of the dividend must be distributed to each class of shares for each of the three scenarios.
b. Are there any dividends in arrears after the declaration and payment of the dividend in Scenario 3? If so, how much?
c. Prepare the required journal entries for the declaration and payment of the dividends for Scenario 1.

A·S·P·E

P13-32. Accounting for contributed capital and retained earnings

(L.O. 13-3, L.O. 13-4) (Difficult – 30 minutes)

Fenwick Ltd. began operations in 2016. Its fiscal year-end is December 31. Components of the condensed balance sheet as at December 31, 2018, are as follows:

Current liabilities	$ 400,000
Bonds payable—7%, mature 2022	8,000,000
Total liabilities	$8,400,000
Common shares—500,000 authorized, 300,000 issued and outstanding	$6,000,000
Contributed surplus—common shares, from share repurchases and resales	400,000
Retained earnings (deficit)	(200,000)
Total shareholders' equity	$6,200,000

During 2019, Fenwick had the following activities:

i. January 1: Issued 40,000 preferred shares with cumulative dividends of $1.25 per share. Proceeds were $480,000, or $12 per share.
ii. July 1: Repurchased and cancelled 50,000 common shares at a cost of $18 per share.
iii. Net income for the year was $1,700,000.

During 2020, the company had the following activities:

i. July 1: Repurchased and cancelled 60,000 common shares at a cost of $30 each.
ii. December 31: Fenwick declared dividends totalling $400,000.
iii. Net income for the year was $800,000.

Required:

a. Assume that Fenwick follows the guidance in ASPE pertaining to accounting for equity transactions. Prepare the journal entries required for 2019.
b. Prepare the equity section of the balance sheet as at December 31, 2019, including any notes that would be required.
c. Prepare the journal entries required for 2020.
d. Prepare the equity section of the balance sheet as at December 31, 2020, including any notes that would be required.

P13-33. Statement of changes in equity

(L.O. 13-5) (Medium – 15 minutes)

Below are details relating to balances for the equity accounts of Barrie Company and changes to those balances (note that AOCI is accumulated other comprehensive income).

Balances or changes	Amount ($000's)
Common shares, Jan. 1, 2021	$20,000
Unappropriated retained earnings, Jan. 1, 2021	11,000
Appropriated retained earnings for sinking fund reserve, Jan. 1, 2021	2,000
AOCI from revaluations, Jan. 1, 2021	1,000
Net income for 2021	3,000
Retained earnings appropriated for sinking fund reserve during 2021	1,300
AOCI from revaluations in 2021	500
Dividends declared during 2021	1,000
Net income for 2022	4,000
Retained earnings appropriated for sinking fund reserve during 2022	400
AOCI from revaluations in 2022	(200)
Dividends declared during 2022	1,200

Required:

Prepare a statement of changes in equity for the years ended December 31, 2021 and 2022. The following format will be helpful for preparing this statement for each of the two years.

	Common shares	Retained earnings	Appropriated retained earnings	AOCI	Total
Changes during year 20XX:					
Balance Jan. 1, 20XX					
Balance Dec. 31, 20XX					

P13-34. Statement of changes in equity (L.O. 13-5) (Medium – 15 minutes)

Below are details relating to balances for the equity accounts of PICSR Company and changes to those balances (note that AOCI is accumulated other comprehensive income).

Balances or changes	Amount ($000's)
Common shares, Jan. 1, 2021	$50,000
Unappropriated retained earnings, Jan. 1, 2021	15,000
Appropriated retained earnings for sinking fund reserve, Jan. 1, 2021	4,000
AOCI from revaluations, Jan. 1, 2021	(2,000)
Net income for 2021	4,000
Retained earnings appropriated for sinking fund reserve during 2021	2,500
AOCI from revaluations in 2021	1,000
Dividends declared during 2021	3,000
Net income for 2021	6,000
Retained earnings appropriated for sinking fund reserve during 2022	600
AOCI from revaluations in 2022	500
Dividends declared during 2022	1,500

Required:

Prepare a statement of changes in equity for the years ended December 31, 2021 and 2022. The following format will be helpful for preparing this statement for each of the two years.

	Common shares	Retained earnings	Appropriated retained earnings	AOCI	Total
Changes during year 20XX:					
Balance Jan. 1, 20XX					
Balance Dec. 31, 20XX					

P13-35. Statement of changes in equity (L.O. 13-5) (Difficult – 30 minutes)

Below are details relating to balances for the equity accounts of Mark's Photography Company and changes to those balances (note that AOCI is accumulated other comprehensive income).

Balances or changes	Amount ($000's)
Preferred shares, Jan. 1, 2021	100,000
Common shares, Jan. 1, 2021	200,000
Contributed surplus, Jan. 1, 2021	5,000
Retained earnings, Jan. 1, 2021	150,000
AOCI from revaluations, Jan. 1, 2021	10,000

(Continued)

Balances or changes	Amount ($000's)
AOCI from foreign currency translation adjustment (FCTA), Jan. 1, 2021	12,000
Net income for 2021	10,000
AOCI from revaluations in 2021	3,000
AOCI from foreign currency translation adjustments (FCTA) in 2021	(2,000)
Dividends declared on preferred shares during 2021	2,000
Dividends declared on common shares during 2021	3,000
Common shares issued during 2021	10,000
Net income for 2022	(4,000)
AOCI from revaluations in 2022	(1,000)
AOCI from foreign currency translation adjustments (FCTA) in 2022	2,000
Dividends declared on preferred shares during 2022	1,800
Dividends declared on common shares during 2022	2,000
Preferred shares redeemed during 2022	5,000
Increase in contributed surplus from redemption of preferred shares 2022	500

Required:

Prepare a statement of changes in equity for the years ended December 31, 2021 and 2022. The following format will be helpful for preparing this statement for each of the two years.

	Common shares	Preferred shares	Contributed surplus	Total capital	Retained earnings	AOCI from revaluations	AOCI from FCTA	Total AOCI	Total
Changes during year 20XX:									
Balance Jan. 1, 20XX									
Balance Dec. 31, 20XX									

APPENDIX PROBLEMS

P13A-36. Types of share equity and their characteristics 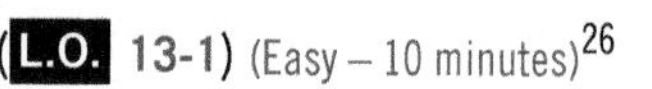 (L.O. 13-1) (Easy – 10 minutes)[26]

Canada and many other countries discourage and even prohibit the use of "par value" for common shares because it could be a misleading label.

Required:

Why is the term "par value" for *common* shares a misleading idea for many investors?

26. Based on CGA-Canada FA3 examination, 2009.

P13A-37. Accounting for contributed capital

(L.O. 13-3) (Easy – 5 minutes)

When shares are repurchased at more than their original issue price, then held in treasury or cancelled, the journal entry potentially includes which of the following components?

Account	Transaction potentially affects this account in the manner indicated (Yes / No)
Debit to share capital	
Debit to contributed surplus	
Debit to treasury shares	
Debit to loss on share retirement	
Debit to retained earnings	
Debit to accumulated other comprehensive income (AOCI)	

P13A-38. Accounting for contributed capital

(L.O. 13-3) (Easy – 5 minutes)

When shares are repurchased and held in treasury, and the purchase is at more than the original issue price, the journal entry to record the repurchase potentially includes which of the following components under the single-transaction method?

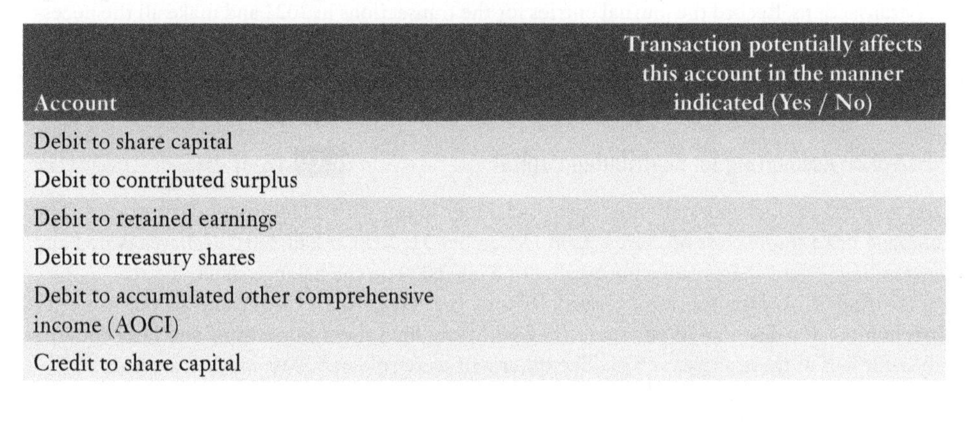

Account	Transaction potentially affects this account in the manner indicated (Yes / No)
Debit to share capital	
Debit to contributed surplus	
Debit to retained earnings	
Debit to treasury shares	
Debit to accumulated other comprehensive income (AOCI)	
Credit to share capital	

P13A-39. Accounting for contributed capital

(L.O. 13-3) (Easy – 10 minutes) A·S·P·E

Canaan Corp. (CC) is a private corporation that elects to report its financial results in accordance with ASPE. On January 1, 2021, CC, a newly incorporated company, issued (sold) 10,000, $2 par value, common shares for $50 each. On January 1, 2022, CC paid $47,000 to repurchase 1,000 of its shares.

Required:

a. Prepare the journal entry to record the sale of the shares.
b. Prepare the journal entry to record the repurchase of the shares.

P13A-40. Accounting for contributed capital

(L.O. 13-3) (Easy – 10 minutes)

Belle Ltd. (BL) is a private corporation that elects to report its financial results in accordance with ASPE. On January 1, 2021, BL, a newly incorporated company, issued (sold) 5,000, $10 par value, common shares for $25 each. On January 1, 2022, BL paid $27,000 to repurchase 1,000 of its shares.

Required:

a. Prepare the journal entry to record the sale of the shares.
b. Prepare the journal entry to record the repurchase of the shares.

A·S·P·E

P13A-41. Accounting for contributed capital (L.O. 13-3, L.O. 13-4) (Medium – 20 minutes)

Utopia Is A Destination Inc. had the following shareholders' equity account balances on December 31, 2021:

Common stock, no par, 60,000 shares authorized, 40,000 issued	$ 800,000
Contributed surplus on repurchases and resales	20,000
Treasury stock, 3,000 shares	(90,000)
Retained earnings	400,000
Total shareholders' equity	$1,130,000

During 2022, the following transactions occurred:

i. March 1: Utopia resold 500 of the treasury shares at $40 per share.
ii. May 15: Utopia issued (sold) 5,000 common shares for $25 each.
iii. December 15: The board of directors declared cash dividends of $4 per share, payable on January 15, 2023.
iv. December 31: Net income for the year ended December 31, 2022, was $200,000.

Utopia uses the single-transaction method for treasury shares.

Required:

a. Assume that Utopia follows the guidance in ASPE pertaining to accounting for equity transactions. Record the journal entries for the transactions in 2022 and make all the necessary year-end entries relating to shareholders' equity accounts.
b. Prepare the presentation of the shareholders' equity section of Utopia's balance sheet as at December 31, 2022.

P13A-42. Accounting for contributed capital (L.O. 13-3) (Medium – 15 minutes)

Drayton Inc. was incorporated under provincial legislation with a December 31 year-end. The company has a single class of shares. As at December 31, 2020, it had 200,000 shares issued and outstanding. These shares had a book value of $5,000,000 on the balance sheet.

During 2021, Drayton repurchased 10% of the issued shares from one of the minority shareholders at a cost of $30 per share. The company held these in treasury and later found a buyer for half of these shares at $35. The other half were sold at $28 to another investor.

Required:

Assume that Drayton follows the guidance in ASPE pertaining to accounting for equity transactions. Record the share transactions using the single-transaction method for treasury shares, which is the preferred accounting method.

A·S·P·E

P13A-43. Accounting for contributed capital (L.O. 13-3) (Medium – 15 minutes)

Refer to the facts for Drayton Inc. presented in problem P13A-42.

Required:

Assume that Drayton follows the guidance in ASPE pertaining to accounting for equity transactions. Record the share transactions using the alternative two-transaction method for treasury shares.

P13A-44. Accounting for contributed capital (L.O. 13-3, L.O. 13-4) (Medium – 15 minutes)

Elgin Company had the following shareholders' equity account balances on December 31, 2021:

Common stock, no par, 40,000 shares authorized, 30,000 issued	$720,000
Contributed surplus on repurchases and resales	25,000
Treasury shares, 5,000 shares	(165,000)
Retained earnings	350,000
Total shareholders' equity	$930,000

During 2022, the following transactions occurred:

i. May 1: Elgin resold 800 of the treasury shares at $48 per share.
ii. December 30: The board of directors declared cash dividends of $2 per share payable on January 15, 2023.
iii. December 31: Net income for the year ended December 31, 2022, was $120,000.

Elgin uses the single-transaction method for treasury shares.

Required:

a. Assume that Elgin follows the guidance in ASPE pertaining to accounting for equity transactions. Record the journal entries for the transactions in 2022 and make all the necessary year-end entries relating to shareholders' equity accounts.
b. Prepare the presentation of the shareholders' equity section of Elgin's balance sheet as at December 31, 2022.

P13A-45. Accounting for contributed capital (L.O. 13-3, L.O. 13-4) (Difficult – 30 minutes) A·S·P·E

Liway's Cleaning Emporium Corp. had the following shareholders' equity account balances on December 31, 2021:

Preferred shares A, $100, 4% cumulative, 10,000 authorized, 2,000 issued and outstanding	$ 200,000
Preferred shares B, $100, 5% non-cumulative, 10,000 authorized, 1,000 issued and outstanding	100,000
Common shares, no par, 50,000 authorized, 40,000 issued	4,000,000
Contributed surplus on repurchases and resales	100,000
Treasury shares—common, 2,000 shares	(200,000)
Retained earnings	1,400,000
Accumulated other comprehensive income	300,000
Total shareholders' equity	$5,900,000

During 2022, the following transactions occurred:

i. February 1: Liway's resold the 2,000 treasury shares at $90 per share.
ii. May 20: Liway's bought back 500 common shares for $95 each and retired them.
iii. December 1: The board of directors declared cash dividends of $600,000 payable on January 2, 2023. (There were no dividends in arrears.)
iv. December 31: Other comprehensive income for the year ended December 31, 2022, was $50,000.
v. December 31: Net income for the year ended December 31, 2022, was $1,000,000.

Liway's uses the single-transaction method for treasury shares and follows the guidance in ASPE pertaining to the issuance and redemption of share capital.

Required:

a. Record the journal entries for the transactions in 2022 and make all the necessary year-end entries relating to shareholders' equity accounts.
b. Prepare the presentation of the shareholders' equity section of Liway's balance sheet as at December 31, 2022.
c. How much is the dividend per share paid to the common shareholders?

P13A-46. Dividends preference (L.O. 13-4) (Easy – 10 minutes)

Stanger's Secure Storage Inc.'s capital structure includes the following equity instruments:

- No par value common shares, 1,000,000 shares issued and outstanding
- Class A, $100 par value, 4% cumulative preferred shares, 100,000 shares issued and outstanding
- Class B, $100 par value, 6% non-cumulative preferred shares, 50,000 shares issued and outstanding

The dividends on the Class B shares are subordinated to the Class A shares; dividends must be up to date on the Class A shares before dividends can be declared on Class B shares. In 2021, Stanger's declared $1,300,000 in dividends.

- Scenario 1—there are no dividends in arrears.
- Scenario 2—dividends were neither declared nor paid in 2020.
- Scenario 3—dividends were neither declared nor paid in 2019 or 2020.

Required:

Determine how much of the dividend must be distributed to each class of shares for each of the three scenarios.

P13A-47. Accounting for retained earnings

(L.O. 13-4) (Easy – 10 minutes)

Acton Company has two classes of shares that were both issued on January 1, 2019:

- Class A, $100 par value, 5% preferred shares, 100,000 shares issued and outstanding
- Class B, no par value common shares issued at $50 per share, 1,000,000 shares issued and outstanding

Due to challenging start-up problems in 2019 and 2020, there were no dividends paid; in 2021, dividends of $6,000,000 were paid. For 2022, dividends paid totalled $17,000,000, and for 2023 total dividends paid were $15,000,000.

Required:

How much was the amount of dividends paid to preferred and common shares in 2019 to 2023? First assume that the preferred shares are non-cumulative, then assume that they are cumulative. Use the following table for your answer.

(in $000's)	2019	2020	2021	2022	2023
Total dividends	0	0	$6,000	$17,000	$15,000
Non-cumulative preferred dividends					
Common dividends					
Total dividends	0	0	$6,000	$17,000	$15,000
Cumulative preferred dividends					
Common dividends					

A·S·P·E

P13A-48. Accounting for contributed capital and retained earnings

(L.O. 13-3, L.O. 13-4) (Medium – 30 minutes)

As of January 1, 2021, the equity section of Smokey The Cat Corp.'s balance sheet contained the following:

Class A preferred stock, $1 cumulative dividend, 100,000 shares authorized, 1,000 issued and outstanding	$ 10,000
Class B preferred stock, $2 cumulative dividend, 100,000 shares authorized, 2,000 issued and outstanding	40,000
Common stock, no par, unlimited shares authorized, 10,000 issued and outstanding	200,000
Contributed surplus—from repurchase and cancellation of common shares	5,000
Contributed surplus—from repurchase and cancellation of Class A preferred shares	5,000
Contributed surplus—from repurchase and cancellation of Class B preferred shares	5,000
Retained earnings	135,000
Total shareholders' equity	$400,000

- Smokey uses the single-transaction method to account for treasury shares.
- Dividends were last paid in 2017. There were no arrears at that time.
- On February 1, 2021, Smokey repurchased 1,000 common shares for $25,000 cash and held them as treasury shares.
- On March 1, 2021, Smokey issued a 10% stock dividend on common shares. Smokey's stock traded at $22 per share after the dividend.
- On April 1, 2021, Smokey repurchased and cancelled 1,000 Class B preferred shares at $23 per share.
- On June 1, 2021, Smokey declared and distributed a two-for-one stock split on the common shares.
- On July 1, 2021, Smokey declared $25,000 in cash dividends, payable on August 1, 2021.
- On August 1, 2021, Smokey paid the dividends declared on July 1.
- On September 1, 2021, Smokey resold the common shares in treasury for $28 each.

Required:

a. Assume that Smokey follows the guidance in ASPE pertaining to accounting for equity transactions. Record the journal entries for the above transactions occurring in 2021.
b. How much was the dividend per share amount paid to the common shareholder?
c. Ignoring income for the year, what is the total capitalization of the company on August 2, 2021?

P13A-49. Accounting for contributed capital and retained earnings (L.O. 13-3, L.O. 13-4) (Difficult – 20 minutes)

A·S·P·E

The following is an extract from the balance sheet of Devlin Ltd. as at December 31, 2021:

Shareholders' equity	
Preferred shares, $1 per share non-cumulative dividend, redeemable at $12 per share, 500,000 authorized, 50,000 issued and outstanding	$ 500,000
Contributed surplus—preferred shares, from share repurchases and resales	150,000
Common shares, 10,000,000 authorized, 1,000,000 issued and outstanding	2,637,489
Retained earnings	12,649,187
Total shareholders' equity	$15,936,676

The company did not declare dividends on preferred shares in 2021. Transactions in 2022 include the following:

i. March 15: Devlin purchased 10,000 preferred shares on the stock exchange for $11.50 per share and held these in treasury.
ii. March 28: The company redeemed 15,000 preferred shares directly from shareholders for $12.00 per share and immediately cancelled them.
iii. July 1: The market price of common shares shot up to $45 per share, so Devlin decided to split the common shares four to one.
iv. August 1: Devlin cancelled 8,000 preferred shares that were held in treasury.
v. December 31: The company declared dividends of $1.00 per preferred share and $0.10 per common share.

Required:

Assume that Devlin follows the guidance in ASPE pertaining to accounting for equity transactions. Prepare the journal entries to record the above transactions. The company uses the single-transaction method to account for treasury shares.

A·S·P·E

P13A-50. Accounting for contributed capital and retained earnings

(L.O. 13-3, L.O. 13-4) (Difficult –30 minutes)

Hamilton Holdings had the following balances in shareholders' equity as at December 31, 2021:

Preferred shares, $1 cumulative dividend, 1,000,000 authorized, 700,000 issued and outstanding	$17,500,000
Common shares, no par value, unlimited number authorized, 1,200,000 issued	9,600,000
Contributed surplus—common shares, from share repurchases and resales	120,000
Treasury shares, 320,000 common shares	(1,920,000)
Retained earnings	23,450,000
Total shareholders' equity	$48,750,000

In addition, the financial statement notes on this date indicated that two years of preferred share dividends were in arrears, totalling $1,400,000.

The following transactions occurred during 2022:

i. January 31: Hamilton resold half of the shares held in treasury for proceeds of $7.50 each.
ii. March 30: The company repurchased and immediately cancelled 200,000 common shares at a cost of $1,620,000.
iii. June 1: The company repurchased and retired 175,000 preferred shares at a price of $30 each. Note that repurchased shares lose any rights to dividends.
iv. July 13: The company issued 250,000 common shares in exchange for some heavy machinery. The market price of the shares was $9 on this day.
v. August 1: The remaining shares held in treasury were cancelled. The share price was $9.50.
vi. September 30: The board of directors declared and issued a 10% stock dividend on common shares. The shares were trading at $11 per share on this day. On the ex-dividend date of October 31, the share price was $10. To issue this stock dividend, the board also declared dividends on preferred shares for the current year and the two years in arrears.

Required:

Assume that Hamilton follows the guidance in ASPE pertaining to accounting for equity transactions. Prepare the journal entries to reflect Hamilton's equity transactions in 2022. It may be helpful to use a tabular schedule similar to Exhibit 13-16 to track the number of shares and dollar amounts.

0. MINI-CASES

CASE 1
Peterborough Printers
(30 minutes)

Peterborough Printers specializes in high-volume reproduction of advertising leaflets, such as those distributed by direct mail or inserted in newspapers. Located in Scarborough and founded by Peter Pang over 40 years ago, the company has been publicly traded for the past 20 years. Through its history, the company has successfully attracted and retained a solid and stable base of business clients largely as a result of Peter's savvy salesmanship.

Peterborough has two classes of shares, common and preferred. The common shares are listed on the Toronto Stock Exchange, and Peter still holds 20% of these shares. The preferred shares are privately held by five individuals and pay cumulative dividends.

You are the CFO of Peterborough Printers. You recently met with Peter to discuss financial matters. The following is an excerpt from that conversation:

PETER: This recession is a lot deeper and lasting a lot longer than I and many others had anticipated. Our sales are way down and I'm becoming more and more worried.

YOU: There's no doubt about it. We'll need to be on our toes to come out of this in one piece.

PETER: On top of the recession, there has been a gradual but noticeable drop in our printing volume over the past decade.

YOU: I think it has a lot to do with companies relying less on print media and switching to online advertising.

PETER: That's probably right. I'm working on adjusting our production capabilities in light of this long-term trend.

YOU: That's good to hear.

PETER: So, the reason we're meeting today is to see what we might do on the financial side of things to help us cope with the current economic pressures. In hindsight, we have been very fortunate, having built up a substantial cushion of cash and short-term investments during the good years. We are still in good shape now, but I expect another one or two lean years will take us to the breaking point.

As you know, Peterborough has been able to consistently maintain and increase dividends to our common shareholders over the past 20 years. Under the circumstances, we need to seriously think about whether we can continue with this policy. I wonder if there is anything we can do to maintain our financial health while not disappointing our shareholders. I've heard that some companies pay stock dividends. I'm not exactly sure how they work, but I've been told that paying these dividends doesn't cost us any cash.

YOU: What are your thoughts on the dividends on the preferred shares?

PETER: I'm not as concerned about maintaining those dividends. As it is, the dividends are cumulative, so these shareholders will get their money sooner or later, even if we have to miss paying them this year or next year.

YOU: Well, let me think about these dividend issues and get back to you tomorrow.

Required:

Draft a short report discussing the dividend policy alternatives and your recommendations.

CASE 2
Thamesford Tubs
(45 minutes)

A relaxing bath represents a busy day's more enjoyable moments for many people. For over a hundred years, Thamesford Tubs has been fulfilling this need, manufacturing bathtubs of all shapes and sizes and in all quality ranges. The company enjoyed decades of success along with North America's burgeoning population, which created great demand for new homes and new bathtubs. At the company's peak, production reached 500,000 tubs a year.

In more recent years, however, demand for the company's products has decreased significantly due to a confluence of many factors. Consumer tastes have evolved toward a preference for showers over baths for several reasons: people have become more aware of the lower water consumption of showers compared to baths; increasing numbers of people live in condominiums/apartments in which space is at a premium compared to detached homes; fewer consumers value distinctive and high-quality tubs; and there was a bursting of the housing bubble that dramatically lowered the rate of new home construction. Due to the significant drop in sales, Thamesford has experienced three consecutive years of losses, and management expects a net loss of around $2 million this year before business recovers to profitability.

It is mid-September, almost three-quarters of the way to Thamesford's fiscal year-end of December 31. The company has a $20 million bank loan coming due next March 30. Given recent years' operating results, the company's financial resources have been stretched, and there is little available to repay this loan in seven months' time.

In addition to this $20 million loan, Thamesford has another long-term loan outstanding for $16 million, which is due in five years, bearing interest at 8%. This loan requires Thamesford to maintain a current ratio of at least 1.0 and a debt-to-equity ratio less than 3:1 at each fiscal year-end. Violating these covenants would make the loan immediately due and payable. As of the previous fiscal year-end, the company was in compliance with these covenants. Other liabilities, which consist primarily of accounts payable, stood at $14 million, so liabilities totalled $50 million. These figures resulted in a current ratio of 1.5 and a debt-to-equity ratio of 2.5:1.

Top management is considering the options available to the company. The bank that lent the $20 million due next March is willing to refinance the loan for another three years, but at a considerably higher interest rate of 15% plus a pledge of the company manufacturing facilities as collateral. Alternatively, the company could issue preferred shares with a cumulative dividend rate of 12%. The investment firm proposing this option also suggested that the dividend rate could be lowered to 10% if Thamesford added a provision to give the preferred shareholders the right to retract the shares at the issuance price (i.e., the company must redeem the shares if a shareholder demanded it). A third alternative is to issue common shares, although Thamesford's share price is understandably depressed under the circumstances.

Required:

Play the role of Thamesford's chief financial officer and analyze the three financing alternatives. Provide a recommendation to your CEO and board of directors.

CASE 3

Equities

(30 minutes)

Out2B Corporation is a public company that manufactures high quality camping and outdoor equipment. Out2B has been able to maintain its leadership position within the industry for many years due to its innovative products and aggressive marketing strategy.

You are John Quinn, the CFO of Out2B. It is now January 17, 2018, and you are in the process of closing the books for 2017. On January 24, there will be a meeting of the board of directors to discuss and to decide on the annual dividend. The dividend then will be announced the following day, and will be paid two weeks later. As the CFO, you will be presenting your recommendations for the annual dividend. It is a common practice to send the directors a short memo prior to the meeting with the recommendations you will be delivering during the meeting.

In preparation for your meeting, the employees of the accounting department have compiled the expected annual balance sheet and annual income statements, which are presented below:

Balance Sheet			
Current assets		**Current liabilities**	
Cash	$ 4,000,000	Accounts payable	$ 2,000,000
Accounts receivable	5,000,000	Provisions	3,000,000
Inventory	2,000,000	Short-term loan	2,000,000
Others	3,700,000	Others	2,000,000
Total current assets	14,700,000	Total current liabilities	9,000,000
Investments (market value)	7,000,000	Bonds Payable	16,000,000
Non-current assets		**Shareholders' equity**	
PP&E	10,500,000	Common stock	1,000,000
Intangible assets	3,500,000	Contributed surplus	4,900,000
Other assets	3,000,000	Retained earnings	7,800,000
Total non-current assets	17,000,000	Total shareholders' equity	13,700,000
Total assets	$38,700,000	Total liabilities and equity	$38,700,000

Income Statement	
Sales	$44,000,000
Cost of goods sold	29,400,000
Gross profit	14,600,000
Sales, general, and administration costs	6,000,000
Operating income before interest	8,600,000
Interest expenses	1,000,000
Income before tax	7,600,000
Income tax (30%)	2,300,000
Income after tax	$ 5,300,000

As part of your preparation, you have also collected some other relevant information:

- Last year, net income was $4.4 million and the firm distributed $3.3 million in cash dividends.
- The firm has two loan agreements (reported under "bonds payable") that require the firm to maintain at least $2.5 million in retained earnings and to maintain a debt-to-total assets ratio no higher than 0.7:1.
- There was no change in the number of outstanding shares during the year.
- Out2B has distributed dividends for many years, and as the profit increased over the years, dividends were increased as well.

Since you were appointed CFO only six months ago, this is your first significant interaction with the board of directors, and you want to impress them by providing them with solid recommendations.

Required:

a. What is the maximum amount that can be currently distributed as cash dividend?
b. What are important issues that may influence your decision? How are those issues going to affect your recommendations?
c. Given your answers in (a) and (b), write a short memo to the board of directors with your recommendations.
d. Prepare any journal entries that are related to your recommendations.

Bbourdages/Fotolia

CHAPTER 14

Complex Financial Instruments

LEARNING OBJECTIVES

After studying this chapter, you should be able to:

L.O. 14-1. Describe the nature of standard financial instruments, derivatives, and compound financial instruments, and identify when transactions involve such instruments.

L.O. 14-2. Apply the accounting standards for compound financial instruments from the perspective of the issuer.

L.O. 14-3. Apply the accounting standards for employee stock compensation plans from the perspective of the issuer.

L.O. 14-4. Apply the accounting standards for derivatives.

L.O. 14-5. Apply the accounting standards for hedges and identify situations in which hedge accounting may be appropriate.

CPA competencies addressed in this chapter:

1.1.2 Evaluates the appropriateness of the basis of financial accounting (Level B)

1.2.1 Develops or evaluates appropriate accounting policies and procedures (Level B)

1.2.2 Evaluates treatment for routine transactions (Level A)
k. Financial instruments

1.2.3 Evaluates treatment for non-routine transactions (Level B)
d. Fair value and cash flow hedges

1.2.4 Analyzes treatment for complex events or transactions (Level C)

1.3.2 Prepares routine financial statement note disclosure (Level B)

1.4.1 Analyzes complex financial statement note disclosure (Level C)

As every school-aged child knows (or should know), Christopher Columbus "discovered" the Americas in 1492 while searching for a westerly route from Europe to Asia. Venturing across the oceans at the time was dangerous at best, and unimaginably more treacherous when done over territory that was literally uncharted. Such voyages were also expensive. If you were Columbus asking Queen Isabella of Spain to finance this expedition, what would you propose? If you were the Queen, what proposal would you accept?

In this scenario, there are immense information problems. How far would the ships have to travel westward to reach any type of land? Columbus had some crude estimates, and the Queen and her counsel knew even less. How large should the ships be; how many ships should be sent; and what quantity of supplies should be provided? These all factor into the financing required, and there was no assurance that the Queen would recover any of these funds. More funds can increase the chances of success to some extent, but what if the Queen advanced too much to Columbus—would that just increase her losses? Would Columbus misspend the funds or perhaps even run off with the bounty to some unknown land? These questions suggest that the problems of adverse selection and moral hazard are pervasive in this situation.

While the voyage of Christopher Columbus is unique in many respects, the financing problem is not. Consider a company mining for gold. Funds are required for geological tests to determine whether there are gold deposits at a particular site. If the results are promising, the company will require further funds to drill ore samples to determine whether the ore concentration is high enough. The final stages of ore extraction and refinement also require a lot of equipment and financing. How much should investors advance to a gold mining company? Too much financing and the funds could be wasted on unpromising projects. Too little financing and a good project may never be completed.

14 CONTENTS

A. INTRODUCTION 691
B. TYPES OF FINANCIAL INSTRUMENTS 692
1. Basic financial assets, financial liabilities, and equity instruments 692
2. Derivative financial instruments 693
3. Compound financial instruments 695
C. ACCOUNTING FOR COMPOUND FINANCIAL INSTRUMENTS 696
1. Initial measurement 697
2. Subsequent measurement 698
3. Derecognition of debt prior to maturity or conversion into equity 700
4. Derecognition of debt through exercise of the conversion option 703
5. Derecognition of debt at maturity 705
D. ACCOUNTING FOR WARRANTS 705
1. Initial measurement 705
2. Subsequent measurement 706
3. Derecognition through exercise of the warrants 706
4. Derecognition when the warrants expire 707
E. ACCOUNTING FOR STOCK COMPENSATION PLANS 707
1. Employee stock option plans (ESOPs) 708
2. Stock appreciation rights (SARs) 710
F. PRESENTATION AND DISCLOSURE 716
G. SUBSTANTIVE DIFFERENCES BETWEEN RELEVANT IFRS AND ASPE 716
H. APPENDIX: DERIVATIVES AND HEDGING 717
1. Derivatives—Forwards, futures, and swaps 717
2. Accounting for derivatives 719
3. Hedging overview 720
4. Hedge accounting 722
5. Fair value hedges 722
6. Cash flow hedges 724
I. SUMMARY 726
J. ANSWERS TO CHECKPOINT QUESTIONS 726
K. GLOSSARY 727
L. REFERENCES 728
M. PROBLEMS 729
N. MINI-CASES 748

One solution is to provide financing in stages—supplying an initial amount but committing to provide further funds if the project is successful (or at least looks increasingly promising). Such staged financing can be accomplished by the use of compound financial instruments, such as convertible debt and stock warrants issued along with shares, which automatically result in additional financing when a project proves to be successful. How do we account for such compound financial instruments? How do we account for financial instruments other than a simple liability or equity instrument?

A. INTRODUCTION

Accounting for financial instruments is complex. The accounting standards for financial instruments have been almost continuously deliberated and re-deliberated for over two decades, with frequent revisions during that time. The frequent modifications reflect the rapid changes in the field of finance, which seems to know no bounds when it comes to the creation of new financial instruments. Many of these new financial instruments are innovative and meet the needs of financial market participants. However, not all financial innovations are beneficial, as amply demonstrated during the financial crisis of 2008 (see Chapter 1 for a discussion of this crisis). In particular, some financial innovations are designed to circumvent accounting standards to achieve desired results for accounting purposes. For this reason, it is important to understand the economic substance of each financial instrument so that the reported results ultimately reflect the transaction's substance rather than its form.

This chapter will first look at the economic characteristics of different financial instruments before turning to the accounting for these instruments. We will focus on the central ideas in the accounting standards for financial instruments. These fundamentals will be applicable for enterprises applying IFRS or ASPE. More advanced study is required for a full appreciation of all the requirements in IFRS, which are contained in IAS 39 (recognition and measurement), IAS 32 (presentation), and IFRS 7 (disclosures).

B. TYPES OF FINANCIAL INSTRUMENTS

L.O. 14-1. Describe the nature of standard financial instruments, derivatives, and compound financial instruments, and identify when transactions involve such instruments.

This section identifies and distinguishes among the different types of financial instruments. First, we review the relatively basic financial assets, financial liabilities, and equity instruments. We then discuss derivatives. Finally, we look at compound financial instruments, which comprise more than one basic financial instrument or derivative in some combination.

1. Basic financial assets, financial liabilities, and equity instruments

Previous chapters in this text discussed the three basic types of financial instruments:

- Chapter 7 discussed financial assets;
- Chapters 11 and 12 discussed financial liabilities; and
- Chapter 13 discussed equity instruments.

As Chapter 7 notes, a holder of a financial asset has a counterparty that has either a financial liability or an equity instrument. An investor holding a bond has a financial asset, while the bond issuer has a financial liability. An investor holding a share has a financial asset, while the company that issued the share has an equity instrument outstanding. As discussed in those chapters, we can summarize the accounting for these financial instruments as follows:

Exhibit 14-1 Summary of accounting for simple financial assets, financial liabilities, and equity instruments

Financial assets can be accounted for using	*Financial liabilities can be accounted for using*	*Equity instruments are accounted for using*
■ consolidation for controlled subsidiaries ■ a modified form of proportionate consolidation for joint operations ■ equity method for joint ventures ■ equity method for associates ■ fair value through profit or loss for investments in financial assets at FVPL* ■ fair value through OCI** for investments in financial assets at FVOCI*** ■ amortized cost for investments in financial assets at amortized cost	■ amortized cost (most financial liabilities for non-financial companies) ■ fair value through profit or loss for liabilities designated at FVPL*	■ historical cost

*FVPL = fair value through profit or loss
**OCI = other comprehensive income
***FVOCI = fair value through other comprehensive income

Since other chapters have dealt with these basic financial instruments in some depth, there is no need to repeat that material here. Instead, we will proceed with other types of financial instruments.

2. Derivative financial instruments

A **derivative** is a financial instrument that is derived from some other underlying quantity. That **underlying quantity** can be the value of an asset, an index value, or an event. (In technical jargon, finance and accounting professionals will often use the expedient but grammatically incorrect term "underlying," which omits the required noun.) For example, a derivative can be based on the price of a share, the value of the Toronto Stock Exchange Index, or the exchange rate between Canadian and US dollars.

derivative A financial instrument that is derived from some other underlying quantity.

underlying quantity The value of an asset, an index value, or an event that helps determine the value of a derivative.

The underlying quantity need not be financial in nature. For example, a derivative can be based on the minimum temperature in Florida in January. Such a derivative can be useful to orange producers, who face large losses when temperatures drop below freezing. If orange growers are able to buy derivatives that pay them when the temperature drops below zero degrees Celsius, they would be able to reduce their losses under those circumstances. For a reasonable price, there will be other people willing to take on the other side of that derivative contract. Thus, even though there is little we can do about the weather, financial innovation allows for risk sharing through the use of derivatives.

Having described what a derivative is, we will briefly explore why entities buy and sell derivatives before describing some of their more common forms. Fundamentally, parties enter into derivative contracts for two reasons: to hedge or to speculate.

Hedging involves identifying a risk and trying to mitigate that risk by using derivative contracts (or possibly other means). For example, a Canadian manufacturer that purchases inventory from a US supplier on credit is subject to the risk that the US dollar may strengthen (appreciate) against the Canadian dollar between the time the order is placed and when the payable is settled. If this occurs, the Canadian firm's inventory will cost more in Canadian dollars than originally expected, ultimately increasing its cost of goods sold and reducing profitability. The manufacturer can reduce the foreign exchange risk by entering into a derivative contract. For example, it can enter into a forward contract to buy US dollars at a future date at a specified exchange rate, effectively locking in its cost of inventory at the time of purchase.

Speculation is purposely taking on an identified risk with a view to making a profit. For instance, one can take a gamble that the exchange rate will move in his/her favour by entering into a forward exchange agreement. In the manufacturer example above, the counterparty to the forward contract is betting that the US dollar will weaken (depreciate) against the Canadian dollar. If this counterparty is not hedging an exchange risk exposure, then it is speculating. Now assume that the forward contract calls for the speculator to deliver US$100,000 in one month's time at a rate of US$1 to C$1.02, or C$102,000. If the US dollar weakens and the spot rate changes to US$1 = C$0.99, the speculator will make a profit of C$3,000 (buy at the spot rate and sell under the forward agreement—$100,000 × [$1.02 – $0.99]). Of course, if the US dollar strengthens in the intervening period the speculator will lose money.

Below, we discuss the nature of options and warrants, deferring discussion of forwards, futures, and swaps to the appendix of this chapter.

a. Options

option A derivative contract that gives the holder the right, but not the obligation, to buy or sell an underlying financial instrument at a specified price. A **call option** gives the right to buy, whereas a **put option** provides the right to sell.

An **option** contract gives the holder the right, but not the obligation, to buy or sell something at a specified price. The most common type of option is a call option, which gives the holder the *right to acquire* an underlying instrument at a pre-specified price

out-of-the-money When the value of the underlying instrument in an option contract is unfavourable to the holder exercising the option compared with letting the option expire. In the case of a call option, this is when the underlying price is lower than the strike price; for a put option, it is when the underlying price is higher than the strike price.

in-the-money When the value of the underlying instrument in an option contract is favourable to the holder exercising the option compared with letting the option expire. In the case of a call option, this occurs when the underlying price exceeds the strike price; for a put option, it is when the underlying price is below the strike price.

intrinsic value of an option In a call option, the greater of zero and $(S-K)$, which is the difference between the market price and the strike price.

within a defined period of time. The pre-specified price is called the *exercise price* or *strike price*. A put option has the opposite characteristic, giving the holder the *right to sell* at a specified price. Other more exotic options are also possible. We focus our discussion on the call option because it is the most frequently encountered. For concreteness, we will assume that the underlying instrument is a share of common stock.

The option holder's decision to exercise an option is dependent on the difference between the exercise price, which is fixed, and the market price of the underlying instrument. For a call option on a share, if the market price of the share (S) is less than the exercise price (K), the option is **out-of-the-money** and, of course, the holder of the option would not exercise the option. On the other hand, if the market price exceeds the strike price ($S > K$), the call option is **in-the-money** and the option holder may choose to exercise the option, but need not do so.

The value of an option (V) can be decomposed into two parts: its intrinsic value and its time value. The **intrinsic value of a call option** is the greater of zero and $(S-K)$, the difference between the market price and the strike price. When $S = K$, the intrinsic value is exactly zero. Graphically, the value of call and put options prior to expiration can be depicted as shown in Exhibit 14-2.

Exhibit 14-2 Graphical depictions of option values and their components prior to expiration

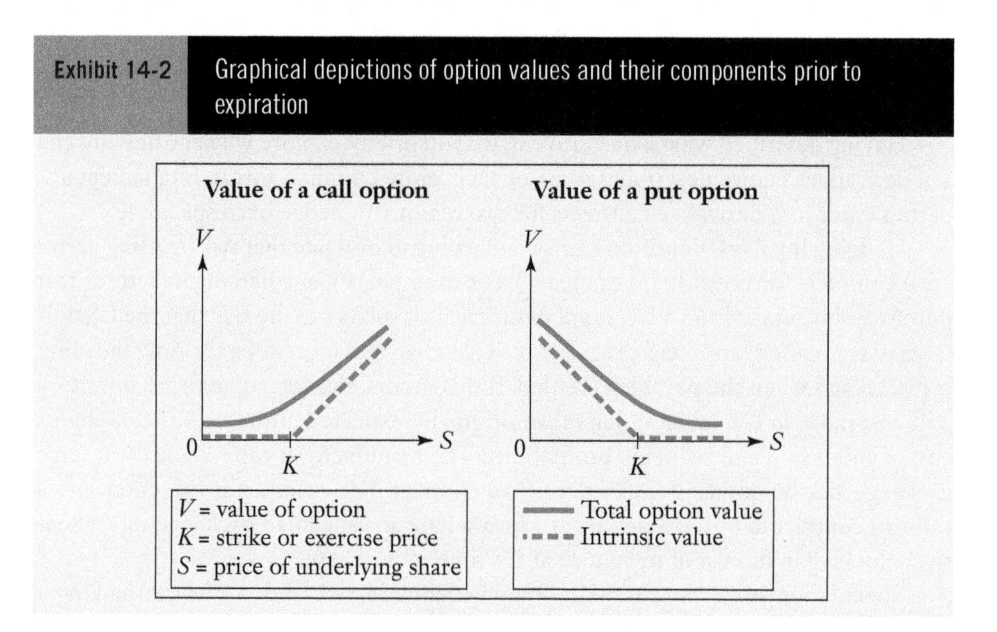

time value of an option The portion of an option's value that reflects the probability that the future market price of the underlying instrument will exceed the strike price.

As the graph for a call option shows, above the strike price K, the intrinsic value of the option increases 1:1 with the share price S. The **time value of an option** reflects the probability that the future market price of the underlying instrument will exceed the strike price. The time value increases with the length of time to expiration and the volatility of the underlying instrument (such as the share price). The time value is always positive until the option expires, so the total value of an unexpired option is always greater than the intrinsic value. At expiration, there is no longer any time value left, so total value equals the intrinsic value.

In contrast to a call, the put option's intrinsic value increases when the underlying share price declines below the strike price because a put allows the holder to sell at the strike price. For example, if the strike price $K = \$10$ and the underlying share price $S = \$6$, then a holder of a put can buy a share for \$6 and exercise the put option to sell the share at \$10, for a profit of \$4.

employee stock option An option a company issues to its employees giving them the right to buy shares in the enterprise at a pre-specified price.

An important type of call option is an **employee stock option**, which a company issues to its employees, giving them the right to buy shares in the enterprise at a pre-specified price. Companies often use employee stock options as a form of compensation and to reduce the moral hazard inherent in an employer–employee relationship. (See Chapter 1 for more on moral hazard.)

More generally, options on a company's shares can be issued not only by the company itself, but also by others outside the company. For larger public companies, there are many call and put options written on their share prices. For example, in mid-October 2017, when the Royal Bank of Canada's common shares were trading for around $101, there were about 400 different call and put options with maturities ranging from October 2017 to January 2020 and strike prices ranging from $38 to $120.

b. Warrants

Warrants provide the holder with the right, but not the obligation, to buy a company's shares at a specified price over a specified period of time. Thus, warrants are similar to call options. The main differences are that warrants are issued only by the company whose shares are the underlying instrument. Compared with options, warrants also tend to have longer times to maturity (typically three to ten years), and they tend to be issued in combination with other financial instruments such as bonds, preferred shares, and common shares.

warrant A right, but not the obligation, to buy a share at a specified price over a specified period of time. Can be considered a type of call option.

3. Compound financial instruments

As introduced in the opening vignette about the voyages of Columbus, sometimes companies require financial instruments that are more than just debt or equity. There are situations when it is beneficial to commit to staged financing, and this can often be accomplished with **compound financial instruments**—those that have more than one financial instrument component.

compound financial instruments Those financial instruments with more than one financial instrument component.

For instance, a frequently used compound financial instrument is a convertible bond. Typically, these bonds allow the holder to convert the bond into shares at a specific conversion rate. For example, a convertible bond might specify that the holder can convert each $1,000 bond (where $1,000 refers to the face value of the bond) into 50 common shares. Another common compound financial instrument is the issuance of warrants attached to shares or bonds. For example, a common share may be issued for $20 per share and include a warrant to purchase another share within five years at $30 per share.

The conversion feature and the warrants are commonly referred to as "sweeteners" that enhance the attractiveness of an offering of bonds or shares. However, that description does not adequately explain why companies use these compound financial instruments. If these additions "sweeten" an offer, why don't all companies issue bonds and shares with these additional features?

A more compelling explanation is that these compound financial instruments solve problems of information asymmetry. A company that issues common shares sends a negative signal to investors, because the share issuance indicates a lack of confidence in the future prospects of the company. If management were more confident, it would instead use internally generated cash flow, issue debt, or perhaps issue preferred shares. Indeed, announcements of common share issuances are usually greeted with significant declines in the share price. As a result, companies issue shares as a last resort; adverse selection poses a significant cost to issuing equity.

A compound financial instrument such as a convertible bond alleviates this adverse selection problem. With such a bond, the company is initially issuing debt, which does not send the negative signal that share issuances do. Investors who hold these bonds will exercise the conversion option only when it is beneficial to them; that is, when converting to common shares becomes more valuable than holding the debt. Thus, conversion would occur when the firm performs well. The conversion decreases debt and increases equity, thereby decreasing leverage and increasing debt capacity. Should the company wish to bring in additional financing at this point, it can do so by issuing additional debt. Through this entire process, the company did not have to directly issue shares, which would have sent a negative signal to the market. Instead, it issued shares indirectly via the conversion of bonds into shares.

A similar thought process can explain the usefulness of a debt or an equity instrument with warrants attached. Holders of the warrants would exercise the warrants only if they are in-the-money, which is when the company is doing well. Upon exercise, the warrant holders contribute to the firm an amount of cash equal to the exercise price. Just as for convertible bonds, the company increases equity not by issuing shares directly, but by issuing shares indirectly via investors exercising their warrants to purchase shares.

THRESHOLD CONCEPT
INFORMATION ASYMMETRY

Another useful function of these compound financial instruments is that they provide the company with funds in more than one stage, which is helpful at alleviating moral hazard. Investors do not want to give too much money to management when outcomes are highly uncertain, because management may misspend the funds. At the same time, the conversion option and warrants are a commitment from investors to provide additional funding—but only if the company performs well. If the company performs poorly, the conversion option or warrant will be out-of-the-money and investors will choose to not exercise these rights.

Compound financial instruments are suitable and therefore commonly used when operational uncertainty is relatively high, such as for early-stage companies and mining companies. In fact, some 200 companies have tradable warrants listed on the TSX Venture Exchange, which specializes in early-stage public companies and those in the mining sector.

CHECKPOINT **CP14-1**

What is a derivative?

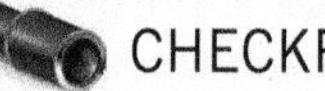

CHECKPOINT **CP14-2**

Briefly describe two reasons why entities buy and sell derivatives.

CHECKPOINT **CP14-3**

Briefly describe an option. What is the difference between a call option and a put option?

CHECKPOINT **CP14-4**

How do warrants differ from call options?

CHECKPOINT **CP14-5**

Briefly describe a compound financial instrument.

C. ACCOUNTING FOR COMPOUND FINANCIAL INSTRUMENTS

The previous section discussed the nature of compound financial instruments. Now we turn to how we treat these instruments for accounting purposes. These compound financial instruments often involve one or more equity components. As noted in Chapter 13, IFRS is not specific regarding which equity account should be used. Thus, the following discussion uses the more specific terminology available in ASPE for equity accounts, as described in Chapter 13.

1. Initial measurement

L.O. 14-2. Apply the accounting standards for compound financial instruments from the perspective of the issuer.

Compound financial instruments include at least two components: (i) the underlying financial instrument and (ii) the investors' option to convert the financial instrument purchased into a different type of financial instrument. If the components of the compound instrument are all equity, for example a preferred share that is convertible into a common share, the component parts need not be accounted for separately. Rather, the journal entry to record the transaction would normally include a debit to cash or other asset received and a credit to preferred shares. The conversion option would then be disclosed in accordance with IAS 1 paragraph 79. If, however, the compound financial instrument includes the ability to convert debt into equity, the enterprise needs to account for each component separately. For example, when a bond is convertible into common shares, IAS 32 paragraph 29 requires that the entity separately recognize the bond (debt) and the conversion option (equity) in its financial statements.

When a compound financial instrument includes both debt and an equity, the question arises as to how one should allocate amounts to each of the two or more components. There are three reasonable methods:

1. *Proportional method:* Estimate the fair values of all components and allocate them proportionally to all components. This approach is similar to that used to allocate the cost of bundled purchases of property, plant, and equipment discussed in Chapter 8. The proportional method is also known as the relative fair value method.
2. *Incremental method:* Estimate the fair value of all but one of the components and allocate the balance (the residual) to the remaining component. For compound financial instruments that are comprised of both debt and equity, paragraph 32 of IAS 32 requires that the debt component be initially recognized at its fair value with the residual of the consideration received ascribed to the equity component. The incremental method is also known as the residual value method.
3. *Zero common equity method:* No value is ascribed to the common equity component. Rather, 100% of the fair value of the consideration received is reported as a liability.

IFRS requires method (2). ASPE permits both methods (2) and (3).[1]

Exhibit 14-3 illustrates accounting for the sale of compound financial instruments.

Exhibit 14-3a Accounting for the sale of compound financial instruments—Example

Facts: $100,000 of five-year, 6% convertible bonds that pay interest semi-annually are issued (sold) on January 1, 2018. The bonds are sold to yield a 5% return to the investors. At the option of the investor, each $1,000 bond may be converted into 50 common shares any time after December 31, 2021. The market rate for similar bonds without a conversion option is 6%.

Required:

1. Record the issuance of the bonds using the incremental method.
2. Record the issuance of the bonds using the zero common equity method.

For the incremental method, we need to determine the price of the bonds that include the conversion option and the price of the comparable bonds that do not include the option. In this instance, the bonds without a conversion option will sell at par—$100,000—as the market rate equals the coupon rate. The actual bond with the conversion option sells for $104,376, as calculated in Exhibit 14-3b.

[1] US GAAP requires method (3).

Exhibit14-3b	Computation of sales price—convertible bonds
Maturity value	$100,000
Interest payments	$3,000 ($100,000 × 6% / 2)
Number of payments	10 (5 × 2)
Effective rate (yield) per period	2.5% (5% / 2)
Price paid for the bond	$104,376 as per the computations below
Calculation of sales price when the effective rate of interest is known:	
Using a BA II Plus financial calculator:	
10 **N** 2.5 **I/Y** 3000 **PMT** 100000 **FV** **CPT** **PV** = −104,376 (rounded)	

The next step is to allocate the purchase price. Using the incremental method, a liability is recognized for the debt element. The debt is initially measured at the fair value of a similar liability without a conversion option, less any applicable transaction costs. As set out above, the fair value of the debt without the conversion feature is $100,000. The $4,330 difference between the sales price and this amount is allocated to the conversion option ($104,376 − $100,000 = $4,376). Having determined the value of the components, the journal entry to record the issuance can be prepared.

Exhibit 14-3c	Journal entry to record issuance of bonds—incremental method (IFRS and ASPE)	
Dr. Cash	104,376	
Cr. Bonds payable		100,000
Cr. Contributed surplus—conversion option		4,376

To prepare the journal entry for the zero common equity method as permitted under ASPE, we only need to know the sales price of the financial instrument—$104,376.

Exhibit 14-3d	Journal entry to record issuance of bonds—zero common equity method (ASPE)	
Dr. Cash	104,376	
Cr. Bonds payable		104,376

2. Subsequent measurement

Once a compound financial instrument has been separated into its components, the accounting for each component follows the standards applicable to that component. Enterprises would report a financial liability for a convertible bond at amortized cost; it would report the contributed surplus for the conversion option in equity at historical cost. This is consistent with how other financial liabilities and equity were measured in Chapters 12 and 13, respectively.

Refer back to the incremental method journal entry in Exhibit 14-3c and assume that no bonds were redeemed in the interim. On December 31, 2021, the issuing entity would continue to report a liability of $100,000[2] for the bonds and equity of $4,376 for the conversion option as there is no premium or discount to amortize.

2. Accrued interest of $6,000 would also be reported in the normal manner.

Transaction costs that directly relate to the issuance of compound financial instruments are allocated to debt and equity on a pro-rata basis in accordance with paragraph 38 of IAS 32. Briefly:

1. Calculate the fair value of an equivalent bond without the conversion feature.
2. Recognize a bond liability for the fair value of the equivalent bond determined in step 1, less a pro-rata share of the transaction costs.
3. Allocate the difference between the fair value of the compound financial instrument and the fair value of the equivalent bond without the conversion to the conversion option.
4. Recognize contributed surplus—conversion option for the amount determined in step 3 less a pro-rata share of the transaction costs.

This process is illustrated in Exhibit 14-4.

Exhibit 14-4a Accounting for the sale of compound financial instruments—Example

Facts: $1,000,000 of 10-year, 6% convertible bonds that pay interest semi-annually are issued (sold) on January 1, 2018. At the option of the investor, each $1,000 bond may be converted into 50 common shares any time after December 31, 2021. The sales proceeds realized were $1,200,000 less a $50,000 transaction fee. The market rate for similar bonds without the conversion feature is 5%. The issuing corporation reports its financial results in accordance with IFRS.

Required:

1. Allocate the sales proceeds to the liability and equity components of the convertible bond.
2. Record the issuance of the bonds.
2. Determine the effective interest rate per period on the bond liability.

Exhibit 14-4b illustrates how to allocate the sales proceeds received from the sale of a convertible bond in the presence of issuance costs.

Exhibit 14-4b Allocation of sales proceeds of a convertible bond with transaction costs

Maturity value of bonds	$1,000,000	
Gross sales proceeds	$1,200,000	
Less: Transaction costs	50,000	
Net sales proceeds	$1,150,000	
Semi-annual coupon rate (6% / 2)	3%	
Semi-annual payment	$ 30,000	
Yield on non-convertible bonds (5% / 2)	2.5%	
Number of periods to maturity (10 × 2)	20	
PV of stand-alone bond at issuance before transaction costs	$1,077,946	
Using a financial calculator: 20 **N** 2.5 **I/Y** 30000 **PMT** 1000000 **FV** **CPT** **PV** → = −1,077,946 (rounded)		
Residual value of conversion option before transaction costs	**$**	%
Gross sales proceeds	$1,200,000	
Less: PV of stand-alone bond at issuance before transaction costs	1,077,946	89.83%
Conversion rights	$ 122,054	10.17%
		100.00%

(Continued)

Exhibit 14-4b Continued

Allocation of transaction costs	$ 50,000	
To liability	44,915	89.83%
To equity	5,085	10.17%
	$ 50,000	
Allocation of sale proceeds		
Bond liability	$1,077,946	
Less: Transaction costs	44,915	
Net amount allocated to bond liability	$1,033,031	$1,033,031
Contributed surplus	$ 122,054	
Less: Transaction costs	5,085	
Net amount allocated to contributed surplus	$ 116,969	116,969
		$1,150,000

Once the sales proceeds have been allocated, the journal entries can be readily constructed as follows:

Exhibit 14-4c Journal entry to record issuance of bonds with transaction costs

Journal entry on issuance		
Dr. Cash ($1,200,000 − $50,000)	1,150,000	
Cr. Bonds payable		1,033,031
Cr. Contributed surplus—conversion option		116,969

Note that the transaction costs for the two components are accounted for in the same manner as illustrated in Chapters 12 and 13. Recall that in Chapter 12, transaction costs for other financial liabilities were deducted from the bond liability and then subsequently charged to interest expense through application of the effective interest method. In Chapter 13, one option for accounting for transaction costs was the offset method. Under this method, the costs of issuing the securities were deducted from the related equity account.

The effective interest rate must be calculated to subsequently measure interest expense as demonstrated below:

Exhibit 14-4d Calculation of effective interest rate per period

Using a financial calculator: **+/−** 1033031 **PV** 20 **N** 30000 **PMT** 1000000 **FV** **CPT** **I/Y**
➜ = 2.7824% (rounded) *per period*

3. Derecognition of debt prior to maturity or conversion into equity

When an entity repurchases a convertible bond and retires it before maturity or conversion, the accounting treatment depends on whether the entity initially measured the debt and equity components using the incremental method or the zero common equity method.[3]

[3] Recall that the incremental method is required by IFRS but that under ASPE the entity can elect to initially measure the component parts of the convertible bond using either the incremental method or the zero common equity method.

a. Incremental method used to initially measure the convertible bond components (IFRS and ASPE)

If the incremental method was used to initially measure the convertible bond components, both IFRS and ASPE require that the consideration paid to extinguish the debt be allocated to the debt and equity components on the same basis that was used to allocate the sales price received.[4] Recall that the bond liability was initially recognized at the fair value of the stand-alone debt instrument and that the difference between the sales price of the convertible bond and the fair value of the debt component was recognized in equity as contributed surplus—conversion option. From a practical perspective, this means that:

- The fair value of the stand-alone debt when repurchased will be allocated to the debt component and the residual amount paid will be allocated to equity.
- The difference between the book value and the fair value of the debt is recognized as a gain or loss on derecognition of the liability reported on the income statement.
- The consideration paid that was allocated to equity is recognized in equity. As this is a capital transaction, the loss, if any, will be charged directly to equity, rather than flow through the income statement.[5] If the consideration allocated to equity on derecognition exceeds the amount originally credited to the contributed surplus—conversion option at recognition—then the excess is charged to retained earnings.[6]

Exhibit 14-5 illustrates the application of the forgoing.

Exhibit 14-5a Accounting for the derecognition of compound financial instruments prior to maturity or conversion—Incremental method example

Facts: The amortized cost of convertible bonds on repurchase date was $535,000 including accrued interest, and the contributed surplus—conversion option was $25,000. The fair value of the debt without the conversion option on repurchase date was estimated to be $520,000.

Required:

1. Assume that the bonds were repurchased on the open market for $580,000 and immediately cancelled. Prepare the journal entry to record the derecognition of the convertible bond.
2. Assume that the bonds were repurchased on the open market for $540,000 and immediately cancelled. Prepare the journal entry to record the derecognition of the convertible bond.

Exhibit 14-5b illustrates how to allocate the consideration paid to redeem convertible bonds prior to maturity to the debt and equity components.

Exhibit 14-5b Journal entry to record the derecognition of the convertible bond

Repurchased for $580,000		
Dr. Bonds payable	535,000	
Dr. Contributed surplus—conversion option	25,000	
Dr. Retained earnings[(a)]	35,000	
Cr. Gain on derecognition of bonds[(b)]		15,000
Cr. Cash		580,000

(Continued)

[4] See AG 33 and AG 34 of IAS 32 of Part I and paragraph 3586.A36(b) of Part II of the CPA Canada Handbook—Accounting.

[5] Given the requisite accounting treatment, when debt is retired prior to maturity or conversion, there can never be a gain on the equity component.

[6] As established in Chapter 13, IFRS provides little guidance with respect to specific categories of equity to be used for transactions relating to contributed capital. Thus, in this chapter, we use the account titles commonly seen in ASPE.

Exhibit 14-5b Continued

Calculations:

(a) \$580,000 total consideration − \$520,000 fair value of stand-alone debt = \$60,000; \$60,000 − \$25,000 contributed surplus = \$35,000 loss to be charged directly to retained earnings
(b) \$520,000 fair value − \$535,000 amortized cost = \$15,000 gain

Repurchased for \$540,000

Dr. Bonds payable	535,000	
Dr. Contributed surplus—conversion option	20,000	
Cr. Gain on derecognition of bonds(c)		15,000
Cr. Cash		540,000

Calculations:

(c) \$520,000 fair value − \$535,000 amortized cost = \$15,000 gain

b. Zero common equity method used to initially measure the convertible bond components (ASPE)

If the zero common equity method was used to initially measure the convertible bond components, ASPE requires that the consideration paid to extinguish the debt be allocated first to debt, to the carrying amount (amortized cost) of the debt including accrued interest, with the balance, if any, recognized in equity.[7] From a practical perspective this means that:

- When the cash paid to redeem the debt is less than the amortized cost of the debt, a gain on derecognition will be recognized in net income.
- When the cash paid to redeem the debt is more than the amortized cost of the debt, the excess is charged to retained earnings. Note that the loss is charged directly to equity, rather than flowing through the income statement.

Exhibit 14-6 illustrates the application of the forgoing.

Exhibit 14-6a Accounting for the derecognition of compound financial instruments prior to maturity or conversion—Zero common equity example

Facts: The amortized cost of convertible bonds on repurchase date was \$560,000 including accrued interest. The fair value of the debt without the conversion option on the repurchase date was estimated to be \$520,000.

Required:

1. Assume that the bonds were repurchased on the open market for \$580,000 and immediately cancelled. Prepare the journal entry to record the derecognition of the convertible bond.
2. Assume that the bonds were repurchased on the open market for \$540,000 and immediately cancelled. Prepare the journal entry to record the derecognition of the convertible bond.

Exhibit 14-6b illustrates how to allocate the consideration paid to redeem convertible bonds prior to maturity when the debt and equity components were initially measured using the zero common equity approach available under ASPE.

7. See paragraph 3586.A36(a) of Part II of the CPA Canada Handbook—Accounting.

Exhibit 14-6b Journal entry to record the derecognition of the convertible bond

Repurchased for $580,000		
Dr. Bonds payable	560,000	
Dr. Retained earnings	20,000	
Cr. Cash		580,000
Repurchased for $540,000		
Dr. Bonds payable	560,000	
Cr. Gain on derecognition of bonds		20,000
Cr. Cash		540,000

4. Derecognition of debt through exercise of the conversion option

Conceptually, there are two ways to record the conversion of bonds or preferred shares into an equity instrument (most often common shares): the book value and the market value methods.

The book value method records the common shares at the current book value of the preferred shares or the convertible bond and related contributed surplus; no gain or loss is recorded. In contrast, the market value method records the shares at their fair value at date of conversion, recording a loss[8] for the difference between the market value and the book value as determined above.

IFRS and ASPE both mandate the use of the book value method. In particular, IAS 32 indicates the following in its application guidance:

> AG32 On conversion of a convertible instrument at maturity, the entity derecognizes the liability component and recognizes it as equity. The original equity component remains as equity (although it may be transferred from one line item within equity to another). There is no gain or loss on conversion at maturity.[9]

In this paragraph, the word "maturity" should be interpreted to include the date of exercise, which could be before the expiry date of the conversion option. That is, the act of conversion by the investor causes the instrument to mature.

Similarly, the appendix of ASPE 3856 provides the following guidance:

> A34 When an option to convert a financial liability to equity is exercised and the issuer settles the obligation by issuing shares in accordance with the original terms of the instrument, the carrying amount of the equity element, if any, plus the carrying amount of the liability element (including any accrued but unpaid interest), are transferred to share capital. No gain or loss is recognized on this form of conversion because it is according to the original terms of the instrument.[10]

---

8. There is unlikely to be a gain in such instances. Investors exercise their conversion rights only when it is to their own benefit, meaning that the market price of shares must be high relative to the bond value for the conversion to occur.

9. Copyright © 2012 IFRS Foundation.

10. ASPE at a glance Section 3856—Financial Instruments 2011, with permission Chartered Professional Accountants of Canada, Toronto, Canada.

Continuing on with the incremental method example in Exhibit 14-3, assume that the bondholders all elected to convert their bonds on January 2, 2022. The journal entry to record this exercise of warrants using the book value method is illustrated in Exhibit 14-7. Note that the amount credited to the common stock account represents the book value of the bonds and the contributed surplus that arose upon recognition of the compound financial instrument.

Exhibit 14-7 Journal entry to record the conversion of bonds—incremental method

Dr. Bonds payable	100,000	
Dr. Contributed surplus—conversion option	4,376	
Cr. Common stock		104,376

Contrast this result with that of the conversion of the convertible bond accounted for with the zero common equity method in Exhibit 14-8:

Exhibit 14-8 Journal entry to record the conversion of bonds—zero common equity method

Dr. Bonds payable	104,376	
Cr. Common stock		104,376

To further illustrate the application of the book value method, suppose Dante Corp. issued convertible bonds with a face value of $10 million in 2018, and the share price at this time was $15. Each $1,000 bond can be converted into 50 shares. In 2022, the company's stock price increased significantly to $25, such that investors found it attractive to convert all the bonds to shares. (The 50 shares converted from each $1,000 bond would be worth 50 × $25 = $1,250.) At the time of conversion, we assume Dante's account balances to be as follows:

Exhibit 14-9 Accounts prior to bond conversion for Dante Corp. ($000's)

Bond payable face value	$10,000 Cr
Bond discount[11]	1,000 Dr
Bond payable net of bond discount	9,000 Cr
Contributed surplus—convertible bond	2,000 Cr
Total book value of convertible bond	$11,000 Cr

The conversion would be recorded as follows:

Exhibit 14-10 Book value method for bond conversion of Dante Corp. ($000's)

Book value method		
Dr. Bonds payable	9,000	
Dr. Contributed surplus—convertible bond	2,000	
Cr. Common stock		11,000

Conceptually, the book value method acknowledges the compound nature of the convertible bond and the reason for its issuance in the first place. The issuance of

[11] Note that there would normally be a discount on a convertible bond. The coupon rate is typically lower than the market rate of interest at the date of issuance; the addition of the conversion option adds value to the convertible bond, allowing the issuing company to lower the coupon rate.

shares at a below market price for the conversion is not a loss, per se, but rather the consequence of successful operations that have driven up the market price of common shares.

5. Derecognition of debt at maturity

The mechanics of derecognizing non-convertible bonds at maturity was demonstrated in Chapter 12. Recall that the procedure is to:

- Update the entity's records to account for interest expense, including the amortization of discounts or premiums up to the derecognition date.
- Record the derecognition of the liability. Note that the amortized cost of the bonds to be derecognized now equals their par value.
- Record the outflow of cash paid to redeem the bonds. As the amount paid to redeem the matured bond equals the par value of the bond, there will not be a gain or loss on derecognition.

The procedure to derecognize convertible bonds at maturity is substantially the same. The amount previously credited to contributed surplus—conversion option remains in equity. To facilitate disclosure, however, the company may choose to record a housekeeping journal entry removing the contributed surplus relating to the convertible bond by transferring the amount to contributed surplus—expired conversion option. Exhibit 14-11 illustrates the optional journal entry that could be passed, if the convertible bond in Exhibit 14-3 was not converted prior to maturity.

Exhibit 14-11 Optional journal entry to record the expiry of the conversion option

Dr. Contributed surplus—conversion option	4,376	
Cr. Contributed surplus—expired conversion option		4,376

This transfer of contributed surplus is cosmetic and does not changes total equity, however, recording the contributed surplus as expired provides meaningful information to users of the financial statements. Note that all increases and decreases to contributed surplus arising from convertible bonds are classified as contributed surplus-other. Recall from Chapter 13 that this is because they are not related to the proceeds of stock issued in excess of par, nor do they pertain to repurchase and resale transactions.

D. ACCOUNTING FOR WARRANTS

Warrants are typically offered in a bundled sale of financial instruments as described in Chapter 13. That is, the warrants will be packaged with other financial instruments such as common shares or a bond and sold as a unit for one price.

1. Initial measurement

The manner in which the sales proceeds of the bundle is allocated is determined by the nature of the securities included in the bundle. If the financial instruments include a debt instrument (e.g., a bond) and an equity instrument (e.g., a warrant), then the incremental method must be used to allocate the sales proceeds. If, however, all financial instruments in the bundle are equity instruments (e.g., a common share and a warrant), the entity may elect to allocate the sales proceeds using either the incremental method or the proportional method.

As the mechanics of both methods are discussed in Chapter 13 and revisited in Section C, subsection 1 of this chapter, they will not be repeated here; rather, the application of the methods are demonstrated in the example that follows.

Exhibit 14-12a Allocating the sales proceeds of a bundle of securities using the incremental method and proportional method—example

Facts: Callisto Corp. sold 500,000 packages of equity securities consisting of one common share and one warrant. Each package sold for $10; total proceeds were $5,000,000. At the time of sale, the market price of the common shares was $9.80 and the estimated fair value of the warrants was $0.30.

Required:

1. Assume that Callisto uses the incremental method to allocate the sales price of the securities to the two components. Prepare the journal entry to record the sale (issuance) of the packages of financial instruments.
2. Assume that Callisto uses the proportional method to allocate the sales price of the securities to the two components. Prepare the journal entry to record the sale (issuance) of the packages of financial instruments.

Exhibit 14-12b illustrates how to allocate the consideration received from the sale of the packages of equity securities to the component parts.

Exhibit 14-12b Journal entry to record the sale of a package of equity securities

Incremental method		
Dr. Cash	5,000,000	
Cr. Common shares (500,000 × $9.80)		4,900,000
Cr. Contributed surplus—warrants ($5,000,000 − $4,900,000)		100,000
Proportional method		
Dr. Cash	5,000,000	
Cr. Common shares[(a)]		4,851,485
Cr. Contributed surplus—warrants[(b)]		148,515

Calculations:

(a) $9.80 / ($9.80 + $0.30) × $5,000,000 = $4,851,485 (rounded)

(b) $0.30 / ($9.80 + $0.30) × $5,000,000 = $148,515 (rounded)

2. Subsequent measurement

Contributed surplus arising from the sale of warrants is subsequently measured at historical cost in the same manner as was demonstrated in Chapter 13 for other equity instruments.

3. Derecognition through exercise of the warrants

The accounting for this type of transaction is fairly straightforward. The company derecognizes the warrants when exercised and recognizes the shares issued and the cash received. For instance, suppose that the warrants issued by Callisto Corp. in Exhibit 14-12a each allow the investors to buy a common share in the company for $15, and that investors exercised 200,000 warrants when Callisto's share price increased to $18. Assuming that Callisto used the incremental method to initially allocate the sales price of the securities, the journal entry to record this exercise of warrants would be as follows:

Exhibit 14-13 Journal entry to record the exercise of warrants for Callisto Corp.

Dr. Cash (200,000 warrants × 1 share/warrant × $15/share)	3,000,000	
Dr. Contributed surplus—warrants	40,000	
(200,000 / 500,000 × $100,000 or		
200,000 warrants × $0.20/warrant)		
Cr. Common shares		3,040,000

Note that the market price of the shares issued is not considered when recognizing the issuance of the shares due to the exercise of the warrants. Rather, the common shares issued are initially measured at the sum of the cash received and the contributed surplus derecognized. This is an application of the book value method described in Section C, subsection 4 of this chapter.

4. Derecognition when the warrants expire

In the same manner as that demonstrated for unexercised conversion options on convertible bonds, the company may choose to record a housekeeping journal entry transferring the amount of the contributed surplus arising from the sale of the warrants to contributed surplus—expired warrants.

Assuming that the remainder of the warrants in Exhibit 14-12 were not exercised, the optional journal entry to record this expiry of the warrants would be as follows:

Exhibit 14-14 Optional journal entry to record the expiry of the warrants

Dr. Contributed surplus—warrants ($100,000 − $40,000)	60,000	
Cr. Contributed surplus—expired warrants		60,000

CHECKPOINT **CP14-6**

Briefly describe three potential methods to allocate values to the component parts of a compound financial instrument. Which method(s) are acceptable under IFRS? Under ASPE?

CHECKPOINT **CP14-7**

Briefly describe two potential methods to record the conversion of bonds or preferred shares into common equity. Which method(s) are acceptable under IFRS? Under ASPE?

E. ACCOUNTING FOR STOCK COMPENSATION PLANS

L.O. 14-3. Apply the accounting standards for employee stock compensation plans from the perspective of the issuer.

A common form of remuneration for employees is stock compensation plans. The underlying theory behind stock compensation plans is that if employees own shares in the company, then they will have a vested interest in working hard to ensure the company does well—thus aligning their interest with that of the other shareholders. As discussed in Section B, subsection 2a, this alignment of interests serves to reduce moral

THRESHOLD CONCEPT
INFORMATION ASYMMETRY

hazard. Stock compensation plans can represent a significant component of employees' total compensation packages, particularly for senior executives. Two common stock compensation plans are employee stock option plans (ESOPs) and stock appreciation rights (SARs). Similar to stock options, employees benefit from SARs when the actual stock price rises above a pre-determined benchmark price.

How should a company account for them? In this respect, there are three items that need to be addressed. First, how should we value ESOPs and SARs for financial reporting purposes? Second, over what period of time and on what basis should the cost be allocated? Third, how do we account for the exercise or expiration of the ESOPs and SARs?

1. Employee stock option plans (ESOPs)

The mechanics of how an ESOP works are much the same as that of purchased call stock options described in Section B, subsection 2. The primary differences between ESOPs and purchased exchange traded call options are illustrated below:

Exhibit 14-15 Differences between ESOPs and exchange traded call options

	ESOPs	Exchange traded call options
How obtained	Company grants as part of employee's compensation package at no cost to the employee.	Purchased on an exchange.
Selling	Cannot normally be resold to an outside party.	Can be resold to an outside party.
Restrictions on exercise	Typically, have vesting conditions that must be satisfied before the options can be exercised.	No restrictions on exercise.
Time to expiry	Typically, do not expire for a number of years.	Typically expire in a relatively short period, normally less than one year.

For each ESOP exercised, the employee pays the company the purchase price[12] stipulated in the option and the company issues the employee one common share for each option exercised. A discussion of how to account for ESOPs from the issuing company's perspective follows.

a. Initial measurement

ESOPs are measured at their fair value on the "grant" date as shown in Exhibit 14-16. As discussed in Section B, the fair value of the options includes both an intrinsic value and time value component.[13] This method of valuation is required by both IFRS and ASPE. As employee stock options are not traded like other options, their fair value must be estimated using techniques such as the Black–Scholes or binomial pricing models.

Exhibit 14-16 Important dates for stock compensation plans

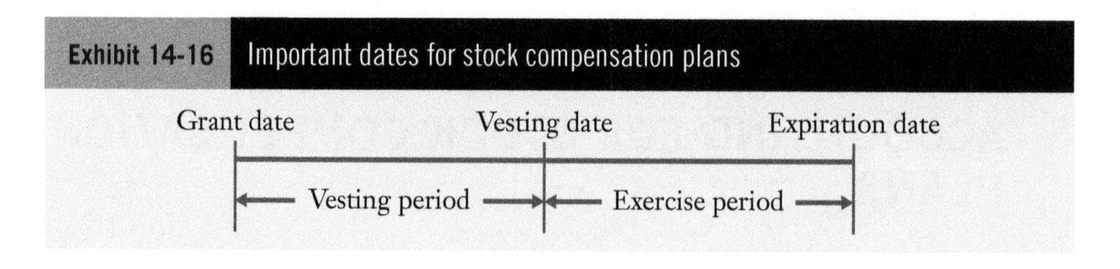

12. Commonly referred to as the exercise price or the strike price.

13. Prior to 2003, it was acceptable to use the intrinsic value method, which records only the intrinsic value of an option at the date the company grants the options. Most often, this intrinsic value is zero.

Typically, employees must fulfill certain conditions, including continuing to work for the company for a specified period, before they can exercise their options. These requirements are referred to as **vesting conditions**. Vesting conditions are not considered when determining the fair value of individual options. Rather, compensation expense is adjusted to reflect the number of options that are estimated to eventually vest. For example, if 1,000 options are granted with a fair value of $10 each, and the estimated forfeiture rate is 5% due to non-fulfillment of the vesting conditions, then the compensation expense to be recognized for the ESOPs is 1,000 options × (1 − 5%) = 950 options; 950 × $10 = $9,500.

vesting conditions Conditions that determine whether the employee is entitled to exercise the option or redeem the SAR under a share-based payment arrangement.

b. Subsequent measurement

Employee stock options typically cannot be exercised until they have vested. The value of the employee stock options granted is determined at the grant date and allocated as an expense over the **vesting period**.[14] The vesting period is the minimum length of time for which an option must be held before it can be exercised. It is the span of time between the date that the options are granted and the date they vest, as illustrated in Exhibit 14-16.

vesting period The minimum length of time for which an option must be held before it can be exercised.

Paragraph 19 of IFRS 2—Share-based Payment stipulates that the total amount recognized as an expense over the life of the options shall be based upon the number of options that eventually vest. This requirement is fulfilled by updating the estimated forfeiture rate at each period end, between the grant date and the vesting date, to reflect the additional knowledge gained from the passage of time. On vesting date, the estimate is revised to equal the number of options that actually vested.

The cost of options that can be exercised immediately are fully expensed in the period granted since the vesting period is nil.

c. Derecognition

Accounting for the exercise of ESOPs does not pose any special challenges.

If employees exercise their options, they pay the company the exercise price, surrender the options, and receive the shares. The accounting for the company reflects these three components by recording the cash received, a reduction of contributed surplus relating to the stock options, and an increase in the common share account for the balance. Again, this is an application of the book value method.

To facilitate disclosure, if options expire, the company may choose to record a housekeeping journal entry removing the contributed surplus relating to the stock options by transferring the amount to contributed surplus—expired stock options.

d. ESOPs illustrated

To illustrate accounting for employee stock options, suppose Enchanted Forest grants 10,000 options to its employees on January 1, 2021, giving them the right to buy shares at $60 each. The options may be exercised at any time between January 1, 2023, and December 31, 2024. The fair value estimate for these options is $220,000 on the date of grant, which is $22 per option. On December 31, 2021, the company estimated an ESOP forfeiture rate of 10%. On December 31, 2022, 96% of the options actually vested. Assuming a fiscal year-end of December 31, the following journal entries would be recorded to recognize the expense:

---

14. ASPE 3870.07(p) provides that the expense is recognized over the service period, but notes that if the service period is not defined as an earlier or shorter period, then the service period is presumed to be the vesting period. For ease of reference, we will use the term "vesting period" throughout the rest of this chapter.

Exhibit 14-17 Journal entries to record the granting of employee stock options for Enchanted Forest

December 31, 2021		
Dr. Compensation expense (10,000 options × \$22/option × (1 − 10%) ÷ 2 years)	99,000	
Cr. Contributed surplus—stock options		99,000
December 31, 2022		
Dr. Compensation expense (10,000 options × \$22/option × 96% − \$99,000)	112,200	
Cr. Contributed surplus—stock options		112,200

Note that a journal entry is not required at the date of the grant. Rather, a memorandum to the company's books would be made specifying the details of the plan. As part of the adjusting entry process, a journal entry is made at each period-end to record compensation expense.

If employees exercise 2,000 options on March 15, 2023, the employees are required to pay the exercise price of \$60 per share. The journal entry would be:

Exhibit 14-18 Journal entry to record the exercise of employee stock options for Enchanted Forest

Dr. Cash (2,000 options × 1 share/option × \$60/share)	120,000	
Dr. Contributed surplus—stock options (2,000 options × \$22/option)	44,000	
Cr. Common shares (balance)		164,000

If the remaining 7,600 options expire unexercised, the following entry may be recorded to transfer the contributed surplus:

Exhibit 14-19 Optional journal entry to record the expiration of employee stock options for Enchanted Forest

Dr. Contributed surplus—stock options (\$211,200 − \$44,000)	167,200	
Cr. Contributed surplus—expired stock options		167,200

Again, this transfer of contributed surplus is cosmetic and does not change total equity. All increases and decreases to contributed surplus arising from ESOPs are also classified as contributed surplus-other, because they are not related to the proceeds of stock issued in excess of par, nor do they pertain to repurchase and resale transactions.

2. Stock appreciation rights (SARs)

Stock appreciation rights, like employee stock options, are a form of share-based compensation. The essence of SARs is that if the shares appreciate in value, the employee is entitled to receive the difference between the market price of the shares at the date of settlement and the benchmark price. (The benchmark price for SARs is analogous to the exercise price for options.) Unlike stock options, though, the employee need not make a cash outlay at the exercise date. Rather, they receive an amount equal to the appreciation.

There are different types of stock appreciation rights, including those that are settled in cash, those that can be settled in cash or shares at the option of the granting entity, and those that can be settled in cash or shares at the option of the employee. The following focuses on cash-settled SARs but does include a brief overview of the accounting requirements for SARs with multiple settlement options.

Similar to stock option plans, the expense of SAR plans is allocated over the vesting period. Unlike stock option plans, though, compensation expense needs to be updated at the end of each period to reflect the change in the fair value of the SARs.

a. Initial and subsequent measurement

While there are some similarities between how the obligation arising from ESOPs and SARs are measured and reported, there are distinct differences as well, as summarized below:

	SARs	ESOPs
Obligation	Reported as a liability[15]	Reported as equity[16]
Basis of subsequent measurement	Fair value of SARs at period end	Fair value of ESOPs determined at grant date
Measurement of obligation after vesting	Updated to reflect changes in the fair value of the SARs	Not updated to reflect changes in the fair value of the ESOPs

The SAR liability at period end is determined using the equation:

(SARs granted − SARs satisfied through performance − SARs estimated to be forfeited) × fair value of each SAR at period end × % of vesting period worked by employees since grant date.[17]

The process of determining the SARs liability and compensation expense to be reported at each period end on the company's financial statements is illustrated below.

Refer back to the example illustrated in Exhibits 14-17 to 14-19. Assume that Enchanted Forest granted its employees 10,000 SARs with a benchmark price of $60 on January 1, rather than the 10,000 options. The two-year vesting period and the expiry date of the plan remain unchanged, as do the estimated and actual forfeiture rates. The fair value of the SARs and the market price of the shares are as detailed below:

Exhibit 14-20 Fair value of SARs and market value of shares

	Fair value of 1 SAR	Market price of 1 share
January 1, 2021	Not required	$60
December 31, 2021	$25	72
December 31, 2022	15	68
March 15, 2023	13	71
December 31, 2023	5	64
December 31, 2024	0	59

15. The obligation under a cash-based SAR meets the definition of a liability as the obligation is settled in cash.

16. The obligation under an ESOP meets the definition of equity as the obligation is settled by issuing common shares.

17. The number of years in the vesting period worked since the grant date of the SARs divided by the vesting period (in years). Once the SARs have vested, this equals 100%.

Note that while the market price of the shares affects the fair value of the SARs, it does not directly affect the valuation of the liability. It is the fair value of the SARs that determines the value of the obligation.

In the previous Enchanted Forest example, the compensation expense was allocated over the two-year vesting period. While the underlying process is the same for SARs, we must also make provision for changes in the fair value of the SARs between the time they are granted and when they are exercised or expire. A table like the one in Exhibit 14-21 is useful to track the amount to be expensed in each period.

The process for determining compensation expense in each period is as follows:

1. Determine the estimated remaining number of SARs eligible for exercise (column C). This is the number of SARs granted, less the number of SARs that have been exercised to date, less the number of SARs that are expected to be forfeited.[18]
2. Determine the percentage to be accrued (column D). This is determined by dividing the time that has passed since the SARs were granted by the total time that it takes for the SARs to vest.
3. Determine the required liability for the end of the period. This equals the fair value of each SAR (column B) times the estimated remaining number of SARs eligible for exercise (column C) times the percentage to be accrued (column D).
4. Compare the required liability for the end of the period (column E) to the liability at the beginning of the period (column F) and prepare a journal entry for the difference. If the liability has increased, debit compensation expense and credit the obligation; if the liability has decreased, debit the liability and credit compensation expense.

Changes in the fair value of the SARs and the estimated forfeiture rate represent changes in estimates that are accounted for prospectively, as discussed in Chapter 19.

Exhibit 14-21 Cash-settled stock appreciation rights—compensation expense (IFRS)

Column A	B	C	D	E = B × C × D	F	G = E − F
Date	Fair value per SAR	Number of SARs[(a)]	Percentage accrued[(b)]	Cumulative liability—ending balance	Cumulative liability—beginning balance	Compensation expense
Dec. 31, 2021	$25	9,000	50%	$ 112,500	$ 0	$112,500
Dec. 31, 2022	15	9,600	100	144,000	112,500	31,500
Mar. 15, 2023	—	(2,000)[(c)]	100	(22,000)	Partial exercise of SARs	
		7,600		122,000		
Dec. 31, 2023	5	7,600	100	38,000	$ 122,000	$ (84,000)
Dec. 31, 2024	0	7,600	100	0	38,000	(38,000)
						$ 22,000[(d)]

[(a)] SARs granted − SARs satisfied through performance − SARs estimated to be forfeited

[(b)] Number of years passed since grant date ÷ Total number of years required for plan to vest. In year one, this is 1 ÷ 2 = 50%; in year two, 2 ÷ 2 = 100%.

[(c)] Exercise of 2,000 of the SARs. A journal entry is required to record the outflow of cash and to reduce the obligation. # SARs exercised × (Market price − Benchmark price) = 2,000 × ($71 − $60) = $22,000.

[(d)] Note that the cumulative compensation expense for SARs will always equal the amount of cash paid to the employees when the SARs are exercised. In this example, the cumulative compensation expense of $22,000 equals the cash paid of $22,000.

[18] Once the SARs have vested, this equation becomes either: number of SARs vested − number of SARs exercised = remaining number of SARs eligible for exercise; or, number of SARs granted − number of SARs forfeited − number of SARs exercised = remaining number of SARs eligible for exercise.

Briefly, we use the updated information to adjust our accounting records for the current and future periods, but we do not go back and change prior period financial statements.

Under no circumstances will the fair value of the SARs ever be less than $0, as employees are not required to exercise them. Hence, the cumulative obligation can never have a debit balance.

When SARs are exercised, the obligation is reduced by the amount of cash paid to the employees, rather than a pro-rata share of the outstanding liability.[19] The debit to the SARs liability is equal to the intrinsic value of the SARs (market value of shares – benchmark price) × the number of SARs exercised.

Journal entries are made at each redemption to record the cash outflow, and at the end of each reporting period to record the change in the underlying obligation. The journal entries pertaining to the forgoing example are presented in Exhibit 14-22.

Exhibit 14-22 Journal entries pertaining to the SARs for Enchanted Forest (IFRS)

December 31, 2021		
Dr. Compensation expense	112,500	
Cr. Liability for stock appreciation rights		112,500
December 31, 2022		
Dr. Compensation expense	31,500	
Cr. Liability for stock appreciation rights		31,500
March 15, 2023		
Dr. Liability for stock appreciation rights	22,000	
Cr. Cash		22,000
December 31, 2023		
Dr. Liability for stock appreciation rights	84,000	
Cr. Compensation expense		84,000
December 31, 2024		
Dr. Liability for stock appreciation rights	38,000	
Cr. Compensation expense		38,000

b. Derecognition

The liability can be derecognized through exercise, expiry, or both. In the Enchanted Forest example above, the liability was reduced by the $22,000 cash paid on March 15, 2023, when 2,000 SARs were exercised. The remaining liability of $38,000 was then derecognized on December 31, 2024, when the SARs expired.

c. Stock appreciation rights with multiple settlement options

Stock appreciation rights that may be settled in cash or shares are governed by paragraphs 34 to 43 of IFRS 2. Briefly, when an entity grants an employee the right to choose to receive cash or shares from a share-payment plan, they have issued a compound financial instrument. As discussed in Section C, subsection 1a, the fair value of the financial instrument must be allocated to its component parts, namely, debt and equity (contributed surplus).

When an entity retains the right to determine whether settlement will be in cash or by issuing equity instruments, it will normally account for the arrangement in the same manner as equity-settled share-based payments (e.g., employee stock options

19. The difference between the cash paid and the proportionate share of the SARs liability at redemption date will be captured in the determination of compensation expense at the next period end.

discussed in Section E, subsection 1). Certain exceptions do apply, for example, if the entity is legally prohibited from issuing shares or if they have a stated policy of settling in cash. In circumstances like these, the entity accounts for the arrangement in the same manner as cash-settled share-based payments (i.e., cash-settled SARs discussed in Section E, subsection 2).

d. Accounting for SARs under ASPE

Accounting for SARs under ASPE differs from that under IFRS, as ASPE 3870.37 requires the use of the intrinsic value of the SARs to determine the obligation until settlement. Exhibits 14-23 and 14-24 illustrate the required accounting for the Enchanted Forest SAR plan under ASPE using the market price data previously set out in Exhibit 14-20.[20]

Exhibit 14-23 Cash-settled stock appreciation rights—compensation expense (ASPE)

Column A	B	C	D	E	F = (B − C) × D × E	G	H = F − G
Date	Market value per share	Benchmark price	Number of SARs[(a)]	Percentage accrued	Cumulative liability—ending balance (≥ 0)[(b)]	Cumulative liability—beginning balance	Compensation expense
Dec. 31, 2021	$72	$60	9,000	50%	$ 54,000	$ 0	$54,000
Dec. 31, 2022	68	60	9,600	100	76,800	54,000	22,800
Mar. 15, 2023	71	60	(2,000)[(c)]	100	(22,000)	Partial exercise of SARs	
			7,600		54,800		
Dec. 31, 2023	64	60	7,600	100	30,400	$54,800	$(24,400)
Dec. 31, 2024	59	60	7,600	100	0	30,400	(30,400)
							$ 22,000[(d)]

[(a)] SARs granted − SARs satisfied through performance − SARs estimated to be forfeited.
[(b)] If the market price of the shares is less than the benchmark price, the cumulative obligation is reported at $0 as employees do not have to exercise the SARs at a loss.
[(c)] Exercise of 20% of the SARs. A journal entry is required to record the outflow of cash and reduce the obligation. # SARs exercised × (Market price − Benchmark price) = 2,000 × ($71 − $60) = $22,000.
[(d)] Note that the cumulative compensation expense for SARs will always equal the amount of cash paid to the employees when the SARs are exercised. In this example, the cumulative compensation expense of $22,000 equals the cash paid of $22,000.

Comparing this schedule of compensation expense with that in Exhibit 14-21 for IFRS, you can see that while the period-by-period compensation expense and the SAR-related obligation do differ under the two methods, both methods produce the same ending obligation ($0), and total compensation expense over the life of the SARs ($22,000). This result is not unexpected as it is analogous to using different methods to value inventory. If a company values inventory using FIFO, its asset balances and cost of goods sold expense will differ every period from what they would be if they valued inventory at average cost. Over the life of the company, however, the total cost of goods sold expense will be the same under both methods, as will be the ending asset balance of $0. This is an issue of timing of recognition, as discussed in Chapter 3.

THRESHOLD CONCEPT
TIMING OF RECOGNITION

[20] Under ASPE, the company can either estimate forfeiture rates in the same manner required by IFRS, or it can assume that all options/SARs will vest and recognize actual forfeitures when they occur. To facilitate comparison, this example assumes that the company estimates forfeiture rates at each period end as required by IFRS.

Exhibit 14-24 Journal entries pertaining to the SARs for Enchanted Forest (ASPE)

December 31, 2021		
Dr. Compensation expense	54,000	
Cr. Liability for stock appreciation rights		54,000
December 31, 2022		
Dr. Compensation expense	22,800	
Cr. Liability for stock appreciation rights		22,800
March 15, 2023		
Dr. Liability for stock appreciation rights	22,000	
Cr. Cash		22,000
December 31, 2023		
Dr. Liability for stock appreciation rights	24,400	
Cr. Compensation expense		24,400
December 31, 2024		
Dr. Liability for stock appreciation rights	30,400	
Cr. Compensation expense		30,400

We conclude this discussion with Exhibit 14-25, which contrasts the accounting treatment for the various types of stock compensation plans discussed in this section.

Exhibit 14-25 Contrasting the accounting for employee stock options and cash-settled SARs

	Employee stock options	Cash-settled SARs—IFRS	Cash-settled SARs—ASPE
Nature of the obligation	Deliver shares	Pay cash	Pay cash
Balance sheet category	Equity	Liability	Liability
Basis of measurement of the obligation	Fair value of options at grant date	Fair value of SARs at period end	Intrinsic value of SARs at period end

CHECKPOINT **CP14-8**

Briefly describe how the obligation to deliver shares under employee stock option plans is measured under IFRS and ASPE.

CHECKPOINT **CP14-9**

Briefly describe how the liability for cash-settled stock appreciation rights is measured under IFRS and ASPE.

F. PRESENTATION AND DISCLOSURE

IFRS 2 does not set out any specific standards with respect to the presentation of information on share-based payments. Rather, presentation is governed by IAS 1—Presentation of Financial Statements and IAS 32—Financial Instruments: Presentation.

IFRS 2 paragraphs 44–52 establish extensive disclosure provisions with respect to employee stock options and stock appreciation rights. The resultant financial statement disclosure can be lengthy—for example, Canadian Tire's disclosure includes two pages of notes in its 2016 financial statements. A brief summary of the statutory disclosure requirements is listed below:

- Information that enables users to understand the nature and extent of share-based payment arrangements (¶44)
- Information that enables users to understand how fair values were determined (¶46)
- Information that enables users to understand the effect of share-based payments on the entity's income statement and balance sheet (¶50)

To meet these requirements, an entity must provide complete details about each plan, the number and average exercise price of options that were outstanding at the beginning and end of the year, and details about the changes throughout the year categorized as to source (e.g., options granted, forfeited, exercised, and expired). Canadian Tire's disclosure relative to the impact of its share-based payment plans is set out in note 26, Share-based payments. The first portion of the note is shown in Exhibit 14-26; for the remainder, please refer to the full financial statements in Appendix C.

Exhibit 14-26 Excerpt from Canadian Tire's 2016 financial statements, Note 26

26. Share-based payments
The Company's share-based payment plans are described below.

Stock options
The Company has granted stock options to certain employees that enable such employees to exercise their stock options and subscribe for Class A Non-Voting Shares or surrender their options and receive a cash payment. Such cash payment is calculated as the difference between the fair market value of Class A Non-Voting Shares as at the surrender date and the exercise price of the option. Stock options granted prior to 2012 vested on the third anniversary of their grant. Stock options that were granted in 2012 and later vest over a three-year period. All outstanding stock options have a term of seven years. At December 31, 2016, the aggregate number of Class A Non-Voting Shares that were authorized for issuance under the stock option plan was 3.4 million.

Source: From Canadian Tire Corporation 2016 Report to Shareholders. Copyright ©2016 by Canadian Tire Corporation, Limited. Reprinted by permission.

G. SUBSTANTIVE DIFFERENCES BETWEEN RELEVANT IFRS AND ASPE

ISSUE	IFRS	ASPE
Initial recognition of compound financial instruments	Use the residual value method. The debt component is initially recognized at fair value; the residual of the consideration received is ascribed to the equity component.	Use either the residual value method or the zero value method. The latter assigns a zero value to the common equity component.
Measurement of the value of cash-settled stock appreciation rights	Measures the obligation at the fair value of the stock appreciation rights (time value + intrinsic value = fair value).	Measures the obligation at the intrinsic value of the stock appreciation rights.

(*Continued*)

ISSUE	IFRS	ASPE
Estimated forfeiture rates for share-based payments	Updated at each period end, between the grant date and the vesting date, at which time the estimate is revised to equal the number of options that actually vested.	Accruals based on best available estimate of forfeiture rates and revised if it appears that actual forfeitures will differ from initial estimates. Alternatively, accruals based on expectation of a forfeiture rate of 0% with actual forfeitures recognized as they occur.
Hedge accounting[21]	Employs a fair value–based model for hedge accounting that requires quantitative assessments for effectiveness.	Relies on a narrowly described set of hedging relationships.
Types of hedges[21]	Identifies hedges as fair value hedges and cash flow hedges and prescribes the accounting treatment for each.	Does not use the terms fair value hedge or cash flow hedge. Rather, lists five specific transactions that qualify for hedge accounting and specifies the accounting treatment for each.
Eligible hedging instruments for fair value and cash flow hedges[21]	Derivatives and, in certain instances, non-derivative financial assets and liabilities.	Only forward instruments and interest rate swaps can be used as hedging instruments.
Gains and losses on hedging items[21]	Gains and losses on fair value hedging items normally flow through net income, while gains and losses on cash flow hedging items flow through other comprehensive income.	Gains and losses on all hedges flow through net income; ASPE does not permit the reporting of other comprehensive income.

H. APPENDIX: DERIVATIVES AND HEDGING

1. Derivatives—Forwards, futures, and swaps

a. Forwards

In a **forward** contract, one party to the contract commits to buy something at a specified price at a specified future date. A forward differs from an option, discussed earlier in this chapter, because a party to a forward contract does not have a choice in the purchase or sale of the future. For example, suppose on December 15, 2018, Axel Inc. agrees to buy US$1 million for C$1.05 million in 90 days from Bluebird Corp. The underlying quantity is the USD:CAD exchange rate. Axel Inc. enters into this forward because it expects the US dollar to appreciate in value; hence, it wants to make sure that for each US dollar it pays only C$1.05 and no more. For Bluebird Corp., the expectation is the opposite: it is concerned that the US dollar might have a value less than C$1.05. Forwards are possible only if the two parties to the agreement have different expectations or risk tolerances regarding future price changes.

forward A contract in which one party commits upfront to buy or sell something at a defined price at a defined future date.

The two parties to a forward contract can specify any price and any maturity date agreeable to both. Thus, forwards are quite flexible in their contractual terms in contrast to futures, which we discuss next.

Exhibit 14-27 A foreign currency forward contract between Axel Inc. and Bluebird Corp.

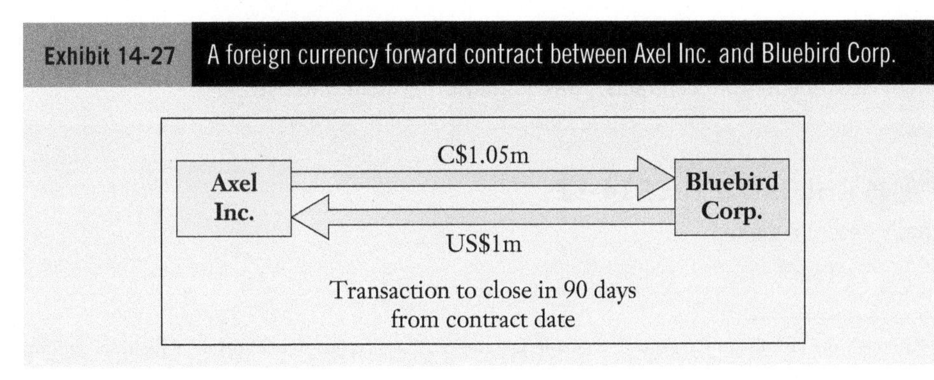

21. This item refers to a topic covered in the appendix, Section H.

b. Futures

future Similar to a forward but the contract is written in more standardized terms (e.g., prices, maturity dates) and involves commonly traded items (e.g., commodities, currencies).

A **future** is similar to a forward, except that a future contract is written in more standardized terms (e.g., prices, maturity dates) and they involve commonly traded items (e.g., commodities, currencies). The reason for the standardized terms is that futures are tradeable in organized markets, and standardization increases liquidity since more investors are trading the same contracts. For example, a commodities futures contract on gold could specify a price of $1,300 per ounce to be settled in December 2018.[22] In contrast, a forward contract can be more specific, such as $1,301.22 per ounce to be settled on December 12, 2018.

c. Swaps

swap A derivative contract in which two parties agree to exchange cash flows.

A **swap** is a derivative contract in which two parties agree to exchange cash flows. For example, if Beowulf Company has $100 million in debt that has a floating rate of prime + 2%, it could arrange a swap with another company (such as an investment bank) to fix the interest rate at 6%. The ability to complete a swap depends, of course, on whether one party desires to have the cash flow stream of the other party.

Exhibit 14-28 An interest rate swap

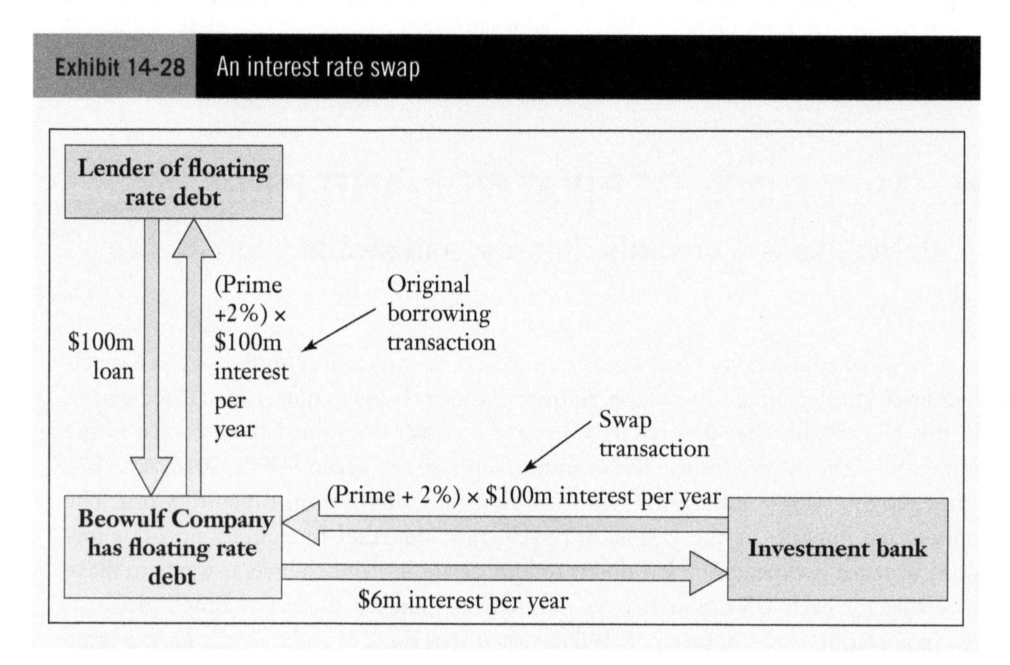

CHECKPOINT **CP14-10**

List the five common derivatives identified in this chapter.

CHECKPOINT **CP14-11**

Briefly describe forward contracts. How do they differ from futures?

CHECKPOINT **CP14-12**

Briefly describe a swap.

22. Although the futures contract specifies simply December 2018, it refers to one specific date in the month, depending on the exchange. On North American exchanges, that day is the third Friday of the month. Also, many futures contracts use only one expiration per quarterly period (i.e., March, June, September, and December) to further concentrate trading and liquidity.

2. Accounting for derivatives

L.O. 14-4. Apply the accounting standards for derivatives.

We now look at how to account for the derivatives discussed in the previous topic.

As discussed in Chapter 7, we generally classify derivative investments at fair value through profit or loss (FVPL) and measure them at fair value, with changes in fair value recorded through income. This general rule applies to both sides of a derivative transaction. There are two exceptions to this general rule. The first is for derivatives that are part of hedging transactions, which we discuss in the next section. The second exception is for derivatives that relate to the reporting entity's own equity, which should be recorded at historical cost. Warrants on common shares and employee stock options, discussed earlier in this chapter, are examples of derivatives on the company's own equity.

To illustrate the general treatment of derivatives, recall the example of the forward contract involving Axel Inc. and Bluebird Corp. Axel agrees to buy US$1 million for C$1.05 million from Bluebird. The contract was made on December 15, 2018, and closes 90 days later. At inception, neither company records the forward, because nothing changes hands at this date.

At the companies' year-end of December 31, 2018, the exchange rate is US$1 to C$0.98. This exchange rate means that US$1,000,000 is worth only C$980,000. However, Axel has committed to pay C$1,050,000 to buy the US$1,000,000, so it has a mark-to-market[23] loss of C$70,000 ($1,050,000 – $980,000). Correspondingly, Bluebird would record a gain of C$70,000.

Exhibit 14-29 Journal entries to record fair value changes in the currency forward contract between Axel and Bluebird

Axel Inc.			Bluebird Corp.		
Dr. Loss on currency derivative	70,000		Dr. Foreign currency derivative	70,000	
Cr. Foreign currency derivative		70,000	Cr. Gain on currency derivative		70,000

This example illustrates a derivative involving no transfers on the contract initiation, so neither party records a journal entry at that time. Other derivatives do require entries upon initiation. For example, suppose that, instead of a forward, Axel had bought a futures contract that entitles the company to buy US$1 million at a cost of C$1.05 million on March 15, 2019. Axel may have incurred a cost to buy this futures contract. Supposing that cost is $10,000, the company would record the following entry for the purchase:

Exhibit 14-30 Journal entry to record Axel's purchase of a foreign currency futures contract

Dr. Foreign currency derivative (classified as at fair value through profit or loss financial asset)	10,000	
Cr. Cash		10,000

This futures contract becomes more valuable if the US dollar appreciates, and less valuable if the US dollar depreciates. In fact, if the US dollar depreciates enough, Axel's currency futures contract will have negative value (i.e., it becomes a liability). Consider two scenarios in which the exchange rates increase or decrease by C$0.03 to either US$1:C$1.08 or US$1:C$1.02 on December 31, 2018, which causes the futures

[23] Briefly, mark-to-market involves regularly revaluing assets and liabilities to reflect their current market value, rather than the acquisition price.

contract price to increase or decrease to either $40,000 or ($20,000).[24] In these scenarios, Axel would record one of the following journal entries:

Exhibit 14-31 Two scenarios and journal entries to account for changes in value in Axel's US dollar foreign currency futures contract

Scenario	Resulting exchange rate Dec. 31, 2018	Value of futures contract	Journal entry		
USD appreciates			Dr. Foreign currency derivative	30,000	
by C$0.03	US$1:C$1.08	$40,000	Cr. Gain on currency derivative		30,000
USD depreciates			Dr. Loss on foreign currency derivative	30,000	
by C$0.03	US$1:C$1.02	($20,000)	Cr. Foreign currency derivative		30,000

In the second scenario, notice that the $30,000 Cr. adjustment to the foreign currency derivative account combined with the original balance of $10,000 Dr. results in a net credit of $20,000, so Axel would report this amount as a liability on its December 31, 2018, financial statements.

3. Hedging overview

L.O. 14-5. Apply the accounting standards for hedges and identify situations in which hedge accounting may be appropriate.

The application of hedge accounting can be very complex and is primarily the purview of advanced financial accounting. Indeed, another accounting academic made the comment, "a book on how to account for hedges published by PWC runs nearly 600 pages and is not totally comprehensive in coverage." The discussion that follows is meant only to provide an overview of some of the basic considerations of hedging and hedge accounting.

Before proceeding further, a clear understanding of a few basic definitions is needed:

- Hedging is a risk management strategy used to transfer risks arising from fluctuations in the price of foreign exchange, interest rates, or commodities from parties who prefer to avoid it to those who are willing to take it on.
- Hedge accounting recognizes income or loss on the hedging item and the related hedged item in the same period when they would otherwise be recognized in net income in different periods.
- A hedged item is what you are trying to protect from changes in value. IFRS 9 permits both financial and non-financial items (such as the price of jet fuel) to be hedged, provided that the risk component is separately identifiable and readily measurable.
- A hedging item is the financial instrument you are using to protect the value of the hedged item. To qualify for hedge accounting, the hedging instrument must normally be either a derivative financial instrument or a non-derivative financial instrument measured at FVPL. Additionally, non-derivative financial instruments measured at other than FVPL may also be used to hedge the risk of a change in foreign currency exchange rates.[25]

It is important to recognize that hedging and hedge accounting are not the same thing. As described above, hedging is a risk management strategy, while hedge

24. Actual prices of futures contracts do not move in lockstep with exchange rates. We assume these figures for simplicity.

25. IFRS 9 paragraphs 6.2.1 to 6.2.3 set out limited exceptions to the forgoing list of permitted hedging instruments.

accounting is a method of accounting for hedging activities. Entities may elect to use hedge accounting as an accounting policy choice but they are not required to do so, as the adoption of hedge accounting is optional.

Enterprises often use financial instruments to reduce risk. For example, a company could enter into a forward contract to buy US dollars not for the purpose of speculation, but in anticipation of a liability that needs to be settled in US dollars. In the Axel–Bluebird example given in the previous topic, Axel's purchase of a forward for US$1 million in exchange for C$1.05 million would reduce Axel's risk if it also had a US dollar obligation due in 90 days, such as an account payable to a US supplier. Buying the forward ensures that the company pays exactly C$1.05 million. In other words, the forward hedges the exchange rate risk arising from the US dollar obligation. This is a hedge of the foreign currency risk arising from a firm commitment to pay in US dollars. However, if Axel didn't have such an obligation, then the purchase of the forward would be simply a speculative investment that bets on the direction of currency movements, which increases the company's risk.

Generally speaking, one item hedges another if their values tend to move in opposite directions. For accounting purposes, a hedge can be either a fair value hedge or a cash flow hedge.[26] A **fair value hedge** reduces the exposure to changes in the fair value of a recognized asset or liability or a firm commitment. The Axel–Bluebird example can be accounted for as a fair value hedge, since Axel's purchase of the forward contract limits its exposure to changes in the value of its accounts payable.

fair value hedge A financial instrument that reduces an entity's exposure to changes in fair value.

A **cash flow hedge** reduces the exposure to changes in future cash flows, including highly probable forecast transactions. An example of a cash flow hedge is an interest-rate swap. The Axel–Bluebird example can also be accounted for as a cash flow hedge since it reduces the exposure to changes in future cash flows (the amount required to settle the accounts payable).[27]

cash flow hedge A financial instrument that reduces an entity's exposure to changes in future cash flows.

To qualify for hedge accounting, enterprises need to take three steps: (i) identify the risk exposure (i.e., the item that needs to be hedged); (ii) designate the hedging instrument; and (iii) demonstrate that the hedge will likely be effective.

A natural question to ask is, "Why do we need hedge accounting?" If the hedging instrument and the hedged item experience changes in opposite directions, wouldn't other accounting procedures result in the desired outcome of no (or little) net change? The reason is that in the absence of hedge accounting, profit or loss attributable to the hedging instrument and the hedged item may be reported in different periods or in different parts of the statement of comprehensive income (i.e., net income or other comprehensive income [OCI]). For instance, assume that one month before year-end, a company issues a purchase order to buy inventory for delivery in three months' time priced in a foreign currency. To limit its exposure to foreign exchange risk, the company prudently enters into a forward contract to purchase the required currency at a later date. At year-end, in the absence of hedge accounting, the company would recognize the change in value of the forward contract in profit or loss, but it would not recognize the change in value of the purchase order until payment was made in the following period.

As another example, an at fair value through OCI financial asset would be marked-to-market, with fair value changes flowing through OCI; a derivative that offsets those fair value changes would have its gains and losses flowing through net income (as is required for most derivatives). Hedge accounting allows the hedged item and the hedging instrument to be treated in the same way so that the effects offset, at least

26. There is a third category, hedge of a net investment in a foreign operation. As this category relates to foreign operations, it is a topic for advanced financial accounting and is not addressed in this text.

27. As discussed in subsection 4, IFRS 9 paragraph 6.5.4 provides that a hedge of foreign currency risk of a firm commitment may be accounted for either as a fair value or cash flow hedge.

partially. (A perfect hedge would have completely offsetting effects, but hedges need not be 100% perfect.)

For fair value hedges, the changes in fair value for both the hedged item and the hedging instrument normally[28] flow through income. For cash flow hedges, the change in the fair value of the hedging instrument passes through OCI.

4. Hedge accounting

For entities that elect to use hedge accounting, IFRS 9 details the requisite accounting treatment for fair value and cash flow hedges. It does not mandate, however, the specific manner in which the transactions are to be recorded. This is normal, as IFRS speaks to financial reporting (the basis on which financial statements are prepared), rather than recording (the bookkeeping function characterized by journal entries).

As a result, two divergent methods have evolved in practice: the gross method and the memorandum or net method. While a full discussion of hedge accounting is beyond the scope of this text, briefly, under the gross method the full amount of the hedging item is recorded, whereas under the net method it is not. Proponents of the gross method note that if the hedging item (e.g., a forward contract) is not explicitly recognized in the books, it is easy to overlook and the necessary adjustments may not be made at period end. Moreover, they note that the hedging item is a financial instrument that must be accounted for. Advocates of the net method note that at the outset the hedge represents a mutually unexecuted contract and as such it need not be recorded. For illustrative purposes, we will use the net method, which is more commonly seen in practice.

5. Fair value hedges

As previously outlined, a fair value hedge reduces an entity's exposure to changes in the fair value of a recognized asset or liability or of a firm commitment. A firm commitment is a contractual agreement for future delivery where the quantity, price, and dates are specified. Examples of recognized assets, liabilities, and firm commitments are, respectively, a euro-denominated accounts receivable or an investment in marketable securities designated as at fair value through OCI; a trade payable denominated in Swiss francs or a US-dollar denominated bond; and accepted purchase orders, both incoming and outgoing.

An important outcome of fair value hedging is that when a foreign currency–denominated asset is hedged, it is usually reported in Canadian dollars at the exchange rate specified in the forward agreement, rather than at the spot rate. This is because the change in value in the fair value hedge offsets the gains and losses from the asset being hedged; the exchange rate on the hedged asset does not change with the spot rate but is fixed at the forward rate. (Refer to IFRS 9 paragraphs 6.5.8(b) and 6.5.9 for more information.)

As foreign currency exposure to a firm commitment affects both the fair value of the item and future cash flows, IFRS 9 paragraph 6.5.4 provides that a hedge of the foreign currency risk of a firm commitment may be accounted for either as a fair value hedge or as a cash flow hedge.

Exhibit 14-32 illustrates accounting for fair value hedges.

28. An exception to this rule is when the hedged item is an equity item for which the entity elected to present the changes of fair value in OCI. In this instance, the gain or loss on the hedging instrument remains in OCI as per IFRS 9 paragraph 6.5.8(b).

Exhibit 14-32a Fair value hedge example

Facts: On November 1, 2018, Ian and Catherine Champion Enterprises Inc. (ICCE) signed a contract to purchase property in Britain at a cost of £400,000. The company takes title to the property on January 31, 2019, and pays for it at that time.

- On November 1, 2018, ICCE entered into a forward contract with its bank to receive £400,000 on January 31, 2019.
- The hedging item qualifies for hedge accounting. ICCE designates the forward contract as a fair value hedge.
- A schedule setting out exchange rates of significance follows:

Date		Spot rate C$ per £	Forward rate to Jan. 31, 2019, C$ per £
November 1, 2018	Contract signed	1.5000	1.5100
December 31, 2018	Year-end	1.5050	1.5130
January 31, 2019	Title obtained	1.5340	1.5340

Required: Prepare all entries relative to this transaction using the net method.

No entry is required on November 1 as the contract to purchase the property and the forward contract are both mutually unexecuted contracts.

Exhibit 14-32b Journal entries to record year-end adjusting entries

Dr. Forward contract receivable (pounds)	1,200	
Cr. Foreign exchange gains and losses		1,200
Dr. Foreign exchange gains and losses	1,200	
Cr. Contract commitment liability		
[£400,000 × (1.5130−1.5100)]		1,200

At year-end, the hedge is adjusted to fair value using the forward rate as at December 31. The additional cost of meeting the contractual commitment because of an increase in the forward rate is recognized as a liability. The resultant gain and loss from these adjustments both flow through net income and offset each other.

Exhibit 14-32c Journal entries to record transfer of title to the land

Dr. Forward contract receivable (pounds)	8,400	
Cr. Foreign exchange gains and losses		8,400
Dr. Foreign exchange gains and losses	8,400	
Cr. Contract commitment liability		
[£400,000 × (1.5340 − 1.5130)]		8,400
Dr. Cash (£) (£400,000 × 1.5340)	613,600	
Cr. Cash ($) (£400,000 × 1.5100)		604,000
Cr. Forward contract receivable (pounds) (1,200 + 8,400)		9,600
Dr. Land (£400,000 × 1.5100)	604,000	
Dr. Contract commitment liability (£1,200 + £8,400)	9,600	
Cr. Cash (£) (£400,000 × 1.5340)		613,600

When title to the property is transferred on January 31, 2019:

- The hedge is again adjusted to fair value using the forward rate as at January 31.
- The forward contract with the bank is closed out. ICCE pays the bank $604,000, which was the amount agreed to in the forward agreement (£400,000 × 1.5100).

In exchange it receives £400,000 from the bank, which is now worth $613,600, as the spot rate is 1.5340 (£400,000 × 1.5340 = $613,600). The $9,600 difference between the Canadian equivalent of the amount received and the amount paid ($613,600 − $604,000) represents the foreign exchange gain on the forward over the life of the contract.

- ICCE uses the £400,000 received from the bank to pay for the land. The contract commitment liability is closed out, as the obligation is concurrently being settled.
- The land is valued at the rate contracted for in the forward agreement (£400,000 × 1.5100 = $604,000).

6. Cash flow hedges

As already discussed, a cash flow hedge reduces an entity's exposure to changes in future cash flows, including highly probable forecast transactions. A highly probable forecast transaction is one that the entity expects to take place but for which no firm commitment exists. Examples of exposure to changes in future cash flows and highly probable forecast transactions include, respectively, future interest payments on variable rate debt or interest payments on foreign-denominated debt; and an expected inventory purchase priced in a foreign currency or the anticipated sale of offshore property.

Exhibit 14-33 illustrates accounting for cash flow hedges. To facilitate comparison of the results with that of fair value hedges, we will keep all the facts the same as those used in Exhibit 14-32 except that ICCE now designates the forward contract as a cash flow hedge.

Exhibit 14-33a Cash flow hedge example

Facts: On November 1, 2018, Ian and Catherine Champion Enterprises Inc. (ICCE) signed a contract to purchase property in Britain at a cost of £400,000. The company takes title to the property on January 31, 2019, and pays for it at that time.

- On November 1, 2018, ICCE entered into a forward contract with its bank to receive £400,000 on January 31, 2019.
- The hedging item qualifies for hedge accounting. ICCE designates the forward contract as a fair value hedge.
- A schedule setting out exchange rates of significance follows:

Date		Spot rate C$ per £	Forward rate to Jan. 31, 2019, C$ per £
November 1, 2018	Contract signed	1.5000	1.5100
December 31, 2018	Year-end	1.5050	1.5130
January 31, 2019	Title obtained	1.5340	1.5340

Required: Prepare all entries relative to this transaction using the net method.

As with the fair value hedge, no entry is required on November 1 as the contract to purchase the property and the forward contract are both mutually unexecuted contracts.

Exhibit 14-33b Journal entries to record year-end adjusting entries

Dr. Forward contract receivable (pounds)	1,200	
Cr. Other comprehensive income		
[£400,000 × (1.5130 − 1.5100)]		1,200

At year-end the hedge is adjusted to fair value using the forward rate as at December 31. The gain is deferred in OCI, so net income is not affected.

Exhibit 14-33c	Journal entries to record transfer of title to the land	
Dr. Forward contract receivable (pounds)	8,400	
Cr. Other comprehensive income [£400,000 × (1.5340 – 1.5130)]		8,400
Dr. Cash (£) (£400,000 × 1.5340)	613,600	
Cr. Cash ($) (£400,000 × 1.5100)		604,000
Cr. Forward contract receivable (pounds) (1,200 + 8,400)		9,600
Dr. Land	613,600	
Cr. Cash (£) (£400,000 × 1.5340)		613,600
Dr. Accumulated other comprehensive income (1,200 + 8,400)	9,600	
Cr. Land		9,600

The mechanics of this transaction are much the same as for the fair value hedge as shown above in Exhibit 14-32c. The final entry adjusts the value of the land by the amount of accumulated other comprehensive income (AOCI). Observed similarities and differences in the outcome include those shown in Exhibit 14-34.

Exhibit 14-34 Fair value and cash flow hedge results contrasted

Item	Fair value hedge	Cash flow hedge
Gains and losses on hedging items	Flow through net income	Initially flow through OCI
Asset (land) value	Reported at the cost in foreign currency × the contracted forward rate	Reported at the cost in foreign currency × the contracted forward rate

CHECKPOINT **CP14-13**

Briefly describe hedging and contrast it with hedge accounting.

CHECKPOINT **CP14-14**

Briefly describe fair value hedges and cash flow hedges and summarize the accounting for each.

I. SUMMARY

L.O. 14-1. Describe the nature of standard financial instruments, derivatives, and compound financial instruments, and identify when transactions involve such instruments.

- Standard financial instruments are financial liabilities and equity instruments.
- Derivatives are financial instruments whose values derive from other financial instruments.
- Compound financial instruments have more than one component. Use of such instruments in the right context can help alleviate information asymmetries.

L.O. 14-2. Apply the accounting standards for compound financial instruments from the perspective of the issuer.

- Enterprises need to separately account for the components of compound financial instruments. Under IFRS, the common equity component should be allocated the residual value after allocation to all other components.

L.O. 14-3. Apply the accounting standards for employee stock compensation plans from the perspective of the issuer.

- When an enterprise grants stock options or stock appreciation rights to employees, it needs to estimate the fair value of the obligation and allocate that amount to expense over the vesting period. The liability pertaining to stock appreciation rights must be continually revalued to the earlier of exercise or expiry to allow for changes in the market value of the underlying shares.

L.O. 14-4. Apply the accounting standards for derivatives.

- Enterprises should generally report derivatives at fair value, with changes in fair value reported through net income.

L.O. 14-5. Apply the accounting standards for hedges and identify situations in which hedge accounting may be appropriate.

- Enterprises can identify specific transactions and items as hedges, but must demonstrate that the hedge is effective.
- Gains and losses on fair value hedging items normally flow through net income.
- Gains and losses on cash flow hedging items flow through other comprehensive income.

J. ANSWERS TO CHECKPOINT QUESTIONS

CP14-1: A derivative is a financial instrument that is derived from some other underlying quantity.

CP14-2: Entities buy and sell derivatives to hedge and to speculate. Hedging involves entering into derivative contracts to mitigate identified risks, while speculating involves purposely taking on an identified risk with a view to making a profit.

CP14-3: An option gives the holder the right, but not the obligation, to buy or sell an identified item at a specified price. A call option gives the holder the right to buy the item; a put option gives the holder the right to sell.

CP14-4: Warrants differ from call options in that they are only issued by the company whose shares are the underlying instrument, and they tend to have a longer time to maturity.

CP14-5: A compound financial instrument is one that has more than one component, for example, debt and equity.

CP14-6: Three potential methods to allocate values to the component parts of a compound financial instrument are the proportional method (relative fair value method), the incremental method (residual value method), and the zero common equity method. The proportional method estimates the fair value of all components and allocates them proportionally.

The incremental method estimates the fair value of all but one of the components and allocates the balance (the residual) to the remaining component. For compound financial instruments that are comprised of both debt and equity, the debt component is initially recognized at its fair value with the residual of the consideration received ascribed to the equity component. The zero common equity method assigns a zero value to the common equity component. IFRS mandates the use of the incremental method, while ASPE permits both the incremental method and zero common equity method to be used.

CP14-7: Two potential methods to record the conversion of bonds or preferred shares into common equity are the book value method and the market value method. The book value method records the common shares at the current book value of the preferred shares, or the convertible bond and related contributed surplus. No gain or loss is recorded upon conversion. In contrast, the market value method records the shares at their fair value at the date of conversion, recording a loss for the difference between the market value and the book value as determined above. Both IFRS and ASPE require that the book value method be used.

CP14-8: Under both IFRS and ASPE, the obligation to deliver shares under employee stock option plans is measured using the formula: fair value of an option at grant date × # of options × percentage accrued = contributed surplus—stock options.

CP14-9: Under IFRS, the liability for cash-settled stock appreciation rights is measured using the formula: fair value of SAR × # of SARs × percentage accrued = cumulative liability for SARs. Under ASPE, the liability is measured slightly differently as the intrinsic value of the SAR is used rather than the fair value. Thus, the formula becomes: (market price of share − benchmark price) × # of SARs × percentage accrued = cumulative liability for SARs.

CP14-10: Five common derivatives are options, warrants, forwards, futures, and swaps.

CP14-11: In a forward contract, the two counterparties agree to exchange a specified item for an agreed-upon price on an identified date. Forwards differ from futures because futures are traded in organized markets, are written in more standardized terms, and involve only commonly traded items such as commodities and currencies.

CP14-12: A swap is a derivative contract in which the counterparties agree to exchange cash flows.

CP14-13: Hedging is a risk management strategy designed to transfer risks arising from fluctuations in the price of foreign exchange, interest rates, or commodities from parties who prefer to avoid it to those that are willing to assume it. Hedge accounting is a method of accounting for hedging activities.

CP14-14: A fair value hedge reduces an entity's exposure to the changes in fair value of a recognized asset or liability or a firm commitment. A cash flow hedge reduces an entity's exposure to changes in future cash flows, including highly probable forecast transactions. For fair value hedges, the changes in fair value for both the hedged item and the hedging instrument normally flow through income. For cash flow hedges, the change in the fair value of the hedging instrument passes through OCI.

K. GLOSSARY

call option: See **option.**

cash flow hedge: A financial instrument that reduces an entity's exposure to changes in future cash flows.

compound financial instruments: Those financial instruments with more than one financial instrument component.

derivative: A financial instrument that is derived from some other underlying quantity.

employee stock option: An option a company issues to its employees giving them the right to buy shares in the enterprise at a pre-specified price.

fair value hedge: A financial instrument that reduces an entity's exposure to changes in fair value.

forward: A contract in which one party commits upfront to buy or sell something at a defined price at a defined future date.

future: Similar to a forward but the contract is written in more standardized terms (e.g., prices, maturity dates) and involves commonly traded items (e.g., commodities, currencies).

in-the-money: When the value of the underlying instrument in an option contract is favourable to the holder exercising the option compared with letting the option expire. In the case of a call option, this occurs when the underlying price exceeds the strike price; for a put option, it is when the underlying price is below the strike price.

intrinsic value of an option: In a call option, the greater of zero and $(S - K)$, which is the difference between the market price and the strike price.

option: A derivative contract that gives the holder the right, but not the obligation, to buy or sell an underlying financial instrument at a specified price. A **call option** gives the right to buy, whereas a **put option** provides the right to sell.

out-of-the-money: When the value of the underlying instrument in an option contract is unfavourable to the holder exercising the option compared with letting the option expire. In the case of a call option, this is when the underlying price is lower than the strike price; for a put option, it is when the underlying price is higher than the strike price.

put option: See option.

swap: A derivative contract in which two parties agree to exchange cash flows.

time value of an option: The portion of an option's value that reflects the probability that the future market price of the underlying instrument will exceed the strike price.

underlying quantity: The value of an asset, an index value, or an event that helps determine the value of a derivative.

vesting conditions: Conditions that determine whether the employee is entitled to exercise the option or redeem the SAR under a share-based payment arrangement.

vesting period: The minimum length of time for which an option must be held before it can be exercised.

warrant: A right, but not the obligation, to buy a share at a specified price over a specified period of time. Can be considered a type of call option.

L. REFERENCES

Authoritative standards:

IFRS	ASPE Section
IAS 39—Financial Instruments: Recognition and Measurement	3856—Financial Instruments (includes recognition, measurement, presentation, and disclosure)
IAS 32—Financial Instruments: Presentation	
IFRS 7—Financial Instruments: Disclosures	
IAS 1—Presentation of Financial Statements	1400—General Standards of Financial Statement Presentation
IFRS 2—Share-based Payment	3870—Stock-based Compensation and Other Stock-based Payments
IFRS 9—Financial Instruments	

M. PROBLEMS

P14-1. Nature and identification of financial instruments (L.O. 14-1) (Easy – 5 minutes)

Identify whether each of the following is a financial instrument.

a. Account payable
b. Note payable
c. Warranty provision
d. Long-term debt
e. Common share

P14-2. Nature and identification of financial instruments (L.O. 14-1) (Easy – 5 minutes)

Identify whether each of the following is a financial liability.

a. Account payable
b. Note payable
c. Warranty provision
d. Long-term debt
e. Deferred tax liability

P14-3. Nature and identification of financial instruments (L.O. 14-1) (Easy – 5 minutes)

Identify whether the following financial instruments are (i) a basic financial asset, financial liability, or equity instrument; (ii) a derivative; or (iii) a compound financial instrument.

Item	Basic financial asset, financial liability, or equity instrument	Derivative	Compound financial instrument
a. 10-year bond payable			
b. Convertible debenture			
c. Preferred shares			
d. Convertible preferred shares			
e. Stock warrants			
f. Interest rate swap			

P14-4. Nature and identification of financial instruments (L.O. 14-1) (Easy – 5 minutes)

Identify whether the following financial instruments are (i) a basic financial asset, financial liability, or equity instrument; (ii) a derivative; or (iii) a compound financial instrument.

Item	Basic financial asset, financial liability, or equity instrument	Derivative	Compound financial instrument
a. Employee stock option			
b. Shares with warrants			
c. Bank loan			
d. Convertible bond			
e. Currency forward			

P14-5. Nature and identification of financial instruments (L.O. 14-1) (Easy – 10 minutes)

In relation to stock options, identify whether each of the following statements is true or false.

	Item	True/False
a.	A stock option provides a right to buy but not a right to sell a share.	
b.	An option's fair value is at least as high as its intrinsic value.	
c.	A stock option's fair value increases with the volatility of the underlying stock.	
d.	A stock option's exercise price is the price of the share at the time of exercise.	
e.	An option's intrinsic value cannot be negative.	
f.	An option's intrinsic value increases with the length of time until the option matures.	
g.	An in-the-money option is one in which the exercise price is higher than the market price.	

P14-6. Nature and identification of financial instruments (L.O. 14-1) (Medium – 10 minutes)

In the table below, choose the derivative instrument on the left side that best matches the example on the right side. There is one example for each instrument.

Type of derivative	Example
Option	A company contracts to sell 10,000 ounces of gold at $1,100/ounce on March 15, 2021, on the Chicago Mercantile Exchange.
Warrant	A company contracts with an investment bank to pay the bank 5% interest on $25 million of debt in exchange for receiving LIBOR + 1% from the bank. (LIBOR is the London Interbank Offered Rate, similar to the prime rate.)
Forward	A company purchases the right, but not the obligation, to purchase US dollars for C$1.02/US$1 within a 90-day period.
Future	Company X contracts to buy 10,000 ounces of gold at $1,100/ounce on March 15, 2021, from Company Y.
Swap	An investor purchases a bundle of securities that includes 100 common (ordinary) shares and the right, but not the obligation, to purchase another 100 shares in the same company at $20 each in five years' time.

P14-7. Nature and identification of financial instruments (L.O. 14-1) (Medium – 10 minutes)

Identify the examples of derivatives that follow as one of the following:

- Forward contract
- Future contract
- Option
- Warrant
- Swap

a. Canadian Inc. (which has some US operations) contracts with American Corp. (which has some Canadian operations) to pay the interest and principal on a US$20,000,000 loan in exchange for American Corp. making the payments on a Canadian dollar loan of equal value.
b. Marianne Corp. contracts with its bank to sell them US$100,000 cash in December 2018 at a rate of C$1.15/US$1.00.
c. An investor purchases a bundle of securities that includes a $1,000 bond issued by Starlight Inc. and the right, but not the obligation, to purchase 20 common (ordinary) shares in the company for $38 each in three to five years' time.

d. Jakeman Corp. purchases the right, but not the obligation, to sell €100,000 for C$1.40/€ for a 30-day period.
e. Irene Ltd. purchases 100 BAX (Canadian Banker's acceptance contracts that mature in three months) on the TMX.

P14-8. Accounting for compound financial instruments (L.O. 14-2) (Easy – 5 minutes)

A company issues convertible bonds with a face value of $6,000,000 and receives proceeds of $6,540,000. Each $1,000 bond can be converted, at the option of the holder, into 40 common shares. The underwriter estimated the market value of the bonds alone, excluding the conversion rights, to be approximately $6,200,000.

Required:

Record the journal entry for the issuance of these bonds.

P14-9. Accounting for compound financial instruments (L.O. 14-2) (Easy – 5 minutes)

A company issued 100,000 preferred shares and received proceeds of $6,540,000. These shares have a par value of $60 per share and pay cumulative dividends of 8%. Buyers of the preferred shares also received a detachable warrant with each share purchased. Each warrant gives the holder the right to buy one common share at $30 per share within 10 years. The underwriter estimated that the market value of the preferred shares alone, excluding the conversion rights, is approximately $62 per share. Shortly after the issuance of the preferred shares, the detachable warrants traded at $2 each.

Required:

Record the journal entry for the issuance of these shares and warrants.

P14-10. Accounting for compound financial instruments (L.O. 14-2) (Easy – 5 minutes)[29]

A company had a debt-to-equity ratio of 1.52 before issuing convertible bonds. This ratio included $400,000 in equity. The company issued convertible bonds. The value reported for the bonds on the balance sheet is $254,000, and the conversion rights are valued at $21,000.

Required:

After the issuance of the convertible bonds, what is the debt-to-equity ratio?

P14-11. Accounting for compound financial instruments (L.O. 14-2) (Easy – 5 minutes)[30]

On June 18, 2018, Gail Fisher Ltd. issued for $102 per share, 30,000 no par value, $4 cumulative, convertible preferred shares. Each preferred share could be converted into five no par value common shares at the option of the preferred shareholder. At the time of the share sale, similar non-convertible preferred shares were selling for $100 each. On August 17, 2021, all of the preferred shares were converted into common shares. The market value of the common shares at the date of the conversion was $30 per share.

Required:

Prepare journal entries to record:
a. The issuance of the convertible preferred shares on June 18, 2018.
b. Declaration and payment of the annual dividend on June 18, 2019.
c. Conversion of the preferred shares on August 17, 2021.

29. Uniform Final Examination June 2009, with permission Chartered Professional Accountants of Canada, Toronto, Canada.

30. CGA-Canada FA3 Examination, June 2010, with permission Chartered Professional Accountants of Canada, Toronto, Canada.

P14-12. Accounting for compound financial instruments (L.O. 14-2) (Medium – 10 minutes)[31]

Complete the following table by indicating whether the listed transactions would improve, worsen, or have no effect on the financial ratios listed below. Consider each transaction independently. The answer for the first transaction is presented as an example.

Ratio	Return on common shareholders' equity	Current ratio	Operating margin
Ratio definition	(Net income – Preferred dividends) / Common equity	Current assets / Current liabilities	Operating profit / Revenue
Ratio without transaction	16%	1.25	10%
Repayment of a bond on the first day of the fiscal year	No effect	Worsen	No effect
Conversion of a bond with a 10% stated rate into common shares			
Sale of 2,000 common shares for cash			
Sale of $5,000 of inventory on credit for $6,000 revenue			

P14-13. Accounting for compound financial instruments (L.O. 14-2) (Medium – 15 minutes)[32]

JKD Company reported the following amounts on its balance sheet at July 31, 2021:

Liabilities	
Convertible bonds payable, $4,000,000 face value, 10%, due July 31, 2022	$3,859,649
Equity	
Contributed surplus—common stock conversion rights	345,000
Preferred shares, no par value, 3,100,000 shares authorized, 20,000 outstanding	2,000,000
Common shares, no par value, 1,000,000 shares authorized, 120,000 outstanding	6,000,000
Additional information	
1. The bonds pay interest each July 31. Each $1,000 bond is convertible into 15 common shares. The bonds were originally issued to yield 14%. On July 31, 2022, all the bonds were converted after the final interest payment was made. JKD uses the book value method to record bond conversions as recommended under IFRS.	
2. No other share or bond transactions occurred during the year.	

Required:

a. Prepare the journal entry to record the bond interest payment on July 31, 2022.
b. Calculate the total number of common shares outstanding after the bonds' conversion on July 31, 2022.
c. Prepare the journal entry to record the bond conversion.

31. CGA-Canada FA3 examination, June 2009, with permission Chartered Professional Accountants of Canada, Toronto, Canada.

32. CGA-Canada FA3 Examination, 2009, with permission Chartered Professional Accountants of Canada, Toronto, Canada.

P14-14. Accounting for compound financial instruments (L.O. 14-2) (Medium – 20 minutes)

On September 30, 2018, Niagara Co. issued a $2 million, 8%, 10-year convertible bond maturing on September 30, 2028, with semi-annual coupon payments on March 31 and September 30. Each $1,000 bond can be converted into 80 no par value common shares. In addition, each $1,000 bond included 20 detachable common stock warrants with an exercise price of $20 each. Immediately after issuance, the warrants traded at $4 each on the open market. Gross proceeds on issuance were $2,555,000. Without the warrants and conversion features the bond would be expected to yield 6% annually. Niagara's year-end is December 31.

On February 22, 2021, warrant holders exercised one-half of the warrants. The shares of Niagara traded at $44 each on this day.

Required:

a. Determine how Niagara should allocate the $2,555,000 proceeds into its components. Assume that the warrants are initially recognized at the market value of $4 each.
b. Prepare all the journal entries for fiscal year 2018.
c. Record the journal entry for the exercise of stock warrants on February 22, 2021.

P14-15. Accounting for compound financial instruments (L.O. 14-2) (Medium – 20 minutes)[33]

On January 1, 2021, Portside Co. issued a $10 million, 8%, nine-year convertible bond with annual coupon payments. Each $1,000 bond was convertible into 25 shares of Portside's common shares. Starboard Investments purchased the entire bond issue for $10.2 million on January 1, 2021. Portside estimated that without the conversion feature, the bonds would have sold for $9,400,475 (to yield 9%).

On January 1, 2023, Starboard converted bonds with a par value of $4 million. At the time of conversion, the shares were selling at $45 each.

Required:

a. Prepare the journal entry to record the issuance of the convertible bonds.
b. Prepare the journal entry to record the conversion according to IFRS (book value method).

P14-16. Accounting for compound financial instruments (L.O. 14-2) (Medium – 20 minutes)

On January 1, 2021, Christine and Ian Hacker Inc. issued (sold) $600,000 of 8%, six-year, convertible bonds for gross proceeds of $660,000. Each $1,000 bond was convertible into 20 no par value common shares. Similar non-convertible bonds were yielding 9% at that time. Interest was payable semi-annually on June 30 and December 31.

On July 1, 2025, all bondholders exercised the conversion option and converted the bonds to common shares. The interest payment had been made on June 30, 2025, in the normal fashion.

The company prepares its financial statements in accordance with IFRS. The market price of the common shares was $65 at the date of conversion.

Required:

Prepare journal entries to record:

a. The issuance of the convertible bonds on January 1, 2021.
b. Payment of interest and related amortization on June 30, 2021.
c. Payment of interest and related amortization on June 30, 2025.
d. Conversion of the bonds on July 1, 2025.

P14-17. Accounting for compound financial instruments (L.O. 14-2) (Medium – 15 minutes) A·S·P·E

On January 1, 2021, Christine and Ian Hacker Inc. (CIHI) issued (sold) $600,000 of 8%, six-year, convertible bonds for gross proceeds of $660,000. Each $1,000 bond was convertible into 20 no

[33] CGA-Canada FA3 Examination, March 2010, with permission Chartered Professional Accountants of Canada, Toronto, Canada.

par value common shares. Similar non-convertible bonds were yielding 9% at that time. Interest was payable semi-annually on June 30 and December 31.

On July 1, 2025, all bondholders exercised the conversion option and converted the bonds to common shares. The interest payment had been made on June 30, 2025, in the normal fashion.

The company prepares its financial statements in accordance with ASPE. CIHI elects to determine interest expense using the straight-line method and account for the conversion option using the zero common equity method.

Required:

Prepare journal entries to record:

a. The issuance of the convertible bonds on January 1, 2021.
b. Payment of interest and related amortization on June 30, 2021.
c. Payment of interest and related amortization on June 30, 2025.
d. Conversion of the bonds on July 1, 2025.

P14-18. Accounting for compound financial instruments (L.O. 14-2) (Difficult – 30 minutes)

On January 1, 2021, Gretta Cat Co. (GCC) issued (sold) $2,000,000 of five-year, 5% convertible bonds that pay interest semi-annually on June 30 and December 31. At the investor's option, each $1,000 bond may be converted into 10 common shares any time after December 31, 2024. The sales proceeds realized were $2,100,000 less a $40,000 fee charged by GCC's investment banker. Similar bonds without the conversion feature were yielding 6% at that time. GCC reports its financial results in accordance with IFRS.

Required:

a. Allocate the sales proceeds to the liability and equity components of the convertible bond.
b. Record the issuance of the bonds.
c. Determine the effective interest rate per period on the bond liability.

A·S·P·E

P14-19. Accounting for compound financial instruments (L.O. 14-2) (Difficult – 45 minutes)

Storoshenko Inc. previously sold $1,000,000 in convertible bonds for $1,050,000. At time of issuance, the fair value of the equivalent non-convertible bond was $1,000,000. Interest on the bonds was last paid on August 31, 2021. On September 1, 2021, Storoshenko Inc. repurchased 100% of the outstanding bonds on the open market.

Required:

Prepare the journal entries to record the derecognition of the bonds in each of the following independent scenarios:

Storoshenko Inc. reports its financial results in accordance with IFRS.

a. Storoshenko Inc. paid $1,020,000 to repurchase the bonds. The fair value of a similar bond without the conversion option at the time of repurchase was estimated to be $980,000.
b. Storoshenko Inc. paid $1,080,000 to repurchase the bonds. The fair value of a similar bond without the conversion option at the time of repurchase was estimated to be $1,005,000.

Storoshenko Inc. reports its financial results in accordance with ASPE and used the zero common equity method to initially measure the convertible bond components.

c. Storoshenko Inc. paid $1,020,000 to repurchase the bonds. The amortized cost (book value) of the debt at the time of repurchase was $1,025,000.
d. Storoshenko Inc. paid $1,080,000 to repurchase the bonds. The amortized cost (book value) of the debt at the time of repurchase was $1,025,000.

P14-20. Accounting for compound financial instruments (L.O. 14-2) (Difficult – 45 minutes)

On January 1, 2021, Luv-U-2bits Ltd. sold $500,000 of 6%, five-year convertible bonds for $520,000. Each $1,000 bond was convertible into 40 no par value common shares. Similar non-convertible bonds were yielding 7% at that time. Interest was paid semi-annually on June 30 and December 31.

On July 1, 2024, bondholders converted 60% of the bonds to common shares. The interest payment had been made on June 30, 2024, in the normal fashion.

The company prepares its financial statements in accordance with IFRS.

Required:

Prepare journal entries to record:

a. The issuance of the convertible bonds on January 1, 2021.
b. Payment of interest and related amortization on June 30, 2021.
c. Payment of interest and related amortization on June 30, 2024.
d. Conversion of the bonds on July 1, 2024.
e. Payment of interest and related amortization on December 31, 2025.
f. Derecognition of the bond on January 1, 2026.
g. Briefly explain the process of applying the incremental method of accounting for convertible bonds.

P14-21. Accounting for compound financial instruments (L.O. 14-2) (Difficult – 45 minutes)

On January 1, 2021, Weddings-R-Us Inc. raised $5.5 million by issuing $5 million of 4%, eight-year convertible bonds maturing on January 1, 2029. Interest was paid semi-annually on June 30 and December 31. Each $1,000 bond could be converted into 32 no par value common shares. In addition, each $1,000 bond included 40 detachable common stock warrants with an exercise price of $35 each. Immediately after issuance, the warrants, which expire on January 1, 2029, traded at $3 each on the open market. Similar non-convertible bonds issued without warrants were yielding 5% at that time.

On July 1, 2025, warrant holders exercised 80% of the warrants. The shares of Weddings-R-Us traded at $40 each on that day.

On July 1, 2026, bondholders converted 70% of the bonds to common shares. The interest payment had been made on June 30, 2026, in the normal fashion. The shares of Weddings-R-Us traded at $42 each on that day.

Weddings-R-Us prepares its financial statements in accordance with IFRS.

Required:

Prepare journal entries to record:

a. The issuance of the convertible bonds on January 1, 2021.
b. Payment of interest and related amortization on June 30, 2021.
c. Exercise of the warrants on July 1, 2025.
d. Payment of interest and related amortization on June 30, 2026.
e. Conversion of the bonds on July 1, 2026.
f. Derecognition of the bonds on January 1, 2029.

P14-22. Accounting for compound financial instruments (L.O. 14-2) (Difficult – 45 minutes)[34]

On August 1, 2021, LOL Corporation issued 15-year, $5,000,000, 8%, convertible bonds for proceeds of $5,325,000. The bonds pay interest annually each July 31. Each $1,000 bond is convertible into 50 common shares at the investor's option. If the bond had been sold without the conversion feature, it would have sold for $4,240,000, reflecting a market interest rate of 10%.

LOL's controller recorded the bond issuance on August 1 as follows:

Dr. Cash	5,325,000	
Cr. Bonds payable		5,325,000

The controller did not make any other journal entries related to the bonds as of the company's year-end, December 31.

LOL closed its general ledger accounts and is now preparing its December 31, 2021, financial statements. Upon reviewing the long-term liabilities, you come across the convertible bond journal entry shown above. You know LOL has debt covenants that specify its debt-to-equity ratio cannot exceed 1.20. The preliminary financial statements show total liabilities to be $25,000,000 and total equity of $20,000,000.

---

34. CGA-Canada FA3 Examination, June 2010, with permission Chartered Professional Accountants of Canada, Toronto, Canada.

Required:

a. Prepare the correcting journal entry or entries related to the issuance of the convertible bonds.
b. Prepare the correcting journal entry or entries for the interest on the convertible bonds. Ignore any tax implications. (Remember that the general ledger accounts have been closed for the year.)
c. Discuss the effect of any corrections to the bond recording on the debt-to-equity ratio. However, you do not need to recalculate the ratio.

 P14-23. Accounting for stock compensation plans (L.O. 14-3) (Easy – 10 minutes)[35]

Oshawa Motor Parts issued 100,000 stock options to its employees. The company granted the stock options at-the-money, when the share price was $30. These options have no vesting conditions. By year-end, the share price had increased to $32. Oshawa's management estimates the value of these options at the grant date to be $1.50 each.

Required:

Record the issuance of the stock options.

 P14-24. Accounting for stock compensation plans (L.O. 14-3) (Easy – 5 minutes)

Pelham Farms granted 200,000 stock options to its employees. The options expire 10 years after the grant date of January 1, 2018, when the share price was $25. Employees still employed by Pelham five years after the grant date may exercise the option to purchase shares at $50 each; that is, the options vest to the employees after five years. A consultant estimated the value of each option at the date of grant to be $1 each.

Required:

Record the journal entries relating to the issuance of stock options.

 P14-25. Accounting for stock compensation plans (L.O. 14-3) (Easy – 10 minutes)

Rainy Lake Lodge issued 30,000 at-the-money stock options to its management on January 1, 2021. These options vest on January 1, 2024. Rainy Lake's share price was $12 on the grant date and $18 on the vesting date. Estimates of the fair value of the options showed that they were worth $2 on the grant date and $7 on the vesting date. On the vesting date, management exercised all 30,000 options. Rainy Lake has a December 31 year-end.

Required:

Record all of the journal entries relating to the stock options.

P14-26. Accounting for stock compensation plans 

On January 1, 2021, Unbelievable Golf Inc. granted stock options to various employees for past service. The options, which vested immediately and expired in four years, entitled the employees to purchase 50,000 no par value common shares for $27 each. The market price of Unbelievable's common shares at grant date was $27. Using the Black–Scholes option pricing model, the company estimated the fair value of the options to be $250,000.

On May 31, 2021, 30,000 of the options were exercised when the market value of the shares was $32; the balance was exercised on June 30, 2021, when the market value was $31.

Required:

Record all required journal entries for Unbelievable Golf's stock options.

---

35. CGA-Canada FA3 Examination, June 2009, with permission Chartered Professional Accountants of Canada, Toronto, Canada.

P14-27. Accounting for stock compensation plans ( L.O. 14-3) (Medium – 15 minutes)

On January 1, 2018, Thomasburg Inc. granted stock options to officers and key employees for the purchase of 200,000 of the company's no par value common shares at $25 each. The options were exercisable between January 1, 2020, and December 31, 2024, by grantees still employed by the company. The market price of Thomasburg's common shares was $20 per share at the date of grant. Using the Black–Scholes option pricing model, the company estimated the value of each option on January 1, 2018, to be $3.

On March 31, 2020, 120,000 options were exercised when the market value of the company's common shares was $40 per share. The remainder of the options expired unexercised. The company has a December 31 year-end.

Required:

Record the journal entries for Thomasburg's stock options.

P14-28. Accounting for stock compensation plans (L.O. 14-3) (Medium – 15 minutes)

Refer to the 2016 financial statements for Canadian Tire Corporation in Appendix C.

Required:

a. How many stock options were outstanding at the end of 2016? Reconcile the change in the outstanding options for the year using the same categories that the company reports in its notes to the financial statements.
b. What was the weighted average exercise price of stock options outstanding at the end of 2016? What was the weighted average price of the company's shares when the options were exercised?
c. What were the four categories of share-based payments that Canadian Tire offered to its employees, directors, and executive officers? Describe how each of the categories is settled.
d. What was the intrinsic value of the liability for vested benefits arising from share-based payment plans as at December 31, 2016? What was the carrying value of the liability for share-based payments at the same date? Identify the two most probable factors contributing to the difference.

P14-29. Accounting for compound financial instruments and employee stock options (L.O. 14-2, L.O. 14-3) (Medium – 15 minutes)[36]

On July 1, 2018, Ameri-Can Limited issued $3,000,000 of convertible bonds. The bonds pay annual interest of 10% on June 30. Each $1,000 bond is convertible into 75 common shares, at the investor's option, between July 1, 2023, and July 1, 2028, at which time the bonds mature. The financial instrument was issued for total proceeds of $3,402,605, yielding 8%. The bonds without the conversion feature were valued at $2,660,987, yielding 12%.

Ameri-Can also has a stock option plan. On October 1, 2018, the company issued 5,000 options to employees to buy common shares at $20 per share. An option pricing model valued these options at $50,000. The vesting period is five years. On December 31, 2018, $5,000 worth of options that had been granted in previous years expired unexercised.

Ameri-Can has a December 31 year-end.

Required:

a. Prepare the journal entry to record the issuance of the bonds on July 1, 2018.
b. Prepare the journal entries to record the issuance and expiration of stock options.

P14-30. Accounting for stock compensation plans (L.O. 14-3) (Medium – 20 minutes)

On January 1, 2018, The Ultimate Accountant Inc. granted stock options to officers and key employees for the purchase of 150,000 of the company's no par value common shares at $22 each. The options were exercisable between January 1, 2021, and December 31, 2025, by grantees still

36. CGA-Canada FA3 Examination, 2009, with permission Chartered Professional Accountants of Canada, Toronto, Canada.

employed by the company. The market price of The Ultimate Accountant's common shares was $22 per share at the date of grant. Using the Black–Scholes option pricing model, the company estimated the fair value of the options to be $450,000.

On April 30, 2021, 90,000 options were exercised when the market value of common stock was $29 per share. An additional 50,000 options were exercised on June 30, 2021, when the market value of the shares was $30 each. The remainder of the options expired unexercised. The company has a December 31 year-end.

Required:

Record all required journal entries for The Ultimate Accountant's stock options.

P14-31. Accounting for stock compensation plans (L.O. 14-3) (Medium – 20 minutes)

On January 1, 2021, Honeymoon Corp. established a cash-settled stock appreciation rights plan for its senior employees, the details of which are listed below:

- 100,000 stock appreciation rights (SARs) were granted.
- Each SAR entitled the employees to receive cash equal to the difference between the market price of the common shares and a benchmark price of $10.
- The SARs vested after two years of service; they expired on December 31, 2025.
- On January 1, 2023, 60,000 SARs were exercised. The market price of the shares remained at $12.
- On January 1, 2024, the balance of the SARs were exercised. The market price of the shares remained at $13.
- Pertinent stock-related data are set out below:

	Fair value of each SAR	Market price of share
January 1, 2021		$10
December 31, 2021	$5	11
December 31, 2022	4	12
December 31, 2023	7	13
December 31, 2024	6	14
December 31, 2025	5	15

Required:

a. Complete the schedule below showing the amount of compensation expense for each of the five years, starting with 2021. If necessary, refer to the example illustrated in Exhibit 14-21 for guidance.
b. Prepare the journal entry at December 31, 2021, to record compensation expense.
c. Prepare the journal entry at December 31, 2022, to record compensation expense.
d. Prepare the journal entry at January 1, 2023, to record the partial exercise of the SARs.
e. Prepare the journal entry at December 31, 2023, to record compensation expense.
f. Prepare the journal entry at January 1, 2024, to record the exercise of the balance of the SARs.
g. Prepare the journal entry at December 31, 2024, to record compensation expense.
h. Prepare the journal entry at December 31, 2025 to record compensation expense.

Cash-Settled Stock Appreciation Rights—Compensation Expense (IFRS)						
A	B	C	D	E = B × C × D	F	G = E − F
Date	Fair value	Number of SARs	Percentage accrued	Cumulative liability close	Cumulative liability open	Compensation expense
Dec. 31, 2021						
Dec. 31, 2022						

(Continued)

Cash-Settled Stock Appreciation Rights—Compensation Expense (IFRS)						
A	B	C	D	$E = B \times C \times D$	F	$G = E - F$
Jan. 1, 2023	X				Partial exercise of SARs	
Jan. 1, 2023	X					
Dec. 31, 2023						
Jan. 1, 2024	X				Partial exercise of SARs	
Jan. 1, 2024	X					
Dec. 31, 2024						
Dec. 31, 2025						

P14-32. Accounting for stock compensation plans

(L.O. 14-3) (Medium – 20 minutes) **A·S·P·E**

Refer to P14-31 above. Assume Honeymoon Corp. reports its financial results in accordance with ASPE.

Required:

a. Complete the schedule below showing the amount of compensation expense for each of the five years, starting with 2021. If necessary, refer to the example illustrated in Exhibit 14-23 for guidance.
b. Prepare the journal entry at December 31, 2021, to record compensation expense.
c. Prepare the journal entry at December 31, 2022, to record compensation expense.
d. Prepare the journal entry at January 1, 2023, to record the partial exercise of the SARs.
e. Prepare the journal entry at December 31, 2023, to record compensation expense.
f. Prepare the journal entry at January 1, 2024, to record the exercise of the balance of the SARs.
g. Prepare the journal entry at December 31, 2024, to record compensation expense.
h. Prepare the journal entry at December 31, 2025, to record compensation expense.

Cash-Settled Stock Appreciation Rights—Compensation Expense (ASPE)							
A	B	C	D	E	$F = (B - C) \times D \times E$ subject to liability ≥ \$0	G	$H = F - G$
Date	Market value	Benchmark price	Number of SARs	Percentage accrued	Cumulative liability close	Cumulative liability open	Compensation expense
Dec. 31, 2021							
Dec. 31, 2022							
Jan. 1, 2023						Partial exercise of SARs	
Jan. 1, 2023	X						
Dec. 31, 2023							
Jan. 1, 2024						Exercise of balance of SARs	
Jan. 1, 2024	X						
Dec. 31, 2024							
Dec. 31, 2025							

P14-33. Accounting for stock compensation plans with forfeiture

(L.O. 14-3) (Difficult – 25 minutes)

Taj Singh Corp. (TSC) reports its financial results in accordance with IFRS. It has a December 31 year-end.

On January 1, 2021, TSC granted stock options to officers and key employees that entitled them to collectively purchase 10,000 of the company's no par value common shares for $30 each. The options vest on December 31, 2023. On the grant date, TSC estimated the fair value of the options to be $100,000.

On December 31, 2021, TSC estimated the forfeiture rate on the options would be 5%. On December 31, 2022, TSC updated the estimated forfeiture rate to 7%. On December 31, 2023, 94% of the options actually vested.

On January 15, 2024, when the company stock was trading at $48, 100% of eligible employees exercised their stock options.

Required:

Record all required journal entries pertaining to the employee stock options issued by Taj Singh Corp.

P14-34. Accounting for stock compensation plans (L.O. 14-3) (Difficult – 30 minutes)

On January 1, 2021, Stephanie Place Inc. established a cash-settled stock appreciation rights plan for its executives, the details of which are listed below:

- 180,000 stock appreciation rights (SARs) were granted.
- Each SAR entitled the executives to receive cash equal to the difference between the market price of the common shares and a benchmark price of $16.
- The SARs vested after three years of service; they expired on December 31, 2026.
- On January 1, 2024, 80,000 SARs are exercised. The market price of the shares remained at $20.
- On January 1, 2025, 60,000 SARs are exercised. The market price of the shares remained at $22.
- The remaining SARs expired.
- Pertinent stock-related data are set out below:

	Fair value of each SAR	Market price of share
January 1, 2021		$16
December 31, 2021	$10	21
December 31, 2022	6	18
December 31, 2023	7	20
December 31, 2024	8	22
December 31, 2025	1	15
December 31, 2026	0	14

Required:

a. Complete the schedule below showing the amount of compensation expense for each of the six years, starting with 2021. If necessary, refer to the example illustrated in Exhibit 14-21 for guidance.
b. Prepare the journal entry at December 31, 2021, to record compensation expense.
c. Prepare the journal entry at January 1, 2024, to record the partial exercise of the SARs.
d. Prepare the journal entry at January 1, 2025, to record the partial exercise of the SARs.
e. Prepare the journal entry at December 31, 2026, to record compensation expense.

Cash-Settled Stock Appreciation Rights—Compensation Expense (IFRS)						
A	B	C	D	E = B × C × D	F	G = E − F
Date	Fair value	Number of SARs	Percentage accrued	Cumulative liability close	Cumulative liability open	Compensation expense
Dec. 31, 2021						
Dec. 31, 2022						
Dec. 31, 2023						

(Continued)

Cash-Settled Stock Appreciation Rights—Compensation Expense (IFRS)						
A	B	C	D	E = B × C × D	F	G = E − F
Jan. 1, 2024	X				Partial exercise of SARs	
Jan. 1, 2024	X					
Dec. 31, 2024						
Jan. 1, 2025	X				Partial exercise of SARs	
Jan. 1, 2025	X					
Dec. 31, 2025						
Dec. 31, 2026						

P14-35. Accounting for stock compensation plans (L.O. 14-3) (Difficult – 30 minutes)

Refer to P14-34 above. Assume that Stephanie Place Inc. reports its financial results in accordance with ASPE.

A·S·P·E

Required:

a. Complete the schedule below showing the amount of compensation expense for each of the six years, starting with 2021. If necessary, refer to the example illustrated in Exhibit 14-23 for guidance.
b. Prepare the journal entry at December 31, 2021, to record compensation expense.
c. Prepare the journal entry at January 1, 2024, to record the partial exercise of the SARs.
d. Prepare the journal entry at January 1, 2025, to record the partial exercise of the SARs.
e. Prepare the journal entry at December 31, 2025, to record compensation expense.

Cash-Settled Stock Appreciation Rights—Compensation Expense (ASPE)							
A	B	C	D	E	F = (B − C) × D × E subject to liability ≥ $0	G	H = F − G
Date	Market value	Benchmark price	Number of SARs	Percentage accrued	Cumulative liability close	Cumulative liability open	Compensation expense
Dec. 31, 2021							
Dec. 31, 2022							
Dec. 31, 2023							
Jan. 1, 2024						Partial exercise of SARs	
Jan. 1, 2024	X						
Dec. 31, 2024							
Jan. 1, 2025						Partial exercise of SARs	
Jan. 1, 2025	X						
Dec. 31, 2025							
Dec. 31, 2026							

P14-36. Accounting for stock compensation plans with forfeiture (L.O. 14-3) (Difficult – 35 minutes)

Sam's Kennel Corp (SKC) maintains an employee stock option plan for its senior executive. On January 1, 2021, SKC awarded its employees a total of 20,000 options that are first exercisable on January 1, 2025. Each option, which expires on December 31, 2029, enables the employees to buy one common share of SKC, which was trading at $20 on the grant date. On the grant date, SKC estimated the fair value of the options to be $5 each.

SKC reports its financial results in accordance with IFRS. It has a December 31 year-end. Estimated and actual forfeiture rates appear below:

Date	Forfeiture rate
December 31, 2021	12%
December 31, 2022	10%
December 31, 2023	8%
December 31, 2024	9%

On January 31, 2025, when the company stock was trading at $32 and the fair value of the options was $15 each, employees exercised 12,000 of the stock options.

Required:

Prepare journal entries to record compensation expense for each of December 31, 2021, 2022, 2023, and 2024, and the exercise of the stock options on January 31, 2025.

Cash-Settled Stock Appreciation Rights—Compensation Expense (IFRS)

A	B	C	D	E	F = (B − C) × D × E	G	H = F − G
Date	**Market value per share**	**Benchmark price**	**Number of SARs**	**Percentage accrued**	**Cumulative liability ending balance**	**Cumulative liability beginning balance**	**Compensation expense**
Dec. 31, 2021							
Dec. 31, 2022							
Dec. 31, 2023							
Dec. 31, 2024							
Jan. 31, 2025	X					Partial exercise of SARS	

P14-37. Accounting for stock compensation plans with forfeiture

(L.O. 14-3) (Difficult – 45 minutes)

On January 1, 2021, Samantha Clark Corp. established a cash-settled stock appreciation rights plan for its executives, the details of which are listed below:

- 100,000 stock appreciation rights (SARs) were granted.
- Each SAR entitled the executives to receive cash equal to the difference between the market price of the common shares and a benchmark price of $12.
- The SARs vested after three years of service; they expired on December 31, 2025.
- On June 15, 2025, 40,000 SARs are exercised. The market price of the shares at time of exercise was $17.
- On December 15, 2025, the remaining SARs are exercised. The market price of the shares at time of exercise was $18.
- Estimated and actual forfeiture rates follow:

	Forfeiture rate
December 31, 2021	7%
December 31, 2022	6%
December 31, 2023	9%

- Stock price related data follows:

	Fair value of each SAR	Market price of share
January 1, 2021	NA	$12
December 31, 2021	$8	15
December 31, 2022	5	13
December 31, 2023	7	17
December 31, 2024	6	16
December 31, 2025	0	19

Required:

a. Complete the schedule below showing the amount of compensation expense for each of the five years, starting with 2021. If necessary, refer to the example illustrated in Exhibit 14-21 for guidance.
b. Prepare the journal entry at December 31, 2021, to record compensation expense.
c. Prepare the journal entry at June 15, 2025, to record the partial exercise of the SARs.
d. Prepare the journal entry at December 15, 2025, to record the exercise of the remaining SARs.
e. Prepare the journal entry at December 31, 2025, to record the required adjustment to compensation expense.

Cash-Settled Stock Appreciation Rights—Compensation Expense (IFRS)						
A	B	C	D	E = B × C × D	F	G = E − F
Date	Fair value	Number of SARs	Percentage accrued	Cumulative liability close	Cumulative liability open	Compensation expense
Dec. 31, 2021						
Dec. 31, 2022						
Dec. 31, 2023						
Dec. 31, 2024						
June 15, 2025	X				Partial exercise of SARs	
Dec. 15, 2025	X				Exercise of remaining SARs	
Dec. 31, 2025						

P14-38. Accounting for equity transactions, complex financial instruments, and employee stock options (L.O. 14-2, L.O. 14-3) (Difficult – 60 minutes)

Corus Manufacturing Ltd., a sailboat manufacturer, is preparing its financial statements for the year ended August 31, 2018. It is September 15 and your CFO presents you (the controller) with a list of issues that require additional attention:

i. The company repurchased 100,000 common shares at $17/share on March 31, 2018. Of these, 70,000 were put into treasury and the remainder were cancelled.
ii. Corus has a stock option plan for its management team. At the beginning of fiscal year 2018, the company had outstanding 200,000 stock options with an exercise price of $12; the value of these options at the grant date was $1.50 per option. On April 30, 2018, 150,000 of these options were exercised and 50,000 expired. The company used treasury shares to supply the shares for the stock option exercises.
iii. On May 1, 2018, the company granted to management employees another 50,000 stock options for services to be rendered from the grant date until April 30, 2020. These options had an exercise price of $18, vest with the employees on April 30, 2022, and expire on April 30, 2027. These options had an estimated fair value of $2.40 per option on the grant date.
iv. Corus had a two-for-one stock split on May 31, 2018. Relevant conditions of convertible securities and stock options were adjusted for this split.

v. The company issued long-term bonds to a group of private investors. The bonds were issued on June 30, 2018, had maturity value of $20 million on June 30, 2024, and pay semi-annual interest at a rate of 7% per year. Each $1,000 bond is convertible into 50 common shares. Proceeds of the issuance were $21.5 million. Without the conversion feature, the bond would have been priced to yield 8% per annum, resulting in proceeds of $18,640,967.

The company had net income of $10.5 million for fiscal 2018, a tax rate of 30%, and $16 average stock price.

The equity section of the company's balance sheet on August 31, 2017 (end of the prior fiscal year), showed the following:

Preferred stock ($200 par, 6% cumulative, 50 million authorized, 100,000 issued and outstanding)	$ 20,000,000
Common stock (no par value, unlimited number authorized, 9.5 million issued, 9.42 million outstanding)	57,000,000
Treasury stock (80,000 common shares)	(1,200,000)
Contributed surplus—issuance of preferred shares	800,000
Contributed surplus—repurchases/resales of common shares	300,000
Contributed surplus—stock options	475,000
Contributed surplus—expired stock options	285,000
Contributed surplus—conversion rights*	950,000
Retained earnings	34,500,000
Total shareholders' equity	$113,110,000

* The bonds with these conversion rights were issued in fiscal 2008, had face value of $5 million and coupon payments of 8% per year payable semi-annually, yielded 6%, and mature on September 30, 2022. Each $100 bond is convertible into 10 common shares. On April 1, 2018, all of these bonds were converted into common shares.

Required:

a. Record the repurchase of 100,000 shares on March 31, 2018. Use the number of shares issued (rather than outstanding) to compute any per share amounts of contributed surplus. [*Hint:* You need two separate journal entries.]
b. Compute the April 1, 2018 carrying value of the debt portion of the convertible bond issued in fiscal 2008.
c. Record the conversion of the $5 million of bonds into common shares on April 1, 2018. Use the book value method.
d. Record the exercise of stock options and the related sale of treasury shares on April 30, 2018.
e. Record the entry to reflect stock option expiration on April 30, 2018.
f. Record the issuance of stock options on May 1, 2018.
g. Record the $20 million security issuance of bonds on June 30, 2018.
h. Show in good form the equity section of the balance sheet for Corus as at August 31, 2018.

APPENDIX PROBLEMS

P14A-39. Accounting for derivatives (L.O. 14-4) (Easy – 5 minutes)

On December 15, a company enters into a foreign currency forward to buy €200,000 at C$1.32 per euro in 30 days. The exchange rate on the day of the company's year-end of December 31 was C$1.30:€1.

Required:

Record the journal entries related to this forward contract.

P14A-40. Accounting for derivatives (L.O. 14-4) (Easy – 5 minutes)

A company pays $8,000 to purchase futures contracts to buy 200 ounces of gold at $1,200/ounce. At the company's year-end, the price of gold was $1,230/ounce and the value of the company's futures contracts increased to $12,000.

Required:

Record the journal entries related to these futures.

P14A-41. Accounting for derivatives (L.O. 14-4) (Medium – 10 minutes)

On August 15, 2018, Jarvis Company issued 50,000 options on the shares of RBC (Royal Bank Corporation). Each option gives the option holder the right to buy one share of RBC at $60 each until March 16, 2019. Jarvis received $150,000 for issuing these options. At the company's year-end of December 31, 2018, the options contracts traded on the Montreal Exchange at $2.50 per contract. On March 16, 2019, RBC shares closed at $58 per share, so none of the options was exercised.

Required:

Record the journal entries related to these call options.

P14A-42. Accounting for derivatives (L.O. 14-4) (Medium – 15 minutes)

Kearney Corporation issued call options on 20,000 shares of BCE Inc. on October 21, 2021. These options give the holder the right to buy BCE shares at $33 per share until May 17, 2022. For issuing these options, Kearney received $30,000. On December 31, 2021 (Kearney's fiscal year-end), the options traded on the Montreal Exchange for $3.50 per option. On May 17, 2022, BCE's share price increased to $37 and the option holders exercised their options. Kearney had no holdings of BCE shares.

Required:

For Kearney Corporation, record the journal entries related to these call options.

P14A-43. Accounting for derivatives (L.O. 14-4) (Medium – 20 minutes)

On December 19, 2018, Enchanted Inc. sold 1,000 put options on the common shares of CIBC. Each option gives the option holder the right to sell one share of CIBC at $100 each until March 19, 2019. Enchanted received $1,000 for issuing these options. At the company's year-end of December 31, 2018, the options contracts traded on the TMX at $1.50 per contract. On March 19, 2019, CIBC shares closed at $98 per share, and the options were exercised.

Required:

Record the journal entries related to these put options.

P14A-44. Nature of hedges (L.O. 14-5) (Easy – 5 minutes)

Identify whether each of the following derivatives provides a fair value hedge or a cash flow hedge if it is used as a hedging instrument.

Item	Fair value hedge or cash flow hedge?
a. A forward contract to buy US$1 million for C$1.05 million.	
b. A swap of investment with a variable interest rate with one providing a fixed return.	
c. A swap of a foreign-denominated bond payable for one denominated in Canadian dollars.	
d. A futures contract to sell 10,000 ounces of gold at US$1,150/ounce.	

P14A-45. Nature of hedges (L.O. 14-5) (Medium – 10 minutes)

A company located in Canada spends $6,000 to purchase a foreign currency futures contract to buy US$500,000 at C$1.02:US$1.00. The contract matures 90 days later. Under which of the following circumstances could the company consider this future contract to be a fair value hedge for accounting purposes?

Circumstance	Futures contract to buy USD can be considered as a fair value hedge?
a. The company has an account receivable of US$500,000 due in 90 days.	
b. The company has an account payable of US$500,000 due in 90 days.	
c. The company has an investment in shares traded on a US stock exchange and plans to sell these shares in 90 days.	
d. The company intends to buy US$500,000 of inventories for which it must pay 90 days later.	

P14A-46. Nature of hedges (L.O. 14-5) (Medium – 10 minutes)

The following is selected balance sheet information for Taylor Company, which has operations located primarily in Canada. Amounts are in Canadian dollars unless otherwise indicated.

Assets	Amount	Liabilities and equity	Amount
Cash	$ 30,000	Accounts payable	$ 350,000
Cash (US$)	200,000	Accounts payable (US$)	300,000
Accounts receivable	500,000	Long-term debt, 6% interest	1,000,000
Property, plant, and equipment	1,200,000	Common shares	600,000
Goodwill	400,000	Retained earnings	250,000

Required:

Taking into account the above information, first identify whether Taylor Company could potentially identify the following items as hedging instruments for accounting purposes. If it is a potential hedging instrument, identify the item being hedged. If not, explain why not.

Item	Potential hedging instrument?	Item being hedged or explanation
a.	A forward contract to sell US$200,000	
b.	A forward contract to sell US$100,000	
c.	A forward contract to buy US$100,000	
d.	An interest rate swap involving future payments of 6% interest and receipts of prime + 2% on $1,000,000 principal	

P14A-47. Accounting for hedges (L.O. 14-5) (Medium – 20 minutes)

On December 1, 2021, Aaron Brandon Ltd. entered into a binding agreement to buy inventory costing US$200,000 for delivery on February 16, 2022. Terms of the sale were COD (cash on delivery). Aaron, which has a December 31 year-end, decided to hedge its foreign exchange risk and entered into a forward agreement to receive US$200,000 at that time. Aaron designated the forward a fair value hedge. Pertinent exchange rates follow:

Date	Spot rate C$ per US$1	Forward rate for delivery on February 2, 2022, C$ per US$1
December 1, 2021	1.010	1.000
December 31, 2021	0.980	0.995
February 2, 2022	0.990	0.990

Required:

Record the required journal entries for December 1, December 31, and February 2 using the net method. If no entries are required, state "no entry required" and indicate why.

P14A-48. Accounting for hedges (L.O. 14-5) (Medium – 20 minutes)

Refer to P14A-47 above. Assume that Aaron designated the forward as a cash flow hedge.

Required:

Record the required journal entries for December 1, December 31, and February 2, using the net method. If no entries are required, state "no entry required" and indicate why.

P14A-49. Accounting for hedges (L.O. 14-5) (Medium – 20 minutes)

On June 18, 2021, Jamie Banfied Inc. signed a contract to sell machinery for €100,000 (inventoried cost C$110,000) for delivery on August 12, 2021. Terms of the sale were COD (cash on delivery). Jamie, which has a June 30 year-end, entered into a forward agreement to sell €100,000 on August 12 to mitigate its foreign exchange risk. Jamie designated the forward a fair value hedge. Pertinent exchange rates follow:

Date	Spot rate C$ per €1	Forward rate for delivery on August 12, 2021, C$ per €1
June 18, 2021	1.300	1.305
June 30, 2021	1.310	1.310
August 12, 2021	1.290	1.290

Required:

Record the required journal entries for June 18, June 30, and August 12 using the net method. If no entries are required, state "no entry required" and indicate why.

P14A-50. Accounting for hedges (L.O. 14-5) (Medium – 20 minutes)

Refer to P14A-49 above. Assume that Jamie designated the forward as a cash flow hedge.

Required:

Record the required journal entries for June 18, June 30, and August 12, using the net method. If no entries are required, state "no entry required" and indicate why.

N. MINI-CASES

CASE 1
Ultramart
(30 minutes)

Ultramart is a chain of large discount supermarkets with 30 locations primarily in southern Ontario. The company was founded about 40 years ago. Although the company is now publicly traded, the founding family still has 30% of the 50 million common shares outstanding, which are trading around $40 per share. The second generation of the family holds the important posts in management.

The CEO, Theodor (Ted) Chamberlain, has bold plans to expand Ultramart beyond the Ontario border. Recently, he attended a conference on finance and strategy where there was much discussion about less conventional types of financial instruments. After the conference, he comes to you, the CFO of Ultramart, to talk about some of what he heard and saw.

Ted: The investment bankers went over quite a few financial instruments. In keeping with the theme of the conference, they didn't spend much time on traditional stocks and bonds. Instead, they talked a lot about options, swaps, and so on. I didn't find much of it relevant, but one thing that did catch my eye was the idea of hybrids. They said that hybrids, or compound financial instruments, are a combination of different instruments, such as a bond that is convertible into shares. I know that hybrid cars are very popular these days, and it seems that the trend is catching on in finance as well.

You: Yes, I have heard of hybrid instruments before.

Ted: As you know, we are going to ramp up our expansion plans. To do that, we need to bring in a lot more financing, probably $500 million or so. I am wondering whether these hybrids are a good alternative. We could go the traditional way and issue more shares or bonds to the public. The speakers at the conference talked about convertible bonds benefiting from lower interest rates of 3–4% because of the sweeteners in the deal. If this works, we could save quite a bit of money. What do you think? Could you write me a memo explaining these hybrids and whether we should go with some sort of hybrid or more traditional financing sources?

Required:

Prepare the memo requested by the CEO.

CASE 2
Canadian Development Limited
(30 minutes)[37]

Stephanie Baker is an audit senior with the public accounting firm of Wilson & Lang. It is February 2022, and the audit of Canadian Development Limited (CDL) for the year ended December 31, 2021, is proceeding. Stephanie has identified several transactions that occurred in the 2021 fiscal year that have major accounting implications. The engagement partner has asked Stephanie to draft a memo to him addressing the accounting implications of these transactions.

CDL is an important player in many sectors of the economy. The company has both debt and equity securities that trade on a Canadian stock exchange. Except for a controlling interest (53%) owned by the Robichaud family, CDL's shares are widely held. The company has interests in the natural resources, commercial and residential real estate, construction, transportation, and technology development sectors, among others.

Changes in Capital Structure

During 2021, CDL's underwriters recommended some changes to the company's capital structure. As a result, the company raised $250 million by issuing 1 million convertible,

[37] Uniform Final Examination 1989, with permission Chartered Professional Accountants of Canada, Toronto, Canada.

redeemable debentures at $250 each. Each debenture is convertible into one common share at any time. A sizable block of the 1 million debentures issued was acquired by CDL's controlling shareholders; the remainder were taken up by a few large institutional investors like pension funds.

The company proposes to partition the balance sheet in a manner that will include a section entitled "Shareholders' Equity and Convertible Debentures." The company views this classification as appropriate because the convertible debt, being much more akin to equity than debt, represents a part of the company's permanent capital. Maurice Richard, the controller of CDL, has emphasized that the interest rate on the debentures is considerably lower than on normal convertible issues and that it is expected that the majority of investors will exercise their conversion privilege. The company has the option of repaying the debt at maturity in 20 years' time through the issuance of common shares. The company's intention is to raise additional permanent capital, and convertible debt was chosen because of the attractive tax savings from the deductibility of interest payments.

The debentures are redeemable at the option of the holder at $250 from January 1, 2027, to January 1, 2030.

At the same time as the company issued the convertible debentures, 2 million common shares were converted into 2 million preferred, redeemable shares. The net book value of the 2 million common shares was $20 million. The preferred shares do not bear dividends and are mandatorily redeemable in five years at $15 per share. They have been recorded at their redemption value of $30 million; the difference between this redemption value and the net book value of the common shares (a difference of $10 million) has been charged against retained earnings.

Required:

Take the role of Stephanie Baker and prepare the memo for the partner.

CASE 3

Convertible debt

(20 minutes)

Lord Motor Co. is a large carmaker famous for the high-quality automobiles it manufactures. The Company recently completed a debt restructuring initiative that substantially reduced its debt and lowered its interest expense.

The company previously issued $50 million in 5% convertible bonds on January 1, 2021 for net proceeds of $46,869,892. The market interest rate for similar non-convertible debt at that time was 8%. The bonds mature on January 1, 2029, and pay interest semi-annually on January 1 and July 1.

On October 1, 2023, Lord Motor Co. announced a conversion offer proposing to pay a cash premium to induce the holders of the bonds to convert them into shares of Lord's common stock. Bondholders had until December 31, 2023, to tender their bonds for conversion under the enhanced offer. Bonds with a face amount of $42 million were tendered resulting in the payment of accrued interest on the bonds; the issuance of an aggregate 2.52 million shares of Lord's common stock; and the payment of an aggregate $1.26 million in cash for the inducement.

On December 31, 2023, Lord Motor's shares traded at $15.50 and the convertible bonds at $95. Lord Motor reports its financial results in accordance with IFRS.

Required:

a. What are some reasons why Lord Motor offered bondholders the option to convert their debt to equity? Why did they offer the cash as an inducement?
b. What percentage of bondholders accepted the offer?
c. What was the conversion rate expressed as 1 share per $x.xx dollars of bonds?
d. For each $10,000 in bonds (face value) converted, how much cash did the holder receive as an inducement to convert?
e. Prepare the journal entries required on December 31, 2023.
f. What will the interest expense be in 2024? How much was expensed in 2023?
g. Was the cash inducement necessary to make bondholders convert? Explain your reasoning.

Torontonian/Alamy Stock Photo; Pat Holmes/Alamy Stock Photo; Brent Lewin/Bloomberg/Getty Images

CHAPTER 15
Earnings per Share

LEARNING OBJECTIVES

After studying this chapter, you should be able to:

L.O. 15-1. Describe the reasons for reporting basic and diluted earnings per share.

L.O. 15-2. Calculate basic earnings per share.

L.O. 15-3. Differentiate between dilutive and antidilutive potential ordinary shares.

L.O. 15-4. Calculate diluted earnings per share.

CPA competencies addressed in this chapter:

1.2.2 Evaluates treatment for routine transactions (Level A)
j. Earnings per share (basic and diluted)

1.2.4 Analyzes treatment for complex events or transactions (Level C)
a. Complex financial instruments

1.3.1 Prepares financial statements (Level A)

1.3.2 Prepares routine financial statement note disclosure (Level B)

Canadian Tire Corporation's (CTC) operations include Canadian Tire's retail and automotive service operations, as well as CT REIT and Financial Services; FGL's sporting goods retail chains, including Sport Chek and Sports Experts; and Mark's, the clothing retailer.

For the year ended December 31, 2016, CTC reported basic and diluted earnings per share (EPS) of $9.25 and $9.22, respectively. These results were up from the $8.66 (basic) and $8.61 (diluted) reported the previous year-end.

Why does CTC report EPS in its financial statements? Why does it report both basic and diluted EPS? What is the difference between basic and diluted EPS, and how is each calculated?

15 CONTENTS

A. INTRODUCTION TO BASIC AND DILUTED EARNINGS PER SHARE 751
B. CALCULATING BASIC EPS 752
1. Numerator: Net income available to ordinary shareholders 753
2. Denominator: Weighted average number of ordinary shares outstanding 755
3. Complicating factors 756
4. Basic EPS 759
C. CALCULATING DILUTED EPS 760
1. Identify all potential ordinary shares 761
2. Compute incremental EPS for all potential ordinary shares 762
3. Rank order incremental EPS 764
4. Sequentially compare incremental EPS to provisional EPS to determine diluted EPS 764
5. Effect of discontinued operations 769
6. Diluted EPS when basic EPS is negative 770
7. Other considerations 771
8. Putting it all together: A comprehensive example 772
D. PRESENTATION AND DISCLOSURE 774
1. Presentation 774
2. Disclosure 774
E. SUBSTANTIVE DIFFERENCES BETWEEN RELEVANT IFRS AND ASPE 775
F. SUMMARY 775
G. ANSWERS TO CHECKPOINT QUESTIONS 776
H. GLOSSARY 776
I. REFERENCES 777
J. PROBLEMS 778
K. MINI-CASES 797

A. INTRODUCTION TO BASIC AND DILUTED EARNINGS PER SHARE

For the year ended December 31, 2016, Canadian Tire's consolidated net income totalled \$747.5 million. If you owned a CTC common share, a natural question to ask when you read this information would be, "How much of the profit belongs to me?" As one among many thousands of shareholders, the total amount CTC earns is not as meaningful to you as your share of profit. In this case, each share in CTC earned \$9.25, which is CTC's **earnings per share (EPS)**. EPS measures each common share's interest in a company's earnings. (IFRS uses the term "ordinary share" to refer to what traditionally have been known as common shares in Canada. This chapter will use the IFRS terminology.)

L.O. 15-1. Describe the reasons for reporting basic and diluted earnings per share.

earnings per share (EPS) Measures each ordinary share's interest in a company's earnings.

The EPS figure is frequently quoted in the financial press. It is used by investors and analysts to assess company performance, to predict future earnings, and to estimate the value of the firm's shares. (Section C of Appendix A to this text describes some basic approaches for valuing a company.) There are two EPS statistics: basic and diluted.

- Basic EPS communicates "ownership" of earnings based on the average number of ordinary shares *actually* outstanding during the period.
- Diluted EPS is more abstract in nature as it conveys a *hypothetical* worst-case scenario that considers the effect of potentially dilutive securities—securities that could lead to the issuance of additional ordinary shares. Examples of securities that are potentially dilutive include convertible securities and stock options, discussed in Chapter 14.

simple capital structures A capital structure that does not include potentially dilutive securities.

complex capital structures A capital structure that includes potentially dilutive securities.

Capital structures that do not include potentially dilutive securities are commonly referred to as **simple capital structures**; those that have such securities are known as **complex capital structures**. All publicly accountable entities must report basic EPS information in their financial statements. Moreover, companies with a complex financial structure must also report diluted EPS. The IASB's reasons for requiring disclosure of EPS information are set out in IAS 33—Earnings per Share:

> ¶1 The objective of this Standard is to prescribe principles for the determination and presentation of earnings per share, so as to improve performance comparisons between different entities in the same reporting period and between different reporting periods for the same entity.
>
> ¶11 The objective of basic earnings per share information is to provide a measure of the interests of each ordinary share of a parent entity in the performance of the entity over the reporting period.
>
> ¶32 The objective of diluted earnings per share is consistent with that of basic earnings per share—to provide a measure of the interest of each ordinary share in the performance of an entity—while giving effect to all dilutive potential ordinary shares outstanding during the period.[1]

The need for basic EPS is simply to increase the understandability and comparability of the earnings number. The need for diluted EPS is to prevent moral hazard, which was discussed in Chapter 1. In the absence of diluted EPS, it would be easier for management to mislead shareholders regarding the profitability of the company by issuing securities such as convertible bonds and stock options that do not entail the issuance of ordinary shares immediately, but which could lead to share issuances in the future.

THRESHOLD CONCEPT
INFORMATION ASYMMETRY

Accounting Standards for Private Enterprises (ASPE) in Canada do not require companies to report EPS information in their financial statements because the owners of such private enterprises normally have substantial ownerships such that per share amounts are no more informative than the aggregate earnings.[2] For private companies that choose to apply international standards, IFRS also does not require such companies to disclose EPS information unless they are in the process of going public (IAS 33 paragraph 2).

CHECKPOINT **CP15-1**

Briefly contrast a simple capital structure with that of a complex capital structure.

B. CALCULATING BASIC EPS

basic EPS An indicator of profitability that measures how much of the company's earnings are attributable (belong) to each ordinary share.

L.O. 15-2. Calculate basic earnings per share.

Basic EPS is an indicator of profitability that measures how much of the company's earnings are attributable (belong) to each ordinary share. Recall from the opening vignette that CTC's basic EPS for 2016 was $9.25. The equation for basic EPS is simply the following ratio:

1. Copyright © 2012 IFRS Foundation.

2. Recall that a private enterprise is a profit-oriented entity that is neither a publicly accountable enterprise nor an entity in the public sector.

Exhibit 15-1 Formula for basic EPS

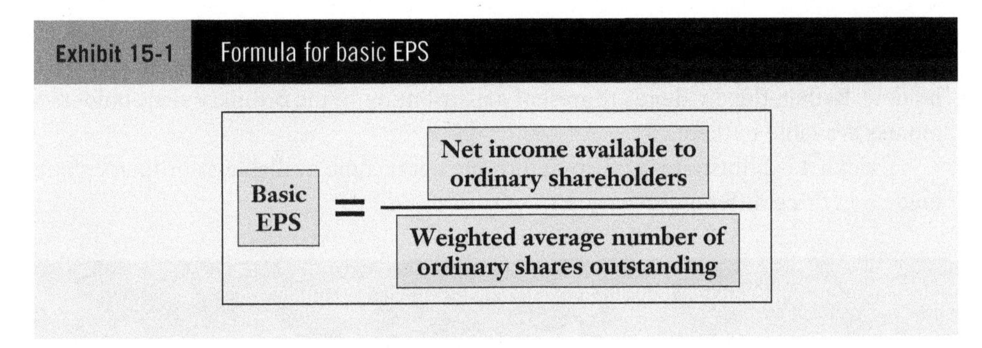

The ratio that is basic EPS is certainly intuitive. However, the components of the ratio require some more exploration, as detailed below.

1. Numerator: Net income available to ordinary shareholders

For purposes of EPS, the measure of earnings is not net income but a slightly different measure called **net income available to ordinary shareholders**, which is net income less dividends on preferred shares. There are two key points regarding the numerator. First, it is important to note that we exclude other comprehensive income (OCI) from the numerator because EPS is intended to measure performance (see IAS 33 paragraph 1 above); items in OCI are deemed not to be a part of current period performance. For example, OCI contains unrealized gains or losses on financial assets at fair value through other comprehensive income (Chapter 7), which are classified as FVOCI because it is in accordance with the objective of the entity's business model.

net income available to ordinary shareholders The company's net income less dividends on preferred shares.

Second, we need to adjust for dividends on preferred shares. There are two shareholder groups that have claims on a company's profit: ordinary shareholders and preferred shareholders. While dividend payments made to the preferred shareholders do not flow through the income statement, these monies are not available to ordinary shareholders and must be deducted for EPS purposes. The amount subtracted reflects either the stated dividend rate or actual dividends, depending on whether the preferred shares are cumulative or non-cumulative.

- For cumulative preferred shares, deduct the preferred shareholders' entitlement to dividends according to the stated dividend rate regardless of whether they were declared or paid. If there are dividends in arrears, only the current period's dividend rate should be considered.
- For non-cumulative preferred shares, deduct the dividends declared (whether paid or not) without considering the stated entitlement.

The logic underlying these requirements is rooted in the matching concept.

1. The obligation to pay dividends on cumulative preferred shares arises from the passage of time. The responsibility cannot be avoided, as the preferred shareholders must receive all dividends due before any monies are distributed to ordinary shareholders. As such, it is appropriate to deduct the dividend entitlement from net income for the corresponding period even if they have not been declared.
2. The company is not required to pay non-cumulative preferred dividends unless the board of directors declares them. Accordingly, it is proper to deduct dividends from net income only if they have been declared.
3. EPS is based on profit or loss for the period, rather than cash flow; accordingly, we deduct dividends in the period to which they relate rather than when they are paid.

Note that dividends declared or paid to common shareholders are not deducted from net income as they do not affect the net income available to ordinary shareholders. Rather, the dividends represent a distribution to the ordinary shareholders of monies available to them.

Exhibit 15-2 illustrates how to determine net income available to ordinary shareholders in three different scenarios.

Exhibit 15-2a Example for computing net income available to ordinary shareholders (basic EPS numerator)

Facts:

- For the year ended December 31, 2021, Stewart Hyder Co. earned $5,000,000.
- Stewart Hyder had $1,000,000 in cumulative preferred shares outstanding the entire year. The dividend rate is 4% (i.e., $40,000 per year).
- The dividends on the cumulative preferred shares were not declared in 2020.
- Stewart Hyder had $2,000,000 in non-cumulative preferred shares outstanding for the entire year. The dividend rate is 5% (i.e., $100,000 per year)
- Dividend declaration and payment dates are noted as follows:

	Scenario 1	Scenario 2	Scenario 3
Cumulative preferred shares			
Amount declared in 2021	$80,000(a)	$40,000(b)	$0
Amount paid	60,000	0	0
Dividend payment date	Jan. 15, 2022	Oct. 15, 2021	NA
Non-cumulative preferred shares			
Amount declared in 2021	$100,000	$100,000	$0
Amount paid	100,000	30,000	0
Dividend payment date	Jan. 15, 2022	Oct. 15, 2021	NA

Notes:

(a) Scenario 1: The $80,000 declaration includes $40,000 for 2020 and $40,000 for 2021.

(b) Scenario 2: The dividends declared on the cumulative preferred shares pertain to 2020.

Recall that to determine net income available to ordinary shareholders, we use net income as a starting point and then (i) deduct the dividend entitlement on cumulative preferred shares and (ii) deduct the dividends declared on non-cumulative preferred shares. Applying this process to the facts above, we observe that:

- The *annual* entitlement to cumulative preferred dividends must be deducted from net income in all three scenarios. Whether the dividends were declared and the amount and date paid are irrelevant.
- The amount of non-cumulative preferred dividends declared in 2021 are deducted from net income in Scenarios 1 and 2. A deduction is not made in Scenario 3 as non-cumulative dividends were not declared during the year. The stated entitlement and the amount and date they were paid are of no conse quence.

Exhibit 15-2b Computation of net income available to ordinary shareholders

	Scenario 1	Scenario 2	Scenario 3
Net income	$5,000,000	$5,000,000	$5,000,000
Less: Cumulative preferred dividends	40,000	40,000	40,000
Non-cumulative preferred dividends	100,000	100,000	0
Net income available to ordinary shareholders	$4,860,000	$4,860,000	$4,960,000

2. Denominator: Weighted average number of ordinary shares outstanding

The denominator in the EPS formula is the weighted average number of ordinary shares outstanding (WASO). We need to determine a weighted average rather than the number at the year-end because the number of ordinary shares outstanding may change significantly during the year. Reasons for the change in the number of shares are many. For example, a company issues new shares to raise capital, to meet its commitment under employee share purchase agreements, or for a stock split or stock dividend. Sometimes, companies will repurchase shares on the open market.

Subject to some special rules discussed below, computing WASO is no different from computing any other weighted average. In the case of WASO, the weights are the number of days a particular share has been outstanding during the fiscal year. A share that has been outstanding for 12 months has 12 times the weight of a share that was outstanding for one month. To reduce computational complexity the examples that follow use monthly figures. In practice, though, the number of ordinary shares outstanding is based on daily balances.

Exhibit 15-3a illustrates how to compute WASO in the absence of complicating factors using the table method.

Exhibit 15-3a Computing weighted average ordinary shares outstanding (WASO)—table method

Facts:

- Stewart Hyder Co. had 120,000 ordinary shares outstanding on January 1, 2021.
- On March 1, 2021, Stewart Hyder issued an additional 60,000 ordinary shares.
- On June 1, 2021, Stewart Hyder repurchased 30,000 ordinary shares and cancelled them.
- On November 1, 2021, Stewart Hyder issued an additional 90,000 ordinary shares.

Date (2021)	Activity	Shares outstanding (A)	Fraction of year (B)	Contribution to WASO (A × B)
Jan. 1–Feb. 28	Opening balance	120,000	2/12	20,000
Mar. 1	Issue 60,000 shares	+60,000		
Mar. 1–May 31	Balance	180,000	3/12	45,000
June 1	Repurchase 30,000 shares	−30,000		
June 1–Oct. 31	Balance	150,000	5/12	62,500
Nov. 1	Issue 90,000 shares	+90,000		
Nov. 1–Dec. 31	Balance	240,000	2/12	40,000
			12/12	
Weighted average number of ordinary shares outstanding (WASO)				167,500

Thus, the computation multiplies each balance by the amount of time for which that balance is valid (e.g., 120,000 shares × 2 / 12). The sum of these products is WASO, which amounts to 167,500 in this example. Note in the above table that the fractions of the year must sum up to one. And as with any type of average, the weighted average must be between the lowest and highest balances (120,000 and 240,000 in this example).

Some students find it easier to calculate WASO using an alternative technique. The methodology follows:

- The opening number of ordinary shares are the starting point.
- Ordinary shares issued during the year, adjusted for the period that they were actually outstanding, are added to this amount.
- Ordinary shares repurchased during the year, adjusted for the period that they were no longer outstanding, are subtracted from this amount.

Exhibit 15-3b, which is based on the same facts used in Exhibit 15-3a, illustrates how to compute WASO in the absence of complicating factors using the alternative approach.

Exhibit 15-3b Computing weighted average ordinary shares outstanding (WASO)—alternative method

Activity	Shares	WASO
Shares outstanding—January 1, 2021	120,000	120,000
Weighted shares issued—March 1, 2021	60,000 × 10 / 12	50,000
Weighted shares repurchased—June 1, 2021	30,000 × 7 / 12	(17,500)
Weighted shares issued—November 1, 2021	90,000 × 2 / 12	15,000
Weighted average number of ordinary shares outstanding		167,500

Observe how WASO is the same irrespective of the method used to determine the result.

A graphical depiction of the shares outstanding may help understanding. In the following bar chart, each bar represents the number of shares outstanding for that month. The weighted average is the average height of the 12 bars. That average height is equal to the height of a rectangle with the same width as the 12 bars covering the same amount of area as the 12 bars combined.[3]

Exhibit 15-4 Graphical depiction of the number of shares outstanding for Stewart Hyder Co. during 2021—table method

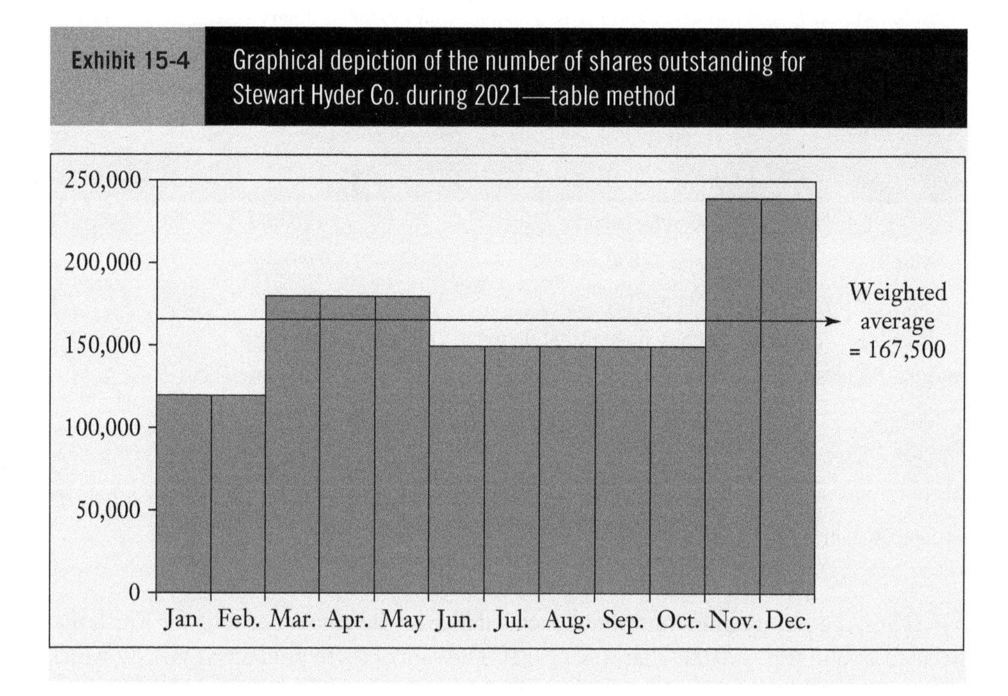

3. Complicating factors

There are two factors that complicate the computation of WASO: (i) treasury shares, and (ii) stock splits and stock dividends.

[3] The graphical representation of the table method uses the *balance* of the number of shares after each transaction and determines the area covered by summing the vertical strips. The alternative method described computes the same area by summing (and sometimes subtracting, in cases of share repurchases) horizontal strips.

a. Treasury shares

As discussed in Chapter 13, while the *Canada Business Corporations Act* no longer allows companies to hold treasury shares, some provincial jurisdictions still permit them. Shares in treasury are issued but not outstanding, so they are not included in WASO.

Exhibit 15-5 illustrates the computation of WASO when treasury shares are involved.

Exhibit 15-5 Computing WASO when there are treasury share transactions—table method

Facts:

- Stewart Hyder Co. had 120,000 ordinary shares outstanding on January 1, 2021.
- On March 1, 2021, Stewart Hyder issued an additional 60,000 ordinary shares.
- On June 1, 2021, Stewart Hyder repurchased 30,000 ordinary shares *and held them as treasury shares.*
- On November 1, 2021, Stewart Hyder sold 90,000 ordinary shares including the 30,000 shares held in treasury.

Date (2021)	Activity	Shares outstanding (A)	Fraction of year (B)	Contribution to WASO (A × B)
Jan. 1–Feb. 28	Opening balance	120,000	2/12	20,000
Mar. 1	Issue 60,000 shares	+60,000		
Mar. 1–May 31	Balance	180,000	3/12	45,000
June 1	Repurchase 30,000 shares	−30,000		
June 1–Oct. 31	Balance	150,000	5/12	62,500
Nov. 1	Issue 90,000 shares	+90,000		
Nov. 1–Dec. 31	Balance	240,000	2/12	40,000
			12/12	
Weighted average number of ordinary shares outstanding (WASO)				167,500

Comments:

- When the shares are repurchased and held as treasury shares, they are issued but not outstanding and are disregarded for WASO purposes.
- Note that the only difference between Exhibit 15-3a and this one is whether the repurchased shares were cancelled or held in treasury. The resulting WASOs are the same in both scenarios (167,500) as treasury shares are ignored in the calculations.

b. Stock splits and stock dividends

Stock splits and stock dividends affect EPS because they increase the number of shares outstanding.[4] Note that neither stock splits nor stock dividends bring about any changes in company resources and obligations. These types of changes are different from the changes in shares discussed earlier, such as share issuances, because those transactions increase the EPS denominator number of shares as well as contribute resources to the enterprise, which should increase the earnings in the numerator. The only change from stock splits and stock dividends is the number of shares, which is an entirely cosmetic change. Having one share that is at some point split into two is not any different from exchanging a single $20 bill for two $10 bills.

Unlike share issuances or repurchases, the actual date of the stock split or dividend is not considered for computing WASO. Instead, we convert all shares to end-of-year equivalents. For example, if a company has 100 shares at the beginning of

4. We do not explicitly discuss instances where companies engage in reverse stock splits (also called share consolidations) that reduce the number of shares outstanding. The effect is similar but of course opposite to what we discuss here.

the year and there is a two-for-one stock split on July 1, each of the 100 shares outstanding from January 1 to June 30 would be considered to be two shares, while each of the 200 shares outstanding from July 1 to December 31 would be just one share. Thus, it is as if the company for the whole year had 200 shares outstanding in terms of end-of-year shares. It is of course possible to state the number of shares as beginning-of-year equivalents (100 shares in this example). However, using end-of-year equivalents makes more sense because financial statement readers are evaluating EPS after the end of the year, so the share basis closest to the end of the year is the most relevant to them.

The requirement to use end-of-year equivalents for EPS also extends to all comparative periods presented in the financial statements and annual report. In this respect IAS 33 states the following (emphasis added):

> ¶26 The weighted average number of ordinary shares outstanding during the period and *for all periods presented* shall be adjusted for events . . . that have changed the number of ordinary shares outstanding without a corresponding change in resources.[5]

The reasons for standardizing the adjustment date for splits and dividends are to preclude possible manipulation of EPS through discretionary timing, to ensure that EPS is prepared on a consistent basis by all companies, and to enhance comparability. Exhibits 15-6a and 15-6b illustrate the effect of stock splits and stock dividends using the table method and alternative method, respectively.

Exhibit 15-6a Computing WASO when there are stock splits or stock dividends—table method

Facts:

- Stewart Hyder Co. had 120,000 ordinary shares outstanding on January 1, 2021.
- On March 1, 2021, Stewart Hyder issued an additional 60,000 ordinary shares.
- On April 1, 2021, Stewart Hyder *declared and issued a two-for-one stock split.*
- On June 1, 2021, Stewart Hyder repurchased 60,000 ordinary shares.
- On November 1, 2021, Stewart Hyder sold 180,000 ordinary shares.
- On December 1, 2021, Stewart Hyder *declared and issued a 10% stock dividend.*

Date (2021)	Activity	Shares outstanding (A)	Share adjustment factor (B)[(a)]	Fraction of year (C)	Contribution to WASO (A × B × C)
Jan. 1–Feb. 28	Opening balance	120,000	2 × 1.1[(b)]	2/12	44,000
Mar. 1	Issue 60,000 shares	+60,000			
Mar. 1–Mar. 31	Balance	180,000	2 × 1.1[(b)]	1/12	33,000
Apr. 1	**2:1 stock split**	**× 2**			
Apr. 1–May 31	Balance	360,000	1.1[(c)]	2/12	66,000
June 1	Repurchase 60,000 shares	−60,000			
June 1–Oct. 31	Balance	300,000	1.1[(c)]	5/12	137,500
Nov. 1	Issue 180,000 shares	+180,000			
Nov. 1–Nov. 30	Balance	480,000	1.1[(c)]	1/12	44,000
Dec. 1	**10% stock dividend**	**× 1.1**			
Dec. 1–Dec. 31	Balance	528,000	1[(d)]	1/12	44,000
				12/12	
Weighted average number of ordinary shares outstanding (WASO)					368,500[(e)]

(Continued)

[5] Copyright © 2012 IFRS Foundation.

Exhibit 15-6a Continued

Supporting comments and computations:

(a) We only need to adjust the shares outstanding *before* the stock split or stock dividend to incorporate the effect of the split or dividend; the shares outstanding after the split or dividend already include the additional shares issued.

(b) For WASO purposes we assume that the stock split and stock dividend both took place at the beginning of the year. We adjust for this by multiplying the actual number of shares outstanding by 2 (two-for-one stock split) and then again by 1.1 (1 + 10% stock dividend).

(c) As the actual number of shares already includes those issued in the stock split, we need only adjust it for the stock dividend.

(d) As the outstanding number of shares includes those issued in the stock split and stock dividend, we need not make any further adjustments.

(e) Notice that the WASO of 368,500 is exactly 2.2 times 167,500, the result obtained in Exhibit 15-3a. This is expected because all the transactions are the same in the two examples except for the stock split and the stock dividend.

Exhibit 15-6b, which is based on the same facts used in Exhibit 15-6a, illustrates how to compute WASO using the alternative approach when there are stock splits and/or stock dividends.

Exhibit 15-6b Computing weighted average ordinary shares outstanding (WASO)—alternative method

Activity	Shares	WASO
Shares outstanding—January 1, 2021	120,000 × 2.0 × 1.1	264,000
Weighted shares issued—March 1, 2021	60,000 × 2.0 × 1.1 × 10/12	110,000
Weighted shares repurchased—June 1, 2021	60,000 × 1.1 × 7/12	(38,500)
Weighted shares issued—November 1, 2021	180,000 × 1.1 × 2/12	33,000
Weighted average number of ordinary shares outstanding		368,500

Again, observe how WASO is the same irrespective of the method used to determine the result.

4. Basic EPS

Having demonstrated how to calculate the numerator (the net income available to ordinary shareholders) and the denominator (the weighted average number of ordinary shares outstanding), we use this information to compute EPS. Select information from Exhibits 15-2 and 15-6a is reproduced below and used to calculate EPS.

Exhibit 15-7 Computing basic EPS for Stewart Hyder Co.*

Numerator information from Exhibit 15-2 (Scenario 1)	
Net income	$5,000,000
Less: Cumulative preferred dividends	40,000
Non-cumulative preferred dividends	100,000
Net income available to ordinary shareholders	$4,860,000
Denominator information from Exhibit 15-6a	
Weighted average number of ordinary shares outstanding	368,500
Basic EPS	
$4,860,000 ÷ 368,500 shares	$ 13.19/sh

*In Canada, EPS is always rounded to the nearest whole cent and expressed in dollars and cents ($X.xx).

CHECKPOINT **CP15-2**

What information does the basic EPS figure provide?

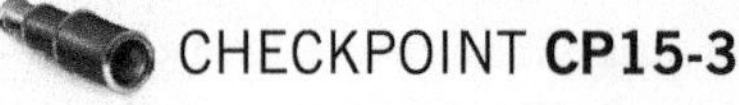

CHECKPOINT **CP15-3**

How is net income available to ordinary shareholders determined?

CHECKPOINT **CP15-4**

What are three reasons for standardizing the adjustment dates for stock splits and stock dividends?

L.O. 15-3. Differentiate between dilutive and antidilutive potential ordinary shares.

L.O. 15-4. Calculate diluted earnings per share.

C. CALCULATING DILUTED EPS

As previously established, publicly accountable enterprises with a complex capital structure must report diluted EPS even if it is the same as basic EPS. **Diluted EPS** measures the amount of the company's earnings attributable to each ordinary shareholder in a hypothetical scenario in which all dilutive securities are converted to ordinary shares. It is a conservative metric that reports the lowest possible EPS. The procedures for calculating diluted EPS ensure that it will always be less than or equal to basic EPS. Recall from the opening vignette that CTC's diluted EPS for 2016 was $9.22. The formula for diluted EPS is as follows:

diluted EPS Measures the amount of the company's earnings attributable to each ordinary shareholder in a hypothetical scenario in which all dilutive securities are converted to ordinary shares.

Exhibit 15-8 Formula for calculating diluted EPS

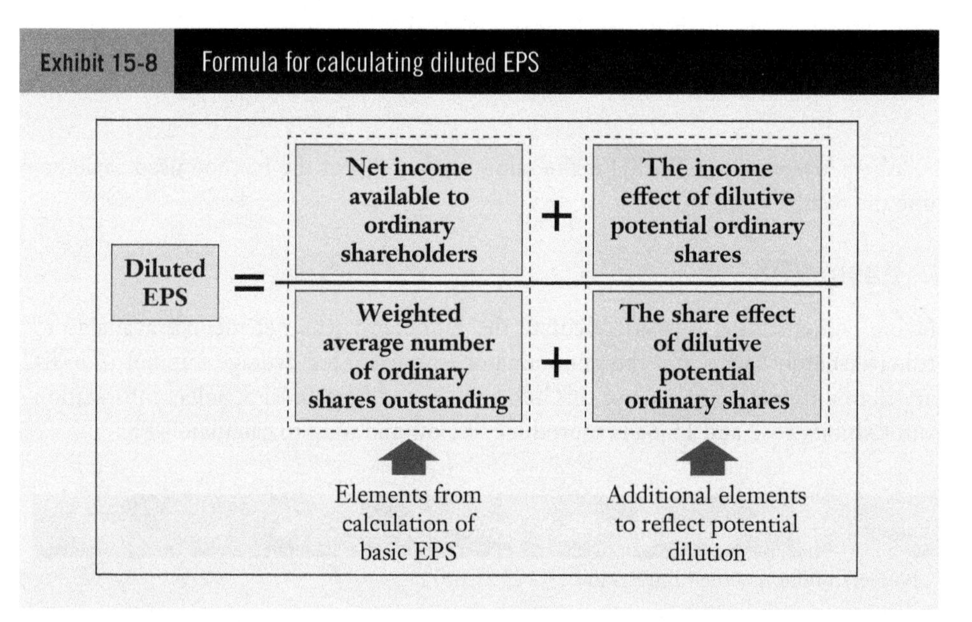

As shown in this formula, the calculation of diluted EPS begins with the numerator and denominator of basic EPS. We then adjust each of these two elements for the effect of "dilutive potential ordinary shares," which is the technical term IFRS uses to describe potentially dilutive securities. A **potential ordinary share (POS)** is a "financial instrument or other contract that may entitle its holder to ordinary shares" (IAS 33 paragraph 5).[6]

potential ordinary share (POS) A financial instrument or other contract that may entitle its holder to ordinary shares.

[6] Copyright © 2012 IFRS Foundation.

Not all POS are dilutive; some are antidilutive. Thus, **dilutive potential ordinary shares** are those POS that decrease EPS or increase the loss per share from continuing operations. Since the objective of reporting diluted EPS is to provide the lowest possible EPS figure, we include all dilutive POS but exclude any **antidilutive potential ordinary shares**. If there is a combination of many (or even just a handful of) potentially dilutive factors, it could be quite laborious to determine which combination would produce the lowest EPS. Fortunately, there is an algorithm that guarantees that we are able to determine the lowest EPS. There are four steps in the process to separate dilutive from antidilutive POS and to calculate diluted EPS:

dilutive potential ordinary shares Potential ordinary shares whose conversion to ordinary shares would decrease EPS or increase loss per share from continuing operations.

antidilutive potential ordinary shares Potential ordinary shares whose conversion to ordinary shares would increase EPS or decrease the loss per share from continuing operations.

1. Identify all potential ordinary shares.
2. Compute "incremental EPS" for each category of potential ordinary shares.
3. Rank order incremental EPS on potential ordinary shares from the lowest (the most dilutive) to the highest (least dilutive).
4. Sequentially compare incremental EPS to "provisional EPS"[7] to determine diluted EPS.

We now examine each of these four steps in more detail.

1. Identify all potential ordinary shares

This step is fairly straightforward. Go through the company's records to identify financial instruments or other contracts that entitle the holder to obtain ordinary shares at a later date on predefined terms. The shares that the company may have to issue under these agreements are referred to as potential ordinary shares. Financial instruments that give rise to POS include the following:

- convertible bonds that can be exchanged for ordinary shares;
- convertible preferred shares that can be exchanged for ordinary shares; and
- stock options and warrants that permit the holder to buy ordinary shares from the company at a predetermined price.

The terms of conversion or purchase are specified in the original financial instrument. These terms include:

- the date or range of dates when the exchange may take place;
- the conversion ratio (e.g., one $1,000 bond can be traded for 60 ordinary shares); or
- the price to be paid (e.g., an ordinary share can be purchased for $17).

When the holder exchanges convertible securities for ordinary shares, the company's obligations under the original instrument are extinguished, and the firm is no longer required to pay interest or dividends on those securities.

2. Compute incremental EPS for all potential ordinary shares

Incremental EPS is used to rank order the securities in terms of their dilutiveness. As we will show, this information is needed to identify dilutive and antidilutive POS and ensure that we obtain the lowest diluted EPS. Computing incremental EPS involves taking the ratio of the income effect to the share effect arising from dilutive POS. Exhibit 15-9 shows this formula.

incremental EPS Quantifies the relationship between the income effect and the share effect for each class of potential ordinary shares.

Income effect: In this formula, the **income effect** indicates the incremental after-tax income available to ordinary shareholders if a category of POS had been converted into ordinary shares. There is a different income effect for each class of POS.

income effect Indicates the incremental after-tax income available to ordinary shareholders if a category of potential ordinary shares had been converted into ordinary shares.

7. "Provisional EPS" is not a defined term in IFRS nor is it reported in the financial statements. Rather, it is used to establish whether a given POS is dilutive or antidilutive.

Exhibit 15-9 Formula for calculating incremental EPS

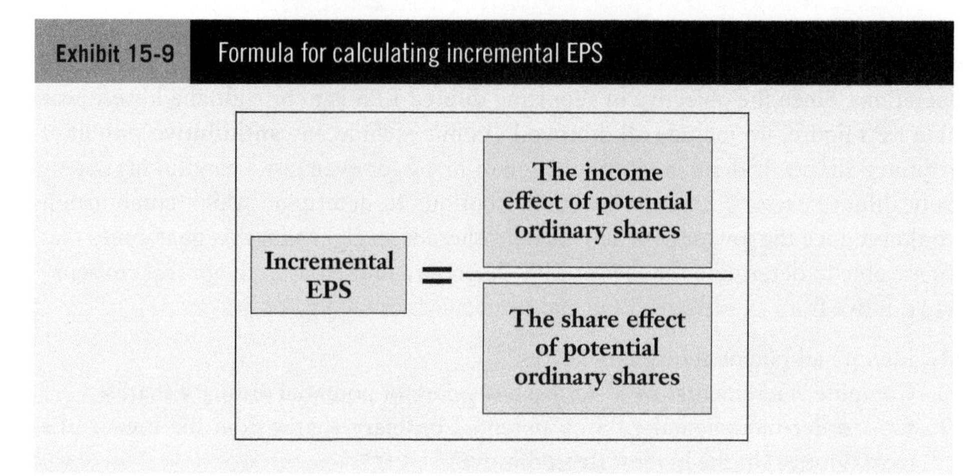

share effect Indicates the incremental number of ordinary shares outstanding if a category of potential ordinary shares had been converted into ordinary shares.

Share effect: The **share effect** indicates the incremental number of ordinary shares outstanding if a category of POS had been converted into ordinary shares. There is a different share effect for each class of POS. In addition, it is necessary to treat convertible securities differently from options and warrants because of the different nature of the two types of securities.

a. Convertible bonds and preferred shares: The if-converted method

if-converted method Assumes (i) that the security was converted into ordinary shares at the beginning of the period, and (ii) interest and/or dividends were not paid on the security during the year.

We calculate incremental EPS on convertible bonds and preferred shares using the if-converted method. The **if-converted method** assumes (i) that the security had been converted into ordinary shares at the beginning of the period and (ii) that the company had not paid interest or preferred dividends on the security during the year because the security had already been converted. The purpose is to determine what the effect would be had the securities been converted. This is accomplished by isolating the after-tax increase in income that would accrue to ordinary shareholders had the POS been converted, and then dividing this amount by the additional number of ordinary shares that would be issued upon conversion.

Interest on bonds payable is usually a tax-deductible expense, while dividends on preferred shares are not. For convertible securities, we are interested in the after-tax effect on income, calculated as shown in Exhibit 15-10.[8]

Exhibit 15-10 Computing the after-tax effect on income using the if-converted method

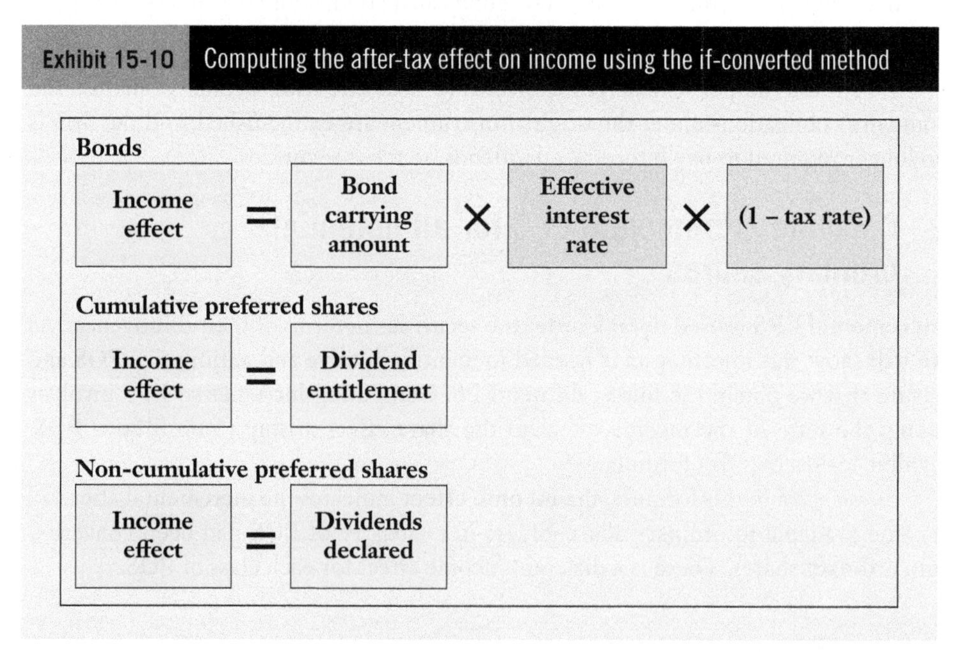

[8] IAS 33 refers to the after-tax amount of the dividends. In Canada, however, dividends paid are not normally tax deductible, so the before- and after-tax effects are the same.

For cumulative preferred shares, the income effect is the dividend entitlement for the period for that class of share, irrespective of the amounts declared and paid. For non-cumulative preferred shares, the income effect is the amount of dividends declared during the period on that class of share. If dividends are not declared, the income effect will be $0.

The following provides two examples showing the calculation of incremental EPS, one for convertible bonds and the other for convertible preferred shares.

Exhibit 15-11 Example for computing incremental EPS for convertible bonds

Facts:

- Smithers Rupert Co. has $1,000,000 in 6% bonds outstanding.
- The bonds' carrying amount equals their face value; therefore, the yield equals the coupon rate.
- The bonds were issued on January 1, 2021, and mature on January 1, 2029.
- Each $1,000 bond is convertible into 20 ordinary shares.
- The company's income tax rate is 30%.

Required:

Determine the incremental EPS of the bond issue for the year ended December 31, 2022.

Analysis:

Income effect	= Carrying amount × Yield × (1 − Tax rate) = $1,000,000 × 6% × (1 − 30%)	$42,000
Share effect	= $1,000,000 ÷ $1,000/bond × 20 shares/bond	20,000
Incremental EPS	Income effect ÷ share effect	$ 2.10

Exhibit 15-12 Example for computing incremental EPS for convertible preferred shares

Facts:

- Smithers Rupert Co. has 10,000 cumulative preferred shares outstanding with par value of $1,000,000 and dividend rate of 5%.
- The preferred shares were issued on January 1, 2021, and do not mature.
- Each $100 preferred share is convertible into three ordinary shares.
- Smithers Rupert's income tax rate is 30%.

Required:

Determine the incremental EPS of the preferred share issue for the year ended December 31, 2022.

Analysis:

Income effect	Dividend entitlement = $1,000,000 × 5%	$50,000
Share effect	10,000 pfd × 3 ordinary/pfd	30,000
Incremental EPS	Income effect ÷ Share effect	$ 1.67

b. Options and warrants: The treasury stock method

Similar to the treatment of convertible securities, we assume that options or warrants are exercised at the beginning of the period (or date of issuance if the security was issued during the period). While the amount of interest saved when convertible debt is converted can be easily determined, it is not as clear what the corresponding adjustment for options and warrants should be. The amount of income that could be earned from funds received from the exercise of options and warrants is, at best, an educated

treasury stock method The process used to determine the share effect for call options and warrants.

in-the-money When the value of the underlying instrument in an option contract is favourable to the holder exercising the option compared with letting the option expire. In the case of a call option, this occurs when the underlying price exceeds the strike price; for a put option, it is when the underlying price is below the strike price.

out-of-the-money When the value of the underlying instrument in an option contract is unfavourable to the holder exercising the option compared with letting the option expire. In the case of a call option, this is when the underlying price is lower than the strike price; for a put option, it is when the underlying price is higher than the strike price.

at-the-money An option is at the money if the market price of the share equals the exercise price.

guess. To avoid making such subjective adjustments to the numerator, which could be subject to manipulation, the required approach completely reflects the dilution in the denominator using the **treasury stock method**.

For purposes of computing diluted EPS, we consider only call options and warrants that are **in-the-money**, which is when the market price of the underlying security exceeds the exercise price (also called the strike price). They are said to be in-the-money as the holder could pay the agreed-upon exercise price (say $20) and immediately resell the security for the market price (say $22) and earn a profit. Call options and warrants are **out-of-the-money** when the market price of the security is less than the exercise price. They are said to be out-of-the-money because the holder would have to pay more for the security (say $24) than he or she could simultaneously sell it for in the market (say $22), and as such would generate a loss if this suboptimal strategy were pursued. Options and warrants are **at-the-money** when the market price of the security is equal to the exercise price.

Note that the *average* market price for the reporting period, rather than the period-end price, is used to determine whether an option is in the money. The underlying rationale for this approach is that EPS covers a period of time.

In this method, the proceeds from the assumed option exercise are used to purchase common shares from the market. However, since the exercise price of an in-the-money call option or warrant is below the average market price in the year, the number of shares that could be repurchased using the proceeds from the option exercise must be less than the number of shares issued for the options. The difference between the number of shares needed for full exercise and the number of shares that could be repurchased represents the incremental shares that the company would have had to issue to cover the exercise. It is the incremental shares needed that is added to the weighted average number of shares outstanding in the denominator.[9] Out-of-the money and at-the-money options are ignored since holders of these options would not have exercised their options.

As set out in the opening vignette, CTC reported basic and diluted earnings per share (EPS) of $9.25 and $9.22, respectively. While not evident from this statement, the difference is due entirely to the dilutive effect of in-the-money stock options. CTC's weighted average number of shares outstanding for basic EPS purposes was 72.360 million common (ordinary) shares, which was diluted (i.e., increased) by the 0.195 million share effect of the stock options.

The application of the treasury stock method is summarized in Exhibit 15-13.

Exhibit 15-14 provides an example to demonstrate the calculation of incremental EPS for options and warrants.

3. Rank order incremental EPS

The third step is to rank order incremental EPS on POS from the lowest (the most dilutive) to the highest (the least dilutive). This step is easy to perform, as demonstrated in Exhibit 15-15. Note that in-the-money stock options and warrants are always the most dilutive because they have incremental EPS of zero. If there is more than one in-the-money option or warrant, the in-the-money options and warrants may be ranked in any order.

4. Sequentially compare incremental EPS to provisional EPS to determine diluted EPS

As stated previously, when calculating diluted EPS the goal is to identify the scenario that maximizes dilution. Using the rankings just obtained in Step 3, compare incremental EPS of the most dilutive POS to basic EPS. If incremental EPS is lower than

9. The dilutive effect of company-issued put options is calculated using the reverse treasury stock method. Discussion of this process is beyond the scope of this text.

Exhibit 15-13 Computing incremental shares from options (or warrants)

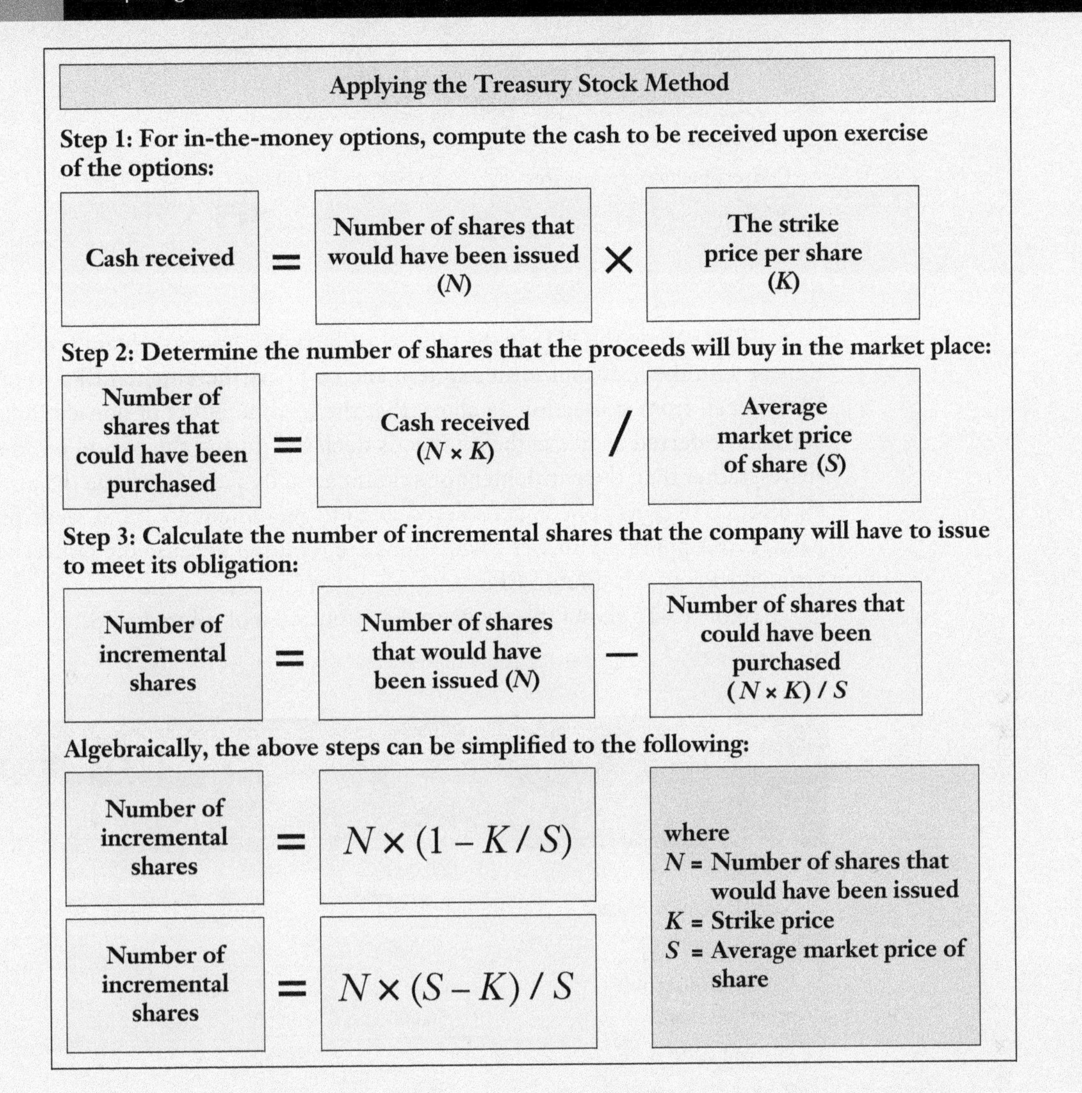

Applying the Treasury Stock Method
Step 1: For in-the-money options, compute the cash to be received upon exercise of the options:
Cash received = Number of shares that would have been issued (N) × The strike price per share (K)
Step 2: Determine the number of shares that the proceeds will buy in the market place:
Number of shares that could have been purchased = Cash received (N × K) / Average market price of share (S)
Step 3: Calculate the number of incremental shares that the company will have to issue to meet its obligation:
Number of incremental shares = Number of shares that would have been issued (N) – Number of shares that could have been purchased (N × K) / S
Algebraically, the above steps can be simplified to the following:
Number of incremental shares = N × (1 – K / S)
Number of incremental shares = N × (S – K) / S
where
N = Number of shares that would have been issued
K = Strike price
S = Average market price of share

Exhibit 15-14 Example showing the calculation of incremental EPS for options and warrants

Facts:

- Smithers Rupert Co. has options outstanding that entitle the holders to purchase 10,000 ordinary shares for $42 each.
- The options were issued on January 1, 2021, and expire on January 1, 2027.
- The average market price of Smithers Rupert's ordinary shares during 2022 was $48.
- The company's income tax rate is 30%.

Required:

- Determine the incremental number of shares that may be issued for diluted EPS purposes.
- Determine the incremental EPS for the year ended December 31, 2022.

Analysis:

Were options in the money?	Average market price ($48) > Option price ($42)	Options are in the money
# of shares that would have been issued		10,000
# of shares that could have been purchased	Proceeds = 10,000 × $42 = $420,000 # shares purchased = $420,000 ÷ $48 = 8,750	8,750
Incremental shares	10,000 – 8,750	1,250*
Incremental EPS	Income effect ÷ Share effect = $0 ÷ 1,250	$ 0.00

* We can compute this figure directly by formula: N(1 – K/S) = 10,000 × (1 – $42 / $48) = 1,250.

Exhibit 15-15 Rank ordering incremental EPS computed in Exhibits 15-11, 15-12, and 15-14

Potential ordinary shares	Income effect	Share effect	Incremental EPS	Rank order
Convertible bonds	$42,000	20,000	$2.10	3rd
Convertible preferred shares	50,000	30,000	1.67	2nd
Stock options	0	1,250	0.00	1st

basic EPS, include the POS in the diluted EPS computation to obtain provisional EPS. Repeat with the next rank-ordered item and compare incremental EPS to provisional EPS. Recall from subsection 2a above that the income effect of non-cumulative convertible preferred shares is the dividends declared during the period on that class of shares, rather than the entitlement or amount actually paid. Continue the process until all dilutive POS have been considered or until incremental EPS exceeds provisional EPS. At this point, no further calculations are required because the last recorded provisional EPS equals diluted EPS.

Exhibit 15-16 shows this sequential computation of diluted EPS.

Exhibit 15-16 Calculating diluted EPS (Step 4)

	Income	Shares	Incremental EPS	EPS
Basic EPS	$4,860,000	368,500		$13.19
Rank 1: Stock options	0	1,250	$0.00	
Provisional EPS	4,860,000	369,750		$13.14
Rank 2: Convertible preferred shares	50,000	30,000	$1.67	
Provisional EPS	4,910,000	399,750		$12.28
Rank 3: Convertible bonds	42,000	20,000	$2.10	
Diluted earnings per share	$4,952,000	419,750		$11.80

- As previously discussed, in-the-money stock options are always dilutive; when included they reduce provisional EPS from $13.19 to $13.14.
- Convertible preferred shares are dilutive since the incremental EPS of $1.67 is less than the EPS just computed. Adding in the convertible preferred shares using the if-converted method results in an EPS of $12.28.
- The incremental EPS on convertible bonds of $2.10 is lower than the EPS just computed. Adding in the effect of convertible bonds reduces the EPS to $11.80.
- Diluted EPS is $11.80 as there are not any remaining POS left to consider.

In the preceding example, all POS were dilutive. While this will not always be the case, the process used in Exhibit 15-16 remains the same. The following example illustrates the importance of the sequential inclusion of dilutive factors according to the ranking of incremental EPS.

Exhibit 15-17a Illustration of the importance of sequential inclusion of dilutive factors—Bob Beanery Ltd.

Facts:	
Bob Beanery Ltd.'s net income for the year ended December 31, 2018	$500,000
Weighted average number of ordinary shares outstanding	390,000
Average market price of ordinary shares in 2018	$ 25
Fiscal 2018 year-end market price of ordinary shares	$ 28
Bob Beanery Ltd.'s income tax rate for 2018	30%

Potential Ordinary Shares (POS)

- 10% convertible bonds: $100,000 convertible bonds were sold at par on January 1, 2012, maturing January 1, 2025. Each $1,000 bond is convertible into 60 ordinary shares at the option of the holder at any time after January 1, 2020.
- 8% cumulative convertible preferred shares: $200,000 convertible preferred shares were sold at par on July 1, 2011. Each $100 preferred share is convertible into 20 ordinary shares at the option of the holder at any time after issuance. Dividends were not declared in 2018.
- Stock options A: Option to purchase 20,000 shares for $20 per share, expiring December 31, 2024. The options may be exercised at any time prior to expiry.
- Stock options B: Option to purchase 10,000 shares for $30 per share, expiring June 30, 2019. The options may be exercised at any time prior to expiry.

Required: Compute Bob's basic and diluted earnings per share for 2018.

First, calculate basic EPS.

Exhibit 15-17b Calculating basic EPS

Basic EPS	
Net income available to ordinary shareholders = Net income − Dividends = $500,000 − ($200,000 × 0.08) (From second bullet point in Exhibit 15-17a)	$484,000
Basic EPS = Net income available to ordinary shareholders ÷ Weighted average number of ordinary shares outstanding = $484,000 ÷ 390,000	$ 1.24

Identify POS and compute the incremental EPS.

Exhibit 15-17c Calculating diluted EPS (Steps 1 and 2)

Diluted EPS		
Step 1 Identify all potential ordinary shares—there are four potential ordinary shares as set out in the fact section above ("Facts")		
Step 2 Compute the incremental EPS for all potential ordinary shares		
Convertible bonds		
Income effect	Face amount of bonds × Coupon rate × (1 − Income tax rate) = $100,000 × 10% × (1 − 30%)	$ 7,000
Share effect	Conversion factor = ($100,000 ÷ $1,000) × 60	6,000
Incremental EPS	Income effect ÷ Share effect = $7,000 ÷ 6,000	$ 1.17
Convertible preferred shares		
Income effect	Dividend entitlement = $200,000 × 8%	$ 16,000
Share effect	Conversion factor = ($200,000 ÷ $100) × 20	40,000
Incremental EPS	Income effect ÷ Share effect = $16,000 ÷ 40,000	$ 0.40
Stock Options A		
Dilutive or antidilutive?	Average market price ($25) > Option price ($20)	Options are dilutive
Incremental shares	N(1 − K/S) = 20,000 × (1 − $20/$25) = 4,000	4,000
Stock Options B		
Dilutive or antidilutive?	Average market price ($25) < Option price ($30)	Options are antidilutive

Rank order the potential ordinary shares.

Exhibit 15-17d Calculating diluted EPS (Step 3)

Step 3. Rank order the incremental EPS on potential ordinary shares from the lowest (the most dilutive) to the highest (the least dilutive)

Potential ordinary shares	Incremental EPS	Rank order
Convertible bonds	$1.17	3rd
Convertible preferred shares	0.40	2nd
Stock options A	0.00	1st
Stock options B	antidilutive	—

Calculate diluted EPS while considering the points listed below.

- **Point 1:** The preferred shares are cumulative; thus, the dividend entitlement is deducted even though dividends were not declared.
- **Point 2:** The convertible bonds are included in the 2018 dilution calculations even though the earliest that it can be converted is January 1, 2020.
- **Point 3:** For stock options, the average price throughout the year is used, not the year-end price.
- **Point 4:** The bonds are antidilutive as the incremental EPS of $1.17 is greater than provisional EPS of $1.15. To determine whether POS are dilutive, compare their incremental EPS to provisional EPS, rather than basic EPS.

Exhibit 15-17e Calculating diluted EPS (Step 4)

Step 4. Sequentially compare the incremental EPS to the provisional EPS to determine diluted EPS

Diluted earnings per share	Income	Shares	Incremental EPS	Diluted EPS
Basic EPS	$484,000	390,000		$1.24
Stock options A	0	4,000	$0.00	
Provisional EPS	484,000	394,000		1.23
Convertible preferred shares	16,000	40,000	$0.40	
Provisional EPS	500,000	434,000		1.15
Convertible bonds—antidilutive (Point 4)	0	0	$1.17 > $1.15	
Diluted earnings per share	$500,000	434,000		$1.15

This example demonstrates why it is imperative to check POS for dilution potential in the prescribed manner. Had we first compared the bond's incremental EPS of $1.17 to the basic EPS of $1.24, we would have incorrectly concluded that the bonds were dilutive.

As discussed in Section D, subsection 1 later in this chapter, basic EPS and, if applicable, diluted EPS must be presented on the face of the income statement. Exhibit 15-17f illustrates the required presentation.

Exhibit 15-17f Presentation of earnings per share on the income statement

Net income	$500,000
Earnings per share:	
Basic earnings per share	$ 1.24
Diluted earnings per share	$ 1.15

CHECKPOINT **CP15-5**

Itemize the four-step process to calculate diluted EPS.

CHECKPOINT **CP15-6**

List three financial instruments that give rise to potential ordinary shares.

5. Effect of discontinued operations

Profit or loss has potentially two distinct components when a company reports discontinued operations in a period. IFRS requires EPS to be separately calculated and reported for continuing operations and for discontinued operations. For computing diluted EPS, net income or loss available to ordinary shareholders from continuing operations (which excludes the effect of discontinued operations) is used as the control number (starting point) for determining the dilutiveness of POS. This requirement is set out in IAS 33, which reads:

> ¶42 An entity uses profit or loss from continuing operations attributable to the parent entity as the control number to establish whether potential ordinary shares are dilutive or antidilutive.[10]

We will amend the facts in Exhibit 15-17 to illustrate the presentation of EPS for discontinued operations. Assume that Bob's net income for the year ended December 31, 2018, was $400,000, composed of income from continuing operations of $500,000 and a loss from discontinued operations, net of tax, of $100,000.

Basic EPS from continuing operations is $1.24 and diluted EPS from continuing operations is $1.15, with these amounts determined in the same manner as illustrated in Exhibit 15-17. The basic loss per share from discontinued operations is ($0.26) [($100,000) ÷ 390,000 = ($0.26)]; and diluted loss per share from discontinued operations is ($0.23) [($100,000) ÷ 434,000 = ($0.23)]. The impact on EPS is summarized in Exhibit 15-18a.

Exhibit 15-18a Computation of EPS amounts

Basic EPS	Net income available to ordinary shareholders	WASO	EPS
Income from continuing operations	$484,000	390,000	$1.24
Loss from discontinued operations, net of tax	(100,000)	390,000	(0.26)
Net income	$384,000	390,000	$0.98
Diluted EPS			
Income from continuing operations	$500,000	434,000	$1.15
Loss from discontinued operations, net of tax	(100,000)	434,000	(0.23)
Net income	$400,000	434,000	$0.92

10. Copyright © 2012 IFRS Foundation.

As discussed in Section D, subsection 1, EPS from discontinued operations may be either presented on the face of the income statement or disclosed in the notes to the financial statement. Exhibit 15-18b illustrates the presentation of this information on the income statement.

Exhibit 15-18b	Presentation of earnings per share on the income statement (discontinued operations)
Income from continuing operations	$500,000
Loss from discontinued operations, net of tax	100,000
Net income	$400,000
Earnings per share:	
Basic earnings per share:	
From continuing operations	$ 1.24
From discontinued operations	(0.26)
Basic earnings per share	$ 0.98
Diluted earnings per share:	
From continuing operations	$ 1.15
From discontinued operations	(0.23)
Diluted earnings per share	$ 0.92

6. Diluted EPS when basic EPS is negative

When a company loses money during the year, or preferred dividends exceed income, basic EPS is negative, meaning that there is a loss per ordinary share. When basic EPS is less than zero, POS that would otherwise be dilutive are antidilutive, as illustrated in the example in Exhibit 15-19. For this reason, when basic EPS from continuing operations is negative, all POS are deemed to be antidilutive.[11]

Exhibit 15-19 Illustration of diluted EPS when basic EPS is negative

Facts:

- There is a single ordinary share outstanding.
- There is one bond outstanding that can be converted into one ordinary share. The after-tax income effect is $2.
- In Scenario 1, the firm earns a profit of $3.
- In Scenario 2, the firm suffers a loss of $3.

	Scenario 1			Scenario 2		
	Income	Shares	EPS	Income	Shares	EPS
Basic EPS	$3.00	1	$3.00	$(3.00)	1	$(3.00)
Convertible bond	2.00	1		2.00	1	
Diluted EPS if bond included	$5.00	2	2.50	$(1.00)	2	(0.50)
Observation	Bond is dilutive: EPS decreases from $3.00 to $2.50			Bond is antidilutive: loss per share decreases from $(3.00) to $(0.50)		

11. This conclusion is not explicitly stated in IAS 33; rather, it must be gleaned by carefully reading and interpreting the governing standard. For example, paragraph 50 establishes that convertible debt and preferred shares are antidilutive when their incremental EPS exceeds basic EPS. As incremental EPS is always a positive number, all convertible securities are thus antidilutive when basic EPS is negative.

There are situations where a company can report a loss from continuing operations and still be profitable overall in terms of net income. For example, a company may report net income of $50,000, consisting of a $100,000 loss from continuing operations and a $150,000 gain from discontinued operations. In these circumstances, all POS are antidilutive as there is a loss from continuing operations. As noted above, it is income available to ordinary shareholders from continuing operations that determines the dilutiveness of POS.

7. Other considerations

a. Convertible securities issued, redeemed, or exchanged during the year

The preceding examples assumed that the securities giving rise to POS were outstanding the entire year. This may not always be the case. During the year, dilutive securities may have been issued, redeemed, or converted into ordinary shares; or the right of exchange may have lapsed. How are these events reflected in the computation of diluted EPS?

- *Issued during the year.* If convertible securities are issued during the year, both the income and share effect are pro-rated to reflect the date of issuance. For example, if the preferred shares in Exhibit 15-17 had been issued on April 1, 2018, the income effect would be $16,000 × 9 / 12 = $12,000 and the share effect 40,000 shares × 9 / 12 = 30,000 shares. The incremental EPS remains unchanged at $0.40/share ($12,000 ÷ 30,000 shares).
- *Redeemed or lapsed during the year.* If a convertible security is redeemed or the right to convert expires during the year, the income and share effects are pro-rated to include only the portion of the year for which the security was outstanding.
- *Converted during the year.* If a convertible security is exchanged during the year, the income effect is the after-tax amount expensed during the period the security was outstanding.[12] The POS are included until the date of conversion. The shares issued for the conversion would have already been included in the basic EPS calculation.

Thus, the general idea is to reflect the amount of time during the year for which the convertible securities were available to be converted into ordinary shares.

b. Convertible securities with more than one conversion option

Some securities have multiple conversion options. For example, a convertible bond might permit the holder to exchange it for five ordinary shares on December 31, 2022, or four ordinary shares on December 31, 2024. For EPS purposes, we use the most dilutive alternative available (IAS 33 paragraph 39). In fiscal 2021, this would be five ordinary shares. In fiscal 2023, the conversion option would reduce to four ordinary shares, though, as the opportunity to convert the bond to five ordinary shares has expired.

c. Potential ordinary shares that are not yet eligible to be converted/exercised

Many POS can be exchanged or exercised only at specific times or after a specific date. For example, a convertible bond may allow for conversion into 50 ordinary shares three years after the issue date but not before. For diluted EPS purposes, we include the POS in the computation of diluted EPS regardless of when the conversion option becomes effective. This approach is entirely consistent with the treatment of "convertible securities with more than one conversion option" discussed above. Specifically, we

---

12. Because bonds can be issued at a discount or premium, the income effect reflects the after-tax amount of interest expensed rather than paid.

can think of the conversion privilege of the bond as currently zero but increasing to 50 ordinary shares three years after the issue date. Accordingly, we use the most dilutive alternative (the 50 ordinary shares) for EPS purposes.

d. Bonds sold at a discount or premium

When a bond's carrying amount and its face value differ, the effective interest rate differs from the coupon rate. Since it is the effective interest rate—rather than the coupon rate—that determines the amount of interest expense, we use the effective interest rate to determine the income effect of the bond.

e. Purchased options versus written options

To date, the discussion of options concentrated on call options granted (written) by the company, which may be dilutive or antidilutive. If the company is on the other side of the transaction, buying call options on its own shares from an outside party, then its role is reversed from that discussed previously. Whereas issued options are potentially dilutive, purchased options are always antidilutive (see IAS 33 paragraph 62).

8. Putting it all together: A comprehensive example

In this chapter, we have set out the steps to compute both basic and diluted EPS. You now have an opportunity to work through a comprehensive example to confirm your knowledge of the topic. When complete, compare your answer to the solution that follows.

Exhibit 15-20 Comprehensive example

Scenario

- Zero Tolerance Accounting Inc.'s (ZTA) ordinary shares are actively traded on the Toronto Stock Exchange.
- The company accountant has been asked to calculate ZTA's basic and diluted EPS for the year ended December 31, 2021.

Facts

- There were 75,000 ordinary shares outstanding at January 1, 2021. An additional 150,000 shares were issued on July 1, 2021.
- A two-for-one stock split was declared and distributed on October 1, 2021.[a]
- On January 1, 2020, ZTA issued at par $300,000 in 8% bonds that mature on January 1, 2028. Each $1,000 bond is convertible into 55 common shares. Assume that the effective interest rate is 8%.
- There are 15,000 outstanding cumulative preferred shares that are each entitled to an annual dividend of $0.30. Dividends were not declared or paid during 2021. Each preferred share is convertible into two ordinary shares.
- ZTA previously granted its employees options to acquire 5,000 ordinary shares at an exercise price of $25 each. These options expire on June 30, 2026.
- ZTA previously granted its executives options to acquire 1,800 ordinary shares at an exercise price of $20 each. These options expire on August 31, 2027.
- ZTA's net income for the year ended December 31, 2021 was $183,000. Its income tax rate is 30%. The average market price of its shares during 2021 was $24.

[a] Convertible securities and options normally include a clause that adjusts the conversion rate or exercise price to counteract the effect of stock splits and stock dividends. Otherwise, these securities would be worthless—the board of directors can always keep the securities out-of-the-money by artificially lowering the stock price with stock splits and stock dividends. For purposes of this exercise, assume that the conversion rates and the exercise prices set out in the facts section have already been adjusted for the stock split.

Solution:

Zero Tolerance Accounting Inc.'s basic and diluted EPS are \$0.60 and \$0.55, respectively. These amounts were determined using the procedures discussed earlier in the chapter and shown in Exhibit 15-21.

Exhibit 15-21 Computations supporting the solution to comprehensive example

Calculation of Basic EPS

Calculation of numerator

Net income		\$183,000
Less: Preferred dividends (cumulative)	(15,000 × \$0.30)	(4,500)
Net income to ordinary shareholders		\$178,500

Calculation of denominator

Date (2021)	Activity	Shares O/S	Adjustment factor	Fraction of year	WASO
Jan. 1–Jun. 30	Opening balance	75,000	2.0	6/12	75,000
Jul. 1	Issue 150,000 sh.	150,000			
Jul. 1–Sep. 30	Balance	225,000	2.0	3/12	112,500
Oct. 1	2:1 stock split	225,000			
Oct. 1–Dec. 31	Balance	450,000	1.0	3/12	112,500
Weighted average number of ordinary shares outstanding					300,000
Basic EPS	= \$178,500 ÷ 300,000				\$0.60

Calculation of Diluted EPS

Computation of incremental EPS and ranking of dilutiveness

Potential ordinary shares	Income effect	Share effect	Incremental EPS	Rank order
Convertible bonds	(\$300,000 × 0.08) × (1 − 30%) = \$16,800	(\$300,000 ÷ \$1,000) × 55 = 16,500	\$1.02	3rd
Convertible preferred shares	15,000 × \$0.30 = \$4,500	15,000 × 2 = 30,000	0.15	2nd
Stock options–employees	Exercise price (\$25) > Average market price (\$24), therefore *antidilutive*		—	—
Stock options–executives	N(1 − K / S) = 1,800 × (1 − \$20 / \$24) = 300		0.00	1st

Sequentially compare the incremental EPS to the provisional EPS to determine diluted EPS

	Income	Shares	Incremental EPS	Diluted EPS
Basic EPS	\$178,500	300,000		\$0.60
Stock options – executives	0	300	\$0.00	
Provisional EPS	\$178,500	300,300		\$0.59
Convertible preferred shares	4,500	30,000	\$0.15	
Provisional EPS	\$183,000	330,300		\$0.55
Convertible bonds–antidilutive	0	0	\$1.02 > \$0.55	
Diluted earnings per share	\$183,000	330,300		\$0.55

CHECKPOINT **CP15-7**

What does the income effect indicate? The share effect?

CHECKPOINT **CP15-8**

What adjustment, if any, is made to the income and the share effect when convertible securities are issued during the year?

CHECKPOINT **CP15-9**

When a convertible security has multiple conversion options, which alternative is used to compute diluted EPS?

D. PRESENTATION AND DISCLOSURE

The following summarizes the requirements for presenting and disclosing EPS information according to IAS 33 paragraphs 66–73A.

1. Presentation

Information to be presented on the income statement[13] includes:

- basic EPS;
- diluted EPS if the company has any POS, even if it is the same as basic EPS; and
- basic and diluted EPS arising from operations, continuing operations, and discontinued operations if the company has discontinued operations. Alternatively, EPS from discontinued operations may be disclosed in the notes to the financial statements.

2. Disclosure

Particulars that must be included in the notes to the financial statements include the following items:

- the income available to ordinary shareholders used to calculate both basic and diluted EPS;
- the weighted average number of ordinary shares used to calculate both basic and diluted EPS;
- particulars of POS that were not included in the diluted EPS calculations as they were antidilutive for the period;
- details of post-balance sheet date transactions that significantly change either the number of ordinary shares outstanding or the number of POS; and
- information regarding stock splits or dividends that occur after year-end but before the statements are authorized for issue. Note that basic and diluted EPS for the year is based on the new number of outstanding shares.

As an example, EPS related information disclosed in Canadian Tire Corporation's 2016 consolidated income statement is reproduced in Exhibit 15-22.

13. Companies can present income in an income statement or as part of a single statement of comprehensive income. In this section, the term "the income statement" encompasses "the single statement of comprehensive income."

Exhibit 15-22 Excerpts from Canadian Tire Corporation's 2016 financial statements

Canadian Tire Corporation Consolidated Income Statement		
For the years ended (C$ in millions, except per share amounts)	December 31, 2016	January 2, 2016
Net income	**$ 747.5**	$ 735.9
Net income attributable to:		
Shareholders of Canadian Tire Corporation	$ 669.1	$ 659.4
Non-controlling interests	78.4	76.5
	$ 747.5	$ 735.9
Basic EPS	$ 9.25	$ 8.66
Diluted EPS	$ 9.22	$ 8.61
Weighted average number of Common and Class A Non-Voting		
Shares outstanding: Basic	72,360,303	76,151,321
Diluted	72,555,732	76,581,602

Source: From Canadian Tire Corporation 2016 Report to Shareholders. Copyright ©2016 by Canadian Tire Corporation, Limited. Reprinted by permission.

E. SUBSTANTIVE DIFFERENCES BETWEEN RELEVANT IFRS AND ASPE

Issue	IFRS	ASPE
Requirement to present EPS information	IFRS requires publicly accountable enterprises or private entities in the process of going public to present EPS information in accordance with IAS 33.	ASPE does not require entities to present EPS information.

F. SUMMARY

L.O. 15-1. Describe the reasons for reporting basic and diluted earnings per share.

- EPS provides information about how much of the reported earnings belongs to each ordinary shareholder.
- EPS facilitates comparison of an entity's performance to that of other companies and to the entity's accomplishments in other reporting periods.

L.O. 15-2. Calculate basic earnings per share.

- Basic EPS = Net income available to ordinary shareholders ÷ Weighted average number of ordinary shares outstanding.

L.O. 15-3. Differentiate between dilutive and antidilutive potential ordinary shares.

- Dilutive potential ordinary shares, if converted, will decrease EPS or increase the loss per share from continuing operations.
- Antidilutive potential ordinary shares, if converted, will increase EPS or decrease the loss per share from continuing operations.

L.O. 15-4. Calculate diluted earnings per share.

- Diluted EPS = (Net income available to ordinary shareholders + The income effect of dilutive potential ordinary shares) ÷ (Weighted average number of ordinary shares outstanding + The share effect of dilutive potential ordinary shares).

G. ANSWERS TO CHECKPOINT QUESTIONS

CP15-1: Capital structures that do not include potentially dilutive securities are commonly referred to as simple capital structures; those that have such securities are known as complex capital structures.

CP15-2: Basic EPS is an indicator of profitability that measures how much of a company's earnings are attributable to each ordinary share.

CP15-3: To determine net income available to ordinary shareholders, start with net income and then subtract the dividend entitlement on cumulative preferred shares and the dividends declared on non-cumulative preferred shares.

CP15-4: Three reasons for standardizing the adjustment dates for stock splits and stock dividends include (i) to preclude possible manipulation of EPS through discretionary timing, (ii) to ensure that EPS is prepared on a consistent basis by all companies, and (iii) to enhance comparability.

CP15-5: The four steps in the process to calculate diluted EPS are (i) identify all potential ordinary shares; (ii) compute "incremental EPS" for each category of potential ordinary shares; (iii) rank order incremental EPS on potential ordinary shares from the lowest (the most dilutive) to the highest (the least dilutive); and (iv) sequentially compare incremental EPS to "provisional EPS" to determine diluted EPS.

CP15-6: Financial instruments that give rise to potential ordinary shares include (i) convertible bonds that can be exchanged for ordinary shares, (ii) convertible preferred shares that can be exchanged for ordinary shares, and (iii) stock options and warrants that permit the holder to buy ordinary shares from the company at a predetermined price.

CP15-7: The income effect indicates the incremental after-tax income available to ordinary shareholders if a category of potential ordinary shares had been converted into ordinary shares. The share effect indicates the incremental number of ordinary shares outstanding if a category of potential ordinary shares had been converted into ordinary shares.

CP15-8: When convertible securities are issued during the year, both the income and the share effect are pro-rated to reflect the date of issuance.

CP15-9: When a convertible security has multiple conversion options, we use the most dilutive alternative for EPS purposes.

H. GLOSSARY

antidilutive potential ordinary shares: Potential ordinary shares whose conversion to ordinary shares would increase EPS or decrease the loss per share from continuing operations.

at-the-money (options or warrants): An option is at the money if the market price of the share equals the exercise price. Compare with **in-the-money** and **out-of-the-money**.

basic EPS: An indicator of profitability that measures how much of the company's earnings are attributable (belong) to each ordinary share.

complex capital structure: A capital structure that includes potentially dilutive securities. Contrast with **simple capital structure**.

diluted EPS: Measures the amount of the company's earnings attributable to each ordinary shareholder in a hypothetical scenario in which all dilutive securities are converted to ordinary shares.

dilutive potential ordinary shares: Potential ordinary shares whose conversion to ordinary shares would decrease EPS or increase loss per share from continuing operations.

earnings per share (EPS): Measures each ordinary share's interest in a company's earnings.

if-converted method: Assumes (i) that the security was converted into ordinary shares at the beginning of the period and (ii) interest and/or dividends were not paid on the security during the year.

income effect: Indicates the incremental after-tax income available to ordinary shareholders if a category of potential ordinary shares had been converted into ordinary shares.

incremental EPS: Quantifies the relationship between the income effect and the share effect for each class of potential ordinary shares.

in-the-money (options or warrants): When the value of the underlying instrument in an option contract is favourable to the holder exercising the option compared with letting the option expire. In the case of a call option, this occurs when the underlying price exceeds the strike price; for a put option, it is when the underlying price is below the strike price. Contrast with **out-of-the-money**.

net income available to ordinary shareholders: The company's net income less dividends on preferred shares.

out-of-the-money (options or warrants): When the value of the underlying instrument in an option contract is unfavourable to the holder exercising the option compared with letting the option expire. In the case of a call option, this is when the underlying price is lower than the strike price; for a put option, it is when the underlying price is higher than the strike price. Contrast with **in-the-money**.

potential ordinary share (POS): A financial instrument or other contract that may entitle its holder to ordinary shares.

share effect: Indicates the incremental number of ordinary shares outstanding if a category of potential ordinary shares had been converted into ordinary shares.

simple capital structure: A capital structure that does not include potentially dilutive securities. Contrast with **complex capital structure**.

treasury stock method: The process used to determine the share effect for call options and warrants.

I. REFERENCES

Authoritative standards:

IFRS	ASPE Section
IAS 33—Earnings per Share	No equivalent guidance
IAS 1— Presentation of Financial Statements	1400— General Standards of Financial Statement Presentation 1520—Income Statement

MyLab Accounting Make the grade with **MyLab Accounting:** The problems marked with a 🌐 can be found on **MyLab Accounting.** You can practise them as often as you want, and most feature step-by-step guided instructions to help you find the right answer.

J. PROBLEMS

P15-1. Earnings per share (EPS) concepts

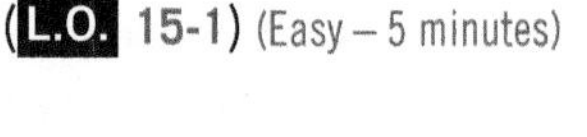

(L.O. 15-1) (Easy – 5 minutes)

a. What information does EPS communicate to investors?
b. Describe the difference between basic and diluted EPS.
c. What are potential ordinary shares?
d. Provide three examples of potential ordinary shares.

P15-2. Basic EPS concepts

(L.O. 15-2) (Easy – 5 minutes)

a. What is the formula for basic EPS?
b. How is net income available to ordinary shareholders determined?
c. How does other comprehensive income affect the calculation of EPS?

P15-3. Net income available to ordinary shareholders

(L.O. 15-2) (Medium – 10 minutes)

a. Discuss how declared and undeclared dividends on cumulative preferred shares and on non-cumulative preferred shares affect the computation of net income available to ordinary shareholders.
b. Explain the underlying logic for these requirements.

P15-4. Net income available to ordinary shareholders

(L.O. 15-2) (Easy – 5 minutes)

For the year ended December 31, 2018, Ghostly Productions Inc. earned $5,000,000. Outstanding preferred shares included $1,000,000 in 3% cumulative preferred shares issued on January 1, 2017, and $2,000,000 in 6% non-cumulative preferred shares issued on January 1, 2018. Dividends on the cumulative preferred shares were not declared in 2017.

The following are three independent situations:

a. On December 15, 2018, Ghostly declared and paid $60,000 in dividends on the 3% cumulative shares including the arrears. Ghostly also declared and paid the $120,000 dividends on the non-cumulative shares.
b. Ghostly did not declare any dividends during 2018.
c. On December 15, 2018, Ghostly declared $120,000 in dividends on the non-cumulative preferred shares, payable on January 15, 2019. Dividends on the cumulative preferred shares are neither declared nor paid.

Required:

For each of these three independent situations, determine the net income available to ordinary shareholders for the year ended December 31, 2018.

P15-5. Net income available to ordinary shareholders

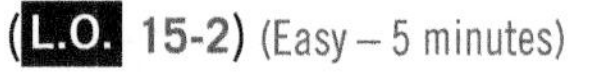

(L.O. 15-2) (Easy – 5 minutes)

For the year ended December 31, 2021, Mixed Up Productions Inc. earned $10,000,000. Outstanding preferred shares included $2,000,000 in 4% cumulative preferred shares issued on January 1, 2019, and 30,000 $100 non-cumulative preferred shares issued on January 1, 2020, that are each entitled to dividends of $6 per annum. Dividends were neither declared nor paid on either class of the preferred shares in 2019 or 2020.

The following are three independent situations:

a. On December 15, 2021, Mixed Up declared and paid the $160,000 dividends in arrears on the 4% cumulative preferred shares. Mixed Up also declared and paid $180,000 dividends on the non-cumulative preferred shares.
b. On December 15, 2021, Mixed Up declared and paid $140,000 of the dividends in arrears on the 4% cumulative preferred shares.
c. On December 15, 2021, Mixed Up declared $150,000 dividends on the 4% cumulative preferred shares and $120,000 in dividends on the non-cumulative preferred shares, both payable on January 15, 2022.

Required:

For each of these three independent situations, determine the net income available to ordinary shareholders for the year ended December 31, 2021.

P15-6. Net income available to ordinary shareholders (L.O. 15-2) (Medium – 5 minutes)

For each of the years ended December 31, 2021 and 2022, Accountants Without Borders Corp. earned $7,000,000. Outstanding preferred shares included 10,000, $100 cumulative preferred shares "A" that are each entitled to dividends of $1 per quarter and 15,000, $100 non-cumulative preferred shares "B" that are each entitled to dividends of $1.25 per quarter. The "A" and "B" preferred shares were issued on July 1, 2021, and January 1, 2020, respectively. Dividends were neither declared nor paid in either 2020 or 2021.

On December 15, 2022, Accountants declared $50,000 dividends on the cumulative preferred shares and $15,000 in dividends on the non-cumulative preferred shares, both payable on January 15, 2023.

Required:

Determine the net income available to ordinary shareholders for the years ended December 31, 2021 and 2022.

P15-7. Weighted average number of shares outstanding

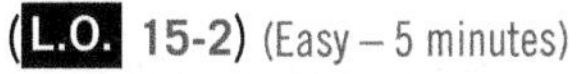

(L.O. 15-2) (Easy – 5 minutes)

a. Describe how each of the following affects the determination of the weighted average number of shares outstanding (WASO):
   i. Treasury shares (ordinary)
   ii. Stock splits
   iii. Stock dividends
b. Provide three reasons why IFRS requires a standardized adjustment date for stock splits and stock dividends.

P15-8. Weighted average number of shares outstanding (L.O. 15-2) (Easy – 10 minutes)

Potatohead Corporation had 150,000 ordinary shares outstanding on January 1, 2018. On April 1, 2018, Potatohead issued an additional 80,000 shares. On July 1, 2018, Potatohead repurchased 60,000 ordinary shares and cancelled them. On October 1, 2018, Potatohead issued an additional 20,000 ordinary shares.

Required:

a. What was the weighted average number of ordinary shares outstanding in 2018?
b. Assume that on July 1, 2018, Potatohead repurchased the shares and held them as treasury shares. Will the weighted average number of ordinary shares outstanding in 2018 change from the amount in part (a)? Why or why not?

P15-9. Weighted average number of shares outstanding (L.O. 15-2) (Easy – 10 minutes)

Eggplant Solutions Inc. had 150,000 ordinary shares outstanding on January 1, 2018. On April 1, 2018, Eggplant issued an additional 80,000 shares. On June 1, 2018, the company declared and issued a two-for-one stock split. On July 1, 2018, Eggplant repurchased 60,000 ordinary shares and cancelled them. On October 1, 2018, Eggplant issued an additional 20,000 ordinary shares. On November 1, 2018, Eggplant declared and issued a 10% stock dividend.

Required:

What was the weighted average number of ordinary shares outstanding in 2018?

P15-10. Weighted average number of shares outstanding

(L.O. 15-2) (Medium – 15 minutes)

Corporate Financial Innovations Inc. had 100,000 ordinary shares outstanding on January 1, 2018. On February 1, 2018, Corporate repurchased 50,000 shares, cancelling 30,000 and holding the balance as treasury shares. On June 1, 2018, the company declared and issued a 1.5-for-1 stock split. On July 1, 2018, Corporate issued an additional 80,000 shares, 10,000 of which were from treasury. On October 1, 2018, Corporate issued an additional 20,000 ordinary shares. On November 1, 2018, Corporate declared and issued a 20% stock dividend.

Required:

What was the weighted average number of ordinary shares outstanding in 2018?

P15-11. Weighted average number of shares outstanding

(**L.O.** 15-2) (Medium – 15 minutes)

On January 1, 2018, Barbara Lee Innovations Inc.'s (BLI) share capital included 220,000 issued ordinary shares of which 200,000 were outstanding. On February 1, 2018, the company declared and distributed a three-for-one stock split. On March 1, 2018, BLI issued an additional 60,000 shares, 20,000 of which were from treasury. On October 1, 2018, BLI issued an additional 40,000 ordinary shares. On December 1, 2018, BLI declared and distributed a 30% stock dividend.

Required:

Determine the weighted average number of ordinary shares outstanding in 2018.

P15-12. Calculating basic EPS

(**L.O.** 15-2) (Easy – 10 minutes)

Wong's Lingerie Inc. (WLI) has been in business for over 10 years. As at January 1, 2018, its capital structure consisted of 200,000 ordinary shares; $500,000 of 4% non-cumulative preferred shares; and 20,000, $100, 3% cumulative preferred shares. Net income for the year ended December 31, 2018, was $800,000. Dividends were last declared and paid in full in 2016. During 2018, WLI declared and paid a total of $180,000 in dividends.

Required:

a. Compute WLI's basic EPS for 2018.
b. How much in dividends did each ordinary shareholder receive in 2018?

P15-13. Calculating basic EPS

(**L.O.** 15-2) (Easy – 10 minutes)

Trust Me Renovations Corp. (TMRC) was incorporated on January 1, 2018. At that time, it issued 100,000 ordinary shares; 10,000, $100, 4% preferred shares "A"; and 20,000, $100, 5% preferred shares "B." Net income for the year ended December 31, 2018, was $400,000. TMRC declares and pays a total of $200,000 in dividends.

The following are three independent situations:

a. Both the preferred shares series A and B are cumulative in nature. Series A shareholders must be fully paid their current entitlement as well as any arrears before any monies are paid to the Series B shareholders.
b. The Series A preferred shares are cumulative and the Series B preferred shares are non-cumulative. Series A shareholders must be fully paid their current entitlement before any monies are paid to the Series B shareholders.
c. Both the preferred shares Series A and B are non-cumulative in nature. Series A shareholders must be fully paid their current entitlement before any monies are paid to the Series B shareholders.

Required:

For each of these three independent situations, compute basic EPS.

P15-14. Calculating basic EPS

(**L.O.** 15-2) (Easy – 10 minutes)

Balloons Aloft Inc. (BAI) was incorporated on January 1, 2018. At that time, it issued 100,000 ordinary shares; 10,000, $100, 4% preferred shares "A"; and 20,000, $100, 5% preferred shares "B." Net income for the year ended December 31, 2018, was $300,000. BAI declares and pays a total of $100,000 in dividends.

The following are three independent situations:

a. Both the preferred shares Series A and B are cumulative in nature. Series A shareholders must be fully paid their current entitlement as well as any arrears before any monies are paid to the Series B shareholders.
b. The Series A preferred shares are cumulative and the Series B preferred shares are non-cumulative. Series A shareholders must be fully paid their current entitlement before any monies are paid to the Series B shareholders.
c. Both the preferred shares Series A and B are non-cumulative in nature. Series A shareholders must be fully paid their current entitlement before any monies are paid to the Series B shareholders.

Required:

For each of these three independent situations, compute basic EPS.

P15-15. Calculating basic EPS (L.O. 15-2) (Easy – 10 minutes)

Umbrellas Unlimited Ltd. (UUL) was incorporated on January 1, 2018. At that time, it issued 100,000 ordinary shares; 10,000, $100, 4% preferred shares "A"; and 20,000, $100, 5% preferred shares "B." Net income for the year ended December 31, 2018, was $200,000. UUL neither declares nor pays dividends during the year.

The following are three independent situations:

a. Both the preferred shares Series A and B are cumulative in nature. Series A must be fully paid their current entitlement as well as any arrears before any monies are paid to the Series B shareholders.
b. The Series A preferred shares are cumulative and the Series B preferred shares are non-cumulative. Series A must be fully paid their current entitlement before any monies are paid to the Series B shareholders.
c. Both the preferred shares Series A and B are non-cumulative in nature. Series A must be fully paid their current entitlement before any monies are paid to the Series B shareholders.

Required:

For each of these three independent situations, compute basic EPS.

P15-16. Calculating basic EPS (L.O. 15-2) (Medium – 15 minutes)

Burlington Bathrooms Inc. (BBI) had 100,000 ordinary shares outstanding on January 1, 2021. Transactions throughout 2021 affecting its shareholdings follow:

- February 1: BBI issued 10,000, $100, cumulative 5% preferred shares.
- March 1: BBI issued 30,000 ordinary shares.
- April 1: BBI declared and issued a 10% stock dividend on the ordinary shares.
- July 1: BBI repurchased and cancelled 20,000 ordinary shares.
- October 1: BBI declared and issued a three-for-one stock split on the ordinary shares.
- December 31: BBI declared and paid $50,000 in dividends on the ordinary shares.
- BBI's net income for the year ended December 31, 2021, was $250,000. Its tax rate was 40%.

Required:

a. What was BBI's weighted average number of ordinary shares outstanding in 2021?
b. What was BBI's basic EPS in 2021?
c. If the preferred shares issued on February 1, 2021, were non-cumulative, what would BBI's basic EPS for 2021 have been?

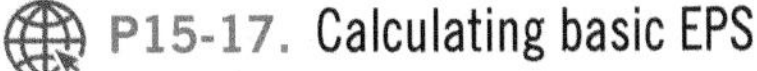

P15-17. Calculating basic EPS (L.O. 15-2) (Medium – 20 minutes)

Princess and Frog Corp. was formed on January 1, 2017. At that time, it issued 50,000 ordinary shares and 50,000, $100, cumulative 4% preferred shares. Subsequent transactions affecting its shareholdings follow:

2017

- September 1: Princess issued 20,000, $100, non-cumulative 6% preferred shares.
- December 1: Princess issued 10,000 ordinary shares.
- Dividends were not declared in 2017.

2018

- February 1: Princess issued 15,000 ordinary shares.
- June 1: Princess repurchased 20,000 shares and held them as treasury shares.
- July 1: Princess declared and paid $300,000 in dividends on the cumulative preferred shares, $60,000 on the non-cumulative preferred shares, and $50,000 on the ordinary shares.
- September 1: Princess reissued (sold) the 20,000 shares held in treasury.
- October 1: Princess declared and issued a two-for-one stock split on the ordinary shares.
- December 1: Princess declared and paid $100,000 in dividends on the cumulative preferred shares, $60,000 on the non-cumulative preferred shares, and $50,000 on the ordinary shares.
- Princess's net income for the year ended December 31, 2018, was $500,000. Its tax rate was 30%.

Required:

a. What was Princess's weighted average number of ordinary shares outstanding in 2018?
b. What was Princess's basic EPS in 2018?

P15-18. Calculating basic EPS (L.O. 15-2) (Difficult – 30 minutes)

The ordinary share transactions of Caltown Financing Inc. and net income for its latest three years are summarized below:

	2021	2022	2023
Net income	$300,000	$250,000	$350,000
Ordinary shares			
Outstanding January 1	100,000	125,000	103,500
Issued April 1, 2021	25,000		
Repurchased February 1, 2022		(35,000)	
15% stock dividend May 1, 2022		13,500	
Issued April 1, 2023			46,500
1.5-for-1 stock split October 1, 2023			75,000
Outstanding December 31	125,000	103,500	225,000

Caltown does not have any preferred shares outstanding.

Required:

a. Calculate the weighted average number of ordinary shares outstanding in each of 2021, 2022, and 2023.
b. Calculate basic EPS for each of 2021, 2022, and 2023.
c. Assume that Caltown includes three years of financial statement data in its annual report. Calculate the weighted average number of ordinary shares that would be used to calculate basic EPS in 2021, 2022, and 2023 as reported in Caltown's annual report for the year ended December 31, 2023.
d. Calculate basic EPS for each of 2021, 2022, and 2023 based on the weighted average number of ordinary shares outstanding that you determined in part (c).
e. Your answers to part (b) and part (d) represent two sets of EPS statistics for the same company. Does the unadjusted or adjusted set of EPS statistics provide investors with better information for decision-making purposes? Why?

P15-19. Calculating basic EPS (L.O. 15-2) (Difficult – 20 minutes)

Manjit's Mannequin Supply Inc. (MMSI) was incorporated on January 1, 2017. At that time, it issued 50,000 ordinary shares and 30,000, $100, 5% non-cumulative preferred shares. Transactions throughout 2018 affecting MMSI's shareholdings follow:

a. March 1: MMSI issued 20,000 ordinary shares.
b. April 1: MMSI issued $2,000,000 in 3% cumulative preferred shares.
c. July 1: MMSI declared and issued a 15% stock dividend on the ordinary shares.
d. August 1: MMSI repurchased 30,500 ordinary shares and held them as treasury shares.
e. October 1: MMSI declared and issued a two-for-one stock split on the ordinary shares.
f. MMSI's net income for the year ended December 31, 2018, was $500,000. It neither declared nor paid dividends during the year.

Required:

a. What was MMSI's weighted average number of ordinary shares outstanding in 2018? (Round each period's WASO to the nearest whole share.)
b. What was MMSI's basic EPS for 2018?
c. If the preferred shares issued on April 1, 2018, were non-cumulative, what would MMSI's basic EPS for 2018 have been?
d. Based on your answer to part (b), what would the price–earnings ratio be if the market price of the stock was $30? [*Hint:* P/E ratio = Stock price ÷ Basic EPS]

P15-20. Calculating basic EPS (L.O. 15-2) (Difficult – 25 minutes)

Blue Riding Stables Corp. has been in business for over 20 years. Its capital structure as at January 1, 2021, consisted of 25,000 ordinary shares and $200,000, 4%, non-cumulative preferred shares. Subsequent transactions affecting its shareholdings follow:

2021

- March 1: Blue issued $100,000 of cumulative 3% preferred shares.
- October 1: Blue purchased and cancelled 10,000 ordinary shares.
- December 15: $50,000 dividends were declared, payable on January 2, 2022.
- Blue's net income for the year ended December 31, 2021, was $200,000.

2022

- March 1: Blue issued 20,000 ordinary shares.
- June 1: Blue repurchased 10,000 shares and held them as treasury shares.
- September 1: Blue reissued (sold) 5,000 of the shares held in treasury.
- October 1: Blue declared and issued a three-for-one stock split on the ordinary shares.
- Blue did not declare dividends in 2022.
- Blue's net income for the year ended December 31, 2022, was $500,000.

Required:

a. What was Blue's weighted average number of ordinary shares outstanding in 2021?
b. What was Blue's weighted average number of ordinary shares outstanding in 2022?
c. What was Blue's basic EPS in 2021?
d. What was Blue's basic EPS in 2022?
e. What was Blue's basic EPS in 2021 as reported in Blue's 2022 comparative financial statements?

P15-21. Definitions relating to potential dilution (L.O. 15-3) (Easy – 5 minutes)

a. Define a simple capital structure.
b. Define a complex capital structure.
c. Define in-the-money call options.
d. Define at-the-money call options.
e. Define out-of-the-money call options.

P15-22. Differentiating between dilutive and antidilutive potential ordinary shares

(L.O. 15-3) (Easy – 10 minutes)

Four different companies have many similarities, including the following:

1. They all earned net income of $2,000,000 for the year ended December 31, 2021.
2. They are all subject to a 30% tax rate.
3. The average price of all four companies' ordinary shares during the year was $35.
4. Each company had 1,000,000 ordinary shares outstanding during the year.

They do have slightly different complex capital structures, however. Specifically:

- Company A had stock options outstanding the entire year that allowed employees to buy 10,000 ordinary shares for $32 each until December 31, 2023.
- Company B had stock options outstanding the entire year that allowed employees to buy 5,000 ordinary shares for $30 each between January 1, 2022, and December 31, 2023.
- Company C had $1,000,000 in 4% non-cumulative preferred shares outstanding the entire year. Each $100 share is convertible into three ordinary shares. Dividends were not declared in 2021.
- Company D had $2,000,000 in 5% bonds maturing on December 31, 2023, that were outstanding the entire year. Each $1,000 bond is convertible into 15 ordinary shares anytime before expiry.

Required:

a. Calculate the basic EPS of the four companies.
b. Prepare a schedule that sets out the income effect, share effect, and incremental EPS for each company's security that is convertible into ordinary shares.
c. Consider each company's POS and determine whether it is dilutive or antidilutive. For Company D assume that the effective rate of interest on the bonds equals the coupon rate.

P15-23. Differentiating between dilutive and antidilutive potential ordinary shares

(L.O. 15-3) (Easy – 10 minutes)

Four different companies have many similarities, including the following:

1. They all earned net income of $1,000,000 for the year ended December 31, 2021.
2. They are all subject to a 40% tax rate.
3. The average price of all four companies' ordinary shares during the year was $25.
4. Each company had 600,000 ordinary shares outstanding during the year.

They do have slightly different complex capital structures, however. Specifically:

- Company A had stock options outstanding the entire year that allowed employees to buy 20,000 ordinary shares for $20 each until December 31, 2023.
- Company B had stock options outstanding the entire year that allowed employees to buy 10,000 ordinary shares for $26 each between January 1, 2022, and December 31, 2023.
- Company C had $1,000,000 in 5% bonds maturing on December 31, 2023, that were outstanding the entire year. Each $1,000 bond is convertible into 20 ordinary shares anytime before expiry.
- Company D had $800,000 in 4%, non-cumulative preferred shares outstanding the entire year. Each $100 share is convertible into two ordinary shares. Dividends were declared and paid in 2021.

Required:

a. Calculate the basic EPS of the four companies.
b. Prepare a schedule that sets out the income effect, share effect, and incremental EPS for each company's security that is convertible into ordinary shares.
c. Consider each company's potential ordinary shares and determine whether it is dilutive or antidilutive. For Company C assume that the effective rate of interest on the bonds equals the coupon rate.

P15-24. Diluted EPS concepts (L.O. 15-3, L.O. 15-4) (Medium – 15 minutes)

a. What is the formula for diluted EPS?
b. What are dilutive potential ordinary shares? Antidilutive potential ordinary shares? How do they each impact the computation of diluted EPS?
c. Describe the procedure for identifying dilutive and antidilutive potential ordinary shares and calculating diluted EPS.

P15-25. If-converted method and diluted EPS (L.O. 15-2, L.O. 15-3, L.O. 15-4) (Medium – 20 minutes)

The net income for Rip's Curling Corp. for the year ended December 31, 2021, was $700,000. Rip had 50,000 ordinary shares outstanding at the beginning of the year. Rip declared and distributed a three-for-one stock split on May 1, 2021, and issued (sold) 30,000 ordinary shares on November 1, 2021. Select details of Rip's liabilities and equities follow:

- Bonds A—$1,000,000, 6%, 10-year, semi-annual bonds issued on July 1, 2021. At the option of the holder, each $1,000 bond can be converted into 14 ordinary shares at any time before expiry.
- Bonds B—$1,000,000, 5%, semi-annual bonds maturing September 30, 2025. The owners of the bonds elect to convert them into 12,000 ordinary shares on December 1, 2021.
- 100,000 cumulative preferred shares that are each entitled to dividends of $2 per annum. Dividends are not declared in 2021.

Rip's corporate tax rate was 40%. The recorded conversion factor for the convertible bonds has already been adjusted for the stock split.

Required:

Assuming that the effective rate of interest on the bonds equals the coupon rate:

a. Calculate Rip's basic earnings per share for 2021.
b. Prepare a schedule that sets out the income effect, share effect, and incremental EPS for each security that is convertible into ordinary shares. Rank the potential ordinary shares by their dilutiveness.
c. Calculate Rip's diluted earnings per share for 2021.

P15-26. If-converted method and diluted EPS (L.O. 15-2, L.O. 15-3, L.O. 15-4) (Medium – 20 minutes)

Jamie's Golf Ltd.'s net income for the year ended December 31, 2021, was $900,000. Jamie had 100,000 ordinary shares outstanding at the beginning of the year. Jamie declared and distributed a 10% stock dividend on June 1, 2021, and issued (sold) 10,000 ordinary shares on October 1, 2021. Select details of Jamie's liabilities and equities follow:

- Bonds A—$500,000, 4%, 12-year, semi-annual bonds issued on July 1, 2020. At the option of the holder, each $1,000 bond can be converted into 10 ordinary shares at any time before expiry.
- Bonds B—$500,000, 3%, semi-annual bonds maturing September 30, 2028. At the option of the holder, each $1,000 bond can be converted into 12 ordinary shares at any time before expiry.
- 100,000 convertible, cumulative preferred shares that are each entitled to dividends of $3 per annum. Dividends were not declared in 2020. Dividends of $600,000 were declared and paid in 2021. At the option of the holder, each preferred share can be converted into one ordinary share at any time between January 1, 2026, and December 31, 2031.
- Jamie's corporate tax rate was 30%. The recorded conversion factor for the convertible bonds has already been adjusted for the stock dividend.

Required:

Assuming that the effective rate of interest on the bonds equals the coupon rate:

a. Calculate Jamie's basic earnings per share for 2021.
b. Prepare a schedule that sets out the income effect, share effect, and incremental EPS for each security that is convertible into ordinary shares. Rank the potential ordinary shares by their dilutiveness.

c. Calculate Jamie's diluted earnings per share for 2021.
d. Based on your answer to part (a), what would the price–earnings ratio be if the market price of the stock were $60? [*Hint:* P/E ratio = Stock price ÷ Basic EPS]

P15-27. If-converted method and diluted EPS

(L.O. 15-2, L.O. 15-3, L.O. 15-4) (Medium – 20 minutes)

Ron's Squash Inc.'s net income for the year ended December 31, 2021, was $140,000. Ron had 60,000 ordinary shares outstanding at the beginning of the year. Ron wanted to consolidate the number of shares outstanding and so declared a one-for-two stock split effective June 1, 2021. The company then repurchased an additional 10,000 ordinary shares on October 1, 2021, and held them in treasury. Select details of Ron's liabilities and equities follow:

- Bonds A—$2,000,000, 3%, five-year, semi-annual bonds issued on October 1, 2021. At the option of the holder, each $1,000 bond can be converted into eight ordinary shares at any time before expiry.
- Bonds B—$1,000,000, 4%, semi-annual bonds maturing September 30, 2036. At the option of the holder, each $1,000 bond can be converted into six-and-a-half ordinary shares at any time before expiry.
- 10,000, $100 non-cumulative preferred shares that are each entitled to dividends of $1 per annum. Dividends are not declared in 2021.
- Ron's corporate tax rate was 20%. The recorded conversion factor for the convertible bonds has already been adjusted for the stock split.

Required:

Assuming that the effective rate of interest on the bonds equals the coupon rate:

a. Calculate Ron's basic earnings per share for 2021.
b. Prepare a schedule that sets out the income effect, share effect, and incremental EPS for each security that is convertible into ordinary shares. Rank the potential ordinary shares by their dilutiveness.
c. Calculate Ron's diluted earnings per share for 2021.

P15-28. Treasury stock method

(L.O. 15-4) (Easy – 10 minutes)

a. What is the treasury stock method and when is it used?
b. Briefly describe the application of the treasury stock method.
c. What does the treasury stock method assume about the exercise date? What is the exception to the rule with respect to the assumed exercise date? What alternative procedure is employed in this instance?

P15-29. Treasury stock method

(L.O. 15-4) (Easy – 10 minutes)

During 2021, Fun with Numbers Inc. (FWNI) had four series of employee stock options outstanding, the details of which follow:

1. Options A entitle employees to purchase 10,000 ordinary shares for $19 each. This series of options was granted on February 1, 2019, and expires on December 31, 2023.
2. Options B entitle employees to purchase 15,000 ordinary shares for $20 each. This series of options was granted on June 1, 2018, and expires on December 31, 2022.
3. Options C entitle employees to purchase 20,000 ordinary shares for $21 each. This series of options was granted on April 1, 2020, and expires on December 31, 2024.
4. Options D entitle employees to purchase 20,000 ordinary shares for $18 each. This series of options was granted on April 1, 2021, and expires on December 31, 2024.

The average market price of FWNI's ordinary shares for the year ended December 31, 2021, was $20.

Required:

a. For each of the options series, indicate whether they are dilutive or antidilutive in nature in 2021 and provide the reason why.
b. For each of the options series that are dilutive, determine the number of incremental shares to be notionally issued.
c. For each of the options series, determine the incremental EPS.

P15-30. Treasury stock method (L.O. 15-3, L.O. 15-4) (Medium – 10 minutes)

I Am Free Corp. has three stock option plans outstanding on December 31, 2021. They provide the holders with the following entitlements:

1. Stock option A—The holders may purchase 30,000 ordinary shares at any time on or before December 31, 2025, for $20 each.
2. Stock option B—The holders may purchase 6,000 ordinary shares at any time on or before December 31, 2022, for $22 each. From January 1, 2023, to December 31, 2025, the holders may purchase 10,000 ordinary shares for $25 each.
3. Stock option C—The holders may purchase 5,000 ordinary shares at any time on or before December 31, 2023, for $26 each.

The average price of ordinary shares in 2021 was $24. I Am Free's basic EPS from continuing operations for the year was $1.22.

Required:

a. Which of the stock options are dilutive and which are antidilutive in 2021? What is the rule in this respect?
b. Assuming that all three option plans have been in place the entire year, for each plan determine the incremental number of shares, if any, that need to be considered for diluted EPS purposes.
c. Assume that stock option A was issued on April 1, 2021. Does this change your answer to part (b)? If so, what is the revised number of incremental shares for option A that need to be considered for diluted EPS purposes?

P15-31. Treasury stock method (L.O. 15-3, L.O. 15-4) (Medium – 10 minutes)

During 2021, Fuzzy Pandas Inc. (FPI) had three series of employee stock options outstanding, details of which follow:

1. Option A entitle employees to purchase 10,000 ordinary shares for $22 each. This series of options was granted on February 1, 2019, and expires on June 30, 2021.
2. Option B entitle employees to purchase 15,000 ordinary shares for $26 each until December 31, 2022, and $23 thereafter. This series of options was granted on June 1, 2018, and expires on December 31, 2025.
3. Option C entitle employees to purchase 20,000 ordinary shares for $21 each. This series of options was granted on April 1, 2021, and expires on December 31, 2024.

The average market price of FPI's ordinary shares for the year ended December 31, 2021, was $25.

Required:

a. For each of the options series, indicate whether they are dilutive or antidilutive in nature, and provide the reason why.
b. For each of the options series that are dilutive, determine the number of incremental shares to be notionally issued.

P15-32. Treasury stock method (L.O. 15-2, L.O. 15-3, L.O. 15-4) (Medium – 15 minutes)

In 2018, TC Ash Inc.'s net income was $150,000. Ash had 100,000 ordinary shares outstanding at year-end. There were two ordinary share transactions during the year: (i) Ash declared and distributed a two-for-one stock split on March 1, 2018; and (ii) Option C was exercised on April 1, 2018. Details of Ash's stock option plans follow:

- Option A entitles employees to purchase 10,000 ordinary shares for $15 each. This option was granted during 2017 and expires in 2020.
- Option B entitles employees to purchase 10,000 ordinary shares for $25 each. This option was granted on July 1, 2018, and expires in 2021.
- Option C entitles employees to purchase 10,000 ordinary shares for $18 each. This option was granted during 2016 and was exercised on April 1, 2018.
- Option D entitles employees to purchase 10,000 ordinary shares for $16 each. This option was granted on September 1, 2018, and expires in 2021.

The average market price of Ash's ordinary shares for the year is $20. Ash does not have any preferred shares or convertible bonds outstanding. The recorded exercise prices and number of shares that can be acquired under the stock option plans have already been adjusted for the stock split.

Required:

a. Calculate Ash's basic earnings per share for the year ended December 31, 2018.
b. Calculate Ash's diluted earnings per share for the year ended December 31, 2018.

P15-33. Calculating basic and diluted EPS

(L.O. 15-2, L.O. 15-3, L.O. 15-4) (Medium – 10 minutes)

Broken Man Inc. had 100,000 ordinary shares outstanding in all of 2021. On January 1, 2019, Broken issued at par $500,000 in 7% bonds maturing on January 1, 2027. Each $1,000 bond is convertible into 30 ordinary shares. Assume that the effective interest rate is 7%.

There are 10,000 outstanding cumulative preferred shares that are each entitled to an annual dividend of $0.32. Dividends were not declared or paid during 2021. Each preferred share is convertible into two ordinary shares.

Broken's net income for the year ended December 31, 2021, was $150,000. Its income tax rate was 25%.

Required:

a. Calculate Broken's basic EPS for 2021.
b. Are the convertible bonds dilutive or antidilutive in nature? The convertible preferred shares?
c. Calculate Broken's diluted EPS for 2021.

P15-34. Calculating basic and diluted EPS

(L.O. 15-2, L.O. 15-3, L.O. 15-4) (Medium – 15 minutes)

Select information for George's Dive Adventures Corp. (GDAC) follows:

- GDAC earned net income of $4,000,000 for the year ended December 31, 2021.
- GDAC was subject to a 30% tax rate.
- GDAC had 2,000,000 ordinary shares outstanding during the entire year; their average market price was $17.
- GDAC had $1,000,000 in 5% non-cumulative preferred shares outstanding during the entire year. Each $100 share is convertible into two ordinary shares.
- GDAC declared and paid the stated dividend on the preferred shares as well as $400,000 of dividends on the ordinary shares.
- GDAC had series A stock options outstanding the entire year that allowed employees to buy 5,000 ordinary shares for $15 each until December 31, 2024.
- GDAC had series B stock options outstanding the entire year that allowed employees to buy 10,000 ordinary shares for $20 each until December 31, 2024.
- GDAC had $5,000,000 in 7% bonds maturing on December 31, 2024, that were outstanding the entire year. Each $1,000 bond is convertible into 40 ordinary shares anytime before expiry.

Assume that the effective rate of interest on the bonds equals the coupon rate.

Required:

a. Calculate GDAC's basic EPS for the year ended December 31, 2021.
b. Prepare a schedule that sets out the income effect, share effect, and incremental EPS for each security that is convertible into ordinary shares. Rank order the shares by their dilutiveness.
c. Calculate GDAC's diluted EPS for the year ended December 31, 2021.

P15-35. Calculating basic and diluted EPS

(L.O. 15-2, L.O. 15-3, L.O. 15-4) (Medium – 20 minutes)

The following information is available for Jill's Emporium Ltd., which reports its financial results in accordance with IFRS:

Net income for 2018	$ 800,000
Income tax rate during 2018	32%
Liabilities and equity outstanding as at December 31, 2018	
8% bonds	$1,000,000
7% convertible bonds—each $1,000 bond is convertible into 7.5 ordinary shares	850,000
5% non-cumulative preferred shares	500,000
4% cumulative preferred shares—each $100 preferred share is convertible into four ordinary shares	400,000
Ordinary shares	1,000,000
The bonds and preferred shares were outstanding for the entire year	
Dividends were not declared on either series of the preferred shares in 2018	

	Activity	Ordinary shares outstanding
January 1, 2018	Opening balance	50,000
March 1, 2018	20% stock dividend	60,000
June 1, 2018	Two-for-one stock split	120,000
December 1, 2018	Repurchased 30,000 shares	90,000

Required:

a. Compute Jill's basic EPS for the year ended December 31, 2018.
b. Prepare a schedule that sets out the income effect, share effect, and incremental EPS for each security that is convertible into ordinary shares. Rank the potential ordinary shares by their dilutiveness.
c. Compute Jill's diluted EPS for the year ended December 31, 2018.

P15-36. Calculating basic and diluted EPS

(L.O. 15-2, L.O. 15-3, L.O. 15-4) (Medium – 20 minutes)

The following information is available for Bobby's Baubles Corp., which reports its financial results in accordance with IFRS:

Net income for 2021	$500,000
Income tax rate during 2021	35%
Liabilities and equity outstanding as at December 31, 2021	
6% convertible bonds—each $1,000 bond is convertible into eight ordinary shares	$500,000
5% convertible bonds—each $1,000 bond is convertible into six ordinary shares	700,000
4% cumulative preferred shares—each $100 preferred share is convertible into five ordinary shares	200,000
Ordinary shares	500,000

(Continued)

The bonds and preferred shares were outstanding for the entire year

Dividends were not declared on the preferred shares in 2020

$16,000 dividends were declared and paid on the preferred shares in 2021

	Activity	Ordinary shares outstanding
January 1, 2021	Opening balance	50,000
April 1, 2021	Sold 20,000 shares	70,000
May 1, 2021	Repurchased 10,000 shares	60,000
December 1, 2021	Sold 20,000 shares	80,000

Required:

a. Compute Bobby's basic EPS for the year ended December 31, 2021.
b. Prepare a schedule that sets out the income effect, share effect, and incremental EPS for each security that is convertible into ordinary shares. Rank the potential ordinary shares by their dilutiveness.
c. Compute Bobby's diluted EPS for the year ended December 31, 2021.
d. Show the required presentation of the EPS data on the income statement.

P15-37. Calculating basic and diluted EPS

(L.O. 15-2, L.O. 15-3, L.O. 15-4) (Medium – 10 minutes)

Catronic Ltd. had 80,000 ordinary shares outstanding in all of 2021. On January 1, 2019, Catronic issued at par $300,000 in 4% bonds maturing on January 1, 2031. Each $1,000 bond is convertible into 20 ordinary shares. Assume that the effective interest rate is 4%.

There are 4,000, $100, outstanding cumulative preferred shares that are each entitled to an annual dividend of $2. Dividends of $5,000 were declared on December 15, 2021, and paid on January 6, 2022. Each preferred share is convertible into three ordinary shares.

Catronic's net income for the year ended December 31, 2021, was $300,000. Its income tax rate was 30%.

Required:

a. Calculate Catronic's basic EPS for 2021.
b. Are the convertible bonds dilutive or antidilutive in nature? The convertible preferred shares?
c. Calculate Catronic's diluted EPS for 2021.

P15-38. Calculating basic and diluted EPS

(L.O. 15-2, L.O. 15-3, L.O. 15-4) (Medium – 10 minutes)

Brandy Dudas Maternity Wear Ltd. (BDM) had 100,000 ordinary shares outstanding during all of 2019. In 2017, BDM issued $500,000, 3% non-cumulative preferred shares. Each $100 preferred share is convertible into one ordinary share. BDM also had 6,000, $100 cumulative preferred shares outstanding that are each entitled to an annual dividend of $1.60. Each preferred share is convertible into two ordinary shares.

BDM's net income for the year ended December 31, 2019, was $400,000. Its income tax rate was 20%. The annual dividend was declared and paid during 2019 on the cumulative preferred shares but not on the non-cumulative shares.

Required:

a. Calculate BDM's basic EPS for 2019.
b. Are the non-cumulative convertible preferred shares dilutive or antidilutive in nature? The cumulative convertible preferred shares?
c. Calculate BDM's diluted EPS for 2019.

P15-39. Calculating basic and diluted EPS

(L.O. 15-2, L.O. 15-3, L.O. 15-4) (Medium – 15 minutes)

Select information for Gail's Play School Corp. (GPSC) follows:

- GPSC earned net income of $9,000,000 for the year ended December 31, 2021.
- GPSC was subject to a 40% tax rate.
- GPSC had 5,000,000 ordinary shares outstanding during the entire year; their average market price was $15.
- GPSC had $1,000,000 in 4% cumulative preferred shares outstanding during the entire year. At the option of the holder, each $100 share is convertible into four ordinary shares anytime after December 31, 2024.
- GPSC did not declare dividends in 2021, but paid out $400,000 in dividends declared in 2020.
- GPSC had series A stock options outstanding the entire year that allowed employees to buy 20,000 ordinary shares for $16 each until December 31, 2023, and for $14 each from January 1, 2024, until December 31, 2025.
- GPSC had series B stock options outstanding the entire year that allowed employees to buy 5,000 ordinary shares for $13 each until December 31, 2023.
- GPSC had $3,000,000 in 5% bonds maturing on December 31, 2026, that were outstanding the entire year. Each $1,000 bond is convertible into 16 ordinary shares anytime before expiry.
- Assume that the effective rate of interest on the bonds equals the coupon rate.

Required:

a. Calculate GPSC's basic EPS for the year ended December 31, 2021.
b. Prepare a schedule that sets out the income effect, share effect, and incremental EPS for each security that is convertible into ordinary shares. Rank the potential ordinary shares by their dilutiveness.
c. Calculate GPSC's diluted EPS for the year ended December 31, 2021.

P15-40. EPS when there is a loss

(L.O. 15-2, L.O. 15-3, L.O. 15-4) (Medium – 10 minutes)

Pendulum Toys Corp. (PTC) was incorporated on January 1, 2018. At that time, it issued 50,000 ordinary shares; 5,000, $100, 5% cumulative preferred shares "A"; and 30,000, $100, 6% non-cumulative preferred shares "B." Dividends were not declared or paid during 2018. PTC also issued at par $500,000 in 7% bonds maturing on January 1, 2021. Each $1,000 bond is convertible into 30 ordinary shares. Assume that the effective interest rate is 7%. PTC's net income (loss) for the year ended December 31, 2018, was ($400,000). Its income tax rate was 25%.

Required:

a. Calculate PTC's basic EPS for 2018.
b. Are the convertible bonds dilutive or antidilutive in nature? Why?
c. Calculate PTC's diluted EPS for 2018.

P15-41. EPS when there is a loss

(L.O. 15-2, L.O. 15-3, L.O. 15-4) (Medium – 10 minutes)

During all of 2018, Sandhawalia Computer Corp.'s (SCC) capital structure included the following:

- 200,000 ordinary shares outstanding
- 15,000, $100, 4% non-cumulative Series 1 preferred shares
- 12,000, $100, 3% cumulative Series 2 preferred shares
- $1,000,000, 5% bonds maturing on January 1, 2021. The bonds were issued at par. Each $1,000 bond is convertible into 18 ordinary shares.

SCC's net income (loss) for the year ended December 31, 2018, was ($250,000). Its income tax rate was 35%. The preferred shareholders received their full dividend entitlement in 2016; however, dividends were neither declared nor paid during 2017. During 2018, the company declared and paid a total of $132,000 in dividends.

Required:

a. Calculate SCC's basic EPS for 2018.
b. Are the convertible bonds dilutive or antidilutive in nature? Why?
c. Calculate SCC's diluted EPS for 2018.

P15-42. EPS when there is a loss

(L.O. 15-2, L.O. 15-3, L.O. 15-4) (Medium – 10 minutes)

Details of Crothers Aussie Corp.'s (CAC) capital structure during 2018 follow:

- 300,000 ordinary shares were outstanding on January 1, 2018; 100,000 additional ordinary shares were issued on July 1, 2018.
- $2,000,000, 4.5% bonds maturing on December 31, 2024. The bonds were issued at par. Each $1,000 bond is convertible into 22 ordinary shares.
- 40,000, $100, 3% cumulative preferred shares. Dividends were last declared and paid in 2015.

CAC's net income for the year ended December 31, 2018, was $50,000. Its income tax rate was 18%.

Required:

a. Calculate CAC's basic EPS for 2018.
b. Are the convertible bonds dilutive or antidilutive in nature? Why?
c. Calculate CAC's diluted EPS for 2018.

P15-43. EPS when there are discontinued operations

(L.O. 15-2, L.O. 15-3, L.O. 15-4) (Medium – 10 minutes)

Sherbrook Pizza Inc. (SPI) was incorporated on January 1, 2018. Its capital structure included 5,000 ordinary shares; 1,000, $100, 4%, non-cumulative preferred shares; and 10,000 options on ordinary shares with a strike price of $10. SPI's net income (loss) for the year ended December 31, 2018, was ($10,000), consisting of a loss from continuing operations of ($50,000) and earnings from discontinued operations of $40,000. Dividends were neither declared nor paid in 2018. The average market price of its shares during the year was $12.50.

Required:

Compute basic earnings per share and diluted earnings per share from each of continuing operations, discontinued operations, and operations.

P15-44. EPS when there are discontinued operations

(L.O. 15-2, L.O. 15-3, L.O. 15-4) (Medium – 15 minutes)

Dartmouth Subs Ltd. (DSL) was incorporated on January 1, 2018. Its capital structure includes 5,000 ordinary shares; 2,000, $100, 3% cumulative preferred shares; and 6,000 options on ordinary shares with a strike price of $15. DSL's net income (loss) for the year ended December 31, 2018, was ($10,000), consisting of a profit from continuing operations of $50,000 and a loss from discontinued operations of ($60,000). Dividends were neither declared nor paid in 2018. The average market price of its shares during the year was $18.

Required:

Compute basic earnings per share and diluted earnings per share from each of continuing operations, discontinued operations, and operations.

P15-45. EPS when there are discontinued operations

(L.O. 15-2, L.O. 15-3, L.O. 15-4) (Medium – 15 minutes)

During all of 2018, Josh's Sportswear Inc.'s (JSI) capital structure included the following:

- 20,000 ordinary shares outstanding
- 3,000, $100, 5% cumulative preferred shares
- $500,000, 6% bonds maturing on January 1, 2023. The bonds were issued at par. Each $1,000 bond is convertible into 12 ordinary shares.

JSI's net income for the year ended December 31, 2018, was $190,000, comprised of earnings from continuing operations and discontinued operations of $172,000 and $18,000, respectively. Dividends were not declared in 2017. However, $30,000 in dividends were declared on the preferred shares in 2018. JSI's income tax rate was 27%.

Required:

Compute basic earnings per share and diluted earnings per share arising from each of continuing operations, discontinued operations, and operations.

P15-46. Calculating basic and diluted EPS (comprehensive)

(L.O. 15-2, L.O. 15-3, L.O. 15-4) (Difficult – 30 minutes)

The following are selected details of Kitchener Fasteners Inc.'s capital structure as at January 1, 2021:

- 100,000 ordinary shares issued and outstanding.
- 10,000, $100 cumulative preferred shares "A" with a stated dividend rate of 2% per annum. At the option of the holder, two preferred shares can be exchanged for one ordinary share on or before December 31, 2026.
- 50,000 non-cumulative shares "B" that are each entitled to dividends of $3 per annum.
- Bonds A—$1,000,000, 5%, semi-annual bonds maturing December 31, 2026.
- Bonds B—$1,000,000, 4%, semi-annual bonds maturing September 30, 2028. At the option of the holder, each $1,000 bond can be converted into 10 ordinary shares at any time between January 1, 2025, and December 31, 2025, and into 11 ordinary shares thereafter.
- Bonds C—$800,000, 3%, semi-annual bonds maturing December 31, 2027. At the option of the holder, each $1,000 bond can be converted into nine ordinary shares.
- Option A—grants the holder the right to purchase 20,000 ordinary shares at any time before December 31, 2025, for $26 per share.
- Option B—grants the holder the right to purchase 15,000 ordinary shares for $15 per share. The option expires on December 31, 2025.

During the year, Kitchener's ordinary shareholdings changed as follows:

- February 1, 2021—repurchased 20,000 ordinary shares and held them as treasury shares.
- September 1, 2021—issued (sold) 10,000 ordinary shares from treasury.
- November 1, 2021—declared and distributed a two-for-one stock split.

Kitchener was subject to a 20% tax rate. Net income for the year ended December 31, 2021, was $800,000. During the year, dividends were neither declared nor paid. The average market rate in 2021 for Kitchener's ordinary shares was $17.

The recorded exercise prices and number of shares under the stock options plans that can be acquired have already been adjusted for the stock split. Similarly, the recorded conversion factor for the convertible bonds and preferred shares has already been adjusted for the stock dividend.

Assume that the effective rate of interest on the bonds equals the coupon rate.

Required:

a. Calculate Kitchener's basic EPS for the year ended December 31, 2021.
b. Prepare a schedule that sets out the income effect, share effect, and incremental EPS for each security that is convertible into ordinary shares. Rank the potential ordinary shares by their dilutiveness.
c. Calculate Kitchener's diluted EPS for the year ended December 31, 2021.

P15-47. Calculating basic and diluted EPS (comprehensive)

(L.O. 15-2, L.O. 15-3, L.O. 15-4) (Difficult – 35 minutes)

The following are selected details of Complex Capital Structures Inc.'s capital structure as at January 1, 2018:

- 400,000 ordinary shares were issued; 200,000 were outstanding.
- Bonds A—$2,000,000, 4%, semi-annual bonds maturing December 31, 2026. At the option of the holder, each $1,000 bond can be converted into five ordinary shares at any time prior to maturity.

- Bonds B—$1,000,000, 6%, semi-annual bonds maturing December 31, 2024. At the option of the holder, each $1,000 bond can be converted into eight ordinary shares at any time prior to maturity.
- 30,000 non-cumulative preferred shares "A" that are each entitled to dividends of $2 per annum. At the option of the holder, each preferred share can be converted into one ordinary share.
- 50,000, $100, non-cumulative shares "B" with a stated dividend rate of 5% per annum. At the option of the holder, each preferred share can be converted into two ordinary shares.
- Employee stock option—grants the holder the right to purchase 10,000 ordinary shares at any time before December 31, 2022, for $11 per share.
- Warrant—grants the holder the right to purchase 1,200 ordinary shares for $7 per share. The warrant, which can be exercised at any time, expires on December 31, 2024.

During the year, Complex Capital Structures Inc. issued and redeemed ordinary shares as follows:

- March 1, 2018—declared and issued a three-for-one stock split.
- July 1, 2018—repurchased 20,000 ordinary shares and held them as treasury shares.
- September 1, 2018—sold 10,000 ordinary shares from treasury.
- October 1, 2018—sold 40,000 ordinary shares from treasury.

Complex was subject to a 35% tax rate. Its net income for the year ended December 31, 2018, totalled $2,800,000. In 2018 the average market price for Complex's ordinary shares was $10.

Complex declared and paid the dividends on both classes of preferred shares in 2018.

The recorded exercise prices and number of shares under the stock options plans that can be acquired have already been adjusted for the stock split. Similarly, the recorded conversion factors for the convertible bonds and preferred shares have already been adjusted for the stock split.

Assume that the effective rate of interest on the bonds equals the coupon rate.

Required:

a. Calculate Complex's basic EPS for the year ended December 31, 2018.
b. Prepare a schedule that sets out the income effect, share effect, and incremental EPS for each security that is convertible into ordinary shares. Rank the potential ordinary shares by their dilutiveness.
c. Calculate Complex's diluted EPS for the year ended December 31, 2018.

P15-48. Calculating basic and diluted EPS (comprehensive)

(L.O. 15-2, L.O. 15-3, L.O. 15-4) (Difficult – 30 minutes)

The following are selected details of Kingston Objects Inc.'s capital structure as at January 1, 2018:

- 200,000 ordinary shares issued and outstanding.
- 100,000 cumulative preferred shares "A" that are each entitled to dividends of $4 per annum.
- 50,000, $100 non-cumulative shares "B" with a stated dividend rate of 3% per annum. At the option of the holder, each preferred share can be converted into two ordinary shares on December 31, 2023.
- Bonds A—$1,000,000, 6%, semi-annual bonds maturing December 31, 2022.
- Bonds B—$2,000,000, 5%, semi-annual bonds maturing June 30, 2028. At the option of the holder, each $1,000 bond can be converted into 10 ordinary shares at any time between January 1, 2023, and December 31, 2023.
- Bonds C—$500,000, 3%, semi-annual bonds maturing December 31, 2023. At the option of the holder, each $1,000 bond can be converted into eight ordinary shares.
- Option A—grants the holder the right to purchase 10,000 ordinary shares at any time before December 31, 2021, for $20 per share.
- Option B—grants the holder the right to purchase 5,000 ordinary shares for $12 per share. The option expires on December 31, 2019.

During the year, Kingston issued ordinary shares as follows:

- March 1, 2018—issued (sold) 20,000 ordinary shares.
- October 1, 2018—issued (sold) 10,000 ordinary shares.
- December 1, 2018—declared and distributed a 20% stock dividend.

Kingston was subject to a 30% tax rate. Its net income for the year ended December 31, 2018, totalled $1,339,000. During the year, Kingston declared and paid the stated dividends on both classes of preferred shares as well as $200,000 of dividends on its ordinary shares. The average market rate in 2018 for Kingston's ordinary shares was $15.

The recorded exercise prices and number of shares under the stock options plans that can be acquired have already been adjusted for the stock dividend. Similarly, the recorded conversion factors for the convertible bonds and preferred shares have already been adjusted for the stock dividend.

Assume that the effective rate of interest on the bonds equals the coupon rate.

Required:

a. Calculate Kingston's basic EPS for the year ended December 31, 2018.
b. Prepare a schedule that sets out the income effect, share effect, and incremental EPS for each security that is convertible into ordinary shares. Rank the potential ordinary shares by their dilutiveness.
c. Calculate Kingston's diluted EPS for the year ended December 31, 2018.

P15-49. Calculating basic and diluted EPS (comprehensive)

(L.O. 15-2, L.O. 15-3, L.O. 15-4) (Difficult – 35 minutes)

The following are selected details of Simple Objects Inc.'s capital structure as at January 1, 2018:

- 300,000 ordinary shares were issued; 250,000 were outstanding.
- Bonds A—$1,000,000, 3%, semi-annual bonds maturing December 31, 2026. At the option of the holder, each $1,000 bond can be converted into seven ordinary shares at any time prior to maturity.
- Bonds B—$2,000,000, 5%, semi-annual bonds maturing December 31, 2024. At the option of the holder, each $1,000 bond can be converted into six ordinary shares at any time prior to maturity.
- 10,000 non-cumulative preferred shares "A" that are each entitled to dividends of $3 per annum. At the option of the holder, each preferred share can be converted into two ordinary shares.
- 100,000, $100 non-cumulative shares "B" with a stated dividend rate of 4% per annum. At the option of the holder, each preferred share can be converted into three ordinary shares.
- Employee stock option—grants the holder the right to purchase 8,000 ordinary shares at any time before December 31, 2022, for $10 per share.
- Warrant—grants the holder the right to purchase 5,000 ordinary shares for $8 per share.

The warrant, which can be exercised at any time, expires on December 31, 2024.

During the year, Simple Objects issued and redeemed ordinary shares as follows:

- March 1, 2018—declared and issued a two-for-one stock split.
- July 1, 2018—sold 20,000 ordinary shares from treasury.
- September 1, 2018—repurchased 10,000 ordinary shares and held them as treasury shares.
- October 1, 2018—sold 30,000 ordinary shares from treasury.

Simple was subject to a 25% tax rate. Its net income for the year ended December 31, 2018, totalled $3,300,000. In 2018 the average market price for Simple's ordinary shares was $12.

Simple declared dividends totalling $500,000 on December 15, 2017, payable on January 15, 2018. Of the $500,000, $30,000 pertained to the preferred "A" shares; $400,000 related to the preferred "B" shares; with the balance being allocated to the ordinary shares. Dividends were not declared in 2018.

The recorded exercise prices and number of shares under the stock options plans that can be acquired have already been adjusted for the stock split. Similarly, the recorded conversion factors for the convertible bonds and preferred shares have already been adjusted for the stock split.

Assume that the effective rate of interest on the bonds equals the coupon rate.

Required:

a. Calculate Simple's basic EPS for the year ended December 31, 2018.
b. Prepare a schedule that sets out the income effect, share effect, and incremental EPS for each security that is convertible into ordinary shares. Rank the potential ordinary shares by their dilutiveness.
c. Calculate Simple's diluted EPS for the year ended December 31, 2018.

P15-50. EPS when there are discontinued operations

(L.O. 15-2, L.O. 15-3, L.O. 15-4) (Difficult – 30 minutes)

Four independent situations follow:

	Situation 1	Situation 2	Situation 3	Situation 4
Earnings (loss) from continuing operations	$500,000	$(500,000)	$(50,000)	$ 50,000
Earnings (loss) from discontinued operations	100,000	100,000	100,000	(100,000)
Net income (loss)	$600,000	$(400,000)	$ 50,000	$ (50,000)
Weighted average number of ordinary shares outstanding	100,000	100,000	100,000	100,000
Preference shares	None outstanding	None outstanding	None outstanding	None outstanding
Potential ordinary shares	10,000 options on ordinary shares—exercise price $20, average market price $25	10,000 options on ordinary shares—exercise price $20, average market price $25	10,000 options on ordinary shares—exercise price $20, average market price $25	10,000 options on ordinary shares—exercise price $20, average market price $25

Required:

a. For each of the four independent situations, compute basic earnings per share and diluted earnings per share from each of continuing operations, discontinued operations, and operations.
b. Summarize IFRS requirements with respect to determining diluted EPS when there is a loss from continuing operations.
c. Summarize IFRS requirements with respect to determining diluted EPS when there is a net loss; however, earnings from continuing operations is positive.
d. Describe the presentation requirement for EPS including permissible alternatives.

K. MINI-CASES

CASE 1
XYZ Company
(20 minutes)[14]

XYZ, a public company, is required to disclose earnings per share information in its financial statements for the year ended December 31, 2021. The facts about XYZ's situation are as follows:

- At the beginning of fiscal 2021, 450,000 ordinary shares, issued for $5.75 million, were outstanding. The authorized number of ordinary shares is 1 million. On January 1, 2021, 50,000, 10% cumulative preferred shares were also outstanding. They had been issued for $500,000.
- On September 30, 2021, XYZ issued 100,000 ordinary shares for $1.5 million cash.
- On January 15, 2022, XYZ made a private share placement of 25,000 ordinary shares, raising $350,000 cash.
- XYZ reported net income of $2.5 million for the year ended December 31, 2021.
- Managers of XYZ hold options to purchase 20,000 ordinary shares of XYZ at a price of $11.50 per share. The options expire on July 31, 2024.
- At January 1, 2021, XYZ had outstanding $1 million of 8% convertible bonds ($1,000 face value), with interest payable on June 30 and December 31 of each year. Each bond is convertible into 65 ordinary shares at the option of the holder, before December 31, 2026. On June 30, 2021, $400,000 of the bonds were converted.
- XYZ has an effective tax rate of 40% and has an average after-tax rate of return of 10%. The average market price in 2021 for XYZ's ordinary shares was $13.

Required:

Calculate the basic and diluted earnings per share figures for 2021.

CASE 2
Mom and Dot Reid Inc.
(45 minutes)

Mom and Dot Reid Inc. (MDRI) is a Canadian company listed on the Toronto Stock Exchange that manufactures component parts for automobiles. MDRI, like many public companies, has various stock option plans for its executives and employees. Charlotte Ash, the CEO of MDRI, is scheduled to retire on March 31, 2019. Charlotte is concerned about the recent drop in the company's share price as her various stock options all expire on her retirement date. While Ms. Ash is a brilliant ideas person and has spearheaded the launch of many successful new products, her financial savvy is mediocre at best.

Charlotte has heard that a firm's stock price is affected to some degree by both the reported earnings per share (EPS) and the magnitude of the change from the previous year. It is now September 15, 2018, and Charlotte is contemplating ways of increasing MDRI's reported EPS for the year ending December 31, 2018, so as to improve the company's share price before she retires. In this respect, Charlotte has a number of proposals, summarized below, and has called you, Gail Fisher, a chartered professional accountant and the CFO of MDRI, into her office to solicit your input. To prepare for the meeting you have summarized MDRI's currently projected EPS and other pertinent information as set out in Exhibit I below.

Charlotte's proposals

1. MDRI could purchase 5 million of its own ordinary shares on the open market for $325 million and retire them. While the company would have to borrow to do this, it does have several underutilized credit facilities with its banking consortium and accessing the necessary funds would not be difficult.

---

14. Uniform Final Examination 1991, with permission Chartered Professional Accountants of Canada, Toronto, Canada.

2. MDRI has $300 million in 3% bonds outstanding that mature in three years. The bonds were issued several years ago at par when interest rates were at historical lows. Rates have recently risen due to inflationary pressures and as such Charlotte believes that the bonds can be redeemed on the open market for about $276 million. Her thoughts are that the $24 million gain on redemption will improve earnings and hence EPS. Charlotte suggests that the redemption be financed by issuing a new series of bonds at the current market rate of 6%.
3. MDRI closed and sold one of its plants during the year, suffering a pre-tax loss of $20 million. The autonomously run plant was one of three plants located in Windsor, Ontario, that produced automobile engines. It was closed due to a prolonged drop in demand due to stagnant new car sales. Charlotte suggests that this loss be classified as arising from discontinued operations so as to remove the loss from "core" EPS.
4. MDRI has an opportunity to sell one of its plants for a pre-tax gain of $50 million, providing that they irrevocably agree to lease back the property for a 20-year period. The lease rates would initially be market based and subsequently adjusted every four years to reflect the change in the consumer price index during the intervening period. If MDRI enters into this transaction, it will close on December 31, 2018.
5. MDRI could complete a reverse stock split in which it would issue one new ordinary share for each two old ordinary shares currently outstanding. Charlotte knows that EPS measures income available to the ordinary shareholders divided by the weighted average number of ordinary shares outstanding and expects that reducing the number of outstanding shares will increase the reported EPS.

After the meeting, you reflect on the legitimacy of the proposals, which you know have not been discussed with the board of directors.

Required:

Prepare a memo addressed to Charlotte Ash analyzing the effect on EPS for each of her proposals. Discuss any concerns that you may have with respect to the manner in which Charlotte has proposed to increase EPS.

Exhibit I MDRI projected earnings per share for the year ending December 31, 2018

	Actual 2017	Projected 2018 (existing)
Basic EPS		
Net income		$140,000,000
Preferred dividends		10,000,000
Net income available to ordinary shareholders		$130,000,000
Weighted average number of ordinary shares outstanding (WASO)		40,000,000
Basic EPS	$3.35	$ 3.25
Corporate income tax rate		30%
MDRI stock price September 15, 2018		65.00
Interest rate on the bank consortium credit facilities		5%

CASE 3 Canadian Tire Corporation

(15 minutes)

Refer to Appendix C for the Canadian Tire Corporation's financial statements for the year ended December 31, 2016.

Required:

a. Does Canadian Tire Corporation have potential ordinary (common) shares in its capital structure? How can you quickly determine this?
b. Identify the type(s) of potential ordinary (common) shares that Canadian Tire Corporation has outstanding.

CASE 4
EPS
(30 minutes)

You, Sarina Felmeguchi, are the chief financial officer of SPE Corporation, a public company whose shares are traded on the Toronto Stock Exchange. You are in the process of finalizing the financial statements for 2021. SPE's chief executive officer, Margaret D. Tale, is a very hands-on manager and usually reviews the details of the financial statements before they are published. You previously provided Ms. Tale with the details of your calculations of the firm's earnings per share (EPS). Ms. Tale returned your calculations to you on January 14, 2022, with her comments:

Comment 1: I heard that EPS is a commonly used measure by market participants such as investors and financial analysts. Why is this statistic so popular?

Comment 2: I realize that many companies report both basic and diluted EPS. I understand that a popular view of diluted EPS is that it is a "worst case scenario." Given the popularity of this measure, is there another way to interpret the additional information provided by diluted EPS?

Comment 3: I noticed that you use the weighted average number of outstanding shares during the year to calculate EPS rather than the number of shares outstanding at year-end. Please explain the logic of this methodology.

Comment 4: I understand that a company's earnings can increase compared to the previous year but its basic EPS may remain unchanged and its diluted EPS may be lower. How is this possible?

Required:

Write a memo to Ms. Tale addressing her comments.

FMUA/Fotolia

CHAPTER 16

Pensions and Other Employee Future Benefits

LEARNING OBJECTIVES

After studying this chapter, you should be able to:

L.O. 16-1. Explain the nature of pension plans and distinguish between defined contribution and defined benefit plans.

L.O. 16-2. Apply the accounting standards for defined contribution pension plans.

L.O. 16-3. Analyze an array of pension plan data to determine the amount of pension expense and other comprehensive income for defined benefit pension plans.

L.O. 16-4. Analyze the effect of actuarial assumptions on the financial statement assets, liabilities, and income, and evaluate the appropriateness of assumptions used to account for pensions.

L.O. 16-5. Integrate pension plan information by preparing the relevant note disclosures.

CPA competencies addressed in this chapter:

1.1.2 Evaluates the appropriateness of the basis of financial reporting (Level B)
b. Methods of measurement

1.2.3 Evaluates treatment for non-routine transactions (Level B)
b. Pension plans and other employee future benefits

1.4.1 Analyzes complex financial statement note disclosure (Level C)

In 2016, more than 6 million people in Canada participated in over 19,000 pension plans, covering 38% of all workers. In the public sector, this percentage rises to 86%, but even in the private sector it is a significant 25% of the total. Clearly, pension plans are important to a large segment of the population.[1]

Of the 6 million people covered by pension plans, the vast majority (67%) are in defined benefit plans, although this percentage is a significant drop from rates of over 90% in the 1980s. What are defined benefit plans? How do they differ from other pension plans?

One prominent company that offers defined benefit pension plans is Air Canada, which as of 2016 employed some 24,000 staff. The company has more than 10 separate pension plans covering various groups of staff ranging from pilots to machinists to management personnel.

At the end of 2016, the company disclosed that it had $19.1 billion in pension obligations, yet the company reported only $1.2 billion in pension liabilities on the balance sheet. What explains the difference between the $19.1 billion obligation and the $1.2 billion liability? How does Air Canada derive this information, and how should we interpret it?

[1] Statistics Canada, *The Daily*, July 21, 2017.

16 CONTENTS

A. INTRODUCTION 801
B. NATURE OF PENSION PLANS 802
1. Defined contribution plans 802
2. Defined benefit plans 803
C. ACCOUNTING FOR DEFINED CONTRIBUTION PLANS 803
D. ACCOUNTING FOR DEFINED BENEFIT PLANS 804
1. What to account for in defined benefit plans 806
2. Implementing pension accounting for defined benefit plans 811
3. Presentation and disclosure 816
E. OTHER ISSUES 818
1. Settlements 818
2. Asset ceiling 818
3. Multi-employer plans 818
4. Other long-term employee benefits 819
F. A PRACTICAL ILLUSTRATION: CANADIAN TIRE CORPORATION 819
G. SUBSTANTIVE DIFFERENCES BETWEEN RELEVANT IFRS AND ASPE 821
H. SUMMARY 821
I. ANSWERS TO CHECKPOINT QUESTIONS 822
J. GLOSSARY 822
K. REFERENCES 823
L. PROBLEMS 823
M. MINI-CASES 837

A. INTRODUCTION

Companies frequently offer benefits to their employees in addition to cash pay. Benefits such as extended health and dental plans, life insurance, counselling services, and so on can comprise a significant portion of employees' total pay packages (sometimes up to one-third). There are many reasons for having these benefit arrangements instead of wage payments, but the two most important are risk sharing and tax advantages.

First, different people will require services such as health care at different times. Since people are generally risk-averse, it is efficient for a group of people to pay into a health plan that defrays their costs when they subsequently need health services. Fundamentally, this is the reason for universal health care that is funded by the Canadian federal and provincial governments through taxes. The same logic applies to extended health plans that cover services beyond basic health needs (such as dental services and prescription glasses), as well as to other non–health benefit plans.

Second, many employee benefit plans are tax advantageous relative to cash payments to employees. Cash wages are of course deductible to employers and taxable to employees. However, a number of non-cash benefits are deductible to employers but *non*-taxable to employees. Extended health benefits, dental plans, and disability insurance are examples of these deductible but non-taxable benefits.

From the employer's perspective, it is fairly straightforward to account for employee benefits that are consumed in the same period in which the employees earn them (such as extended health coverage). That is, the employer records an expense for the amount of benefits employees earn in a year, similar to the recording of compensation expense for wages earned. However, the accounting becomes more complicated

when employees *earn* the rights to benefits *now* but *consume* those benefits far into the *future*. Pension benefits are one obvious example, which is the focus of this chapter. Sometimes, employers also commit to provide other types of benefits to their employees, such as health care, even after employees have retired; we address this issue toward the end of this chapter.

B. NATURE OF PENSION PLANS

L.O. 16-1. Explain the nature of pension plans and distinguish between defined contribution and defined benefit plans.

pension trust The legal entity that holds the investments and discharges the obligations of a pension plan.

Pension plans involve three parties: the employer, the employees, and the pension trust. The **pension trust** is the legal entity that holds the investments and discharges the obligations of a pension plan; it is managed by a trustee who is independent of the company. A number of flows occur among these three parties:

1. Employees provide services to their employer. To partially compensate for employees' services, the employer pays wages to them.
2. As part of the employees' compensation, the employer also pays into a pension plan, which will pay employees in the future when they retire.
3. In many pension plans, employees must also contribute to the pension plan; in other plans, employees have the option to contribute to the pension plan to increase the future benefits that they expect to receive.

The following diagram summarizes the relationship among the parties, along with the flows of services and dollars. The dotted arrows indicate flows that are not of particular interest to our discussion in this chapter.

Exhibit 16-1 Schematic of the parties involved in a pension plan and flows between them

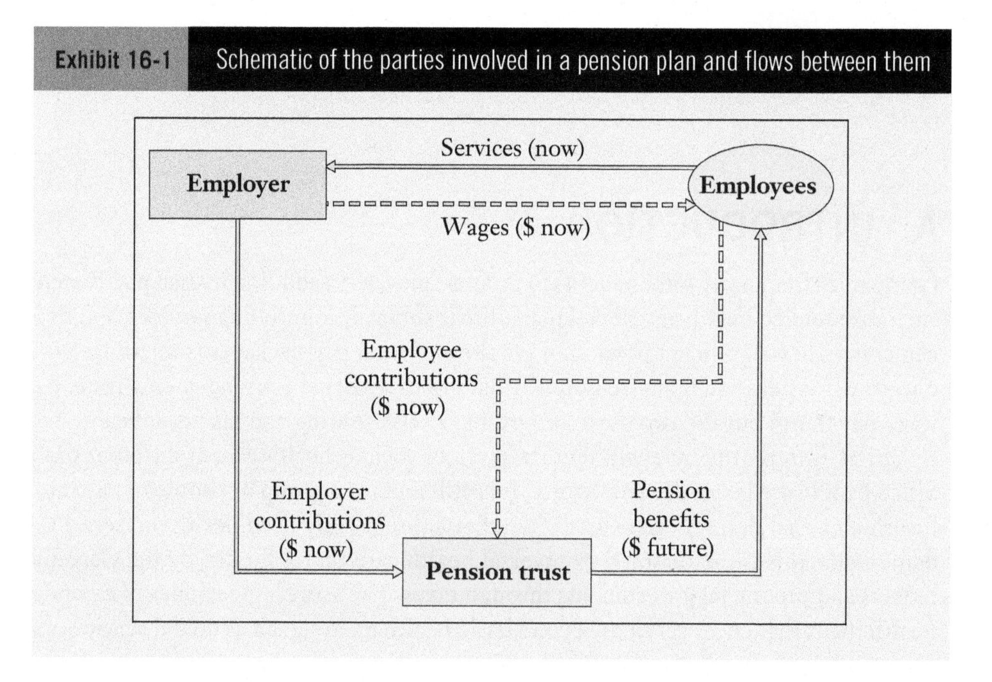

This diagram also helps to identify the two main types of pension plans. The two types reflect whether the pension plan specifies the *inflows* to the pension trust or the *outflows* from it.

1. Defined contribution plans

defined contribution plan A pension plan that specifies how much funds the employer needs to contribute.

A **defined contribution plan** specifies how much money the employer needs to contribute to the pension plan. For example, a plan may require the employer to contribute $10 per hour worked by an employee, or it may require the employer to contribute

$1 for every $1 the employee contributes to the plan. These plans place investment risk on employees. That is, poor returns on the pension trust's investments correspondingly reduce the pension benefits that will be paid to employees (future retirees). On the other hand, high returns will result in higher benefit payments to the employees in the future.

2. Defined benefit plans

A **defined benefit plan** specifies how much in pension payments employees will receive during their retirement. For example, a plan may require the employer to pay $200 per month for each year of service provided by the employee, so that someone who has worked 30 years for the employer would receive $6,000 per month. These plans place investment risk on employers since the eventual outflows from the pension trust to employees are pre-specified. Inadequate contributions by the pension plan sponsor (i.e., the employer) or poor investment returns will result in an underfunded pension where pension assets are insufficient to cover pension obligations. In this case, the sponsor needs to increase its contributions to the pension trust. In contrast, if the pension plan is overfunded, then the employer can reduce its contributions.[2]

defined benefit plan A pension plan that specifies how much in pension payments employees will receive during their retirement.

CHECKPOINT **CP16-1**

What is the fundamental difference between a defined contribution and a defined benefit pension plan?

C. ACCOUNTING FOR DEFINED CONTRIBUTION PLANS

L.O. 16-2. Apply the accounting standards for defined contribution pension plans.

When a company uses a defined contribution plan, its rights and obligations begin and end with making the specified contribution according to the contribution formula. The company faces neither the risks nor the benefits of low or high investment returns earned by the pension trust. Given the economics of this type of pension plan, the accounting is fairly straightforward: the company records compensation expense for the amount of contribution it owes according to the contribution formula.

For example, suppose Panorama Cameras provides its 300 employees with a defined contribution plan. The plan requires the company to contribute to the pension an amount equal to 10% of the employee's gross wages. During the year, these employees earned a total of $15 million. As a result, Panorama would record the following entry:

Exhibit 16-2	Journal entry to record pension expense for Panorama Cameras' defined contribution plan	
Dr. Pension expense ($15,000,000 × 10%)	1,500,000	
Cr. Cash or pension contribution payable		1,500,000

[2] In some instances, the employer may even be able to withdraw surpluses from the pension trust. However, the law in this area is complex and remains unsettled, so it is not clear whether surpluses can be withdrawn by the employer or whether such funds are stranded within the pension plan.

Keep in mind that the pension cost could be capitalized instead of expensed. For example, if the employees are engaged in manufacturing products, then the debit would be capitalized into the labour component of inventories. This is no different from capitalizing the cost of production wages into inventories. Wages and pension cost incurred on employees engaged in constructing a building would be capitalized into property, plant, and equipment. For ease of exposition, this chapter will simply assume that the pension cost will be expensed with the understanding that, under the appropriate circumstances, that cost could be capitalized into various assets.

L.O. 16-3. Analyze an array of pension plan data to determine the amount of pension expense and other comprehensive income for defined benefit pension plans.

L.O. 16-4. Analyze the effect of actuarial assumptions on the financial statement assets, liabilities, and income, and evaluate the appropriateness of assumptions used to account for pensions.

D. ACCOUNTING FOR DEFINED BENEFIT PLANS

In this type of plan, the employer guarantees to employees a certain amount of benefits in the future. Since pension benefit payments could be decades away from the services the company receives now, there is a severe mismatch in the timing of the future cash payments to employees and when they earn those benefits. Thus, cash accounting is obviously inappropriate and accrual accounting is needed. However, the computations of the amounts to be accrued are complex due to the need to forecast decades into the future. In particular, we need to estimate (at least) the following:

1. When will each employee be entitled to retire and receive pension payments?
2. For how long will each employee be entitled to pension payments? That is, how long will employees live (how long is their life expectancy)?
3. How much will be the periodic pension payments for each employee?
4. What part of the expected benefit payments relate to services provided in the current year?
5. What is the value of the pension obligation at retirement?
6. How much in plan assets are required now to satisfy the pension obligation at retirement?

actuary A professional who specializes in the estimation of risks and uncertainties.

Fortunately, accountants can rely on actuaries for these forecasts. An **actuary** is a professional who specializes in the estimation of risks and uncertainties. Nevertheless, accountants need to be familiar with the basics of the computations to assess the reasonability of the actuarial amounts, because these amounts will form the basis of the accounting for the pension plan.

To illustrate the actuarial computations, we focus on a single employee, Mabel Lam, who works for Peachland Canners. (The results for one person can be extrapolated to many people by simple multiplication.) Mabel has worked for Peachland for the past 25 years and she has just turned 55 at the end of 2021. Upon retirement at age 65, the pension specifies that Mabel will be entitled to receive pension payments of $2,000 per year for each year of service provided. Life expectancy tables indicate that a non-smoking female such as Mabel is expected to live until the age of 85. Peachland's management estimates that any assets invested in the pension plan will earn 8% on average, and this is the same rate used to discount her pension obligation.

Exhibit 16-3 Timeline of events for Mabel Lam

End of year:	1996	2021	2031	2051	
Age:	30	55	65	85	→ Time
Event:	Mabel begins working for Peachland	Now	Retirement	Expected end of pension payments (i.e., death)	

Ultimately, we need to determine the expense relating to the benefits Mabel has earned for 2021. To do this, we need to carry out the following steps:

1. Estimate the pension payments Mabel is entitled to receive during retirement for the services she provided during the year (2021).
2. Estimate the amount of pension assets that will be required when Mabel turns 65 to fund these pension payments from age 65 to age 85, identified in Step 1.
3. Estimate the amount of pension assets required now (at the end of 2021) to obtain the amount of assets required at age 65, calculated in Step 2. This amount is the current service cost, which will be more precisely defined below.

The following diagram shows these three steps along with the calculations for Mabel Lam.

Exhibit 16-4 Calculations for estimating the current service cost for Mabel Lam

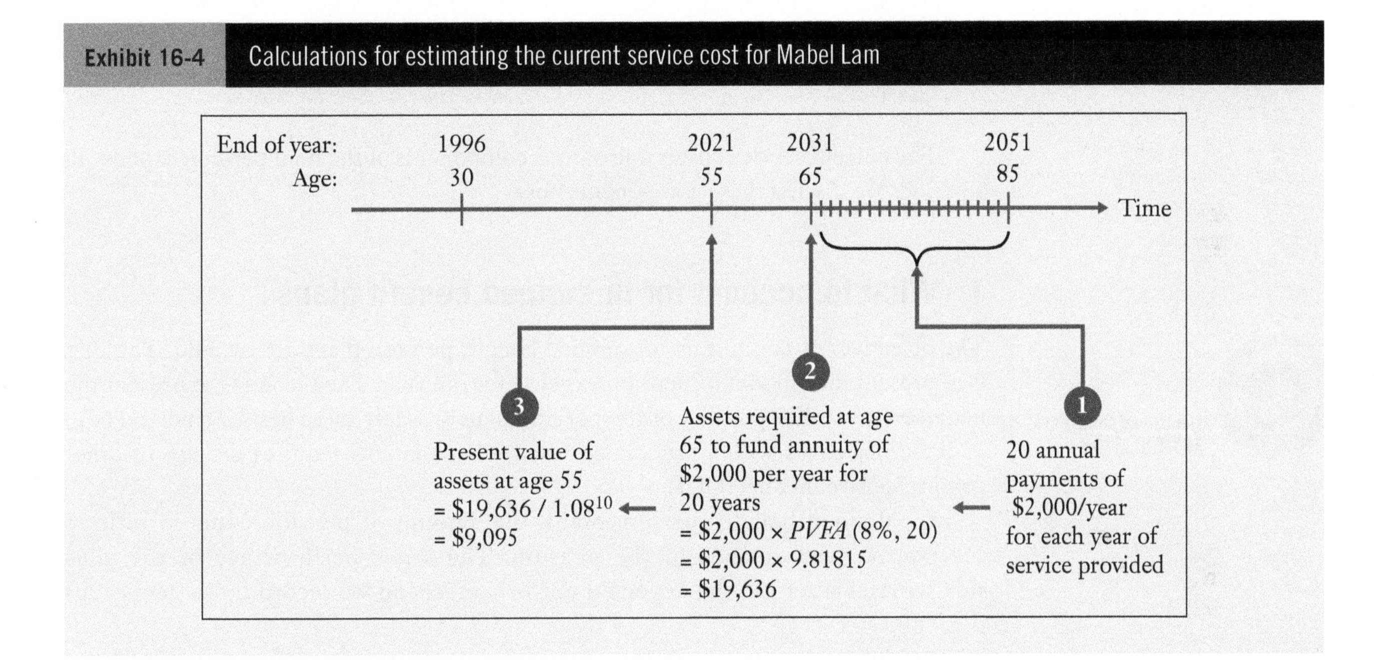

These calculations show that it will cost $9,095, in terms of 2021 dollars, to provide Mabel with pension payments of $2,000 per year over 20 years from 2031 to 2051. As these pension payments are what Mabel earns by working one year, in 2021, this is the amount of expense that Peachland Canners should record in that year. This expense is called the current service cost, which is technically defined in IAS 19 as follows:

> ¶8 **current service cost** is the increase in the present value of a defined benefit obligation resulting from employee service in the current period.

current service cost The increase in the present value of pension obligations due to an employee's provision of services during the current period.

For each additional year that Mabel works, she earns an additional $2,000 per year during her retirement, and Peachland would record an expense for the current service cost for that year of service received. In 2021, this amount was $9,095. In the following year, the amount would increase to $9,823 ($19,636 ÷ 1.08^9) because the number of years until retirement reduces by one, from 10 years to nine years. Thus, the current service cost increases from year to year according to the discount rate; the amount for 2022 is 8% higher than the amount for 2021 ($9,095 × 1.08 = $9,823).

accrued benefit obligation The present value of pension benefits that employees have earned.

When we add together all the benefits that Mabel has earned through all her years of employment with Peachland Canners, we obtain the **accrued benefit obligation** that Peachland has promised to Mabel. This obligation represents the present value of pension benefits that employees have earned.

Actual pension plans provide benefit formulas that are more complex than illustrated by this example. Plans will often specify that the pension payments depend on the highest salary earned over a number of years (e.g., the highest three years). There can also be adjustments for inflation in the consumer price index.

CHECKPOINT **CP16-2**

What is the key objective in the accounting for defined benefit plans that is achieved by estimating and recording current service cost?

The current service cost is one of four components of the total pension expense in a period. We discuss these components next.

1. What to account for in defined benefit plans

The objectives of accounting for defined benefit pension plans are twofold. The first is to present the amount of pension expense for the year. The second is to present the net asset or liability position of the pension plan on a fair value basis. Achieving both of these objectives within articulated financial statements requires the use of other comprehensive income (OCI).

For defined benefit pension plans, the amount of pension expense reflects the *expected* performance of the pension. The *actual* performance of the pension will deviate from the expected performance, and we record those deviations through OCI.

For defined benefit plans, there are four components of pension expense and two components of OCI that are important and common across most plans (see IAS 19 paragraph 57):

Pension expense

a. current service cost
b. past service cost
c. interest cost on pension obligations
d. expected income from plan assets[3]

Other comprehensive income

e. actuarial gains and losses on plan obligations
f. unexpected gains and losses on plan assets

We can relate these six components directly to the three parties in a pension plan as shown in Exhibit 16-1. We repeat that diagram here with some additions:

[3] Technically, IAS 19 combines items (c) and (d) as the net interest on the net liability (asset). Conceptually, it is easier to keep these separate to understand items (e) and (f).

Exhibit 16-5 The six components of pension expense and OCI in relation to the three parties in a defined benefit pension plan

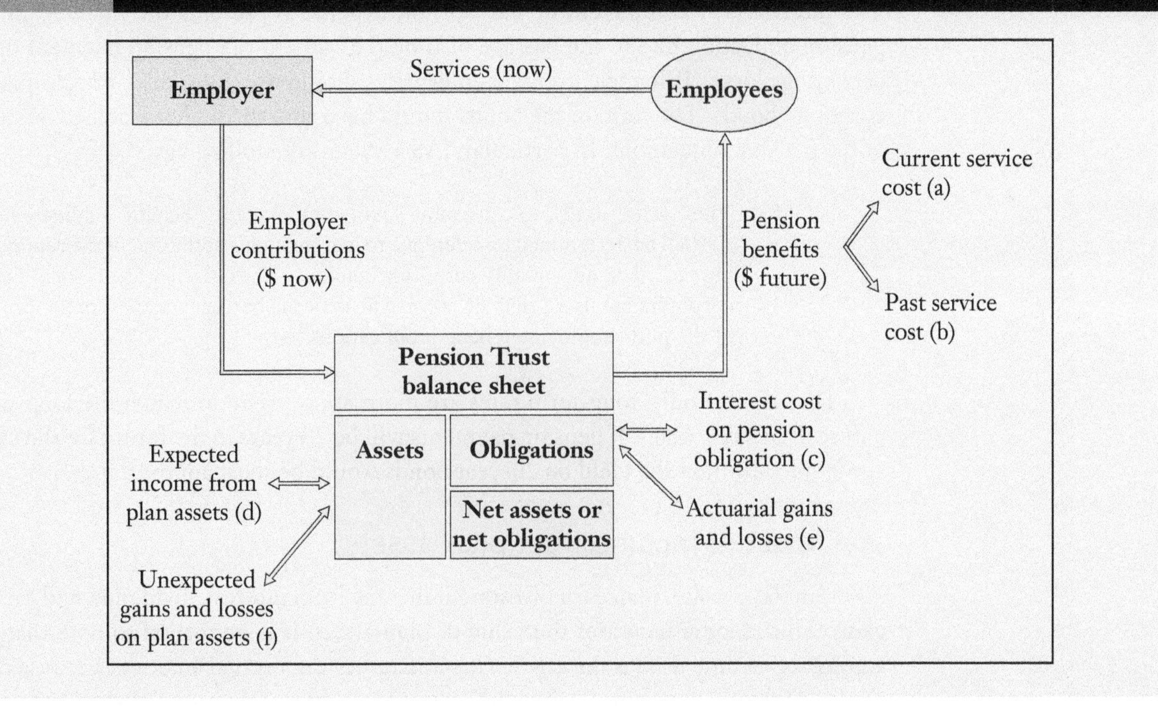

As shown in this diagram, components (a) and (b) relate to the benefits earned by employees, and such benefits arise from services they provided in the current period (current service cost) or in prior periods (past service cost). The other four components relate to the assets and liabilities held in the pension trust. On the liability side of the pension trust, the pension obligations incur interest charges (c), which in turn increase the pension obligations. The assets of the trust produce investment income (d), which in turn flows back into the trust to increase asset values. The last two components (e and f), reflect the deviations of fair values from the expected values of the pension plan assets and liabilities. We now look at each of these six components in more detail.

a. Current service cost

As explained in the last section, this portion of the pension expense is the increase in the present value of the pension obligation that results from the employees' current services. In any active pension plan, this component will always be present. Information on current service cost is provided by the pension plan's actuary.

b. Past service cost

Past service costs arise from plan initiations, amendments to the plan, and curtailments. Introducing a new pension plan gives rise to a positive amount for past service cost that increases pension expense. An amendment to an existing plan can result in a positive or negative past service cost, depending on whether the change improves or reduces the benefits offered. A **curtailment** is a reduction in the number of employees covered by a pension plan. A curtailment has an effect that is similar to a plan amendment that reduces benefits—whether there is a decrease in the number of employees covered or the amount of benefits per employee, both result in a reduced cost to the sponsor and therefore a reduction in pension expense.

past service cost The change in the present value of pension obligations due to initiation, amendment, or curtailment of a pension.

curtailment A reduction in the number of employees or the amount of benefits they will receive in the future.

c. Interest cost

The interest cost component of the pension expense represents the increase in the pension obligation due to the passage of time (i.e., due to the pension payment dates becoming closer). IFRS specifies that enterprises should use the yields on high-quality corporate bonds. The term of the bonds should have a maturity that matches the term of the pension obligations. In particular, IAS 19 states the following:

> ¶83 The rate used to discount post-employment benefit obligations . . . shall be determined by reference to market yields at the end of the reporting period on high quality corporate bonds. . . . The currency and term of the corporate bonds . . . shall be consistent with the currency and estimate term of the post-employment benefit obligations.[4]

That is, generally, long-term rates are more appropriate to match the long-term nature of pension plans. If pension payments will be 20 years in the future for the average employee, then the yield on 20-year bonds would be most appropriate.

d. Expected income from plan assets

Assets in the pension plan earn investment income from interest, dividends, and capital gains. This income increases the value of plan assets. It is important to note that the amount of income used is the *expected* income rather than actual amounts, because over the long life of a pension plan it is the expected amounts that are relevant. Deviations of actual investment results and the expected income are dealt with under subsection (f) below. For purposes of estimating expected income, the rate of return is the same as the discount rate used to compute the interest cost on pension obligations in subsection (c) above. In fact, IAS 19 reads as follows:

> ¶123 Net interest on the net defined benefit liability (asset) shall be determined by multiplying the net defined benefit liability (asset) by the discount rate specified in paragraph 83. . . .[5]

In other words, IAS 19 refers to a single calculation for the net interest, using one discount rate multiplied by the net liability or asset. This is equivalent to saying that the same discount rate must be applied to both the pension assets and the pension liability. Indeed, IAS 19 reiterates this point:

> ¶125 Interest income on plan assets . . . is determined by multiplying the fair value of the plan assets by the discount rate specified in paragraph 83. . . .[6]

e. Actuarial gains and losses

actuarial gain A favourable difference between actual and expected amounts for pension obligations.

actuarial loss An unfavourable difference between actual and expected amounts for pension obligations.

Actuarial gains and losses arise from the obligations of a pension plan. These gains and losses derive from differences between the actual and expected values of the obligation. IFRS requires actuarial gains and losses to be recorded through OCI without recycling through the income statement. For instance, if $10 million is the projected obligation factoring in current service cost, past service cost, and interest on the obligation for the year, and the fair value of the pension obligation amounts to $12 million, then there would be a $2 million actuarial loss recorded through OCI.

---

4. Copyright © 2012 IFRS Foundation.

5. Copyright © 2012 IFRS Foundation.

6. Copyright © 2012 IFRS Foundation.

f. Unexpected gains and losses on plan assets

Unexpected gains and losses on plan assets are deviations of fair value from the expected value of plan assets. These gains and losses are also recorded through OCI without recycling through income. For example, if plan assets are projected to be $20 million at the end of the year but the fair value turns out to be $23 million, then there would be a $3 million gain recorded through OCI.

unexpected gain on plan assets A favourable difference between actual and expected amounts of income from pension assets.

unexpected loss on plan assets An unfavourable difference between actual and expected amounts of income from pension assets.

ECONOMIC EFFICIENCY OF IMMEDIATE RECOGNITION OF ACTUARIAL GAINS AND LOSSES

Prior to 2013, enterprises applying IFRS had the option of using the immediate recognition approach as described above or the "corridor approach." The latter approach recognized gains and losses only if they exceeded the "corridor limit," being 10% of the value of plan assets or liabilities, whichever was higher. Furthermore, the gains and losses were amortized over a number of years reflecting how long employees were expected to remain in the employment of the enterprise. This corridor approach absorbed temporary shocks to the value of pension assets and obligations by (i) ignoring small gains and losses that fell within the corridor limit and (ii) spreading out over many years any gains and losses that exceeded the corridor limit.

Without the corridor limit and amortization process acting as shock absorbers, companies would be less willing to use defined benefit pension plans because management generally dislikes volatility in income. As noted in the introduction, the use of defined benefit plans is economically efficient from a risk-sharing point of view. In other words, employees are less able to bear the risks of uncertain life expectancy and investment returns in comparison to employers, who are able to diversify this risk across many employees as well as over time. Transferring risk from employees to employers produces an economic gain, so defined benefit plans increase societal welfare. The willingness of companies to take on these risks is dependent on their management. When accounting standards reduce the willingness of management to offer defined benefit pension plans to employees, societal welfare decreases.

THRESHOLD CONCEPT
DECISION MAKING UNDER UNCERTAINTY

Recognizing that immediate recognition of changes in the fair value of pension assets and liabilities could lead to adverse behavioural consequences, IAS 19 did not require the fair value changes to flow through net income, but instead they would flow through OCI. This approach ensures that the balance sheet reflects the fair value of pension assets and liabilities without increasing the volatility of net income.

THRESHOLD CONCEPT
ECONOMIC CONSEQUENCES OF ACCOUNTING CHOICE

g. Summary

To sum up, the accounting for defined benefit pension plans involves three steps:

1. Determine the fair values of the asset and liabilities of the pension plan at the end of year. The net balance will be the amount reported on the balance sheet.
2. Determine the net amount of the pension expense to be reported on the income statement. The pension expense adjusted by the amount of funds contributed to the pension plan is the expected change in the pension plan assets and liabilities.

For example, if the pension expense is $3 million and the company contributed only $2 million to the pension, then the pension liability would increase by the difference of $1 million.

3. Determine the expected values of pension assets and liabilities using the opening fair value plus the expected change from (2). The differences between the actual fair values from (1) and these expected fair values are the re-measurement adjustments that flow through OCI. The OCI can be accumulated in the equity section of the balance sheet as a separate component of accumulated other comprehensive income (AOCI) or transferred to retained earnings without recycling through the income statement.

For example, suppose Farro Company has a defined benefit pension plan. At the end of 2019, the fair value of the assets and liabilities in the pension amounted to a net liability of $6 million. During 2020, the pension expense amounted to $10 million, while the company contributed $8 million to the pension plan. By the end of 2020, the fair value of the pension assets and liabilities amounted to a net liability of $9 million.

To reflect these events, Farro would record the follow entries:

Exhibit 16-6 Journal entries for Farro Company's defined benefit pension plan in 2020

To record cash contribution to pension plan		
Dr. Defined benefit pension liability	8,000,000	
Cr. Cash		8,000,000
To record pension expense		
Dr. Pension expense	10,000,000	
Cr. Defined benefit pension liability		10,000,000
To adjust pension liability (or asset) to fair value		
Dr. Other comprehensive income	1,000,000	
Cr. Net defined benefit liability (see T-account below)		1,000,000

The first entry is straightforward to reflect the cash contributed to the pension plan. A cash contribution increases the assets in the pension plan and therefore reduces the net liability. Note that this entry would be recorded whenever the cash transaction occurred during the year, whereas the next two entries are adjusting entries recorded at year-end. The next entry is to record the pension expense for the year, which increases the pension liability. The third entry adjusts the balance of the pension liability to fair value. To determine the amount of this adjustment, a simple T-account for the defined benefit liability would be helpful, as shown in Exhibit 16-7:

Exhibit 16-7 T-account for Farro Company's defined benefit liability in 2020

	Net defined benefit liability (Dr.)	Net defined benefit liability (Cr.)	
		6,000,000	Opening balance at fair value
Cash contribution	8,000,000		
		10,000,000	Pension expense
		8,000,000	Expected balance
		1,000,000	**Re-measurement adjustment**
		9,000,000	Ending balance at fair value

After taking account of the opening fair value, cash contribution, and pension expense, the expected balance of the net pension liability amounts to $8 million. However, the actual fair value at the end of the year is $9 million, so the liability needs to be increased by $1 million.

In this example, we have shown the journal entries in summary format. We now look more carefully at recording the six specific components of pension expense and OCI.

CHECKPOINT **CP16-3**

What is the key distinction between amounts recorded through income as pension expense versus amounts recorded through OCI?

2. Implementing pension accounting for defined benefit plans

As noted above, the three steps in pension accounting are the determination of the fair value of the pension assets and liabilities; the pension expense, which has four components; and the amount of OCI for the fair value re-measurement, which has two components. This section explains how one goes about collecting the necessary information and synthesizing that information to compute these components.

Two reports will contain much of the necessary information. The first is the pension trustee's report on the pension plan assets. This report provides information about the changes in the assets of the pension plan. Among the information items are:

- contribution to the plan;
- expected income on plan assets;
- benefits paid out of the plan to retirees; and
- actual value of the plan assets at end of year.

The second report is the pension actuary's report on the pension plan obligations. This report provides information about the changes in the obligations of the pension plan. Among the items in this report are:

- current service cost;
- past service cost;
- interest cost on the pension obligations;
- benefits paid out of the plan to retirees; and
- actual value of the pension obligation at end of year.

Putting all this information together, we construct the six components of pension expense and OCI, as illustrated in the following schematic showing the connections between two reports from the pension plan and the T-account for the defined benefit asset or liability.

To illustrate the process of synthesizing the information shown in Exhibit 16-8, consider the following example of GB Corp. The example will proceed through two years, one at a time, to highlight different aspects of pension accounting.

Exhibit 16-8 Sources of information for the components of pension expense and OCI along with a T-account for the net pension asset or liability

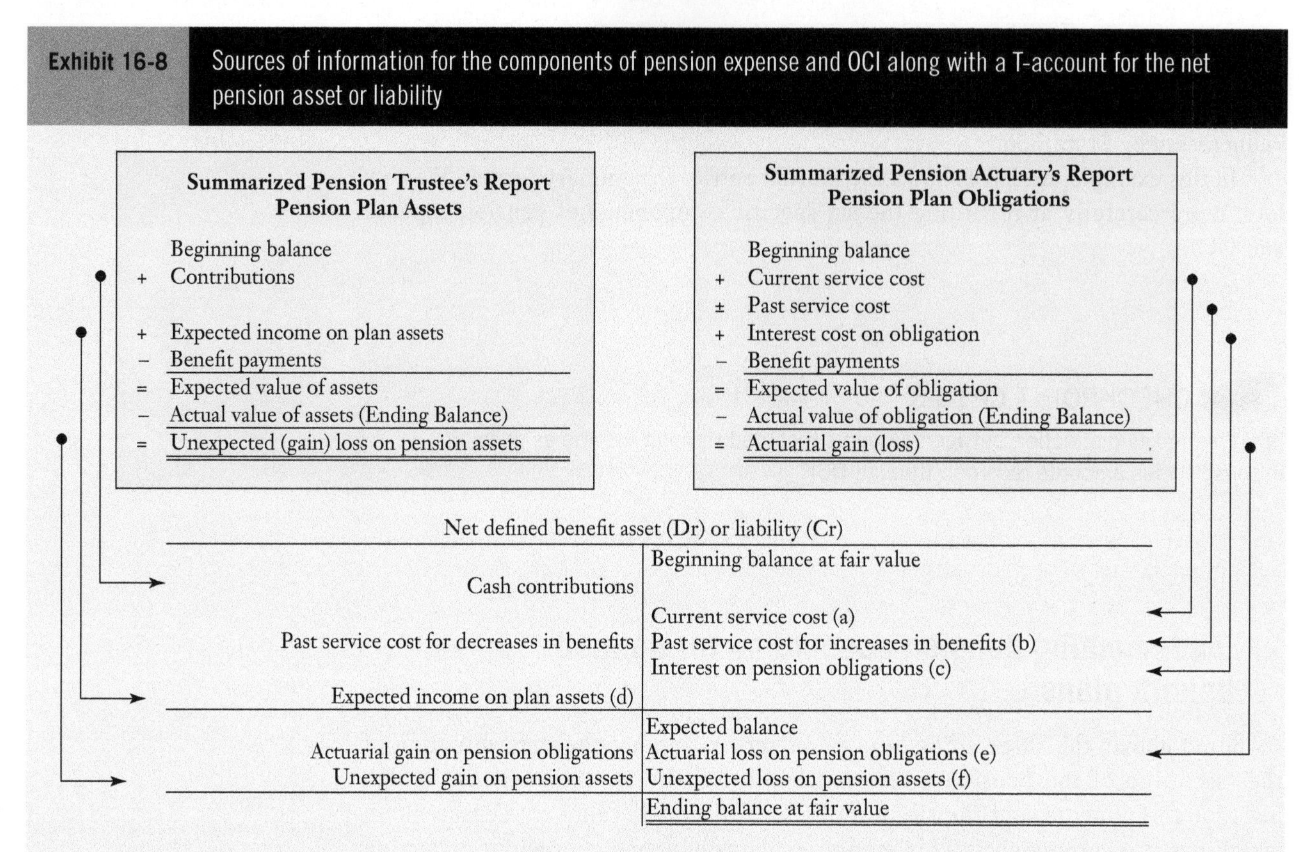

Note: Letters (a) through (f) indicate the six components of pension expense and OCI.

Exhibit 16-9 Information compiled for GB Corp. to illustrate computation of pension expense

GB Corp. has provided a defined benefit pension plan for the past two decades. The company has been trying very hard to keep its pension assets up to a level that is sufficient to cover its pension obligations, but it has not been completely successful, as its pension plan remains underfunded (see tables below). Fortunately, returns on invested securities have been exceeding expectations recently, alleviating some of the pressure.

Your files show that GB had a net defined benefit pension liability of $5,000,000 as at December 31, 2019.

Table 1—Pension trustee's report on plan assets	2020
Beginning balance, January 1, 2020	$ 50,000,000
Expected income on plan assets @ 8%*	4,000,000
Contributions (received at end of year)	13,000,000
Benefit payments (paid at end of year)	(11,000,000)
Expected value of assets, December 31, 2020	56,000,000
Actual value of assets, December 31, 2020	60,000,000
Unexpected (gain) loss on plan assets	$ (4,000,000)

*8% × beginning balance

(Continued)

Exhibit 16-9 Continued

Table 2—Actuary's report on pension obligations	2020
Beginning balance	$55,000,000
Interest cost on obligation @ 8%†	4,400,000
Current service cost	15,900,000
Benefit payments (paid at end of year)	(11,000,000)
Expected value of obligation, December 31, 2020	64,300,000
Actual value of obligation, December 31, 2020	62,500,000
Actuarial gain (loss) on plan obligations	$ 1,800,000
†8% of beginning balance	

Based on the above information, the computation of the pension expense and OCI relating to the pension plan would be as shown in Exhibit 16-10.

Exhibit 16-10 Calculation of pension expense in 2020 for GB Corp.

Calculation of pension expense	Dr. (Cr.)
a. Current service cost (Table 2)	$15,900,000
b. Past service cost	0
c. Interest cost on obligation (Table 2)	4,400,000
d. Expected income on plan assets (Table 1)	(4,000,000)
Pension expense	$16,300,000
Calculation of OCI	**Dr. (Cr.)**
e. Actuarial (gains) and losses (Table 2)	$ (1,800,000)
f. Unexpected (gains) and losses on plan assets (Table 1)	(4,000,000)
Other comprehensive (income) loss	$ (5,800,000)

Based on these amounts of pension expense and OCI, GB Corp. would record the following journal entries:

Exhibit 16-11 GB Corp. example: Journal entries

To record cash contribution		
Dr. Net defined benefit liability	13,000,000	
Cr. Cash		13,000,000
To record pension expense in 2020		
Dr. Pension expense—current service cost	15,900,000	
Dr. Pension expense—interest on obligation	4,400,000	
Cr. Pension expense—expected income on plan assets		4,000,000
Cr. Net defined benefit asset or liability		16,300,000
To adjust net pension asset or liability		
Dr. Net defined benefit asset or liability	5,800,000	
Cr. OCI—actuarial gains and losses		1,800,000
Cr. OCI—unexpected gains and losses on plan assets		4,000,000

After recording these journal entries, the balance of the net pension is as follows:

Exhibit 16-12 GB Corp. example: Balance of the net defined benefit asset or liability account

	Dr (Cr)
Balance, December 31, 2019 (given in Exhibit 16-9)	$ (5,000,000)
Adjustment due to cash contribution (Exhibit 16-9)	13,000,000
Adjustment due to pension expense (Exhibit 16-10)	(16,300,000)
Adjustment recorded in OCI (Exhibit 16-10)	5,800,000
Balance, December 31, 2020	$ (2,500,000)

Notice that the balance in the net defined benefit asset or liability account reconciles to the net financial position of the pension plan. Using the information provided by the reports from the pension trustee and pension actuary, we have the following amount:

Exhibit 16-13 GB Corp. example: Net financial position of pension plan at December 31, 2020

	Dr. (Cr.)
Fair value of pension plan assets (Exhibit 16-9 Table 1)	$ 60,000,000
Fair value of pension plan obligations (Exhibit 16-9 Table 2)	(62,500,000)
Net financial position of pension plan, December 31, 2020	$ (2,500,000)

The example thus far demonstrates probably the simplest scenario in which a company has only three of the four components of pension expense. That is, GB did not have any past service cost (component b). Furthermore, the cash contributed to the pension as well as the benefit payments both occurred at the end of the year, simplifying the calculations. We now add these two additional issues by following GB's pension plan through a second year.

Exhibit 16-14 Information compiled for GB Corp., second year

Effective January 1, 2021, the company increased the future benefit payments for all existing employees. The actuarial cost of this plan amendment was $10 million.

The following tables summarize information provided by the pension plan trustee and actuary.

Table 1—Pension trustee's report on plan assets	2021
Beginning balance, January 1, 2021	$60,000,000
Expected income on plan assets @ 8%*	5,100,000
Contributions (received October 1, 2021)	15,000,000
Benefit payments (paid end of year)	(12,000,000)
Expected value of assets, December 31, 2021	68,100,000
Actual value of assets, December 31, 2021	72,000,000
Unexpected (gain) loss on plan assets	$(3,900,000)

*(8% × $60,000,0000 + 3 / 12 × 8% × $15,000,000) = $4,800,000 + $300,000 = $5,100,000

(Continued)

Exhibit 16-14 Continued

Table 2—Actuary's report on pension obligations	2021
Beginning balance, January 1, 2021	$ 62,500,000
Plan amendment, effective January 1, 2021	10,000,000
Beginning balance adjusted for plan amendment	72,500,000
Interest cost on obligation @ 8%†	5,800,000
Current service cost	16,200,000
Benefit payments (paid end of year)	(12,000,000)
Expected value of obligation, December 31, 2021	82,500,000
Actual value of obligation, December 31, 2021	82,000,000
Actuarial gain (loss)	$ 500,000

†8% of beginning balance including plan amendment at beginning of year.

Notice that the expected income on the pension plan assets needs to factor in the cash contribution from GB to the pension trust during the year. Since $15 million was transferred on October 1, that amount is available to earn income for the remaining three months of the year.

Based on the above information, the computation of the pension expense and the journal entries for 2021 would be as shown in Exhibit 16-15.

Exhibit 16-15 Calculation of pension expense for GB Corp., second year (2021)

Calculation of pension expense	Dr. (Cr.)
a. Current service cost (Table 2)	$ 16,200,000
b. Past service cost (Table 2)	10,000,000
c. Interest cost on obligation (Table 2)	5,800,000
d. Expected income on plan assets (Table 1)	(5,100,000)
Pension expense	$26,900,000
Calculation of OCI	**Dr. (Cr.)**
e. Actuarial (gains) and losses (Table 2)	$ (500,000)
f. Unexpected (gains) and losses on plan assets (Table 1)	(3,900,000)
Other comprehensive (income) loss	$ (4,400,000)

Based on these amounts of pension expense and OCI, GB Corp. would record the following journal entries:

Exhibit 16-16 GB Corp. example: Journal entries, second year (2021)

To record cash contribution		
Dr. Net defined benefit liability	15,000,000	
Cr. Cash		15,000,000
To record pension expense in 2021		
Dr. Pension expense—current service cost	16,200,000	
Dr. Pension expense—past service cost	10,000,000	

(Continued)

Exhibit 16-16 Continued		
Dr. Pension expense—interest on obligation	5,800,000	
Cr. Pension expense—expected income on plan assets		5,100,000
Cr. Net defined benefit asset or liability		26,900,000
To adjust net pension asset or liability		
Dr. Net defined benefit asset or liability	4,400,000	
Cr. OCI—actuarial gains and losses		500,000
Cr. OCI—unexpected gains and losses on plan assets		3,900,000

After recording these journal entries, the balance of the net pension asset or liability will be $10,000,000, reconciling with the net financial position of the pension plan:

Exhibit 16-17 GB Corp. example: Balance of the net defined benefit asset or liability account and net financial position of pension plan

Net defined benefit asset or liability account	Dr. (Cr.)
Balance, December 31, 2020 (Exhibit 16-13)	$ (2,500,000)
Adjustment due to cash contribution (Exhibit 16-15)	15,000,000
Adjustment due to pension expense (Exhibit 16-15)	(26,900,000)
Adjustment recorded in OCI (Exhibit 16-15)	4,400,000
Balance, December 31, 2021	$(10,000,000)
Net financial position of pension plan	**Dr. (Cr.)**
Fair value of pension plan assets (Exhibit 16-14, Table 1)	$ 72,000,000
Fair value of pension plan obligations (Exhibit 16-14, Table 2)	(82,000,000)
Net financial position of pension plan, December 31, 2021	$(10,000,000)

To recap, the accounting for defined benefit pension plans involves three interrelated steps. The first establishes the fair value of the net pension asset or liability to be reported on the balance sheet. The second step determines the amount of pension expense to record through the income statement. This pension expense goes into the calculation of the expected balance of the net pension asset or liability account. The third step resolves the discrepancy between the expected and actual values of the net financial position of the pension plan by recording an adjustment to the net pension asset or liability account and this adjustment flows through OCI.

CHECKPOINT **CP16-4**

What are the two components of OCI related to pensions? What is the conceptual reason for recognizing these two components through OCI rather than net income?

3. Presentation and disclosure

L.O. 16-5. Integrate pension plan information by preparing the relevant note disclosures.

The accounting for defined benefit pension plans affects only four accounts: cash, pension expense, OCI, and the defined benefit asset or liability. The latter three amounts, if they are not separately identified on the face of the financial statements, must be disclosed in the notes. In addition, enterprises need to disclose the components of pension expense.

When a company has more than one defined benefit plan, IFRS does not permit the offsetting of pension asset and pension liability amounts, in accordance with the general prohibition against offsetting assets and liabilities. If an enterprise has a pension plan with a defined benefit liability and another plan with a defined benefit asset, the two amounts would be shown separately in the balance sheet. (Exceptional cases in which offsetting would be permitted are rare; refer to IAS 19 for discussion of these conditions.) Two plans that both have net liability positions can be added together, and likewise if they both have net asset balances.

Note that the reporting on the employer's books reflects the net asset or net liability position of the pension plans. Consequently, information about the total assets separate from the total liabilities of the pension plan would be useful to readers, so this information needs to be disclosed. Enterprises also need to present schedules showing the movements in plan assets and liabilities from the beginning of the year to the end of the year; this information is similar to that received from the pension trustee and pension actuary.

In Exhibit 16-18, we use GB Corp. to illustrate the main note disclosures for defined benefit pension plans.

Exhibit 16-18 Key note disclosures for GB Corp.

The following components comprise the pension expense recorded through income:		
Dr. (Cr.)	2020	2021
Current service cost	$ 15,900,000	$ 16,200,000
Past service cost	—	10,000,000
Interest cost on obligation	4,400,000	5,800,000
Expected income on plan assets	(4,000,000)	(5,100,000)
Pension expense	$ 16,300,000	$ 26,900,000
The company's pension plan had assets and liabilities as follows:		
	2020	2021
Fair value of pension assets	$ 60,000,000	$ 72,000,000
Accrued pension obligation	62,500,000	82,000,000
Pension plan surplus (deficit)	$ (2,500,000)	$ (10,000,000)
The following shows the changes in plan assets:		
	2020	2021
Opening balance, January 1	$ 50,000,000	$ 60,000,000
Contributions	13,000,000	15,000,000
Benefit payments	(11,000,000)	(12,000,000)
Expected income on plan assets	4,000,000	5,100,000
Unexpected gain (loss) on plan assets	4,000,000	3,900,000
Closing balance	$ 60,000,000	$ 72,000,000
The following shows the changes in plan obligations:		
	2020	2021
Opening balance, January 1	$ 55,000,000	$ 62,500,000
Benefit payments	(11,000,000)	(12,000,000)
Current service cost	15,900,000	16,200,000
Past service cost	—	10,000,000
Interest on obligations	4,400,000	5,800,000
Actuarial (gain) loss	(1,800,000)	(500,000)
Closing balance	$ 62,500,000	$ 82,000,000

Notice that the disclosures provide details of the composition of pension expense. Therefore, to facilitate the compilation of information for the note disclosures, it is useful when recording journal entries to identify the component of pension expense being recorded rather than generically referring to "pension expense." Exhibits 16-11 and 16-16 illustrated the use of the specific pension expense accounts (e.g., "Pension expense—current service cost").

E. OTHER ISSUES

1. Settlements

settlement The extinguishment of all or part of an enterprise's pension obligations.

A **settlement** occurs when an enterprise extinguishes all or part of its pension obligations. One way to do this is through a lump sum cash payment in lieu of the future stream of payments. Any gains or losses from settlements would flow through income in a way similar to curtailments.

2. Asset ceiling

In recent years, most defined benefit pension plans have been underfunded. Even under these conditions, there are some pensions that are overfunded. If an enterprise can afford the cash flow, overfunding a pension plan is a tax efficient method of investment since the return on the investment accumulates tax free. Overfunding is usually not a problem for financial reporting purposes, since we reflect that overfunding as an asset on the balance sheet. However, there are rare situations in which the overfunding is of such a large extent that we need to consider whether all of the defined benefit pension assets can be recovered by the enterprise in the future.

Going back to the basics of what constitutes an asset, an overfunded pension plan is an asset to the sponsor because the sponsor can reduce the amount of cash it needs to contribute to the pension in future years. In some instances, the employer may even be able to withdraw surpluses from the pension trust. However, the law in this area is complex and remains unsettled. In cases where the sponsor cannot withdraw the surplus funds, those funds are stranded within the pension plan, and the maximum benefit from the surplus would be the future contribution not required to be made.

asset ceiling The present value of the reduction in future contributions plus the amount of refunds from the pension plan, if any.

The **asset ceiling** is the present value of (i) the reduction in future contributions plus (ii) the amount of refunds from the pension plan, if any. When the sponsor is permitted to access the funds in the pension plan, then the asset ceiling would be unlimited. When the sponsor cannot access the funds in the pension, then the maximum benefit of the overfunding to the sponsor is the amount of cash saved by not contributing *any* funds to the pension plan in any future year. If the defined benefit pension asset is limited by the asset ceiling, we record the amount of the reduction through OCI. Information relating to the asset ceiling would also need to be disclosed.

3. Multi-employer plans

Pension plans typically have a single sponsor company. In some instances, a pension plan will have several sponsoring companies. This happens most commonly with small and medium-sized enterprises because each enterprise does not have a sufficiently large employee base to establish a pension plan on its own.

For *defined contribution* plans, a multi-employer plan adds no additional complexity because the risk relating to the performance of the pension plan rests with the employees. However, multi-employer *defined benefit* plans face an obvious problem: how do the different employers share the risk of the pension plan? If one company is unable to provide the funds necessary for the provision of the defined benefits, would the others have to make up the shortfall?

In general, IAS 19 requires a company participating in a multi-employer defined benefit plan to account for its proportionate share as a defined benefit plan. In exceptional circumstances, where there is insufficient information available to apply defined benefit accounting, the company can account for the multi-employer plan as a *defined contribution* plan with accompanying disclosures regarding the plan as noted in IAS 19 paragraphs 36 and 148.

4. Other long-term employee benefits

Some companies provide other employee benefits that are similar to pension benefits in that employees receive these benefits in the future rather than during their employment. For example, many companies in the United States continue to pay for health services used by former employees who have retired; similar benefits are less common and less significant in Canada, given that basic health services are government-funded. Nevertheless, Air Canada, for example, reported a liability of $1.3 billion for non-pension employee future benefits in addition to the $1.2 billion in pension liabilities (see opening vignette). In contrast to the requirement to fund pension benefits, non-pension benefits are unfunded (meaning there are no assets set aside to pay for these benefits).

Following the logic of accounting for pension benefits, if an enterprise offers employees other future benefits, it should also account for those benefits in a way that is similar to defined benefit pension plans. That is, the company should accrue an expense for benefits earned by employees in the year they earn those benefits, and a liability for the provision of those benefits in the future.

While the basic idea is straightforward, the implementation requires many estimates that are even more subjective than for pension benefits.

- The benefits promised are often in terms of services (e.g., health care), not dollars as for pensions.
- Costs for promised services such as health care change considerably over time.
- Employees' use of those future services is irregular compared with periodic payments for pension plans.
- Whereas pension plans have formal and explicit contracts, there are usually no contractual obligations to pay for the promised services. The obligation is constructive rather than contractual, so the range and amount of services covered may be expanded or curtailed unilaterally by the company.

Due to all these factors, amounts reported for such future benefits should be interpreted with a considerable amount of caution.

CHECKPOINT **CP16-5**

From an accounting perspective, what is one important similarity and one important difference between defined benefit pension plans and post-employment health benefits?

F. A PRACTICAL ILLUSTRATION: CANADIAN TIRE CORPORATION

The 2016 financial statements for Canadian Tire Corporation contained in Appendix C do not explicitly show any defined benefit pension amounts on the balance sheet and income statement. Instead, that information is found in Note 24.

Note 24 includes the following disclosure for Canadian Tire's post-employment benefits:

Exhibit 16-19 Canadian Tire's 2016 financial statements: Excerpt from Note 24

Defined benefit plan

The Company provides certain health care, dental care, life insurance and other benefits for certain retired employees pursuant to Company policy. The Company does not have a pension plan. Information about the Company's defined benefit plan is as follows:

(C$ in millions)	2016	2015
Change in the present value of defined benefit obligation		
Defined benefit obligation, beginning of year	$141.2	$137.5
Current service cost	1.7	2.3
Interest cost	5.7	5.4
Actuarial loss (gain) arising from changes in demographic assumptions	–	(0.2)
Actuarial (gain) loss arising from changes in financial assumptions	4.8	(4.6)
Actuarial (gain) loss arising from experience assumptions	(1.0)	3.8
Benefits paid	(3.1)	(3.0)
Defined benefit obligation, end of year[1]	$149.3	$141.2

[1] The accrued benefit obligation is not funded because funding is provided when benefits are paid. Accordingly, there are no plan assets.

Source: From Canadian Tire Corporation 2016 Report to Shareholders. Copyright ©2016 by Canadian Tire Corporation, Limited. Reprinted by permission.

The first thing to note is that the company does not have a pension plan for its employees. Rather, the post-employment benefits relate to health care, dental care, life insurance, etc. Second, these benefits are unfunded, so the defined benefit obligation is also the net benefit obligation since plan assets are zero. Third, this table identifies the items that resulted in the benefit obligation increasing by $8.1 million, from $141.2 to $149.3 million. Out of the six items, only the $3.1 million in benefits paid does not affect comprehensive income. We can tabulate the income impact in the following table:

Exhibit 16-20 Income impact of Canadian Tire's defined benefit plans

Components of non-pension post-retirement benefit cost	2016	2015
Amounts recognized in net income:		
Current service cost	$ 1.7	$ 2.3
Interest cost	5.7	5.4
Total recognized in income	7.4	$ 7.7
Amount recognized in other comprehensive income		
Actuarial (loss) gain arising from changes in demographic assumptions	$ –	$ 0.2
Actuarial gain (loss) arising from changes in financial assumptions	(4.8)	4.6
Actuarial gain (loss) arising from experience assumptions	1.0	(3.8)
Total recognized in other comprehensive income	$ (3.8)	$ 1.0

Source: From Canadian Tire Corporation 2016 Report to Shareholders. Copyright ©2016 by Canadian Tire Corporation, Limited. Reprinted by permission.

Note 24 goes on further to describe the assumptions used in the estimation of the defined benefit obligation, and to provide sensitivity analysis for those assumptions.

G. SUBSTANTIVE DIFFERENCES BETWEEN RELEVANT IFRS AND ASPE

ISSUE	IFRS	ASPE
Actuarial gains and losses on defined benefit obligation and unexpected gains and losses on plan assets	Flow through other comprehensive income (OCI).	Flow through net income (since ASPE has no concept of OCI)

H. SUMMARY

L.O. 16-1. Explain the nature of pension plans and distinguish between defined contribution and defined benefit plans.

- Pension plans provide future cash flow benefits to employees in partial exchange for current services.
- Defined contribution plans specify the inflow of funds that the sponsoring company needs to contribute to the plan, whereas defined benefit plans specify the outflows to retirees.

L.O. 16-2. Apply the accounting standards for defined contribution pension plans.

- An enterprise should record an expense for the contribution it is required to make to the pension plan corresponding to the services provided by employees.

L.O. 16-3. Analyze an array of pension plan data to determine the amount of pension expense and other comprehensive income for defined benefit pension plans.

- There are six common components to the pension expense and other comprehensive income (OCI) for a defined benefit plan: current service cost, past service cost, interest on the obligation, and expected income on plan assets flow through income. Items of OCI include actuarial gains and losses and unexpected gains and losses on plan assets.
- One can determine these six components by using two reports from the pension trustee and the pension actuary.

L.O. 16-4. Analyze the effect of actuarial assumptions on the financial statement assets, liabilities, and income, and evaluate the appropriateness of assumptions used to account for pensions.

- Pension accounting involves many estimates regarding uncertain future outcomes. These estimates can change significantly with small changes in assumptions about the interest/discount rate, life expectancy, employee turnover rates, inflation, and so on.

L.O. 16-5. Integrate pension plan information by preparing the relevant note disclosures.

- To enable users to gain an understanding of how pension plans affect the financial statements, enterprises need to provide information on the components of pension expense, as well as the assets and liabilities in the pension plan(s), among other disclosures.

I. ANSWERS TO CHECKPOINT QUESTIONS

CP16-1: The fundamental difference between a defined contribution and defined benefit pension plan is the party who carries the risk related to the pension. A defined contribution plan puts the risk on the beneficiaries (employees) while a defined benefit plan puts the risk on the pension plan sponsor (the employer).

CP16-2: Estimating and recording current service cost achieves the key objective of matching the employment expense with the services received from employees in the same period. Not doing so results in expenses being recorded much later than the services received.

CP16-3: The key distinction between amounts recorded through income as pension expense versus amounts recorded through OCI is that the amount recorded through income reflects the expected outcomes, while the amount recorded through OCI reflects the difference between the actual and expected outcomes.

CP16-4: The two components of OCI related to pensions are (i) actuarial gains and losses on pension obligations and (ii) unexpected gains and losses on pension assets. Standards specify that these two amounts should flow through OCI because management generally dislikes volatility in net income; allowing these gains and losses to bypass the income statement avoids unnecessarily deterring the use of defined benefit plans by companies.

CP16-5: Comparing pension plans and post-employment health benefits, one important similarity is that the accounting needs to consider the vast difference in timing of benefit payments and services received from employees. An important difference is that pension payments are clearly specified by some contractual formula, whereas the costs for health services are not known in advance with much accuracy.

J. GLOSSARY

accrued benefit obligation: The present value of pension benefits that employees have earned.

actuarial gain: A favourable difference between actual and expected amounts for pension obligations.

actuarial loss: An unfavourable difference between actual and expected amounts for pension obligations.

actuary: A professional who specializes in the estimation of risks and uncertainties.

asset ceiling: The present value of the reduction in future contributions plus the amount of refunds from the pension plan, if any.

current service cost: The increase in the present value of pension obligations due to an employee's provision of services during the current period.

curtailment: A reduction in the number of employees or the amount of benefits they will receive in the future.

defined benefit plan: A pension plan that specifies how much in pension payments employees will receive during their retirement.

defined contribution plan: A pension plan that specifies how much funds the employer needs to contribute.

past service cost: The change in the present value of pension obligations due to initiation, amendment, or curtailment of a pension.

pension trust: The legal entity that holds the investments and discharges the obligations of a pension plan.

settlement (of a pension): The extinguishment of all or part of an enterprise's pension obligations.

unexpected gain on plan assets: A favourable difference between actual and expected amounts of income from pension assets.

unexpected loss on plan assets: An unfavourable difference between actual and expected amounts of income from pension assets.

K. REFERENCES

Authoritative standards:

IFRS	ASPE Section
IAS 19—Employee benefits	3462—Employee future benefits

MyLab Accounting Make the grade with **MyLab Accounting:** The problems marked with a [globe icon] can be found on **MyLab Accounting.** You can practise them as often as you want, and most feature step-by-step guided instructions to help you find the right answer.

L. PROBLEMS

P16-1. Nature of pension plans

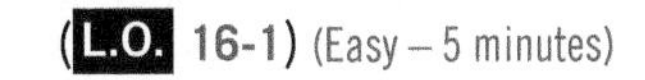
(L.O. 16-1) (Easy – 5 minutes)

Identify whether each of the following descriptions of pension plans describes defined contribution plans, defined benefit plans, or both.

	Defined contribution plans	Defined benefit plans
a. Must use a pension trust to hold the plan's assets.		
b. Transfers risk from retirees to plan sponsors.		
c. Allows employees to contribute to a pension plan.		
d. Can be underfunded or overfunded.		
e. Provides a guaranteed amount of retirement income.		
f. Provides a guaranteed amount of plan funding.		

P16-2. Nature of pension plans

(L.O. 16-1) (Easy – 3 minutes)

Peter is currently 30 years old and he plans to retire early, in 25 years' time. He would like to have an income of $50,000 per year during his retirement, which he anticipates will last for 30 years. Assume that Peter receives the retirement income at the end of each of the 30 years.

Required:

Determine the amount of money Peter will need to have accumulated by the time he starts his retirement. Assume a discount rate of 9%.

P16-3. Nature of pension plans

(L.O. 16-1) (Easy – 5 minutes)

A pension plan promises to pay $30,000 at the end of each year for 25 years of the retirement period.

Required:

Compute the funds required to fund this pension plan at the start of the retirement period assuming:

a. a discount rate of 8%
b. a discount rate of 6%

P16-4. Nature of pensions plans 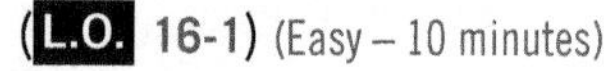 (L.O. 16-1) (Easy – 10 minutes)

Hamilton Steel provides a defined benefit pension plan for its employees. One of its employees, Sue Cameron, who just turned 45 years old, expects to retire at age 65. At that time, the pension plan will pay Sue annual pension payments equal to 3% of her final year's salary for each year of services she rendered. The pension payments will continue until Sue's death, which actuaries expect to be when she turns 80. Sue is currently earning $50,000 per year, and this rate is not expected to increase because of the poor state of the steel industry. Hamilton Steel uses a 10% interest rate for its pension obligations.

Required:

Determine the current service cost for Sue Cameron's pension for the past year (the year just before she turned 45).

P16-5. Nature of pension plans (L.O. 16-1) (Medium – 10 minutes)

Sue Cameron (see P16-4) has a twin brother, Tom, who works for the Government of Alberta. Tom is covered by a defined benefit pension plan. Tom just turned 45 years old, and expects to retire at age 65. At that time, the pension plan will pay Tom annual pension payments equal to 3% of his final year's salary for each year of services rendered. The pension payments will continue until Tom's death, which actuaries expect to be when he turns 80. For the current year, Tom will earn $50,000 and this rate is expected to increase by 8% per year. Assume that the Alberta government uses a 10% interest rate for its pension obligations.

Required:

Determine the current service cost for Tom Cameron's pension for the past year (the year just before he turned 45).

P16-6. Accounting for defined contribution plans 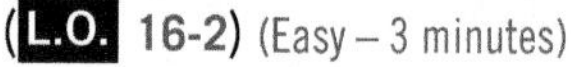 (L.O. 16-2) (Easy – 3 minutes)

Templeton Company sponsors a defined contribution pension plan for its employees. The plan specifies that the company will contribute $2 for every dollar that an employee contributes to the plan. Employees are eligible to contribute up to 5% of their salary to the pension plan.

During the current year, employees covered by the pension plan earned salaries totalling $40 million. Employee contributions to the pension totalled $1.8 million. Templeton contributed $3 million to the plan during the year.

Required:

Provide the summary journal entry for Templeton's pension plan for the year.

P16-7. Accounting for defined contribution plans (L.O. 16-2) (Easy – 5 minutes)

Umbria Products has a defined contribution pension plan for its employees. The plan requires the company to contribute 15% of these employees' salaries to the pension. For the current year, total salary for employees covered by the pension plan amounted to $60 million, of which 80% is attributable to employees involved in manufacturing while the remaining 20% of salaries relate to administrative staff. The company contributed $7 million to the pension plan during the year.

Required:

Provide the summary journal entry for Umbria's pension plan for the year.

P16-8. Accounting for defined contribution plans (L.O. 16-2) (Easy – 5 minutes)

Gidget's Cat Emporium Inc. (GCE) maintains a defined contribution pension plan for its employees. GCE is required to contribute 8% of qualifying employees' salaries to the pension. GCE's year-end is December 31. Other pertinent information follows:

- On February 15, 2019, GCE remitted $400,000 to the pension trust pertaining to the funding of its pension obligation for 2018.

- For the year ended December 31, 2019, GCE's wage expense totalled $15.1 million, $13.4 million of which were qualifying salaries.
- On December 31, 2019, GCE remitted $1 million to the pension trust.

Required:

Provide the journal entry for Gidget's Cat Emporium Inc.'s pension plan for 2019.

P16-9. Accounting for defined benefit plans (L.O. 16-2) (Easy – 3 minutes)[7]

A company reported $350,000 of pension expense in its income statement. The balance sheet showed that the pension liability increased by $20,000 over the year. No amounts were recorded in other comprehensive income for the pension plan for the year.

Required:

How much cash was paid to the pension trustee during the period?

P16-10. Accounting for defined benefit plans (L.O. 16-3) (Easy – 5 minutes)

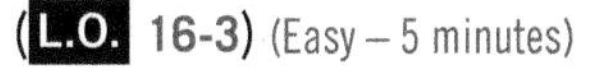

A company has a defined benefit pension liability of $600,000 at the beginning of the year. The company contributes $3,800,000 to the pension during the year and records a pension expense of $3,600,000.

Required:

Determine the value of the defined benefit pension liability prior to fair value re-measurements.

P16-11. Accounting for defined benefit plans (L.O. 16-3) (Easy – 5 minutes)

A company's defined benefit pension plan incurs a current service cost of $2,200,000. Expected income on the pension plan's assets amounted to $8,700,000, while actual income was $8,800,000. The interest on the pension obligation was $9,500,000, which matched the actuarial estimates. No past service costs arose during the year.

Required:

Compute the amount of pension expense for the year.

P16-12. Accounting for defined benefit plans (L.O. 16-3) (Easy – 5 minutes)

Current service cost for a defined benefit pension plan amounted to $6,800,000. This pension plan's assets generated $5,500,000 of income, which exceeded expectations by $500,000. Pension obligations incurred an interest cost of $4,800,000, which was above expectations by $200,000. During the year, the company increased benefits in the pension plan and incurred $300,000 for past service cost.

Required:

Compute the amount of pension expense for the year.

P16-13. Accounting for defined benefit plans—fair value re-measurements (L.O. 16-3) (Easy – 5 minutes)

At the beginning of the current year, a pension has assets of $45,600,000 and accrued benefit obligation of $57,500,000. During the year, the sponsor recorded $3,200,000 in pension expense and contributed $5,000,000 to the pension plan. At the end of the year, the plan assets had a fair value of $49,400,000 while the plan obligations had a present value of $59,000,000.

Required:

Compute the amount of other comprehensive income relating to the pension plan for the year.

---

7. Reprinted from Financial Accounting Exam 2009, with permission Chartered Professional Accountants of Canada, Toronto, Canada.

P16-14. Accounting for defined benefit plans (L.O. 16-3) (Easy – 10 minutes)

The following table provides information for a defined benefit pension plan:

End-of-year balances, in $000's	2017	2018	2019	2020
Pension assets at fair value	$60,000	$67,000	$71,000	$ 60,000
Pension obligations at present value	56,000	60,000	65,000	75,000
Net pension surplus (deficit)	$ 4,000	$ 7,000	$ 6,000	$(15,000)
Transactions for the year				
Employer's contribution to pension	4,000	4,000	4,000	4,000
Payments to retirees	2,000	3,000	4,000	5,000

Required:

Compute the amount of other comprehensive income for 2018 to 2020.

P16-15. Accounting for defined benefit plans—settlements (L.O. 16-3) (Easy – 5 minutes)

On December 31, 2019, the pension trust for Taj Singh Consulting Corp. (TSC) made a settlement payment of $450,000 to a recently terminated employee of TSC. The accrued benefit obligation pertaining to the terminated employee was $500,000.

Required:

Assume that the journal entries relating to the normal accruals for pension expense for the year have already been passed. Prepare the journal entry for Taj Singh Consulting Corp. to record this settlement.

P16-16. Accounting for defined benefit plans—settlements (L.O. 16-3) (Easy – 5 minutes)

Sam's Golden Lab Corp. (SGL) maintains a defined benefit pension plan for its employees. On January 1, 2019, SGL finalized the sale of a business segment to Gretta's Great Kittens Ltd. (GGK). Terms of the sale required SGL's pension trust to pay $1,600,000 to GGK's pension trust, to provide for the pension obligation relating to the group of employees that continued to work for the business unit that was sold. The accrued benefit obligation pertaining to these employees was $1,400,000.

Required:

Prepare the journal entry for Sam's Golden Lab Corp. to record this settlement.

P16-17. Accounting for defined benefit plans (L.O. 16-3) (Medium – 10 minutes)

Mika Imports Ltd. provided the following pension plan information:

Fair value of pension plan assets, January 1, 2021	$4,235,000
Fair value of pension plan assets, December 31, 2021	4,614,500
Contributions to the plan—beginning of year	233,000
Benefits paid to retirees—end of year	246,000
Expected rate of return in 2021	7.0%

Required:

a. Calculate the expected value of the plan assets on December 31, 2021.
b. Calculate the actual rate of return on plan assets earned in 2021.
c. Prepare the journal entry to account for the deviation between the expected and actual return for the year.

P16-18. Accounting for defined benefit plans (L.O. 16-3) (Medium – 10 minutes)

Jaxxen Exports Ltd. provided the following pension plan information:

Present value of plan obligations, December 31, 2020	$6,854,500
Plan amendment effective January 1, 2021	1,450,000
Current service costs—accrued at end of year	500,000
Benefits paid to retirees—end of year	420,000
Actual value of plan obligations, December 31, 2021	8,772,000
Interest costs on opening balance	4.0%

Required:

a. Calculate the expected value of the obligation on December 31, 2021.
b. Prepare the journal entry to account for the deviation between the expected and actual value of the plan obligation at year-end.

P16-19. Accounting for defined benefit plans (L.O. 16-3) (Medium – 10 minutes)

Niagara Inns provides a modest defined benefit pension for its employees. At the end of the current fiscal year, which ended on December 31, the pension plan supplied Niagara with information about the pension, which is summarized in the following tables:

Pension trustee report	
Opening assets, January 1	$2,100,000
+ Funding	400,000
+ Expected return on assets	168,000
− Payments to retirees	(40,000)
Expected value, December 31	$2,628,000
Actual market value, December 31	2,410,000
Unexpected gain (loss)	$ (218,000)

Pension actuary report	
Opening accrued benefit obligation, January 1	$3,000,000
+ Current service cost	225,000
+ Interest	240,000
− Payments to retirees	(40,000)
Expected value, December 31	$3,425,000
Actual obligation, December 31	2,964,000
Actuarial gain (loss)	$ 461,000

The company did not have any past service costs.

Required:

Provide the journal entries for Niagara's pension plan for the year.

P16-20. Accounting for defined benefit plans (L.O. 16-3) (Medium – 10 minutes)[8]

PEP Corporation has a defined benefit pension plan. As of January 1, the following balances exist:

Accrued benefit obligation	$2,400,000
Plan assets (at market value)	1,440,000
Interest rate on obligations	5%

8. Reprinted from Financial Accounting Exam 2010, with permission Chartered Professional Accountants of Canada, Toronto, Canada.

For the year ended December 31, the current service cost as determined by an appropriate actuarial cost method was $330,000. Improvements in benefits created a past service cost of $800,000. A change in actuarial assumptions created a gain of $15,000 in the year. The expected return on plan assets was $72,000; however, the actual return is $70,000. PEP paid $325,000 to the pension trustee in December.

Required:

Prepare the journal entries for the pension for the year.

P16-21. Accounting for defined benefit plans (L.O. 16-3) (Medium – 10 minutes)[9]

Koffee Corporation provides its employees with a defined benefit pension plan. As of January 1, the following balances exist:

Accrued benefit obligation	$8,000,000
Plan assets (at market value)	8,160,000
Interest rate on obligations	5%

For the year ended December 31, the current service cost as determined by an appropriate actuarial cost method was $570,000. A negotiated curtailment of the pension plan resulted in a past service cost of $500,000 to Koffee's benefit. A change in actuarial assumptions created a loss of $15,000. The expected return on plan assets was $408,000. However, the actual return is $395,000. Koffee paid $730,000 to the pension trustee in December of the prior year and made no further contributions.

Required:

Record the journal entries for the pension for the year.

P16-22. Accounting for defined benefit plans (L.O. 16-3) (Medium – 10 minutes)

Muskoka Canoes has had a defined benefit pension plan for three decades. Two years ago, the company improved the benefits at a cost of $2,800,000.

Pension plan assets were $84,000,000 while pension obligations were $76,000,000 at the beginning of the year.

For the current year, Muskoka's pension plan incurred a current service cost of $5,400,000 and interest of $7,600,000. The pension's assets earned $8,000,000, which is $400,000 below expectations. There were no actuarial gains or losses for the year.

Required:

a. Compute the pension expense for the year.
b. Record the journal entries for Muskoka's pension plan.

P16-23. Accounting for defined benefit plans (L.O. 16-3) (Medium – 10 minutes)

The following tables are the reports of the pension trustee and pension actuary for Timmins Industries, which started the defined benefit pension plan at the beginning of 2018:

Pension trustee report	2018	2019
Opening assets, January 1	$ 0	$ 476,000
+ Funding	500,000	545,000
− Payments to retirees	0	(20,000)
+ Expected return on assets	40,000	81,000
Expected value, December 31	$ 540,000	1,082,000
Actual market value, December 31	476,000	1,038,000
Unexpected gain (loss)	$ (64,000)	$ (44,000)

9. Reprinted from Financial Accounting Exam 2009, with permission Chartered Professional Accountants of Canada, Toronto, Canada.

Pension actuary report	2018	2019
Opening accrued benefit obligation, January 1	$ 0	$ 520,000
+ Current service cost (accrued evenly during year)	500,000	580,000
− Payments to retirees (paid evenly through year)	0	(20,000)
+ Interest	22,000	64,000
Expected value, December 31	$ 522,000	$1,144,000
Actual obligation, December 31	520,000	1,150,000
Actuarial gain (loss)	$ 2,000	$ (6,000)

Required:

Compute the pension expense and the amount of OCI for the two years.

P16-24. Accounting for defined benefit plans (L.O. 16-3) (Medium – 15 minutes)

The following tables are the reports of the pension trustee and pension actuary for Macpherson Massage Corp., which started the defined benefit pension plan at the beginning of 2018:

Pension trustee report	2018	2019
Opening assets, January 1	$ 0	$1,050,000
+ Funding (received beginning of year)	1,000,000	1,100,000
− Payments to retirees (paid at end of year)	(50,000)	(120,000)
+ Expected return on assets	60,000	107,500
Expected value, December 31	$1,010,000	2,137,500
Actual market value, December 31	1,050,000	2,100,000
Unexpected gain (loss)	$ 40,000	$ (37,500)

Pension actuary report	2018	2019
Opening accrued benefit obligation, January 1	$ 0	$4,000,000
+ Current service cost (accrued at end of year)	1,500,000	1,650,000
+ Past service cost (accrued at beginning of year)	2,400,000	0
− Payments to retirees (paid at end of year)	(50,000)	(120,000)
+ Interest	144,000	200,000
Expected value, December 31	$3,994,000	$5,730,000
Actual obligation, December 31	4,000,000	5,700,000
Actuarial gain (loss)	$ (6,000)	$ 30,000

Required:

a. Prepare the journal entries for Macpherson's pension plan in 2018. Record each item of pension expense and OCI separately.
b. Prepare the journal entries for Macpherson's pension plan in 2019. Record each item of pension expense and OCI separately.

P16-25. Accounting for defined benefit plans (L.O. 16-3) (Medium – 15 minutes)

The following tables are the reports of the pension trustee and pension actuary for Golf is Good Inc., which started the defined benefit pension plan at the beginning of 2018:

Pension trustee report	2018	2019
Opening assets, January 1	$ 0	$1,900,000
+ Funding (received beginning of year)	2,000,000	2,000,000
− Payments to retirees (paid at end of year)	(100,000)	(130,000)

(*Continued*)

Pension trustee report	2018	2019
+ Expected return on assets	80,000	195,000
Expected value, December 31	$1,980,000	3,965,000
Actual market value, December 31	1,900,000	4,000,000
Unexpected gain (loss)	$ (80,000)	$ 35,000

Pension actuary report	2018	2019
Opening accrued benefit obligation, January 1	$ 0	$5,660,000
+ Current service cost (accrued at end of year)	1,800,000	2,100,000
+ Past service cost (accrued at beginning of year)	3,800,000	0
− Payments to retirees (paid at end of year)	(100,000)	(130,000)
+ Interest	152,000	283,000
Expected value, December 31	$5,652,000	$7,913,000
Actual obligation, December 31	5,660,000	7,900,000
Actuarial gain (loss)	$ (8,000)	$ 13,000

Required:

a. Prepare the journal entries for Golf is Good's pension plan in 2018. Record each item of pension expense and OCI separately.
b. Prepare the journal entries for Golf is Good's pension plan in 2019. Record each item of pension expense and OCI separately.

P16-26. Accounting for defined benefit plans (L.O. 16-3) (Medium – 15 minutes)

Belle Fragrances Inc. provided the following pension plan information:

Fair value of pension plan assets, January 1, 2021	$6,984,000
Fair value of pension plan assets, December 31, 2021	7,011,500
Contributions to the plan—evenly throughout the year	740,000
Benefits paid to retirees—evenly throughout the year	920,000
Expected rate of return in 2021	5.0%

Required:

a. Calculate the expected value of the plan assets on December 31, 2021.
b. Approximate the actual rate of return earned on plan assets in 2021.
c. Prepare the journal entry to account for the deviation between the expected and actual return for the year.

P16-27. Accounting for defined benefit plans (L.O. 16-3) (Medium – 15 minutes)

Zachary Motors Corp. provided the following pension plan information:

Present value of plan obligations, December 31, 2020	$9,844,750
Plan curtailment effective January 1, 2021	2,355,750
Current service costs—accrued evenly throughout the year	400,000
Benefits paid to retirees—paid evenly throughout the year	290,000
Actual value of plan obligations, December 31, 2021	7,750,000
Interest costs on average balance	4.5%

Required:

a. Calculate the expected value of the obligation on December 31, 2021.
b. Prepare the journal entry to account for the deviation between the expected and actual value of the plan obligation at year-end.

P16-28. Assumptions for defined benefit plans ( 16-4) (Medium – 5 minutes)

The actuarial valuation and accounting for defined benefit pension plans involve a number of different estimates. For each of the following changes in assumptions, identify the likely effect on the amount of pension expense in the current period (increase, decrease, or no effect). For this question, ignore the requirement to use the same rate for return on assets and interest on obligations.

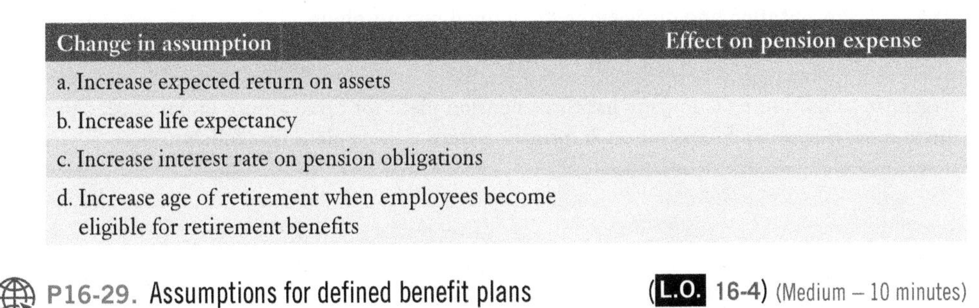

Change in assumption	Effect on pension expense
a. Increase expected return on assets	
b. Increase life expectancy	
c. Increase interest rate on pension obligations	
d. Increase age of retirement when employees become eligible for retirement benefits	

P16-29. Assumptions for defined benefit plans (L.O. 16-4) (Medium – 10 minutes)

The actuarial valuation and accounting for defined benefit pension plans involves a number of different estimates. For each of the following changes in assumptions, identify the likely effect on the indicated items at the end of the current year (increase, decrease, or no effect). Assume that the sponsor's balance sheet has a net defined benefit pension asset.

Change in assumption	Defined benefit pension asset
a. Increase expected return on assets	
b. Increase interest rate on pension obligations	
c. Increase life expectancy of employees/retirees	
d. Increase age of retirement when employees become eligible for retirement benefits	
e. Increase rate of wage increase when pension benefits are specified relative to employees' wages	

P16-30. Assumptions for defined benefit plans (L.O. 16-4) (Medium – 20 minutes)

Changing Assumptions Ltd. has the following details related to its defined benefit pension plan as at December 31, 2019:

Pension fund assets	$ 800,000
Actuarial obligation	790,264

The actuarial obligation represents the present value of a single benefit payment of $1,400,000 that is due on December 31, 2025, discounted at an interest rate of 10%; that is, $\$1{,}400{,}000 \div 1.10^6 = \$790{,}264$.

Funding during 2020 was $65,000. The actual value of pension fund assets at the end of 2020 was $950,000. As a result of the current services received from employees, the single payment due on December 31, 2025, had increased from $1,400,000 to $1,500,000.

Required:

a. Compute the current service cost for 2020 and the amount of the accrued benefit obligation at December 31, 2020. Perform this computation for interest rates of 8%, 10%, and 12%.
b. Ignore the requirement to use the same rate for return on assets and interest on obligations. Derive the pension expense for 2020 under various assumptions about (i) the expected return, and (ii) the discount rate, by completing the following table:

	Case 1	Case 2	Case 3	Case 4	Case 5	Case 6
Expected return assumption	8%	8%	10%	10%	12%	12%
Discount rate assumption	8%	10%	8%	10%	12%	8%
Current service cost						
Interest on obligation						
Expected return on assets						
Total pension expense						

c. Briefly comment on the different amounts of pension expense in relation to the assumptions for expected return and discount rate.
d. Comment on why IAS 19 requires the use of a discount rate that is the same as the rate of return on assets.
e. How does a change in the discount rate affect the accrued benefit obligation?

P16-31. Presentation and disclosures for defined benefit plans

(L.O. 16-5) (Easy – 5 minutes)

Aegis Air Conditioning Company has three pension plans for three groups of employees: production, service, and administration. Information for the three plans is as follows:

	Production	Service	Administration	Total
Pension assets	$ 4,500,000	$ 3,000,000	$ 2,000,000	$ 9,500,000
Pension obligations	(5,000,000)	(3,200,000)	(1,400,000)	9,600,000
Net pension surplus (deficit)	$ (500,000)	$ (200,000)	$ 600,000	$ (100,000)

Required:

Provide an excerpt of Aegis's balance sheet showing the presentation of its pension plans.

P16-32. Note disclosures for defined benefit plans (L.O. 16-5) (Easy – 5 minutes)

Brockstone Masons' balance sheet shows a net defined benefit liability of $1,790,000. Relating to this amount are pension assets of $5,450,000 and pension obligations of $7,240,000. At the beginning of the year, pension assets were $4,900,000 while pension obligations were $5,500,000. For the year, current service cost was $850,000 and interest cost was $580,000. The assets were expected to earn $420,000 while actual return amounted to $480,000. A decrease in discount rate caused the pension obligation to increase by $900,000 above expectations. Brockstone contributed $660,000 to the pension.

Required:

Prepare the two schedules that would be presented in the notes to reconcile the opening and closing balances of Brockstone's pension assets and liabilities.

P16-33. Note disclosures for defined benefit plans (L.O. 16-5) (Medium – 10 minutes)

Cornwall has a defined benefit pension plan. The company's balance sheet shows a defined benefit asset of $650,000 at year-end. This balance was composed of $22,800,000 of assets and $22,150,000 of pension obligations. During the year, the company contributed $7,500,000 to the pension, while $3,450,000 was paid out to retirees. The pension assets earned $3,350,000, which was $1,500,000 above expectations. Current service cost was $2,800,000 and interest cost was $1,700,000. The actuaries calculated an actuarial loss of $1,250,000 for the year.

Required:

Prepare the two schedules that would be presented in the notes to reconcile the opening and closing balances of Cornwall's pension assets and liabilities.

P16-34. Note disclosures for defined benefit plans—asset ceiling

(L.O. 16-5) (Medium – 10 minutes)

Dovetail Furnishings produces quality household furniture. The company has only one defined benefit pension plan, which covers its 30 carpenters. The company has completed its accounting for the year and closed its books. The draft financial statements show a defined benefit asset of $25,000,000. This net asset is the result of $72,500,000 of pension assets and $38,300,000 of pension obligations. The remainder was determined to be not recoverable.

During the year, $1,150,000 was paid out to retirees. The pension assets earned $9,450,000, which was $3,450,000 above expectations. Current service cost was $2,400,000 and interest cost was $2,700,000. The actuaries calculated an actuarial gain of $1,500,000 for the year.

Required:

Prepare the two schedules that would be presented in the notes to reconcile the opening and closing balances of Dovetail's pension assets and liabilities.

P16-35. Accounting for defined benefit plans and note disclosures

(L.O. 16-3, L.O. 16-5) (Medium – 20 minutes)

As of January 1, 2019, Microbyte Computer Company began a defined benefit pension plan that covers all 300 of its employees. Employment levels have remained constant and are expected to remain so in the future. Prior to 2019, rather than having a defined benefit plan, the company had a defined contribution plan that had accumulated assets of $2,100,000 at market value. All employees were retroactively grandfathered as to the defined benefit entitlements they would receive under the new plan (i.e., the employees had been participating in the defined contribution plan and are now part of the defined benefit plan). The company's insurance company, which is administering the pension plan, determined the following values effective on January 1, 2019:

Plan assets at market value	$2,100,000
Accrued benefit obligation	3,000,000
Initial net asset (obligation)	$ (900,000)

The company's funding policy is to contribute annually on December 31 at a rate of 15% of covered employees' payroll. The annual payroll of employees covered by the pension plan amounted to $2,500,000 in 2019. Assume that all other cash flows as well as expense accruals occur on the last day of the year.

The insurance company provided the following information for 2019:

Plan assets at market value, December 31	$2,424,000
Accrued benefit obligation, December 31	2,964,000
Present value of pension benefits earned by employees during year	125,000
Payments to retirees	40,000
Discount rate on obligations and expected return on assets	10%

Required:

a. Using the above information, complete the missing information in the note disclosures reconciling the opening and closing positions of pension assets and liabilities for 2019.

Pension assets schedule	
Opening assets, January 1	$2,100,000
+ Funding (occurs at end of year)	
+ Expected return on assets	
− Payments to retirees	
Unexpected gain (loss) on plan assets	
Actual market value, December 31	
Pension obligations schedule	
Opening accrued benefit obligation, January 1	$3,000,000
+ Current service cost (accrued at end of year)	
+ Interest	
− Payments to retirees	
Actuarial (gain) loss	
Actual obligation, December 31	

b. Calculate the pension expense to be recognized in 2019 and show the individual components making up the pension expense.

c. Record the journal entries for Microbyte's pension in 2019. Use separate accounts for each item of pension expense and OCI.

P16-36. Accounting for defined benefit plans and note disclosures

(L.O. 16-3, L.O. 16-5) (Medium – 20 minutes)

DB Company operates a defined benefit pension plan. Until January 1, 2017, DB Company had a defined contribution plan that had been retroactively changed to a defined benefit plan. The plan was on this date underfunded by $1,000,000. DB Company has a December 31 year-end.

On January 1, 2019, valuations were completed with the following results:

Plan assets at market value	$1,750,000
Accrued benefit obligation	2,500,000
Net asset (obligation)	$ (750,000)

The company uses the following assumptions for its pension plan:

- Discount rate on obligations and expected rate of investment return: 8%
- All accruals and payments take place at mid-year.

The following data are relevant for 2019:

Plan assets at market value, December 31	$2,075,000
Accrued benefit obligation, December 31	2,850,000
Present value of pension benefits earned by employees during year	125,000
Funding contribution	150,000
Payments to retirees	50,000

Required:

a. Using the above information, complete the following note disclosures reconciling the opening and closing balances of pension assets and liabilities for 2019.

Pension assets schedule	
Opening assets	
+ Funding (occurs mid-year)	
− Payments to retirees (paid mid-year)	
+ Expected return on assets	
+ Unexpected gain (loss) on plan assets	
Closing balance	

Pension obligations schedule	
Opening accrued benefit obligation	
+ Current service cost (accrued mid-year)	
− Payments to retirees (paid mid-year)	
+ Interest	
+ Actuarial (gain) loss	
Closing balance	

b. Calculate the pension expense to be recognized in 2019 and show the individual components making up the pension expense.

c. Record the journal entries for DB's pension in 2019.

P16-37. Accounting for defined benefit plans and note disclosures

(L.O. 16-3, L.O. 16-5) (Medium – 15 minutes)

Corus Manufacturing Ltd. has a defined benefit pension plan that covers its production employees. On September 1, 2008, Corus initiated this plan and had immediately contributed $12 million toward covering the costs of the plan because the plan provided for retroactive benefits. The actuary valued these retroactive benefits at $12 million.

You have the following information with respect to the plan as at August 31, 2018 (10 years after the plan initiation):

Plan assets at market value	$29,000,000
Accrued benefit obligation	25,800,000
Balance sheet defined benefit pension asset	3,200,000

Information for fiscal year ended August 31, 2019:

Pension benefit obligation at year-end	$27,500,000
Market value of plan assets at year-end	33,000,000
Current service cost (accrued evenly through year)	2,700,000
Contributions to plan assets, made mid-year (February 28, 2019)	1,800,000
Benefit payments (paid evenly through year)	900,000
Expected earnings rate on plan assets and discount rate on obligations	8%

Required:

a. Using the above information, prepare the schedules in the note disclosures reconciling the beginning and ending balances of the pension's assets and liabilities for the 2019 fiscal year.
b. Derive the pension expense for the fiscal year ended August 31, 2019.
c. Record the journal entries relating to the pension plan for the 2019 fiscal year.

P16-38. Accounting for defined benefit plans and note disclosures

(L.O. 16-3, L.O. 16-5) (Medium – 15 minutes)

Dayton Products Ltd. has a separate pension plan for its management. This pension plan was put in place on January 1, 2010. The plan initiation created a pension obligation of $3 million. However, only $1 million was put into the plan initially. On January 1, 2020, the company improved the benefits for the plan, which increased the actuarial obligation by $750,000.

The pension plan's trustee and actuary provided the following information for the fiscal year ended December 31, 2020:

Pension benefit obligation at year-end	$8,500,000
Market value of plan assets at year-end	6,600,000
Current service cost	240,000
Benefit payments (no employees have yet retired)	none
Discount rate on pension obligation and rate of return on plan assets	9%

Financial statements for the pension trust show that, as at December 31, 2019, plan assets were $5.4 million and the pension obligation was $7.2 million.

The accounting department's records indicate that $250,000 was contributed into the pension fund during 2020.

For purposes of interest calculations, management assumes that all accruals and cash flows occur at the beginning of the fiscal year.

Required:

a. Prepare the schedules showing the movements in the pension assets and liabilities during fiscal 2020.
b. Derive the pension expense for the fiscal year ended December 31, 2020. Please show your work.
c. Record the journal entries relating to the pension plan for the 2020 fiscal year.

P16-39. Accounting for defined benefit plans and note disclosures

(L.O. 16-3, L.O. 16-5) (Difficult – 30 minutes)

Generous Co. Ltd. (Gen) operates a defined benefit pension plan that offers its employees an annual retirement income based on years of service and average of the final five years' earnings prior to retirement.

On January 1, 2019, Gen improved the pension benefits by increasing the percentage of the last five years' earnings from 2.1% to 2.2%. This enhancement has been retroactively applied to all actively employed workers on January 1, 2019. The amendment gave rise to an increase in the accrued benefit obligation of $100,000 on January 1, 2019.

On January 1, 2020, the balance of the accrued benefit obligation is $600,000 and the pension fund assets total $420,000.

The following amounts relate to Gen's pension plan experience as determined by annual valuations in 2020 and 2021:

	2020	2021
Plan assets at market value, December 31	$ 591,250	$ 802,000
Accrued benefit obligation, December 31	724,500	865,000
Pension benefits earned by employees during year*	75,000	80,000
Payments to retirees*	15,000	20,000
Funding contribution (at end of year)	100,000	115,000
Expected return on assets and interest rate on obligations	10%	10%

* The company assumes that pension benefits are earned and paid evenly through the year.

Required:

a. Determine the balance of the net defined benefit pension asset or liability as at January 1, 2020.
b. Using the above information, prepare the schedules to reconcile the opening and closing balances of pension assets and liabilities for 2020 and 2021.
c. Calculate the pension expense to be recognized in 2020 and 2021, and show the individual components making up the pension expense.
d. Record the journal entries for Gen's pension in 2020 and 2021.
e. Determine the balance of the net defined benefit pension liability as at December 31, 2020 and 2021. Reconcile these balances with the transactions recorded to this account in the two years.

P16-40. Accounting for defined benefit plans and note disclosures

(L.O. 16-3, L.O. 16-5) (Medium – 15 minutes)

Refer to the 2016 financial statements for Canadian Tire Corporation in Appendix C.

Required:

a. What was the amount of the post-employment obligation reported in Canadian Tire's financial statements as at December 31, 2016?
b. What was the nature of this obligation (e.g., what benefits are provided)?
c. What was the total cost of maintaining the post-employment obligation during 2016? How much of this was expensed and how much was reported in other comprehensive income?
d. Why does the amount reported as an actuarial gain or loss on the Consolidated Statement of Comprehensive Income appear to differ from that reported in Note 24?

M. MINI-CASES

CASE 1

ESL Teachers Union

(30 minutes)

English as a second language (ESL) has been a significant part of the Canadian education landscape for several decades, and its importance continues to grow with the increasing amount of immigration from countries where English is not the mother tongue. In addition, many individuals visit Canada for the primary purpose of learning English. This demand has spawned a thriving industry of dozens of private ESL schools, which range in size from those that operate with a handful of teachers to those with several dozen teachers. A few of the larger schools have multiple locations in different cities. These ESL schools exist separately from the conventional educational system of primary, secondary, and post-secondary schools.

While practically all instructors in the conventional education system are covered by pension plans—be they defined benefit or defined contribution plans—the same cannot be said for teachers at ESL schools. While the number of ESL teachers is large and growing, there has been little coordination among teachers within and across schools.

Five years ago, a group of ESL teachers formed the ESL Teachers Union (ETU) at a school in Vancouver. The idea quickly spread and the union now represents a significant proportion of ESL teachers across the country. One of the key reasons for the formation of the union is to increase the bargaining position of its member teachers to improve working conditions and compensation. After five years solidifying its position, the union executive decided the time had come to push for pension benefits for its members.

So far, the ETU has had a good working relationship with the representatives of the ESL schools' management, and the two sides have been able to resolve issues amicably. For the current pension negotiations, the ETU and the affected ESL schools have jointly hired you to prepare a preliminary report that provides fair and independent advice that will aid them in their negotiations.

1. What amount should be contributed to the pension plan for each teacher? To be useful, this amount should be expressed as a percentage of a teacher's salary. For this purpose, the two parties have agreed that reasonable parameters for estimating this amount are for a teacher at the beginning of his or her career who will spend 30 years as a teacher, 20 years in retirement, and annual pension payments that equal 2% of the final year's salary for each year of service (i.e., a teacher who earns pension benefits for 30 years would expect to receive 60% of his or her final year's salary). The average salary of an ESL teacher at the beginning of the 30-year working period is $35,000 and increasing by 2% in real terms. Inflation can be ignored.
2. Should the pension be a defined benefit or defined contribution plan? How does this choice affect issue 1 above?
3. The representative of the ESL schools proposes that the teachers be provided with an "opt-in" clause, whereby the teachers would by default receive their full salary as they have in the past, but if they choose to be part of the pension plan then their salary payments would be reduced in exchange for the future pension benefits. On the other hand, the ETU has proposed an "opt-out" clause, whereby the teachers would by default be enrolled in the pension plan; if they choose to opt out, they can receive the full salary as they do currently.

Required:

Prepare the report requested by the ETU and the ESL schools. Assume an interest rate of 6% for both investment returns and discounting.

CASE 2

Tubular Ltd.

(60 minutes)[10]

Syntax Inc., a public company, has undertaken to purchase Tubular Ltd., a manufacturer of home heating units and industrial heating systems. Your firm, Cox & Williams LLP, is the current auditor of Syntax and is advising the company on the acquisition of Tubular.

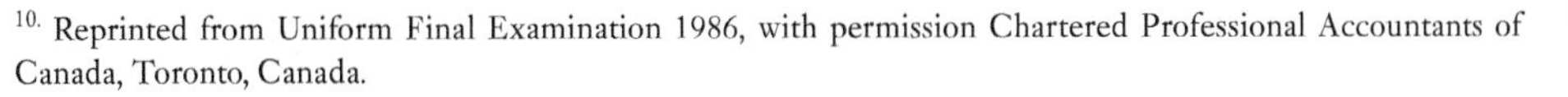

[10] Reprinted from Uniform Final Examination 1986, with permission Chartered Professional Accountants of Canada, Toronto, Canada.

Tubular is a private corporation owned by Jason Kent and other members of the Kent family. The company's original business was casting and assembling wood stoves. Subsequently, Tubular improved its line to cast new energy-efficient wood and coal stoves. In the past decade, under the management of the eldest son, Allen, the company expanded its plant for the fabrication of industrial heating systems for installation in large industrial and commercial complexes. Because of recent high interest charges and rigorous competition, cash flow has been poor, and the company is about to report the first large loss in its history, amounting to $500,000.

To become more competitive, Tubular will have to purchase new machinery and equipment and obtain additional financing. The Kent family considered the financing requirement too great and therefore decided to sell its common shares to Syntax. Syntax has sufficient cash to purchase the common shares and, if so desired, to extinguish the outstanding debt of Tubular.

Extracts from the share purchase agreement that Syntax and Tubular negotiated are provided below:

1. Tubular is to provide financial statements for the year ending June 30, 2021. These financial statements are to be audited by the current auditors of Tubular (Robert & Rosberg LLP).
2. The closing date of the agreement is to be July 31, 2021, and a balance sheet at that date is to be prepared by Cox & Williams. This "closing balance sheet" will be used to determine the final purchase price.
3. The preliminary purchase price is $7 million, based on the audited financial statements of June 30, 2020. The price is to be adjusted upward or downward, dollar for dollar, based on the change in retained earnings during the 13-month period between June 30, 2020 and July 31, 2021.
4. The closing balance sheet will be prepared in accordance with generally accepted accounting principles applied on a basis consistent with the preceding period. Tubular has been reporting under IFRS.

The partner on this engagement at Cox & Williams informed you, a staff member at Cox & Williams, that Robert & Rosberg had completed their field work on the audit of Tubular for the year ending June 30, 2021, but had not yet issued their report. Because of the time constraint, the partner has asked you to conduct a preliminary review of the audit working papers. Your notes are presented in Exhibit I, and extracts from Tubular's balance sheet are given in Exhibit II.

Exhibit I Notes on Tubular's audit file for the year ended June 30, 2021

1. Tubular started a pension plan for its employees in 1980. The last valuation report from the actuary, dated September 30, 2020, shows a surplus amounting to $97,000. This surplus occurred due to a better return on investment than anticipated. On June 30, 2021, Tubular recognized the surplus with a journal entry offsetting the amount against current-year service costs.

   Management adopted this treatment because the surplus relates to the business prior to the date of sale. Furthermore, management said that, according to generally accepted accounting principles, actuarial revaluations can be immediately recognized in the current period instead of being amortized.
2. In May 2020, the company paid a $60,000 deposit on a tube-bending machine costing $200,000. The machine was delivered in July 2020. The balance of the purchase price was to be paid by September 2020; however, before the final payment was made, the manufacturer of the tube-bending machine went into bankruptcy. The trustees of the bankrupt company have not made any claim.

   Management feels that no additional liability should be set up since the manufacturer has breached the contract, which warranted that the manufacturer would service the machine for two years. Up to June 30, 2021, the company incurred and expensed $20,000 of service costs that should have been covered under the warranty. Management has determined that the machine has four years of service remaining as at June 30, 2021.
3. The deferred income taxes have resulted primarily from temporary differences in the recognition of capital cost allowance (CCA) claimed in excess of depreciation recorded. Management is reasonably certain that the tax benefits of the tax losses carried forward can

(Continued)

Exhibit I Continued

be realized by claiming less CCA than depreciation. It has therefore reduced the current year's losses by recognizing the deferred income tax benefit. The average tax rate of the company is 30%.

When filing its income tax return for the past five years, the company reported no taxable income as a result of claiming enough CCA to offset its net income. This year, no CCA has been claimed because of the significant loss. Depreciation is calculated at 20% declining balance.

Exhibit II Summarized balance sheet

($000's)	2021 (unaudited)	2020 (audited)
Current assets		
Accounts receivable, net	$11,350,000	$10,000,000
Deferred income tax on losses carried forward	233,000	—
Other	9,300,000	5,600,000
Property, plant, and equipment (net)	320,000	400,000
Total assets	$21,203,000	$16,000,000
Current liabilities		
Bank indebtedness	$ 8,000,000	$ 7,000,000
Maintenance reserve	—	120,000
Other	6,241,000	3,544,000
Long-term debt	2,000,000	—
Deferred income taxes*	72,000	96,000
Common shares	1,000,000	1,000,000
Retained earnings	3,890,000	4,240,000
Total liabilities and equity	$21,203,000	$16,000,000

*Due to CCA in excess of depreciation.

Required:

Prepare a report to the partner analyzing the significant issues relating to the engagement.

CASE 3

Pensions

(30 minutes)

In the consulting firm where you are employed, you are considered the "pensions guru." Whenever a client has a question related to pensions, he or she is referred to you for advice. Recently, two clients approached you with the following unrelated issues:

Case 1: This year the stock market took a big plunge. Your client is worried that not only did they lose significant sums on their investments, but also their net pension obligations will sky rocket. The client is also wondering if this will have a negative effect on the company's net income.

Case 2: The client is a software company. It is February 2020 now, and its pension plan specifies that upon retirement, an employee will receive 2% of the last annual salary per year, for each year of service provided. Similar plans are common with most other software companies. During the last year (2019), most software companies amended their pension plan to increase the pay at retirement from 2% to 2.5%, retroactively. Your client company has not made such a change yet. However, the union is very eager to have this change implemented, and was already asking for a meeting to discuss the issue. Your client is asking for your advice on whether the pension liability for 2019 should be calculated based on 2% or 2.5%.

Required:

Prepare a separate report for each client addressing their concerns.

Russell Hart/Alamy Stock Photo

CHAPTER 17
Accounting for Leases

LEARNING OBJECTIVES

After studying this chapter, you should be able to:

L.O. 17-1. Apply the criteria for lessors for classifying leases as finance (capital) or operating leases, and apply the appropriate accounting method.

L.O. 17-2. Analyze a lease to determine the present value of lease payments, the interest rate implicit in the lease, and the lease payments required from the lessee.

L.O. 17-3. Apply the appropriate accounting method for lessees' right-of-use assets.

L.O. 17-4. Analyze a lease to determine whether practical expedients are available to lessees and, if available, apply the appropriate accounting methods.

L.O. 17-5. Apply the presentation and disclosure requirements applicable to leases.

L.O. 17-6. Describe the nature of sale and leaseback transactions and account for these transactions.

CPA competencies addressed in this chapter:

1.1.2 Evaluates the appropriateness of the basis of financial reporting (Level B)
- a. Fundamental accounting concepts and principles (qualitative characteristics of accounting information, basic elements)
- b. Methods of measurement
- c. Differences between accrual accounting compared to cash accounting

1.2.2 Evaluates treatment for routine transactions (Level A)
- d. Property, plant, and equipment
- h. Long-term liabilities
- n. Leases

1.3.2 Prepares routine financial statement note disclosure (Level B)*

Sir David Tweedie, the former chair of the International Accounting Standards Board (IASB), once said that he would like to fly on an aircraft that actually appeared on the airline's balance sheet. Of course, there is no question that airlines use aircraft in their operations, so the implicit claim expressed by the former IASB chair was that airlines and other companies were able to avoid recording certain assets (and liabilities) on their balance sheets.

The spirit of IAS 17—Leases, the predecessor standard for leasing, was for entities to report the economic substance of lease transactions rather than their legal form on their financial statements. In this regard, a lease agreement typically conveys the rights and responsibilities of ownership of the asset to the lessee coupled with a financing agreement. Tweedie's and others' concern was that the spirit of the accounting standard was being circumvented by creative leasing agreements designed specifically to ensure that lessees could classify leases as "operating leases," thus keeping a considerable portion of their airline fleets and corresponding liabilities off-balance-sheet.

To address this concern, the IASB substantively revised the leasing standard. The new standard, IFRS 16—Leases, ensures that virtually all right-of-use assets and the associated liabilities are reported by lessees on their balance sheets.

What are the economics of leasing? What is the difference between an operating lease and a finance lease? What are right-of-use assets? How do we account for lease contracts from the perspective of the lessor and the lessee?

The lessee accounting section is self-contained for those who prefer to focus on lessee accounting and skip lessor accounting. The lessor accounting sections C, D, E, F, I, and J parts 1 and 2 of this chapter can be skipped by those who want to focus on the lessee's accounting for leases.

---

*From Chartered Professional Accountants of Canada (CPA Canada).

CONTENTS

A. INTRODUCTION 842
B. ECONOMICS OF LEASING 842
C. CLASSIFICATION OF LEASES—LESSOR 846
1. The primary consideration when classifying leases 846
2. Indicators supporting the classification of leases 847
3. Additional considerations for classification of real estate leases 849
D. ACCOUNTING FOR OPERATING LEASES—LESSOR 849
E. ACCOUNTING FOR FINANCE LEASES—LESSOR 851
1. Recognition and initial measurement 852
2. Subsequent measurement 860
3. Derecognition 864
4. Lessor's preference for classifying leases as finance leases, rather than operating leases 865
F. PRESENTATION AND DISCLOSURE OF LEASES—LESSOR 865
1. Presentation 865
2. Disclosure 866
G. ACCOUNTING FOR LEASES—LESSEE 867
1. Recognition and initial measurement of lease liabilities 867
2. Recognition and initial measurement of right-of-use assets 869
3. Applying the recognition and initial measurement criteria for right-of-use assets and lease liabilities 870
4. Subsequent measurement of lease liabilities 873
5. Subsequent measurement of right-of-use assets 873
6. Applying the subsequent measurement criteria for right-of-use assets and lease liabilities 874
7. Practical expedients 879
8. Derecognition 882
H. PRESENTATION AND DISCLOSURE OF LEASES—LESSEE 885
1. Presentation 885
2. Disclosure 885
I. ACCOUNTING FOR SALE AND LEASEBACK TRANSACTIONS 885
1. Accounting for a sale and leaseback transaction—Sales criteria met 887
2. Accounting for a sale and leaseback transaction—Sales criteria not met 889
J. SUBSTANTIVE DIFFERENCES BETWEEN RELEVANT IFRS AND ASPE 891
1. Lessor's lease capitalization criteria 892
2. Lessor's classification of finance (capital) leases 892
3. Lessee's lease capitalization criteria 892
4. Lessee's discount rate for present value calculations 893
5. Lessee's inclusion of residual value guarantees in the determination of lease payments 893
6. Lessee's accounting for the lease and related non-lease components in the lease contract 893
K. SUMMARY 894
L. ANSWERS TO CHECKPOINT QUESTIONS 895
M. GLOSSARY 895
N. REFERENCES 897
O. PROBLEMS 897
P. MINI-CASES 915

A. INTRODUCTION

lease A contract, or part of a contract, that conveys the right to use an asset (the underlying asset) for a period of time in exchange for consideration.

lessor The owner of the asset in a lease.

lessee The renter in a lease contract. This is the party that has the right to use the underlying asset during the lease term.

finance lease A lease that transfers substantially all the risks and rewards incidental to ownership of an underlying asset. Depending on its nature, the lessor accounts for a finance lease as either a financing arrangement or as an asset sale with vendor-provided financing.

operating lease A lease that does not transfer substantially all the risks and rewards incidental to ownership of an underlying asset. An operating lease is accounted for by the lessor as a rental agreement.

underlying asset The asset stipulated in the lease agreement that the lessor rents to the lessee.

right-of-use (ROU) asset An asset that represents a lessee's right to use an underlying asset for the lease term. This is the asset that the lessor rents to the lessee.

Whether we are aware or not, we have all leased assets before. A **lease** is simply a contract (whether written or verbal) in which the property owner permits another person to use that property in exchange for something else (usually money). Most readers will be familiar with apartment leases. In that case, the landlord is the **lessor**, and the renter is the **lessee**. Other everyday transactions that involve leases include renting a car for the day for $40 and using a photocopier to make 20 copies at 10¢ per page.

Legally, all leases are rental agreements. The lessor (the owner of the asset) leases (rents) the asset to the lessee (the user of the asset). As mentioned in the opening vignette, accounting for leases is based on the substance of the lease agreement, rather than its legal form.

There are always at least two parties to a business transaction, each of which accounts for the transaction independently of the other. For example, a furniture retailer that sells office furnishings to a business for cash would debit cash and credit revenue, and debit cost of goods sold and credit inventory (assuming a perpetual inventory system). The purchaser, though, debits furniture and fixtures and credits cash. The seller and the buyer account for the same transaction very differently. There is no symmetry in the accounting—the buyer's accounting is not the mirror image of the seller's accounting. This asymmetry applies to accounting for leases as well, as the lessor's accounting differs from the lessee's in many respects.

While the lessor and lessee usually negotiate rates, payment dates, and the like, it is ultimately the lessor (the lender) who establishes the terms of the lease including the payment schedule. As such, this chapter first examines accounting for leases from the lessor's perspective. We then consider how the lessee accounts for the lease agreement given the stipulated lease terms.

As will be discussed later in this chapter, the lessor evaluates the nature of the lease to determine whether it is a **finance lease**[1] or an **operating lease**. Briefly, a finance lease bears many of the characteristics of an asset sale coupled with vendor-provided financing, while an operating lease more closely resembles typical short-term rental arrangements like those mentioned above (apartment lease, daily car rental, photocopier rental).

Unlike the lessor, the lessee does not distinguish between finance leases and operating leases. The **underlying asset** that the lessee is entitled to use during the lease term is known as a **right-of-use (ROU) asset**, while the liability arising from the lease contract is referred to as a lease liability.

B. ECONOMICS OF LEASING

Those who are in the leasing business often identify many advantages of leasing to attract customers (e.g., potential lessees), including the following:

- "100%" financing of the asset's purchase price, which is often more than the amount that can be obtained from a loan.
- Payment schedules that are more flexible in comparison to loans and that can be tailored to match the lessee's anticipated cash flows.
- 100% deductibility of the lease payments from the lessee's taxable income.[2]

---

1. "Finance lease" is the term used in IFRS; the equivalent term in ASPE is "capital lease." Substantive differences between IFRS and ASPE leasing standards are contrasted in Section J of this chapter.

2. The lessee claims the lease payment as a deductible expense, rather than interest expense and capital cost allowance (CCA). The lessor claims CCA on the leased asset. In limited circumstances, CRA permits the parties to file a joint election that entitles the lessee to deduct CCA and interest expense, rather than the lease payment. A full discussion of this aspect is beyond the scope of this text.

- The after-tax cost of financing may be less under a lease than a traditional loan, particularly for not-for-profit organizations as the tax deduction available for the capital cost allowance (CCA) is worth more to the lessor than the lessee. Similarly, after-tax costs may be lower due to differences in tax rates for the lessor and lessee.[3]

Given these advantages, there must be some significant disadvantage to leasing; otherwise, everyone would lease and no one would purchase any of the assets that they use, which is clearly not descriptive of reality.

As previously mentioned, a lease transfers usage and property rights from the lessor to the lessee for the duration of the lease. This type of contract creates an agency relationship, resulting in a moral hazard problem: the user who controls the asset during the lease (the lessee) is not the owner of the asset (because the lessor still owns it).[4] When the lessor relinquishes control of the leased property to the lessee, the lessor must bear the risk that the lessee will not take the utmost care of the leased property (or as much care as the lessor would). This reduced level of care due to the separation of an asset's ownership and its control is the **agency cost of leasing**—see Exhibit 17-1 for a graphical illustration. As shown in this diagram, the value of an asset normally declines over time with usage, deterioration, and so on. However, the rate of decline depends on whether the asset is owned or leased, and to what extent the lease transfers risks and rewards of ownership.

THRESHOLD CONCEPT
INFORMATION ASYMMETRY

agency cost of leasing The reduced level of care due to the separation of an asset's ownership and its control.

If the lessor does not expect to regain control of the asset at the end of the lease, then the agency cost of leasing is nil because the lessee, rather than the lessor, bears the consequences of neglect. However, if the lease does transfer the property back to the lessor at the end of the lease, then the agency cost of leasing could be significant, and it must factor into the lessor's pricing decision. In other words, the lessor should anticipate that the lease will lower the property's value at the end of the lease to an amount below what it would be without the lease. As a result, the lessor must raise the required rental payments accordingly to compensate for the agency cost of leasing.

Exhibit 17-1 Stylized illustration of the agency cost of leasing

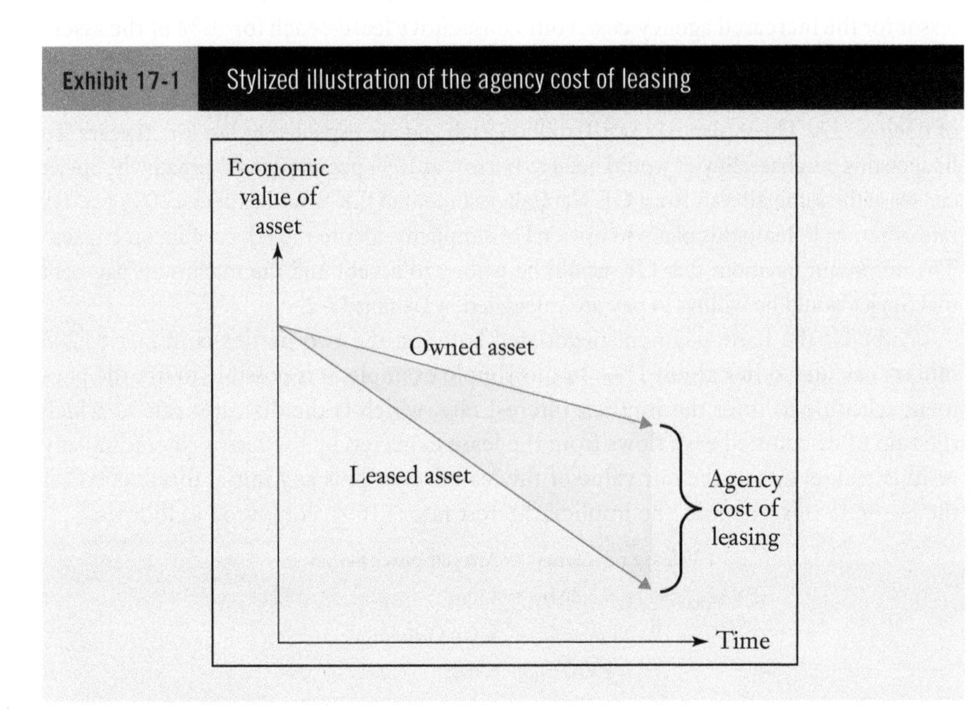

---

[3] These are examples of an advanced tax planning topic known as "tax arbitrage," the details of which are beyond the scope of this text.

[4] Refer to Chapter 1 for a discussion of moral hazard and agency theory.

The degree to which this agency cost matters depends on many factors, including:

1. *The inherent nature of the asset that is leased.* Assets that are robust and difficult to damage have lower agency costs and are better candidates for leasing.
2. *The incentives of the lessee to maintain the condition of the leased asset.* Some types of lessees are more motivated to maintain the leased asset than others. For example, airlines are very keen to ensure that their leased aircraft are safe for their customers since the consequences of equipment failure are severe in terms of both the airlines' business and human lives.
3. *Regulations that require a high degree of care.* Airlines again are a good example here. Regulators have stringent requirements for maintaining commercial passenger aircraft.
4. *Conditions negotiated between the lessor and lessee.* Lease agreements often contain conditions that mitigate agency costs. For example, damage deposits for apartments deter renters from harming the property, and long-term car leases often limit the amount of mileage that can be driven annually. A particularly important contract provision that reduces or even eliminates agency costs is a **bargain purchase option (BPO)** that allows the lessee to purchase the asset at a price below the market value expected at the end of the lease. Also important is a **residual value guarantee**, whereby the lessee must ensure that the leased asset retains a certain value at the end of the lease.
5. *The length of the lease contract.* As mentioned previously, if the lease transfers ownership to the lessee at the end of the lease, then no agency costs arise. Similarly, if the length of the lease contract covers substantially the entire useful life of the asset, then agency costs will be minimal since the lessee bears the cost of neglecting or abusing the property. As the duration of the lease shortens, agency costs increase.

bargain purchase option (BPO) An option given to the lessee to purchase the leased asset at a price that is below the expected fair value at a future date; the assessment of whether a bargain exists is made at the time of entering the lease arrangement.

residual value guarantee A guarantee made to the lessor by the lessee or an independent third party that the value of the leased asset at the end of the lease will be greater than or equal to the guaranteed amount.

This last factor has important implications for the rental price. For example, suppose the rental rate for a lease that covers 100% of an asset's life is $400,000 in present value terms. In comparison, two consecutive lease terms each for 50% of the asset's life must have present value higher than $400,000 because the leases must compensate the lessor for the increased agency cost. Four consecutive leases, each for 25% of the asset's life, would cost even more.

To illustrate, consider Spyjet, a Canadian airline that is considering expanding its fleet of Boeing 737s. These planes cost $30 million each and are expected to last for 20 years. To finance this purchase, Spyjet would need to borrow at 10% per annum. Alternatively, Spyjet can lease the same aircraft from GE Capital. Assume that GE would expect a 10% pre-tax rate of return to lease this plane to Spyjet. For simplicity, ignore the effect of income taxes.[5] The minimum payment that GE would be willing to accept and the maximum payment that Spyjet would be willing to pay are calculated in Exhibit 17-2.

Suppose the lease payment negotiated between the two parties is in fact $3.203 million calculated in Exhibit 17-2. In this simple example, it is possible to use the payment schedule to infer the implicit interest rate, which is the discount rate at which the sum of discounted cash flows from the lease expected by the lessor (including any residual value) equals the fair value of the leased asset plus any initial direct costs[6] of the lessor. In this example, the implicit interest rate is 10%, computed as follows:

$$\begin{aligned} \text{PV(lease payments)} &= \text{Aircraft purchase price} \\ (\text{PVAF}_{x,19} + 1) \times 3.203\text{m} &= \$30\text{m} \\ (\text{PVAF}_{x,19} + 1) &= \$30\text{m}/3.203\text{m} \\ \text{PVAF}_{x,19} &= 8.3662 \\ x &= 10\% \end{aligned}$$

5. For capital cost allowance purposes, aircraft are Class 9 assets with a 25% CCA rate.

6. Initial direct costs are outlays by the lessor, other than a manufacturer/dealer lessor, that are directly attributable to arranging and negotiating the lease. Accounting for initial direct costs is first examined in Section E on page 854.

Exhibit 17-2 Determining the lease payment for GE Capital and Spyjet

Based on this information, GE determines that the *lowest* lease payment it can accept is \$3.203 million, received at the beginning of each of 20 years, computed as follows (LP = lease payment; PVFA = present value factor for an annuity; PVFAD = present value factor for an annuity due):

$$\text{Present value of lease payments} \geq \text{Aircraft purchase price}$$

$$\text{PVFAD}_{10\%, 20} + \text{LP} \geq \$30\text{m}$$

$$(\text{PVFA}_{10\%, 19} + 1) \times \text{LP} \geq \$30\text{m}$$

$$9.3649 \times \text{LP} \geq \$30\text{m}$$

$$\text{LP} \geq \$3.203\text{m}$$

Using a BA II Plus financial calculator: **2ND** **BGN** **2ND** **SET** **2ND** **QUIT** 20 **N** 10 **I/Y** 30000000 **+/−** **PV** **CPT** **PMT** → PMT = 3,203,444

Meanwhile, Spyjet computes the *highest* lease payment it is willing to pay:

$$\text{PV(lease payments)} \leq \text{Aircraft purchase price}$$

$$(\text{PVAF}_{10\%,19} + 1) \times \text{LP} \leq \$30\text{m}$$

$$9.3649 \times \text{LP} \leq \$30\text{m}$$

$$\text{LP} \leq \$3.203\text{m}$$

2ND **BGN** **2ND** **SET** **2ND** **QUIT** 20 **N** 10 **I/Y** 30000000 **+/−** **PV** **CPT** **PMT** → PMT = 3,203,444

Therefore, lease payments must equal \$3.203 million for both parties to agree to the lease contract.

Of course, the implicit interest rate need not be a whole number as in this example. Implicit interest rates can be computed using a financial calculator if payments are constant: **2ND** **BGN** **2ND** **SET** **2ND** **QUIT** 20 **N** 30000000 **+/−** **PV** 3203444 **PMT** **CPT** **I/Y** → I/Y = 10%.

A computer spreadsheet, like Excel, can also be used to solve for the implicit interest for any pattern of payments. In Excel, this is done by using the "solver" tool, illustrated in Exhibit 17-3.

Exhibit 17-3 Spreadsheet solver to compute implicit interest rate

Implicit interest rate			10.0000%
Year	Lease payment	PV Factor	PV of lease payment
1	\$ 3,203,444	1.00000	\$ 3,203,444
2	3,203,444	0.90909	2,912,222
3	3,203,444	0.82645	2,647,474
4	3,203,444	0.75131	2,406,795
5	3,203,444	0.68301	2,187,995
6	3,203,444	0.62092	1,989,087
7	3,203,444	0.56447	1,808,261
8	3,203,444	0.51316	1,643,873
9	3,203,444	0.46651	1,494,430
10	3,203,444	0.42410	1,358,573
11	3,203,444	0.38554	1,235,067
12	3,203,444	0.35049	1,122,788
13	3,203,444	0.31863	1,020,716
14	3,203,444	0.28966	927,924
15	3,203,444	0.26333	843,567
16	3,203,444	0.23939	766,879
17	3,203,444	0.21763	697,163
18	3,203,444	0.19784	633,784
19	3,203,444	0.17986	576,168
20	3,203,444	0.16351	523,789
Present value of lease			\$ 30,000,000

Solver Parameters
Set Target Cell: \$D\$24
Equal To: Max Min Value of: 30000000
By Changing Cells: \$D\$1
Subject to the Constraints:
Solve Close Guess Options Add Change Delete Reset All Help

In this simple example, there are no economic gains or losses from the leasing arrangement for either party. However, due to some of the advantages of leasing, the lessee (Spyjet) may be willing to pay more than the minimum amount that the lessor (GE) is willing to accept. For example, this would occur if GE requires a rate of return that is lower than Spyjet's borrowing rate, or if GE has a higher tax rate than Spyjet (and therefore GE values the tax shields more highly). These effects are clearly important as leases are so prevalent in the economy; however, further exploration of these additional effects of leases is beyond the scope of this text.

CHECKPOINT **CP17-1**

What is the principal economic loss from a leasing transaction? Why do leases exist despite this loss?

L.O. 17-1. Apply the criteria for lessors for classifying leases as finance (capital) or operating leases, and apply the appropriate accounting method.

C. CLASSIFICATION OF LEASES—LESSOR

The above discussion highlights the important issue of who bears the risks and rewards of ownership, which is at the crux of lease accounting for the lessor. The discussion below first explains how these criteria are applied to distinguish an operating lease from a finance lease, and then describes the accounting procedures for the lessor that follow the classification decision.

The process of accounting for leases from the lessor's perspective can be grouped into three stages, as illustrated in Exhibit 17-4.

L.O. 17-2. Analyze a lease to determine the present value of lease payments, the interest rate implicit in the lease, and the lease payments required from the lessee.

1. The primary consideration when classifying leases

International Financial Reporting Standards (IFRS), as described in IFRS 16 (and similarly described in ASPE Section 3065), recommend the following for the lessor:

> ¶62 A lease is classified as a finance lease if it transfers substantially all the risks and rewards incidental to ownership of an underlying asset. A lease is classified as an operating lease if it does not transfer substantially all the risks and rewards incidental to ownership of an underlying asset.

The risks and rewards of ownership include but are not limited to the following:

- the risk of breakage and the reward of a longer-than-expected useful life;
- the risk of obsolescence and the reward of high resale value;
- the risks and rewards of changes in rental prices; and
- the risks and rewards of changes in demand for the usage of the property.

In the three examples presented in the introduction (apartment, car, and photocopier rentals), the lessor retains the risks and rewards of ownership since the leases are for short durations relative to the items' useful lives. Therefore, we normally consider

Exhibit 17-4 Stages of accounting for leases from the lessor's perspective

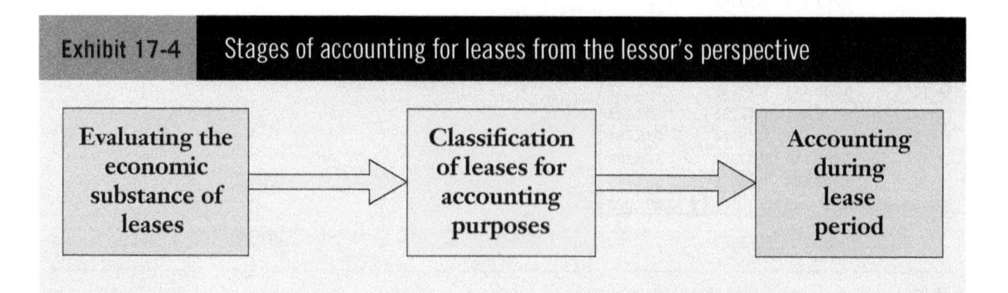

these leases to be operating leases for the lessor's accounting purposes. Accounting for operating leases from the lessor's perspective is discussed in Section D of this chapter.

At the other extreme, some leases transfer almost all of the risks and rewards of ownership to the lessee. For example, suppose Spyjet, in the example in Section B, does sign a 20-year lease with GE for payments of $3.203 million at the beginning of each year. Since the lease term covers the asset's entire expected useful life of 20 years, it is quite clear that the lessee (Spyjet) has incentives to maintain the aircraft to ensure that it operates as it should for the full 20 years. Therefore, Spyjet bears practically all the risks and rewards of ownership.[7] Since the lease transfers substantially all the risks and rewards of ownership, from the perspective of the lessor, GE, the lease between GE and Spyjet would be considered a finance lease. Accounting for finance leases from the lessor's perspective is discussed in Section E of this chapter.

CHECKPOINT **CP17-2**

What are the general criteria used by the lessor to determine whether a lease is an operating or a finance lease?

2. Indicators supporting the classification of leases

In addition to the general idea that a lease transferring substantially all the risks and rewards of ownership should be classified as a finance lease, IFRS 16 provides additional guidance to help make this determination:

1. Ownership of the leased asset transfers to the lessee at the end of the lease.
2. The lease includes a bargain purchase option (BPO).
3. The lease term is a major part of the **economic life** of the asset. What constitutes a "major part" is a matter of professional judgement as IFRS does not quantify this term. ASPE, however, establishes that a "major part" is ≥ 75% of the asset's economic life.
4. The present value of the **lease payments** (PVLP) comprises substantially all of the fair value of the leased asset. Again, "substantially all" is a matter of professional judgement as IFRS does not quantify this term. ASPE, though, establishes that "substantially all" is ≥ 90% of the asset's fair value.
5. The leased asset is so specialized that, without major modification, it cannot be used by anyone other than the lessee.

economic life The time period or units of output during which the asset is expected to be economically usable.

lease payments Payments over the lease term that the lessee makes to the lessor, including: fixed payments; variable payments that depend on an index or rate; the exercise price of a BPO; and in certain circumstances, penalties for early termination of the lease. For the lessor, lease payments normally include residual value guarantees. For the lessee, lease payments include the amount expected to be paid out under residual value guarantees.

The foregoing indicators, individually or together, normally constitute sufficient evidence that substantially all the risks and rewards of ownership have transferred. *Thus, if one or more of these factors are present, the lessor will normally classify the lease as a finance lease.*

IFRS 16 also provides an additional three indicators to assist lessors in determining how to classify the lease. The presence of one or more of these factors, which are not as conclusive as the first five, *may* warrant the lessor classifying the lease as a finance lease:

1. The lessee can cancel the lease, but if it does so, it is responsible for the lessor's losses arising from the cancellation.
2. The lessee enjoys the benefit but suffers the loss from fluctuations in the fair value of the residual value of the leased asset.
3. The lessee can renew the lease for a further period at a rate substantially lower than the market rate.

[7] Even in this case, however, the transfer of risks and rewards is not absolute as the useful life is just an estimate. The actual useful life could turn out to be substantially more or less than 20 years.

IFRS acknowledges that the foregoing criteria may not always be conclusive. In these limited circumstances, professional judgement must be exercised in determining how the lessor should classify the lease.

a. Rationale as to why the supporting indicators confirm that substantially all the risks and rewards of ownership have transferred

These indicators augment the general criteria and help to determine whether there is a transfer of the risks and rewards of ownership from the lessor to the lessee. Regarding the first indicator, if there is an automatic transfer of ownership then clearly the lessee bears the risks and rewards of ownership. Likewise, a bargain purchase option has the same effect: the lessee is almost certain to exercise the option given that the asset can be purchased at a price below market. We can think of a bargain purchase option as providing a future transfer of ownership, since the likelihood of eventual ownership, while not 100%, is still very high.

The third and fourth indicators capture leases that do not have clear-cut transfers of ownership. Instead, they identify cases when there are, *in substance*, transfers of economic risks and rewards.

Some believe that the fifth indicator, which is not included in ASPE, is superfluous as presumably a rational, profit-motivated lessor will structure the lease in a manner that ensures that it will earn its required rate of return without having to retake possession of the specialized asset. As such, at least one of the other indicators, for example the present value of the lease payments or the economic life test, would normally be met.

To illustrate the manner in which a lease is analyzed for classification purposes, suppose that on January 1, 2019, Marianne RMT Corp. purchased drafting equipment for $60,000 cash and immediately leased it for the three years ending December 31, 2021, to Eli Inc. Eli made a payment of $8,000 when it took delivery of the equipment, and is required to make payments of $9,500 each on January 1, 2020, and January 1, 2021.

Other pertinent information:

- The equipment is non-specialized and can be used by other entities without significant modification.
- At the end of the lease term, Eli Inc. must return the equipment to Marianne RMT Corp.
- The economic life of the equipment is estimated to be 10 years.
- The expected **residual value** of the equipment is $0.
- Both companies have a December 31 year end.
- Marianne RMT Corp. paid $3,000 cash for equipment maintenance on June 30, 2020.
- Marianne RMT Corp. depreciates all equipment on a straight-line basis.
- The present value of the lease payments (PVLP) using Marianne RMT Corp.'s expected rate of return on transactions of this nature is approximately $24,000.

residual value The estimated value of the asset at the end of the asset's economic (useful) life.

The terms of the lease must be analyzed to determine whether Marianne RMT Corp. should classify this lease as an operating or finance lease as set out in Exhibit 17-5.

Exhibit 17-5 Analysis of Marianne RMT Corp. lease transaction

Criteria	Analysis
Transfer of title	Not met—asset returned to lessor
Bargain purchase option (BPO)	Not met—BPO not indicated
Economic life	Not met—3 years / 10 years = 30%
Present value of the lease payments (PVLP)	Not met—$24,000 / $60,000 = 40%
Specialized asset	Not met—not specialized
Conclusion – Marianne RMT Corp. should classify this lease as an operating lease.	

Having determined that the equipment leased to Eli Inc. should be classified as an operating lease, Marianne RMT Corp. will prepare journal entries throughout the term of the lease as set out in Exhibits 17-6a to 17-6c in the next section.

CHECKPOINT **CP17-3**

What is the key issue in the accounting for leases from the lessor's perspective?

3. Additional considerations for classification of real estate leases

Leases of real estate can include the lessor renting out a parcel of land, for use as say a parking lot, or of land and building for use as say an office.

A lease of land and buildings has two elements: the rental of the land and the rental of the buildings. Unless the amount of the land element is immaterial to the lease,[8] the lessor must separately determine whether the lease of the land and the lease of the buildings is an operating lease or a financing lease.

For leases of land and buildings, the lessor assesses whether the building lease is a finance lease or an operating lease in the same manner described for other assets. For leases of short duration in relation to the expected life of the buildings, and in the absence of a transfer of title or a BPO, building leases will usually be accounted for as operating leases. The land element of a "land and buildings" lease is assessed in the same manner as a stand-alone parcel of land.

For leases of land, the third criterion based on time is largely irrelevant because land has an indefinite economic life.[9] Similarly, the fifth criterion is not relevant to land, as land is not a specialized asset. The fourth criterion relating to the present value of the lease will seldom be met—the present value of land leases will seldom approach 75% of the land value because of the indefinite life of land and the substantial residual value at the end of the lease. Therefore, in the absence of a transfer of title or a BPO, leases of land will normally be accounted for as an operating lease.

Perusal of some of Canada's largest commercial landlords' financial statements confirms that the lessors all classify their leases of land and buildings as operating leases.

D. ACCOUNTING FOR OPERATING LEASES—LESSOR

The IFRS requirements for accounting for operating leases from the lessor's perspective are relatively straightforward. They include the following:

- Irrespective of the timing of the cash flows, income earned from operating leases is normally recognized on the statement of comprehensive income on a straight-line basis over the term of the lease.[10]

---

8. The basis of conclusions BCZ247 accompanying IFRS 16 establishes that for purpose of this determination that the allocation of the lease payments is weighted to reflect their role in compensating the lessor, and not by reference to the relative fair value of the land and buildings. Further discussion of this highly technical aspect is beyond the scope of this text.

9. Up until 2009, IFRS previously stated that a land lease would normally be classified as an operating lease. This guidance was removed, however, and replaced with a statement that in determining whether the land element is an operating lease or finance lease, an important consideration is that land normally has an indefinite economic life. The guidance was changed to allow for extreme circumstances such as a 999-year lease of land and buildings. Further discussion of this aspect is beyond the scope of this text.

10. Paragraph 81 of IFRS 16 provides that revenue can be recognized on either a straight-line or other systematic basis if the latter is more representative of the pattern of use of the leased asset.

- Costs incurred to earn the lease income (e.g., maintenance, insurance, and depreciation) are expensed in the normal manner.
- Costs associated with negotiating and arranging the lease are initially added to the carrying amount of the asset (capitalized) and subsequently recognized as an expense over the lease term on the same basis as lease income.
- The lessor reports assets leased out under operating leases on its statement of financial position in the same manner as similar assets acquired for the company's own use.
- Assets under operating leases are depreciated or amortized over their useful lives in the same manner as those held for the company's own use.[11]

We will now use the facts considered in the analysis in Exhibit 17-5 in the previous section to prepare the journal entries over the life of the lease for Marianne RMT Corp.'s lease of drafting equipment to Eli Inc. The journal entries appear in Exhibits 17-6a to 17-6c.

Exhibit 17-6a Journal entries to record Marianne RMT Corp.'s lease-related transactions during 2019

January 1, 2019		
Dr. Property, plant, and equipment (drafting equipment)	60,000	
Cr. Cash		60,000
Dr. Cash	8,000	
Dr. Lease receivable	1,000	
Cr. Lease revenue		9,000
December 31, 2019		
Dr. Depreciation expense—drafting equipment	6,000	
Cr. Accumulated depreciation—drafting equipment		6,000

Revenue is typically recognized on a straight-line basis over the lease term irrespective of the payment schedule (($8,000 + ($9,500 × 2)) / 3 = $9,000 per year). Assets are depreciated in the same manner as those used by the company in its own operations (($60,000 − 0) / 10 = $6,000 per year, straight-line).

Exhibit 17-6b Journal entries to record Marianne RMT Corp.'s lease-related transactions during 2020

January 1, 2020		
Dr. Cash	9,500	
Cr. Lease receivable		500
Cr. Lease revenue		9,000
June 30, 2020		
Dr. Maintenance and repair expense	3,000	
Cr. Cash		3,000
December 31, 2020		
Dr. Depreciation expense—drafting equipment	6,000	
Cr. Accumulated depreciation—drafting equipment		6,000

11. Typically, depreciation or amortization of the leased asset will be governed by IAS 16—Property, Plant and Equipment or IAS 38—Intangible Assets.

Repairs and maintenance expenses are recognized in the same manner as those that relate to assets used by the company in its own operations.

Exhibit 17-6c Journal entries to record Marianne RMT Corp.'s lease-related transactions during 2021

January 1, 2021		
Dr. Cash	9,500	
Cr. Lease receivable		500
Cr. Lease revenue		9,000
December 31, 2021		
Dr. Depreciation expense—drafting equipment	6,000	
Cr. Accumulated depreciation—drafting equipment		6,000

Exhibit 17-7 summarizes the lessor's accounting for operating leases.

Exhibit 17-7 Summary of lessor's journal entries for operating leases

Operating lease—lessor	
Timing	**Journal entries**
At start of lease	None required unless lease payment received
During lease	Lease payments received Revenue recognition* Depreciation/amortization Maintenance and repair expense
At end of lease	None required

* The amount of revenue may differ from the lease payments received. Revenue is typically recognized on a straight-line basis over the lease term irrespective of the payment schedule.

E. ACCOUNTING FOR FINANCE LEASES—LESSOR

Exhibit 17-8 summarizes the analysis that the lessor conducts as a prelude to determining how to account for a given lease.

First determine whether the lease is an operating lease or financing lease. The process used to make this decision was discussed in Section C above.

Exhibit 17-8 Decision tree for lease classification for lessor

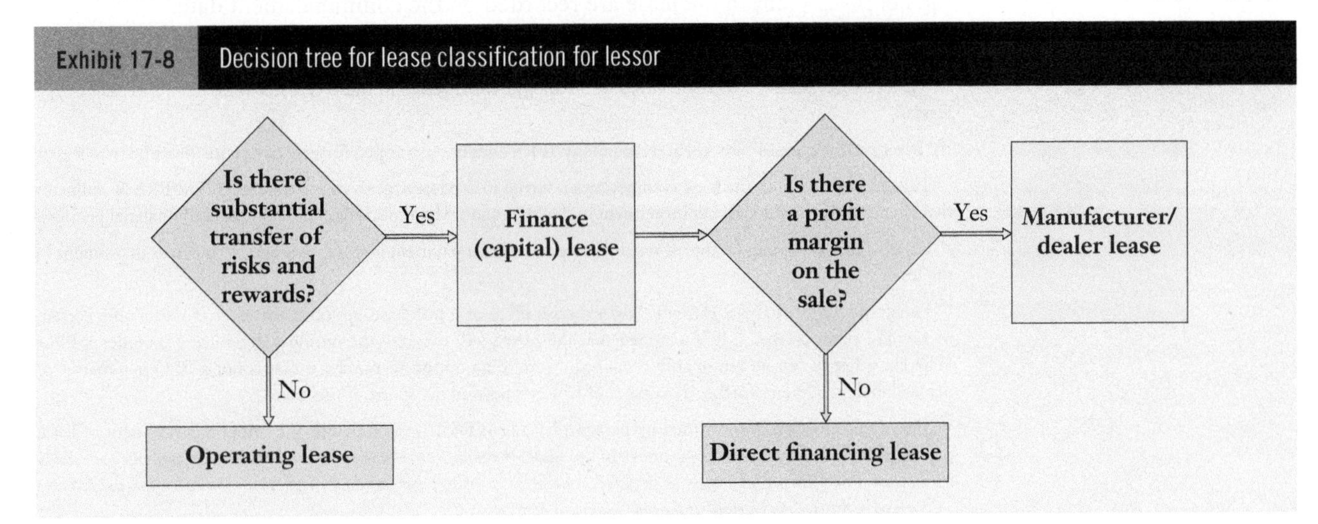

manufacturer/dealer lease A lease offered by the lessor as a financing mechanism to facilitate the sale of its own products.

direct financing lease A lease offered by a finance company or other lender. The lessor does not have a prior interest in the asset to be leased; rather, it purchases the asset at fair value and leases it out immediately. In the absence of initial direct costs, the lessor's carrying amount of the leased property is the same as its fair value at the commencement of the lease.

If the lease is a finance lease, the initial accounting for the lease is affected by whether there is a profit margin on the sale of the asset. Since a finance lease for a lessor is treated as a sale of the asset (plus a financing arrangement), there is potentially a profit margin on that sale. If there is a profit margin, the lease is a **manufacturer/dealer lease.**[12] If the sale price is equal to the cost of the asset to the lessor, then the lease is a **direct financing lease.**[13]

For example, a car dealership offering a long-term lease arrangement would have a profit margin on the sale and finance income over the life of the lease. In contrast, a finance company such as GE Capital that acts solely as a financial intermediary and does not take possession of the leased property (such as an aircraft) would usually not have a profit margin. Rather, its earnings consist of the finance incomes over the life of the lease. In other words, the profit margin is usually associated with the seller bearing some risk of holding inventory.

1. Recognition and initial measurement

net investment in the lease The gross investment in the lease discounted using the interest rate implicit in the lease. Each payment within the gross investment, which is the total of the lease payments receivable under a finance lease and any unguaranteed residual value, must be discounted to reflect the risk and timing of the related cash flow. The net investment in the lease is also referred to as a *lease receivable.*

gross investment in the lease The undiscounted lease payments receivable plus the undiscounted unguaranteed residual value of the leased asset.

unguaranteed residual value The expected value of the leased asset that will be returned to the lessor at the end of the lease term that is not guaranteed by the lessee or an outside party.

commencement date of the lease The date that the leased asset is first available to the lessee.

For manufacturer/dealer leases, the lessor recognizes a sale of the asset under lease, accounted for in the same manner as the lessor accounts for outright sales.

Irrespective of whether the lease is a manufacturer/dealer lease or a direct financing lease, on the commencement date, the lessor recognizes an asset on its statement of financial position equal to its **net investment in the lease**. The net investment in the lease[14] is the discounted value of **gross investment in the lease**, which consists of the *receivable* arising from the lease payments described below, together with the undiscounted value of any **unguaranteed residual value.**[15]

Lease payments include the following cash flows:

- fixed payments less lease incentives;
- certain variable lease payments;
- any guaranteed residual value of the asset;
- the exercise price of a bargain purchase option[16]; and
- some penalties for terminating the lease.

It is important to note that the gross investment in the lease includes lease payments *receivables*.[17] As such, the initial measurement of the net investment in the lease excludes payments made before, or on the same day as the **commencement date of the lease**, which is the date on which the leased asset is first available for use by the lessee. As such, any deposits made by the lessee to secure delivery of the asset or, more commonly, payments made on the first day of the lease, are excluded from this calculation.

This requirement does not create any special challenges. Rather, it is something that accountants need to be aware of as it affects the way that journal entries to recognize the net investment in the lease are recorded on the commencement date.

12. Manufacturer/dealer leases are IFRS terminology. ASPE refers to these types of transactions as "sales-type leases."

13. "Direct finance leases" are ASPE terminology. IFRS does not use a specific term to denote direct finance leases.

14. The net investment in the lease is sometimes referred to as a lease receivable; paragraph 67 of IFRS 16 indicates that a receivable equal to the net investment in the lease should be reported on the statement of financial position.

15. For sake of clarity, unguaranteed residuals are not a lease payment but are included in the gross investment in the lease.

16. Paragraph 70(d) of IFRS 16 reads "the exercise price of a purchase option if the lease is reasonably certain to exercise that option…". It is assumed that the lessee will exercise the option when a lease includes a BPO. Whether a lessee can be reasonably certain to exercise an option to purchase that is not a BPO is a matter of professional judgement, further discussion of which is beyond the scope of this text.

17. This determination is confirmed by paragraph 70 of IFRS 16 which details the initial measurement of lease payments included in the net investment in the lease. It reads *"At the commencement date, the lease payments included in the measurement of the net investment in the lease comprise the following payments for the right to use the underlying asset during the lease term that are not received at the commencement date"*.

Fixed lease payments are the amount stipulated in the lease contract that are paid on a regular basis (e.g., monthly or annually) for the right to use the underlying asset. The payment includes in-substance fixed lease payments[18] but excludes lease incentives and consideration for any **non-lease components** included in the lease contract.[19]

non-lease components Include services provided for or arranged by the lessor that would be purchased by the lessee independent of whether the lessee had purchased or leased the asset. The lessor excludes payments for non-lease components from the fixed payment amount when calculating the total lease payments, accounting for the non-lease component separately.

A lease incentive is a payment made by the lessor to the lessee as an incentive to enter into the lease contract or to reimburse the lessee for costs incurred. For example, a lessor reimbursing the lessee for $5,000 in legal costs associated with reviewing the lease document would be an example of a lease incentive. Similarly, a $20,000 signing bonus paid to the lessee for entering into the lease would be a lease incentive.

Non-lease components[20] include services provided by the lessor that would be purchased by the lessee independent of whether the lessee had purchased or leased the asset. For example, a lease contract that requires the lessee to pay a certain amount to the lessor on a regular basis to repair and maintain the leased property is a non-lease component. Such maintenance costs would be incurred whether the lessee bought or leased the property. The lessor excludes payments for non-lease components from the fixed payment amount when calculating the total lease payments, accounting for the non-lease component separately. ASPE includes these items in its definition of executory costs.

Amounts paid by the lessee to the lessor for services provided by outside suppliers (e.g., property taxes or insurance) that the lessor purchases or pays for on behalf of the lessee are also excluded from the fixed payment amount. The reason for this exclusion is that it does not meet the definition of a fixed payment, as the amount paid is for something other than the right to use the underlying asset. These amounts are also excluded from the total lease payments and are accounted for separately. ASPE includes these items in its definition of executory costs.

Variable lease payments are lease payments where the amount may change depending on facts or circumstances occurring after the commencement date of the lease. For example, leases of retail space often include a requirement that the lessee pay the lessor a percentage of its sales; the variable amount required to be paid depends on future sales, which are not known until after the commencement date. Variable lease payments are only included in the lease payment and net investment in the lease if they are linked to a rate or an index (e.g., the overnight money market financing rate or the commodity price index). The lessor recognizes variable lease payments that are not linked to a rate or an index (e.g., percentage of retail sales), in income when earned.

Section B discussed the economics behind leasing arrangements, with an emphasis on the agency costs of leasing. Among the various tools that can be used to mitigate moral hazard is the use of a residual value guarantee. By agreeing to provide a guarantee that the leased property will be worth at least a certain amount at the end of the lease, the lessee assures the lessor that the property will be treated with due care, since the lessee is responsible for compensating the lessor for any shortfall.

Since the lessor is assured of receiving the guaranteed amount (or more), the guaranteed residual value is included in the lease payments. Note, however, that if the lease contract includes both a BPO and a guaranteed residual, only the BPO is included in the lease payments. The guaranteed residual is not usually relevant as it is assumed that the BPO will be exercised and the ROU asset will be retained by the lessee.

---

18. In-substance fixed lease payments are payments that appear to be variable but in fact are fixed and unavoidable. Further discussion of in-substance fixed lease payments is beyond the scope of this text.

19. The lessor allocates revenue to the lease and non-lease components on the contract based on the guidance in IFRS 15—Revenue from Contracts with Customers pertaining to allocating the transaction price to the performance obligations. Recall from Chapter 4 that this allocation is made on the observable or estimated relative standalone selling prices of the performance obligations.

20. ASPE does not use the term non-lease component; rather, it refers to executory costs, which are costs related to the operation of the leased property, citing examples of insurance, property taxes, and maintenance costs. Executory costs are excluded from the determination of the lessor's fixed lease payment.

By its nature, a BPO is almost certain to be exercised. As a result, the lessee's cost of exercising the option is another cash flow that the lessor expects to receive from the lessee, and therefore the BPO is included in the lease payments.

Penalties for terminating the lease are only included if the lessee is expected to exercise its option to cancel. In this respect, some lease contracts allow the lessee to cancel the lease providing that it pays a cancellation penalty. For example, the lease may be for four years with a mandatory renewal term of three years. If the lease provides that the lessee may cancel the lease at the end of the original four-year term, and if the lessee is expected to exercise its option to cancel, then the termination penalty will be included in the lease payments.[21]

Unguaranteed residual values are not included in the lease payments as the lessee is not responsible for ensuring that the lease asset is worth this amount, and is not obligated to make any additional payments to the lessor regardless of the eventual value of the leased property. The amount expected to be realized from the leased asset, however, is included in the gross investment in the lease and the present value of the unguaranteed residual is included in the net investment in the lease.

a. Initial direct costs

Initial direct costs are outlays by the lessor, other than a manufacturer/dealer lessor, that are directly attributable to arranging and negotiating the lease. Examples of initial direct costs include legal fees, realtor commissions, and internal costs excluding general overhead. The accounting treatment of costs associated with arranging and negotiating a lease is described below:

- Direct finance leases—costs that are attributable to arranging and negotiating the lease meet the IFRS definition of initial direct costs (IDC). Paragraph 69 of IFRS 16 requires that IDCs be included in the initial measurement of the net investment in the lease and they reduce the amount of (interest) income recognized over the lease term.[22]
- Manufacturer/dealer leases—costs that are attributable to arranging and negotiating the lease *do not* meet the IFRS definition of initial direct costs. Therefore, the costs are *not* included in the net investment in the lease. Rather, they are expensed in the same period as sales revenue is recognized following the normal "matching" principle.

Exhibit 17-9 summarizes the components of lease payments, and the gross and net investment in the lease when accounting for the lessor.

To confirm the manner in which leases are analyzed for classification purposes, and to demonstrate the accounting for various finance leases, suppose that on January 1, 2019, J. L. Hornstein Inc. (JLH) purchased a customized dental X-ray machine for $230,000 from Taj Singh Ltd. (TSL) and immediately leased it for nine years to Canaan Dental Corp. (CDC). The equipment could not be used elsewhere without significant modification. Pertinent details follow:

- Payments are due annually with the first payment due on January 1, 2019.
- CDC has the option to purchase the equipment for $10,000 at the end of the lease. The estimated residual value at that time is $20,000.

---

21. Further discussion of penalties for cancelling the lease is beyond the scope of this text.

22. (Fair value of asset + initial direct costs) = (each lease payment discounted using the implicit rate of interest + unguaranteed residual discounted using the implicit rate of interest). All other things being equal, if there are IDCs, by definition,* the implicit rate of interest, and hence interest income, will be lower than that in the absence of IDCs. The practical outcome of this is that the initial direct costs have been "charged" (used to reduce) interest income. Further discussion of this point is beyond the scope of the text.

*In the presence of IDCs, the value of the left side of the equation will be higher than otherwise. To preserve the equality, the value of the right side of the equation must be increased by the same amount. As the lease payments and the unguaranteed residual are fixed, the only way to achieve a higher value for the right side of the equation is to decrease the discount rate used (the implicit rate of interest in the lease).

Exhibit 17-9 Lease payment summary—accounting for the lessor

Lease payments	Gross investment in lease	Net investment in lease*
Fixed payments less: lease incentives and non-lease components	Lease payments receivable	Present value of the remaining individual payments included in the lease payments
+	+	+
Variable lease payments (some, not all)	Unguaranteed residual value	Present value of the unguaranteed residual value
+	=	+
Guaranteed residual value of the asset (unless bargain purchase option)	Gross investment in lease	Unamortized initial direct costs (direct finance leases only)[23]
+		=
Bargain purchase option		Net investment in lease
+		
Penalties for terminating the lease (some, not all)		
=		
Lease payments		

*. The interest rate implicit in the lease is used to discount each remaining payment in the lease, together with the unguaranteed residual back to the commencement date, to determine the net investment in the lease at initial recognition. Similarly, the implicit rate in the lease is used to discount the remaining payments and the unguaranteed residual back to the statement of financial position (SFP) date to determine the net investment in the lease at the SFP date.

- The fair value of the equipment is $230,000.
- The economic life of the equipment is 10 years.
- JLH's required rate of return for transactions of this nature, exclusive of initial direct costs, is 7%.
- JLH paid its account manager a $3,000 commission for arranging the lease.
- All companies have December 31 year ends.

The terms of the lease first must be analyzed to determine whether JLH should classify this lease as an operating or finance lease as shown in Exhibit 17-10a.

Exhibit 17-10a Analysis of customized dental X-ray machine lease transaction

Criteria	Analysis
Transfer of title	Not met—asset returned to lessor
Bargain purchase option	Met—$10,000 purchase option is a bargain, given the $20,000 estimated residual value
Economic life	Met—9 years / 10 years = 90%
Present value of lease payments	Met—$229,999* / $230,000 = 100%
Specialized asset	Met—specialized equipment

*Using a financial calculator:

2ND BGN 2ND SET 2ND QUIT 9 N 7 I/Y 230000 +/− PV 10000 FV CPT PMT → PMT = 32,212 (rounded)†;

2ND BGN 2ND SET 2ND QUIT 9 N 7 I/Y 32212 PMT 10000 FV CPT PV → PV = −229,999 (rounded)

†The lessor will always structure the lease so that it expects to recover 100% of the fair value of the asset plus its required rate of return on the lease receivable.

Conclusion: JLH should classify this lease as a direct finance lease.

23. The mechanics of exactly how initial direct costs (IDCs) are included in the net investment in the lease is a very complex topic, a full discussion of which is beyond the scope of this text. For expositional purposes, we have explicitly included IDCs in the computation of the net investment in the lease. While the process used in the text differs slightly from the manner detailed in IFRS 16, the end result is the same, and, as importantly, tends to be more easily understood by accounting students.

As this is a direct finance lease, the journal entries at the commencement date of the lease, ignoring the purchase of the equipment, will be recorded as shown in Exhibit 17-10b.

Exhibit 17-10b Direct finance lease—lessor journal entries at commencement date (January 1, 2019)

January 1, 2019		
Dr. Net investment in lease (lease receivable) ($230,000 − $32,212)	197,788	
Dr. Cash	32,212	
Cr. Equipment		230,000
Dr. Net investment in lease (initial direct costs)	3,000	
Cr. Cash		3,000

For reasons previously explained, the net investment in the lease at the commencement date is $200,788 comprised of the $230,000 present value of the lease payments less the $32,212 payment made on the commencement date plus the $3,000 in IDCs. It is not $233,000.

As this is a direct finance lease, the initial direct costs are added to the net investment in the lease. Thus for subsequent measurement purposes we need to calculate the **interest rate implicit in the lease**, which will differ from the interest rate used by the lessor to determine the required payment. Using a financial calculator: **2ND** **BGN** **2ND** **SET** **2ND** **QUIT** 9 **N** 233000* **+/−** **PV** 10000 **FV** **PMT** 32212, **CPT** **I/Y** → I/Y = 6.6250% (rounded) (*$230,000 PVLP + $3,000 initial direct costs = $233,000).

interest rate implicit in the lease The rate of interest that causes the present value of (a) the lease payments and (b) the unguaranteed residual value to equal the sum of (i) the fair value of the underlying asset and (ii) any initial direct costs of the lessor. In the absence of initial direct costs, this will be the discount rate used by the lessor in determining the payments in the lease.

It is important to note that the implicit rate of interest is determined based on the present value of the lease payments (and the unguaranteed residual), rather than the present value of the lease payment receivable used to determine the net investment in the lease.

To illustrate the difference between the recognition and initial measurement of direct finance leases and manufacturer/dealer leases, assume that TSL manufactured the equipment at a cost of $200,000 and then leased the asset directly to CDC. The analysis of the lease carried out in Exhibit 17-10a remains largely unchanged. The conclusion needs to be amended to indicate that TSL should classify the lease as a manufacturer/dealer lease, however, as TSL is now using the lease to facilitate the sale of its own products and earns a profit on the sale. The journal entries at the commencement date of the lease will be recorded as shown in Exhibit 17-11.

Exhibit 17-11 Manufacturer/dealer lease—lessor journal entries at commencement date (January 1, 2019)

January 1, 2019		
Dr. Net investment in lease (lease receivable) ($230,000 − $32,212)	197,788	
Dr. Cash	32,212	
Cr. Sales		230,000
Dr. Cost of goods sold	200,000	
Cr. Inventory		200,000
Dr. Sales commission	3,000	
Cr. Cash		3,000

Note that, as this is a manufacturer/dealer lease, the sales commission is expensed in the same period that the sales proceeds are recognized.

b. Unguaranteed residual values in manufacturer/dealer leases

When the lessor leases an asset that includes an unguaranteed residual value, its net investment in the lease includes the present value of the lease payments and the present value of the unguaranteed residual value. Sales revenue, though, is recognized at the lower of the asset's fair value and the present value of the lease payments. The rationale for this approach is that the unguaranteed residual should not be included in the transaction price as it is a form of variable consideration.[24] The profit on sale remains the same, however, as the reduction in sales revenue is offset by decreasing the cost of goods sold by the same amount, normally the present value of the unguaranteed residual.

Refer to the fact pattern used for Exhibit 17-11 and amend this information to reflect a situation in which CDC does not have an option to purchase the equipment at the end of the lease term; rather, the unguaranteed residual is $10,000. The journal entries required to recognize the lease can then be compared to those in Exhibit 17-11 to contrast the difference between the recognition and initial measurement of a sale that includes a BPO to one that includes an unguaranteed residual.

An updated version of the analysis of the lease carried out in Exhibit 17-10a is shown in Exhibit 17-12a.

Exhibit 17-12a Analysis of the lease transaction with no option to purchase

Criteria	Analysis
Transfer of title	Not met—asset returned to lessor
Bargain purchase option	Not met—no purchase option
Economic life	Met—9 years / 10 years = 90%
PVLP	Met—$224,559* / $230,000 = 97.6%
Specialized asset	Met—specialized equipment

*Using a financial calculator: **2ND** **BGN** **2ND** **SET** **2ND** **QUIT** 9 **N** 7 **I/Y** 32212 **PMT** 0 **FV** **CPT** **PV** → PV = −224,559 (rounded)

We can confirm that the present value of the $10,000 unguaranteed residual = $229,999 − $224,559 = $5,440. Using a financial calculator: **2ND** **BGN** **2ND** **SET** **2ND** **QUIT** 9 **N** 7 **I/Y** 10000 **FV** **CPT** **PV** → PV = −5,439 (rounded) or more simply 9 **N** 7 **I/Y** 10000 **FV** **CPT** **PV** → PV = −5,439 (small difference due to rounding).

Having confirmed the amount to be deducted from both the sale amount and the cost of goods sold, we can now prepare the journal entries at the commencement date of the lease, as shown in Exhibit 17-12b.

Exhibit 17-12b Manufacturer/dealer lease unguaranteed residual—lessor journal entries at commencement date (January 1, 2019)

January 1, 2019		
Dr. Net investment in lease (lease receivable) ($230,000 − $32,212)	197,788	
Dr. Cash	32,212	
Dr. Cost of goods sold ($200,000 − $5,440)	194,560	
Cr. Sales ($230,000 − $5,440)		224,560
Cr. Inventory		200,000
Dr. Sales commission	3,000	
Cr. Cash		3,000

24. The unguaranteed residual does not meet the definition of a lease payment as it is a form of variable consideration that is not linked to a rate or an index.

Note how only the sales and cost of goods sold amounts recognized have changed from the previous example, and that they have both been reduced by $5,440, which is the present value of the unguaranteed residual.

As previously indicated, it is important that the lessor structure the lease in a manner that allows it to recoup the fair value of the asset and earn its required rate of return on the lease receivable. A critical step in this process is calculating the required lease payment once the rest of the lease terms have been agreed upon. The example that follows demonstrates the method of determining the required lease payment under various scenarios, as well as the initial recognition of the lease transaction. While not every conceivable circumstance is covered, the situations are sufficiently diverse that you should gain a strong understanding on how to determine the required lease payment and how to recognize the lease asset on the commencement date.

Suppose that on January 1, 2019, Rachel Corp. leased an asset to Daniel Inc. for five years. The fair value of the equipment, which could not be used elsewhere without significant modification, was $250,000. The estimated economic life of the equipment is six years. Rachel Corp.'s required rate of return on leases is 5%. Daniel Inc.'s incremental borrowing cost (IBC) is 6%. Both companies have a December 31 year end.

Scenario 1

- Rachel Corp. is a finance company and the lease is a direct financing lease.
- Payments are due annually with the first payment due on the commencement date of the lease.
- Daniel Inc. has an option to purchase the asset at the end of the lease term for $20,000. The estimated residual value at that time is $30,000.
- Daniel Inc. does not know the interest rate implicit in the lease.

Scenario 2

- Rachel Corp. is a finance company and the lease is a direct financing lease.
- Payments are due annually with the first payment due on December 31, 2019.
- Daniel Inc. provides a residual value guarantee of $35,000.
- Daniel Inc. expects to pay out $5,000 on the residual value guarantee.
- Daniel Inc. knows the interest rate implicit in the lease.

Scenario 3

- Rachel Corp. is a finance company and the lease is a direct financing lease.
- Payments are due annually with the first payment due on the commencement date of the lease.
- The lease contract provides that Rachel Corp. will maintain the asset during the life of the lease. Rachel Corp. normally charges $3,000 per year for this service, which is a non-lease component. Rachel Corp. adds $3,000 to the payment for the lease component calculated in the normal manner and includes the total amount in the lease contract.
- Daniel Inc. does not elect to adopt the practical expedient available to it regarding accounting for the lease component and related non-lease component as a single lease component.[25]
- Ownership of the asset transfers automatically to Daniel Inc. at the end of the lease term.
- Daniel Inc. does not know the interest rate implicit in the lease.

Scenario 4

- Rachel Corp. is a manufacturer and the lease is a manufacturer/dealer lease.
- The asset cost Rachel Corp. $200,000 to manufacture.
- Payments are due annually with the first payment due on December 31, 2019.

25. Practical expedients available to the lessee and how to account for them are discussed in Section G.

- Daniel Inc. has an option to purchase the asset at the end of the lease term for $10,000. The estimated residual value at that time is $15,000.
- Daniel Inc. pays its lawyers $2,000 to review the lease documents. The $2,000 paid is an initial direct cost (IDC).
- Daniel Inc. knows the interest rate implicit in the lease.

Scenario 5

- Rachel Corp. is a manufacturer and the lease is a manufacturer/dealer lease.
- The asset cost Rachel Corp. $190,000 to manufacture.
- Payments are due annually with the first payment due on the commencement date of the lease.
- The unguaranteed residual value of the asset is $25,000.
- Daniel Inc. does not know the interest rate implicit in the lease.

As the leased asset cannot be used elsewhere without significant modification, the lease in each of the five scenarios is a finance lease. While it is good practice to fully analyze the terms of the lease in the manner demonstrated in Exhibit 17-10a, we have omitted this step in the analysis, as it is not the point of this example. The process for determining the fixed lease payment and recognizing the lease transaction is illustrated in Exhibit 17-13.

Exhibit 17-13 Lessor determining the fixed lease payment and recognizing the lease transaction for Scenarios 1 to 5

Scenario 1—lessor determining the fixed lease payment

Using a financial calculator: 2ND BGN 2ND SET 2ND QUIT 5 N 5 I/Y 250000 +/– PV 20000 FV CPT PMT → PMT = 51,547 (rounded).

Rationale: Payments are at the beginning of the period first due on the commencement date; lessor uses required rate of return to determine the lease payments; BPO expected to be exercised ($20,000 option price versus $30,000 expected residual value).

Scenario 1—lessor recognition

January 1, 2019

Dr. Net investment in lease (lease receivable) ($250,000 – $51,547)	198,453	
Dr. Cash	51,547	
Cr. Equipment		250,000

Scenario 2—lessor determining the fixed lease payment

Using a financial calculator: 5 N 5 I/Y 250000 +/– PV 35000 FV CPT PMT → PMT = 51,410 (rounded).

Rationale: Payments are at the end of the period; lessor uses required rate of return to determine the lease payments; lessor includes full amount of guaranteed residual.

Scenario 2—lessor recognition

January 1, 2019

Dr. Net investment in lease (lease receivable)	250,000	
Cr. Equipment		250,000

Scenario 3—lessor determining the fixed lease payment

Using a financial calculator: 2ND BGN 2ND SET 2ND QUIT 5 N 5 I/Y 250000 +/– PV 0 FV CPT PMT → PMT = 54,994 (rounded). Stipulated payment = $54,994 + $3,000 = $57,994.

Rationale: Payments are at the beginning of the period first due on the commencement date; lessor uses required rate of return to determine the lease payments; ownership transfers to lessee at end of lease term; the $3,000 for maintenance is a non-lease component that the lessor must account for separately.

(Continued)

Exhibit 17-13 Continued

Scenario 3—lessor recognition		
January 1, 2019		
Dr. Net investment in lease (lease receivable) ($250,000 – $54,994)	195,006	
Dr. Cash	57,994	
Cr. Equipment		250,000
Cr. Service revenue[26]		3,000

Scenario 4—lessor determining the fixed lease payment

Using a financial calculator: 5 N 5 I/Y 250000 +/– PV 10000 FV CPT PMT → PMT = 55,934 (rounded).

Rationale: Payments are at the end of the period; lessor uses required rate of return to determine the lease payments; BPO expected to be exercised ($10,000 option price versus $15,000 expected residual value); IDCs pertain to lessee, not lessor.

Scenario 4—lessor recognition		
January 1, 2019		
Dr. Net investment in lease (lease receivable) ($250,000 – $55,934)	194,066	
Dr. Cash	55,934	
Cr. Sales		250,000
Dr. Cost of goods sold	200,000	
Cr. Inventory		200,000

Scenario 5—lessor determining the fixed lease payment

Using a financial calculator: 2ND BGN 2ND SET 2ND QUIT 5 N 5 I/Y 250000 +/– PV 25000 FV CPT PMT → PMT = 50,685 (rounded).

Rationale: Payments are at the beginning of the period including commencement date; lessor uses required rate of return to determine the lease payments; unguaranteed residual included in net investment in the lease.

Scenario 5—lessor determining the present value of the unguaranteed residual

Using a financial calculator: 2ND BGN 2ND SET 2ND QUIT 5 N 5 I/Y 25000 FV CPT PV → PV = –19,588 (rounded); or more simply 5 N, 5 I/Y, 25000 FV, CPT PV → PV = –19,588

Rationale: Unguaranteed residual deducted from both sales and cost of goods sold.

Scenario 5—lessor recognition		
January 1, 2019		
Dr. Net investment in lease (lease receivable) ($250,000 – $50,685)	199,315	
Dr. Cash	50,685	
Dr. Cost of goods sold ($190,000 – $19,588)	170,412	
Cr. Sales ($250,000 – $19,588)		230,412
Cr. Inventory		190,000

2. Subsequent measurement

Finance income is recognized by the lessor using the effective interest method (discussed in Chapters 7 and 12), as IFRS 16 requires income to be recognized on a basis that results in a constant periodic rate of return on the lessor's net investment in the

[26] Technically this is revenue received in advance and could be credited to a liability account. We have prepared the journal entry in this way as the revenue will be earned during the year. In real life, a company will either credit all such amounts to revenue or revenue received in advance. It will then make the necessary adjustments at period end to ensure that revenue earned and the remaining revenue received in advance liability are properly reported on its statement of comprehensive income and statement of financial position.

lease.[27] For lessors, the effective interest rate is the interest rate implicit in the lease. Finance income is recognized using the following formula:

> Finance income for the period = net investment in the lease × the effective rate of interest (the interest rate implicit in the lease) × number of months in period / 12

The way that manufacturer/dealer leases and direct financing leases are subsequently measured is virtually the same and this similarity is unaffected by unguaranteed residual values.[28] From a practical perspective, it is beneficial to use an Excel spreadsheet to create an amortization chart to track the net investment in the lease and other important information. To demonstrate the process, we return to the J. L. Hornstein Inc. example that formed the basis for the analysis in Exhibits 17-10a to 17-12b.

The Excel spreadsheet in Exhibit 17-14a is based on the facts used to prepare the journal entries for Exhibit 17-10b upon initial recognition of the lease. It has been included to illustrate how a spreadsheet can be used to track information that is needed to properly account for finance leases.

Exhibit 17-14a Direct financing lease—lessor spreadsheet based on facts used in Exhibit 17-10b

				Notes:
Present value of lease payments			$230,000	
Less: payment made at commencement date			32,212	
Lease receivable			$197,788	
Unguaranteed residual			0	
Initial direct costs			3,000	
Net investment in lease			$200,788	
Implicit rate of interest in lease			6.6250%	1
Date	**Payment**	**Finance income**	**Net investment in lease**	
01/01/2019			$200,788	
12/31/2019		$13,302	214,090	
01/01/2020	32,212		181,878	
12/31/2020		12,049	193,928	
01/01/2021	32,212		161,716	
12/31/2021		10,714	172,429	
01/01/2022	32,212		140,217	
12/31/2022		9,289	149,507	
01/01/2023	32,212		117,295	
12/31/2023		7,771	125,065	
01/01/2024	32,212		92,853	
12/31/2024		6,152	99,005	
01/01/2025	32,212		66,793	
12/31/2025		4,425	71,218	

(Continued)

27. This is the amortized value of the net investment in the lease. It will decline each period as payments are received. The amortized balance is easily tracked using an Excel spreadsheet.

28. IFRS 16 mandates that unguaranteed residuals be regularly reviewed. If the residual value declines, the decrease is accounted for prospectively as a change in estimate in the manner described in Chapter 19.

Exhibit 17-14a	Continued			
Date	**Payment**	**Finance income**	**Net investment in lease**	
01/01/2026	32,212		39,006	
12/31/2026		2,584	41,590	
01/01/2027	32,212		9,378	
12/31/2027		621	10,000	
01/01/2028	10,000		0	2
Total	$267,696	$66,907		

1. When there are initial direct costs, the implicit interest rate must be calculated. From before, using a financial calculator: **2ND** **BGN** **2ND** **SET** **2ND** **QUIT** 9 **N** 233000 **+/–** **PV** 10000 **FV** 32212 **PMT** **CPT** **I/Y** → I/Y = 6.6250% (rounded)
2. Exercise of purchase option
Small differences due to rounding

This information can be used as a basis for preparing the required journal entries throughout the lease term. To illustrate, the information on the spreadsheet in Exhibit 17-14a has been used to prepare the journal entries in Exhibit 17-14b, namely, the entry on December 31, 2019, to accrue finance income and January 1, 2020, to record the receipt of the lease payment:

Exhibit 17-14b	Direct financing lease—subsequent measurement journal entries	
December 31, 2019		
Dr. Net investment in lease (lease receivable)	13,302	
Cr. Finance income		13,302
January 1, 2020		
Dr. Cash	32,212	
Cr. Net investment in lease (lease receivable)		32,212

Note that the accrued interest is added to the net investment in the lease account, rather than debited to an interest receivable or similar account.

You can also determine the balance of the net investment in the lease at a given point in time by using a financial calculator. For example, on December 31, 2021, there are six years remaining on the lease. Using a financial calculator: **2ND** **BGN** **2ND** **SET** **2ND** **QUIT** 6 **N** 6.6250 **I/Y** 32212 **PMT** 10000 **FV** **CPT** **PV** → PV = −172,430. Note how this amount matches the December 31, 2021, balance of the net investment in the lease of $172,429 on the spreadsheet in Exhibit 17-14a (small difference due to rounding).

By way of contrast, Exhibit 17-15a shows the spreadsheet based on the facts used to prepare the journal entries upon initial recognition in Exhibit 17-11.

Exhibit 17-15a	Manufacturer/dealer lease—lessor spreadsheet based on facts used in Exhibit 17-11	
		Notes:
Present value of lease payments	$230,000	
Less: payment made at commencement date	32,212	
Lease receivable	$197,788	
Unguaranteed residual	0	
Initial direct costs	0	
Net investment in lease	$197,788	
Implicit rate of interest in lease	7.0%	

(Continued)

Exhibit 17-15a Continued

Date	Payment	Finance income	Net investment in lease	Notes:
01/01/2019			$197,788	
12/31/2019		$13,845	211,633	
01/01/2020	32,212		179,421	
12/31/2020		12,559	191,981	
01/01/2021	32,212		159,769	
12/31/2021		11,184	170,952	
01/01/2022	32,212		138,740	
12/31/2022		9,712	148,452	
01/01/2023	32,212		116,240	
12/31/2023		8,137	124,377	
01/01/2024	32,212		92,165	
12/31/2024		6,452	98,617	
01/01/2025	32,212		66,405	
12/31/2025		4,648	71,053	
01/01/2026	32,212		38,841	
12/31/2026		2,719	41,560	
01/01/2027	32,212		9,348	
12/31/2027		652	10,000	
01/01/2028	10,000		0	1
Total	$267,696	$69,908		

1. Exercise of purchase option
Small differences due to rounding

Again, for illustrative purposes, we used the information from the spreadsheet in Exhibit 17-15a to prepare the journal entries in Exhibit 17-15b. The journal entry on December 31, 2019, is to accrue finance income and the journal entry on January 1, 2020, is to record the receipt of the lease payment.

Exhibit 17-15b Manufacturer/dealer lease—subsequent measurement journal entries

December 31, 2019		
Dr. Net investment in lease (lease receivable)	13,845	
Cr. Finance income		13,845
January 1, 2020		
Dr. Cash	32,212	
Cr. Net investment in lease (lease receivable)		32,212

Items of note:

- In both examples, finance income is calculated using the same formula: Net investment in the lease × Interest rate implicit in the lease = Finance income.
- In the first example (the direct financing lease), the 6.625% implicit rate of interest differs from the 7.0% required return due to the inclusion of initial direct costs in the net investment in the lease.

- In the first example (the direct financing lease), the finance income realized in each period is less than that earned in the second example (the manufacturer/dealer lease); for example, $13,302 versus $13,845 for the year ended December 31, 2019. The difference represents part of the $3,000 sales commission that is indirectly being charged to finance income, over the life of the lease, through a reduction in the implicit rate of interest in the lease.
- In the first example (the direct financing lease), the total finance income realized over the life of the lease is $66,908, which is $3,000 less than the $69,907 earned in the second example (the manufacturer/dealer lease). Recall, though, that in the second example we expensed the $3,000 sales commission at the time of sale as this was a manufacturer/dealer lease. As such, the finance income earned less the sales commission paid to earn that revenue is the same for both leases ($66,608 = $69,907 − $3,000) (small difference due to rounding).

3. Derecognition

Practically speaking, the net investment in the lease is usually derecognized (removed from the statement of financial position) at the end of the lease term. The process of derecognition is the same as that prescribed for other financial assets governed by IFRS 9—Financial Instruments, discussed in Chapter 7. Recall that when a financial asset was derecognized, the difference between the net book value of the asset (its carrying cost) and the consideration received was recognized in profit or loss.

For leases, there are various possibilities that need to be considered:

1. The lease includes a provision that the title of the asset transfers to the lessee at the end of the lease term, or includes an option to purchase and the option is exercised.
   - The consideration received by the lessor equals the carrying value of the asset; there is no need to recognize a gain or loss on derecognition.
2. At the end of the lease term, the lessee returns the asset to the lessor.
   - The lessor recognizes the asset in accordance with IAS 16—Property, Plant and Equipment or IAS 38—Intangible assets.
     - Upon disposition, if the consideration received exceeds the carrying cost of the asset, the lessor recognizes a gain on derecognition.
     - Upon disposition, if the consideration received is less than the carrying cost of the asset, the lessor recognizes a loss on derecognition, unless the value of the asset is guaranteed. In the latter instance, as the lessee or third-party guarantor is required to cover the shortfall, the total consideration received by the lessor equals the carrying value of the asset and, as such, there is no need to recognize a loss on derecognition.

Exhibit 17-16 summarizes the lessor's accounting for finance leases.

Exhibit 17-16 Summary of lessor's journal entries for finance leases

Finance lease—lessor		
Timing	Journal entries	
	Direct finance lease	Manufacturer/dealer lease
At start of lease	Disposition of asset	Revenue recognition (sales price − cost of goods sold)
	Recognize net investment in lease (lease receivable)	Recognize net investment in lease (lease receivable)
	Lease payment received, if applicable	Lease payment received, if applicable
During lease	Lease payments received	Lease payments received
	Finance income	Finance income
At end of lease	Depends on terms of lease	Depends on terms of lease

4. Lessor's preference for classifying leases as finance leases rather than operating leases

Contrast the accounting under the operating and finance lease methods. If you were the lessor, which classification would you prefer and why? Lessors generally prefer to classify leases as finance leases. Reasons for this include:

- On the statement of financial position, a non-monetary item (inventory or capital asset) is converted to a monetary item (loan receivable), which is generally considered to be more liquid.
- On the statement of comprehensive income, any profit from the asset sale is recognized immediately.
- In the early years of a lease, the finance income earned from a finance lease will usually be more than the net of lease revenue less depreciation for an operating lease. This outcome is illustrated in Exhibit 17-17, which is based on the facts in the Spyjet example in Section B.

Exhibit 17-17 Comparison of the income stream from leases based on the Spyjet example in Section B

Finance lease	
Finance income (($30 million − $3.203 million) × 10%)	$2.680 million
Operating lease	
Lease revenue	$3.203 million
Depreciation ($30 million cost straight-line over 20 years)	1.500 million
Revenue net of expense for operating lease	$1.703 million

This effect reverses later in the lease for the lessor as finance income decreases over time as the loan balance is partially repaid each year. While, over the life of the lease, the cumulative net income under both lease treatments is exactly the same, management usually prefers to report income sooner rather than later.

CHECKPOINT **CP17-4**

Why do the supporting indicators for lease classification use "major part" and "substantially all" rather than "all" in reference to the amount of time and value contained in the lease?

F. PRESENTATION AND DISCLOSURE OF LEASES—LESSOR

L.O. 17-5. Apply the presentation and disclosure requirements applicable to leases—lessors.

1. Presentation

The lessor needs to determine the current and non-current portions of its lease receivables as the two parts must be reported separately on the company's statement of financial position. As previously noted, the total (current plus non-current) lease receivable equals the net investment in the lease.

The simplest way to make this classification is to understand that the lease receivable reflects the financing component of the lease. For the lease receivable, the current amount is the principal due within a year, plus any interest that has been accrued up to the year end (but not any interest to be incurred in the future). This will be the same amount as the lease payment *only if* the lease payment date falls on the first day of the next fiscal year as in the illustration in Exhibit 17-18. The exhibit reconciles the amounts that Mitchell Co. should present on its statement of financial position on December 31, 2020.

Exhibit 17-18 Determining the current and non-current portions of lease receivables

Lessor—Mitchell Co.	Annual lease payment*	Finance income @ 12%	Ending balance of lease receivable
12/31/2019			$50,000
12/31/2020	$12,830	$4,460	**41,631**
12/31/2021	**12,830**	3,456	32,257
12/31/2022	12,830	2,331	21,758
12/31/2023	12,830	1,071	10,000
Presentation by Mitchell Co. on December 31, 2020			
Current portion of lease receivable (for payment due in 2021)			$12,830
Non-current lease receivable†			28,801
Total lease receivable			$41,631

*Payments on the lease are due January 1 each year

†Total lease receivable − current portion of lease receivable = non-current lease receivable

This example has payments occurring immediately following the fiscal year end. In all other instances, the amount in current receivables will be smaller. In the extreme case where the next lease payment occurs at the end of the next fiscal year, then the current portion of the lease is only the amount of the principal portion of the payment in the following year (which excludes the interest portion of that payment).

2. Disclosure

Leases potentially bind lessors for many years. Consequently, accounting standards require significant disclosures so that users can understand to what extent and how a company has used leases. Exhibit 17-19 summarizes some of the more important disclosures. For a complete list of disclosures, the reader should refer to IFRS 16.

Exhibit 17-19 Summary of lessor disclosure requirements for leases

Operating leases	■ Lease income for the period arising from operating leases. ■ Lease payments to be received for each of the first five years and the total of the amounts to be received for the remaining years. These amounts are not adjusted for time value of money.
Finance leases	■ Lease income for the period arising from finance leases segregated into its component parts (e.g., any profit on sale of assets, finance income on the net investment in the lease, and variable lease payments not included in the net investment in the lease). ■ Lease payments to be received for each of the first five years and the total of the amounts to be received for the remaining years. These amounts are not adjusted for time value of money. ■ A reconciliation of the net investment in finance leases to the undiscounted lease payments to be received. Unearned finance income and any discounted unguaranteed residual values must be identified.

G. ACCOUNTING FOR LEASES—LESSEE

L.O. 17-3. Apply the appropriate accounting method for lessees' right-of-use assets.

IFRS 16 requires the lessee to account for the lease contract in the same manner irrespective of whether the lessor accounts for the lease as an operating lease or finance lease.[29] Lessees must employ a capitalization approach in which they recognize a right-of-use asset and a lease liability for virtually all leases.

The IASB did provide limited exceptions to the capitalization approach, referred to as **practical expedients**, which permit lessees to adopt simplified rules of accounting for leases. These practical expedients, discussed in Topic 7 below are permitted as the IASB wanted to provide options to ensure that the cost of providing the required accounting information does not exceed the benefit to the users of that information.

practical expedient An alternative method of accounting that simplifies the accounting for a given transaction. Practical expedients are made available in limited circumstances as a measure to protect against the cost of providing the accounting information exceeding the benefit provided by that same information.

1. Recognition and initial measurement of lease liabilities

The lessee's liability for a lease at any point in time is the present value of the lease payments not yet made. The lease liability initially recognized consists of the present value of the lease payments that have not yet been paid at the commencement date of the lease,[30] which is the date on which the leased asset is first available for use by the lessee. Lease payments include:

- fixed payments less lease incentives;
- certain variable lease payments;
- the amount, if any, expected to be paid out under residual value guarantees;
- the exercise price of a bargain purchase option;[31] and
- some penalties for terminating the lease.

The discussion that follows provides some background on these items.

Fixed lease payments are the amount stipulated in the lease contract that are paid on a regular basis (e.g., monthly or annually) for the right to use the underlying asset. These payments include in-substance fixed lease payments[32] but exclude lease incentives and consideration for any non-lease components included in the lease contract.

Non-lease components include services provided by the lessor that would be purchased by the lessee independent of whether the lessee had purchased or leased the asset. For example, a lease contract that requires the lessee to pay some amount to the lessor on a regular basis to repair and maintain the leased property is a non-lease component. The maintenance costs would be incurred whether the lessee bought or leased the property. Non-lease costs are normally *excluded* from the fixed payment amount, although lessees can elect to adopt a practical expedient that permits them to include the related non-lease components in the lease payment rather than separately account for them (see Topic 7 below).

Amounts paid by the lessee to the lessor for services provided by outside suppliers (e.g., property taxes or insurance) that the lessor purchases or pays for on behalf of the lessee are also excluded from the fixed payment amount. The reason for this exclusion

29. ASPE still makes a distinction between operating and finance leases for lessees. This aspect is addressed in the Substantive Differences outlined in Section J of this chapter.

30. This determination is confirmed by paragraph 26 of IFRS 16, which details the initial measurement of lease payments included in the lease liability. It reads *"At the commencement date, a lessee shall measure the lease liability at the present value of the lease payments that are not paid at that date."*

31. Paragraph 70(d) of IFRS 16 reads "the exercise price of a purchase option if the lease is reasonably certain to exercise that option…". It is assumed that the lessee will exercise the option when a lease includes a BPO. Whether a lessee can be reasonably certain to exercise an option to purchase that is not a BPO is a matter of professional judgement, further discussion of which is beyond the scope of this text.

32. In-substance fixed lease payments are payments that appear to be variable but in fact are fixed and unavoidable. Further discussion of in-substance fixed lease payments is beyond the scope of this text.

is that it does not meet the definition of a fixed payment, as the amount paid is for something other than the right to use the underlying asset. These amounts are also excluded from the total lease payments and are accounted for separately. ASPE collectively describes services provided by outside suppliers and non-lease components as executory costs.

Variable lease payments are lease payments where the amount may change depending on facts or circumstances occurring after the commencement date of the lease. For example, leases of retail space often include a requirement that the lessee pay the lessor a percentage of its sales; the variable amount required to be paid depends on future sales, which are not known until after the commencement date. Variable lease payments are only included in the lease payment and lease liability if they are linked to a rate or an index (e.g., the overnight money market financing rate or the commodity price index). The lessee recognizes variable lease payments that are not linked to a rate or an index (e.g., percentage of retail sales) as an expense when incurred.

Residual value guarantees are guarantees made by the lessee to the lessor that the value of the leased asset at the end of the lease will be greater than or equal to the guaranteed amount. The lessee includes only amounts that it expects to payout under residual value guarantees in its determination of lease payments, rather than the full amount of the guarantees.[33] The underlying rationale for including only the present value of amounts expected to be paid out under residual value guarantees in the lease liability is described below:

THRESHOLD CONCEPT
CONCEPTUAL FRAMEWORK

The IFRS Conceptual Framework (discussed in Chapter 2) notes that a substantial degree of estimation is required to measure some liabilities. Obligations of this nature, including warranties and contingent liabilities (discussed in Chapter 11) are reported on the statement of financial position at their estimated amount. The requirement that lessees include the amount expected to be paid out under the residual guarantee is entirely consistent with the approach used to value other provisions.[34]

As the lessee is not responsible for paying any unguaranteed residual value that the lessor may include in its valuation of its net investment in the lease, the lessee *does not* include unguaranteed residuals in its determination of the lease payments.

Bargain purchase options (BPO) allow the lessee to purchase leased assets at a price below their expected market value at the end of the lease. The exercise price of a BPO is included as a lease payment as it is expected that the option will be exercised. If the lease includes both a BPO and a residual value guarantee, the amount expected to be paid out under the guarantee is $0 given the expectation that the lessee will gain title to the asset, rather than return it to the lessor.

Penalties for terminating the lease are only included if the lessee is expected to exercise its option to cancel. In this respect, some lease contracts allow the lessee to cancel the lease providing that it pays a cancellation penalty. For example, the lease may be for four years with a mandatory renewal term of three years. If the lease provides that the lessee may cancel the lease at the end of the original four-year term, and if the lessee expects to exercise its option to cancel, then it will include the termination penalty in the lease payments.[35]

incremental borrowing rate The interest rate that the lessee would have to pay on a similar lease or loan.

The interest rate used to discount the lease payments is the implicit interest rate in the lease, if readily determinable; otherwise, the lessee uses its **incremental borrowing rate**—the interest rate that the lessee would have to pay on a similar lease or loan. A discussion of the rationale for this requirement follows.

33. This differs from the lessor which includes the present value of the full amount of the guarantee in its net investment in the lease.

34. Recall from Chapter 11 that provisions include liabilities of uncertain amounts.

35. Further discussion of penalties for cancelling the lease is beyond the scope of this text.

a. Interest rate used by the lessee in present-value calculations

Finance theory suggests that the appropriate discount/interest rate is the risk-adjusted rate. However, there is some uncertainty as to the type of risk that should be factored into this rate: the risk associated with the asset being leased, or the risk of the lessee? Ideally, both types of risk should be considered.

How does one quantify these risks and risk-adjusted interest rates? First, note that a rational lessor should factor in risks of both the asset and the risk of the lessee in setting the terms of the lease, especially the lease payments. Thus, we can infer the appropriate risk-adjusted interest rate from the cash flow stream expected by the lessor and the fair value of the leased property; this is called the *interest rate implicit in the lease,* or simply the "implicit rate," as first mentioned in Section B. The lessor should always be able to determine this rate, so *the lessor must use the implicit rate.* The *lessee,* on the other hand, may not always have sufficient information to calculate the implicit rate. For example, it may not know the lessor's initial direct costs and/or the residual value that the lessor expects to realize from the right-of-use asset at the end of the lease term. In this case, under IFRS, the lessee uses its incremental borrowing rate. Thus, under IFRS, the interest rate for the lessee is determined on a hierarchical basis: use the implicit rate if available; otherwise, use the incremental rate.

2. Recognition and initial measurement of right-of-use assets

The lessee initially measures its right-of-use asset (ROU asset) at cost. This approach is conceptually the same as for the initial measurement of property, plant, and equipment discussed in Chapter 8. However, whereas the purchase of property, plant, and equipment usually involves a single payment, the nature of a lease involves a number of payments over time, and therefore determining the cost of a ROU asset is somewhat more complex. Conceptually, the cost of a ROU asset is the present value of payments necessary to "acquire" the ROU asset and to "dispose" of it at the end of the lease.[36] Technically, IFRS 16 defines the cost of an ROU asset as the sum of the following components:

- the initial measurement of the lease liability;
- lease payments made at or before the commencement date of the lease, less any lease incentives received;
- any initial direct costs incurred by the lessee; and
- the estimated costs of decommissioning and site restoration obligations.

You may find it more intuitive, though to calculate the cost of as ROU asset as follows:

- the present value of the lease payments; plus
- any initial direct costs incurred by the lessee; plus
- the estimated costs of decommissioning and site restoration obligations, less
- lease incentives received.

The discussion that follows provides some background on these items.

The present value of the lease liability (PVLP) includes all payments due under the lease. It can differ from the lease liability initially recognized as the PVLP includes any deposits made prior to delivery and payments made on the first day of the lease. Payments made on or before commencement date are also included in the determination of the cost of the ROU asset. From a practical perspective, in the absence of initial direct costs, the cost of the ROU asset usually equals the PVLP.

---

36. Legally, title does not transfer to the lessee, so "acquire" and "dispose" are only in the economic sense, not in the legal sense.

Initial direct costs (IDCs) are the incremental costs of obtaining a lease that were incurred to obtain the lease. Examples include legal fees and realtor commissions.

The nature of decommissioning and site restorations costs was discussed in Chapters 8 and 12. Recall that when the acquisition of an asset includes an obligation to incur the future costs of dismantling and removing the asset, and/or restoring the installation site to a predefined condition, the present value of the estimated decommissioning cost is added to the cost of the asset.

Lease incentives are payments made by the lessor to the lessee as an incentive to enter into the lease contract or to reimburse the lessee for costs incurred. Caution must be exercised as the nature of the reimbursement dictates its accounting treatment:

- If the lessee is reimbursed for costs included in the ROU asset, such as initial direct costs, then the lease incentive is deducted from the cost of the ROU asset. An example of this would be the lessor reimbursing the lessee for the lessee's cost of having its lawyers reviewing the lease contract.
- If the lessee is reimbursed for expenditures not included in the ROU asset, then the incentive is accounted for in accordance with other relevant standards. For example, if the lessor reimbursed the lessee for the cost of moving to its newly leased premises, then the monies received would offset the related moving expense.

Unlike ASPE, IFRS does not impose a "fair value ceiling" on the amount that can be recognized as a ROU asset. Thus, it is possible that the amount recognized as an ROU asset by the lessee will exceed its fair value.[37] This may occur if the lessee discounts the lease payments using an incremental borrowing rate that is lower than the implicit rate in the lease, or if it adopts the practical expedient to report the lease and related non-lease components as a single lease component.

3. Applying the recognition and initial measurement criteria for right-of-use assets and lease liabilities

Upon commencement of the lease, the lessee initially measures and recognizes a ROU asset and lease liability given the terms stipulated in the lease contract. The following example demonstrates how to record these entries on the commencement date. The illustration that follows is based on the information used in Exhibit 17-13. For ease of reference, the key points have been replicated here, including the required lease payment.

Suppose that on January 1, 2019, Rachel Corp. leased an asset to Daniel Inc. for five years. The fair value of the equipment, which could not be used elsewhere without significant modification, was $250,000. The estimated economic life of the equipment is six years. Rachel Corp.'s required rate of return on leases is 5%. Daniel Inc.'s incremental borrowing cost is 6%. Both companies have a December 31 year end.

Scenario 1

- Rachel Corp. is a finance company and the lease is a direct financing lease.
- Payments of $51,547 are due annually with the first payment due on the commencement date of the lease.
- Daniel Inc. has an option to purchase the asset at the end of the lease term for $20,000. The estimated residual value at that time is $30,000.
- Daniel Inc. does not know the interest rate implicit in the lease.

Scenario 2

- Rachel Corp. is a finance company and the lease is a direct financing lease.
- Payments of $51,410 are due annually with the first payment due on December 31, 2019.

37. The equity section of the lessee is not affected by the amount initially recognized. The valuation of the ROU asset is determined by the (simplified) formula: lease liability at initial recognition + lease payment on or before commencement date = ROU asset. As the lease liability and ROU asset, at initial recognition, move in tandem, equity is not affected.

- Daniel Inc. provides a residual value guarantee of $35,000.
- Daniel Inc. expects to pay out $5,000 on the residual value guarantee.
- Daniel Inc. knows the interest rate implicit in the lease.

Scenario 3

- Rachel Corp. is a finance company and the lease is a direct financing lease.
- Payments of $57,994 are due annually with the first payment due on the commencement date of the lease. The $57,994 includes the $3,000 for the non-lease component described below.
- The lease contract provides that Rachel Corp. will maintain the asset during the life of the lease. Rachel Corp. normally charges $3,000 per year for this service, which is a non-lease component.
- Daniel Inc. does not elect to adopt the practical expedient available to it regarding accounting for the lease component and related non-lease component as a single lease component.
- Ownership of the asset transfers automatically to Daniel Inc. at the end of the lease term.
- Daniel Inc. does not know the interest rate implicit in the lease.

Scenario 4

- Rachel Corp. is a manufacturer and the lease is a manufacturer/dealer lease.
- The asset cost Rachel Corp. $200,000 to manufacture.
- Payments of $55,934 are due annually with the first payment due on December 31, 2019.
- Daniel Inc. has an option to purchase the asset at the end of the lease term for $10,000. The estimated residual value at that time is $15,000.
- Daniel Inc. pays its lawyers $2,000 to review the lease documents. The $2,000 paid is an initial direct cost (IDC).
- Daniel Inc. knows the interest rate implicit in the lease.

Scenario 5

- Rachel Corp. is a manufacturer and the lease is a manufacturer/dealer lease.
- The asset cost Rachel Corp. $190,000 to manufacture.
- Payments of $50,685 are due annually with the first payment due on the commencement date of the lease.
- The unguaranteed residual value of the asset is $25,000.
- Daniel Inc. does not know the interest rate implicit in the lease.

Exhibit 17-20 shows how the lessee initially measures and recognizes these five lease transactions.

Exhibit 17-20 Lessee recognizing the lease transaction in Scenarios 1 to 5

Scenario 1—lessee determining the ROU asset and lease liability

Using a financial calculator[38]: **2ND** **BGN** **2ND** **SET** **2ND** **QUIT** 5 **N** 6 **I/Y** 51547 **PMT** 20000 **FV** **CPT** **PV** → PV = −245,108 (rounded). Lease liability $245,108 − $51,547 = $193,561; ROU asset = $245,108.

Rationale: Payments are at the beginning of the period first due on the commencement date; the lessee uses IBC as the implicit rate in the lease is not known; and the BPO is expected to be exercised ($20,000 option price versus $30,000 expected residual value).

(Continued)

[38] As there is a future value to consider, you cannot calculate the present value of the liability immediately after receiving the first payment by simply adjusting the remaining payments (e.g., **2ND** **BGN** **2ND** **SET** **2ND** **QUIT** 4 **N** 6 **I/Y** 51547 **PMT** 20000 **FV** **CPT** **PV** → PV = −205,175 (rounded)), rather than the correct answer of $193,561. While there are other ways to correctly calculate the present value of the liability, the method illustrated in this exhibit is the most straightforward, and will be used throughout the text and supporting materials.

Exhibit 17-20 Continued

Scenario 1—lessee recognition		
January 1, 2019		
Dr. ROU asset	245,108	
Cr. Lease liability		193,561
Cr. Cash		51,547

Scenario 2—lessee determining the ROU asset and lease liability

Using a financial calculator: 5 N 5 I/Y 51410 PMT 5000 FV CPT PV → PV = −226,496 (rounded). Lease liability = $226,496; ROU asset = $226,496.

Rationale: Payments are at the end of the period; lessee uses implicit rate since it is known; and the lessee includes the amount expected to be paid out under the guaranteed residual.

Scenario 2—lessee recognition		
January 1, 2019		
Dr. ROU asset	226,496	
Cr. Lease liability		226,496

Scenario 3—lessee determining the ROU asset and lease liability

Using a financial calculator: 2ND BGN 2ND SET 2ND QUIT 5 N 6 I/Y 54994 PMT 0 FV CPT PV → PV = −245,554 (rounded). Lease liability $245,554 − $54,994 = $190,560; ROU asset = $245,554.

Rationale: Payments are at the beginning of the period first due on the commencement date; the payment must be segregated into its lease and non-lease components ($57,994 − $3,000 = $54,994); and the lessee uses IBC as implicit rate in the lease is not known.

Scenario 3—lessee recognition		
January 1, 2019		
Dr. ROU asset	245,554	
Dr. Maintenance expense	3,000	
Cr. Lease liability		190,560
Cr. Cash		57,994

Scenario 4—lessee determining the ROU asset and lease liability

Using a financial calculator: 5 N 5 I/Y 55934 PMT 10000 FV CPT PV → PV = −250,000 (rounded). Lease liability = $250,000; ROU asset = $250,000 + $2,000 = $252,000.

Rationale: Payments are at the end of the period; lessee uses implicit rate since it is known; BPO expected to be exercised ($10,000 option price versus $15,000 expected residual value); IDCs included in ROU asset.

Scenario 4—lessee recognition		
January 1, 2019		
Dr. ROU asset	252,000	
Cr. Lease liability		250,000
Cr. Cash (payment of initial direct costs)		2,000

Scenario 5—lessee determining the ROU asset and lease liability

Using a financial calculator: 2ND BGN 2ND SET 2ND QUIT 5 N 6 I/Y 50685 PMT 0 FV CPT PV → PV = −226,314 (rounded). Lease liability $226,314 − $50,685 = $175,629; ROU asset = $226,314.

Rationale: Payments are at the beginning of the period first due on the commencement date; the lessee uses IBC as implicit rate in the lease is not known; and the lessee does not include unguaranteed residuals in the lease payments as lessee is not responsible for payment of non-guaranteed amounts.

Scenario 5—lessee recognition		
January 1, 2019		
Dr. ROU asset	226,314	
Cr. Lease liability		175,629
Cr. Cash		50,685

You may wish to compare the amounts initially recognized by the lessee in Exhibit 17-20 to those of the lessor in Exhibit 17-13, which were determined based on the same fact patterns. It should be readily apparent that the lessee's lease liability usually differs from the lessor's net investment in the lease. This is to be expected as while there are many similarities in the procedures followed to determine these two amounts, there are distinct differences as well. They are independent processes that are governed by different rules.

CHECKPOINT **CP17-5**

How would you describe the lessee's approach to accounting for leases in general terms?

4. Subsequent measurement of lease liabilities

Subsequent to the commencement date, the lessee must re-measure the two statement of financial position items that arise from lease contracts: the ROU asset and the corresponding lease liability.

Lease liabilities are subsequently measured at amortized cost using the effective interest method in the same manner as other financial liabilities discussed in Chapter 12. For lessees, the effective rate of interest is the same rate used to measure the lease liability initially: the implicit rate, if readily determinable by the lessee, or else the incremental borrowing rate. Interest expense is recognized using the following formula:

> Interest expense for the period = Opening lease liability × The effective rate of interest × Number of months in period / 12.

Re-measurements: Lease liabilities need to be re-measured if lease payments change from those originally envisaged. These changes can be due to reassessments or modifications of the lease. Briefly, a reassessment occurs when the variable lease consideration differs from that originally estimated and a modification of the lease transpires when the lessor and lessee agree to change the original terms. In both instances, the lease liability must be adjusted to reflect the amended payment stream and the ROU asset must be changed by the same amount. For example, if a lease modification results in the lease liability increasing by $3,000, the ROU asset would be increased by $3,000 as well.[39]

5. Subsequent measurement of right-of-use assets

Right-of-use assets will normally be subsequently measured using the cost model,[40] which is:

- its original cost,
- less accumulated depreciation,
- less accumulated impairment losses, and
- adjusted for re-measurements of the lease liability.

Recall from Chapter 8 that owned property, plant, and equipment subsequently valued using the cost model is valued at cost less accumulated depreciation less accumulated impairment losses, so the process for ROU assets is much the same. The primary

---

39. Further discussion of the details on how to determine the re-measurement amounts, and the resultant impact on the subsequent measurement of ROU assets and lease liabilities is beyond the scope of this text.

40. If the lessee applies IAS 40—Investment Property to its investment property, and the ROU asset meets the definition of investment property, then the lessee will subsequently measure the ROU asset using the fair value model discussed in Chapter 10. Moreover, at the lessee's option, ROU assets for which the lessee applies IAS 16—Property, Plant and Equipment can be subsequently measured using the revaluation model, also discussed in Chapter 10.

difference is the additional requirement to adjust for any re-measurements of the lease liability. This latter aspect was discussed briefly in the subsequent measurement of lease liabilities section above. As impairments and re-measurements occur infrequently, however, most ROU assets are subsequently measured at cost less accumulated depreciation.

While there is not a specific requirement to do so, most lessees depreciate the ROU asset using the straight-line method. The two aspects that must be considered are:

- What residual value should be used when determining the depreciable amount?

  and

- What is an appropriate depreciation period?

a. Depreciable amount

The depreciable amount of an asset is its cost less its residual value (see Chapter 8). The residual value is the value of the asset, less disposal costs, *that the entity expects to obtain* at the end of the asset's useful life. The italicized words are very important when determining an appropriate residual value for the lessee to use, as the lessee is only entitled to the residual value if it gains ownership of the asset at the end of the lease term. The practical outcome of this point follows:

- If the leased asset transfers to the lessee at the end of the lease term, either explicitly through a provision in the lease terms, or implicitly through the inclusion of a BPO, then the residual value at the end of the asset's useful life should be used to determine the ROU asset's depreciable amount. The rationale for this approach is that, since the lessee gains ownership of the asset, the lessee will be entitled to the residual.
- If the leased asset does not transfer to the lessee at the end of the lease term, then a residual value of $0 should be used to determine the ROU asset's depreciable amount. Since the lessee does not gain ownership of the ROU asset, the lessor, rather than the lessee, will realize the residual value. Note that a $0 residual should be used even if there is a residual value guarantee in place or if it is likely that there will be an unguaranteed residual.

b. Depreciation period

As explained in Chapter 8, the process of depreciation is a method of allocating the depreciable amount of the asset over its useful life, where useful life is defined as the period over which an asset is expected to be *available for use by the entity*. The requirement that ROU assets be depreciated over their period of expected use, as detailed below, is entirely consistent with this concept:

- When the lessee gains title to the asset at the end of the lease term, either explicitly through a provision in the lease terms or a BPO, then the period of expected use is the asset's useful life.
- If title does not transfer, the ROU asset is depreciated over the shorter of the lease term and its useful life. Since it is highly unusual to have a lease term that is longer than the useful life of the underlying asset, the ROU asset is normally depreciated over the lease term.

6. Applying the subsequent measurement criteria for right-of-use assets and lease liabilities

Having discussed the manner in which ROU assets and lease liabilities are to be subsequently measured, we now apply this knowledge to the first two scenarios initially measured in Topic 3 above. From a practical perspective, it is beneficial to use a spreadsheet to create an amortization chart to track the lease liability and other important information.

The Excel spreadsheet in Exhibit 17-21a is based on the facts used to prepare the journal entries in Scenario 1 in Exhibit 17-20 upon initial recognition of the ROU asset and lease liability. It has been included to illustrate how a spreadsheet can be used to track information that is needed to properly account for ROU assets and lease liabilities.

Exhibit 17-21a Lessee spreadsheet based on facts used in Scenario 1 in Exhibit 17-20

Scenario 1				Notes:
Present value of lease payments			$245,108	1
Less: payment made at commencement date			51,547	
Lease liability			$193,561	
Payment made at commencement date			51,547	
ROU asset			$245,108	
IBC as implicit rate not known			6.0%	
Date	**Payment**	**Interest expense**	**Lease liability**	
01/01/2019			$193,561	
12/31/2019		$11,614	205,175	
01/01/2020	$51,547		153,628	
12/31/2020		9,218	162,845	
01/01/2021	51,547		111,298	
12/31/2021		6,678	117,976	
01/01/2022	51,547		66,429	
12/31/2022		3,986	70,415	
01/01/2023	51,547		18,868	
12/31/2023		1,132	20,000	
01/01/2024	20,000		0	2
	$226,188	$32,628		

1. From before, **2ND** **BGN** **2ND** **SET** **2ND** **QUIT** 5 **N** 6 **I/Y** 20000 **FV** 51547 **PMT** **CPT** **PV** → PV = −245,108 (rounded)

2. Exercise of purchase option

Small differences due to rounding

Lease term (years)			5	
Economic life (years)			6	
Depreciate over economic life given BPO			6	
Date	**Depreciation expense**	**Accumulated depreciation**	**ROU asset**	
01/01/2019			$245,108	
12/31/2019	$40,851	$40,851	204,257	
12/31/2020	40,851	81,703	163,405	
12/31/2021	40,851	122,554	122,554	
12/31/2022	40,851	163,405	81,703	
12/31/2023	40,851	204,257	40,851	
12/31/2024	40,851	245,108	0	

Small differences due to rounding

Having prepared the spreadsheet to track Daniel Inc.'s ROU asset and lease liability in Scenario 1, we can now use this information to prepare the journal entries required at the company's December 31, 2019, year end, and receipt of the payment on January 1, 2020, as set out in Exhibit 17-21b.

Exhibit 17-21b Lessee subsequent measurement journal entries: Scenario 1 (December 31, 2019, and January 1, 2020)

Scenario 1—lessee subsequent measurement		
December 31, 2019		
Dr. Interest expense	11,614	
Cr. Lease liability*		11,614
Dr. Depreciation expense†	40,851	
Cr. Accumulated depreciation		40,851
*Note that interest expense is added to the lease liability, rather than crediting interest payable or a similar account in accordance with paragraph 36(a) of IFRS 16.		
†The ROU asset is depreciated over the estimated economic life of six years, rather than the lease term of five years as transfer of ownership is assumed since there is a BPO.		
January 1, 2020		
Dr. Lease liability	51,547	
Cr. Cash		51,547

The Excel spreadsheet in Exhibit 17-22a is based on the facts used to prepare the journal entries in Scenario 3 in Exhibit 17-20 upon initial recognition of the ROU asset and lease liability. It has been included to reaffirm how a spreadsheet can be used to track information that is needed to properly account for ROU assets and lease liabilities. Scenario 3 was chosen as it illustrates how the lessee accounts for non-lease components of the lease contract when it has not elected to adopt the practical expedient available to it regarding accounting for the lease component and related non-lease component as a single lease component. We will then use this example later in this section to contrast accounting for lease and related non-lease components separately and as a single lease component.

Exhibit 17-22a Lessee spreadsheet based on facts used in Scenario 3 in Exhibit 17-20

				Notes:
Present value of lease payments			$245,554	1
Less: payment made at commencement date			54,994	
Lease liability			$190,560	
Payment made at commencement date			54,994	
ROU asset			$245,554	
Lease payment ($57,994 − $3,000)			$54,994	2
IBC as implicit rate is not known			6.0%	
Date	**Payment**	**Interest expense**	**Lease liability**	
01/01/2019			$190,560	
12/31/2019		$11,434	201,994	
01/01/2020	$54,994		147,000	
12/31/2020		8,820	155,820	
01/01/2021	$54,994		100,826	
12/31/2021		6,050	106,875	

(Continued)

Exhibit 17-22a Continued

Date	Payment	Interest expense	Lease liability
01/01/2022	$54,994		51,881
12/31/2022		3,113	54,994
01/01/2023	$54,994		0
	$219,976	$29,417	

1. From before, 2ND BGN 2ND SET 2ND QUIT 5 N 6 I/Y 0 FV 54994 PMT CPT PV → PV = −245,554 (rounded)
2. Lease payments exclude payments for related non-lease components unless the lessee elects to adopt the practical expedient available to it.
Small differences due to rounding

Lease term (years)	5
Economic life (years)	6
Depreciate over economic life as ownership transfers (years)	6

Date	Depreciation expense	Accumulated depreciation	ROU asset
01/01/2019			$245,554
12/31/2019	$40,926	$40,926	204,628
12/31/2020	40,926	81,851	163,703
12/31/2021	40,926	122,777	122,777
12/31/2022	40,926	163,703	81,851
12/31/2023	40,926	204,628	40,926
12/31/2024	40,926	245,554	0

Small differences due to rounding

Having prepared the spreadsheet to track Daniel Inc.'s ROU asset and lease liability in Scenario 3, we can now use this information to prepare the journal entries required at the company's December 31, 2019, year end, and for the payment on January 1, 2020, as set out in Exhibit 17-22b.

Exhibit 17-22b Lessee subsequent measurement journal entries: Scenario 3 (December 31, 2019, and January 1, 2020)

Scenario 3—lessee subsequent measurement		
December 31, 2019		
Dr. Interest expense	11,434	
Cr. Lease liability*		11,434
Dr. Depreciation expense†	40,926	
Cr. Accumulated depreciation		40,926

*Interest expense is added to the lease liability, rather than crediting interest payable or a similar account.

†The ROU asset is depreciated over the estimated economic life of six years, rather than the lease term of five years as ownership transfers at the end of the lease term.

January 1, 2020		
Dr. Lease liability	54,994	
Dr. Maintenance expense[41]‡	3,000	
Cr. Cash		57,994

‡The non-lease component of the lease payment is accounted for separately.

[41] Technically this is a prepaid expense, the value of which will be used up by year end.

For expository purposes, we have included an additional Excel spreadsheet in Exhibit 17-23a. It is based on the facts used to prepare the journal entries in Scenario 4 in Exhibit 17-20 upon initial recognition of the ROU asset and lease liability. It differs from the previous two examples in that it includes lessee initial direct costs and the lease payment is at the end of the period.

Exhibit 17-23a Lessee spreadsheet based on facts used in Scenario 4 in Exhibit 17-20

				Notes:
Present value of lease payments			$250,000	1
Less: payment made at commencement date			0	
Lease liability			$250,000	
Initial direct costs			2,000	2
ROU asset			$252,000	
Interest rate implicit in lease is known			5.0%	
Date	**Payment**	**Interest expense**	**Lease liability**	
01/01/2019			$250,000	
12/31/2019		$12,500	262,500	
12/31/2019	$55,934		206,566	
12/31/2020		10,328	216,894	
12/31/2020	55,934		160,960	
12/31/2021		8,048	169,008	
12/31/2021	55,934		113,074	
12/31/2022		5,654	118,728	
12/31/2022	55,934		62,794	
12/31/2023		3,140	65,934	
12/31/2023	55,934		10,000	
12/31/2023	10,000		0	3
	$289,670	$39,670		

1. From before, 5 **N** 5 **I/Y** 10000 **FV** 55934 **PMT** **CPT** **PV** → PV = –250,000 (rounded)
2. Initial direct costs are added to the cost of the ROU asset
3. Exercise of BPO

Lease term (years)			5	
Economic life (years)			6	
Depreciate over economic life since there is a BPO (years)			6	
Date	**Depreciation expense**	**Accumulated depreciation**	**ROU asset**	
01/01/2019			$252,000	2
12/31/2019	$42,000	$42,000	210,000	
12/31/2020	42,000	84,000	168,000	
12/31/2021	42,000	126,000	126,000	
12/31/2022	42,000	168,000	84,000	
12/31/2023	42,000	210,000	42,000	
12/31/2024	42,000	252,000	0	

We can now use this information to prepare the journal entries required at the company's December 31, 2019, year end, as set out in Exhibit 17-23b.

Exhibit 17-23b Lessee subsequent measurement journal entries: Scenario 4 (December 31, 2019)

Scenario 4—lessee subsequent measurement		
December 31, 2019		
Dr. Interest expense	12,500	
Cr. Lease liability*,†		12,500
Dr. Lease liability†	55,934	
Cr. Cash		55,934
Dr. Depreciation expense‡	42,000	
Cr. Accumulated depreciation		42,000

*Interest expense is added to the lease liability, rather than crediting interest payable or a similar account.
†The journal entries to the lease liability could be combined for a net debit of $43,434 ($55,934 − $12,500).
‡The ROU asset is depreciated over the estimated economic life of six years, rather than the lease term of five years as transfer of ownership is assumed since there is a BPO.

7. Practical expedients

L.O. 17-4. Analyze a lease to determine whether practical expedients are available to lessees and, if available, apply the appropriate accounting methods.

As discussed above, the lessee normally accounts for leases by recognizing a right-of-use asset and a lease liability. In limited circumstances, however, IFRS permits the lessee to deviate from this approach and simply expense the entire lease payment. Additionally, lessees may elect to account for the lease and related non-lease components as a combined item, rather than accounting for them separately. These options are referred to as practical expedients.

a. The lessee may elect to expense short-term leases

Lessees may elect to expense short-term leases. Typically, the total expense for the lease is recognized as an expense using the straight-line method over the term of the lease.[42] A short-term lease is defined as one that, at the commencement date:

- has a maximum term of one year, including renewal options that the lessee is reasonably certain to exercise; and
- does not include an option to purchase. Note that this restriction includes all options to purchase, not just bargain purchase options.

As previously mentioned, the IASB offered an exemption to lessees from the normal capitalization requirements for short-term leases due to cost-benefit considerations. The IASB, though, clearly defined what constitutes "short-term" to restrict entities from structuring leases in a manner that allows them to elect to use the short-term practical expedient for leases that are, in substance, longer-term leases.

If a lessee elects to adopt the "short-term" practical expedient for a particular lease, it must adopt the expedient for all qualifying leases in that asset class (e.g., computers). However, the lessee is not required to adopt the expedient for dissimilar asset classes (e.g., if it adopts the expedient for computers, it need not adopt it for automobiles).

42. Another systematic basis should be used if it is more representative of the pattern of use of the leased asset.

Exhibit 17-24 contrasts a lessee's accounting for the following lease under the assumptions that (i) it does not elect to adopt the practical expedient; and (ii) it elects to adopt the practical expedient for short-term leases.

Canaan Corp. (CC) leases office furnishings from an office supply outlet for a one-year period. The lease does not include a renewal option, nor does it include an option to purchase. Payments of $1,000 per month are first due on January 1, 2019, the commencement date of the lease. CC has a 6% incremental borrowing rate for this type of asset (0.5% per month) and cannot easily determine the interest rate implicit in the lease.

Exhibit 17-24 Contrasting the accounting for the lessee's accounting for a lease using a capitalization approach and the short-term practical expedient

Capitalization approach		
January 1, 2019		
Dr. Right-of-use asset*	11,677	
Cr. Lease liability		10,677
Cr. Cash		1,000
* Using a financial calculator: **2ND** **BGN** **2ND** **SET** **2ND** **QUIT** 12 **N** 0.5 **I/Y** 0 **FV** 1000 **PMT** **CPT** **PV** → PV = −11,677 (rounded); Lease liability = $11,677 − $1,000 = $10,677; ROU Asset = $11,677.		
January 31, 2019		
Dr. Interest expense ($10,677 × 0.5%)	53	
Cr. Lease liability		53
Dr. Depreciation expense—ROU asset ($11,677/12)	973	
Cr. Accumulated depreciation—ROU asset		973
February 1, 2019		
Dr. Lease liability	1,000	
Cr. Cash		1,000
Practical expedient		
January 1, 2019		
Dr. Furniture rental expense	1,000	
Cr. Cash		1,000
February 1, 2019		
Dr. Furniture rental expense	1,000	
Cr. Cash		1,000

Looking at the journal entries in Exhibit 17-24, it is readily apparent that the practical expedient option is much easier to account for. As such, it is expected that many lessees will choose this option when it is available. While not readily apparent, as the journal entries only cover part of the lease term, the total expense recognized under both approaches is $12,000 (ROU asset approach is $11,677 depreciation expense + $323 interest expense = $12,000; practical expedient is 12 × $1,000 = $12,000 rental expense).

b. The lessee may elect to expense leases of low-value assets

THRESHOLD CONCEPT
ECONOMIC CONSEQUENCE OF ACCOUNTING CHOICES

Lessees may also elect to expense leases of low-value assets, although this option is subject to a number of restrictions. Again, the IASB's reason for limiting the use of this option is to prevent the lessee from using use the low-value practical expedient for assets that are, in substance, higher-value assets.

IFRS 16 does not specifically define what a low-value asset is, although the supporting basis of conclusion suggests that an appropriate threshold is US$5,000. As this number is not formalized within the standards, however, what constitutes "low-value" is a matter of professional judgement. This monetary threshold pertains to the value of the right-to-use asset when new, even if the asset is used when first leased. For example, a lease of a used computerized sheet metal cutter that costs US$10,000 new does not qualify as a low-value asset even if it is worth only US$4,000 on the commencement date of the lease.[43]

Low-value leases are also subject to an additional restriction that the ROU asset cannot be dependent on, or highly interrelated with, other assets. For example, consider a lessee that enters into separate leases for a computer ($3,500), computer monitor ($600), and all-in-one printer ($1,000). Since the three assets are highly interrelated and their collective value is $5,100, none of the three leases qualify for the low-value asset practical expedient.

Lessees that elect to adopt the low-value practical expedient for a particular lease are not obligated to adopt the expedient for any other leases; the lessee is permitted to make a different election for each lease involving a low-value ROU asset.

Lessees who elect to use the low value practical expedient expense the lease payments in the same manner as that for short-term leases, illustrated in Exhibit 17-24.

c. The lessee need not separately account for the lease and related non-lease components in a lease contract

As mentioned in Section E, lease contracts often include two or more components. Sometimes, the other component is another lease. For example, a contract that includes the right to use a semi-tractor and a trailer contains two leases: the semi-tractor and the trailer. In this case, the semi-tractor and trailer will be accounted for as two separate ROU assets, with the ROU asset and lease liability for each being determined on the relative stand-alone values of each asset.

Other leases can include a lease and a related non-lease component. For example, a lease of office equipment often includes a clause that the lessor will regularly service the equipment. This maintenance agreement is an example of a service that the lessee would purchase irrespective of whether it leased or purchased the asset. Without this practical expedient, the lessee excludes payments for the service component from the equipment component when calculating the total lease payments. The single lease component practical expedient allows the equipment lease and service contract to be combined for accounting purposes.

Consider a lease payment of $2,000 per month of which $1,800 pertains to the ROU asset and $200 to a maintenance agreement. If the practical expedient is adopted, the $2,000 per month will be included in the lease payment used to initially measure the ROU asset and lease liability. If, however, the practical expedient is not adopted, $1,800 per month will be included in the lease payment, and the remaining $200 will be separately accounted for as repair and maintenance expense.

In contrast, amounts paid by the lessee to the lessor for services provided by outside suppliers (e.g., property taxes or insurance) are excluded from the lessee's payment amount. This exclusion reflects the fact that the payment is made for something other than the right to use the underlying asset. Payments of this nature are not eligible for the single lease component practical expedient, however, as they do not meet the definition of a non-lease component of the contract.

Exhibit 17-25 contrasts a lessee's accounting for the following lease under the assumptions that (i) it accounts for the lease and non-lease components separately; and (ii) it elects to adopt the practical expedient and accounts for the lease and related non-lease components as a single lease component. This example is based on the facts in Scenario 3 in Exhibit 17-20.

---

43. For ease of exposition, we will drop the US dollar prefix when referring to both the low-value threshold amount and the value of the assets under consideration for the related practical expedient.

Exhibit 17-25 Contrasting the lessee's accounting for the lease component and related non-lease component of the contract separately and as a single lease component

Based on facts in scenario 3 in Exhibit 17-20

Accounted for as separate components			Accounted for as a single component–adoption of practical expedient		
Using a financial calculator: **2ND** **BGN** **2ND** **SET** **2ND** **QUIT** 5 **N** 6 **I/Y** 54994 **PMT** 0 **FV** **CPT** **PV** → PV = −245,554 (rounded). Lease liability $245,554 − $54,994 = $190,560; ROU asset = $245,554.			Using a financial calculator: **2ND** **BGN** **2ND** **SET** **2ND** **QUIT** 5 **N** 6 **I/Y** 57994 **PMT** 0 **FV** **CPT** **PV** → PV = −258,949 (rounded). Lease liability $258,949 − $57,994 = $200,955; ROU asset = $258,949.		
January 1, 2019					
Dr. Rou asset	245,554		Dr. Rou asset	258,949	
Dr. Maintenance expense	3,000		Dr. Maintenance expense	0	
Cr. Lease liability		190,560	Cr. Lease liability		200,955
Cr. Cash		57,994	Cr. Cash		57,994

Observe how both the ROU asset and lease liability are initially recognized at a higher amount when this expedient is adopted than otherwise. While not readily apparent, the total amount expensed over the life of the lease will be the same under both options. If the practical expedient is adopted, the $3,000 per year that would otherwise be reported as maintenance expense will result in increased expenses being reported for both depreciation and interest.

The ROU assets and lease liabilities that arise when the single lease component expedient is adopted are subsequently measured in the same manner as those that are initially measured using the separate component approach.

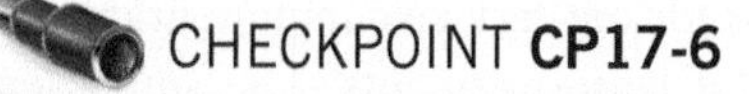

CHECKPOINT **CP17-6**

What are the three practical expedients available to lessees, and what was the IASB's reason for including these options in IFRS 16?

8. Derecognition

Derecognition of ROU assets and lease liabilities is not specifically addressed in IFRS 16. Moreover, for the most part, IAS 16—Property, Plant and Equipment, does not apply to ROU assets. Lacking specific guidance, it is prudent to review the underlying circumstances with a view to determining an appropriate accounting treatment. In this regard, the three most common scenarios at the end of the lease term are:

- the asset is returned to the lessor;
- the lessee obtains title to the ROU asset; or
- the lease term is extended and the lessee continues to lease the ROU asset.

a. Asset returned to the lessor

In the absence of a BPO or residual value guarantee, the lease liability should have a $0 balance and a fully depreciated asset will be returned to the lessor. Derecognition of the ROU assets involves debiting the accumulated depreciation account—ROU asset and crediting the ROU asset account for the same amount. For example, when an ROU asset that was originally recognized at $20,000 is returned to the lessor, the journal entry to derecognize the ROU asset is:

Dr. Accumulated depreciation—ROU asset	20,000	
Cr. ROU asset		20,000

There will be no gain or loss realized upon the derecognition of the ROU asset and the lease liability.

If the lease agreement includes a BPO, but the lessee does not elect to exercise the option, the ROU asset will have not been fully depreciated and the balance of the lease liability will be the option exercise price. The procedure is to remove the ROU asset and accumulated depreciation from the lessee's books and derecognize the remaining lease liability. The difference, if any, will be reported as a gain or loss on derecognition of the lease liability.[44] For example, assuming balances of: ROU asset $50,000; accumulated depreciation $40,000; and lease liability (the option exercise price) $6,000, the entry to derecognize the ROU asset and liability is:

Dr. Lease liability	6,000	
Dr. Accumulated depreciation—ROU asset	40,000	
Dr. Loss on derecognition of lease liability ($50,000 − $6,000 − $40,000)	4,000	
Cr. ROU asset		50,000

If a lease agreement includes a residual value guarantee, the amount to be paid out under the guarantee, if any, may differ from that previously expected. Similar to the BPO scenario above, the process for derecognition is to remove the ROU asset and accumulated depreciation from the lessee's books, and derecognize the remaining lease liability. In this respect:

- A gain or loss will never be recorded on disposition of the asset as the asset has been fully depreciated and its net book value, when returned, is $0. If the residual asset is worth more than the guaranteed amount, the excess accrues to the lessor, rather than the lessee.
- The cash payment required under the guarantee, if any, must be recognized with the net difference between it and the remaining liability—the previously expected payout under the guarantee—being reported as a gain or loss on derecognition of the lease liability.

For example, consider the situation when the lessee is required to pay out $12,000 under a residual value guarantee, which is more than the $7,000 previously estimated. Assuming an ROU asset balance of $50,000 and accumulated depreciation of $50,000, the entry to derecognize the ROU asset and liability is:

Dr. Lease liability (the amount expected to be paid out under the residual guarantee)	7,000	
Dr. Loss on derecognition of lease liability	5,000	
Cr. Cash (the actual amount paid out under the residual guarantee)		12,000
Dr. Accumulated depreciation—ROU asset	50,000	
Cr. ROU asset		50,000

44. In typical circumstances, the net book value of the ROU asset will be greater than the remaining lease liability (the option exercise price) when the lessee does not exercise the BPO. As a result, derecognition usually results in a loss.

Now consider the situation above but assume that the required payout is only $4,000. The entry to derecognize the ROU asset and liability is:

Dr. Lease liability (the amount expected to be paid out under the residual guarantee)	7,000	
Cr. Gain on derecognition of lease liability		3,000
Cr. Cash (the actual amount paid out under the residual guarantee)		4,000
Dr. Accumulated depreciation—ROU asset	50,000	
Cr. ROU asset		50,000

b. The lessee gains title to the ROU asset

The lessee can gain title to the ROU asset at the end of the lease term when there is a contract provision that provides for the transfer, or when the lessee exercises an option to purchase, which is not necessarily a bargain purchase option.

The accounting treatment for title transfers is to derecognize the ROU asset and related accumulated depreciation and to recognize an owned asset for the net of these amounts. For BPOs, the remaining lease liability will equal the option exercise price and the liability will be derecognized when the lessee pays this amount to the lessor. For explicit transfers, the lease liability should be $0 as it would have been derecognized when the last payment was made.

For example, consider the situation when there is a $10,000 BPO. Assume an ROU asset balance of $50,000 and accumulated depreciation of $35,000. The entry to derecognize the ROU asset and liability is:

Dr. Lease liability	10,000	
Cr. Cash (the option price under the BPO)		10,000
Dr. Accumulated depreciation—ROU asset	35,000	
Dr. Property, plant and equipment ($50,000 − $35,000)	15,000	
Cr. ROU asset		50,000

c. The lease term is extended

When the lease term is extended, neither the ROU asset or lease liability is derecognized. Rather, the lease liability is re-measured as set out in IFRS 16 and the ROU asset is revalued.[45]

Exhibit 17-26 summarizes the lessee's accounting for ROU assets.

Exhibit 17-26 Summary of lessee's journal entries for ROU assets

Lessee Timing	Journal entries
At start of lease	Recognize ROU asset
	Recognize lease liability
	Lease payment paid, if applicable
During lease	Lease payments paid
	Interest expense
	Depreciation/amortization expense
At end of lease	Derecognize ROU asset and accumulated depreciation
	Derecognize lease liability, if applicable

45. As discussed elsewhere in this chapter, accounting for remeasurements is beyond the scope of the text.

H. PRESENTATION AND DISCLOSURE OF LEASES—LESSEE

L.O. 17-5. Apply the presentation and disclosure requirements applicable to leases—lessees.

1. Presentation

Right-of-use assets are either reported separately on the statement of financial position (SFP) or included with other assets that are owned. If the ROU assets are not separately reported, then the lessee must disclose which line items on the SFP include ROU assets.

The current and non-current portion of the lease liability are either reported separately on the SFP or included with other liabilities. If the lease liabilities are not separately reported, then the lessee must disclose which line items on the SFP include lease liabilities. The determination of the current and non-current portion of the lease liability is made in the same manner as that of the lessor's lease receivable discussed in Section F.

2. Disclosure

Lessees must report comprehensive information about the nature of the leases they are party to. Exhibit 17-27 lists some of the more important disclosures. Readers should refer to IFRS 16 for a complete list of the lessee's required disclosures.

Exhibit 17-27 Summary of lessee disclosure requirements for leases

Statement of financial position (SFP)

- A schedule setting out the maturity dates of lease liabilities grouped into appropriate time bands (e.g., not later than one year; later than one year and not greater than two years…).
- Additions to ROU assets during the year.
- The carrying value of ROU assets at SFP date segregated as to class of asset.

Statement of comprehensive income

- Depreciation expense segregated as to class of asset.
- Interest expense on lease liabilities.
- Expense for short-term leases accounted for using the practical expedient.
- Expense for leases of low-value assets accounted for using the practical expedient.
- Gains and losses on sales-leaseback transactions.

I. ACCOUNTING FOR SALE AND LEASEBACK TRANSACTIONS

L.O. 17-6. Describe the nature of sale and leaseback transactions and account for these transactions.

A company that is short of cash but that has substantial fixed assets can obtain financing through sale and leaseback arrangements without affecting its operating capabilities. As the label suggests, a sale and leaseback involves the sale of an asset and immediate leasing of that asset from the new owner. The prior owner of the asset becomes the lessee, and the buyer is the lessor. Exhibit 17-28 illustrates these relationships.

If the sale transaction were separate from the leasing transaction, there would not be any additional accounting issues. That is, first record the asset sale transaction and its consequent gain or loss, then record the lease transaction. The problem in a sale and leaseback is that the two transactions are bundled, with the same two parties involved in both transactions. As a result, the sales price may not reflect the fair value of the asset, as the buyer-lessor can adjust the future lease payments to compensate for the difference. For example, if the sales price of the asset is $100,000 more than its fair value, then the lease could be structured so that the present value of the lease payments is $100,000 more than the market rent for an equivalent asset. To prevent manipulation of this nature, IFRS 16 and supporting materials clearly prescribe how to treat any gain or loss on sale and leaseback transactions.

Exhibit 17-28 Schematic of a sale and leaseback transaction

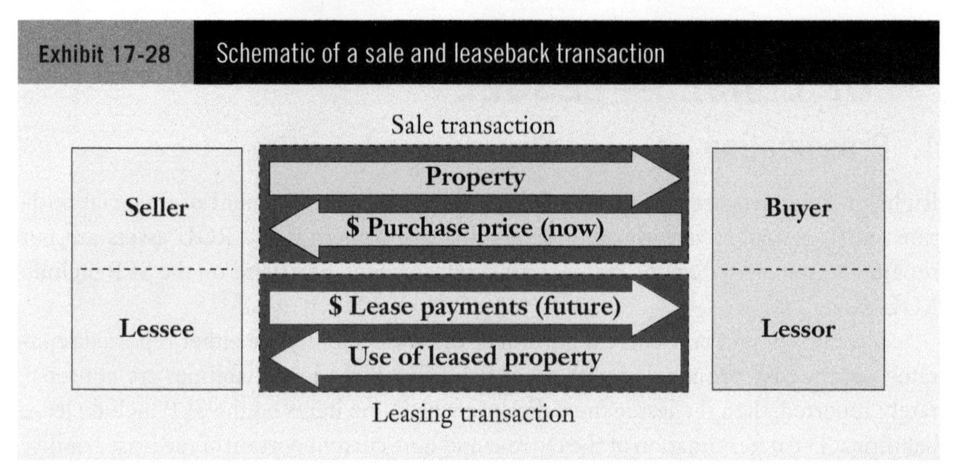

There are two important determinations that need to be made for a sale and leaseback contract as the answers to these questions determine how the transaction is accounted for. The questions are:

- Does the transfer of assets in the sale and leaseback arrangement qualify as a sale? and
- If the transfer of assets is a sale, does the buyer/lessor account for the lease as an operating lease or finance lease?

a. Does the transfer of assets in the sale and leaseback agreement qualify as a sale?

The basis of conclusions supporting IFRS 16 indicates that while a seller-lessee is not precluded from recognizing a sale due solely to a leaseback provision, a sale can only be recognized if the transfer meets the requirements of IFRS 15—Revenue from Contracts with Customers. Per the discussion in Chapter 4, sales revenue is recognized when the vendor (the seller-lessee) satisfies the performance obligation by transferring the promised good or service (the asset in the sale leaseback agreement) to the customer (the buyer-lessor) and the customer takes control of the asset.

The revenue recognition requirement set out above essentially has two parts: (i) the seller-lessee transfers the asset and (ii) the buyer-lessor takes control. Typically, there is no question that the first requirement is met because the seller-lessee and buyer-lessor have entered into an agreement that legally transfers ownership of the asset. The control requirement is not so straightforward, however, as the seller-lessee continues to use the asset. The application guidance supporting IFRS 15—Revenue from Contracts with Customers, which was prepared to assist accountants in making this determination, itemizes several factors that indicate that control has *not* been transferred. Consequently, a sale is *not* recognized if the sale and leaseback agreement includes *any* of the following:

- The seller-lessee has an option to repurchase the asset at a price stipulated in the sale and leaseback agreement.
- The seller-lessee must subsequently repurchase the asset at a price stipulated in the sale and leaseback agreement.
- The seller-lessee must repurchase the asset if requested to do so by the buyer-lessor and the stipulated price is lower than the original selling price of the asset.
- The seller-lessee must repurchase the asset if requested to do so by the buyer-lessor and the stipulated price is equal to or greater than the original selling price and is more than the expected market value of the asset at the time of repurchase.[46]

46. When comparing the repurchase price to the selling price, the time value of money must be considered.

b. Assuming the transfer of assets is a sale, does the buyer/lessor account for the lease as an operating lease or finance lease?

The answer to this question is straightforward: the buyer-lessor uses the same criteria to determine whether the lease is an operating lease or a finance lease as those used by other lessors, as detailed in Section C.

1. Accounting for a sale and leaseback transaction—Sales criteria met

a. Buyer-lessor

When the sales criteria are met in a sale and leaseback transaction, the buyer-lessor records the purchase in the normal manner. The buyer-lessor accounts for the leaseback as an operating lease or finance lease using the same criteria discussed in Section C.[47]

To illustrate how these requirements are accounted for, consider a situation where IAF Corp. (IAF), the buyer-lessor, purchased equipment from JLH Inc. (JLH), the seller-lessee, for $500,000 cash on January 1, 2019, and entered into an agreement that grants JLH the right to use that equipment for five years. Relevant information includes:

- Payments under the lease are $80,000 per year, first payable on December 31, 2019.
- The interest rate implicit in the lease is 6%, and JLH is able to readily determine this.
- The fair value of the equipment at the time of sale was $500,000.
- The required lease payments reflect market rates.
- The estimated remaining useful life of the equipment at the time of sale was 10 years. The estimated residual value at the end of its useful life is $0.
- The book value of the equipment at the time of sale was $600,000 cost less $200,000 accumulated depreciation.
- Both companies have December 31 year ends.
- In Scenario 1, JLH must return the leased asset to IAF at the end of the lease term; however, the residual value is not guaranteed.
- In Scenario 2, JLH must return the leased asset to IAF at the end of the lease term and guarantees the residual value of the asset will be $218,145. The expected payout under the guarantee is $0.

In analyzing the lease for classification purposes, it is clear that the BPO, transfer of title, or significant modification tests are not met. Similarly, the economic life test is not met as 50% (5 years lease / 10 years expected life = 50%) is not a major part of the asset's life.

In Scenario 1, the present value test *is not met* (Using a financial calculator: 5 **N** 6 **I/Y** 80000 **PMT** 0 **FV** **CPT** **PV** → PV = 336,989 (rounded); $336,989 / $500,000 = 67.4%).

In Scenario 2, the present value test *is met* (Using a financial calculator: 5 **N** 6 **I/Y** 80000 **PMT** 218145 **FV** **CPT** **PV** → PV = 500,000 (rounded); $500,000 / $500,000 = 100.0%).

Based on the foregoing analysis, IAF should account for the lease in Scenario 1 as an operating lease, and the lease in Scenario 2 as a finance lease. The journal entries to record this transaction at the commencement date of the lease and December 31, 2019, for IAF the buyer-lessor are set out in Exhibit 17-29.

---

47. This assumes that the asset was sold for its market value and the lease payments reflect market rents. If otherwise, the buyer-lessor recognizes a financial asset or liability for the difference. Further discussion of this complication is beyond the scope of this text.

Exhibit 17-29 Buyer-lessor journal entries for a sale and leaseback transaction when sales criteria are met

IAF (buyer-lessor)—Scenario 1—Operating lease		
January 1, 2019		
Dr. Equipment	500,000	
Cr. Cash		500,000
December 31, 2019		
Dr. Cash	80,000	
Cr. Lease rental revenue		80,000
Dr. Depreciation expense – equipment (($500,000 – $0)/10)*	50,000	
Cr. Accumulated depreciation – equipment		50,000
*The asset remains on the lessor's books as the lease was classified as an operating lease. As such, the lessor depreciates the asset over its useful life, rather than the lease term.		
IAF (buyer-lessor)—Scenario 2—Finance lease		
January 1, 2019		
Dr. Equipment	500,000	
Cr. Cash		500,000
Dr. Net investment in lease (lease receivable)	500,000	
Cr. Equipment		500,000
December 31, 2019		
Dr. Cash	80,000	
Cr. Finance income on lease ($500,000 × 6%)		30,000
Cr. Net investment in lease (lease receivable) ($80,000 – $30,000)		50,000

Note how the lessor accounts for both operating and finance leases in a sale and leaseback agreement that meets the sales criteria in the same manner as illustrated in Section C.

b. Seller-lessee

The seller-lessee's accounting for sales and leaseback transactions is a bit more involved than that of the buyer-lessor. The reason for this is that, after the sale and leaseback transaction, there are two separate interests that must be considered:

- the seller-lessee's right to use the asset during the lease term, and
- the remaining ownership claim of the buyer-lessor.

Fundamentally, because of its right to use the asset during the lease term, the seller-lessee has not transferred 100% of its claim on the asset to the purchaser-lessor. Thus, the seller-lessee can only recognize the portion of the gain on sale that relates to the ownership rights that were transferred to the buyer-lessor. In other words, the seller-lessee cannot recognize a gain on sale on its remaining right to use the asset during the lease period.

Allocating the gain on sale between the two claims is accomplished by following the methodology set out in the governing standards. This process is illustrated below by applying it to the facts in Scenario 1 of the example used in Exhibit 17-29:

1. Determine the value of the ROU asset: ROU asset = (Present value of lease payments/Fair value of asset given up) × Net book value of asset given up.
   - ROU asset = $336,989 / $500,000 × $400,000* = $269,591.

   *Net book value = $600,000 cost – $200,000 accumulated depreciation = $400,000.
2. Calculate the seller-lessee's remaining interest in the equipment: Seller-lessee's remaining interest = Present value of lease payments / Fair value of the asset.
   - Seller-lessee's remaining interest = $336,989 / $500,000 = 67.3978%.

3. Determine the buyer-lessor's interest in the equipment: Buyer-lessor's interest = 100% − Seller-lessee's interest.
   - Buyer-lessor's interest = 100% − 67.3978% = 32.6022%.
4. Compute the gain on sale relating to the rights transferred to the buyer-lessor to be recognized by the seller-lessee: The buyer-lessor's interest × (Sales price − Net book value of asset).
   - Gain on sale to be recognized upon initial recognition of the sales leaseback = 32.6022% × ($500,000 − $400,000) = $32,602.

We now use this information to prepare the seller-lessee's journal entries at the commencement date of the lease and December 31, 2019, as set out in Exhibit 17-30.

Exhibit 17-30 Seller-lessee journal entries for a sale and leaseback transaction when sales criteria are met

Using a financial calculator: 5 **N** 6 **I/Y** 80000 **PMT** 0 **FV** **CPT** **PV** → PV = 336,989 (rounded). Lease liability = PVLP − payment made at commencement date = $336,989 − $0 = $336,989.

January 1, 2019		
Dr. Cash (given in facts)	500,000	
Dr. ROU asset—equipment (as calculated)	269,591	
Dr. Accumulated depreciation—equipment (given in facts)	200,000	
Cr. Equipment (given in facts)		600,000
Cr. Lease liability (as calculated)		336,989
Cr. Gain on sale of equipment (as calculated)		32,602
December 31, 2019		
Dr. Interest expense ($336,989 × 6%)	20,219	
Dr. Lease liability ($80,000 − $20,219)	59,781	
Cr. Cash		80,000
Dr. Depreciation expense—ROU asset ($269,591 / 5)*	53,918	
Cr. Accumulated depreciation—ROU asset		53,918

* Depreciated over the lease term as the asset reverts to the lessor at the end of the lease term.

Note how the seller-lessee's lease liability is subsequently measured in the same manner as those illustrated in Section G.

The seller-lessee realizes a gain on sale of $32,602 versus the $100,000 that would be recognized had it just sold the asset for $500,000 and not leased it back. While not readily evident, the remaining $67,398 ($100,000 − $32,602) will be recognized in profit over the life of the lease through decreased depreciation expense. That is to say, the gain on disposition is deferred and (indirectly) taken into income over the life of the lease.[48]

2. Accounting for a sale and leaseback transaction—Sales criteria not met

When the sales criteria are not met in a sale and leaseback transaction, it is accounted for as discussed below.

[48] 1) For a stand-alone lease independent of a sale and leaseback (SL) transaction, a $336,989 ROU asset would be recognized (the PVLP). 2) The $336,989 cost of the ROU asset would be recognized as depreciation expense over the lease term. 3) The $269,591 ROU cost of the ROU asset under the SL will be recognized in depreciation expense over the lease term. 4) The lessee's profitability is $67,398 ($336,989 − $269,591) higher during the lease term under the SL scenario than the independent lease scenario. 5) The $32,602 (gain on sale) + $67,398 (deferred gain) = $100,000, which is the amount that would be recognized as a gain on an independent sale.

a. Buyer-lessor

The buyer-lessor does not recognize either a lease receivable or an asset purchase. Rather, it recognizes a financial asset under IFRS 9—Financial Instruments for the consideration paid to the seller-lessee for the sale. Typically, the buyer-lessor will report the financial asset at amortized cost. The lease payments stipulated in the lease agreement are accounted for as payments received on the loan.

b. Seller-lessee

The seller-lessee does not recognize a sale. Rather, it continues to report the underlying asset on its statement of financial position and depreciates it in the same manner as before. The consideration received from the buyer-lessor for the sale is accounted for as a loan. A financial liability is recognized under IFRS 9—Financial Instruments and is normally reported at amortized cost. The lease payments stipulated in the lease agreement are accounted for as payments made on the loan.

To illustrate how these requirements are accounted for, consider the situation in which Graydon Hunnicutt LLP (GHL) previously owned its land and office building. On January 1, 2019, the firm entered into a sale and leaseback arrangement on the building with W. Archibald Inc. (WBI) to secure the funds required to buy out two retiring partners. Pertinent details follow:

- The sales price was $16 million, which was the fair market value of the asset.
- GHL must repurchase the land and building at the end of the lease term for $5 million.
- GHL committed to rent the space for the remaining 20 years of the building's useful life for $1,297,497 per year first due on the commencement date. These payments imply an interest rate implicit in the lease of 7.0%, which is known to both parties. This lease payment reflects market rents.
- Before the sale and leaseback, the respective net book value of GHL's land and building were $1 million and $2 million ($5 million cost, less accumulated depreciation of $3 million). GHL depreciates its building using the straight-line method; the estimated residual value at the end of its useful life is $0.
- Both companies' year ends are December 31.

As GHL has a downstream obligation to repurchase the land and buildings at a pre-established price, the sales criteria have not been made. As such, WBI will recognize a financial asset for the $16 million transaction price and GHL will recognize a financial liability for the same amount. The journal entries to record this transaction at the commencement date of the lease and December 31, 2019, for both the buyer-lessor and the seller-lessee are set out in Exhibit 17-31.

Exhibit 17-31	Journal entries for a sale and leaseback transaction when sales criteria not met	
Using a financial calculator[49]: **2ND** **BGN** **2ND** **SET** **2ND** **QUIT** −16000000 **+/−** **PV** 20 **N** 1297497 **PMT** 5000000 **FV** **CPT** **I/Y** → I/Y = 7.0% (rounded).		
WBI (buyer-lessor)		
January 1, 2019		
Dr. Financial asset under sale and leaseback agreement	16,000,000	
Cr. Cash		16,000,000

(*Continued*)

[49] Note that the interest rate on the loan is the same as the interest rate implicit in the lease.

Exhibit 17-31 Continued		
Dr. Cash	1,297,497	
Cr. Financial asset under sale and leaseback agreement		1,297,497
December 31, 2019		
Dr. Financial asset under sale and leaseback agreement	1,029,175	
Cr. Finance income (($16,000,000 − $1,297,497) × 7.0%)		1,029,175
GHL (seller-lessee)		
January 1, 2019		
Dr. Cash	16,000,000	
Cr. Financial liability under sale and leaseback agreement		16,000,000
Dr. Financial liability under sale and leaseback agreement	1,297,497	
Cr. Cash		1,297,497
December 31, 2019		
Dr. Interest expense (($16,000,000 − $1,297,497) × 7.0%)	1,029,175	
Cr. Financial liability under sale and leaseback agreement		1,029,175

CHECKPOINT **CP17-7**

Why are there special rules for sale and leaseback transactions?

J. SUBSTANTIVE DIFFERENCES BETWEEN RELEVANT IFRS AND ASPE

The following table summarizes the key differences between IFRS and ASPE standards for leasing. Additional discussion of these issues follows the table.

ISSUE	IFRS	ASPE
Lessor's lease capitalization criteria	Based on qualitative considerations of whether the lease transfers substantially all the risks and rewards of ownership.	In addition to the criteria for the lessee, the lessor must also consider the credit risk of the lessee and whether non-reimbursable costs are reasonably estimable.
Lessor's classification of finance (capital) leases	No sub-classification of finance leases.	Capital leases are further sub-classified into sales-type and direct financing leases depending on whether there is a profit margin on the sale.
Lessee's lease capitalization criteria	The lessee recognizes a ROU asset and lease liability for virtually all leases.[50]	Based on both qualitative and quantitative considerations of whether the lease transfers substantially all the risks and rewards of ownership.
Lessee's discount rate for present value calculations	Use interest rate implicit in the lease if readily determinable by the lessee. Otherwise, use the incremental borrowing rate.	If the interest rate implicit in the lease is known to lessee, use the lower of the implicit rate and the incremental borrowing rate. Otherwise, use the incremental borrowing rate.
Lessee's inclusion of residual value guarantees in the determination of lease payments	Lessee includes the amount expected to be paid out under the guarantee in its determination of lease payments.	Lessee includes the full amount of the residual value guarantee in its determination of minimum lease payments.
Lessee's accounting for the lease and non-lease components in a lease contract	When the lessee adopts the available practical expedient, it accounts for the lease and related non-lease components in a lease contract as a single lease component.	Lease and executory costs must be accounted for separately.

50. The exceptions are short-term leases and leases of low-value assets for which the lessee has elected to adopt the available practical expedient.

1. Lessor's lease capitalization criteria

IFRS uses the term *finance leases* while ASPE uses the term *capital leases*.

IFRS and ASPE share most of the same qualitative criteria for lease classification. Specifically, both use the general criteria of whether there is a transfer of risks and rewards of ownership. Both also use the specific criteria relating to (i) a transfer of ownership; (ii) a bargain purchase option; (iii) the length of the lease relative to the life of the asset; and (iv) the present value of the lease payments[51] relative to fair value. IFRS, but not ASPE, includes an additional criterion: the asset is of such a specialized nature that only the lessee can use it without major modification.

With respect to criteria (iii) and (iv) just listed, ASPE provides specific quantitative guidance. Under ASPE, if a lease covers 75% or more of the asset's useful life, or if the present value of the minimum lease payments covers 90% or more of the asset's fair value, then it would be a capital lease.

For lessors, ASPE includes two additional indicators to determine whether a lease is a capital lease or an operating lease:

- *The lessee's credit risk is normal:* This indicator asks whether the particular lessee under consideration has a risk of default that is materially different from the lessor's other customers. Unusually high credit risk suggests a higher-than-normal chance that the lessor will repossess the leased property and the retention of significant risk of ownership.
- *Any non-reimbursable costs arising from the lease are reasonably estimable:* This indicator is consistent with the general recognition criteria regarding measurability. For instance, one of the revenue recognition criteria is that the amount ultimately collectible needs to be reasonably measurable; otherwise, the revenue would be deferred to a later date when collection occurs (see Chapter 4). Likewise, the lessor needs to be able to estimate costs to fulfill the lease in order to record the lease as a capital lease (i.e., as a sale of an asset).

Both indicators, together with at least one of the first four criteria, must be satisfied for a lease to be considered a capital lease. These latter indicators are consistent with the general idea that the lessor must have assurance that the risks (and rewards) of ownership have indeed been transferred.

2. Lessor's classification of finance (capital) leases

ASPE further sub-classifies a capital lease into two types. Since a capital lease for a lessor is treated as a sale of the asset, there is potentially a profit margin on that sale. When there is such a profit, the lease is a **sales type lease**. These leases are usually offered by manufacturers and dealers as a method of selling their product. If the sale price is equal to the cost of the asset to the lessor, then the lease is a **direct financing lease**. These leases are usually offered by financial institutions that provide the funds to acquire the leased asset.

sales type lease A type of finance lease in which the lessor obtains a profit margin on the sale of the leased asset (used in ASPE).

direct financing lease A type of finance lease in which the sale price is equal to the cost of the asset to the lessor (used in ASPE).

3. Lessee's lease capitalization criteria

IFRS uses the term *right-of-use assets* while ASPE uses the term *assets under capital lease*. The key difference between IFRS and ASPE pertains to the lessee's accounting for leases. IFRS employs a capitalization approach in which the lessees account for almost all leases as finance leases, recognizing a right-of-use asset and a lease liability. IFRS permits lessees to adopt practical expedients that allow them to expense short-term leases and leases of low-value assets.

51. IFRS refers to lease payments, whereas ASPE refers to minimum lease payments.

ASPE differentiates between finance leases and operating leases for lessees in much the same manner as that used to classify leases for the lessor. The one difference is the additional criteria pertaining to the lessee's credit risk and the estimability of non-reimbursable costs do not apply to lessees. The primary reason for this differentiation is the additional criteria relate to risks faced by lessors but not lessees.

4. Lessee's discount rate for present value calculations

As previously noted, the lessor should always be able to determine the interest rate implicit in the lease since by definition that is the rate it used to price the lease, so *the lessor must use the implicit rate.* The *lessee,* on the other hand, may not always have sufficient information to calculate the implicit rate. In this case, under IFRS, the lessee uses its incremental borrowing rate, the interest rate that the lessee would have to pay on a similar lease or loan. Thus, under IFRS, the interest rate for the lessee is determined on a hierarchical basis: use the implicit rate if readily determinable; otherwise, use the incremental rate.

For lessees, ASPE takes a somewhat different approach. While ASPE also refers to the implicit interest rate and the incremental borrowing rate, it recommends that the lessee use the *lower* of the two rates when both are known. What is the rationale for this rule? The reason is related to the lessee's preference for operating lease treatment: the lessee wants to use the highest interest rate justifiable to minimize the present value of the minimum lease payments, which is one of the quantitative criteria for lease classification. Recognizing the lessee's tendency to have this bias, ASPE requires the use of the lower of the two interest rates to maximize the present value of the minimum lease payments, making it more difficult for the lessee to escape finance lease treatment. Note however that under ASPE the amount recognized for the asset under capital lease may not be more than its fair value.

5. Lessee's inclusion of residual value guarantees in the determination of lease payments

Both IFRS and ASPE require that the lessee include residual value guarantees in its determination of lease payments. IFRS requires that the lessee include the amount expected to be paid out under the guarantee, whereas ASPE requires that the lessee include the full amount of the guarantee.

6. Lessee's accounting for the lease and related non-lease components in the lease contract

IFRS and ASPE both require that the lessee account for the lease and non-lease components[52] in the lease contract separately. IFRS, though, permits the lessee to elect to account for the lease and related non-lease components as a single lease component. Related non-lease costs include goods and services transferred to the lessee that it would purchase irrespective of whether it leased or purchased the underlying asset. For example, a lease of an automobile includes a clause that the lessor will regularly service the vehicle, which is a non-lease cost.

52. ASPE does not use the term *non-lease component,* rather it refers to *executory costs,* which are costs related to the operation of the leased property. Examples cited include insurance, property taxes, and maintenance costs.

K. SUMMARY

L.O. 17-1. Apply the criteria for lessors for classifying leases as finance (capital) or operating leases, and apply the appropriate accounting method.

- The general criteria for classifying a lease as finance or operating reflect the economic substance of the transaction: is there a transfer of risks and rewards of ownership?
- There are a number of indicators to help assess whether there is a transfer of risks and rewards.
- Clear-cut indicators are an outright transfer of ownership or a bargain purchase option in the lease agreement.
- Other indicators are the fraction of the property's useful life covered by the lease and the proportion of the property's fair value represented by the lease payments. While ASPE (though not IFRS) provides quantitative guidelines with respect to lease term and present value, it is difficult to argue that a lease term or present value of 1 percent less automatically changes a lease from a finance lease into an operating lease. So, assessing these two quantitative indicators requires accountants to exercise professional judgment that considers all the lease's characteristics.

L.O. 17-2. Analyze a lease to determine the present value of lease payments, the interest rate implicit in the lease, and the lease payments required from the lessee.

- Accounting for leases requires numerous figures and computations.
- Pay particular attention to residual values that are unguaranteed; payments required under residual value guarantees; payments to exercise bargain purchase options; non-lease components in the lease; and initial direct costs. Also, remain cognizant of the interest rate to be used to discount the cash flows that flow from the lease or that flow from the property outside the lease term.

L.O. 17-3. Apply the appropriate accounting method for lessees' right-of-use assets.

- ROU assets are recognized initially for the cost of the ROU asset, which is the sum of the present value of the lease payments, initial direct costs, and the estimated costs of decommissioning and site-restoration obligations, less lease incentives received.
- ROU assets are subsequently measured at cost less accumulated depreciation and impairment losses, adjusted for remeasurements of the lease liability.
- Lease liabilities are initially recognized for the present value of lease payments not yet made at the commencement date.
- Lease liabilities are subsequently measured at amortized cost using the effective interest method.

L.O. 17-4. Analyze a lease to determine whether practical expedients are available to lessees and, if available, apply the appropriate accounting methods.

- In limited circumstances, IFRS permits lessees to elect to expense the entire lease payment, rather than recognize a ROU asset and lease liability as a practical expedient. Exceptions are available for short-term leases of twelve months or less, and leases of low-value assets.
- As a practical expedient, IFRS permits lessees to elect to account for the lease and related non-lease components as a single lease component, rather than accounting for the non-lease component separately.

L.O. 17-5. Apply the presentation and disclosure requirements applicable to leases.

- Lessees and lessors need to present the current and non-current portions of lease liabilities or receivables separately.
- Accounting standards require significant disclosures so that users can understand whether, to what extent, and how a company has used leases.

L.O. 17-6. Describe the nature of sale and leaseback transactions and account for these transactions.

- A sale and leaseback transaction involves the sale of an asset and immediate leasing of that asset from the new owner. The prior owner of the asset becomes the lessee, and the buyer is the lessor.
- Accounting for the transaction is governed by whether the transaction meets the revenue recognition criteria in IFRS 15—Revenue from Contracts with Customers and, if so, whether the lease from the lessor's perspective is classified as a finance lease or an operating lease.

L. ANSWERS TO CHECKPOINT QUESTIONS

CP17-1: The principal economic loss in leasing is the agency cost of leasing. The separation of ownership and control/use of the asset creates a moral hazard. Leases exist despite this agency cost because of other compensating benefits of leasing, such as flexibility in lease contract terms and tax benefits.

CP17-2: The general criterion used by the lessor to determine whether a lease is an operating or a finance lease is whether the lease transfers substantially all the risks and rewards of ownership from the lessor to the lessee. If yes, the lessor classifies the contract as a finance lease. If no, the lessor classifies it as an operating lease.

CP17-3: The key issue in the accounting for leases from the lessor's perspective is the classification of the lease as an operating lease or a finance lease. That classification depends on the degree to which the risks and rewards of ownership have transferred from the lessor to the lessee.

CP17-4: The supporting indicators use wording that is less than "all" because the standards setters anticipate a certain amount of earnings management in the subjective estimates of useful life and fair value. Lessors prefer financing lease treatment, so they will tend to bias these estimates downwards.

CP17-5: The lessee's approach to accounting for leases is to recognize an asset purchase financed by debt.

CP17-6: The three practical expedients available to lessees are that they may elect to: (i) expense short-term leases; (ii) expense leases of low-value assets; and (iii) account for the lease component and related non-lease component as a single lease component. Cost-versus-benefit considerations were why the IASB made these options available to lessees.

CP17-7: Sale and leaseback transactions require special rules because they involve two related transactions that, if treated separately, could lead to undesirable outcomes such as artificial gains being reported on the entity's statement of comprehensive income.

M. GLOSSARY

agency cost of leasing: The reduced level of care due to the separation of an asset's ownership and its control.

bargain purchase option (BPO): An option given to the lessee to purchase the leased asset at a price that is below expected fair value at a future date; the assessment of whether a bargain exists is made at the time of entering the lease arrangement.

commencement date of the lease: The date that the leased asset is first available to the lessee.

direct financing lease: A type of finance lease in which the sale price is equal to the cost of the asset to the lessor (used in ASPE).

economic life: The time period or units of output during which the asset is expected to be economically usable.

finance lease (also capital lease): A lease that transfers substantially all the risks and rewards incidental to ownership of an underlying asset. Depending on its nature, the lessor accounts for a finance lease as either a financing arrangement or as an asset sale with vendor-provided financing.

gross investment in the lease: The undiscounted lease payments receivable plus the undiscounted unguaranteed residual value of the leased asset.

incremental borrowing rate: The interest rate that the lessee would have to pay on a similar lease or loan.

interest rate implicit in the lease: The discount rate that is used, or implied to be used, by the lessor in the determination of the payments in a lease. Formally, it is the rate of interest that causes the present value of (a) the lease payments and (b) the unguaranteed residual value to equal the sum of (i) the fair value of the underlying asset and (ii) any initial direct costs of the lessor. In the absence of initial direct costs, this will be the discount rate used by the lessor in determining the payments in the lease.

lease: A contract, or part of a contract, that conveys the right to use an asset (the underlying asset) for a period of time in exchange for consideration.

lease payments: Payments over the lease term that the lessee makes to the lessor, including: fixed payments; variable payments that depend on an index or rate; the exercise price of a BPO; and in certain circumstances, penalties for early termination of the lease. For the lessor, lease payments normally include residual value guarantees. For the lessee, lease payments include the amount expected to be paid out under residual value guarantees.

lessee: The renter in a lease contract. This is the party that has the right to use the underlying asset during the lease term.

lessor: The owner of the asset in a lease.

manufacturer/dealer lease: A lease offered by the lessor as a financing mechanism to facilitate the sale of its own products.

net investment in the lease: The gross investment in the lease discounted using the interest rate implicit in the lease. Each payment within the gross investment, which is the total of the lease payments receivable under a finance lease and any unguaranteed residual value, must be discounted to reflect the risk and timing of the related cash flow. The net investment in the lease is also referred to as a *lease receivable*.

non-lease components: Include services provided for or arranged by the lessor that would be purchased by the lessee independent of whether the lessee had purchased or leased the asset. The lessor excludes payments for non-lease components from the fixed payment amount when calculating the total lease payments, accounting for the non-lease component separately.

operating lease: A lease that does not transfer substantially all the risks and rewards incidental to ownership of an underlying asset. An operating lease is accounted for by the lessor as a rental agreement.

practical expedient: An alternative method of accounting that simplifies the accounting for a given transaction. Practical expedients are made available in limited circumstances as a measure to protect against the cost of providing the accounting information exceeding the benefit provided by that same information.

residual value: The estimated value of the asset at the end of the asset's economic (useful) life.

residual value guarantee: A guarantee made to the lessor by the lessee or an independent third party that the value of the leased asset at the end of the lease will be greater than or equal to the guaranteed amount.

right-of-use (ROU) asset: An asset that represents a lessee's right to use an underlying asset for the lease term. This is the asset that the lessor rents to the lessee.

sales type lease: A type of finance lease in which the lessor obtains a profit margin on the sale of the leased asset (used in ASPE).

underlying asset: The asset stipulated in the lease agreement that the lessor rents to the lessee.

unguaranteed residual value: The expected value of the leased asset that will be returned to the lessor at the end of the lease term that is not guaranteed by the lessee or an outside party.

N. REFERENCES

Authoritative standards:

IFRS	ASPE Section
IFRS 16—Leases	3065—Leases
IFRS 9—Financial Instruments	3856—Financial Instruments
IAS16—Property, Plant and Equipment	3061—Property, Plant and Equipment
IAS 38—Intangible Assets	3064—Goodwill and Intangible Assets
IFRS 15—Revenue from Contracts with Customers	3400—Revenue

O. PROBLEMS

P17-1. Substance of lease arrangements and classification—lessor

(L.O. 17-1) (Easy – 5 minutes)

Identify whether the following are lease characteristics relevant to the classification of a lease as a finance (capital) lease for the lessor.

		Yes/No
a.	Lease transfers title to the lessee at the end of the lease.	
b.	Lease payments include payments for related non-lease components.	
c.	Lease transfers substantially all risks and rewards of ownership.	
d.	Lease is for tangible property.	
e.	Lease is for intangible property.	
f.	Lease is considered long term.	

P17-2. Substance of lease arrangements and classification—lessor

(L.O. 17-2) (Easy – 5 minutes)

Identify whether the following are characteristics relevant to the classification of a lease as a finance (capital) lease for the lessor.

		Yes/No
a.	Present value of minimum lease payments comprise at least 75% of the fair value of the leased asset (under ASPE).	
b.	Present value of lease payments comprise substantially all of the fair value of the lease asset.	
c.	The lease is a lease of land.	
d.	The lease contains a bargain purchase option.	
e.	The lease term comprises a major part of the economic life of the asset.	
f.	The lease term comprises at least 75% of the economic life of the asset (under ASPE).	

P17-3. Substance of lease arrangements and classification (L.O. 17-1) (Easy – 5 minutes)

Accounting standards for leases require an assessment of whether the lease transfers substantially all the risks and rewards of ownership.

Required:

Discuss how these standards relate to the definition of assets in the IFRS Framework.

P17-4. Substance of lease arrangements and classification—lessor (L.O. 17-1) (Medium – 10 minutes)

Accounting standards for leases require an assessment of whether the lease transfers substantially all the risks and rewards of ownership.

Required:

Discuss how these standards relate to the concept of information asymmetry in financial accounting theory.

P17-5. Lease classification and accounting—lessor (L.O. 17-1) (Medium – 10 minutes)

On January 1, 2019, Hanover Company (lessor) entered a lease to rent out office space. The lease requires the lessee to pay Hanover $200,000 per year, at the beginning of each year, for 10 years. The lease is non-cancellable and non-renewable. The land and building's cost and current fair value is $5 million, with $2 million allocated to the land and $3 million to the building. The building's estimated residual value at the end of its 30-year useful life is $0. The interest rate implicit in the lease is 10%.

Required:

Classify this lease for Hanover Company and record its journal entries for the first year of the lease.

P17-6. Lease classification and accounting—lessor (L.O. 17-1) (Medium – 10 minutes)

The following are characteristics of a lease:

Price of leased asset from manufacturer	$500,000
Lease payments	$92,823
Lease term	7 years
Payment frequency	Annual
Payment timing	End of year
Guaranteed residual value at end of lease term	$60,000
Interest rate implicit in the lease	9%

Required:

Determine the appropriate classification for this lease for the lessor (who is not the manufacturer), and record the journal entries for the lessor for the first year of the lease.

P17-7. Substance of lease arrangements and classification—lessor

The following are the characteristics of a lease:

Fair value of leased asset	$100,000
Lease payments	$26,380
Lease term	5 years
Payment frequency	Annual
Payment timing	End of year
Guaranteed residual value	None
Interest rate implicit in the lease	10%

Required:

Determine the present value of the lease payments and the appropriate classification of this lease for the lessor.

P17-8. Substance of lease arrangement and classification—lessor

(L.O. 17-1, L.O. 17-2) (Easy – 5 minutes)

The following are the characteristics of a lease:

Fair value of leased asset	$600,000
Lease payments	$80,000
Lease term	5 years
Payment frequency	Annual
Payment timing	End of year
Guaranteed residual value	None
Interest rate implicit in the lease	8%

Required:

Determine the present value of the lease payments and the appropriate classification of this lease for the lessor.

P17-9. Substance of lease arrangement—lessor

(L.O. 17-1, L.O. 17-2) (Medium – 10 minutes)

The following are characteristics of a lease:

Fair value of leased asset	$500,000
Lease payments	$90,000
Lease term	7 years
Payment frequency	Annual
Payment timing	End of year
Guaranteed residual value at end of lease term	$60,000
Interest rate implicit in the lease	9%

Required:

Determine the present value of the lease payments and the appropriate classification for this lease for the lessor.

P17-10. Analysis of leases—ASPE (L.O. 17-1, L.O. 17-2) (Medium – 10 minutes)

A·S·P·E

The following are some of the characteristics of an asset available for lease:

Fair value of leased asset	$100,000
Lease term	5 years
Payment frequency	Annual
Payment timing	Beginning of year
Guaranteed residual value	$20,000
Expected payout under guaranteed residual	$10,000
Interest rate implicit in the lease (not known by lessee)	8%
Lessee's incremental borrowing rate	9%

Assume that the lessor and lessee apply ASPE.

Required:

a. Determine the amount of lease payment that the lessor would require to lease the asset.
b. Compute the present value of the minimum lease payments for the lessor.
c. Evaluate whether the lessee should classify the lease as an operating or capital lease.
d. Compute the value of the lessee's leased asset at initial recognition.

A·S·P·E

P17-11. Analysis of leases—ASPE (L.O. 17-1, L.O. 17-2) (Medium – 10 minutes)

The following are some of the characteristics of an asset available for lease:

Fair value of leased asset	$100,000
Lease term	5 years
Payment frequency	Annual
Payment timing	End of year
Guaranteed residual value	$20,000
Expected payout under guaranteed residual	$10,000
Interest rate implicit in the lease (known to lessee)	10%
Lessee's incremental borrowing rate	8%

Assume that the lessor and lessee apply ASPE.

Required:

a. Determine the amount of lease payment that the lessor would require to lease the asset.
b. Compute the present value of minimum lease payments for the lessor.
c. Compute the present value of minimum lease payments for the lessee.
d. Evaluate whether the lessee should classify the lease as an operating or capital lease.

A·S·P·E

P17-12. Accounting for leases—ASPE (L.O. 17-1, L.O. 17-2) (Medium – 10 minutes)

The following are some of the characteristics of an asset available for lease:

Inception date of lease	January 1, 2019
Fair value of leased asset	$100,000
Useful life	15 years
Lease term	5 years
Payment amount	$13,000
Payment frequency	Annual
Payment timing	Beginning of year
Residual value at end of lease term (unguaranteed)	$50,000
Interest rate implicit in the lease (not known by the lessee)	7%
Lessee's incremental borrowing rate	8%
Company year end	December 31
Depreciation method	Straight-line

Assume that the lessee applies ASPE.

Required:

a. Evaluate whether the lessee should account for this lease as a capital lease or an operating lease.
b. Prepare the lessee's journal entries for the lease for 2019 and January 1, 2020.

P17-13. Accounting for leases—ASPE (L.O. 17-1, L.O. 17-2) (Medium – 15 minutes)

A·S·P·E

The following are some of the characteristics of an asset available for lease:

Inception date of lease	January 1, 2019
Fair value of leased asset	$100,000
Useful life	15 years
Lease term	10 years
Payment amount	$11,000
Payment frequency	Annual
Payment timing	Beginning of year
Residual value at end of lease term (guaranteed)	$20,000
Interest rate implicit in the lease (known by the lessee)	7%
Lessee's incremental borrowing rate	8%
Company year end	December 31
Depreciation method	Straight-line

Assume that the lessee applies ASPE.

Required:

a. Evaluate whether the lessee should account for this lease as a capital lease or an operating lease.
b. Prepare the lessee's journal entries for the lease for 2019 and January 1, 2020.

P17-14. Analysis of leases—ASPE (L.O. 17-1, L.O. 17-2) (Medium – 15 minutes)

A·S·P·E

The following are some of the characteristics of an asset available for lease:

Fair value of leased asset	$100,000
Useful life	8 years
Lease term	5 years
Payment frequency	Annual
Payment timing	Beginning of year
Residual value (unguaranteed)	$20,000
Interest rate implicit in the lease (not known by the lessee)	10%
Lessee's incremental borrowing rate	8%

Assume that the lessor and lessee apply ASPE.

Required:

a. Determine the amount of lease payment that the lessor would require to lease the asset.
b. Compute the present value of minimum lease payments for the lessor.
c. Compute the present value of minimum lease payments for the lessee.
d. Evaluate whether the lessor should classify the lease as an operating or capital lease.
e. Evaluate whether the lessee should classify the lease as an operating or capital lease.

P17-15. Accounting for right-of-use assets (L.O. 17-2, L.O. 17-3) (Medium – 10 minutes)

On January 1, 2019, Star Company leased equipment to Planet Company. The terms of the lease are as follows:

Lease term	6 years
Economic life of equipment	8 years
Fair market value of equipment	$80,000
Guaranteed residual value	$5,000
Expected payout under guaranteed residual	$5,000
Expected residual value at end of economic life	$0
Annual lease payment, due each January 1	$16,000
Interest rate implicit in the lease (known by lessee)	10%

Planet uses straight-line depreciation for its property, plant, and equipment, and its year end is December 31.

Required:

Prepare Planet's journal entries for the lease for 2019.

P17-16. Analysis of lease that includes lessor initial direct costs

(L.O. 17-2, L.O. 17-3) (Medium – 15 minutes)

The following are some of the characteristics of an asset available for lease:

Fair value of asset	$100,000
Lease term	5 years
Payment frequency	Annual
Payment timing	End of year
Lessor initial direct costs	$2,000
Guaranteed residual value	None
Required return by lessor exclusive of initial direct costs	10%
Lessee's incremental borrowing rate	11%

Required:

Assume that the lessee cannot readily determine the interest rate implicit in the lease.

a. Determine the amount of lease payment that the lessor would require to lease the asset.
b. Compute the lessor's net investment in the lease at initial recognition.
c. Compute the value of the lessee's ROU asset at initial recognition.
d. Compute the lessee's lease liability at initial recognition.

P17-17. Analysis of leases

(L.O. 17-2, L.O. 17-3) (Medium – 15 minutes)

The following are some of the characteristics of an asset available for lease:

Fair value of leased asset	$100,000
Lease term	5 years
Payment frequency	Annual
Payment timing	Beginning of year
Guaranteed residual value	$20,000
Expected payout under guaranteed residual	$10,000
Interest rate implicit in the lease (not readily determinable by the lessee)	8%
Lessee's incremental borrowing rate	9%

Required:

a. Determine the amount of lease payment that the lessor would require to lease the asset.
b. Compute the lessor's net investment in the lease at initial recognition.
c. Compute the value of the lessee's ROU asset at initial recognition.
d. Compute the lessee's lease liability at initial recognition.

P17-18. Analysis of leases

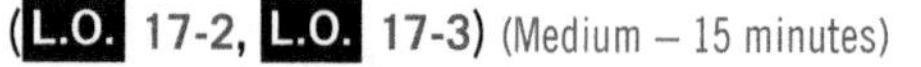

The following are some of the characteristics of an asset available for lease:

Fair value of leased asset	$100,000
Lease term	6 years
Payment frequency	Annual
Payment timing	Beginning of year
Guaranteed residual value	$20,000
Amount expected to be paid out under the guaranteed residual	$15,000
Interest rate implicit in the lease (not readily determinable by the lessee)	10%
Lessee's incremental borrowing rate	8%

Required:

a. Determine the amount of lease payment that the lessor would require to lease the asset.
b. Compute the lessor's net investment in the lease at initial recognition.
c. Compute the value of the lessee's ROU asset at initial recognition.
d. Compute the lessee's lease liability at initial recognition.

P17-19. Reporting consequences of ROU assets

(L.O. 17-2, L.O. 17-3) (Medium – 20 minutes)[53]

Longview Corporation started operations on March 1, 2019. It needs to acquire a special piece of equipment for its manufacturing operations. It is evaluating the following two options:

Option 1: Lease the equipment for eight years. Lease payments would be $11,950 per year, due at the beginning of each fiscal year (March 1). Longview's incremental borrowing rate is 6%. The interest rate implicit in the lease is not readily determinable. There is no bargain purchase or renewal option. Longview is responsible for all costs of operating the equipment.
Option 2: Purchase the equipment for $78,900 by borrowing the full purchase amount at 6% over eight years. This price is considered the fair value of the equipment. Payments are due at the end of each fiscal year (February 28).

The equipment has a useful life of eight years and would be depreciated on a straight-line basis. No residual value is expected to exist at the end of eight years.

Required:

a. Calculate the present value of the lease payments under Option 1.
b. Calculate the payment that would be required under the purchase option (Option 2).
c. Calculate and briefly discuss the financial impact of each option on the non-current assets, total liabilities, and net income of Longview for the first year of operations. Assume all payments were made when due. Show your calculations.
d. Indicate which option you would recommend for Longview. Provide one explanation to support your recommendation.

P17-20. Accounting for right-of-use assets—derecognition

(L.O. 17-3) (Medium – 10 minutes)

Five years ago, Tobey's Well Being Inc. recognized an ROU asset for $50,000. Today, on January 1, 2019, Tobey exercised its option to purchase the equipment for $10,000. This ROU asset has been depreciated over its economic life of eight years on a straight-line basis. At the commencement date of the lease, the option to purchase was determined to represent a bargain purchase and the expected residual value of the asset at the end of its useful life was $0.

Required:

Prepare the journal entries to derecognize the ROU asset and lease liability on January 1, 2019.

P17-21. Accounting for right-of-use assets—derecognition

(L.O. 17-3) (Medium – 10 minutes)

Six years ago, Tidball Valuations Corp. leased office equipment. A $30,000 ROU asset was recognized at that time. Tidball depreciated the asset on a straight-line basis over the lease term. Provisions of the lease included a requirement to provide a $10,000 residual value guarantee. Tidball previously expected to pay out $7,000 under this guarantee. It is now January 1, 2019, and Tidball returned the leased equipment to the lessor. As the value of the equipment was only $4,000, Tidball paid $6,000 cash to settle the guarantee.

---

53. From Chartered Professional Accountants of Canada (CPA Canada).

Required:

Prepare the journal entries to derecognize the right-of-use asset and lease liability on January 1, 2019.

P17-22. Accounting for right-of-use assets with payments for services provided by an outside supplier (**L.O.** 17-3) (Medium – 10 minutes)

On January 1, 2019, Archibald Industries entered into an agreement to lease office space for a five-year period. Details of the lease are:

- Payments: $55,000 per annum first due at the commencement date.
- Payment includes: $50,000 for office rental and $5,000 for property taxes.
- Interest rate implicit in the lease: Not readily determinable.
- Incremental borrowing rate: 8%.
- Depreciation method: Straight-line.
- Year end: December 31.

Required:

Prepare Archibald Industries' journal entries for 2019 and January 1, 2020.

P17-23. Accounting for right-of-use assets with payments for services provided by an outside supplier (**L.O.** 17-3) (Medium – 15 minutes)

On January 1, 2019, Mackenzie Yoga Studios leased exercise equipment for a four-year period. Payments are $10,000 per year, first payable at the commencement date. Of this, $9,900 of the payment is for the lease of the equipment and $100 is for liability insurance forwarded by the lessor on behalf of the lessee to the insurance agency. Mackenzie provided a $20,000 residual value guarantee to the lessor. At the end of the lease term, Mackenzie can either return the equipment, which is expected to be worth $15,000 at that time, or purchase it for $12,000. The interest rate implicit in the lease is not readily determinable. Mackenzie's incremental borrowing rate is 4%. The expected residual value of the equipment at the end of its eight-year economic life is $0. Mackenzie, which uses the straight-line method to depreciate similar assets, has a December 31 year end.

Required:

Prepare Mackenzie Yoga Studios' journal entries for 2019 and January 1, 2020.

P17-24. Accounting for right-of-use assets with initial direct costs (**L.O.** 17-3) (Medium – 15 minutes)

Hornstein Finance Co. (lessor) leased an asset on January 1, 2019, to HPQ Fishing (lessee). The lease agreement calls for eight annual lease payments of $60,000 beginning on the commencement date. The interest rate implicit in the lease is 7%; however, HPQ cannot readily determine this. HPQ's incremental borrowing rate is 6%. The asset has an estimated value of $30,000 at the end of the lease; however, this is not guaranteed. HPQ must return the asset to the lessor at the end of the lease. The leased equipment has an estimated useful life of 10 years and no residual value at that time. HPQ paid its lawyers $4,000 to review the lease agreement. HPQ uses the straight-line method to depreciate similar equipment that it owns and has a December 31 year end.

Required:

Prepare HPQ Fishing's journal entries for 2019 and January 1, 2020.

P17-25. Accounting for right-of-use assets with initial direct costs (**L.O.** 17-3) (Medium – 15 minutes)

Brow Corp. leased equipment from Rachel Finance, with the following details:

- Commencement date: January 1, 2019.
- Term of lease: 4 years.

- Payments: $45,000 per annum first due at the commencement date.
- Residual guarantee: $15,000. Expected payout is $5,000.
- Interest rate implicit in the lease: 5%. Lessee is able to readily determine this.
- Incremental borrowing rate: 7%.
- Estimated useful life of equipment: 8 years.
- Initial direct costs—lessee: $7,000.
- Depreciation method: Straight-line.
- Year end: December 31.

Required:

Prepare Brow Corp's journal entries for 2019 and January 1, 2020.

P17-26. Accounting for right-of-use assets (L.O. 17-3) (Medium – 15 minutes)

Cappy Ltd. leased equipment to Swen Company on July 1, 2019. The terms of the lease are:

Lease term	8 years
Economic life of equipment	10 years
Fair market value of equipment	$120,000
Guaranteed residual value	$15,000
Expected payout under guaranteed residual	$0
Expected residual at end of economic life	$0
Annual lease payment, due each July 1	$16,000
Lessee's incremental borrowing rate (implicit rate unknown)	6%

Swen uses straight-line depreciation for its property, plant, and equipment, and its year end is December 31.

Required:

a. Prepare Swen's journal entries for the lease for 2019.
b. You are the director of finance for Swen Company. You are concerned about the impact the lease will have on your key performance indicator, which is the ratio of total debt to total assets. Discuss the impact the lease will have on this performance indicator.

P17-27. Accounting for right-of-use assets

LaSalle Leasing Company (lessor) agrees on January 1, 2019, to rent Rockwood Winery (lessee) the equipment that Rockwood requires to expand its production capacity to meet customers' demands for its products. The lease agreement calls for five annual lease payments of $200,000 at the end of each year. Rockwood has determined that the present value of the lease payments, discounted at 15%, is $670,431. The leased equipment has an estimated useful life of five years and no residual value. Rockwood uses the straight-line method for depreciating similar equipment that it owns.

Required:

a. Prepare a lease amortization schedule for this lease for the lessee.
b. Prepare the necessary journal entries for the first year of the lease for the lessee.

P17-28. Accounting for right-of-use assets (L.O. 17-3) (Medium – 15 minutes)

Adams Leasing (lessor) agrees on January 1, 2019, to rent Healthy Diner (HD) (lessee) the equipment that HD requires to expand its restaurant. The lease agreement calls for 10 annual lease payments of $50,000 at the beginning of each year. HD determined that the present value of the lease payments, discounted at 11%, is $326,852. The leased equipment has an estimated useful life of 10 years and no residual value. HD uses the straight-line method for depreciating similar equipment that it owns.

Required:

a. Prepare a lease amortization schedule for this lease for the lessee.
b. Prepare the necessary journal entries for 2019 and January 1, 2020, for the lessee.

P17-29. Accounting for right-of-use assets with initial direct costs

(L.O. 17-3) (Medium – 20 minutes)

Yucatil Leasing (lessor) signs a lease on January 1, 2019, with Zebra Charters (lessee). The lease agreement calls for five annual lease payments of $80,000 at the beginning of each year. Yucatil's implicit rate in the lease is 6%. Zebra, whose incremental borrowing rate is 5%, cannot readily determine the interest rate implicit in the lease. The asset (a boat) has an estimated value of $50,000 at the end of the lease. Zebra has an option to purchase the boat at the end of the lease for $30,000. The leased equipment has an estimated useful life of eight years and no residual value at that time. Zebra paid its lawyers $5,000 to review the lease agreement. Zebra uses the straight-line method to depreciate similar equipment that it owns and has a December 31 year end.

Required:

a. Prepare a lease amortization schedule for this lease for Zebra Charters.
b. Prepare Zebra Charters' journal entries for 2019 and January 1, 2020.

P17-30. Presentation and disclosure of leases for right-of-use assets

(L.O. 17-5) (Medium – 10 minutes)

A lessee has the following amortization schedule for a particular lease:

Present value of lease payments			$150,000
Less: payment made at commencement date			33,594
Lease liability			$116,406
Payment made at commencement date			33,594
Initial direct costs			0
ROU asset			$150,000
Interest rate implicit in lease as known			6.0%
Date	**Payment**	**Interest expense**	**Lease liability**
01/01/2019			$116,406
12/31/2019		$6,984	123,390
01/01/2020	$33,594		89,796
12/31/2020		5,388	95,184
01/01/2021	33,594		61,590
12/31/2021		3,695	65,286
01/01/2022	33,594		31,692
12/31/2022		1,902	33,594
01/01/2023	33,594		0
Small differences due to rounding			

The company entered into the lease at the beginning of its fiscal year, on January 1, 2019. Depreciation follows the straight-line method.

Required:

Provide the appropriate presentation of this lease in the lessee's statement of financial position for December 31, 2020, distinguishing amounts that are current from those that are non-current.

P17-31. Presentation and disclosure of leases for right-of-use assets (L.O. 17-5) (Medium – 10 minutes)

A lessee has the following amortization schedule for a particular lease:

Period	Interest for year @ 12%	Payments at end of year	Reduction in principal	Principal after interest and payments
01/01/2019				$142,389
12/31/2019	$17,087	$31,200	$14,113	128,276
12/31/2020	15,393	31,200	15,807	112,469
12/31/2021	13,496	31,200	17,704	94,765
12/31/2022	11,372	31,200	19,828	74,937
12/31/2023	8,992	31,200	22,208	52,729
12/31/2024	6,328	31,200	24,872	27,857
12/31/2025	3,343	31,200	27,857	0

The company entered into the lease at the beginning of its fiscal year, on January 1, 2019. Depreciation follows the straight-line method.

Required:

Provide the appropriate presentation of this lease in the lessee's statement of financial position for December 31, 2021, distinguishing amounts that are current from those that are non-current.

P17-32. Accounting and presentation and disclosure for right-of-use assets (L.O. 17-2, L.O. 17-3, L.O. 17-5) (Medium – 15 minutes)

On April 1, 2019, Help Company entered into a five-year lease for equipment. Annual lease payments are $25,000, payable at the beginning of each lease year (April 1). At the end of the lease, possession of the equipment will revert to the lessor. The equipment has an expected useful life of five years.

Similar equipment could be purchased for $170,000 cash. Help's incremental borrowing rate is 6%. The interest rate implicit in the lease is not readily determinable. The company has a March 31 year end and it uses straight-line depreciation for its property, plant, and equipment.

Required:

a. Prepare the journal entries relating to the lease and leased asset for Help's fiscal year ending March 31, 2020.
b. State the amounts related to the lease that would be reported on the statement of financial position (SFP) as at March 31, 2020, indicating the SFP classifications, account names, and amounts.

P17-33. Accounting for right-of-use assets—practical expedients (L.O. 17-3, L.O. 17-4) (Medium – 10 minutes)

The details of the equipment lease agreement that Taj Corp. (lessee) recently entered into with Stanger Leasing (lessor) are:

- Commencement date: January 1, 2019.
- Term of lease: 12 months.
- Payments: $1,000 per month first due at the commencement date.
- Other: Title does not transfer and the lease does not include any renewal or purchase options.
- Interest rate implicit in the lease: Lessee not able to readily determine.
- Incremental borrowing rate: 9% per annum (0.75% per month).
- Estimated useful life of equipment: 8 years.
- Depreciation method: Straight-line.
- Year end: December 31.

Required:

a. Assume that Taj Corp. elects to expense leases of a short-term nature. Prepare the journal entries for the month of January 2019 and February 1, 2019.
b. Assume that Taj Corp. *does not* elect to expense leases of a short-term nature. Prepare the journal entries for the month of January 2019 and February 1, 2019.

P17-34. Accounting for right-of-use assets—practical expedients

(L.O. 17-3, L.O. 17-4) (Medium – 10 minutes)

On January 1, 2019, Dudas Inc. entered into a 12-month, non-renewable lease to rent office equipment. The lease payment is $1,500 per month first due on January 31, 2019. The interest rate implicit in the lease is 4.8% per annum (0.4% per month) and Dudas, which has an incremental borrowing rate of 4.0% per year, knows this. Dudas has a December 31 year end and depreciates similar equipment on a straight-line basis.

Required:

a. Assume that Dudas Inc. elects to expense leases of a short-term nature. Prepare the journal entries for the month of January 2019.
b. Assume that Dudas Inc. *does not* elect to expense leases of a short-term nature. Prepare the journal entries for the month of January 2019.

P17-35. Accounting for right-of-use assets—practical expedients

(L.O. 17-3, L.O. 17-4) (Medium – 10 minutes)

Hicks Co. leased a new computer for three years on January 1, 2019, with the following details:

- Payments: $1,200 per annum first due at the commencement date.
- Interest rate implicit in the lease: 5% and lessee is able to readily determine.
- Incremental borrowing rate: 7% per annum.
- Estimated useful life of equipment: 3 years.
- Other: Title does not transfer. The leased item is not dependent upon or highly interrelated with other assets.
- Depreciation method: Straight-line.
- Year end: December 31.

Required:

a. Assume that Hicks Co. elects to expense leases of low-value assets. Prepare the journal entries for 2019 and January 1, 2020.
b. Assume that Hicks Co. *does not* elect to expense leases of low-value assets. Prepare the journal entries for 2019 and January 1, 2020.

P17-36. Accounting for right-of-use assets—practical expedients

(L.O. 17-3, L.O. 17-4) (Medium – 10 minutes)

Gail Inc. leased new office furniture for two years on January 1, 2019, with the following details:

- Payments: $2,000 per annum first due at the commencement date.
- Interest rate implicit in the lease: 5%; however, lessee is not able to readily determine this.
- Incremental borrowing rate: 4% per annum.
- Estimated useful life of equipment: 5 years.
- Other: Title does not transfer. The leased item is not dependent upon or highly interrelated with other assets.
- Depreciation method: Straight-line.
- Year end: December 31.

Required:

a. Assume that Gail Inc. elects to expense leases of low-value assets. Prepare the journal entries for 2019 and January 1, 2020.
b. Assume that Gail Inc. *does not* elect to expense leases of low-value assets. Prepare the journal entries for 2019 and January 1, 2020.

P17-37. Accounting for right-of-use assets—practical expedients
(L.O. 17-3, L.O. 17-4) (Medium – 15 minutes)

Gidget Corp. entered into a lease on January 1, 2019, to rent a car for a three-year period. Payments are $700 per month, $600 of which is for the car rental and $100 of which is for a repairs and maintenance service agreement. The first payment is due on the commencement date. Gidget has the option to purchase the vehicle at the end of the lease period for $20,000, which approximates its estimated fair value at the end of the lease term. The residual value of the leased asset is estimated to be $5,000 at the end of its expected economic life of 10 years. Gidget, which has an incremental borrowing rate of 6% per annum (0.5% per month), is unable to readily identify the interest rate implicit in the lease. Gidget depreciates all assets on a straight-line basis and has a December 31 year end.

Required:

a. Assume that Gidget Corp. elects to account for the lease and non-lease components of the contract as a single lease component. Prepare the journal entries for January 2019 and February 1, 2019.
b. Assume that Gidget Corp. *does not* elect to account for the lease and non-lease components of the contract as a single lease component. Prepare the journal entries for January 2019 and February 1, 2019.

P17-38. Accounting for right-of-use assets—practical expedients
(L.O. 17-3, L.O. 17-4) (Difficult – 20 minutes)

Sam Inc. leased a photocopier on January 1, 2019, for a three-year period. Payments, which are first due on the commencement date, are $3,000 per year. The $3,000 is comprised of $2,500 for the photocopier rental, $400 for a maintenance agreement, and $100 for an environmental tax that the lessor collects on behalf of the federal government. The first payment is due on the commencement date. The asset returns to the lessor at the end of the lease term. Sam, which has an incremental borrowing rate of 5% per annum, is unable to readily identify the interest rate implicit in the lease. Sam has a December 31 year end and depreciates all assets on a straight-line basis.

Required:

a. Assume that Sam Inc. elects to account for the lease and non-lease components of the contract as a single lease component. Prepare the journal entries for 2019 and January 1, 2020.
b. Assume that Sam Inc. *does not* elect to account for the lease and non-lease components of the contract as a single lease component. Prepare the journal entries for 2019 and January 1, 2020.

P17-39. Comprehensive lease question—manufacturer/dealer lease
(L.O. 17-1, L.O. 17-2, L.O. 17-3) (Difficult – 25 minutes)

Trucks for Sale Corp. (TFS) manufactures tractor-trailer units at a cost of $89,000 per unit. On January 1, 2019, TFS offered Nate's Trucking Inc. (NTI) the option of buying a unit for $122,000 cash or leasing it from TFS. Pertinent details are:

- The lease offered was a four-year, non-cancellable agreement with the first payment due at the beginning of each year starting January 1, 2019.
- The estimated economic life of the tractor-trailer is 10 years. Its estimated residual value is $0.
- The lease does not include a renewal option. NTI has the option to purchase the unit at the expiration of the lease for $40,000. The estimated value at that time is $50,000.
- NTI's incremental borrowing rate is 7.0%. It knows that the interest rate implicit in the lease is 6.0%.
- NTI depreciates similar equipment that it owns on a straight-line basis.
- Both companies have December 31 year ends.

Required:

a. Determine the amount of the lease payment that TFS will include in the lease agreement.
b. Evaluate how TFS (the lessor) should account for the lease transaction.

c. Prepare the journal entries on January 1, 2019, December 31, 2019, and January 1, 2020, for TFS, the lessor.
d. Prepare the journal entries on January 1, 2019, December 31, 2019, and January 1, 2020, for NTI, the lessee.

P17-40. Comprehensive lease question—direct financing lease, including lessor and lessee initial direct costs (L.O. 17-1, L.O. 17-2, L.O. 17-3) (Difficult – 40 minutes)

William Corp. (the lessee) leased equipment from Daniel Finance (the lessor), details of which are:

- Commencement date: January 1, 2019.
- Fair value of equipment: $150,000.
- Cost of equipment to William Corp.: $150,000.
- Term of lease: 6 years.
- Payments due: beginning of year commencing January 1, 2019.
- Purchase option: $40,000.
- Estimated value of asset at end of lease: $50,000.
- Required return by lessor exclusive of initial direct costs: 6%.
- Implicit rate used to determine lease payments: Lessee unable to readily determine.
- Incremental borrowing rate: 6%.
- Estimated economic life of equipment: 10 years.
- Estimated residual value: $0.
- Lessee's initial direct costs: $3,000.
- Lessor's initial direct costs: $4,000.
- Depreciation methods: Straight-line.
- Year ends: December 31.

Required:

a. Evaluate how the lessor (Daniel Finance) should account for the lease transaction.
b. Prepare a lease amortization schedule for this lease for Daniel Finance, the lessor.
c. Prepare a lease amortization schedule for this lease for William Corp., the lessee.
d. Prepare the journal entries on January 1, 2019, December 31, 2019, and January 1, 2020, for Daniel Finance, the lessor.
e. Prepare the journal entries on January 1, 2019, December 31, 2019, and January 1, 2020, for William Corp., the lessee.

P17-41. Comprehensive lease question—direct financing lease (L.O. 17-1, L.O. 17-2, L.O. 17-3) (Difficult – 40 minutes)

Salem Creamery (lessee) leases its ice cream making equipment from Big City Finance Company (lessor) under the following lease terms:

- The lease term is five years, non-cancellable, and requires equal rental payments of $46,498 first payable on the commencement date of the lease (January 1, 2019).
- On January 1, 2019, Big City purchased the equipment at its fair value of $200,100 and immediately transferred it to Salem Creamery. The equipment has an estimated economic life of five years and a $10,000 residual value that is guaranteed by Salem Creamery. Salem expects to pay out the entire $10,000 on the guarantee.
- The lease does not include a renewal option and the equipment reverts to Big City Finance Company upon termination of the lease.
- Salem's incremental borrowing rate is 10%; the interest rate implicit in the lease is also 10%.
- Salem depreciates similar equipment that it owns on a straight-line basis.
- Both companies have December 31 year ends.

Required:

a. Evaluate how the lessor (Big City) should account for the lease transaction.
b. Prepare a lease amortization schedule for this lease for Salem Creamery, the lessee.
c. Prepare the journal entries on January 1, 2019, December 31, 2019, and January 1, 2020, for Big City, the lessor.

d. Prepare the journal entries on January 1, 2019, December 31, 2019, and January 1, 2020, for Salem Creamery, the lessee.
e. On December 31, 2023, the actual residual value of the equipment is $4,000. Salem returns the equipment to Big City and pays the required amount under the residual value guarantee. Prepare the journal entry for this final transaction on Salem's books.

P17-42. Comprehensive lease question—manufacturer dealer lease (L.O. 17-1, L.O. 17-2, L.O. 17-3) (Difficult – 40 minutes)

Thornhill Equipment (lessor) leased a construction crane to Vanier Construction (lessee) on January 1, 2019. The following information relates to the leased asset and the lease agreement:

Cost of crane to lessor	$100,000
Thornhill's normal selling price for crane	$146,913
Useful life	10 years
Estimated value at end of useful life	$4,000
Lease provisions	
Lease term	7 years
Payment frequency	Annual
Payment timing	December 31
Annual payments, at end of year	$31,200
Estimated residual value at end of lease (unguaranteed)	$10,000
Ownership of crane reverts to lessor at end of lease term.	
Interest rate implicit in the lease (readily determinable by lessee)	12%
Lessee's incremental borrowing rate	13%

Both companies use the straight-line depreciation method for cranes, and they both have December 31 year ends.

Required:

a. Evaluate how the lessor (Thornhill Equipment) should account for the lease transaction.
b. Prepare a lease amortization schedule for this lease for Thornhill Equipment, the lessor.
c. Prepare a lease amortization schedule for this lease for Vanier Construction, the lessee.
d. Prepare the journal entries on January 1, 2019, and December 31, 2019, for Thornhill Equipment, the lessor.
e. Prepare the journal entries on January 1, 2019, and December 31, 2019, for Vanier Construction, the lessee.

P17-43. Comprehensive lease question—manufacturer/dealer lease (L.O. 17-1, L.O. 17-2, L.O. 17-3) (Difficult – 45 minutes)

On January 1, 2019, a lessor agrees to rent a truck with fair value and carrying value of $129,999 for a period of four years at an annual rental of $34,478 first payable at the commencement date. The truck's residual value is estimated to be $20,000. The interest rate implicit in the lease is 12%, and the lessee cannot readily determine this. The lessee's incremental borrowing rate is 10%. Previous analysis has already concluded that this is a direct financing lease for the lessor.

Required:

For parts (a) through (e), assume that the lessee has guaranteed the residual value and that the expected payout under the guarantee was $20,000.

a. Compute the lessor's net investment in the lease at initial recognition.
b. Compute the value of the lessee's ROU asset and lease liability at initial recognition.
c. Prepare the lessor's journal entries for each of January 1, 2019, December 31, 2019, and January 1, 2020.
d. Prepare the lessee's journal entries for each of January 1, 2019, December 31, 2019, and January 1, 2020.

e. Record the lessor's journal entries on January 1, 2023, to derecognize the net investment in the lease assuming that the truck's actual residual value is (i) $20,000; (ii) $4,000; or (iii) $35,000.
f. Record the lessee's journal entries on January 1, 2023, to derecognize the net investment in the lease assuming that the truck's actual residual value is (i) $20,000; (ii) $4,000; or (iii) $35,000.
For part (g), assume that the residual value is not guaranteed.
g. Prepare the lessee's journal entries for each of January 1, 2019, December 31, 2019, and January 1, 2020.

P17-44. Comprehensive lease question—manufacturer/dealer lease including disclosure (L.O. 17-1, L.O. 17-2, L.O. 17-3, L.O. 17-5) (Difficult – 45 minutes)

Prairie Railroad Inc. (PRI) (the lessee) and Loco-Motive Corporation (LMC) (the lessor) enter into an agreement that requires LMC to build a diesel-electric engine to PRI's specifications. Upon completion of the engine, PRI has agreed to lease it for a period of 12 years and to assume all costs and risks of ownership. The lease is non-cancellable, becomes effective on January 1, 2019, and requires annual rental payments of $280,000 first due on the commencement date of the lease.

PRI's incremental borrowing rate is 13%, and the implicit interest rate used by LMC, which is not readily determinable by PRI, is 12%. The total cost of building the engine is $1,550,000. The economic life of the engine is estimated to be 12 years with residual value set at zero. PRI depreciates similar equipment on a straight-line basis. At the end of the lease, PRI obtains title to the engine.

Required:

a. Evaluate how the lessor (LMC) should account for the lease transaction.
b. Prepare a lease amortization schedule for this lease for LMC, the lessor.
c. Prepare a lease amortization schedule for this lease for PRI, the lessee.
d. Prepare the journal entries on January 1, 2019, and December 31, 2019, for LMC, the lessor.
e. Prepare the journal entries on January 1, 2019, and December 31, 2019, for PRI, the lessee.
f. Show the items and amounts that would be reported for both parties as at December 31, 2019. Clearly distinguish current from non-current items.

P17-45. Sale and leaseback transactions—buyer-lessor (L.O. 17-6) (Medium – 15 minutes)

On January 1, 2019, Amelia Company (seller-lessee) sold a plane to Lewis Financial (buyer-lessor) for its fair value of $14,000,000 and immediately leased it back under a 10-year lease at $1,676,199 per year, payable at the beginning of each year. The lease payment reflects market rents. Amelia must repurchase the plane from Lewis at the end of the lease term for $4,000,000. The plane is expected to have a residual value of $0 at the end of its remaining useful life of 20 years. The interest rate implicit in the lease is 8% and Amelia is able to readily determine this. At the time of sale, the carrying cost of the plane was $20,000,000 less accumulated depreciation of $12,000,000. Both companies have a December 31 year end and both companies depreciate this type of asset on a straight-line basis.

Required:

a. Evaluate how the buyer-lessor (Lewis) should account for the lease transaction.
b. Prepare the journal entries on January 1, 2019, December 31, 2019, and January 1, 2020, for Lewis, the buyer-lessor, pertaining to this sale and leaseback transaction.

P17-46. Sale and leaseback transactions—seller-lessee (L.O. 17-6) (Medium – 15 minutes)

On January 1, 2019, Amelia Company (seller-lessee) sold a plane to Lewis Financial (buyer-lessor) for its fair value of $14,000,000 and immediately leased it back under a 10-year lease at $1,676,199 per year, payable at the beginning of each year. The lease payment reflects market rents. Amelia must repurchase the plane from Lewis at the end of the lease term for $4,000,000. The plane is expected to have a residual value of $0 at the end of its remaining useful life of 20 years. The interest rate implicit in the lease is 8% and Amelia is able to readily determine this. At the time of sale, the carrying cost of the plane was $20,000,000 less accumulated depreciation of $12,000,000. Both companies have a December 31 year end and both companies depreciate this type of asset on a straight-line basis.

Required:

a. Evaluate how the seller-lessee (Amelia) should account for the lease transaction.
b. Prepare the journal entries on January 1, 2019, December 31, 2019, and January 1, 2020, for Amelia, the seller-lessee, pertaining to this sale and leaseback transaction.

P17-47. Sale and leaseback transactions—buyer-lessor

(L.O. 17-1, L.O. 17-2, L.O. 17-6) (Medium – 15 minutes)

On January 1, 2019, Devlin Company (seller-lessee) sold heavy-duty equipment to Bancroft Bank (buyer-lessor) for its fair market value of $6,400,000 and immediately leased it back under a 20-year non-cancellable lease at $765,022 per year, first payable on the commencement date. The remaining useful life of the equipment is 20 years, at which time its residual value is expected to be $0. Devlin Company must return the asset to Bancroft at the end of the lease term. Bancroft used an implicit rate of 12% to determine the lease payments and this is readily determinable by Devlin. The equipment had a carrying value of $4,000,000 on Devlin's books. Both companies have a December 31 year end and both companies depreciate this type of asset on a straight-line basis.

Required:

a. Evaluate how the buyer-lessor (Bancroft) should account for the lease transaction.
b. Prepare the journal entries on January 1, 2019, December 31, 2019, and January 1, 2020, for Bancroft, the buyer-lessor.

P17-48. Sale and leaseback transactions—seller-lessee

(L.O. 17-3, L.O. 17-6) (Difficult – 20 minutes)

On January 1, 2019, Devlin Company (seller-lessee) sold heavy-duty equipment to Bancroft Bank (buyer-lessor) for its fair market value of $6,400,000 and immediately leased it back under a 20-year non-cancellable lease at $765,022 per year, first payable on the commencement date. The remaining useful life of the equipment is 20 years, at which time its residual value is expected to be $0. Devlin Company must return the asset to Bancroft at the end of the lease term. Bancroft used an implicit rate of 12% to determine the lease payments and this is readily determinable by Devlin. The equipment had a carrying value of $4,000,000 on Devlin's books. Both companies have a December 31 year end and both companies depreciate this type of asset on a straight-line basis.

Required:

a. Evaluate how Devlin, the seller-lessee, should account for the lease transaction.
b. For Devlin, the seller-lessee, determine the value of the ROU asset and lease liability at initial recognition.
c. Prepare the journal entries on January 1, 2019, December 31, 2019, and January 1, 2020, for Devlin, the seller-lessee.

P17-49. Sale and leaseback transactions—seller-lessee

(L.O. 17-3, L.O. 17-6) (Difficult – 20 minutes)

On January 1, 2019, Tobey Company (seller-lessee) sold excavating equipment to Eli Bank (buyer-lessor) for its fair market value of $6,400,000 and immediately leased it back under a five-year non-cancellable lease at $1,023,021 per year, first payable on the commencement date. The remaining useful life of the equipment is 20 years, at which time its residual value is expected to be $0. Tobey has provided a residual guarantee for $4,000,000, although the expected payout under this guarantee is only $500,000. Tobey Company must return the asset to Eli at the end of the lease term. Eli used an implicit rate of 12% to determine the lease payments and this is readily determinable by Tobey. The equipment had a carrying value of $4,000,000 on Tobey's books. Both companies have a December 31 year end and both companies depreciate this type of asset on a straight-line basis.

Required:

a. Evaluate how Tobey, the seller-lessee, should account for the lease transaction.
b. Determine the value of the ROU asset and lease liability at initial recognition for Tobey, the seller-lessee.
c. Prepare the journal entries on January 1, 2019, December 31, 2019, and January 1, 2020, for Tobey, the seller-lessee.

P17-50. Sale and leaseback transactions—buyer-lessor and seller-lessee (L.O. 17-1, L.O. 17-2, L.O. 17-3, L.O. 17-6) (Difficult – 30 minutes)

On January 1, 2019, Archibald Inc. (seller-lessee) sold a cargo ship to MacPherson Capital (buyer-lessor) for its fair value of $24,000,000 and immediately leased it back under a 10-year non-cancellable lease at $2,250,758 per year, first payable on the commencement date of the lease. Archibald must return the asset to the buyer-lessor at the end of the lease term. The expected residual guarantee at the end of the lease term of $16,600,000 is not guaranteed. The ship has a remaining useful life of 20 years and its expected residual value at the end of its useful life is $0. Archibald is able to readily determine the 8% interest rate implicit in the lease. The ship had a gross carrying value of $30,000,000 and accumulated depreciation of $10,000,000 on Archibald's books. Both companies have a December 31 year end and both companies depreciate this type of asset on a straight-line basis.

Required:

a. Evaluate how the buyer-lessor (MacPherson) should account for the lease transaction.
b. Prepare the journal entries on January 1, 2019, December 31, 2019, and January 1, 2020, for MacPherson, the buyer-lessor.
c. Evaluate how the seller-lessee (Archibald) should account for the lease transaction.
d. Determine the value of the ROU asset and lease liability at initial recognition for Archibald, the seller-lessee.
e. Prepare the journal entries on January 1, 2019, December 31, 2019, and January 1, 2020, for Archibald, the seller-lessee.

P. MINI-CASES

CASE 1

Debt Laden Inc.

(45 minutes)

It is January, and Ms. Deb. T. Laden, president of Debt Laden Inc. (Debt Laden), has just returned from an annual visit with the company's banker, Mr. Green, to present Debt Laden's December financial statements. Mr. Green expressed concern over Debt Laden's profitability and debt level. In an effort to alleviate Mr. Green's concerns, Ms. Laden proposed to sell a major piece of production equipment to a local finance company, provided Debt Laden is able to lease it back. The equipment was purchased two years ago from a Japanese manufacturer for $1,000,000 and is being depreciated at 15% per year on a declining-balance basis. Due to the rise in the value of the Japanese yen relative to the Canadian dollar, Ms. Laden estimates that the machinery is currently worth $1,500,000.

She has approached Mr. Fin, president of Sharky's Financial Services Ltd. (Sharky's), who indicated that he would be willing to purchase the equipment for $1,500,000 and lease it back to Debt Laden for $274,252 per year for the next 10 years, payable at the end of each year. Debt Laden would have the option to repurchase the asset at the end of the lease term at its estimated fair value of $500,000, as it would be usable for at least another five years. Ms. Laden thinks Sharky's is getting a pretty good deal, as she estimates Debt Laden's cost of capital to be 12%. However, Mr. Fin indicated over lunch, "Hey, I gotta earn 15% or I just don't make no money on this lease!"

Ms. Laden is eager to complete the transaction in an effort to improve the company's profitability (by recording the gain on the sale of the equipment) and to concurrently reduce the company's debt level (by using the sale proceeds to pay down a loan of $1,500,000 with a 12% interest rate).

Required:

Analyze the above information and provide your recommendation to Ms. Laden as to whether she should undertake the proposed transaction.

CASE 2

PDQ Leasing Options

(30 minutes)

Parcels Delivered Quickly (PDQ) is a public company that provides shipping and delivery services for household and commercial parcels ranging from a few grams to several hundred kilograms. The company uses a fleet of 800 trucks and vans to pick up and deliver parcels. For inter-city shipping, the company has an arrangement with commercial airlines to ship parcels using airlines' cargo capacity.

The volume of parcel shipments has been increasing steadily since the start of online shopping in the late 1990s, as consumers search for the best deals regardless of physical location. As a result, PDQ needs to expand its fleet capacity by 200 vehicles to meet the increasing demand. In addition, 200 of the existing vehicles will need to be replaced over the next two years as they come to the end of their service lives.

Management is concerned about the potential for adverse reactions from investors should the company's leverage become too high or if profitability suffers as a result of this program to replace and expand the vehicle fleet. As a result, instead of borrowing and buying the needed vehicles outright, PDQ's management is considering two other alternatives:

Option 1: Lease the trucks and vans with short-term leases, one year at a time and elect to expense these short-term leases. For a truck with a cost of $80,000, the annual lease payment would amount to $15,000, due in advance.
Option 2: Lease the vehicles with long-term leases that last for the 10 years of the expected useful life. For a truck with a cost of $80,000, the annual payments would be $11,000. These leases would transfer title to PDQ at the end of the lease.

With either option, PDQ would be responsible for maintenance and repairs on the vehicles.

PDQ currently has about $32 million in total assets and $19 million in liabilities. Debt on the balance sheet carries an average interest rate of 7%. The company's bank has quoted a 9% interest rate for additional borrowing.

Required:

Analyze the alternatives relevant to the fleet replacement and expansion and provide your recommendation to management for the best course of action. Assume that PDQ depreciates vehicles using the declining-balance method at a 20% rate.

CASE 3

Lilliput Transport Authority—ASPE

(30 minutes)

Part 1

The Lilliput Transport Authority (LTA) provides public transport services in a major metropolitan area. On October 1, 2019, it entered a deal with Bus Finance Co. (BFC) to lease 100 new buses with the following terms:

- Lease term is 9 years.
- Useful life is 13 years.
- Executory (maintenance) costs for each bus are $1,500 per year and are to be included as part of the lease payment.
- Unguaranteed residual value at the end of the lease term is $14,500 per bus.
- By the end of the contract, the bus fleet reverts to BFC.
- Estimated residual value, end of useful life, is $3,600 per bus.
- BFC's interest rate implicit in the lease is 9%, which is known by LTA and the same as LTA's incremental borrowing rate.
- Each bus sells for $60,000. BFC only leases the fleet of buses and is not a bus manufacturer.
- Annual lease and maintenance payments are made on October 1 of each year, with the first payment made on the inception date.
- LTA, which has a December 31 year end, is a private firm that elects to account for its financial results in accordance with ASPE.

Required:

a. Calculate the annual payment required by BFC.
b. Explain how LTA would classify this lease.
c. Independent of your answer to part (b), assume this is a finance lease for both companies. Prepare all required journal entries for BFC for 2019.
d. Independent of your answer to part (b), assume this is a finance lease for both companies. Prepare all required journal entries for LTA for 2019.

Part 2

LTA also entered into a deal with Swift Transport Inc. to lease new cars for its metro system. The LTA metro cars use a wheel technology. Most rubber-tired trains, including the one used by LTA, are purpose-built and designed for the system on which they operate. The terms of the deal are the following:

- Lease term is eight years.
- Useful life is 20 years.
- Unguaranteed residual value at the end of the lease term is $500,000 per car.
- By the end of the contract, the cars revert to Swift Transport.
- Estimated salvage value, end of useful life, is $0.
- Swift Transport's interest rate implicit in the lease is 7% and this is known by LTA. LTA's incremental borrowing rate is 9%.
- Each car sells for $1,000,000.
- Annual lease payment of $110,966 per car and maintenance payment of $25,000 per car are made on October 1 of each year, with the first payment made on the inception date.

Required:

Discuss how LTA would classify this lease.

Margoe Edwards/Shutterstock

CHAPTER 18

Accounting for Income Taxes

CPA competencies addressed in this chapter:

1.1.2 Evaluates the appropriateness of the basis of financial reporting (Level B)
  b. Methods of measurement
  c. Differences between accrual accounting compared to cash accounting

1.2.2 Evaluates treatment for routine transactions (Level A)
  o. Changes in accounting policies and estimates, and errors
  q. Accounting for income taxes

1.3.2 Prepares routine financial statement note disclosure (Level B)

1.4.1 Analyzes complex financial statement note disclosure (Level C)

For many decades, Canadian corporations have reported on their balance sheets large amounts of liabilities for "deferred taxes" or "future income taxes." These amounts had surpassed the $100 billion mark by 2006, even counting only those corporations that are publicly traded, and the amount continues to grow.[1] To put this figure in context, total corporate income taxes collected by the federal and provincial governments are about $50 billion per year for all corporations, public and private. From time to time, politicians cite these figures, in aggregate and for specific corporations, to suggest that the government is providing "corporate welfare" to companies by allowing them to defer tax payments that are owing to the government.

Is this interpretation justified? What are deferred taxes and future income taxes that appear on companies' balance sheets? What causes these amounts to arise and build up to such large magnitudes? If companies report these amounts as liabilities on the balance sheet, are they taxes owing to the government and not yet paid?

LEARNING OBJECTIVES

After studying this chapter, you should be able to:

L.O. 18-1. Describe the conceptual differences among the three methods of accounting for income taxes, and apply the taxes payable method under ASPE.

L.O. 18-2. Analyze the effect of permanent and temporary differences on income tax expense and income tax liabilities under IFRS.

L.O. 18-3. Analyze the effect of changes in tax rates on income tax expenses, assets, and liabilities, and account for these effects under IFRS.

L.O. 18-4. Analyze the effect of tax losses on past and future income taxes, and evaluate whether and how much of these tax loss benefits can be recognized as assets under IFRS.

L.O. 18-5. Apply the presentation and disclosure standards for income taxes.

[1] Amount computed from Compustat database.

18 CONTENTS

A. INTRODUCTION 918

B. METHODS OF ACCOUNTING FOR INCOME TAXES 919
 1. Taxes payable method 920
 2. Tax allocation methods 920
 3. Summary of alternative approaches 924

C. APPLYING THE ACCRUAL METHOD: PERMANENT AND TEMPORARY DIFFERENCES 925
 1. Permanent differences 925
 2. Temporary differences 927
 3. Disposals of depreciable assets 930
 4. Schedule for analyzing permanent and temporary differences 933

D. CHANGES IN TAX RATES 934

E. TAX LOSSES 936
 1. Carryback of tax losses 937
 2. Carryforward of tax losses 938

F. MEASUREMENT: NO DISCOUNTING FOR TIME VALUE OF MONEY 940

G. PRESENTATION AND DISCLOSURE 940
 1. Presentation and disclosure of income tax expense 940
 2. Presentation and disclosure of income tax assets and liabilities 941

H. A PRACTICAL ILLUSTRATION: CANADIAN TIRE CORPORATION 941

I. SUBSTANTIVE DIFFERENCES BETWEEN RELEVANT IFRS AND ASPE 943

J. SUMMARY 944

K. ANSWERS TO CHECKPOINT QUESTIONS 945

L. GLOSSARY 945

M. REFERENCES 946

N. PROBLEMS 946

O. MINI-CASES 963

A. INTRODUCTION

Accounting for income taxes is a complex topic that involves the interaction of financial reporting and tax reporting. The complexity arises because financial reporting rules differ from tax rules, resulting in accounting income that differs from taxable income. While we will not identify every one of these differences, we can say that, as a rule of thumb, tax rules tend to more closely follow cash flows than accrual accounting. The tendency for this difference exists because the fair enforcement of laws in general requires a higher standard of verifiability than required for financial reporting.

To see the difference in financial and tax reporting, consider Tahsis Company. In each of 2019 and 2020, the company records $100,000 of revenue on long-term contracts using the percentage of completion method for financial reporting purposes (see Chapter 4 for an overview of this method of revenue recognition). Meanwhile, for tax purposes, the company uses the completed contract method and records revenue of $80,000 and $120,000 for 2019 and 2020, respectively. For simplicity of illustration, assume that Tahsis incurs no expenses other than income taxes. If Tahsis faces a tax rate of 40%, it would have a tax payable for the year 2019 of $32,000 (40% × $80,000). *If one were to account only for the amount of taxes payable*, the journal entry would be as follows:

Exhibit 18-1	Journal entry to record Tahsis Company's income tax payable in 2019	
Dr. Income tax expense	32,000	
Cr. Income tax payable		32,000

We call the method just illustrated the **taxes payable method**, which records an amount for income tax expense equal to the tax payments required for the fiscal year. However, this method has an obvious problem: there is a mismatch of income and income tax expense. We can see this mismatch by looking at the amounts Tahsis would report under this method for 2019 and 2020, assuming no other transactions in either year:

taxes payable method A method that records an amount for income tax expense equal to the tax payments for the current period.

Exhibit 18-2 Reporting outcome using the taxes payable method for Tahsis Company

	2019	2020	Total
Income before tax	$100,000	$100,000	$200,000
Income tax expense*	(32,000)	(48,000)	(80,000)
Net income	$ 68,000	$ 52,000	$120,000
Effective tax rate (Income tax expense ÷ income before tax)	32%	48%	40%

*Equals amount of tax payable

As shown in Exhibit 18-2, even though the amount of income before tax is the same in both years, the taxes payable method results in different amounts of income tax expense, so there is poor matching of tax expense to the revenue recognized in the period. The tax expense is $32,000 for $100,000 of pre-tax income in the first year—representing a rate of only 32%. The next year, the $48,000 of income tax results in an effective tax rate of 48%, since the tax payable is based on $120,000 of taxable income. Only when both years are combined do we see the expected result of 40% for the tax rate.

The difference in timing between (i) the accrual accounting income recognized for financial reporting and (ii) income recognized for tax purposes is the crux of the problem in accounting for income taxes. The next section addresses this issue conceptually. After that, we will discuss the specific approaches permitted by accounting standards.

This chapter addresses only issues related to the accounting for taxes based on income. Other government levies such as sales tax, carbon tax, goods and services tax, and import tax are outside the scope of this chapter.

B. METHODS OF ACCOUNTING FOR INCOME TAXES

Conceptually, there are three possible ways to account for income taxes:

1. taxes payable method;
2. income statement approach (deferral method); and
3. balance sheet approach (accrual method).

The latter two methods are considered "tax allocation" approaches. We will discuss each of these three methods in more detail below.

L.O. 18-1. Describe the conceptual differences among the three methods of accounting for income taxes, and apply the taxes payable method under ASPE.

1. Taxes payable method

This is the simplest method of accounting for income taxes. The introductory section has already described the essence of this approach, which is to record the income statement expense for income taxes and the corresponding liability according to the amount payable to the tax authorities. In Canada, we have income tax assessed at both the federal and provincial levels, so the amount of income taxes needs to account for both levels of tax.

It is also important to note that the label "taxes payable method" should not be interpreted too literally. If a company makes installment payments on its income taxes during the year, the amount of tax payment due when it files its tax return at the end of a year could be very small or even negative (i.e., the company is entitled to a refund because its installments exceeded the tax due). The amount of tax expense recorded is the sum of the installments and the final payment or refund expected when the enterprise files its tax return.

For example, if Tahsis Company, which has a tax payable of $32,000 for 2019, had paid tax installments totalling $30,000 during the year, then it would need to pay just the final $2,000 when it files its tax return. The journal entries would be as follows:

Exhibit 18-3	Journal entries to record Tahsis Company's income taxes using the taxes payable method		
During 2019	Dr. Income tax installments (asset)	30,000	
	Cr. Cash		30,000
Dec. 31, 2019	Dr. Income tax expense	32,000	
	Cr. Income tax installments		30,000
	Cr. Income tax payable		2,000

The taxes payable method is simple and the least costly of the three methods. There is no need to make further computations or to keep track of numerous other figures required for the other methods discussed below. However, this method does not satisfy the matching principle, as illustrated in Exhibit 18-2, and it potentially omits significant assets and liabilities for future taxes. The other two methods below will address these problems.

accounting income The amount of income (before subtracting income tax) recognized for financial reporting purposes.

taxable income The amount of income recognized for tax purposes used to compute taxes payable.

deferral method Focuses on obtaining the income statement value for income tax expense that best matches the amount of income recognized for the year.

accrual method Focuses on obtaining the balance sheet value for the income tax liability (or asset) that best reflects the assets and liabilities recognized on the balance sheet.

2. Tax allocation methods

As mentioned in the introduction, income for financial reporting purposes (**accounting income**) will generally differ from income for tax purposes (**taxable income**). As a result, the amount of income taxes payable derived from taxable income can be higher or lower than the amount of tax expense attributable to the amount of income reported on the *income statement* for a particular year. On a cumulative basis, the *balance sheet* amount of assets and liabilities will also differ between the tax report and accounting reports.

Conceptually, there are two methods to help account for these temporary differences between accounting income and taxable income. (Section C below will define temporary differences precisely.) The **deferral method** focuses on obtaining the income statement value for income tax expense that best matches the amount of income recognized for the year. In contrast, the **accrual method** focuses on obtaining the balance sheet value for the income tax liability (or asset) that best reflects the assets and liabilities recognized on the balance sheet. Collectively, these two methods are called tax allocation methods because they allocate the tax effects to periods in which the enterprise recognizes the related financial reporting amounts (in contrast to the taxes payable method, which simply records the tax effect in the period the tax is payable).

THRESHOLD CONCEPT
ARTICULATION

a. Income statement approach—Deferral method

The deferral method focuses on the income statement in order to best match the income tax expense to the revenues, expenses, gains, and losses recognized in that period, regardless of when the cash flows occur. Take the example of Tahsis Company given in the introduction. Recall that Tahsis recognized $100,000 of accounting income in the first of two years, but the company reported only $80,000 of taxable income. Since the tax rate is 40%, the income tax expense that best matches this amount of accounting income is $100,000 × 40% = $40,000. However, the tax payable due is 40% × $80,000 = $32,000. The $8,000 difference between the tax expense and tax payable goes to an account for deferred tax. In this case, the deferred tax is a liability, but in other circumstances, it can be an asset.

Exhibit 18-4 Journal entry to record Tahsis Company's income tax expense under the deferral method

Dr. Income tax expense[2] (40% × $100,000)	40,000	
Cr. Deferred tax liability (balancing figure)		8,000
Cr. Income tax payable (40% × $80,000)		32,000

In the following year, Tahsis also reports $100,000 of accounting income and the $40,000 (40% × $100,000) of tax expense. Thus, the result of the deferral method on the income statement is as follows (with taxes payable method also shown for comparison):

Exhibit 18-5 Reporting outcome using the deferral method for Tahsis Company (with taxes payable method also shown for comparison)

Deferral method	2019	2020	Total
Income before tax	$100,000	$100,000	$200,000
Income tax expense	(40,000)	(40,000)	(80,000)
Net income	$ 60,000	$ 60,000	$120,000
Effective tax rate (Income tax expense ÷ Income before tax)	40%	40%	40%
Taxes payable method (see Exhibit 18-2)	**2019**	**2020**	**Total**
Income before tax	$100,000	$100,000	$200,000
Income tax expense	(32,000)	(48,000)	(80,000)
Net income	$ 68,000	$ 52,000	$120,000
Effective tax rate (Income tax expense ÷ Income before tax)	32%	48%	40%

2. At this point, we do not separate this income tax expense into its current and deferred components. We will make that distinction later in this chapter.

THRESHOLD CONCEPT
CONCEPTUAL FRAMEWORK

Notice that the deferral method produces an effective tax rate that is consistently 40% in both years, which is the rate expected based on the assumed statutory tax rate. In contrast, the taxes payable method results in fluctuating tax rates even though the statutory rate remains constant. Thus, the deferral method better matches the income tax expense to the amount of income recorded because it applies the appropriate current tax rate to the income recognized. The resulting tax expense and net income are more relevant and representationally more faithful of performance in each year.

b. Balance sheet approach—Accrual method

As noted before, the accrual method focuses on obtaining the balance sheet value for the tax liability (or asset) that best reflects the assets and liabilities recognized on the balance sheet. When there are no changes in tax rates, the accrual method and the deferral method both produce the same results, although the sequence of logic and computations differ.

To illustrate, again consider Tahsis Company. The company recorded $100,000 of revenue on its construction contracts in the first of two years using the percentage of completion method, but only $80,000 worth was completed in the year. Further assume that the company invoices its clients at the end of each contract. The following journal entry summarizes the entries that would have been made during the first year:

Exhibit 18-6 Journal entry to record Tahsis Company's construction contracts

Dr. Cash and accounts receivable	80,000	
Dr. Construction in progress (inventory)	20,000	
Cr. Revenue on long-term contracts		100,000

As a result, $20,000 remains in inventory at year-end. The balance sheet for Tahsis at December 31, 2019, before taking account of tax effects would be as follows:

Exhibit 18-7 Balance sheet for Tahsis Company as at December 31, 2019, before accounting for income tax

Cash and accounts receivable	$ 80,000
Construction in progress	20,000
Total assets	$100,000
Equity (retained earnings)	$100,000
Total liabilities and equity	$100,000

The accrual method computes the amount of taxes that relate to the construction in progress of $20,000. At a tax rate of 40%, this amount is $8,000. Furthermore, this amount is a liability, because when the $20,000 of inventory is later recognized into income in 2020, there will be tax payable of $8,000.

Under the accrual method, Tahsis would record the following journal entry for income taxes:

Exhibit 18-8 Journal entry to record Tahsis Company's income tax expense under the accrual method

Dr. Income tax expense (balancing figure)	40,000	
Cr. Deferred tax liability (40% × $20,000)		8,000
Cr. Income tax payable (40% × $80,000)		32,000

Notice that this entry looks exactly the same as the one shown in Exhibit 18-4. The only difference is the order in which the figures are computed. The accrual method just described computes the balance sheet amount first (the $8,000 for the deferred tax liability), leaving the income statement expense as the residual "plug" figure; the deferral method calculation goes in the opposite order.

While the results of the deferral and accrual methods are the same for the example just illustrated, the two methods are equal only when tax rates remain constant from year to year. When tax rates change, the two methods will produce different results. The difference in results arises because when there is a change in tax rates:

- the deferral method focuses on the income statement and applies the new tax rate to the current year's income only and ignores the effect on accumulated balances; whereas
- the accrual method focuses on the balance sheet and applies the new tax rate to the accumulated tax amounts on the balance sheet as well as any new amounts for the current year.

To illustrate, we take the example of Tahsis Company and modify it slightly. As before, assume the company recorded $100,000 in revenue in 2019 and the tax rate in 2019 was 40%. Now also assume that the company had a deferred tax liability of $35,000 at the end of the prior year (2018). This liability was recorded when the tax rate was 35%. Under the deferral method, the journal entry to record income taxes would be no different from that shown in Exhibit 18-4, which is as follows.

Exhibit 18-9 Journal entry to record Tahsis Company's income tax expense under the deferral method

Dr. Income tax expense (40% × $100,000)	40,000	
Cr. Deferred tax asset (balancing figure)		8,000
Cr. Income tax payable (40% × $80,000)		32,000

There is no change in the journal entry from that previously recorded because the deferral method does not reflect the effect of the change in tax rate from 35% to 40% on any balances carried forward from 2018 to 2019.

In contrast, under the accrual method, the deferred tax liability of $35,000 needs to be revalued from the original tax rate of 35% to the new tax rate of 40%. At the old tax rate of 35%, the $35,000 deferred tax liability corresponds to a $100,000 taxable temporary difference. At the new tax rate of 40%, this temporary difference translates into a $40,000 liability. Thus, the change in tax rate increases the deferred tax liability by $5,000, from $35,000 to $40,000. (A general formula for computing the effect of tax rate changes will follow in Section D.)

For Tahsis, the journal entry to record its tax expense in 2019, including the effect of the tax rate change, would be as shown in Exhibit 18-10.

Exhibit 18-10 Journal entry to record Tahsis Company's income tax expense under the accrual method

Dr. Income tax expense (balancing figure)	45,000	
Cr. Deferred tax liability (40% × $20,000)		8,000
Cr. Deferred tax liability ($40,000 − $35,000)		5,000
Cr. Income tax payable (40% × $80,000)		32,000

As a result of the increase in deferred tax liability by $5,000, the income tax expense also increases by that amount, going from $40,000 to $45,000. The resulting effective tax rate is then $45,000 ÷ $100,000 = 45%, which is higher than the 40% prevailing tax rate for 2019.

It is often useful to separate the above journal entry into two separate entries to reflect the different sources of the income tax expense. Exhibit 18-11 shows journal entries that separate out the effect of the tax rate change from the effect of the current-year temporary difference.

Exhibit 18-11 Separate journal entries for temporary differences and tax rate change for Tahsis Company

Dr. Income tax expense	40,000	
Cr. Deferred tax liability (40% × $20,000)		8,000
Cr. Income tax payable (40% × $80,000)		32,000
Dr. Income tax expense	5,000	
Cr. Deferred tax liability ($40,000 − $35,000)		5,000

3. Summary of alternative approaches

These three methods of accounting for income taxes roughly parallel the three methods of accounting for bad debts, as shown in Exhibit 18-12.

Exhibit 18-12 Comparison of accounting methods for income taxes and for bad debts

Conceptual focus	Accounting method for income taxes	Accounting method for bad debts
Cash basis	Taxes payable method	Direct write-off
Income statement approach	Deferral method	Percentage of sales
Balance sheet approach	Accrual method	Aging of accounts receivable

THRESHOLD CONCEPT
TIMING OF RECOGNITION

The taxes payable method is close to cash basis accounting because the tax effect is recorded in the period in which the tax becomes due/payable.[3] This is similar to recognizing bad debts only when the enterprise determines that the accounts are uncollectible. The deferral method and the percentage of sales method are similar in that they both apply a percentage to an income statement amount to determine an expense (tax rate × income before tax; bad debt percentage × credit sales). The accrual method and aging of accounts receivable are similar because they both use information from the balance sheet to compute the amounts to recognize.

Exhibit 18-13 is another way to summarize these three methods of accounting for income taxes.

3. For the taxes payable method to be strictly cash accounting, the tax effect would be recorded only when the tax is paid, not when it is due/payable.

Exhibit 18-13 Conceptual methods of accounting for income taxes

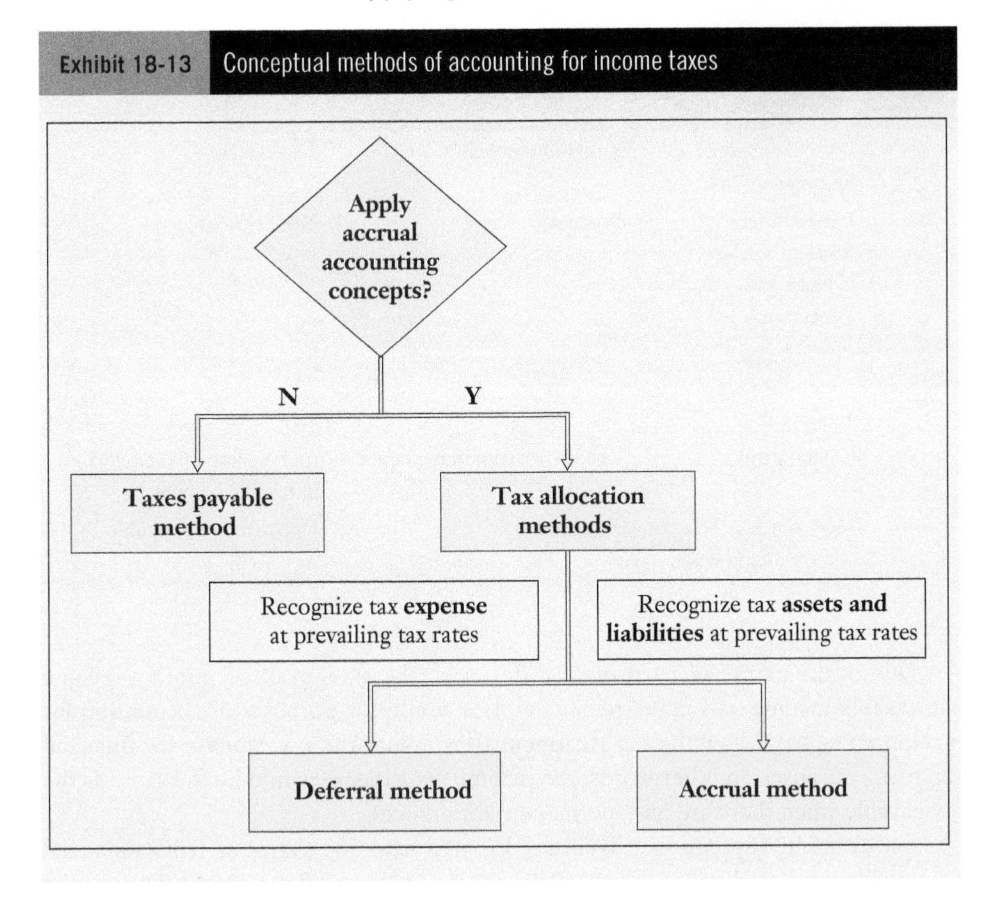

Currently, the *accrual method is the accepted approach* in both IFRS and ASPE. The deferral method had been the accepted approach in the past, but is not currently accepted.[4] However, that method has left a legacy of some terminology that continues to be used, as we will see below. The taxes payable method is an accepted alternative to the accrual method under ASPE.

CHECKPOINT **CP18-1**

Why is the taxes payable method not an accepted approach under IFRS? What difference explains why ASPE permits this approach in addition to the accrual approach?

C. APPLYING THE ACCRUAL METHOD: PERMANENT AND TEMPORARY DIFFERENCES

L.O. 18-2. Analyze the effect of permanent and temporary differences on income tax expense and income tax liabilities under IFRS.

As the introduction already indicated, the complexity in accounting for income taxes is due to the differences between (i) how we record transactions and events for financial reporting purposes and (ii) how tax rules treat these transactions and events. These differences come in two varieties: permanent and temporary.

1. Permanent differences

permanent difference Arises from a transaction or event that affects accounting income but never taxable income, or vice versa.

A **permanent difference** arises from a transaction or event that affects accounting income but never taxable income, or vice versa. For example, lottery winnings in Canada are not taxable, but are nonetheless income for financial reporting purposes. While we do not expect to see this particular item very often in companies, there are some more common examples of permanent differences:

[4] The deferral method was the accepted approach in Canada until the end of 1999.

Exhibit 18-14 Common examples of permanent differences

	Item	Accounting treatment	Tax treatment
a.	Dividends received by corporations	Include in income	Not taxable
b.	Initiation fees for membership in clubs and associations	Expense	Not deductible
c.	Life insurance premiums for employees	Expense	Not deductible
d.	Capital gains	Include full gain in income	Include half of capital gain in taxable income
e.	Meal and entertainment costs	Expense	Only half is deductible

Due to the nature of permanent differences, the amount of accounting income and taxable income will never reconcile. As a result, for purposes of accounting for income taxes, we follow the tax treatment to compute the tax expense for financial reporting purposes. In other words, the income tax expense would be the same as the tax payable when there are only permanent differences.

For example, suppose that Wynndel Limited held 500 shares of RBC Financial previously purchased at $60/share (RBC is also known as Royal Bank). During the year, Wynndel receives dividend income of $4/share from RBC. At the end of the year, Wynndel sells all 500 shares at $80/share. For the year, Wynndel's sales revenue and operating expenses are $500,000 and $420,000, respectively. The combined federal and provincial tax rate is 40%. Note that only one-half of the capital gain on the sale of shares is taxable.

Based on these facts, Wynndel would report the following results:

Exhibit 18-15 Accounting and taxable income for Wynndel Limited

	Accounting income	Taxable income
Sales revenue	$ 500,000	$ 500,000
Operating expenses	(420,000)	(420,000)
Dividend income (500 shares × $4/share; non-taxable)	2,000	0
Gain on sale of shares (500 shares @ $20/share; ½ taxable)	10,000	5,000
Income before tax or taxable income	92,000	$ 85,000
Tax rate		× 40%
Income tax payable		$ 34,000
Income tax expense (= income tax payable)	(34,000)	
Net income	$ 58,000	

Since all of the differences between accounting and taxable income are permanent, the $34,000 in taxes payable is the amount of the income tax expense. In practice, rather than going through all the items in accounting income and taxable income in parallel as just shown, it is more expedient to start with the accounting income number and then make the necessary adjustments for the permanent differences. Exhibit 18-16 shows this approach.

Exhibit 18-16 Computation of income tax expense	
Income before tax	$92,000
Less: Non-taxable dividends	(2,000)
Less: Non-taxable portion of capital gains	(5,000)
Income for computing tax expense	$85,000
Tax rate	× 40%
Income tax expense	$34,000

Focusing on the items where there are differences is useful not only for permanent differences, but also for temporary differences, which we discuss next.

2. Temporary differences

A **temporary difference** is a difference between the carrying amount of an asset or liability in the balance sheet and its tax base (IAS 12 paragraph 5). Most (but not all) temporary differences arise from transactions and events that affect both accounting income and taxable income but *just in different reporting periods.*[5] The different timing of revenue recognition for Tahsis Company given in the introduction is an example of a temporary difference. Let's review and explore that example in more depth.

temporary difference Arises from a transaction or event that affects both accounting income and taxable income, but in different reporting periods.

- Accounting income of $100,000 *is more than* taxable income of $80,000 in 2019. The difference of $20,000 is reflected in construction in process inventory on the balance sheet, but this asset has zero value on a tax basis because taxable income includes only the $80,000 of revenue from completed contracts.
- Since taxable income is $20,000 less in 2019, the amount of tax payable is less than the income tax expense by $8,000 based on a tax rate of 40%. However, this $8,000 will become payable in the future when the $20,000 is recognized in taxable income. In other words, the temporary difference of $20,000 will reverse in the future.
- In this example, the temporary difference reverses in 2020, resulting in taxable income of $120,000 exceeding accounting income of $100,000. As a result, tax payable exceeds income tax expense by $8,000. That future tax payment of $8,000 constitutes a liability at the end of 2019. We call this $8,000 a **deferred tax liability** in IFRS and "future income tax liability" in ASPE.

deferred tax liability The amount of income tax payable in future periods as a result of taxable temporary differences.

This example illustrates a case when *future* taxable income will be higher than accounting income; thus, we call this a **taxable temporary difference**.

taxable temporary difference A temporary difference that results in future taxable income being higher than accounting income.

The opposite case involves a **deductible temporary difference**, which occurs when the temporary difference results in future taxable income that will be lower than accounting income. In this case, we should record an asset for the reduction in taxes payable in the future. We call this asset a **deferred tax asset** in IFRS and a "future income tax asset" in ASPE.

deductible temporary difference A temporary difference that results in *future* taxable income being less than accounting income.

Exhibit 18-17 summarizes permanent and temporary differences.

deferred tax asset The amount of income tax recoverable in future periods as a result of deductible temporary differences, losses carried forward, or tax credits carried forward.

5. There are rare instances of temporary differences that do not involve different timing of income or expense recognition, which are beyond the scope of this text.

Exhibit 18-17 Summary of accounting/tax differences and resulting asset or liability

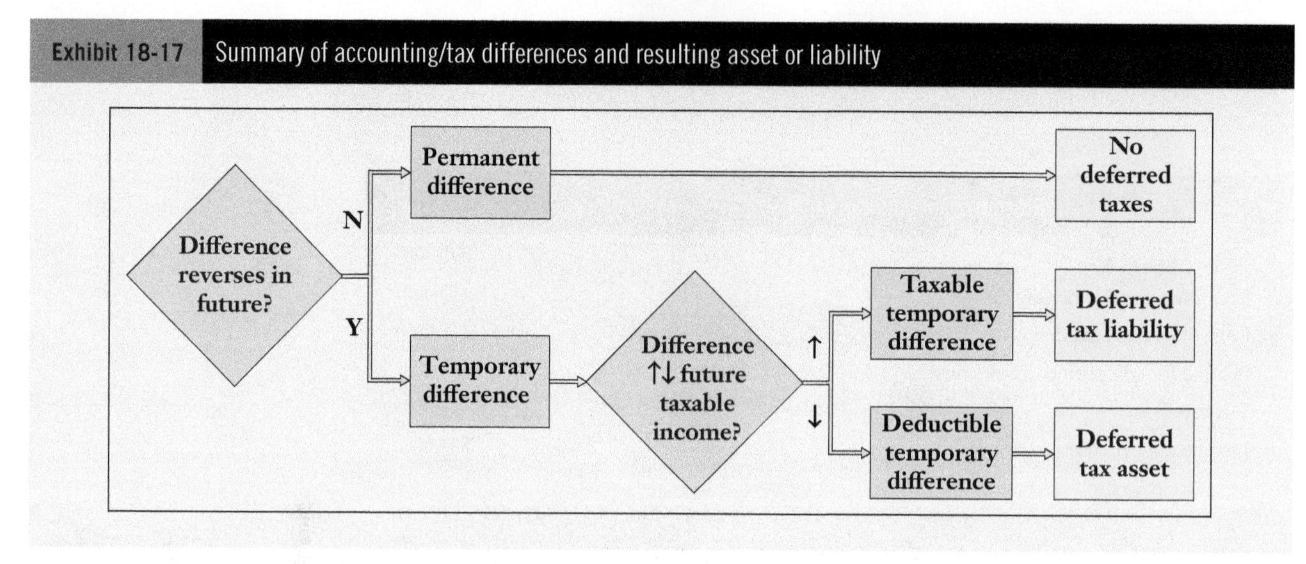

TERMINOLOGY FOR TAX ASSETS AND LIABILITIES

Canadian GAAP prior to 2000 also used the term "deferred tax liability," because the term is consistent with the deferral method. The change to the accrual method in 2000, which has a balance sheet focus, resulted in a change in terminology to "future income tax" to de-emphasize the idea of deferral, which is an income statement concept. However, IFRS continues to use the terms "deferred tax liability" and "deferred tax asset." Given the different terminology used in different standards and during different time periods, accountants tend to use the two sets of terms interchangeably. In this text, we will use "deferred tax" asset or liability.

CHECKPOINT **CP18-2**

Why is it necessary to distinguish permanent differences from temporary differences?

a. Common temporary differences

THRESHOLD CONCEPT
CONCEPTUAL FRAMEWORK

A difference in revenue recognition on long-term contracts is just one example of temporary differences. There are potentially many temporary differences due to the fact that politicians/governments set tax rules with objectives that differ from the objectives of accounting standard setters and financial statement preparers. Some of these temporary differences include the following:

Exhibit 18-18 Common examples of temporary differences

	Item	Accounting treatment	Tax treatment
a.	Revenue on construction contracts	Recognize using percentage of completion method	Can use completed contract method
b.	Fair value increase on biological assets (e.g., grape vines, cattle, trees)	Recognize fair value gains through income	Recognize income upon disposal of or production from biological assets
c.	Warranty costs	Accrue expense to match revenue recognition	Deduct when actual costs are incurred
d.	Finance leases	Record interest and depreciation expense (see Chapter 17)	Deduct lease payment
e.	Depreciation, depletion, and amortization	Record expenses using methods and rates according to company's accounting policy	Deduct capital cost allowance using rates and methods specified in tax rules

For most enterprises, the last item in this table—depreciation—is the largest temporary difference. We examine this temporary difference in more detail next.

b. Temporary differences due to depreciation

Usually, the amount of depreciation for tax purposes, or **capital cost allowance (CCA)**, exceeds the amount of depreciation for accounting purposes. This tendency is due to governments' desire to encourage investment in capital assets: high CCA deductions decrease the present value of taxes because less taxes are due in the early periods of the assets' lives. As a result, taxable income tends to be less than accounting income, and companies tend to report significant amounts of deferred tax liabilities. To see this result, consider the following example of Yale Company.

capital cost allowance (CCA) Depreciation for tax purposes.

Exhibit 18-19 Yale Company: An example to illustrate temporary differences due to depreciation

Yale Company has a single depreciable asset purchased at a cost of $300,000 at the beginning of Year 1. The asset has a useful life of three years and residual value of zero. The capital cost allowance (CCA) for the asset is $150,000, $100,000, and $50,000 for Year 1, Year 2, and Year 3, respectively.[6] In each of the three years, Yale Company has $500,000 of income before taxes (after subtracting depreciation), and the company uses the straight-line depreciation method for financial reporting purposes. The company faces a 40% tax rate in all years.

Computation of tax expense and taxes payable	Year 1	Year 2	Year 3	Total
Income before taxes	$500,000	$500,000	$500,000	$1,500,000
Add back: non-deductible depreciation	100,000	100,000	100,000	300,000
Subtract: CCA	(150,000)	(100,000)	(50,000)	(300,000)
Taxable income	$ 450,000	$ 500,000	$ 550,000	$1,500,000
Income tax expense (40% × income before taxes)	$ 200,000	$ 200,000	$ 200,000	$ 600,000
Taxes payable (40% × taxable income)	$ 180,000	$ 200,000	$ 220,000	$ 600,000

Journal entries	Year 1 Dr.	Year 1 Cr.	Year 2 Dr.	Year 2 Cr.	Year 3 Dr.	Year 3 Cr.
Current income tax expense	180,000		200,000		220,000	
Income tax payable		180,000		200,000		220,000
Deferred income tax expense	20,000					20,000
Deferred tax liability		20,000			20,000	

Balance sheet at Dec. 31	Year 1	Year 2	Year 3
Deferred tax liability	20,000 Cr.	20,000 Cr.	0

As shown in this example, the fact that CCA exceeds depreciation in Year 1 results in a taxable temporary difference of $50,000, which, at a tax rate of 40%, translates into a deferred tax liability of $20,000. In Year 2, CCA equals depreciation, so the current-year temporary difference is zero. However, the *cumulative* temporary difference is $50,000, and the balance sheet amount for deferred tax liability is $20,000, which is the amount carried forward from Year 1. In Year 3, the temporary difference reverses because CCA is less than depreciation, resulting in a drawdown (debit) of the deferred tax liability of $20,000.

[6] For ease of illustration, the CCA amounts for this example differ from the typical pattern, which uses a declining-balance method. What is important is that CCA tends to be higher in the early years of asset ownership.

originating difference A temporary difference that widens the gap between accounting and tax values of an asset or liability.

reversing difference A temporary difference that narrows the gap between accounting and tax values of an asset or liability.

This example also illustrates the idea of originating and reversing differences. An **originating difference** is a temporary difference that widens the gap between accounting and tax values of an asset or liability. A **reversing difference** narrows that gap. The $50,000 difference between CCA and accounting depreciation in Year 1 is an originating difference. The $50,000 difference in Year 3 is a reversing difference.

Note that we distinguish the income tax expense into a current component and a deferred component. The current component is for taxes payable for the year, while the deferred portion relates to taxes in future years. For example, in Year 1, the total income tax expense is $200,000, separated into $180,000 for the current tax expense and $20,000 for future tax expense.

In substance, temporary differences for depreciation are distinct from other temporary differences only in their magnitude and duration. In the example of Yale Company, the temporary difference reverses over three years—the useful life of the asset. In reality, depreciable assets can have much longer useful lives—10, 20, 40 years or even longer. Thus, the reversal of temporary differences due to depreciation can take decades. In fact, temporary differences due to depreciation tend to build up over time because enterprises continually acquire assets to augment those that are aging and to expand capacity for growth. This accumulation of temporary differences explains the large and growing amount of deferred tax liabilities on corporations' balance sheets mentioned in the opening vignette.

CHECKPOINT **CP18-3**

What is the relationship between (i) taxable temporary differences and deductible temporary differences, and (ii) deferred tax assets and deferred tax liabilities?

3. Disposals of depreciable assets

A sale or other disposal of a depreciable asset can result in a gain or loss for financial reporting purposes. That gain or loss is equal to the proceeds less the carrying value of the asset. For tax purposes, the amount of gain or loss will tend to differ from the amount for financial reporting purposes because of differences between the depreciation and CCA previously recorded. Furthermore, the tax gain or loss potentially has two components: one relating to regular income and the other relating to capital. The distinction is important because only one-half of capital gains are taxable. As a result, disposals of depreciable assets can involve both temporary and permanent differences. To account for the temporary and permanent differences requires some detailed knowledge of the *Income Tax Act* that is potentially beyond your knowledge base and the scope of this text. Nevertheless, the following summarizes these issues at a basic level.

a. Disposal of an asset from an asset pool

undepreciated capital cost (UCC) The net carrying amount of an asset or asset class for tax purposes.

For tax purposes, depreciable assets are generally put into classes according to their type. For example, aircraft would be put into Class 9, while trucks would be put into Class 10. An important concept in tax depreciation is the **undepreciated capital cost (UCC)**, which is the tax version of carrying amount in financial accounting. In other words, UCC is cost less accumulated CCA. For most asset classes, the UCC is treated as a "pool" such that the costs are not specifically identified with a particular asset. For such assets, disposals simply reduce the balance of UCC of the class, resulting in no gain or loss for tax purposes. However, future CCA will be less due to the reduced

UCC. The result of a disposal from a UCC pool is a temporary difference equal to the amount of gain or loss recognized for accounting purposes.[7]

b. Disposal of specifically identified assets

Tax rules specify that some depreciable assets need to be specifically identified rather than put into a pool. For example, buildings are Class 1 assets for tax purposes, but each building must be treated as a separate class (i.e., specifically identified). This treatment is similar to the specific identification method for inventory accounting, while the asset pools discussed above are comparable to the non-specific methods (weighted-average cost and first-in, first-out). The disposal of a specifically identified asset can result in one of three cases. The different cases arise because of the different tax treatments of regular income and capital gains. Exhibit 18-20 provides an overview of these three cases, after which we will look at each case individually.

Exhibit 18-20 Three possible cases for disposals of specifically identified depreciable assets

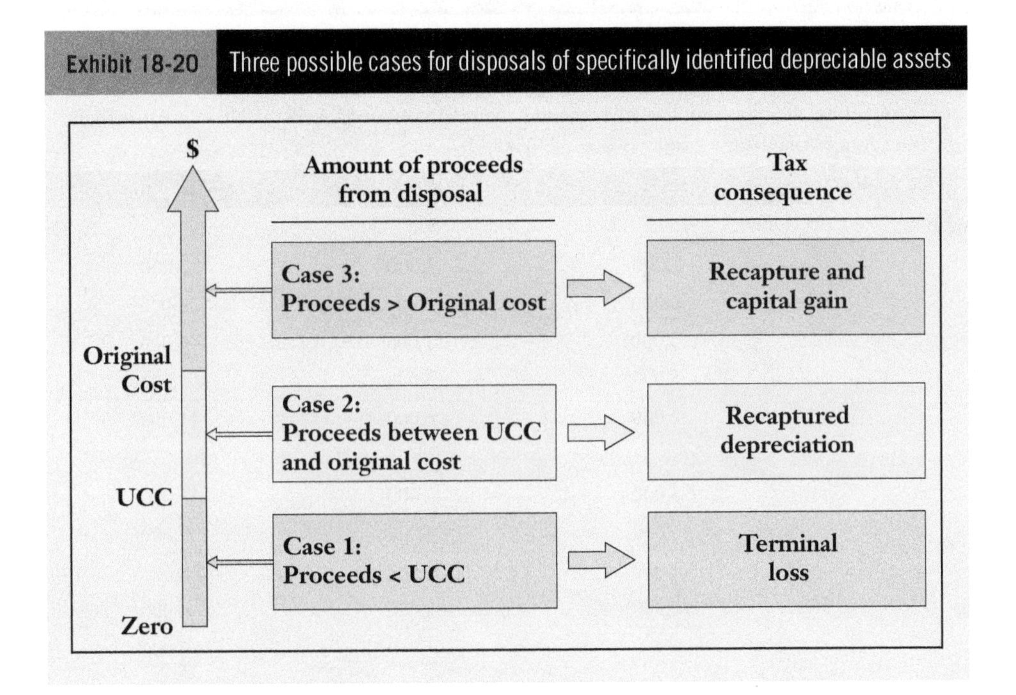

Case 1: When the proceeds from disposal are less than the UCC of the asset, there is a loss for tax purposes called a **terminal loss**. A terminal loss is deductible against other income in full, in contrast to capital losses, which are only one-half deductible (just as capital gains are one-half taxable). This case results in a temporary difference equal to the difference between the accounting gain or loss and the amount of the terminal loss.

terminal loss The tax loss arising from the sale of an asset for proceeds below its undepreciated capital cost. Applies to assets separately identified for tax purposes.

Case 2: When the proceeds from disposal are more than the UCC of the asset but less than the original cost, the enterprise records income for tax purposes called **recaptured depreciation**, or simply "recapture." This label reflects the fact that the amount of tax depreciation (CCA) has been too generous, resulting in a UCC that is below the asset's market value at time of disposal. Recapture is fully taxable, just as CCA is fully deductible. The difference between the accounting gain or loss and the amount of recapture is a temporary difference.

recaptured depreciation The taxable income recorded for the reversal of previously taken capital cost allowances when the sale proceeds of an asset exceed its undepreciated capital cost. Applies to assets separately identified for tax purposes.

[7] For assets treated in a pool, there are special cases such as the disposal of the last asset in the class and when the disposal proceeds exceed the amount of UCC in the class. We do not explicitly address these cases, but their treatment is similar to the following discussion for specifically identified assets.

Case 3: When the proceeds from disposal are more than the original cost of the asset, there will be both recapture and a capital gain. The amount of recapture equals the difference between the original cost and UCC, while the amount of capital gains equals the difference between the sale proceeds and original cost. Recapture is fully taxable, but only one-half of capital gain is included in taxable income. This case results in a permanent difference for the one-half of the capital gains that is non-taxable. There will also be a temporary difference for the difference between the carrying amount and UCC.

The example in Exhibit 18-21 illustrates these three cases.

Exhibit 18-21 Illustration of tax effects of disposals of specifically identified depreciable assets, Comox Co.

Comox Co. sells a building with a cost of $10 million and undepreciated capital cost (UCC) of $4 million for tax purposes. For financial reporting, the building has a carrying amount of $6 million. The sale price of the building is one of three values: $3, $7, or $12 million. Aside from the sale of the building, the company has other income (before taxes) of $5 million. There are no other permanent or temporary differences. The company faces an income tax rate of 30%.

($000's)	Case 1		Case 2		Case 3	
Computation of accounting income						
Proceeds from sale of building		**3,000**		**7,000**		**12,000**
Carrying amount		6,000		6,000		6,000
Accounting gain (loss)		(3,000)		1,000		6,000
Other accounting income		5,000		5,000		5,000
Accounting income before tax		2,000		6,000		11,000
Computation of taxable income						
Proceeds from sale		3,000		7,000		12,000
UCC		4,000		4,000		4,000
Tax basis gain (loss)		(1,000)		3,000		8,000
Portion for recapture (terminal loss)		(1,000)		3,000		6,000
Portion for capital gain		0		0		2,000
Recapture (terminal loss)		(1,000)		3,000		6,000
Capital gain		0		0		2,000
Less: non-taxable portion of capital gain		0		0		(1,000)
Taxable income (loss) due to sale		(1,000)		3,000		7,000
Other taxable income		5,000		5,000		5,000
Total taxable income		4,000		8,000		12,000
Accounting vs. tax basis						
Permanent difference		—		—		(1,000)
Temporary difference*		2,000		2,000		2,000
Journal entries						
Dr. Current income tax expense	1,200		2,400		3,600	
Cr. Taxes payable[a]		1,200		2,400		3,600
Dr. Deferred tax liability[b]	600		600		600	
Cr. Deferred income tax recovery		600		600		600

*Temporary differences can be defined in either direction. For convenience, we define the differences as (taxable income − accounting income) for the particular temporary difference. When defined this way, positive temporary differences correspond to debits and negative temporary differences correspond to credits of deferred taxes.

[a]Taxes payable = Taxable income × 30%

[b]Reduction in deferred tax liability = Reversing taxable temporary difference × 30%

4. Schedule for analyzing permanent and temporary differences

Due to the variety of sources of permanent and temporary differences, it is often useful to systematically organize the analysis in a schedule. To illustrate, consider the example of Cramer Company in Exhibit 18-22.

Exhibit 18-22 Illustration of schedule for analysis of permanent and temporary differences

Cramer Company earned $500,000 of income before taxes in the fiscal year ended December 31, 2020. During the year, the company recorded depreciation of $160,000 while for tax purposes it claimed CCA of $250,000. The company also rented out a portion of its unused office space and received $20,000 in payment for a year starting July 1, 2020, and this amount is taxable in the year received. Cramer also received dividends from other taxable Canadian corporations totalling $20,000 during the year. In September, the company sold a piece of land with a cost of $300,000 for proceeds of $700,000. The statutory tax rate applicable to Cramer is 30%.

Item/transaction	Amounts for tax purposes	Amounts for financial accounting purposes	Temporary difference	× Tax rate	Debit (credit) to deferred tax account on balance sheet
Income before taxes	$ 500,000	$500,000	$ —	30%	—
Add back depreciation[a]	160,000		(90,000)	30%	$(27,000)
Deduct CCA[a]	(250,000)				
Unearned rent revenue[b]	10,000		10,000	30%	3,000
Dividend income[c]	(20,000)	(20,000)	—	30%	
Non-taxable portion of capital gain[d]	(200,000)	(200,000)	—	30%	
Subtotal	$ 200,000	$ 280,000	$ (80,000)	30%	$(24,000)
Tax rate	30%	30%	30%		
Tax payable or tax expense	$ 60,000	$ 84,000	$ (24,000)		

Notes:

[a]Depreciation is not deductible for tax purposes; add back to taxable income; deduct CCA from taxable income instead.

[b]Received $20,000 for one year of rent starting July 1, 2020; only one-half was earned and recognized in accounting income, but the full amount is taxable, so $10,000 is added to taxable income.

[c]Dividend income is not taxable; this is a permanent difference that should be removed from both taxable income and the accounting income number used to compute income tax expense.

[d]Capital gain of $400,000 was realized; only one-half is taxable.

In this schedule, the first numeric column itemizes the amounts for tax purposes (e.g., taxable income, tax payable). The second column itemizes the amounts for financial reporting purposes (e.g., income tax expense). Notice that temporary differences appear in only one of these two columns, whereas permanent differences appear in both columns.

In addition to systematically organizing the information on temporary and permanent differences, this schedule produces useful accounting information. The bottom of the schedule identifies the amounts of taxes payable as $60,000 and the amount of income tax expense as $84,000. The difference of $(24,000) represents the net deferred tax adjustment on the balance sheet, with the negative figure meaning a credit adjustment. This $24,000 credit adjustment is explained by the figures on the far right column: the depreciation/CCA adjustments amount to a $27,000 credit to deferred tax liability. The $3,000 debit is for unearned rent revenue that will be earned in the following year, so it should be recorded as a deferred tax asset. With this schedule in hand, the journal entries can be readily constructed, as shown in Exhibit 18-23.

Exhibit 18-23 Journal entry to record income taxes for Cramer Company

Dr. Income tax expense—current	60,000	
Cr. Income tax payable		60,000
Dr. Income tax expense—deferred	24,000	
Dr. Deferred income tax asset	3,000	
Cr. Deferred income tax liability		27,000

The total income tax expense, current and deferred, is $84,000 as identified at the bottom of Exhibit 18-22.

Notice in these journal entries that income tax expense is either current taxes payable or deferred taxes relating to future years. *On the balance sheet*, the deferred tax asset and liability accounts are always non-current under IFRS.

D. CHANGES IN TAX RATES

L.O. 18-3. Analyze the effect of changes in tax rates on income tax expenses, assets, and liabilities, and account for these effects under IFRS.

The discussion in Section C is valid for transactions and events occurring in each year, using the tax rates appropriate for that year. However, tax amounts on the balance sheet (deferred tax assets and deferred tax liabilities) carry forward from year to year. If tax rates change from one year to another, the values of these balances need to be adjusted.

In fact, tax rates do change from time to time, and sometimes frequently. For instance, the federal corporate tax rate declined from 22.5% to 19.5% as of January 1, 2008, and further by 0.5%, 1%, 1.5%, and 1.5% at the beginning of each of the next four years to reach 15% at the beginning of 2012. These are just the changes at the federal level. Provinces also change their provincial income tax rates. Such changes in tax rates are important when we use the accrual method, discussed in Section B.

To illustrate the effect of tax rate changes, consider the following example of Delta Inc. in Exhibit 18-24. Assume that, at the beginning of the year, the company had taxable temporary differences amounting to $400,000, corresponding to $100,000 of deferred tax liabilities at a tax rate of 25%. Also suppose that the government increased the tax rate to 30% at the beginning of the year. During the year, Delta had additional temporary differences resulting from taxable income being $100,000 less than accounting income. The following table shows the results of the above assumed facts on Delta's deferred taxes.

Exhibit 18-24 Illustration of change in tax rates, Delta Inc.

($000's)	Deductible (taxable) temporary differences	×	Tax rate	=	Deferred tax Dr. (Cr.)
Beginning balance, Jan. 1	(400)		25%		(100)
Adjustment for change in tax rate	—		+5%		(20)
Adjusted balance	(400)		30%		(120)
Temporary differences during the year	(100)		30%		(30)
Ending balance, Dec. 31	(500)		30%		(150)

As this example illustrates, the value of deferred tax assets and liabilities will increase and decrease along with income tax rates. The \$100,000 of deferred tax liability at the beginning of the year needs to be adjusted upward due to the 5% increase in tax rates. Given the old tax rate and the new tax rate, we can compute the amount of the adjusted deferred tax balance using either the beginning balance of deferred tax or the balance of temporary differences.

Exhibit 18-25 Formula to calculate adjusted balance of deferred taxes when tax rates change

$$\text{Adjusted deferred tax balance} = \frac{\text{Beginning deferred tax balance}}{\text{Old tax rate}} \times \text{New tax rate}$$
$$= \text{Beginning temporary difference balance} \times \text{New tax rate}$$

For Delta Inc., the calculations are as follows:

Exhibit 18-26 Computing adjusted balance of deferred taxes after a tax rate change for Delta Inc.

$$\text{Adjusted deferred tax balance} = \frac{\text{Beginning deferred tax balance}}{\text{Old tax rate}} \times \text{New tax rate}$$
$$= \frac{\$100{,}000 \text{ Cr.}}{25\%} \times 30\%$$
$$= \$120{,}000 \text{ Cr.}$$

$$\text{Adjusted deferred tax balance} = \text{Beginning temporary difference balance} \times \text{New tax rate}$$
$$= \$(400{,}000) \times 30\%$$
$$= \$120{,}000 \text{ Cr.}$$

Given that the opening deferred tax liability balance is \$100,000 Cr., the amount of adjustment is \$20,000 Cr., recorded as follows:

Exhibit 18-27 Journal entry to record change in tax rate for Delta Inc.

	Dr.	Cr.
Dr. Deferred income tax expense	20,000	
Cr. Deferred tax liability		20,000

Based on the above analysis, a somewhat more direct computation of the amount required for the journal entry is as follows:

Exhibit 18-28 Formula to calculate adjustment to deferred tax balance for tax rate changes

$$\text{Adjustment} = \text{Beg. deferred tax balance} \times \frac{\text{New tax rate}}{\text{Old tax rate}} - \text{Beg. deferred tax balance}$$
$$= \text{Beg. deferred tax balance} \times \left(\frac{\text{New tax rate}}{\text{Old tax rate}} - 1\right)$$
$$= \$100{,}000 \text{ Cr.} \times \left(\frac{30\%}{25\%} - 1\right)$$
$$= \$100{,}000 \text{ Cr.} \times (1.2 - 1)$$
$$= \$20{,}000 \text{ Cr.}$$

Looking at the term in parentheses, we see that the term is positive if the tax rate increases and negative if the tax rate decreases. Thus, if the deferred tax balance is an asset, that asset becomes more valuable if the tax rate increases and less so if the tax rate decreases. Likewise, if the deferred tax balance is a liability, that liability becomes more costly if the tax rate increases and less costly if the tax rate decreases.

Other issues relating to changes in tax rates are that enterprises should use tax rates that have been "enacted or substantively enacted" (IAS 12 paragraph 46), and measure deferred tax assets and liabilities at the tax rates that are expected to apply when the difference is anticipated to reverse (IAS 12 paragraph 47). This means enterprises need to take account of changes in future tax rates if such changes have already been put into legislation. Even legislation that has not yet received royal assent, but which is almost certain to pass through the legislative process, needs to be considered because such legislation is considered "substantively enacted."

CHECKPOINT **CP18-4**

Supposing that a company makes no sales and incurs no expenses such that it has no income before tax. Why would a change in tax rate result in non-zero net income?

E. TAX LOSSES

L.O. 18-4. Analyze the effect of tax losses on past and future income taxes, and evaluate whether and how much of these tax loss benefits can be recognized as assets under IFRS.

When a business is profitable, it pays taxes according to its taxable income multiplied by the tax rate. If the tax system were symmetric for profits and losses, a business that has a loss in a year would receive a tax payment from the government equal to the amount of loss multiplied by the tax rate. However, the income tax system treats income and losses asymmetrically. The government will pay the company sometimes, but not at other times, as we will see shortly.

Income tax laws in many countries permit a corporation with a loss for tax purposes (i.e., negative taxable income) to carry that loss to surrounding years. Currently, Canadian tax laws allow corporations to carry an operating loss backward for three years and forward for 20 years, and capital losses backward for three years and forward indefinitely.[8] Carrying a loss back to offset taxable income in a prior year produces a tax refund. However, carrying a loss forward has no immediate cash flow benefits; the company realizes the benefit in the future when it earns income.

WHY DOES THE TAX SYSTEM TREAT PROFITS AND LOSSES ASYMMETRICALLY?

On the surface, it may seem unfair for the government to treat profits and losses asymmetrically for tax purposes. Supposing the tax rate were 30%, each dollar of profit would require the payment of 30 cents, so shouldn't the government compensate the corporation 30 cents for each dollar of loss?

THRESHOLD CONCEPT
INFORMATION ASYMMETRY

The reason for the asymmetric treatment is rooted in the concept of moral hazard, discussed in Chapter 1. Moral hazard is relevant because we can think of the government as a silent partner who holds an equity interest in the corporation and moral hazard is a concern for any equity interest holder. The government's equity interest is equal to the tax rate (say 30%) because for each dollar of pre-tax profits, 30 cents goes to the government and 70 cents goes to the non-government owners.

[8] The carryforward period for operating losses was 10 years for losses incurred prior to 2006 and 7 years prior to March 23, 2004.

When the business is profitable, the government is happy to receive its 30% share. However, the government is reluctant to contribute its 30% share for losses because it may not have reliable information on the source of that loss. For example, the loss may have been incurred because management has consumed the business resources, and the government does not wish to subsidize consumption. Furthermore, the business may not even be a bona fide business that could be expected to earn a profit. Given the limited liability of corporations, the government would not be able to recover funds that it has contributed toward losses, even if those losses were illegitimate. Consequently, the government is only willing to provide refunds on taxes previously paid for losses carried back, but it is unwilling to pay for losses in the absence of prior profits.

1. Carryback of tax losses

When a company incurs a tax loss and also has taxable income in past years, it is eligible to apply the loss to offset income in those prior years. Currently, that carryback period is three years. Technically, the carryback works as follows:

- The company chooses one of the previous three years to apply the loss. Normally, the optimal choice is the earliest of the three years. The loss reduces the taxable income in that prior year, but cannot create or increase a loss in that prior year.
- The company recalculates the tax payable for that prior year using the revised taxable income that includes the effect of the loss carried back. It uses the tax rate in force for that prior tax year.
- The difference between the recalculated tax payable and the tax actually paid previously for that prior year is the amount of refund owing to the company.

For example, suppose Esquimalt Company has taxable income of $10 million in 2017 and pays taxes of $3 million (i.e., its tax rate was 30%). Later, in year 2020, the company incurs an operating tax loss of $8 million when the tax rate is 35%. For financial reporting purposes, Esquimalt's loss before tax is $6 million.

Based on these facts, Esquimalt would be entitled to claim a tax refund of $2.4 million by carrying the $8 million loss back to reduce the taxable income in 2017. Exhibit 18-29 summarizes the effect of the loss carryback.

Exhibit 18-29 Effect of losses carried back for Esquimalt Company

($ millions)	Taxable income	×	Tax rate	=	Taxes payable
2017 as previously filed	10		30%		3.0
Losses carried back from 2020 to 2017	(8)		30%		(2.4)
2017 after losses carried back	2		30%		0.6

The amount of the refund is determined by the tax rate of 30%, which was the rate in force for 2017. The 35% tax rate in 2020 is not relevant. In other words, the company previously paid $3 million on $10 million of taxable income for 2017. After carrying the 2020 loss of $8 million back to 2017, the taxable income reduces to $2 million, and the tax at 30% is only $0.6 million. The reduction in tax for 2017 from $3 million to $0.6 million is $2.4 million.

Esquimalt would record the following journal entries. Note that "income tax recovery" is an income statement account for a negative income tax expense.

Exhibit 18-30 Journal entries to record tax recovery for Esquimalt Company

Dr. Income tax receivable ($8,000,000 loss × 30%)	2,400,000	
Cr. Current income tax recovery		2,400,000
Dr. Deferred income tax expense ($2,000,000 × 35%)	700,000	
Cr. Deferred income tax liability		700,000

The second entry reflects temporary differences totalling $2 million, since the accounting loss is $6 million while the tax loss is $8 million.

2. Carryforward of tax losses

Whereas carrying back losses results in a *definite and immediate* cash inflow, carrying losses forward only results in *uncertain future* cash flows because the loss has a benefit in the future only if future years have taxable income. Therefore, if a company has taxable income in prior years, it would generally prefer to first carry any losses back rather than forward. Nevertheless, it is frequently the case that a company will need to carry losses forward because it has exhausted its ability to carry losses backward, or it simply did not have prior taxable income. For example, companies in the start-up phase typically incur losses for a number of years before turning a profit.

THRESHOLD CONCEPT
CONCEPTUAL FRAMEWORK

The fact that losses carried back have benefits that are definite and immediate means there is no issue as to whether an enterprise should record an asset for the tax refund receivable, such as that shown in Exhibit 18-30. In contrast, losses carried forward have uncertain future benefits, so there is an issue as to whether an enterprise should record an asset for a loss carried forward. IAS 12 indicates the following:

> ¶34 A deferred tax asset shall be recognized for the carryforward of unused tax losses and unused tax credits to the extent that it is probable that future taxable profit will be available against which the unused tax losses and unused tax credits can be utilized.[9]

This paragraph suggests that whether an enterprise recognizes an asset for the tax loss carryforward depends on a probability assessment, with "probable" usually interpreted to mean "more likely than not" or greater than 50%. This is the same interpretation of "probable" in reference to contingencies discussed in Chapter 11. However, the standard goes on to state the following:

> ¶35 . . . the existence of unused tax losses is strong evidence that future taxable profit may not be available. Therefore, when an entity has a history of recent losses, the entity recognizes a deferred tax asset arising from unused tax losses or tax credits only to the extent that the entity has sufficient taxable temporary differences or there is convincing other evidence that sufficient taxable profit will be available . . . [10]

This paragraph suggests that the very fact that the enterprise needs to carry losses forward creates a presumption that it will not be able to realize the benefits of the losses. Management has the burden of proof to show that it will be profitable enough in the future to use up these losses.

To illustrate the accounting for a loss carryforward, suppose Esquimalt Company, discussed above, did not have prior years with taxable income against which it could use the $8 million tax loss incurred in 2020. As a result, it must carry the loss forward. If Esquimalt's management believes that the loss will be used against taxable income in future years (up to 20 years based on current legislation), then it can record the following entry for its income tax in 2020 (note that the tax rate in 2020 is 35%):

Exhibit 18-31 Entries to record taxes when there are probable future benefits of tax losses carried forward

Dr. Deferred tax asset ($8,000,000 loss × 35%)	2,800,000	
Cr. Deferred income tax recovery		2,800,000
Dr. Deferred income tax expense ($2,000,000 × 35%)	700,000	
Cr. Deferred income tax liability		700,000

Notice that the second journal entry for the temporary difference remains the same as in Exhibit 18-30. The first entry records the deferred tax asset using the current tax rate of 35%. As noted earlier, if future tax rates have been enacted or substantially enacted, the enterprise should use those future rates to determine the value of the deferred tax asset due to the losses carried forward. For instance, if Esquimalt expects to use the tax loss in the year 2021, and legislation indicates that the tax rate applicable to 2021 will be 40%, then the deferred tax asset would be $8,000,000 × 40% = $3,200,000, instead of $2,800,000 as shown in Exhibit 18-31.

If Esquimalt's management believes that it is *not* probable that the tax loss will be used in the future, then it would not record the deferred tax asset. The impact on financial results is clearly significant, since the loss before tax is not mitigated by any tax recovery. That is, the full $6 million loss before tax would be the net loss after tax for the year. In comparison, recognizing the tax loss benefit results in a net loss of $3.9 million ($6,000,000 − $2,800,000 + $700,000).

Probability assessments need to be updated annually. Deteriorating economic conditions may require the writedown or write-off of deferred tax assets previously recognized for tax losses carried forward. Likewise, if circumstances improve, the enterprise could record deferred tax assets for previously unrecognized tax losses.

In practice, enterprises use a valuation allowance account to record the adjustments to the deferred tax asset for tax losses. This valuation allowance is a contra account that works in much the same way as the allowance for bad debts. The objective of both allowance accounts is the same: to preserve the information of the gross carrying amount while also measuring the net carrying value for reporting purposes.

For example, let's say a tax loss carried forward has a full value of $100,000 if the enterprise expects to be able to use all of the loss to offset future income. If the company's financial condition worsens, such that it only anticipates being able to recover $60,000 in the future, then the enterprise would record a credit of $40,000 to the deferred tax valuation allowance. The gross carrying value of $100,000 net of the valuation allowance then gives the net carrying value of $60,000 for the deferred tax asset.

CHECKPOINT **CP18-5**

Why do we account for tax losses carried forward differently from tax losses carried back?

F. MEASUREMENT: NO DISCOUNTING FOR TIME VALUE OF MONEY

The discussion above has not made mention of the time value of money and computations of present value. The absence of this discussion should be somewhat surprising given that we are dealing with amounts that can vary in timing for many years, such as temporary differences for depreciable assets and tax losses carried forward. However, IAS 12 indicates the following:

> ¶53 Deferred tax assets and liabilities shall not be discounted.

The rationale for this requirement is based on considerations of costs and benefits as well as comparability among enterprises.

> ¶54 The reliable determination of deferred tax assets and liabilities on a discounted basis requires detailed scheduling of the timing of the reversal of each temporary difference. In many cases such scheduling is impracticable or highly complex. Therefore, it is inappropriate to require discounting of deferred tax assets and liabilities. To permit, but not to require, discounting would result in deferred tax assets and liabilities which would not be comparable between entities. Therefore, this Standard does not require or permit the discounting of deferred tax assets and liabilities.[11]

G. PRESENTATION AND DISCLOSURE

1. Presentation and disclosure of income tax expense

L.O. 18-5. Apply the presentation and disclosure standards for income taxes.

The amount of tax expense is obviously important to financial statement readers for performance evaluation. Thus, the total income tax expense must be shown as a line item on the income statement. In addition to this aggregate amount, enterprises need to explain the composition of this tax expense in the note disclosures. In particular, the notes should distinguish the amount for current versus deferred tax:

- current tax expense;
- deferred tax expense due to temporary difference; and
- deferred tax expense due to changes in tax rates.

In addition, a writedown of a deferred tax asset or recognition of a previously unrecognized deferred tax asset can significantly increase or decrease the tax expense. Enterprises need to disclose the impact of these changes of deferred tax assets on current and deferred tax expense.

As noted in a number of other chapters, the income tax expense on the income statement relates only to ordinary activities. Taxes on discontinued operations would be presented with those discontinued operations (or netted against those operations with additional note disclosure of the related income tax). Any taxes on items relating to other comprehensive income would be presented in other comprehensive income rather than in profit or loss.

A particularly useful disclosure relates to the difference between (i) the actual tax expense and (ii) the tax expense expected based on the before-tax income multiplied

[11] Copyright © 2012 IFRS Foundation.

by the statutory tax rate. Essentially, this disclosure identifies all the permanent differences impacting the tax expense for the year. Enterprises have a choice of explaining in terms of either the dollar amounts of taxes involved or the tax rates (i.e., dollar amount of taxes divided by before-tax income).

2. Presentation and disclosure of income tax assets and liabilities

As shown earlier in this chapter, the accounting for income taxes produces a number of different items on the balance sheet: current tax payables or recoveries, deferred tax assets, and deferred tax liabilities. Enterprises must present these items separately (i.e., not offset an asset against a liability). In addition, enterprises face multiple tax jurisdictions, such as the Canadian federal government, provincial governments, and foreign governments. Since each jurisdiction demands compliance with its own tax laws, enterprises cannot offset tax assets for one jurisdiction against liabilities relating to another jurisdiction. Likewise, governments usually assess taxes according to the legal entity, so an enterprise consisting of two or more component entities (e.g., corporations) cannot offset the tax liabilities of one component entity with tax assets of another. In general, then, an enterprise is prohibited from offsetting unless it is legally authorized to offset.

In terms of disclosure, enterprises need to identify deferred tax assets or liabilities according to their sources. For example, a deferred tax asset from warranty costs would be disclosed separately from another deferred tax asset from unearned revenue. Also, enterprises need to disclose the amount of deferred tax assets recognized for tax losses carried forward. Regardless of the source of the deferred tax asset or liability, enterprises must classify them as non-current items when the enterprises use the current/non-current presentation for the balance sheet (IAS 1 paragraph 56).

Under ASPE, Section 3465 indicates less onerous disclosures. Private enterprises using the accrual method need to disclose the following amounts (if not already presented elsewhere):

1. current income tax expense
2. future income tax expense
3. income taxes related to capital transactions
4. unrecognized tax assets arising from unused tax losses or deductible temporary differences

As noted earlier in the chapter, private enterprises can simplify their accounting for income taxes by choosing to use the taxes payable method. Doing so also removes the disclosures related to future income tax expense, deferred tax assets, and deferred tax liabilities. On the other hand, an enterprise using the taxes payable method needs to provide a reconciliation of (i) the effective income tax rate corresponding to the income tax expense to (ii) the statutory tax rate. This disclosure would identify the permanent and temporary differences arising in the year. (This reconciliation under the accrual method would not identify temporary differences.)

H. A PRACTICAL ILLUSTRATION: CANADIAN TIRE CORPORATION

Canadian Tire's financial statements in Appendix C provide two pages of disclosures relating to its deferred taxes. In particular, Note 15 shows the following:

Exhibit 18-32 Disclosures for Canadian Tire Corporation

15.1 Deferred income tax assets and liabilities

The amount of deferred tax assets or liabilities recognized in the Consolidated Balance Sheets and the corresponding movement recognized in the Consolidated Statements of Income, Consolidated Statements of Changes in Equity, or resulting from a business combination is as follows:

					2016
(C$ in millions)	Balance, beginning of year	Recognized in profit or loss	Recognized in other comprehensive income	Other adjustments	Balance, end of year
Provisions, deferred revenue and reserves	$ 143.8	$ 8.8	$ –	$ 0.2	$ 152.8
Property and equipment	(43.8)	5.9	–	–	(37.9)
Intangible assets	(153.5)	(17.1)	–	–	(170.6)
Employee benefits	37.5	1.1	1.1	–	39.7
Cash flow hedges	(53.3)	–	40.1	–	(13.2)
Other	6.3	1.0	–	–	7.3
Net deferred tax asset (liability)[1]	$ (63.0)	$ (0.3)	$ 41.2	$ 0.2	$ (21.9)

[1]Includes the net amount of deferred tax asset of $82.3 million and deferred tax liabilities of $104.2 million.

(Note: Table with comparative figures for 2015 omitted for brevity.)

15.2 Income tax expense

The following are the major components of the income tax expense:

(C$ in millions)	2016	2015
Current tax expense		
Current period	**$ 261.9**	$ 258.9
Adjustments with respect of prior years	**1.3**	21.6
	$ 263.2	$ 280.5
Deferred tax expense (benefit)		
Deferred income tax expense (benefit) relating to the origination and reversal of temporary difference	**$ 2.9**	$ (0.3)
Deferred income tax (benefit) adjustments with respect to prior years	**(2.6)**	(16.6)
Deferred income tax expense resulting from change in tax rate	–	1.8
	0.3	(15.1)
Total Income tax expense	**$ 263.5**	$ 265.4

Income tax (benefit) expense recognized in Other Comprehensive Income was as follows:

(C$ in millions)	2016	2015
(Losses) gains on derivatives designated as cash flow hedges and available-for-sale financial assets	**$ (14.7)**	$ 99.8
Reclassification of gains to non-financial assets of derivatives designated as cash flow hedges	**(24.8)**	(74.9)
Reclassification of gains to income on derivatives designated as cash flow hedges and available-for-sale financial assets	**(0.6)**	(1.1)
Actuarial (losses) gains	**(1.1)**	0.2
Total income tax (benefit) expense	**$ (41.2)**	$ 24.0

Reconciliation of income tax expense

Income taxes in the Consolidated Statements of Income vary from amounts that would be computed by applying the statutory income tax rate for the following reasons:

Exhibit 18-32 Continued

(C$ in millions)	2016	2015
Income before income taxes	$ 1,011.0	$ 1,001.3
Income taxes based on the applicable statutory tax rate of 26.67% (2015—26.56%)	**$ 269.6**	$ 266.0
Adjustment to income taxes resulting from:		
Non-deductibility of stock option expense	**5.0**	2.5
Non-taxable portions of capital gains	**(2.0)**	(6.8)
Income attributable to non-controlling interest in flow-through entities	**(7.0)**	(6.3)
Other	**(2.1)**	10.0
Income tax expense	**$ 263.5**	$ 265.4

The applicable statutory tax rate is the aggregate of the Canadian federal income tax rate of 15.0 percent (2015—15.0 percent) and the Canadian provincial income tax rate of 11.67 percent (2015—11.56 percent). The increase in the applicable rate from 2015 is primarily due to changes in the provincial tax rates in the year.

In the ordinary course of business, the Company is subject to ongoing audits by tax authorities. While the Company has determined that its tax filing positions are appropriate and supportable, from time to time certain matters are reviewed and challenged by the tax authorities.

The Company regularly reviews the potential for adverse outcomes with respect to tax matters. The Company believes that the ultimate disposition of these will not have a material adverse effect on its liquidity, consolidated financial position, or net income because the Company has determined that it has adequate provision for these tax matters. Should the ultimate tax liability materially differ from the provision, the Company's effective tax rate and its earnings could be affected positively or negatively in the period in which the matters are resolved.

Source: From Canadian Tire Corporation 2016 Report to Shareholders. Copyright ©2016 by Canadian Tire Corporation, Limited. Reprinted by permission.

The first table shows that Canadian Tire Corporation had net deferred tax liabilities of $21.9 million, which is $41.1 million lower than the balance at the beginning of the year. This amount of net liability is comprised of $221.7 million of deferred tax liabilities, reduced by $199.8 million in deferred tax assets. The largest sources of these deferred tax balances are "intangible assets" ($170.6 million deferred tax liability) and "provisions, deferred revenue, and reserves" ($152.8 million deferred tax asset).

The second table identifies the tax expense at $263.5 million, of which $263.2 million is current tax while only $0.3 million is deferred tax. The third table identifies the tax effects of items recognized in OCI, totalling $41.2 million of tax benefits (i.e., negative tax expense).

The fourth table reconciles the $269.6 million income tax amount that would result if the statutory tax rate of 26.67% were to apply, to the actual income tax expense of $263.5 million. The reconciling items include the non-deductible stock option expense and the non-taxable portion of capital gains, which are permanent differences.

I. SUBSTANTIVE DIFFERENCES BETWEEN RELEVANT IFRS AND ASPE

ISSUE	IFRS	ASPE
Method of accounting for income taxes	Entities should use the accrual method of accounting.	Entities can use either the accrual method or the taxes payable method.
Presentation and disclosures	Deferred tax assets and liabilities need to be identified by source.	There is no requirement to identify tax assets and liabilities by source. Entities choosing the taxes payable method need to reconcile their effective tax rate to the statutory tax rate.

(*Continued*)

ISSUE	IFRS	ASPE
Terminology	Deferred income tax	Future income tax
Presentation	All deferred tax assets and liabilities are classified as non-current.	Future income tax assets and liabilities are classified as current or non-current according to the nature of the asset or liability that generated the future income tax.

J. SUMMARY

L.O. 18-1. Describe the conceptual differences among the three methods of accounting for income taxes, and apply the taxes payable method under ASPE.

- The taxes payable method records a tax expense equal to the taxes payable for the current period. This method is not conceptually appealing, but is an accepted alternative for private enterprises in Canada due to its simplicity.
- The deferral and accrual methods try to allocate an amount of tax expense to the period in which the relevant event or transaction occurs.
- The deferral method focuses on obtaining the tax expense on the income statement that best matches the income recognized in the period.
- The accrual method focuses on obtaining balance sheet values of tax assets and liabilities that best reflect the amount of tax benefit or obligation ultimately due.
- The accrual method is the only acceptable method in IFRS and is also an accepted alternative for private enterprises in Canada.

L.O. 18-2. Analyze the effect of permanent and temporary differences on income tax expense and income tax liabilities under IFRS.

- Permanent differences relate to events and transactions that impact accounting income but never taxable income, or vice versa.
- Temporary differences reverse in future years.
- Deductible temporary differences are those that result in future taxable income being *lower* than accounting income.
- Taxable temporary differences are those that result in future taxable income being *higher* than accounting income.

L.O. 18-3. Analyze the effect of changes in tax rates on income tax expenses, assets, and liabilities, and account for these effects under IFRS.

- Enterprises need to revalue deferred tax assets and liabilities for changes in tax rates. These increases and decreases in assets and liabilities result in a corresponding change in income tax expense.

L.O. 18-4. Analyze the effect of tax losses on past and future income taxes, and evaluate whether and how much of these tax loss benefits can be recognized as assets under IFRS.

- Enterprises can carry losses back three years and forward for up to 20 years.
- Losses carried back result in a definite and immediate cash inflow and are therefore immediately recognized as tax recoveries and receivables.
- Losses carried forward result in uncertain future reductions in taxes payable, so enterprises should recognize deferred tax assets for these losses only if it will be probable that such losses can be used in future years.

L.O. 18-5. **Apply the presentation and disclosure standards for income taxes.**

- Income taxes pervasively affect business transactions in different ways. Presentation and disclosure standards try to ensure that users are able to determine the effect of tax laws on the enterprise's operations.

K. ANSWERS TO CHECKPOINT QUESTIONS

CP18-1: IFRS does not allow the taxes payable method because it is neither consistent with accrual accounting generally nor with the Conceptual Framework. The taxes payable method is similar to cash basis accounting and does not reflect the effect of transactions when they occur. Not recording the effect of deferred taxes is inconsistent with the definition and recognition criteria for assets and liabilities. ASPE permits the taxes payable approach because of the different costs and benefits faced by private enterprises. This method is less costly, and the limited user base, being primarily owners and lenders, are more concerned about cash flows and can obtain information about deferred taxes should they need it.

CP18-2: It is necessary to distinguish permanent differences from temporary differences because the latter will reverse while the former will not. Temporary differences reflect differences in timing of recognition in financial reporting standards versus tax laws (when something is taxed). Permanent differences reflect differences in the tax base (i.e., what is and is not taxed).

CP18-3: Temporary differences relate to deferred tax assets/liabilities through the statutory tax rate. That is, temporary difference × tax rate = deferred tax. Taxable temporary differences give rise to deferred tax liabilities because such differences increase tax payments in the future. Deductible temporary differences give rise to deferred tax assets because such differences reduce future tax payments.

CP18-4: A change in tax rate results in non-zero net income even if pre-tax income is zero because the tax rate change causes a revaluation of deferred tax assets and liabilities. When the tax rate increases, the increase in deferred tax assets results in negative tax expense, while the increase in deferred tax liabilities creates tax expense. The opposite occurs with tax rate decreases.

CP18-5: We account for tax losses carried forward differently from tax losses carried back because of the difference in uncertainty. Losses carried back have little uncertainty regarding the amount of future benefits since those future benefits are in the form of tax refunds of taxes previously paid on prior years' income. In contrast, the benefits of losses carried forward have much more uncertainty because the use of these losses depends on the entity's ability to generate taxable income in future years.

L. GLOSSARY

accounting income: The amount of income (before subtracting income tax) recognized for financial reporting purposes; contrast with **taxable income**.

accrual method (of accounting for income tax): Focuses on obtaining the balance sheet value for the income tax liability (or asset) that best reflects the assets and liabilities recognized on the balance sheet.

capital cost allowance (CCA): Depreciation for tax purposes.

deductible temporary difference: A temporary difference that results in *future* taxable income being less than accounting income; contrast with **taxable temporary difference**.

deferral method (of accounting for income tax): Focuses on obtaining the income statement value for income tax expense that best matches the amount of income recognized for the year.

deferred tax asset: The amount of income tax recoverable in future periods as a result of deductible temporary differences, losses carried forward, or tax credits carried forward.

deferred tax liability: The amount of income tax payable in future periods as a result of taxable temporary differences.

originating difference: A temporary difference that widens the gap between accounting and tax values of an asset or liability; contrast with **reversing difference.**

permanent difference: Arises from a transaction or event that affects accounting income but never taxable income, or vice versa; contrast with **temporary difference.**

recaptured depreciation: The taxable income recorded for the reversal of previously taken capital cost allowances when the sale proceeds of an asset exceed its undepreciated capital cost. Applies to assets separately identified for tax purposes.

reversing difference: A temporary difference that narrows the gap between accounting and tax values of an asset or liability; contrast with **originating difference.**

taxable income: The amount of income recognized for tax purposes used to compute taxes payable; contrast with **accounting income.**

taxable temporary difference: A temporary difference that results in future taxable income being higher than accounting income; contrast with **deductible temporary difference.**

taxes payable method: A method that records an amount for income tax expense equal to the tax payments for the current period.

temporary difference: Arises from a transaction or event that affects both accounting income and taxable income but in different reporting periods. Contrast with **permanent difference**.

terminal loss: The tax loss arising from the sale of an asset for proceeds below its undepreciated capital cost. Applies to assets separately identified for tax purposes.

undepreciated capital cost (UCC): The net carrying amount of an asset or asset class for tax purposes.

M. REFERENCES

Authoritative standards:

IFRS	ASPE Section
IAS 12—Income Taxes	3465—Income Taxes

MyLab Accounting Make the grade with **MyLab Accounting:** The problems marked with a [globe icon] can be found on **MyLab Accounting.** You can practise them as often as you want, and most feature step-by-step guided instructions to help you find the right answer.

N. PROBLEMS

A·S·P·E **P18-1. Methods of accounting for income taxes** (L.O. 18-1) (Easy – 3 minutes)

A company earns $300,000 in pre-tax income, while its tax return shows taxable income of $250,000. At a tax rate of 30%, how much is the income tax expense under the taxes payable method permitted under ASPE?

 **P18-2. Methods of accounting for income taxes** (L.O. 18-1) (Easy – 3 minutes)

A company uses the accrual method and reports $600,000 for income tax expense for the year. The company does not have any transactions that would create permanent differences. Assume that the statutory tax rate is 25% and this rate is constant from year to year.

Required:

How much was the company's pre-tax income?

P18-3. Methods of accounting for income taxes

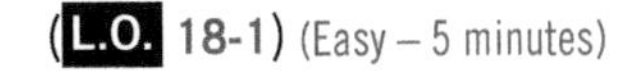

(L.O. 18-1) (Easy – 5 minutes)

A company facing a 25% tax rate has calculated its taxable income for the year to be $2,400,000. It made installment payments during the year totalling $650,000; this amount has been recorded in an asset account as "income tax installments."

Required:

Prepare the journal entry to record the adjusting entry for income taxes at the end of the year under the taxes payable method.

P18-4. Methods of accounting for income taxes

(L.O. 18-1) (Easy – 5 minutes)[12]

PLC Company reported $400,000 in income tax expense for the year under the accrual method. Its balance sheet reported an overall increase in deferred income tax liability of $10,000 and a decrease in income tax payable of $15,000.

Required:

How much would PLC report as income tax expense had it used the taxes payable method?

P18-5. Methods of accounting for income taxes

(L.O. 18-1) (Easy – 5 minutes)

For each of the following characteristics, identify which of the three methods of accounting for income tax (taxes payable, deferral, or accrual) best matches that characteristic.

Characteristic	Accounting method
Closest to cash basis accounting	
Focuses on the balance sheet values of deferred tax	
Similar to direct write-off method for bad debts	
Focuses on the income statement tax expense	
Records an income tax expense adjustment when tax rates change	
Analogous to percentage of sales method for estimating bad debts	
Analogous to aging of accounts receivable approach for estimating bad debts	
Income tax asset and liability balances reflecting the prevailing tax rate	
Income tax expense for the period reflecting the prevailing tax rate	

P18-6. Methods of accounting for income taxes

(L.O. 18-1) (Medium – 10 minutes)

Earlton Inc. began operations in 2019. Due to the untimely death of its founder, Earl Davies, the company was wound up in 2021. The following table provides information on Earlton's income over the three years:

	2019	2020	2021
Income before tax	$10,000	$80,000	$50,000
Taxable income	nil	60,000	80,000

The statutory income tax rate remained at 30% throughout the three years.

Required:

a. For each year and for the three years combined, compute the following:
   i. Income tax expense under the taxes payable method
   ii. The effective tax rate (tax expense ÷ pre-tax income) under the taxes payable method

---

12. Reprinted from Financial Accounting Exam 2010, with permission Chartered Professional Accountants of Canada, Toronto, Canada.

iii. Income tax expense under the accrual method
iv. The effective tax rate under the accrual method

b. Briefly comment on any differences between the effective tax rates and the statutory rate of 30%.

P18-7. Permanent and temporary differences (L.O. 18-2) (Easy 7 – 5 minutes)[13]

Identify whether each of the following items is a permanent or a temporary difference.

	Item	Permanent	Temporary
a.	Golf club dues that are not deductible for tax purposes		
b.	Depreciation of property, plant, and equipment versus the tax method of CCA*		
c.	Warranty liabilities for which only the actual amount of cash paid is deductible for tax purposes		
d.	Percentage of completion income that is taxable only once the contract is complete		
e.	Dividends received that are not taxable		

*CCA = capital cost allowance

P18-8. Permanent and temporary differences (L.O. 18-2) (Easy – 5 minutes)

Identify whether each of the following items would cause income taxes payable to be higher or lower than income tax expense.

	Item	Higher	Lower	Neither
a.	Rent revenue collected in advance that is taxable in the year received			
b.	CCA* that exceeds depreciation expense for property, plant, and equipment			
c.	Membership dues that are not deductible			
d.	Percentage of completion income that is taxable only once the contract is complete			
e.	Dividends received that are not taxable			

*CCA = capital cost allowance

P18-9. Permanent and temporary differences (L.O. 18-2) (Easy – 5 minutes)

Identify whether the following items relate to a deductible temporary difference, a taxable temporary difference, or neither.

	Item	Deductible temporary difference	Taxable temporary difference	Neither
a.	Warranty expense accrued but not deductible until actual costs are incurred			
b.	CCA* that exceeds depreciation expense for property, plant, and equipment			
c.	Dividends received that are not taxable			

13. Reprinted from Financial Accounting Exam 2010, with permission Chartered Professional Accountants of Canada, Toronto, Canada.

	Item	Deductible temporary difference	Taxable temporary difference	Neither
d.	A deferred tax asset for rent revenue received in advance and taxed upon receipt			
e.	Equipment that has a carrying value above undepreciated capital cost			

*CCA = capital cost allowance

P18-10. Permanent and temporary differences  (L.O. 18-2) (Easy – 3 minutes)

A company has income before tax of $300,000, which includes a permanent difference of $60,000 relating to non-taxable dividend income. There are no other permanent or temporary differences. The income tax rate is 20%.

Required:

Compute the amount of taxes payable and income tax expense.

P18-11. Permanent and temporary differences (L.O. 18-2) (Easy – 3 minutes)

A company has income before tax of $300,000. The company also has a temporary difference of $60,000 relating to capital cost allowance in excess of depreciation expense recorded for the year. There are no other permanent or temporary differences. The income tax rate is 20%.

Required:

Compute the amount of taxes payable and income tax expense.

P18-12. Permanent and temporary differences (L.O. 18-2) (Easy – 10 minutes)

The following summarizes information relating to Grafton Corporation's operations for the current year:

Sales revenue	$ 4,500,000
Dividend income (not taxable)	100,000
Operating expenses other than depreciation	(3,200,000)
Depreciation	(800,000)
Income before tax	$ 600,000
Capital cost allowance claimed	$ 1,000,000
Income tax rate	25%

Required:

Compute the amount of taxes payable and income tax expense for Grafton Corporation.

P18-13. Permanent and temporary differences (L.O. 18-2) (Easy – 10 minutes)

For each of the following differences between the amount of taxable income and income recorded for financial reporting purposes, compute the effect of each difference on deferred taxes balances on the balance sheet. Treat each item independently of the others. Assume a tax rate of 25%.

Item	Amount
Depreciation for financial reporting purposes	$20,000
Depreciation for tax purposes (CCA*)	30,000
Non-taxable dividends	40,000
Provision for warranty	60,000
Unearned rent revenue	80,000
CCA in excess of depreciation	10,000

*CCA = capital cost allowance

P18-14. Permanent and temporary differences (L.O. 18-2) (Medium – 15 minutes)[14]

At the beginning of the current fiscal year, Vation Corporation had a deferred income tax liability balance of $15,000, which relates to depreciable assets. During the year, Vation reported the following information:

- Income before income taxes for the year was $550,000 and the tax rate was 30%.
- Depreciation expense was $45,000 and capital cost allowance was $30,000.
- Unearned rent revenue was reported at $40,000. Rent revenue is taxable when the cash is received. There was no opening balance in the unearned rent revenue account at the beginning of the year.
- No other items affected deferred tax amounts other than these transactions.

Required:

Prepare the journal entry or entries to record income taxes for the year.

P18-15. Permanent and temporary differences (L.O. 18-2) (Medium – 20 minutes)

The following data represent the differences between accounting and tax income for Oriental Imports Inc., whose pre-tax accounting income is $860,000 for the year ended December 31. The company's income tax rate is 40%. Additional information relevant to income taxes includes the following:

- Capital cost allowance of $202,500 exceeded accounting depreciation expense of $100,000 in the current year.
- Rents of $5,000, applicable to next year, had been collected in December and deferred for financial statement purposes but are taxable in the year received.
- In a previous year, the company established a provision for product warranty expense. A summary of the current year's transactions appears below:

Provision for warranties, January 1 balance	$ 96,300
Provision for the year	35,600
Payments made to fulfill product warranties	(26,000)
Provision for warranties, December 31 balance	$105,900

  For tax purposes, only actual amounts paid for warranties are deductible.
- Insurance expense to cover the company's executive officers was $5,200 for the year, and you have determined that this expense is not deductible for tax purposes.

Required:

Prepare the journal entries to record income taxes for Oriental Imports.

P18-16. Permanent and temporary differences (L.O. 18-2) (Medium – 15 minutes)

Occidental Exports has income before tax of $660,000 for the year ended December 31. The company's income tax rate is 30%. Additional information relevant to income taxes includes the following:

- Capital cost allowance of $160,000 exceeded accounting depreciation expense of $120,000 in the current year.
- The company received non-taxable dividends of $50,000.
- The company paid $20,000 for club memberships for its executives. These membership costs are not tax deductible.
- The company guarantees its products for three years after sale. For tax purposes, only actual amounts paid for warranties are deductible. Information on the warranty provision is as follows:

---

14. Reprinted from Financial Accounting Exam 2010, with permission Chartered Professional Accountants of Canada, Toronto, Canada.

Provision for warranties, January 1 balance	$ 88,000
Provision for the year	32,000
Payments made to fulfill product warranties	(30,000)
Provision for warranties, December 31 balance	$ 90,000

Required:

Prepare the journal entries to record income taxes for Occidental Exports.

P18-17. Permanent and temporary differences (L.O. 18-2) (Medium – 15 minutes)

Northland Water Inc. has taxable income of $316,000 for the year ended December 31. The company's income tax rate is 25%. Additional information relevant to income taxes includes the following:

- Capital cost allowance was $80,000 while depreciation expense was $120,000 in the current year. Entering the year, the company had a deferred tax liability on property, plant, and equipment of $50,000 Cr.
- Dividends from taxable Canadian corporations amounted to $60,000.
- The company expensed $16,000 on life insurance for its management. This expense is not deductible for tax purposes.

Required:

Prepare the journal entries to record income taxes for Northland Water.

P18-18. Permanent and temporary differences (L.O. 18-2) (Medium – 15 minutes)

The following information is available for Meagan's Counselling Inc. for its year ended December 31, 2019:

- Accounting income before taxes was $1,500,000.
- Dividends received from a taxable Canadian corporation during the year totalled $75,000.
- Warranty expense for the year was $125,000. Costs that were incurred to service the warranties totalled $85,000.
- Depreciation expense for the company's property, plant, and equipment for the year was $205,000; Meagan's claimed $225,000 of CCA on its tax return.
- Equipment was disposed of during the year for $180,000. The net book value of the equipment sold was $110,000.
- Meagan's paid Canada Revenue Agency $7,000 in interest and penalties for failing to remit its 2018 taxes due in a timely manner.
- The enacted tax rate was 40%.

Required:

Prepare the journal entries to record income taxes for Meagan's Counselling Inc. for 2019.

P18-19. Permanent and temporary differences (L.O. 18-2) (Medium – 15 minutes)

The following information is available for Angela's Special Needs Inc. (ASN) for its year ended December 31, 2019:

- Accounting income before taxes was $900,000.
- The company paid $18,000 for a golf club membership for one of its executives.
- Warranty expense for the year was $72,000. Costs that were incurred to service the warranties totalled $85,000.
- Depreciation expense for the company's property, plant, and equipment for the year was $35,000; ASN claimed $30,000 of CCA on its tax return. At December 31, 2019, the net book value of the PPE was $265,000; its UCC was $230,000.
- During the year, ASN sold investments for $125,000. The book value and the cost of the investments sold was $55,000. The $70,000 gain was a capital gain.
- ASN reported meals and entertainment expenses of $14,000 on its income statement.
- The enacted tax rate was 30%.

Required:

Prepare the journal entries to record income taxes for Angela's Special Needs Inc. for 2019.

P18-20. Permanent and temporary differences (L.O. 18-2) (Medium – 15 minutes)

The following information is available for Eli Corp. for its year ended December 31, 2019:

- Accounting income before taxes was $600,000.
- The company is a contractor. It uses the percentage of completion method to report revenue on its financial statements and the completed contract method to report revenue on its tax return. In 2019, Eli Corp. reported revenue of $1,200,000 on its financial statements and revenue of $1,050,000 on its tax return.
- During the year, Eli Corp. paid $3,000 for key person life insurance coverage of its senior executives.
- The company paid the local health spa $5,000 to enable its executives to use the recreational facilities during the year.
- Depreciation expense for the company's property, plant, and equipment for the year was $120,000; Eli Corp. claimed $130,000 CCA on its tax return.
- The company reported pension expense of $85,000 on its income statement; during the year, it remitted a total of $65,000 to the pension trust.
- Eli Corp. reported meals and entertainment expenses of $18,000 on its income statement.
- The enacted tax rate was 20%.

Required:

Prepare the journal entries to record income taxes for Eli Corp. for 2019.

P18-21. Permanent and temporary differences (L.O. 18-2) (Medium – 20 minutes)

Southern Solar earned taxable income of $995,000 for the year ended December 31. As an environmental technology company, Southern Solar's income tax rate is only 20%. Additional information relevant to income taxes includes the following:

- Capital cost allowance of $350,000 exceeded accounting depreciation expense of $170,000 in the current year.
- The company provides warranties on its solar panels for a period of five years. A summary of the current year's transactions appears below:

Provision for warranties, January 1 balance	$450,000
Provision for the year	120,000
Payments made to fulfill product warranties	(90,000)
Provision for warranties, December 31 balance	$480,000

- During the year, the company sold a parcel of unused land. Proceeds on the sale were $1,500,000 while the purchase cost was $600,000. For tax purposes, one-half of capital gains is taxable.

Required:

Prepare the journal entries to record income taxes for Southern Solar.

P18-22. Permanent and temporary differences with asset impairment (L.O. 18-2) (Difficult – 20 minutes)

The following information relates to the accounting income for Manitoba Press Company (MPC) for the current year ended December 31:

Accounting income before income taxes	$210,000
Dividend income (non-taxable)	30,000
Depreciation expense	100,000
Capital cost allowance claimed	70,000
Impairment loss on land—see additional information below	200,000
Income tax rate	35%

The company had purchased land some years ago for $500,000. Recently, it was discovered that this land is contaminated by industrial pollution. Because of the soil remediation costs required, the value of the land has decreased. For tax purposes, the impairment loss is not currently deductible. In the future, when the land is sold, half of any losses is deductible against taxable capital gains (i.e., the other half that is not taxable or deductible is a permanent difference).

The deferred income tax liability account on January 1 had a credit balance of $76,000. This balance is entirely related to property, plant, and equipment.

Required:

Prepare the journal entries to record income taxes for MPC.

P18-23. Permanent and temporary differences with disposal of a depreciable asset (L.O. 18-2) (Medium – 15 minutes)

The following information relates to the accounting income for Saskatchewan Uranium Enterprises (SUE) for the current year ended December 31:

Accounting income before income taxes	$840,000
Depreciation and depletion expense	450,000
Capital cost allowance claimed	570,000
Membership initiation fees (not deductible)	5,000
Loss on disposal of equipment—see additional information below	40,000
Income tax rate	30%

During the year, the company sold one of its machines with a carrying value of $60,000 for proceeds of $20,000, resulting in an accounting loss of $40,000. This loss has been included in the pre-tax income figure of $840,000 shown above. For tax purposes, the proceeds from the disposal were removed from the undepreciated capital cost (UCC) of Class 8 assets.

The deferred income tax liability account on January 1 had a credit balance of $150,000. This balance is entirely related to property, plant, and equipment.

Required:

Prepare the journal entries to record income taxes for SUE.

P18-24. Permanent and temporary differences with disposal of a specifically identified depreciable asset (L.O. 18-2) (Difficult – 15 minutes)

The following information relates to the accounting income for Alberta Real Estate Company (AREC) for the current year ended December 31:

Accounting income before income taxes	$600,000
Depreciation and depletion expense	300,000
Capital cost allowance (CCA) excluding recapture on building disposal	300,000
Gain on disposal of building—see additional information below	240,000
Income tax rate	25%

During the year, the company sold one of its buildings with a carrying value of $720,000 for proceeds of $960,000, resulting in an accounting gain of $240,000. This gain has been included in the pre-tax income figure of $600,000 shown above. For tax purposes, the acquisition cost of the building was $800,000. For purposes of CCA, it is a Class 1 asset, which treats each building as a separate class. The undepreciated capital cost on the building at the time of disposal was $600,000.

Required:

Prepare the journal entries to record income taxes for AREC.

P18-25. Effect of tax rate changes (L.O. 18-3) (Easy – 3 minutes)

A company has a deferred tax liability of $40,000 at the beginning of the fiscal year relating to a taxable temporary difference of $100,000. The tax rate for the year increased from 40% to 45%.

Required:

Provide the journal entry to reflect the tax rate change.

P18-26. Effect of tax rate changes  (L.O. 18-3) (Easy – 5 minutes)

A company has a deferred tax liability of $29,900 at the beginning of the fiscal year. The company's records show that it had taxable temporary differences totalling $115,000 entering the year. In the current fiscal year, the tax rate is 24%.

Required:

Provide the journal entry to reflect the tax rate change (if any).

P18-27. Effect of tax rate changes (L.O. 18-3) (Medium – 10 minutes)

Jay Company has a deferred tax asset of $20,000 at the beginning and $55,000 at the end of the year. The end-of-year balance corresponds to $250,000 of deductible temporary differences. During the year, the company recorded $33,000 into deferred tax asset. The tax rate was 2% higher than the rate in the prior year.

Required:

Determine the following:

a. The opening balance of deductible temporary differences for the year.
b. The tax rate in the prior year.
c. The amount of change in deductible temporary differences during the year.

P18-28. Effect of tax rate changes (L.O. 18-3) (Medium – 10 minutes)

Kay Company has a deferred tax liability of $55,000 at the beginning of the year. At the end of the year, the deferred tax liability was $90,000. During the year, the company had taxable temporary differences of $80,000. For this year, the tax rate is 30%.

Required:

Determine the balance of temporary differences at the beginning and at the end of the year and the tax rate effective in the prior year.

P18-29. Effect of tax rate changes (L.O. 18-2, L.O. 18-3) (Medium – 20 minutes)[15]

RCD Company started operations in 2019. The financial statements of RCD reflected the following pre-tax amounts for its December 31 year-end:

	2019	2020
Income statement (summarized)		
Revenues	$200,000	$230,000
Depreciation expense	25,000	25,000
Other operating expenses	110,000	120,000
Pre-tax accounting income	65,000	85,000

15. Reprinted from Financial Accounting Exam 2009, with permission Chartered Professional Accountants of Canada, Toronto, Canada.

	2019	2020
Balance sheet (partial)		
Property, plant, and equipment, cost	$250,000	$250,000
Accumulated depreciation	(25,000)	(50,000)
Net property, plant, and equipment	$225,000	$200,000
Unearned rent revenue	—	7,000

RCD had a tax rate of 30% in 2019 and 35% in 2020, enacted in February each year. The unearned rent revenue represents cash received from a tenant that will be moving into the building February 1, 2021. For tax purposes, any cash received for future rent is taxed when the cash is received. RCD claimed capital cost allowance for income tax purposes of $12,500 in 2019 and $23,500 in 2020.

Required:

a. Calculate the income taxes payable for 2020.
b. For each year (2019 and 2020), calculate the deferred tax balance on the balance sheet at the end of the year. Indicate whether the amount is an asset or a liability.

P18-30. Permanent and temporary differences with a change in tax rates

(L.O. 18-2, L.O. 18-3) (Medium – 20 minutes)

Maui Sun Inc.'s accounting income before income taxes was $625,000 for the year ended December 31, 2021. Additional information pertaining to income taxes follows:

- Depreciation on capital assets was $287,000. Capital cost allowance claimed was $395,000.
- Warranty claims paid out for the year were $45,000. Provision for warranty expense was $22,000.
- Dividends received from a taxable Canadian corporation were $5,000.
- Golf club membership dues paid for company executives amounted to $20,000. This expense is not deductible for tax purposes.
- On January 1, 2021, the government unexpectedly changed the income tax rate from 35% to 40%, effective immediately. At that time Maui Sun Inc. had a $56,000 provision for warranty liability balance on its statement of financial position and the net book value of its capital assets (accounting basis) was $1,276,000, while the undepreciated capital cost (tax basis) was $856,000.

Required:

Prepare all income tax related journal entries for Maui Sun Inc. for 2021.

P18-31. Permanent and temporary differences with a change in tax rates

(L.O. 18-2, L.O. 18-3) (Medium – 20 minutes)

Australian Koala Inc.'s (AKI) accounting income before income taxes was $405,000 for the year ended December 31, 2021. Additional information pertaining to income taxes follows:

- Depreciation on capital assets was $205,000. Capital cost allowance claimed was $194,000.
- Cash remitted to the pension trustee for the year by AKI was $270,000. Pension expense was $280,000. For income tax purposes, pension costs are deductible when cash is remitted to the trustee.
- Dividends received from a taxable Canadian corporation were $15,000.
- Life insurance premiums on the lives of the AKI's chief executive officer paid by the company were $12,000. This expense is not deductible for tax purposes.
- On January 1, 2021, the government unexpectedly changed the income tax rate from 30% to 25%, effective immediately. At that time, Australian Koala Inc. had a $200,000 net defined pension liability balance on its statement of financial position and the net book value of its capital assets (accounting basis) was $800,000 while the undepreciated capital cost (tax basis) was $750,000. (Note that the pension liability represents the accumulated difference between pension expense and cash remitted to the pension trustee. A liability exists as the cumulative pension expense exceeded the cumulative cash remittance.)

Required:

Prepare the journal entries to record income taxes for Australian Koala Inc. for 2021.

P18-32. Permanent and temporary differences with a change in tax rates (L.O. 18-2, L.O. 18-3) (Medium – 20 minutes)

Gidget Cat Co.'s (GCC) accounting income before taxes was $500,000 in 2019, its first year of operations. Select information from the company's financial records follow:

- The company paid $10,000 for a golf club membership in 2019.
- The net book value of GCC's equipment at December 31, 2019, was $350,000; its undepreciated capital cost (UCC) was $320,000. GCC expects that this temporary difference will reverse in 2022.
- GCC offers a two-year warranty on all products it sells. The balance of the provision for warranty at the end of 2019 was $45,000. GCC expects that $35,000 of the provision for warranty will be settled in 2020 and the remaining $10,000 will be settled in 2021.
- The income tax rate for 2019 was 20%. During 2019, suppose the federal government announced that the tax rate would increase to 25% for 2020 and 30% for 2021.

Required:

Prepare the journal entries to record income tax expense for Gidget Cat Co.

P18-33. Effect of tax rate changes (L.O. 18-2, L.O. 18-3) (Difficult – 20 minutes)[16]

Vanier Corporation reported the following information at the beginning of its current fiscal year:

Deferred income tax asset (warranties)	$ 2,400 Dr.
Deferred income tax liability (depreciable assets)	10,500 Cr.

During the year, Vanier reported the following information:

- Income before income taxes for the year was $850,000 and the tax rate was 32%.
- Depreciation expense was $75,000 and the capital cost allowance was $80,000. The carrying amount of property, plant, and equipment at the end of the year was $420,000, while the undepreciated capital cost was $380,000.
- Warranty expense was reported at $40,000, while actual cash paid out was $38,000. The warranty liability had a year-end balance of $10,000.
- No other items have affected deferred tax amounts other than these transactions.

Required:

Prepare the journal entry or entries to record income tax for the year.

P18-34. Effect of tax rate changes (L.O. 18-2, L.O. 18-3) (Difficult – 20 minutes)

Singh Corporation reported the following information at the beginning of its current fiscal year:

Deferred income tax asset (defined benefit pension plan)	$ 20,000 Dr.
Deferred income tax liability (equipment)	10,000 Cr.

During the year, Singh reported the following information:

- Income before income taxes for the year was $600,000.
- Depreciation expense was $50,000 and capital cost allowance was $60,000. The carrying amount of property, plant, and equipment at the end of the year was $490,000, while its undepreciated capital cost was $440,000.

[16] Reprinted from Financial Accounting Exam 2009, with permission Chartered Professional Accountants of Canada, Toronto, Canada.

- Defined benefit pension plan expense was $190,000, while the cash paid to the pension plan trustee was $205,000. The defined benefit pension plan liability had a year-end balance of $65,000.

The tax rate was 20%. No other items affected the deferred tax amounts during the year.

Required:

Prepare the journal entries to record income tax for the year.

P18-35. Permanent and temporary differences with a change in tax rates

(L.O. 18-2, L.O. 18-3) (Difficult – 30 minutes)

Gretta Corp. was formed in 2019. Accounting and tax information for its first three years of operations follows:

	2019	2020	2021
Accounting income before taxes	$150,000	$225,000	$310,000
Tax rate	30%	40%	35%
Dividend income from Canadian corporations	3,000	2,000	4,000
Depreciation on PPE—original cost $250,000	25,000	25,000	25,000
Capital cost allowance	50,000	40,000	30,000
Pension expense	25,000	18,000	22,000
Payments to pension trustee	20,000	20,000	20,000
Warranty expense	6,000	5,000	4,000
Warranty costs	4,000	3,000	5,000

The change in tax rates was not enacted until the year of the tax change. That is to say that in 2019, Gretta Corp. did not know that the tax rate in 2020 would be 40%; in 2020, it did not know that the tax rate in 2021 would be 35%.

Required:

Prepare all journal entries related to income taxes for Gretta Corp. from 2019 to 2021.

P18-36. Accounting for tax losses

(L.O. 18-4) (Easy – 5 minutes)

In the first two years of operations, a company reported taxable income of $100,000 and $150,000, respectively. In these two years, the company paid $20,000 and $36,000, respectively, in income taxes. It is now the end of the third year, and the company has a loss of $220,000 for tax purposes. The company carries losses to the earliest year possible. The tax rate is currently 25%.

Required:

Compute the amount of income tax payable or receivable in the current (third) year.

P18-37. Accounting for tax losses

(L.O. 18-4) (Easy – 5 minutes)

In the first year of operations, a company reported taxable income of $160,000 and paid $32,000 of income taxes. It is now the end of the second year, and the company has a loss of $300,000 for tax purposes. The company's management believes it is probable the company will be able to use up its tax losses. The tax rate is currently 25%.

Required:

Compute the amounts of income tax receivable and/or deferred income tax asset in the current (second) year.

P18-38. Accounting for tax losses

(L.O. 18-4) (Medium – 10 minutes)

In 2016 to 2018, respectively, Flotsam Beachcombers earned taxable income of $50,000, $200,000, and $30,000. The tax rate for each year was 20%, 25%, and 10%. It is now the end of 2019 and the company has incurred a loss of $380,000 for tax purposes and has earned an accounting loss before tax of $200,000. The difference between accounting and taxable income is due to capital cost allowance exceeding depreciation expense. The tax rate is currently 25%.

Required:

Record the journal entries for income tax expense and income tax payable or receivable for 2019.

P18-39. Accounting for tax losses

(L.O. 18-4) (Medium – 10 minutes)

In 2016 to 2018, respectively, Bonwick Company earned taxable income of $500,000, $800,000, and $700,000, and paid income tax of $150,000, $260,000, and $200,000. It is now the end of 2019 and the company has incurred a loss of $3,500,000 for tax purposes and earns an accounting loss before tax of $3,000,000. The difference between accounting and taxable income is due to capital cost allowance exceeding depreciation expense. The tax rate is currently 30%. Bonwick anticipates using only 60% of the losses carried forward within the allowable carryforward period.

Required:

Record the journal entries for income tax expense and income tax payable or receivable for 2019. Use a valuation account for the unrecognized portion of losses carried forward.

P18-40. Permanent and temporary differences; losses

(L.O. 18-2, L.O. 18-4) (Medium – 20 minutes)[17]

During its first year of operations, Kinkle Corporation reported the following information:

- Income before income taxes for the year was $450,000 and the tax rate was 30%.
- Depreciation expense was $195,000 and capital cost allowance was $97,500. The carrying amount of property, plant, and equipment at the end of the year was $620,000, while undepreciated capital cost was $717,500.
- Warranty expense was reported at $160,000, while actual cash paid out was $75,000.
- $45,000 of expenses included in income were not deductible for tax purposes.
- No other items affected deferred tax amounts besides these transactions.

Required:

a. Prepare the journal entries to record income tax expense for the year.
b. Assume Kinkle reported a loss instead of income in its first year of operations. Explain what accounting policy choices are available to Kinkle to record the tax implications of the loss, and provide a recommendation.

P18-41. Permanent and temporary differences; losses

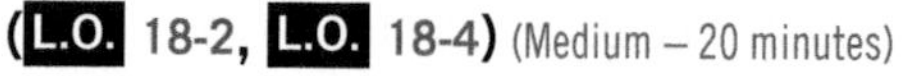
(L.O. 18-2, L.O. 18-4) (Medium – 20 minutes)

Simone Corp. was incorporated on January 1, 2020. For the year ended December 31, 2020, Simone Corp.'s taxable income was $105,000. There were no temporary differences. Income tax paid was $31,500. Additional information pertaining to income taxes for the year ended December 31, 2021, follows:

- Simone Corp. suffered a loss before income taxes of $210,000.
- Depreciation expense was $50,000. Capital cost allowance was not claimed given the loss situation.

---

17. Reprinted from Uniform Final Examination 1999, with permission Chartered Professional Accountants of Canada, Toronto, Canada. Any changes to the original material are the sole responsibility of the author (and/or publisher) and have not been reviewed or endorsed by the Chartered Professional Accountants of Canada.

- Meal and entertainment expenses for the year were $8,000. Only $4,000 of this expense is deductible for tax purposes.
- Simone Corp. expensed $10,000 on life insurance policies for its key personnel. This expense is not deductible for tax purposes.
- On January 1, 2021, the government increased the income tax rate to 35% effective immediately and announced that it would increase to 40% effective January 1, 2022.
- Management elects to carry back the loss to the greatest extent possible and anticipates that it will use 100% of the loss carryforward within the allowable carryforward period.

Required:

Prepare the journal entries to record income tax expense for the year.

P18-42. Accounting for tax losses and tax rate changes

(L.O. 18-3, L.O. 18-4) (Medium – 10 minutes)

In 2019, Compton Inc. incurred a loss of $12,600,000 for tax purposes, when the tax rate was 30%. Because the company had no prior taxable income, it carried the entire loss forward. Considering the size of the loss, Compton management expected to recover only three-quarters of the loss by applying the loss to future income. In 2020, the income tax rate increased from 30% to 32%.

Required:

Record the 2019 and 2020 journal entries relating to Compton's tax loss. Use a valuation account for the unrecognized portion of losses carried forward.

P18-43. Accounting for tax losses with tax rate changes

(L.O. 18-3, L.O. 18-4) (Difficult – 30 minutes)

West Limited reported the following amounts and information for four years ended on December 31 as follows:

	2016	2017	2018	2019
Accounting income (loss)	$ 550,000	$(1,400,000)	$ 200,000	$1,900,000
Add: depreciation	100,000	100,000	100,000	100,000
Less: CCA	(170,000)	(170,000)	(170,000)	(250,000)
Taxable income (loss)	$ 480,000	$ (1,470,000)	$ 130,000	$ 1,750,000
Tax rate	40%	45%	50%	55%

Deferred tax relating to property, plant, and equipment on December 31, 2015, was $200,000 Cr. This is the only tax account on the balance sheet. It relates to the difference between the undepreciated capital cost of $1,000,000 and net carrying value of $1,400,000 of depreciable assets. The taxable income in the two years prior to 2016 was $0. Assume any changes to future tax rates are not enacted until the year of the tax change. West's management is confident that it is probable the company will be able to use the losses carried forward.

Required:

Prepare all journal entries related to income taxes for the four years from 2016 to 2019.

P18-44. Permanent and temporary differences with a change in tax rates; presentation and disclosure

(L.O. 18-2, L.O. 18-3, L.O. 18-5) (Difficult – 40 minutes)

Storoshenko Yoga Ltd.'s (SYL) accounting income before income taxes was $650,000 for the year ended December 31, 2019, and $950,000 for the year ended December 31, 2020. Additional information pertaining to income taxes follows:

- The net book value of the SYL's property, plant, and equipment at January 1, 2019, was $1,000,000; the UCC was $800,000.
- SYL paid $175,000 cash in 2019 to purchase equipment.

- SYL received $70,000 cash in 2020 from the sale of equipment; the net book value of the equipment sold was $45,000.
- $100,000 of depreciation expense was reported on the 2019 income statement versus the $150,000 of CCA claimed for income tax purposes.
- $125,000 of depreciation expense was reported on the 2020 income statement versus the $131,000 of CCA claimed for income tax purposes.
- SYL's 2019 revenues included $18,000 in dividends from a taxable Canadian corporation; 2020 revenues included $24,000 in dividends from a taxable Canadian corporation.
- SYL's 2019 expenses included $30,000 in meal and entertainment expenses; 2020 expenses included $20,000 in meal and entertainment expenses.
- SYL's tax rate for 2018 and 2019 was 32%. On January 1, 2020, the government unexpectedly increased the tax rate to 35%, effective immediately.

Required:

a. Prepare all journal entries related to income taxes for Storoshenko Yoga Ltd. for 2019.
b. Prepare all journal entries related to income taxes for Storoshenko Yoga Ltd. for 2020.
c. Prepare income statement excerpts for 2020, including line items between income before tax and net income.

P18-45. Accounting for tax losses and tax rate changes

(L.O. 18-3, L.O. 18-4, L.O. 18-5) (Difficult – 40 minutes)

	2016	2017	2018	2019
Accounting income (loss)	$ 250,000	$(900,000)	$200,000	$ 800,000
Add: depreciation	250,000	60,000	50,000	50,000
Less: CCA*	(110,000)	0	0	(120,000)
Taxable income (loss)	$ 390,000	$(840,000)	$250,000	$ 730,000
Tax rate	40%	45%	45%	45%

*CCA = capital cost allowance

Taxable income in the two years prior to 2016 was $0. At the beginning of 2016, the company had a deferred income tax liability of $160,000, which relates to property, plant, and equipment whose carrying value of $1,500,000 exceeded its undepreciated capital cost of $1,100,000.

Required:

a. Case A: Prepare the income tax journal entries for the four years, assuming that it is probable the company will realize the benefits of tax losses carried forward.
b. Case B: Prepare the income tax journal entries for the four years, assuming that it is *not* probable the company will realize the benefits of tax losses carried forward.
c. For both Cases A and B, prepare income statement excerpts including line items between income before tax and net income.
d. Compute the effective tax rate (total tax expense or recovery ÷ income before tax) for each year for both Cases A and B. Comment on any differences or patterns in the effective tax rates.

P18-46. Comprehensive question with temporary differences, tax rate changes, and tax losses

(L.O. 18-2, L.O. 18-3, L.O. 18-4) (Difficult – 30 minutes)

Coastal Forests International began operations in 2016. Selected information relating to the company's operations is shown in the following table (DIT denotes deferred income tax. Amounts other than percentages are in $000's):

Fiscal years ending December 31:	2016	2017	2018	2019	2020
Pre-tax accounting income (loss)	200	50	(360)	(200)	320
Temporary differences	(40)	(30)	(20)	50	(20)
Taxable income (loss) before carryforward or back	160	20	(380)	(150)	300
Cumulative balance of deductible (taxable) temporary differences	(40)	(70)	(90)	(40)	(60)
Statutory tax rate (rate changes not known before the year to which they apply)	35%	30%	30%	30%	30%
End-of-year assessment of the degree of likelihood that the benefit of accumulated tax losses will be realized in the future (each year's likelihood is not known before that year)	N/A	N/A	70%	20%	90%
Tax losses carried back to prior years	—	—			
Beginning balance of tax losses carried forward	—	—			
Current-year tax losses carried forward	—	—			
Use of tax losses carried forward from prior years	—	—			
End-of-year balance of tax losses carried forward	—	—			
End-of-year DIT asset for losses carried forward	—	—			
End-of-year DIT liability for temporary differences					(18)
Journal entry [Please show credit amounts in (parentheses)]					
Income tax expense (recovery)	70		(116)		
Income tax receivable (payable)	(56)			0	0
DIT asset for losses carried forward	—				
DIT liability for temporary differences	(14)				

Required:

Complete the missing information in the table.

P18-47. Presentation and disclosure (L.O. 18-5) (Medium – 15 minutes)

For the year ended October 31, 2017, BMO Financial Group (Bank of Montreal) reported income before tax of $6,646 million and income tax expense of $1,296 million for an effective tax rate of 19.5%. In the notes to the financial statements, BMO's disclosures included the following information:

Reconciliation of statutory and effective tax rates	Amount ($ millions)	Rate (%)
Combined Canadian federal and provincial income taxes at the statutory tax rate	$1,768	26.6%
Increase (decrease) resulting from:		
Tax-exempt income from securities	(409)	(6.2)
Foreign operations subject to different tax rates	22	0.3
Previously unrecognized tax loss, tax credit, or temporary difference of a prior period	(54)	(0.8)
Income attributable to investments in associates and joint ventures	(103)	(1.5)
Change in tax rate for deferred income taxes	(2)	–
Adjustments in respect of current tax for prior periods	18	0.2
Other	56	0.9
Provision for income tax and effective tax rate	$1,296	19.5%
(in $ millions)	**2017**	**2016**
Deferred income tax assets	$3,705	$3,722
Deferred income tax liabilities	1,073	863

Required:

a. From BMO's disclosures provided above, identify any permanent differences.
b. In which direction did the tax rate change?
c. Refer to the line "Adjustments in respect of current tax for prior periods" in the above disclosures. What does this information imply about BMO's treatment of tax losses in prior years?

P18-48. Presentation and disclosure (L.O. 18-5) (Medium – 15 minutes)

Refer to the 2016 financial statements for Canadian Tire Corporation in Appendix C.

Required:

a. Of the $263.5 million in income tax expense reported on the 2016 income statement, how much was current and how much was deferred?
b. How much was the average effective tax rate faced by Canadian Tire (calculated as income tax expense divided by pre-tax income)? How does this figure compare with the statutory tax rate according to the company?
c. How much would tax expense have been in 2016 had the statutory tax rate applied to pre-tax income?
d. By how much did the rate increase or decrease from 2015 to 2016? What effect did this change have on income tax expense in 2016?
e. How much in assets and liabilities relating to deferred taxes did the company have at the end of 2016?

P18-49. Presentation and disclosure (L.O. 18-5) (Medium – 20 minutes)

Obtain the 2016 annual report for Telus Corporation either through the company's website or from SEDAR (www.sedar.com).

Required:

a. How much was income tax expense in 2016? How much was current and how much was deferred?
b. How much was the average effective tax rate faced by the company (calculated as income tax expense divided by pre-tax income)? How does this figure compare with the statutory tax rate according to the company?
c. How much would tax expense have been in 2016 had the statutory tax rate applied to pre-tax income?
d. What was the most significant factor in explaining the difference between the effective and statutory tax rates?
e. How much was the amount of deferred income tax liability on the balance sheet at the end of 2016?
f. What was the source of the largest temporary difference contributing to the deferred income tax liability? Explain the nature of this temporary difference; that is, how does this temporary difference arise?
g. Compute the amount of the temporary difference identified in part (f).

P18-50. Presentation and disclosure (L.O. 18-5) (Medium – 20 minutes)

Obtain the 2016 annual report for Bombardier Inc. either through the company's website or from SEDAR (www.sedar.com).

Required:

a. How much was income tax expense in 2016? How much was current and how much was deferred?
b. How much was the average effective tax rate faced by the company (calculated as income tax expense divided by pre-tax income)? How does this figure compare with the statutory tax rate according to the company?
c. How much would tax expense have been in 2016 had the statutory tax rate applied to pre-tax income?
d. What was the most significant factor in explaining the difference between the effective and statutory tax rates?
e. How much were the amounts of deferred income tax asset and deferred income tax liability on the balance sheet at the end of 2016?
f. What was the most significant source of deferred income tax assets?
g. How much was the valuation allowance on deferred tax assets?

O. MINI-CASES

CASE 1
The political economy of income tax reporting
(30 minutes)

Income taxes came into being in Canada in 1917 as a "temporary" measure to finance the costly World War I. Ever since then, as surely as night follows day, complaints about income taxation have been frequent but expected. These complaints come from all directions, varying from cries that tax rates are too high, or that governments waste tax revenues, to allegations that certain taxpayers do not pay their fair share of taxes.

The global recession in 2008–2009 threw the budgets of most governments in the world out of balance. Canadian governments were not spared. For example, the federal government's budget swung from a modest surplus of $3 billion in the fiscal year ended March 31, 2008, to a deficit of $54 billion for the year ended March 31, 2010. Under these circumstances, the government sought any means possible to reverse the dramatic deficits.

Your good friend Clark Stevens, a (fictitious) member of parliament, has heeded the call for ideas and is examining ways for the government to obtain higher revenues. Stevens is, of course, aware that raising the tax rate will help to increase revenues, but higher tax rates will also dampen economic activity, which has already suffered due to the recession. Thus, Stevens is looking for more creative alternatives.

Knowing that you are an expert in financial reporting, Stevens meets with you to discuss his ideas:

STEVENS: I have two ideas to raise more tax revenue, but I don't know if they'll work.

YOU: I'll see if I can help.

STEVENS: Well, for my first idea, I want to close down some of the bigger tax loopholes that are unfairly rewarding some taxpayers, especially large corporations. For example, I was looking at the financial statements of Toronto Dominion Bank (TD), one of Canada's largest financial institutions. The bank seems to pay an amazingly small amount of tax and that's not right!

He hands you the financial statements for the year ended October 31, 2009, with the following excerpt in Note 28 highlighted:

Exhibit I Reconciliation to statutory tax rate

	Amount ($ millions)	Rate (%)
Income taxes at Canadian statutory income tax rate	$1,006	31.8%
Increase (decrease) resulting from:		
Dividends received	(333)	(10.5)
Rate differentials on international operations	(448)	(14.1)
Other	16	0.4
Provision for income taxes and effective income tax rate	$ 241	7.6%

STEVENS: Look at that—7.6%. Who do you know pays only 7.6% in taxes?

YOU: Hmm. Interesting.

STEVENS: Not only that, but take a look at this.

(He points to the following excerpt.)

Exhibit II	Deferred income tax liabilities[18]
	Amount ($ millions)
Intangible assets	$ 898
Deferred income	72
Employee benefits	323
Other	519
Deferred income tax liabilities	$1,812

STEVENS: Looks like TD has paid only $241 million and owes the government another $1.8 billion that it hasn't paid. I don't know how these guys are getting away with it, but I want to put a stop to it. And I don't think it's just TD—there are probably dozens or even hundreds of other companies in similar situations. If we could get even half of what's owed to us, we could cut the deficit down to size in a hurry.

YOU: Well, it's not quite that straightforward.

STEVENS: Why don't you think about it carefully and then write me a short report so I fully understand the issues? Then I'll know how to approach Cabinet about this.

YOU: All right, I'll do my best.

Required:

Draft the report requested by Clark Stevens.

CASE 2 Whitney Equity Partners

(30 minutes)

Whitney Equity Partners (WEP) is a private equity firm that specializes in buying underperforming firms, installing new management or implementing improved management techniques, and then selling the companies at a higher price.

You are one of the analysts at WEP who specialize in financial analysis. The firm has identified two potential targets. Your colleagues have provided you with the financial reports from these two targets. In particular, they have brought to your attention the note disclosures relating to income taxes; Exhibit I and II are excerpts from relevant parts of these disclosures.

Exhibit I	Income tax note excerpt for Nieman Inc.	
	%	$000's
Combined federal and provincial income tax at statutory rate	31.0%	$4,510
Increase (decrease) resulting from:		
Tax-exempt dividend income	(4.5)	(655)
Income tax expense	26.5%	$3,855

Exhibit II	Income tax note excerpt for Marcus Company
	$000's
Current tax expense	$2,110
Deferred income tax relating to increases in tax rates	610
Income tax expense*	$2,720

*This income tax expense of $2,720,000 represents 40% of Marcus's pre-tax income.

18. Denoted as "Future income tax liabilities" in original financial statements. Adapted here to match contemporary terminology.

Your colleague, Jane, who supports the buyout of Nieman Inc., argues that the company must have a management team that is adept at minimizing tax costs. She argues that the low effective tax rate of 26.5% is proof. "Nieman doesn't fit our typical profile for a buyout, but it would be ideal if we are able to get that tax management talent and apply it to all the companies that we buy," she notes.

Kevin, another of your colleagues who supports the buyout of Marcus Company, argues that Marcus fits perfectly with WEP's strategy of buying poorly run companies. He notes that the effective tax rate of 40% is much higher than the current statutory rate of 31%. He argues, "The management of Marcus must not be very savvy at tax planning, which suggests that they are probably not that great at management more generally."

Required:

Prepare a memo to respond to the issues raised by your colleagues.

CASE 3
Oddities in the Accounting for Income Tax

(30 minutes)

Dale, a colleague of yours who has a rudimentary understanding of income tax reporting, has come to you for your expert advice on a number of issues that have confounded him. Specifically, he has three questions.

a. Is it possible for a company to report a loss before income taxes and income tax expense (current and future) together? Said differently, is it possible for a company to report the following?

Loss from continuing operations	(3,000,000)
Income tax expense (current and future)	2,000,000
Net loss	(5,000,000)

b. SunRise Ltd. made an investment in SunSet Inc. and classified it as available for sale. SunRise purchased 30,000 shares on August 1 of the current fiscal year for $12 per share. By the end of the fiscal year (December 31), shares of SunSet traded at $14 per share. Dale is wondering how to account for this investment and its related tax effects.

c. Suppose a company opts to carry a loss forward rather than to carry it back to past years. Would it be rational to do so and when would it be optimal?

Assume the tax rate is 40%.

Required:

Draft a response to Dale that explains these issues to your colleague.

Mikhail Tchkheidze/123RF

CHAPTER 19
Accounting Changes

LEARNING OBJECTIVES

After studying this chapter, you should be able to:

L.O. 19-1. Evaluate whether an accounting change is an error correction, a change in accounting policy, or a change in estimate.

L.O. 19-2. Apply the prospective and retrospective treatments for accounting changes.

L.O. 19-3. Evaluate the effects of retrospective adjustments and record those effects in the accounting records.

CPA competencies addressed in this chapter:

1.1.2 Evaluates the appropriateness of the basis of financial reporting (Level B)
a. Fundamental accounting concepts and principles (qualitative characteristics of accounting information, basic elements)

1.2.2 Evaluates treatment for routine transactions (Level A)
o. Changes in accounting policies and estimates, and errors

1.3.2 Prepares routine financial statement note disclosure (Level B)

In July 2006, the United States Government Accountability Office published a widely cited report, *Financial Restatements*, which identified 1,390 restatements of financial reports made by public companies between 2002 and September 2005. The report noted that "the proportion of listed companies restating grew from 3.7 percent in 2002 to 6.8 percent in 2005" (p. 12). Evidently, the frequency with which companies need to correct their published financial statements is not trivial.

The report further identified the principal reason for each restatement. The three most common reasons were to correct the recording of costs and expenses (35.2%), revenue recognition (20.1%), and recording securities-related transactions (14.1%). These are all topics that have been addressed in previous chapters of this text. The aggregate impact of these restatement announcements on the share values of these companies ranges from a low of US$36 billion to a high of US$126 billion. (Dollar amounts and percentages are from Tables 3, 5, and 6 and Figure 4 of the report.)

Closer to home is the case of Nortel Networks, a maker of telecommunications equipment. At one time, the company employed over 90,000 employees and was the most valuable company in Canada, with shares valued at almost $400 billion in September 2000. In the wake of the bursting of the Internet bubble in 2000, the company faced severe declines in its revenue and stock price. The company changed its top management several times and undertook a number of restructuring efforts without success. In January 2009, the company filed for bankruptcy. In the midst of this turmoil, investigations found that Nortel had improperly recorded about $3 billion in revenue between 1998 and 2000, at the height of the company's apparent success. It is hard to say precisely the extent to which the misstated revenues contributed to the high valuation of Nortel's shares in the period leading up to September 2000. Nevertheless, it is likely that the misstated financial statements played some part in influencing investors' perceptions of the company.[1]

1. Further information can be found on Wikipedia under the topic "Nortel."

19 CONTENTS

A. TYPES OF ACCOUNTING CHANGES 967
 1. Changes in accounting policy 967
 2. Corrections of errors from prior periods 968
 3. Changes in accounting estimates 969
 4. Summary 970
B. TREATMENTS FOR ACCOUNTING CHANGES 971
 1. Prospective adjustment 971
 2. Retrospective adjustment 973
C. CHANGES IN ACCOUNTING STANDARDS 975
D. IMPLEMENTING RETROSPECTIVE ADJUSTMENTS 976
 1. Retrospective adjustments involving only presentation 977
 2. Retrospective adjustments affecting only temporary accounts 977
 3. Retrospective adjustments affecting both permanent and temporary accounts 978
E. SUMMARY 984
F. ANSWERS TO CHECKPOINT QUESTIONS 984
G. GLOSSARY 985
H. REFERENCES 985
I. PROBLEMS 985
J. MINI-CASE 1002

In the restatements mentioned above, how should companies report the corrections? How many accounting periods do they need to adjust? Under what circumstances should restatements be made? How should companies reflect new information that changes their assessment of estimates previously made?

A. TYPES OF ACCOUNTING CHANGES

Early in this textbook, Chapter 3 introduced the topic of accounting changes. This chapter reviews this topic and explores it in further depth.

L.O. 19-1. Evaluate whether an accounting change is an error correction, a change in accounting policy, or a change in estimate.

As noted in Chapter 3, there are three types of accounting changes: changes in accounting policy, correction of errors from prior periods (such as the restatements mentioned in the opening vignette), and changes in accounting estimates. These accounting changes are fundamentally different from each other because they arise for different reasons. Briefly, they differ according to (i) whether the trigger for the accounting change is a matter of choice or a matter of fact, and (ii) if it is a matter of fact, whether that information was known or should have been known in the past. The following discussion explores each of these three accounting changes in more detail. In this discussion, we assume that the amounts involved are material.

1. Changes in accounting policy

A **change in accounting policy** is an accounting change made at the discretion of management. A change in accounting policy is purely a matter of management choice among acceptable alternatives. For instance, both weighted-average cost and first-in, first-out (FIFO) are acceptable cost flow assumptions—an enterprise can use one or the other method, and can also choose to switch from one method to the other.

change in accounting policy An accounting change made at the discretion of management.

Changes in accounting policy are relatively infrequent compared to changes in estimates. This is due in part to accounting standard setters being wary of

THRESHOLD CONCEPT
QUALITY OF EARNINGS

management choosing accounting policies opportunistically for earnings management. Over time, the number of areas where management has a free choice over accounting policies has diminished. For instance, Canadian companies could have chosen the last-in, first-out (LIFO) cost flow assumption for inventories in the past but are no longer permitted to do so.

The following table provides examples of changes in accounting policy:

Exhibit 19-1 Examples of changes in accounting policy

Financial statement items	Changes in accounting policy
Revenue	On long-term contracts, a company changes from using the cost ratio to using engineering estimates to determine the percentage completed.
Operating expenses	A company changes the presentation of operating expenses from "by function" to "by nature."
Receivables	A company changes from the gross method to the net method of recording cash discounts.
Property, plant, and equipment (PPE)	A company changes from the cost model to the revaluation model of measuring the value of land.
Government assistance	An enterprise switches from the gross method to the net method of presenting government grants.

CHECKPOINT **CP19-1**

What is the essential characteristic that distinguishes a change in accounting policy from either an error correction or a change in estimate?

2. Corrections of errors from prior periods

correction of an error An accounting change made necessary by the discovery of an incorrect amount given the information available at the time the amount was reported.

A **correction of an error** is, as intuition suggests, an accounting change that is made necessary by the discovery of an incorrect amount, given the information available at the time the amount was reported. Such errors can be as simple and clear-cut as arithmetic errors in the computation of depreciation or bad debts expense. They can also be more complex errors of judgment from the misapplication of accounting standards, such as recording revenue when the criteria for revenue recognition had not yet been satisfied (as in the case of Nortel described in the opening vignette) or omitting some relevant indicators in the analysis of whether a cash generating unit is potentially impaired.

THRESHOLD CONCEPT
DECISION MAKING UNDER UNCERTAINTY

It is important to emphasize that an accounting error is a mistake *given the information that was available at the time of reporting.* In other words, one must not use hindsight to judge whether there is an accounting error that requires correction. An accounting error is not just an estimate that subsequently turns out to be wrong. Much of accounting involves uncertainty and predictions of future outcomes, so inevitably estimates will differ from actual outcomes.

For example, the allowance for doubtful accounts of $50,000 is just an estimate of the amount that will not be collected in the future; an actual outcome of $45,000 of bad debts does not mean that we need to correct the estimate of $50,000 because the $45,000 is based on hindsight (i.e., information subsequent to the time of reporting). On the other hand, if the $50,000 resulted from a multiplication error, and the correct amount without the multiplication error should have been $60,000, then there would be an error of $10,000. The information necessary to identify the error was available at the time of reporting. The following table provides a few other examples of errors that require correction, as well as other events that do not require correction.

Exhibit 19-2 Examples of errors that require correction and events that do not require correction

Financial statement items	Errors that require correction	Events that are not errors and do not require correction
Revenue	The full sale price was recognized in revenue for a sale arrangement involving a sale of a good and the provision of services over three future years; the multiple performance obligation should have been separated into its components, with the service component deferred to future years.	The cost on a long-term contract turned out to be $15,325,000 instead of the $15,000,000 originally estimated.
Inventories	Inventory was not written down to the lower of cost and net realizable value even though actual sales made in the subsequent events period indicated impairment in inventories.	Inventory was sold below carrying amount even though the inventory had been previously written down to the lower of cost and net realizable value.
Property, plant, and equipment (PPE)	Costs not related to the construction of a building were included in the building cost.	The useful life on a building was originally estimated to be 20 years but the building turned out to be useful for only 15 years.
Intangible assets	Development costs were capitalized when only five of six criteria for capitalization had been satisfied.	A patent was expected to provide protection of intellectual property for the full legal life of 20 years, but technological advances made the patent obsolete after only 12 years.
Current liabilities and long-term debt	The company failed to report as current liabilities the portion of long-term debt that was repayable within 12 months of the fiscal year-end.	A contingency for a lawsuit that was evaluated to be unlikely to lead to an outflow of resources was ultimately resolved against the reporting entity.
Deferred income tax	A temporary difference was treated as a permanent difference.	A deferred tax asset for a loss carried forward became worthless when the government reduced the length of the carryforward period.
Earnings per share (EPS)	The company miscalculated the weighted average number of ordinary shares outstanding because it used the wrong date for a share issuance.	Convertible securities that were identified as dilutive for computing diluted EPS were not converted by the expiration date.

CHECKPOINT **CP19-2**

What distinguishes an error correction from a change in accounting estimate?

3. Changes in accounting estimates

The nature of accrual accounting requires forecasts of some future events, such as the amount that will be collectible from customers. Since the future is inherently uncertain, these forecasts can change over time as better information arrives. Indeed, management should revise estimates as time goes on to reflect more accurate information so as to reduce information asymmetry and uncertainty faced by financial statement users. This type of accounting change, made necessary by the arrival of new information, is a **change in estimate**.

change in estimate An accounting change made necessary by the arrival of new information.

It is important to highlight the words "made necessary" in the above definition in that a change in estimate is not optional. When management is aware of material new information that is relevant to an estimate used in a published financial report, it has an obligation to revise the estimates used in its next financial report. For example, if a piece of equipment was anticipated to have a useful life of seven years in the 2019 financial statements, but during 2020 new technological developments shortened the useful life to five years, then the 2020 financial statements must reflect the five-year useful life, not the seven-year estimate. Indeed, ignoring the new information would constitute an error.

Changes in accounting estimates are pervasive and occur frequently because management receives new and better information over time and economic conditions change all the time. The following table provides a small sample of the many changes in estimates that are possible.

Exhibit 19-3 Examples of changes in accounting estimates

Financial statement items	Changes in accounting estimates
Revenue	For a long-term contract, a change in the estimated total cost of the contract from $12 million to $13 million.
Receivables	A change in the percentage of sales used to estimate bad debts expense from 0.5% to 0.6%.
Property, plant, and equipment (PPE)	A company using the straight-line method of depreciation changes the estimated useful life of a building from 20 years to 15 years remaining as at the beginning of the year.
Goodwill	A change in economic conditions resulted in the fair value of goodwill declining from $15 million to $10 million.
Current liabilities and long-term debt	A change in the terms of a loan from repayment on demand to a fixed repayment date two years after the fiscal year-end.
Deferred income taxes	A change in income tax rates from 32% to 33%.
Employee future benefits	Change in life expectancy from 78 to 80 years for beneficiaries of a defined benefit pension plan.

This list is but a small sample of the endless possibilities for changes in estimates.

In some instances, it is difficult to distinguish a change in accounting policy from a change in estimate. For example, a change in depreciation pattern from straight-line to declining-balance is usually considered a change in estimate because the depreciation pattern is not a free choice among acceptable alternatives. IAS 16 requires enterprises to choose the pattern of depreciation that best reflects the pattern of economic benefits expected from the asset, so a change from straight-line to declining-balance is presumed to reflect a change in the estimated pattern of benefits.

4. Summary

The beginning of this section identified two characteristics that distinguish the type of accounting change. Therefore, answering the following two questions will identify the type of accounting change:

1. *Is the accounting change due to management choice, or is it due to new information?* If the change is due to management choice, then it is a change in accounting policy. Otherwise, it is a correction of an error or change in estimate.

2. *Is the accounting change a result of new information, or old information that was known or should have been known in a prior period?* If the accounting change is due to old information (the information was known or should have been known to management), then it is a correction of an error. If the accounting change is due to new information (it could not have been previously known to management), then it is a change in estimate. The following decision tree summarizes the application of these two questions.

Exhibit 19-4 Decision tree to identify types of accounting changes

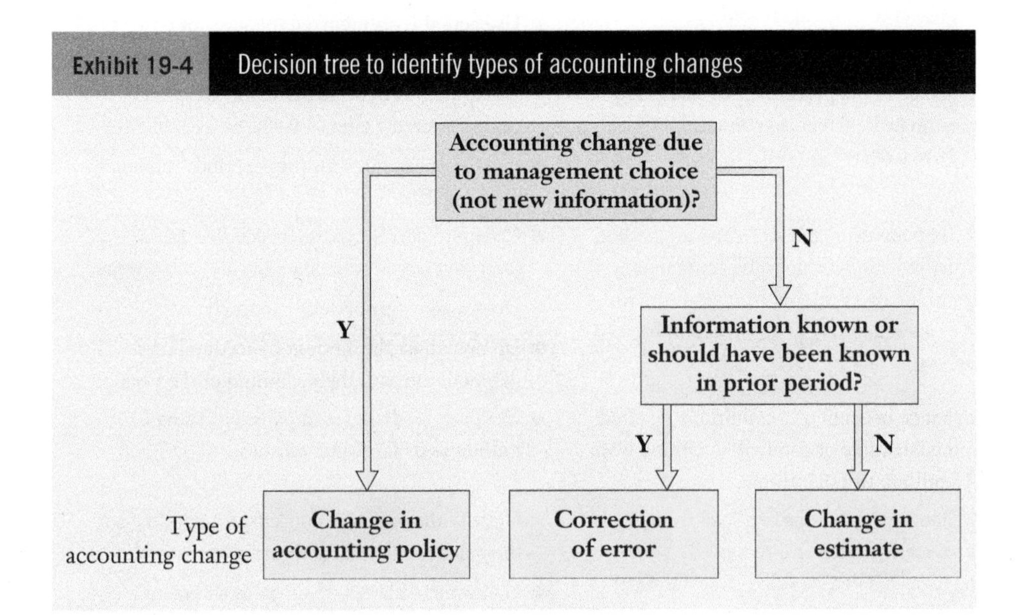

B. TREATMENTS FOR ACCOUNTING CHANGES

L.O. 19-2. Apply the prospective and retrospective treatments for accounting changes.

Once the type of accounting change has been identified, there will be a corresponding treatment for that accounting change. In general terms, we can report accounting changes in two ways: prospectively (looking forward) or retrospectively (looking backward).

1. Prospective adjustment

prospective adjustment Applies an accounting change only to the current and future periods without any changes to past financial statements.

The **prospective adjustment** approach applies an accounting change only to the current and future periods without any changes to past financial statements. This is the appropriate treatment for changes in estimates because this type of change is triggered by new information. Since this information was not previously known, it does not make sense to go back in time and amend prior financial statements. Consider the alternative: if we were to adjust already published financial statements for new information that arrives later, then we would be constantly adjusting past financial statements; it would be cumbersome for preparers and confusing to readers. For these reasons, it makes sense to reflect new information on a prospective basis.

Reflecting this intuitively appealing approach, we have already explicitly or implicitly applied prospective adjustments to changes in estimates on many occasions. Consider the sample of changes in estimates shown in Exhibit 19-3. The corresponding treatments of these changes using the prospective method are as follows:

Exhibit 19-5 Examples of changes in accounting estimates with description of prospective adjustments

Financial statement items	Changes in accounting estimates	Prospective adjustments
Revenue	For a long-term contract, a change in the estimated total cost of the contract from $12 million to $13 million.	■ Re-evaluate whether the contract remains profitable. ■ Compute the percentage completed using the new cost total (if the company uses the cost ratio to estimate percentage completed). ■ Use actual costs incurred to date, not cost estimates at the beginning of the contract.
Receivables	A change in the percentage of sales used to estimate bad debts expense from 0.5% to 0.6%.	■ Compute bad debts expense for the current period as credit sales × 0.6%. ■ Bad debts expenses for prior periods remain unchanged.
Property, plant, and equipment (PPE)	A company using the straight-line method of depreciation changes the estimated useful life of a building from 20 years to 15 years remaining as at the beginning of the year.	■ Compute current year depreciation as (carrying amount − residual value) ÷ 15 years. ■ Do not adjust prior year's depreciation. ■ Do not adjust the amount of accumulated depreciation as at the beginning of the year.
Goodwill	A change in economic conditions resulted in the fair value of goodwill declining from $15 million to $10 million.	■ Evaluate goodwill for impairment using $10 million as its fair value estimate.
Current liabilities and long-term debt	A change in the terms of a loan from repayment on demand to a fixed repayment date two years after the fiscal year-end.	■ Classify the loan as a non-current liability on the balance sheet for the current year-end. ■ Continue to classify the loan as a current liability on the balance sheet for the prior year-end.
Deferred income taxes	A change in income tax rates from 32% to 33%.	■ Compute the amount for deferred tax assets or liabilities for the current year-end using the new 33% rate. ■ Do not adjust the value of deferred tax assets or liabilities reported in prior years.
Employee future benefits	Change in life expectancy from 78 to 80 years for beneficiaries of a defined benefit pension plan.	■ This change will increase the projected benefit obligation estimated by the actuary, which will increase the net pension liability (or decrease the net pension asset). ■ Do not adjust pension liabilities or assets reported in prior years.

THRESHOLD CONCEPT
TIMING OF RECOGNITION

These examples are just a small subset of the many changes in estimates because these changes arise simply as a matter of accrual accounting. Accruals anticipate the future outcomes of operating, investing, and financing cash cycles, so changes in conditions over time necessitate changes in the accruals. Under cash accounting, there is no need to forecast the future outcomes since the accounting follows cash flows.

The implementation of the prospective method for specific changes in estimates has been demonstrated in many prior chapters and is not repeated here to avoid redundancy.

CHECKPOINT **CP19-3**

Why is the prospective treatment conceptually appropriate for changes in estimates?

2. Retrospective adjustment

In contrast to a prospective adjustment, which is forward-looking, a **retrospective adjustment** applies an accounting change to all periods affected in the past, present, and future. Since a prospective adjustment affects just the current and future periods, the difference between prospective and retrospective adjustments is in the adjustment of past financial statements—hence the term "retrospective."

retrospective adjustment Applies an accounting change to all periods affected in the past, present, and future.

Retrospective adjustment is the appropriate treatment for both corrections of errors and changes in accounting policy. For errors made in previously published financial statements, it is common sense that we should reflect the corrections in the period when those mistakes occurred rather than in the period when the mistakes were discovered. For changes in accounting policy, the benefit of adjusting prior periods using the retrospective approach is the consistency/comparability in the financial reports presented over time. If the retrospective approach were not used, then the financial statements for one year would be presented using one set of accounting policies, while the next year could be presented using quite a different set of policies, making inter-year comparisons difficult and possibly meaningless.

THRESHOLD CONCEPT
CONCEPTUAL FRAMEWORK

When there is a change in accounting policy, IAS 1 requires the presentation of three balance sheets (i.e., for the end of the current fiscal year and the two preceding years) compared with the normal requirement of two balance sheets (see Exhibit 19-6). Requirements for the other (flow) financial statements remain at two years. The end of the second preceding year is of course the beginning of the comparative year. The objective of the requirement to present the extra balance sheet is to allow users to follow the articulation of the financial statements for a full two-year cycle.

THRESHOLD CONCEPT
ARTICULATION

Exhibit 19-6 Presentation requirements when there are changes in accounting policy or error corrections

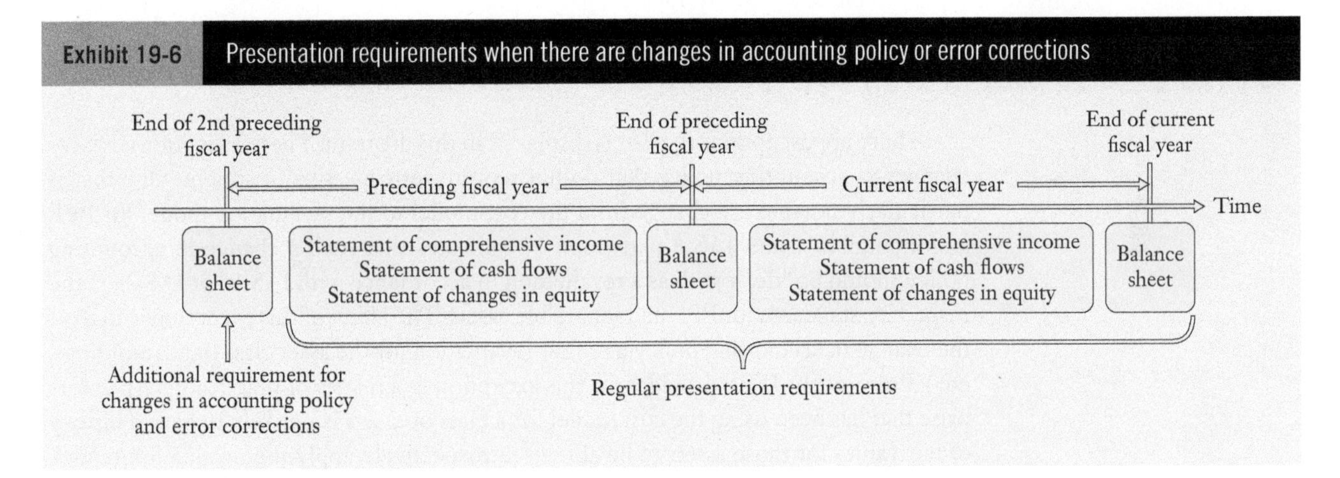

Care must be taken in interpreting Exhibit 19-6. This exhibit merely shows the *presentation* requirement to show two complete years of financial statements, beginning with the balance sheet from the beginning of the preceding year. However, it does *not* indicate how far back the *accounting records* should be adjusted to fully reflect the retrospective adjustments for a change in accounting policy or error correction. Generally speaking, the changes need to go as far back as necessary. For example, in the simple case where the current financial report is for the fiscal year ended December 31, 2020, and the company discovers an error in the 2017 financial statements in which a $10 million site restoration obligation was not recorded, the 2017 financial statements would be corrected to show that liability, with any consequential changes in 2018, 2019, and 2020 (for interest and depreciation) also made. In this case, the change affects four years, not just two. (More specific numerical examples along with journal entries will follow in Section D.)

Expanding on Exhibit 19-4, Exhibit 19-7 summarizes the relationship among the three different types of accounting changes and two accounting treatments for these changes.

Exhibit 19-7 Decision tree to identify types of accounting changes and corresponding treatment

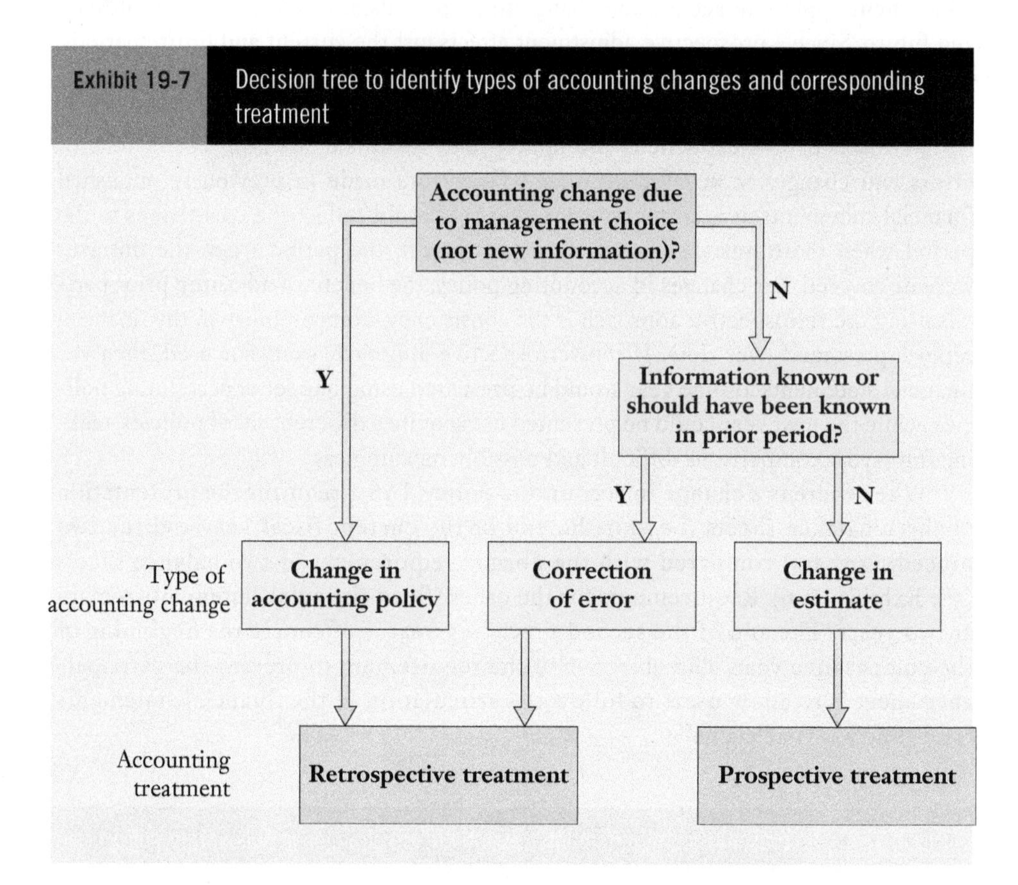

There are exceptions to what is displayed in this diagram. These exceptions involve changes in accounting policy that do not require retrospective treatment. One that is particularly notable is a change from the cost model to the revaluation model for PPE and intangible assets. IAS 8 paragraph 17 indicates that such a change in accounting policy should be "dealt with as a revaluation in accordance with IAS 16 or IAS 38,"[2] the respective standards for PPE and intangible assets. The effect of this exception is to treat the change in accounting policy as a first revaluation for the asset class (land, buildings, etc.). Presumably, IFRS provides for this exception as a matter of practicality. An enterprise that has been using the cost model for a class of assets is unlikely to have a history of fair values for those assets to be able to retrospectively apply the revaluation model. For PPE and intangible assets, that history could be decades long. Requiring retrospective adjustments in this instance would mean that practically no one would be able to switch from the cost model to the revaluation model. Note that the reverse switch, from the revaluation model to the cost model, does not have the same practical limitations. Enterprises do have the necessary cost information, even when they had been applying the revaluation model. Consequently, switching from the revaluation model to the cost model *does* need to follow the general requirement of retrospective adjustment.

CHECKPOINT **CP19-4**

Why is the retrospective approach conceptually appropriate for changes in accounting policy?

[2] Copyright © 2012 IFRS Foundation.

C. CHANGES IN ACCOUNTING STANDARDS

Accounting standards evolve over time. When changes in standards occur, how should enterprises reflect those changes? Should the treatment be prospective because changes in accounting standards represent events and information that could not be known in the past? Or should the treatment be retrospective so that the same set of standards applies to all figures presented in the financial statements?

In reality, there is no "one size fits all" solution to this issue. Depending on the particular accounting standard undergoing change, the treatment could be prospective, retrospective, or a modified version of these approaches. Many new standards prescribe the treatment for the change in a section called "transitional provisions" positioned near the end of the standard. Whether enterprises are likely to have the information necessary to restate past financial statements plays a large part in the prescribed approach. When that information is readily available, then retrospective treatment will be the norm. When it is likely that enterprises do not have the necessary information to restate, or that it will be costly to obtain that information, prospective treatment will be the norm. In cases when a particular standard does not specify the transitional provision, IAS 8 paragraph 19 states that default treatment is retrospective adjustment.

For example, consider the revision of IAS 19—Employee Benefits, which became effective as of January 1, 2013. The most significant change in this standard was the requirement to immediately recognize changes in the value of pension assets and liabilities. (Prior to the revision, there was an option to defer and amortize the changes in value.) The standard provides the following transitional provision:

> ¶173 An entity shall apply this Standard retrospectively, in accordance with IAS 8 *Accounting Policies, Changes in Accounting Estimates and Errors*, except that:
>
> (a) an entity need not adjust the carrying amount of assets outside the scope of this Standard for changes in employee benefit costs that were included in the carrying amount before the date of initial application. The date of initial application is the beginning of the earliest prior period presented in the first financial statements in which the entity adopts this Standard.
>
> (b) in financial statements for periods beginning before 1 January 2014, an entity need not present comparative information for the disclosures required by paragraph 145 about the sensitivity of the defined benefit obligation.[3]

This is an example of a modified retrospective treatment. The overall requirement is retrospective adjustment but with two exceptions. The first exception in clause (a) reflects the high cost of tracing labour costs through inventories, PPE, and other assets when the enterprise has capitalized labour costs to those assets. In particular, for inventories, full retrospective adjustment would require changing the rates of labour cost allocated to each unit of production, which could be difficult and time consuming to determine for companies that manufacture a variety of products. The second exception in clause (b) reflects the high likelihood that enterprises do not have the information necessary for the disclosure.

[3] Copyright © 2012 IFRS Foundation.

For comparison, another example is IAS 16—Property, Plant and Equipment. The transitional provisions state the following regarding the measurement of non-monetary transactions that came into force on January 1, 2005:

> ¶80 The requirements of paragraphs 24–26 regarding the initial measurement of an item of property, plant and equipment acquired in an exchange of assets transaction shall be applied prospectively only to future transactions.[4]

In this instance, the prospective treatment makes sense to the extent that it would be impractical to obtain fair value information on non-monetary exchanges that took place prior to 2005.

CHECKPOINT **CP19-5**

How should enterprises reflect changes in accounting standards?

D. IMPLEMENTING RETROSPECTIVE ADJUSTMENTS

L.O. 19-3. Evaluate the effects of retrospective adjustments and record those effects in the accounting records.

The previous two sections discussed situations when the prospective and retrospective methods should be used. In terms of implementation, the prospective method does not pose particular complications because one only needs to be mindful of the new method going forward. As noted earlier, prospective adjustments are pervasive and have been previously illustrated in many different contexts in previous chapters. Here are a few examples:

- Chapter 4—changes in the estimated costs of a long-term contract
- Chapter 5—changes in estimates for bad debts
- Chapter 8—changes in estimated useful lives
- Chapter 18—changes in tax rates

In comparison, the retrospective method is significantly more complex because of the changes that need to be made to past reporting periods. The task is made even more difficult by the fact that the accounting system has permanent and temporary accounts, which are affected differently by retrospective restatements. This section discusses the technical procedures for making retrospective adjustments.

Since we need to amend past financial reports, we first need to address an important question: how far back in time must we go? There is no single quantifiable answer in terms of the number of years. Generally speaking, retrospective changes need to go *as far back as is necessary so that the next set of financial statements will be presented correctly.* Applying this principle does not mean that the adjustments need to go into the infinite past. For instance, if the current fiscal year is 2021, then comparative figures for 2020 also need to be presented when the enterprise issues the 2021 financial report. If a potential adjustment involves transactions before 2020 but has no impact on the accounts in 2020 (and by implication any subsequent year), then there is no need to adjust any financial statement nor is there a need to record journal entries for the adjustments. On the other hand, if a potential adjustment involves transactions before 2020 but has follow-through implications for the accounts in 2020 or subsequent years, then adjustments will need to be made to the financial statements and records. For example, a change in the amount recorded for PPE in 2019 would have follow-through effects on depreciation in 2020 and later years.

---

4. Copyright © 2012 IFRS Foundation.

Note that for retrospective adjustments, we need to distinguish between changes in the presentation of financial statements and changes in the accounting records. There are certain adjustments that cannot be recorded in the accounts, but nonetheless need to be reflected in the financial statements. Below we will see why and how this occurs. The discussion first covers two types of adjustments that are relatively simple but infrequent in occurrence. Then we move on to the procedures for the third type of retrospective adjustment, which is more complex but also more common.

1. Retrospective adjustments involving only presentation

The easiest type of retrospective adjustment involves matters of financial statement presentation only, with no changes required in the accounting records. For instance, suppose that Pailco borrowed $100,000 during 2020 and the loan requires $20,000 principal repayment in June of each year for five years. The company has a December 31 year-end. In 2021, Pailco discovered that it did not correctly separate the loan between current and non-current portions. In the accounts, there would normally be only one account for the loan balance, which would show $100,000 at the end of 2020. The allocation of this amount between current and non-current liabilities occurs only during the preparation of the financial statements. This retrospective adjustment simply requires the correction of presentation in the next set of published financial statements. No journal entries are required to carry out this retrospective adjustment.

Exhibit 19-8 Partial balance sheet and adjustment for Pailco's retrospective adjustment

Original (incorrect) presentation in 2020			Corrected presentation in 2021			
	2020	2019		2021	**2020**	2019
Current liabilities			Current liabilities			
—			Current portion of long-term debt	20,000	**20,000**	—
Non-current liabilities			Non-current liabilities			
Long-term debt	**100,000**	—	Long-term debt	60,000	**80,000**	—
Journal entries for retrospective adjustment						
None needed.						

Notice the corrected presentation includes the balance sheet at the end of the second preceding year as required by IAS 1, which was discussed earlier.

2. Retrospective adjustments affecting only temporary accounts

This type of retrospective adjustment is also easy to correct because only presentation is affected. Conceptually, the accounts need to be adjusted, but due to the affected accounts being temporary, those accounts cannot be adjusted by journal entries. For example, suppose Ticco Inc. misreported a $50,000 interest expense as administrative expense in 2020, and the company discovered the error in 2021. Administrative expenses would have been $180,000 otherwise. However, since these accounts are temporary, the 2020 accounts would already be closed when the error was discovered in 2021. The accounts for "interest expense" and "administrative expense" would be for the current year (2021), not 2020. Thus, even though Ticco should conceptually transfer

$50,000 of expenses between accounts, no journal entries would be made; only the presentation would be changed to reflect the retrospective adjustment. Exhibit 19-9 summarizes this example.

Exhibit 19-9 Partial income statement and adjustment for Ticco Inc.'s retrospective adjustment

Original (incorrect) presentation in 2020			Corrected presentation in 2021		
	2020	2019		2021	**2020**
...			...		
Operating expenses			Operating expenses		
Administrative expense [other operating expenses]	**230,000**		Administrative expense [other operating expenses]		**180,000**
...			...		
			Interest expense		**50,000**
Journal entries for retrospective adjustment					
None possible since 2020 temporary accounts already closed.					

3. Retrospective adjustments affecting both permanent and temporary accounts

The most common type of retrospective adjustment involves both permanent and temporary accounts. The reason is due to the nature of accrual accounting. As explained in Chapter 3, all items in the balance sheet (i.e., the permanent accounts) other than cash arise from accruals. These accruals are generally associated with one or more flows measured by the temporary accounts. For instance, we record accounts receivable for revenue that precedes the collection of cash (permanent account—receivables; temporary account—revenue). Similarly, we record cash outflows on the purchase of equipment into PPE and later depreciate it as well as record any gain or loss on disposal (permanent account—PPE; temporary accounts—depreciation expense and gains/losses). Because of the articulation between permanent and temporary accounts, most retrospective adjustments affect both types of accounts.

While we can record journal entries to the permanent accounts to reflect retrospective adjustment, we cannot do the same with the temporary accounts, as noted above. At the end of each period, we close temporary accounts relating to net income to retained earnings and we close temporary accounts relating to other comprehensive income (OCI) to accumulated other comprehensive income (AOCI). Therefore, the effects of retrospective adjustments on the temporary accounts of prior years need to be recorded through retained earnings and AOCI rather than the temporary accounts themselves.

To further analyze this type of retrospective adjustment, we separate the adjustments according to whether they relate to accruals that (i) reverse in the immediately subsequent periods or (ii) reverse over a longer time frame.

a. Retrospective adjustments for accruals that reverse in the immediately subsequent period

Accruals that reverse in the immediately subsequent period generally involve operating activities such as the purchase and sale of goods, provision of services, and so on. For example, suppose Radon Company recorded $300,000 in sales too early, in 2019 instead of 2020. The related receivable was ultimately collected in 2021. In this case, Radon has overstated revenue and accounts receivable by $300,000 in 2019. In 2020, that overstatement will reverse, resulting in 2020 revenue being understated. By the end of 2020, the balance in accounts receivable will be correct because the $300,000 of accounts receivable was ultimately recorded by that time as it should have been.

Since the accrual and its reversal occur over two consecutive periods, we only need to be concerned about making adjustments if the second year (the reversal year) overlaps with either the current fiscal year or the comparative year or years presented. (Recall that IAS 1 requires only one year of comparative figures, but enterprises can choose to present more years.) If the relevant accrual and reversal occur prior to the beginning of the earliest comparative year, then no adjustments are necessary. Exhibit 19-10 summarizes when adjustments are required for accruals that reverse in the immediately subsequent period (using the minimum of one comparative year).

Exhibit 19-10 When adjustments are required for accruals that reverse in the immediately subsequent period

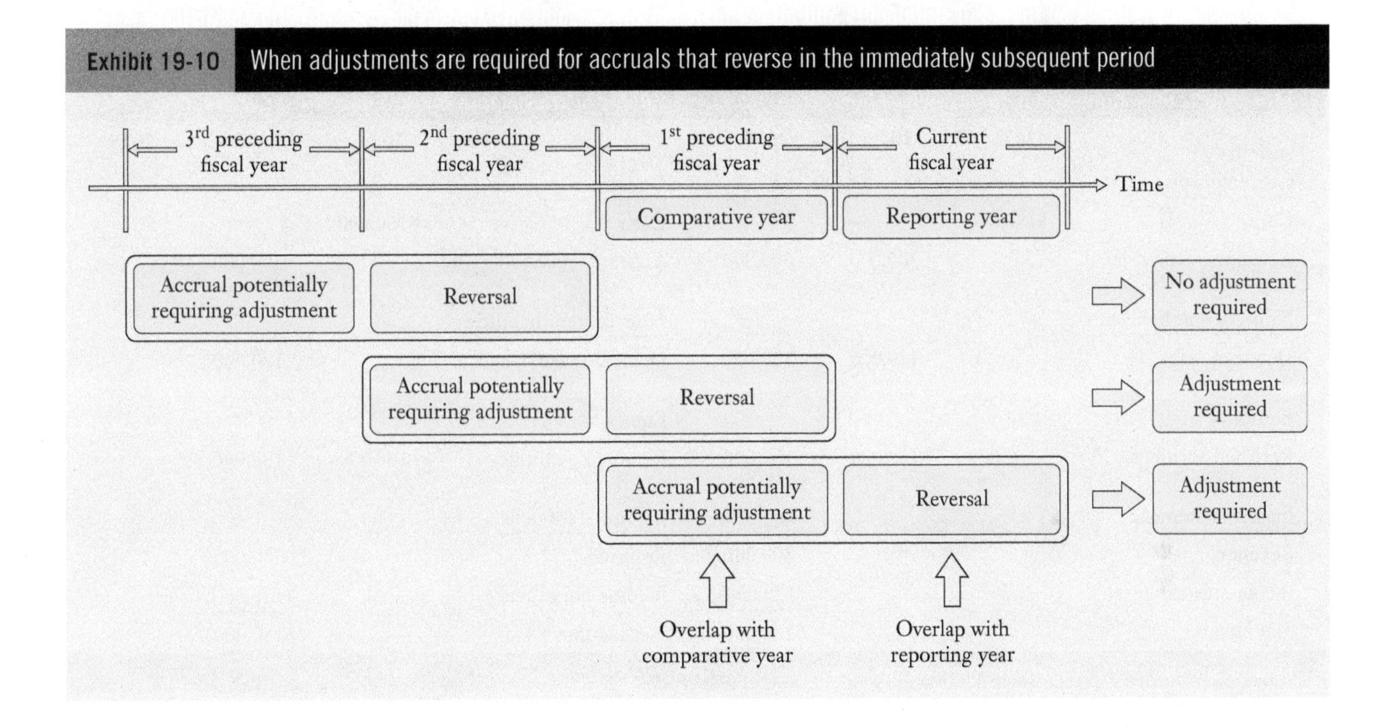

Applying this graphic to Radon Company, we observe the following:

- If 2022 is the current fiscal year, then no adjustments would be required because the initial accrual and its reversal occurred in 2019 and 2020, prior to the start of the comparative year of 2021.
- If 2021 is the current fiscal year, then the error in the 2019 accrual needs to be corrected because its reversal in 2020 is in the comparative year.
- If 2020 is the current fiscal year, then the error in the 2019 accrual needs to be corrected because it is in the comparative year and its reversal is in the current reporting year.

Now that we know adjustments are required in the second and third cases, we need to figure out the specifics of how to make those adjustments. For this purpose, assume that the income tax rate is 40% and constant through the years. Since revenue was recorded too early, in 2019, revenue and accounts receivable were both overstated by $300,000. As well, income tax expense was overstated by $120,000 in 2019

($300,000 × 40%). Net income and retained earnings at the end of 2019 would have been overstated by $180,000 ($300,000 − $120,000). Since the revenue and tax expense should have been recorded later, in 2020, revenue in that year was understated by $300,000 and income tax expense was understated by $120,000, so net income was understated by $180,000. The balance sheet amounts at the end of 2020 are correctly stated: accounts receivable at $300,000 since it was not collected until 2021; deferred tax liability of $120,000; and retained earnings of $180,000.[5] The correction needs to shift the $300,000 revenue from 2019 to 2020, along with the related tax expense. To proceed further, we need to know the year when we identified the error (i.e., what is the current fiscal year).

If 2021 is the current fiscal year, then the effects of the sale transactions can be summarized as shown in Exhibit 19-11. The exhibit also identifies the needed journal entries at the bottom.

Exhibit 19-11 Effects on financial statements and adjustment for Radon Company's retrospective correction of an error discovered in 2021

Effects of transaction on statements before correction				Effects of transaction on statements after correction			
	2021	2020	2019		2021	2020	2019
Current assets				Current assets			
Cash	$180,000	$ —	$ —	Cash	$180,000	$ —	$ —
Accounts receivable		300,000	300,000	Accounts receivable		300,000	—
Non-current liabilities				Non-current liabilities			
Deferred taxes		120,000	120,000	Deferred taxes		120,000	—
Equity				Equity			
Retained earnings	180,000	180,000	180,000	Retained earnings	180,000	180,000	—
Income statement				Income statement			
Revenue			300,000	Revenue		300,000	
Income tax expense			(120,000)	Income tax expense		(120,000)	
Net income			$180,000	Net income		$180,000	

Journal entries in 2021 for retrospective adjustment

Temporary accounts for 2020 are already closed, so adjustments are not possible in 2021.
Permanent accounts are correctly stated and require no adjustments.

When the reversal occurs in the comparative year, the adjustment cannot be made using journal entries. The required adjustments involve temporary income statement accounts in 2020, which were closed at the end of 2020 and not available for journal entries in 2021. Instead, the changes need to be made separately during financial statement preparation.

If 2020 is the current fiscal year, then Exhibit 19-12 summarizes the effects of the error and related correcting journal entries.

---

5. In general, we assume that errors made in financial reports are not also errors in the tax returns, so any effect on accounting income for the computation of income tax expense results in deferred tax liabilities or assets rather than current taxes payable or receivable.

Exhibit 19-12 Effects on financial statements and adjustment for Radon Company's retrospective correction of an error discovered in 2020

Effects of transaction on statements before correction			Effects of transaction on statements after correction		
	2020	2019		2020	2019
Current assets			Current assets		
Cash	$ —	$ —	Cash	$ —	$ —
Accounts receivable	300,000	300,000	Accounts receivable	300,000	—
Deferred taxes	120,000	120,000	Deferred taxes	120,000	—
Equity			Equity		
Retained earnings	180,000	180,000	Retained earnings	180,000	—
Income statement			Income statement		
Revenue	—	300,000	Revenue	300,000	—
Income tax expense	—	(120,000)	Income tax expense	(120,000)	—
Net income		$ 180,000	Net income	$ 180,000	
Journal entries in 2020 for retrospective adjustment					
Dr. Retained earnings—opening balance				180,000	
Dr. Income tax expense				120,000	
Cr. Revenue					300,000

When the error occurs in the prior year and the reversal of the error occurs in the current year, we are able to make the adjustments to the income statement accounts for the current year, recording $300,000 of revenue and $120,000 of tax expense in 2020. However, note that the correcting journal entry cannot undo the revenue and tax expense recorded in 2019 because those accounts were closed at the end of 2019. Instead, we can only undo the net effect of $180,000 on retained earnings. The correction of the comparative figures for revenue and income tax expense for 2019 will need to be made during financial statement preparation.

So that users can understand the difference in the retained earnings figure originally reported at the end of 2019 and the revised comparative figure reported in the 2020 financial statements, enterprises need to identify three specific amounts in the statement of changes in equity: the amount of retained earnings originally reported, the amount of the retrospective adjustment, and the revised amount of retained earnings. For Radon Company, the portion of the statement of changes in equity relating to retained earnings would appear as follows (assuming no other transactions occurred):

Exhibit 19-13 Partial statement of changes in equity

	Common stock	Retained earnings	AOCI
Balance, January 1, 2020 (as originally reported)		$ 180,000	
Correction of error		(180,000)	
Balance, January 1, 2020 (as restated)		0	
Net income for the year		180,000	
Dividends declared		(0)	
Balance, December 31, 2020		$ 180,000	

This example of Radon Company involves items affecting net income and retained earnings. Retrospective adjustment involving items of OCI and AOCI involve similar procedures.

b. Retrospective adjustments for accruals that reverse over more than two periods

THRESHOLD CONCEPT
TIMING OF RECOGNITION

The nature of accrual accounting is that accruals will reverse when cash cycles are complete. Accruals and their reversals that occur in consecutive periods have relatively short cash cycles. Operating activities generally have this characteristic. However, investing and financing activities often involve longer cash cycles. For example, the purchase of equipment involves an initial accrual to record the asset followed by accrual reversals in the form of depreciation expense and derecognition of the asset upon disposal. Consequently, errors or changes in accounting policy that affect non-current items like equipment will result in follow-through changes over many accounting periods. While the time frame involved is longer, the basic mechanics of the retrospective adjustment remain the same as for accruals that reverse the next period.

For example, suppose Impact Demolition purchased a piece of demolition equipment for $20 million in early 2011. The company depreciates the equipment using the straight-line method over its useful life of 10 years, when it will have zero residual value. Impact's income tax rate is 40%. At the end of 2014, after four years of depreciation, the company wrote down the carrying amount of the equipment from $12 million to $9 million after performing an impairment test on the cash generating unit (CGU) to which the equipment belonged. As a result of the impairment, the annual depreciation declined from $2 million to $1.5 million. In 2017, prior to recording depreciation for that year, the company's staff discovered an error in one of the formulas in the spreadsheet used to compute the value in use for the impairment test carried out in 2014. Removing the error in the spreadsheet, the value in use for the CGU exceeded its carrying value. Therefore, the CGU was in fact not impaired, and Impact should not have recorded an impairment writedown on the demolition equipment in 2014.

Due to the multi-year effects of PPE investments and errors, it is useful to first tabulate the amounts involved year by year, as shown in Exhibit 19-14, with the years of the impairment error and its subsequent discovery highlighted.

Exhibit 19-14 Schedule for Impact Demolition's $20 million of equipment purchased in 2011 (in $000's)

	As originally recorded				Corrected amounts			
Year	Depr. and impairment	Accum. depr.	Net carrying amount	Tax effect of depr.	Depr. and impairment	Accum. depr.	Net carrying amount	Tax effect of depr.
2011	$2,000	$ 2,000	$18,000	$ 800	$2,000	$ 2,000	$18,000	$800
2012	2,000	4,000	16,000	800	2,000	4,000	16,000	800
2013	2,000	6,000	14,000	800	2,000	6,000	14,000	800
2014	2,000	8,000	12,000	800	2,000	8,000	12,000	800
	3,000*	11,000	9,000	1,200	—			—
2015	1,500	12,500	7,500	600	2,000	10,000	10,000	800
2016	1,500	14,000	6,000	600	2,000	12,000	8,000	800
2017	Year error was discovered; amounts not yet recorded				2,000	14,000	6,000	800
2018					2,000	16,000	4,000	800
2019					2,000	18,000	2,000	800
2020					2,000	20,000	0	800

* Impairment charge

With this information in hand, we can readily determine the journal entries that need to be recorded to make the retrospective adjustment. Comparing what was recorded and what should have been recorded in 2014, we see that two adjustments are required:

1. Accumulated depreciation should be reduced by $3,000,000, from $11,000,000 to $8,000,000. The impairment loss of $3,000,000 should be reversed, but this correction must be recorded through retained earnings since the 2014 impairment loss account is closed.
2. The tax effect associated with the impairment loss should be reversed. These two corrections are the first two journal entries in Exhibit 19-15.

Exhibit 19-15 Journal entries in 2017 to correct error in impairment writedown recorded in 2014

1. Reversal of impairment		
Dr. Accumulated depreciation	3,000,000	
Cr. Retained earnings		3,000,000
2. Reversal of tax effect on impairment		
Dr. Retained earnings	1,200,000	
Cr. Deferred tax liability		1,200,000
3. Reversal of depreciation decrease in years following impairment		
Dr. Retained earnings—opening balance (for 2015 depr. expense)	500,000	
Dr. Retained earnings—opening balance (for 2016 depr. expense)	500,000	
Cr. Accumulated depreciation		1,000,000
4. Adjust for tax effect of additional depreciation		
Dr. Deferred tax liability	400,000	
Cr. Retained earnings—opening balance (for 2015 tax expense)		200,000
Cr. Retained earnings—opening balance (for 2016 tax expense)		200,000

As a result of the correction of the impairment, subsequent years' depreciation and related tax effects need to be adjusted as well. Since the 2014 error was discovered in 2017, prior to the recording of depreciation for 2017, we need to correct the depreciation recorded in 2015 and 2016. Exhibit 19-15 shows these corrections in entry #3 and the related adjustment of tax expense in entry #4.

CHECKPOINT **CP19-6**

Why are retrospective adjustments to past years' income and expenses recorded directly in retained earnings?

E. SUMMARY

L.O. 19-1. Evaluate whether an accounting change is an error correction, a change in accounting policy, or a change in estimate.

- A change in accounting policy is a choice made at the discretion of management, while the other two accounting changes are not discretionary.
- An error correction is required when there exists material information relevant to financial reports that management knew or should have known but was not reflected in the financial reports.
- A change in estimates is required when new information indicates that prior estimates are no longer valid.

L.O. 19-2. Apply the prospective and retrospective treatments for accounting changes.

- The prospective treatment makes accounting adjustments in current and future periods. This treatment is appropriate for changes in estimates.
- The retrospective treatment makes accounting adjustments in past, current, and future periods. This treatment is appropriate for corrections of errors and changes in accounting policies.

L.O. 19-3. Evaluate the effects of retrospective adjustments and record those effects in the accounting records.

- Retrospective adjustments require careful analysis of the effects of those adjustments and a clear understanding of the accounting system. Retrospective changes to permanent (balance sheet) accounts can be made directly to those accounts. However, because temporary accounts are closed each period, retrospective changes to temporary accounts cannot be recorded in those accounts. Instead, we record the adjustments through retained earnings and accumulated other comprehensive income.

F. ANSWERS TO CHECKPOINT QUESTIONS

CP19-1: The essential characteristic that distinguishes a change in accounting policy from either an error correction or a change in estimate is that a change in accounting policy involves a management choice among acceptable alternatives. Management does not have a choice as to whether it corrects an error or changes an estimate to reflect new information.

CP19-2: We can distinguish an error correction from a change in accounting estimate based on whether the relevant information triggering the change was known or should have been known previously. If so, then there exists an error requiring correction. If not, then the information merely updates the accounting estimates going forward.

CP19-3: The prospective approach is conceptually appropriate for changes in estimates because such changes arise from new information that was not previously known.

CP19-4: The retrospective approach is conceptually appropriate for changes in accounting policy because it results in financial statements that are comparable over time. Comparability enhances the usefulness of financial reports.

CP19-5: Enterprises should reflect changes in accounting standards according to the transitional provisions of each standard. Where there are no specific transitional provisions, retrospective adjustments should be made to reflect the change in accounting standard.

CP19-6: We record retrospective adjustments to past years' income and expenses directly in retained earnings because prior years' income and expense accounts (i.e., temporary accounts) have been closed to retained earnings, so no entries can be made to those accounts; instead the net effect on income must be reflected directly in retained earnings.

G. GLOSSARY

change in accounting policy: An accounting change made at the discretion of management.

change in estimate: An accounting change made necessary by the arrival of new information.

correction of an error: An accounting change made necessary by the discovery of an incorrect amount given the information available at the time the amount was reported.

prospective adjustment: Applies an accounting change only to the current and future periods without any changes to past financial statements.

retrospective adjustment: Applies an accounting change to all periods affected in the past, present, and future.

H. REFERENCES

Authoritative standards:

IFRS	ASPE Section
IAS 1—Presentation of Financial Statements	1400—General Standards of Financial Statement Presentation
IAS 8—Accounting Policies, Changes in Accounting Estimates, and Errors	1506—Accounting Changes

MyLab Accounting Make the grade with **MyLab Accounting:** The problems marked with a 🌐 can be found on **MyLab Accounting.** You can practise them as often as you want, and most feature step-by-step guided instructions to help you find the right answer.

I. PROBLEMS

P19-1. Types of accounting changes (L.O. 19-1) (Easy – 3 minutes)

For the following types of accounting changes, identify the appropriate treatment under IFRS.

Type of accounting change	Accounting treatment
a. Change in estimate	
b. Change in accounting policy	
c. Correction of an error	

P19-2. Types of accounting changes (L.O. 19-1) (Easy – 3 minutes)

For the following types of accounting changes, identify the relevant criteria for each accounting change by selecting "yes," "no," or "n/a" (not applicable).

Type of accounting change	Accounting change due to management choice?	Information known (or should have been known) in prior period?
a. Change in estimate	Yes No n/a	Yes No n/a
b. Change in accounting policy	Yes No n/a	Yes No n/a
c. Correction of an error	Yes No n/a	Yes No n/a

P19-3. Types of accounting changes (L.O. 19-1) (Medium – 10 minutes)

The discussion in IAS 16 paragraphs 60–62 indicates that a change in depreciation method is usually a change in accounting estimate. Explain the logic behind why a change in depreciation method is normally considered a change in estimate.

P19-4. Types of accounting changes (L.O. 19-1) (Medium – 15 minutes)

A company changes the depreciation for a piece of equipment from 20% declining-balance to units-of-production. Describe a plausible circumstance that would support this change for each of the following: (i) an error, (ii) a change in estimate, or (iii) a change in accounting policy.

P19-5. Types of accounting changes and treatments  (L.O. 19-4) (Easy – 10 minutes)

Explain why a change in accounting policy requires the adjustment of both prior and future periods, whereas a change in estimate requires only adjustment of future periods.

P19-6. Types of accounting changes and treatments (L.O. 19-4) (Medium – 15 minutes)

Accrual accounting necessarily involves professional judgment, because accruals depend on decisions about uncertain future events. These judgments and decisions include the choices of accounting policies that management determines to be most appropriate for the circumstances.

Required:

Using the conceptual frameworks and other ideas, discuss whether a change in accounting policy should be treated prospectively or retrospectively.

P19-7. Types of accounting changes and treatments (L.O. 19-1, L.O. 19-2) (Medium – 15 minutes)

Evaluate each of the following independent situations to determine the type of accounting change (correction of error, change in accounting policy, or change in estimate) and the appropriate accounting treatment (retrospective or prospective).

a. A furniture maker decreases bad debts expense from 3% to 2% of credit sales.
b. A manufacturer determines that credit losses are becoming material due to deteriorating economic conditions. As a result, it decides to set up an allowance for doubtful accounts at 5% of amounts over 90 days.
c. A parking service estimates bad debts to be 10% of the value of parking violations issued. In the current year, management changed its approach to estimating the allowance for bad debts to be equal to 20% of accounts 30 to 90 days and 50% of accounts over 90 days.
d. A shipbuilder changes its revenue recognition policy from the point of receipt by the customer to when the ship leaves the factory shipyard. This change results from a change in shipping policy from F.O.B. destination to F.O.B. shipping point. (Recall from introductory accounting that F.O.B. means "free on board," and it refers to the point at which custody transfers from seller to buyer.)
e. An electronics retailer has never accrued for warranties or product guarantees. A new consumer protection law comes into effect, giving buyers of electronic products a guarantee against defects for 180 days after purchase and the ability to return defective products to the retailer.
f. A clothing company that has been operating for 20 years decides to obtain an external audit for the first time to meet the bank's demands. The audit firm recommends that management report inventories at the lower of cost and net realizable value, whereas the company has previously only tracked and reported inventory figures at cost.

P19-8. Types of accounting changes and treatments (L.O. 19-1, L.O. 19-2) (Medium – 15 minutes)

Evaluate each of the following independent situations to determine the type of accounting change (correction of error, change in accounting policy, or change in estimate) and the appropriate accounting treatment (retrospective or prospective). Assume that all amounts are material and the companies follow IFRS.

a. A retail sporting goods store changed from using a weighted average inventory cost flow assumption to the first-in, first-out (FIFO) method used by its major competitors.
b. An entity increased its liability for post-employment benefits due to decreased employee turnover.
c. A building contractor changed from the completed contract method of accounting for its revenues to the percentage of completion method used by its major competitors.
d. A company previously deferred and amortized actuarial gains and losses on its defined benefit pension plan using the corridor method. As a result of amendments to IAS 19, Employment Benefits, the company now recognizes actuarial gains and losses in other comprehensive income as they occur.
e. A company accounts for its real estate holdings using the cost model. Previously, due to rapidly escalating real estate prices, the company did not depreciate its buildings. The company began depreciating its buildings this year using the straight-line method as real estate prices have stabilized.

P19-9. Types of accounting changes and treatments

(L.O. 19-1, L.O. 19-2) (Medium – 15 minutes)

Evaluate each of the following independent situations to determine the type of accounting change (correction of error, change in accounting policy, or change in estimate) and the appropriate accounting treatment (retrospective or prospective).

a. A building contractor changes from using engineering estimates to the cost-to-cost approach to determine the percentage completed on long-term contracts.
b. A company's actuary advises that the expected income from pension plan assets be increased from 4% to 5% per annum.
c. A clothing retailer switches from using the taxes payable method to the accrual method of accounting for income taxes, which is the same method used by the rest of the industry.
d. A manufacturing company switches from using the net method to the gross method of presenting government grants, which is the same method used by the majority of its competitors.
e. A company changes from using the straight-line method to the declining-balance method of depreciating its computer systems.

P19-10. Types of accounting changes and treatments

(L.O. 19-1, L.O. 19-2) (Medium – 15 minutes)

Evaluate each of the following independent situations to determine the type of accounting change (correction of error, change in accounting policy, or change in estimate) and the appropriate accounting treatment (retrospective or prospective).

a. A company changes from the net method to the gross method of recording cash discounts offered for early payment of accounts receivable.
b. A company changes from the cost model to the revaluation model to subsequently measure the value of its real estate holdings.
c. An electronics company is no longer the industry leader in product development. It determines that the value of its goodwill has decreased from $1,500,000 to $900,000.
d. A franchisor sells a five-year franchise agreement to a franchisee for $200,000. It recognized revenue for this amount at the time of sale. Terms of the franchise agreement require the franchisor to provide operational support over the life of the franchisee.
e. A company previously paid $5 million for a trademark that was expected to substantively contribute to its income stream for the foreseeable future. The company now values the trademark at only $500,000 due to negative media coverage highlighting the company's employment of children in third world countries.

P19-11. Types of accounting changes and treatments

(L.O. 19-1, L.O. 19-2) (Medium – 10 minutes)

For each of the following scenarios, determine the effects (if any) of the accounting change (correction of error, change in accounting policy, or change in estimate) on the relevant asset or liability, equity, and comprehensive income in the year of change and the prior year. Use the following table for your response:

			Year prior to change			Year of accounting change		
	Type of accounting change	Treatment	Asset or liability	Equity	Income	Asset or liability	Equity	Income
a.								
b.								
c.								

a. Company A increases the allowance for doubtful accounts (ADA). Using the old estimate, ADA would have been $40,000. The new estimate is $45,000.
b. Company B omitted to record an invoice for an $8,000 sale made on credit at the end of the previous year and incorrectly recorded the sale in the current year. The related inventory sold has been accounted for.
c. Company C changes its revenue recognition to a more conservative policy. The result is a decrease in prior-year revenue by $3,000 and a decrease in current-year revenue by $4,000 relative to the amounts under the old policy.

P19-12. Types of accounting changes and treatments

(L.O. 19-1, L.O. 19-2) (Medium – 10 minutes)

During the audit of Keats Island Brewery for the fiscal year ended June 30, 2019, the auditors identified the following issues:

a. The company sells beer for $1 each plus $0.10 deposit on each bottle. The deposit collected is payable to the provincial recycling agency. During 2019, the company recorded $8,000 of deposits as revenue. The auditors believe this amount should have been recorded as a liability.
b. The company had been using the first-in, first-out cost flow assumption for its inventories. In fiscal 2019, management decided to switch to the weighted-average method. This change reduced inventory by $20,000 at June 30, 2018, and $35,000 at June 30, 2019.
c. The company has equipment costing $5,000,000 that it has been depreciating over 10 years on a straight-line basis. The depreciation for fiscal 2018 was $500,000 and accumulated depreciation on June 30, 2018, was $1,000,000. During 2019, management revises the estimate of useful life to 12 years, reducing the amount of depreciation to $400,000 per year.

Required:

For each of the three issues described above, using the following table, identify:

i. the type of accounting change;
ii the treatment required; and
iii. the effect of the accounting change on the financial statements dated June 30, 2019.

For (iii), identify both the direction (increase or decrease) and the amount of the effect relative to the amount without the accounting change.

			Effect of accounting change on financial statements dated June 30, 2019 (indicate both direction and amount)			
	Type of accounting change	Treatment	Assets	Liabilities	Equity	Income
a.						
b.						
c.						

P19-13. Recording retrospective adjustments—receivables

(L.O. 19-3) (Medium – 5 minutes)

Aylmer Company is analyzing its accounts receivable for purposes of preparing its financial report for the year ended December 31, 2020. The company uses the aging method to estimate bad debts. During this analysis, Aylmer discovered that staff had written off a $53,000 account in 2020 even though the company had received information about the bankruptcy of the client in late 2019.

The company has already recorded bad debts expense for 2020, but the general ledger for the year has not yet been closed. The following table provides information relating to Aylmer's accounts receivables just prior to the discovery of the $53,000 error:

	2019	2020
Accounts receivable—gross	$2,240,000	$2,460,000
Allowance for doubtful accounts	(123,000)	(145,000)
Accounts receivable—net	$2,117,000	$2,315,000
Bad debts expense	$ 225,000	$ 236,000

Required:

Record any adjusting journal entries necessary to correct the error in Aylmer's accounts receivable.

P19-14. Recording retrospective adjustments—receivables

(L.O. 19-3) (Medium – 5 minutes)

Bayfield Corp. is analyzing its accounts receivable for purposes of preparing its second-quarter financial report for June 30, 2020. For interim reporting, the company uses the percentage-of-sales method to estimate bad debts. During this analysis, Bayfield identified an account for $22,000 that should have been written off in the first quarter ended March 31, 2020, but was actually written off in May 2020.

The following table provides information relating to Bayfield's accounts receivables after recording the provision for bad debts for the quarter but prior to the discovery of the $22,000 error:

	March 31, 2020	June 30, 2020
Accounts receivable—gross	$1,480,000	$1,560,000
Allowance for doubtful accounts	(83,000)	(95,000)
Accounts receivable—net	$1,397,000	$1,465,000
Bad debts expense	$ 145,000	$ 178,000

Required:

Record any adjusting journal entry or entries necessary to correct the error in Bayfield's accounts receivable.

P19-15. Recording retrospective adjustments—receivables

(L.O. 19-3) (Medium – 5 minutes)

Cardiff Company has a December 31 year-end. The company uses the aging method to estimate bad debts at year-end. For interim reporting, the company uses the percentage-of-sales method because it is simpler.

In March of 2021, the company identified a $78,000 receivable from Dashwood Inc. as uncollectible. Upon further consideration, staff concluded that the write-off should have occurred in the 2020 fiscal year because the information about the uncollectibility of the account was available at the time. The general ledger accounts for 2020 have already been closed.

Required:

a. Record the entry to write off the uncollectible account.
b. Record any adjusting journal entries necessary to correct the error in Cardiff's accounts receivable.

P19-16. Recording retrospective adjustments—receivables

(L.O. 19-3) (Medium – 15 minutes)

On December 15, 2019, Dutton Furnishings factored $800,000 of accounts receivable for proceeds of $750,000. The company recorded the transaction as being without recourse, with $50,000 recorded to interest expense. During the preparation of the financial statements dated December 31, 2020, staff concluded that the factoring arrangement should have been classified as being with recourse. Additional information about the factoring is as follows:

- The factor withheld $20,000 for potential uncollectible accounts.
- Actual uncollectible accounts amounted to $25,000; Dutton paid the additional $5,000 to the factor on August 7, 2020, and recorded this amount as "miscellaneous expense."

Required:

a. Reproduce the incorrect journal entry that was recorded on December 15, 2019, and on August 7, 2020.
b. Provide the correct journal entries that should have been recorded on December 15, 2019, and on August 7, 2020.
c. Record any adjusting journal entries necessary to correct the error in Dutton's accounts.

P19-17. Recording retrospective adjustments—receivables

(L.O. 19-3) (Medium – 10 minutes)

On June 30, 2016, Elgin Company received $50,000 from Foxboro Finance Inc. in exchange for a promissory note. The terms of the note required Elgin to repay Foxboro on June 30, 2018, the principal amount plus interest at 6% per annum compounded semi-annually.

Due to financial difficulties, Elgin could not make the repayment as scheduled. On June 30, 2018, Foxboro agreed to extend the terms of repayment by one year, to June 30, 2019. However, accounting staff at Foxboro was unaware of the change in repayment terms and did not record the effects of the note restructuring during 2018. The error was discovered on June 30, 2019, when Elgin paid Foxboro $56,275 in fulfillment of the terms of the restructured note.

Foxboro has a December 31 year-end. No interest had been accrued between the original repayment date and the extended repayment date.

Required:

Record any adjusting journal entries necessary to correct the error in Foxboro's accounting for the note receivable from Elgin Company.

P19-18. Recording retrospective adjustments—receivables

(L.O. 19-3) (Medium – 10 minutes)

Geralton Marine Services overhauled a commercial transport vessel for Highgate Shipping. For the services completed on March 31, 2020, Geralton received a promissory note for $200,000 due and payable on March 31, 2021. Highgate paid the amount as scheduled. Geralton staff recorded the full amount as revenue on March 31, 2020.

It is now May 20, 2021. The accounting staff at Geralton just realized that the note was improperly recorded, and that no interest income had been recognized. The controller believes that an 8% interest rate would be appropriate.

Required:

Record any adjusting journal entries necessary to correct Geralton's accounts in relation to the note receivable from Highgate.

P19-19. Recording retrospective adjustments—inventories

(L.O. 19-3) (Medium – 10 minutes)

In early 2021, Darwin's Pet Shop discovered that some of its inventory of dogs was not what the supplier purported it to be. More than 300 puppies that were supposed to be purebred (and therefore expensive) were in fact sired by parents with unknown history. As at the fiscal year ended December 31, 2020, 210 of these puppies had been sold while 90 remained in inventory. Purebred puppies cost $150 each and they would retail for $400. Non-purebreds have a replacement cost of $40 each, and the estimated sale price is $100 each. Darwin is pursuing the supplier to obtain a refund for the cost difference. However, whether there will be compensation is uncertain.

Required:

a. Record the journal entry for the writedown of puppy inventory on December 31, 2020. Note any assumptions necessary.
b. Suppose the error (non-purebreds treated as purebreds) had not been discovered. Indicate the effect of this error on the following accounts (i.e., were they over- or understated, and by how much?):
   i. Inventory, December 31, 2020
   ii. Cost of goods sold, year 2020
   iii. Cost of goods sold, year 2021

P19-20. Recording retrospective adjustments—inventories

(L.O. 19-3) (Medium – 10 minutes)

For each of the following independent scenarios, indicate the effect of the error (if any) on:

i. 2020 net income
ii. 2021 net income
iii. 2021 closing retained earnings

The company uses the periodic system of inventory and its fiscal year-end is December 31. Ignore income tax effects.

a. Your analysis of inventory indicates that inventory at the end of 2020 was overstated by $15,000 due to an inventory count error. Inventory at the end of 2021 was correctly stated.[6]
b. Invoices in the amount of $24,000 for inventory received in December 2020 were not entered on the books in 2020. They were recorded as purchases in January 2021 when they were paid. The goods were counted in the 2020 inventory count and included in ending inventory on the 2020 financial statements.[6]
c. Goods received on consignment amounting to $37,000 were included in the physical count of goods at the end of 2021 and included in ending inventory on the 2021 financial statements.[6]

P19-21. Recording retrospective adjustments—inventories

(L.O. 19-3) (Medium – 10 minutes)

For each of the three scenarios in P19-20, provide the journal entry that should be recorded in 2021 to correct the error.

P19-22. Recording retrospective adjustments—inventories

(L.O. 19-3) (Medium – 15 minutes)

Brow Corp. commenced operations on January 1, 2019. The company initially elected to value its inventories using the first-in first-out (FIFO) method. When preparing its 2021 financial statements, Brow decided to switch to the weighted-average cost method to enhance the comparability of its financial statements to those of its competitors. Pertinent information follows:

- Brow's tax rate is 30%.
- Brow employs a perpetual inventory system.
- During 2021, FIFO was initially used to value inventory and determine cost of goods sold.
- The 2021 draft financial statements were prepared using the FIFO cost flow assumption and include adjusting entries for the preliminary estimate of income tax expense for 2021.

	FIFO	Weighted average
December 31, 2019	$400,000	$410,000
December 31, 2020	650,000	620,000
December 31, 2021	920,000	880,000

[6] Reprinted from CGA-Canada FA2 examination, March & June 2009, with permission Chartered Professional Accountants of Canada, Toronto, Canada. Any changes to the original material are the sole responsibility of the author (and/or publisher) and have not been reviewed or endorsed by the Chartered Professional Accountants of Canada.

Required:

a. Prepare the journal entry to retrospectively account for this change in accounting policy. Include the effect of income taxes.
b. Prepare the journal entry required on December 31, 2021, to adjust Brow Corp.'s accounting records to properly reflect the use of the weighted-average cost method to value inventories during 2021. Include the effect of income taxes.

P19-23. Recording retrospective adjustments—inventories

(L.O. 19-3) (Difficult – 10 minutes)

Knoclew Inc. is a subsidiary of a US publicly traded manufacturer of murder mystery games. The company uses the last-in, first-out (LIFO) cost flow assumption. Additional information on inventory during Year 1 includes the following:

Beginning-of-year finished goods inventory	20,000 units
Units finished during Year 1	200,000 units
End-of-year finished goods inventory	15,000 units
Beginning-of-year work in process (in equivalent units*)	10,000 units
Ending work in process (in equivalent units*)	10,000 units

(*For example, 10 units that are each 40% complete are equal to 4 equivalent units.)

a. One of Knoclew's products became obsolete and worthless during Year 1, but the inventory writedown did not occur until Year 2. The cost of this inventory was $25,000.
b. In the Year 1 closing inventory count, employees improperly included 1,000 units of finished goods that had already been sold to customers. These units had a cost of $8,000 under LIFO.
c. An invoice for $15,000 of material received and used in production arrived after the year-end. Neither the purchase nor the accounts payable was recorded. However, the amount of raw materials in ending inventory was correct based on the inventory count.
d. In Year 1, Knoclew incurred the following expenditures:

Factory labour	$1,000,000
Materials used in manufacturing	800,000
Variable overhead	300,000
Subtotal	2,100,000
Transportation cost of raw materials	200,000
Factory depreciation	700,000
Salary of production vice-president	100,000
Salary of marketing vice-president	120,000
Advertising cost for new game	200,000
	$3,420,000

Knoclew's accountants debited only $2,100,000 into the inventory (work in process) account. The remainder was expensed as period costs.

Required:

For each of the above independent scenarios (a) through (d), indicate in the following table the effect of the accounting errors on the books of Knoclew Inc. Specifically, identify the *amount* and *direction* of over- or understatement of inventory and income for Year 1 and Year 2. If an account requires no adjustment, indicate that the account is "correct."

	Year 1		Year 2	
Scenario	Inventory	Income	Inventory	Income
a.				
b.				
c.				
d.				

P19-24. Recording retrospective adjustments—inventories

(L.O. 19-3) (Difficult – 20 minutes)

Monster Bikes manufactures off-road bicycles. In 2021, the company's accountant recorded the following costs into the inventory account:

Variable costs (raw materials, labour, variable overhead)	$10,680,000
Fixed manufacturing overhead	2,000,000
Salary of factory manager	100,000
Salary of company president	300,000
Advertising and promotion	500,000
Total	$13,580,000

The company had no work in process at the end of both 2020 and 2021. Finished goods at the end of 2020 amounted to 6,000 bikes at $250 per bike. Production was 50,000 bikes and 4,000 bikes remained in inventory at December 31, 2021. The company uses a periodic inventory system and the FIFO cost flow assumption.

Required:

a. Of the $13,580,000, how much should have been capitalized into inventories?
b. Compute the ending value of inventory and the cost of goods sold for 2021.
c. If the error in inventory costing had not been corrected as per part (a), by how much would inventory be overstated at the end of 2021?
d. Record the journal entry to correct the error in inventory costing.
e. If the company uses the weighted-average cost method, how much would be the ending value of inventory and cost of goods sold for 2021?

P19-25. Recording retrospective adjustments—inventories

(L.O. 19-3) (Difficult – 40 minutes)

Oculus is a proprietorship that produces a specialized type of round windows. It is after the fiscal year-end for 2018, and the owner has drafted the financial statements for the business for presentation to the bank and for tax purposes. The following provides a summary of those financial statements, along with comparative information for the prior year:

Balances as at December 31	2018	2017
Cash	$ 8,900	$ 7,600
Accounts receivable	42,600	40,900
Inventories: raw materials	7,900	5,500
Inventories: work in process	5,100	6,200
Inventories: finished goods	48,400	29,400
Other assets	320,000	310,000
Total assets	$432,900	$399,600
Total liabilities	$113,800	$137,900
Contributed capital	5,000	5,000
Retained earnings	314,100	256,700
Total liabilities and equity	$432,900	$399,600

For the year ended December 31	2018	2017
Sales	$561,000	$529,000
Cost of goods sold	321,200	305,000
Gross margin	$239,800	$224,000
Operating expenses	182,600	178,300
Net income	$ 57,200	$ 45,700

Raw materials consist of glass and aluminum. Due to their nature, these inventories cannot be specifically identified. Consequently, Oculus has used the first-in, first-out (FIFO) method for all of its inventories. Oculus uses a periodic inventory system, and the above financial information has been prepared using FIFO.

Input prices had been reasonably stable prior to 2017. However, as a result of rapidly rising prices for raw material inputs, the owner of Oculus feels that the FIFO method is overstating income. He wonders whether and by how much his financial results would change if he were to use the weighted-average cost method for inventories. To help address this issue, he has assembled additional information on the inventories for Oculus (raw material quantities are expressed in units equivalent to one standard finished window):

	2018		2017	
	Quantity	$	Quantity	$
Glass: beginning inventory	75	$ 3,400	80	$ 2,500
Glass: purchases	1,235	74,700	1,297	53,500
Glass: used in production	(1,250)	(73,200)	(1,302)	(52,600)
Glass: ending inventory	60	$ 4,900	75	$ 3,400
Aluminum: beginning inventory	75	$ 2,100	80	$ 1,600
Aluminum: purchases	1,235	50,700	1,297	33,500
Aluminum: used in production	(1,250)	(49,800)	(1,302)	(33,000)
Aluminum: ending inventory	60	$ 3,000	75	$ 2,100
WIP: beginning inventory	25	$ 6,200	23	$ 4,600
WIP: materials, labour, overhead used	1,250	339,100	1,302	311,800
WIP: cost of goods completed	(1,260)	(340,200)	(1,300)	(310,200)
WIP: ending inventory	15	$ 5,100	25	$ 6,200
Finished goods: beginning inventory	120	$ 29,400	121	$ 24,200
Finished goods: production	1,260	340,200	1,300	310,200
Finished goods: cost of goods sold	(1,230)	(321,200)	(1,301)	(305,000)
Finished goods: ending inventory	150	$ 48,400	120	$ 29,400

Required:

Prepare the revised balance sheets and income statements for Oculus under the weighted-average cost method. [*Hint:* Pay attention to how cost flows between raw materials to WIP to finished goods.]

P19-26. Recording prospective adjustments—PPE (L.O. 19-3) (Easy – 5 minutes)

On January 1, 2019, Golden Lab Corp. purchased equipment costing $1,000,000. The company has been depreciating the asset on a straight-line basis over its initially estimated useful life of 12 years and residual value of $100,000. When preparing its adjusting entries for its year ended December 31, 2020, management determined that it was now appropriate to depreciate the equipment over a total of 10 years. It also downwardly adjusted its estimated residual value to $0. Golden Lab Corp.'s tax rate is 30%. The company has already prepared journal entries for its preliminary estimate of depreciation expense and income tax expense for the year.

Required:

Prepare the journal entries in 2020 to account for this change in estimate. Include the effect of income taxes.

P19-27. Recording retrospective adjustments—PPE

(L.O. 19-3) (Medium – 15 minutes)

Kingfisher Inc. purchased a piece of real estate in early 2017 for $4,000,000. The company initially allocated the purchase price 40% to land, 50% to building, and 10% to fixtures. Subsequently, Kingfisher recorded straight-line depreciation based on useful lives of 20 years and

5 years on the building and fixtures, respectively. No residual value was assigned to either depreciable asset. The company has a policy of recording a full year of depreciation in the year of acquisition, and none in the year of disposal.

It is now 2021. During a review of its legal contracts, Kingfisher staff noted that the property purchased in 2017 included an adjacent lot whose value was omitted from the initial purchase price allocation. Based on the land that was included, the excluded land had a fair value of $1,000,000.

Required:

a. Determine the balance of accumulated depreciation for each of the depreciable assets as at the end of 2020. Do this twice, once with and once without including the effects from the discovery of the error in 2021.
b. Record any adjusting entries required to correct the accounts.

P19-28. Recording retrospective adjustments—PPE (L.O. 19-3) (Medium – 15 minutes)

LaSalle Company purchased a building in 2011 at a cost of $5,000,000. The company previously purchased the land on which the building is located, so the entire purchase price was allocated to the building account and none was allocated to land. At the time of purchase, the estimated useful life of the building was 25 years. The company depreciates the building on a straight-line basis and has chosen to record a full year of depreciation in the year of acquisition, and none in the year of disposal.

It is now 2021. LaSalle has found it necessary to replace all of the windows in this building at a cost of $800,000. Upon further review, management concluded that the windows should have been recorded as a separate component because, as of 2011, their useful lives did not extend for 25 years—the manufacturer's specifications indicate that the windows would be expected to remain in functioning condition until 2021. The estimated value of the windows when the building was purchased was $600,000.

Required:

a. Prepare the journal entry to record the replacement of the windows assuming that the windows were recorded as a separate component.
b. Assume that LaSalle committed an error in not componentizing the windows separately from the building. Record the adjusting journal entry or entries required to correct this error.
c. Prepare the journal entry to record the replacement of the windows after having properly recorded the windows as a separate component in part (b).
d. Assume retained earnings at the beginning of 2021 were $9,000,000. With the retrospective componentization of the building and windows, by how much did the following amounts change in 2021: opening retained earnings, income, and closing retained earnings?

P19-29. Recording retrospective and prospective adjustments—PPE (L.O. 19-3) (Medium – 20 minutes)

In 2021, before its books were closed off, Tyabi Corp. determined that a machine it purchased on January 1, 2019, at a cost of $250,000, was expensed and appeared on both the company's income statement and tax return. As the amount of the expenditure was material, it should have been capitalized and depreciated on a straight-line basis over 10 years. The estimated residual value at the purchase date was $25,000. Other information follows:

- Notwithstanding that it expensed the cost of the machine on its 2019 tax return, Tyabi Corp. properly claimed CCA for the machine on its tax return from January 1, 2019, onward.
- Tyabi Corp.'s tax rate is 20%.
- In 2022, Tyabi estimated that the useful life of the machine was now only a total of eight years, and the residual value at the end of the useful life would be nil.

Required:

a. Prepare the journal entry in 2021 necessary to correct the prior-year error. Include the effect of income taxes.
b. Calculate the amount of depreciation expense for the machine to be reported on Tyabi Corp.'s 2022 income statement.

P19-30. Recording retrospective adjustments—intangibles

(L.O. 19-3) (Medium – 10 minutes)

McGregor Biomed undertook a research and development project in 2014. As of May 1 of that year, management concluded that the project had met the requirements for the capitalization of development costs. For the remainder of 2014 and 2015, the company capitalized $3.4 million of development costs for the project. Capitalizing these costs helped McGregor to remain profitable; had these costs been expensed, the company would have reported losses. In 2016, McGregor began amortizing the development cost over the estimated useful life of 10 years, beginning with a full year of amortization in 2016.

In 2019, in preparation for an initial public offering (IPO), the company engaged a public accounting firm to conduct an external audit of its financial statements. The auditors concluded that the development cost did not meet the criteria for capitalization. Specifically, it was their opinion that McGregor, at the time, did not demonstrate that the company had sufficient financial resources to complete the development project due to the recurring operating losses incurred. After some heated debate, McGregor's management agreed with the auditors' position in order to obtain an unqualified audit opinion. The company had not yet recorded any amortization for 2019 when it agreed to correct the error. The company's tax rate is 20%.

Required:

Record the journal entries necessary to correct McGregor's accounts. Include the effect of income taxes.

P19-31. Recording retrospective adjustments—revaluation

(L.O. 19-3) (Easy – 10 minutes)

In 2015, Meagan Inc. purchased a parcel of land for future expansion of its manufacturing plant for $10 million. The company initially opted to value the asset using the revaluation model. The land was subsequently revalued at year-end as set out below:

Date	Fair market value
December 31, 2015	$11.0 million
December 31, 2016	$10.5 million
December 31, 2017	$11.5 million

In December 2018, before the books for the year were closed, the company elected to account for the land using the cost model as it provided more relevant information about its financial performance.

Required:

Record any adjusting journal entries required to reflect the change in accounting policy. Include the effect of income taxes, assuming that Meagan Inc.'s tax rate was 25% for all years.

P19-32. Recording retrospective adjustments—revaluation

(L.O. 19-3) (Easy – 10 minutes)

On September 20, 2020, Marshall Inc., whose year-end is December 31, paid $2,000,000 to purchase land. Marshall Inc. initially elected to subsequently measure the land using the revaluation model. In 2023, the company decided to use the cost model to subsequently measure its land to enhance the comparability of its financial statements to those of its competitors. Its tax rate is 20%.

Revaluation date	Book value of land
December 31, 2020	$1,950,000
December 31, 2021	2,080,000
December 31, 2022	2,200,000

Required:

Prepare the journal entry to retrospectively account for this change in accounting policy. Include the effect of income taxes.

P19-33. Recording retrospective adjustments—revaluation

(L.O. 19-3) (Medium – 15 minutes)

Norwich Company purchased real estate property in 2017 for $18 million ($8 million for land and $10 million for a building). The building had a useful life of 20 years at the time of purchase. The company's policy is to use the straight-line method to depreciate buildings and to take a full year of depreciation in the year of acquisition and none in the year of disposal.

The company opted to use the revaluation model for its property holdings, with a fair value estimate every three years. At the end of 2020, an independent appraisal valued the property at $18 million, which management allocated to the land and building in proportion to their net carrying amounts (after including the effect of depreciation for 2020). For revaluations, Norwich's policy is to use the proportional method to adjust the gross carrying amount and accumulated depreciation.

It is now March 2022. The audit for the year ended December 31, 2021, identified an error in the revaluation recorded in 2020. Specifically, detailed examination of the appraisal documents shows that the increase in value was entirely attributable to the land and none to the building. Depreciation for 2021 had been recorded prior to the discovery of the error. However, the books for 2021 have not yet been closed.

Required:

a. Reproduce the journal entries that Norwich used to record the property revaluation at the end of 2020.
b. Provide the journal entries that Norwich should have recorded for the revaluation.
c. Record the journal entries necessary to correct Norwich's accounts.

P19-34. Recording retrospective adjustments—warranties

(L.O. 19-3) (Medium – 15 minutes)

Prescott Appliances is a relatively new producer of commercial grade appliances. To enhance the competitiveness of its products, on July 2, 2017, the company introduced a warranty against defects for 12 months from the date of installation.

The company's products are of a sufficiently high quality such that no warranty claims were received in 2017. However, in February 2019, when the auditors examined the records for the year ended December 31, 2018, they noted a small number of warranty claims in 2018 amounting to $163,000, which was recorded as miscellaneous expense. These claims alerted the auditors to the fact that the company should have but did not accrue for the expected warranty costs starting in 2017.

Prescott's management estimates warranty fulfillment costs to be 0.5% of revenue. The company recorded revenue of $41,528,000 in 2017 and $46,321,000 in 2018. There is very little seasonality in the sales pattern through the year. The company's tax rate is 30%. The general ledger for 2018 has not yet been closed.

Required:

Record any adjusting journal entries required to correct Prescott's books. Include the effect of income taxes.

P19-35. Recording retrospective adjustments—warranties

(L.O. 19-3) (Medium – 15 minutes)

Quitzau Ltd. commenced operations on January 1, 2019. It has a December 31 year-end. The company's tax rate is 40%. The company offers a four-year warranty on all the products it sells. Historically, it expensed warranty costs when incurred, rather than making a provision for them each year. During the audit of its 2021 year-end results, though, the external accountants discovered this oversight, and as they believed the amounts to be material, required Quitzau Ltd. to correct its error. Pertinent details of the warranty follow:

Year	Costs expensed	Estimated provision required*
2019	$178,000	$520,000
2020	388,000	580,000
2021	622,000	680,000

* This is the amount that should have been originally recognized as a provision for warranty claims for the given year.

Assume that the rest of the adjusting entries, including those related to tax expense, have been journalized, but that closing entries have not yet been made.

Required:

a. Prepare the journal entry to retrospectively account for this correction of an error. Include the effect of income taxes.
b. Prepare the journal entry required on December 31, 2021, to adjust Quitzau Ltd.'s accounting records to properly recognize the provision for warranty expense required for 2021. Include the effect of income taxes.

P19-36. Recording retrospective adjustments—warranties

(L.O. 19-3) (Difficult – 20 minutes)

Luk Enterprises Corp. (LEC) manufactures and distributes high quality bicycles. In 2019, as part of a promotional campaign, LEC offered a three-year warranty on all products it sells.

The company engaged new auditors in 2018. During the course of its investigation, the CPA firm inquired about the $19,000 charged to warranty expense during 2018 (before the launch of the warranty program). LEC explained that, while it had not previously offered a formal warranty, the company's longstanding policy had been to repair or replace defective parts on a no-charge basis for three years from date of purchase. It charged the cost of the labour and parts at time of service to warranty expense. Pertinent information follows:

	2015	2016	2017	2018
Sales	$1,100,000	$1,200,000	$1,300,000	$1,400,000
Warranty expense:				
For sales made in 2015	5,000	8,000	7,000	3,000
For sales made in 2016		6,000	8,000	4,000
For sales made in 2017			7,000	7,000
For sales made in 2018				5,000

LEC estimates that the cost of the warranty program is 2% of sales. Its tax rate is 20%. The general ledger for 2018 has not yet been closed.

Required:

a. Briefly explain the nature of the accounting change and how it must be accounted for. Assume that all amounts are material.
b. Record any adjusting journal entries required to correct LEC's books. Include the effect of income taxes.

P19-37. Recording retrospective adjustments—long-term debt

(L.O. 19-3) (Medium – 15 minutes)

Selkirk Inc. issued a 10-year bond on July 1, 2017. The $20,000,000 par bond pays $600,000 of interest on December 31 and June 30. The company has a calendar year-end.

It is now February 2021. During the audit of the 2020 financial statements, it was discovered that the bond indenture allowed holders to convert the bonds to common shares. The terms of the conversion allow each $1,000 bond to be converted into 50 shares. Additional investigation concluded that the bond would have yielded 10% per annum had it not included the conversion option.

Required:

Record any adjusting journal entries required to correct Selkirk's accounts. The books for 2020 have not yet been closed.

P19-38. Effects of accounting changes—leases

(L.O. 19-1, L.O. 19-2, L.O. 19-3) (Medium – 20 minutes)

On January 1, 2017, Timmins Resorts signed a long-term rental agreement with Uxbridge Properties. The agreement gave Timmins the exclusive right to use the specified property for a period of 10 years at a rental rate of $1.5 million per year paid at the beginning of each year. Timmins' accounting staff concluded that the lease period did not constitute a major part of the 30-year useful life of the property, and that the present value of lease payments did not amount to substantially all of the $20 million fair value of the property. As a result, Timmins treated this transaction as an operating lease.

In 2019, management realized that the lease agreement was incomplete. In preliminary discussions, which were documented, Timmins and Uxbridge negotiators discussed the inclusion of an option for Timmins to purchase the property for $20 million at the end of the lease, when the property would be expected to increase in value to $30 million. As both parties agreed that the omission of the purchase option was accidental, the lease agreement was amended on December 31, 2019, to include the purchase option.

Timmins has a calendar year-end. The books for 2019 have not been closed. The company has an incremental borrowing rate of 8%, and depreciates similar property on a straight-line basis.

Required:

a. Briefly discuss why the amendment to the lease agreement could be considered either a change in estimate or an error correction.
b. Assume that the lease amendment is a change in estimate. Record the entries necessary to reflect the amendment and the adjusting entries on December 31, 2019.
c. Assume that the lease amendment is an error correction. Record the entries necessary to reflect the amendment and the adjusting entries on December 31, 2019.

P19-39. Effects of accounting changes

(L.O. 19-1, L.O. 19-2, L.O. 19-3) (Medium – 30 minutes)

Cross Company Limited, a private company, was started on January 1, 2017. For the first year, the chief accountant prepared the financial statements and a local accountant completed the necessary review of these statements. However, for the year ended December 31, 2018, an external auditor was appointed. The income statement for 2017 and the preliminary amounts for 2018 are as follows:

	2017	2018
Long-term contract income	$3,000,000	$4,000,000
Other income (loss)	(800,000)	(900,000)
Bad debt expense	(400,000)	(500,000)
Depreciation expense—machine	(500,000)	(500,000)
Depreciation expense—building	(300,000)	(270,000)
Warranty expense	(200,000)	(320,000)
Income before taxes	800,000	1,510,000
Income taxes (at 30%)	(240,000)	(453,000)
Net income	$ 560,000	$1,057,000

In the process of examining the accounting records, the auditor noted the following issues:

i. **Long-term contracts:** Cross Company used the completed contract method for revenue recognition in 2017. Management now believes that the percentage of completion method would be better. Income under the completed contract method for 2017 was $3,000,000 and for 2018 it was $4,000,000. If the percentage of completion method had been used, the incomes would have been $4,200,000 (2017) and $3,700,000 (2018).

ii. **Accounts receivable:** The accounts receivable on December 31, 2017, included a $100,000 account that was not provided for but subsequently was written off during 2018 as the customer went bankrupt after the issuance of the financial statements. Cross Company would like to adjust 2017 for this oversight as it sees this as an error.

iii. **Machine depreciation:** Cross Company has one huge machine that cost $5,000,000 and was depreciated over an estimated useful life of 10 years. Upon reviewing the manufacturer's reports in 2018, management now firmly believes the machine will last a total of 15 years from date of purchase. They would like to change last year's depreciation charge based on this analysis. Depreciation expense of $500,000 has been recorded for 2018.

iv. **Building depreciation:** The company's building (cost $3,000,000, estimated salvage value $0, useful life 20 years) was depreciated last year using the 10% declining-balance method. The company and auditor now agree that the straight-line method would be a more appropriate method to use. A depreciation provision of $270,000 has been made for 2018.

v. **Inventories:** The accountant last year failed to apply the lower of cost and net realizable value test to ending inventory. Upon review, the inventory balance for last year should have been reduced by $200,000. The closing inventory allowance for this year-end should be $300,000. No entry has been made for this matter.

vi. **Warranties:** Cross Company does not accrue for warranties; rather it records the warranty expense when amounts are paid. Cross provides a one-year warranty for defective goods. Payments to satisfy warranty claims were $200,000 in 2017, and $320,000 in 2018. Out of the $320,000 paid in 2018, $150,000 related to 2017 sales. A reasonable estimate of warranties payable at the end of 2018 is $275,000.

Required:

a. As the audit senior on this engagement, what is your recommended treatment for each of these matters in terms of whether they are errors, changes in accounting policy, or changes in estimate? Explain your conclusion.

b. Assume that management of Cross Company agrees with your recommendations. Prepare the corrected statements of comprehensive income for 2017 and 2018.

P19-40. Recording retrospective adjustments—revenue (L.O. 19-3) (Difficult – 30 minutes)

Arthur and Doyle Ltd. is a company involved in the construction of small residential complexes. Until the end of 2017, the company used the cost ratio method to estimate the percentage complete. After that point, the company switched to using estimates from architectural engineers to estimate the degree of completion. To prepare the financial report for the 2018 fiscal year, you have gathered the following data on projects that were in progress at the end of fiscal years 2016, 2017, and 2018:

	2016	2017	2018
Project Opal (started 2016)			
Contract price	$15,000,000	$15,000,000	—
Estimated total cost	$12,000,000	$12,400,000	—
% complete at year-end (cost ratio)	38%	100%	—
% complete at year-end (engineering estimate)	40%	100%	—
Project Sapphire (started 2017)			
Contract price	$20,000,000	$20,000,000	$20,000,000
Estimated total cost	$16,000,000	$16,800,000	$16,700,000
% complete using cost ratio	15%	60%	100%
% complete using engineering estimate	10%	50%	100%

	2016	2017	2018
Project Emerald (started 2018)			
Contract price	—	$10,000,000	$10,000,000
Estimated total cost	—	$ 8,000,000	$ 7,200,000
% complete using cost ratio	—	20%	70%
% complete using engineering estimate	—	25%	75%

Required:

a. Compute the amount of revenue and cost of sales that was recognized in 2016 and 2017 using the old accounting policy.
b. Compute the amount of revenue and cost of sales that should be recognized in each year using the new accounting policy.
c. Record the adjusting journal entries to reflect the change in accounting policy from using the cost ratio to using engineering estimates. The general ledger accounts for 2018 have not yet been closed. Ignore income tax effects.

J. MINI-CASE

CASE 1
Accounting Changes
(40 minutes)

You are the external auditor of Iron Company.

During the 2021 year-end audit, the following items come to your attention:

1. On January 1, 2018, the company capitalized an amount of $90,000 related to interest on a loan it took to finance the construction of a production asset it fabricated by itself. Because the asset was completed by the end of 2017 and immediately became productive, the interest should have been expensed. The company has depreciated the asset using the straight-line method since January 1, 2018, assuming a six-year life, and no residual value. This issue was discovered after depreciation for 2021 was recorded.
2. During 2021, Iron changed from the straight-line method of depreciating its machinery to the double-declining-balance method. The following calculations present depreciation on both bases:

	2021	2020	2019
Straight-line	$23,000	$23,000	$23,000
Double-declining-balance	28,100	35,000	41,000

The net income for 2021 already reflects the double-declining-balance method.

3. Iron, in reviewing its provision for uncollectible accounts during 2021, has determined that 2% is the appropriate amount of bad debt expense to be charged to operations. The company had used 1% as its rate in 2020 and 2019 when the expense had been $9,000 and $6,000, respectively. The company recorded bad debt expense under the new rate for 2021. The company would have recorded $3,000 less of bad debt expense on December 31, 2021, under the old rate.

Net income for the most recent three years is presented below:

2021	2020	2019
$200,000	$180,000	$160,000

Required:

a. Prepare, in general journal form, the entries necessary to correct the books for the transactions described above, assuming that the books have not been closed for the current year. Describe the situation for each transaction and support the appropriate accounting treatment according to GAAP, if any, for the change. Ignore all income tax effects.
b. Present comparative income statement data for the years 2019 to 2021, starting with income before cumulative effect of accounting changes and adjusting the net income balance based on your analysis in part (a).
c. Assume that the beginning retained earnings balance (unadjusted) for 2021 is $800,000 and that non-comparative financial statements are prepared. Show the adjusted amount of the beginning retained earnings balance.
d. Suppose that, when you looked into the increase in the estimates of uncollectible accounts, you learned that by 2019 all other companies in Iron Company's industry were using 2%. Would this change your treatment of the change? Explain (no need to provide calculations).

Brent Lewin/Bloomberg/Getty Images

CHAPTER 20
Statement of Cash Flows

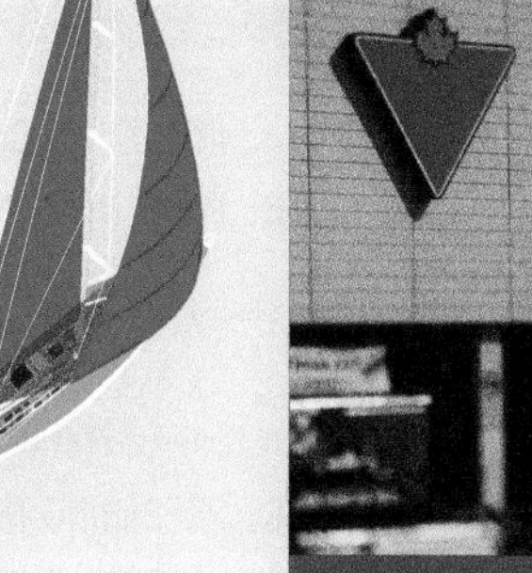

LEARNING OBJECTIVES

After studying this chapter, you should be able to:

L.O. 20-1. Describe the purpose of the statement of cash flows and the information it conveys.

L.O. 20-2. Define cash and cash equivalents.

L.O. 20-3. Differentiate among cash flows from operating activities, investing activities, and financing activities.

L.O. 20-4. Describe the difference between the direct and indirect methods of calculating cash flows from operating activities.

L.O. 20-5. Prepare a statement of cash flows using both the direct and indirect methods.

CPA competencies addressed in this chapter:

1.1.2 Evaluates the appropriateness on the basis of financial reporting (Level B)
  c. Differences between accrual accounting compared to cash accounting

1.2.1 Develops or evaluates appropriate accounting policies and procedures (Level B)

1.2.2 Evaluates treatment for routine transactions (Level A)
  a. Cash and cash equivalents and numerous others

1.2.3 Evaluates treatment for non-routine transactions (Level B)
  Exchange of assets

1.3.1 Prepares financial statements (Level A)

1.3.2 Prepares routine financial statement note disclosure (Level B)

1.4.1 Analyzes complex financial statement note disclosure (Level C)

Canadian Tire Corporation (CTC), which bills itself as "one of Canada's most trusted companies," is a well-established Canadian retail chain.

For the year ended December 31, 2016, CTC reported comprehensive income of $634.4 million. Despite this reported profit, CTC's statement of cash flows disclosed a net decrease in cash of $76.8 million for the year. How are these seemingly inconsistent results possible?

The statement of cash flows indicates that the net decrease of $76.8 million was due to cash inflows of $986.4 million from operating activities, offset by a $782.8 million outflow from investing activities and a $280.4 million outflow from financing activities. Moreover, CTC presented operating cash flows using the indirect method, in contrast to the direct method used for investing and financing cash flows. Why does the company categorize cash flows as arising from operating, investing, or financing activities? What is the difference between the direct and indirect methods of reporting cash flows from operating activities? Why does CTC produce a statement of cash flows? What information does this statement provide?

20 CONTENTS

A. INTRODUCTION 1004
B. PRESENTATION OF THE STATEMENT OF CASH FLOWS 1005
1. Cash and cash equivalents defined 1005
2. Classifying cash flows 1006
3. Format of the statement of cash flows 1010
4. Format of the statement of cash flows under ASPE 1014
C. PREPARING THE STATEMENT OF CASH FLOWS 1016
1. Sources of information 1017
2. The process—Indirect method 1017
3. The process—Direct method 1027
4. Effects of specific items on the statement of cash flows 1031
5. Putting it all together—Comprehensive examples 1036
D. PRESENTATION AND DISCLOSURE 1047
E. SUBSTANTIVE DIFFERENCES BETWEEN IFRS AND ASPE 1048
F. SUMMARY 1049
G. ANSWERS TO CHECKPOINT QUESTIONS 1049
H. GLOSSARY 1050
I. REFERENCES 1050
J. PROBLEMS 1051
K. MINI-CASES 1075

A. INTRODUCTION

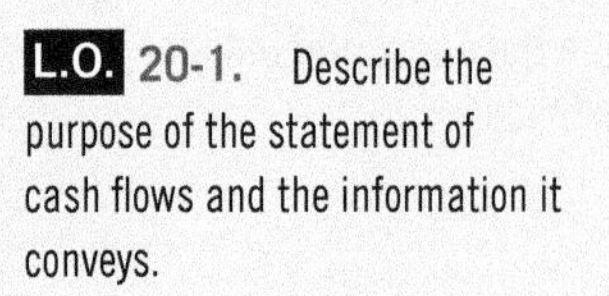
L.O. 20-1. Describe the purpose of the statement of cash flows and the information it conveys.

Net income is an important metric as it measures the financial performance of the company. Equally important is the firm's ability to generate cash—because it is ultimately cash, not income, that pays employees, suppliers, creditors, investors, and governments. Income statements are prepared on an accrual basis, and consequently net income seldom equals the change in cash during the period.

In the opening vignette, CTC's cash decreased by $76.8 million in 2016 despite the reported profit of $634.4 million. While CTC's affairs are complex, its financial statements do give some insight into sources of the substantive gap between the decrease in cash and comprehensive income. For example, CTC reported net cash outflows for investing and financing activities of $782.8 million and $280.4 million, respectively. These amounts represent outflows of cash that are not included in comprehensive income.

Investors, creditors, and managers are interested in how entities generate and use cash. Responding to this demand, IAS 1—Presentation of Financial Statements requires all companies to present both an income statement and a statement of cash flows (SCF). The SCF speaks to the capacity of a business to generate cash and the business's need for cash resources. Managing cash flow to ensure that the company has sufficient monies to pay bills when due is an essential function. Larger companies have a treasury department dedicated to managing cash resources.

To provide information useful to decision makers, IAS 1 requires companies to report cash inflows and outflows using standardized categories: operations, investments, and financing. Second, the SCF provides information on why the change in cash for a period differs from its reported income. Moreover, comparative SCFs provide a historical record of both the firm's ability to generate cash and its ongoing need for funds. The SCF thus provides useful information that is not available in other financial statements (i.e., the balance sheet, income statement, and so on).

The SCF is useful for evaluating a company's liquidity—its ability to generate sufficient cash to meet its obligations when due. Users can also glean valuable information about the timing and uncertainty of cash flows by analyzing past relationships between items like sales and cash flow from operations. Using these facts facilitates more accurate forecasts of future cash flows than relying solely on the income statement. Lastly, the SCF can also be used to ascertain the firm's quality of earnings. As discussed in Chapter 3, the quality of earnings refers to how closely reported earnings correspond to earnings that would be reported in the absence of managerial bias. One way to evaluate earnings quality is to compare the company's net income with cash from operating activities, because cash flows are less subject to managerial bias compared with accrual income. If the reported net income is consistently close to or less than cash from operating activities, the company's net income or earnings are said to be of a "high quality." If net income is consistently more than cash from operating activities, further investigation is needed to ascertain why the reported net income is not matched by an increase in cash.

THRESHOLD CONCEPT
QUALITY OF EARNINGS

For all of the reasons above, the SCF is a useful and important component of an enterprise's financial report. The next section discusses *what* should appear on the SCF. Section C will then describe the procedures for *how* one goes about compiling the figures that appear in the SCF.

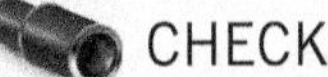
CHECKPOINT **CP20-1**

List three reasons why the statement of cash flows is a useful component of an enterprise's financial statements.

B. PRESENTATION OF THE STATEMENT OF CASH FLOWS

The general standards for the presentation of the SCF appear in IAS 1—Presentation of Financial Statements, with more specific standards provided by IAS 7—Statement of Cash Flows. To properly specify the reporting requirements for the SCF, it is necessary to identify what is a "cash flow." To do so, we need to review what are considered to be cash and cash equivalents (see also Chapter 5).

1. Cash and cash equivalents defined

In IAS 7, "cash and cash equivalents" is an important concept. The standard defines the two components separately as follows:

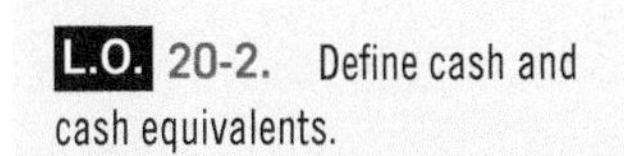
L.O. 20-2. Define cash and cash equivalents.

> ¶6 ... *Cash* comprises cash on hand and demand deposits.
> ... **Cash equivalents** are short-term, highly liquid investments that are readily convertible to known amounts of cash and which are subject to an insignificant risk of changes in value.[1]

cash equivalents Short-term, highly liquid investments that are readily convertible to known amounts of cash and which are subject to an insignificant risk of changes in value.

The reference to "demand deposits" means funds in accounts with financial institutions that can be withdrawn without notice or penalty; for example, a chequing account.

To qualify as a cash equivalent, an item must meet both requirements of *convertibility* and *insignificant risk*. Many items meet one but not both criteria. For example, an investment in widely traded stock is readily convertible to cash because it can be sold on a stock exchange, but its price is subject to significant risk of change. A non-redeemable term deposit is not subject to significant risk of change in value, but cannot be readily converted to cash if the maturity date is far in the future. Neither the stock investment nor the term deposit would be considered cash equivalents. In contrast, Treasury bills (which are government bonds with maturity under a year) that mature within 90 days of acquisition could be considered a cash equivalent because they can be readily sold in a public market and their value does not fluctuate significantly. Likewise, a term deposit with a short enough maturity also meets the criteria of convertibility and insignificant risk; IAS 7 paragraph 7 suggests that three months or less would be a short enough duration.

Note that investments in securities that satisfy the criteria of a cash equivalent are not always reported as such. In this respect, if an investment in a qualifying security is held for the purpose of meeting short-term cash commitments, then it is reported as a cash equivalent. If, though, the qualifying investment is held for other reasons, then the cash flows resulting from the purchase and sale of the investment are classified as follows:

- an operating activity, if the investment is held for trading purposes; or
- an investing activity, if the investment is held for purposes other than trading.

Cash is an idle asset that does not earn income. Consequently, most enterprises try to keep cash holdings close to zero, so it is common for bank balances to be in overdraft (i.e., to be negative). When a bank's overdraft facility is an integral part of an enterprise's cash management system, and if the balance often fluctuates between a positive balance and an overdraft, the overdraft is included in the balance of cash and cash equivalents.

The reason for considering the details of "cash" and "cash equivalents" above is that the two are considered together in the definition of cash flows. IAS 7 indicates the following:

> ¶9 Cash flows exclude movements between items that constitute cash or cash equivalents because these components are part of the cash management of an entity rather than part of its operating, investing and financing activities. Cash management includes the investment of excess cash in cash equivalents.[2]

Thus, for purposes of the SCF, we do not look at cash versus cash equivalents as two separate items but rather as a single unit of "cash and cash equivalents." For brevity, the remainder of this chapter will simply use "cash" to mean "cash and cash equivalents."

 CHECKPOINT **CP20-2**

Briefly describe cash equivalents.

L.O. 20-3. Differentiate among cash flows from operating activities, investing activities, and financing activities.

2. Classifying cash flows

As discussed in Chapter 3, there are three distinct cash cycles. The shortest cash cycle relates to operations, followed by investments, with the financial cycle being the longest. Consistent with these cash cycles, IAS 7 classifies cash flows into three categories: operating activities, investing activities, and financing activities.

---

[2] Copyright © 2012 IFRS Foundation.

a. Operating activities

Cash flows from operating activities arise from the day-to-day running of the business. Technically, IAS 7 defines operating activities as follows:

> ¶6 **Operating activities** are the principal revenue-producing activities of the entity and other activities that are not investing or financing activities.[3]

operating activities The principal revenue-producing activities of the entity and other activities that are not investing or financing activities.

Cash flows from operating activities give considerable insight into a firm's ability to generate sufficient cash to maintain its business operations, repay loans, and make new investments without having to arrange external financing. Exhibit 20-1 lists some of the most common operating activities.

b. Investing activities

IAS 7 defines investing activities as follows:

> ¶6 **Investing activities** are the acquisition and disposal of long-term assets and other investments not included in cash equivalents.[4]

investing activities The acquisition and disposal of long-term assets and other investments not included in cash equivalents.

Cash flows related to investing summarizes the net expenditure on assets meant to generate future income. There are two distinct components of investing activities: (i) the acquisition and disposition of fixed assets; and (ii) the purchase and resale of financial assets. The first type of investing encompasses companies purchasing and selling property, plant, and equipment (PPE) to establish and maintain the infrastructure necessary to run their businesses. The second includes companies buying and selling debt and equity securities.

While most dealings in debt and equity securities are reported in the investing activity section, there are two exceptions to this:

- For reasons previously discussed, the purchase and resale of investments classified as cash equivalents are not reported as cash flows.
- Transactions involving the purchase and sale of investments at FVPL held for trading purposes are reported as operating activities, as they are similar to inventory held specifically for resale. The ASPE requirements in this respect are virtually identical to those of IFRS.

c. Financing activities

Companies raise money by issuing debt and by selling equity, using the proceeds to acquire fixed assets or for operating purposes. Financing activities record the cash flows associated with the issuance and retirement of debt and equity. Technically, IAS 7 defines financing activities as follows:

> ¶6 **Financing activities** are activities that result in changes in the size and composition of the contributed equity and borrowings of the entity.[5]

financing activities Activities that result in changes in the size and composition of the contributed equity and borrowings of the entity.

For purposes of the SCF, financing activities do not include financing resulting from ordinary operations. For example, supplier financing through accounts payable is an operating rather than a financing activity.

Exhibit 20-1 Common examples of cash flows by type of activity

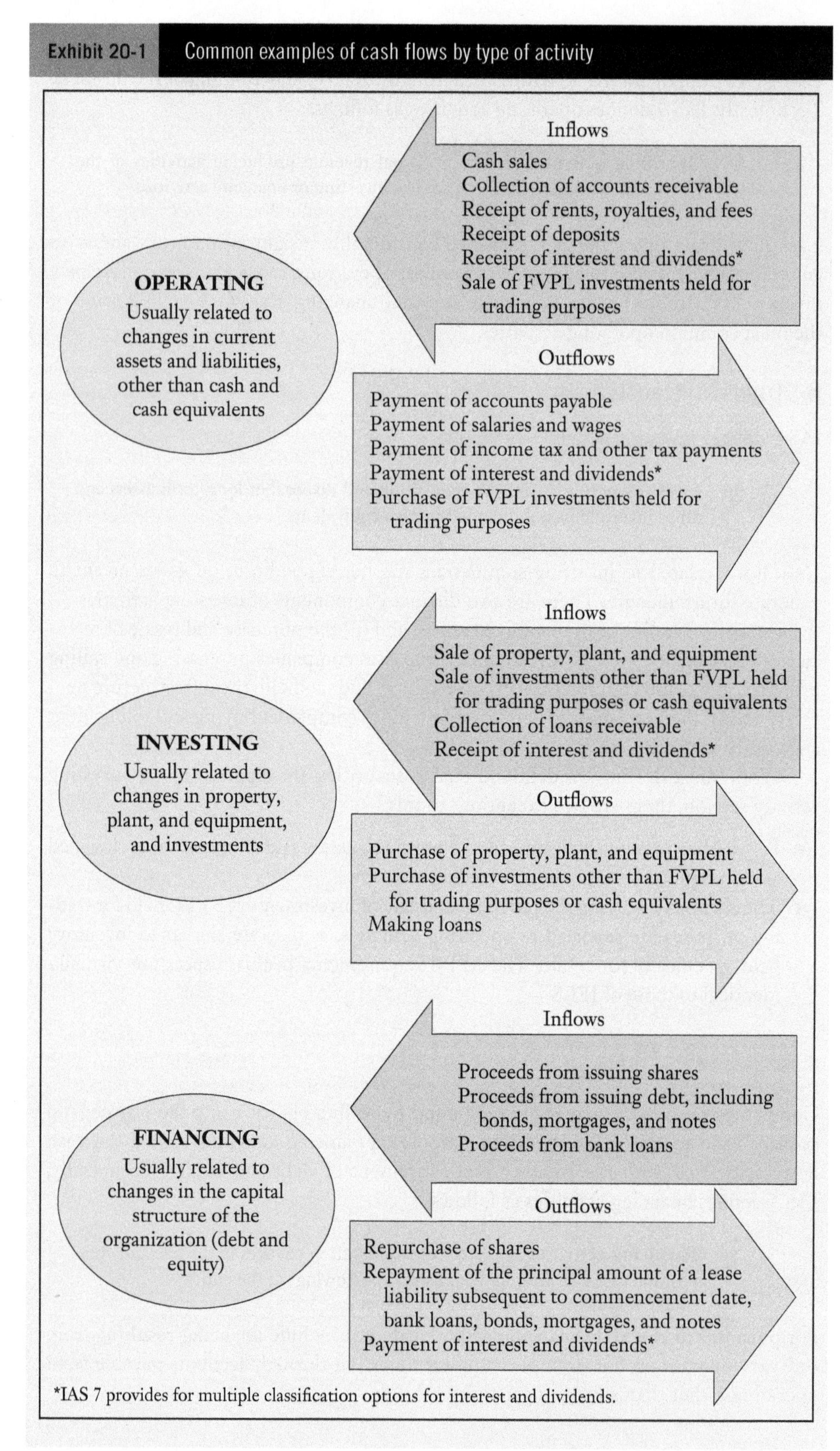

OPERATING
Usually related to changes in current assets and liabilities, other than cash and cash equivalents
Inflows
Cash sales
Collection of accounts receivable
Receipt of rents, royalties, and fees
Receipt of deposits
Receipt of interest and dividends*
Sale of FVPL investments held for trading purposes
Outflows
Payment of accounts payable
Payment of salaries and wages
Payment of income tax and other tax payments
Payment of interest and dividends*
Purchase of FVPL investments held for trading purposes
INVESTING
Usually related to changes in property, plant, and equipment, and investments
Inflows
Sale of property, plant, and equipment
Sale of investments other than FVPL held for trading purposes or cash equivalents
Collection of loans receivable
Receipt of interest and dividends*
Outflows
Purchase of property, plant, and equipment
Purchase of investments other than FVPL held for trading purposes or cash equivalents
Making loans
FINANCING
Usually related to changes in the capital structure of the organization (debt and equity)
Inflows
Proceeds from issuing shares
Proceeds from issuing debt, including bonds, mortgages, and notes
Proceeds from bank loans
Outflows
Repurchase of shares
Repayment of the principal amount of a lease liability subsequent to commencement date, bank loans, bonds, mortgages, and notes
Payment of interest and dividends*

*IAS 7 provides for multiple classification options for interest and dividends.

To illustrate these three classes of cash flows, consider an electronics retail store. Some of the operating activities include cash received from customers, payments for inventories, wages of the sales staff, and taxes to the government. Investing activities include purchasing cash registers and computer systems, buying a long-term bond issued by another entity, and selling a delivery vehicle. Financing activities include issuing bonds, repurchasing preferred shares, and reducing the principal on an outstanding lease liability.

d. Cash flows with classification options

For most transactions, the classification of a cash flow is unambiguous. However, there are two situations where the standards allow a choice of classification (IAS 7 paragraphs 31–34).

- *Interest and dividends received*: An enterprise may classify the receipt of interest and dividends as either an operating or an investing activity. The ambiguity here arises because it is not clear-cut whether this type of income is part of an enterprise's normal operations or part of its investments.
- *Interest and dividends paid:* An enterprise may choose to report the payment of interest and dividends as either an operating or a financing activity. The ambiguity occurs because, even though interest and dividend payments both arise from financing activities (issuance of debt and equity), interest is recorded through income, while dividends are not.

Note that a separate policy may be adopted for each type of cash flow. For example, a company may classify interest received as an operating activity and dividends received as an investing activity. Regardless of the choice for this accounting policy, the enterprise must apply it consistently to all similar transactions.

Accounting Standards for Private Enterprises (ASPE) does not provide options. Rather, the receipt of interest and dividends and the payment of interest are operating activities; the payment of dividends is a financing activity. This mandated treatment is illustrated in Section B, subsection 4.

Exhibit 20-1 categorizes common cash inflows and outflows.

e. Non-cash transactions

When a company borrows money from the bank and then uses the funds to purchase a vehicle, the loan is recorded as a cash inflow from financing activities, and the automobile purchase as a cash outflow from investing activities. However, if the company leases this vehicle from the automobile dealer, the transaction is not recorded on the statement of cash flows as this is a non-cash transaction. **Non-cash transactions** are activities that do not involve cash. Investing and financing activities that involve non-cash transactions are not recorded on the SCF because the SCF reports only the cash effect of a company's activities. Common non-cash transactions include the following:

non-cash transactions Activities that do not involve cash.

- exchanging assets such as parcels of land with another company
- converting bonds or preferred shares into common shares
- stock dividends
- leasing a right-of-use asset

Certain transactions are only partially settled in cash; for example, a company acquires a building for $1,000,000 by paying $200,000 in cash and signing an $800,000 note payable. The SCF records only the $200,000 cash paid as an outflow in the investing activities section. Similarly, lease payments made on or before the commencement date are reported as a cash outflow in the investing activities section.

While the effect of non-cash transactions does not appear as line items in the SCF, enterprises must disclose significant non-cash transactions in the notes to the financial statements.

CHECKPOINT **CP20-3**

Briefly describe how the classification of cash flows arising from the purchase and sale of investments at FVPL is determined.

CHECKPOINT **CP20-4**

List the three categories of cash flows reported on the statement of cash flows.

CHECKPOINT **CP20-5**

Briefly describe the options available under IFRS with respect to classifying the receipt and payment of interest and dividends.

CHECKPOINT **CP20-6**

Briefly describe non-cash transactions and how they are reported on the statement of cash flows.

3. Format of the statement of cash flows

a. Illustrative example

L.O. 20-4. Describe the difference between the direct and indirect methods of calculating cash flows from operating activities.

Exhibit 20-2 reproduces the 2016 statement of cash flows for CTC. Preliminary comments about the structure and format of the statement are provided as a prelude to a full discussion of these points later in the chapter:

- The cash flows are grouped by type of activity: operating, investing, and financing.
- Cash inflows and outflows are not netted against each other. Rather, they are presented separately; for example, CTC reports "issuance of loans payable" and "repayment of loans payable."
- The amount of dividends paid is presented as a line item in the SCF. CTC elected to present these amounts as a financing activity.
- The amount of interest paid and received is presented as a line item in the statement. CTC elected to present these amounts as an operating activity.
- The amount of income taxes paid is presented as a line item in the statement. CTC reported these as operating cash flow, which was consistent with their nature.
- The opening and closing cash and cash equivalents balances at the bottom of the SCF match those presented on the accompanying balance sheet net of bank indebtedness. While not reproduced here, these amounts are reconciled in note 7 to the financial statements. As previously discussed, including short-term bank indebtedness as part of cash and cash equivalents is consistent with paragraph 8 of IAS 7.
- CTC used the indirect method to present its cash flows from operating activities. The company could have also used the direct method. We discuss these two methods next.

Exhibit 20-2 Canadian Tire's 2016 statement of cash flows

Canadian Tire Corporation, Limited

Consolidated Statements of Cash Flows

For the years ended (C$ in millions)	December 31, 2016	January 2, 2016
Cash (used for) generated from: Operating activities		
Net income	$ 747.5	$ 735.9
Adjustments for:		
Depreciation of property and equipment and investment property (Notes 28 and 29)	330.8	312.8
Income tax expense	263.5	265.4
Net finance costs (Note 30)	93.9	92.8
Amortization of intangible assets (Note 29)	126.1	111.9
Changes in fair value of derivative instruments	(15.8)	6.9
(Gain) on disposal of property and equipment, investment property, assets held for sale, intangible assets, and lease terminations	(14.9)	(43.9)
Interest paid	(114.0)	(101.4)
Interest received	6.5	8.4
Income taxes paid	(262.8)	(284.0)
Other	5.6	14.6
Total adjustments, except as noted below	1,166.4	1,119.4
Change in operating working capital and other (Note 31)	126.1	(115.3)
Change in loans receivable	(306.1)	(25.2)
Cash generated from operating activities	986.4	978.9
Investing activities		
Additions to property and equipment and investment property	(617.3)	(515.9)
Additions to intangible assets		
Total additions	(163.5)	(94.7)
	(780.8)	(610.6)
Acquisition of short-term investments	(422.3)	(177.4)
Proceeds from the maturity and disposition of short-term investments	441.4	426.6
Acquisition of long-term investments	(61.4)	(35.0)
Proceeds on disposition of property and equipment, investment property, and assets held for sale	32.8	101.5
Other	7.5	(4.1)
Cash (used for) investing activities	(782.8)	(299.0)
Financing activities		
Dividends paid	(157.5)	(152.2)
Distributions paid to non-controlling interests	(76.4)	(53.8)
Total dividends and distributions paid	(233.9)	(206.0)
Net issuance (repayment) of short-term borrowings	110.7	(111.2)
Issuance of loans payable	288.3	270.1
Repayment of loans payable	(243.5)	(219.0)
Issuance of long-term debt (Note 22)	350.0	856.1
Repayment of long-term debt and finance lease liabilities (Note 22)	(24.5)	588.5
Payment of transaction costs related to long-term debt	(3.2)	(6.5)

(Continued)

Exhibit 20-2 Continued

Canadian Tire Corporation, Limited
Consolidated Statements of Cash Flows

Repurchase of share capital (Note 25)	(449.4)	(434.6)
Change in deposits	(74.9)	12.5
Cash (used for) financing activities	(280.4)	(427.1)
Cash (used) generated in the period	(76.8)	252.8
Cash and cash equivalents, net of bank indebtedness, beginning of period	900.6	647.8
Cash and cash equivalents, net of bank indebtedness, end of period (Note 7)	$ 823.6	$ 900.6

The related notes form an integral part of these consolidated financial statements.

Source: From Canadian Tire Corporation 2016 Report to Shareholders. Copyright ©2016 by Canadian Tire Corporation, Limited. Reprinted by permission.

b. Direct and indirect methods of reporting cash flows from operating activities

Cash flows from operations can be reported using either the direct or indirect method. IAS 7 states the following:

> ¶18 An entity shall report cash flows from operating activities using either:
>
> (a) the **direct method**, whereby major classes of gross cash receipts and gross cash payments are disclosed; or
>
> (b) the **indirect method**, whereby profit or loss is adjusted for the effects of transactions of a non-cash nature, any deferrals or accruals of past or future operating cash receipts or payments, and items of income or expense associated with investing or financing cash flows.[6]

direct method A method of presenting the statement of cash flows by showing major classes of gross cash receipts and gross cash payments.

indirect method A method of presenting the statement of cash flows by adjusting profit or loss for the effects of transactions of a non-cash nature, any deferrals or accruals of past or future operating cash receipts or payments, and items of income or expense associated with investing or financing cash flows.

Although the net amount of operating cash flows remains the same, the direct and indirect methods involve different line items within cash flows from operating activities. Moreover, the choice of the direct or indirect method does not affect the reporting of cash flows from investing and financing activities as cash flows from investing and financing are presented using the direct method.

The International Accounting Standards Board (IASB) and the Accounting Standards Board in Canada (AcSB) have long favoured the direct method of reporting because, they argue, this method provides more useful information than the indirect method. Indeed, the first sentence of IAS 7 paragraph 19 reads "Entities are encouraged to report cash flows from operating activities using the direct method."[7] Notwithstanding this support, the vast majority of companies choose to use the indirect method of presentation. While hard statistics are not readily available, it is estimated that less than 1% of entities use the direct method of presentation in Canada. To reflect common practice, we focus on the indirect method in this chapter.

As IAS 7 provides only general guidance on the format of the statement of cash flows, users will observe that entities do present their results in different ways. The two exhibits that follow illustrate the general form of presentation. (Ignore the "Reference" column for now; these references will be used later in the chapter.)

---

[6] Copyright © 2012 IFRS Foundation.

[7] Copyright © 2012 IFRS Foundation.

Some observations about these two exhibits:

- Notice that net cash from operating activities of $590 is the same under both the direct and indirect methods.
- The format employed of separately disclosing related items together (e.g., income tax expense and income taxes paid) facilitates meeting disclosure requirements discussed elsewhere in this chapter.
- As set out above, paragraph 18 of IAS provides that the starting point for the indirect method is profit or loss. Profit or loss as defined in paragraph 7 of IAS 1 specifically excludes other comprehensive income. Notwithstanding that the illustrative example in Chapter 20 to IAS 7 uses profit before taxation as a starting point, we begin with net income as this is analogous to profit or loss and is consistent with past practice in Canada. As set out in Exhibit 20-2, the first line of CTC's SCF is net income.

The above discussion reveals some flexibility in the presentation of the SCF. For the sake of consistency, unless specifically stated otherwise, the remainder of this chapter assumes that the company has adopted the following conventions:

- Net income is the starting point for determining cash flow from operating activities using the indirect method.
- Interest paid, interest received, dividends paid, and dividends received are all classified as operating activities.

Exhibit 20-3 Sample operating section of a statement of cash flows using the indirect method

Illustrative Company (Partial) Statement of Cash Flows
Year Ended December 31, 2021

Cash flow from operating activities		Reference
Net income	$ 3,050	(i)
Adjustments for:		
Depreciation	450	(ii)
Gain on sale	(50)	
Investment income	(400)	
Interest expense	400	(iii)
Income tax expense	300	
Subtotal	3,750	
Increase in trade and other receivables	(500)	
Decrease in inventories	1,050	(iv)
Decrease in trade payables	(1,740)	
Cash generated from operating activities	2,560	
Dividends received*	200	
Interest received*	200	
Dividends paid†	(1,200)	(v)
Interest paid†	(270)	
Income taxes paid	(900)	
Net cash from operating activities	$ 590	(vi)

*Can also be shown as cash flows from investment.

†Can also be shown as cash outflows for financing.

Exhibit 20-4 Sample operating section of a statement of cash flows using the direct method

Illustrative Company (Partial) Statement of Cash Flows Year Ended December 31, 2021	
Cash flow from operating activities	
Cash receipts from customers	$ 30,360
Cash paid to suppliers and employees	(27,800)
Cash generated from operating activities	2,560
Dividends received*	200
Interest received*	200
Dividends paid†	(1,200)
Interest paid†	(270)
Income taxes paid	(900)
Net cash from operating activities	$ 590

*Can also be shown as cash flows from investment.

†Can also be shown as cash outflows for financing.

4. Format of the statement of cash flows under ASPE

Section 1540 of Part II of the *CPA Canada Handbook*—Accounting governs the preparation of the statement of cash flows under ASPE. While Section 1540 is substantively the same as IAS 7, small differences do exist. These include the following:

- ASPE refers to this statement as a cash flow statement, rather than the statement of cash flows.
- Under ASPE, the receipt of interest and dividends and the payment of interest are normally classified as operating activities and the payment of dividends is reported as a financing activity. Unlike IFRS, ASPE does not permit choice in this respect.
- ASPE only requires that the amount of interest and dividends paid and charged directly to retained earnings be separately presented as financing activities. Unlike IFRS, it does not require separate disclosure of the amount of interest and dividends received and paid. Disclosure of this information is not prohibited, however, and many private companies choose to provide some or all of this information.
- Under ASPE the amount of income taxes paid need not be disclosed.

Exhibits 20-5a and 20-5b present two versions of ASPE cash flow statements using the same set of facts. (The underlying facts will be given in Section C.) The two versions differ as to whether there is separate disclosure of the amounts of interest and dividends received/paid and the amount of income taxes paid.

Contrasting this statement to that presented under IFRS in Exhibit 20-10, you should note the following:

- The statement is referred to as a cash flow statement (i).
- The payment of interest is reported as an operating activity (ii). Under ASPE this is normally mandatory. Separate disclosure of this amount is not required, however.
- Separate disclosure of income taxes paid is not required under ASPE (iii).
- The payment of dividends is reported as a financing activity (iv). Under ASPE this is mandatory.
- While the net increase in cash ($48,000) is the same under ASPE and IFRS, the categorization of cash flows may differ. The determining factor is the entity's choice of accounting policy under IFRS with respect to reporting cash received and paid for interest and dividends. In this example, under ASPE the amount reported as net cash from operating activities is $46,000 more than that under IFRS; net cash from financing activities $46,000 less.

Exhibit 20-5a Result of applying procedures for cash flow statement, Example 1 (ASPE and IFRS compliant)

Kimzoo Fireworks Ltd. Cash Flow Statement Year Ended December 31, 2021			
Cash flows from operating activities			**Reference**
Net income	$ 67,000		(i)
Adjustments for:			
Depreciation and amortization	32,000		
Interest expense	5,000		
Income tax expense	33,000		
Subtotal	137,000		
Increase in trade and other receivables	(14,000)		
Decrease in inventory	10,000		
Decrease in prepaid expenses	3,000		
Increase in trade payables	1,000		
Cash generated from operating activities	137,000		
Interest paid	(5,000)		(ii)
Income taxes paid	(33,000)		(iii)
Net cash from operating activities		$ 99,000	
Cash flows from investing activities			
Purchase of plant assets	(70,000)		
Net cash used in investing activities		(70,000)	
Cash flows from financing activities			
Dividends paid	(46,000)		(iv)
Retirement of mortgage payable	(150,000)		
Sale of preferred shares	215,000		
Net cash from financing activities		19,000	
Net increase in cash		48,000	
Cash and cash equivalents, January 1, 2021		51,000	
Cash and cash equivalents, December 31, 2021		$ 99,000	

Note that the amounts reported as cash flows arising from operating, investing, and financing activities in Exhibit 20-5b are identical to those reported in Exhibit 20-5a. The two statements differ only in the amount of information provided to the reader. Both statements are acceptable under ASPE as the governing standards primarily address the categorization of cash flows and establish the minimum amount of information that must be provided.

Having discussed what should be presented in the statement of cash flows, we now turn to how one goes about preparing this financial statement. Whereas the standards specify the required presentation, little guidance is provided with respect to the preparation and formatting of the statement of cash flows.

CHECKPOINT **CP20-7**

Briefly describe the primary difference between IFRS and ASPE with respect to the presentation of the statement of cash flows.

Exhibit 20-5b Result of applying procedures for cash flow statement, Example 1 (ASPE)

Kimzoo Fireworks Ltd. Cash Flow Statement Year Ended December 31, 2021		
Cash flows from operating activities		
Net income	$ 67,000	
Adjustments for:		
Depreciation and amortization	32,000	
Increase in trade and other receivables	(14,000)	
Decrease in inventory	10,000	
Decrease in prepaid expenses	3,000	
Increase in trade payables	1,000	
Net cash from operating activities		$ 99,000
Cash flows from investing activities		
Purchase of plant assets	(70,000)	
Net cash used in investing activities		(70,000)
Cash flows from financing activities		
Dividends paid	(46,000)	
Retirement of mortgage payable	(150,000)	
Sale of preferred shares	215,000	
Net cash from financing activities		19,000
Net increase in cash		48,000
Cash and cash equivalents, January 1, 2021		51,000
Cash and cash equivalents, December 31, 2021		$ 99,000

C. PREPARING THE STATEMENT OF CASH FLOWS

L.O. 20-5. Prepare a statement of cash flows using both the direct and indirect methods.

The SCF explains the change in cash and cash equivalents during the year, categorizing the cash flows by activity: operating, investing, or financing. The general format of the SCF is shown in Exhibit 20-6.

Exhibit 20-6 General format of the statement of cash flows

Company Name Statement of Cash Flows Period Ended	
Cash flow from operating activities	
Details of the adjustments to profit or loss by category (indirect method)	
Details of cash inflows and outflows by category (direct method)	
Net cash from (used in) operating activities	$ xx
Cash flow from investing activities	
Details of cash inflows and outflows by category	
Net cash from (used in) investing activities	xx
Cash flow from financing activities	
Details of cash inflows and outflows by category	
Net cash from (used in) financing activities	xx
Net increase (decrease) in cash and cash equivalents	xx
Cash and cash equivalents at beginning of period	xx
Cash and cash equivalents at end of period	$ xx

Observe how the net increase (decrease) in cash and cash equivalents explains the difference between the opening and ending balance of cash and cash equivalents.

1. Sources of information

The balance sheet and income statement are prepared directly from the adjusted trial balance, as they each present select components of the general ledger. In contrast, preparing the SCF requires additional information outside of the trial balance, which only contains information about the ending cash balance but not changes in that balance. The required information comes from three primary sources:

- *Comparative balance sheets:* The change in cash for the year can be explained by the net change of all the non-cash accounts on the balance sheet.
- *The income statement for the period:* The income statement is a necessary starting point to determine cash from operating activities under the indirect method. It also provides information about the change in retained earnings.
- *Select transaction data:* The income statement and comparative balance sheets provide aggregated information that is insufficient for identifying some cash flows. For example, the purchase of furniture for $50,000 and the sale of land originally costing $20,000 would result in a net change of $30,000 in PPE on the balance sheet. The $30,000 net figure is inadequate for SCF purposes because the standards require that cash flows used for the purchase of assets be presented separately from cash arising from the sale of assets. Moreover, the cost of assets sold does not directly correlate to the proceeds from their sale.

2. The process—Indirect method

a. When are adjustments required?

When preparing the SCF, we consider the net change in each balance sheet account during the year. Nevertheless, it is instructive to contemplate individual transactions to gain greater insight into the underlying mechanics of preparing the SCF. There are four types of straightforward transactions to be considered, depending on whether each half of the transaction involves income/expenses or cash inflows/outflows:

As shown in Exhibit 20-7, whenever the amount reflected in the income statement differs from the amount of cash flow for a transaction, there needs to be an adjustment

Exhibit 20-7 Types of transactions according to impact on income/expense and cash inflows/outflows

One-half of transaction involves income or expenses	Yes	No	Yes	No
One-half of transaction involves cash inflows or outflows	No	Yes	Yes	No
Label for convenience	Transaction type 1	Transaction type 2	Transaction type 3	Transaction type 4
Example transaction	Sale to a customer on credit	Purchase of equipment using cash	Cash sale	Purchase of equipment using note payable
Example journal entry	Dr. Accounts receivable Cr. Sales revenue	Dr. Equipment Cr. Cash	Dr. Cash Cr. Sales revenue	Dr. Equipment Cr. Notes payable
Adjustment required in indirect method	Yes	Yes	No	No
Reason	Income or expense recorded but not received/paid in cash	Cash received or paid but not reflected in income or expenses	Cash flow equals income or expense	No cash involved

in the SCF using the indirect method (transaction types 1 and 2). When the effect is the same on the income statement and on cash flows, then an adjustment would not be required (transaction types 3 and 4).

b. The indirect method described

The indirect method of compiling the SCF involves converting the company's accrual-based income statement to a cash-based statement. Net income, rather than comprehensive income, is the starting point as items that are included in other comprehensive income do not affect cash flows. The opening balance of cash plus (or minus) cash generated from (used in) operating, investing, and financing activities results in the closing balance, which should match the amount on the balance sheet. The process of preparing the SCF is as follows:[8]

Step 1: Determine the change in cash that needs to be explained. This is a simple matter of comparing this year's closing cash and cash equivalents balance to the prior year's balance.

Step 2: The numerical references below (i to vi) correspond to the noted areas of Exhibit 20-3. Adjust net income as necessary to determine net cash from operating activities:

- **i.** The starting point is the company's recorded profit or loss.
- **ii.** Adjust net income for all non-cash items including depreciation and gains and losses on the sale of assets or the settlement of debt.
- **iii.** Add back interest and income tax expense and subtract investment income from interest and dividends.
- **iv.** Adjust for the unexplained changes in working capital accounts representing operating activities, for example, trade receivables, inventory, trade payables, and prepaid expenses, amongst others. (Note that changes in interest and dividends receivable, interest and dividends payable, and income taxes payable accounts are adjusted for in (iii) and (v).)
- **v.** Add dividends and interest received and subtract dividends, interest, and income taxes paid. Separately itemizing these cash flows meets the disclosure requirements set out in paragraphs 31 and 35 of IAS 7.
- **vi.** The total of items (i) to (v) equals net cash from operating activities for the year.

Step 3: Account for the changes in remaining balance sheet accounts. The reconciling items are recorded in the financing or investing activities section of the SCF according to their nature.

Step 4: Calculate subtotals for operating, investing, and financing activities and ensure the net change in cash and cash equivalents thus determined is equal to the actual change for the period computed from Step 1.

c. The indirect method illustrated—Example 1

The process of preparing a relatively straightforward SCF using the steps outlined above is set out in the three exhibits that follow. Exhibits 20-8a and 20-8b show the information necessary for compiling the SCF for Kimzoo Fireworks for the year 2021, Exhibits 20-9a to 20-9d illustrate the process to prepare the SCF, and Exhibit 20-10 presents the results.

[8] The procedure discussed relates to the example of the indirect method SCF set out in Exhibit 20-10. The process will vary slightly for companies that present their SCF differently.

Exhibit 20-8a Information necessary for the indirect method: Income statement, Example 1

Kimzoo Fireworks Ltd. Income Statement Year Ended December 31, 2021	
Sales	$660,000
Cost of sales	363,000
Gross profit	297,000
Operating expenses	160,000
Interest expense	5,000
Amortization and depreciation expense	32,000
Income before income taxes	100,000
Income tax expense	33,000
Net income	$ 67,000

Exhibit 20-8b Balance sheet and supplemental information, Example 1

Balance Sheets with Change in Balances Computed As at December 31	2021	2020	Change
Assets			
Cash and cash equivalents	$ 99,000	$ 51,000	$ 48,000
Accounts receivable	53,000	39,000	14,000
Inventory	50,000	60,000	(10,000)
Prepaid expenses	6,000	9,000	(3,000)
Property, plant, and equipment at cost	420,000	350,000	70,000
Accumulated depreciation	(150,000)	(125,000)	(25,000)
Patents	51,000	58,000	(7,000)
Total assets	$529,000	$442,000	
Liabilities			
Dividends payable	$ 2,000	$ 2,000	$ 0
Trade payables	69,000	68,000	1,000
Mortgage payable	0	150,000	(150,000)
Total liabilities	71,000	220,000	
Shareholders' Equity			
Preferred shares	215,000	0	215,000
Common shares	200,000	200,000	0
Retained earnings	43,000	22,000	21,000
Total shareholders' equity	458,000	222,000	
Total liabilities and shareholders' equity	$529,000	$442,000	

Supplemental information: The company's policy is to report interest and dividends paid as cash outflows from operating activities.

The first step is to determine the change in cash that needs to be reconciled. The process is illustrated in Exhibits 20-9a to 20-9d.

Exhibit 20-9a Applying the process for preparing a statement of cash flows using the indirect method, Step 1, Example 1

Step 1: Determine the change in cash that needs to be explained.

From the comparative balance sheet, the company's closing cash and cash equivalents balance was $99,000, an increase of $48,000 over the opening balance of $51,000.

Having determined the change in cash that needs to be explained, we adjust net income as necessary to determine net cash from operations. This process is illustrated in Step 2.

Exhibit 20-9b Process for the indirect method, Step 2, Example 1

Step 2: Adjust net income as necessary to determine net cash from operating activities.

i. Start with the company's net income.

The income statement shows net income of $67,000.

ii. Adjust for all non-cash items.

Depreciation and amortization expense reported on the income statement totalled $32,000. This amount is added to net income as the expense did not involve a cash outflow.

iii. Add back interest and income tax expense and subtract investment income.

The income statement reports interest expense of $5,000 and income tax expense of $33,000.

iv. Adjust for the unexplained changes in working capital accounts representing operating activities.

The working capital accounts included on the balance sheet requiring adjustment are accounts receivable, inventory, prepaid expenses, and trade payables.

Accounts receivable *increased* $14,000 during the year as the cash collected was *less* than the revenue recognized. While the $14,000 increase was the aggregate change for the year, to help visualize the required adjustment it is sometimes instructive to think of events that could have caused the noted difference in terms of an originating journal entry.

Dr. Accounts receivable	14,000	
Cr. Sales revenue		14,000

Revenue and income *exceeds* the amount of cash collected by $14,000 so, starting with net income, we need to deduct this $14,000 difference.

Once you understand this, you can apply a more straightforward method to determine the amount and direction of adjustment: think of what the cash balance must do in response to a change in a non-cash account on the balance sheet. If a non-cash asset increases, holding all else constant, the cash account must decline to keep the balance sheet in balance. Likewise, an increase in a liability results in an increase in cash. The increase in accounts receivable requires a –$14,000 adjustment in the SCF.

Inventory *decreased* $10,000 during the year. A decrease in a non-cash asset is accompanied by an increase in cash, so this requires a +$10,000 adjustment in the SCF.

Prepaid expenses *decreased* $3,000 during the year. A decrease in a non-cash asset is accompanied by an increase in cash, so this requires a +$3,000 adjustment in the SCF.

Trade payables *increased* $1,000 during the year. An increase in a liability is accompanied by an increase in cash, so this requires a +$1,000 adjustment in the SCF.

v. Add dividends and interest received and subtract dividends, interest, and income taxes paid.

Interest paid = interest expense − change in interest payable. Interest payable for both years was $0, so interest paid equals interest expense, which was $5,000 as shown in the income statement.

Income taxes paid = income tax expense − change in income taxes payable. Income taxes payable for both years was $0, so income taxes paid equals income tax expense, which was $33,000 as shown on the income statement.

Dividends paid = dividends declared − change in dividends payable. The balance in the dividends payable account remains unchanged, so dividends payable equals dividends declared. However, the amount of dividends declared is not directly apparent from the balance sheet and income statement. In the absence of capital transactions that directly affect retained earnings (see Chapters 13 and 14), changes in retained earnings are due to net income and dividends declared.

Retained earnings, beginning of year (from balance sheet)	$22,000
Plus: net income (from income statement)	67,000
Less: dividends declared (solve)	(46,000)
Retained earnings, end of year (from balance sheet)	$43,000

In practice, the amount of dividends declared can be determined from the general ledger. We show this analysis here to demonstrate the relationship between income, dividends, and retained earnings.

In all three of the above formulas, "change" is a positive number for increases and a negative number for decreases.

(*Continued*)

Exhibit 20-9b Continued

vi. The total of items (i) to (v) equals net cash from operating activities.

$67,000 + $32,000 + $5,000 + $33,000 − $14,000 + $10,000 + $3,000 + $1,000 − $5,000 − $33,000 − $46,000 = $53,000.

From a practical perspective, this step is fulfilled by completing the cash flows from operating activities section of the SCF.

As outlined in Step 3, we then account for the changes in the remaining balance sheet accounts.

Exhibit 20-9c Process for the indirect method, Step 3, Example 1

Step 3: Account for the changes in remaining balance sheet accounts. The reconciling items are recorded in the financing or investing activities section according to their nature.

The remaining account balances requiring adjustment are property, plant, and equipment (PPE) at cost, mortgage payable, and preferred shares. From the comparative balance sheet, the respective changes are a $70,000 increase, a $150,000 decrease, and a $215,000 increase. Note that the change in accumulated depreciation and patents was dealt with when depreciation and amortization was added back in the operating activities section. Similarly, the change in retained earnings was explained by net income and dividends declared, both of which were allowed for in cash flow from operating activities. Unless provided with specific information to the contrary, assume that these transactions are all cash based.

- The company paid $70,000 to acquire the PPE, so record a $70,000 cash outflow in the investing activities section.
- To reflect the $150,000 paid to extinguish the mortgage obligation, record a $150,000 cash outflow in the financing activities section.
- The sale of preferred shares raised $215,000, so record a $215,000 cash inflow in the financing activities section.

We now complete the process as detailed in Step 4.

Exhibit 20-9d Process for the indirect method, Step 4, Example 1

Step 4: Calculate subtotals for operating, investing, and financing activities and ensure the net change in cash and cash equivalents thus determined is equal to the actual change for the period computed from Step 1.

The completed SCF follows. Note how the $48,000 increase in cash corresponds to the amount from Step 1.

Exhibit 20-10 Result of applying procedures for statement of cash flows, Example 1 (IFRS)

Kimzoo Fireworks Ltd. Statement of Cash Flows Year Ended December 31, 2021	
Cash flows from operating activities	
Net income	$ 67,000
Adjustments for:	
Depreciation and amortization	32,000
Interest expense	5,000
Income tax expense	33,000
Subtotal	137,000
Increase in trade and other receivables	(14,000)
Decrease in inventory	10,000

(Continued)

Exhibit 20-10 Continued

Kimzoo Fireworks Ltd. Statement of Cash Flows Year Ended December 31, 2021		
Decrease in prepaid expenses	3,000	
Increase in trade payables	1,000	
Cash generated from operating activities	137,000	
Dividends paid	(46,000)	
Interest paid	(5,000)	
Income taxes paid	(33,000)	
Net cash from operating activities		$53,000
Cash flows from investing activities		
Purchase of plant assets	(70,000)	
Net cash used in investing activities		(70,000)
Cash flows from financing activities		
Retirement of mortgage payable	(150,000)	
Sale of preferred shares	215,000	
Net cash from financing activities		65,000
Net increase in cash		48,000
Cash and cash equivalents, January 1, 2021		51,000
Cash and cash equivalents, December 31, 2021		$ 99,000

d. The indirect method illustrated—Example 2

To help you master the process for preparing a statement of cash flows, we use the same steps to work through a more complex example, Fred's Fajitas Ltd. (FFL).

Exhibit 20-11a Information necessary for the indirect method: Income statement, Example 2

Fred's Fajitas Ltd. Income Statement Year Ended December 31, 2021	
Sales	$1,000,000
Cost of sales	400,000
Gross profit	600,000
General and administrative expenses	175,000
Interest expense	10,000
Depreciation expense	110,000
Operating income	305,000
Recycled loss on FVOCI* investments	2,000
Loss on sale of land	50,000
Income before income taxes	253,000
Income tax expense	107,000
Net income	$ 146,000

*FVOCI = at fair value through other comprehensive income

Exhibit 20-11b Balance sheet and supplemental information, Example 2

Balance Sheets with Change in Balances Computed As at December 31			
Assets	**2021**	**2020**	**Change**
Cash and cash equivalents	$ 17,000	$ 43,000	$ (26,000)
Accounts receivable	104,000	90,000	14,000
Inventory	80,000	65,000	15,000
Prepaid expenses	48,000	45,000	3,000
Current assets	249,000	243,000	
Land	551,000	310,000	241,000
Buildings at cost	860,000	810,000	50,000
Accumulated depreciation	(250,000)	(220,000)	(30,000)
Investments (FVOCI*)	84,000	90,000	(6,000)
Total assets	$1,494,000	$1,233,000	
Liabilities			
Trade payables	$ 52,000	$ 65,000	(13,000)
Dividends payable	7,000	12,000	(5,000)
Income tax payable	9,000	4,000	5,000
Notes payable	129,000	116,000	13,000
Current liabilities	197,000	197,000	
Bank loan	620,000	410,000	210,000
Total liabilities	817,000	607,000	
Shareholders' Equity			
Preferred shares	0	100,000	(100,000)
Common shares	265,000	210,000	55,000
Retained earnings	412,000	316,000	96,000
Total shareholders' equity	677,000	626,000	
Total liabilities and shareholders' equity	$1,494,000	$1,233,000	

*FVOCI = at fair value through other comprehensive income

Supplemental information:

- FFL's policy is to report interest and dividends paid as cash outflows from operating activities.
- During the year, FFL bought and sold land. The historical cost of the land sold was $250,000.
- FFL sold a building originally costing $250,000 for proceeds equal to its carrying value.
- The cost of the investment at FVOCI sold during the year was $6,000. This was also its carrying cost immediately prior to sale.

Recall that the first step is to determine the change in cash that needs to be reconciled as demonstrated in Step 1.

Exhibit 20-12a Applying the process for preparing a statement of cash flows using the indirect method, Step 1, Example 2

Step 1: Determine the change in cash that needs to be explained.

From the comparative balance sheet, the company's closing cash balance was $17,000, a decrease of $26,000 from the opening balance of $43,000.

The second step requires that we determine the net cash from operating activities. While this example is more involved than example 1, the process remains the same.

Exhibit 20-12b Process for the indirect method, Step 2, Example 2

Step 2: Adjust net income as necessary to determine net cash from operating activities.

i. Record the company's net income.

The income statement reported net income for the year of $146,000.

ii. Adjust for all non-cash items.

Depreciation expense reported on the income statement was $110,000. This amount is added back on the SCF because the expense did not involve a cash outflow.

The income statement recorded a loss *on the sale of investments* of $2,000 and *a loss on the sale of land* of $50,000.

These losses are the difference between the sales price of the assets and their respective carrying values. It may be instructive to consider one of the underlying transactions to help visualize the required adjustments.

Dr. Cash	200,000	
Dr. Loss on sale of land	50,000	
Cr. Land		250,000

The $200,000 cash received is a cash inflow from investing activities. Since this $200,000 fully reflects the cash flow from this transaction, we need to add back $50,000 to cash flow from operating activities for the loss included in income.

iii. Add back interest and income tax expense and subtract investment income.

The income statement reports interest expense of $10,000 and income tax expense of $107,000.

iv. Adjust for the unexplained changes in working capital accounts representing operating activities.

The working capital accounts included on the balance sheet requiring adjustment are accounts receivable, inventory, prepaid expenses, trade payables, and notes payable.

Accounts receivable increased $14,000 during the year. Cash collected was less than the revenue recognized on the income statement, so this is a cash outflow from operating activities.

Inventory increased $15,000 during the year. The cash outflow was more than the related expense (cost of goods sold), so this is a cash outflow from operating activities.

Prepaid expenses increased $3,000. The cash outflow was more than the related expense, so this is a cash outflow from operating activities.

Trade payables decreased $13,000. The cash outflow was more than the related expense, so this is a cash outflow from operating activities.

v. Add dividends and interest received and subtract dividends, interest, and income taxes paid.

Interest paid = Interest expense − Change in interest payable. Interest payable for both years was $0, so interest paid equals interest expense of $10,000.

Income taxes paid = Income tax expense − Change in income taxes payable. The balance of the income taxes payable account increased $5,000. Therefore, income taxes paid equals $107,000 − $5,000 = $102,000.

Dividends paid = Dividends declared − Change in dividends payable. First, the amount of dividends declared can be determined from the change in retained earnings and net income.

Retained earnings, beginning of year (from balance sheet)	$316,000
Plus: net income (from income statement)	146,000
Less: dividends declared (solve)	(50,000)
Retained earnings, end of year (from balance sheet)	$412,000

Second, the balance of the dividends payable account decreased $5,000 during the year. Dividends paid were thus $50,000 − (−$5,000) = $55,000.

vi. The total of items (i) to (v) equals net cash from operating activities for the year.

Cash flow from operating activities totalled $213,000 as set out on the SCF in Exhibit 20-13.

Step 3 requires that we account for the changes in the remaining balance sheet accounts. Again, while this illustration is more complex than the preceding example, the process to prepare a statement of cash flows using the indirect method remains unchanged.

Exhibit 20-12c Process for the indirect method, Step 3, Example 2

Step 3: Account for the changes in remaining balance sheet accounts. The reconciling items are recorded in the financing or investing activities section according to their nature.

The remaining account balances requiring adjustment are land, building at cost, accumulated depreciation, investments, bank loan, preferred shares, and common shares. Note that the change in accumulated depreciation was only partially explained when depreciation was added back in the operating activities section. The change in retained earnings was fully explained by net income and dividends declared, both of which were allowed for in cash flow from operating activities.

We first deal with transactions that do not require supplemental calculations.

Notes payable increased $13,000 during the year and is recorded as a cash inflow from financing.

The *increased bank loan* is recorded as a cash inflow of $210,000 in the financing section.

The *retirement of preferred shares* is recorded as a cash outflow of $100,000 in the financing section.

The *issuance of common shares* is recorded as a cash inflow of $55,000 in the financing section.

Sale of investments at FVOCI: From the income statement, we know that the net realized loss of $2,000 on the sale of investments at FVOCI was recycled through net income. From the supplemental information, we know that the cost of the investment was $6,000 as was the carrying cost of the investment immediately prior to sale. Therefore, the sales proceeds were $4,000, which is recorded as a cash inflow from investing activities.

Journal entry immediately prior to sale of investment

Dr. OCI unrealized loss on investment at FVOCI	2,000	
Cr. Investments (FVOCI)		2,000

Journal entry at time of sale of investment

Dr. Cash	4,000	
Cr. Investments (FVOCI)		4,000

Journal entry to recycle the realized loss at period-end*

Dr. Loss on sale of investment at FVOCI†	2,000	
Cr. OCI		2,000

*OCI will be closed to AOCI as part of the closing entry process.
†Reported in net income.

Land: There were two transactions involving land. The historical cost of the land sold is known ($250,000 from the supplemental information section) as is the loss on sale ($50,000 from the income statement). Therefore, as already established in point ii in Exhibit 20-12b, the sales proceeds were $200,000. This amount is recorded as a cash inflow from investing.

A T-account can be used to solve for the cost of the land purchased. The $491,000 purchase price (from the T-account) is recorded as a cash outflow from investing.

	Land (Dr.)	Land (Cr.)	
Jan. 1 balance	310,000		
		250,000	Cost of land sold
Cost of land purchased	**491,000**		
Dec. 31 balance	551,000		

Buildings: There were two transactions involving buildings, a sale and a purchase. For the building sold, the historical cost is known ($250,000 from the supplemental information section), but the related accumulated depreciation must be found by analyzing the T-account for accumulated depreciation. The T-account below shows that the building sold had accumulated depreciation of $80,000, so the carrying value of the building sold was $250,000 − $80,000 = $170,000. This is also the amount of the sale proceeds since there was no gain or loss on the sale. This amount is recorded as a cash inflow from investing.

(*Continued*)

Exhibit 20-12c Continued

For the building purchased in the year, analysis of the T-account for buildings shows that the purchase price was $300,000. This amount is recorded as a cash outflow from investing.

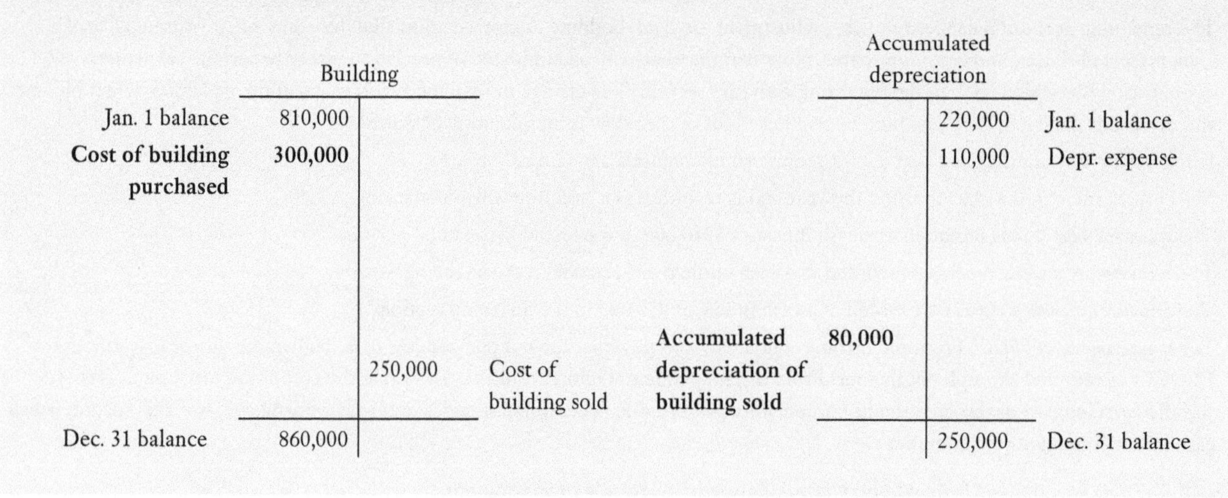

Building
Jan. 1 balance 810,000
Cost of building purchased 300,000
250,000 Cost of building sold
Dec. 31 balance 860,000
Accumulated depreciation
220,000 Jan. 1 balance
110,000 Depr. expense
Accumulated depreciation of building sold 80,000
250,000 Dec. 31 balance

The process is then completed in Step 4.

Exhibit 20-12d Process for the indirect method, Step 4, Example 2

Step 4: Calculate subtotals for operating, investing, and financing activities and ensure the net change in cash and cash equivalents thus determined is equal to the actual change for the period computed from Step 1.

The completed SCF is shown in Exhibit 20-13. Note how the $26,000 decrease in cash from Step 1 has been explained.

Exhibit 20-13 Result of applying procedures for statement of cash flow, Example 2

Fred's Fajitas Ltd. Statement of Cash Flows Year Ended December 31, 2021	
Cash flows from operating activities	
Net income	$ 146,000
Adjustments for:	
Loss on sale of investment	2,000
Loss on sale of land	50,000
Depreciation and amortization	110,000
Interest expense	10,000
Income tax expense	107,000
Subtotal	425,000
Increase in accounts receivable	(14,000)
Increase in inventory	(15,000)
Increase in prepaid expenses	(3,000)
Decrease in trade payables	(13,000)

Exhibit 20-13 Continued

Fred's Fajitas Ltd. Statement of Cash Flows Year Ended December 31, 2021		
Cash generated from operating activities	380,000	
Dividends paid	(55,000)	
Interest paid	(10,000)	
Income taxes paid	(102,000)	
Net cash from operating activities		$ 213,000
Cash flows from investing activities		
Purchase of land	(491,000)	
Sale of land	200,000	
Purchase of building	(300,000)	
Sale of building	170,000	
Sale of FVOCI* investment	4,000	
Net cash used in investing activities		(417,000)
Cash flows from financing activities		
Issuance of notes payable	13,000	
Proceeds of bank loan	210,000	
Retirement of preferred shares	(100,000)	
Issuance of ordinary shares	55,000	
Net cash from financing activities		178,000
Net increase in cash		(26,000)
Cash and cash equivalents, January 1, 2021		43,000
Cash and cash equivalents, December 31, 2021		$ 17,000

*FVOCI = at fair value through other comprehensive income

 CHECKPOINT **CP20-8**

Itemize the four-step process to prepare a statement of cash flows using the indirect method.

3. The process—Direct method

The indirect method just described and illustrated refers only to cash flows from operating activities. Cash flows from investing and financing activities are always presented using the direct method. We now apply the direct method also to operating activities. Moreover, the method of determining dividends and interest received and dividends, interest, and income taxes paid is the same for both methods. Therefore, discussion is confined to how to ascertain cash receipts from customers and cash paid to suppliers and employees.

a. The direct method described

The direct method differs from the indirect method as it does not directly consider net income; rather, it focuses on cash received from sales and cash paid to suppliers and employees to generate those sales.

The general format for presenting cash flows from operating activities, as first presented in Exhibit 20-4, is partially reproduced below.

Exhibit 20-14 Sample of operating section of statement of cash flows

Illustrative Company Statement of Cash Flows (Partial) Year Ended December 31, 2021		
Cash flow from operating activities		
Cash receipts from customers	$ 30,360	Described below
Cash paid to suppliers and employees	(27,800)	Described below
Cash generated from operating activities	2,560	
Dividends received	200	These amounts are determined in the same manner whether the direct or indirect method is used.
Interest received	200	
Dividends paid	(1,200)	
Interest paid	(270)	
Income taxes paid	(900)	
Net cash from operating activities	$ 590	

This example shows only two lines other than those involving dividends, interest, and taxes. This presentation is the minimum required since inflows should not be netted against outflows. Enterprises can choose to provide more details by using additional lines. For example, "cash paid to suppliers and employees" could be divided into "cash paid to suppliers," "cash paid to employees," and "other operating expenses." There is no concrete guidance as to what level of detail should be provided, so professional judgment is required. In the discussion and illustrations below, we will use this two-line presentation.

CASH RECEIPTS FROM CUSTOMERS The starting point for determining cash receipts from customers is sales. This accrual-based number is transformed to a cash-based figure by adjusting for the net change in accounts receivable (AR) during the period. If AR increased during the year, sales exceeded cash collections; if AR decreased during the year, sales were less than cash collections. Thus,

$$\text{Cash receipts from customers} = \text{Sales} - \text{Change in accounts receivable}$$

In this formula, "change" can be an increase or decrease, with increases being positive amounts and decreases being negative ones.

It may be instructive to consider the underlying summary journal entry of a simple example and compare it with the formula solution.

Exhibit 20-15 Illustration for computing cash receipts from customers

Facts:

- Zil Baguettes Ltd.'s sales for the year totalled $1,000,000.
- Zil's receivables increased $10,000 during the year.

Summary journal entry		
Dr. Cash	990,000	
Dr. Accounts receivable	10,000	
Cr. Sales		1,000,000

Direct computation

Cash receipts from customers = Sales – Change in accounts receivable
= $1,000,000 – $10,000 = $990,000

CASH PAID TO SUPPLIERS AND EMPLOYEES Cash paid to suppliers and employees is the sum of the cash paid for inventory and cash paid for operating expenses.

Cash paid for inventory is determined in two steps: (i) establishing the cost of inventory purchased; and (ii) ascertaining the cash paid for the purchases. We first compute cost of inventory purchased (or produced) using the formula:

$$\text{Purchases} = \text{Cost of goods sold} + \text{Change in inventory}$$

Second, cash paid for purchases is:

$$\text{Cash paid for inventory} = \text{Purchases} - \text{Change in accounts payable}$$

We can then combine these into one calculation (COGS denotes cost of goods sold):

$$\text{Cash paid for inventory} = \text{COGS} + \text{Change in inventory} - \text{Change in accounts payable}$$

Cash paid for operating expenses is determined in much the same manner as just illustrated for inventories; that is, adjust the accrual-based income statement number to determine the cash outflow for the year:

$$\text{Cash paid for operating expenses} = \text{Operating expenses} + \text{Change in prepaid expenses}$$

In all of the above formulas, "change" is a positive number for increases and a negative number for decreases. The foregoing points are summarized in Exhibit 20-16.

Exhibit 20-16 Determining direct cash flows from operating activities

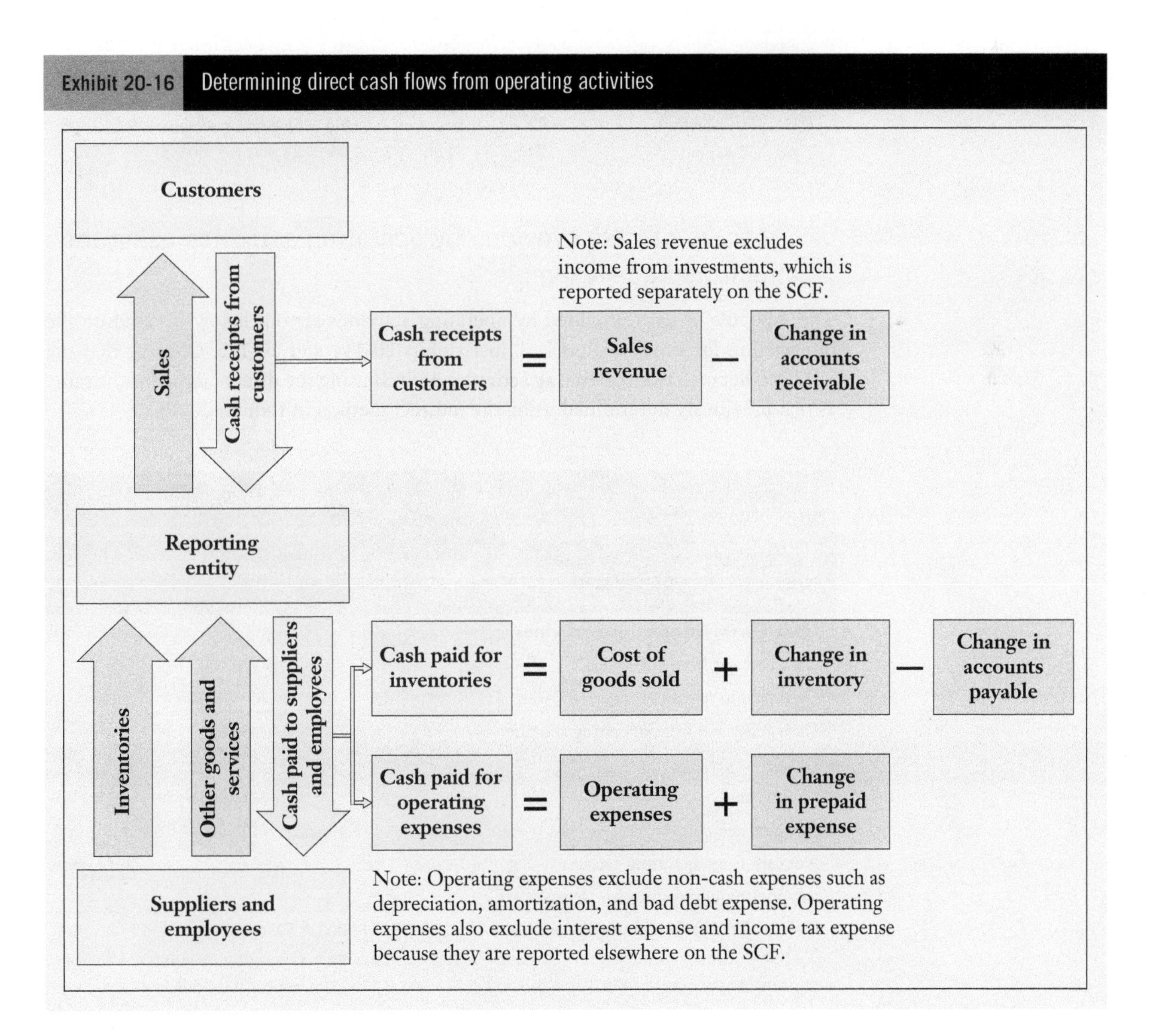

b. Schedule of cash provided by operating activities using the direct method—Example 1

The schedule of cash provided by operating activities set out below is based on the information for Kimzoo Fireworks in Exhibits 20-8a and 20-8b. Observe that the $53,000 net cash from operating activities derived using the direct method is the same as that previously determined using the indirect method in Exhibit 20-10.

Exhibit 20-17 Schedule of cash provided by operating activities using direct method, Example 1

Kimzoo Fireworks Ltd. Schedule of Cash Provided by Operating Activities Year Ended December 31, 2021		
Cash flows from operating activities		
Cash receipts from customers*	$ 646,000	
Cash paid to suppliers and employees†	(509,000)	
Cash generated from operating activities	137,000	
Dividends paid	(46,000)	
Interest paid	(5,000)	
Income taxes paid	(33,000)	
Net cash from operating activities		$53,000
Supporting computations		
*Sales − Change in accounts receivable = $660,000 − $14,000 = $646,000		
†COGS + Change in inventory − Change in accounts payable + Operating expenses + Change in prepaid expenses = $363,000 − $10,000 − $1,000 + $160,000 − $3,000 = $509,000		

c. Schedule of cash provided by operating activities using the direct method—Example 2

The schedule of cash provided by operating activities set out below is based on the information for Fred's Fajitas Ltd. in Exhibits 20-11a and 20-11b. Observe that the $213,000 net cash from operating activities derived using the direct method is the same as that previously determined using the indirect method in Exhibit 20-13.

Exhibit 20-18 Schedule of cash provided by operating activities using the direct method, Example 2

Fred's Fajitas Ltd. Schedule of Cash Provided by Operating Activities Year Ended December 31, 2021		
Cash flows from operating activities		
Cash receipts from customers*	$ 986,000	
Cash paid to suppliers and employees†	(606,000)	
Cash generated from operating activities	380,000	
Dividends paid	(55,000)	
Interest paid	(10,000)	
Income taxes paid	(102,000)	
Net cash from operating activities		$213,000
Supporting computations:		
*Sales − Change in accounts receivable = $1,000,000 − $14,000 = $986,000		
†COGS + Change in inventory − Change in accounts payable + Operating expenses + Change in prepaid expenses = $400,000 + $15,000 + $13,000 + $175,000 + $3,000 = $606,000		

CHECKPOINT **CP20-9**

Describe the process of determining cash receipts from customers and cash paid to suppliers and employees.

4. Effects of specific items on the statement of cash flows

The process for preparing the SCF as described above provides general guidance on how to deal with common situations. The list that follows provides additional direction on select items not already addressed.

a. Accounts receivable—Allowance for bad debts

Companies often report receivables at the gross amount less an allowance. To obtain the amount of operating cash flow, the indirect method simply adjusts for the change in the net receivables. For the direct method of presentation, the calculation is a bit more involved. Cash receipts from sales is adjusted for the change in the gross amount of the receivables less the amount of receivables written off during the period. Thus,

Cash receipts from customers = Sales − Change in gross accounts receivables − Write offs

Alternatively, cash from sales may be calculated as

Cash receipts from customers = Sales − Change in net receivables − Bad debt expense

b. Complex financial instruments

As discussed in Chapter 14, complex financial instruments frequently include components of both debt and equity. As the cash received for the issuance of both debt and equity are classified as cash inflows from financing, reporting complex financial instruments on the SCF does not present any special challenges.

- *At time of issuance:* The consideration received for the issuance of the complex financial instrument is allocated to the constituent parts as per the guidance in Chapter 14. The elements are then normally reported separately as cash inflows in the financing activities section.
- *While the instruments are outstanding:* Cash inflows and outflows relative to the component parts are reported in the normal manner. In the event that a cash inflow or outflow contains multiple elements, they are each classified according to their nature. Paragraph 12 of IAS 7 indicates "*A single transaction may include cash flows that are classified differently . . .*"
- *At time of conversion:* The conversion is reported as a non-cash transaction. For example, a convertible bond is received in exchange for ordinary shares. If cash is involved, the cash received is reported as a cash inflow in the appropriate category, normally financing. For example, when warrants and cash are received in exchange for ordinary shares, the cash received is reported as a cash inflow from financing.
- *At time of derecognition:* The cash consideration paid is categorized according to its nature, normally financing.

c. Discontinued operations

Cash flows from discontinued operations are shown separately in the operating, investing, and financing sections of the SCF according to their nature. Alternatively, as per paragraph 33(c) of IFRS 5, Non-current Assets Held for Sale and Discontinued Operations, this information may be disclosed in the notes to the financial statements.

d. Discounts and premiums on bonds and other financial instruments

IAS 7 does not address the classification of the amortization of discounts and premiums on investments in debt instruments or financial liabilities. Recall that interest received may be classified as a cash inflow from operating or investing, while interest paid may be categorized as a cash outflow from operating or financing. The lack of specific guidance in this area does not present any particular difficulties, however, as the amortization of discounts and premiums does not involve cash flows, the SCF is adjusted as follows:

- For the direct method of presentation—report the amount of interest received or paid in the designated category.
- For the indirect method of presentation—subtract interest revenue and/or add back interest expense from/to net income in the operating activities section. Then report the amount of interest received and/or paid in the chosen category.

IFRS differs from ASPE. When the indirect method is used, ASPE requires that the amortization of discounts on both financial assets and liabilities be reported in the operating activities section. ASPE also requires that the amortization of premiums on financial assets and liabilities be included in the investing and financing activities sections respectively.

Exhibit 20-19 and Exhibit 20-20 illustrate the process of reporting the amortization of a bond premium and discount under IFRS. As previously established, the reporting entity can elect to classify cash outflows for interest payments as either an operating activity or a financing activity; we have presented both options for illustrative purposes. This is a simplified example that isolates the required treatment of the amortization of the premium and discount.

Exhibit 20-19a Amortization of bonds issued at a premium

Facts:

- Georgina's Stables Inc.'s (GSI) net income for the year ended December 31, 2018, was $100,000.
- GSI interest expense for the year was $10,000; interest paid was $12,000. The $2,000 difference is due to the amortization of a premium on a bond payable.
- Opening cash was $25,000; closing cash $123,000.
- There were no other items that needed to be reported on GSI's statement of cash flows.

Exhibit 20-19b Interest payments classified as an operating activity; indirect method

Georgina's Stables Inc. Statement of Cash Flows Year Ended December 31, 2018		
Cash flows from operating activities		
Net income	$100,000	
Interest expense	10,000	
Interest paid	(12,000)	
Net cash from operating activities		$ 98,000
Cash flows from investing activities		0
Cash flows from financing activities		0
Net increase (decrease) in cash		98,000
Cash, January 1, 2018		25,000
Cash, December 31, 2018		$123,000

Exhibit 20-19c Interest payments classified as a financing activity

Georgina's Stables Inc. Statement of Cash Flows Year Ended December 31, 2018		
Cash flows from operating activities		
Net income	$100,000	
Interest expense	10,000	
Net cash from operating activities		$ 110,000
Cash flows from investing activities		0
Cash flows from financing activities		
Interest paid	(12,000)	
Net cash from financing activities		(12,000)
Net increase (decrease) in cash		98,000
Cash, January 1, 2018		25,000
Cash, December 31, 2018		$ 123,000

Exhibit 20-20a Amortization of bonds issued at a discount

Facts:

- Georgina's Stables Inc.'s (GSI) net income for the year ended December 31, 2018, was $100,000.
- GSI interest expense for the year was $12,000; interest paid was $10,000. The $2,000 difference is due to the amortization of a discount on a bond payable.
- Opening cash was $25,000; closing cash $127,000.
- There were no other items that needed to be reported on GSI's statement of cash flows.

Exhibit 20-20b Interest payments classified as an operating activity; indirect method

Georgina's Stables Inc. Statement of Cash Flows Year Ended December 31, 2018		
Cash flows from operating activities		
Net income	$100,000	
Interest expense	12,000	
Interest paid	(10,000)	
Net cash from operating activities		$102,000
Cash flows from investing activities		0
Cash flows from financing activities		0
Net increase (decrease) in cash		102,000
Cash, January 1, 2018		25,000
Cash, December 31, 2018		$127,000

Exhibit 20-20c Interest payments classified as a financing activity

Georgina's Stables Inc. Statement of Cash Flows Year Ended December 31, 2018		
Cash flows from operating activities		
Net income	$100,000	
Interest expense	12,000	
Net cash from operating activities		$112,000
Cash flows from investing activities		0
Cash flows from financing activities		

(Continued)

Exhibit 20-20c Continued

Georgina's Stables Inc. Statement of Cash Flows Year Ended December 31, 2018		
Interest paid	(10,000)	
Net cash from financing activities		(10,000)
Net increase (decrease) in cash		102,000
Cash, January 1, 2018		25,000
Cash, December 31, 2018		$127,000

e. At fair value through profit or loss investments—Unrealized and realized gains and losses

The unrealized profit or loss on an investment at FVPL is reported in the income statement. When the indirect method of presentation is used, the unrealized profit or loss must be reversed in the cash flows from operating activities section of the SCF. No adjustment is required when the direct method of presentation is used.

The realized profit or loss on the sale of an investment at FVPL is a non-cash item and is treated in the same manner as gains and losses arising on the sale of other assets. When the indirect method of presentation is used, the realized profit or loss must be reversed in the cash flows from operating activities section of the SCF. No adjustment is required when the direct method of presentation is used.

The sales proceeds of an investment at FVPL held for trading purposes is reported as a cash inflow from operating activities under both the direct and indirect methods of presentation. The sales proceeds of an investment at FVPL held for other than trading purposes is reported as a cash inflow from investing activities under both the direct and indirect methods of presentation.

f. At fair value through other comprehensive income investments—Unrealized and realized gains and losses

The unrealized profit or loss on an investment at FVOCI is reported in other comprehensive income rather than in net income. As such, an adjustment is not necessary under either the direct or indirect methods of presentation. The unrealized gain or loss for the period needs to be factored in when reconciling that change in the value of investments at FVOCI reported on the comparative balance sheet, however.

As illustrated in Chapter 7, immediately prior to derecognizing (selling) an investment at FVOCI, the carrying value of the asset may be updated to the current market value with the as-yet-unrealized gains or losses reported in other comprehensive income. These unrealized gains and losses are treated in the same manner as those just described.

When an investment at FVOCI is derecognized, accumulated holding gains or losses on the investment are recycled (transferred) to profit or loss and are reported in net income.[9] This recycled income is a non-cash item and is treated in the same manner as gains and losses arising on the sale of other assets. When the indirect method

[9] As discussed in Chapter 7, the accumulated holding gains and losses on an investment in an equity security for which the investee elected to report the holding gains and losses in OCI are not recycled when the investment is derecognized. As such, the previously unrealized gain or loss is not reported in net income and, accordingly, an adjustment is not required when preparing the statement of cash flows.

of presentation is used, the realized profit or loss must be reversed in the cash flows from operating activities section of the SCF. No adjustment is required when the direct method of presentation is used.

The sales proceeds of an investment at FVOCI are reported as a cash inflow from investing activities under both the direct and indirect methods of presentation.

g. Income taxes—Classification

IAS 7 paragraph 35 requires that "taxes on income . . . shall be classified as cash flows from operating activities unless they can be specifically identified with financing and investing activities." In this text, all cash flows arising from income taxes are classified as operating activities.

h. Income taxes—Current and deferred

There are two components of income tax on both the balance sheet and the income statement—current and deferred. We compute cash paid for income taxes using the formula:

$$\text{Income taxes paid} = \text{Income tax expense} - \text{Change in income taxes payable}$$

This equation still holds provided you recognize that income tax expense includes both current and deferred tax expense and that taxes payable encompasses the current and deferred portions.

i. Investments in associates

Investments in associates are typically accounted for using the equity method. The SCF is concerned only with the cash received or advanced, rather than investment income. The required adjustment for the indirect method of presentation entails deducting income from investments in the operating section and recording dividends received in either the operating or investing section.

Exhibits 20-21a and 20-21b give a simplified example that isolates the illustration of the process of reporting cash flows arising from investments in associates using the indirect method of presentation of cash flows from operating activities.

Exhibit 20-21a Cash flows from investment in associates

Facts:

- Jaxxen's Hot Cars (JHC) Ltd.'s net income (including investment income) for the year ended December 31, 2018, was $100,000.
- JHC accounts for its investment in its associate, Belle's Racing Inc. (BRI), using the equity method. In 2018, JHC reported earning $20,000 from its investment in BRI.
- In 2018, BRI declared and paid $5,000 in dividends to JHC.
- JHC elects to report dividends received as an operating activity.
- Opening cash was $25,000; closing cash $110,000.
- There were no other items that had to be reported on JHC's statement of cash flows.

The $20,000 investment income is deducted from the SCF because the income did not involve a cash inflow. Similarly, the $5,000 dividend received is reported on the SCF as the cash received is not included in income. Note that JHC could also elect to report the dividend received as an investment activity.

Exhibit 20-21b Dividends received classified as an operating activity; indirect method

Jaxxen's Hot Cars Ltd. Statement of Cash Flows Year Ended December 31, 2018		
Cash flows from operating activities		
Net income	$100,000	
Investment income (investments in associates)	(20,000)	
Dividends received	5,000	
Net cash from operating activities		$ 85,000
Cash flows from investing activities		0
Cash flows from financing activities		0
Net increase (decrease) in cash		85,000
Cash, January 1, 2018		25,000
Cash, December 31, 2018		$110,000

j. Other comprehensive income

Other comprehensive income (OCI) is not reported on the SCF, as OCI does not affect cash since it records only unrealized gains and losses on select items.

k. Stock splits and dividends

Stock splits and dividends are non-cash transactions. They are not recorded on the SCF.

l. Treasury shares

Cash flows from the purchase and sale of treasury shares are reported as a financing activity.

5. Putting it all together—Comprehensive examples

This section has described the process for preparing the SCF using both the direct and indirect methods. You now have an opportunity to work through two comprehensive examples to confirm your knowledge of the topic. Many aspects of these examples are more involved than the previous two examples provided above. To solve, you will need to supplement the material in this chapter with your general knowledge of accounting. When complete, compare your answers to the solutions that follow.

a. Comprehensive example #1

Zippo Hosiery Inc.'s income statement, comparative balance sheet, and supplemental information follow:

Exhibit 20-22a Zippo Hosiery Inc.'s income statement

Zippo Hosiery Inc. Income Statement For the year ended December 31, 2021	
Sales	$1,432,000
Cost of sales	756,000
Gross profit	676,000
Other expenses	256,600

(Continued)

Exhibit 20-22a Continued

Zippo Hosiery Inc. Income Statement For the year ended December 31, 2021	
Interest expense	75,000
Depreciation expense	334,400
Income before income taxes	10,000
Income tax expense	4,000
Net income before discontinued operations	6,000
Discontinued operations, net of taxes ($100,000)	283,100
Net income	$ 289,100

Exhibit 20-22b Zippo Hosiery Inc.'s balance sheet

Zippo Hosiery Inc.
Comparative Balance Sheet
As at December 31

	2021	2020	Change
Assets			
Cash and cash equivalents	$ 172,000	$ 210,000	$ (38,000)
Accounts receivable	150,000	170,000	(20,000)
Inventory	575,000	498,000	77,000
Investments—FVPL held for trading purposes	140,000	190,000	(50,000)
Current assets	1,037,000	1,068,000	
Property, plant, and equipment at cost	1,984,000	1,396,000	588,000
Accumulated depreciation	(650,400)	(487,000)	(163,400)
Patents	690,000	552,000	138,000
Total assets	$3,060,600	$2,529,000	
Liabilities			
Trade payables	$ 93,000	$ 86,000	$ 7,000
Current liabilities	93,000	86,000	
Bank loan	0	100,000	(100,000)
Bonds payable	659,500	674,000	(14,500)
Total liabilities	752,500	860,000	
Shareholders' Equity			
Ordinary shares	1,150,000	700,000	450,000
Retained earnings	1,158,100	969,000	189,100
Total shareholders' equity	2,308,100	1,669,000	
Total liabilities and shareholders' equity	$3,060,600	$2,529,000	

Exhibit 20-22c Zippo Hosiery Inc.'s supplemental information

- The decrease in bonds payable is due entirely to the amortization of the related premium.
- Zippo's policy is to report interest and dividends paid as a cash outflow from operating activities.

(Continued)

Exhibit 20-22c Continued

- $10,000 of FVPL investments were purchased during the year; none was sold.
- Property, plant, and equipment costing $570,000 was sold for $422,000.
- 100,000 ordinary shares were issued to acquire $450,000 of property, plant, and equipment.
- The $212,000 cost of successfully suing a competitor for patent infringement was capitalized during the year.
- "Other Expenses" includes gains and losses on asset sales, holding losses, and patent amortization.
- Cash was received or paid for all revenues and expenses other than those relating to inventories, sales, depreciation, and amortization.
- Income from discontinued operations represents the operating profits of a plant that is in the process of being decommissioned. The recorded profit was received in cash.

Required:

1. Prepare Zippo Hosiery Inc.'s statement of cash flows for the year ended December 31, 2021, using the indirect method, including disclosure of non-cash activities.
2. Prepare a schedule of Zippo's cash provided by operating activities for the year ended December 31, 2021, using the direct method.

Solution to comprehensive example #1

For the year ended December 31, 2021, Zippo Hosiery Inc.'s cash inflows from operating activities totalled $560,000. Zippo's investing and financing activities for the year resulted in cash outflows of $498,000 and $100,000, respectively. These amounts were determined using the procedures illustrated in the chapter. Note that both the direct and indirect methods established that the aggregate cash inflows from operating activities were $560,000. Note that the references column is for expository purposes only. It would not normally be included in a formal statement of cash flows.

Exhibit 20-23a Solution to comprehensive example #1

Zippo Hosiery Inc. Statement of Cash Flows
For the year ended December 31, 2021

Cash flows from operating activities		**References**
Net income from continuing operations	$ 6,000	
Net income from discontinued operations	283,100	1
Adjustments for:		
Holding loss on FVPL investment	60,000	5
Gain on sale of property, plant, and equipment	(23,000)	3, 8
Depreciation and amortization expense	408,400	2, 7
Interest expense	75,000	
Income tax expense—continuing operations	100,000	
Income tax expense—discontinued operations	4,000	
Subtotal	913,500	
Purchase of FVPL investment held for trading purposes	(10,000)	
Decrease in accounts receivable	20,000	
Increase in inventory	(77,000)	
Increase in trade payables	7,000	
Cash generated from operating activities	853,500	

(Continued)

Exhibit 20-23a Continued

Zippo Hosiery Inc. Statement of Cash Flows For the year ended December 31, 2021			
Cash flows from operating activities			**References**
Dividends paid	(100,000)		6
Interest paid	(89,500)		4
Income taxes paid—continuing operations	(100,000)		
Income taxes paid—discontinued operations	(4,000)		1
Net cash from operating activities		$ 560,000	
Cash flows from investing activities			
Purchase of property, plant, and equipment	(708,000)		8
Sale of property, plant, and equipment	422,000		
Patent	(212,000)		
Net cash used in investing activities		(498,000)	
Cash flows from financing activities			
Retire bank loan	(100,000)		
Net cash from financing activities		(100,000)	
Net increase (decrease) in cash		(38,000)	
Cash, January 1, 2021		210,000	
Cash, December 31, 2021		$ 172,000	

Exhibit 20-23b Required disclosure—Notes to financial statement

Note: During the year, the company issued $450,000 of ordinary shares in exchange for property, plant, and equipment having a fair market value of $450,000.

Exhibit 20-23c Supporting comments calculations as per the references in SCF

1. Income and income taxes pertaining to discontinued operations must be separately disclosed.
2. $334,400 depreciation (PPE) + $74,000 amortization (patent) = $408,400.
   Depreciation is reported on the income statement, while amortization is determined using a T-account (see #7 below).
3. Gain on sale = Sales proceeds − Net book value = $422,000 − ($570,000 − $171,000) = $23,000.
   The accumulated depreciation on the PPE sold is determined using a T-account (see #8 below).
4. Interest paid = Interest expense + Amortization of the bond premium = $75,000 + $14,500 = $89,500.
   Amortization of the bond premium is the change in the bonds payable balance from the comparative balance sheet.
5. Investment (FVPL—held for trading purposes)

	Debit	Credit	
Jan. 1 balance	190,000		
Cost of investments purchased	10,000		
		60,000	**Unrealized holding loss**
Dec. 31 balance	140,000		

6. Retained earnings

	Debit	Credit	
		969,000	Jan. 1 balance
		289,100	Net income
Dividends declared	**100,000**		
		1,158,100	Dec. 31 balance

(Continued)

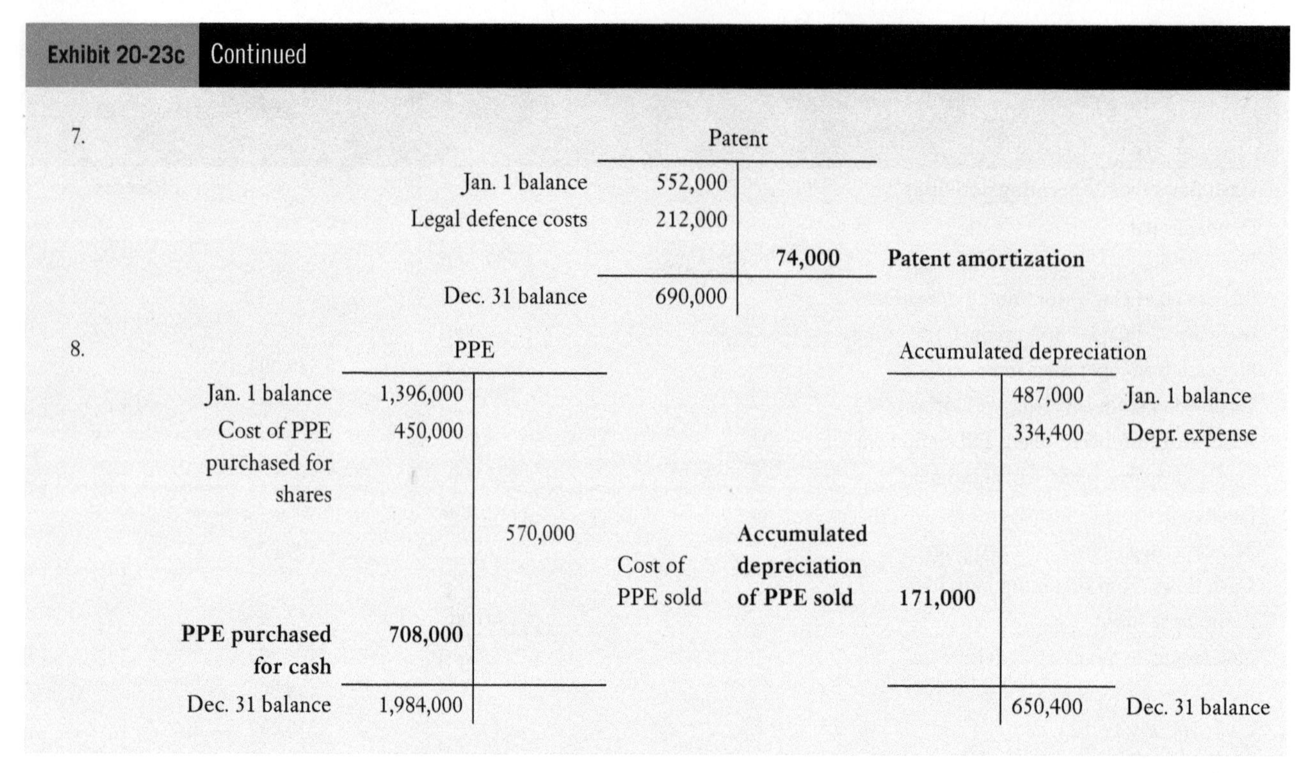

Exhibit 20-23c Continued
7.
Patent
Jan. 1 balance 552,000
Legal defence costs 212,000
74,000 Patent amortization
Dec. 31 balance 690,000
8.
PPE
Jan. 1 balance 1,396,000
Cost of PPE purchased for shares 450,000
570,000 Cost of PPE sold
PPE purchased for cash 708,000
Dec. 31 balance 1,984,000
Accumulated depreciation
487,000 Jan. 1 balance
334,400 Depr. expense
Accumulated depreciation of PPE sold 171,000
650,400 Dec. 31 balance

Exhibit 20-23d Cash flow from operations: Direct method

Zippo Hosiery Inc. Schedule of Cash Provided by Operating Activities For the year ended December 31, 2021		
Cash flows from operating activities		
Cash receipts from customers (1)	$1,452,000	
Cash receipts from discontinued operations (2)	383,100	
Cash paid to suppliers and employees (3)	(971,600)	
Cash paid to acquire FVPL investment held for trading purposes	(10,000)	
Cash generated from operating activities	853,500	
Dividends paid	(100,000)	
Interest paid	(89,500)	
Income taxes paid—continuing operations	(4,000)	
Income taxes paid—discontinued operations	(100,000)	
Net cash from operating activities		$560,000

Supporting computations

1. \$1,432,000 (sales) + \$20,000 (decrease in accounts receivable) = \$1,452,000
2. \$283,100 (income net of tax from discontinued operations) + \$100,000 (income tax paid—discontinued operations) = \$383,100
3. \$756,000 (COGS) + \$256,600 (other expenses) + \$77,000 (increase in inventory) − \$7,000 (increase in trade payables) − \$74,000 (amortization included in other expenses) − \$60,000 (holding loss included in other expenses) + \$23,000 (gain on sale included in other expenses) = \$971,600

b. Comprehensive example #2

Gretta's Cat Products (GCP) Inc.'s statement of comprehensive income, statement of financial position, and supplemental information follow:

Exhibit 20-24a GCP's statement of comprehensive income

Gretta's Cat Products Inc. Statement of Comprehensive Income For the year ended December 31, 2021	
Sales	$5,000,000
Cost of sales	3,500,000
Gross profit	1,500,000
Bad debt expense	(50,000)
Depreciation and amortization expense	(75,000)
Gain on sale of investments at FVPL	15,000
Holding gain on investments at FVPL	5,000
Interest expense	(60,000)
Loss on sale of property, plant, and equipment	(25,000)
Recycled loss on disposal of assets at FVOCI	(30,000)
Other expenses	(1,000,000)
Income before income from associates and income taxes	280,000
Income from associates	95,000
Income before income taxes	375,000
Current income tax expense	(125,000)
Deferred income tax expense	(80,000)
Net income	$ 170,000
Other comprehensive income, net of taxes	
Items that may subsequently be reclassified to net income:	
Holding loss on investment at FVOCI	$ (20,000)
Reclassification of holding losses to income	30,000
Other comprehensive income, net of taxes	$ 10,000
Comprehensive income	$ 180,000

Exhibit 20-24b GCP's statement of financial position

Gretta's Cat Products Inc. Comparative Statement of Financial Position As at December 31			
	2021	**2020**	**Change**
Assets			
Cash	$ 758,000	$ 612,000	146,000
Investments for purpose of meeting short-term cash commitments	136,000	124,000	12,000
Investments at FVPL held for trading purposes	154,000	221,000	(67,000)
Accounts receivable (net)	492,000	474,000	18,000
Inventory	822,000	839,000	(17,000)
Prepaid expenses	28,000	26,000	2,000
Investments at FVPL held for other than trading purposes	83,000	85,000	(2,000)
Investments at FVOCI	91,000	84,000	7,000

(Continued)

Exhibit 20-24b Continued

Gretta's Cat Products Inc. Comparative Statement of Financial Position As at December 31			
	2021	**2020**	**Change**
Investments in associates	412,000	365,000	47,000
Property, plant, and equipment (net)	1,064,000	1,226,000	(162,000)
ROU asset (net)	65,000	0	65,000
Intangible assets (net)	26,000	29,000	(3,000)
Total assets	$4,131,000	$4,085,000	
Liabilities			
Accounts payable and accruals	$ 372,000	$ 383,000	(11,000)
Interest payable	14,000	11,000	3,000
Income taxes payable	6,000	22,000	(16,000)
Dividends payable	121,000	129,000	(8,000)
Bank loan payable	640,000	1,250,000	(610,000)
Lease payable	57,000	0	57,000
Bonds payable	783,000	291,000	492,000
Deferred income taxes	126,000	114,000	12,000
Total debt	2,119,000	2,200,000	
Shareholders' equity			
Preferred shares	225,000	200,000	25,000
Common shares	950,000	1,000,000	(50,000)
Contributed surplus—conversion option	75,000	0	75,000
Retained earnings	712,000	645,000	67,000
Accumulated other comprehensive income	50,000	40,000	10,000
Total shareholders' equity	2,012,000	1,885,000	
Total debt and shareholders' equity	$4,131,000	$4,085,000	

Exhibit 20-24c GCP's supplemental information

- GCP's policy is to report interest and dividends received and paid as operating activities.
- GCP sold investments at FVPL held for trading purposes during the year.
- GCP did not buy or sell any investments held for other than trading purposes during the year.
- GCP purchased investments at FVOCI during the year.
- GCP sold an investment at FVOCI for $62,000 cash.
- GCP's shareholdings in its associate did not change during the year.
- GCP acquired an ROU asset valued at $70,000 during the year which was financed 100% by the lessor. Lease payments were made subsequent to the commencement date of the lease.
- GCP paid $5,000 in legal fees to successfully defend its patent (intangible asset) during the year.
- GCP borrowed an additional $220,000 from the bank during the year.
- GCP's interest expense included amortization of an $8,000 premium on its bonds payable.
- GCP issued $50,000 of preferred shares during the year in exchange for equipment with a fair value of $50,000.
- GCP distributed a common stock dividend during the year valued at $82,000.
- GCP issued a convertible bond during the year.

Solution to comprehensive example #2

For the year ended December 31, 2021, GCP's cash inflows from operating activities totalled $270,000. GCP's investing activities for the year resulted in cash inflows of $93,000, while its financing activities resulted in cash outflows of $205,000. These amounts were determined using the procedures illustrated in the chapter. Note that both the direct and indirect methods established that the aggregate cash inflows from operating activities were $270,000. The references column is for expository purposes only. It would not normally be included in a formal statement of cash flows.

Exhibit 20-25a Solution to comprehensive example #2

Gretta's Cat Products Inc. Statement of Cash Flows For the year ended December 31, 2021			
Cash flows from operating activities	**References**		
Net income	1	$170,000	
Adjustments for:			
Gain on sale of investments at FVPL	2	(15,000)	
Holding gain on investments at FVPL	2	(5,000)	
Loss on sale of property, plant, and equipment	2	25,000	
Recycled loss on disposal of assets at FVOCI	2	30,000	
Income from associates	3	(95,000)	
Depreciation and amortization expense		75,000	
Interest expense		60,000	
Current income tax expense		125,000	
Deferred income tax expense		80,000	
Subtotal		450,000	
Sale of FVPL investment held for trading purposes	4	89,000	
Increase in accounts receivable		(18,000)	
Decrease in inventory		17,000	
Increase in prepaid expenses		(2,000)	
Decrease in accounts payable and accruals		(11,000)	
Cash generated from operating activities		525,000	
Dividends received	3	48,000	
Dividends paid	5	(29,000)	
Interest paid	6	(65,000)	
Income taxes paid	7	(209,000)	
Net cash from operating activities			$270,000
Cash flows from investing activities			
Purchase of investment at FVOCI	8	(89,000)	
Sale of investment at FVOCI		62,000	
Sale of property, plant, and equipment	9	125,000	
Capitalization of legal fees on intangible assets		(5,000)	
Net cash used in investing activities			93,000
Cash flows from financing activities			
Borrow by way of bank loan		220,000	
Payment on bank loan	10	(830,000)	
Payment on lease liability	11	(13,000)	
Sale of bonds	12	575,000	
Repurchase of preferred shares	13	(25,000)	
Repurchase of common shares	14	(132,000)	

(Continued)

Exhibit 20-25a Continued

Gretta's Cat Products Inc. Statement of Cash Flows For the year ended December 31, 2021		
Net cash from financing activities		(205,000)
Net increase in cash		158,000
Cash and cash equivalents, January 1, 2021	15	736,000
Cash and cash equivalents, December 31, 2021	16	$ 894,000

Exhibit 20-25b Required disclosure—Notes to financial statement

Notes:

- During the year, the company issued $50,000 of preferred shares in exchange for equipment having a fair market value of $50,000.
- During the year, the company acquired a right-of-use asset valued at $70,000, financed by a lease liability of the same amount.
- During the year, the company declared and distributed an $82,000 stock dividend on its common shares.
- The cash and cash equivalents of $894,000 as at December 31, 2021, were comprised of $758,000 in demand deposits with a local bank and a short-term money market investment valued at $136,000 that is held to meet short-term cash commitments.

Exhibit 20-25c Supporting comments calculations as per the references in SCF

1. Net income, rather than comprehensive income, is the starting point for determining cash flows from operations (indirect method).
2. Gains and losses on investments are not cash flows and must be adjusted in the cash flows from operating activities section (indirect method).
3. Income from associates are not cash flows and must be adjusted in the cash flows from operating activities section (indirect method). Dividends received are cash flows and must be reported as a cash inflow from either operating or investing activities in accordance with the company's policy in this respect. See T-account in #20 below for determination of the amount of dividends received.
4. The sale of an investment at FVPL held for trading purposes is reported as a cash inflow in the cash flows from operating activities section. See T-account in #17 below and supporting commentary for determination of the sales proceeds.
5. Dividends paid = Cash dividends declared + Decrease in dividends payable account = $21,000 + $8,000 = $29,000. See T-account in #30 below for determination of the amount of dividends declared.
6. Interest paid = Interest expense − Increase in interest payable account + Amortization of bond premium = $60,000 − $3,000 + $8,000 = $65,000.
7. Income taxes paid = Current income tax expense + Deferred income tax expense + Decrease in income taxes payable − Increase in deferred taxes payable = $125,000 + $80,000 + $16,000 − $12,000 = $209,000.
8. The purchase of an investment at FVOCI is reported as a cash outflow in the cash flows from investing activities section. See T-account in #19 below for determination of the purchase price.
9. The sale of PPE is reported as a cash inflow in the cash flows from investing activities section. See T-account in #21 below and supporting commentary for determination of the sales proceeds.
10. The repayment of bank loans is reported as a cash outflow in the cash flows from financing activities section. See T-account in #24 below for determination of the amount repaid.
11. The repayment of the lease liability is reported as a cash outflow in the cash flows from financing activities section. See T-account in #25 below for determination of the amount repaid.
12. The sale of bonds is reported as a cash inflow in the cash flows from financing activities section. See T-account in #26 below and supporting commentary for determination of the sales proceeds.

(Continued)

Exhibit 20-25c Continued

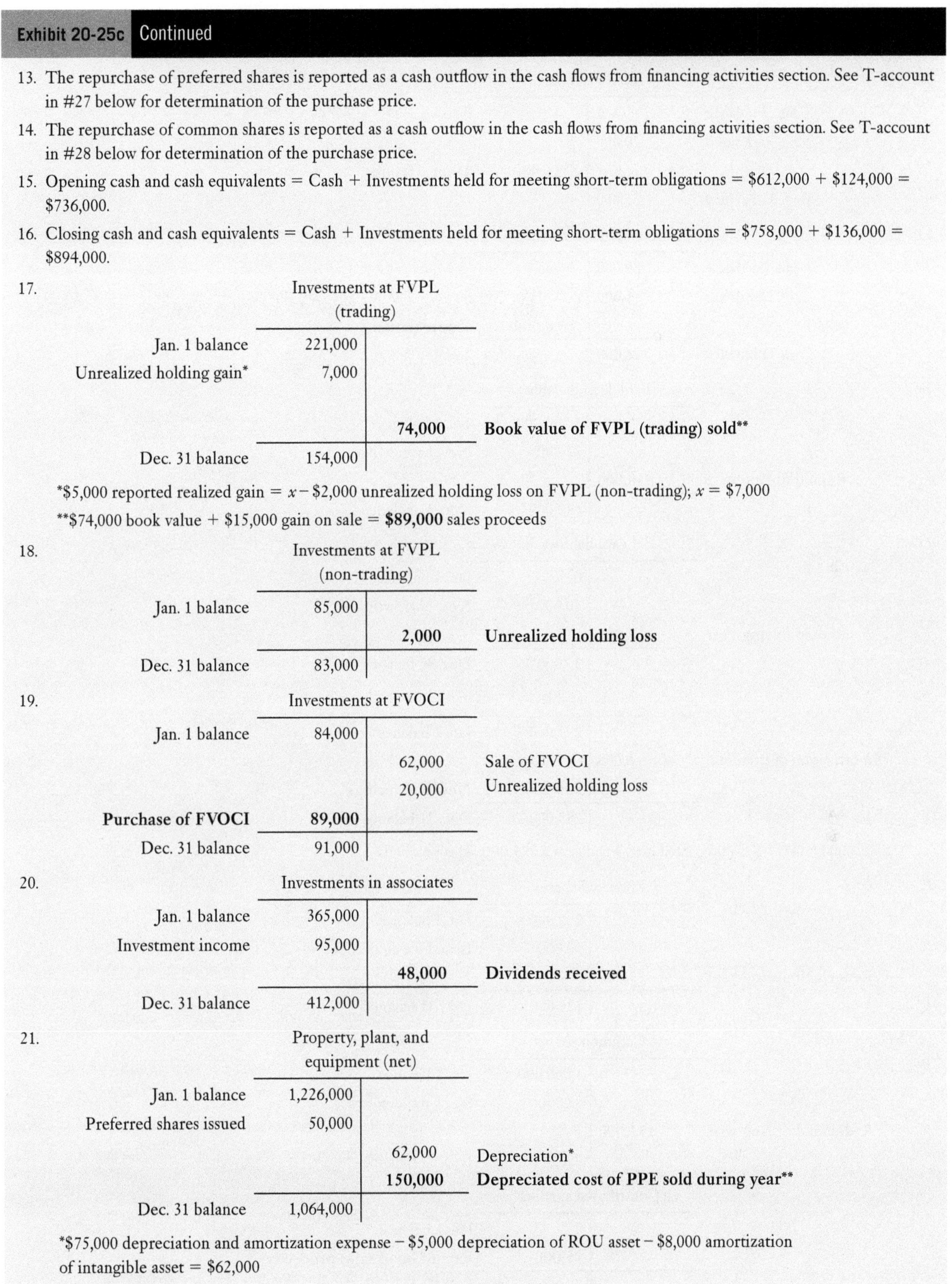

13. The repurchase of preferred shares is reported as a cash outflow in the cash flows from financing activities section. See T-account in #27 below for determination of the purchase price.
14. The repurchase of common shares is reported as a cash outflow in the cash flows from financing activities section. See T-account in #28 below for determination of the purchase price.
15. Opening cash and cash equivalents = Cash + Investments held for meeting short-term obligations = $612,000 + $124,000 = $736,000.
16. Closing cash and cash equivalents = Cash + Investments held for meeting short-term obligations = $758,000 + $136,000 = $894,000.
17. Investments at FVPL (trading)

	Debit	Credit	
Jan. 1 balance	221,000		
Unrealized holding gain*	7,000		
		74,000	**Book value of FVPL (trading) sold****
Dec. 31 balance	154,000		

*$5,000 reported realized gain = x − $2,000 unrealized holding loss on FVPL (non-trading); x = $7,000

$74,000 book value + $15,000 gain on sale = **$89,000 sales proceeds

18. Investments at FVPL (non-trading)

	Debit	Credit	
Jan. 1 balance	85,000		
		2,000	**Unrealized holding loss**
Dec. 31 balance	83,000		

19. Investments at FVOCI

	Debit	Credit	
Jan. 1 balance	84,000		
		62,000	Sale of FVOCI
		20,000	Unrealized holding loss
Purchase of FVOCI	**89,000**		
Dec. 31 balance	91,000		

20. Investments in associates

	Debit	Credit	
Jan. 1 balance	365,000		
Investment income	95,000		
		48,000	**Dividends received**
Dec. 31 balance	412,000		

21. Property, plant, and equipment (net)

	Debit	Credit	
Jan. 1 balance	1,226,000		
Preferred shares issued	50,000		
		62,000	Depreciation*
		150,000	**Depreciated cost of PPE sold during year****
Dec. 31 balance	1,064,000		

*$75,000 depreciation and amortization expense − $5,000 depreciation of ROU asset − $8,000 amortization of intangible asset = $62,000

$150,000 depreciated cost − $25,000 loss on sale = **$125,000 sales proceeds

(Continued)

Exhibit 20-25c Continued

22. ROU asset (net)

Jan. 1 balance	0		
Leased	70,000		
		5,000	**Depreciation**
Dec. 31 balance	65,000		

23. Intangible assets (net)

Jan. 1 balance	29,000		
Legal fees	5,000		
		8,000	**Depreciation**
Dec. 31 balance	26,000		

24. Bank loan payable

		1,250,000	Jan. 1 balance
		220,000	New borrowings
Repaid during year	**830,000**		
		640,000	Dec. 31 balance

25. Lease liability

		0	Jan. 1 balance
		70,000	New borrowings
Repaid during year	**13,000**		
		57,000	Dec. 31 balance

26. Bonds payable

		291,000	Jan. 1 balance
Amortization of premium	8,000		
		500,000	**New borrowings***
		783,000	Dec. 31 balance

*$500,000 bonds + $75,000 contributed surplus = **$575,000** sales proceeds

27. Preferred shares

		200,000	Jan. 1 balance
		50,000	Issued for equipment
Redeemed during year	**25,000**		
		225,000	Dec. 31 balance

28. Common shares

		1,000,000	Jan. 1 balance
		82,000	Stock dividend
Redeemed during year	**132,000**		
		950,000	Dec. 31 balance

29. Contributed surplus

		0	Jan. 1 balance
		75,000	**Part of bond sales proceeds**
		75,000	Dec. 31 balance

(Continued)

Exhibit 20-25c Continued

30.

	Retained earnings		
		645,000	Jan. 1 balance
Net income		170,000	
Stock dividend distributed	82,000		
Cash dividend declared	**21,000**		
		712,000	Dec. 31 balance

31.

	AOCI		
		40,000	Jan. 1 balance
		10,000	**OCI 2021**
		50,000	Dec. 31 balance

Exhibit 20-25d Cash flow from operations: Direct method

Gretta's Cat Products Inc. Schedule of Cash Provided by Operating Activities For the year ended December 31, 2021		
Cash flows from operating activities		
Cash receipts from customers (1)	$4,932,000	
Cash paid to suppliers and employees (2)	(4,496,000)	
Cash received from sale of FVPL investment held for trading purposes	89,000	
Cash generated from operating activities	525,000	
Dividends received	48,000	
Dividends paid	(29,000)	
Interest paid	(65,000)	
Income taxes paid	(209,000)	
Net cash from operating activities		**$270,000**
Supporting computations		
1. $5,000,000 (sales) – $18,000 (increase in accounts receivable) – $50,000 (bad debt expense) = $4,932,000		
2. $3,500,000 (COGS) + $1,000,000 (other expenses) – $17,000 (decrease in inventory) + $11,000 (decrease in trade payables) + $2,000 (increase in prepaid expenses) = $4,496,000		

D. PRESENTATION AND DISCLOSURE

The previous sections of this chapter have described the presentation and disclosure requirements regarding the SCF. These requirements are primarily contained in IAS 1 and IAS 7. The following table provides a summary of the principal requirements:

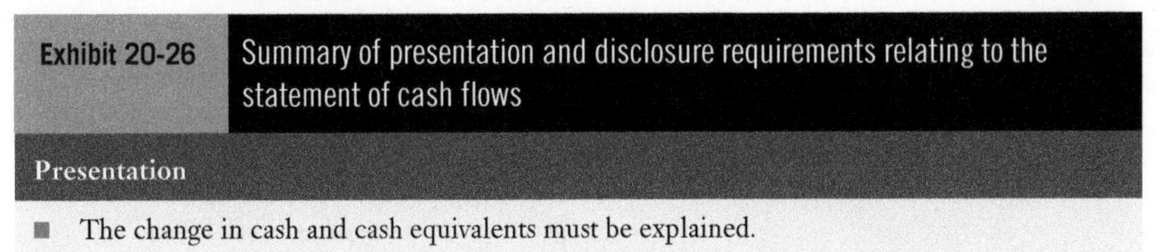

Exhibit 20-26 Summary of presentation and disclosure requirements relating to the statement of cash flows

Presentation

- The change in cash and cash equivalents must be explained.
- Cash flows must be classified as arising from operating, investing, or financing activities.

(Continued)

Exhibit 20-26 Continued

Presentation

- Cash flows from operating activities may be reported using either the direct or indirect method.
- Major classes of cash inflows and outflows for both investing and financing activities must be separately reported.
- Cash flows from interest paid and received, dividends paid and received, and income taxes paid must be individually disclosed. This information may be included directly on the statement of cash flows or discussed in the supporting notes to the financial statements.

Disclosure

- The components of cash and cash equivalents must be disclosed.
- The policy adopted to determine the composition of cash and cash equivalents must be disclosed.
- Non-cash investing and financing transactions are not reported on the statement of cash flows, but must be disclosed elsewhere in the financial statements.
- Sufficient information must be provided to enable users to evaluate changes in liabilities arising from financing activities, including both cash and non-cash transactions.

E. SUBSTANTIVE DIFFERENCES BETWEEN IFRS AND ASPE

ISSUE	IFRS	ASPE
Cash equivalents	Qualifying investments held to meet the entity's short-term cash commitments are reported as a cash equivalent.	Qualifying investments may be reported as (i) a cash equivalent or (ii) a trading asset or investment. The entity establishes a policy concerning which of these assets will be reported as cash equivalents.
Interest and dividends received	Enterprises may classify cash inflows arising from the receipt of interest and dividends as either an operating or an investing activity.	Cash inflows arising from the receipt of interest and dividends must be classified as an operating activity.
Interest paid	Enterprises may classify cash outflows arising from the payment of interest as either an operating or a financing activity.	Cash outflows arising from the payment of interest is normally classified as an operating activity.
Dividends paid	Enterprises may classify cash outflows arising from the payment of dividends as either an operating or a financing activity.	Cash outflows arising from the payment of dividends must be classified as a financing activity.
Interest and dividends received and paid	IFRS requires separate disclosure of the amount of interest and dividends both received and paid.	ASPE requires that interest and dividends paid and charged directly to retained earnings be separately presented as cash outflows from financing.
Income taxes paid	IFRS requires disclosure of the amount of income taxes paid.	ASPE does not require disclosure of the amount of income taxes paid.
Amortization of discounts on financial assets and financial liabilities	IFRS is silent on this matter.	ASPE requires that the amortization be accounted for as an adjustment to net income in the operating section (indirect method).
Amortization of premiums on financial assets	IFRS is silent on this matter.	ASPE requires that the amortization of the premium be reported as a cash inflow from investing.
Amortization of premiums on financial liabilities	IFRS is silent on this matter.	ASPE requires that the amortization of the premium be reported as a cash outflow from financing.

F. SUMMARY

L.O. 20-1. **Describe the purpose of the statement of cash flows and the information it conveys.**

- The statement of cash flows helps users determine the entity's ability to make payments when due and to pay dividends.
- It also helps users assess the company's quality of earnings.

L.O. 20-2. **Define cash and cash equivalents.**

- Cash is cash on hand and demand deposits.
- Cash equivalents are short-term, highly liquid investments that are easily convertible to a known amount of cash and which are subject to an insignificant risk of changes in value.

L.O. 20-3. **Differentiate among cash flows from operating activities, investing activities, and financing activities.**

- Operating cash flows arise from the day-to-day running of the business.
- Cash flows from investing result from the acquisition and disposal of non-current assets and other investments.
- Cash flows from financing activities stem from issuing and retiring debt and equity.

L.O. 20-4. **Describe the difference between the direct and indirect methods of calculating cash flows from operating activities.**

- Net income is the starting point for the indirect method of presenting cash flows from operating activities. Profit and loss is adjusted for non-cash transactions, deferrals and accruals, and income or expense items related to investing and financing activities.
- The direct method of presenting cash flows from operating activities discloses the gross amount of cash receipts and cash payments by category.

L.O. 20-5. **Prepare a statement of cash flows using both the direct and indirect methods.**

- The statement of cash flows is prepared in accordance with the methodology outlined in this chapter.

G. ANSWERS TO CHECKPOINT QUESTIONS

CP20-1: Three reasons why the statement of cash flows is a useful component of an enterprise's financial statements include (i) it is useful for evaluating a company's liquidity, (ii) it provides information about the timing and uncertainty of cash flows, and (iii) it can be used to ascertain the firm's quality of earnings.

CP20-2: Cash equivalents are short-term, highly liquid investments that are readily convertible to a known amount of cash and which are subject to an insignificant risk of changes in value.

CP20-3: Cash flows arising from the purchase and sale of investments at FVPL are classified as operating activities if the investments are held for trading purposes, and as investing activities if held for other than trading purposes.

CP20-4: The three categories of cash flows reported on the statement of cash flows are those arising from operating activities, investing activities, and financing activities.

CP20-5: IFRS permits an enterprise to classify interest and dividends received as an operating or investing activity and interest and dividends paid as an operating or financing activity.

CP20-6: A non-cash transaction is one that does not involve cash. Non-cash financing and investing activities are not reported on the statement of cash flows. If significant, however, they are disclosed in the notes to the financial statements.

CP20-7: The primary differences between the two sets of standards governing the preparation of the statement of cash flows are as follows:

- ASPE refers to a cash flow statement; IFRS a statement of cash flows.
- ASPE does not normally provide options with respect to the classification of interest and dividends received and paid.
- ASPE does not require separate disclosure of the amount of interest and dividends paid and received. Rather, ASPE only requires separate disclosure of the amount of interest and dividends charged directly to retained earnings.
- ASPE does not require disclosure of the amount of income taxes paid.

CP20-8: The four-step process to prepare a statement of cash flows using the indirect method is as follows:

1. Determine the change in cash that needs to be explained.
2. Adjust net income as necessary to determine net cash from operating activities.
3. Account for the changes in remaining balance sheet accounts. The reconciling items are recorded in the financing or investing activities section according to their nature.
4. Calculate subtotals for operating, investing, and financing activities and ensure the net change in cash and cash equivalents thus determined is equal to the actual change for the period computed in the first step.

CP20-9: The process of determining cash receipts from customers is to start with sales and then deduct the net increase in accounts receivable (or add the net decrease) to determine the cash received. Cash paid to suppliers and employees is the sum of cash paid for inventory and cash paid for operating expenses. The cash paid for inventory is cost of goods sold plus the increase in inventory (or minus the decrease) minus the increase in accounts payable (or plus the decrease); the cash paid for operating expenses is operating expenses plus the increase in prepaid expenses (or minus the decrease in prepaid expenses).

H. GLOSSARY

cash equivalents: Short-term, highly liquid investments that are readily convertible to known amounts of cash and which are subject to an insignificant risk of changes in value.

direct method: A method of presenting the statement of cash flows by showing major classes of gross cash receipts and gross cash payments.

financing activities: Activities that result in changes in the size and composition of the contributed equity and borrowings of the entity.

indirect method: A method of presenting the statement of cash flows by adjusting profit or loss for the effects of transactions of a non-cash nature, any deferrals or accruals of past or future operating cash receipts or payments, and items of income or expense associated with investing or financing cash flows.

investing activities: The acquisition and disposal of long-term assets and other investments not included in cash equivalents.

non-cash transactions: Activities that do not involve cash.

operating activities: The principal revenue-producing activities of the entity and other activities that are not investing or financing activities.

I. REFERENCES

Authoritative standards:

IFRS	ASPE Section
IAS 1—Presentation of Financial Statements	1400—General Standards of Financial Statement Presentation
IAS 7—Statement of Cash Flows	1540—Cash Flow Statement
IFRS 5—Non-current Assets Held for Sale and Discontinued Operations	3475—Disposal of Long-lived Assets and Discontinued Operations
IAS 8—Accounting Policies, Changes in Accounting Estimates and Errors	1506—Accounting Changes

MyLab Accounting Make the grade with **MyLab Accounting:** The problems marked with a 🌐 can be found on **MyLab Accounting.** You can practise them as often as you want, and most feature step-by-step guided instructions to help you find the right answer.

J. PROBLEMS

P20-1. Purpose of the statement of cash flows (L.O. 20-1) (Easy – 5 minutes)

Describe in a general way the purpose of the statement of cash flows and the information that it conveys.

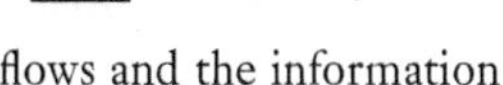

P20-2. Usefulness of the statement of cash flows (L.O. 20-1) (Easy – 5 minutes)

The statement of cash flows provides information relative to the entity's cash inflows and outflows for the period. List three ways that stakeholders may use this information.

P20-3. Cash and cash equivalents (L.O. 20-2) (Easy – 10 minutes)

a. Describe cash equivalents.
b. Briefly discuss the factors that determine how investments that meet the criteria of cash equivalents are reported on the statement of cash flows.
c. What guidance does IFRS provide with respect to reporting bank overdrafts on the statement of cash flows?

P20-4. Classifying cash flows (L.O. 20-3) (Medium – 10 minutes)

a. Describe operating activities, investing activities, and financing activities and provide three examples of each.
b. Describe in a general way what information each category of cash flows provides.
c. Describe the options available with respect to classifying the receipt and payment of interest and dividends under IFRS. Contrast this with the options available, if any, under ASPE. A·S·P·E

P20-5. Classifying cash flows—indirect method (L.O. 20-3) (Medium – 15 minutes)

A list of items that may affect an IFRS-based statement of cash flows prepared using the *indirect* method follows. Assume that the transactions are for cash unless stated otherwise. For each item, indicate by using the associated letter whether it is:

A—a cash receipt reported as an operating activity or an amount added to net income in the cash flows from operating activities section
B—a cash outflow reported as an operating activity or an amount deducted from net income in the cash flows from operating activities section
C—a cash receipt in the cash flows from investments section
D—a cash outflow in the cash flows from investments section
E—a cash receipt in the cash flows from financing section
F—a cash outflow in the cash flows from financing section
G—not reported on the statement of cash flows
H—an item for which there is more than one alternative for reporting

Item	Transaction	Categorization on the statement of cash flows
1.	Receipt of dividends	
2.	Increase in accounts receivable	
3.	Decrease in deferred income taxes payable	
4.	Sale of an at fair value through profit or loss investment held for trading purposes	
5.	Issuing (selling) shares	
6.	Depreciation expense	
7.	Loss on the sale of a financial asset at amortized cost investment	
8.	Payment of interest	
9.	Goodwill impairment loss	
10.	Purchase of an at fair value through other comprehensive income investment	
11.	Decrease in accounts payable	
12.	Conversion of bonds to ordinary shares	
13.	Borrowing money from the bank	
14.	Sale of a computer at book value	
15.	Retirement of bonds	

P20-6. Classifying cash flows—direct method (L.O. 20-3) (Easy – 10 minutes)

A list of items that may affect an IFRS-based statement of cash flows prepared using the *direct* method follows. Assume that the transactions are for cash unless stated otherwise. For each item indicate by using the associated letter whether it is:

A—a cash receipt in the cash flows from operations section
B—a cash outflow in the cash flows from operations section
C—a cash receipt in the cash flows from investments section
D—a cash outflow in the cash flows from investments section
E—a cash receipt in the cash flows from financing section
F—a cash outflow in the cash flows from financing section
G—not reported on the statement of cash flows
H—an item for which there is more than one alternative for reporting
I—none of the above

Item	Transaction	Categorization on the statement of cash flows
1.	Sale of land at a loss	
2.	Gain on the sale of equipment	
3.	Repurchasing own shares	
4.	Receipt of interest	
5.	Purchase of an investment that meets the criteria of a cash equivalent held to meet short-term cash commitments	
6.	Depreciation expense	
7.	Leased right-of-use equipment	
8.	Payment of dividends	
9.	Other comprehensive income	
10.	Impairment loss on a patent	

P20-7. Analysis of changes in account balances—effects of specific transactions (L.O. 20-3) (Medium – 10 minutes)

Select financial information for Aaron and Jamie Ltd. appears below:

Aaron and Jamie Ltd. Select Financial Information As at December 31		
	2019	2018
Plant assets	$ 800,000	$ 500,000
Accumulated depreciation	(140,000)	(180,000)
Dividends payable	35,000	52,000
Retained earnings	1,058,000	1,029,000
		2019
Net income		$ 400,000
Depreciation—plant assets		74,000

- The company issued 20,000 ordinary shares to a supplier in exchange for plant assets having a fair value of $200,000.
- The company sold equipment (plant assets) with a net book value of $125,000 for $90,000 cash.
- The company declared and issued an ordinary stock dividend valued at $30,000.

Required:

a. Determine the amount of cash inflows from investing that should be reported on the statement of cash flows.
b. Determine the amount of cash outflows from investing that should be reported on the statement of cash flows.
c. Determine the amount of cash dividends declared and paid during the year.

P20-8. Classifying cash flows—Other comprehensive income and non-cash transactions (L.O. 20-3, L.O. 20-4) (Medium – 5 minutes)

a. Describe how other comprehensive income is reported on the statement of cash flows prepared using the direct method of presenting cash flows from operating activities.
b. Describe how other comprehensive income is reported on the statement of cash flows prepared using the indirect method of presenting cash flows from operating activities.
c. Describe how the statement of cash flows reports non-cash investing and financing transactions.
d. Provide three examples of non-cash investing or financing transactions.

P20-9. Identifying and determining cash flows from operating activities—indirect method (L.O. 20-3, L.O. 20-5) (Medium – 10 minutes)

Hobnob Corp.'s policy is to report all cash flows arising from interest and dividends in the operating activities section. Hobnob's activities for the year ended December 31, 2018, included the following:

- Net income after taxes for 2018 totalled $125,000.
- Declared and issued a stock dividend valued at $50,000.
- Accounts receivable decreased $32,000 in 2018.
- Sold an at fair value through profit or loss investment that was held for trading purposes for $12,000. The book value was $10,000.
- Interest revenue for the period was $12,000. The interest receivable account decreased $3,000.
- Declared a $20,000 dividend payable. The dividends payable account decreased $12,000 in 2018.
- Sold an at fair value through other comprehensive income investment for $8,000. The cost of the investment and its book value immediately prior to sale was $9,000.

- Hobnob recorded a $10,000 goodwill impairment loss during the year.
- Depreciation expense for the year was $8,000.

Required:

a. Prepare the cash flows from operating activities section of the statement of cash flows using the indirect method.
b. Identify how the activities listed above that are not operating activities would be reported in the statement of cash flows.

A·S·P·E

P20-10. Identifying and determining cash flows from operating activities—indirect method

(L.O. 20-3, L.O. 20-5) (Medium – 10 minutes)

Refer to the information presented in P20-9. Assume that Hobnob Corp. is a private corporation that elects to report its financial results in accordance with ASPE.

Required:

a. Prepare the cash flows from operating activities section of the cash flow statement using the indirect method.
b. Identify how the activities listed above that are not operating activities would be reported in the cash flow statement.

Note: At fair value through profit or loss (FVPL) and at fair value through other comprehensive income (FVOCI) are IFRS terminology that is not used in Part II of the *CPA Canada Handbook*—Accounting (ASPE). For the purpose of this question, assume that the FVPL item is an equity instrument acquired for trading purposes and the FVOCI item is an equity instrument that was not acquired for trading purposes.

P20-11. Cash flows from operating activities—direct method

(L.O. 20-3, L.O. 20-5) (Medium – 10 minutes)

Jill K. Ltd.'s policy is to report all cash flows arising from interest and dividends in the operating section. Jill's activities for the year ended December 31, 2018, included the following:

- Income tax expense for the year was $30,000.
- Sales for the year were $650,000.
- Accounts payable decreased $10,000 in 2018.
- Selling and administration expenses for the year totalled $200,000.
- Accounts receivable increased $20,000 in 2018.
- Jill's cost of goods sold in 2018 was $325,000.
- Jill's inventory decreased $15,000 during the year.
- Interest expense for the period was $12,000. The interest payable account increased $1,000.
- Dividends were not declared during the year; however, the dividends payable account decreased $10,000.
- Sold an at fair value through other comprehensive income investment for $8,000. The cost of the investment and its book value immediately prior to sale was $9,000.
- Depreciation expense for the year was $13,000.

Required:

a. Prepare the cash flows from operating activities section of the statement of cash flows using the direct method.
b. Identify how the activities listed above that are not operating activities would be reported in the statement of cash flows.

A·S·P·E

P20-12. Cash flows from operating activities—direct method

(L.O. 20-3, L.O. 20-5) (Medium – 10 minutes)

Refer to the information presented in P20-11. Assume that Jill K. Ltd. is a private corporation that elects to report its financial results in accordance with ASPE.

Required:

a. Prepare the cash flows from operating activities section of the cash flow statement using the direct method.
b. Identify how the activities listed above that are not operating activities would be reported in the cash flow statement.

Note: At fair value through other comprehensive income (FVOCI) is IFRS terminology that is not used in Part II of the *CPA Canada Handbook*—Accounting (ASPE). For the purpose of this question, assume that the FVOCI item is an equity instrument that was not acquired for trading purposes.

P20-13. Identifying and determining cash flows from operating activities—indirect method (L.O. 20-3, L.O. 20-5) (Medium – 10 minutes)

Meagan's Psychologist Practice Ltd. is a private corporation that elects to report its financial results in accordance with ASPE. Meagan's activities for the year ended December 31, 2018, included the following:

- Meagan's paid $20,000 in income taxes on its 2018 income before income taxes of $110,000.
- Retained earnings increased $52,000 during the year.
- Accounts receivable decreased $15,000 in 2018.
- Accounts payable increased $16,000 in 2018.
- Prepaid expenses decreased $2,000 in 2018.
- Depreciation expense for the year was $10,000.
- Purchased an investment for trading purposes for $5,000 that is not designated as a cash equivalent.
- Repaid $100,000 in bank indebtedness plus $5,000 in interest.
- Bond interest expense for the period was $14,000. The bonds were previously issued at a discount; $2,000 of the discount was amortized during the year.

Required:

a. Prepare the cash flows from operating activities section of the cash flow statement using the indirect method.
b. Identify how the activities listed above that are not operating activities would be reported in the cash flow statement.

P20-14. Identifying and determining cash flows from operating activities—indirect method (L.O. 20-3, L.O. 20-5) (Medium – 10 minutes)

A·S·P·E

Gail's Restaurant Ltd. is a private corporation that elects to report its financial results in accordance with ASPE. Gail's activities for the year ended December 31, 2018, included the following:

- Net income after taxes for 2018 totalled $75,000.
- Declared and issued a two-for-one stock split.
- Accounts receivable increased $18,000 in 2018.
- Accounts payable increased $12,000 in 2018.
- Depreciation expense for the year was $15,000.
- Sold an investment acquired for trading purposes for its book value of $9,000.
- Sold an investment not acquired for trading purposes for its book value of $10,000.
- Interest expense for the period was $10,000. The bonds to which this interest expense relates were previously issued at a premium; $2,000 of the premium was amortized during the year. The interest payable account increased $6,000.
- Declared a $20,000 cash dividend payable on January 15, 2019. The dividends payable account increased $15,000 in 2018.
- Gail's recorded a $5,000 impairment loss on a patent it owns.

Required:

a. Prepare the cash flows from operating activities section of the cash flow statement using the indirect method.
b. Identify how the activities listed above that are not operating activities would be reported in the cash flow statement.

P20-15. Identifying and determining cash flows from investing

(L.O. 20-3, L.O. 20-5) (Medium – 10 minutes)

Anne Gapper Crafts Inc.'s policy is to report all cash inflows from interest and dividends in the investing section and cash outflows arising from interest and dividends in the financing section. Anne Gapper Crafts' activities for the year ended December 31, 2021, included the following:

- Purchased an investment for $11,000. The investment, which met the criteria of a cash equivalent, was held for the purpose of meeting short-term cash commitments.
- Purchased an at fair value through other comprehensive income investment for $10,000.
- Paid $85,000 cash for $90,000 in bonds.
- Repaid a $20,000 investment loan plus $1,000 in interest to the bank.
- Sold equipment for $20,000 that originally cost $40,000. The net book value of this item at time of sale was $30,000.
- Received $10,000 in interest and $5,000 in dividends on sundry investments.
- Acquired land and buildings valued at $200,000 by paying $110,000 cash and issuing a $90,000 note payable for the balance.

Required:

a. Prepare the cash flows from investing activities section of the statement of cash flows.
b. Identify how the activities listed above that are not investing activities would be reported in the statement of cash flows assuming that the statement is prepared using the indirect method.

P20-16. Identifying and determining cash flows from investing

(L.O. 20-3) (Medium – 10 minutes)

Recon Cile Ltd.'s policy is to report all cash flows arising from interest and dividends in the operating section. Recon Cile's activities for the year ended December 31, 2018, included the following:

- Sold an at fair value through profit or loss investment for $11,000. The book value of this investment, which was held for trading purposes, was $10,000.
- Purchased an at fair value through other comprehensive income investment for $16,000.
- Borrowed $50,000 from the bank for investment purposes.
- Sold equipment for $20,000 that originally cost $30,000. The net book value of this item at time of sale was $25,000.
- Purchased inventory costing $45,000 for cash.
- Received $10,000 in interest and $5,000 in dividends on sundry investments.
- Leased a right-of-use forklift valued at $24,000.
- Acquired land and buildings valued at $300,000 by issuing ordinary shares.
- Bought $100,000 in bonds at a discount, paying $95,000 cash.

Required:

a. Prepare the cash flows from investing activities section of the statement of cash flows.
b. Identify how the activities listed above that are not investing activities would be reported in the statement of cash flows assuming that the statement is prepared using the indirect method.

P20-17. Identifying and determining cash flows from investing

(L.O. 20-3, L.O. 20-5) (Medium – 10 minutes)

Jamie Bleay Law Ltd.'s policy is to report all cash inflows from interest and dividends in the investing section and cash outflows arising from interest and dividends in the financing section. Jamie Bleay Law's activities for the year ended December 31, 2021, included the following:

- Sold an at fair value through profit or loss investment for $11,000. The book value of this investment, which was not held for trading purposes, was $11,000.
- Sold an at fair value through other comprehensive income investment for $12,000. The cost of the investment was $10,000. Its book value immediately prior to sale was $13,000.

- Borrowed $40,000 from the bank for investment purposes.
- Sold equipment for $30,000 that originally cost $50,000. The net book value of this item at time of sale was $20,000.
- Received $8,000 in interest and $9,000 in dividends on sundry investments.
- Paid $2,000 interest on the investment loan.
- Acquired land and buildings valued at $500,000 by paying $300,000 cash and issuing ordinary shares for the balance.
- Bought $100,000 in bonds at a premium, paying $105,000 cash.

Required:

a. Prepare the cash flows from investing activities section of the statement of cash flows.
b. Identify how the activities listed above that are not investing activities would be reported in the statement of cash flows assuming that the statement is prepared using the indirect method.

P20-18. Identifying and determining cash flows from financing

(L.O. 20-3, L.O. 20-5) (Medium – 10 minutes)

Angela's Angels Corp.'s policy is to report all cash inflows from interest and dividends in the investing section and cash outflows arising from interest and dividends in the financing section. Angela's activities for the year ended December 31, 2021, included the following:

- Declared and issued a stock dividend valued at $50,000.
- Issued $500,000 in ordinary shares.
- Accounts payable decreased $28,000 during the year.
- Paid $985,000 to repurchase bonds. The book value of the bonds was $1,000,000.
- Made a $10,000 principal payment on a bank loan.
- Interest expense for the period was $18,000. The interest payable account increased $2,000.
- Declared a $10,000 cash dividend payable on January 15, 2022.
- Leased a right-of-use automobile valued at $40,000.

Required:

a. Prepare the cash flows from financing activities section of the statement of cash flows.
b. Identify how the activities listed above that are not financing activities would be reported in the statement of cash flows assuming that the statement is prepared using the indirect method.

P20-19. Identifying and determining cash flows from financing

(L.O. 20-3) (Medium – 10 minutes)

Boboto Inc.'s policy is to report all cash flows arising from interest and dividends in the operating section. Boboto's activities for the year ended December 31, 2018, included the following:

- Declared and issued a stock dividend valued at $100,000.
- Paid $40,000 to repurchase ordinary shares and cancelled them. The book value was $30,000.
- Accounts payable increased $32,000 during the year.
- Issued $1,000,000 in bonds. The cash proceeds were $985,000.
- Interest expense for the period was $15,000. The interest payable account decreased $2,000.
- Made a $20,000 principal payment on a bank loan.
- Declared a $20,000 cash dividend payable on January 15, 2019.

Required:

a. Prepare the cash flows from financing activities section of the statement of cash flows.
b. Identify how the activities listed above that are not financing activities would be reported in the statement of cash flows assuming that the statement is prepared using the indirect method.

P20-20. Identifying and determining cash flows from financing

(L.O. 20-3, L.O. 20-5) (Medium – 10 minutes)

Jane's Bookkeeping Services Inc.'s policy is to report all cash inflows from interest and dividends in the investing section and cash outflows arising from interest and dividends in the financing section. Jane's activities for the year ended December 31, 2021, included the following:

- Declared and issued a two-for-one stock split.
- Converted $300,000 of preferred shares into ordinary shares.
- Accounts payable increased $5,000 during the year.
- Paid $505,000 to repurchase bonds. The book value of the bonds was $500,000.
- Interest expense for the period was $10,000. The interest payable account decreased $2,000.
- Paid a $20,000 cash dividend declared in 2020.
- Distributed a stock dividend valued at $25,000.
- Borrowed $40,000 from the bank. $30,000 of the proceeds were used to pay off a lease liability.

Required:

a. Prepare the cash flows from financing activities section of the statement of cash flows.
b. Identify how the activities listed above that are not financing activities would be reported in the statement of cash flows assuming that the statement is prepared using the indirect method.

P20-21. Statement of cash flows—indirect method—classification of transactions

(L.O. 20-3) (Difficult – 30 minutes)

Select transactions of Mark Fisher Taxidermy Inc. (MFTI) are listed below. MFTI is a publicly accountable company that uses the indirect method to determine cash flows from operating activities.

1. MFTI purchased a $15,000 bond at a discount, paying $14,500 cash. Management classified the investment as a financial asset at amortized cost.
2. MFTI's comprehensive income for the year totalled $150,000 consisting of $200,000 net income and other comprehensive income of $(50,000).
3. MFTI declared and distributed a stock dividend valued at $20,000.
4. MFTI's retained earnings increased $150,000. The dividends payable account decreased $40,000.
5. MFTI made a payment of $20,000 on a lease liability including interest of $6,000.
6. MFTI exchanged equipment valued at $100,000 for a patent and $40,000 cash.
7. MFTI's income tax expense totalled $10,000. Its income tax payable account decreased $5,000, while its deferred income tax liability account increased $8,000.
8. At year-end, MFTI wrote off $40,000 in bad debts.
9. MFTI amortized $10,000 of the premium on bonds payable.
10. MFTI sold a maturing Treasury bill held to meet short-term cash commitments for $100,000. The book value of the investment equalled the market value.

Required:

Discuss how the activities listed above would be reported in the statement of cash flows. For items with multiple reporting options, identify all available options. For items not reported on the statement of cash flows, indicate the disclosure requirements, if any.

P20-22. Statement of cash flows—indirect method—classification of transactions

(L.O. 20-3) (Medium – 30 minutes)

Select transactions of Jack Lin Accounting Inc. (JLAI) are listed below. JLAI is a publicly accountable company that uses the indirect method to determine cash flows from operating activities.

1. JLAI purchased a $100,000, 60-day Treasury bill at fair value through profit or loss investment. The investment was held for trading purposes.
2. JLAI amortized $30,000 of the discount on bonds payable.
3. At year-end, JLAI increased its allowance for bad debts by $50,000.
4. JLAI's income tax expense totalled $40,000. Its income tax payable account increased $7,000, while its deferred income tax liability account decreased $10,000.

5. JLAI leased right-of-use equipment valued at $100,000.
6. JLAI declared and distributed a stock dividend valued at $30,000.
7. JLAI declared a cash dividend of $20,000. The dividends payable account increased $15,000.
8. JLAI's comprehensive income for the year totalled $200,000 consisting of $150,000 net income and $50,000 other comprehensive income.
9. JLAI sold a financial asset at amortized cost investment for $12,000. The investment's amortized cost was $10,000.

Required:

Discuss how the activities listed above would be reported in the statement of cash flows. For items with multiple reporting options, identify all available options. For items not reported on the statement of cash flows, indicate the disclosure requirements, if any.

P20-23. Analysis of changes in account balances—effects of specific transactions (L.O. 20-3, L.O. 20-4) (Difficult – 30 minutes)

Information pertaining to select activities of Rosamelia Corp. during 2021 is set out below:

1. On January 1, 2021, Rosamelia leased right-of-use equipment. The lease calls for five annual payments of $20,000 due at the beginning of the year. Rosamelia must return the equipment to the lessor at the end of the lease. The payment due on January 1, 2021, was made as agreed. The implicit rate in the lease is 4%; the present value of the lease payments is $92,598.
2. The opening balance in the computer account was $70,000; the closing balance was $80,000. The corresponding balances in the accumulated depreciation accounts were $42,000 and $53,000. During the year, Rosamelia scrapped a computer originally costing $10,000 having a remaining net book value of $2,000 and purchased a replacement machine for cash.
3. The opening balance in the land account was $250,000; the closing balance was $300,000. During the year, land costing $40,000 was given to a creditor in full settlement of a $50,000 loan. The fair value of the land at the time of the exchange was $50,000. The company also purchased a separate parcel of land for cash during the year.

Required:

a. Prepare the underlying journal entries to record the transactions and record events stemming from the transactions (e.g., the accrual of interest at year-end).
b. For each entry, identify the cash flow effects, if any, under both the direct and indirect methods of presentation and classify the cash flow according to its nature.
c. Why does the IASB require that companies classify cash flows as arising from operations, investing, or financing activities?

P20-24. Analysis of changes in account balances—effects of specific transactions (L.O. 20-3, L.O. 20-4) (Medium – 15 minutes)

Information pertaining to select activities of Extravaganza Inc. during 2019 is set out below:

1. Extravaganza converted $2,000,000 in bonds payable into 10,000 ordinary shares. At time of conversion, the book value of the bonds was $1,950,000; the contributed surplus–conversion option was $75,000; and the interest paid was $8,000. The interest had not previously been accrued.
2. During the year, Extravaganza sold production equipment that originally cost $20,000 for $8,000. The net book value at time of sale was $5,000.
3. The opening balance in the land account was $200,000; the closing balance $225,000. During the year, land costing $60,000 was given to a creditor in full settlement of a $70,000 loan. The fair value of the land at the time of the exchange was $70,000. The company also purchased a separate parcel of land for cash during the year.

Required:

a. Prepare the underlying journal entries to record the transactions.
b. For each entry, identify the cash flow effects, if any, under both the direct and indirect methods of presentation and classify the cash flow according to its nature.

P20-25. Contrast the direct and indirect methods of preparing the statement of cash flows

(L.O. 20-4) (Easy – 5 minutes)

a. What are the similarities and differences between the direct and indirect methods of preparing the statement of cash flows?
b. In practice, do more companies use the direct or indirect method of preparation?
c. Does the IASB encourage the use of the direct or indirect method of presenting the statement of cash flows?

P20-26. Presentation and disclosure of cash flows

(L.O. 20-5) (Easy – 5 minutes)

Summarize the principal presentation, reporting, and disclosure requirements for the statement of cash flows.

P20-27. Preparing a statement of cash flows

(L.O. 20-5) (Easy – 10 minutes)

a. Briefly discuss how unrealized gains and losses arising from at fair value through profit or loss investments that are held for trading are reported on the statement of cash flows.
b. Briefly discuss how cash flows arising from income taxes are reported on the statement of cash flows.
c. Briefly discuss how stock splits and stock dividends are reported on the statement of cash flows.
d. Briefly discuss how cash flows arising from the purchase and sale of treasury shares are reported on the statement of cash flows.

P20-28. Preparing a statement of cash flows

(L.O. 20-5) (Medium – 15 minutes)

a. Briefly discuss how the amortization of discounts and premiums on financial instruments are classified in an IFRS-based statement of cash flows.
b. Briefly discuss how other comprehensive income is reported on the statement of cash flows.
c. Briefly discuss how cash flows arising from investments in associates are reported on the statement of cash flows.

A·S·P·E

d. Briefly discuss how the amortization of discounts and premiums on financial instruments are classified in an ASPE-based cash flow statement.

P20-29. Preparing a statement of cash flows

(L.O. 20-4, L.O. 20-5) (Easy – 10 minutes)

a. List the three primary sources of information required to prepare a statement of cash flows.
b. A company may report its accounts receivable at the gross amount less an allowance for bad debts. Contrast the direct and indirect methods of adjusting for accounts receivable reported at the gross amount.
c. Briefly discuss the alternatives for reporting discontinued operations in the statement of cash flows.

P20-30. Cash flows from operating activities—indirect method

(L.O. 20-3, L.O. 20-5) (Medium – 10 minutes)

Coastal Cares Inc.'s (CCI) policy is to report all cash flows arising from interest and dividends in the operating section. The company's activities for the year ended December 31, 2021, included the following:

- Comprehensive income totalled $350,000, including $50,000 in other comprehensive income.
- Paid a cash dividend of $50,000 that was declared in 2020.
- Interest expense for the year was $30,000; the opening and closing balances in the interest payable account were $25,000 and $10,000, respectively.
- Accounts receivable increased $24,000 and accounts payable decreased $18,000 during the year.
- CCI paid $47,000 cash for equipment.
- CCI sold a financial asset at amortized cost investments for $18,000. The book value of the investment was $20,000.
- Depreciation expense for the year totalled $37,000.
- CCI suffered an impairment loss on patents of $12,000.
- Declared and issued a two-for-one stock split. There were 10,000 ordinary shares outstanding before the split with a collective market value of $2,500,000.

Required:

a. Prepare the cash flows from operating activities section of the statement of cash flows using the indirect method.
b. Identify how the activities detailed above that are not operating activities would be reported in the statement of cash flows.

P20-31. Cash flows from operating activities—indirect method

(L.O. 20-5) (Medium – 5 minutes)

Refer to the information presented in P20-30.

Required:

Prepare the cash flows from operating activities section of the statement of cash flows using the indirect method, assuming that Coastal Cares Inc.'s policy is to report interest and dividends received as an investing activity and interest and dividends paid as a financing activity.

P20-32. Cash flows from operating activities—indirect method

(L.O. 20-3, L.O. 20-5) (Medium – 15 minutes)

Liz Hicks Accounting Ltd.'s (LHA) policy is to report all cash flows arising from interest and dividends in the operating section. LHA owns a 30% interest in an associated company, LH Bookkeeping Inc. (LHB), and accounts for this investment using the equity method. LHA's activities for the year ended December 31, 2019, included the following:

- Net income totalled $625,000, including $60,000 in investment income arising from its investment in LHB.
- Received $20,000 in dividends from LHB that were declared in 2018.
- Declared a cash dividend of $40,000 that was payable on January 5, 2020.
- Interest expense for the year was $28,000; the opening and closing balances in the interest payable account were $17,000 and $21,000, respectively.
- Total income tax expense for the year was $65,000; the current taxes payable account increased $3,000 and the deferred taxes liability increased $5,000.
- Accounts receivable decreased $16,000 and accounts payable decreased $14,000 during the year.
- LHA sold equipment for $15,000 cash that had a net book value of $14,000.
- Depreciation expense for the year totalled $62,000.
- LHA leased right-of-use equipment valued at $39,000. The company made one payment of $4,500 during the year; $2,900 was allocated to interest expense with the remaining $1,600 reducing the lease liability.

Required:

a. Prepare the cash flows from operating activities section of the statement of cash flows for LHA using the indirect method.
b. Identify how the activities detailed above that are not operating activities would be reported in the statement of cash flows.

P20-33. Cash flows from operating activities—indirect method

(L.O. 20-3, L.O. 20-5) (Medium – 10 minutes)

Valley Hospitality Ltd.'s (VHL) policy is to report all cash flows arising from interest and dividends as operating activities. The company's activities for the year ended December 31, 2021, included the following:

- VHL reported income before income taxes of $400,000. Current income tax expense was $40,000; deferred income tax expense was $10,000.
- Retained earnings increased $340,000 for the year; the dividends payable account increased $5,000.
- Current income taxes payable decreased $4,000; deferred income taxes payable increased $6,000.
- Interest expense for the year was $20,000; the interest payable account increased $12,000.

- Accounts receivable decreased $18,000 and accounts payable increased $40,000 during the year.
- Inventory increased $14,000.
- VHL sold equipment with a net book value of $40,000 for $42,000 cash.
- VHL sold at fair value through other comprehensive income investments for $12,000. The investment cost was $15,000. The book value of the investment immediately preceding the sale was $11,000.
- Depreciation expense for the year totalled $22,000.
- VHL recorded a goodwill impairment loss of $15,000.
- Leased right-of-use equipment valued at $200,000 by way of a $20,000 cash down payment and a $180,000 lease liability.

Required:

a. Prepare the cash flows from operating activities section of the statement of cash flows using the indirect method.
b. Identify how the activities detailed above that are not operating activities would be reported in the statement of cash flows.

P20-34. Cash flows from operating activities—indirect method

(L.O. 20-5) (Medium – 5 minutes)

Refer to the information presented in P20-33.

Required:

Prepare the cash flows from operating activities section of the statement of cash flows using the indirect method, assuming that Valley Hospitality Ltd.'s policy is to report interest and dividends received as an investing activity and interest and dividends paid as a financing activity.

P20-35. Cash flows from operating activities—indirect method

(L.O. 20-5) (Medium – 5 minutes)

Refer to the information presented in P20-33.

Required:

Prepare the cash flows from operating activities section of the cash flow statement using the indirect method, assuming that Valley Hospitality Ltd. is a private enterprise that elects to report its financial results in accordance with ASPE.

Note: Under ASPE, deferred income taxes are referred to as future income taxes. Also, at fair value through other comprehensive income (FVOCI) is IFRS terminology that is not used in Part II of the *CPA Canada Handbook*—Accounting. For the purposes of this question, assume that the FVOCI is an equity instrument that was not acquired for trading purposes.

P20-36. Statement of cash flows—indirect method—comprehensive

(L.O. 20-3, L.O. 20-5) (Difficult – 60 minutes)

Brigitte's Bathrooms Ltd.'s balance sheet for the year ended December 31, 2021, follows:

Brigitte's Bathrooms Ltd. Comparative Balance Sheet As at December 31	2021	2020
Assets		
Cash	$ 17,000	$ 43,000
Accounts receivable	104,000	90,000

(*Continued*)

Brigitte's Bathrooms Ltd. Comparative Balance Sheet As at December 31		
	2021	2020
Inventory	80,000	65,000
Prepaid expenses	48,000	45,000
Current assets	249,000	243,000
Land	551,000	310,000
Buildings	860,000	810,000
Accumulated depreciation	(250,000)	(220,000)
Long-term investment (equity)	84,000	90,000
Total assets	$1,494,000	$1,233,000
Liabilities and shareholders' equity		
Accounts payable	$ 50,000	$ 60,000
Accrued interest payable	2,000	5,000
Notes payable	145,000	132,000
Current liabilities	197,000	197,000
Long-term bank loan	600,000	400,000
Deferred income taxes payable	20,000	10,000
Total liabilities	817,000	607,000
Preferred shares	0	100,000
Ordinary shares	285,000	210,000
Retained earnings	392,000	316,000
Total equity	677,000	626,000
Total liabilities and shareholders' equity	$1,494,000	$1,233,000

Additional information:

- During the year, Brigitte declared and paid cash dividends of $50,000. They also declared and distributed stock dividends valued at $20,000.
- Brigitte bought and sold land during the year. The land that was sold for $200,000 originally cost $250,000.
- Brigitte's long-term investment consists of holding ordinary shares in one company (GFF Services Inc.). For most of the year, Brigitte owned 50,000 of the 200,000 ordinary shares outstanding. GFF's net income for the year (which ended December 15) was $40,000. GFF's income from December 16 to December 31 was not material. The company paid dividends of $100,000 on December 15. Brigitte bought additional shares in GFF on December 31.
- A gain of $25,000 was realized on the sale of a building that cost $200,000. Accumulated depreciation at time of sale was $150,000.
- Brigitte borrowed money from a finance company, which accounted for the increase in notes payable.
- The company's expenses for the year included $40,000 for income tax and $30,000 for interest.
- Brigitte's policy is to report investment income and interest paid in the cash flows from operating activities section, while dividends paid are classified as a cash outflow from financing activities.

Required:

a. Prepare a statement of cash flows for Brigitte's Bathrooms Ltd. for 2021 using the indirect method.
b. Identify what supplemental disclosure, if any, is required.

P20-37. Prepare statement of cash flows from transactions

(L.O. 20-3, L.O. 20-5) (Difficult – 30 minutes)

Golf Is Great Corp.'s condensed balance sheet for the year ended December 31, 2017, follows:

Golf Is Great Corp. Balance Sheet As at December 31, 2017			
Cash	$ 30,000	Accounts payable	$ 20,000
Inventory	50,000	Other current liabilities	60,000
Other current assets	60,000	Bank loans	50,000
Investments—at fair value through other comprehensive income	40,000	Bonds payable	100,000
Plant and equipment (net)	100,000	Share capital	10,000
Land	80,000	Retained earnings	120,000
	$360,000		$360,000

Golf Is Great's 2018 transactions are as follows:

1. Net income for the year was $27,000 after recording $20,000 in depreciation expense on the plant and equipment.
2. Received cash proceeds of $20,000 from the issuance of preferred shares.
3. Purchased $10,000 inventory on account.
4. Received $19,000 cash from the sale of at fair value through other comprehensive income investments. The investment originally cost $22,000. Its book value immediately preceding the sale was $22,000.
5. Issued $100,000 in bonds to acquire land having a fair value of $100,000.
6. Declared and paid dividends totalling $25,000. Golf Is Great has a policy of including dividends paid in the financing section.
7. Made a $10,000 principal payment on the bank loan.

Required:

a. Prepare a statement of cash flows for 2018 using the indirect method.
b. Discuss how the transaction(s) above that are not reported on the statement of cash flows are reported in the financial statements.
c. Prepare a balance sheet as at December 31, 2018. Assume that other current assets and other current liabilities remain unchanged.
d. Golf's policy is to report dividends paid as a cash outflow from financing activity. What are its alternatives in this respect? How would the statement of cash flows that you prepared in (a) differ if Golf had adopted the alternative presentation method?

P20-38. Prepare statement of cash flows from transactions

(L.O. 20-3, L.O. 20-5) (Difficult – 45 minutes)

Squash Forever Corp.'s first year of operations was 2018. Its transactions for the year are as follows:

1. Sold ordinary shares for $50,000 cash and preferred shares for $20,000 cash.
2. Paid $20,000 to acquire at fair value through other comprehensive income securities.
3. Net income for the year was $29,000 after recording $10,000 in depreciation expense on the plant and equipment.
4. Purchased $200,000 inventory on account.
5. Recorded $300,000 in sales on account; cost of goods sold was $140,000.
6. Received $190,000 from customers previously sold to on account.
7. Paid $40,000 cash to a supplier in partial settlement of the inventory purchased in transaction #4.
8. Paid $20,000 cash to redeem ordinary shares redeemed at book value.
9. Received $23,000 cash from the sale of at fair value through other comprehensive income investments purchased in transaction #2.

10. Leased right-of-use equipment valued at $80,000.
11. Declared and paid dividends totalling $20,000. Squash has a policy of reporting dividends as a cash outflow from financing activities.
12. Made a $15,000 payment on the lease liability including $4,000 in interest. Squash has a policy of reporting interest paid as a cash outflow from operating activities.
13. Paid $100,000 cash for various administrative expenses.
14. Paid $20,000 cash in income taxes; cash paid equals income tax expense.

Required:

a. Prepare a statement of cash flows for 2018 using the indirect method.
b. Prepare an income statement for the year ended December 31, 2018.
c. Prepare a balance sheet as at December 31, 2018.
d. Discuss how the transaction(s) above that are not reported on the statement of cash flows are reported in the financial statements.
e. Squash's policy is to report interest paid as a cash outflow from operating activities and dividends paid as a cash outflow from financing activity. What are its alternatives in this respect? How would the statement of cash flows that you prepared in (a) differ if Squash had adopted a policy of reporting the receipt and payment of interest and dividends as operating activities?

P20-39. Statement of cash flows—operating activities—direct method

(L.O. 20-3, L.O. 20-5) (Medium – 15 minutes)

Quitzau's Supplies Inc.'s income statement for the year ended December 31, 2021, follows:

Quitzau's Supplies Inc. Income Statement Year Ended December 31, 2021		
Sales		$1,000,000
Cost of goods sold		
Beginning inventory	$500,000	
Purchases	400,000	
Cost of goods available for sale	900,000	
Ending inventory	300,000	
Cost of goods sold		600,000
Gross profit		400,000
Operating expenses		200,000
Interest expense		10,000
Amortization and depreciation expense		30,000
Income before income taxes		160,000
Income tax expense		40,000
Net income		$ 120,000

Additional information:

- Accounts receivable decreased $20,000 during the year.
- Accounts payable increased $15,000 during the year.
- Prepaid expenses increased $5,000 during the year.
- Income taxes payable decreased $3,000 during the year.
- Accrued interest payable increased $2,000 during the year.
- Quitzau has adopted a policy of reporting the cash flows arising from the receipt and payment of dividends and interest as an operating activity.

Required:

Prepare the operating section of Quitzau's statement of cash flows for the year ended December 31, 2021, using the direct method.

P20-40. Statement of cash flows—indirect method

(L.O. 20-3, L.O. 20-5) (Difficult – 40 minutes)

Financial information for Solnickova Inc. follows:

Solnickova Inc. Balance Sheets As at December 31		
	2021	**2020**
Assets		
Cash	$ 150,000	$ 500,000
Accounts receivable	1,400,000	1,500,000
Inventory	600,000	400,000
Investments—at fair value through profit or loss	100,000	
Investments—financial asset at amortized cost	200,000	—
Property, plant, and equipment	3,250,000	3,250,000
Accumulated depreciation	(1,950,000)	(1,700,000)
Total	$ 3,750,000	$ 3,950,000
Liabilities and shareholders' equity		
Accounts payable	$ 320,000	$ 100,000
Bank loans	1,967,200	2,550,000
Bonds payable	382,800	380,000
Preferred shares	—	10,000
Ordinary shares	600,000	500,000
Retained earnings	480,000	410,000
Total	$ 3,750,000	$ 3,950,000

Additional information:

- Preferred shares were converted to common shares during the year at their book value.
- The face value of the bonds is $400,000; they pay a coupon rate of 5% per annum. The effective rate of interest is 6% per annum.
- Net income was $80,000.
- There was an ordinary stock dividend valued at $4,000 and cash dividends were also paid.
- Interest expense for the year was $125,000. Income tax expense was $20,000.
- Solnickova arranged for a $250,000 bank loan to finance the purchase of the held-to-maturity investments.
- Solnickova has adopted a policy of reporting cash flows arising from the payment of interest and dividends as operating and financing activities, respectively.
- The at fair value through profit or loss investments are held for trading purposes.

Required:

a. Prepare a statement of cash flows for the year ended December 31, 2021, using the indirect method.
b. Discuss how the transaction(s) above that are not reported on the statement of cash flows are reported in the financial statements.
c. Independent of part (a), assume that Solnickova held the $100,000 investment to meet short-term cash commitments. Summarize the impact of this change on the company's statement of cash flows for the year ended December 31, 2021.

P20-41. Statement of cash flows—operating activities—direct method

(L.O. 20-4, L.O. 20-5) (Medium – 20 minutes)

Refer to the information presented in P20-40 and the supplemental information below:

Sales	$1,600,000
Cost of goods sold	600,000
Sales and administrative expenses	525,000

Required:

a. Prepare the cash flows from operating activities section of the statement of cash flows using the direct method.

b. Compare and contrast the cash flows from operating activities prepared in this question using the direct method with that prepared in P20-40 part (a) using the indirect method. Which statement do you feel provides investors and other users of the financial statements with more useful information? Why?

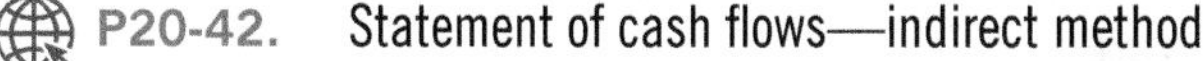

P20-42. Statement of cash flows—indirect method

(L.O. 20-3, L.O. 20-5) (Difficult – 40 minutes)

Financial information for Robinson Inc. follows:

Robinson Inc. Balance Sheets As at December 31		
	2021	**2020**
Assets		
Cash	$ 600,000	$ 400,000
Accounts receivable	1,100,000	1,300,000
Inventory	400,000	600,000
Investments—held to meet short-term cash commitments	200,000	—
Investments—financial asset at amortized cost	100,000	—
Property, plant, and equipment	4,200,000	3,400,000
Accumulated depreciation	(2,000,000)	(1,500,000)
Total	$ 4,600,000	$ 4,200,000
Liabilities and shareholders' equity		
Accounts payable	$ 100,000	$ 150,000
Bank loans	2,700,000	2,400,000
Bonds payable	413,860	416,849
Preferred shares	300,000	—
Ordinary shares	300,000	400,000
Retained earnings	786,140	833,151
Total	$ 4,600,000	$ 4,200,000

Additional information:

- Ordinary shares were redeemed during the year at their book value.
- The face value of the bonds is $400,000; they pay a coupon rate of 7% per annum. The effective rate of interest is 6% per annum.
- Net income was $100,000.
- There was an ordinary stock dividend valued at $20,000 and cash dividends were also paid.
- Interest expense for the year was $100,000. Income tax expense was $50,000.
- Robinson arranged for a $500,000 bank loan to finance the purchase of equipment.

- Robinson sold equipment with a net book value of $150,000 (original cost $200,000) for $180,000 cash.
- Robinson leased right-of-use equipment valued at $250,000.
- Robinson has adopted a policy of reporting cash flows arising from the payment of interest and dividends as operating activities.

Required:

a. Prepare a statement of cash flows for the year ended December 31, 2021, using the indirect method.
b. Discuss how the transaction(s) above that are not reported on the statement of cash flows are reported in the financial statements.

P20-43. Statement of cash flows—operating activities—direct method

(L.O. 20-5) (Medium – 15 minutes)

Refer to the information presented in P20-42 and the supplemental information below:

Sales	$2,000,000
Cost of goods sold	1,200,000
Sales and administrative expenses	30,000

Required:

Prepare the cash flows from operating activities section of the statement of cash flows using the direct method.

P20-44. Statement of cash flows—indirect method—comprehensive

(L.O. 20-3, L.O. 20-5) (Difficult – 60 minutes)

Zippo's financial statements as at December 31, 2021, appear below:

Zippo Ltd. Comparative Balance Sheet As at December 31		
	2021	2020
Cash	$ 160,000	$ 100,000
Investments held to meet short-term cash commitments	12,000	10,000
Accounts receivable	300,000	375,000
Less allowance for bad debts and doubtful accounts	(10,000)	(15,000)
Inventory	575,000	498,000
Property, plant, and equipment	1,984,000	1,396,000
Less accumulated depreciation	(650,400)	(487,000)
Intangibles, net	126,000	135,000
Deferred product development costs	564,000	417,000
	3,060,600	2,429,000
Accounts payable	81,000	84,000
Income taxes payable	12,000	2,000
Bonds payable	659,500	674,000
Ordinary shares	1,150,000	700,000
Retained earnings	1,158,100	969,000
	$3,060,600	$2,429,000

Zippo Ltd. Income Statement For the Year Ended December 31, 2021	
Sales	$2,511,100
Cost of goods sold	1,256,000
Gross profit	1,255,100
Depreciation of property, plant, and equipment	334,400
Interest expense	75,000
Other expenses	256,600
Income before income taxes	589,100
Income taxes	300,000
Net income	$ 289,100

Additional information:

- Property, plant, and equipment costing $570,000 was sold for $422,000.
- 100,000 ordinary shares were issued to acquire $450,000 of property, plant, and equipment.
- $212,000 of deferred development costs were capitalized during the year.
- The company nets many items to "Other Expenses," for example, gains and losses on fixed asset sales and some amortization.
- Bad debt expense for the year was $8,000.
- The deferred product development expenditures were all paid in cash.
- The decrease in the bonds payable account was due to the amortization of the premium.
- Zippo has adopted a policy of classifying cash outflows from interest and dividends as financing activities.

Required:

a. Prepare a statement of cash flows for Zippo Ltd. for 2021 using the indirect method.
b. Identify what supplemental disclosure, if any, is required
c. Based on your analysis of Zippo's cash flow activities during the year, do you think that you should consider investing in the company? Why or why not?

P20-45. Statement of cash flows—operating activities—direct method

(L.O. 20-5) (Medium – 15 minutes)

Based on the information set out in P20-44 above, prepare the cash flows from operating activities section of the statement of cash flows using the direct method.

P20-46. Statement of cash flows—indirect method—comprehensive

(L.O. 20-3, L.O. 20-5) (Difficult – 45 minutes)

Tymen's financial statements as at December 31, 2019, appear below (PPE denotes property, plant, and equipment):

Tymen Ltd. Comparative Balance Sheet As at December 31		
	2019	2018
Cash	$ 91,000	$ 85,000
Investments at fair value through profit or loss	11,000	13,000
Accounts receivable (net)	406,000	374,000
Inventory	501,000	522,000

(Continued)

Tymen Ltd. Comparative Balance Sheet As at December 31		
	2019	**2018**
Property, plant, and equipment (owned and right-of-use)	1,645,000	1,344,000
Less accumulated depreciation	(412,000)	(389,000)
Patent (net)	140,000	162,000
Investment in associate	465,000	312,000
	$2,847,000	$2,423,000
Accounts payable	$ 74,000	$ 77,000
Income taxes payable	12,000	16,000
Lease liability	93,000	0
Bonds payable	608,000	625,000
Deferred tax liability	396,000	442,000
Ordinary shares	329,000	239,000
Preferred shares	400,000	380,000
Retained earnings	935,000	644,000
	$2,847,000	$2,423,000

Tymen Ltd. Income Statement For the Year Ended December 31, 2019	
Sales	$3,218,575
Cost of goods sold	1,649,125
Gross profit	1,569,450
Depreciation of PPE	318,700
Patent impairment	40,000
Interest expense—bonds	36,000
Interest expense—lease liability	4,500
Other expenses	735,750
Operating income	434,500
Investment income—associate	288,000
Income before income taxes	722,500
Income taxes	293,000
Net income	$ 429,500

Additional information:

- Tymen has adopted a policy of classifying cash inflows and outflows from interest and dividends as operating activities.
- The investments at fair value through profit or loss were purchased for other than trading purposes.
- Tymen accounts for its investment in an associate using the equity method.
- The company nets many items to "Other Expenses"; for example, gains and losses on fixed asset sales.
- During the year, Tymen leased a right-of-use asset valued at $100,000. The payment made on the lease liability was made after the commencement date.
- 90,000 ordinary shares and 10,000 preferred shares were issued to acquire $110,000 of PPE.

- Tymen successfully defended its right to a patent. Related expenditures totalled $18,000.
- The decrease in the bonds payable account was due to the amortization of the premium.
- Property, plant, and equipment costing $420,000 was sold for $75,000.

Required:

a. Prepare a statement of cash flows for Tymen Ltd. for 2019 using the indirect method.
b. Identify what supplemental disclosure, if any, is required.

P20-47. Statement of cash flows—operating activities—direct method

(L.O. 20-5) (Medium – 15 minutes)

Based on the information set out in problem P20-46 above, prepare the cash flows from operating activities section of the statement of cash flows using the direct method.

P20-48. Statement of cash flows—indirect method—comprehensive income

(L.O. 20-3, L.O. 20-5) (Difficult – 60 minutes)

Luke and Angie Inc.'s financial statements as at December 31, 2021, appear below:

Luke and Angie Inc.
Comparative Balance Sheet
As at December 31

	2021	2020
Cash	$ 85,000	$ 102,000
Investments—held for meeting short-term cash commitments	26,000	26,000
Investments—at fair value through other comprehensive income	33,000	38,000
Accounts receivable	52,000	59,000
Inventory	45,000	39,000
Prepaid expenses	12,000	10,000
Investments—financial asset at amortized cost	90,000	100,000
Plant assets	850,000	490,000
Accumulated depreciation	(160,000)	(110,000)
Goodwill	42,000	82,000
	$1,075,000	$836,000
Accounts payable	$ 48,000	$ 44,000
Accrued liabilities	27,000	30,000
Cash dividends payable	10,000	18,000
Bonds payable	52,000	54,000
Mortgage payable	100,000	—
Lease liability	90,000	
Deferred income tax liability	9,000	4,000
Preferred shares	150,000	—
Ordinary shares	536,000	400,000
Retained earnings	58,000	286,000
Reserves	(5,000)	—
	$1,075,000	$836,000

Luke and Angie Inc. Statement of Comprehensive Income For the Year Ended December 31, 2021	
Sales	$860,000
Cost of sales	(422,000)
Gross profit	438,000
Interest expense	(10,000)
Depreciation expense	(70,000)
Operating expenses	(180,000)
Other gains and losses	(29,000)
Income before income tax	149,000
Income tax expense	(42,000)
Net income	107,000
Other comprehensive income: Holding loss on at fair value through other comprehensive income securities	(5,000)
Comprehensive income	$102,000

Supplemental financial information for the year ended December 31, 2021:

- Luke and Angie exchanged 1,500 preferred shares for plant assets having a fair value of $150,000.
- Luke and Angie declared and issued 1,000 ordinary shares as a stock dividend valued at $10,000.
- Goodwill was determined to be impaired and was written down $40,000.
- Luke and Angie paid $10,000 cash and signed a lease agreement for $90,000 to acquire an ROU asset valued at $100,000.
- Luke and Angie sold equipment (plant assets) with a net book value of $70,000 for $80,000 cash.
- Luke and Angie did not buy or sell any at fair value through other comprehensive income securities during the year.
- Financial asset at amortized cost securities with a book value of $10,000 were called for redemption during the year; $11,000 cash was received.
- The recorded decrease in the bonds payable account was due to the amortization of the premium.
- The deferred income tax liability represents temporary differences relating to the use of capital cost allowance for income tax reporting and straight-line depreciation for financial statement reporting.
- Luke and Angie elects to record interest and dividends paid as an operating activity.

Required:

a. From the information provided, prepare Luke and Angie's statement of cash flows for the year ended December 31, 2021, using the indirect method.
b. Prepare note disclosure(s) for non-cash transactions.

P20-49. Statement of cash flows—operating activities—direct method

(L.O. 20-5) (Medium – 15 minutes)

Based on the information presented in P20-48, prepare the cash flows from operating activities section of the statement of cash flows using the direct method.

P20-50. Statement of cash flows—indirect and direct methods—comprehensive income

(L.O. 20-3, L.O. 20-4, L.O. 20-5) (Difficult – 75 minutes)

Valli Ltd.'s financial statements as at December 31, 2021, appear below:

Valli Ltd. Comparative Balance Sheet As at December 31		
	2021	2020
Cash	$ 69,000	$ 21,000
Investments—at fair value through profit or loss held for trading purposes	25,000	22,000
Investments—at fair value through other comprehensive income	30,000	25,000
Accounts receivable	53,000	39,000
Inventory	50,000	60,000
Prepaid expenses	6,000	9,000
Plant assets	540,000	380,000
Accumulated depreciation	(140,000)	(125,000)
Goodwill	51,000	58,000
	$684,000	$489,000
Accounts payable	$ 41,000	$ 46,000
Accrued liabilities	33,000	24,000
Cash dividends payable	8,000	6,000
Bonds payable	50,000	47,000
Mortgage payable	—	136,000
Deferred income tax liability	5,000	8,000
Preferred shares	201,000	—
Ordinary shares	320,000	200,000
Retained earnings	21,000	22,000
Reserves	5,000	—
	$684,000	$489,000

Valli Ltd. Statement of Comprehensive Income For the Year Ended December 31, 2021	
Sales	$660,000
Cost of sales	(359,000)
Gross profit	301,000
Interest expense, long term	(6,000)
Depreciation expense	(25,000)
Operating expenses	(160,000)
Other gains and losses	(4,000)
Income before income tax	106,000
Income tax expense	(39,000)
Net income	67,000
Other comprehensive income: Holding gain on at fair value through other comprehensive income securities	5,000
Comprehensive income	$ 72,000

Supplemental information:

- During the year, Valli exchanged 5,000 ordinary shares for plant assets having a fair value of $100,000.
- During the year, Valli declared and issued a stock dividend of 1,000 ordinary shares. The transaction was valued at $20,000.
- During the year, goodwill was written down $7,000 to reflect a permanent impairment of the asset.
- The deferred income tax liability represents temporary differences relating to the use of capital cost allowance for income tax reporting and straight-line depreciation for financial statement reporting.
- Valli did not buy or sell any at fair value through profit or loss or at fair value through other comprehensive income securities during the year.
- The recorded increase in the bonds payable account was due to the amortization of the discount.
- Valli elects to record interest paid as an operating activity and dividends paid as a financing activity.
- During the year, Valli sold equipment (plant assets) that originally cost $40,000 for $30,000 cash.

Required:

a. From the information above, prepare Valli's statement of cash flows for the year ended December 31, 2021, using the indirect method.
b. Prepare Valli's cash flows from operating activities for the year ended December 31, 2021, using the direct method.
c. Prepare note disclosure(s) for non-cash transactions.

K. MINI-CASES

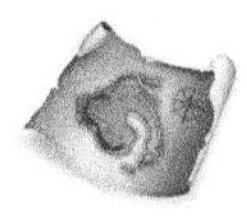

CASE 1
CompuCo Ltd.
(45 minutes)[10]

You have been asked to prepare a statement of cash flows using the balance sheet provided in Exhibit I, the income statement in Exhibit II, and the extracts from the notes provided in Exhibit III. Assume that the term deposits are cash equivalents. Further assume that CompuCo elects to report both the payment and collection of interest as operating activities.

Required:

1. Use the indirect method to prepare a statement of cash flows for 2021 on a non-comparative basis in good form from the information provided.
2. Use the direct method to prepare the cash flows from operations section of the statement of cash flows for 2021.
3. What are the objectives of a statement of cash flows prepared in accordance with generally accepted accounting principles?

Exhibit I Extracts from consolidated balance sheet

CompuCo Ltd.
Extracts from Consolidated Balance Sheet
As at December 31
($000's)

	2021	2020
Assets		
Current		
Cash and term deposits	$ 3,265	$ 3,739
Accounts receivable	23,744	18,399
Inventories	26,083	21,561
Income taxes recoverable	145	0
Prepaid expenses	1,402	1,613
	54,639	45,312
Investments (note 1)	5,960	6,962
Property, plant, and equipment (note 2)	37,332	45,700
Deferred income taxes	4,875	2,245
Goodwill	0	12,737
Intangible assets (note 3)	4,391	1,911
	$107,197	$114,867
Liabilities		
Current		
Bank indebtedness	$ 6,844	$ 6,280
Accounts payable	3,243	4,712
Current portion of long-term debt	1,800	1,200
	11,887	12,192
Long-term debt (note 4)	14,900	14,500
Total liabilities	26,787	26,692

(Continued)

[10] Reprinted from Uniform Final Examination 1999, with permission from Chartered Professional Accountants of Canada, Toronto, Canada. Any changes to the original material are the sole responsibility of the author (and/or publisher) and have not been reviewed or endorsed by the Chartered Professional Accountants of Canada.

Exhibit I Continued

CompuCo Ltd.
Extracts from Consolidated Balance Sheet
As at December 31
($000's)

	2021	2020
Shareholders' equity		
Share capital (Note 5)	79,257	62,965
Retained earnings	1,153	25,210
Total shareholders' equity	80,410	88,175
	$107,197	$114,867

Exhibit II Extracts from consolidated income statement

CompuCo Ltd.
Extracts from the Consolidated Income Statement
For the Years Ended December 31
(in $000's)

	2021	2020
Revenue		
Operating	$ 89,821	$ 68,820
Interest	1,310	446
	91,131	69,266
Expenses		
Operating	76,766	62,355
General and administrative	13,039	12,482
Depreciation and amortization	10,220	11,709
Goodwill write-off	12,737	0
Interest	1,289	1,521
Loss on sale of property, plant, and equipment	394	0
	114,445	88,067
Income (loss) before income from associates and income taxes	(23,314)	(18,801)
Income (loss) from associates (Note 1)	(2,518)	0
Income (loss) before income taxes	(25,832)	(18,801)
Recovery of income taxes	2,775	5,161
Net loss	$(23,057)	$(13,640)

Exhibit III Extracts from notes to financial statements

CompuCo Ltd.
Extracts from Notes to Financial Statements
For the Year Ended December 31
(in $000's)

1. Investments

The company's investments at December 31 are as follows:

	2021	2020
XYZ Inc. (investment in associate)		
Shares	$ 5,962	$ 5,962

(Continued)

Exhibit III Continued

CompuCo Ltd.
Extracts from Notes to Financial Statements
For the Year Ended December 31
(in $000's)

Income (loss) from associates	(2,518)	—
	3,444	$ 5,962
Other investments (financial asset at amortized cost)	2,516	1,000
	$ 5,960	$ 6,962

2. Property, plant, and equipment (PPE)

Additions to PPE for the current year amounted to $2.29 million and proceeds from the disposal of PPE amounted to $250,000.

3. Intangible assets

Qualifying development costs of intangible assets are capitalized.

4. Long-term debt

	2021	2020
Debentures	$12,500	$12,500
Bank term loans, due December 31, 2028; principal repayable $150,000 a month (2020, $100,000 a month)	4,200	3,200
	16,700	15,700
Current maturities	(1,800)	(1,200)
	$14,900	$14,500

Debentures bear interest at 12% per annum and are due in 2024. Bank term loans bear interest at 8% and the bank advanced $2.2 million during the year.

5. Share capital

On May 14, 2021, CompuCo Ltd. issued 3.8 million shares with special warrants. Net proceeds from issuing 3.8 million shares amounted to $14.393 million. Net proceeds from issuing 3.8 million warrants amounted to $899,000. On December 31, 2021, a stock dividend of $1 million was distributed.

CASE 2
Big City Gymnastics
(60 minutes)[11]

Big City Gymnastics (BCG or the Club) is a not-for-profit organization that operates a gymnastics club. BCG was incorporated in May 1983 and has operated the Club at the same facility since that time. BCG was started with a generous donation of equipment after a gymnastics competition that was held in April 1983.

BCG is governed by an elected board of directors of 10 members, all of whom are parents of athletes who train at the Club.

BCG trains both male and female athletes, from preschool to young adult. Its programs are preschool gymnastics, recreational gymnastics, and competitive gymnastics. BCG's athletes have qualified for national and international gymnastics meets, with some even going on to full scholarships at Canadian and American universities. BCG's coaches and programs are recognized by the Canadian gymnastics community as being of high quality.

Like most gymnastics clubs, BCG has paid coaching staff. Salaried staff, paid in total $20,000 a month including all required government remittances, include an office

[11] Reprinted from Uniform Final Examination 2005, with permission from Chartered Professional Accountants of Canada, Toronto, Canada. Any changes to the original material are the sole responsibility of the author (and/or publisher) and have not been reviewed or endorsed by the Chartered Professional Accountants of Canada.

manager, a program director who coaches and also oversees the program and staffing, and three head coaches who oversee, respectively, the women's competitive, men's competitive, and recreational/preschool programs.

You are the parent of a gymnast. You were appointed to the board of BCG as treasurer three-and-a-half weeks ago. During your short time as treasurer, you have interviewed the office manager (Exhibit I) to become familiar with the workings of BCG, and gathered some historical financial information (Exhibit II).

Today, July 23, 2021, the president of BCG, Jim Taylor, approached you while you were watching your daughter train at BCG's facility. He informed you that the treasurer is responsible for preparing and presenting a financial report to the BCG board of directors at each monthly board meeting. Jim mentioned that, in the past, the report usually consisted of a quick update on the cash balance in the Club's bank account. At the May 2021 board meeting, the report stated a cash balance of $19,823. At the board meeting on June 30, 2021, the cash balance was $4,324. The board was concerned about the deteriorating cash situation and wondered how it would look at the end of the fiscal year.

At previous board meetings, members often asked for more financial information but the previous treasurer was unable to provide it. Jim let you know that the lack of information caused some frustration among the board members and asks you to recommend reporting improvements to the board.

As you think about Jim's comments, you remember that, as a parent of a BCG athlete, you had your own questions about the financial situation of BCG, the success of the various programs and of the fundraisers, and so on. You tell Jim that your report will be different. You will report to the board the findings from your recent discussions and recommendations for improvement, and you will provide some insights into BCG's current financial situation.

Required:

Prepare the report, paying specific attention to (i) BCG's cash flow and (ii) the sufficiency of the financial reports currently being produced.

Exhibit I Notes from interview with office manager

The office manager is Joan Epp. She was hired three weeks ago to replace the outgoing office manager, Tom Dickens, who quit after only 11 months on the job. Joan's role as office manager:

- Receive payments from athletes' families for their gymnastics fees. These fees are paid monthly in advance. BCG accepts cash, cheques, and credit card payments. Receipts are issued upon request.
- Tally the cash received and credit card slips on a deposit sheet and enter the amounts monthly into the accounting records. Deposits are made on an occasional basis at the nearby bank branch, once sufficient cash has been accumulated to warrant making a deposit.
- Receive and pay suppliers' invoices. One signature is required for all cheques. Signing officers are the office manager, the treasurer, and the president.

Joan reviewed the records on her first day. She had examined the paid invoices, stored in a filing cabinet, to become familiar with BCG's operations. Joan mentioned that there were several small cheques, most of which were posted as debits to the revenue accounts, that did not have corresponding invoices. Most of those cheques were made out to Tom Dickens. Also, one large cheque for $5,617 had a note that it was to reimburse Tom for the purchase of a trampoline, but no supporting invoice was attached. Joan also noted there were several cheques to suppliers, totalling $820, that are still outstanding.

As far as Joan is aware, there is no formal policy established for approval of spending. Joan can order what she needs for her job. Coaches can order the equipment or other gymnastics materials that they believe are needed for BCG's various programs.

(*Continued*)

Exhibit I Continued

BCG has a chocolate fundraiser where athletes sell chocolate bars for $3 apiece. An envelope marked Chocolate Fundraiser was in Joan's desk. It had $3,750 cash in it, with various notes on who had paid for chocolate bars. The drawer is locked when Joan is out of the office. Joan will deposit the money as soon as all the chocolate bars are sold, so that she will know the exact amount raised. The chocolate supplier shipped 1,500 chocolate bars. Joan received an invoice for $3,300, dated July 20, from the chocolate supplier. The terms on the invoice are that any unsold chocolate bars cannot be returned and, if payment is made within 30 days, the supplier's discount is 20%.

Exhibit II CA's notes on BCG's historical financial information

The fiscal year-end of the Club is August 31.

Revenues are seasonal. The fall and winter recreational sessions are busy. The competitive season starts in September and runs through June. The spring recreational session appears to have one-third less revenue than the other two sessions due to the start of competing outdoor sports in the spring (baseball, football, soccer, etc.). The two summer months provide approximately 10% of BCG's annual revenue because of school summer holidays. Some weekly gymnastics camps are run, but attendance is muted due to athletes being away or taking time off. In addition to the chocolate fundraiser, BCG holds two other fundraisers during the year.

BCG receives a grant of $1,200 per month from the citywide gymnastics organization.

General and administrative costs include building rent and utilities, which combined are approximately $2,000 per month.

The net book value of BCG's equipment was $54,563 as of August 31, 2020.

BCG does not have any bank loans or lines of credit because it has never needed credit.

Exhibit III BCG financial data produced by the system

	10 months ended June 30, 2021	12 months ended August 31, 2020
Cash Receipts		
Donations/grants	$ 20,549	$ 22,547
Facility rentals	9,094	12,402
Fundraising activities	68,685	73,158
Fees, recreational and competitive	201,864	209,402
	300,192	317,509
Cash Disbursements		
General and administrative	45,301	45,465
Repairs and maintenance	50,281	50,419
Salaries, benefits, and travel	220,603	217,056
Fundraising activities	6,635	9,219
	322,820	322,159
Net change in cash	(22,628)	(4,650)
Beginning cash	26,952	31,602
Ending cash	$ 4,324	$ 26,952

CASE 3 Community Care Services

(60 minutes)[12]

Community Care Services (CCS) is a not-for-profit organization formed in January 2021 and is located in the rural community of Thomas County. CCS is dedicated to serving the needs of seniors. CCS's informational literature and website contain the following statement:

> Our mission is to provide a secure retirement community in a carefully selected location in the heart of our beloved Thomas County. Our organization provides a warm, attractive setting as the surroundings for a vibrant, healthy living space—one that our residents deserve. Our vision is to serve the community, and it encompasses accommodation and leisure as well as the provision of health care.

Background information on CCS is provided in Exhibit I, and some details of CCS's operations are included in Exhibit II. The executive director, Janet Admer, joined the organization in the last month and was recruited from a nearby city. Janet has extensive experience in managing the construction and operations of a major hotel. It was the board of directors' view that, even though Janet's salary of $120,000 seemed high, her hospitality-industry skills would be a good contribution to the operation of CCS.

It is now November 15, 2021. You have known Janet Admer for many years, and she has approached you for advice. Janet has asked your firm, Yelt and Rerdan, Chartered Professional Accountants, to advise her and the board on the issues facing CCS as it moves from the construction phase to the operating phase. Janet has prepared a cash budget, included in Exhibit III, and she is very pleased that her estimate indicates that a surplus will exist in the first year of full operation. Because the board members would like to make sure that CCS will have sufficient cash to meet its obligations as it starts to operate the residences, Janet wants you to look at her budget. The board had approved obtaining a bank loan to complete the construction phase but is still concerned that there is a risk that CCS will run out of cash by the end of the year.

CCS has already appointed KZY, Chartered Professional Accountants, as the auditor, and KZY will be reporting on the first fiscal year-end of December 31, 2021. Janet has deliberately not assigned the engagement to you and your firm so that the functions of auditor and advisor will be independent.

The board is made up of highly respected individuals in the community; however, the members have very little experience in running an operation such as CCS. Janet would like you to help her determine the kind of information, financial and otherwise, that would be useful to them to evaluate the performance of CCS in meeting its goals.

You are pleased at the prospect of bringing in a client to the firm, and you have discussed the engagement with a partner at Yelt and Rerdan. The partner has agreed to accept the engagement and has asked you to prepare a draft report addressing Janet's requests.

Required:

Prepare the draft report addressing Janet's requests, including a comprehensive analysis of CCS's cash flow situation and an analysis of CCS's information needs.

Exhibit I Background information

In the last decade, foreign investors who believed that land was a bargain as a result of the weak Canadian dollar have purchased many of the farms in Thomas County. The community was concerned that there were no residential alternatives in the county for older farmers who left their farms as a result of a sale or retirement.

Mr. MacDougall, an advocate for the local farmers and seniors, started with the idea of providing residential options to the families. He was instrumental in setting up CCS and was appointed the chairman of the board. He donated 10 acres of land from his farm for the facility.

(*Continued*)

[12] Reprinted from Uniform Final Examination 2003, with permission from Chartered Professional Accountants of Canada, Toronto, Canada. Any changes to the original material are the sole responsibility of the author (and/or publisher) and have not been reviewed or endorsed by the Chartered Professional Accountants of Canada.

Exhibit I Continued

He also donated $1 million for the construction of the residential units. The conditions of the donations were as follows:

1. The land can never be sold.
2. At least one-third of all residential units must be provided to low-income seniors who must meet an annual income test, and the rent charged cannot generate a surplus on the operational costs of these units. (These units have been designated as Building C.)
3. At least one-third of all residential units must provide full health care services. (These units have been designated as Building A, commonly referred to as the "Nursing Home.")
4. One-half of the sales proceeds from the retirement home sales units must be maintained in a separate account to be used for the maintenance and capital repairs of the complex.

If these terms are not met, the land reverts to Mr. MacDougall, or to a special MacDougall trust if the breach occurs after the death of Mr. MacDougall.

The layout of the complex is as follows:

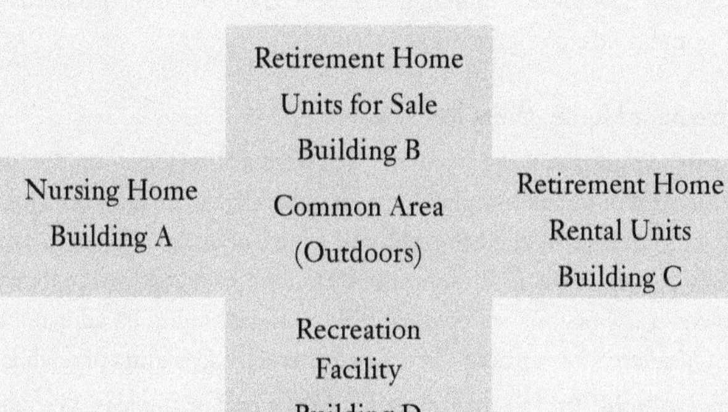

Construction began in February 2021 and is almost complete. The nursing home and both retirement homes are completed. The recreation facility is scheduled to be completed by December 31. All of the units in the nursing home and the rental retirement home have been assigned to residents. Sales contracts have been signed for all of the units in the other retirement home. These sales are expected to close in January 2022. The complex is expected to be fully operational in early January 2022.

The costs of construction and the budget are as follows:

	Original budget	Estimate to December 2021*
Land Improvements	$ 170,000	$ 168,000
Building A – Nursing Home	300,000	421,000
Building B – Retirement Homes for Sale	250,000	250,000
Building C – Retirement Homes for Rent	275,000	270,000
Building D – Recreation Facility	150,000	100,000
Equipment and Furniture	150,000	150,000
	$1,295,000	$1,359,000

* Total actual cost incurred plus revised estimates to complete

(Continued)

Exhibit I Continued

Source of funds	
Mr. MacDougall	$1,000,000
Thomas County Grant	200,000
Bank loan—no interest until January 1, 2022, then payments of $20,000 per month, plus annual interest of 5%.	200,000
	$1,400,000

Exhibit II Additional information

Building A—Nursing Home

This building has 20 beds and its operations will be funded by the provincial government's Ministry of Community and Social Services (the ministry). The funding formula is $130 per day per bed, and any surplus from operations must be returned to the ministry. To determine the surplus, the ministry will allow direct costs plus a reasonable allocation of overheads. The ministry, which provides some funding, has requested the audit of the annual financial statements as part of the funding requirement.

Building B—Retirement Home, Units for Sale

There are 10 unfurnished units and the residents will have a "life-lease" on the land, which means that the residents will have the right to use the portion of the land on which the building is located but they will not own it, and the right will expire at either the death of the resident or sooner if mutually agreed to. In addition to the purchase price, the residents will also pay $550 per month to cover the occupancy costs, and this amount could be adjusted to meet actual costs if necessary. There are two types of "sales" and there are five units of each type:

Type I—The units are "sold" for fair market value. At the end of the lease (i.e., death or resident moves out), CCS must pay back the full price paid.

Type II—The units are "sold" for 120% of fair market value. At the end of the lease (i.e., death or resident moves out), CCS must pay back the fair market value at the date the resident purchased the unit plus 50% of any increase in value.

For both types, CCS has the right to select the next occupant, and the price to be charged for the unit is to be based on fair market value and must be supported by an independent opinion. The fair market value for all the initial sales was determined to be $100,000. The board is confident that the value of these units will increase. These units are designed to appeal to those who want a "premium" unit and can afford to pay for it.

Building C—Retirement Home, Rental Units

There are 15 unfurnished units. The rent will be approximately $400 per month per unit and includes all utilities, cable, etc. To be eligible for these units, the applicants must prove that the combined annual income available to them is not more than $20,000. CCS will receive an annual operating grant of $200,000 from the ministry.

Building D—Recreation Facility

When it is completed, Building D will hold the administration offices and a recreation facility to be used for social activities. The residents of all buildings can use the common area and recreation facility.

Other

Each of the four buildings has a staff member employed as the "Program Director." Each program director has an annual salary of $60,000. The total administrative costs incurred in 2021 are expected to be limited to $115,000.

Exhibit III Budgeted cash flows

Budgeted operating cash flows for the Year Ending December 31, 2022 (in $000's)	
Cash inflows	
Government funding—Nursing Home (20 beds × $130 × 365 days)	$ 949
Government funding—Retirement Home rental units	200
Sales proceeds—Retirement Home sales units	1,100
Occupancy fees—Retirement Home sales units (10 units × $550 × 12 months)	66
Rent—Retirement Home rental units (15 units × $400 × 12 months)	72
Interest (same amount as earned in 2021)	29
	2,416
Cash outflows	
Salaries and benefits (including medical staff costs of $260)	850
Medical supplies	55
Furniture and equipment (Nursing Home and Administration)	44
Food costs—Nursing Home	160
Staff training (one-time cost)	34
Repairs and maintenance	23
Communications, office, etc.	15
Utilities and property taxes	23
Insurance	10
	1,214
Excess of cash inflows over cash outflows	$1,202

CASE 4 Enviro Ltd.

(60 minutes)[13]

You are employed by McDowell and Partners, Chartered Professional Accountants (M&P). A new client, Community Finance Corporation (CFC), approached M&P for assistance. Enviro Ltd. (Enviro) has asked CFC for a loan of $10 million in the form of long-term debt to fund capital expenditures and other operating requirements. CFC has already conducted a general assessment of Enviro but now needs an accounting firm to look closely at the financial aspects, including the areas of financial risk. In particular, CFC needs to be assured that it will receive the payments of principal and interest over the term of the loan. M&P has accepted the engagement and is responsible for preparing a report to CFC.

It is now August 2021. Enviro's board of directors have provided both CFC and M&P with recent financial statements (Exhibit I) and extracts from the working papers of Enviro's auditors, Y&Z, for the most recent year-end (Exhibit II). The engagement partner wants you to prepare a memo addressing CFC's concerns.

Required:

Prepare the memo requested by the engagement partner.

[13] Reprinted from Uniform Final Examination 2002, with permission from Chartered Professional Accountants of Canada, Toronto, Canada. Any changes to the original material are the sole responsibility of the author (and/ or publisher) and have not been reviewed or endorsed by the Chartered Professional Accountants of Canada.

Exhibit I Extracts from financial statements

Extracts from the Financial Statements of Enviro Ltd.
Consolidated Balance Sheet
As at June 30
(audited, in $000's)

	2021	2020	2019
Assets			
Current assets			
Cash	$ 15	$ 105	$ 655
Marketable securities	0	870	1,495
Accounts receivable	3,870	3,705	3,580
Inventory			
Metals and scrap	7,775	5,260	4,005
Other	610	585	570
Prepaid expenses	130	120	110
	12,400	10,645	10,415
Land	910	1,160	1,160
Building and equipment	8,985	8,720	8,570
Accumulated depreciation	(2,880)	(2,290)	(1,720)
Waste disposal equipment, net of depreciation	2,060	1,435	1,410
Development cost, net of depreciation	330	240	390
Goodwill	640	700	770
Investment in Klens & Breeth	4,990	3,730	3,160
	$27,435	$24,340	$24,155
Liabilities			
Current liabilities			
Bank demand loan, secured	$ 3,000	$ 2,000	$ 2 ,200
Accounts payable and accrued liabilities	3,815	1,880	1,185
Other liabilities	790	580	315
	7,605	4,460	3,700
Mortgage payable, 12%, due 2022	2,310	2,490	2,670
Notes payable, 13%, due 2022	4,000	4,000	4,000
Bank term loan, 12%, due 2023	2,500	2,200	2,400
	16,415	13,150	12,770
Shareholders' equity			
Ordinary shares	5,000	5,000	5,000
Preferred shares, 11% cumulative dividend	4,000	4,000	4,000
Retained earnings	2,020	2,190	2,385
	11,020	11,190	11,385
	$27,435	$24,340	$24,155

(*Continued*)

Exhibit I Continued

Enviro Ltd.
Extracts from the Financial Statements
Consolidated Income Statements
For the Year Ended June 30
(audited, in $000's)

	2021	2020	2019
Revenues	$ 9,660	$10,450	$ 8,795
Expenses			
Cost of goods sold	3,180	3,360	2,265
Wages and benefits	3,420	3,210	2,370
Depreciation	950	790	615
Maintenance and insurance	1,440	1,470	1,305
General and administrative	1,335	1,165	865
Gain on disposal of securities	(360)	(910)	0
Gain on sale of land	(1,105)	0	0
	8,860	9,085	7,420
Income before income from associates	800	1,365	1,375
Income from associate—Klens & Breeth	1,260	570	490
Income before interest and income tax expenses	2,060	1,935	1,865
Interest expense	1,670	1,590	1,005
Income tax expense	120	100	320
Net income	$ 270	$ 245	$ 540

Exhibit II Extracts from working papers

Extracts from Y&Z's Working Papers
For the Year Ended June 30, 2021

Enviro

1. Enviro is a holding company that was incorporated under federal legislation several years ago as an investment company for a small group of investors. Enviro owns the following:
   - 100% of the voting shares of Waste Disposal Corporation (WDC), which collects and disposes of environmentally hazardous chemicals.
   - 50% of a partnership that specializes in designing advertisements for organizations that promote improvements to the environment. The partnership is called Klens & Breeth (KB). KB in turn owns all the voting shares of two corporations involved in advertising design and development.
   - 100% of the voting shares of Scrap Metal Enterprises Ltd. (SMEL), which deals in the collection and sale of non-precious metals (copper, iron, and others).
2. Enviro's existing bank loans are secured by a first charge on receivables. The mortgage payable is secured by a first mortgage on the land and building. The notes payable are secured by inventory and are due in August 2022. The notes payable cannot be renewed because payment in full has been demanded.
3. Enviro is insured for liability and accidents but not for theft and fire.
4. Enviro paid dividends on preferred shares of $440,000 in each of 2019, 2020, and 2021. In addition, the company paid $100,000 of dividends on common shares in 2019.

(*Continued*)

Exhibit II Continued

WDC

1. To meet government requirements, WDC's disposal equipment has to be upgraded by October 1, 2022; otherwise, large segments of the operations will have to be suspended and other safe disposal methods will have to be found—an unlikely prospect. Upgrading is really the only alternative if WDC is to avoid having to cancel contracts and incur significant cancellation penalties. Approximately $7 million is needed as soon as possible.

2. Using its own waste disposal technology, WDC builds some of the equipment that it needs to process certain wastes. During fiscal 2021, the following expenditures were capitalized:

Components and parts	$322,100
Wages and benefits	208,220
Overhead costs	208,000
Interest on borrowings	12,680
	$751,000

The overhead costs are allocated based on roughly 100% of wages and benefits.

KB

1. We do not audit KB but have reviewed the audit working papers and have had discussions with KB's auditors. KB's income for the year ended March 31, 2021, was $2,520,000, and Enviro has appropriately accounted for its share using the equity method of accounting. Enviro is a silent partner. However, Enviro provides major assistance in developing new client contracts for KB. The other partner needs the partnership form of ownership for various purposes. Among the more significant transactions during fiscal 2021 were the following:
   a. KB accounts for its investments on an equity basis; its subsidiaries paid cash dividends in fiscal 2021 of $1,200,000. KB retained these funds to develop new technology.
   b. KB earned $1,875,000 from a federal government contract that has expired this month. Most of the fee was recognized in income in 2021 because the ideas had already been generated for another project and few additional costs were necessary.
   c. The other partner of KB operates an advertising firm for non-environmental promotion. KB paid this firm $895,000 for a variety of services.

SMEL

1. SMEL's scrap metal piles are large, and it is difficult to estimate the quantity of metal in the piles. To satisfy ourselves, we photographed the piles, compared them geometrically to photographs of previous years, and discussed important issues with management. We also conducted extra checks of the perpetual inventory system against arrival and departure weights of trucks. The system was operating satisfactorily, but estimates were necessary for wastage.
2. The scrap metal is recorded at cost because resale prices of scrap vary considerably. If prices are low, SMEL stores the metals until selling prices improve. Management believes there is no need to sell at a loss.
3. The government requires a soil test of SMEL's scrap yard every five years. The most recent soil test was conducted four years ago.

CASE 5
Statement of Cash Flows
(20 minutes)

You are the assistant controller for StrongBar Ltd., a company that specializes in making energy bars and other high-protein snacks. The company's CFO, Diana Cash, has just stopped by your office. She is meeting with a consortium of banks this afternoon regarding StrongBar's upcoming public debt issue. The bankers have asked her to present the statement of cash flows for 2021 in the meeting. She further states that the controller,

Exhibit I Balance sheets at December 31

	2021	2020
Cash	$ 69,000	$ 41,000
Trading securities	30,000	26,500
Accounts receivable	86,000	68,000
Inventory	36,000	50,000
Prepaid expenses	6,000	9,000
Plant assets	450,000	380,000
Accumulated depreciation	(150,000)	(125,000)
	$ 527,000	$ 449,500
Accounts payable	$ 60,032	$ 53,000
Accrued liabilities	18,000	19,000
Deferred tax liability	5,000	8,000
Bonds	0	146,500
Convertible bonds	154,968	0
Common shares	230,000	200,000
Retained earnings	31,000	22,000
Reserves—conversion rights	25,000	0
Reserves—accumulated other comprehensive income	3,000	1,000
	$ 527,000	$ 449,500

James Well, was supposed to provide her the statement of cash flows, but this morning he called in sick. She is wondering if you can prepare the report for her. She remembers that yesterday Mr. Well started working on the report and suggests that you check his desk for his notes. You tell Ms. Cash that you will try to help her, and promise to update her in a few hours. Nervously you walk to Mr. Well's office and, searching his desk, you find the following information.

Additional information:

1. In the beginning of 2021, StrongBar had 20,000 shares outstanding.
2. On March 1, the company declared and distributed a 5% stock dividend. At that date StrongBar's shares were trading for $10.
3. A cash dividend of $18,000 was declared and paid in October 2021.
4. On May 1, the company issued common shares for cash.
5. On January 1, 2021, StrongBar extinguished all of its outstanding bonds and replaced them with a new issue of convertible bonds. The old bonds had a face value of 150,000. To induce the retirement of the bonds, it offered bondholders $10,000 above the market value of the bonds. At that date the bonds were trading at $0.99. On the same day, StrongBar issued 150,000, 9%, five-year convertible bonds. The bonds pay interest *annually* on December 31 each year. Similar bonds without conversion options are traded to yield 8%. The company does not remember what the proceeds from the issue were, but the controller's notes say that the fair value of the conversion rights at issuance was $25,000. Because the terms of the old bonds and the new bonds were substantially different, those transactions are not considered a modification of debt.

6. StrongBar has two investments, as follows:

Name	Initial Investment	Fair Value Dec. 31, 2020	Fair Value Dec. 31, 2021	Classification
Prot-In	$13,000	$13,500	$15,000	At fair value through profit or loss
ProBar	12,000	13,000	15,000	At fair value through other comprehensive income

7. In 2021, the company sold plant assets with a gross book value of $30,000 and accumulated depreciation of $25,000. There was no gain or loss on the sale.

One thing that you are unable to locate is the income statement or information about the company's net income. At first you are worried that this will mean you will not be able to prepare the statement of cash flows. However, after carefully examining the information, you feel relief as you realize that this is not going to be a problem, and you start preparing the report.

StrongBar is a public Canadian company located in Vancouver. StrongBar uses the indirect method for reporting the operating activities section of the statement of cash flows. StrongBar's policy is to classify interest expense as an operating activity, dividends paid as a financing activity, and interest and dividends received as investing activities.

Required:

1. Explain how it is possible to prepare the statement of cash flows without having the income statement.
2. Prepare the statement of cash flows. Assume that the bond premium is included in the same category as the underlying interest expense. Ignore the disclosure requirements pertaining to interest and dividends paid and received, income taxes paid, and non-cash transactions.
3. Now assume that the company classified the dividends paid as an operating activity. Without regenerating the entire report again, explain what will change in the statement of cash flows. Be specific.
4. Suppose investors are unaware that companies can choose how to classify interest expense and dividends paid. How can this affect their assessment of StrongBar's statement of cash flows?

APPENDIX A
Time Value of Money and Simple Valuation Techniques

This appendix reviews several aspects of the time value of money, which is covered in introductory finance. The first section looks at the basic relationships and formulas for future and present values. The second section goes through the practical approaches (formulas, calculators, and spreadsheets) to make computations frequently encountered in accounting applications. The third section briefly discusses simple valuation techniques used to estimate the value of assets and enterprises. The end of this appendix includes present and future value tables.

A. FUTURE VALUES AND PRESENT VALUES

The time value of money is a concept that will be useful for many parts of this text. It is simply the idea that people value a dollar received today more than a dollar received tomorrow, next week, or next year. We can ask the question, "In order to be as satisfied as being paid a dollar now, how much would you need to be paid in one year's time?" If the answer is \$1.10, then the interest rate you demand is 10% (i.e., 10% more than \$1). We usually use "*r*" to denote the interest rate, also called the discount rate. Once we have an interest rate, we can express the value of money at any point in time, at the present time or in the future, giving rise to the concepts of present value and future value.

1. Future value of a single sum received now

In the example just given, \$1.10 is the future value in one year's time of \$1 today. Changing the example slightly, if you invest \$100 now, you expect to obtain \$110 in a year's time because you would earn 10% interest. If you invest for two years, you would have $\$100 \times 1.10 \times 1.10 = \$100 \times 1.10^2 = \$121$. Formally, we can express this relationship by the following equation:

Exhibit A-1 Future value of a single sum

$$FV_t = PV_0 \times (1 + r)^t$$

In this equation, FV_t denotes future value (a dollar amount) at time t, PV_0 denotes present value (a dollar amount) at time 0, and r is the interest rate per period. Time is usually measured in years, but it could be any length of time, as long as the interest rate is defined accordingly.

2. Present value of a single sum to be received in the future

We can rearrange the equation in Exhibit A-1 to isolate PV_0, the present value at time 0, as follows:

Exhibit A-2 Present value of a single sum

$$PV_0 = \frac{FV_t}{(1 + r)^t}$$

Thus, the present value of \$121 to be received in two years' time when the interest rate is 10% per year is $PV_0 = \$121 \div 1.10^2 = \$121 \div 1.21 = \$100$. The diagram in Exhibit A-3 summarizes the relationship between the present and future values just calculated.

Exhibit A-3 Timeline illustrating the relationship between present and future values

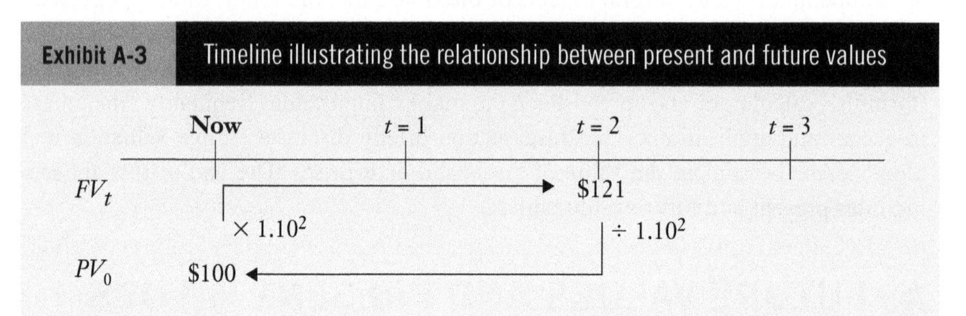

One reason for computing future and present values is to allow us to add together cash flows that occur at different times. For example, if you were to receive \$100 next year, \$100 in two years, and \$100 three years from now, how much are you really receiving? Simply adding together the three cash flows is not appropriate because the cash flows occur at different times and each cash flow has a different time value of money. Instead, all the cash flows need to be expressed in terms of one particular point in time. In most instances, it is most convenient to choose the present time as the point of reference. If the interest rate is 10%, we can compute the present value of each of the three cash flows and then they can be summed up, as follows:

Exhibit A-4 Computation of present value of three cash flows of \$100 each

$$\begin{aligned} PV_0 &= \$100/1.1 + \$100/1.1^2 + \$100/1.1^3 \\ &= \$90.91 + \$82.64 + \$75.13 \\ &= \$248.68 \end{aligned}$$

As you can see, the present value (\$248.68) is considerably less than the simple sum of the three cash flows (\$300). The diagram in Exhibit A-5 illustrates this computation.

Exhibit A-5 Timeline showing the computation of present value of three cash flows

	Now	$t = 1$	$t = 2$	$t = 3$
CF_t		\$100	\$100	\$100
PV_0	\$ 90.91	÷ 1.10		
PV_0	\$ 82.64		÷ 1.10^2	
PV_0	\$ 75.13			÷ 1.10^3
PV_0	\$248.68			

3. Present value of a perpetuity

A **perpetuity** is a series of cash flows in equal amounts occurring at regular intervals for an infinite number of periods. The present value of a perpetuity is not infinite, even though the cash flows occur for an infinite number of periods. In fact, we can compute the value of a perpetuity using the following formula, where each cash flow occurs at the end of period *t*:

perpetuity A series of cash flows in equal amounts occurring at regular intervals for an infinite number of periods.

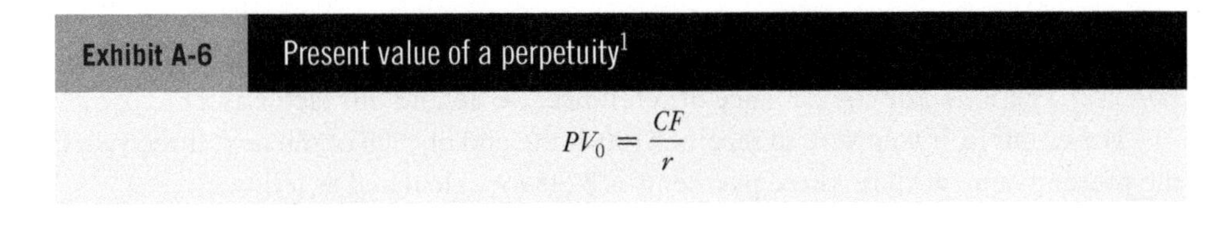

Exhibit A-6 Present value of a perpetuity[1]

$$PV_0 = \frac{CF}{r}$$

For example, if each cash flow, denoted *CF* in the formula, is $100 and received at the end of each year forever into the future, and the discount rate is 10%, then $PV =$ $100 ÷ 0.10 = $1,000.

4. Present value of a perpetuity with growth

Instead of the same cash flow every period, a **perpetuity with growth** is one in which the cash flows grow at a constant rate. The present value of a perpetuity with the cash flow CF_1 occurring at the end of one year and growing at rate *g*, discounted at rate *r*, is given by the following formula:

perpetuity with growth A series of cash flows occurring at regular intervals for an infinite number of periods with cash flows that grow at a constant rate.

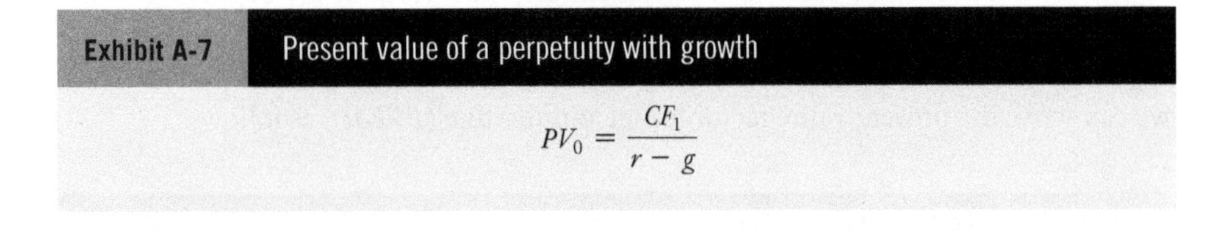

Exhibit A-7 Present value of a perpetuity with growth

$$PV_0 = \frac{CF_1}{r - g}$$

5. Present value of an ordinary annuity

The pattern of cash flows illustrated by the computation in Exhibit A-5 is an example of an **annuity**, which is a series of cash flows in equal amounts occurring at regular intervals (i.e., $CF_1 = CF_2 = \ldots$). In this example, $100 is received at the end of each of three years. In addition, this is an **ordinary annuity** because the cash flows occur at the *end* of each period. In comparison, an **annuity due** is one in which the cash flows occur at the *beginning* of each period.

annuity A series of cash flows in equal amounts occurring at regular intervals.

ordinary annuity An annuity with cash flows at the *end* of each period.

annuity due An annuity with cash flows at the *beginning* of each period.

In cases where there are a small number of cash flows, as in the example illustrated in Exhibit A-5, we can compute the present value by computing the present value of each individual cash flow and then adding them up. However, this approach is laborious even using a spreadsheet if the number of cash flows in the annuity is large. Instead, using the following formula is often more efficient:

[1] For those curious as to the source of this formula, it is an application of the general formula for the sum of an infinite series from high school algebra: $\Sigma_{t=1}^{\infty}(1/a^t) = 1/(a-1)$. For example, if $a = 2$, then ½ + ¼ + ... = 1, which is $1/(a-1) = 1/(2-1)$. If $a = 10$, then 0.1 + 0.01 + 0.001 + ... = 0.111 ... = 1/9. If $a = 1 + r$, then $[1/(1+r)] + [1/(1+r)^2] + \ldots = 1/(1 + r - 1) = 1/r$.

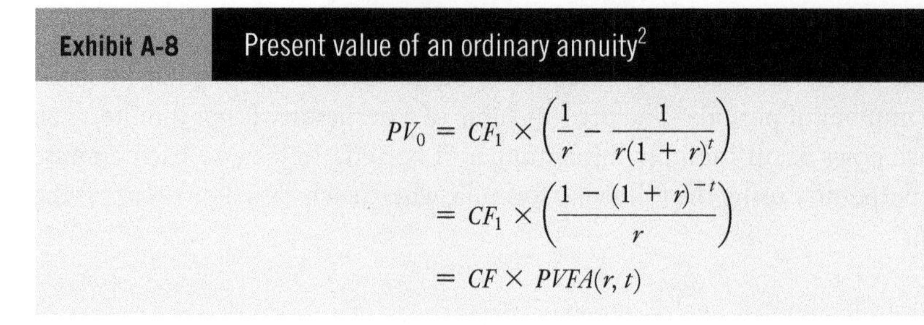

Exhibit A-8 Present value of an ordinary annuity[2]

$$PV_0 = CF_1 \times \left(\frac{1}{r} - \frac{1}{r(1+r)^t}\right)$$
$$= CF_1 \times \left(\frac{1-(1+r)^{-t}}{r}\right)$$
$$= CF \times PVFA(r, t)$$

The term in parentheses is known as the *present value factor for an annuity* at discount rate r for t periods. For convenience of reference, we denote this factor as $PVFA(r, t)$.

For example, if you were to receive \$100 at the end of each of the next three years, the present value of those three payments is \$248.69, calculated as follows:

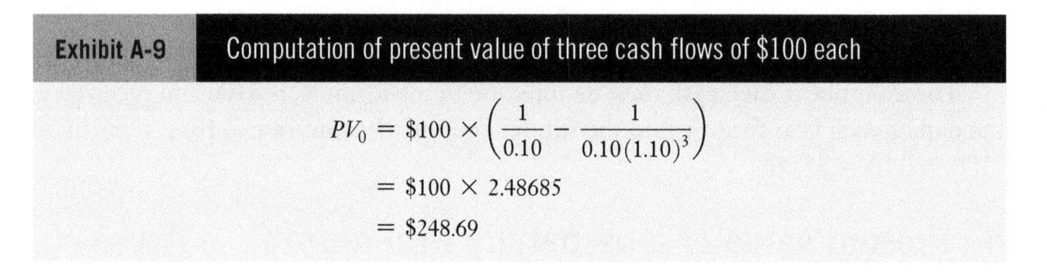

Exhibit A-9 Computation of present value of three cash flows of \$100 each

$$PV_0 = \$100 \times \left(\frac{1}{0.10} - \frac{1}{0.10(1.10)^3}\right)$$
$$= \$100 \times 2.48685$$
$$= \$248.69$$

Of course, this is the same as the answer obtained using the calculations in Exhibit A-5.

6. Present value of an annuity due

As mentioned above, the cash flows for an annuity due occur at the beginning of the period. The simplest way to deal with such annuities is to recognize that, setting aside the first cash flow, the remainder is just an ordinary annuity with one less period. Thus, we can write the present value factor for an annuity due ($PVFAD$) as follows:

Exhibit A-10 Present value factor for an annuity due *(PVFAD)*

$$PVFAD(r, t) = 1 + PVFA(r, t-1)$$
$$= 1 + \left(\frac{1}{r} - \frac{1}{r(1+r)^{t-1}}\right)$$

For example, if you receive three cash flows of \$100 each at the beginning of each of three years, and the discount rate is 10%, then:

Exhibit A-11 Present value of \$100 received at the beginning of each of three years

$$PV_0 = CF \times PVFAD(10\%, 3)$$
$$= \$100 \times \left(1 + \frac{1}{0.10} - \frac{1}{0.10\,(1.10)^2}\right)$$
$$= \$100 \times 2.73554$$
$$= \$273.55$$

[2] This formula is derived from the perpetuity formula. A \$1 annuity of t periods is equivalent to a \$1 perpetuity minus a \$1 perpetuity that starts at the end of period t. The first perpetuity has value $1/r$. The second perpetuity starts after t periods, so it has value $(1/r) \times 1/(1+r)^t = 1/r(1+r)^t$. Thus, $PVAF = (1/r) - 1/r(1+r)^t$.

Notice that this present value of \$273.55 is 10% more than \$248.69, the value of the ordinary annuity (\$248.69 × 1.1 = \$273.55). So another way to think of an annuity due is to imagine that it is like an ordinary annuity with every payment shifted by one period closer to the present time. Thus, we can also express the present value annuity factor for an annuity due as follows:

Exhibit A-12 Alternate formula for present value factor for an annuity due

$$PVFAD(r, t) = PVFA(r, t) \times (1 + r)$$
$$= \left(\frac{1}{r} - \frac{1}{r(1 + r)^t}\right) \times (1 + r)$$

B. COMPUTATION TECHNIQUES

The previous section reviewed the fundamentals of present and future values, as well as the formulas for computing these values. Exhibit A-13 summarizes techniques to make these computations using formulas, a financial calculator (Texas Instruments BA II Plus), or a spreadsheet (Microsoft Excel). Notation is as follows:

- FV = future value
- PV = present value
- CF = cash flow
- r = interest rate per period
- t = number of periods
- g = growth rate
- $PVFA$ = present value factor for an annuity

Exhibit A-13 Basic computation techniques for future and present values

Objective	Example	Formula calculation	Texas Instruments BA II Plus	Microsoft Excel
FV of a single sum	A \$100 investment earns 5% interest compounded annually. Compute the future value of this investment at the end of 10 years.	$FV_t = PV_0 \times (1 + r)^t$ $FV_{10} = 100\,(1.05)^{10}$ $= \$162.89$	−100 [PV] 5 [I/Y] 10 [N] [CPT] [FV] [Output] 162.89	Input: =FV (5%, 10, , −100) Output: 162.89
PV of a single sum	You agree to pay \$162.89 at the end of 10 years. If the interest rate is 5%, how much would you need to set aside today to fund that future payment?	$PV_0 = \frac{FV_t}{(1 + r)^t}$ $PV_0 = \frac{162.89}{(1.05)^{10}}$ $= 100.00$	−162.89 [FV] 5 [I/Y] 10 [N] [CPT] [PV] [Output] 100.00	Input: =PV (5%, 10, , −162.89) Output: 100.00

(*Continued*)

Exhibit A-13 Continued

PV of a perpetuity	An investment promises to pay \$100 at the end of each year indefinitely. If the discount rate is 5%, how much would it cost to buy the investment?	$PV_0 = \frac{CF_t}{r}$ $PV_0 = \frac{100}{0.05}$ $= 2{,}000$	No special financial functions. Use normal arithmetic functions.	No special financial function. Input according to formula.
PV of a perpetuity with growth	An investment promises to make a stream of payments indefinitely, with payments starting at \$100 at the end of the first year and growing at 1% each year. If the interest rate is 5%, how much would it cost to buy the investment?	$PV_0 = \frac{CF_1}{r - g}$ $PV_0 = \frac{100}{0.05 - 0.01}$ $= 2{,}500$	No special financial functions. Use normal arithmetic functions.	No special financial function. Input according to formula.
PV of an ordinary annuity	You promise to pay \$100 at the end of each year for 10 years. If the interest rate is 5%, how much would you need to set aside now to fund these 10 payments?	$PV_0 = CF_1 \times PVFA(r, t)$ $= CF_1 \times \left(\frac{1}{r} - \frac{1}{r(1 + r)^t}\right)$ $PV_0 = 100 \times PVFA(5\%, 10)$ $= 100 \times \left(\frac{1}{0.05} - \frac{1}{0.05(1.05)^{10}}\right)$ $= 100 \times 7.7217$ $= 772.17$	−100 PMT 5 I/Y 10 N CPT PV [Output] 772.17	Input: =PV(5%, 10, −100) Output: -772.17
PV of an annuity due	You promise to pay \$100 at the beginning of each year for 10 years. If the interest rate is 5%, how much would you need to set aside now to fund these 10 payments?	$PV_0 = CF_1 \times [1 + PVFA(r, t - 1)]$ $= CF_1 \times \left(1 + \frac{1}{r} - \frac{1}{r(1 + r)^{t-1}}\right)$ $PV_0 = 100 \times [1 + PVFA(5\%, 9)]$ $= 100 \times \left(1 + \frac{1}{0.05} - \frac{1}{0.05(1.05)^9}\right)$ $= 100 \times 8.1078$ $= 810.78$	2ND BGN 2ND SET 2ND QUIT −100 PMT 5 I/Y 10 N CPT PV [Output] 810.78	Input: =PV (5%, 10, −100, , 1) Output: 810.78

- Subscripts denote the timing of a variable (e.g., 0 is the present, 1 is one period in the future)
- For the calculator entries, keystrokes are either numbers or function keys denoted by ▭; items in [square brackets] are informational and not for keying

In addition to the above future and present value computations, it is sometimes necessary to determine the interest rate or yield of an annuity or a bond. It is not generally possible to calculate yields using algebraic formulas. Instead, a financial calculator or a spreadsheet is necessary.

Exhibit A-14 Techniques for computing yields on annuities and bonds

Objective	Example	Formula	Texas Instruments BA II Plus			Microsoft Excel
Interest rate or yield of an annuity	An ordinary annuity has annual cash payments of $100 for 10 periods. The present value of the annuity is $772.17. Compute the interest rate of the annuity.	No formula	−100	PMT		Input: =RATE (10, −100, 772.17)
			10	N		
			772.17	PV		
			CPT	I/Y		Output: 5.00%
			[Output]	5.00		
Annual yield of a bond	You purchase a bond on Jan. 1, 2013. The bond has an annual coupon rate of 6% and semi-annual coupon payments until maturity on Dec. 31, 2022, at which time it will repay the principal of $1,000. You paid $900 for this bond.	No formula	[Start bond functions]	2ND	BOND	Input cell A1: 2013/01/01
			[Purchase date]	1.0111	ENTER ↓	Input cell A2: 2022/12/31
			[Coupon rate]	6	ENTER ↓	Input cell A3: = YIELD(A1, A2, 6%, 90, 100, 2, 0)
			[Maturity date]	12.3120	ENTER ↓	Output cell A3: 7.44%
			[Maturity payment per $100 face value]	100	ENTER ↓	
			[Display shows ACT]		↓	
			[Display shows 2/Y]		↓	
			[Display shows YLD]		↓	
			[Price per $100 face value]	90	ENTER ↑	
			[Display shows YLD]		CPT	
			[Output]		7.44	

The above table shows an example of a bond with standard characteristics, but the number of steps in the calculator is already becoming unwieldy. For more complex bonds, it is advisable to use a spreadsheet that identifies the timing and amount of all cash flows, and then sum the present value of each cash flow.

C. SIMPLE VALUATION METHODS

As noted in Chapter 1, the demand for accounting information arises from uncertainty about the future. Due to this uncertainty, equity investors are only able to make imperfect forecasts about the future prices of shares, which influence whether and in which companies they invest. Given the importance of this topic, it is the subject of many books in finance and investments. The following discussion touches on the basic approaches to equity valuation using accounting information. This will provide a basis for understanding why accounting information is important in equity markets.

In all the methods discussed below, our goal is to estimate a fundamental value (V). If prevailing stock price (P) in the market is below V, then the valuation suggests that the stock is underpriced. In contrast, $P > V$ suggests that the stock is overpriced. However, it is important to recognize that these estimates of V are just that: estimates. Each estimation approach has its limitations because of the assumptions required. Below, we will discuss approaches using book value, dividends, and earnings.

1. Valuation using book value

The simplest method of share valuation is to use a company's book value per share ($BVPS$). "Book value" in this context refers to the amount for common shares, retained earnings, and any other amounts in equity on the balance sheet that pertain to the common shareholders. We divide book value by the number of shares outstanding[3] to obtain a value comparable to the company's stock price, which is naturally expressed on a per share basis.

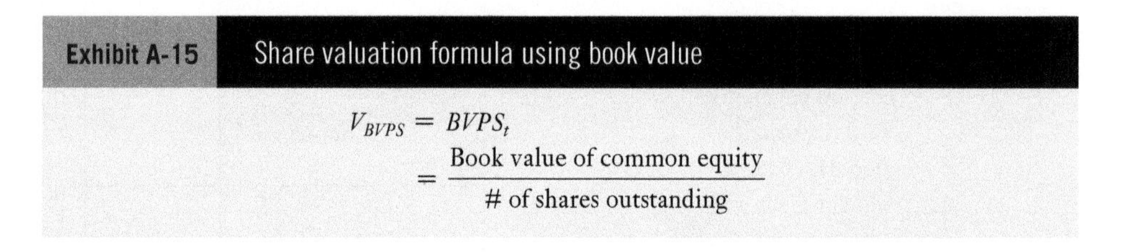

Exhibit A-15 Share valuation formula using book value

$$V_{BVPS} = BVPS_t = \frac{\text{Book value of common equity}}{\text{\# of shares outstanding}}$$

While this method is simple, it is useful in very limited circumstances. Specifically, this valuation approach requires the following assumptions to be approximately correct:

- *Completeness:* The company's balance sheet has recorded all significant assets and liabilities. That is, the company cannot have unrecorded assets such as patents, or unrecorded liabilities such as pending lawsuits.
- *Neutrality:* Accounting policies are neutral such that the recorded values of assets and liabilities on the balance sheet approximate their current values. In other words, the accounting can be neither conservative nor aggressive.
- *Stability:* The company's operations are stable rather than growing (or declining). Usually, this also requires that the company's industry be mature and stable.

Using the book value method, the estimate V will usually be substantially below stock price P because (1) the balance sheet does not show all economic assets such as valuable patents and internally generated goodwill; (2) accounting tends to be conservative; and (3) firms tend to grow over time along with growth in the overall economy. Despite these limitations, the book value method often provides a reliable lower bound estimate of fundamental value, and it is a good starting point to gauge the reasonability of the other methods discussed below. For instance, if another valuation method produces a value estimate that is four times book value, is the 300% difference reasonably explained by incomplete accounting of assets, conservative accounting, or future growth?

2. Valuation using dividends

Finance theory suggests that the value of common equity is equal to the present value of expected future dividends. This idea is summarized by the following formula:

[3] There are some complexities relating to the number of shares that should be used in the denominator. These issues are addressed in Chapter 15 on earnings per share. For simplicity, we use the number of shares outstanding.

Exhibit A-16 Valuation formula using expected dividends

$$V_{Div} = \sum_{t=1}^{\infty} \frac{E(DPS_t)}{(1 + t)^t}$$

$E(DPS_t)$ is the expected dividends per share in period t. This formula is just an application of basic discounted cash flow analysis. However, the difficulty with applying this approach is that dividends are hard to predict: they are at the discretion of companies' boards of directors, and some companies have no history of dividends to help forecast future dividends. One way to overcome these difficulties is to replace expected dividends with another measure of expected cash flow, such as cash flow from operations. Another approach is to use earnings forecasts in place of expected dividends, because earnings eventually result in cash inflows, from which the firm pays dividends.

3. Valuation using earnings and earnings multiples

The earnings forecasting process can be quite elaborate and complex. A good starting point is to use the most recent reported earnings per share. For valuation purposes, it is useful to "normalize" the earnings per share: adjusting the actual earnings for temporary fluctuations so as to obtain a better forecast of permanent earnings. We can then use this normalized earnings per share (EPS_0) as an indicator for future dividend-paying capacity, and apply the perpetuity with growth formula (see Exhibit A-7) to obtain the following formula:

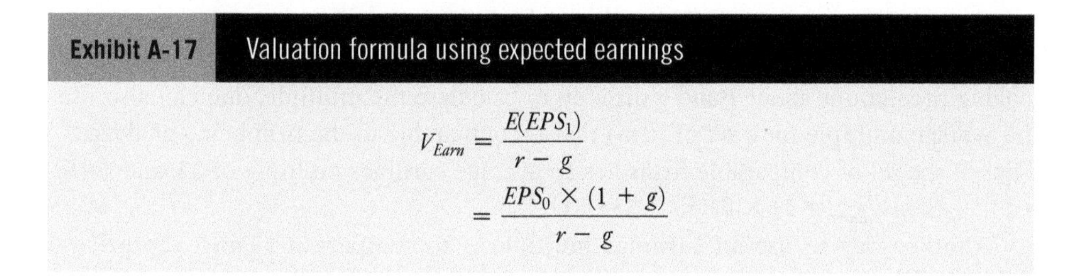

Exhibit A-17 Valuation formula using expected earnings

$$V_{Earn} = \frac{E(EPS_1)}{r - g} = \frac{EPS_0 \times (1 + g)}{r - g}$$

In this equation, $E(EPS_1)$ is the expected earnings per share next year. If growth is zero ($g = 0$), then the formula is particularly simple: $V_{Earn} = EPS_0 / r$.

To illustrate this approach and the related computations below, assume the following for Alpha Corporation:

Exhibit A-18 Assumptions about Alpha Corporation

Item description	Notation	Amount
Current stock price	P_0	\$39.00
Most recent year's earnings per share	EPS_0	\$1.50
Discount rate	r	9%
Growth rate in earnings per share	g	4%

Applying the equation in Exhibit A-17, we obtain $V_{Earn} = \$1.50 \times 1.04 \div (0.09 - 0.04) = \$1.56 \div 0.05 = \$31.20$ as the estimated value per share for Alpha Corporation.

earnings multiple A number that, when multiplied with earnings, provides an estimate of a share's value. When earnings are expected to grow at rate g and the discount rate is r, the earnings multiple is equal to $(1 + g)/(r - g)$.

It is also useful to write the formula for V_{Earn} from Exhibit A-17 in a slightly different way to emphasize what is commonly known as an **earnings multiple**:

Exhibit A-19 Valuation formula using earnings multiples

$$V_{Earn} = EPS_0 \times \frac{1 + g}{r - g}$$
$$= EPS_0 \times \text{Earnings multiple}$$

Using the assumptions for Alpha Corporation shown above in Exhibit A-18, we have the following results:

Exhibit A-20 Valuation of Alpha Corporation using multiples

Earnings multiple	Value estimate
Earnings multiple $= \frac{1 + g}{r - g} = \frac{1.04}{0.09 - 0.04} = 20.8$	$V_{Earn} = EPS_0 \times$ Earnings multiple $= \$1.50 \times 20.8$ $= \$31.20$

Of course, the estimated value of \$31.20 is the same as computing the value using the perpetuity with growth formula in Exhibit A-7.

One of the reasons for isolating the multiple in the earnings valuation method is that it allows for comparisons among different firms. Along the same line, instead of making predictions about r and g directly to calculate the multiple, one can also use the average multiple for a set of firms that is comparable to the firm being analyzed.[4] Thus, if the set of comparable firms has an average earnings multiple of 23, and $EPS_0 = \$1.50$, then $V_{Earn} = 23 \times \$1.50 = \$34.50$.

Another way to use an earnings multiple is to compare it against the price–earnings ratio, or P/E ratio, which is simply the share price divided by earnings per share:

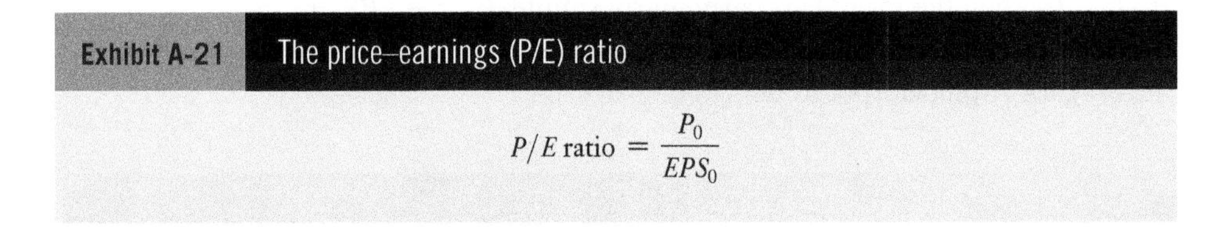

If the prevailing stock price (P_0) is \$39, then the P/E ratio is \$39 ÷ \$1.50 = 26. This ratio exceeds the earnings multiple of 20.8, as well as the average multiple of 23 for comparable firms. This analysis suggests that the stock is overpriced. The same inference of overpricing would be drawn by comparing the actual price of \$39 with the estimated value of \$31.20.

4. This method of using earnings multiples of comparable firms is one application of an approach called the method of comparable multiples. This method involves using multiples of earnings, sales, book value, cash flow, or any other measure that helps to predict share price.

Exhibit A-22 Summary of earnings valuation for Alpha Corporation

Earnings multiple for the firm (estimated):	$\frac{1+g}{r-g} = 20.8$	The actual P/E ratio of 26 exceeds the earnings multiple corresponding to the discount rate and growth rate estimated for the firm. The P/E ratio also exceeds the earnings multiple for comparable firms.
Earnings multiple for comparable firms (given):	23	
Actual P/E ratio:	$\frac{P_0}{EPS_0} = \frac{\$39}{\$1.50} = 26$	
Value estimate:	$V_{Earn} = \$31.20$	The actual market price for the shares at \$39 exceeds estimated value of \$31.20. Therefore, this analysis suggests that the shares are overvalued.
Actual price:	$P_0 = \$39$	

D. GLOSSARY

annuity: A series of cash flows in equal amounts occurring at regular intervals.

annuity due: An annuity that has cash flows at the *beginning* of each period.

earnings multiple: A number that, when multiplied with earnings, provides an estimate of a share's value. When earnings are expected to grow at rate g and the discount rate is r, the earnings multiple is equal to $(1 + g) / (r - g)$.

ordinary annuity: An annuity that has cash flows at the *end* of each period.

perpetuity: A series of cash flows in equal amounts occurring at regular intervals for an infinite number of periods.

perpetuity with growth: A series of cash flows occurring at regular intervals for an infinite number of periods with cash flows that grow at a constant rate.

E. TABLES OF PRESENT VALUE AND FUTURE VALUE FACTORS

1. Present value factors for a single sum of $1 (PVF)

Periods	Interest rate per period (r)											
(t)	2%	3%	4%	5%	6%	7%	8%	9%	10%	11%	12%	15%
1	0.9804	0.9709	0.9615	0.9524	0.9434	0.9346	0.9259	0.9174	0.9091	0.9009	0.8929	0.8696
2	0.9612	0.9426	0.9246	0.9070	0.8900	0.8734	0.8573	0.8417	0.8264	0.8116	0.7972	0.7561
3	0.9423	0.9151	0.8890	0.8638	0.8396	0.8163	0.7938	0.7722	0.7513	0.7312	0.7118	0.6575
4	0.9238	0.8885	0.8548	0.8227	0.7921	0.7629	0.7350	0.7084	0.6830	0.6587	0.6355	0.5718
5	0.9057	0.8626	0.8219	0.7835	0.7473	0.7130	0.6806	0.6499	0.6209	0.5935	0.5674	0.4972
6	0.8880	0.8375	0.7903	0.7462	0.7050	0.6663	0.6302	0.5963	0.5645	0.5346	0.5066	0.4323
7	0.8706	0.8131	0.7599	0.7107	0.6651	0.6227	0.5835	0.5470	0.5132	0.4817	0.4523	0.3759
8	0.8535	0.7894	0.7307	0.6768	0.6274	0.5820	0.5403	0.5019	0.4665	0.4339	0.4039	0.3269
9	0.8368	0.7664	0.7026	0.6446	0.5919	0.5439	0.5002	0.4604	0.4241	0.3909	0.3606	0.2843
10	0.8203	0.7441	0.6756	0.6139	0.5584	0.5083	0.4632	0.4224	0.3855	0.3522	0.3220	0.2472
11	0.8043	0.7224	0.6496	0.5847	0.5268	0.4751	0.4289	0.3875	0.3505	0.3173	0.2875	0.2149
12	0.7885	0.7014	0.6246	0.5568	0.4970	0.4440	0.3971	0.3555	0.3186	0.2858	0.2567	0.1869
13	0.7730	0.6810	0.6006	0.5303	0.4688	0.4150	0.3677	0.3262	0.2897	0.2575	0.2292	0.1625
14	0.7579	0.6611	0.5775	0.5051	0.4423	0.3878	0.3405	0.2992	0.2633	0.2320	0.2046	0.1413
15	0.7430	0.6419	0.5553	0.4810	0.4173	0.3624	0.3152	0.2745	0.2394	0.2090	0.1827	0.1229
16	0.7284	0.6232	0.5339	0.4581	0.3936	0.3387	0.2919	0.2519	0.2176	0.1883	0.1631	0.1069
17	0.7142	0.6050	0.5134	0.4363	0.3714	0.3166	0.2703	0.2311	0.1978	0.1696	0.1456	0.0929
18	0.7002	0.5874	0.4936	0.4155	0.3503	0.2959	0.2502	0.2120	0.1799	0.1528	0.1300	0.0808
19	0.6864	0.5703	0.4746	0.3957	0.3305	0.2765	0.2317	0.1945	0.1635	0.1377	0.1161	0.0703
20	0.6730	0.5537	0.4564	0.3769	0.3118	0.2584	0.2145	0.1784	0.1486	0.1240	0.1037	0.0611
21	0.6598	0.5375	0.4388	0.3589	0.2942	0.2415	0.1987	0.1637	0.1351	0.1117	0.0926	0.0531
22	0.6468	0.5219	0.4220	0.3418	0.2775	0.2257	0.1839	0.1502	0.1228	0.1007	0.0826	0.0462
23	0.6342	0.5067	0.4057	0.3256	0.2618	0.2109	0.1703	0.1378	0.1117	0.0907	0.0738	0.0402
24	0.6217	0.4919	0.3901	0.3101	0.2470	0.1971	0.1577	0.1264	0.1015	0.0817	0.0659	0.0349
25	0.6095	0.4776	0.3751	0.2953	0.2330	0.1842	0.1460	0.1160	0.0923	0.0736	0.0588	0.0304
26	0.5976	0.4637	0.3607	0.2812	0.2198	0.1722	0.1352	0.1064	0.0839	0.0663	0.0525	0.0264
27	0.5859	0.4502	0.3468	0.2678	0.2074	0.1609	0.1252	0.0976	0.0763	0.0597	0.0469	0.0230
28	0.5744	0.4371	0.3335	0.2551	0.1956	0.1504	0.1159	0.0895	0.0693	0.0538	0.0419	0.0200
29	0.5631	0.4243	0.3207	0.2429	0.1846	0.1406	0.1073	0.0822	0.0630	0.0485	0.0374	0.0174
30	0.5521	0.4120	0.3083	0.2314	0.1741	0.1314	0.0994	0.0754	0.0573	0.0437	0.0334	0.0151
31	0.5412	0.4000	0.2965	0.2204	0.1643	0.1228	0.0920	0.0691	0.0521	0.0394	0.0298	0.0131
32	0.5306	0.3883	0.2851	0.2099	0.1550	0.1147	0.0852	0.0634	0.0474	0.0355	0.0266	0.0114
33	0.5202	0.3770	0.2741	0.1999	0.1462	0.1072	0.0789	0.0582	0.0431	0.0319	0.0238	0.0099
34	0.5100	0.3660	0.2636	0.1904	0.1379	0.1002	0.0730	0.0534	0.0391	0.0288	0.0212	0.0086
35	0.5000	0.3554	0.2534	0.1813	0.1301	0.0937	0.0676	0.0490	0.0356	0.0259	0.0189	0.0075
36	0.4902	0.3450	0.2437	0.1727	0.1227	0.0875	0.0626	0.0449	0.0323	0.0234	0.0169	0.0065
37	0.4806	0.3350	0.2343	0.1644	0.1158	0.0818	0.0580	0.0412	0.0294	0.0210	0.0151	0.0057
38	0.4712	0.3252	0.2253	0.1566	0.1092	0.0765	0.0537	0.0378	0.0267	0.0190	0.0135	0.0049
39	0.4619	0.3158	0.2166	0.1491	0.1031	0.0715	0.0497	0.0347	0.0243	0.0171	0.0120	0.0043
40	0.4529	0.3066	0.2083	0.1420	0.0972	0.0668	0.0460	0.0318	0.0221	0.0154	0.0107	0.0037
45	0.4102	0.2644	0.1712	0.1113	0.0727	0.0476	0.0313	0.0207	0.0137	0.0091	0.0061	0.0019
50	0.3715	0.2281	0.1407	0.0872	0.0543	0.0339	0.0213	0.0134	0.0085	0.0054	0.0035	0.0009

2. Present value factors for an ordinary annuity of $1 (PVFA)

Periods	Interest rate per period (r)											
(t)	2%	3%	4%	5%	6%	7%	8%	9%	10%	11%	12%	15%
1	0.9804	0.9709	0.9615	0.9524	0.9434	0.9346	0.9259	0.9174	0.9091	0.9009	0.8929	0.8696
2	1.9416	1.9135	1.8861	1.8594	1.8334	1.8080	1.7833	1.7591	1.7355	1.7125	1.6901	1.6257
3	2.8839	2.8286	2.7751	2.7232	2.6730	2.6243	2.5771	2.5313	2.4869	2.4437	2.4018	2.2832
4	3.8077	3.7171	3.6299	3.5460	3.4651	3.3872	3.3121	3.2397	3.1699	3.1024	3.0373	2.8550
5	4.7135	4.5797	4.4518	4.3295	4.2124	4.1002	3.9927	3.8897	3.7908	3.6959	3.6048	3.3522
6	5.6014	5.4172	5.2421	5.0757	4.9173	4.7665	4.6229	4.4859	4.3553	4.2305	4.1114	3.7845
7	6.4720	6.2303	6.0021	5.7864	5.5824	5.3893	5.2064	5.0330	4.8684	4.7122	4.5638	4.1604
8	7.3255	7.0197	6.7327	6.4632	6.2098	5.9713	5.7466	5.5348	5.3349	5.1461	4.9676	4.4873
9	8.1622	7.7861	7.4353	7.1078	6.8017	6.5152	6.2469	5.9952	5.7590	5.5370	5.3282	4.7716
10	8.9826	8.5302	8.1109	7.7217	7.3601	7.0236	6.7101	6.4177	6.1446	5.8892	5.6502	5.0188
11	9.7868	9.2526	8.7605	8.3064	7.8869	7.4987	7.1390	6.8052	6.4951	6.2065	5.9377	5.2337
12	10.5753	9.9540	9.3851	8.8633	8.3838	7.9427	7.5361	7.1607	6.8137	6.4924	6.1944	5.4206
13	11.3484	10.6350	9.9856	9.3936	8.8527	8.3577	7.9038	7.4869	7.1034	6.7499	6.4235	5.5831
14	12.1062	11.2961	10.5631	9.8986	9.2950	8.7455	8.2442	7.7862	7.3667	6.9819	6.6282	5.7245
15	12.8493	11.9379	11.1184	10.3797	9.7122	9.1079	8.5595	8.0607	7.6061	7.1909	6.8109	5.8474
16	13.5777	12.5611	11.6523	10.8378	10.1059	9.4466	8.8514	8.3126	7.8237	7.3792	6.9740	5.9542
17	14.2919	13.1661	12.1657	11.2741	10.4773	9.7632	9.1216	8.5436	8.0216	7.5488	7.1196	6.0472
18	14.9920	13.7535	12.6593	11.6896	10.8276	10.0591	9.3719	8.7556	8.2014	7.7016	7.2497	6.1280
19	15.6785	14.3238	13.1339	12.0853	11.1581	10.3356	9.6036	8.9501	8.3649	7.8393	7.3658	6.1982
20	16.3514	14.8775	13.5903	12.4622	11.4699	10.5940	9.8181	9.1285	8.5136	7.9633	7.4694	6.2593
21	17.0112	15.4150	14.0292	12.8212	11.7641	10.8355	10.0168	9.2922	8.6487	8.0751	7.5620	6.3125
22	17.6580	15.9369	14.4511	13.1630	12.0416	11.0612	10.2007	9.4424	8.7715	8.1757	7.6446	6.3587
23	18.2922	16.4436	14.8568	13.4886	12.3034	11.2722	10.3711	9.5802	8.8832	8.2664	7.7184	6.3988
24	18.9139	16.9355	15.2470	13.7986	12.5504	11.4693	10.5288	9.7066	8.9847	8.3481	7.7843	6.4338
25	19.5235	17.4131	15.6221	14.0939	12.7834	11.6536	10.6748	9.8226	9.0770	8.4217	7.8431	6.4641
26	20.1210	17.8768	15.9828	14.3752	13.0032	11.8258	10.8100	9.9290	9.1609	8.4881	7.8957	6.4906
27	20.7069	18.3270	16.3296	14.6430	13.2105	11.9867	10.9352	10.0266	9.2372	8.5478	7.9426	6.5135
28	21.2813	18.7641	16.6631	14.8981	13.4062	12.1371	11.0511	10.1161	9.3066	8.6016	7.9844	6.5335
29	21.8444	19.1885	16.9837	15.1411	13.5907	12.2777	11.1584	10.1983	9.3696	8.6501	8.0218	6.5509
30	22.3965	19.6004	17.2920	15.3725	13.7648	12.4090	11.2578	10.2737	9.4269	8.6938	8.0552	6.5660
31	22.9377	20.0004	17.5885	15.5928	13.9291	12.5318	11.3498	10.3428	9.4790	8.7331	8.0850	6.5791
32	23.4683	20.3888	17.8736	15.8027	14.0840	12.6466	11.4350	10.4062	9.5264	8.7686	8.1116	6.5905
33	23.9886	20.7658	18.1476	16.0025	14.2302	12.7538	11.5139	10.4644	9.5694	8.8005	8.1354	6.6005
34	24.4986	21.1318	18.4112	16.1929	14.3681	12.8540	11.5869	10.5178	9.6086	8.8293	8.1566	6.6091
35	24.9986	21.4872	18.6646	16.3742	14.4982	12.9477	11.6546	10.5668	9.6442	8.8552	8.1755	6.6166
36	25.4888	21.8323	18.9083	16.5469	14.6210	13.0352	11.7172	10.6118	9.6765	8.8786	8.1924	6.6231
37	25.9695	22.1672	19.1426	16.7113	14.7368	13.1170	11.7752	10.6530	9.7059	8.8996	8.2075	6.6288
38	26.4406	22.4925	19.3679	16.8679	14.8460	13.1935	11.8289	10.6908	9.7327	8.9186	8.2210	6.6338
39	26.9026	22.8082	19.5845	17.0170	14.9491	13.2649	11.8786	10.7255	9.7570	8.9357	8.2330	6.6380
40	27.3555	23.1148	19.7928	17.1591	15.0463	13.3317	11.9246	10.7574	9.7791	8.9511	8.2438	6.6418
45	29.4902	24.5187	20.7200	17.7741	15.4558	13.6055	12.1084	10.8812	9.8628	9.0079	8.2825	6.6543
50	31.4236	25.7298	21.4822	18.2559	15.7619	13.8007	12.2335	10.9617	9.9148	9.0417	8.3045	6.6605

3. Present value factors for an annuity due of $1 (PVFAD)

Periods	Interest rate per period (r)											
(t)	2%	3%	4%	5%	6%	7%	8%	9%	10%	11%	12%	15%
1	1.0000	1.0000	1.0000	1.0000	1.0000	1.0000	1.0000	1.0000	1.0000	1.0000	1.0000	1.0000
2	1.9804	1.9709	1.9615	1.9524	1.9434	1.9346	1.9259	1.9174	1.9091	1.9009	1.8929	1.8696
3	2.9416	2.9135	2.8861	2.8594	2.8334	2.8080	2.7833	2.7591	2.7355	2.7125	2.6901	2.6257
4	3.8839	3.8286	3.7751	3.7232	3.6730	3.6243	3.5771	3.5313	3.4869	3.4437	3.4018	3.2832
5	4.8077	4.7171	4.6299	4.5460	4.4651	4.3872	4.3121	4.2397	4.1699	4.1024	4.0373	3.8550
6	5.7135	5.5797	5.4518	5.3295	5.2124	5.1002	4.9927	4.8897	4.7908	4.6959	4.6048	4.3522
7	6.6014	6.4172	6.2421	6.0757	5.9173	5.7665	5.6229	5.4859	5.3553	5.2305	5.1114	4.7845
8	7.4720	7.2303	7.0021	6.7864	6.5824	6.3893	6.2064	6.0330	5.8684	5.7122	5.5638	5.1604
9	8.3255	8.0197	7.7327	7.4632	7.2098	6.9713	6.7466	6.5348	6.3349	6.1461	5.9676	5.4873
10	9.1622	8.7861	8.4353	8.1078	7.8017	7.5152	7.2469	6.9952	6.7590	6.5370	6.3282	5.7716
11	9.9826	9.5302	9.1109	8.7217	8.3601	8.0236	7.7101	7.4177	7.1446	6.8892	6.6502	6.0188
12	10.7868	10.2526	9.7605	9.3064	8.8869	8.4987	8.1390	7.8052	7.4951	7.2065	6.9377	6.2337
13	11.5753	10.9540	10.3851	9.8633	9.3838	8.9427	8.5361	8.1607	7.8137	7.4924	7.1944	6.4206
14	12.3484	11.6350	10.9856	10.3936	9.8527	9.3577	8.9038	8.4869	8.1034	7.7499	7.4235	6.5831
15	13.1062	12.2961	11.5631	10.8986	10.2950	9.7455	9.2442	8.7862	8.3667	7.9819	7.6282	6.7245
16	13.8493	12.9379	12.1184	11.3797	10.7122	10.1079	9.5595	9.0607	8.6061	8.1909	7.8109	6.8474
17	14.5777	13.5611	12.6523	11.8378	11.1059	10.4466	9.8514	9.3126	8.8237	8.3792	7.9740	6.9542
18	15.2919	14.1661	13.1657	12.2741	11.4773	10.7632	10.1216	9.5436	9.0216	8.5488	8.1196	7.0472
19	15.9920	14.7535	13.6593	12.6896	11.8276	11.0591	10.3719	9.7556	9.2014	8.7016	8.2497	7.1280
20	16.6785	15.3238	14.1339	13.0853	12.1581	11.3356	10.6036	9.9501	9.3649	8.8393	8.3658	7.1982
21	17.3514	15.8775	14.5903	13.4622	12.4699	11.5940	10.8181	10.1285	9.5136	8.9633	8.4694	7.2593
22	18.0112	16.4150	15.0292	13.8212	12.7641	11.8355	11.0168	10.2922	9.6487	9.0751	8.5620	7.3125
23	18.6580	16.9369	15.4511	14.1630	13.0416	12.0612	11.2007	10.4424	9.7715	9.1757	8.6446	7.3587
24	19.2922	17.4436	15.8568	14.4886	13.3034	12.2722	11.3711	10.5802	9.8832	9.2664	8.7184	7.3988
25	19.9139	17.9355	16.2470	14.7986	13.5504	12.4693	11.5288	10.7066	9.9847	9.3481	8.7843	7.4338
26	20.5235	18.4131	16.6221	15.0939	13.7834	12.6536	11.6748	10.8226	10.0770	9.4217	8.8431	7.4641
27	21.1210	18.8768	16.9828	15.3752	14.0032	12.8258	11.8100	10.9290	10.1609	9.4881	8.8957	7.4906
28	21.7069	19.3270	17.3296	15.6430	14.2105	12.9867	11.9352	11.0266	10.2372	9.5478	8.9426	7.5135
29	22.2813	19.7641	17.6631	15.8981	14.4062	13.1371	12.0511	11.1161	10.3066	9.6016	8.9844	7.5335
30	22.8444	20.1885	17.9837	16.1411	14.5907	13.2777	12.1584	11.1983	10.3696	9.6501	9.0218	7.5509
31	23.3965	20.6004	18.2920	16.3725	14.7648	13.4090	12.2578	11.2737	10.4269	9.6938	9.0552	7.5660
32	23.9377	21.0004	18.5885	16.5928	14.9291	13.5318	12.3498	11.3428	10.4790	9.7331	9.0850	7.5791
33	24.4683	21.3888	18.8736	16.8027	15.0840	13.6466	12.4350	11.4062	10.5264	9.7686	9.1116	7.5905
34	24.9886	21.7658	19.1476	17.0025	15.2302	13.7538	12.5139	11.4644	10.5694	9.8005	9.1354	7.6005
35	25.4986	22.1318	19.4112	17.1929	15.3681	13.8540	12.5869	11.5178	10.6086	9.8293	9.1566	7.6091
36	25.9986	22.4872	19.6646	17.3742	15.4982	13.9477	12.6546	11.5668	10.6442	9.8552	9.1755	7.6166
37	26.4888	22.8323	19.9083	17.5469	15.6210	14.0352	12.7172	11.6118	10.6765	9.8786	9.1924	7.6231
38	26.9695	23.1672	20.1426	17.7113	15.7368	14.1170	12.7752	11.6530	10.7059	9.8996	9.2075	7.6288
39	27.4406	23.4925	20.3679	17.8679	15.8460	14.1935	12.8289	11.6908	10.7327	9.9186	9.2210	7.6338
40	27.9026	23.8082	20.5845	18.0170	15.9491	14.2649	12.8786	11.7255	10.7570	9.9357	9.2330	7.6380
45	30.0800	25.2543	21.5488	18.6628	16.3832	14.5579	13.0771	11.8605	10.8491	9.9988	9.2764	7.6524
50	32.0521	26.5017	22.3415	19.1687	16.7076	14.7668	13.2122	11.9482	10.9063	10.0362	9.3010	7.6596

4. Future value factors for a single sum of $1 (FVF)

Periods	Interest rate per period (r)										
(t)	2%	3%	4%	5%	6%	7%	8%	9%	10%	11%	12%	15%
1	1.0200	1.0300	1.0400	1.0500	1.0600	1.0700	1.0800	1.0900	1.1000	1.1100	1.1200	1.1500
2	1.0404	1.0609	1.0816	1.1025	1.1236	1.1449	1.1664	1.1881	1.2100	1.2321	1.2544	1.3225
3	1.0612	1.0927	1.1249	1.1576	1.1910	1.2250	1.2597	1.2950	1.3310	1.3676	1.4049	1.5209
4	1.0824	1.1255	1.1699	1.2155	1.2625	1.3108	1.3605	1.4116	1.4641	1.5181	1.5735	1.7490
5	1.1041	1.1593	1.2167	1.2763	1.3382	1.4026	1.4693	1.5386	1.6105	1.6851	1.7623	2.0114
6	1.1262	1.1941	1.2653	1.3401	1.4185	1.5007	1.5869	1.6771	1.7716	1.8704	1.9738	2.3131
7	1.1487	1.2299	1.3159	1.4071	1.5036	1.6058	1.7138	1.8280	1.9487	2.0762	2.2107	2.6600
8	1.1717	1.2668	1.3686	1.4775	1.5938	1.7182	1.8509	1.9926	2.1436	2.3045	2.4760	3.0590
9	1.1951	1.3048	1.4233	1.5513	1.6895	1.8385	1.9990	2.1719	2.3579	2.5580	2.7731	3.5179
10	1.2190	1.3439	1.4802	1.6289	1.7908	1.9672	2.1589	2.3674	2.5937	2.8394	3.1058	4.0456
11	1.2434	1.3842	1.5395	1.7103	1.8983	2.1049	2.3316	2.5804	2.8531	3.1518	3.4785	4.6524
12	1.2682	1.4258	1.6010	1.7959	2.0122	2.2522	2.5182	2.8127	3.1384	3.4985	3.8960	5.3503
13	1.2936	1.4685	1.6651	1.8856	2.1329	2.4098	2.7196	3.0658	3.4523	3.8833	4.3635	6.1528
14	1.3195	1.5126	1.7317	1.9799	2.2609	2.5785	2.9372	3.3417	3.7975	4.3104	4.8871	7.0757
15	1.3459	1.5580	1.8009	2.0789	2.3966	2.7590	3.1722	3.6425	4.1772	4.7846	5.4736	8.1371
16	1.3728	1.6047	1.8730	2.1829	2.5404	2.9522	3.4259	3.9703	4.5950	5.3109	6.1304	9.3576
17	1.4002	1.6528	1.9479	2.2920	2.6928	3.1588	3.7000	4.3276	5.0545	5.8951	6.8660	10.7613
18	1.4282	1.7024	2.0258	2.4066	2.8543	3.3799	3.9960	4.7171	5.5599	6.5436	7.6900	12.3755
19	1.4568	1.7535	2.1068	2.5270	3.0256	3.6165	4.3157	5.1417	6.1159	7.2633	8.6128	14.2318
20	1.4859	1.8061	2.1911	2.6533	3.2071	3.8697	4.6610	5.6044	6.7275	8.0623	9.6463	16.3665
21	1.5157	1.8603	2.2788	2.7860	3.3996	4.1406	5.0338	6.1088	7.4002	8.9492	10.8038	18.8215
22	1.5460	1.9161	2.3699	2.9253	3.6035	4.4304	5.4365	6.6586	8.1403	9.9336	12.1003	21.6447
23	1.5769	1.9736	2.4647	3.0715	3.8197	4.7405	5.8715	7.2579	8.9543	11.0263	13.5523	24.8915
24	1.6084	2.0328	2.5633	3.2251	4.0489	5.0724	6.3412	7.9111	9.8497	12.2392	15.1786	28.6252
25	1.6406	2.0938	2.6658	3.3864	4.2919	5.4274	6.8485	8.6231	10.8347	13.5855	17.0001	32.9190
26	1.6734	2.1566	2.7725	3.5557	4.5494	5.8074	7.3964	9.3992	11.9182	15.0799	19.0401	37.8568
27	1.7069	2.2213	2.8834	3.7335	4.8223	6.2139	7.9881	10.2451	13.1100	16.7386	21.3249	43.5353
28	1.7410	2.2879	2.9987	3.9201	5.1117	6.6488	8.6271	11.1671	14.4210	18.5799	23.8839	50.0656
29	1.7758	2.3566	3.1187	4.1161	5.4184	7.1143	9.3173	12.1722	15.8631	20.6237	26.7499	57.5755
30	1.8114	2.4273	3.2434	4.3219	5.7435	7.6123	10.0627	13.2677	17.4494	22.8923	29.9599	66.2118
31	1.8476	2.5001	3.3731	4.5380	6.0881	8.1451	10.8677	14.4618	19.1943	25.4104	33.5551	76.1435
32	1.8845	2.5751	3.5081	4.7649	6.4534	8.7153	11.7371	15.7633	21.1138	28.2056	37.5817	87.5651
33	1.9222	2.6523	3.6484	5.0032	6.8406	9.3253	12.6760	17.1820	23.2252	31.3082	42.0915	100.6998
34	1.9607	2.7319	3.7943	5.2533	7.2510	9.9781	13.6901	18.7284	25.5477	34.7521	47.1425	115.8048
35	1.9999	2.8139	3.9461	5.5160	7.6861	10.6766	14.7853	20.4140	28.1024	38.5749	52.7996	133.1755
36	2.0399	2.8983	4.1039	5.7918	8.1473	11.4239	15.9682	22.2512	30.9127	42.8181	59.1356	153.1519
37	2.0807	2.9852	4.2681	6.0814	8.6361	12.2236	17.2456	24.2538	34.0039	47.5281	66.2318	176.1246
38	2.1223	3.0748	4.4388	6.3855	9.1543	13.0793	18.6253	26.4367	37.4043	52.7562	74.1797	202.5433
39	2.1647	3.1670	4.6164	6.7048	9.7035	13.9948	20.1153	28.8160	41.1448	58.5593	83.0812	232.9248
40	2.2080	3.2620	4.8010	7.0400	10.2857	14.9745	21.7245	31.4094	45.2593	65.0009	93.0510	267.8635
45	2.4379	3.7816	5.8412	8.9850	13.7646	21.0025	31.9204	48.3273	72.8905	109.5302	163.9876	538.7693
50	2.6916	4.3839	7.1067	11.4674	18.4202	29.4570	46.9016	74.3575	117.3909	184.5648	289.0022	1,083.6574

5. Future value factors for an ordinary annuity of $1 (FVFA)

Periods	Interest rate per period (r)											
(t)	2%	3%	4%	5%	6%	7%	8%	9%	10%	11%	12%	15%
1	1.0000	1.0000	1.0000	1.0000	1.0000	1.0000	1.0000	1.0000	1.0000	1.0000	1.0000	1.0000
2	2.0200	2.0300	2.0400	2.0500	2.0600	2.0700	2.0800	2.0900	2.1000	2.1100	2.1200	2.1500
3	3.0604	3.0909	3.1216	3.1525	3.1836	3.2149	3.2464	3.2781	3.3100	3.3421	3.3744	3.4725
4	4.1216	4.1836	4.2465	4.3101	4.3746	4.4399	4.5061	4.5731	4.6410	4.7097	4.7793	4.9934
5	5.2040	5.3091	5.4163	5.5256	5.6371	5.7507	5.8666	5.9847	6.1051	6.2278	6.3528	6.7424
6	6.3081	6.4684	6.6330	6.8019	6.9753	7.1533	7.3359	7.5233	7.7156	7.9129	8.1152	8.7537
7	7.4343	7.6625	7.8983	8.1420	8.3938	8.6540	8.9228	9.2004	9.4872	9.7833	10.0890	11.0668
8	8.5830	8.8923	9.2142	9.5491	9.8975	10.2598	10.6366	11.0285	11.4359	11.8594	12.2997	13.7268
9	9.7546	10.1591	10.5828	11.0266	11.4913	11.9780	12.4876	13.0210	13.5795	14.1640	14.7757	16.7858
10	10.9497	11.4639	12.0061	12.5779	13.1808	13.8164	14.4866	15.1929	15.9374	16.7220	17.5487	20.3037
11	12.1687	12.8078	13.4864	14.2068	14.9716	15.7836	16.6455	17.5603	18.5312	19.5614	20.6546	24.3493
12	13.4121	14.1920	15.0258	15.9171	16.8699	17.8885	18.9771	20.1407	21.3843	22.7132	24.1331	29.0017
13	14.6803	15.6178	16.6268	17.7130	18.8821	20.1406	21.4953	22.9534	24.5227	26.2116	28.0291	34.3519
14	15.9739	17.0863	18.2919	19.5986	21.0151	22.5505	24.2149	26.0192	27.9750	30.0949	32.3926	40.5047
15	17.2934	18.5989	20.0236	21.5786	23.2760	25.1290	27.1521	29.3609	31.7725	34.4054	37.2797	47.5804
16	18.6393	20.1569	21.8245	23.6575	25.6725	27.8881	30.3243	33.0034	35.9497	39.1899	42.7533	55.7175
17	20.0121	21.7616	23.6975	25.8404	28.2129	30.8402	33.7502	36.9737	40.5447	44.5008	48.8837	65.0751
18	21.4123	23.4144	25.6454	28.1324	30.9057	33.9990	37.4502	41.3013	45.5992	50.3959	55.7497	75.8364
19	22.8406	25.1169	27.6712	30.5390	33.7600	37.3790	41.4463	46.0185	51.1591	56.9395	63.4397	88.2118
20	24.2974	26.8704	29.7781	33.0660	36.7856	40.9955	45.7620	51.1601	57.2750	64.2028	72.0524	102.4436
21	25.7833	28.6765	31.9692	35.7193	39.9927	44.8652	50.4229	56.7645	64.0025	72.2651	81.6987	118.8101
22	27.2990	30.5368	34.2480	38.5052	43.3923	49.0057	55.4568	62.8733	71.4027	81.2143	92.5026	137.6316
23	28.8450	32.4529	36.6179	41.4305	46.9958	53.4361	60.8933	69.5319	79.5430	91.1479	104.6029	159.2764
24	30.4219	34.4265	39.0826	44.5020	50.8156	58.1767	66.7648	76.7898	88.4973	102.1742	118.1552	184.1678
25	32.0303	36.4593	41.6459	47.7271	54.8645	63.2490	73.1059	84.7009	98.3471	114.4133	133.3339	212.7930
26	33.6709	38.5530	44.3117	51.1135	59.1564	68.6765	79.9544	93.3240	109.1818	127.9988	150.3339	245.7120
27	35.3443	40.7096	47.0842	54.6691	63.7058	74.4838	87.3508	102.7231	121.0999	143.0786	169.3740	283.5688
28	37.0512	42.9309	49.9676	58.4026	68.5281	80.6977	95.3388	112.9682	134.2099	159.8173	190.6989	327.1041
29	38.7922	45.2189	52.9663	62.3227	73.6398	87.3465	103.9659	124.1354	148.6309	178.3972	214.5828	377.1697
30	40.5681	47.5754	56.0849	66.4388	79.0582	94.4608	113.2832	136.3075	164.4940	199.0209	241.3327	434.7451
31	42.3794	50.0027	59.3283	70.7608	84.8017	102.0730	123.3459	149.5752	181.9434	221.9132	271.2926	500.9569
32	44.2270	52.5028	62.7015	75.2988	90.8898	110.2182	134.2135	164.0370	201.1378	247.3236	304.8477	577.1005
33	46.1116	55.0778	66.2095	80.0638	97.3432	118.9334	145.9506	179.8003	222.2515	275.5292	342.4294	664.6655
34	48.0338	57.7302	69.8579	85.0670	104.1838	128.2588	158.6267	196.9823	245.4767	306.8374	384.5210	765.3654
35	49.9945	60.4621	73.6522	90.3203	111.4348	138.2369	172.3168	215.7108	271.0244	341.5896	431.6635	881.1702
36	51.9944	63.2759	77.5983	95.8363	119.1209	148.9135	187.1021	236.1247	299.1268	380.1644	484.4631	1,014.3457
37	54.0343	66.1742	81.7022	101.6281	127.2681	160.3374	203.0703	258.3759	330.0395	422.9825	543.5987	1,167.4975
38	56.1149	69.1594	85.9703	107.7095	135.9042	172.5610	220.3159	282.6298	364.0434	470.5106	609.8305	1,343.6222
39	58.2372	72.2342	90.4091	114.0950	145.0585	185.6403	238.9412	309.0665	401.4478	523.2667	684.0102	1,546.1655
40	60.4020	75.4013	95.0255	120.7998	154.7620	199.6351	259.0565	337.8824	442.5926	581.8261	767.0914	1,779.0903
45	71.8927	92.7199	121.0294	159.7002	212.7435	285.7493	386.5056	525.8587	718.9048	986.6386	1,358.2300	3,585.1285
50	84.5794	112.7969	152.6671	209.3480	290.3359	406.5289	573.7702	815.0836	1,163.9085	1,668.7712	2,400.0182	7,217.7163

6. Future value factors for an annuity due of $1 (FVFAD)

Periods	Interest rate per period (r)											
(t)	2%	3%	4%	5%	6%	7%	8%	9%	10%	11%	12%	15%
1	1.0200	1.0300	1.0400	1.0500	1.0600	1.0700	1.0800	1.0900	1.1000	1.1100	1.1200	1.1500
2	2.0604	2.0909	2.1216	2.1525	2.1836	2.2149	2.2464	2.2781	2.3100	2.3421	2.3744	2.4725
3	3.1216	3.1836	3.2465	3.3101	3.3746	3.4399	3.5061	3.5731	3.6410	3.7097	3.7793	3.9934
4	4.2040	4.3091	4.4163	4.5256	4.6371	4.7507	4.8666	4.9847	5.1051	5.2278	5.3528	5.7424
5	5.3081	5.4684	5.6330	5.8019	5.9753	6.1533	6.3359	6.5233	6.7156	6.9129	7.1152	7.7537
6	6.4343	6.6625	6.8983	7.1420	7.3938	7.6540	7.9228	8.2004	8.4872	8.7833	9.0890	10.0668
7	7.5830	7.8923	8.2142	8.5491	8.8975	9.2598	9.6366	10.0285	10.4359	10.8594	11.2997	12.7268
8	8.7546	9.1591	9.5828	10.0266	10.4913	10.9780	11.4876	12.0210	12.5795	13.1640	13.7757	15.7858
9	9.9497	10.4639	11.0061	11.5779	12.1808	12.8164	13.4866	14.1929	14.9374	15.7220	16.5487	19.3037
10	11.1687	11.8078	12.4864	13.2068	13.9716	14.7836	15.6455	16.5603	17.5312	18.5614	19.6546	23.3493
11	12.4121	13.1920	14.0258	14.9171	15.8699	16.8885	17.9771	19.1407	20.3843	21.7132	23.1331	28.0017
12	13.6803	14.6178	15.6268	16.7130	17.8821	19.1406	20.4953	21.9534	23.5227	25.2116	27.0291	33.3519
13	14.9739	16.0863	17.2919	18.5986	20.0151	21.5505	23.2149	25.0192	26.9750	29.0949	31.3926	39.5047
14	16.2934	17.5989	19.0236	20.5786	22.2760	24.1290	26.1521	28.3609	30.7725	33.4054	36.2797	46.5804
15	17.6393	19.1569	20.8245	22.6575	24.6725	26.8881	29.3243	32.0034	34.9497	38.1899	41.7533	54.7175
16	19.0121	20.7616	22.6975	24.8404	27.2129	29.8402	32.7502	35.9737	39.5447	43.5008	47.8837	64.0751
17	20.4123	22.4144	24.6454	27.1324	29.9057	32.9990	36.4502	40.3013	44.5992	49.3959	54.7497	74.8364
18	21.8406	24.1169	26.6712	29.5390	32.7600	36.3790	40.4463	45.0185	50.1591	55.9395	62.4397	87.2118
19	23.2974	25.8704	28.7781	32.0660	35.7856	39.9955	44.7620	50.1601	56.2750	63.2028	71.0524	101.4436
20	24.7833	27.6765	30.9692	34.7193	38.9927	43.8652	49.4229	55.7645	63.0025	71.2651	80.6987	117.8101
21	26.2990	29.5368	33.2480	37.5052	42.3923	48.0057	54.4568	61.8733	70.4027	80.2143	91.5026	136.6316
22	27.8450	31.4529	35.6179	40.4305	45.9958	52.4361	59.8933	68.5319	78.5430	90.1479	103.6029	158.2764
23	29.4219	33.4265	38.0826	43.5020	49.8156	57.1767	65.7648	75.7898	87.4973	101.1742	117.1552	183.1678
24	31.0303	35.4593	40.6459	46.7271	53.8645	62.2490	72.1059	83.7009	97.3471	113.4133	132.3339	211.7930
25	32.6709	37.5530	43.3117	50.1135	58.1564	67.6765	78.9544	92.3240	108.1818	126.9988	149.3339	244.7120
26	34.3443	39.7096	46.0842	53.6691	62.7058	73.4838	86.3508	101.7231	120.0999	142.0786	168.3740	282.5688
27	36.0512	41.9309	48.9676	57.4026	67.5281	79.6977	94.3388	111.9682	133.2099	158.8173	189.6989	326.1041
28	37.7922	44.2189	51.9663	61.3227	72.6398	86.3465	102.9659	123.1354	147.6309	177.3972	213.5828	376.1697
29	39.5681	46.5754	55.0849	65.4388	78.0582	93.4608	112.2832	135.3075	163.4940	198.0209	240.3327	433.7451
30	41.3794	49.0027	58.3283	69.7608	83.8017	101.0730	122.3459	148.5752	180.9434	220.9132	270.2926	499.9569
31	43.2270	51.5028	61.7015	74.2988	89.8898	109.2182	133.2135	163.0370	200.1378	246.3236	303.8477	576.1005
32	45.1116	54.0778	65.2095	79.0638	96.3432	117.9334	144.9506	178.8003	221.2515	274.5292	341.4294	663.6655
33	47.0338	56.7302	68.8579	84.0670	103.1838	127.2588	157.6267	195.9823	244.4767	305.8374	383.5210	764.3654
34	48.9945	59.4621	72.6522	89.3203	110.4348	137.2369	171.3168	214.7108	270.0244	340.5896	430.6635	880.1702
35	50.9944	62.2759	76.5983	94.8363	118.1209	147.9135	186.1021	235.1247	298.1268	379.1644	483.4631	1,013.3457
36	53.0343	65.1742	80.7022	100.6281	126.2681	159.3374	202.0703	257.3759	329.0395	421.9825	542.5987	1,166.4975
37	55.1149	68.1594	84.9703	106.7095	134.9042	171.5610	219.3159	281.6298	363.0434	469.5106	608.8305	1,342.6222
38	57.2372	71.2342	89.4091	113.0950	144.0585	184.6403	237.9412	308.0665	400.4478	522.2667	683.0102	1,545.1655
39	59.4020	74.4013	94.0255	119.7998	153.7620	198.6351	258.0565	336.8824	441.5926	580.8261	766.0914	1,778.0903
40	61.6100	77.6633	98.8265	126.8398	164.0477	213.6096	279.7810	368.2919	486.8518	645.8269	859.1424	2,045.9539
45	73.3306	95.5015	125.8706	167.6852	225.5081	305.7518	417.4261	573.1860	790.7953	1,095.1688	1,521.2176	4,122.8977
50	86.2710	116.1808	158.7738	219.8154	307.7561	434.9860	619.6718	888.4411	1,280.2994	1,852.3360	2,688.0204	8,300.3737

APPENDIX B

Case Solving, Comprehensive Cases, and Capstone Cases

A. INTRODUCTION

If you are like most other business students, you are excited about cases while at the same time intimidated by them. The excitement comes from the realistic context a case provides in which you can apply the skills and knowledge you have learned in the classroom. This realism adds a dimension of difficulty that may be new to you. This difficulty does not arise from the technical nature of the issue—in most instances, cases involve issues that are technically no more demanding than non-case problems—but rather the difficulty results from the complex interplay among issues, facts, alternatives, and decision makers. As a result, case solving is not a linear process (like solving a simple calculation problem).[1]

Given the non-linear, context-specific nature of cases, there can be no universal one-size-fits-all recipe for solving them. However, there are some elements, or ingredients, that are often useful. This appendix lays out a number of these ingredients. Depending on the situation, you will need to use your judgment to use more or less of some ingredients (i.e., to emphasize different elements in different situations) and to omit other ingredients altogether.

B. APPROACHING A CASE

1. Role-playing

Whether explicitly or implicitly, most cases require you to play a role in the scenario rather than act as a passive external observer. To solve a case effectively, you need to take your role seriously. Your role determines the scope of your authority: which decisions can you or can't you make? In some cases, you are an advisor who can only provide suggestions or recommendations, and it is up to the ultimate decision maker to follow or to reject those recommendations. At other times, you are the ultimate decision maker.

The role that you play also determines to what extent different issues are relevant to you. For example, intricate audit issues may be highly relevant to an auditor, but less so to a small business owner. Finally, your role also determines the type of language you need to use (will the reader understand technical terms?) and the form of your communication (should the response be an internal memo or a letter to the client?).

2. Identification of issues

One of the skills required of professional accountants is the ability to identify issues. While some cases clearly lay out issues that you need to address, other cases involve

[1] Some case authors and publications differentiate between a "case" and a "simulation." When there is such a differentiation, a case refers to a real, historically accurate account of facts and circumstances, whereas a simulation refers to an imagined but realistic scenario that mimics real business situations. In this appendix and in the text, a "case" refers to both real case studies and simulated scenarios.

issues that are not readily apparent from a superficial reading of the case. In real life, clients hire professional accountants precisely because the clients do not know all the relevant issues. In some cases, analysis of one issue results in the identification of additional issues that warrant further investigation.

3. Ranking

Related to the identification of issues is the need to rank order them. The rank of an issue affects how much time you devote to addressing the issue and the priority it has in your memo, letter, or report (higher ranking issues should appear earlier in the report). When there are logical or chronological connections between issues, where one issue must be considered before another, the ranking is clear-cut. For example, in a case that involves the recognition and measurement of inventories, the issue of recognition should be addressed before measurement, because recognition is about whether the inventories are recorded on the balance sheet while measurement involves how much should be recorded if the inventories were to be recognized.

When there are no clear logical or chronological connections among issues, ranking should consider two factors: urgency and importance. Your case analysis should address more urgent matters before less urgent ones, and more important matters before less important ones. An issue that is both urgent and important has even more priority. For example, an issue relating to a cash shortage in the short term would be both urgent and important, because not resolving the issue satisfactorily will jeopardize the survival of the enterprise.

Take note that the amount of information relating to an issue is not necessarily indicative of the importance of an issue. Some cases deliberately provide extraneous information that is not relevant to the most urgent or important issue to examine your ability to determine what is actually urgent and important.

4. Analysis (including consideration of alternatives)

Analysis involves applying the facts of the situation and relevant accounting standards. For example, in a particular situation, is it appropriate to record a transaction using a particular accounting policy; or which of several possible accounting policies is more appropriate under the circumstances? Analysis implicitly includes the consideration of alternative courses of action, including the status quo.

The extent of the analysis (i.e., how much time you devote to the issue) depends on the ranking of the issue you made earlier. An issue with high priority will generally require extensive analysis, while some issues with low priority can be dealt with in as little as a sentence or two.

5. Evaluation/conclusion/recommendation

After analyzing the potential alternatives, you must evaluate the overall attractiveness of those alternatives in order to draw a conclusion regarding which is the best alternative under the circumstances. If your role is to provide advice to the decision maker, then these conclusions would be in the form of recommendations.

While most cases require you to draw conclusions, be careful not to jump to conclusions. Conclusions need to logically follow and flow from the analysis with full consideration of the relevant facts. Avoid rushing to a conclusion and then selectively using facts from the case to support that conclusion.

6. Action plan

If the case involves a large number of issues, it would be helpful to lay out an action plan that outlines the sequence in which those issues would be resolved. An action plan explains who does what and when. It chronologically lists the actions required, and it is helpful to identify the person or people responsible for each particular task. Depending on the case, the timing may need to be precise (with specific dates) or general (short, medium, and long term).

C. SUMMARY

The above discussion lays out the ingredients that are useful for solving a variety of styles of cases. You will need to use your judgment to put more or less emphasis on different components. With practice, you will be able to master the art of case solving.

D. COMPREHENSIVE CASES

CASE 1

Marathon Petroleum Inc.

Chapters 11–13

(90 minutes)

Marathon Petroleum Inc. commenced operations on January 2, 2018, and has a year-end of December 31. It operates an oil refinery located on the Seaway and a chain of 36 gasoline stations in eastern Canada. It is privately owned and reports under IFRS. The refinery supplies gasoline and home heating oil retailers as well as all the gasoline stations it owns. Most of the capital came from a single bond issue due January 2, 2028, (10-year, $200 million face value, 6% coupon, issued to yield 8%) on which interest is paid semi-annually, and through shares issued to the owners ($40 million). A 7% note payable for $40 million to a bank was also issued in 2018, due in May 2020. Retained earnings was $15 million as at December 31, 2018, and no dividends were paid in 2018.

You work for a mid-sized CPA firm in Toronto and have been asked by a partner to look into the accounting by Marathon's accounting team. The controller, Tom Tesarski, CPA, is concerned about the loan covenants included on the debt issue and whether the financial results for the 2019 fiscal year will fall short of their requirements. Specifically, it requires that, beginning with the fiscal year ended December 31, 2019, the following loan covenants need to be met:

1. The long-term debt-to-equity ratio must not exceed 4:1.
2. Times interest earned must exceed 2 times.

The draft 2019 earnings are an improvement over last year's: net income after tax was $16 million with $4 million of dividends having been declared and paid.

The following may impact the financial position and 2019 earnings:

- Tom mentions that, to simplify matters, he accounted for the bond interest using the straight 6% rate on the $200 million principal amount in 2019. The financial statements for 2018 were audited by your firm and the bond accounting to the end of that year was in accordance with IFRS.
- The refinery has a 30-year life starting in 2018. It was expected then that site restoration would cost $75 million and a separate property, plant, and equipment account for this ARO (asset retirement obligation) was set up. A 6% discount rate was used to value the related ARO. At the beginning of 2019, an external geo-technical evaluation showed that the eventual cost will be $90 million. Tom recorded the same amounts for 2019 as for 2018 for interest on the ARO and depreciation, and otherwise did not update any accounting for the ARO in 2019 nor did he include the impact if any from the ARO revaluation.
- In December 2019, Marathon obtained an extension on $20 million of the 7% note payable to the bank with a new maturity date in 2021. A contractual arrangement was also made with one of the shareholders to purchase an additional $20 million in shares in April 2020, with the funds being used to pay the remaining $20 million of the 7% bank note in May 2020.
- Starting in February 2019, Marathon offered customers the option of buying a prepaid card for gasoline. The cards are loaded with "gasoline dollars" and offer a discount to encourage their popularity and to "lock in" future sales. For $100, a customer can obtain $115 in gas from one of Marathon's gasoline stations. Tom mentions that he has considered the cash received on sale of the cards as unearned revenue, and then has recognized the revenue as the cards were used to purchase gasoline. The notes made by the audit partner in your 2019 audit file state the proper accounting would be: "When a card is sold, a liability for $115 is recognized; then when the card is used, the retail value of gasoline is credited to revenue. The $15 discount is included in promotion expense."

- Up to December 31, 2019, cards with a retail value (exchangeable for gasoline) of $12 million have been issued and gasoline with a retail value of $6.5 million has been paid for using the cards. It is expected that the remaining amount will be redeemed equally over the next two years to the end of December 2021.

Required:

You are a CPA working for a medium-sized CPA firm in Toronto and have been asked by your senior to draft a report to respond to Tom Tesarski's concerns.

CASE 2
Allied Produce Inc.
Chapters 11–15
(85 minutes)

Allied Produce Inc. is a major seller and distributor of fresh food products with annual sales of more than $900 million. Average net income and gross profit margins for the most recent five years have been only 1% and 1.5% of sales respectively, which is below industry norms. The tax rate is 30%. Excerpts from the draft 2019 financial statements (11-month actual, 1-month estimate) for the current year ended December 31, 2019, and estimated for 2020 are provided in Exhibit I. Based on this situation, the company's president, Thomas Lowe, desperately needs to enhance the investment performance and shareholder value for Allied's common shareholders because the share price has fallen from $18 five years ago to about half that now. According to listing requirements with the TSX, Allied is prevented from repurchasing common shares until 2024 and can only issue new shares until that time. He advises you that, during 2021, new and renegotiated existing contracts will be in effect to prevent further erosion in earnings; however, his main concern is for estimated 2020 earnings per share numbers, since he wants to consider a share offering in early 2021 to finance expansion into new markets. However, if the share price does not improve, this may not be possible and thus it will be important to maximize 2020 diluted earnings per share.

You are advised that the shares are generally priced to trade at 20 times diluted total earnings per share. Currently, 12,500,000 common shares are issued and outstanding.

Allied has sufficient cash reserves to undertake one of the following two alternative courses of action, which could potentially increase earnings per share in 2020:

Option 1: Allied has outstanding $125 million of 6% convertible, redeemable bonds payable to mature in 12 years from their date of issue on January 1, 2018. The bonds, without the convertible feature, would have been priced to yield 7% (i.e., $115,072,500); however, they were issued for $120 million. Each $1,000 bond is convertible into 100 shares of common stock. Allied's underwriter estimates that if the bond issue could be refunded on January 1, 2020, and that the fair value reflects that the yield has increased to 9%, an inducement of $14 million in cash would need to be offered for all the bonds to be redeemed. According to the indenture, the bond issue would have to be redeemed in its entirety.

Option 2: Allied also has $75 million in 4.5% cumulative, convertible preferred shares outstanding, redeemable at $102. The underwriter says that they could be redeemed on January 1, 2020. Dividends were declared and paid in July 2019. Each $100 preferred share is currently convertible into eight common shares, which will increase to 12 common shares by 2022. This conversion ratio has enabled Allied to offer a relatively low dividend yield.

Required:

Mr. Lowe asks you, CPA to (i) compute the 2019 basic and diluted earnings per share, and (ii) determine which of the two courses of action above should be entered into based on maximizing projected diluted earnings per share for 2020. Ignore any return difference on cash reserves from the two options.

Exhibit I

Allied Produce Inc. Estimated Net Income For years ended December 31	2019	2020
Net income before interest and tax	$22,200,000	$19,200,000
Interest	8,100,000	8,150,000
Net income before tax	14,100,000	11,050,000
Income tax	4,230,000	3,315,000
Net income after tax	$ 9,870,000	$ 7,735,000

CASE 3
Longhorn Casuals Ltd.
Chapters 15–18
(70 minutes)

Longhorn Casuals Ltd. is a retail operation, the shares of which have been publically traded since it was incorporated. The company has prepared the following draft income statement. You work for Benson and Associates, CPAs, and will conduct the audit of the financial statements. Bill Benson, partner, provides you with the following information provided by the client and asks you to prepare an adjusted income statement including the tax provision. He would also like you to outline any necessary note disclosures and to include the journal entries required to adjust the draft income statement.

Longhorn Casuals Ltd. Draft Income Statement For the year ended December 31, 2019 (000s)			
Sales			$100,000
Cost of goods sold			50,000
Gross profit			50,000
Expenses:			
Depreciation		$6,000	
Pension		2,000	
Operating		28,000	36,000
Net pretax income			14,000
Income tax-estimate	30%		4,200
Net income			$ 9,800
Earnings per share	($9,800,000/2,000,000) = $4.90		

Additional information:

1. The company introduced a pension plan at the beginning of 2019. Past service costs were paid in full in the amount of $2 million. Current service costs for 2019 were $500,000 and were not funded in the year. Amounts funded were the only amounts included in pension expense (operating expense). The actual return on plan assets was 9% and the discount rate used 7% for the pension plan obligation, which is equivalent to the expected return on plan assets. Only funding is recognized by CRA as tax deductible. No benefits were paid because there were no retirees as of December 31, 2019.
2. At the date of incorporation, the company had issued 2,000,000 common shares for $10 per share. On February 1, 2019, 20,000 of the shares were repurchased and cancelled by the company. The controller included the $1 million cost of this repurchase in operating expenses. The company had issued a call option in 2018, expiring in 2020 and allowing the holder to purchase 40,000 shares for $40 per share. The average share price in 2019 was $51.

3. On January 1, 2019, the company leased its administrative building under a contract wherein the company will obtain ownership of the building at the end of the 20-year lease for a nominal amount. Management decided to expense the lease payment of $3,000,000 for 2019 (paid on January 1, 2019). The building would have been capitalized at $30 million if treated as a capital lease. The building has a remaining economic life of 25 years. The interest for 2019 would have amounted to $2.45 million. The company has adopted IFRS 16 for lease accounting.
4. The depreciation expense was $2 million lower than CCA in 2019, not including any impact from transaction 3. The tax rate enacted for 2020 and beyond was increased to 32%.

Required:

Prepare the report.

E. CAPSTONE CASES

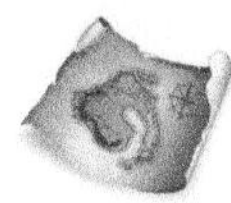

CASE 1 Gibraltar Enterprises[2]

Gibraltar Enterprises Ltd. (GEL, or the company) was incorporated under federal legislation in 1999. GEL began operations as a land development company, but over the years expanded its operations to include a construction division and a panel manufacturing division. The company currently follows International Financial Reporting Standards (IFRS).

The land development division (real estate division) purchases large plots of raw land. It holds some land for resale, but most of the land is subdivided into smaller parcels upon which GEL builds commercial and industrial buildings. GEL retains ownership of these buildings and rents units of the buildings to various businesses and individuals.

The construction division commenced operations in 2004 and handles building and construction activity for the company. Initially, the construction division's activities were limited to construction projects for GEL. Since 2010, the construction division has also contracted to do construction work for unrelated parties.

The panel manufacturing division (panel division), which was acquired in 2009, fabricates products incorporating new technology for the high-rise construction industry. Its primary product is wall panels used to finish the exterior of office buildings, apartment buildings, and shopping centres.

From its inception, GEL was owned by four individuals, each of whom was actively involved in managing the operations of the company. As a result of growing disagreements among the owners, the company was sold in September 2014 to Mutual Investment Corporation (MIC), which is owned by a group of investors.

MIC was provided with an "information package" by the previous owners. The information package was dated August 31, 2014, and contained the fiscal 2012, 2013, and 2014 audited financial statements of GEL, a two-year cash flow forecast, and a brief description of the business, including its history.

It is now June 2015, and GEL is experiencing financial difficulties. MIC has allowed the bank to foreclose on several GEL properties as part of a restructuring of GEL that was necessary to satisfy GEL's creditors.

MIC intends to commence legal action against GEL's previous owners and the preparers of the information package. MIC contends that the price it paid for GEL was excessive because it was misled as to GEL's true financial status by the information package that had been provided.

Charles Brown & Company (CB), Chartered Professional Accountants, was involved in the preparation of the information that was made available to prospective purchasers of GEL. Specifically, the information package included CB's audit reports on the financial statements presented and CB's Notice to Reader on GEL's cash flow forecast.[3] All other contents of the information package were reviewed by CB. CB was also involved in discussions with potential purchasers, including MIC.

Since legal action may be taken against CB, CB and its lawyers have engaged your firm, Anthony & Matthews (A&M), Chartered Professional Accountants, to assist them.

CB's lawyers have informed the A&M partner responsible for this assignment that MIC is alleging that the contents of the information package were improperly prepared and that CB's conduct was not in keeping with professional standards. CB's legal liability will depend on the degree to which the damages suffered by MIC can be reasonably attributed to the quality of the work done by CB on the information package.

You are employed by A&M and have been assigned to this engagement. The partner has asked you to draft a report to CB's lawyers addressing MIC's allegations. Your report should highlight those issues that will be of greatest significance to CB's lawyers.

---

2. Reprinted from Uniform Final Examination 2002, with permission Chartered Professional Accountants of Canada, Toronto, Canada. Any changes to the original material are the sole responsibility of the author (and/or publisher) and have not been reviewed or endorsed by the Chartered Professional Accountants of Canada.

3. A "Notice to Reader" is the professional accountant's letter that accompanies financial information that has been prepared, or compiled, by the accountant based on information supplied by the client. Among other things, this letter cautions readers of the financial information that the information has not been audited or reviewed. Professional standards simply require that the accountant not present information that is false or misleading to the best of his or her knowledge.

CB has provided A&M with all its working papers and a copy of the information package. It has allowed A&M to interview its partners and staff as necessary. As a result of your review and discussions, you have assembled the data included in Exhibits I to IV.

Required:

Prepare the report.

Exhibit I

Gibraltar Enterprises Ltd.
Balance Sheets
As of June 30
(audited, in 000's)

	2014	2013	2012
Assets			
Cash	$ 300	$ 590	$ 880
Accounts receivable	12,690	12,885	11,970
Inventory (Note 2a)	43,510	62,755	70,470
Investments, at cost	—	3,370	6,925
Capital assets, less depreciation	9,825	8,690	10,295
Land (Note 2b)	9,700	13,342	21,835
Revenue-producing properties	100,900	97,890	95,770
Tenant inducements, less amortization (Note 2c)	8,520	3,595	878
Deferred charges, less amortization (Note 2d)	13,715	8,853	4,085
Investment in joint venture (Note 3)	10,000	—	—
Goodwill	3,500	3,500	3,500
	$212,660	$215,470	$226,608
Liabilities			
Accounts payable	$ 6,535	$ 5,305	$ 6,328
Demand bank loan, prime + 1%	22,610	14,100	18,935
Debenture, 12%, due 2015	20,000	20,000	20,000
Unearned revenue	40,810	51,975	61,895
Mortgages payable (Note 4)	87,740	89,255	84,875
	177,695	180,635	192,033
Shareholders' Equity			
Common shares	20,000	20,000	20,000
Preferred shares, 12%, non-cumulative	10,000	10,000	10,000
Retained earnings	4,965	4,835	4,575
	34,965	34,835	34,575
	$212,660	$215,470	$226,608

Gibraltar Enterprises Ltd.
Income And Retained Earnings Statements
For the years ended June 30 (audited, in 000's)

	2014	2013	2012
Revenue			
Panel division	$22,520	$19,460	$17,410
Real estate division			
Rental	10,105	10,695	11,690

(Continued)

Exhibit I Continued

Gain on sales of land	3,795	3,710	320
Gain on sale of building	890	—	—
Construction division	47,475	34,080	38,655
Investments	1,395	970	235
	86,180	68,915	68,310
Expenses			
Panel	13,165	11,880	11,140
Rental	4,170	4,040	4,005
Construction	38,905	26,440	27,500
Selling and administrative	3,575	3,540	3,550
Amortization of capital assets	4,258	4,870	3,600
Other amortization	3,922	2,105	900
Interest	14,010	13,440	13,860
Writedown of revenue-producing properties	1,795	—	—
	83,800	66,315	64,555
Income before income tax	2,380	2,600	3,755
Income tax	1,050	1,140	1,710
Net income	1,230	1,460	2,045
Opening retained earnings	4,935	4,575	3,730
	6,165	6,035	5,775
Dividends on preferred shares	1,200	1,200	1,200
Closing retained earnings	$ 4,965	$ 4,835	$ 4,575

Gibraltar Enterprises Ltd.
Excerpts From Notes To Financial Statements
For the years ended June 30
(audited)

You reviewed all the notes to GEL's financial statements and noted the following pertinent information:

1. **Significant accounting policies**

   a. Real estate division

   Revenues from sale of land are recorded at the time that title transfers.

   All property taxes, interest, and similar costs are capitalized to revenue-producing properties until the project generates sufficient cash flows to pay all expenses except interest and amortization. During fiscal 2014, the division capitalized $677,400 of these costs.

   Payments to improve or alter revenue-producing properties for tenants are amortized over the lease period. Such leasehold payments are amortized over an average period of 10 years.

   Rent revenue is recorded on a straight-line basis over the lease period. A sum of $2.615 million was recognized as rental revenue in 2014 on new lease contracts that did not require tenants to pay rent because of "free rent" incentives included in the lease.

   b. Panel division

   Development costs are capitalized and amortized over five years on a straight-line basis.

2. **Details of certain assets**

a. Inventory	2014	2013 (in 000's)	2012
Panel inventory	$ 4,925	$ 5,560	$ 5,900
Construction work in progress	38,585	57,195	64,570
	$43,510	$62,755	$70,470

(Continued)

Exhibit I Continued

b. Land	2014	2013	2012
		(in 000's)	
Raw land held for resale, at lower of cost or market	$ 6,390	$10,312	$16,315
Land improvements	2,110	3,030	4,670
Land held for future development, at cost	1,200	—	850
	$ 9,700	$ 13,342	$ 21,835

During 2014, $1.2 million of land inventory was reclassified from land held for resale to land held for future development. At the date of transfer, the net realizable value of the land was $900,000. Management intends to hold the land for future development instead of continuing to offer it for sale.

c. Tenant inducements	2014	2013	2012
		(in 000's)	
Leasehold, less amortization	$ 5,800	$ 2,795	$ 878
Free rent, less amortization	2,720	800	878
	$ 8,520	$ 3,595	$ 1,756

d. Deferred charges	2014	2013	2012
		(in 000's)	
Deferred charges, less amortization	$ 4,375	$ 3,382	$ 1,755
Development costs, less amortization	9,340	5,471	2,330
	$13,715	$ 8,853	$ 4,085

3. Investment in joint venture

In fiscal 2014, GEL entered into a joint venture with an unrelated party to develop a 40-unit commercial property. GEL has a 60% interest in the venture, which is accounted for on the equity basis.

4. Mortgages payable

Mortgages payable represent first mortgages secured by revenue-producing properties, repayable by monthly principal installments totalling $130,000 plus interest ranging from 9% to 12%. These mortgages mature in years ranging from 2015 to 2019.

Exhibit II Operational information gathered by A&M from CB regarding Gibraltar Enterprises Ltd.

1. **Bank loans**

   GEL's loans are secured by accounts receivable, inventory, and a general charge on the company's assets.

   In the real estate industry, new sources of financing are difficult to find, which is causing many companies to experience problems. Lenders tend to want more collateral and increased interest rates. Some lenders want personal guarantees from the shareholders of the borrowing corporations.

2. **Panel division**

   a. A considerable amount of research and development activity has been occurring in the panel division to improve the variety and quality of the products. To continue offering state-of-the-art products so that sales levels can be maintained, management has stated that research and development must continue at 2014 levels. The company has claimed significant investment tax credits in respect of these expenditures.

   b. Panels are costed on a full-costing basis using a budgeted overhead application rate that is based on the plant being used at 50% of its capacity.

   c. Many panels are made to order, conforming to the specifications prescribed by the general contractor. The division frequently produces more than the number of panels ordered so that it can use the extras for display purposes. The average actual manufacturing cost is used to assign a cost to these extras. The extra panels are treated as capital assets. As of June 30, 2014, the cost less amortization of the extra panels amounted to $362,735.

   Standard-size panels are also manufactured. These standard panels are colour-coated once a sales order has been placed by a customer.

(*Continued*)

Exhibit II Continued

d. The division records revenue on receipt of an order for standard panels whenever the inventory is "in stock" and "can be delivered within 30 days." A liability is set up for colour-coating when revenue is recorded. Revenue for made-to-order panels is recognized upon completion of production.

e. The division also installs both standard and made-to-order panels. Revenue for the installation work is recognized on a percentage of completion basis.

f. The division has to bid for most of its contracts. As a matter of policy, the division bids for combined manufacturing and installation contracts in such a way as to break even on the installation portion and make a profit on the manufacturing portion. The division is aware that there is strong competition for installation work.

g. During fiscal 2014, the manufacturing overhead that was charged to units produced exceeded the actual manufacturing overhead by $488,290 because the division was operating at 100% capacity.

h. The history of the outstanding orders at the end of each fiscal year that were filled from production in the next fiscal year is as follows (in $000's):

Fiscal year	Outstanding orders
2013	$6,075
2012	5,020
2011	4,000

At June 30, 2014, there were outstanding orders worth $2.2 million.

3. **Real estate division**

a. Financial information on the revenue-producing properties at June 30, 2014, is as follows (in 000's):

Property number	Cost	Accumulated amortization	Estimated market value	Mortgage principal	Mortgage due date
1	$ 23,650	$ 4,730	$ 19,300	$15,305	April 2016
2	15,795	3,185	11,500	10,725	October 2014
3	22,290	2,970	19,500	17,900	December 2014
4	20,680	2,665	16,600	14,600	May 2015
5	17,340	1,620	15,800	14,500	November 2017
6	18,210	100	18,200	14,710	August 2019
	$117,965	$15,270	$100,900	$87,740	

All mortgages represent first mortgages on the properties. On commercial properties, mortgage companies are permitted to lend 75% of the current fair market value of the property.

Second mortgages are generally available for up to 10% of the estimated market value. Current interest rates for second mortgages are 17–20% per annum for terms of repayment of three to five years.

b. During fiscal 2014, a variety of incentives were offered to potential tenants, including partial payments for leasehold improvements, free rent, and subsidized cleaning and maintenance costs. Most new tenants signed one of the following two types of leases:

i. A 10-year lease with the first year rent free, and 50% of the leasehold improvements to be paid by GEL.

ii. A 5-year lease with the first six months rent free, and 25% of the leasehold improvements to be paid by GEL.

c. In August 2013, the division arranged a mortgage for a new shopping centre it had developed (property #5). The mortgage contains a participation clause that allows the mortgage company to receive more than the stipulated interest on the mortgage if rental income of the shopping centre exceeds a stipulated threshold. GEL has decided to account for participation payments on a cash basis because payments are unlikely to be calculated until late September each year.

d. The major tenant in one of the office buildings moved after its 10-year lease had expired in September 2013. To date no replacement tenant has been found for the vacated space, which amounts to two-thirds of the eight-storey building. Five floors in the building are being renovated at a cost of $800,000, and all other costs (including property taxes, insurance, interest, cleaning, heating, ventilation, etc.) are to be capitalized until a tenant has been found and has signed a lease. During 2014, $490,000 of renovation costs and $317,200 of other costs were capitalized as tenant inducements.

(Continued)

Exhibit II Continued

e. The division expects business and economic conditions in fiscal years 2015 and 2016 to be similar to those that it experienced in fiscal 2014.

f. In May 2014, a commercial rental building was traded for a similar commercial building located in the same area with an unrelated real estate company. The mortgages were included in the trade.

	Building given up by GEL (in 000's)	Building acquired by GEL (property #6) (in 000's)
Fair market value	$ 18,870	$ 18,210
Mortgage		
12% due August 2019		14,710
10% due August 2014	13,870	
Cost to transferor company	17,700	19,800
Ac cumulated amortization on transferor company's building	1,120	970
Undepreciated capital cost of the building	4,890	915

As part of the transaction, GEL received $100,000 in addition to the traded building.

g. A joint venture construction project was undertaken between GEL and an unrelated party. Total costs of the project were originally expected to be $26.2 million and the project was scheduled to be completed by August 2016. As at June 30, 2014, $16.7 million had been invested in the joint venture, of which $10 million was invested by GEL. The venture is high risk, and it has been difficult for GEL to obtain financing. The real estate division's 40% partner in the venture withdrew from the project in July 2014. As of July 31, 2014, financing for the completion of the project had not been arranged, but GEL was confident that financing could be obtained.

4. **Construction division**

a. As of June 30, 2014, the division had the following contracts in progress with unrelated parties (in 000's):

Year contract commenced	Contract number	Expected revenue	Costs to date	Additional expected costs	Expected completion date
2012	12-A	$ 19,850	$13,840	$ 4,150	2015
2012	12-B	12,990	9,670	3,430	2015
2013	13-C	9,220	5,115	3,200	2015
2013	13-D	11,100	9,960	1,290	2015
2014	14-E	18,670	7,200	8,500	2016
2014	14-F	17,700	4,800	11,200	2017

The completed contract method of accounting is being used for contracts entered into prior to 2014. For contracts commencing in 2014, the percentage of completion method, based on costs, is being used for revenue recognition.

b. Customers receive progress billings in accordance with the terms of their contract with GEL. The progress billing also includes charges for "extra" work not included in signed construction contracts. All billings by the division are credited to unearned revenue until revenue is recognized.

Customers are entitled to withhold 15% of invoiced amounts as a "holdback" until work has been satisfactorily completed.

Exhibit III Notes from review of 2014 GEL audit files of Charles Brown & Company Chartered Professional Accountants

Your review of CB's working papers for GEL has produced the following information. Nothing else came to your attention that warranted notation.

1. **You noted the following matters from your review of the general section of the audit file.**

a. CB's unqualified audit report on GEL's financial statements of June 30, 2014, was dated August 16, 2014.

(Continued)

Exhibit III Continued

b. Notations in the audit planning memo were as follows:
   i. "Materiality is set as 1% of net assets, consistent with prior years."
   ii. "The general audit approach is to rely on internal controls, based on past assessment of the reliability of controls."
   iii. "Risk of the engagement is assessed as higher than normal based on the pending sale of GEL."
   iv. "Additional service opportunity: we have been asked to assist GEL in preparing forecasts that are to be included in an information package GEL will provide to prospective purchasers. Procedures for the cash flow forecast will be limited to a check of the compilation of the numbers, and we will issue a Notice to Reader report."

c. The unadjusted misstatement schedule affecting income before tax for the 2014 year-end audit of GEL is summarized below:

Unadjusted misstatements carried forward from previous year	
Net understatement of 2013	$206,000
2014 audit: unadjusted mortgage participation interest	10,000
Total unadjusted misstatements, June 30, 2014	$216,000

d. CB advised GEL on its corporate income tax filing. A summary of the reconciliation of accounting income to taxable income is as follows (in $000's):

Net income per fi nancial statements	$ 1,330
Add:	
Income tax	1,050
Amortization per financial statements	8,180
Taxable capital gains on raw land and buildings	3,514
Writedown of revenue-producing properties per financial statements	1,795
Deduct:	
Gain on disposal of assets per financial statements—raw land	(3,795)
Gain on disposal of assets per financial statements—building	(890)
Construction contracts (adjust to completed contract basis)	(1,872)
Capital cost allowance	(5,365)
Net income for tax purposes, being taxable income	$ 3,947

e. Calculation of income tax expense (in $000's):

Current taxes for 2014 fiscal year before deductions	$ 1,500
Less: scientifi c research and experimental development tax credits (arising from panel division development activities)	(450)
	$ 1,050

f. The auditor identified the following significant issues in the 2014 year-end audit summary memo:
   i. The construction division's revenue recognition policy for contracts was changed from the completed contract method to the percentage of completion method in 2014 due to the increasing length of contracts.

      Conclusion: Change in facts (i.e., commercial circumstances of contracts); therefore, retroactive treatment is not necessary for reporting purposes.

      A note explaining the change has been included in the notes to financial statements.
   ii. Demand loan

      The company's demand loan agreement expires September 30, 2014, and negotiations with the bank have begun. The bank has stated that it will renew the demand loan if the total amount currently outstanding is reduced and the rate of interest is increased to prime +3%.

      Conclusion: Based on a review of management's estimated future cash flows, we conclude that the company can continue to operate with the terms proposed.

(Continued)

Exhibit III Continued

iii. Revenue-producing properties

Given the tough economy, we examined the need to write down revenue-producing properties.

Conclusion: Based on the fair market value of the property portfolio, a writedown of $1.795 million was determined to be necessary.

2. **Panel division**

   a. In March 2014, tests of controls were performed on the purchases/payables, payroll, and sales/receivables control systems and several errors were detected. The working papers state: "Errors appear to be due to staff turnover; therefore, there are no problems with relying on internal controls."

   b. The division purchases metals from a company owned by two of the original owners of GEL. In order to "obtain assured supply," GEL pays fair market value for the metals. CB requested that a standard related party note be included in the financial statements; this request was agreed to by GEL's directors.

   c. In the last two business days of June 2014, orders were received for the entire inventory of excess standard panels—both finished goods and work in progress. The revenue was recorded, and a liability was recorded for estimated completion costs. Gross profit on these two days of sales was approximately $500,000. CB's working papers noted that approximately half of these orders were not shipped until August. A notation in the working papers indicates "Not material."

   d. CB's audit staff examined over one-half of the external invoices and payroll vouchers that supported the additions to development costs and discussed the "nature of additions" with management.

   e. The working papers state that "management requested that accounts receivable confirmations not be sent to some customers. We decided to verify these receivables by checking subsequent cash receipts, shipping documents, and sales invoices, as well as discussing these accounts with management."

   f. CB's staff observed the physical inventory count as of June 30, 2014. In light of the low dollar value of raw materials inventory, the auditor tested costing by referring to recent purchase prices to assess the reasonability of the per-unit costs. The working papers state that "recent prices of raw materials have varied considerably, and pricing tests were inconclusive."

   g. CB's staff tested the value of raw material and labour included in work in progress for made-to-order panel inventory and noted that "no items were considered obsolete or required a writedown since most items pertained to installation contracts, which earn significantly higher margins than contracts that do not include installations."

3. **Real estate division**

   a. At the request of its lenders, GEL adopted a policy several years ago of having its revenue-producing properties appraised every three years. GEL instructs appraisers to adopt a long-term perspective, considering growth in the community and any potential rezoning or other beneficial developments. CB used the appraisers' valuation figures in establishing market value for auditing purposes because "this information was considered appropriate for establishing the value of the properties and the appraisal date coincided with the year-end date."

   b. The procedures performed in relation to capitalized property taxes, interest, and similar costs consisted of an examination of all invoices and bank statements.

   c. Audit work on the joint venture consisted of an examination of the joint venture file. The auditor came across correspondence from the Provincial Environmental Protection Department requesting that an environmental assessment of the property be scheduled in accordance with the new Environmental Protection Act. The audit files note that "the issue was discussed with management, and they stated that GEL is in compliance with all environmental regulations."

   d. The working papers show that "in late fiscal 2014, GEL was awarded $1 million in a lawsuit against a former tenant for rent owed as a result of a breach of a rental contract. GEL believes it will likely collect the awarded amount; however, we insisted that the amount not be accrued until it is received, which is expected in 2015."

   e. Other notations in the working papers are as follows:

      i. "All receivables over $5,000 were verified by direct confirmation, subsequent receipts, or analytical review."

      ii. "All additions to capital assets in excess of $10,000 were checked to invoices."

      iii. "The company is making lump sum payments to new tenants for leasehold improvements made by the tenants to the leased premises. We have not seen invoices from these tenants, but have read the lease agreements."

4. **Construction division**

   a. The construction contracts for all work in progress at June 30, 2014, were examined.

   b. The status of each contract was discussed with management.

(Continued)

Exhibit III Continued

c. Receivables at June 30, 2014, were verified by examination of subsequent receipts and confirmations with customers. Some confirmations returned by customers excluded the amount billed for extra work (not included in the original contract). The auditor vouched such invoiced amounts to GEL's work in progress to ensure that the work had indeed been performed by GEL.

d. Additions to work in progress at June 30, 2014, were test-checked for the month of June 2014, and no material errors were found.

e. The additional expected costs to complete work in progress at year-end were agreed to the original cost estimates that were compiled for bidding purposes.

Exhibit IV

Excerpts From Cash Flow Forecast Included in the Information Package (in 000's)

		2015	2016
Cash receipts			
Divisional revenue net of expenses			
Panel division	(Note 1)	$10,208	$11,408
Real estate division			
—rental	(Note 2)	6,000	6,500
—sales of land	(Note 3)	1,000	1,000
Construction division	(Note 4)	8,570	8,570
		25,778	27,478
Cash disbursements			
Selling and administrative costs	(Note 4)	3,575	3,575
Interest charges	(Note 4)	14,010	14,010
		17,585	17,585
Cash flow before income tax and dividends		8,193	9,893
Less: income taxes	(Note 5)	(1,500)	(2,000)
Less: dividends		(1,200)	(1,200)
Forecasted cash flow		$ 5,493	$ 6,693

Excerpts from notes:

1. An annual increase in sales of $3 million is estimated by management (at 40% gross margin).
2. Rental income is based on improved occupancy rates (2015—75%, 2016—80%).
3. Management intends to sell some land over the next two years for $2 million.
4. It is the opinion of management that economic conditions existing in 2014 will continue; therefore, activity will remain constant and profit margins (revenues and costs) for 2014 will be maintained.
5. Income taxes were calculated on the basis of expected taxable income for the year.

CASE 2 Netconnect Inc.[4]

Netconnect Inc. (NI) is a mid-sized internet service provider, supplying internet connection and related services in two Canadian provinces. NI is privately owned by four wealthy Canadian investors who are not active in the business. The company's board of directors consists of the investors, two friends, and the CEO of NI.

[4] Adapted with permission from Densmore Consulting Services Inc., Fall River, Nova Scotia. Any changes to the original material are the sole responsibility of the author and have not been reviewed or endorsed by Densmore Consulting Services.

NI offers a wide variety of services to meet consumer and business needs, including the latest high-speed connections. In this competitive industry, the company has only been marginally profitable and losses for income tax purposes have been recorded most years. The company has a May 31 year-end and has been audited since it was incorporated.

In early spring 2014, management of NI saw an opportunity to diversify the business by purchasing Plastok Corporation (PC). PC was originally an industrial plastic forming company, founded by Vulcan Vostival. Vostival passed away in 1998 and the company was taken over by his only son, Peter. By the early 2010s, Peter had transformed the company from the original plastics business to software systems development and internet consulting. By this time, the company had over 50 employees but it was still operating out of the original plastics factory and warehouse complex, which it had converted into office space. PC developed a product that sped up the movement of internet traffic and other data around corporate internal networks. Version 1.0 of the NetworkAccelerator, a six-inch by six-inch box that is plugged into corporate networks, was released to the market in January 2014.

With the proliferation of the internet, many companies, from the largest software and hardware firms to small outfits, had opened internet consultancy ventures. At the same time, the internet consulting market was growing rapidly, as every business and not-for-profit organization wanted a first-time or improved presence on the internet. In parallel with this, faster internet access and greater bandwidth, inside and outside corporate networks, were being sought by many companies. In 2013, PC obtained a few internet consulting contracts with blue-chip customers, as well as contracts with lesser-known companies.

In April 2014, NI management was introduced to Peter. They liked the NetworkAccelerator, the consulting revenue stream, and the potential of PC. A leveraged buyout, financed by the Notional Bank of Canada (the banker for both companies), was closed on June 30, 2014. The deal was financed by a $4 million, 18% term loan from Notional Bank and $1 million of cash from NI, which had just been injected by the four investors. Stating tax reasons, Peter refused to sell assets. PC shares were purchased and an indemnity clause was signed to protect NI. PC has a May 31 year-end. A regional firm of CPAs has looked after its tax and accounting needs since 1970. The company underwent its first audit in 2014 due to the pending sale, and a clean audit opinion was issued. PC chose to follow IFRS to meet the needs of the buyer (NI).

Prior to closing the purchase, NI engaged merchant banker, Salmon Brothers Inc. (SB), to provide a "solvency opinion" on whether PC would be solvent and able to discharge its liabilities after the close of the transaction. Legal counsel for the Notional Bank insisted on this. A solvency opinion dated June 24, 2014, was made available to NI on June 27, 2014.

The actual share price was negotiated on the basis of a 1.5 times multiplier of last year's annual audited sales plus a negotiated amount reflecting the technology and sales potential of the NetworkAccelerator product. NI's management under no circumstances wanted to pay more than 10 times the book value of the company. Final NI board of directors' approval of the transaction and term loan financing was given at a meeting held on June 27, 2014. Peter was appointed general manager of PC after the purchase. NI laid off PC's controller and both accounting clerks within a month of closing. NI's auditors were appointed auditors of PC.

Peter resigned from the company six months after NI took over. NI has initiated legal action against him, as a departure this early was not provided for in his employment contract. His position was not filled, so the company has operated with an ad hoc management structure. NI injected an additional $500,000 into the company seven months after the initial purchase, but this has not been enough to meet the company's needs. The stock market crash of April 2015 and the economic adjustments that took place thereafter drove the prime rate up to 9%. The company was unable to make its end-of-May loan payment, is negotiating with the Notional Bank, and has sought creditor protection. A third party has tentatively offered to purchase the company's assets for $800,000 (land and buildings) and $300,000 for all other assets including intangibles, subject to creditor approval. NI's management believes that creditor approval will not be difficult to obtain.

It is now June 17, 2015. As a result of PC's failure, the investors who own NI have engaged the law firm McLean & Patterson (M&P). M&P have been asked to prepare claims against all negligent parties involved and to advise the company what to do about its current situation. M&P has engaged Wolfe & Naish (WN), Chartered Professional Accountants, to prepare a report on financial and other aspects of the investigation.

M&P has asked WN to go in and "determine what went wrong and, from a business perspective, who is responsible." They said, "We will sue them all. We lawyers will figure out exactly how. We want to know what went wrong, who was negligent in causing NI damages, and why. We also want to know if any of NI's personnel need to share responsibility for this mess and how similar situations could be prevented in the future." If the legal actions initiated are not settled out of court, WN's report will be re-drafted for use in court.

Salmon Brothers' legal counsel has taken the position that any claim by NI is "entirely without merit" and SB intends to "vigorously defend" itself. She notes that SB has "nothing to hide" and that its work will withstand "professional scrutiny." After extensive negotiations, SB's counsel agreed to make the solvency opinion file available to NI's legal counsel for examination.

You work for Wolfe & Naish, and have been put in charge of the M&P assignment. As a result of your review and discussions to date, you have assembled the data included in Exhibits I to VI.

Required:

Prepare the draft report to M&P.

Exhibit I Selected financial statements and notes for Plastok Corporation.

Balance Sheets
As of May 31
(in 000's)

	2015 (unaudited)	2014 (audited)	2013 (unaudited)
Assets			
Cash and liquid investments	—	—	$ 5
Accounts receivable and accrued revenue	102	212	168
Inventory	125	59	28
Prepaid expenses	26	38	11
	253	309	212
Goodwill	2,766	—	—
Deferred development costs	1,600	265	4
Capital assets	945	866	744
Accumulated depreciation	(561)	(511)	(464)
	$5,003	$ 929	$ 496
Liabilities and Shareholders' Equity			
Accounts payable and accrued liabilities	$1,502	$ 84	$ 131
Line of credit	139	98	110
	1,641	182	241
Long term – preferred shares	200	200	200
– product warranty	—	46	—
– term loan	3,500	—	—
Common shares (note 2)	1,633	633	175
Deficit	(1,971)	(132)	(120)
	(338)	501	55
	$5,003	$ 929	$ 496
Commitment (note 3)			

(Continued)

Exhibit I Continued

Income Statements
For the years ended May 31
(in 000's)

	2015 (unaudited)	2014 (audited)	2013 (unaudited)
Consulting revenues	$ 948	$1,344	$1,101
Product sales	4,345	256	56
Total sales	5,293	1,600	1,157
Cost of product sold	3,302	161	39
	1,991	1,439	1,118
Expenses			
Selling, administration, R&D, and other	960	458	298
Direct consulting costs	756	852	602
Network survey costs	782	56	—
Depreciation and amortization	751	47	39
Interest expense	581	38	35
	3,830	1,451	974
Net income (loss) before taxes	(1,839)	(12)	144
Income tax provision (note 4)	—	—	—
Net income (loss)	$(1,839)	$ (12)	$ 144

EXCERPTS FROM NOTES TO THE FINANCIAL STATEMENTS
For the years ended May 31

1. **Significant accounting policies**

   Revenue recognition

   The company uses the percentage completion method to account for long-term contracts.

   Inventory

   Inventory is valued at the lower of cost or market.

   Deferred development costs

   Development costs associated with the development of software are deferred and amortized over 10 years.

   Depreciation and amortization

   The company uses the straight-line method to depreciate capital assets as follows: computers, equipment, and vehicles, 5 years; buildings, 40 years.

2. **Common share capital**

   The company has authorized and issued 1,000,000 Class A common shares.

3. **Commitment**

   Under relevant federal and provincial environmental legislation, the company is responsible for annual payments to the provincial government for the containment of historical effluent at the original plastics factory location. The amount of the payment for 2014 was set at $14,456 per annum and is escalated based on the Statistics Canada Industrial Materials Index.

4. **Income tax losses**

   The benefit of income tax losses amounting to approximately $200,000 has not been recorded in the accounts.

Exhibit II Leveraged buyout information

The key points of the purchase and sale agreement were as follows:

1. Deal agreed to on June 28, 2014, and closed June 30, 2014, with the delivery of $5 million to the vendor's counsel.
2. PC's management signed off on a series of standard representations stating that all material facts and liabilities had been disclosed, the audited financial statements of May 31, 2014, fairly represented the financial position of the company, and the company's environmental liabilities were fully disclosed in the audited financial statements.
3. Peter to indemnify NI dollar for dollar for net unfavourable working capital changes greater than $100,000 and up to $500,000 for errors or omissions found in PC's financial statements dated May 31, 2014.
4. Peter's aunt did not want to sell her $200,000, 7% preferred shares, retractable on demand by the holder at face value. She signed a letter to PC dated May 29, 2014, stating that she would not request retraction for five years from that date, conditional on the sale of PC's common shares within 60 days.

The key extracts from the Notional Bank's "Offer to Finance" dated June 10, 2014, were as follows:

1. Loan amount of $4 million to PC, interest rate 18% calculated annually, to be repaid in equal monthly installments of $50,000 principal plus interest for the month. Loan amount will be used to complete purchase of Peter's shares. There is a one-time bank set-up fee of $40,000.
2. The term loan was secured by a fixed and floating charge on all assets of PC and an unlimited cross-guarantee from NI.
3. Maximum consolidated debt-to-equity ratio must be 2.5 and minimum current ratio must be 1.5 to 1 in PC.
4. Quarterly statements are required to be sent to the bank 30 days after month-end, and audited annual financials of PC and NI consolidated are to be sent 60 days after year-end.
5. Bank approval must be obtained for all dividends and capital additions over $50,000 in either company.

Exhibit III Plastok Corporation solvency opinion

To: Board of Directors, Netconnect Inc.

We performed an analysis of Plastok Corporation's historical accounting records, audited financial statements, projections prepared by Plastok Corporation management, industry trends and forecasts, and other relevant information. We are not aware of any factors that would cause Plastok Corporation to become insolvent or unable to pay its liabilities as they come due. Plastok Corporation will have adequate capital upon completion of the transaction set out in the "Offer to Finance" dated June 10, 2014, from the Notional Bank of Canada and the injection of $1 million of capital by Netconnect Inc.

Salmon Brothers Inc.
June 24, 2014

Exhibit IV Extracts from Salmon Brothers Inc. solvency files

1. Salmon Brothers Inc. representatives met with PC's auditors on June 23, 2014.
2. The manager in charge of the solvency opinion engagement was Christine Bedard, CA.
3. Christine Bedard signed the solvency opinion.
4. A pro forma, post-debt working capital calculation was prepared as follows (amounts in 000's):

Accounts receivable and accrued revenue	$212
Inventory	59
Prepaid expenses	38
	309
Accounts payable and accruals	84
Line of credit	139
Net working capital	$ 86

Conclusion: Plastok Corporation is solvent.

(Continued)

Exhibit IV Continued

5. An interest coverage calculation was prepared. Projected Year 1 income before interest and taxes is $2,706,000, divided by interest expense of $615,000 = 4.4.

   Conclusion: Plastok Corporation has adequate earnings to cover interest charges.

6. The earnings and cash flow projections, supplied by PC's management to SB, were copied from the files and are attached.

Plastok Corporation
Earnings and Cash Flow Projection
For the Years Ended May 31 (unaudited, in 000's, see assumptions attached)

	2015	2016
Consulting revenues	$ 2,016	$ 3,024
Product sales	8,000	12,000
Total sales	10,016	15,024
Cost of product sold	4,200	6,300
	5,816	8,724
Expenses		
Selling, administration, R&D, and other	1,000	1,500
Direct consulting costs	1,210	1,814
Network survey costs	100	150
Depreciation and amortization	800	820
Interest expense	615	550
	3,725	4,834
Net income (loss) before taxes	2,091	3,890
Income tax provision	—	1,556
Net income (loss)	$ 2,091	$ 2,334
Cash flow adjustments		
Add: depreciation and amortization	800	820
increase in prepaid expenses	50	75
increase in income tax payable	—	1,556
Less: capital asset purchases	(200)	(200)
decrease in line of credit	(139)	—
accounts receivable increase	(1,000)	(1,500)
inventory increase	(400)	(600)
Net cash flow	$ 1,502	$ 2,885

EARNINGS AND CASH FLOW PROJECTION ASSUMPTIONS

1. Projections and assumptions were prepared on June 22, 2014, by PC management. Two years was considered a reasonable projection period.
2. NetworkAccelerator selling price per unit, $4,000, per PC's VP of product sales.
3. Unit sales are estimated by PC's management.
4. NetworkAccelerator unit cost is estimated at $2,100 by PC's management.
5. Consulting business expected to grow 50% annually.
6. Operating and financing costs estimated by PC's management based on historical information and cost behaviour.

Exhibit V Information from NI's due diligence files

1. The due diligence was primarily carried out by NI's VP of business development, who became the proposed acquisition's champion along with NI's controller. His due diligence work consisted primarily of interviewing Peter and the two other most senior executives of the company.
2. On June 1, 2014, Certified Real Estate Appraisers Inc. provided an independent appraisal of the real property of PC to NI. The real property was appraised in the range of $1.1 to $1.3 million.
3. According to the VP of business development's notes: "PC's long-time consulting customer, Berkshire Limited, gave a glowing evaluation of the NetworkAccelerator product as used in a standard corporate network. This has convinced me that the product will achieve the wider market breakthrough Peter has forecasted."
4. A May 2014 forecast from the Gardiner Group said that the internet consulting market would grow from US$4 billion in 2014 to US$11 billion in 2017. A February 2014 market estimate from Spice Waterhouse Goobers said the market for internet speed and bandwidth acceleration software and hardware was growing at over 300% a year.
5. PC's customers for the NetworkAccelerator product are located primarily in Canada. The average selling price to date has been $3,500 and the full cost of a unit is about $2,050, consisting primarily of a subcontractor-produced printed circuit board and computer chips.
6. Prior to each installation of a NetworkAccelerator, consultants of the company must do a "network review" to ensure that the device will be configured and installed properly.
7. The company can borrow amounts up to 75% of accounts receivable, to a maximum of $250,000, and 50% of finished goods inventory up to $75,000, under its Notional Bank operating line facility, which the bank agreed to keep in place after the change in ownership.
8. The NI due diligence team had access to the audit working paper files for the year ended May 31, 2014. The following information was collected:
   - The auditors used analytical review techniques and analysis of subsequent payments to audit accrued liabilities and accounts payable.
   - The auditors confirmed the line of credit and attended the inventory count.
   - The audit report was dated June 20, 2014.
   - The audit staff reviewed all correspondence with the federal and provincial governments in assessing the company's commitment note and confirmed the amount of the annual payment in writing.
   - The auditors footed and recalculated the percentage completion schedule below, prepared by the client and agreed total budgeted contract amounts to the relevant contract files. PC has always accounted for long-term consulting contracts under the percentage of completion method, whereby actual hours incurred versus budgeted hours are used to track progress toward completion.

Contract	Budgeted hours	Hours to date	% completed	Budgeted total revenue	Revenue recorded	Billed to date	Accrued revenue
IDN contract 5	36,450	18,560	50.9%	$400,000	$203,676	$180,000	$ 23,676
Coracle	800	400	50.0	8,000	4,000	4,000	—
KO assignment	24,000	11,453	47.7	260,450	124,289	84,000	40,289
Carabella Inc.	35	25	71.4	140,000	100,000	—	100,000
Nortena Corp.	13,600	5,420	39.9	150,000	59,779	18,000	41,779
Makeup Inc.	169	171	101.2	19,100	19,100	19,100	—
snorton.com	4,400	860	19.5	4,600	899	—	899
The S Foundation	990	800	80.8	10,000	8,081	8,000	81
	80,444	37,689		$992,150	$519,824	$313,100	$206,724

Exhibit VI Other information gathered by you

1. On May 26, 2015, the federal and provincial environment departments jointly requested a payment of $189,000 within 21 days to settle the environmental commitment for the old plastics factory site, or $29,789 per annum in perpetuity. Failure to pay could result in seizure of the property.
2. On July 30, 2014, PC's consulting contract with IDN (Canada) Inc. was cancelled unilaterally by written notice. In PC's IDN file, with a received stamp dated June 20, 2014, was a letter from IDN dated June 18, 2014. The letter stated that IDN "intended to cancel the contract for the reasons related to delivery milestones set out below" and requested the refund of $180,000 already paid by IDN in April 2014. IDN did not follow up on PC's failure to pay until June 4, 2015. On that date, a letter demanding immediate payment or legal action would be taken was received. The contract manager says the company has no choice but to pay, given the terms of the contract.
3. Peter's aunt made a written request for the retraction of her preferred shares on January 3, 2015. PC claimed that she had agreed in writing not to redeem the shares. A lower court has ruled that the written note is not valid due to lack of consideration, and she has the right to request retraction.
4. PC had cash on hand of $18,000 at June 17, 2015.
5. PC recorded $990,678 of consulting fee revenue from various IDN (Canada) Inc. contracts during the 2014 fiscal year.
6. In fiscal 2015, PC's customer demographics were as follows: 93% from Canada, 4% United States, and 3% other.
7. During fiscal 2014, 50,000 stock options were granted to various senior employees to purchase PC's common shares for between $0.50 and $1. In addition, 45,000 stock options to purchase PC's common shares at an exercise price of $0.10 were issued to Berkshire Limited in March 2014.
8. SB's specialty is investment banking and related services to the financial industry. The fee for the solvency letter provided to NI was $29,500.
9. On October 12, 2014, MightySoft Limited sued PC for a patent infringement in relation to PC's development of real-time, packet switching internet protocol software in the NetworkAccelerator. The lawsuit is still pending.
10. In late July 2014, PC started to experience more severe indirect competition in the market for the NetworkAccelerator and the price had to be dropped from $4,000 to $2,700. The product has a six-month warranty.
11. Management was surprised at the shortfall in consulting revenue in Q1, fiscal 2015.
12. NI does not have a vice-president of finance or a chief financial officer.
13. Currently, tax losses are worth about 5–10 cents on the dollar—if after the change in control the purchaser can argue that the purchaser and the target company have the same or similar businesses.
14. The Carabella contract is almost entirely subcontracted to The GSi Group Inc. PC's only significant time spent on the project is the project manager's time at the beginning of the project. The contract's margin was originally estimated to be 35% and at May 31, 2014, $25,467 in charges from GSi had been incurred.
15. PC had the following breakdown of employees:

	June 30, 2014	May 31, 2015
Executives	3	2
Consulting	27	31
Marketing & sales	2	3
R&D	8	12
Production	10	14
Admin & other	7	4
Total	57	66

16. In early June 2015, 21 PC employees were laid off due to the shortage of funds.
17. Unit sales of the NetworkAccelerator declined from a high of 110 in the month of August 2014 to only 38 in the month of May 2015.
18. Management of NI are evaluated and paid bonuses based on the compensation committee's judgmental performance evaluation (60%) and net income after taxes (40%).

(Continued)

Exhibit VI Continued

19. The PC timesheet clerk, who was hired July 4, 2014, has provided the accrued revenue schedule below, which she insists is accurate at May 31, 2015. The only projects to span fiscal years 2014 to 2016 are the KO assignment and the Nortena Corp. project. The company recorded 4,322 hours on the former assignment and 850 hours on the latter in fiscal 2015 according to her records. She has pieced together the multi-year numbers from the poor 2014 records.

Contract	Budgeted hours	Hours to-date	Percentage completion	Budget total	Revenue recorded	Billed to date	Accrued revenue
ACB Manufacturing	1,256	800	63.7%	$ 13,000	$ 8,280	$ 6,000	$ 2,280
Congklin	802	325	40.5	8,000	3,242	3,000	242
KO assignment	24,000	7,800	32.5	260,450	84,646	84,000	646
Ongor Inc.	865	170	19.7	10,000	1,965	1,200	765
Nortena Corp.	13,600	1,701	12.5	150,000	18,761	18,000	761
Snack Corporation	400	350	87.5	5,000	4,375	4,000	375
Stepsi	4,400	2,101	47.8	46,000	21,965	1,000	20,965
Will St. Hospital	1,990	1,600	80.4	10,000	8,040	8,000	40
	47,313	14,847		$502,450	$151,275	$125,200	$26,075

APPENDIX C

Canadian Tire Corporation 2016 Consolidated Financial Statements

Index to the Consolidated Financial Statements and Notes

MANAGEMENT'S RESPONSIBILITY FOR FINANCIAL STATEMENTS 56

INDEPENDENT AUDITOR'S REPORT 57

CONSOLIDATED FINANCIAL STATEMENTS:

Consolidated Balance Sheets 58
Consolidated Statements of Income 59
Consolidated Statements of Comprehensive Income 60
Consolidated Statements of Cash Flows 61
Consolidated Statements of Changes in Equity 62

NOTES TO THE CONSOLIDATED FINANCIAL STATEMENTS:

Note 1. The Company and its operations 63
Note 2. Basis of preparation 63
Note 3. Significant accounting policies 66
Note 4. Capital management 75
Note 5. Financial risk management 76
Note 6. Operating segments 78
Note 7 Cash and cash equivalents 80
Note 8. Trade and other receivables 80
Note 9. Loans receivable 80
Note 10. Long-term receivables and other assets 82
Note 11. Goodwill and intangible assets 82
Note 12. Investment property 84
Note 13. Property and equipment 85
Note 14. Subsidiaries 86
Note 15. Income taxes 87
Note 16. Deposits 89
Note 17. Trade and other payables 89
Note 18. Provisions 90
Note 19. Contingencies 90
Note 20. Short-term borrowings 90
Note 21. Loans payable 90
Note 22. Long-term debt 91
Note 23. Other long-term liabilities 92
Note 24. Employment benefits 93
Note 25. Share capital 94
Note 26. Share-based payments 95
Note 27. Revenue 97
Note 28. Cost of producing revenue 97
Note 29. Selling, general and administrative expenses 97
Note 30. Net finance costs 98
Note 31. Notes to the consolidated statements of cash flows 98
Note 32. Financial instruments 99
Note 33. Operating leases 101
Note 34. Guarantees and commitments 101
Note 35. Related parties 103
Note 36. Comparative figures 103

Management's Responsibility for Financial Statements

The Management of Canadian Tire Corporation, Limited (the "Company") is responsible for the integrity and reliability of the accompanying consolidated financial statements. These consolidated financial statements have been prepared by Management in accordance with International Financial Reporting Standards and include amounts based on judgements and estimates. All financial information in our Management's Discussion and Analysis is consistent with these consolidated financial statements.

Management is responsible for establishing and maintaining adequate systems of internal control over financial reporting. These systems are designed to provide reasonable assurance that the financial records are reliable and form a proper basis for the timely and accurate preparation of financial statements. Management has assessed the effectiveness of the Company's internal control over financial reporting based on the framework in Internal Control – Integrated Framework (2013) issued by the Committee of Sponsoring Organizations of the Treadway Commission (COSO) and concluded that the Company's internal controls over financial reporting were effective as at the date of these consolidated financial statements.

The Board of Directors oversees Management's responsibilities for the consolidated financial statements primarily through the activities of its Audit Committee, which is comprised solely of directors who are neither officers nor employees of the Company. This Committee meets with Management and the Company's independent auditors, Deloitte LLP, to review the consolidated financial statements and recommend approval by the Board of Directors. The Audit Committee is responsible for making recommendations to the Board of Directors with respect to the appointment of and, subject to the approval of the shareholders authorizing the Board of Directors to do so, approving the remuneration and terms of engagement of the Company's auditors. The Audit Committee also meets with the auditors, without the presence of Management, to discuss the results of their audit.

The consolidated financial statements have been audited by Deloitte LLP, in accordance with Canadian generally accepted auditing standards. Their report is presented below.

Stephen G. Wetmore
President and Chief Executive Officer

Dean McCann
Executive Vice-President and
Chief Financial Officer

February 15, 2017

Independent Auditor's Report

To the Shareholders of Canadian Tire Corporation, Limited

We have audited the accompanying consolidated financial statements of Canadian Tire Corporation, Limited, which comprise the consolidated balance sheets as at December 31, 2016 and January 2, 2016, and the consolidated statements of income, consolidated statements of comprehensive income, consolidated statements of cash flows and consolidated statements of changes in equity for the years ended December 31, 2016 and January 2, 2016, and a summary of significant accounting policies and other explanatory information.

Management's Responsibility for the Consolidated Financial Statements

Management is responsible for the preparation and fair presentation of these consolidated financial statements in accordance with International Financial Reporting Standards, and for such internal control as management determines is necessary to enable the preparation of consolidated financial statements that are free from material misstatement, whether due to fraud or error.

Auditor's Responsibility

Our responsibility is to express an opinion on these consolidated financial statements based on our audits. We conducted our audits in accordance with Canadian generally accepted auditing standards. Those standards require that we comply with ethical requirements and plan and perform the audit to obtain reasonable assurance about whether the consolidated financial statements are free from material misstatement.

An audit involves performing procedures to obtain audit evidence about the amounts and disclosures in the consolidated financial statements. The procedures selected depend on the auditor's judgment, including the assessment of the risks of material misstatement of the consolidated financial statements, whether due to fraud or error. In making those risk assessments, the auditor considers internal control relevant to the entity's preparation and fair presentation of the consolidated financial statements in order to design audit procedures that are appropriate in the circumstances, but not for the purpose of expressing an opinion on the effectiveness of the entity's internal control. An audit also includes evaluating the appropriateness of accounting policies used and the reasonableness of accounting estimates made by management, as well as evaluating the overall presentation of the consolidated financial statements.

We believe that the audit evidence we have obtained in our audits is sufficient and appropriate to provide a basis for our audit opinion.

Opinion

In our opinion, the consolidated financial statements present fairly, in all material respects, the financial position of Canadian Tire Corporation, Limited as at December 31, 2016 and January 2, 2016, and its financial performance and its cash flows for the years then ended in accordance with International Financial Reporting Standards.

Deloitte LLP

Chartered Professional Accountants
Licensed Public Accountants

February 15, 2017
Toronto, Ontario

Consolidated Balance Sheets

As at (C$ in millions)	December 31, 2016	January 2, 2016
ASSETS		
Cash and cash equivalents (Note 7)	$ 829.7	$ 900.6
Short-term investments	117.2	96.1
Trade and other receivables (Note 8)	690.8	915.0
Loans receivable (Note 9)	5,138.4	4,875.5
Merchandise inventories	1,710.7	1,764.5
Income taxes recoverable	42.5	42.2
Prepaid expenses and deposits	103.8	96.1
Assets classified as held for sale	4.6	2.3
Total current assets	8,637.7	8,692.3
Long-term receivables and other assets (Note 10)	763.7	731.2
Long-term investments	175.2	153.4
Goodwill and intangible assets (Note 11)	1,280.3	1,246.8
Investment property (Note 12)	266.4	137.8
Property and equipment (Note 13)	4,097.2	3,978.2
Deferred income taxes (Note 15)	82.3	48.1
Total assets	$ 15,302.8	$ 14,987.8
LIABILITIES		
Bank indebtedness (Note 7)	$ 5.9	$ –
Deposits (Note 16)	950.7	880.7
Trade and other payables (Note 17)	1,856.9	1,957.1
Provisions (Note 18)	253.2	216.1
Short-term borrowings (Note 20)	199.4	88.6
Loans payable (Note 21)	700.3	655.5
Income taxes payable	61.1	61.5
Current portion of long-term debt (Note 22)	653.4	24.3
Total current liabilities	4,680.9	3,883.8
Long-term provisions (Note 18)	45.9	45.7
Long-term debt (Note 22)	2,667.1	2,971.4
Long-term deposits (Note 16)	1,230.8	1,372.2
Deferred income taxes (Note 15)	104.2	111.1
Other long-term liabilities (Note 23)	836.6	813.9
Total liabilities	9,565.5	9,198.1
EQUITY		
Share capital (Note 25)	648.1	671.2
Contributed surplus	2.9	2.9
Accumulated other comprehensive income	36.7	148.1
Retained earnings	4,250.9	4,172.0
Equity attributable to shareholders of Canadian Tire Corporation	4,938.6	4,994.2
Non-controlling interests (Note 14)	798.7	795.5
Total equity	5,737.3	5,789.7
Total liabilities and equity	$ 15,302.8	$ 14,987.8

The related notes form an integral part of these consolidated financial statements.

Maureen J. Sabia
Director

Diana L. Chant
Director

Consolidated Statements of Income

For the years ended (C$ in millions, except per share amounts)	December 31, 2016	January 2, 2016
Revenue (Note 27)	$ 12,681.0	$ 12,279.6
Cost of producing revenue (Note 28)	8,288.5	8,144.3
Gross margin	4,392.5	4,135.3
Other (income)	(4.3)	(54.9)
Selling, general and administrative expenses (Note 29)	3,291.9	3,096.1
Net finance costs (Note 30)	93.9	92.8
Income before income taxes	1,011.0	1,001.3
Income taxes (Note 15)	263.5	265.4
Net income	$ 747.5	$ 735.9
Net income attributable to:		
Shareholders of Canadian Tire Corporation	$ 669.1	$ 659.4
Non-controlling interests (Note 14)	78.4	76.5
	$ 747.5	$ 735.9
Basic EPS	$ 9.25	$ 8.66
Diluted EPS	$ 9.22	$ 8.61
Weighted average number of Common and Class A Non-Voting Shares outstanding:		
Basic	72,360,303	76,151,321
Diluted	72,555,732	76,581,602

The related notes form an integral part of these consolidated financial statements.

Consolidated Statements of Comprehensive Income

For the years ended (C$ in millions)	December 31, 2016	January 2, 2016
Net income	$ 747.5	$ 735.9
Other comprehensive (loss) income, net of taxes		
Items that may be reclassified subsequently to net income:		
Cash flow hedges and available-for-sale financial assets:		
(Losses) gains	(40.5)	275.1
Reclassification of gains to non-financial assets	(67.9)	(207.4)
Reclassification of gains to income	(1.7)	(3.0)
Item that will not be reclassified subsequently to net income:		
Actuarial (losses) gains	(3.0)	0.8
Other comprehensive (loss) income	(113.1)	65.5
Other comprehensive (loss) income attributable to:		
Shareholders of Canadian Tire Corporation	$ (114.3)	$ 68.0
Non-controlling interests	1.2	(2.5)
	$ (113.1)	$ 65.5
Comprehensive income	$ 634.4	$ 801.4
Comprehensive income attributable to:		
Shareholders of Canadian Tire Corporation	$ 554.8	$ 727.4
Non-controlling interests	79.6	74.0
	$ 634.4	$ 801.4

The related notes form an integral part of these consolidated financial statements.

Consolidated Statements of Cash Flows

For the years ended (C$ in millions)	December 31, 2016	January 2, 2016
Cash (used for) generated from:		
Operating activities		
Net income	**$ 747.5**	$ 735.9
Adjustments for:		
Depreciation of property and equipment and investment property (Notes 28 and 29)	**330.8**	312.8
Income tax expense	**263.5**	265.4
Net finance costs (Note 30)	**93.9**	92.8
Amortization of intangible assets (Note 29)	**126.1**	111.9
Changes in fair value of derivative instruments	**(15.8)**	6.9
(Gain) on disposal of property and equipment, investment property, assets held for sale, intangible assets, and lease terminations	**(14.9)**	(43.9)
Interest paid	**(114.0)**	(101.4)
Interest received	**6.5**	8.4
Income taxes paid	**(262.8)**	(284.0)
Other	**5.6**	14.6
Total adjustments, except as noted below	**1,166.4**	1,119.4
Change in operating working capital and other (Note 31)	**126.1**	(115.3)
Change in loans receivable	**(306.1)**	(25.2)
Cash generated from operating activities	**986.4**	978.9
Investing activities		
Additions to property and equipment and investment property	**(617.3)**	(515.9)
Additions to intangible assets	**(163.5)**	(94.7)
Total additions	**(780.8)**	(610.6)
Acquisition of short-term investments	**(422.3)**	(177.4)
Proceeds from the maturity and disposition of short-term investments	**441.4**	426.6
Acquisition of long-term investments	**(61.4)**	(35.0)
Proceeds on disposition of property and equipment, investment property, and assets held for sale	**32.8**	101.5
Other	**7.5**	(4.1)
Cash (used for) investing activities	**(782.8)**	(299.0)
Financing activities		
Dividends paid	**(157.5)**	(152.2)
Distributions paid to non-controlling interests	**(76.4)**	(53.8)
Total dividends and distributions paid	**(233.9)**	(206.0)
Net issuance (repayment) of short-term borrowings	**110.7**	(111.2)
Issuance of loans payable	**288.3**	270.1
Repayment of loans payable	**(243.5)**	(219.0)
Issuance of long-term debt (Note 22)	**350.0**	856.1
Repayment of long-term debt and finance lease liabilities (Note 22)	**(24.5)**	(588.5)
Payment of transaction costs related to long-term debt	**(3.2)**	(6.5)
Repurchase of share capital (Note 25)	**(449.4)**	(434.6)
Change in deposits	**(74.9)**	12.5
Cash (used for) financing activities	**(280.4)**	(427.1)
Cash (used) generated in the period	**(76.8)**	252.8
Cash and cash equivalents, net of bank indebtedness, beginning of period	**900.6**	647.8
Cash and cash equivalents, net of bank indebtedness, end of period (Note 7)	**$ 823.8**	$ 900.6

The related notes form an integral part of these consolidated financial statements.

Consolidated Statements of Changes in Equity

(C$ in millions)	Share capital	Contributed surplus	Total accumulated other comprehensive income	Retained earnings	Equity attributable to shareholders of Canadian Tire Corporation	Equity attributable to non-controlling interests	Total equity
Balance at January 2, 2016	**$ 671.2**	**$ 2.9**	**$ 148.1**	**$ 4,172.0**	**$ 4,994.2**	**$ 795.5**	**$ 5,789.7**
Net income	**–**	**–**	**–**	**669.1**	**669.1**	**78.4**	**747.5**
Other comprehensive (loss) income	**–**	**–**	**(111.4)**	**(2.9)**	**(114.3)**	**1.2**	**(113.1)**
Total comprehensive (loss) income	**–**	**–**	**(111.4)**	**666.2**	**554.8**	**79.6**	**634.4**
Contributions and distributions to shareholders of Canadian Tire Corporation							
Issuance of Class A Non-Voting Shares (Note 25)	**9.3**	**–**	**–**	**–**	**9.3**	**–**	**9.3**
Repurchase of Class A Non-Voting Shares (Note 25)	**(449.4)**	**–**	**–**	**–**	**(449.4)**	**–**	**(449.4)**
Excess of purchase price over average cost (Note 25)	**417.0**	**–**	**–**	**(417.0)**	**–**	**–**	**–**
Dividends	**–**	**–**	**–**	**(170.3)**	**(170.3)**	**–**	**(170.3)**
Contributions and distributions to non-controlling interests							
Issuance of trust units to non-controlling interests, net of transaction costs	**–**	**–**	**–**	**–**	**–**	**2.0**	**2.0**
Distributions and dividends to non-controlling interests	**–**	**–**	**–**	**–**	**–**	**(78.4)**	**(78.4)**
Total contributions and distributions	**(23.1)**	**–**	**–**	**(587.3)**	**(610.4)**	**(76.4)**	**(686.8)**
Balance at December 31, 2016	**$ 648.1**	**$ 2.9**	**$ 36.7**	**$ 4,250.9**	**$ 4,938.6**	**$ 798.7**	**$ 5,737.3**

(C$ in millions)	Share capital	Contributed surplus	Total accumulated other comprehensive income	Retained earnings	Equity attributable to shareholders of Canadian Tire Corporation	Equity attributable to non-controlling interests	Total equity
Balance at January 3, 2015	$ 695.5	$ 2.9	$ 82.0	$ 4,075.1	$ 4,855.5	$ 775.3	$ 5,630.8
Net income	–	–	–	659.4	659.4	76.5	735.9
Other comprehensive income (loss)	–	–	66.1	1.9	68.0	(2.5)	65.5
Total comprehensive income	–	–	66.1	661.3	727.4	74.0	801.4
Contributions and distributions to shareholders of Canadian Tire Corporation							
Issuance of Class A Non-Voting Shares (Note 25)	8.3	–	–	–	8.3	–	8.3
Repurchase of Class A Non-Voting Shares (Note 25)	(434.6)	–	–	–	(434.6)	–	(434.6)
Excess of purchase price over average cost (Note 25)	402.0	–	–	(402.0)	–	–	–
Dividends	–	–	–	(162.4)	(162.4)	–	(162.4)
Contributions and distributions to non-controlling interests							
Issuance of trust units to non-controlling interests, net of transaction costs	–	–	–	–	–	1.8	1.8
Distributions and dividends to non-controlling interests	–	–	–	–	–	(55.6)	(55.6)
Total contributions and distributions	(24.3)	–	–	(564.4)	(588.7)	(53.8)	(642.5)
Balance at January 2, 2016	$ 671.2	$ 2.9	$ 148.1	$ 4,172.0	$ 4,994.2	$ 795.5	$ 5,789.7

The related notes form an integral part of these consolidated financial statements.

1. The Company and its operations

Canadian Tire Corporation, Limited is a Canadian public company primarily domiciled in Canada. Its registered office is located at 2180 Yonge Street, Toronto, Ontario, M4P 2V8, Canada. It is listed on the Toronto Stock Exchange (TSX – CTC, CTC.A). Canadian Tire Corporation, Limited and entities it controls are together referred to in these consolidated financial statements as the "Company" or "Canadian Tire Corporation". Refer to Note 14 for the Company's major subsidiaries.

The Company comprises three main business operations, which offer a range of retail goods and services, including general merchandise, apparel, sporting goods, petroleum, financial services including a bank, and real estate operations. Details of its three reportable operating segments are provided in Note 6.

2. Basis of preparation

Fiscal year

The fiscal year of the Company consists of a 52 or 53-week period ending on the Saturday closest to December 31. The fiscal years for the consolidated financial statements and notes presented for 2016 and 2015 are the 52-week periods ended December 31, 2016 and January 2, 2016, respectively.

Statement of compliance

These consolidated financial statements have been prepared in accordance with International Financial Reporting Standards ("IFRS") using the accounting policies described herein.

These consolidated financial statements were authorized for issuance by the Company's Board of Directors on February 15, 2017.

Basis of presentation

These consolidated financial statements have been prepared on the historical cost basis, except for the following items, which are measured at fair value:

- financial instruments at fair value through profit or loss ("FVTPL");
- derivative financial instruments;
- available-for-sale financial assets;
- liabilities for share-based payment plans; and
- initial recognition of assets acquired and liabilities assumed in a business combination.

In addition, the post-employment defined benefit obligation is recorded at its discounted present value.

Functional and presentation currency

These consolidated financial statements are presented in Canadian dollars ("C$"), the Company's functional currency.

Judgments and estimates

The preparation of these consolidated financial statements in accordance with IFRS requires Management to make judgments and estimates that affect:

- the application of accounting policies;
- the reported amounts of assets and liabilities;
- disclosures of contingent assets and liabilities; and
- the reported amounts of revenue and expenses during the reporting periods.

Actual results may differ from estimates made in these consolidated financial statements.

Judgments are made in the selection and assessment of the Company's accounting policies. Estimates are used mainly in determining the measurement of recognized transactions and balances. Estimates are based on historical experience and other factors, including expectations of future events believed to be reasonable under the circumstances. Judgments and estimates are often interrelated. The Company's judgments and estimates are continually re-evaluated to ensure they remain appropriate. Revisions to accounting estimates are recognized in the period in which the estimates are revised and in future periods affected.

Following are the accounting policies that are subject to judgments and estimates that the Company believes could have the most significant impact on the amounts recognized in these consolidated financial statements.

Impairment of assets

Judgment – The Company uses judgment in determining the grouping of assets to identify its Cash Generating Units ("CGUs") for purposes of testing for impairment of property and equipment and goodwill and intangible assets. The Company has determined that its Retail CGUs comprise individual stores or groups of stores within a geographic market. In testing for impairment, goodwill acquired in a business combination is allocated to the CGUs that are expected to benefit from the synergies of the business combination. In testing for impairment of intangibles with indefinite lives, these assets are allocated to the CGUs to which they relate. Furthermore, on a quarterly basis, judgment has been used in determining whether there has been an indication of impairment, which would require the completion of a quarterly impairment test, in addition to the annual requirement.

Estimation – The Company's estimate of a CGU's or group of CGUs' recoverable amount based on value in use ("VIU") involves estimating future cash flows before taxes. Future cash flows are estimated based on multi-year extrapolation of the most recent historical actual results or budgets and a terminal value calculated by discounting the final year in perpetuity. The growth rate applied to the terminal value is based on the Bank of Canada's target inflation rate or Management's estimate of the growth rate specific to the individual item being tested. The future cash flow estimates are then discounted to their present value using an appropriate pre-tax discount rate that incorporates a risk premium specific to each business. The Company's determination of a CGU's or group of CGUs' recoverable amount based on fair value less cost to sell uses factors such as market rental rates for comparable assets.

Fair value measurement of redeemable financial instrument

Judgment – The Company uses judgment in determining the fair value measurement of the redeemable financial instrument issued in conjunction with the sale of a 20 percent equity interest in the Company's Financial Services business. In calculating the fair value, judgment is used when determining the discount and growth rates applied to the forecast earnings in the discounted cash flow valuation. Refer to Note 32 for further information regarding this financial instrument.

Estimation – The inputs to determine the fair value are taken from observable markets where possible, but where they are unavailable, assumptions are required in establishing fair value. The fair value of the redeemable financial instrument is determined based on the Company's best estimate of forecast normalized earnings attributable to the Financial Services business, adjusted for any undistributed earnings.

Merchandise inventories

Estimation – Merchandise inventories are carried at the lower of cost and net realizable value. The estimation of net realizable value is based on the most reliable evidence available of the amount the merchandise inventories are expected to realize. Additionally, estimation is required for inventory provisions due to shrinkage.

Income and other taxes

Judgment – In calculating current and deferred income and other taxes, the Company uses judgment when interpreting the tax rules in jurisdictions where the Company operates. The Company also uses judgment in classifying transactions and assessing probable outcomes of claimed deductions, which considers expectations of future operating results, the timing and reversal of temporary differences, and possible audits of income tax and other tax filings by tax authorities.

Consolidation

Judgment – The Company uses judgment in determining the entities that it controls and accordingly consolidates. An entity is controlled when the Company has power over an entity, exposure or rights to variable returns from its involvement with the entity, and is able to use its power over the entity to affect its return from the entity. The Company has power over an entity when it has existing rights that give it the current ability to direct the relevant activities, which are the activities that significantly affect the investee's returns. Since power comes from rights, power can result from contractual arrangements. However, certain contractual arrangements contain rights that are designed to protect the Company's interest, without giving it power over the entity.

Loans receivable

Estimation – The Company's estimate of allowances on credit card loans receivable is based on a roll-rate methodology that employs analysis of historical data and experience of delinquency and default, to estimate the amount of loans that will eventually be written off as a result of events occurring before the reporting date, with certain adjustments for other relevant circumstances influencing the recoverability of these loans receivable. Default rates, loss rates, and the expected timing of future recoveries are regularly benchmarked against actual outcomes to ensure that they remain appropriate. Future customer behaviour may be affected by a number of factors, including changes in interest and unemployment rates and program design changes.

Post-employment benefits

Estimation – The accounting for the Company's post-employment benefit plan requires the use of assumptions. The accrued benefit liability is calculated using actuarial determined data and the Company's best estimates of future salary escalations, retirement ages of employees, employee turnover, mortality rates, market discount rates, and expected health and dental care costs.

Other

Other estimates include determining the useful lives of property and equipment, investment property, and intangible assets for the purposes of depreciation and amortization; in accounting for and measuring items such as deferred revenue, customer loyalty and other provisions, and purchase price adjustments on business combinations; and in measuring certain fair values, including those related to the valuation of business combinations, share-based payments, and financial instruments.

Standards, amendments, and interpretations issued and adopted

Disclosure initiative (IAS 1)

In December 2014, the International Accounting Standard Board ("IASB") issued *Disclosure Initiative Amendments to IAS 1* as part of the IASB's Disclosure Initiative. These amendments encourage entities to apply professional judgment regarding disclosure and presentation in their financial statements.

These amendments were effective for annual periods beginning on or after January 1, 2016 and were applied prospectively. The implementation of these amendments did not have a significant impact on the Company other than immaterial amendments to current and prior-year note disclosure.

Standards, amendments, and interpretations issued but not yet adopted

The following new standards, amendments, and interpretations have been issued and are expected to impact the Company, but are not effective for the fiscal year ending December 31, 2016 and, accordingly, have not been applied in preparing the consolidated financial statements.

Financial instruments

In July 2014, the IASB issued the final version of IFRS 9 – *Financial Instruments* ("IFRS 9"), which brings together the classification and measurement, impairment, and hedge-accounting phases of the IASB's project to replace IAS 39 – *Financial Instruments: Recognition and Measurement* ("IAS 39").

Classification and measurement – Financial assets are classified and measured based on the business model under which they are managed and the contractual cash flow characteristics of the financial assets. Financial liabilities are classified in a similar manner as under IAS 39, except that financial liabilities measured at fair value will have fair value changes resulting from changes in the entity's own credit risk recognized in Other Comprehensive Income ("OCI") instead of Net Income, unless this would create an accounting mismatch.

Impairment – The measurement of impairment of financial assets is based on an expected credit loss model. It is no longer necessary for a triggering event to have occurred before credit losses are recognized. IFRS 9 also includes new disclosure requirements about expected credit losses and credit risk.

Hedge accounting – The new general hedge accounting model more closely aligns hedge accounting with risk management activities undertaken by entities when hedging their financial and non-financial risk exposures. It will provide more opportunities to apply hedge accounting to reflect actual risk management activities.

IFRS 9 will be applied retrospectively for annual periods beginning on or after January 1, 2018. The impairment requirements of IFRS 9 are expected to have an impact on the Company, particularly with respect to the estimate of allowances on credit card loans receivable. In order to meet the impairment requirements of IFRS 9, a dedicated project team has been established with joint leadership from finance and credit risk. The Company is assessing the potential financial and disclosure impact of this standard.

Revenue from contracts with customers

In May 2014, the IASB issued IFRS 15 – *Revenue from Contracts with Customers* ("IFRS 15"), which replaces IAS 11 – *Construction Contracts*, IAS 18 – *Revenue*, and International Financial Reporting Interpretations Committee 13 – *Customer Loyalty Programmes* ("IFRIC 13"), as well as various other interpretations regarding revenue. IFRS 15 outlines a single comprehensive model for entities to use in accounting for revenue arising from contracts with customers; except for contracts that are within the scope of the standards on leases, insurance contracts, and financial instruments. IFRS 15 also contains enhanced disclosure requirements. IFRS 15 will be applied retrospectively for annual periods beginning on or after January 1, 2018. The Company is assessing the potential impact of this standard.

In April 2016, the IASB published clarifications to IFRS 15 which address three topics (identifying performance obligations, principal versus agent considerations, and licensing) and provide some transition relief for modified contracts and completed contracts. The amendments are effective for annual periods beginning on or after January 1, 2018. Earlier adoption is permitted. The Company is assessing the potential impact of these amendments.

Disclosure initiative (IAS 7)

In January 2016, the IASB issued Disclosure Initiative Amendments to IAS 7 – *Statement of Cash Flows* also as part of the IASB's Disclosure Initiative. These amendments require entities to provide additional disclosures that will enable financial statement users to evaluate changes in liabilities arising from financing activities, including changes from cash flows and non-cash changes.

These amendments are effective for annual periods beginning on or after January 1, 2017. The implementation of these amendments is not expected to have a significant impact on the Company.

Leases

In January 2016, the IASB issued IFRS 16 – *Leases* ("IFRS 16"), which replaced IAS 17 – *Leases* ("IAS 17") and related interpretations. IFRS 16 provides a single lessee accounting model, requiring the recognition of assets and liabilities for all leases, unless the lease term is 12-months or less or the underlying asset has a low value. IFRS 16 substantially carries forward the lessor accounting in IAS 17 with the distinction between operating leases and finance leases being retained.

IFRS 16 is effective for annual periods beginning on or after January 1, 2019. Early adoption is permitted if IFRS 15 has also been applied. The Company is assessing the potential impact of this standard.

Income taxes

In January 2016, the IASB amended IAS 12 – *Income Taxes* by issuing *Recognition of Deferred Tax Assets for Unrealized Losses*. These amendments address the accounting for deferred tax assets for unrealized losses on debt instruments measured at fair value.

These amendments are effective for annual periods beginning on or after January 1, 2017. The implementation of these amendments is not expected to have a significant impact on the Company.

Share-based payment

In June 2016, the IASB issued amendments to IFRS 2 – *Share-based Payment,* clarifying how to account for the effects of vesting and non-vesting conditions on the measurement of cash-settled share-based payments, share-based payment transactions with a net settlement feature, and a modification to the terms and conditions that changes the classification of the transactions.

These amendments are effective for annual periods beginning on or after January 1, 2018. Early adoption is permitted. The Company is assessing the potential impact of these amendments.

Insurance contracts

In September 2016, the IASB issued amendments to IFRS 4 – *Insurance Contracts*, introducing two approaches; an overlay approach and a deferral approach, to address the additional accounting mismatches and volatility that may arise in profit or loss as a result of applying IFRS 9.

The overlay approach can be applied whenever IFRS 9 is applied and the deferral approach permits a company with activities that are predominantly connected with insurance to be exempted from applying IFRS 9 until 2021. The Company is assessing the potential impact of these amendments.

3. Significant accounting policies

The accounting policies set out below have been applied consistently to all periods presented in these consolidated financial statements and have been applied consistently throughout the Company.

Basis of consolidation

These consolidated financial statements include the accounts of Canadian Tire Corporation and entities it controls. An entity is controlled when the Company has the ability to direct the relevant activities of the entity, has exposure or rights to variable returns from its involvement with the entity, and is able to use its power over the entity to affect its returns from the entity.

The results of certain subsidiaries that have different year ends have been included in these consolidated financial statements for the 52-week periods ended December 31, 2016 and January 2, 2016. The year end of CTFS Holdings Limited and its subsidiaries, Franchise Trust, and CT Real Estate Investment Trust ("CT REIT") is December 31.

Income or loss and each component of OCI are attributed to the shareholders of the Company and to the non-controlling interests. Total comprehensive income is attributed to the shareholders of the Company and to the non-controlling interests even if this results in the non-controlling interests having a deficit balance on consolidation.

Business combinations

The Company applies the acquisition method in accounting for business combinations.

The Company measures goodwill as the difference between the fair value of the consideration transferred, including the recognized amount of any non-controlling interests in the acquiree, and the net recognized amount (generally fair value) of the identifiable assets acquired and liabilities assumed, all measured as at the acquisition date.

Consideration transferred includes the fair value of the assets transferred (including cash), liabilities incurred by the Company on behalf of the acquiree, the fair value of any contingent consideration, and equity interests issued by the Company.

Where a business combination is achieved in stages, previously held interests in the acquired entity are remeasured to fair value at the acquisition date, which is the date control is obtained, and the resulting gain or loss, if any, is recognized in net income. Amounts arising from interests in the acquiree prior to the acquisition date that have previously been recognized in OCI are reclassified to net income.

The fair values of property and equipment recognized as a result of a business combination is based on either the cost approach or market approach, as applicable. The market value of property is the estimated amount for which a property could be exchanged on the date of valuation between a willing buyer and a willing seller in an arm's length transaction after proper marketing wherein the parties each act knowledgeably and willingly. For the cost approach, the current replacement cost or reproduction cost for each major asset is calculated.

The fair values of banners and trademarks acquired in a business combination are determined using an income approach. The "relief from royalty" method has been applied to forecast revenue using an appropriate royalty rate. This results in an estimate of the value of the intangible assets acquired by the Company.

The fair values of franchise agreements and other intangibles, such as customer relationships, are determined using an income approach or multi-period excess earnings approach. This method is based on the discounted cash flows expected to be derived from ownership of the assets. The present value of the cash flows represents the value of the intangible asset. The fair value of off-market leases acquired in a business combination is determined based on the present value of the difference between market rates and rates in the existing leases.

The fair values of inventories acquired in a business combination is determined based on the estimated selling price in the ordinary course of business less the estimated costs of sale, and a reasonable profit margin based on the effort required to complete and sell the inventories.

Transaction costs that the Company incurs in connection with a business combination are expensed immediately.

Joint arrangement

A joint arrangement is an arrangement in which two or more parties have joint control. Joint control is the contractually agreed sharing of control whereby decisions about relevant activities require unanimous consent of the parties sharing control. A joint arrangement is classified as a joint operation when the parties that have joint control have rights to the assets and obligations for the liabilities related to the arrangement. The Company records its share of a joint operation's assets, liabilities, revenues, and expenses.

Foreign currency translation

Transactions in foreign currencies are translated into Canadian dollars at rates in effect at the date of the transaction. Monetary assets and liabilities in foreign currencies are translated into Canadian dollars at the closing exchange rate at the balance sheet date. Non-monetary items that are measured in terms of historical cost are translated into Canadian dollars at the exchange rate at the date of the original transaction. Exchange gains or losses arising from translation are recorded in Other income or Cost of producing revenue as applicable in the Consolidated Statements of Income.

Financial instruments

Recognition and measurement

Financial assets and financial liabilities, including derivatives, are recognized in the Consolidated Balance Sheets when the Company becomes a party to the contractual provisions of a financial instrument or non-financial derivative contract. All financial instruments are required to be measured at fair value on initial recognition. Subsequent measurement of these assets and liabilities is based on either fair value or amortized cost using the effective interest method, depending upon their classification.

Transaction costs that are directly attributable to the acquisition or issue of financial assets and financial liabilities (other than financial assets and financial liabilities classified as FVTPL) are added to or deducted from the fair value of the financial assets or financial liabilities, as appropriate, on initial recognition. Transaction costs directly attributable to the acquisition of financial assets or financial liabilities classified as FVTPL are recognized immediately in net income.

The Company classifies financial instruments, at the time of initial recognition, according to their characteristics and Management's choices and intentions related thereto for the purposes of ongoing measurement. Classification choices for financial assets include a) FVTPL, b) held to maturity, c) available for sale, and d) loans and receivables. Classification choices for financial liabilities include a) FVTPL and b) other liabilities.

The Company's financial assets and financial liabilities are generally classified and measured as follows:

Asset/Liability	Category	Measurement
Cash and cash equivalents	Loans and receivables	Amortized cost
Short-term investments[1]	Available for sale	Fair value
Trade and other receivables[2]	Loans and receivables	Amortized cost
Loans receivable	Loans and receivables	Amortized cost
Deposits (recorded in prepaid expenses and deposits)	Loans and receivables	Amortized cost
Long-term receivables and other assets[2]	Loans and receivables	Amortized cost
Long-term investments	Available for sale	Fair value
Bank indebtedness	Other liabilities	Amortized cost
Deposits	Other liabilities	Amortized cost
Trade and other payables[2]	Other liabilities	Amortized cost
Short-term borrowings	Other liabilities	Amortized cost
Loans payable	Other liabilities	Amortized cost
Long-term debt	Other liabilities	Amortized cost
Redeemable financial instrument (recorded in other long-term liabilities)	FVTPL	Fair value

[1] *Certain short-term investments are classified as FVTPL and measured at fair value.*

[2] *Includes derivatives that are classified as FVTPL or are effective hedging instruments, and measured at fair value.*

Financial instruments at fair value through profit or loss

Financial instruments are classified as FVTPL when the financial instrument is either held for trading or designated as such upon initial recognition. Financial instruments are classified as held for trading if acquired principally for the purpose of selling in the near future or if part of an identified portfolio of financial instruments that the Company manages together and has a recent actual pattern of short-term profit-making. Derivatives are classified as FVTPL unless they are designated as effective hedging instruments.

Financial instruments classified as FVTPL are measured at fair value, with changes in fair value recorded in net income in the period in which they arise.

Available-for-sale

Financial assets classified as available-for-sale are measured at fair value with changes in fair value recognized in OCI until realized through disposal or other than temporary impairment, at which point the change in fair value is recognized in net income. Dividend income from available-for-sale financial assets is recognized in net income when the Company's right to receive payments is established. Interest income on available-for-sale financial assets, calculated using the effective interest method, is recognized in net income.

Loans and receivables

Loans and receivables are financial assets with fixed or determinable payments that are not quoted in an active market. Subsequent to initial recognition, loans and receivables are measured at amortized cost using the effective interest method, less any impairment, with gains and losses recognized in net income in the period that the asset is derecognized or impaired.

Other liabilities

Subsequent to initial recognition, other financial liabilities are measured at amortized cost using the effective interest method, with gains and losses recognized in net income in the period that the liability is derecognized.

Derecognition of financial instruments

A financial asset is derecognized when the contractual rights to the cash flows from the asset expire or when the Company transfers the financial asset to another party without retaining control or substantially all the risks and rewards of ownership of the asset. Any interest in transferred financial assets created or retained by the Company is recognized as a separate asset or liability.

A financial liability is derecognized when its contractual obligations are discharged, cancelled, or expire.

Derivative financial instruments

The Company enters into various derivative financial instruments as part of the Company's strategy to manage its foreign currency and interest rate exposures. The Company also enters into equity derivative contracts to hedge certain future share-based payment expenses. The Company does not hold or issue derivative financial instruments for trading purposes.

All derivative financial instruments, including derivatives embedded in financial or non-financial contracts not closely related to the host contracts, are measured at fair value. The gain or loss that results from remeasurement at each reporting period is recognized in net income immediately unless the derivative is designated and effective as a hedging instrument, in which case the timing of the recognition in net income depends on the nature of the hedge relationship.

Hedge accounting

Where hedge accounting can be applied, certain criteria are documented at the inception of the hedge and updated at each reporting date.

Cash flow hedges

For cash flow hedges, the effective portion of the changes in the fair value of the hedging derivative, net of taxes, is recognized in OCI, while the ineffective and unhedged portions are recognized immediately in net income. Amounts recorded in Accumulated Other Comprehensive Income ("AOCI") are reclassified to net income in the periods when the hedged item affects net income. However, when a forecast transaction that is hedged results in the recognition of a non-financial asset or liability, the gains and losses previously recognized in AOCI are reclassified from AOCI and included in the initial measurement of the cost of the non-financial asset or liability.

When hedge accounting is discontinued, the amounts previously recognized in AOCI are reclassified to net income during the periods when the variability in the cash flows of the hedged item affects net income. Gains and losses on derivatives are reclassified immediately to net income when the hedged item is sold or terminated early. If hedge accounting is discontinued due to the hedged item no longer being expected to occur, the amount previously recognized in AOCI is reclassified immediately to net income.

The Company enters into foreign currency contracts to hedge the exposure against foreign currency risk on the future payment of foreign-currency-denominated inventory purchases and certain expenses. The changes in fair value of these contracts are included in OCI to the extent the hedges continue to be effective. Once the inventory is received, the Company reclassifies the related AOCI amount to merchandise inventories and subsequent changes in the fair value of the foreign currency contracts are recorded in net income as they occur. When the expenses are incurred, the Company reclassifies the related AOCI amount to the expense.

The Company enters into interest rate-swap contracts to hedge the exposure against interest rate risk on the future interest payments of debt issuances. The changes in fair value of these contracts are included in OCI to the extent that the hedges continue to be effective. When the interest expense is incurred, the Company reclassifies the related AOCI amount to finance costs.

Cash and cash equivalents

Cash and cash equivalents are defined as cash plus highly liquid and rated certificates of deposit or commercial paper with an original term to maturity of three months or less.

Short-term investments

Short-term investments are investments in highly liquid and rated certificates of deposit, commercial paper or other securities, primarily Canadian and United States ("U.S.") government securities, and notes of other creditworthy parties, with an original term to maturity of more than three months and remaining term to maturity of less than one year.

Trade and other receivables

The allowance for impairment of trade and other receivables is established when there is objective evidence that the Company will not be able to collect all amounts due according to the original terms of the receivables. Significant financial difficulties of the debtor, probability that the debtor will enter bankruptcy or financial reorganization, and default or delinquency in payments are considered indicators that the trade receivable is impaired. The amount of the allowance is calculated as the difference between the asset's carrying amount and the present value of estimated future cash flows, discounted at the original effective interest rate. The carrying amount of the asset is reduced through the use of an allowance account, and the amount of the loss is recognized in Selling, general and administrative expenses in the Consolidated Statements of Income. When a trade receivable is deemed uncollectible, it is written off against the allowance account. Subsequent recoveries of amounts previously written off are recognized as a recovery in Selling, general and administrative expenses in the Consolidated Statements of Income.

Loans receivable

Loans receivable consists of credit card and line of credit loans, as well as loans to Associate Dealers ("Dealers"), who are independent third-party operators of Canadian Tire Retail stores. Loans receivable are recognized when cash is advanced to the borrower. They are derecognized when the borrower repays its obligations, the loans are sold or written off, or substantially all of the risks and rewards of ownership are transferred.

Losses for impaired loans are recognized when there is objective evidence that impairment of the loans has occurred. Impairment allowances are calculated on individual loans and on groups of loans assessed collectively. Impairment losses are recorded in Cost of producing revenue in the Consolidated Statements of Income. The carrying amount of impaired loans in the Consolidated Balance Sheets is reduced through the use of impairment allowance accounts. Losses expected from future events are not recognized.

All individually significant loans receivable are assessed for specific impairment. All individually significant loans receivable found not to be specifically impaired are then collectively assessed for any impairment that has been incurred but not yet identified. Loans receivable not individually significant are collectively assessed for impairment by grouping together loans receivable with similar risk characteristics.

The Company uses a roll-rate methodology to calculate allowances for credit card loans. This methodology employs analysis of historical data, economic indicators, and experience of delinquency and default to estimate the amount of loans that will eventually be written off as a result of events occurring before the reporting date, with certain adjustments for other relevant circumstances influencing the recoverability of the loans receivable. Default rates, loss rates, and cash recoveries are regularly benchmarked against actual outcomes to ensure that they remain appropriate.

Merchandise inventories

Merchandise inventories are carried at the lower of cost and net realizable value.

Cash consideration received from vendors is recognized as a reduction to the cost of related inventory, unless the cash consideration received is either a reimbursement of incremental costs incurred by the Company or a payment for assets or services delivered to the vendor.

The cost of merchandise inventories is determined based on weighted average cost and includes costs incurred in bringing the merchandise inventories to their present location and condition. All inventories are finished goods.

Net realizable value is the estimated selling price of inventory during the normal course of business less estimated selling expenses.

Long-term investments

Investments in highly liquid and rated certificates of deposit, commercial paper, or other securities with a remaining term to maturity of greater than one year are classified as long-term investments. The Company's exposure to credit, currency, and interest rate risks related to other investments is disclosed in Note 5.

Intangible assets

Goodwill

Goodwill represents the excess of the cost of an acquisition over the fair value of the Company's share of the identifiable assets acquired and liabilities assumed in a business combination. Goodwill is measured at cost less any accumulated impairment and is not amortized.

Finite life and indefinite life intangible assets

Intangible assets with finite useful lives are measured at cost and are amortized on a straight-line basis over their estimated useful lives, generally for a period of two to ten years. The estimated useful lives and amortization methods are reviewed annually with the effect of any changes in estimate being accounted for on a prospective basis.

Intangible assets with indefinite useful lives are measured at cost, less any accumulated impairment, and are not amortized.

Expenditures on research activities are expensed as incurred.

Investment property

Investment property is property held to earn rental income or for appreciation of capital or both. The Company has determined that properties it provides to its Dealers, franchisees, and agents are not investment property as these relate to the Company's operating activities. This was determined based on certain criteria such as whether the Company provides significant ancillary services to the lessees of the property. The Company includes property that it leases to third parties (other than Dealers, franchisees, or agents) in investment property. Investment property is measured and depreciated in the same manner as property and equipment.

Property and equipment

Property and equipment is measured at cost less accumulated depreciation and any accumulated impairment. Land is measured at cost less any accumulated impairment. Properties in the course of construction are measured at cost less any accumulated impairment. The cost of an item of property or equipment comprises costs that are directly attributed to its acquisition and initial estimates of the cost of dismantling and removing the item and restoring the site on which it is located.

Buildings, fixtures, and equipment are depreciated using a declining balance method to their estimated residual value over their estimated useful lives. The estimated useful lives, amortization method, and residual values are reviewed annually with the effect of any changes in estimate being accounted for on a prospective basis.

Leasehold improvements are amortized on a straight-line basis over the terms of the respective leases or useful life, if shorter.

Assets held under finance leases are depreciated on the same basis as owned assets. If there is no reasonable certainty that the Company will obtain ownership by the end of the lease term, the asset is depreciated over the shorter of lease term and its useful life.

Depreciation and amortization rates are as follows:

Asset Category	Depreciation rate/term
Buildings	4-20%
Fixtures and equipment	5-40%
Leasehold improvements	Shorter of term of lease or useful life
Assets under finance lease	Shorter of term of lease or useful life

Leased assets

Leases are classified as finance leases whenever the terms of the lease transfer substantially all the risks and rewards of ownership to the lessee. All other leases are classified as operating leases.

Lessor

When the Company is the lessor in an operating lease, rental income and licence fees are recognized in net income on a straight-line basis over the term of the lease.

Lessee

When the Company is the lessee in an operating lease, rent payments are charged to net income on a straight-line basis over the term of the lease. Lease incentives are amortized on a straight-line basis over the terms of the respective leases.

Assets under finance leases are recognized as assets of the Company at their fair value or, if lower, at the present value of the minimum lease payments, each determined at the inception of the lease. The corresponding liability is included in the Consolidated Balance Sheets as a finance lease obligation. Lease payments are apportioned between finance costs and reduction of the lease obligations, so as to achieve a constant rate of interest on the remaining balance of the liability.

Sale and leaseback

The accounting treatment of a sale and leaseback transaction is assessed based upon the substance of the transaction and whether the sale is made at the asset's fair value.

For sale and finance leasebacks, any gain or loss from the sale is deferred and amortized over the lease term. For sale and operating leasebacks, the assets are sold at fair value and, accordingly, the gain or loss from the sale is recognized immediately in net income.

Impairment of assets

The carrying amounts of property and equipment, investment property, and intangible assets with finite useful lives are reviewed at the end of each reporting period to determine whether there are any indicators of impairment. Indicators of impairment may include a significant decline in asset market value, material adverse changes in the external operating environment which affect the manner in which the asset is used or is expected to be used, obsolescence, or physical damage of the asset. If any such indicators exist, then the recoverable amount of the asset is estimated. Goodwill and intangible assets with indefinite useful lives and intangible assets not yet available for use are not amortized but are tested for impairment at least annually or whenever there is an indicator that the asset may be impaired.

Cash generating units

When it is not possible to estimate the recoverable amount of an individual asset, the Company estimates the recoverable amount of the CGU to which the asset belongs. The CGUs correspond to the smallest identifiable group of assets whose continuing use generates cash inflows that are largely independent of the cash inflows from other assets or groups of assets.

Goodwill acquired in a business combination is allocated to each of the CGUs (or groups of CGUs) expected to benefit from the synergies of the combination. Intangible assets with indefinite useful lives are allocated to the CGU to which they relate.

Determining the recoverable amount

An impairment loss is recognized when the carrying amount of an asset, or of the CGU to which it belongs, exceeds the recoverable amount. The recoverable amount of an asset or CGU is defined as the higher of its fair value less costs to sell ("FVLCS") and its VIU.

In assessing VIU, the estimated future cash flows are discounted to their present value. Cash flows are discounted using a pre-tax discount rate that includes a risk premium specific to each line of business. The Company estimates cash flows before taxes based on the most recent actual results or budgets. Cash flows are then extrapolated over a period of up to five years, taking into account a terminal value calculated by discounting the final year in perpetuity. The growth rate applied to the terminal values is based on the Bank of Canada's target inflation rate or a growth rate specific to the individual item being tested based on Management's estimate.

Recording impairments and reversals of impairments

Impairments and reversals of impairments are recognized in Other income in the Consolidated Statements of Income. Any impairment loss is allocated first to reduce the carrying amount of any goodwill allocated to the CGU and then to the other assets of the CGU. Impairments of goodwill cannot be reversed. Impairments of other assets recognized in prior periods are assessed at the end of each reporting period to determine if the indicators of impairment have reversed or no longer exist. An impairment loss is reversed if the estimated recoverable amount exceeds the carrying amount. The increased carrying amount of an asset attributable to a reversal of impairment may not exceed the carrying amount that would have been determined had no impairment been recognized in prior periods.

Assets classified as held for sale

Non-current assets and disposal groups are classified as assets held for sale when their carrying amount is to be recovered principally through a sale transaction rather than through continuing use. This condition is regarded as met only when the sale is highly probable and the asset (or disposal group) is available for immediate sale in its present condition. Management must be committed to the sale, and it should be expected to qualify for recognition as a completed sale within one year from the date of classification. Assets (and disposal groups) classified as held for sale are measured at the lower of the carrying amount or FVLCS and are not depreciated. The fair value measurement of assets held for sale is categorized within Level 2 of fair value hierarchy (refer to Note 32.4 for definition of levels).

Borrowing costs

Borrowing costs directly attributable to the acquisition or construction of a qualifying asset are capitalized. Qualifying assets are those that require a minimum of three months to prepare for their intended use. All other borrowing costs are recognized in Cost of producing revenue or in Net finance costs in the Consolidated Statements of Income in the period in which they are incurred.

Employee benefits

Short-term benefits

Short-term employee benefit obligations are measured on an undiscounted basis and are expensed as the related service is provided.

The Company recognizes a liability and an expense for short-term benefits such as bonuses, profit-sharing, and employee stock purchases if the Company has a present legal obligation or constructive obligation to pay this amount as a result of past service provided by the employees and the obligation can be estimated reasonably.

Post-employment benefits

The Company provides certain health care, dental care, life insurance, and other benefits, but not pensions, for certain retired employees pursuant to Company policy. The Company accrues the cost of these employee benefits over the periods in which the employees earn the benefits. The cost of employee benefits earned by employees is actuarially determined using the projected benefit method pro-rated on length of service and Management's best estimate of salary escalation, retirement ages of employees, employee turnover, life expectancy, and expected health and dental care costs. The costs are discounted at a rate that is based on market rates as at the measurement date. Actuarial gains and losses are immediately recorded in OCI.

The Company also provides post-employment benefits with respect to contributions to a Deferred Profit Sharing Plan ("DPSP").

Termination benefits

Termination benefits are payable when employment is terminated by the Company before the normal retirement date or whenever an employee accepts voluntary redundancy in exchange for these benefits. The Company recognizes a provision for termination benefits when it is demonstrably committed to either terminating the employment of current employees according to a detailed formal plan, without possibility of withdrawal, or providing termination benefits as a result of an offer made to encourage voluntary redundancy.

Share-based payments

Stock options with tandem stock appreciation rights ("stock options") are granted with a feature that enables the employee to exercise the stock option or receive a cash payment equal to the difference between the market price of the Company's Class A Non-Voting Shares as at the exercise date and the exercise price of the stock option. These stock options are considered to be compound instruments. The fair value of compound instruments is measured at each reporting date, taking into account the terms and conditions on which the rights to cash or equity instruments are granted. As the fair value of the settlement in cash is the same as the fair value of the settlement as a traditional stock option, the fair value of the stock option is the same as the fair value of the debt component. The corresponding expense and liability are recognized over the respective vesting period.

The fair value of the amount payable to employees with respect to share unit plans and trust unit plans, which are settled in cash, is recorded as the services are provided over the vesting period. The fair value of the liability is remeasured at each reporting date with the change in the liability being recognized in Selling, general and administrative expenses in the Consolidated Statements of Income.

Insurance reserve

Included in trade and other payables is an insurance reserve that consists of an amount determined from loss reports and individual cases and an amount, based on past experience, for losses incurred but not reported. These estimates are continually reviewed and are subject to the impact of future changes in such factors as claim severity and frequency. While Management believes that the amount is adequate, the ultimate liability may be in excess of or less than the amounts provided, and any adjustment will be reflected in net income during the periods in which they become known.

The Company uses actuarial valuations in determining its reserve for outstanding losses and loss-related expenses using an appropriate reserving methodology for each line of business. The Company does not discount its liabilities for unpaid claims.

Provisions

A provision is recognized if, as a result of a past event, the Company has a present legal or constructive obligation that can be estimated reliably and it is probable that an outflow of economic benefits will be required to settle the obligation. The amount recognized as a provision is the best estimate of the consideration required to settle the present obligation at the end of the reporting period, taking into account risks and uncertainty of cash flows. Where the effect of discounting is material, provisions are determined by discounting the expected future cash flows at a pre-tax rate that reflects current market assessments of the time value of money and the risks specific to the liability.

Sales and warranty returns

The provision for sales and warranty returns relates to the Company's obligation for defective goods in current store inventories and defective goods sold to customers that have yet to be returned, after sales service for replacement parts, and future corporate store sales returns. Accruals for sales and warranty returns are estimated on the basis of historical returns and are recorded so as to allocate them to the same period the corresponding revenue is recognized. These accruals are reviewed regularly and updated to reflect Management's best estimate; however, actual returns could vary from these estimates.

Site restoration and decommissioning

Legal or constructive obligations associated with the removal of underground fuel storage tanks and site remediation costs on the retirement of certain property and equipment and with the termination of certain lease agreements, are recognized in the period in which they are incurred, when it is probable that an outflow of resources embodying economic benefits will be required and a reasonable estimate of the amount of the obligation can be made. The obligations are initially measured at the Company's best estimate, using an expected value approach, and are discounted to present value.

Onerous contracts

A provision for onerous contracts is recognized when the expected benefits to be derived by the Company from a contract are lower than the unavoidable costs of meeting its obligations under the contract. The provision is measured at the present value of the lower of the expected cost of terminating the contract or the expected net cost of continuing with the contract.

Customer loyalty

An obligation arises from the "My Canadian Tire 'Money'™" customer loyalty program when the Company issues electronic Canadian Tire 'Money'® and when the Dealers pay the Company to acquire paper-based Canadian Tire 'Money', as the Dealers retain the right to return paper-based Canadian Tire Money to the Company for refund in cash. These obligations are measured at fair value by reference to the fair value of the awards for which they could be redeemed and based on the estimated probability of their redemption. The expense is recorded in Selling, general and administrative expenses in the Consolidated Statements of Income.

Debt

Debt is classified as current when the Company expects to settle the liability in its normal operating cycle, it holds the liability primarily for the purpose of trading, the liability is due to be settled within 12 months after the date of the Consolidated Balance Sheets, or it does not have an unconditional right to defer settlement of the liability for at least 12 months after the date of the Consolidated Balance Sheets.

Share capital

Shares issued by the Company are recorded at the value of proceeds received. Repurchased shares are removed from equity. No gain or loss is recognized in net income on the purchase, sale, issue, or cancellation of the Company's shares.

Share repurchases are charged to share capital at the average cost per share outstanding and the excess between the repurchase price and the average cost is first allocated to contributed surplus, with any remainder allocated to retained earnings.

Dividends

Dividends declared and payable to the Company's shareholders are recognized as a liability in the Consolidated Balance Sheets in the period in which the dividends are approved by the Company's Board of Directors.

Distributions

Distributions to non-controlling interests are recognized as a liability in the Consolidated Balance Sheets in the period in which the distributions are declared.

Revenue

The Company recognizes revenue when the amount can be reliably measured, when it is probable that future economic benefits will flow to the entity, and when specific criteria have been met for each of the Company's activities described below.

Sale of goods

Revenue from the sale of goods includes merchandise sold to Dealers and Mark's Work Wearhouse Ltd. ("Mark's") and FGL Sports Ltd. ("FGL Sports") franchisees, the sale of gasoline through agents, and the sale of goods by Mark's, PartSource, and FGL Sports corporately-owned stores to the general public. This revenue is recognized when the goods are delivered, less an estimate for the sales and warranty returns. Revenue from the sale of goods is measured at the fair value of the consideration received less an appropriate deduction for actual and expected returns, discounts, rebates, and warranty and loyalty program costs, net of sales taxes.

If there is any uncertainty regarding the right of a customer to return goods, no revenue is recognized until the uncertainty is resolved. However, in the case of warranties, if warranty claims can be reasonably estimated, revenue is recorded for the net amount.

Customer loyalty programs

Loyalty award credits issued as part of a sales transaction relating to the Company's Gas Advantage, Cash Advantage, and Sport Chek MasterCard Rewards credit card programs result in revenue being deferred until the loyalty award is redeemed by the customer. The portion of the revenue that is deferred is the fair value of the award. The fair value of the award takes into account the amount for which the award credits could be sold separately, less the proportion of the award credits that are not expected to be redeemed by customers.

Interest income on loans receivable

Interest income includes interest charged on loans receivable and fees that are an integral part of the effective interest rate on financial instruments. Interest income on financial assets that are classified as loans and receivables is determined using the effective interest method.

Services rendered

Service revenue includes Roadside Assistance Club membership revenue; insurance premiums and reinsurance revenue; extended warranty contract fees; merchant, interchange, and processing fees; cash advance fees; foreign exchange fees; and service charges on the loans receivable of the Financial Services operating segment, as well as Mark's clothing alteration revenue. Service revenue is recognized according to the contractual provisions of the arrangement, which is generally when the service is provided or over the contractual period.

Merchant, interchange, and processing fees, cash advance fees, and foreign exchange fees on credit card transactions are recognized as revenue at the time transactions are completed. Revenue from separately priced extended warranty contracts is recorded on a straight-line basis over the term of the contracts.

Reinsurance premiums are recorded on an accrual basis and are included in net income on a pro rata basis over the life of the insurance contract, with the unearned portion deferred in the Consolidated Balance Sheets. Premiums that are subject to adjustment are estimated based on available information. Any variances from the estimates are recorded in the periods in which they become known.

Royalties and licence fees

Royalties and licence fees include licence fees from petroleum agents and Dealers, and royalties from Mark's and FGL Sports franchisees. Royalties and licence fee revenues are recognized as they are earned in accordance with the substance of the relevant agreement and are measured on an accrual basis.

Rental income

Rental income from operating leases where the Company is the lessor is recognized on a straight-line basis over the terms of the respective leases.

Vendor rebates

The Company records cash consideration received from vendors as a reduction in the price of vendors' products and recognizes it as a reduction to the cost of related inventory or, if the related inventory has been sold, to the cost of producing revenue. Certain exceptions apply where the cash consideration received is either a reimbursement of incremental selling costs incurred by the Company or a payment for assets or services delivered to the vendor, in which case the cost is reflected as a reduction in selling, general and administrative expenses.

The Company recognizes rebates that are at the vendor's discretion when the vendor either pays the rebates or agrees to pay them and payment is considered probable and can be reasonably estimated.

Net finance costs

Finance income comprises interest income on funds invested (including available-for-sale financial assets). Interest income is recognized as it accrues using the effective interest method.

Finance costs comprises interest expense on borrowings (including borrowings relating to the Dealer Loan Program), unwinding of the discount on provisions, and is net of borrowing costs that have been capitalized. Interest on deposits is recorded in Cost of producing revenue in the Consolidated Statements of Income.

Income taxes

The income tax expense for the year comprises current and deferred income tax. Income tax expense is recognized in net income except to the extent that it relates to items recognized either in OCI or directly in equity. In this case, the income tax expense is recognized in OCI or in equity, respectively.

The income tax expense is calculated on the basis of the tax laws enacted or substantively enacted at the date of the Consolidated Balance Sheets in the countries where the Company operates and generates taxable income.

Deferred income tax is recognized using the liability method for unused tax losses, unused tax benefits, and temporary differences arising between the tax bases of assets and liabilities and their carrying amounts in these consolidated financial statements. However, deferred income tax is not accounted for if it arises from the initial recognition of goodwill or the initial recognition of an asset or liability in a transaction, other than a business combination, that at the time of the transaction affects neither accounting nor taxable income. Deferred income tax is determined using tax rates (and laws) that have been enacted or substantively enacted at the date of the Consolidated Balance Sheets and are expected to apply when the related deferred income tax asset is realized or the deferred income tax liability is settled.

Deferred income tax assets are recognized only to the extent that it is probable that future taxable income will be available against which the temporary differences can be utilized. Deferred income tax liabilities are provided on temporary differences arising on investments in subsidiaries and associates, except where the timing of the reversal of the temporary difference is controlled by the Company and it is probable that the temporary difference will not reverse in the foreseeable future.

Earnings per share

Basic earnings per share ("Basic EPS") is calculated by dividing the net income attributable to the shareholders of the Company by the weighted average number of Common and Class A Non-Voting shares outstanding during the reporting period. Diluted earnings per share ("Diluted EPS") is calculated by adjusting the net income attributable to the shareholders of the Company and the weighted average number of shares outstanding for the effects of all potentially dilutive equity instruments, which comprise employee stock options. Net income attributable to the shareholders of the Company is the same for both the Basic EPS and Diluted EPS calculations.

Non-controlling interests

When the proportion of the equity held by non-controlling interests changes, the Company adjusts the carrying amounts of the controlling and non-controlling interests to reflect the changes in their relative interest in the subsidiary. The Company recognizes directly in equity any difference between the amount by which the non-controlling interests are adjusted and the fair value of the consideration paid or received, and attribute it to the shareholders of the Company.

4. Capital management

The Company's objectives when managing capital are:

- ensuring sufficient liquidity to support its financial obligations and execute its operating and strategic plans;
- maintaining healthy liquidity reserves and access to capital; and
- minimizing the after-tax cost of capital while taking into consideration current and future industry, market, and economic risks and conditions.

The definition of capital varies from company to company, industry to industry, and for different purposes. In the process of managing the Company's capital, Management includes the following items in its definition of capital, which includes Glacier Credit Card Trust ("GCCT") indebtedness but excludes Franchise Trust indebtedness:

(C$ in millions)	2016	% of total	2015	% of total
Capital components				
Deposits	$ 950.7	8.5%	$ 880.7	8.2%
Short-term borrowings	199.4	1.8%	88.6	0.8%
Current portion of long-term debt	653.4	5.9%	24.3	0.2%
Long-term debt	2,667.1	24.0%	2,971.4	27.8%
Long-term deposits	1,230.8	11.1%	1,372.2	12.8%
Total debt	$ 5,701.4	51.3%	$ 5,337.2	49.8%
Redeemable financial instrument	517.0	4.7%	517.0	4.9%
Share capital	648.1	5.8%	671.2	6.3%
Contributed surplus	2.9	0.0%	2.9	0.0%
Retained earnings	4,250.9	38.2%	4,172.0	39.0%
Total capital under management	$ 11,120.3	100.0%	$ 10,700.3	100.0%

The Company monitors its capital structure through measuring debt-to-earnings ratios and ensures its ability to service debt and meet other fixed obligations by tracking its interest and other coverage ratios, and forecasting cash flows.

The Company manages its capital structure over the long term to optimize the balance among capital efficiency, financial flexibility, and risk mitigation. Management calculates its ratios to approximate the methodology of debt-rating agencies and other market participants on a current and prospective basis. To assess its effectiveness in managing capital, Management monitors these ratios against targeted ranges.

In order to maintain or adjust the capital structure, the Company has the flexibility to adjust the amount of dividends paid to shareholders, repurchase shares pursuant to a normal course issuer bid ("NCIB") program, repay debt, issue new debt and equity at Canadian Tire Corporation and CT REIT, issue new debt with different characteristics to replace existing debt, engage in additional sale and leaseback transactions of real estate properties, and increase or decrease the amount of sales of co-ownership interests in loans receivable to GCCT.

The Company has a policy in place to manage capital. As part of the overall management of capital, Management and the Audit Committee of the Board of Directors review the Company's compliance with, and performance against, the policy. In addition, periodic review of the policy is performed to ensure consistency with the risk tolerances.

Financial covenants of the existing debt agreements are reviewed by Management on an ongoing basis to monitor compliance with the agreements. The key financial covenant for Canadian Tire Corporation is a requirement for the retail segment to maintain, at all times, a ratio of total indebtedness to total capitalization equal to or lower than a specified maximum ratio (as defined in the applicable bank credit facility agreements, but which excludes consideration of CTFS Holdings, CT REIT, Franchise Trust, and their respective subsidiaries).

The Company was in compliance with this key covenant as at December 31, 2016 and January 2, 2016. Under the covenant, the Company currently has sufficient flexibility to fund business growth.

CT REIT is required to comply with financial covenants established under its Trust Indenture, Bank Credit Agreement, and the Declaration of Trust and was in compliance with the key covenants as at December 31, 2016 and 2015.

In addition, the Company is required to comply with regulatory requirements for capital associated with the operations of Canadian Tire Bank ("CTB" or "the Bank"), a federally chartered bank, and other regulatory requirements that have an impact on its business operations and certain financial covenants established under its unsecured revolving credit facility.

CTB manages its capital under guidelines established by the Office of the Superintendent of Financial Institutions of Canada ("OSFI"). OSFI's regulatory capital guidelines are based on the international Basel Committee on Banking Supervision framework entitled Basel III: A Global Regulatory Framework for More Resilient Banks and Banking Systems ("Basel III"), which came into effect in Canada on January 1, 2013, and measures capital in relation to credit, market, and operational risks. The Bank has various capital policies and procedures and controls, including an Internal Capital Adequacy Assessment Process ("ICAAP"), which it utilizes to achieve its goals and objectives.

The Bank's objectives include:

- providing sufficient capital to maintain the confidence of investors and depositors; and
- being an appropriately capitalized institution, as measured internally, defined by regulatory authorities and compared with the Bank's peers.

OSFI's regulatory capital guidelines under Basel III allow for two tiers of capital. As at December 31, 2016, the Bank's fiscal year end, Common Equity Tier 1 ("CET1") capital includes common shares, retained earnings, and AOCI, less regulatory adjustments including items risk-weighted at 0 percent which are deducted from capital. The Bank currently does not hold any additional Tier 1 or Tier 2 capital instruments. Therefore, the Bank's CET1 is equal to its Tier 1 and total regulatory capital. Risk-weighted assets ("RWA") include a credit risk component for all on-balance-sheet assets weighted for the risk inherent in each type of asset, off-balance sheet financial instruments, an operational risk component based on a percentage of average risk-weighted revenues, and a market-risk component for assets held for trade. For the purposes of calculating RWA, securitization transactions are considered off-balance-sheet transactions and, therefore, securitization assets are not included in the RWA calculation. Assets are classified as held for trade when they are held with trading intent.

The Leverage Ratio prescribed by OSFI's Leverage Requirements Guideline provides an overall measure of the adequacy of an institution's capital and is defined as the all-in Tier 1 capital divided by the leverage ratio exposure. The leverage ratio exposure is the sum of on-balance sheet exposures, derivative exposures, securities financing transaction exposures, and off-balance sheet items.

As at December 31, 2016 and 2015, the Bank complied with all regulatory capital guidelines established by OSFI, its internal targets as determined by its ICAAP, and the financial covenants of its credit facility.

5. Financial risk management

5.1 Overview

The Company has exposure to the following risks from its use of financial instruments:

- credit risk;
- liquidity risk; and
- market risk (including foreign currency and interest rate risk).

This note presents information about the Company's exposure to each of the above risks and the Company's objectives, policy, and processes for measuring and managing risk. Further quantitative disclosures are included throughout these consolidated financial statements and notes thereto.

5.2 Risk management framework

The Company's financial risk management policy serves to identify and analyze the risks faced by the Company, to set acceptable risk tolerance limits and controls, and to monitor risks and adherence to limits. The financial risk management strategies and systems are reviewed regularly to ensure they remain consistent with the objectives and risk tolerance acceptable to the Company and current market trends and conditions. The Company, through its training and management standards and procedures, aims to uphold a disciplined and constructive control environment in which all employees understand their roles and obligations.

5.3 Credit risk

Credit risk is the risk of financial loss to the Company if a customer or counterparty to a financial instrument fails to meet its contractual obligations. Credit risk primarily arises from the Company's credit card customers, Dealer network, and financial instruments held with bank or non-bank counterparties.

5.3.1 Financial instrument counterparty credit risk

The Company has a Board-approved financial risk management policy in place to manage the various risks including counterparty credit risk relating to cash balances, investment activity. and the use of financial derivatives. The Company limits its exposure to counterparty credit risk by transacting only with highly-rated financial institutions and other counterparties and by managing within specific limits for credit exposure and term to maturity. The Company's financial instrument portfolio is spread across financial institutions, provincial and federal governments, and, to a lesser extent, corporate issuers that are dual rated and have a credit rating in the "A" category or better.

5.3.2 Consumer and Dealer credit risk

Through the granting of Canadian Tire credit cards to its customers, the Company assumes certain risks with respect to the ability and willingness of its customers to repay debt. In addition, the Company may be required to provide credit enhancement for individual Dealer's borrowings in the form of standby letters of credit (the "LCs") or guarantees of third-party bank debt agreements, with respect to the financing programs available to the Dealers (Note 34).

The Company's maximum exposure to credit risk, over and above amounts recognized in the Consolidated Balance Sheets, include the following:

(C$ in millions)	**2016**	2015
Undrawn loan commitments	**$ 9,517.4**	$ 9,514.1
Guarantees	**428.5**	482.1
Total	**$ 9,945.9**	$ 9,996.2

Refer to Note 9 for information on the credit quality and performance of loans receivables.

5.4 Liquidity risk

Liquidity risk is the risk that the Company might encounter difficulty in meeting the obligations associated with its financial liabilities that are settled by delivering cash or another financial asset. The Company's approach to managing liquidity is to ensure, as much as possible, that it will always have sufficient liquidity to meet its liabilities when due, under both normal and reasonably stressed conditions. The Company's financial risk management policy serves to manage its exposure to liquidity risk. The Company uses a detailed consolidated cash flow forecast model to regularly monitor its near-term and longer-term cash flow requirements, which assists in optimizing its short-term cash and indebtedness position while evaluating longer-term funding strategies.

In addition, CTB has in place an Asset Liability Management policy. It is CTB's objective to ensure the availability of adequate funds by maintaining a strong liquidity management framework and to satisfy all applicable regulatory and statutory requirements.

As at December 31, 2016, the Company had $4.525 billion in committed bank lines of credit of which $1.975 billion is available to Canadian Tire Corporation under a syndicated credit facility expiring in July 2021, $300.0 million is available to CT REIT under a syndicated credit facility expiring in April 2021, and $2.25 billion is available to CTB expiring October 2019.

In addition to the bank lines of credit, the Company has access to additional funding sources including internal cash generation, access to public and private financial markets, and strategic real estate transactions. Assets of CTB are funded through the securitization of credit card receivables using GCCT, broker guaranteed investment certificate ("GICs") deposits, retail GIC deposits, and high-interest savings ("HIS") account deposits. CTB also holds high quality liquid assets, as required by regulators, which are available to address funding disruptions.

CT REIT filed a base-shelf prospectus on March 5, 2015, under which it may raise up to $1.5 billion of debt and equity capital for the subsequent 25-month period (and under which the Company can sell some of the equity units it owns of CT REIT). On March 31, 2015, GCCT filed a base shelf prospectus permitting it to issue up to $1.5 billion of term notes for the subsequent 25-month period.

Due to the diversification of its funding sources, the Company is not exposed to any concentration risk regarding liquidity.

The following table summarizes the Company's contractual maturity for its financial liabilities, including both principal and interest payments:

(C$ in millions)	2017	2018	2019	2020	2021	Thereafter	Total
Non-derivative financial liabilities							
Deposits[1]	957.8	362.9	413.5	281.9	172.5	–	2,188.6
Trade and other payables	1,626.3	–	–	–	–	–	1,626.3
Short-term borrowings	199.4	–	–	–	–	–	199.4
Loans payable	700.3	–	–	–	–	–	700.3
Long-term debt	636.7	264.6	500.0	500.0	150.0	1,100.0	3,151.3
Finance lease obligations	16.7	14.5	12.7	11.5	11.4	59.0	125.8
Mortgages	1.2	17.1	37.6	–	–	–	55.9
Interest payments[2]	146.0	125.1	103.3	78.7	61.4	437.7	952.2
Total	$ 4,284.4	$ 784.2	$ 1,067.1	$ 872.1	$ 395.3	$ 1,596.7	$ 8,999.8

[1] Deposits exclude the GIC broker fee discount of $7.1 million.

[2] Includes interest payments on deposits, short-term borrowings, loans payable, long-term debt, and finance lease obligations.

It is not expected that the cash flows included in the maturity analysis would occur significantly earlier or at significantly different amounts.

5.5 Market risk

Market risk is the risk that changes in market prices, such as foreign exchange rates, interest rates, and equity prices, will affect the Company's income or the value of its holdings of financial instruments. The objective of market risk management is to manage market risk exposures within acceptable parameters while optimizing the return. The Company's financial risk management policy establishes guidelines on how the Company is to manage the market risk inherent to the business and provides mechanisms to ensure business transactions are executed in accordance with established limits, processes, and procedures.

All such transactions are carried out within the established guidelines and, generally, the Company seeks to apply hedge accounting in order to manage volatility in its net income.

5.5.1 Foreign currency risk

The Company sources its merchandise globally. Approximately 40%, 45%, and 6% of the value of the inventory purchased for the Canadian Tire, Mark's, and FGL Sports banners, respectively, is sourced directly from vendors outside North America, primarily denominated in U.S. dollars. To mitigate the impact of fluctuating foreign exchange rates on the cost of these purchases, the Company has an established foreign exchange risk management program that governs the proportion of forecast U.S. dollar purchases that must be hedged through the purchase of foreign exchange contracts. The purpose of the program is to provide certainty with respect to a portion of the foreign exchange component of future merchandise purchases.

As the Company has hedged a significant portion of the cost of its near-term U.S.-dollar-denominated forecast purchases, a change in foreign currency rates will not impact that portion of the cost of those purchases. Even when a change in rates is sustained, the Company's program to hedge a proportion of forecast U.S. dollar purchases continues. As hedges are placed at current foreign exchange rates, the impact of a sustained change in rate will eventually be reflected in the cost of the Company's U.S. dollar purchases. The hedging program has historically allowed the Company to defer the impact of sudden exchange rate movements on margins and allow it time to develop strategies to mitigate the impact of a sustained change in foreign exchange rates. Some vendors have an underlying exposure to U.S. currency fluctuations which may affect the price they charge the Company for merchandise from time to time; the Company's hedging program does not mitigate that risk. While the Company may be able to pass on changes in foreign currency exchange rates through pricing, any decision to do so will be subject to market conditions.

5.5.2 Interest rate risk

The Company may enter into interest rate swap contracts to manage its current and anticipated exposure to interest rate price risk. The Company's financial risk management policy requires that a minimum of 75 percent of its long-term debt (term greater than one year) and lease obligations must be at fixed interest rates.

A one percent change in interest rates would not materially affect the Company's net income or equity as the Company has minimal floating interest rate exposure given the indebtedness of the Company is predominantly at fixed rates.

The Company's exposure to interest rate changes is predominantly driven by the Financial Services business to the extent that the interest rates on future GIC deposits, HIS account deposits, tax free savings account ("TFSA") deposits, and securitization transactions are market-dependent. Partially offsetting this will be rates charged on credit cards and future liquidity pool investment rates available to the Bank. In addition, the Company has entered into delayed start interest rate swaps to hedge a portion of its planned GCCT term debt issuances in 2017 to 2020.

6. Operating segments

The Company has three reportable operating segments: Retail, CT REIT, and Financial Services. The reportable operating segments are strategic business units offering different products and services. They are separately managed due to their distinct nature. The following summary describes the operations in each of the Company's reportable segments:

- The retail business is conducted under a number of banners including Canadian Tire, Canadian Tire Gas ("Petroleum"), Mark's, PartSource, and various FGL Sports banners. Retail also includes the Dealer Loan Program (the portion [silo] of Franchise Trust that issues loans to Dealers). Non-CT REIT real estate is included in Retail.
- CT REIT is an unincorporated, closed-end real estate investment trust. CT REIT holds a geographically-diversified portfolio of properties comprised largely of Canadian Tire banner stores, Canadian Tire anchored retail developments, mixed-use commercial property, and distribution centres.
- Financial Services markets a range of Canadian Tire branded credit cards including Canadian Tire Options MasterCard, Cash Advantage MasterCard, Gas Advantage MasterCard, and Sport Chek MasterCard and also participates in the Canadian Tire loyalty program. Certain costs associated with these activities were allocated to Financial Services for segment reporting purposes. Financial Services also markets insurance and warranty products and provides settlement services to Canadian Tire affiliates. Financial Services includes CTB, a federally regulated financial institution that manages and finances the Company's consumer MasterCard, Visa, and retail credit card portfolios, as well as an existing block of Canadian Tire-branded line of credit portfolios. CTB also offers high-interest savings deposit accounts, tax free savings accounts, and GIC deposits, both directly and through third-party brokers. Financial Services also includes GCCT, a structured entity established to purchase co-ownership interests in the Company's credit card loans. GCCT issues debt to third-party investors to fund its purchases.

Performance is measured based on segment income before income taxes, as included in the internal management reports. Management has determined that this measure is the most relevant in evaluating segment results and allocating resources. Information regarding the results of each reportable operating segment is as follows:

					2016					2015
(C$ in millions)	**Retail**	**CT REIT**	**Financial Services**	**Eliminations and adjustments**	**Total**	Retail	CT REIT	Financial Services	Eliminations and adjustments	Total
External revenue	**$ 11,447.6**	**$ 24.9**	**$ 1,091.9**	**$ 116.6**	**$ 12,681.0**	$ 11,069.8	$ 16.3	$ 1,087.6	$ 105.9	$ 12,279.6
Intercompany revenue	**5.8**	**382.3**	**15.9**	**(404.0)**	**–**	5.5	361.9	13.6	(381.0)	–
Total revenue	**11,453.4**	**407.2**	**1,107.8**	**(287.4)**	**12,681.0**	11,075.3	378.2	1,101.2	(275.1)	12,279.6
Cost of producing revenue	**7,890.9**	**–**	**449.2**	**(51.6)**	**8,288.5**	7,747.6	–	452.1	(55.4)	8,144.3
Gross margin	**3,562.5**	**407.2**	**658.6**	**(235.8)**	**4,392.5**	3,327.7	378.2	649.1	(219.7)	4,135.3
Other (income) expense	**(120.5)**	**–**	**0.4**	**115.8**	**(4.3)**	(160.7)	–	1.9	103.9	(54.9)
Selling, general and administrative expenses	**3,099.1**	**106.7**	**293.7**	**(207.6)**	**3,291.9**	2,926.0	96.5	274.7	(201.1)	3,096.1
Net finance (income) costs	**(37.9)**	**85.9**	**(0.6)**	**46.5**	**93.9**	(42.5)	87.1	(1.5)	49.7	92.8
Fair value (gain) loss on investment properties	**–**	**(44.5)**	**–**	**44.5**	**–**	–	(39.9)	–	39.9	–
Income before income taxes	**$ 621.8**	**$ 259.1**	**$ 365.1**	**$ (235.0)**	**$ 1,011.0**	$ 604.9	$ 234.5	$ 374.0	$ (212.1)	$ 1,001.3
Items included in the above:										
Depreciation and amortization	**$ 374.9**	**$ –**	**$ 9.3**	**$ 72.7**	**$ 456.9**	$ 350.6	$ –	$ 7.0	$ 67.1	$ 424.7
Interest income	**91.4**	**0.2**	**871.7**	**(72.9)**	**890.4**	101.1	0.3	845.4	(80.6)	866.2
Interest expense	**39.3**	**86.1**	**103.9**	**(73.2)**	**156.1**	45.5	87.4	109.7	(81.2)	161.4

The eliminations and adjustments include the following items:

- reclassifications of certain revenues and costs in the Financial Services segment to net finance costs;
- reclassifications of revenues and operating expenses to reflect loyalty program accounting in accordance with IFRIC 13 for the Company's Loyalty program;
- conversion from CT REIT's fair value investment property valuation policy to the Company's cost model, including the recording of depreciation; and
- inter-segment eliminations and adjustments including intercompany rent, property management fees, and credit card processing fees.

Capital expenditures by reportable operating segment are as follows:

				2016				2015
(C$ in millions)	**Retail**	**CT REIT**[1]	**Financial Services**	**Total**	Retail[2]	CT REIT[1]	Financial Services	Total
Capital expenditures[3]	**$ 568.7**	**$ 176.8**	**$ 9.4**	**$ 754.9**	$ 655.9	$ 42.4	$ 17.8	$ 716.1

[1] *CT REIT capital expenditures include the construction of stores under Mark's and FGL Sports banners of $2.0 million (2015 – $17.7 million).*

[2] *Retail capital expenditures include $17.7 million relating to the acquisition of 12 real estate leases, formerly held by Target Canada which were acquired during 2015, and are recorded in long-term receivables and other assets on the Consolidated Balance Sheets.*

[3] *Capital expenditures are presented on an accrual basis and include software additions.*

Total assets by reporting operating segment are as follows:

(C$ in millions)	**2016**	2015
Retail	**$ 11,024.4**	$ 11,128.0
CT REIT	**5,014.6**	4,350.9
Financial Services	**5,773.5**	5,520.3
Eliminations and adjustments	**(6,509.7)**	(6,011.4)
Total assets[1]	**$ 15,302.8**	$ 14,987.8

[1] *The Company employs a shared-services model for several of its back-office functions, including finance, information technology, human resources, and legal. As a result, expenses relating to these functions are allocated on a systematic and rational basis to the reportable operating segments. The associated assets and liabilities are not allocated among segments in the presented measures of segmented assets and liabilities.*

Total liabilities by reporting operating segment are as follows:

(C$ in millions)	2016	2015
Retail	$ 3,943.9	$ 3,899.1
CT REIT	2,424.0	2,137.5
Financial Services	4,731.6	4,588.4
Eliminations and adjustments	(1,534.0)	(1,426.9)
Total liabilities[1]	$ 9,565.5	$ 9,198.1

[1] *The Company employs a shared-services model for several of its back-office functions, including finance, information technology, human resources, and legal. As a result, expenses relating to these functions are allocated on a systematic and rational basis to the reportable operating segments. The associated assets and liabilities are not allocated among segments in the presented measures of segmented assets and liabilities.*

The eliminations and adjustments include the following items:

- conversion from CT REIT's fair value investment property valuation policy to the Company's cost model, including the recording of depreciation; and
- inter-segment eliminations.

7. Cash and cash equivalents

Cash and cash equivalents comprise the following:

(C$ in millions)	2016	2015
Cash	$ 81.0	$ 192.2
Cash equivalents	738.2	698.6
Restricted cash[1]	10.5	9.8
Total cash and cash equivalents[2]	829.7	900.6
Bank indebtedness	(5.9)	–
Cash and cash equivalents, net of bank indebtedness	$ 823.8	$ 900.6

[1] *Relates to GCCT and is restricted for the purpose of paying out note holders and additional funding costs.*
[2] *Included in cash and cash equivalents are amounts held in reserve in support of Financial Services' liquidity and regulatory requirements. Refer to Note 31.1.*

8. Trade and other receivables

Trade and other receivables include the following:

(C$ in millions)	2016	2015
Trade and other receivables	$ 614.2	$ 673.6
Derivatives (Note 32)	76.6	241.4
Total financial assets	$ 690.8	$ 915.0

Trade receivables are primarily from Dealers and franchisees, a large and geographically-dispersed group whose receivables, individually, generally comprise less than one percent of the total balance outstanding.

Receivables from Dealers are in the normal course of business, and include cost-sharing and financing arrangements. The net average credit period on sale of goods is between 14 and 120 days.

9. Loans receivable

Quantitative information about the Company's loans receivable portfolio is as follows:

	Total principal amount of receivables[1]	
(C$ in millions)	2016	2015
Credit card loans[2]	$ 5,104.6	$ 4,844.3
Dealer loans[3]	705.4	659.6
Total loans receivable	5,810.0	5,503.9
Less: long-term portion[4]	671.6	628.4
Current portion of loans receivable	$ 5,138.4	$ 4,875.5

[1] *Amounts shown are net of allowance for loan impairment.*
[2] *Includes line of credit loans.*
[3] *Dealer loans primarily relate to loans issued by Franchise Trust (refer to Note 21).*
[4] *The long-term portion of loans receivable is included in long-term receivables and other assets and includes Dealer loans of $668.9 million (2015 – $624.9 million).*

For the year ended December 31, 2016, cash received from interest earned on credit cards and loans was $820.2 million (2015 – $789.6 million).

The carrying amount of loans includes loans to Dealers that are secured by the assets of the respective Dealer corporations. The Company's exposure to loans receivable credit risk resides at Franchise Trust and at the Bank. Credit risk at the Bank is influenced mainly by the individual characteristics of each credit card customer. The Bank uses sophisticated credit scoring models, monitoring technology, and collection modelling techniques to implement and manage strategies, policies, and limits that are designed to control risk. Loans receivable are generated by a large and geographically-dispersed group of customers. Current credit exposure is limited to the loss that would be incurred if all of the Bank's counterparties were to default at the same time.

A continuity schedule of the Company's allowances for loans receivable[1] is as follows:

(C$ in millions)	2016	2015
Balance, beginning of year	$ 111.5	$ 113.2
Impairments for credit losses, net of recoveries	293.7	301.9
Recoveries	69.4	65.9
Write-offs	(367.7)	(369.5)
Balance, end of year	$ 106.9	$ 111.5

[1] *Loans include credit card loans and line of credit loans. No allowances for credit losses have been made with respect to Franchise Trust and FGL Sports loans receivable.*

The Company's allowances for credit losses are maintained at levels that are considered adequate to absorb future credit losses.

The Company's aging of the loans receivable that are past due, but not impaired, is as follows:

			2016			2015
(C$ in millions)	1-90 days	> 90 days	Total	1-90 days	> 90 days	Total
Loans receivable	$ 308.6	$ 58.3	$ 366.9	$ 306.3	$ 62.8	$ 369.1

Credit card loans are considered impaired and written off when a payment is 180 days in arrears. Line of credit loans are considered impaired when a payment is over 90 days in arrears and are written off when a payment is 180 days in arrears. No collateral is held against loans receivable, except for loans to Dealers, as discussed above.

Transfers of financial assets

Glacier Credit Card Trust

GCCT is a structured entity that was created to securitize credit card loans receivable. As at December 31, 2016, the Bank has transferred co-ownership interest in credit card loans receivable to GCCT but has retained substantially all the credit risk associated with the transferred assets. Due to the retention of substantially all of the risks and rewards on these assets, the Bank continues to recognize these assets within loans receivable and the transfers are accounted for as secured financing transactions. The associated liability as at December 31, 2016, secured by these assets, includes the commercial paper and term notes on the Consolidated Balance Sheets and is carried at amortized cost. The Bank is exposed to the majority of ownership risks and rewards of GCCT and, hence, it is consolidated. The carrying amount of the assets approximates their fair value. The difference between the credit card loans receivable transferred and the associated liabilities is shown below:

		2016		2015
(C$ in millions)	Carrying amount	Fair value	Carrying amount	Fair value
Credit card loans receivable transferred[1]	$ 1,989.0	$ 1,989.0	$ 1,988.0	$ 1,988.0
Associated liabilities	1,985.0	2,017.0	1,982.3	2,021.4
Net position	$ 4.0	$ (28.0)	$ 5.7	$ (33.4)

[1] *The fair value measurement of credit card loans receivable is categorized within Level 2 of the fair value hierarchy. For a definitions of the levels refer to Note 32.4.*

For legal purposes, the co-ownership interests in the Bank's receivables owned by GCCT have been sold at law to GCCT and are not available to the creditors of the Bank. Furthermore GCCT's liabilities are not legal liabilities of the Company.

The Bank has not identified any factors arising from current market circumstances that could lead to a need for the Bank to extend liquidity and/or credit support to GCCT over and above the existing arrangements or that could otherwise change the substance of the Bank's relationship with GCCT. There have been no relevant changes in the capital structure of GCCT since the Bank's assessment for consolidation.

Franchise Trust

The consolidated financial statements include a portion (silo) of Franchise Trust, a legal entity sponsored by a third-party bank that originates and services loans to Dealers for their purchases of inventory and fixed assets (the "Dealer loans"). The Company has arranged for several major Canadian banks to provide standby LCs to Franchise Trust as credit support for the Dealer loans. Franchise Trust has sold all of its rights in the LCs and outstanding Dealer loans to other independent trusts set up by major Canadian banks (the "Co-owner Trusts") that raise funds in the capital markets to finance their purchase of these undivided co-ownership interests. Due to the retention of substantially all of the risks and rewards relating to these Dealer loans, the transfers are accounted for as secured financing transactions. Accordingly, the Company continues to recognize the current portion of these assets in loans receivable and the long-term portion in long-term receivables and other assets, and records the associated liability secured by these assets as loans payable, being the loans that Franchise Trust has incurred to fund the Dealer loans. The Dealer loans and loans payable are initially recorded at fair value and subsequently carried at amortized cost.

	2016		2015	
(C$ in millions)	Carrying amount	Fair value	Carrying amount	Fair value
Dealer loans[1]	**$ 700.3**	**$ 700.3**	$ 655.5	$ 655.5
Associated liabilities	**700.3**	**700.3**	655.5	655.5
Net position	**$ –**	**$ –**	$ –	$ –

[1] *The fair value measurement of Dealer loans is categorized within Level 2 of the fair value hierarchy. For a definitions of the levels refer to Note 32.4.*

The Dealer loans have been sold at law and are not available to the creditors of the Company. Loans payable are not legal liabilities of the Company.

In the event that a Dealer defaults on a loan, the Company has the right to purchase such loan from the Co-owner Trusts, at which time the Co-owner Trusts will assign such Dealer's debt instrument and related security documentation to the Company. The assignment of this documentation provides the Company with first-priority security rights over all of such Dealer's assets, subject to certain prior ranking statutory claims.

In most cases, the Company would expect to recover any payments made to purchase a defaulted loan, including any associated expenses. In the event the Company does not choose to purchase a defaulted Dealer loan, the Co-owner Trusts may draw against the LCs.

The Co-owner Trusts may also draw against the LCs to cover any shortfalls in certain related fees owing to them. In any case, where a draw is made against the LCs, the Company has agreed to reimburse the bank issuing the LCs for the amount so drawn. Refer to Note 34 for further information.

10. Long-term receivables and other assets

Long-term receivables and other assets include the following:

(C$ in millions)	2016	2015
Loans receivable (Note 9)	**$ 671.6**	$ 628.4
Derivatives (Note 32)	**46.2**	50.2
Mortgages receivable	**17.1**	28.0
Other receivables	**3.6**	5.1
Total long-term receivables	**738.5**	711.7
Other	**25.2**	19.5
	$ 763.7	$ 731.2

11. Goodwill and intangible assets

The following table presents the changes in cost and accumulated amortization and impairment of the Company's intangible assets:

						2016
	Indefinite-life intangible assets and goodwill			**Finite-life intangible assets**		
(C$ in millions)	**Goodwill**	**Banners and trademarks**	**Franchise agreements and other intangibles**	**Software**	**Other intangibles[1]**	**Total**
Cost						
Balance, beginning of year	**$ 438.9**	**$ 267.4**	**$ 158.9**	**$ 1,267.7**	**$ 23.1**	**$ 2,156.0**
Additions[2]	**7.7**	**–**	**–**	**153.8**	**–**	**161.5**
Disposals/retirements	**–**	**–**	**–**	**(10.7)**	**–**	**(10.7)**
Reclassifications and transfers	**–**	**2.9**	**(2.9)**	**–**	**–**	**–**
Balance, end of year	**$ 446.6**	**$ 270.3**	**$ 156.0**	**$ 1,410.8**	**$ 23.1**	**$ 2,306.8**
Accumulated amortization and impairment						
Balance, beginning of year	**$ (1.9)**	**$ –**	**$ –**	**$ (889.6)**	**$ (17.7)**	**$ (909.2)**
Amortization for the year	**–**	**–**	**–**	**(124.6)**	**(1.5)**	**(126.1)**
Impairment	**–**	**(0.6)**	**–**	**–**	**–**	**(0.6)**
Disposals/retirements	**–**	**–**	**–**	**10.7**	**–**	**10.7**
Reclassifications and transfers	**–**	**–**	**–**	**–**	**(1.3)**	**(1.3)**
Balance, end of year	**$ (1.9)**	**$ (0.6)**	**$ –**	**$ (1,003.5)**	**$ (20.5)**	**$ (1,026.5)**
Net carrying amount, end of year	**$ 444.7**	**$ 269.7**	**$ 156.0**	**$ 407.3**	**$ 2.6**	**$ 1,280.3**

[1] *Includes FGL Sports customer relationships, certain private-label brands, and off-market leases.*
[2] *Additions primarily relate to internally developed intangible assets.*

						2015
	Indefinite-life intangible assets and goodwill			Finite-life intangible assets		
(C$ in millions)	Goodwill	Banners and trademarks	Franchise agreements and other intangibles	Software	Other intangibles[1]	Total
Cost						
Balance, beginning of year	$ 438.5	$ 266.6	$ 156.9	$ 1,158.1	$ 23.1	$ 2,043.2
Additions[2]	0.4	0.8	2.0	109.1	–	112.3
Disposals/retirements	–	–	–	0.9	–	0.9
Reclassifications and transfers	–	–	–	(0.4)	–	(0.4)
Balance, end of year	$ 438.9	$ 267.4	$ 158.9	$ 1,267.7	$ 23.1	$ 2,156.0
Accumulated amortization and impairment						
Balance, beginning of year	$ (1.9)	$ –	$ –	$ (775.3)	$ (14.3)	$ (791.5)
Amortization for the year	–	–	–	(109.8)	(2.1)	(111.9)
Disposals/retirements	–	–	–	(4.5)	–	(4.5)
Reclassifications and transfers	–	–	–	–	(1.3)	(1.3)
Balance, end of year	$ (1.9)	$ –	$ –	$ (889.6)	$ (17.7)	$ (909.2)
Net carrying amount, end of year	$ 437.0	$ 267.4	$ 158.9	$ 378.1	$ 5.4	$ 1,246.8

[1] *Includes FGL Sports customer relationships, certain private-label brands, and off-market leases.*
[2] *Additions primarily relate to internally developed intangible assets.*

The following table presents the details of the Company's goodwill:

(C$ in millions)	**2016**	2015
FGL Sports	**$ 364.6**	$ 356.9
Mark's	**56.7**	56.7
Canadian Tire	**23.4**	23.4
Total	**$ 444.7**	$ 437.0

Banners and trademarks includes FGL Sports and Mark's store banners, which represent legal trademarks of the Company with expiry dates ranging from 2017 to 2030. In addition, banners and trademarks include FGL Sports and Mark's private-label brands that have legal expiry dates. As the Company currently has no approved plans to change its store banners and intends to continue to renew all trademarks and private-label brands at each expiry date for the foreseeable future, there is no foreseeable limit to the period over which the assets are expected to generate net cash inflows. Therefore, these intangible assets are considered to have indefinite useful lives.

Franchise agreements have expiry dates with options to renew, or have indefinite lives. As the Company intends to renew these agreements at each renewal date for the foreseeable future, there is no foreseeable limit to the period over which the franchise agreements and franchise locations will generate net cash inflows. Therefore, these assets are considered to have indefinite useful lives.

Finite-life intangible assets are amortized over a term of two to ten years. Off-market leases are amortized over the term of the lease to which they relate.

The amount of borrowing costs capitalized in 2016 was $5.4 million (2015 – $3.4 million). The capitalization rate used to determine the amount of borrowing costs capitalized during the year was 6.1 percent (2015 – 6.0 percent).

Amortization expense of software and other finite-life intangible assets is included in Selling, general and administrative expenses in the Consolidated Statements of Income.

Impairment of intangible assets and subsequent reversal

The Company performed its annual impairment test on goodwill and indefinite-life intangible assets for all CGUs based on VIU using after-tax discount rates ranging from 7.3 to 10.5 percent and growth rates ranging from 1.1 to 10.7 percent per annum.

The amount of impairment of intangible assets in 2016 was $0.6 million (2015 – $nil). There was no reversal of impairments in 2016 or 2015. The impairment on goodwill in 2016 pertains to the Company's Retail operating segment and is reported in Other Income in the Consolidated Statements of Income.

For all goodwill and intangible assets, the estimated recoverable amount is based on VIU exceeding the carrying amount. There is no reasonably possible change in assumptions that would cause the carrying amount to exceed the estimated recoverable amount.

12. Investment property

The following table presents changes in the cost and the accumulated depreciation and impairment on the Company's investment property:

(C$ in millions)	2016	2015
Cost		
Balance, beginning of year	$ 172.4	$ 178.8
Additions	135.1	11.0
Disposals/retirements	(0.9)	(3.8)
Reclassifications and transfers	(0.3)	(13.6)
Balance, end of year	$ 306.3	$ 172.4
Accumulated depreciation and impairment		
Balance, beginning of year	$ (34.6)	$ (30.2)
Depreciation for the year	(6.1)	(4.0)
Reversal of impairment	0.1	–
Disposal/retirements	0.7	1.1
Reclassifications and transfers	–	(1.5)
Balance, end of year	$ (39.9)	$ (34.6)
Net carrying amount, end of year	$ 266.4	$ 137.8

The investment properties generated rental income of $29.7 million (2015 – $19.2 million).

Direct operating expenses (including repairs and maintenance) arising from investment property recognized in net income were $13.0 million (2015 – $9.7 million).

The estimated fair value of investment property was $357.2 million (2015 – $228.2 million). This recurring fair value measurement is categorized within Level 3 of the fair value hierarchy (refer to Note 32.4 for definition of levels). The Company determines the fair value of investment property by applying a pre-tax capitalization rate to the annual rental income for the current leases. The capitalization rate ranged from 4.9 percent to 11.0 percent (2015 – 5.3 percent to 11.0 percent). The cash flows are for a term of five years, including a terminal value. The Company has real estate management expertise that is used to perform the valuation of investment property and has also completed independent appraisals on certain investment property owned by CT REIT.

Impairment of investment property and subsequent reversal

Any impairment or reversals of impairment are reported in Other income in the Consolidated Statements of Income.

13. Property and equipment

The following table presents changes in the cost and the accumulated depreciation and impairment on the Company's property and equipment:

							2016
(C$ in millions)	Land	Buildings	Fixtures and equipment	Leasehold improvements	Assets under finance lease	Construction in progress	Total
Cost							
Balance, beginning of year	$ 874.4	$ 2,915.9	$ 1,216.6	$ 1,140.7	$ 262.8	$ 359.4	$ 6,769.8
Additions	41.8	44.2	156.4	152.7	0.5	72.7	468.3
Disposals/retirements	(2.5)	(5.3)	(19.0)	(8.2)	(4.0)	(6.2)	(45.2)
Reclassifications and transfers	(2.5)	(10.9)	28.0	21.2	(36.3)	–	(0.5)
Balance, end of year	$ 911.2	$ 2,943.9	$ 1,382.0	$ 1,306.4	$ 223.0	$ 425.9	$ 7,192.4
Accumulated depreciation and impairment							
Balance, beginning of year	$ (6.6)	$ (1,385.8)	$ (794.8)	$ (436.2)	$ (168.2)	$ –	$ (2,791.6)
Depreciation for the year	–	(108.5)	(116.9)	(84.0)	(15.5)	–	(324.9)
Impairment	–	–	(3.3)	(0.2)	–	–	(3.5)
Disposals/retirements	–	3.8	17.8	7.3	4.1	–	33.0
Reclassifications and transfers	–	8.9	(21.9)	(21.9)	26.7	–	(8.2)
Balance, end of year	$ (6.6)	$ (1,481.6)	$ (919.1)	$ (535.0)	$ (152.9)	$ –	$ (3,095.2)
Net carrying amount, end of year	$ 904.6	$ 1,462.3	$ 462.9	$ 771.4	$ 70.1	$ 425.9	$ 4,097.2

							2015
(C$ in millions)	Land	Buildings	Fixtures and equipment	Leasehold improvements	Assets under finance lease	Construction in progress	Total
Cost							
Balance, beginning of year	$ 861.0	$ 2,857.7	$ 1,071.9	$ 1,001.1	$ 256.5	$ 224.3	$ 6,272.5
Additions	9.1	63.3	165.8	155.6	14.0	163.2	571.0
Disposals/retirements	(4.2)	(10.5)	(21.4)	(6.7)	(8.0)	(26.3)	(77.1)
Reclassifications and transfers	8.5	5.4	0.3	(9.3)	0.3	(1.8)	3.4
Balance, end of year	$ 874.4	$ 2,915.9	$ 1,216.6	$ 1,140.7	$ 262.8	$ 359.4	$ 6,769.8
Accumulated depreciation and impairment							
Balance, beginning of year	$ (4.4)	$ (1,289.8)	$ (712.0)	$ (365.7)	$ (157.5)	$ –	$ (2,529.4)
Depreciation for the year	–	(108.4)	(103.8)	(80.0)	(16.5)	–	(308.7)
Impairment	–	(0.2)	(0.2)	–	–	–	(0.4)
Reversal of impairment losses	–	–	0.1	0.1	–	–	0.2
Disposals/retirements	0.1	4.8	18.6	7.1	7.4	–	38.0
Reclassifications and transfers	(2.3)	7.8	2.5	2.3	(1.6)	–	8.7
Balance, end of year	$ (6.6)	$ (1,385.8)	$ (794.8)	$ (436.2)	$ (168.2)	$ –	$ (2,791.6)
Net carrying amount, end of year	$ 867.8	$ 1,530.1	$ 421.8	$ 704.5	$ 94.6	$ 359.4	$ 3,978.2

The Company capitalized borrowing costs of $18.0 million (2015 – $11.8 million) on indebtedness relating to property and equipment under construction. The rate used to determine the amount of borrowing costs capitalized during the year was 6.1 percent (2015 – 6.0 percent).

The carrying amount of assets under finance leases at December 31, 2016, comprises $33.4 million (2015 – $39.3 million) in buildings and $36.7 million (2015 – $55.3 million) in fixtures and equipment.

Impairment of property and equipment and subsequent reversal

The amount of impairment of property and equipment in 2016 was $3.5 million (2015 – $0.4 million). There was no reversal of impairment in 2016 (2015 – $0.2 million). The impairment of property and equipment pertain to the Company's Retail operating segment. Any impairment or reversal of impairment is reported in Other income in the Consolidated Statements of Income.

14. Subsidiaries

14.1 Control of subsidiaries and composition of the Company

These consolidated financial statements include entities controlled by Canadian Tire Corporation. Control exists when Canadian Tire Corporation has the ability to direct the relevant activities and the returns of an entity. The financial statements of these entities are included in these consolidated financial statements from the date that control commences until the date that control ceases. Details of the Company's significant entities are as follows:

Name of subsidiary	Principal activity	Country of incorporation and operation	Ownership Interest 2016	Ownership Interest 2015
CTFS Holdings Limited[1]	Marketing of insurance products, processing credit card transactions at Canadian Tire stores, banking, and reinsurance	Canada	**80.0%**	80.0%
Canadian Tire Real Estate Limited	Real estate	Canada	**100.0%**	100.0%
CT Real Estate Investment Trust	Real estate	Canada	**85.1%**	83.8%
FGL Sports Ltd.	Retailer of sporting equipment, apparel and footwear	Canada	**100.0%**	100.0%
Franchise Trust[2]	Canadian Tire Dealer Loan Program	Canada	**0.0%**	0.0%
Glacier Credit Card Trust[3]	Financing program to purchase co-ownership interests in Canadian Tire Bank's credit card loans	Canada	**0.0%**	0.0%
Mark's Work Wearhouse Ltd.	Retailer of clothing and footwear	Canada	**100.0%**	100.0%

[1] *Legal entity CTFS Holdings Limited, incorporated in 2014, is the parent company of CTB and CTFS Bermuda Ltd. CTB's principal activity is banking, marketing of insurance products, and the processing credit card transactions at Canadian Tire stores. CTFS Bermuda Ltd.'s principal activity is reinsurance.*

[2] *Franchise Trust is a legal entity sponsored by a third-party bank that originates loans to Dealers under the Dealer Loan Program. The Company does not have any share ownership in Franchise Trust. However, the Company has determined that it has the ability to direct the relevant activities and returns on the silo of assets and liabilities of Franchise Trust that relate to the Canadian Tire Dealer Loan Program. As the Company has control over this silo of assets and liabilities, it is consolidated in these financial statements.*

[3] *GCCT was formed to meet specific business needs of the Company, namely to buy co-ownership interests in the Company's credit card loans. GCCT issues debt to third-party investors to fund its purchases. The Company does not have any share ownership in GCCT. However, the Company has determined that it has the ability to direct the relevant activities and returns of GCCT. As the Company has control over GCCT, it is consolidated in these financial statements.*

14.2 Details of non-wholly owned subsidiaries that have non-controlling interests

The portion of net assets and income attributable to third parties is reported as non-controlling interests and net income attributable to non-controlling interests in the Consolidated Balance Sheets and Consolidated Statements of Income, respectively. The non-controlling interests of CT REIT and CTFS Holdings Limited were initially measured at fair value on the date of acquisition.

The following table summarizes the information relating to non-controlling interests:

(C$ in millions)	CT REIT[1]	CTFS Holdings Limited[2]	Other[3]	Total 2016
Non-controlling interests	14.9%	20.0%	50.0%	
Current assets	$ 11.1	$ 5,539.4	$ 13.6	$ 5,564.1
Non-current assets	5,003.5	234.1	33.0	5,270.6
Current liabilities	219.3	2,201.9	4.3	2,425.5
Non-current liabilities	2,204.8	2,527.2	23.4	4,755.4
Net assets	2,590.5	1,044.4	18.9	3,653.8
Revenue	$ 407.2	$ 1,180.7	$ 184.9	$ 1,772.8
Net income attributable to non-controlling interests	$ 21.4	$ 52.4	$ 4.6	$ 78.4
Equity attributable to non-controlling interests	288.6	504.1	6.0	798.7
Distributions to non-controlling interests	(20.9)	(53.8)	(3.7)	(78.4)

[1] *Net income attributable to non-controlling interests is based on net income of CT REIT adjusted to convert to the Company's cost method, including recording of depreciation.*

[2] *Net income attributable to non-controlling interests is based on the net income of CTFS Holdings Limited adjusted for contractual requirements as stipulated in the Universal Shareholder agreement.*

[3] *Net income attributable to non-controlling interests is based on net income of the subsidiary adjusted for contractual requirements as stipulated in the ownership agreement.*

(C$ in millions)	CT REIT[1]	CTFS Holdings Limited[2]	Other[3]	2015 Total
Non-controlling interests	16.2%	20.0%	50.0%	
Current assets	$ 29.3	$ 5,364.2	$ 13.2	$ 5,406.7
Non-current assets	4,321.6	209.9	32.2	4,563.7
Current liabilities	245.2	1,226.3	4.3	1,475.8
Non-current liabilities	1,892.4	3,305.8	25.6	5,223.8
Net assets	2,213.3	1,042.0	15.5	3,270.8
Revenue	$ 378.2	$ 1,165.2	$ 181.4	$ 1,724.8
Net income attributable to non-controlling interests	$ 20.6	$ 53.0	$ 2.9	$ 76.5
Equity attributable to non-controlling interests	286.5	504.3	4.7	795.5
Distributions to non-controlling interests	(20.3)	(33.6)	(1.7)	(55.6)

[1] *Net income attributable to non-controlling interests is based on net income of CT REIT adjusted to convert to the Company's cost method, including recording of depreciation.*

[2] *Net income attributable to non-controlling interests is based on the net income of CTFS Holdings Limited adjusted for contractual requirements as stipulated in the Universal Shareholder agreement.*

[3] *Net income attributable to non-controlling interests is based on net income of the subsidiary adjusted for contractual requirements as stipulated in the ownership agreement.*

14.3 Continuity of non-controlling interests

(C$ in millions)	2016	2015
Balance at beginning of year	**$ 795.5**	$ 775.3
Comprehensive income attributable to non-controlling interests for the year[1]	**79.6**	74.0
Issuance of trust units to non-controlling interests, net of transaction costs	**2.0**	1.8
Distributions	**(78.4)**	(55.6)
Balance at end of year	**$ 798.7**	$ 795.5

[1] *Includes $1.2 million [2015 – $(2.5) million] from the Consolidated Statements of Comprehensive Income.*

15. Income taxes

15.1 Deferred income tax assets and liabilities

The amount of deferred tax assets or liabilities recognized in the Consolidated Balance Sheets and the corresponding movement recognized in the Consolidated Statements of Income, Consolidated Statements of Changes in Equity, or resulting from a business combination is as follows:

(C$ in millions)	Balance, beginning of year	Recognized in profit or loss	Recognized in other comprehensive income	Other adjustments	2016 Balance, end of year
Provisions, deferred revenue and reserves	**$ 143.8**	**$ 8.8**	**$ –**	**$ 0.2**	**$ 152.8**
Property and equipment	**(43.8)**	**5.9**	**–**	**–**	**(37.9)**
Intangible assets	**(153.5)**	**(17.1)**	**–**	**–**	**(170.6)**
Employee benefits	**37.5**	**1.1**	**1.1**	**–**	**39.7**
Cash flow hedges	**(53.3)**	**–**	**40.1**	**–**	**(13.2)**
Other	**6.3**	**1.0**	**–**	**–**	**7.3**
Net deferred tax asset (liability)[1]	**$ (63.0)**	**$ (0.3)**	**$ 41.2**	**$ 0.2**	**$ (21.9)**

[1] *Includes the net amount of deferred tax assets of $82.3 million and deferred tax liabilities of $104.2 million.*

					2015
(C$ in millions)	Balance, beginning of year	Recognized in profit or loss	Recognized in other comprehensive income	Other adjustments	Balance, end of year
Provisions, deferred revenue and reserves	$ 139.3	$ 4.5	$ –	$ –	$ 143.8
Property and equipment	(56.7)	12.9	–	–	(43.8)
Intangible assets	(147.5)	(5.7)	–	(0.3)	(153.5)
Employee benefits	36.4	1.3	(0.2)	–	37.5
Cash flow hedges	(29.5)	–	(23.8)	–	(53.3)
Other	3.5	2.1	–	0.7	6.3
Net deferred tax asset (liability)[1]	$ (54.5)	$ 15.1	$ (24.0)	$ 0.4	$ (63.0)

[1] *Includes the net amount of deferred tax assets of $48.1 million and deferred tax liabilities of $111.1 million.*

No deferred tax is recognized on the amount of temporary differences arising from the difference between the carrying amount of the investment in subsidiaries, branches and associates, and interests in joint arrangements accounted for in the financial statements and the cost amount for tax purposes of the investment. The Company is able to control the timing of the reversal of these temporary differences and believes it is probable that they will not reverse in the foreseeable future. The amount of these taxable temporary differences was approximately $2.3 billion at December 31, 2016 (2015 – $2.6 billion).

15.2 Income tax expense

The following are the major components of income tax expense:

(C$ in millions)	2016	2015
Current tax expense		
Current period	**$ 261.9**	$ 258.9
Adjustments with respect to prior years	**1.3**	21.6
	$ 263.2	$ 280.5
Deferred tax expense (benefit)		
Deferred income tax expense (benefit) relating to the origination and reversal of temporary differences	**$ 2.9**	$ (0.3)
Deferred income tax (benefit) adjustments with respect to prior years	**(2.6)**	(16.6)
Deferred income tax expense resulting from change in tax rate	**–**	1.8
	0.3	(15.1)
Total income tax expense	**$ 263.5**	$ 265.4

Income tax (benefit) expense recognized in Other Comprehensive Income was as follows:

(C$ in millions)	2016	2015
(Losses) gains on derivatives designated as cash flow hedges and available-for-sale financial assets	**$ (14.7)**	$ 99.8
Reclassification of gains to non-financial assets on derivatives designated as cash flow hedges	**(24.8)**	(74.9)
Reclassification of gains to income on derivatives designated as cash flow hedges and available-for-sale financial assets	**(0.6)**	(1.1)
Actuarial (losses) gains	**(1.1)**	0.2
Total income tax (benefit) expense	**$ (41.2)**	$ 24.0

Reconciliation of income tax expense

Income taxes in the Consolidated Statements of Income vary from amounts that would be computed by applying the statutory income tax rate for the following reasons:

(C$ in millions)	2016	2015
Income before income taxes	**$ 1,011.0**	$ 1,001.3
Income taxes based on the applicable statutory tax rate of 26.67% (2015 – 26.56%)	**$ 269.6**	$ 266.0
Adjustment to income taxes resulting from:		
Non-deductibility of stock option expense	**5.0**	2.5
Non-taxable portion of capital gains	**(2.0)**	(6.8)
Income attributable to non-controlling interest in flow-through entities	**(7.0)**	(6.3)
Other	**(2.1)**	10.0
Income tax expense	**$ 263.5**	$ 265.4

The applicable statutory tax rate is the aggregate of the Canadian federal income tax rate of 15.0 percent (2015 – 15.0 percent) and the Canadian provincial income tax rate of 11.67 percent (2015 – 11.56 percent). The increase in the applicable rate from 2015 is primarily due to changes in the provincial tax rates in the year.

In the ordinary course of business, the Company is subject to ongoing audits by tax authorities. While the Company has determined that its tax filing positions are appropriate and supportable, from time to time certain matters are reviewed and challenged by the tax authorities.

The Company regularly reviews the potential for adverse outcomes with respect to tax matters. The Company believes that the ultimate disposition of these will not have a material adverse effect on its liquidity, consolidated financial position, or net income because the Company has determined that it has adequate provision for these tax matters. Should the ultimate tax liability materially differ from the provision, the Company's effective tax rate and its earnings could be affected positively or negatively in the period in which the matters are resolved.

16. Deposits

Deposits consist of broker deposits and retail deposits.

Cash from broker deposits is raised through sales of GICs through brokers rather than directly to the retail customer. Broker deposits are offered for varying terms ranging from 30 days to five years and issued broker GICs are non-redeemable prior to maturity (except in certain rare circumstances). Total short-term and long-term broker deposits outstanding at December 31, 2016, were $1,515.7 million (2015 – $1,548.5 million).

Retail deposits consist of HIS deposits, retail GICs, and TFSA deposits. Total retail deposits outstanding at December 31, 2016, were $665.8 million (2015 – $704.4 million).

For repayment requirements of deposits refer to Note 5.4. The following are the effective rates of interest:

	2016	2015
GIC deposits	**2.78%**	2.84%
HIS account deposits	**1.39%**	1.52%

17. Trade and other payables

Trade and other payables include the following:

(C$ in millions)	**2016**	2015
Trade payables and accrued liabilities	**$ 1,626.3**	$ 1,761.2
Derivatives (Note 32)	**13.4**	0.7
Total financial liabilities	**1,639.7**	1,761.9
Deferred revenue	**39.5**	38.4
Insurance reserve	**18.4**	16.9
Other	**159.3**	139.9
	$ 1,856.9	$ 1,957.1

Deferred revenue consists mainly of unearned insurance premiums, unearned roadside assistance revenue, and unearned revenue relating to gift cards.

Other consists primarily of the short-term portion of share based payment transactions and sales taxes payable.

The credit range period on trade payables is three to 270 days (2015 – three to 180 days).

18. Provisions

The following table presents the changes to the Company's provisions:

					2016
(C$ in millions)	Sales and warranty returns	Site restoration and decommissioning	Customer loyalty	Other	Total
Balance, beginning of year	$ 120.5	$ 38.3	$ 86.2	$ 16.8	$ 261.8
Charges, net of reversals	301.9	3.9	176.6	6.0	488.4
Utilizations	(279.5)	(1.3)	(161.5)	(8.0)	(450.3)
Discount adjustments	0.6	(1.6)	–	0.2	(0.8)
Balance, end of year	$ 143.5	$ 39.3	$ 101.3	$ 15.0	$ 299.1
Current provisions	137.1	6.5	101.3	8.3	253.2
Long-term provisions	6.4	32.8	–	6.7	45.9

19. Contingencies

Legal and regulatory matters

The Company is party to a number of legal and regulatory proceedings. The Company believes that each such proceeding constitutes a routine matter incidental to the business conducted by the Company. The Company cannot determine with certainty the ultimate outcome of all the outstanding claims but believes that the ultimate disposition of the proceedings will not have a material adverse effect on its consolidated earnings, cash flow, or financial position.

20. Short-term borrowings

Short-term borrowings include commercial paper notes issued by GCCT and bank line of credit borrowings. Short-term borrowings may bear interest payable at maturity or be sold at a discount and mature at face value.

The commercial paper notes are short-term notes issued with varying original maturities of one year or fewer, typically 90 days or fewer, at interest rates fixed at the time of each renewal, and are recorded at amortized cost. As at December 31, 2016, $89.6 million (2015 – $88.6 million) of commercial paper notes were issued.

As at December 31, 2016, $109.8 million (2015 – $nil) of bank line of credit borrowings had been drawn on CT REIT's Bank Credit Facility.

21. Loans payable

Franchise Trust, a special purpose entity, is a legal entity sponsored by a third-party bank that originates loans to Dealers. Loans payable are the loans that Franchise Trust incurs to fund loans to Dealers. These loans are not direct legal liabilities of the Company but have been consolidated in the accounts of the Company as the Company effectively controls the silo of Franchise Trust containing the Dealer Loan Program.

Loans payable, which are initially recognized at fair value and are subsequently measured at amortized cost, are due within one year.

22. Long-term debt

Long-term debt includes the following:

(C$ in millions)	2016 Face value	2016 Carrying amount	2015 Face value	2015 Carrying amount
Senior notes[1]				
Series 2012-1, 2.807%, May 20, 2017	**$ 200.0**	**$ 199.9**	$ 200.0	$ 199.7
Series 2012-2, 2.394%, October 20, 2017	**400.0**	**399.6**	400.0	399.2
Series 2013-1, 2.755%, November 20, 2018	**250.0**	**249.4**	250.0	249.1
Series 2014-1, 2.568%, September 20, 2019	**472.5**	**471.2**	472.5	470.7
Series 2015-1, 2.237%, September 20, 2020	**465.0**	**463.3**	465.0	462.9
Subordinated notes[1]				
Series 2012-1, 3.827%, May 20, 2017	**11.6**	**11.6**	11.6	11.6
Series 2012-2, 3.174%, October 20, 2017	**23.3**	**23.3**	23.3	23.3
Series 2013-1, 3.275%, November 20, 2018	**14.6**	**14.6**	14.6	14.6
Series 2014-1, 3.068%, September 20, 2019	**27.5**	**27.5**	27.5	27.5
Series 2015-1, 3.237%, September 20, 2020	**35.0**	**35.0**	35.0	35.0
Medium-term notes and debentures				
2.159% due June 1, 2021	**150.0**	**149.1**	–	–
2.85% due June 9, 2022	**150.0**	**149.1**	150.0	149.2
3.53% due June 9, 2025	**200.0**	**198.6**	200.0	198.8
3.289% due June 1, 2026	**200.0**	**198.6**	–	–
6.375% due April 13, 2028	**150.0**	**148.6**	150.0	148.5
6.445% due February 24, 2034	**200.0**	**198.1**	200.0	198.0
5.61% due September 4, 2035	**200.0**	**199.4**	200.0	199.3
Finance lease obligations	**125.8**	**125.8**	145.9	145.9
Mortgages	**55.9**	**56.0**	60.0	60.1
Promissory note	**1.8**	**1.8**	2.3	2.3
Total debt	**$ 3,333.0**	**$ 3,320.5**	$ 3,007.7	$ 2,995.7
Current	**653.4**	**653.4**	24.3	24.3
Non-current	**2,679.6**	**2,667.1**	2,983.4	2,971.4

[1] *Senior and subordinated notes are those of GCCT.*

The carrying amount of long-term debt is net of debt issuance costs of $12.6 million (2015 – $12.0 million).

Senior and subordinated notes

Asset-backed senior and subordinated notes issued by GCCT are recorded at amortized cost using the effective interest method.

Subject to the payment of certain priority amounts, the senior notes have recourse on a priority basis to the related series ownership interest. The subordinated notes have recourse to the related series ownership interests on a subordinated basis to the senior notes in terms of the priority of payment of principal and, in some circumstances, interest. The asset-backed notes, together with certain other permitted obligations of GCCT, are secured by the assets of GCCT. The entitlement of note holders and other parties to such assets is governed by the priority and payment provisions set forth in the GCCT Indenture and the related series supplements under which these series of notes were issued.

Repayment of the principal of the series 2012-1, 2012-2, 2013-1, 2014-1, and 2015-1 notes is scheduled for the expected repayment dates indicated in the preceding table. Subsequent to the expected repayment date, collections distributed to GCCT with respect to the related ownership interest will be applied to pay any remaining amount owing.

Principal repayments may commence earlier than these scheduled commencement dates if certain events occur including:

- the Bank failing to make required payments to GCCT or failing to meet covenant or other contractual terms;
- the performance of the receivables failing to achieve set criteria; and
- insufficient receivables in the pool.

None of these events occurred in the year ended December 31, 2016.

Medium-term notes and debentures

Medium-term notes and debentures are unsecured and are redeemable by the Company, in whole or in part, at any time, at the greater of par or a formula price based upon interest rates at the time of redemption.

Finance lease obligations

Finance leases relate to DCs, fixtures, and equipment. The Company generally has the option to renew such leases or purchase the leased assets at the conclusion of the lease term. During 2016, interest rates on finance leases ranged from 1.09 percent to 11.35 percent. Remaining terms at December 31, 2016, were one to 120 months.

Finance lease obligations are payable as follows:

	2016			2015		
(C$ in millions)	**Future minimum lease payments**	**Interest**	**Present value of future minimum lease payments**	Future minimum lease payments	Interest	Present value of future minimum lease payments
Due in less than one year	**$ 24.2**	**$ 7.5**	**$ 16.7**	$ 27.8	$ 8.2	$ 19.6
Due between one year and two years	**21.0**	**6.5**	**14.5**	24.5	7.2	17.3
Due between two years and three years	**18.5**	**5.8**	**12.7**	21.0	6.5	14.5
Due between three years and four years	**16.6**	**5.1**	**11.5**	18.5	5.8	12.7
Due between four years and five years	**15.7**	**4.3**	**11.4**	16.7	5.1	11.6
Due in more than five years	**69.2**	**10.2**	**59.0**	85.0	14.8	70.2
	$ 165.2	**$ 39.4**	**$ 125.8**	$ 193.5	$ 47.6	$ 145.9

Mortgages

Mortgages bear interest rates ranging from 2.93 percent to 3.60 percent and have maturity dates ranging from January 1, 2018 to December 8, 2019.

Promissory notes

Promissory notes were issued as part of franchise acquisitions in 2015. These notes are non-interest bearing.

Debt covenants

The Company has provided covenants to certain of its lenders. The Company was in compliance with all of its covenants as at December 31, 2016. Refer to Note 4 for details on the Company's debt covenants.

23. Other long-term liabilities

Other long-term liabilities include the following:

(C$ in millions)	**2016**	2015
Redeemable financial instrument[1]	**$ 517.0**	$ 517.0
Employee benefits (Note 24)	**149.3**	141.2
Deferred gains	**15.2**	16.8
Derivatives (Note 32)	**8.3**	12.9
Deferred revenue	**6.1**	8.8
Other	**140.7**	117.2
	$ 836.6	$ 813.9

[1] *A financial liability; refer to Note 32 for further information on the redeemable financial instrument.*

Deferred gains relate to the sale and leaseback of certain distribution centres. The deferred gains are amortized over the terms of the leases.

Other includes the long-term portion of share-based payment transactions, deferred lease inducements, and straight-line rent liabilities.

24. Employment benefits

Profit-sharing program

The Company has a profit-sharing program for certain employees. The amount awarded to employees is contingent on the Company's profitability but shall be equal to at least one percent of the Company's previous year's net profits after income tax. A portion of the award ("Base Award") is contributed to a DPSP for the benefit of the employees. The maximum amount of the Company's Base Award contribution to the DPSP per employee per year is subject to limits set by the Income Tax Act. Each participating employee is required to invest and maintain 10 percent of the Base Award in a Company share fund of the DPSP. The share fund holds both Common Shares and Class A Non-Voting Shares. The Company's contributions to the DPSP with respect to each employee vest 20 percent after one year of continuous service and 100 percent after two years of continuous service.

In 2016, the Company contributed $22.4 million (2015 – $22.1 million) under the terms of the DPSP.

Defined benefit plan

The Company provides certain health care, dental care, life insurance, and other benefits for certain retired employees pursuant to Company policy. The Company does not have a pension plan. Information about the Company's defined benefit plan is as follows:

(C$ in millions)	**2016**	2015
Change in the present value of defined benefit obligation		
Defined benefit obligation, beginning of year	**$ 141.2**	$ 137.5
Current service cost	**1.7**	2.3
Interest cost	**5.7**	5.4
Actuarial (gain) arising from changes in demographic assumptions	**–**	(0.2)
Actuarial loss (gain) arising from changes in financial assumptions	**4.8**	(4.6)
Actuarial (gain) loss arising from changes in experience assumptions	**(1.0)**	3.8
Benefits paid	**(3.1)**	(3.0)
Defined benefit obligation, end of year[1]	**$ 149.3**	$ 141.2

[1] *The accrued benefit obligation is not funded because funding is provided when benefits are paid. Accordingly, there are no plan assets.*

Significant actuarial assumptions used:

	2016	2015
Defined benefit obligation, end of year:		
Discount rate	**3.90%**	4.10%
Net benefit plan expense for the year:		
Discount rate	**4.10%**	4.00%

For measurement purposes, a 4.80 percent weighted average health care cost trend rate is assumed for 2016 (2015 – 4.91 percent). The rate is assumed to decrease gradually to 2.96 percent for 2032 and remain at that level thereafter.

The most recent actuarial valuation of the obligation was performed as of January 2, 2016. The next required valuation will be as of December 29, 2018.

The cumulative amount of actuarial losses before tax recognized in equity at December 31, 2016, was $47.8 million (2015 – $44.1 million).

Sensitivity analysis:

The Company's defined benefit plan is exposed to actuarial risks such as the health care cost trend rate, the discount rate, and the life expectancy assumptions. The following tables provide the sensitivity of the defined benefit obligation to these assumptions. For each sensitivity test, the impact of a reasonably possible change in a single factor is shown with other assumptions left unchanged.

(C$ in millions)		**2016**
Sensitivity analysis	**Accrued benefit obligation**	
	Increase	***Decrease***
A fifty basis point change in assumed discount rates	**$ (11.5)**	**$ 13.1**
A one-percentage-point change in assumed health care cost trend rates	**14.2**	**(11.9)**
A one-year change in assumed life expectancy	**(3.4)**	**3.4**

The weighted-average duration of the defined benefit plan obligation at December 31, 2016 is 16.4 years (2015 – 16.5 years).

25. Share capital

Share capital consists of the following:

(C$ in millions)	2016	2015
Authorized		
3,423,366 Common Shares		
100,000,000 Class A Non-Voting Shares		
Issued		
3,423,366 Common Shares (2015 – 3,423,366)	$ 0.2	$ 0.2
67,323,781 Class A Non-Voting Shares (2015 – 70,637,987)	647.9	671.0
	$ 648.1	$ 671.2

All issued shares are fully paid. The Company does not hold any of its Common or Class A Non-Voting Shares. Neither the Common nor Class A Non-Voting Shares have a par value.

During 2016 and 2015, the Company issued and repurchased Class A Non-Voting Shares. The Company's share repurchases were made pursuant to its NCIB program.

The following transactions occurred with respect to Class A Non-Voting Shares during 2016 and 2015:

		2016		2015
(C$ in millions)	Number	$	Number	$
Shares outstanding at beginning of the year	70,637,987	$ 671.0	74,023,208	$ 695.3
Issued under the dividend reinvestment plan	68,069	9.3	65,760	8.3
Repurchased[1]	(3,382,275)	(449.4)	(3,450,981)	(434.6)
Excess of purchase price over average cost	–	417.0	–	402.0
Shares outstanding at end of the period	67,323,781	$ 647.9	70,637,987	$ 671.0

[1] *Repurchased shares, pursuant to the Company's NCIB program, have been restored to the status of authorized but unissued shares. The Company records shares repurchased on a transaction date basis.*

Conditions of Class A Non-Voting Shares and Common Shares

The holders of Class A Non-Voting Shares are entitled to receive a fixed cumulative preferential dividend at the rate of $0.01 per share per annum. After payment of fixed cumulative preferential dividends at the rate of $0.01 per share per annum on each of the Class A Non-Voting Shares with respect to the current year and each preceding year, and payment of a non-cumulative dividend on each of the Common Shares with respect to the current year at the same rate, the holders of the Class A Non-Voting Shares and the Common Shares are entitled to further dividends declared and paid in equal amounts per share without preference or distinction or priority of one share over another.

In the event of the liquidation, dissolution, or winding up of the Company, all of the property of the Company available for distribution to the holders of the Class A Non-Voting Shares and the Common Shares shall be paid or distributed equally, share for share, to the holders of the Class A Non-Voting Shares, and to the holders of the Common Shares without preference or distinction or priority of one share over another.

The holders of Class A Non-Voting Shares are entitled to receive notice of and to attend all meetings of the shareholders; however, except as provided by the *Business Corporations Act* (Ontario) and as hereinafter noted, they are not entitled to vote at those meetings. Holders of Class A Non-Voting Shares, voting separately as a class, are entitled to elect the greater of (i) three Directors or (ii) one-fifth of the total number of the Company's Directors.

The holders of Common Shares are entitled to receive notice of, to attend, and to have one vote for each Common Share held at all meetings of holders of Common Shares, subject only to the restriction on the right to elect those directors who are elected by the holders of Class A Non-Voting Shares as set out above.

Common Shares can be converted, at any time and at the option of each holder of Common Shares, into Class A Non-Voting Shares on a share-for-share basis. The authorized number of shares of either class cannot be increased without the approval of the holders of at least two-thirds of the shares of each class represented and voted at a meeting of the shareholders called for the purpose of considering such an increase. Neither the Class A Non-Voting Shares nor the Common Shares can be changed in any manner whatsoever whether by way of subdivision, consolidation, reclassification, exchange, or otherwise unless at the same time the other class of shares is also changed in the same manner and in the same proportion.

Should an offer to purchase Common Shares be made to all, or substantially all of the holders of Common Shares, or be required by applicable securities legislation or by the Toronto Stock Exchange to be made to all holders of Common Shares in Ontario and should a majority of the Common Shares then issued and outstanding be tendered and taken up pursuant to such offer, the Class A Non-Voting Shares shall thereupon and thereafter be entitled to one vote per share at all meetings of the shareholders and thereafter the Class A Non-Voting Shares shall be designated as Class A Shares. The foregoing voting entitlement applicable to Class A Non-Voting Shares would not apply in the case where an offer is made to purchase both Class A Non-Voting Shares and Common Shares at the same price per share and on the same terms and conditions.

The foregoing is a summary of certain conditions attached to the Class A Non-Voting Shares of the Company and reference should be made to the Company's articles of amendment dated December 15, 1983 for a full statement of such conditions, which are available on SEDAR at www.sedar.com.

As of December 31, 2016, the Company had dividends declared and payable to holders of Class A Non-Voting Shares and Common Shares of $45.9 million (2015 – $42.6 million) at a rate of $0.650 per share (2015 – $0.575 per share).

On February 15, 2017 the Company's Board of Directors declared a dividend of $0.650 per share payable on June 1, 2017 to shareholders of record as of April 30, 2017.

Dividends per share declared were $2.3750 in 2016 (2015 – $2.1500).

Dilutive effect of employee stock options is 195,429 (2015 – 430,281).

26. Share-based payments

The Company's share-based payment plans are described below.

Stock options

The Company has granted stock options to certain employees that enable such employees to exercise their stock options and subscribe for Class A Non-Voting Shares or surrender their options and receive a cash payment. Such cash payment is calculated as the difference between the fair market value of Class A Non-Voting Shares as at the surrender date and the exercise price of the option. Stock options granted prior to 2012 vested on the third anniversary of their grant. Stock options that were granted in 2012 and later vest over a three-year period. All outstanding stock options have a term of seven years. At December 31, 2016, the aggregate number of Class A Non-Voting Shares that were authorized for issuance under the stock option plan was 3.4 million.

Stock option transactions during 2016 and 2015 were as follows:

	2016		2015	
	Number of options	Weighted average exercise price	Number of options	Weighted average exercise price
Outstanding at beginning of year	**1,010,243**	**$ 97.75**	1,526,343	$ 72.21
Granted	**404,439**	**129.92**	387,234	129.14
Exercised and surrendered	**(337,338)**	**75.12**	(823,888)[1]	65.69
Forfeited	**(115,995)**	**121.13**	(79,446)	92.53
Expired	**–**	**–**	–	–
Outstanding at end of year	**961,349**	**$ 116.41**	1,010,243	$ 97.75
Stock options exercisable at end of year	**395,042**		243,240	

[1] *The weighted average market price of the Company's shares when the options were exercised in 2016 was $131.27 (2015 – $127.12).*

The following table summarizes information about stock options outstanding and exercisable at December 31, 2016:

	Options outstanding			Options exercisable	
Range of exercise prices	**Number of outstanding options**	**Weighted average remaining contractual life[1]**	**Weighted average exercise price**	**Number of exercisable options**	**Weighted average exercise price**
$ 129.14 to 129.92	**658,599**	**5.72**	**$ 129.56**	**166,925**	**$ 129.34**
99.72	**192,241**	**4.19**	**99.72**	**117,608**	**99.72**
53.49 to 69.01	**110,509**	**2.78**	**67.06**	**110,509**	**67.06**
$ 53.49 to 129.92	**961,349**	**5.08**	**$ 116.41**	**395,042**	**$ 103.10**

[1] *Weighted average remaining contractual life is expressed in years.*

Performance share units and performance units

The Company grants Performance Share Units ("PSUs") to certain of its employees that generally vest after three years. Each PSU entitles the participant to receive a cash payment equal to the fair market value of the Company's Class A Non-Voting Shares on the date set out in the Performance Share Unit Plan, multiplied by a factor determined by specific performance-based criteria and, in the case of PSUs granted in 2016, a relative total shareholder return modifier.

CT REIT grants Performance Units ("PUs") to certain of its employees that generally vest after three years. Each PU entitles the participant to receive a cash payment equal to the fair market value of Units of CT REIT on the date set out in the Performance Unit Plan, multiplied by a factor determined by specific performance-based criteria.

Deferred share units and deferred units

The Company offers Deferred Share Unit ("DSU") Plans to certain of its Executives and to members of its Board of Directors. Under the Executives' DSU Plan, eligible Executives may elect to receive all or a portion of their annual bonus in DSUs. The Executives' DSU Plan also provides for the granting of discretionary DSUs. Under the Directors' DSU Plan, eligible directors may defer all or a portion of their annual director fees into DSUs. DSUs received under both the Executives' and Directors' DSU Plans are settled in cash following termination of service with the Company and/or the Board based on the fair market value of the Company's Class A Non-Voting Shares on the settlement date.

CT REIT also offers a Deferred Unit Plan for members of its Board of Trustees. Under this plan, eligible trustees may elect to receive all or a portion of their annual trustee fees in Deferred Units ("DUs"). DUs are settled through the issuance of an equivalent number of Units of CT REIT or, at the election of the trustee, in cash, following termination of service with the Board.

Restricted Unit Plan

CT REIT offers a Restricted Unit Plan for its Executives. Restricted Units ("RUs") may be issued as discretionary grants or, Executives may elect to receive all or a portion of their annual bonus in RUs. At the end of the vesting period, which is generally three years from the date of grant (in the case of discretionary grants) and five years from the annual bonus payment date (in the case of deferred bonus), an Executive receives an equivalent number of Units issued by CT REIT or, at the Executive's election, the cash equivalent thereof.

The fair value of stock options and PSUs at the end of the year was determined using the Black-Scholes option pricing model with the following inputs:

		2016		2015
	Stock options	**PSUs**	Stock options	PSUs
Share price at end of year (C$)	**$ 139.27**	**$ 139.27**	$ 118.16	$ 118.16
Weighted average exercise price[1] (C$)	**$ 116.23**	**N/A**	$ 97.17	N/A
Expected remaining life (years)	**4.1**	**1.1**	4.0	0.9
Expected dividends	**1.8%**	**2.6%**	1.8%	2.6%
Expected volatility[2]	**20.4%**	**19.2%**	22.3%	21.1%
Risk-free interest rate	**1.4%**	**1.0%**	1.1%	0.9%

[1] *Reflects expected forfeitures.*

[2] *Reflects historical volatility over a period of time similar to the remaining life of the stock options, which may not necessarily be the actual outcome.*

Service and non-market performance conditions attached to the transactions are not taken into account in determining fair value.

The Company enters into equity derivative transactions to hedge share-based payments and does not apply hedge accounting. The expense recognized for share-based compensation is summarized as follows:

(C$ in millions)	**2016**	2015
Expense arising from share-based payment transactions	**$ 64.6**	$ 35.6
Effect of hedging arrangements	**(32.0)**	4.1
Total expense included in net income	**$ 32.6**	$ 39.7

The total carrying amount of liabilities for share-based payment transactions at December 31, 2016, was $101.1 million (2015 – $100.0 million).

The intrinsic value of the liability for vested benefits at December 31, 2016, was $30.7 million (2015 – $23.4 million).

27. Revenue

Revenue consists of the following:

(C$ in millions)	2016	2015
Sale of goods	$ 11,002.7	$ 10,649.9
Interest income on loans receivable	881.0	852.1
Royalties and licence fees	400.0	375.6
Services rendered	329.9	342.6
Rental income	67.4	59.4
	$ 12,681.0	$ 12,279.6

Major customers

The Company does not rely on any one customer.

28. Cost of producing revenue

Cost of producing revenue consists of the following:

(C$ in millions)	2016	2015
Inventory cost of sales[1]	$ 7,898.4	$ 7,747.1
Net impairment loss on loans receivable	287.0	297.1
Finance costs on deposits	52.8	54.5
Other	50.3	45.6
	$ 8,288.5	$ 8,144.3

[1] *Inventory cost of sales includes depreciation for the year ended December 31, 2016 of $8.0 million (2015 – $8.9 million).*

Inventory writedowns, as a result of net realizable value being lower than cost, recognized in the year ended December 31, 2016 were $61.5 million (2015 – $52.3 million).

Inventory writedowns recognized in prior periods and reversed in the year ended December 31, 2016 were $5.5 million (2015 – $5.7 million). The reversal of writedowns was the result of actual losses being lower than previously estimated.

The writedowns and reversals are included in inventory cost of sales.

29. Selling, general and administrative expenses

Selling, general and administrative expenses consist of the following:

(C$ in millions)	2016	2015
Personnel expenses[1]	$ 1,169.8	$ 1,127.9
Occupancy[1]	659.6	648.6
Marketing and advertising	400.3	365.3
Depreciation of property and equipment and investment property[2]	322.8	303.9
Information systems	153.3	133.4
Amortization of intangible assets	126.1	111.9
Other[1]	460.0	405.1
	$ 3,291.9	$ 3,096.1

[1] *As a result of certain changes to business processes, costs previously recorded in "Personnel expenses" and "Occupancy" are presented as "Other" in the current year. $9.9 million of Personnel expenses and $2.0 million of Occupancy recorded in 2015 would have been classified as Other under the current year presentation.*

[2] *Refer to Note 28 for depreciation included in cost of producing revenue.*

30. Net finance costs

Net finance costs consists of the following:

(C$ in millions)	2016	2015
Finance (income)[1]	**$ (9.4)**	$ (14.1)
Finance costs		
Subordinated and senior notes	**$ 48.3**	$ 50.2
Medium-term notes	**51.3**	45.9
Loans payable	**12.0**	11.1
Finance leases	**8.3**	9.0
Other[2]	**7.2**	8.6
	127.1	124.8
Less: Capitalized borrowing costs	**23.8**	17.9
Total finance costs	**$ 103.3**	$ 106.9
Net finance costs	**$ 93.9**	$ 92.8

[1] *Primarily includes short and long-term investments, mortgages, and tax installments.*

[2] *Includes $1.2 million of amortization of debt issuance costs (2015 – $1.8 million).*

31. Notes to the consolidated statements of cash flows

Change in operating working capital and other comprise the following:

(C$ in millions)	2016	2015
Change in operating working capital		
Trade and other receivables	**$ 85.0**	$ 83.1
Merchandise inventories	**70.8**	(147.3)
Income taxes	**(1.6)**	(0.6)
Prepaid expenses and deposits	**(7.6)**	8.3
Trade and other payables	**(82.0)**	(80.9)
Total	**64.6**	(137.4)
Change in other		
Provisions	**36.2**	12.7
Long-term provisions	**2.4**	(0.4)
Other long term liabilities	**22.9**	9.8
Total	**61.5**	22.1
Change in operating working capital and other	**$ 126.1**	$ (115.3)

31.1 Cash and marketable investments held in reserve

Cash and marketable investments includes reserves held by the Financial Services segment in support of its liquidity and regulatory requirements. As at December 31, 2016, reserves held by Financial Services totalled $422.1 million (2015 – $275.1 million) and includes restricted cash disclosed in Note 7 as well as short-term investments.

31.2 Supplementary information

During the year ended December 31, 2016, the Company acquired property and equipment and investment property at an aggregate cost of $601.1 million (2015 – $582.0 million). During the year ended December 31, 2016, intangible assets were internally developed or acquired at an aggregate cost of $153.8 million (2015 – $109.9 million).

The amount relating to property and equipment and investment property acquired that is included in trade and other payables at December 31, 2016, is $63.5 million (2015 – $104.1 million). The amount relating to intangible assets that is included in trade and other payables at December 31, 2016, is $28.4 million (2015 – $38.0 million).

During the year ended December 31, 2016, the Company also included in the property and equipment, investment property, and intangible assets acquired non-cash items relating to finance leases, asset retirement obligations, and capitalized interest in the amount of $24.3 million (2015 – $33.7 million).

32. Financial instruments

32.1 Fair value of financial instruments

Fair values have been determined for measurement and/or disclosure purposes based on the following:

The carrying amount of the Company's cash and cash equivalents, trade and other receivables, loans receivable, bank indebtedness, trade and other payables, short-term borrowings, and loans payable approximate their fair value either due to their short-term nature or because they are derivatives, which are carried at fair value.

The carrying amount of the Company's long-term receivables and other assets approximate their fair value either because the interest rates applied to measure their carrying amount approximate current market interest or because they are derivatives, which are carried at fair value.

Fair values of financial instruments reflect the credit risk of the Company and counterparties when appropriate.

Investments in equity and debt securities

The fair values of financial assets at FVTPL, held-to-maturity investments, and available-for-sale financial assets that are traded in active markets are determined by reference to their quoted closing bid price or dealer price quotations at the reporting date. For investments that are not traded in active markets, the Company determines fair values using a combination of discounted cash flow models, comparison to similar instruments for which market-observable prices exist, and other valuation models.

Derivatives

The fair value of a foreign exchange forward contract is estimated by discounting the difference between the contractual forward price and the current forward price for the residual maturity of the contract using a risk-free interest rate (based on government bonds).

The fair value of interest rate swaps is based on counterparty confirmations tested for reasonableness by discounting estimated future cash flows derived from the terms and maturity of each contract, using market interest rates for a similar instrument at the measurement date.

The fair value of equity derivatives is determined by reference to share price movement adjusted for interest using market interest rates specific to the terms of the underlying derivative contracts.

Redeemable financial instrument

On October 1, 2014, The Bank of Nova Scotia ("Scotiabank") acquired a 20.0 percent interest in the Financial Services business from the Company for proceeds of $476.8 million, net of $23.2 million in transaction costs. In conjunction with the transaction, Scotiabank was provided an option to sell and require the Company to purchase all of the interest owned by Scotiabank at any time during the six-month period following the tenth anniversary of the transaction. This obligation gives rise to a liability for the Company (the "redeemable financial instrument") and is recorded on the Company's Consolidated Balance Sheets in Other long-term liabilities. The purchase price will be based on the fair value of the Financial Services business and Scotiabank's proportionate interest in the Financial Services business, at that time.

The redeemable financial instrument was initially recorded at $500.0 million and is subsequently measured at fair value with changes in fair value recorded in net income for the period in which they arise. The subsequent fair value measurements of the redeemable financial instrument are calculated based on a discounted cash flow analysis using normalized earnings attributable to the Financial Services business, adjusted for any undistributed earnings and Scotiabank's proportionate interest in the business. The Company estimates future normalized earnings based on the most recent actual results. The earnings are then forecast over a period of five years, taking into account a terminal value calculated by discounting the final year in perpetuity. The growth rate applied to the terminal value is based on an industry-based estimate of the Financial Services business. The discount rate reflects the cost of equity of the Financial Services business and is based on expected market rates adjusted to reflect the risk profile of the Business. The fair value measurement is performed quarterly using internal estimates and judgment supplemented by periodic input from a third party. This recurring fair value measurement is categorized within Level 3 of the fair value hierarchy (refer to Note 32.4).

32.2 Fair value measurement of debt and deposits

The fair value measurement of debt and deposits is categorized within Level 2 of the fair value hierarchy (refer to Note 32.4). The fair values of the Company's debt and deposits compared to the carrying amounts are as follows:

As at	December 31, 2016		January 2, 2016	
(C$ in millions)	Carrying amount	Fair value	Carrying amount	Fair value
Liabilities carried at amortized cost				
Debt	**$ 3,320.5**	**$ 3,476.9**	$ 2,995.7	$ 3,161.1
Deposits	**$ 2,181.5**	**$ 2,197.9**	$ 2,252.9	$ 2,276.1

The difference between the fair values and the carrying amounts (excluding transaction costs, which are included in the carrying amount of debt) is due to decreases in market interest rates for similar instruments. The fair values are determined by discounting the associated future cash flows using current market interest rates for items of similar risk.

32.3 Items of income, expense, gains or losses

The following table presents certain amounts of income, expense, gains, or losses, arising from financial instruments that were recognized in net income or equity:

(C$ in millions)	2016	2015
Net gain (loss) on:		
Financial instruments designated and/or classified as FVTPL[1]	$ 29.1	$ (7.5)
Interest income (expense):		
Total interest income calculated using effective interest method for financial instruments that are not at FVTPL	888.6	863.0
Total interest expense calculated using effective interest method for financial instruments that are not at FVTPL	(169.5)	(167.4)
Fee expense arising from financial instruments that are not at FVTPL:		
Other fee expense	(13.9)	(11.6)

[1] *Excludes gains (losses) on cash flow hedges, which are effective hedging relationships and gains (losses) on available for sale investments that are both reflected in the Consolidated Statements of Comprehensive Income.*

32.4 Fair value of financial assets and financial liabilities classified using the fair value hierarchy

The Company uses a fair value hierarchy to categorize the inputs used to measure the fair value of financial assets and financial liabilities, the levels of which are:

Level 1 – Inputs are unadjusted quoted prices of identical instruments in active markets;
Level 2 – Inputs are other than quoted prices included in Level 1 but are observable for the asset or liability, either directly or indirectly; and
Level 3 – Inputs are not based on observable market data.

The following table presents the financial instruments measured at fair value classified by the fair value hierarchy:

(C$ in million)		2016		2015	
Balance sheet line	**Category**	**Level**		Level	
Short-term investments	FVTPL	2	$ 38.6	2	$ –
Short-term investments	Available for sale	2	78.6	2	96.1
Long-term investments	Available for sale	2	175.2	2	153.4
Trade and other receivables	FVTPL[1]	2	26.7	2	27.3
Trade and other receivables	Effective hedging instruments	2	49.9	2	214.1
Long-term receivables and other assets	FVTPL[1]	2	26.0	2	25.4
Long-term receivables and other assets	Effective hedging instruments	2	20.2	2	24.8
Trade and other payables	FVTPL[1]	2	1.1	2	0.7
Trade and other payables	Effective hedging instruments	2	12.3	2	–
Redeemable financial instrument	FVTPL	3	517.0	3	517.0
Other long-term liabilities	Effective hedging instruments	2	8.3	2	12.9

[1] *Includes derivatives that are classified as held for trading.*

There were no transfers in either direction between categories in 2016 or 2015.

Changes in fair value measurement for instruments categorized in Level 3

Level 3 financial instruments include a redeemable financial instrument.

As of December 31, 2016, the fair value of the redeemable financial instrument was estimated to be $517.0 million (2015 – $517.0 million). The determination of the fair value of the redeemable financial instrument requires significant judgment on the part of Management. Refer to Note 2 of these consolidated financial statements for further information.

33. Operating leases

The Company as lessee

The Company leases a number of retail stores, distribution centres, petroleum sites, facilities, and office equipment, under operating leases with termination dates extending to March 25, 2060. Generally, the leases have renewal options, primarily at the Company's option.

The annual lease payments for property and equipment under operating leases are as follows:

(C$ in millions)	2016	2015
Less than one year	$ 354.1	$ 343.4
Between one and five years	1,097.7	1,055.5
More than five years	830.2	884.6
	$ 2,282.0	$ 2,283.5

The amounts recognized as an expense are as follows:

(C$ in millions)	2016	2015
Minimum lease payments[1]	$ 369.6	$ 347.0
Sublease payments received	(38.5)	(39.7)
	$ 331.1	$ 307.3

[1] *Minimum lease payments includes contingent rent.*

Due to the redevelopment or replacement of existing properties, certain leased properties are no longer needed for business operations. Where possible, the Company subleases these properties to third parties, receiving sublease payments to reduce costs. In addition, the Company has certain premises where it is on the head lease and subleases the property to franchisees. The total future minimum sublease payments expected under these non-cancellable subleases were $82.6 million as at December 31, 2016 (2015 – $94.9 million).

The Company as lessor

The Company leases out a number of its investment properties, and has certain sublease arrangements, under operating leases (refer to Note 12), with lease terms between one to 20 years with the majority having an option to renew after the expiry date.

The lessee does not have an option to purchase the property at the expiry of the lease period.

The future annual lease payments receivable from lessees under non-cancellable leases are as follows:

(C$ in millions)	2016	2015
Less than one year	$ 35.9	$ 34.4
Between one and five years	90.0	92.3
More than five years	66.5	55.9
	$ 192.4	$ 182.6

34. Guarantees and commitments

Guarantees

In the normal course of business, the Company enters into numerous agreements that may contain features that meet the definition of a guarantee. A guarantee is defined to be a contract (including an indemnity) that contingently requires the Company to make payments to the guaranteed party based on (i) changes in an underlying interest rate, foreign exchange rate, equity or commodity instrument, index or other variable that is related to an asset, a liability or an equity security of the counterparty; (ii) failure of another party to perform under an obligating agreement; or (iii) failure of a third party to pay its indebtedness when due.

The Company has provided the following significant guarantees and other commitments to third parties:

Standby letters of credit

Franchise Trust, a legal entity sponsored by a third-party bank, originates loans to Dealers for their purchase of inventory and fixed assets. While Franchise Trust is consolidated as part of these financial statements, the Company has arranged for several major Canadian banks to provide standby LCs to Franchise Trust to support the credit quality of the Dealer loan portfolio. The banks may also draw against the LCs to cover any shortfalls in certain related fees owing to it. In any case where a draw is made against the LCs, the Company has agreed to reimburse the banks issuing the standby LCs for the amount so drawn. The Company has not recorded any liability for these amounts due to the credit quality of the Dealer loans and to the nature of the underlying collateral represented by the inventory and fixed assets of the borrowing Dealers. In the unlikely event that all the LCs have been fully drawn simultaneously, the maximum payment by the Company under this reimbursement obligation would have been $141.2 million at December 31, 2016 (2015 – $151.0 million).

The Company has obtained documentary and standby letters of credit aggregating $40.4 million (2015 – $32.3 million) relating to the importation of merchandise inventories and to facilitate various real estate activities.

Business and property dispositions

In connection with agreements for the sale of all or part of a business or property and in addition to indemnifications relating to failure to perform covenants and breach of representations and warranties, the Company has agreed to indemnify the purchasers against claims from its past conduct, including environmental remediation. Typically, the term and amount of such indemnification will be determined by the parties in the agreements. The nature of these indemnification agreements prevents the Company from estimating the maximum potential liability it would be required to pay to counterparties. Historically, the Company has not made any significant indemnification payments under such agreements, and no amount has been accrued in the consolidated financial statements with respect to these indemnification agreements.

Lease agreements guarantees

The Company has guaranteed leases on certain franchise stores in the event the franchisees are unable to meet their remaining lease commitments. These lease agreements have expiration dates through November 2023. The maximum amount that the Company may be required to pay under these agreements was $4.6 million (2015 – $5.3 million). In addition, the Company could be required to make payments for percentage rents, realty taxes, and common area costs. No amount has been accrued in the consolidated financial statements with respect to these lease agreements.

Third-party financial guarantees

The Company has guaranteed the debts of certain Dealers. These third-party financial guarantees require the Company to make payments if the Dealer fails to make scheduled debt payments. The majority of these third-party financial guarantees have expiration dates extending up to and including July 2017. The maximum amount that the Company may be required to pay under these debt agreements was $50.0 million (2015 – $50.0 million), of which $23.4 million (2015 – $32.3 million) was issued at December 31, 2016. No amount has been accrued in the consolidated financial statements with respect to these debt agreements.

The Company has entered into agreements to buy back franchise-owned merchandise inventory should the banks foreclose on any of the franchisees. The terms of the guarantees range from less than a year to the lifetime of the particular underlying franchise agreement. The Company's maximum exposure as at December 31, 2016, was $70.4 million (2015 – $88.0 million).

Indemnification of lenders and agents under credit facilities

In the ordinary course of business, the Company has agreed to indemnify its lenders under various credit facilities against costs or losses resulting from changes in laws and regulations that would increase the lenders' costs and from any legal action brought against the lenders related to the use of the loan proceeds. These indemnifications generally extend for the term of the credit facilities and do not provide any limit on the maximum potential liability. Historically, the Company has not made any significant indemnification payments under such agreements, and no amount has been accrued in the consolidated financial statements with respect to these indemnification agreements.

Other indemnification agreements

In the ordinary course of business, the Company provides other additional indemnification agreements to counterparties in transactions such as leasing transactions, service arrangements, investment banking agreements, securitization agreements, indemnification of trustees under indentures for outstanding public debt, director and officer indemnification agreements, escrow agreements, price escalation clauses, sales of assets (other than dispositions of businesses discussed above), and the arrangements with Franchise Trust discussed above. These additional indemnification agreements require the Company to compensate the counterparties for certain amounts and costs incurred, including costs resulting from changes in laws and regulations (including tax legislation) or as a result of litigation claims or statutory sanctions that may be suffered by a counterparty as a consequence of the transaction.

The terms of these additional indemnification agreements vary based on the contract and do not provide any limit on the maximum potential liability. Historically, the Company has not made any significant payments under such additional indemnifications, and no amount has been accrued in the consolidated financial statements with respect to these additional indemnification commitments.

The Company's exposure to credit risks related to the above-noted guarantees are disclosed in Note 5.

Capital commitments

As at December 31, 2016, the Company had capital commitments for the acquisition of property and equipment, investment property, and intangible assets for an aggregate cost of approximately $54.8 million (2015 – $120.2 million).

35. Related parties

The Company's majority shareholder is Ms. Martha G. Billes, who beneficially owns, or controls or directs approximately 61.4 percent of the Common Shares of the Company through two privately held companies, Tire 'N' Me Pty. Ltd. and Albikin Management Inc.

Transactions with members of the Company's Board of Directors who were also Dealers represented less than one percent of the Company's total revenue and were in accordance with established Company policy applicable to all Dealers. Other transactions with related parties, as defined by IFRS, were not significant during the year.

The following outlines the compensation of the Company's Board of Directors and key Management personnel (the Company's Chief Executive Officer, Chief Financial Officer, and certain other Senior Officers):

(C$ in millions)	**2016**	2015
Salaries and short-term employee benefits	**$ 11.0**	$ 12.3
Share-based payments and other	**17.9**	11.7
	$ 28.9	$ 24.0

36. Comparative figures

Certain of the prior period figures have been restated to align with Management's current view of the Company's operations.

Glossary

accounting income The amount of income (before subtracting income tax) recognized for financial reporting purposes. *920*

accrual method Focuses on obtaining the balance sheet value for the income tax liability (or asset) that best reflects the assets and liabilities recognized on the balance sheet. *920*

accrued benefit obligation The present value of pension benefits that employees have earned. *806*

actuarial gain A favourable difference between actual and expected amounts for pension obligations. *808*

actuarial loss An unfavourable difference between actual and expected amounts for pension obligations. *808*

actuary A professional who specializes in the estimation of risks and uncertainties. *804*

agency cost of leasing The reduced level of care due to the separation of an asset's ownership and its control. *843*

amortized cost (of debt) The amount initially recognized for the debt adjusted by subsequent amortization of the net premium or discount. *593*

annuity A series of cash flows in equal amounts occurring at regular intervals. *A3*

annuity due An annuity with cash flows at the *beginning* of each period. *A3*

antidilutive potential ordinary shares Potential ordinary shares whose conversion to ordinary shares would increase EPS or decrease the loss per share from continuing operations. *761*

appropriation The process that allocates a portion of retained earnings to a reserve. *643*

asset ceiling The present value of the reduction in future contributions plus the amount of refunds from the pension plan, if any. *818*

at-the-money An option is at the money if the market price of the share equals the exercise price. *764*

bargain purchase option (BPO) An option given to the lessee to purchase the leased asset at a price that is below the expected fair value at a future date; the assessment of whether a bargain exists is made at the time of entering the lease arrangement. *844*

basic EPS An indicator of profitability that measures how much of the company's earnings are attributable (belong) to each ordinary share. *752*

best efforts approach Occurs when the broker simply agrees to try to sell as much of the (debt) issue as possible to investors. *586*

bond indenture A contract that outlines the terms of the bond, including the maturity date, rate of interest, interest payment dates, security pledged, and financial covenants. *585*

call premium The excess over par value paid to the bondholders when the security is called. *587*

callable bonds Bonds that permit the issuing company to "call" for the bonds to be redeemed before maturity. *587*

capital cost allowance (CCA) Depreciation for tax purposes. *929*

cash equivalents Short-term, highly liquid investments that are readily convertible to known amounts of cash and which are subject to an insignificant risk of changes in value. *1005*

cash flow hedge A financial instrument that reduces an entity's exposure to changes in future cash flows. *721*

change in accounting policy An accounting change made at the discretion of management. *967*

change in estimate An accounting change made necessary by the arrival of new information. *970*

commencement date of the lease The date that the leased asset is first available to the lessee. *852*

common (ordinary) shares An equity interest that has the lowest priority and represents the residual ownership interest in the company. *640*

complex capital structures A capital structure that includes potentially dilutive securities. *752*

compound financial instruments Those financial instruments with more than one financial instrument component. *695*

contingency An existing condition that depends on the outcome of one or more future events. *542*

contingent asset A possible asset that arises from past events and whose existence will be confirmed only by the occurrence or non-occurrence of one or more future events. *547*

contingent liability Is (a) a possible obligation that arises from past events and whose existence depends on one or more future events; or (b) a present obligation that arises from past events that is not recognized as a liability because: (i) it is not probable that an outflow of economic resources will be required to settle the obligation; or (ii) the amount of the obligation cannot be measured with sufficient reliability. *544*

contributed capital The component of equity that reflects amounts received by the reporting entity from transactions with its owners, net of any repayments from capital. *640*

contributed surplus The component of contributed capital in excess of the amount allocated to share capital. *644*

convertible bonds Bonds that allow the holder to exchange or "convert" the bond into other securities in the corporation, usually common shares. *587*

correction of an error An accounting change made necessary by the discovery of an incorrect amount given the information available at the time the amount was reported. *968*

coupon (stated) rate of interest The interest rate specified in the bond indenture. *589*

covenant The borrower's promise to restrict certain activities. *585*

current assets Assets that are expected to be consumed or sold within one year of the balance sheet date or the business's normal operating cycle, whichever is longer. Also includes assets held primarily for trading purposes. *522*

current liabilities Obligations that are expected to be settled within one year of the balance sheet date or the business's normal operating cycle, whichever is longer. Also includes liabilities at fair value through profit or loss, and liabilities that the entity does not have an unconditional right to defer settlement of for at least twelve months after the reporting date. *520*

current service cost The increase in the present value of pension obligations due to an employee's provision of services during the current period. *805*

curtailment A reduction in the number of employees or the amount of benefits they will receive in the future. *807*

debentures Unsecured bonds. *586*

deductible temporary difference A temporary difference that results in *future* taxable income being less than accounting income. *927*

deferral method Focuses on obtaining the income statement value for income tax expense that best matches the amount of income recognized for the year. *920*

deferred revenue A non-financial obligation arising from the collection of revenue that has not yet been earned. *534*

deferred tax asset The amount of income tax recoverable in future periods as a result of deductible temporary differences, losses carried forward, or tax credits carried forward. *927*

deferred tax liability The amount of income tax payable in future periods as a result of taxable temporary differences. *927*

defined benefit plan A pension plan that specifies how much in pension payments employees will receive during their retirement. *803*

defined contribution plan A pension plan that specifies how much funds the employer needs to contribute. *802*

derivative A financial instrument that is derived from some other underlying quantity. *693*

diluted EPS Measures the amount of the company's earnings attributable to each ordinary shareholder in a hypothetical scenario in which all dilutive securities are converted to ordinary shares. *760*

dilutive potential ordinary shares Potential ordinary shares whose conversion to ordinary shares would decrease EPS or increase loss per share from continuing operations. *761*

direct financing lease A lease offered by a finance company or other lender. The lessor does not have a prior interest in the asset to be leased; rather, it purchases the asset at fair value and leases it out immediately. In the absence of initial direct costs, the lessor's carrying amount of the leased property is the same as its fair value at the commencement of the lease. *852*

direct financing lease A type of finance lease in which the sale price is equal to the cost of the asset to the lessor (used in ASPE). *892*

direct method A method of presenting the statement of cash flows by showing major classes of gross cash receipts and gross cash payments. *1012*

earnings multiple A number that, when multiplied with earnings, provides an estimate of a share's value. When earnings are expected to grow at rate g and the discount rate is r, the earnings multiple is equal to $(1 + g)/(r - g)$. *A10*

earnings per share (EPS) Measures each ordinary share's interest in a company's earnings. *751*

economic life The time period or units of output during which the asset is expected to be economically usable. *847*

effective interest rate The rate of interest paid by the borrower that factors in premiums or discounts at issuance and transaction costs. *589*

employee stock option An option a company issues to its employees giving them the right to buy shares in the enterprise at a pre-specified price. *694*

expected value The value determined by weighting possible outcomes by their associated probabilities. *533*

fair value hedge A financial instrument that reduces an entity's exposure to changes in fair value. *721*

fair value The price that would be received to sell an asset or paid to transfer a liability in an orderly transaction between market participants at the measurement date. *521*

finance lease A lease that transfers substantially all the risks and rewards incidental to ownership of an underlying asset. Depending on its nature, the lessor accounts for a finance lease as either a financing arrangement or as an asset sale with vendor-provided financing. *842*

financial guarantee contract A contract that requires the issuer to make specified payments to reimburse the holder for a loss it incurs because a specified debtor fails to make payment when due. *550*

financial leverage Quantifies the relationship between the relative level of a firm's debt and its equity base. *582*

financial liability A contractual obligation to deliver cash or other financial assets to another party. *520, 584*

financing activities Activities that result in changes in the size and composition of the contributed equity and borrowings of the entity. *1007*

firm commitment underwriting Occurs when the investment bank guarantees the borrower a price for the securities. *586*

forward A contract in which one party commits upfront to buy or sell something at a defined price at a defined future date. *717*

future Similar to a forward but the contract is written in more standardized terms (e.g., prices, maturity dates) and involves commonly traded items (e.g., commodities, currencies). *718*

gross investment in the lease The undiscounted lease payments receivable plus the undiscounted unguaranteed residual value of the leased asset. *852*

if-converted method Assumes (i) that the security was converted into ordinary shares at the beginning of the period, and (ii) interest and/or dividends were not paid on the security during the year. *762*

in-substance defeasance An arrangement where funds sufficient to satisfy a liability are placed in trust with a third party to pay directly to the creditor at maturity. *604*

in-the-money When the value of the underlying instrument in an option contract is favourable to the holder exercising the option compared with letting the option expire. In the case of a call option, this occurs when the underlying price exceeds the strike price; for a put option, it is when the underlying price is below the strike price. *694, 764*

income effect Indicates the incremental after-tax income available to ordinary shareholders if a category of potential ordinary shares had been converted into ordinary shares. *761*

incremental borrowing rate The interest rate that the lessee would have to pay on a similar lease or loan. *868*

incremental EPS Quantifies the relationship between the income effect and the share effect for each class of potential ordinary shares. *761*

indirect method A method of presenting the statement of cash flows by adjusting profit or loss for the effects of transactions of a non-cash nature, any deferrals or accruals of past or future operating cash receipts or payments, and items of income or expense associated with investing or financing cash flows. *1012*

interest rate implicit in the lease The rate of interest that causes the present value of (a) the lease payments and (b) the unguaranteed residual value to equal the sum of (i) the fair value of the underlying asset and (ii) any initial direct costs of the lessor. In the absence of initial direct costs, this will be the discount rate used by the lessor in determining the payments in the lease. *856*

intrinsic value of an option In a call option, the greater of zero and $(S - K)$, which is the difference between the market price and the strike price. *694*

investing activities The acquisition and disposal of long-term assets and other investments not included in cash equivalents. *1007*

investment bank A financial institution that acts as an agent or underwriter for corporations and governments issuing securities. *586*

lease A contract, or part of a contract, that conveys the right to use an asset (the underlying asset) for a period of time in exchange for consideration. *842*

lease payments Payments over the lease term that the lessee makes to the lessor, including: fixed payments; variable payments that depend on an index or rate; the exercise price of a BPO; and in certain circumstances, penalties for early termination of the lease. For the lessor, lease payments normally include residual value guarantees. For the lessee, lease payments include the amount expected to be paid out under residual value guarantees. *847*

lessee The renter in a lease contract. This is the party that has the right to use the underlying asset during the lease term. *842*

lessor The owner of the asset in a lease. *842*

liability A present obligation of the entity arising from past events, the settlement of which is expected to result in an outflow of resources. *519*

manufacturer/dealer lease A lease offered by the lessor as a financing mechanism to facilitate the sale of its own products. *852*

market rate of interest (yield) The rate of return (on a bond) actually earned by the investor. *589*

net income available to ordinary shareholders The company's net income less dividends on preferred shares. *753*

net investment in the lease The gross investment in the lease discounted using the interest rate implicit in the lease. Each payment within the gross investment, which is the total of the lease payments receivable under a finance lease and any unguaranteed residual value, must be discounted to reflect the risk and timing of the related cash flow. The net investment in the lease is also referred to as a *lease receivable.* *852*

no par value shares Shares that do not have a stated par value. *641*

non-cash transactions Activities that do not involve cash. *1009*

non-current liabilities Obligations that are expected to be settled more than one year after the balance sheet date or the business's normal operating cycle, whichever is longer. *581*

non-lease components Include services provided for or arranged by the lessor that would be purchased by the lessee independent of whether the lessee had purchased or leased the asset. The lessor excludes payments for non-lease components from the fixed payment amount when calculating the total lease payments, accounting for the non-lease component separately. *853*

onerous contract A contract in which the unavoidable costs of fulfilling it exceed the benefits expected to be received. *549*

operating activities The principal revenue-producing activities of the entity and other activities that are not investing or financing activities. *1007*

operating lease A lease that does not transfer substantially all the risks and rewards incidental to ownership of an underlying asset. An operating lease is accounted for by the lessor as a rental agreement. *842*

option A derivative contract that gives the holder the right, but not the obligation, to buy or sell an underlying financial instrument at a specified price. A **call option** gives the right to buy, whereas a **put option** provides the right to sell. *693*

ordinary annuity An annuity with cash flows at the *end* of each period. *A3*

originating difference A temporary difference that widens the gap between accounting and tax values of an asset or liability. *930*

out-of-the-money When the value of the underlying instrument in an option contract is unfavourable to the holder exercising the option compared with letting the option expire. In the case of a call option, this is when the underlying price is lower than the strike price; for a put option, it is when the underlying price is higher than the strike price. *694, 764*

par value shares Shares with a dollar value stated in the articles of incorporation. *641*

par value The amount to be repaid to the investor at maturity. *590*

past service cost The change in the present value of pension obligations due to initiation, amendment, or curtailment of a pension. *807*

pension trust The legal entity that holds the investments and discharges the obligations of a pension plan. *802*

permanent difference Arises from a transaction or event that affects accounting income but never taxable income, or vice versa. *925*

perpetual bonds Bonds that never mature. *587*

perpetuity A series of cash flows in equal amounts occurring at regular intervals for an infinite number of periods. *A3*

perpetuity with growth A series of cash flows occurring at regular intervals for an infinite number of periods with cash flows that grow at a constant rate. *A3*

possible A probability of 50% or less, but more than remote. *543*

potential ordinary share (POS) A financial instrument or other contract that may entitle its holder to ordinary shares. *760*

practical expedient An alternative method of accounting that simplifies the accounting for a given transaction. Practical expedients are made available in limited circumstances as a measure to protect against the cost of providing the accounting information exceeding the benefit provided by that same information. *867*

preferred shares Any shares that are not common shares. Preferred shares have priority over common shares with respect to the receipt of dividends and a claim on the entity's net assets in liquidation. *641*

priority The rank of a liability or an equity claim when a company liquidates, where higher priority confers preferential payout before other claimants. *639*

probable The probability of occurrence is greater than 50%. *543*

prospective adjustment Applies an accounting change only to the current and future periods without any changes to past financial statements. *971*

provision A liability in which there is some uncertainty as to the timing or amount of payment. *520*

real-return (inflation-linked) bonds Bonds whose cash flows are indexed to the inflation rate. *587*

recaptured depreciation The taxable income recorded for the reversal of previously taken capital cost allowances when the sale proceeds of an asset exceed its undepreciated capital cost. Applies to assets separately identified for tax purposes. *931*

recycling (of OCI) The process of recognizing amounts through OCI, accumulating that OCI in reserves, and later recognizing those amounts through net income and retained earnings. *644*

remote A very low probability of occurrence. *543*

residual value guarantee A guarantee made to the lessor by the lessee or an independent third party that the value of the leased asset at the end of the lease will be greater than or equal to the guaranteed amount. *844*

residual value The estimated value of the asset at the end of the asset's economic (useful) life. *848*

retained earnings A component of equity that reflects the cumulative net income (profit or loss) minus dividends paid. *643*

retrospective adjustment Applies an accounting change to all periods affected in the past, present, and future. *973*

reversing difference A temporary difference that narrows the gap between accounting and tax values of an asset or liability. *930*

right-of-use (ROU) asset An asset that represents a lessee's right to use an underlying asset for the lease term. This is the asset that the lessor rents to the lessee. *842*

sales type lease A type of finance lease in which the lessor obtains a profit margin on the sale of the leased asset (used in ASPE). *892*

secured bonds Bonds backed by specific collateral such as a mortgage on real estate. *586*

serial bonds A set of bonds issued at the same time but that mature at regularly scheduled dates rather than all on the same date. *586*

settlement The extinguishment of all or part of an enterprise's pension obligations. *818*

share effect Indicates the incremental number of ordinary shares outstanding if a category of potential ordinary shares had been converted into ordinary shares. *762*

shares authorized The number of shares that are allowed to be issued by a company's articles of incorporation. *642*

shares issued The number of shares issued by the corporation, whether held by outsiders or by the corporation itself. *642*

shares outstanding Issued shares owned by investors. *642*

simple capital structures A capital structure that does not include potentially dilutive securities. *752*

stock split An increase in the number of shares issued without the issuing company receiving any consideration in return. *649*

stripped (zero-coupon) bonds Bonds that do not pay interest; stripped bonds are sold at a discount and mature at face value. *586*

swap A derivative contract in which two parties agree to exchange cash flows. *718*

taxable income The amount of income recognized for tax purposes used to compute taxes payable. *920*

taxable temporary difference A temporary difference that results in future taxable income being higher than accounting income. *927*

taxes payable method A method that records an amount for income tax expense equal to the tax payments for the current period. *919*

temporary difference Arises from a transaction or event that affects both accounting income and taxable income, but in different reporting periods. *927*

terminal loss The tax loss arising from the sale of an asset for proceeds below its undepreciated capital cost. Applies to assets separately identified for tax purposes. *931*

time value of an option The portion of an option's value that reflects the probability that the future market price of the underlying instrument will exceed the strike price. *694*

trade payables Obligations to pay for goods received or services used. *522*

treasury shares Shares issued but held by the issuing corporation; treasury shares are not outstanding. *642*

treasury stock method The process used to determine the share effect for call options and warrants. *764*

undepreciated capital cost (UCC) The net carrying amount of an asset or asset class for tax purposes. *930*

underlying asset The asset stipulated in the lease agreement that the lessor rents to the lessee. *842*

underlying quantity The value of an asset, an index value, or an event that helps determine the value of a derivative. *693*

unexpected gain on plan assets A favourable difference between actual and expected amounts of income from pension assets. *809*

unexpected loss on plan assets An unfavourable difference between actual and expected amounts of income from pension assets. *809*

unguaranteed residual value The expected value of the leased asset that will be returned to the lessor at the end of the lease term that is not guaranteed by the lessee or an outside party. *852*

vesting conditions Conditions that determine whether the employee is entitled to exercise the option or redeem the SAR under a share-based payment arrangement. *709*

vesting period The minimum length of time for which an option must be held before it can be exercised. *709*

warrant A right, but not the obligation, to buy a share at a specified price over a specified period of time. Can be considered a type of call option. *695*

warranty A guarantee that a product will be free from defects for a specified period. *533*

INDEX

Note: Page numbers followed by '*n*' indicate footnotes.

A

accounting changes
- change in accounting policy, *657, 658, 967–968*
- change in estimate, *967, 969–970*
- changes in accounting standards, *975–976*
- correction of an error, *657, 658, 968–969*
- prospective adjustment, *971–972*
- retrospective adjustment, *973–974, 975, 976–983*
- treatments for, *971–974*
- types of, *967–971*

accounting income, *920*
accounting standards. *See* Accounting Standards for Private Enterprises (ASPE); accounting standards in transition; IAS (International Accounting Standards); IFRS–ASPE differences; International Financial Reporting Standards (IFRS)
Accounting Standards Board (AcSB), *551, 598, 610, 1012*
Accounting Standards for Private Enterprises (ASPE)
- *see also* IFRS–ASPE differences
- accounting for SARs under, *714–715*
- accrual method, *925, 927, 941*
- accumulated other comprehensive income (AOCI), *662*
- asset retirement obligations (AROs), *609*
- book value method, *703, 704*
- capital lease, *842n*
- cash flow statement, *1014–1016*
- contingencies, *548–549*
- contributed surplus, *662–663*
- decommissioning, *609*
- disclosure requirements, *551*
- and earnings per share (EPS), *752*
- employee benefits, *821*
- equity, *647, 661–662, 696*
- financial instruments, *599*
- financial statement concepts, *656*
- future income tax asset, *927*
- future income tax liability, *927*
- income tax assets and liabilities, *941*
- income taxes paid, *1048*
- incremental method, *697*
- interest and dividends paid and received, *1014, 1048*
- lawsuits, *548*
- lease classification, *846*
- loss under, *548*
- property dividends (dividends in kind), *654*
- share purchase loans receivable, *647*
- share repurchases, *651, 663*
- single-transaction method, *665*
- site restoration costs, *609*
- statement of retained earnings, *656*
- stock appreciation rights (SARs), *714*
- stock compensation plans, *708, 709n*
- straight-line method, *599*
- two-transaction method, *664*
- zero common equity method, *697*

accounts receivable, *1031*
accrual accounting, *919, 972, 978*
accrual method (of accounting for income tax), *920–921, 922–924, 925–934, 941*
- permanent difference, *925–927*
- temporary differences, *927–930*

accrual of interest expense, *596, 598*
accrued benefit obligation, *806*
accumulated other comprehensive income (AOCI), *640, 643–644, 644n, 662*
- retrospective adjustment, and temporary accounts, *978*

action plan, case, *B3–B4*
actuarial gains, *808*
actuarial losses, *808*
actuary, *804*
adjustments, and indirect method, *1017–1018*
adverse selection, *695*
Aeroplan, *535, 536*
agency cost of leasing, *843*
agent, *536n*
Aimia, *536*
Air Canada, *536, 800, 819*
Alberta, *528*
Alberta sales tax rates, *524*
allowance for bad debts, *1031*
allowance for doubtful accounts, *968–969*
Altria Group, *654*
amortization
- accounting *vs.* tax treatment, *926*
- of bond premium and discount, *593, 1032*

amortization (*continued*)
- discounts, *613*
- premiums, *613*
- straight-line method, *598–600*
- using effective interest method, *593–598*

amortized cost (of debt), *593, 598 see also* effective interest method; straight-line method
analysis (including consideration of alternatives), case, *B3*
annuity, *A3*
annuity due, *A3*
- present value of, *A4–A5*

appropriation, *643*
asset ceiling, *818*
asset retirement obligations (AROs), *609*
assets
- from asset pool, *930–931*
- biological assets, *928*
- borrowing to acquire assets, *581–582*
- contingent asset, *546, 547*
- current assets, *522*
- deferred tax asset, *927, 928, 940*
- disposal of depreciable assets, *930–932*
- financial assets, *692–693*
- future income tax asset, *927*
- intangible assets, *969, 974*
- non-cash assets, *588*
- right-of-use, *869–879*
- specifically identified assets, *931–932*
- transfer in the sale and leaseback agreement, *886–887*

associates, *1035*
at-the-money, *764*
A&W, *527*

B

balance sheet, *920–921, 933, 934*
balance sheet approach, *922–924*
Bank of Montreal, *640n*
banks, and value-added services, *585*
bargain purchase option, *844*
basic EPS, *752, 759*
- calculation of, *752–760, 767*
- complicating factors, *756–759*
- comprehensive example, *772–774*
- denominator, *755–756*
- disclosure, *774–775*
- end-of-year equivalents, *758*
- introduction to, *751–752*
- negative basic EPS, and diluted EPS, *770–771*
- net income available to ordinary shareholders, *753–754*
- numerator, *753–754*
- presentation, *774*
- stock dividends, *757–759*
- stock splits, *757–759*
- treasury shares, *757*
- weighted average number of ordinary shares outstanding, *755–759*

Bell Canada Enterprises (BCE), *654*
best efforts approach, *586*
best estimate, *521n*
biological assets, *928*
BMO Nesbitt Burns, *586*
bond certificates, *589n*
bond indenture, *585*
bond issuers, *583n*
bond issues outstanding, *583n*
bonds, *585–587, 610–612*
- comprehensive bond example, *604–606*
- conversions of, *703–705*
- denominated in foreign currency, *610–612*
- discount, *593, 772, 1032–1034*
- effective interest method, *593–598*
- interest payment coinciding with fiscal year-end, *593–598*
- interest payment not coinciding with fiscal year-end, *598*
- issuance of, *594–595*
- overview, *585–586*
- premium, *593, 596, 597, 772, 1032–1034*
- safe after specified issue date, *591–593*
- sale between interest payment dates, *592*
- sale on issue date specified in indenture, *591*
- sales price, when yield given, *591*
- straight-line method, *598–600*
- timing of bond issuance, *591–593*
- types of, *586–587*

bonds payable, *762*
book value method, *703–704*
- valuation using, *A8*

borrowing, *581–582*
British Columbia Business Corporations Act, *641n, 663, 663n*
British Columbia sales tax rates, *524*
bundled sales, *648*

C

callable bonds, *587*
call option, *693–695, 764*
call premium, *587*

Canada Business Corporations Act (CBCA), *641, 641n, 650, 650n, 663, 669, 757*
Canadian dollar, *540n, 610n, 693, 722*
Canadian Institute of Chartered Accountants (CICA), *1113n*
Canadian Tire Corporation, Limited (CTC), *550, 638, 642, 750, 764*
    contingencies, *547*
    credit facilities, *532*
    earnings per share (EPS), *774*
    equity, *658–659*
    income taxes, *941–943*
    non-current liabilities, disclosure of, *613*
    pension plans, *819–820*
    share-based compensation, *716*
    statement of cash flows, *1003, 1004, 1010–1012*
cancellation of reacquired shares, *650–652*
capital cost allowance (CCA), *929–930, 844n*
capital structures, *752*
capital transactions, *657, 658*
capitalization of retained earnings, *654*
capstone cases
    Gibraltar Enterprises, *B9–B17*
    Netconnect Inc., *B17–B25*
carryback of tax losses, *937–938*
carryforward of tax losses, *936n, 938–939*
case(es)
    see also capstone cases; comprehensive cases; mini-cases
    action plan, *B3–B4*
    analysis (including consideration of alternatives), *B3*
    defined, *B2n*
    evaluation/conclusion/recommendation, *B3*
    issues identification, *B2–B3*
    ranking, *B3*
    role-playing, *B2*
    solving, *B2–B4*
    vs. simulation, *B2n*
cash, *1005–1006*
    paid to suppliers and employees, *1027, 1028, 1029*
    receipts from customers, *1028*
    schedule of cash, *1030–1031*
    shares sold for, *646*
    vs. retained earnings, *652–653*
cash accounting, *924n*
cash dividends, *652–653*
cash equivalents, *1005–1006*
cash flow hedge, *721, 724–725*
cash flows
    classification of, *1006–1010*
    classification options, *1009*
    definition, *1005–1006*
    financing activities, *1007–1009*
    investing activities, *1007, 1008*
    non-cash transactions, *1009*
    operating activities, *1007, 1008, 1012–1014, 1029*
cash flow statement, *1010 see also* statement of cash flows
cash-settled stock appreciation rights (SARs), *716*
change in accounting policy, *657, 658, 967–968 see also* accounting changes
change in estimate, *967, 969–970*
    see also accounting changes
changes in accounting standards, *975–976*
Chartered Professional Accountants of Canada, *573n, 665n, 903n,* 958*n*
choice of awards, *537*
CIBC Investor's Edge, *586*
Columbus, Christopher, *690*
commencement date of lease, *852*
commitments, *549–550*
common shares, *640–641*
common temporary differences, *928–928*
comparable multiples method, *A10n*
comparative balance sheets, *1017*
compensation expense, *710, 711, 712–713*
complex capital structures, *752*
complex financial instruments
    see also compound financial instruments; derivatives
    disclosure, *716*
    presentation, *716*
    statement of cash flows, *1031*
compound financial instruments, *588–589, 648, 695, 696–705*
    conversions of bonds and preferred shares, *703–704*
    derecognition of debt, *700–705*
    IFRS–ASPE differences, *716*
    initial measurement, *697–698*
    subsequent measurement, *698–700*
comprehensive cases
    Allied Produce Inc., *B6–B7*
    Longhorn Casuals Ltd., *B7–B8*
    Marathon Petroleum Inc., *B5–B6*
comprehensive income, *1018, 1036*
computation techniques, *A5–A7*
consolidation of special purpose entities (SPEs), *610*
construction contracts, *928*
contingencies, *542–549*
    under ASPE, *548–549*
    disclosure as contingent asset, *547*
    disclosure as contingent liability, *544–545*
    IFRS–ASPE differences, *551*
    potential inflows, *546–547*

contingencies (*continued*)
- potential outflows, *543–546*
- probability of future outcomes, *542–543*
- recognition as asset, *546*
- recognition of a provision, *544*
- when no action required, *545–546, 547*

contingent asset, *546, 547*
contingent liability, *544–545*
contra account treatment, *647*
contributed capital, *640–643, 657 see also* shares
contributed capital (common share) account, *654*
contributed capital-related equity transactions, *645–652*
contributed surplus, *644, 662–665*
conversion features, *695*
conversion rights, *703n*
convertibility, *1006*
convertible bonds, *587, 695, 696, 698, 699, 704, 704n, 762–763*
- components, Incremental method to measure, *701–702*
- components, zero common equity method to measure, *702–703*

convertible preferred shares, *766*
convertible securities
- and diluted EPS, *771*
- with more than one conversion option, *771*

correction of an error, *657, 658, 968–969*
see also accounting changes
corridor approach, *809*
cost flow assumptions, *967, 968*
cost model, *608, 974*
costs
- agency cost of leasing, *843–844*
- amortized cost (of debt), *593*
- current service cost, *805–806, 807*
- decommissioning costs, *584, 606–609*
- interest cost component of pension expense, *808*
- past service costs, *807*
- share issuance costs, *649*
- site restoration costs, *584, 606–609, 609*
- transaction costs, *529*

coupon (stated) rate, *589, 704n*
coupons, *539, 589n*
covenants, *586*
CPA Canada Handbook, 640n
credit (loan) facilities, *532*
credit interest expense, *592n*
credit risk, *892*
CTC. *See* Canadian Tire Corporation, Limited (CTC)
cumulative dividends, *641–642*
cumulative preferred dividends, *754*
cumulative preferred shares, *753*
cumulative temporary difference, *929*
current assets, *522*
current liabilities, *520–521*
- change in estimate, *972*
- credit (loan) facilities, *532*
- customer incentives, *535–540*
- customer loyalty programs, *535–539*
- deferred revenues, *534–535*
- disclosure, *551*
- discount vouchers (coupons), *539*
- dividends payable, *527*
- errors, *969*
- foreign currency obligations, *540–541*
- income taxes payable, *527*
- maturing debt to be refinanced, *541*
- non-current debt in default, *541–542*
- non-trade payables, *524–529*
- notes payable, *529–531*
- other current liabilities, *540–542*
- presentation, *551*
- prospective adjustments, *972*
- rebates, *539–540*
- royalty fees payable, *527–529*
- sales tax payable, *524–527*
- trade payables, *522–523*
- *vs.* long-term liabilities, *522*
- warranties, *532–534*

current service cost, *805–806, 807*
curtailment, *807*
customer incentives, *535–540*
- customer loyalty programs, *535–539*
- discount vouchers (coupons), *539*
- rebates, *539–540*

customer loyalty programs, *534, 535–539, 551*
cut-off, *523*

D

date of record, *652*
debentures, *586*
debt
- amortized cost, *593*
- derecognition of, *700–705*
- exchanged for non-cash assets, *588*
- issuance of debt, *588*
- issued at non-market rates of interest, *588*
- long-term debt, *580, 583, 585, 610, 969, 970, 972*
- non-current debt in default, *541–542*
- safe level of debt, *582*

debt exchanged for non-cash assets, *588*
debt issued at non-market rates of interest, *588*
debt-rating agencies, *583–584*

declaration date, *652*
decommissioning costs, *584, 606–609*
deductible temporary difference, *927*
default, noncurrent debt, *541–542*
deferral method, *920, 921–922, 925n*
deferred income tax, *969, 970, 972*
deferred revenues, *534–535*
deferred tax asset, *927, 928, 940*
deferred tax liability, *927, 928*
defined benefit plan, *803, 804–818*
  accrued benefit obligation, *806*
  actuarial computations, *804*
  actuarial gains and losses, *808*
  actuary, *804*
  asset ceiling, *818*
  corridor approach, *809*
  current service cost, *805–806, 807*
  curtailment, *807*
  disclosure, *816–818*
  expected income from plan assets, *808*
  IFRS–ASPE differences, *821*
  interest cost, *808*
  multi-employer plans, *818–819*
  offsetting, *817*
  other comprehensive income (OCI), *806, 807*
  overfunding, *818*
  past service costs, *807*
  pension expense, *806, 807–808*
  practical illustration, *819–820*
  presentation, *816–818*
  settlement, *818*
  underfunding, *818*
  unexpected gains and losses on plan assets, *809*
  what to account for, *806–811*
defined contribution plan, *802–804, 818*
depletion, *928*
depreciation
  accounting *vs.* tax treatment, *928*
  capital cost allowance (CCA), *929–930*
  disposal of depreciable assets, *930–932*
  and land, *607n*
  recaptured depreciation, *931*
  straight-line depreciation, *607n*
  temporary differences due to, *929–930*
  undepreciated capital cost (UCC), *930–931*
  units-of-production method, *607n*
derecognition
  complex financial instruments, *1031*
  of debt, *700–705*
  employee stock option plan (ESOPs), *709*
  in-substance defeasance, *603–604*
  leases, *882–884*
  lessor's accounting for finance leases, *864*
  at maturity, *600*
  non-current liabilities, *600–604*
  offsetting, *603*
  prior to maturity, *600–603*
  stock appreciation rights (SARs), *713*
derivative contracts, *609*
derivatives, *693–695, 717–718, 719–720*
  forward, *717*
  futures, *718*
  option, *693–695*
  swaps, *718*
  warrants, *695, 706–707*
diluted EPS, *752, 760*
  bonds sold at discount or premium, *772*
  calculation of, *760–774*
  comprehensive example, *772–774*
  convertible securities issues, redeemed, or exchanged during year, *771*
  convertible securities with more than one conversion option, *771*
  disclosure, *774–775*
  discontinued operations, *769–770*
  incremental EPS, *761–769*
  introduction to, *751–752*
  other considerations, *771–772*
  potential ordinary shares, *761, 762, 771–772*
  presentation, *774*
  provisional EPS, *761n, 764–769*
  purchased options *vs.* written options, *772*
  rank order incremental EPS, *764*
  sequential comparison of incremental EPS to provisional EPS, *764–769*
  when negative basic EPS, *770–771*
dilutive potential ordinary shares, *761*
direct-financing lease, *852, 854*
direct method, *1012–1014, 1027–1031*
disclosure
  complex financial instruments, *716*
  contingencies as contingent assets, *547*
  contingencies as contingent liabilities, *544–545*
  current liabilities, *551*
  defined benefit plan, *816–818*
  earnings per share (EPS), *752, 774*
  equity, *658–659*
  finance leases, *866*
  financial instruments, *716*
  guarantee, *550*
  income tax assets and liabilities, *941*
  income taxes, *940–941*
  income tax expense, *940–941*

disclosure (*continued*)
- leases, *866*
- liabilities, *551*
- non-current liabilities, *612–613*
- operating lease, *866*
- statement of cash flows, *1048*

discontinued operations, *769–770, 1031*
discount, *593n, 613, 704n, 772, 1032–1034*
discount rate, *893*
discount vouchers, *539*
disposal of depreciable assets, *930–932*
- asset from asset pool, *930–931*
- specifically identified assets, *931–932*

dividends
- cash dividends, *652–653*
- and changes in equity, *657*
- cumulative dividends, *641–642*
- cumulative preferred dividends, *753, 754*
- date of record, *652*
- declaration date, *652*
- dividend preference, *654–656*
- dividends in kind, *654, 662*
- dividends paid, *1009*
- dividends received, *1009*
- ex-dividend date, *652*
- non-cumulative dividends, *641–642*
- non-cumulative preferred dividends, *753, 754*
- property dividends, *654*
- stock dividends, *653–654, 757–759*
- valuation using, *A8–A9*

dividend schedule, *641*
dividends in kind, *654, 662*
dividends payable, *527*
Dominion Bond Rating Service (DBRS), *580, 583*

E

earnings, valuation using, *A9–A11*
earnings management, *968*
earnings multiples, valuation using, *A9–A11, A10n*
earnings per share (EPS), *650, 750, 751*
- basic EPS, *751–760*
- comprehensive example, *772–774*
- diluted EPS, *751–752, 760–774*
- disclosure, *752, 774–775*
- errors, *969*
- IFRS–ASPE differences, *775*
- incremental EPS, *761–769*
- presentation, *774*
- provisional EPS, *761n, 764–769*
- valuation using, *A9*

economic benefits, outflow of, *519, 520*
effective interest method, *521, 593–598*
effective interest rate, *589, 593, 593n, 594, 595, 604, 605*
employee benefit plans, *801–802*
employee future benefits
- change in estimate, *972*
- introduction, *801–802*
- non-pension employee future benefits, *819*
- pension plans (*See* pension plans)
- prospective adjustments, *972*

Employee stock option plan (ESOPs), *708–710*
- derecognition, *709*
- initial measurement, *708–709*
- subsequent measurement, *709*

employee stock options, *694–695, 716*
- *see also* stock compensation plans

endowment reserve account, *643*
Enron, *609–610*
entity-supplied awards, *536*
equity and equity transactions, *639, 650*
- cash dividends, *652–653*
- components, for accounting purposes, *640–645*
- comprehensive illustration, *660–661*
- contributed capital, *640–643*
- contributed capital-related transactions, *645–532*
- disclosure, *658–659*
- dividend preference, *654–656*
- dividends in kind, *654*
- IFRS–ASPE differences, *661–662*
- issuance of shares, *646–649*
- presentation, *658–659*
- priority, *639*
- property dividends, *654*
- reacquisition of shares, *649–652*
- residual nature of, *639*
- retained earnings, *643*
- retained earnings-related transactions, *652–656*
- statement of changes in equity, *656–658*
- stock dividends, *653–654*
- stock splits, *649*

equity instruments, *692–693*
equity method, *698*
errors
- correction of an error, *657, 658, 968–969*
- in financial reports, *980n*
- misinterpretation of facts, *546n*
- multi-year effects of PPE errors, *982–983*
- in tax returns, *980n*

estimate
- best estimate, *521n*
- change in estimate, *967, 969–970*
- of liabilities, *546*

evaluation/conclusion/recommendation, case, *B3*
exchange rates, *540, 610, 720n*
ex-dividend date, *652*
ex-dividend price, *654*
executory costs, *893n*
exercise price, *694*
expected value, *533*
expected value techniques, *533, 539, 544*
exposure draft, *613*
extinguishment of obligation, *600*

F

fair value, *521*
    financial liabilities, *587*
    non-interest bearing notes, *529*
    realized gains and losses, *1034–1035*
    unrealized gains and losses, *1034–1035*
fair value hedge, *721, 722–724*
fair value method, *648*
fair value through profit or loss (FVPL), *521*
finance leases, *842, 846–849, 851–865, 866, 892*
    see also lease
    accounting from lessor's perspective, *851–865*
    classification as, *865*
Financial Accounting Standards Board (FASB), *610, 647*
financial assets, *692–693*
financial crisis of *2008, 692*
financial guarantee contract, *550*
financial instruments
    compound financial instruments, *588–589, 648, 695, 696–705*
    derivatives, *693–695, 719–720*
    disclosure, *716*
    discount, *1032–1034*
    equity instruments, *692–693*
    financial assets, *692–693*
    financial liabilities, *692–693*
    hedging, *720–725*
    premiums, *1032–1034*
    presentation, *716*
    risk reduction, *721*
    statement of comprehensive income, *774n*
    stock compensation plans, *708–710*
    types of, *692–696*
financial leverage, *582–583*
financial liabilities, *520, 584, 692–693 see also* non-current liabilities
Financial Restatements, 966
financial statements
    balance sheet, *920, 933, 934*
    comparative balance sheets, *1017*
    errors made in, *980n*
    income statement, *920, 937, 1004, 1005, 1017*
    statement of cash flows (*See* statement of cash flows)
    statement of changes in equity, *656–658*
    statement of comprehensive income, *721*
financing activities, *1007–1009, 972, 982*
firm commitment underwriting, *586*
Ford Credit Canada, *584*
foreign currency bonds, *610–612*
foreign currency obligations, *540–541*
FortisBC, *517, 542*
forward, *717*
franchises, *527*
Franklin, Benjamin, *524*
functional currency, *540n, 610n*
future income tax asset, *927*
future income tax liability, *927*
futures, *718, 718n, 720n*
future value, of single sum received now, *A1*
future value factors (FVF), *A15*
future value factors for an annuity due (FVFAD), *A17*
future value factors for an ordinary annuity (FVFA), *A16*

G

gains
    actuarial gains, *808*
    hedging items, *717*
    on share repurchase transactions, *651–652*
    unexpected gains on plan assets, *809*
    unrealized gains, *1034–1035*
GE Capital, *844*
goods and services tax (GST), *524–527*
goodwill, *972*
government assistance, *968*
Government of Canada bonds, *586*
gross amount, *523*
gross investment in lease, *852*
Groupe Aeroplan Inc., *536*
guarantee, *550*

H

harmonized sales tax (HST), *524–527*
HBC Rewards™, *535*
hedge accounting, *720–722, 717 see also* hedging
hedge of foreign currency risk of firm commitment, *721n*
hedge of net investment in foreign operation, *721n*
hedging, *693, 720–725*
    cash flow hedge, *721, 724–725*

hedging (*continued*)
- fair value hedge, *721, 722–724*
- hedge accounting, *720–722, 717*
- hedge of foreign currency risk of firm commitment, *721n*
- hedge of net investment in foreign operation, *721n*
- hedging item, *720*
- IFRS–ASPE differences, *717*
- overview, *720–722*

hedging item, *720*
held-for-trading investments, *1034*

I

IAS (International Accounting Standards)
- *see also* International Financial Reporting Standards (IFRS)
- book value method (IAS 32), *703–704*
- carryforward of tax losses, *938*
- change from cost model to revaluation model (IAS 8), *974*
- change in accounting policy, *973*
- classification of cash flows (IAS 7), *1006–1007*
- contingencies, *543*
- contingent asset (IAS 37), *546, 547*
- current liabilities (IAS 1), *520–521*
- current service cost, *805*
- decommissioning and site restoration costs (IAS 37), *547*
- deferred tax assets and liabilities, *941*
- defined benefit plan (IAS 19), *806*
- direct method (IAS 7), *1012–1013*
- earnings per share (IAS 33), *752*
- equity transactions (IAS 1), *645–646*
- errors, *546n*
- expected income from plan assets (IAS 19), *808*
- financial instruments: presentation (IAS 32), *551, 613, 650, 716*
- financial instruments: recognition and measurement (IAS 39), *613*
- financing activities (IAS 7), *1007*
- foreign exchange rate changes (IAS 21), *610*
- income taxes, classification of (IAS 7), *1035*
- income taxes, current and deferred (IAS 7), *1035*
- inventories (IAS 2), *523*
- investing activities (IAS 7), *1007*
- liability (IAS 37), *519, 520*
- multi-employer defined benefit plan (IAS 19), *819*
- mutually unexecuted contracts, *549*
- no discounting of deferred tax assets and liabilities, *940*
- non-current debt in default (IAS 1), *541*
- offsetting (IAS 1, IAS 32), *603*
- onerous contract (IAS 37), *549*
- operating activities (IAS 7), *1007*
- pattern of depreciation (IAS 16), *970*
- possible (IAS 37), *543*
- presentation of financial statements (IAS 1), *551, 656, 716, 1004, 1005*
- probable (IAS 37), *543*
- property, plant and equipment (IAS 16), *976*
- provisions, contingent liabilities and contingent assets (IAS 37), *551, 609*
- rate for discounting post-employment benefit obligations (IAS 19), *808*
- recognition of changes in fair value of pension assets and liabilities (IAS 19), *809*
- remote (IAS 37), *543*
- statement of cash flows (IAS 7), *1006*
- statement of changes in equity, *656*
- tax rates (IAS 12), *936*
- temporary difference (IAS 12), *927*
- warranty (IAS 37), *533*
- weighted average number of ordinary shares outstanding (IAS 33), *758*

if-converted method, *762–763*

IFRIC
- decommissioning, restoration, and similar liabilities, *607–608*
- distribution of non-cash assets to owners, *654*

IFRS–ASPE differences
- compound financial instruments, *716*
- contingencies, *551*
- customer loyalty programs, *551*
- disclosures for liabilities, *551*
- discounts, amortization of, *613*
- dividends in kind, *662*
- earnings per share (EPS), *775*
- equity and equity transactions, *661–662*
- hedge accounting, *717*
- hedging, *717*
- income taxes, *943–944*
- leases, *891–893*
- onerous contracts, *551*
- pension plans, *821*
- premiums, amortization of, *613*
- presentation, *662*
- share repurchases and resale, *661*
- statement of cash flows, *1048*
- stock appreciation rights, *716*
- treasury shares, *661*

IFRS Conceptual Framework, *868*
implicit interest rate, *844*

income
accounting income, *920*
accrual accounting, *919*
accumulated other comprehensive income (AOCI), *640, 643–644, 644n, 662*
comprehensive income, *1018, 1036*
expected income from plan assets, *808*
net income available to ordinary shareholders, *753–754*
other comprehensive income (OCI), *640n, 643–644, 657*
recognized for tax purposes, *919*
taxable income, *920*
income effect, *761*
income statement, *920, 937, 1004, 1005, 1017*
income statement approach, *921–922*
income taxes
accrual method, *920–921, 922–924, 925–934*
asymmetric treatment of profits and losses, *936–937*
balance sheet approach, *922–924*
capital cost allowance (CCA), *929–930*
carryback of tax losses, *937–938*
carryforward of tax losses, *936n, 938–939*
changes in tax rates, *934–936*
deferral method, *920, 921–922, 925n*
deferred income tax, *969, 970, 972*
deferred tax asset, *927, 928, 940*
deferred tax liability, *927, 928*
disclosure, *940–941*
disposal of depreciable assets, *930–932*
errors in tax returns, *980n*
future income tax asset, *927*
future income tax liability, *927*
IFRS–ASPE differences, *943–944*
income statement approach, *921–922*
methods of accounting for, *919–925*
no discounting for time value of money, *940*
practical illustration, *941–943*
presentation, *940–941*
recaptured depreciation, *931*
schedule for analysis of permanent and temporary differences, *933–934*
tax allocation methods, *920–924*
taxes payable method, *920, 924n*
tax losses, *936–939*
tax reporting *vs.* financial reporting, *918–919*
temporary differences, *927–930*
terminal loss, *931*
terminology, *928*
undepreciated capital cost (UCC), *930–931*
income taxes payable, *527*
income tax expense, *921n, 940–941*
incremental borrowing rate, *893*
incremental EPS, *761–769*
if-converted method, *762–763*
rank order incremental EPS, *764*
sequential comparison to provisional EPS, *764–769*
treasury stock method, *763–764*
incremental method, *697, 701–702, 704*
indebtedness, categories of, *521–522*
indirect method, *1012–1014, 1017–1027*
inflation-linked (real-return) bonds, *587*
information asymmetry, *695*
initial measurement. *See* measurement
insignificant risk, *1006*
in-substance defeasance, *603–604*
intangible assets, *969, 974*
interest and interest rate, *589–591*
bonds payable, interest on, *762*
coupon (stated) rate, *589, 704n*
discount rate, *893*
effective interest rate, *589, 590, 593, 594, 595, 604*
implicit interest rate, *844*
incremental borrowing rate, *893*
interest cost component of pension expense, *808*
interest paid, *1009*
interest received, *1009*
market rate, *529n, 589*
non-market interest rates, *588*
present value of lease calculations, interest rate used in, *869*
yield, *589*
interest expense, *594, 596, 597, 598*
interest payment
coinciding with fiscal year-end, *593–598*
not coinciding with fiscal year-end, *598*
interest rate implicit in lease, *856*
International Accounting Standards Board (IASB), *544, 609, 613–614, 752, 840, 1012*
see also IAS (International Accounting Standards); International Financial Reporting Standards (IFRS)
International Financial Reporting Standards (IFRS)
see also IAS (International Accounting Standards); IFRS–ASPE differences
accrual method, *925*
amortized cost, *598*
book value method, *703*
consolidated financial statements, *610*
customer loyalty programs (IFRS 15), *535*
debt exchanged for non-cash assets, *588*
deferred tax asset, *927, 928*

International Financial Reporting Standards (IFRS) (*continued*)
- deferred tax liability, *927, 928*
- discontinued operations, *1031*
- finance lease, *842n*
- earnings per share (EPS), *751, 769*
- effective interest rate, *593, 593n*
- employee stock options, *716*
- equity, *650, 661–662, 696*
- equity transactions, *645*
- extinguishment of obligation, *600*
- fair value hierarchy, *588*
- financial guarantee contract, *550*
- financial instrument disclosures, *613, 716*
- financial instruments, *532*
- financial liabilities, *520*
- guarantee, *550*
- hedge of net investment in foreign operation, *721n*
- income taxes paid, *1048*
- incremental borrowing rate, *893*
- incremental method, *697*
- in-substance defeasance, *603–604*
- interest and dividends paid and received, *1048*
- interest cost component of pension expense, *808*
- key terms, definitions of, *519*
- loss under, *548–549*
- multiple deliverables (IFRS 15), *535, 536*
- non-financial liabilities, *521–522*
- ordinary shares, *582n, 640–641*
- other comprehensive income, *644*
- outstanding lines of credit, *532*
- property dividends (dividends in kind), *654*
- reserves, *644*
- revenue recognition (IFRS 15), *534n*
- separate reporting of assets and liabilities, *603*
- short-term obligations, *521*
- stock appreciation rights (SARs), *714, 716*
- stock compensation plans, *708*
- and straight-line method, *598*

in-the-money, *694, 764, 764, 766*
intrinsic value method, *708n*
intrinsic value of an option, *694*
inventories, *969, 975*
investing activities, *1006, 1008, 972, 982*
investment bank, *586, 586n*
investments
- in associates, *1035*
- hedge of net investment in foreign operation, *721n*
- held-for-trading investments, *1034*
- multi-year effects of PPE investments and errors, *982–983*
- issuance of shares, *646–649*
- issues identification, case, *B2–B3*

K

Kraft Foods, *654*

L

land, and depreciation, *607n*
last-in, first-out (LIFO), *968*
lawsuit, *548*
lease, *842*
- agency cost of leasing, *843*
- bargain purchase option, *844, 868*
- capitalization criteria, *892–893*
- classification of, *847–849*
- classification of real estate, *849*
- commencement date of, *852*
- direct-financing, *852, 854*
- disclosure, *866, 885*
- economics of leasing, *842–846*
- finance leases, *846–849, 851–865, 866, 892*
- gross investment, *852*
- IFRS–ASPE differences, *891–893*
- implicit interest rate, *844*
- incremental borrowing rate, *868, 869*
- interest rate implicit, *856*
- interest rate used in present value calculations, *869*
- lease capitalization criteria, *891*
- lease classification, *846–849, 892*
- lessee's discount rate for present value calculations, *893*
- manufacturer/dealer, *852, 854*
- net investment, *852*
- operating lease, *846–851, 866*
- preference for finance or operating lease treatment, *865*
- presentation, *865–866, 885*
- residual values guarantee, *844, 853*
- supporting indicators for lease classification, *847–849*

lease classification, *846–849*
lessee, *842, 892, 893*
- accounting for leases, *867–884*
- capitalization criteria, *892–893*
- lease and non-lease components, *893*
- lease liabilities, *867–869*
- residual value guarantees, inclusion of, *893*

lessor, *842*
- accounting for finance leases, *851–865*
- accounting for operating leases, *849–851*

capitalization criteria, *892*
classification of finance, *892*
liabilities
contingent liability, *544–545*
current liabilities (*See* current liabilities)
deferred tax liability, *927, 928*
definition, *519, 551–552, 613–614*
disclosures, *551*
financial liabilities, *520, 584, 692–693*
future income tax liability, *927*
key elements, *519–520*
measurement, *521–522*
non-current liabilities (*See* non-current liabilities)
non-financial liabilities, *520, 521–522*
other financial liabilities, *521*
provisions, *520*
recognition, *520*
uncertain in amount or timing, *520*
lines of credit, *532*
liquidity style of presentation, *521n*
loan facilities, *532*
long-term debt, *580, 583, 585, 610*
long-term employee benefits, *819*
see also pension plans
long-term liabilities, *vs.* current liabilities, *522*
loss, *657*
actuarial losses, *808*
hedging items, *717*
operating losses, *936*
tax losses, *936–939*
terminal loss, *931*
under ASPE, *548*
under IFRS, *548–549*
unexpected losses on plan assets, *809*
unrealized losses, *1034*

M

Manitoba sales tax rates, *524*
manufacturer/dealer lease, *852, 854*
unguaranteed residual values. *857–860*
market rate, *529n, 589*
Marriott, *536*
maturing debt to be refinanced, *541*
maturity date, *541*
measurement
compound financial instruments, *698*
liabilities, *521–522*
no discounting for time value of money, *940*
non-current liabilities, *587–593*
non-current liabilities, subsequent measurement, *593–600*
mini-cases
accounting changes, *1002*
Big City Gymnastics, *1077–1079*
Canadian Development Limited, *748–749*
Canadian Tire Corporation, Limited, *798*
Community Care Services, *1080–1083*
CompuCo Ltd., *1075–1077*
Convertible debt, *749*
Cool Look Limited, *573–575*
Debt Laden Inc., *915*
Earth Movers Ltd., *576–578*
ElectroTools Ltd., *579*
Enviro Ltd., *1083–1086*
EPS, *799*
equities, *688–689*
ESL Teachers Union, *837*
Jackson Capital Inc., *633–634*
Kaitlyn's Cats Inc., *636*
Lilliput Transport Authority, *916*
Lisa's Insurance Services Ltd., *578*
Mom and Dot Reid Inc., *797–798*
non-current liabilities, *636–637*
Oddities in the Accounting for Income Tax, *965*
PDQ Leasing Options, *915–916*
Pensions, *839*
Peterborough Printers, *687*
political economy of income tax reporting, *963–964*
statement of cash flows, *1087–1088*
Thamesford Tubs, *687–688*
Total Protection Limited, *635–636*
Tubular Ltd., *837–839*
Ultramart, *748*
Whitney Equity Partners (WEP), *964–965*
XYZ Company, *797*
Moody's Investors Service, *583*
moral hazard, *585, 695, 696, 707–708, 936*
multi-employer plans, *818–819*
multiple deliverables, *535*
mutually unexecuted contracts, *549*

N

net assets, *643n*
net income available to ordinary shareholders, *753–754*
net investment in lease, *852*
net premium, *593n*
New Brunswick sales tax rates, *524*
Newfoundland sales tax rates, *524*
no par value shares, *641, 650–651*
non-cash assets, *588*
non-cash transactions, *1009*
non-controlling interest, *657n*

non-cumulative dividends, *641–642*
non-cumulative preferred dividends, *753, 754*
non-current debt in default, *541–542*
non-current liabilities, *520–521*
  bonds, *585–587, 589–593, 610–612*
  compound financial instruments, *588–589*
  debt exchanged for non-cash assets, *588*
  debt issued at non-market rates of interest, *588*
  debt-rating agencies, *583–584*
  decommissioning costs, *606–609*
  derecognition, *600–604*
  disclosure, *612–613*
  financial leverage, *582–583*
  initial measurement, *587–593*
  notes payable, *584–585*
  off-balance-sheet obligations, *609–610*
  overview, *581–582*
  par value, *590*
  presentation, *612–613*
  site restoration costs, *584, 606–609*
  straight-line method, *598*
  subsequent measurement, *593–600*
non-financial liabilities, *520, 521–522*
non-interest bearing notes, *529*
non-lease components, *853*
  lessee's accounting for, *893*
non-market interest rates, *588*
non-owners, *640*
non-pension employee future benefits, *819*
Nortel Networks Corp., *654, 966, 968*
notes payable, *529–531, 584–585*
not-for-profit organization, *643n*
Nova Scotia sales tax rates, *524*
Nunavut sales tax rates, *524*

O

off-balance-sheet obligations, *609–610*
offsetting, *603*
  defined benefit plan, *817*
oil and gas industry, *528*
onerous contract, *549–550, 551*
Ontario Corporations Act, *641n*
Ontario sales tax rates, *524*
operating activities, *972, 982, 1006, 1007, 1008, 1012–1014, 1029*
operating expenses, *968*
operating lease, *846–851, 866*
  see also lease
  accounting from lessor's perspective, *849–851*
operating losses, *936*
option, *693–695, 763–764, 771*
ordinary annuity, *A3*
  present value, *A3–A4*
ordinary shares, *640–641*
originating difference, *930*
other comprehensive income (OCI), *640n, 643–644, 657*
  see also accumulated other comprehensive income (AOCI)
  actuarial gains and losses, *808*
  defined benefit plan, *806, 807*
  fair value changes flowing through, *721–722*
  statement of cash flows, *1036*
  unexpected gains and losses on plan assets, *809*
out-of-the-money, *694, 764*
outstanding lines of credit, *532*
overfunding, *818*
over-the-counter (OTC) market, *586*
owners, *640*

P

PAEs (publicly accountable enterprises), *551*
par value, *590*
par value shares, *641, 662–663*
past event criterion, *519–520*
past service costs, *807*
payment date, *652*
pension accounting, *811–816*
pension expense, *806, 807–808*
pension plans, *800*
  asset ceiling, *818*
  defined benefit plan, *803–804*
  defined contribution plan, *802–804*
  IFRS-ASPE differences, *821*
  multi-employer plans, *818–819*
  nature of, *802–803*
  pension accounting, *811–816*
  practical illustration, *819–820*
  settlement, *818*
  types of, *802–803*
pension trust, *802*
permanent accounts, *978–983*
permanent difference, *925–927, 933–934*
perpetual bonds, *587*
perpetuity, *A3*
  present value of, *A3*
perpetuity with growth, *A3*
  present value of, *A3*
Philip Morris International Inc., *654*
possible, *543, 543n*
potential ordinary shares (POS), *760, 761–762, 771–772*

practical expedient, *867, 879–882*
preferred shares, *641, 703, 753, 754, 762–763*
premium, *593, 593n, 596, 597, 772, 1032–1034*
presentation
  complex financial instruments, *716*
  current liabilities, *551*
  defined benefit plan, *816–818*
  earnings per share (EPS), *774*
  equity and equity transactions, *658–659*
  financial instruments, *716*
  IFRS–ASPE differences, *662*
  income tax assets and liabilities, *941*
  income taxes, *940–941*
  income tax expense, *940–941*
  leases, *865–866*
  liquidity style of presentation, *521n*
  non-current liabilities, *612–613*
  retrospective adjustments involving only presentation, *977*
  statement of cash flows, *1005–1016, 1048*
  statement of changes in equity, *656*
present obligations, *520*
present value
  of an annuity due, *A4–A5*
  of an ordinary annuity, *A3–A4*
  and leases, *869, 893*
  of a perpetuity, *A3*
  of a perpetuity with growth, *A3*
  of single sum to be received in the future, *A1–A2*
present value factor for an annuity, *A4*
present value factor for an annuity due (PVFAD), *A4, A14*
present value factors (PVF), *A12*
present value factors for an ordinary annuity (PVFA), *A13*
price–earnings (P/E) ratio, *A10–A11*
primary market, *586*
Prince Edward Island sales tax rates, *524*
principal, *536n*
priority, *639*
private enterprise, *752n*
probability assessments, *939*
probable, *543*
profit, *657, 936–937*
profitability, and financial leverage, *582*
property, plant, and equipment (PPE)
  change in accounting policy, *968*
  change in estimate, *972*
  errors, *969*
  multi-year effects of PPE investments and errors, *982*
  prospective adjustments, *972*
  revaluation model, *974*
property dividends, *654*
proportional method, *648, 697*
prospective adjustment, *971–972*
provincial sales tax (PST), *524–527*
provisional EPS, *761n, 764–769*
provisions, *520*
provisions, contingent liabilities and contingent assets (IAS 37), *546*
publicly accountable enterprises (PAEs), *551*
put option. *See* option

Q

Quebec Sales Tax (QST), *524n*

R

ranking, case, *B3*
reacquisition of shares, *649–652, 661*
real-return bonds, *587*
rebates, *539–540*
recaptured depreciation, *931*
receivables, *968, 970, 972*
recognition
  actuarial gains and losses, *809*
  contingency as asset, *546*
  contingency as provision, *544*
  corridor approach, *809*
  liabilities, *520*
recycling, *644*
remote, *543*
reserves, *640n, 644, 657*
residual value, *853*
residual value guarantee, *844, 853*
  lessee's inclusion of, *893*
restoration costs. *See* site restoration costs
retained earnings, *640, 643, 652, 657*
retained earnings-related transactions, *652–656*
retrospective adjustment, *973–974, 975, 976–983*
  accruals that reverse in the immediately subsequent period, *978–982*
  accruals that reverse over more than two periods, *982–983*
  affecting both permanent and temporary accounts, *978–983*
  affecting only temporary accounts, *977–978*
  involving only presentation, *977*
return on equity (ROE), *582*
return to shareholders, *582*
revaluation model, *974*

revenue
- change in accounting policy, *968*
- change in estimate, *927*
- on construction contracts, *928*
- deferred revenues, *534*
- errors, *969*
- prospective adjustments, *972*

reverse stock splits, *757n*
reversing difference, *930*
right to acquire, *693–694*
right to sell, *694*
right-of-use assets, *842, 869–879*
risk reduction, *721*
role-playing, case, *B2*
Royal Bank of Canada, *640n, 695*
royalty fees payable, *527–528*

S

safe level of debt, *582*
sale-leasebacks, *887–891*
- agreement, transfer of assets in, *886–887*
- buyer-lessor accounts, *887–888*
- seller-lessee accounting, *888–889*
- transactions, *885–891*

Sales tax payable, *524–527*
sales-type lease, *892*
Saskatchewan sales tax rates, *524*
Scene™, *535*
schedule for analysis of permanent and temporary differences, *933–934*
schedule of cash, *1030–1031*
secured bonds, *586*
serial bonds, *586*
settlement, *818*
share-based compensation. *See* employee stock options; stock appreciation rights (SARs)
share buybacks, *649–652*
share consolidation, *757n*
share effect, *762*
shareholders
- net income available to ordinary shareholders, *753–754*
- return, *582*

share purchase loans receivable, *647*
share repurchases, *649–652, 661*
shares, *640–642*
- cancellation of reacquired shares, *650–652*
- common shares, *640–641*
- convertible preferred shares, *766*
- cumulative preferred shares, *753, 754*
- cumulative *vs.* non-cumulative dividends, *641–642*
- dilutive potential ordinary shares, *760, 761*
- issuance costs, *649*
- issuance of shares, *646–649*
- issued in exchange for good/services, *646*
- no par value, *641, 650–651*
- non-cumulative preferred shares, *753, 754*
- ordinary shares, *640–641*
- par value shares, *641, 662–663*
- potential ordinary shares, *760, 761–762, 771–772*
- preferred shares, *641, 703, 753, 754, 762–763*
- reacquisition of shares, *649–652, 661*
- share buybacks, *649–652, 661*
- share repurchases, *649–652, 661*
- shares authorized, *642*
- shares issued, *642, 646*
- shares outstanding, *642*
- sold for cash, *646*
- sold on subscription basis, *646–648*
- treasury shares, *642*, 661, *663–665, 756, 757, 1036*
- voting rights, *642*
- weighted average number of ordinary shares outstanding, *755–759*

shares authorized, *642*
shares issued, *642*
shares outstanding, *642*
Shoppers Optimum™, *535*
simple capital structures, *752*
simulation
- defined, *B2n*
- *vs.* case, *B2n*

single-transaction method, *664–665*
site restoration costs, *584, 606–609, 613*
special purpose entities (SPEs), *609–610*
specifically identified assets, *931–932*
speculation, *693, 721*
spread, *584–585*
stated rate. *See* coupon (stated) rate
statement of cash flows
- accounts receivable, *1031*
- allowance for bad debts, *1031*
- amortization of bond premium and discount, *1032*
- associates, investments in, *1035–1036*
- cash and cash equivalents, *1005–1006*
- cash paid to suppliers and employees, *1029*
- cash receipts from customers, *1028*
- classification of cash flows, *1006–1010*
- classification options, *1009*
- complex financial instruments, *1031*
- comprehensive example, *1036–1047*
- direct method, *1012–1014, 1027–1031*
- disclosure, *1047–1048*
- discontinued operations, *1031*

discounts and premiums, *1032–1034*
effects of specific items, *1031–1036*
financing activities, *1007–1009*
format, *1010–1016*
format, under ASPE, *1014–1016*
held-for-trading investments, *1034*
IFRS–ASPE differences, *1048*
income taxes, classification of, *1035*
income taxes, current and deferred, *1035*
indirect method, *1012–1014, 1017–1027*
investing activities, *1007, 1008*
liquidity, evaluation of, *1005*
non-cash transactions, *1009*
operating activities, *1007, 1008, 1012–1014, 1030*
other comprehensive income, *1036*
preparation, *1016–1047*
presentation, *1005–1016, 1047–1048*
requirement, *1004, 1005*
schedule of cash, *1030–1031*
sources of information, *1017*
stock dividends, *1036*
stock splits, *1036*
treasury shares, *1036*
unrealized gains and losses, *1034*
usefulness of, *1004–1005*
statement of changes in equity, *656–658*
statement of comprehensive income, *721, 774n*
stock appreciation rights (SARs), *708*
see also stock compensation plans
accounting under ASPE, *714–715*
cash-settled, *716*
derecognition, *713*
disclosure, *716*
IFRS–ASPE differences, *716*
initial measurement, *711–713*
with multiple settlement options, *713–714*
subsequent measurement, *711–713*
stock compensation plans, *708–710*
accounting for, *707–715*
employee stock option plan (ESOPs), *708–710*
stock appreciation rights (SARs), *708, 710–715*
stock appreciation rights with multiple settlement options, *713*
vesting period, *709, 709n*
stock dividends, *653–654, 757–759, 1036*
stock splits, *649, 757–759, 1036*
straight-line depreciation, *607n*
straight-line method, *598–600*
strike price, *694*
stripped (zero-coupon) bonds, *586*
subscription basis, *646–648*
Subway, *527*
swaps, *718*
sweeteners, *695*
syndicate, *586n*

T

taxable income, *920*
taxable temporary difference, *927*
tax allocation methods, *920–924*
taxes payable method, *919, 920, 924n*
tax losses, *936–939*
tax rates, *934–936*
tax reporting. *See* income taxes
temporary accounts, *977–978*
temporary differences, *927–930*
common temporary differences, *928–929*
cumulative temporary difference, *929*
deductible temporary difference, *927*
due to depreciation, *929–930*
originating difference, *930*
reversing difference, *930*
schedule for analysis of permanent and temporary differences, *933–934*
taxable temporary difference, *927*
Terasen, *517, 518, 520, 524, 545–546, 546n*
terminal loss, *931*
term loans, *541*
third-party awards, *536*
time value of an option, *694*
time value of money, *521n, 940, A1–A17*
Tim Hortons, *527*
Toronto Stock Exchange, *586, 638, 652*
tradable warrants, *696*
trade discounts, *523*
trade payables, *522–523, 540*
trade terms, *523n*
transaction costs, *529, 587, 590, 595n*
transaction data, *1017*
transaction price, *529*
transition (accounting standards). *See* accounting standards in transition
Translink, *580, 583, 583n, 584, 586*
treasury shares, *642, 661, 663–665, 757, 1036*
treasury stock method, *763–764*
TSX Venture Exchange, *696*
Tweedie, David, *840*
two-transaction method, *664*

U

undepreciated capital cost (UCC), *930–931*
underfunding, *818*

underlying asset, *842*
underlying quantity, *693*
unexpected gains on plan assets, *809*
unexpected losses on plan assets, *809*
unguaranteed residual value, *852*
    manufacturer/dealer leases, *857–860*
United States Government Accountability Office, *966*
units-of-production method, *607n*
universities, *643*
unrealized gains and losses, *1034–1035*
US dollar, *610, 693*

V

valuation allowance account, *939*
valuation techniques, *A7–A11*
    using book value, *A8*
    using dividends, *A8–A9*
    using earnings and earnings multiples, *A9–A11*
vesting period, *709, 709n*
virtually certain, *546*
voting rights, *642*

W

warranties, *532–534*
warrants, *695, 706–707, 763–764*
    accounting for, *705–707*
    derecognition, through exercise, *706–707*
    expire, derecognition when, *707*
weighted average number of ordinary shares
    outstanding (WASO), *755–759*

Y

yield (market rate), *589*
Yukon sales tax rates, *524*

Z

zero common equity method, *697, 702–703*

#	Competency and knowledge items	Level at Entry*	Chapter Coverage									
			11	12	13	14	15	16	17	18	19	20
Financial reporting												
1.1.1	Evaluates financial reporting needs	B										
	a. Framework of standard setting (IFRS and ASPE)											
	b. Financial statement users and their broad needs, standard setting, and requirement for accountability											
	c. Objectives of financial reporting											
1.1.2	Evaluates the appropriateness of the basis of financial reporting	B	✓	✓	✓	✓		✓	✓	✓	✓	✓
	a. Fundamental accounting concepts and principles (qualitative characteristics of accounting information, basic elements)								✓		✓	
	b. Methods of measurement							✓	✓	✓		
	c. Difference between accrual accounting compared to cash accounting								✓	✓		✓
1.1.3	Evaluates reporting processes to support reliable financial reporting	B										
	a. Accounting information systems											
	b. The role of IT in the reporting of information, including real-time access, remote access to information, dashboard, spreadsheet, report generator, and XBRL											
1.1.4	Explains implications of current trends and emerging issues in financial reporting	C	✓									
1.1.5	Identifies financial reporting needs for the public sector	C										
	a. Unique concepts in the PSAB handbook											
	b. Internal and external users of government accounting information and the uses of that information											
	c. Identifies financial reporting needs for the public sector—objectives of government reporting and major reporting issues											
1.1.6	Identifies specialized financial reporting requirements for specified regulatory and other filing requirements	C										
	a. Legislation that has an impact on accounting (SOX, Bill 198)											
1.2.1	Develops or evaluates appropriate accounting policies and procedures—Ethical professional judgement	B	✓	✓	✓	✓						✓
1.2.2	Evaluates treatment for routine transactions	A	✓	✓	✓	✓	✓		✓	✓	✓	✓
	a. Cash and cash equivalents											✓
	b. Receivables											
	c. Inventories											
	d. Property, plant, and equipment								✓			
	e. Goodwill and intangible assets											
	f. Depreciation, amortization, impairment, and disposition/derecognition											
	g. Provisions, contingencies, and current liabilities		✓									
	h. Long-term liabilities			✓					✓			
	i. Owners'/shareholders' equity				✓							
	j. Earnings per share (basic, diluted)						✓					
	k. Financial instruments		✓	✓		✓						
	l. Investments in associates/significant influence											
	m. Revenue recognition/revenue from contracts with customers, and accounting for revenue and related expenses											
	n. Leases								✓			
	o. Changes in accounting policies and estimates, and errors									✓	✓	
	p. Foreign currency transactions		✓	✓								
	q. Accounting for income taxes									✓		
	r. Events after the reporting period											
1.2.3	Evaluates treatment for non-routine transactions	B						✓				✓
	a. Uncommon capital assets (e.g., natural resources, exchanges of assets, decommissioning costs)											✓